Aud
78

CW00324491

The
Pub Guide
2003

Welcome to the 2003 edition of the AA Pub
Guide, fully updated with essential information
on nearly 2500 pubs and inns across England,
Scotland, Wales and, new for 2003, the
Channel Islands. We have sought out pubs
that are attractive, interesting or in a good
location, but above all ones that provide good
food and drink in a convivial atmosphere.
Whether you are looking for a good meal or a
delightful place for a drink, our popular guide
will help you find the ideal place.

Produced by AA Publishing
Directory complied by AA Hotel Services Department
Directory generated by the AA Establishment Database,
Information Research, AA Hotel Services
Advertisement Sales: advertisingsales@theAA.com
Editorial: lifestyleguides@theAA.com
Maps prepared by the Cartography Department of
Automobile Association Developments Limited
Maps © The Automobile Association 2002

Ordnance Survey This product includes mapping data licensed from Ordnance Survey® with the permission of the Controller of Her Majesty's Stationery Office.
© Crown copyright 2002.
All rights reserved. Licence number 399221

A CIP catalogue record for this book is available from the British Library Published by AA Publishing, which is a trading name of Automobile Association Developments Limited whose registered office is
Millstream, Maidenhead Road, Windsor, Berkshire, SL4 5GD

Registered number 1878835.
ISBN 0 7495 34354
A1109

Published in the USA by AAA

Design by Richardson Carpenter Advertising Ltd,
Maple Print & Design, Mathew Payne
– Basingstoke, Hampshire

Editor: Jo Sturges
Editorial Contributors: Philip Bryant, Nick Channer, David Foster, Martin Greaves, Julia Hynard, Denise Laing and Jenny White

Cover photographs:
top left; Crooked Billet, Stoke Row
top right; The Angel at Hetton
bottom right; Eagle & Child, Staveley
bottom left; © Photodisc

Contents

Welcome to the Guide

Welcome to the 2003 edition of The AA Pub Guide

We aim to bring you the country's best pubs, selected for their atmosphere, great food and good beer. Ours is the only major pub guide to feature colour photographs, and to highlight the 'Pick of the Pubs', uncovering Britain's finest hostelries. Updated every year, this year you will find lots of old favourites as well as plenty of new destinations for eating and drinking and great places to stay across Britain.

Who's in the Guide?

We make our selection by seeking out pubs that are worth making a detour for – 'destination' pubs – with publicans exhibiting a real enthusiasm for their trade and producing fine food and a good selection of well-kept drinks. Pubs make no payment for their inclusion in our guide. They are included entirely at our discretion.

That Special Place

We look for pubs that are attractive, interesting, unusual or in a good location. Some pubs may be very much a local pub but they have many loyal customers from further afield, others may be included because they are in a particularly exceptional place. Interesting towns and villages, eccentric or historic buildings, and rare settings can all be found within this guide.

Fine Food

We are looking for menus that show a commitment to home-cooking, making good use of local produce wherever possible, and in particular a frequently changing range of freshly prepared dishes. Pubs presenting beautifully prepared traditional dishes, or those offering innovative bar or restaurant food, are all in the running. In keeping with recent trends in pub food, we are keen to include those where particular emphasis is placed on imaginative modern dishes and specialising in fresh fish. At the same time we do not forget traditional pub dishes like ploughman's or pies.

Pick of the Pubs & Full Page Entries

Some of the pubs included in the guide are particularly special and we have highlighted these as Pick of the Pubs. For 2003 over 500 pubs have been chosen by our AA inspectors,

our team's personal knowledge and suggestions from our readers. These pubs have a coloured panel and a more detailed description. From these, over 90 in the 2003 Guide have opted to enhance their entry with two photographs as part of a full-page entry.

Tell us what you think

We welcome your feedback about the pubs included and about the guide itself. We are also delighted to receive suggestions about good pubs you have visited and loved. Reader Report forms appear at the very back of the book, please write in or e-mail to lifestyleguides@theAA.com to help us improve future editions. The Pubs also feature on the AA internet site, www.theAA.com, along with our inspected restaurants, hotels and bed & breakfast accommodation.

AA PUB OF THE YEAR AWARD
for England, Scotland and Wales

Selected with the help of our AA inspectors we have chosen three
worthy winners for this prestigious award.

The winners stand out for being great all-round pubs or inns, combining a great pub
atmosphere, a warm welcome from friendly efficient hosts and staff with excellent food,
well-kept beers and comfortable accommodation. We expect enthusiasm and a
high standard of management from hands-on owners.

The winning entries appear as the opening page for each country section in the guide.

PUB OF THE YEAR FOR ENGLAND
The Rose and Crown
Romaldkirk, Co Durham
see entry on page 181

PUB OF THE YEAR FOR SCOTLAND
The Old Inn
Gairloch, Highland
see entry on page 584

PUB OF THE YEAR FOR WALES
The Bell at Skenfrith
Skenfrith, Monmouthshire
see entry on page 619

Feature:

Inns ain't what they used to be
Have you ever wondered what used
to go on in the pub where you are
eating or what the strange object in
the corner of the bar was used for?
On page 14 Julia Hynard looks at the
unusual, violent and sometimes
macabre history of the many ancient
buildings where we are now offered
hospitality.

Feature:

Trust me I'm a Publican...
How many hundreds of people each
year think that they might like to run
a pub? Would it really be fun or just
a nightmare? Could you cope? Mary
Barnett had the chance to find out
when she and her husband recklessly
launched themselves into buying a
country pub. She lets you in on some
of her experiences on page 20.

About the Editor
Jo Sturges has had many years experience creating lifestyle and travel guides.
She has been editor of the AA's Restaurant Guide as well as writing and editing
travel guides to Britain and France for a number of publishers. Of a restless
nature, among her many ventures were running a pub with her husband and
taking a very, very belated Gap Year to back-pack round the world.

How to use the Guide

1 —NICEPLACE Map 01 TG22 —2

4 — **The Fox Inn** ◆◆◆ 🐷 ♀ **NEW** —3
Sand-next-the-Sea SD23 1NL
5 —☎ 01114 71144444 🖨 01114 71133333 e-mail: foxypub.co.uk
Dir: From A4 to Hambleton, then R on to B161 to Wartham.
Timeless 14th-century village pub within easy reach of the
coast. Unspoilt bars, real ale from the cask, and hearty English
cooking using fresh local ingredients. Typical dishes include
game pie, cheese baked crab, ham and lentil soup, chicken
and rabbit pie and, for pudding, golden syrup sponge. B&B in
adjoining cottage.
6 —**OPEN:** 11.30-2.30, 6-11, closed 25 Dec **BAR MEALS:** Lunch served
all week 12-2,Dinner served Fri & Sat 6.30-8.30. Av main course £6.80. —7
8 —**RESTAURANT:** Dinner Thu-Sat 7-10.30 **BREWERY/COMPANY:** Free
10 — House. **PRINCIPAL BEERS:** Greene King IPA, Woodfordes Wherry, —9
11 — guest beers. **FACILITIES:** Children's licence; family area;. Garden,
12 — outdoor eating. **NOTES:** Parking 10 No credit cards. **ROOMS:** 5
bedrooms 1 en suite. From s £24 d £42 —13

1. Listing Order

Pubs are listed alphabetically by name
(ignoring The) under their village or
town. Towns are listed within their
county (a county map appears at the
back of the guide). The guide has
listings for England, Channel Islands,
Scotland and Wales in that order.

Some village pubs prefer to be initially
located under the nearest town, in
which case the village name is
included in the address and directions.

Pick of the Pubs

Around 500 of the best pubs in
Britain have been selected by the
editor and inspectors and

highlighted. They have longer, more
detailed descriptions and a tinted
background. Around 90 have a full
page entry and two photographs.

Pub Listings

Pubs that have been recommended to
us but general statistics were not
available at the time of going to press
have very short descriptions and no
statistics.

2. Map Reference

The map reference number denotes the map page number in the atlas section at the back of the book and (except for London maps) the National Grid reference. London references help locate their position on the Central London and Greater London maps.

3. Symbols

See Symbols in the column on the right

4. Address and Postcode

This gives the street name and, if necessary the name of the village, which may be up to five miles from the named Location, plus the postcode in case letters need to be sent.

☎   Telephone number
▤   Fax number
email   Wherever possible we have included an email address

5. Directions

Directions are given wherever they have been supplied by the proprietor.

Entry Statistics

6. OPEN indicates the hours when the establishment is open and closed. See box for details on permitted opening times.

7. BAR MEALS indicates the times and days when bar food is available and the average price of a main course as supplied by the proprietor. Last orders may be approximately 30 minutes before the times stated.

8. RESTAURANT indicates the times and days when restaurant food is available. The average cost of a 3-course à la carte meal and a 3- or 4-course fixed-price menu are shown as supplied by the proprietor. Last orders may be approximately 30 minutes before the times stated.

9. BREWERY/COMPANY indicates the name of the Brewery the pub is tied to or the Company the pub is owned by. FREE HOUSE indicates that the pub is independently owned and run.

10. PRINCIPAL BEERS Up to five cask or hand-pulled beers served by each pub are listed. Many pubs have a much greater selection, with several guest beers each week.

11. FACILITIES This section includes information on children i.e. whether or not the pub welcomes children, has a children's licence etc, and gardens (e.g. outdoor eating, floral displays or barbecue area). We also indicate whether dogs are welcome.

12. NOTES

Includes information on parking and credit cards.
CREDIT CARDS NOT TAKEN
As so many establishments take one or more of the major credit cards only those taking no cards are indicated.

13. ROOMS

The number of bedrooms and the number of en suite bedrooms are listed. Accommodation prices indicate the minimum single and double room prices per night. Breakfast is generally included in the price but guests should check when making a reservation.

We cannot vouch for any accommodation that does not have Star or Diamond awards, proving that it has been inspected by the AA. Circumstances and prices may vary during the currency of the Guide so please check when booking.

Symbols

❀   Rosettes – The AA's food award. Explanation of ratings on page 10

★   Stars – The AA's ratings for accommodation. Explanation of ratings on page 9

◆   Diamonds – The AA's ratings for Bed and Breakfast accommodation. Explanation on page 9

🐟   In conjunction with the Seafish Industry Authority, we have introduced a symbol to indicate that a pub serves a minimum of four main course dishes with sea fish as the main ingredient.

♀   Indicates 6 or more wines available by the glass

NEW   Pubs appearing in the guide for the first time in 2003

Opening Hours

Pubs in England and Wales are permitted to open and sell alcohol from 11.00-23.00 on Mondays to Saturdays. On Sundays, licensing hours are 12.00-22.30. You must be 18 years or over to buy and consume alcohol in a bar. Children under 14 years of age are allowed into pubs holding a Children's Certificate. They must be accompanied by an adult and are restricted to those areas certified suitable for young children.

In Scotland pubs and clubs can be open for the sale of alcohol from 11.00-23.00 on Mondays to Saturdays, and 12.30-14.30 and 18.30-23.00 on Sundays. NB: The afternoon gap may be bridged with a regular extension. Occasional or regular extensions to permitted hours may allow premises to open late. For example, in Edinburgh, during the Festival many city centre pubs may remain open to 01.00.

Bank and Public Holidays in England, Scotland & Wales 2003

Remember that many places are very busy on public holidays - it is advisable to book ahead for food and accommodation

New Year's Day	1 January
Bank Holiday	2 January (SCOTLAND ONLY)
Good Friday	18 April
Easter Monday	21 April
May Day Bank Holiday	5 May
Spring Bank Holiday	26 May
Summer Bank Holiday	4 August (SCOTLAND)
Summer Bank Holiday	25 August (EXCLUDING SCOTLAND)
Christmas Day	25 December
Boxing Day	26 December

New Walks for 2003

Following our very popular addition of Pub Walks in last year's guide, we have included 44 brand new circular walks to try. Not too challenging – between 3 and 6 miles in length – perfect for building up a healthy appetite or working off a filling meal.

Walk directions and details are supplied by the pubs featured in these pages. There is a complete list of all the walks on page 648 in the index section at the back of the book.

AA Accommodation Ratings Explained – Stars and Diamonds

When we go away we want to be sure that our establishment offers comfortable well-equipped accommodation and pleasant surroundings. But how do we know in advance that where we stay is going to satisfy our requirements?

Where the following AA ratings appear beside the pub or hotel name in the guide, the establishment has been inspected under nationally recognised Star and Diamond Classification schemes. These ratings ensure that your accommodation meets the AA's highest standards of cleanliness with the emphasis on professionalism proper booking procedures and a prompt and efficient service.

★ AA Star Classification

If you stay in a one-star hotel you should expect a relatively informal yet competent style of service and an adequate range of facilities, including a television in the lounge or bedroom and a reasonable choice of hot and cold dishes. The majority of bedrooms are en suite with a bath or shower room always available.

A two-star hotel is run by smartly and professionally presented management and offers at least one restaurant or dining room for breakfast and dinner, while a three-star hotel includes direct dial telephones, a wide selection of drinks in the bar and last orders for dinner no earlier than 8pm.

A four-star hotel is characterised by uniformed, well-trained staff with additional services, a night porter and a serious approach to cuisine. Finally, and most luxurious of all, is the five-star hotel offering many extra facilities, attentive staff, top quality rooms and a full concierge service. A wide selection of drink, including cocktails, is available in the bar and the impressive menu reflects and complements the hotel's own style of cooking.

The AA's Top 200 Hotels in Britain and Ireland are identified by red stars. These stand out as the very best and range from large luxury destination hotels to snug country inns. To find further details see the AA's internet site at www.theAA.com

◆ AA Diamond Awards

The AA's Diamond Awards cover bed and breakfast establishments only, reflecting guest accommodation at five grades of quality, with one diamond indicating the simplest and five diamonds at the upper end of the scale. The criteria for eligibility is guest care and quality rather than the choice of extra facilities. Establishments are vetted by a team of qualified inspectors to ensure that the accommodation food and hospitality meets the AA's own exacting standards.

Guests should receive a prompt professional check in and check out, comfortable accommodation equipped to modern standards, regularly changed bedding and towels, a sufficient hot water supply at all times, good well-prepared meals and a full English or continental breakfast.

How can I get away without the hassle of finding a place to stay?

Booking a place to stay can be a time-consuming process. You choose a place you like, only to find it's fully booked. That means going back to the drawing board again. Why not ask us to find the place that best suits your needs? No fuss, no worries and no booking fee.

Whatever your preference, we have the place for you. From a rustic farm cottage to a smart city centre hotel - we have them all. Choose from around 8,000 quality rated hotels and B&Bs in Great Britain and Ireland.

Hotel Booking Service

0870 50 50 505
accommodation@aabookings.com
www.theAA.com

You may contact us using a Textphone on 0870 243 2456.
Information is available in large print, audio and Braille on request. Please call for details.

How the AA assesses restaurants for Rosette Awards

The AA's Rosette award scheme was the first nation-wide scheme for assessing the quality of food served by restaurants and hotels. The Rosette scheme is an award scheme not a classification scheme, and although there is necessarily an element of subjectivity when it comes to assessing taste, we aim for a consistent approach to our awards throughout the UK.

Our awards are made solely on the basis of a meal visit or visits by one or more of our hotel and restaurant inspectors, who have an unrivalled breadth and depth of experience in assessing quality. They award Rosettes annually on a rising scale of one to five.

So what makes a restaurant worthy of a Rosette Award?

For our inspectors the top and bottom line is the food. The taste of the food is what counts for them, and whether the dish successfully delivers to the diner what the menu promises. A restaurant is only as good as its worst meal. Although presentation and competent service should be appropriate to the style of the restaurant and the quality of the food, they cannot affect the Rosette assessment as such, either up or down.

The following summaries attempt to explain what our inspectors look for, but are intended only as guidelines. The AA is constantly reviewing its award criteria and competition usually results in an all-round improvement in standards, so it becomes increasingly difficult for restaurants to reach award level.

One Rosette

Excellent local restaurants serving food prepared with care, understanding and skill, using good quality ingredients. These restaurants stand out in their local area. The same expectations apply to hotel restaurants where guests should be able to eat in with confidence and a sense of anticipation. Around 50% of restaurants with Rosettes.

Two Rosettes

The best local restaurants, which aim for and achieve higher standards, better consistency and where a greater precision is apparent in the cooking. There will be obvious attention to the selection of quality ingredients. Around 40% of restaurants with Rosettes.

Three Rosettes

Outstanding restaurants that demand recognition well beyond their local area. The cooking will be underpinned by the selection and sympathetic treatment of the highest quality ingredients. Timing, seasoning and the judgement of flavour combinations will be consistently excellent, supported by other elements such as intelligent service and a well-chosen wine list. Around 150 restaurants (less than 10% of those with Rosettes).

Four Rosettes

Amongst the very best restaurants in the British Isles where the cooking demands national recognition. These restaurants will exhibit intense ambition, a passion for excellence, superb technical skills and remarkable consistency. They will combine appreciation of culinary traditions with a passionate desire for further exploration and improvement. Around a dozen restaurants with four Rosettes.

Five Rosettes

The finest restaurants in the British Isles, where the cooking stands comparison with the best in the world. These restaurants will have highly individual voices, exhibit breathtaking culinary skills and set the standards to which others aspire. Around half a dozen restaurants with five Rosettes.

Pubs with AA Rosette Awards

The pubs listed below are those that have been assessed by the AA's team of highly qualified inspectors and have been awarded one or more Rosettes (the scale runs from one to five) for the notable quality of their food. A full explanation of what the Rosette award means can be found on the previous page.

England

BERKSHIRE
The Red House MARSH BENHAM (1)
Rose & Crown WINKFIELD (1)
Royal Oak Hotel YATTENDON (2)

BUCKINGHAMSHIRE
Green Dragon HADDENHAM (2)
The Angel LONG CRENDON (1)
Chequers Inn WOOBURN COMMON (1)

CAMBRIDGESHIRE
The Anchor Inn ELY (1)
The Old Bridge Hotel HUNTINGDON (1)
Three Horseshoes MADINGLEY (2)
Bell Inn Hotel STILTON (2)

CORNWALL & ISLES OF SCILLY
Trengilly Wartha Inn CONSTANTINE (1)
Old Coastguard Inn MOUSEHOLE (1)
Rising Sun Hotel ST MAWES (1)
New Inn TRESCO (1)

CUMBRIA
Drunken Duck Inn AMBLESIDE (1)
Punch Bowl Inn CROSTHWAITE (1)
Queens Head Hotel TROUTBECK (1)

DERBYSHIRE
Rutland Arms Hotel BAKEWELL (1)

DEVON
Drewe Arms BROADHEMBURY (1)
Rock Inn HAYTOR VALE (1)
Arundell Arms LIFTON (3)
Dartmoor Inn LYDFORD (2)
The Jack In The Green Inn ROCKBEARE (1)
Sea Trout Inn STAVERTON (1)
The Durant Arms TOTNES (1)

DORSET
The Fox Inn CORSCOMBE (1)
The Acorn Inn EVERSHOT (1)

The Museum Arms FARNHAM (2)
The Fox Inn LOWER ANSTY (1)

CO DURHAM
Rose & Crown Hotel ROMALDKIRK (2)

ESSEX
White Hart GREAT YELDHAM (1)

GLOUCESTERSHIRE
The Village Pub BARNSLEY (2)
The Churchill Arms CHIPPING CAMDEN (1)
Noel Arms Hotel CHIPPING CAMPDEN (2)
The Crown Of Crucis CIRENCESTER (1)
The New Inn at Coln COLN ST-ALDWYNS (2)
Wild Duck Inn EWEN (1)
Egypt Mill Hotel NAILSWORTH (1)
The Eagle & Child STOW-ON-THE-WOLD (1)
Halfway Inn STROUD (1)
Trouble House Inn TETBURY (2)

GREATER MANCHESTER
The White Hart Inn OLDHAM (2)

HAMPSHIRE
Bell Inn BROOK (1)
Master Builders House Hotel BUCKLERS HARD (2)
Star Inn EAST TYTHERLEY (2)
The Red House Inn WHITCHURCH (1)
Wykeham Arms WINCHESTER (1)

HEREFORDSHIRE
The Stagg Inn KINGTON (2)
The Feathers Hotel LEDBURY (1)
The Lough Pool Inn SELLACK (2)
Three Crowns Inn ULLINGSWICK (2)

KENT
Dove Inn CANTERBURY (2)
Royal Wells Inn ROYAL TUNBRIDGE WELLS (2)

LANCASHIRE
Millstone Hotel BLACKBURN (1)
Mulberry Tree WRIGHTINGTON (2)

LEICESTERSHIRE
The Sun Inn MARKET HARBOROUGH (1)

LINCOLNSHIRE
Wig & Mitre LINCOLN (1)
The George of Stamford STAMFORD (1)

LONDON POSTAL DISTRICTS
The Bleeding Heart Tavern LONDON EC1 (1)
The Eagle LONDON EC1 (1)
The Fox Reformed LONDON N16 (1)
The Salt House LONDON NW8 (1)
The Fire Station LONDON SE1 (1)
Swag & Tails LONDON SW7 (1)
Anglesea Arms LONDON W6 (1)

NORFOLK
Hoste Arms Hotel BURNHAM MARKET (2)
The Kings Head COLTISHALL (1)
The Rose & Crown SNETTISHAM (1)
Lifeboat Inn THORNHAM (1)
Rococo at The Crown WELLS-NEXT-THE-SEA (2)

NORTHAMPTONSHIRE
The Falcon Hotel CASTLE ASHBY (1)
The Falcon FOTHERINGHAY (2)

NORTHUMBERLAND
Victoria Hotel BAMBURGH (1)
Blue Bell Hotel BELFORD (1)
Linden Tree LONGHORSLEY (2)

OXFORDSHIRE
The Blewbury Inn BLEWBURY (2)
The Goose BRITWELL SALOME (1)
The Inn For All Seasons BURFORD (1)
The Lamb Inn BURFORD (1)
The Sir Charles Napier CHINNOR (2)

The Crown Inn
CHURCH ENSTONE

Deddington Arms
DEDDINGTON

George Hotel
DORCHESTER-ON-THAMES

White Hart Hotel
DORCHESTER-ON-THAMES

The Lamb at Buckland
FARINGDON

The White Hart Hotel
NETTLEBED

The Crazy Bear
STADHAMPTON

Kings Head Inn & Restaurant
WOODSTOCK

RUTLAND
The Olive Branch CLIPSHAM

Barnsdale Lodge Hotel
OAKHAM

Ram Jam Inn STRETTON

SHROPSHIRE
Crown Inn
CLEOBURY MORTIMER

The Waterdine
LLANFAIR WATERDINE

The Roebuck Inn
LUDLOW

Hundred House Hotel
NORTON

SOMERSET
The Woolpack BECKINGTON

Crown Hotel EXFORD

Royal Oak Inn WITHYPOOL

STAFFORDSHIRE
The Three Horseshoes Inn
LEEK

The Moat House
STAFFORD

SUFFOLK
Cornwallis Country Hotel
BROME

Angel Hotel LAVENHAM

The Crown
SOUTHWOLD

St Peter's Hall ST PETER
SOUTH ELMHAM

The Angel Inn
STOKE-BY-NAYLAND

The Westleton Crown
WESTLETON

SURREY
Bryce's at The Old School House
OCKLEY

East SUSSEX
Mermaid Inn RYE

West SUSSEX
George & Dragon BURPHAM

White Horse Inn CHILGROVE

Lickfold Inn LICKFOLD

The Chequers Inn
ROWHOOK

WARWICKSHIRE
Howard Arms ILMINGTON

Fox & Goose Inn
STRATFORD-UPON-AVON

WEST MIDLANDS
The Malt Shovel at Barston
BARSTON

ISLE OF WIGHT
Seaview Hotel & Restaurant
SEAVIEW

WILTSHIRE
Angel Inn HINDON

The Lamb at Hindon
HINDON

The Horse & Groom
MALMESBURY

George & Dragon ROWDE

The Angel Inn WARMINSTER

The Pear Tree WHITLEY

WORCESTERSHIRE
Peacock Inn
TENBURY WELLS

NORTH YORKSHIRE
Crab and Lobster ASENBY

Three Hares Inn
BILBROUGH

The Buck Inn BUCKDEN

Red Lion Hotel BURNSALL

The Star Inn FEVERSHAM

The Boar's Head Hotel
HARROGATE

Feversham Arms Hotel
HELMSLEY

The Angel HETTON

The Worsley Arms Hotel
HOVINGHAM

General Tarleton Inn
KNARESBOROUGH

Three Tuns Inn
OSMOTHERLY

Fox & Hounds Country Inn
PICKERING

White Swan PICKERING

Yorke Arms RAMSGILL

Milburn Arms Hotel
ROSEDALE ABBEY

Wensleydale Heifer Inn
WEST WITTON

WEST YORKSHIRE
Shibden Mill Inn HALIFAX

Channel Islands

GUERNSEY
Hotel Hougue du Pommier
CATEL

Scotland

ARGYLL & BUTE
Loch Melfort Hotel
ARDUAINE

Cairnbaan Hotel
LOCHGILPHEAD

Creggans Inn STRACHUR

Victoria Hotel TARBERT

CITY OF GLASGOW
Ubiquitous Chip
GLASGOW

DUMFRIES & GALLOWAY
Creebridge House Hotel
NEWTON STEWART

Selkirk Arms Hotel
KIRKCUDBRIGHT

FIFE
The Seafood Bar & Restaurant
ST MONANS

HIGHLAND
Summer Isles Hotel
ACHILTIBUIE

Dundonnell Hotel
DUNDONNELL

Moorings Hotel
FORT WILLIAM

Onich Hotel ONICH

PERTH & KINROSS
Killiecrankie Hotel
KILLIECRANKIE

Lomond Country Inn
KINNESSWOOD

SCOTTISH BORDERS
Wheatsheaf SWINTON

Burts Hotel MELROSE

STIRLING
Monachyle Mhor
BALQUIDDER

WEST LOTHIAN
Champany Inn
LINLITHGOW

SCOTTISH ISLANDS
Harbour Inn
BOWMORE, ISLAY

Hotel Eilean Iarmain
ISLE ORNSAY, SKYE

Wales

ISLE OF ANGLESEY
Ye Olde Bulls Head Inn
BEAUMARIS

CARDIFF
Caesars Arms CREIGIAU

GWYNEDD
Penhelig Arms Hotel
ABERDYFI

MONMOUTHSHIRE
Walnut Tree Inn
ABERGAVENNY

The Bell at Skenfrith
SKENFRITH

The Newbidge Inn
TREDUNNOCK

POWYS
The Usk Inn BRECON

White Swan Inn BRECON

The Felin Fach Griffin
BRECON

The Talkhouse CAERSWS

Bear Hotel CRICKHOWELL

Gliffaes Country House Hotel
CRICKHOWELL

Nantyffin Cider Mill Inn
CRICKHOWELL

The Famous Old Black Lion
HAY-ON-WYE

The Bricklayers Arms
MONTGOMERY

Dragon Hotel MONTGOMERY

Seland Newydd PWLLGLOYW

WREXHAM
West Arms Hotel LLANARMON
DYFFRYN CEIRIOG

13

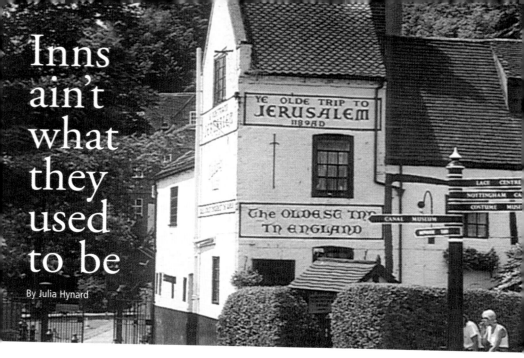

Inns ain't what they used to be

By Julia Hynard

From roses-over-the-door rural to red brick urban chic, however convincing your local pub looks in its current incarnation, have you ever thought about what it used to be? The comforting glow of the fireside bar may conceal a past more macabre or miraculous than you'd ever imagine.

Around 200 years ago the Cambridge Blue, in the city of Cambridge, was the local mortuary – a disturbing thought to some no doubt, but infinitely more restful than the grisly history associated with the Old Bank of England in London's Fleet Street. A pub since 1994, the former Law Courts branch of the bank lies between the site of Sweeney Todd's barbershop and the pie shop owned by his mistress Mrs Lovett. It was in the tunnels and vaults below the present building that the demon barber of Fleet Street's victims were butchered before being cooked and sold in pies to Mrs Lovett's unsuspecting customers.

Spirits in the bar

The Ring O' Bells in Thornton, birthplace of the Brontë sisters, high up in the Yorkshire Pennines, was originally a Wesleyan chapel, and rumour has it that the ghost of a former minister haunts the building still. Locals also talk about the old flint-built barn in the grounds of Oaks Bar, Brasserie & Lodge, a former coaching inn at Walberton, West Sussex, supposedly haunted by a Royal Mail coach driver who lost his head when he forgot to duck under the low entrance to the stables when bringing his horses in to rest. Doors mysteriously open and footsteps are heard in the dead of night.

Waters of recovery

The Dolphin Tavern in Penzance is over 600 years old, so has seen a thing or two over the centuries. Part harbour office and part courthouse in its time, with Judge Jeffreys presiding, it was here that Sir Walter Raleigh enjoyed his first smoke on English soil. The Seafood Bar at St Monans is another well-connected establishment, formerly a fisherman's dwelling dating back 400 years. The legendary King David's Well has pride of place in the conservatory restaurant. It is here that Scotland's King David, sore afflicted by an arrow wound, was miraculously healed by water from this very well.

Right & overleaf: The Highwayman Inn at Sourton in Devon can't be called a typical local. The eccentric exterior is a good indicator of the bizarre collection of furniture, bric-a-brac and paraphernalia inside. Part of the bar is made from an old sailing ship.

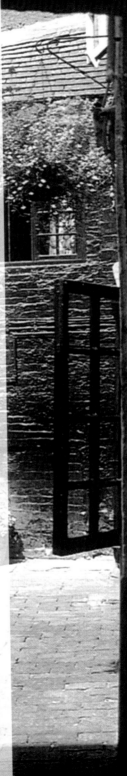

Left & this page: Ye Olde Trip to Jerusalem in Nottingham, is one of many that claims to be the oldest inn in England. Part of the bar is a cave that is part of Castle Rock above, while another part once served as a dungeon. Beware the eerie 'cursed galleon', a model ship hung on the wall. The last three people to clean it all died mysteriously!

Desperate measures

Another inn with ecclesiastical associations is the Star & Eagle at Goudhurst, once an ancient monastery, with relics of vaulted stonework still visible in parts of the building. It stands next to Goudhurst parish church, with one wing projecting into the churchyard, and a tunnel used to run from the cellars to a point underneath the church. The inn was the headquarters of an 18th-century party of desperados called the Goudhurst Gang. Around 1749 these smugglers and robbers terrorised the whole district until the village built up a force of militiamen to resist them. Eventually a battle was fought and the leader of the gang shot dead.

Run of the mill

There's many a more prosaic beginning to the public house of the 21st century. Long ago lots of farmhouses began by selling ale and over time became licensed premises in the way that we now understand them. But other former trade and industry usages are also commonplace – old mills for example, like Nantyffin Cider Mill, Crickhowell, the old mill incorporated into the pub's main dining room, and Hornsbury Mill, Eleighwater, near Chard, a 200-year-old corn mill set in five acres of landscaped water gardens.

Alias Smith

The clue is often in the name – there are more Blacksmiths Arms than you can shake a stick at – like those at Newton Aycliffe, Co Durham, a former blacksmith's shop built into a disused railway embankment, or at Lastingham, North Yorkshire, in the middle of a pretty village. Half of Seland Newydd, at Pwllgloyw, Powys, was the local smithy, and the large fireplace in the centre of the room is part of the old forge.

Riotous postings

There are bank conversions, as we've seen, and post offices turned pubs – like the Armstrong Arms, in the National Trust village of Stackpole in Pembrokeshire, a 17th-century stone-built property still with its original post box set in the wall. The Newfield Inn at Seathwaite, Cumbria, located in Wordsworth's favourite Duddon Valley, dates from early 1600s and has been a farm, inn, post office and hotel during that time. In 1904, navvies working on Seathwaite Tarn were involved in a riot, which began at the Newfield and one man lost his life.

Inset left: An old stable block, now part of the Crown Inn at Pishill.

Inset right: Hard to believe that this was once a Weslyan chapel. The Ring O'Bells at Thornton.

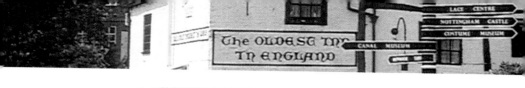

Left: The Barge Inn at Seend, Wiltshire. Once a wharf house serving the Kennet & Avon canal, this is now a barge-style pub, still popular with bargees.

Barging inn

The 17th-century Trout at Tadpole Bridge – by the Thames at Faringdon, Oxfordshire – began life as a humble coal storage house, while one of Chester's more unusual pubs, Old Harkers Arms, is a Victorian warehouse beside the canal. Taking up the canal theme, rather literally, is the Barge Inn at Seend in Wiltshire, converted from a wharf house and elaborately decorated, barge-style, with delicately painted Victorian flowers adorning the ceilings and upper walls. Taking it a stage further, one bar at the Shroppie Fly, a lockside pub by the Shropshire Union Canal at Audlem, Cheshire, is a converted barge.

Right: The Cholmondeley Arms, Cholmondeley. Once the village school, now supplying alcoholic beverages to a village that was officially dry from the 1890s up to 1988.

...Now for the good news

The Cholmondeley Arms, at Cholmondeley in Cheshire, was the village school until 1984. Sad as the locals were to lose the school, they were delighted to see the building re-open as a pub four years later, particularly as the village had been dry for 100 years. In the 1890s the Marquis of Cholmondeley, a passionate teetotaller, had closed all the licensed premises on his estate – in those days a considerable area of some 25,000 acres.

Ultimate conversions

Banks, post offices, mills, smithies – there's a logic to such conversions – convenient size and location for a kick off, but some conversions defy logic. Winning the title for most unlikely pub conversions in this brief survey are the Tram Depot in Cambridge – former tram stables converted in the late 1980s – and the Fire Station in Waterloo Road, London, close to Waterloo Station. The latter a remarkable transformation of an early Edwardian fire station with many of its original trappings left intact.

So next time you're out for a quiet drink, be careful of that pub – you don't know what it's been.

Left: The Highwayman Inn, Sourton, Devon.

Need to find the perfect place?

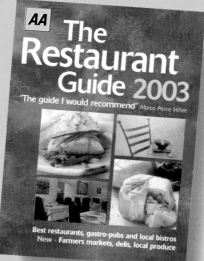

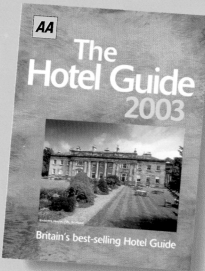

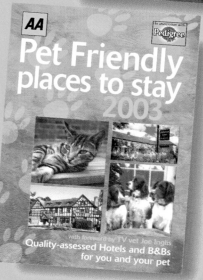

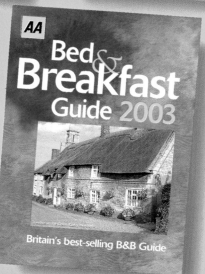

New editions on sale now!

Seafood
- the perfect choice

Whether you're looking for a light and exotic dish or a hearty but healthy meal – seafood is the perfect choice when eating out. You can have it poached, barbecued, fried, stir-fried, baked or steamed, but seafood also tastes great when lightly grilled with a squeeze of lemon.

With up to 100 different species of seafood available in the UK, seafood is a versatile and healthy option, with dishes to suit everyone's taste. From Cullen Skink to Tuna Nicoise or steamed mussels with garlic and white wine, you can find a wide range of succulent and tasty fish and shellfish meals in pubs around Great Britain. So go on, try something new next time you are in a pub and surprise yourself with how wonderful seafood can be.

Good Seafood Served Here

Keen to help you find all the best seafood pub meals, the Sea Fish Industry Authority (Seafish) works with the **AA Pub Guide** to help distinguish the very best pubs in the country. This guide provides you with details of around 800 British pubs that serve excellent seafood dishes. Finding them is easy; your nearest pub is marked with a fish symbol stating 'Good Seafood Served Here' and they have all been visited by AA inspectors to ensure that the menu features a wide range of seafood dishes.

Seafood is delicious and offers oceans of choice when eating out!

Sea Fish Industry Authority, 18 Logie Mill, Logie Green Road, Edinburgh EH7 4HG
Tel: 0131 558 3331 Fax: 0131 558 1442
E-mail: marketing@seafish.co.uk Website: www.seafish.co.uk

Serving the seafood industry

Trust me, I'm a Publican...

by Mary Barnett

'I think I'd like to run a pub' said my husband one day. 'Yes dear,' I replied, my mind on the realities of day to day living. But suddenly I found that was just what we were doing!! In common with many people, he had always entertained the idea of running a pub – he reckoned he'd done enough market research over several decades into what constituted a good pint of beer and knew what the customers were looking for. I, on the other hand, had an enjoyable job and was more than happy to be served a drink and some passable food in any pub without any further thought to the process.

Smiling through

So here we were with a country pub of our own – what was it really going to be like? The first thing I noticed is that we laughed a lot, with customers, with staff, with each other – and my feet hurt terribly – the former carried on but, luckily, the latter improved with the passage of time. It was terribly hard work, but it

was lively and varied and, of course, customers were coming in for a good time, so most people were cheerful. The first days were hectic with everything to learn, from the till, how to change a barrel and wash out pipes, prices of the products, and making sure everything in the kitchen was running smoothly – while smiling all the time and NEVER losing your temper.

Crash course in acting

They say pub life appeals to would-be actors, and it certainly calls upon all one's acting skills to present an always-happy face to the public when Rome is burning in the background. No matter what – power failures when meals have to be cooked by candlelight, or floods in the cellars, or daughters crashing cars or a crushing headache – all have be taken in one's stride and the customers must never know there is a problem.

No bets please

Life in a country pub is totally unpredictable – a large party of walkers might arrive and you'd think hooray, but then they would request four glasses of water – (free)tap will do – and fourteen straws and eat their own sandwiches outside, or a quiet group of four middle-aged women might embark on eating and drinking for England – who could tell. Days when you are sure you will be busy turn out to be quieter than the grave – and you've taken on extra staff because it's a bank holiday – or on a night that is always quiet and there's just you on the bar, one waitress and a skeleton kitchen staff, some large office suddenly decides to make an impromptu outing to a local pub – yours!!

It takes all sorts

One of the joys of running a pub is the variety of clients. In a good country pub you might find local gamekeepers and farmworkers mixing with city gents straight off their commuter trains, walkers with dogs, cyclists, escapees from the local residential home desperate for an outing, retired couples, locals guests at a smart wedding, indeed almost anyone. One day we had a small group of men who looked and sounded as if they had just come off the set of a London gangster movie!! Goodness knows how they found our pub, they looked completely bizarre in the rustic surroundings. Their language was unusually colourful but when my husband suggested we didn't like it (paling at the thought of the weaponry they no doubt had concealed about their persons), they meekly rose and left – as a parting gesture removing a picture from the gent's toilet. But little knowing that it had cost us only a couple of quid in a Sunday market – still it was a nice picture!

Town cousin, country cousin

As in many villages the nearby parish church was the frequent venue for smart weddings and a great boon to us, boosting our B&B trade. The timing of some weddings positively demanded that all the trendy young things out of London should descend on our pub and start on bottles of champagne or large G&T's before the wedding even started. They thought the prices were quaintly low and so drank copiously. It provided us endless amusement watching the girls in their designer frocks carefully avoiding contact with the dairy-farmworkers and their delightful, but over-powering, 'parfum du cow'.

Oops-a-daisy!

Unfortunately you cannot please all the people all of the time and, with the best will in the world, disasters happen. We watched horror-struck as a family of regulars started choosing dishes from the special Christmas menu – as luck would have it a large party of vegetarians had booked out the Christmas menu that night – so no conventional Christmas fare was available. Our regulars had also made a booking, but either failed to point out they wanted the Christmas menu or one of our staff had made a frightful bloomer. Either way it was a disaster! They were not to be placated in spite of our best efforts, apologies and offers of complimentary wine and another booking. We even volunteered to ring our local rival to see if they could accommodate the family. To our chagrin they could, so with much huffing and puffing our customers left – and I'm sorry to say never darkened our door again.

The piper calls the tune

Or the time when one of our staff took the bill to a customer who claimed that he had already paid. As his ticket was still on the board, I tried tactfully to enquire whether there had been some mistake – without more ado he immediately started ranting and accusing me of blackening his name. I backed straight off, thinking discretion was the better part of income, but it made no difference. His departure in high dudgeon was followed up by a lengthy letter – and our till was out at the end of the session by approximately the amount of his bill!!

Mein host

Standing behind the door arguing about which of you is going to spend time with Mr Boring (who has arrived promptly at opening time); or trying not to chat to your favourite clients too long; helping with a difficult crossword on a rainy Thursday or listening to the lonely divorcee who's missing his children, are all part of the challenge. When the pub is buzzing at New Year with happy people, or you introduce some jolly locals to the shy couple who have lived in the village for ten years and still know no one, and they all get on like a house on fire; or you watch strangers meet, become friends and you get an invitation to their wedding, or the schoolchildren who start work in your pub grow in confidence – then you feel truly rewarded. It was certainly the most fun job I ever had.

England

Pub of The Year for England

The Rose & Crown
Romaldkirk, Co Durham

ENGLAND

BEDFORDSHIRE

BEDFORD
Map 06 TL04

The Three Tuns
57 Main Rd, Biddenham MK40 4BD ☎ 01234 354847
A thatched village pub with a large garden, play area and
dovecote. It has a friendly atmosphere, and is popular for its
wide-ranging bar menu. Choose from sandwiches and snacks
or popular main courses like burgers, seafood platter, and
steaks with fries. There's also a range of home-made dishes
such as the daily curry, chicken casserole in a herb and
tomato sauce, and the enduring favourite, steak and kidney
pie. Children's meals are also available.
OPEN: 11–2.30 6–11 (Sun 12–3, 7–10.30) **BAR MEALS:** Lunch
served: all week 12–2 Dinner served: Mon–Sat 6–9 Av main course
£6.50 **RESTAURANT:** Lunch served: all week Dinner served:
Mon–Sat 12–2 6–9.30 **BREWERY/COMPANY:** Greene King
PRINCIPAL BEERS: Greene King IPA, Abbot Ale.
FACILITIES: Children welcome Garden: Food served outside Dogs
allowed **NOTES:** Parking 20 No credit cards

BROOM
Map 06 TL14

The Cock
23 High St SG18 9NA ☎ 01767 314411
Dir: Off B658 SW of Biggleswade
The 17th-century Cock is known as 'The Pub with no Bar',
unspoilt to this day with its intimate, quarry-tiled rooms with
latched doors and panelled walls. Real ales are served straight
from casks racked by the cellar steps. Giant Yorkshire
puddings with several home-made fillings and various steaks
of gammon and beef sirloin are fiercely traditional, finishing
(if not too full) with treacle sponge pudding. For Sunday
roasts require a large appetite (children's portions on offer).
Award winning garden with play area.
OPEN: 12–3 6–11 (Sun 12–4, 7–10.30) **BAR MEALS:** Lunch served:
all week Dinner served: Mon–Sat 12–2.30 7–9 Av main course £5
RESTAURANT: Lunch served: all week 12–2.30 Dinner served:
Mon–Sat 7–9.30 Av 3 course à la carte £14
BREWERY/COMPANY: Greene King **PRINCIPAL BEERS:** Greene
King Abbot Ale, IPA & Ruddles County. **FACILITIES:** Children
welcome Children's licence Garden: Food served outside Dogs
allowed **NOTES:** Parking 30

EATON BRAY
Map 06 SP92

The White Horse
Market Square LU6 2DG ☎ 01525 220231 📠 01525 222485
Dir: Take A5 N of Dunstable then A5050, 1m turn L & follow signs

Splendid 18th-century pub on the village green, with low
beams, brasses and a garden for summer drinking. It is a
family-run business that has developed a reputation over 15
years for good food. This is served in the separate restaurant
and throughout the pub. Dishes range from lunchtime snacks
to main meals of seared tuna loin with roasted vegetables,
tomato coulis and pesto, and braised lamb shank with root
vegetables and creamed potatoes.
OPEN: 11.30–3 6.30–11 (Sun 12–3, 7–11) **BAR MEALS:** Lunch
served: all week Dinner served: all week 12–2.15 7–9.30 Av main
course £8.75 **RESTAURANT:** Lunch served: all week Dinner served:
all week 12–2.15 7.30–9.30 Av 3 course à la carte £18
BREWERY/COMPANY: Punch Taverns
PRINCIPAL BEERS: Scottish Courage Courage Best, Greene King
IPA. **FACILITIES:** Children welcome Garden: Beer garden, patio,
food served outdoors **NOTES:** Parking 40

KEYSOE
Map 06 TL06

Pick of the Pubs

The Chequers
Pertenhall Rd, Brook End MK44 2HR
☎ 01234 708678 📠 01234 708678
e-mail: Chequers.keysoe@tresco.net
Dir: On B660 N of Bedford
In a quiet village, a 15th-century inn characterised by
original beams and an open stone fireplace. Take a ridge-
top walk for fine views of Graffham Water in anticipation
of a warm welcome, good real ale and some fine pub
food. Food served in the bar includes home-made fish
pie, chicken and ham pancakes and hearty steaks either
plain or sauced with peppered or mushroom cream
sauce. A play area in the garden, overlooked by a rear
terrace, is an added summer attraction.
OPEN: 11.30–2.30 6.30–11 **BAR MEALS:** Lunch served:
Wed–Mon Dinner served: Wed–Mon 12–2 7–9.45
BREWERY/COMPANY: Free House
PRINCIPAL BEERS: Hook Norton Best, Fuller's London Pride.
FACILITIES: Children welcome Garden: Patio and outdoor
eating **NOTES:** Parking 50

LINSLADE
Map 06 SP92

The Globe Inn
Globe Ln, Old Linslade LU7 7TA
☎ 01525 373338 📠 01525 850551
Dir: A5 S to Dunstable, follow signs to Leighton Buzzard (A4146)
Licensed in 1830 as an official beer shop, this charming
whitewashed pub stands by the Grand Union Canal, close to
the River Ouzel. It was originally frequented by navvies digging
the canal. Rumoured to be the pub where the nearby Great
Train Robbery was planned in 1963. Character bars and a good
range of ales enhance the interior. Expect seared scallops with
bacon and mango dressing, Thai cod and coconut curry and
shank of lamb Shrewsbury among the interesting main courses.
OPEN: 11–3 6–11 (Sun 12–3.30, 7–10.30 Summer 11–11)
BAR MEALS: Lunch served: all week Dinner served: all week
12–2.30 6.30–9.30 Av main course £5 **RESTAURANT:** Lunch served:
all week Dinner served: all week 12–3 6.30–9.30 Av 3 course £22
BREWERY/COMPANY: Old English Pub Co PLC
PRINCIPAL BEERS: Greene King Abbott Ale, Old Speckled Hen, IPA
& Ruddles County Ale, Wadworth 6X **FACILITIES:** Children welcome
Garden: Patio, BBQ, food served outdoors Dogs allowed (water)
NOTES: Parking 150

continued

MILTON BRYAN   Map 06 SP93

The Red Lion
MK17 9HS ☎ 01525 210044
Nestling in a pretty village close to Woburn Abbey, this
attractive, brick-built pub is festooned with colourful hanging
baskets in the summer. Relaxing, neatly maintained interior,
with beams, rugs on wooden floors, and well-kept ales. Wide-
ranging menu offering grills, casseroles and pies, along with
paella, whole plaice, and nursery puddings.
OPEN: 11–3 6–11 **BAR MEALS:** Lunch served: all week Dinner
served: all week 12–2.30 7–9.30 Av main course £8
RESTAURANT: Lunch served: all week Dinner served: all week
12–2.30 7–9.30 Av 3 course à la carte £17.50
BREWERY/COMPANY: Free House **PRINCIPAL BEERS:** Greene
King IPA & Old Speckled Hen, Ruddles County, Wadworth 6x, plus
guest beers. **FACILITIES:** Children welcome Garden:
NOTES: Parking 40

NORTHILL   Map 06 TL14

The Crown
2 Ickwell Rd SG18 9AA ☎ 01767 627337
New owners are settling in at this delightful 16th century pub,
in its three-acre garden between Northill church and the
village duck pond. This is a popular area with walkers, and the
Shuttleworth Collection of vintage aircraft is just down the
road. Freshly prepared meals include lasagne, cottage pie,
and salmon supreme, as well as main course salads and
chargrilled steaks.
OPEN: 11.30–3 6–11.30 (Summer all day Sat–Sun) Closed: 25 Dec
BAR MEALS: Lunch served: all week Dinner served: all week
12–2.30 7–9.30 Av main course £7.95 **RESTAURANT:** Lunch served:
all week Dinner served: all week 12–2.30 7–9.30 Av 3 course à la carte
£11 **BREWERY/COMPANY:** Greene King
PRINCIPAL BEERS: Greene King IPA, Abbot Ale, plus guest ales.
FACILITIES: Children welcome Garden: Food served outside Dogs
allowed **NOTES:** Parking 30

ODELL   Map 06 SP95

The Bell ♀
Horsefair Ln MK43 7BB ☎ 01234 720254
A Grade II listed 16th-century thatched pub. Within, it
comprises five small inter-linked eating areas all served from a
single long bar, while outside is a patio and aviary next to a
spacious garden that leads down to the River Ouse. It
maintains a high standard of fresh home-made dishes
complemented by fine real ales and a good selection of
wines. Specials posted on chalkboards will likely include
peppery braised steak, chicken in wine sauce, prawn and leek
pasta and home-baked pies.
OPEN: 11–2.30 6–11 (Sun 12–2.30, 7–10.30) **BAR MEALS:** Lunch
served: all week 12–2 Dinner served: Mon–Sat 7–9.30 Av main course
£7 **BREWERY/COMPANY:** Greene King
PRINCIPAL BEERS: Greene King IPA, Abbot Ale & Ruddles County
plus seasonal beers. **FACILITIES:** Children welcome Garden: Patio,
food served outside **NOTES:** Parking 14

RADWELL   Map 06 TL05

The Swan Inn ♀
Felmersham Rd MK43 7HS ☎ 01234 781351
Dir: Off A6 N of Bedford
Stone and thatched listed pub in a quiet country setting
overlooking the River Ouse. The large garden to the rear is
continued

ideal for families. Menu may include salmon fillet, turkey
Roquefort, seafood risotto, beef casserole, crayfish or red
snapper.
OPEN: 11–11 **BAR MEALS:** Dinner served: all week 12–10 Av main
course £6 **RESTAURANT:** Lunch served: Tue–Sun 12–2 Dinner
served: Tue–Sat 6.30–10.00 Av 3 course à la carte £25 Av 3 course
fixed price £12.95 **BREWERY/COMPANY:** Charles Wells
PRINCIPAL BEERS: Wells Eagle & Bombardier.
FACILITIES: Children welcome Garden: Food served outside
NOTES: Parking 25

RISLEY   Map 06 TL06

The Fox & Hounds
High St MK44 1DT ☎ 01234 708240
Busy pub with low beams, a new terrace and comfortable
lounge. Regularly changing guest beers.

SILSOE   Map 06 TL03

The Old George Hotel ♦♦
High St MK45 4EP ☎ 01525 860218 📠 01525 860218
The former ale house, in the heart of the village, for the
workers of the Wrest estate. Many original features survive to
lend atmosphere to the locals' bar, spacious dining room and
simply appointed bedrooms. Nearby places of interest include
Woburn Abbey and Wrest Park itself. Conventional bar meals
use breads, meat and vegetables from local sources, but
meals in the dining room are more adventurous: fruits de mer
platters, pheasant jardinière and beef Wellington. Jazz nights
and an organist every Sunday.
OPEN: all day **BAR MEALS:** Lunch served: all week 12–2.30
Dinner served: Mon–Sat 7–9.30 Av main course £6
RESTAURANT: Lunch served: all week Dinner served: Mon–Sat
12–2.30 7–9.30 Av 3 course à la carte £20 Av 5 course fixed price
£11.95 **BREWERY/COMPANY:** Greene King
PRINCIPAL BEERS: Greene King Old Speckled Hen & IPA.
FACILITIES: Children welcome Garden: Food served outdoors
Dogs allowed (by prior arrangement) **NOTES:** Parking 40
ROOMS: 7 bedrooms from s£35 d£48

STANBRIDGE   Map 06 SP92

Pick of the Pubs

The Five Bells ♀
Station Rd LU7 9JF ☎ 01525 210224 📠 01525 211164
e-mail: fivebells@traditionalfreehouses.com
Dir: M1 10m via Woburn A5 from Dunstable 5m on A5 onto A505
signposted Stambridge Leighton Buzzard 5m

This white painted 400-year-old village inn has been
delightfully renovated and revived to provide a stylish and
continued

England

STANBRIDGE continued

relaxing setting for a drink or a meal. The bar features lots of bare wood, including bare beams, comfortable armchairs and polished, rug strewn floors. The modern decor extends to the bright, airy dining room. Fresh produce is the key to the imaginative menus that draw discerning diners out from Milton Keynes, Aylesbury and Luton. Fish and game feature prominently. Good cask ales, decent coffee and well-chosen wines with six by the glass.
OPEN: 12–3 5–11 (open all day Sat-Sun) **BAR MEALS:** Lunch served: Mon-Sun 12–2.30 Dinner served: Mon-Sat 7–9 Av main course £9 **RESTAURANT:** Lunch served: all week Dinner served: all week 12–2.30 7–9 Av à la carte £23.50
BREWERY/COMPANY: Free House
PRINCIPAL BEERS: Interbrew Bass, Wadworth 6X, Hook Norton Best Bitter, Well's Bombardier. **FACILITIES:** Children welcome Garden: Food served outdoors **NOTES:** Parking 100

TURVEY   Map 06 SP95

The Three Cranes 🍴 ♀
High St Loop MK43 8EP ☎ 01234 881305 📠 01234 881305
Dir: Through Olney, R at rdbt onto A428, then R towards Bedford
Ivy-clad, stone-built inn dating from the 17th-century, in a pretty village setting next to the church. A typical menu offers oven baked salmon fillet, steak, mushroom and ale pie, medallions of chicken breast, lasagne, whole baked seabass, and a choice of steaks. Sandwiches, ploughmans, jacket potatoes, and salad bowls also available. Refer to blackboard for today's specials.
OPEN: 11–2.30 6–11 (Sun 12–3, 7–10.30) **BAR MEALS:** Lunch served: all week Dinner served: all week 12–2 6.30–9.30 Av main course £7.95 **RESTAURANT:** Lunch served: all week Dinner served: all week 12–2 6.30–9.30 Av 3 course à la carte £15
BREWERY/COMPANY: Greene King **PRINCIPAL BEERS:** Hook Norton Best, Fuller's London Pride, Scottish Courage Courage Best & Directors. **FACILITIES:** Children welcome Children's licence Garden: Food served outside **NOTES:** Parking 12 **ROOMS:** 3 bedrooms 3 en suite from s£35 d£45

BERKSHIRE

ALDERMASTON   Map 04 SU56

The Hinds Head ♀
Wasing Ln RG7 4LX ☎ 0118 9712194 📠 0118 9712194
e-mail: aldermaston@hindshead.freeserve.co.uk
Dir: A4 towards Newbury, then L on A340 towards Basingstoke, 2m to village
With its distinctive clock and belltower, this 17th-century inn still has the village lock-up which was last used in 1865. The old brewery (last used in 1921) was recently refurbished to provide a new restaurant. Typical dishes are pan-fried breast of chicken with a fricassee of chorizo sausage, smoked bacon and mushroom, grilled salmon on bubble and squeak glazed with a Béarnaise sauce, or shoulder of lamb on mustard mash with rosemary and garlic jus.
OPEN: 11–11 **BAR MEALS:** Lunch served: all week Dinner served: all week 12–2 6–9.30 Av main course £10 **RESTAURANT:** Lunch served: all week Dinner served: all week 12–2 6–9.30 Av 3 course à la carte £20 **BREWERY/COMPANY:** Gales
PRINCIPAL BEERS: Gales Best, HSB & Guest ale.

FACILITIES: Garden: Food served outside **NOTES:** Parking 50
ROOMS: 16 bedrooms 16 en suite from s£60 d£75

ALDWORTH   Map 04 SU57

Pick of the Pubs

The Bell Inn 🍴
RG8 9SE ☎ 01635 578272
Dir: Just off B4009 (Newbury-Streatley rd)
One of the few truly unspoiled country pubs where many first-time customers could be forgiven for thinking they have stepped back in time to a gentler age where there was no such thing as piped music, mobile phones and games machines. 'Thank God for the Bell,' they exclaim, 'a bit of old England!' Once inside, you'll see that the interior of this 14th-century, cruck-built inn is fascinating. Among its most striking features are a glass-panelled hatch and a shiny ochre ceiling. The landlady's great grandmother installed the triple beer engine in 1902 and the one-handed grandfather clock has been sitting in the tap room for 300 years. The Bell has been family-run for five generations and the present owners have no plans to change it. Plain, simple but appetising food includes hot crusty rolls with ample fillings. Ploughman's lunches and a range of hot and cold puddings are also available. Handy for the Ridgeway Trail which runs nearby.
OPEN: 11–3 6–11 Closed: Dec 25 **BAR MEALS:** Lunch served: Tue-Sun Dinner served: Tue-Sun 11–2.50 6–10.50 Av main course £5 **BREWERY/COMPANY:** Free House
PRINCIPAL BEERS: Arkell's Kingsdown, 3B, West Berkshire Old Tyler. **FACILITIES:** Children welcome Garden: Food served outside Dogs allowed **NOTES:** Parking 12 No credit cards

ASCOT   Map 04 SU96

The Thatched Tavern 🍴 ♀
Cheapside Rd SL5 7QG ☎ 01344 620874 📠 01344 623043
e-mail: thatchedtavern@theoldmonk.co.uk
Dir: Follow signs for Ascot Racecourse drive through Ascot 1st L (Cheapside) drive 1.5m and pub is on the L
Just a mile from the racecourse, a 500-year-old building of original beams, flagstone floors and very low ceilings. In summer the sheltered garden makes a fine spot to enjoy real ales and varied choice of food. In the same safe hands for over ten years, the kitchen produces a range of traditional English food and international dishes. In the bar are home-made soup or anchovy Caesar salad. A la carte there may be fragrant Thai chicken soup and Barbary duck breast with egg noodles and blackcurrant coulis.
OPEN: all day **BAR MEALS:** Lunch served: all week Dinner served: all week 12–3 7–10 Av main course £7.95 **RESTAURANT:** Lunch served: all week Dinner served: all week 12–3 7–10 Av 3 course à la carte £24 **PRINCIPAL BEERS:** Greene King Abbot Ale, Brakspears, Fuller's London Pride, Scottish Courage John Smith's.
FACILITIES: Garden: Food served outside, patio Dogs allowed (water) **NOTES:** Parking 30

> We endeavour to be as accurate as possible but changes to times and other information can occur after we have gone to press

continued

PUB WALK

Burchett's Green
The Crown

THE CROWN,
BURCHETT'S GREEN nr Maidenhead
SL6 6QZ
Tel: 01628 822844
Directions: From M4 take A404(M),
then 3rd exit

Overlooking the village green, in a
large rose garden. Whitewashed walls
and low-beamed ceilings create a
welcoming atmosphere. Do not expect
to pop in for a quick snack, as
everything is cooked to order.
Reservations needed at weekends.
Open: 12–3 6–11
Bar Meals: 12–2.30 7–9.30
Children welcome. Garden and
parking available.

From the Crown this pretty walk crosses the parkland of Hall Place, now the Berkshire College of Agriculture, before reaching the delightful, tree-clad slopes of Ashley Hill.

From the Crown cross over at the junction into Hall Place Lane. When you reach the entrance to Lane End House, follow the footpath to the left of it. Make for a kissing gate and then take the path across the field towards an avenue of limes. Swing left at the avenue and then bear right as the drive forks in front of Hall Place. Pass the vet's surgery before veering half left at the waymark. After the barns and animal enclosures, follow the track down between trees and bushes to a crossroads. Keep left at the fork just beyond it and take the clear track towards High Wood. Make for a gate and cut through the wood to the far side where there are impressive views across the Thames Valley. Swing left and walk along the woodland edge to two gates and a waymark. Bear left here, cutting back through the wood to a gate. Head south across the fields, cross two farm tracks and go through a kissing gate into a field. Take the gate in the far boundary and follow the path through light woodland and up steps to the next gate. Continue ahead in the next field, passing a house with a conservatory before reaching a stile. Turn right and follow the lane. Go straight ahead when it bends right and pass the turning to the Dewdrop Inn. Follow the path ahead at the 'no through road' sign, turn left at a waymarked junction, cross a track and veer left at the fork. Swing left at the house ahead in the trees and follow the drive down through the wood. As it bends right, go forward on a path to the road. Keep right and walk along to a path on the left. Cross two stiles and follow a fence and stream to a track by an oak tree. Go straight on to two stiles by the houses of Burchetts Green. Turn left at the road and return to the Crown.

Distance: 4 miles (6.4km)
Map: OS Landranger 175
Terrain: Parkland and woodland
Paths: Roads, field paths,
woodland tracks
Gradient: Some climbing

Walk submitted and checked
by Nick Channer

England

ASHMORE GREEN
Map 04 SU56

The Sun in the Wood
Stoney Ln RG18 9HF ☎ 01635 42377 📠 01635 528392
e-mail: suninthewood@aol.com
Dir: A34 Robin Hood rndbt, L to Shaw, at mini rndbt R then 7th L into
Stoney Lane, 1.5m, pub on L
Standing in the shadow of tall trees, this popular, extensively
refurbished pub occupies a delightful woodland setting and
yet is only a stone's throw from the centre of Newbury. Stone
floors, plenty of wood panelling and various prints by Renoir
and Monet add to the appeal. Try the braised lambs' liver and
sausages, the salmon fishcakes or perhaps pork in an orange
and fresh basil sauce. Extensive range of starters and a good
choice of Sunday lunch dishes.
OPEN: 12-2.30 6-11 **BAR MEALS:** Lunch served: Tue-Sun 12-2
Dinner served: Tue-Sat 6.30-9.30 Av main course £11
RESTAURANT: Lunch served: Tue-Sun 12-2 Dinner served: Tue-Sat
6.30-9.30 **BREWERY/COMPANY:** Wadworth
PRINCIPAL BEERS: Wadworth 6X & Henrys IPA, Badger Tanglefoot.
FACILITIES: Children welcome Garden: Lovely woodland garden,
food served outside **NOTES:** Parking 60

BINFIELD
Map 04 SU87

Stag & Hounds
Forest Rd RH12 4HA ☎ 01344 483553
Historic old pub, with a collection of sporting prints and a
restaurant. Low beams, log fires, front terrace and a legend
about Elizabeth I and some Morris dancers.

BOXFORD
Map 04 SU47

The Bell at Boxford
Lambourn Rd RG20 8DD ☎ 01488 608721 📠 01488 608749
e-mail: bell.boxford@lycos.co.uk
Dir: A338 toward Wantage, R onto B4000, take 3rd L to Boxford

A Mock Tudor country pub at the heart of the glorious
Lambourn Valley, renowned for its picturesque downland
scenery. The 22-mile Lambourn Valley Way runs through the
village. Relax in the cosy bar with its choice of real ales and
peruse the impressive wine list (champagne by the glass!)
and the bistro-style blackboard menu. Dishes include lemon
chicken risotto, steak fillet à la Bell, lobster, salmon, baked
haddock or Thai fish curry. Heated terraces for alfresco
dining.
OPEN: 11-3 6-11 (Sat 6.30-11, Sun 7-10.30) **BAR MEALS:** Lunch
served: all week Dinner served: all week 12-2 7-10 Av main course £7
RESTAURANT: Lunch served: all week Dinner served: all week 12-2
7-10 Av 3 course à la carte £21 **BREWERY/COMPANY:** Free House
PRINCIPAL BEERS: Morrells Oxford, Badger Tanglefoot, Badger
Best, Scottish Courage Courage Best. **FACILITIES:** Children welcome

Garden: Cosy, heated in evenings, food served outside Dogs allowed
NOTES: Parking 36 **ROOMS:** 10 bedrooms 10 en suite from s£40
d£50

BURCHETT'S GREEN
Map 04 SU88

Pick of the Pubs

The Crown
SL6 6QZ ☎ 01628 822844
Dir: From M4 take A404(M), then 3rd exit
In the middle of a small hamlet and overlooking the
village green, this local stands amid a large rose garden,
bedecked with handsome garden furniture. Nearby Ashley
Hill Woods are a haven for naturalists and walkers, who
often stop by for a pint of real ale. Inside, the
whitewashed walls and low-beamed ceilings create a
welcoming atmosphere, particularly in the intimate
dining-room, whose tables are decorated with vases and
fresh flowers. Do not expect to pop in for a quick snack,
as everything is cooked to order from the freshest
available ingredients. Tempting main dishes on a short,
daily menu may be tuna steak on a nest of leaves, fillet
steak with Roquefort sauce and maybe lobster thermidor
with saffron rissotto. Reservations are advised from Friday
to Sunday to be sure of a table.
OPEN: 12-3 6-11 **BAR MEALS:** Lunch served: all week Dinner
served: all week 12-2.30 7-9.30 Av main course £10
RESTAURANT: Lunch served: all week Dinner served: all week
12-2.30 7-10 Av 3 course à la carte £20
BREWERY/COMPANY: Greene King
PRINCIPAL BEERS: Greene King IPA, Ruddles Best, Wadworth
6X. **FACILITIES:** Children welcome Garden: Food served
outside **NOTES:** Parking 30

See Pub Walk on page 27

CHADDLEWORTH
Map 04 SU47

The Ibex
Main St RG20 7ER ☎ 01488 638311
Dir: A338 towards Wantage, through Great Shefford then R, then 2nd L,
pub is on R in village
Grade II listed building which was originally a bakery and
then an off-licence before finally becoming a pub. Frequented
by the horse-racing fraternity, with many famous stables
close by.

CHIEVELEY
Map 04 SU47

The Blue Boar Inn
North Heath, Wantage Rd RG20 8UE
☎ 01635 248236 📠 01635 248506
Dir: Off B4494 N of Newbury
Oliver Cromwell stayed here before the Battle of Newbury in
1644. His troops left a statue of a wild boar, from which the
inn takes its name. It is an attractive thatched property
offering the likes of poached salmon, char grilled chicken,
local sausages, or lamb and mint pie.
OPEN: 11-3 6-11 (Sun 12-3, 7-10.30) Closed: 25, 26 Dec
BAR MEALS: Lunch served: all week Dinner served: all week 12-1.45
7-9.30 Av main course £7 **BREWERY/COMPANY:** Free House
PRINCIPAL BEERS: Wadworth 6X, Fullers London Pride,
Boddingtons. **FACILITIES:** Children welcome Garden: beer garden,
patio, outdear eating **NOTES:** Parking 60 **ROOMS:** 17 bedrooms 17
en suite from s£57 d£69

continued

COOKHAM **Map 04 SU88**

Pick of the Pubs

Bel and The Dragon
High St SL6 9SQ ☎ 01628 521263 📄 01628 851008
One of the oldest licensed houses in England, built of
wattle and daub. The same menu is offered throughout,
and ranges from sandwiches (at lunchtime) to a full à la
carte selection, with dishes such as roast lamb shank and
chargrilled salmon steak.
OPEN: 11.30-11 (Sun 12-10.30) **BAR MEALS:** Lunch served:
all week Dinner served: all week 12-2.30 7-10 Av main course £8
RESTAURANT: Lunch served: all week Dinner served: all week
12-2.30 7-10 **BREWERY/COMPANY:** Free House
PRINCIPAL BEERS: Brakspear, Marstons Pedigree
FACILITIES: Children welcome Dogs allowed

COOKHAM DEAN **Map 04 SU88**

Pick of the Pubs

Chequers Inn Brasserie 🍴 🍷
Dean Ln SL6 9BQ ☎ 01628 481232 📄 01628 850124
e-mail: info@chequers-inn.com
*Dir: From A4094 in Crookham High St take R fork after r'way bridge
into Dean Lane. Pub in 1m*
You'll find the historic Chequers Inn Brasserie at the heart
of this charming village where Kenneth Grahame, author
of 'The Wind in the Willows', spent his childhood. Striking
Victorian and Edwardian villas around the green set the
tone, whilst the surrounding wooded hills and dales have
earned Cookham Dean the description of a miniature
Switzerland. No wonder Grahame returned to live here
with his wife and family. Today, the Chequers with its oak
beams and open fire is a popular and well-established
meeting point; it offers carefully chosen wines and ales, as
well as a daily-changing blackboard menu. Try pan-fried
pheasant with apples, chestnuts and cider sauce; seared
tuna with roast peppers and avocado salsa; or deep-fried
squid and sweet chilli sauce. Other favourites include
shank of lamb in thyme and port with mashed potatoes,
and roast salmon served with new potatoes, chorizo,
roquette and balsamic jus.
OPEN: 11-3 5.30-11 Closed: Dec 25 **BAR MEALS:** Lunch
served: all week Dinner served: all week 12-2.30 6-9.30 Av main
course £10.95 **BREWERY/COMPANY:** Free House
PRINCIPAL BEERS: Wadworth 6X, Greene King Morland
Original. **FACILITIES:** Children welcome Children's licence
Garden: Patio, food served outside Dogs allowed
NOTES: Parking 50

Pick of the Pubs

Uncle Tom's Cabin 🍴
Hills Ln SL6 9NT ☎ 01628 483339
*Dir: A4 towards Maidenhead, over bridge, R on to Cookham High St,
through town, over r'way, past Whyteladies Ln, pub on L*
Locals' pub in the cosy cottage style, set in beautiful
Berkshire countryside within walking distance of the
Thames. It is surrounded by lovely walks in all directions -
one of the most visited parts of the Thames Valley.
Though the pub was renovated in the late 1980s, it retains
its 17th-century charm and a relaxing atmosphere

throughout a series of little rooms. There is also a lovely
big garden at the rear, set on a hill with shade provided
by mature fruit trees. In many ways it is everyone's idea
of the perfect country pub. The well-kept beers include
Benskins and Fullers, along with Addlestone cider. A good
range of dishes is prepared from fresh ingredients. Fishy
options might be fresh cod, seafood crêpes, and cod and
prawn Creole. Other favourite main courses range
through burgers, beef and ale pie, lamb shank, ribs and
Cajun chicken.

OPEN: 11-3 5.30-11 **BAR MEALS:** Lunch served: all week
Dinner served: all week 12-2 7.30-10 Av main course £6.50
RESTAURANT: Lunch served: all week Dinner served: all week
12-2 7.30-10 **BREWERY/COMPANY:** Carlsberg Tetley
PRINCIPAL BEERS: Benskins, Fuller's London Pride plus guest
ales. **FACILITIES:** Children welcome Garden: Food served
outside Dogs allowed (water, biscuits) **NOTES:** Parking 28

CRAZIES HILL **Map 04 SU78**

Pick of the Pubs

The Horns 🍷
RG10 8LY ☎ 0118 9401416 📄 0118 9404849
Dir: Off A321 NE of Wargrave
Set beside a narrow lane in a small hamlet, this
whitewashed timbered cottage started life in Tudor times
as a hunting lodge to which a barn (now the dining area)
was added some 200 years ago. Sympathetically
refurbished by Brakspear's Brewery, it remains a
delightful country pub that has three interconnecting
rooms complete with old pine tables, exposed beams,
open fires, rugby memorabilia, and a peaceful
atmosphere free of music and electronic games. Dishes
listed on the daily-changing blackboard menus may
include roast guinea fowl with smoked bacon and herb
gravy, whole rainbow trout with lemon and coriander
butter and roasted almonds, chargrilled tuna steak,
mushroom and spinach puff parcels, or rack of limb with
garlic and mint gravy. Fresh filled baguettes and home-
made desserts are also available.
OPEN: 11.30-2.30 6-11 (Sun 12-6, 7-10.30) Closed: 25-26 Dec
BAR MEALS: Lunch served: all week 12-2 Dinner served:
Mon-Sat 7-9.30 Av main course £8 **RESTAURANT:** Lunch
served: all week 12-2 Dinner served: Mon-Sat 7-9.30 Av 3 course
à la carte £18.20 **BREWERY/COMPANY:** Brakspear
PRINCIPAL BEERS: Brakspear Bitter. **FACILITIES:** Children
welcome Garden: Beer garden, outdoor eating Dogs allowed
(garden only, please ask staff) **NOTES:** Parking 45

continued

England

CURRIDGE
Map 04 SU47

The Bunk Traditional Inn ⚘ 🍸
RG18 9DS ☎ 01635 200400 📄 01635 200336
Dir: M4 J13/A34 N towards Oxford then 1st slip Rd then R for 1m. R at T-jnct, 1st R signposted Curridge
Smart and stylish inn dating back about 150 years, with beams, brasses and a log fire in the attractive bar. Informal, friendly atmosphere, pleasant surroundings and good quality menu. Traditional, home-cooked dishes include toad in the hole and cod and chips while Thai fishcakes, crispy duck leg and an excellent choice of fish dishes feature among the specials. Plenty of peaceful woodland walks on the doorstep.
OPEN: 11–11 Closed: 26 Dec, 1 Jan **BAR MEALS:** Lunch served: all week Dinner served: all week 12-2.30 7–10 Av main course £10 **RESTAURANT:** 12-2.30 7-10 **BREWERY/COMPANY:** Free House **PRINCIPAL BEERS:** Arkells 3B, Wadworth 6X, Fuller's London Pride. **FACILITIES:** Children welcome Garden: Patio, Lawn, food served outside Dogs allowed **NOTES:** Parking 38

EAST ILSLEY
Map 04 SU48

The Crown & Horns 🍸 NEW
RG20 7LH ☎ 01635 281205 & 281545 📄 01635 281660
This extended 18th-century pub, just five miles from the M4, might be familiar to you as the Dog & Gun in the BBC TV serial Trainer. The collection of around 160 whiskies from all over the world is an attraction, as is the comprehensive menu, ranging through sandwiches, speciality pies and a vegetarian selection. A house speciality is chicken breast filled with black pudding and finished with sherry cream sauce.
BAR MEALS: Lunch served: all week Dinner served: all week 11.45-2.30 6–10 Av main course £6 **RESTAURANT:** Lunch served: all week Dinner served: all week 11.45-2.30 6-10 Av 3 course à la carte £20 **BREWERY/COMPANY:** Free House **FACILITIES:** Children welcome Garden: Food served outside, patio area Dogs allowed (not overnight in bedrooms) **NOTES:** Parking 35 **ROOMS:** from s£50 d£60

The Swan
RG20 7LF ☎ 01635 281238 📄 01635 281791
e-mail: theswan@east-isley.demon.co.uk
Dir: 5m N of J13 on A34. 18m S of Oxford on A34
16th-century coaching inn nestling in a peaceful downland village close to the long-distance Ridgeway national trail. Enclosed terraced gardens ideal for a drink or lunch. Traditional pub fare includes a selection of pies and cod and chips.
OPEN: 11-2.30 (Sun 12-3, 7-10.30) 6-11 Closed: Dec 25 **BAR MEALS:** Lunch served: all week Dinner served: all week 12-2 6-10 Av main course £8 **BREWERY/COMPANY:** Greene King **PRINCIPAL BEERS:** Greene King, Abbot Ale & IPA. **FACILITIES:** Children welcome Garden: Beer garden with seating, outdoor eating Dogs allowed **NOTES:** Parking 40 **ROOMS:** 5 bedrooms 5 en suite from s£50 d£60

FRILSHAM
Map 04 SU57

Pick of the Pubs

The Pot Kiln
RG18 0XX ☎ 01635 201366
Dir: A34 towards Oxford, 1st L to Chieveley, then 1st R to Hermitage. 2nd L onto B4009, 2nd R to Yattendon, R on sharp L bend, on for 1m
With relaxing views across open fields to woodland from its peaceful garden, this timeless 400-year-old brick pub is

justifiably popular among walkers, cyclists and real ale enthusiasts. Takes its name from being on the site of old brick kilns and the outbuildings now house the West Berkshire Brewery who brew the Brick Kiln Bitter exclusively for the pub. Delightfully old fashioned interior with lobby bar, simple wooden furnishings and warming open fires. Spotlessly kept by long-serving landlords, who also offer well kept Morlands Original and Arkell's 3B on tap. In keeping, food is simple and hearty, including filled rolls, salmon and broccoli fishcakes with fresh vegetables, liver and bacon casserole, and vegetable chilli.

OPEN: 12-3 6.30-11 (Tues 6.30-11 only) Closed: 25 Dec **BAR MEALS:** Lunch served: Wed-Mon Dinner served: Wed-Mon 12-2 7-9.30 Av main course £7 **BREWERY/COMPANY:** Free House **PRINCIPAL BEERS:** West Berkshire Brick Kiln, Morlands Original, Arkells 3B, West Berkshire Resolution. **FACILITIES:** Children welcome Garden: beer garden, outdoor eating, patio. Dogs allowed **NOTES:** Parking 30 No credit cards

GREAT SHEFFORD
Map 04 SU37

The Swan Inn ⚘ 🍸
Newbury Rd RG17 7DS ☎ 01488 648271 📄 01488 648175
e-mail: theswan@greatshefford.fslife.co.uk
Dir: 1.5m north of M4 J14 on A338

Early 19th-century coaching inn situated in the village of Great Shefford in the Lambourn Valley, with river views from both the restaurant and patio. The interior is traditional in style with log-burning fires and a handwritten menu displayed on the blackboard. Favourite dishes include lamb shoulder, spicy cod, tuna penne and chicken Chicago. The Swan is ideal for walkers, with its own circular walk beginning and ending at the pub.
OPEN: 11-3 6-11 (Sun 12-3, 7-10.30) **BAR MEALS:** Lunch served: all week Dinner served: all week 12-2.30 6.30-9.15 Av main course £9.50 **RESTAURANT:** Lunch served: all week Dinner served: all

continued

continued

week 12–2.30 6.30–9.15 **BREWERY/COMPANY:** Eldridge Pope
PRINCIPAL BEERS: Scottish Courage Courage Best, Wadworth 6X
plus Guest Ales. **FACILITIES:** Children welcome Garden: Patio,
food served outside **NOTES:** Parking 25

HARE HATCH   Map 04 SU87

The Queen Victoria ♀
The Holt RG10 9TA ☎ 0118 9402477
Dir: On A4 between Reading & Maidenhead
Situated between Reading and Maidenhead, and dating back
over 300 years, this country-cottage-style inn offers excellent
draught beers, good quality pub food and an interesting
choice of wines. The blackboard menu changes daily, but may
include Cajun chicken butterfly supreme, smoked fish medley,
potato shells with creamed Stilton and bacon and hot nutty
Brie with walnuts.
OPEN: 11–3 5.30–11 (Sun 12–10.30) Closed: Dec 25–26
BAR MEALS: Lunch served: all week Dinner served: all week
12–2.30 6.30–10.30 Av main course £6
BREWERY/COMPANY: Brakspear **PRINCIPAL BEERS:** Brakspear
Bitter, Old, Special & Mild. **FACILITIES:** Children welcome
NOTES: Parking 20

HUNGERFORD   Map 04 SU36

Pick of the Pubs

The Swan Inn ♦♦♦♦ 🏡
Craven Rd, Lower Green, Inkpen RG17 9DX
☎ 01488 668326 🖷 01488 668306
e-mail: enquiries@theswaninn-organics.co.uk
See Pick of the Pubs on page 32

HURLEY   Map 04 SU88

The Rising Sun ♀
High St SL6 5LT ☎ 01628 824274
Dir: Off the A4130 from Maidenhead
Traditional style pub and restaurant with black beams and a
real log fire. Fresh fish and chips on Friday.

HURST   Map 04 SU77

The Green Man 🏡 ♀ NEW
Hinton Rd RG10 0BP ☎ 0118 934 2599 🖷 0118 934 2939
e-mail: info@thegreenman.uk.com
Dir: Between Twyford and Wokingham
The success of this admirable pub revolves around the
dedicated father and son partnership. Low ceilings, open fires
and a host of knick-knacks are on display throughout. The
beers are good, served in surroundings that encourage
conversation as opposed to piped music and fruit machines.
Chalk boards always feature fresh fish such as sea bass, tuna
and monkfish. Alternative choices may include chicken breast
chargrilled with bacon and mushrooms with parmesan cream
sauce and pork fillet served on leek mash.
OPEN: 11–3 5.30–11 (Sun 12–3, 7–10.30) **BAR MEALS:** Lunch
served: all week Dinner served: all week 12–2.30 6.30–9.30 Av main
course £9 **RESTAURANT:** Lunch served: all week Dinner served: all
week 12–2.30 6.30–9.30 **BREWERY/COMPANY:** Brakspear
PRINCIPAL BEERS: Brakspear Bitter, Special, & Seasonal Ales.
FACILITIES: Garden: Large well kept, overlooking fields
NOTES: Parking 40

KINTBURY   Map 04 SU36

Pick of the Pubs

The Dundas Arms
53 Station Rd RG17 9UT ☎ 01488 658263 🖷 01488 658568
e-mail: info@dundasarms.co.uk
*Dir: M4 J13 take A34 to Newbury, then A4 to Hungerford, L to
Kintbury. Pub 1m next to canal and by railway station*

Just outside the front door of this historic inn runs the 87-
mile Kennet & Avon Canal which, having been derelict for
about 40 years, is now one of the south's most popular
waterways – ideal for walking, fishing and studying
wildlife. The pub is on one of the loveliest stretches of the
canal so take a stroll along the towpath before heading
for the pub, named after the first chairman of the canal
company. Both a well-established village local and a
country pub/restaurant of distinction, the Dundas Arms
offers an interesting selection of blackboard specials and
an extensive wine list. Dishes on offer might include duck
confit on home-made baked beans, honey roast ham
hock with grain mustard sauce, spinach and red pepper
lasagne, Thai fish cakes with chilli sauce, Andalucian spicy
stew with baked eggs, grilled rib-eye steak with
mushrooms and chips, or Cumberland sausages with
mash and onion gravy. There are five bedrooms if you
fancy prolonging your visit.
OPEN: 11–2.30 6–11 Closed: 25 & 31Dec **BAR MEALS:** Lunch
served: Mon-Sat 12–2 Dinner served: Tue-Sat 7–9 Av main course
£9.50 **RESTAURANT:** Dinner served: Tue-Sat 7–9 Av 3 course à
la carte £25 **BREWERY/COMPANY:** Free House
PRINCIPAL BEERS: Greene King IPA & Ruddles Best, Ringwood
Best, Butts Barbus Barbus, Shepherd Neame Spitfire.
FACILITIES: Children welcome Garden: Riverside patio, food
served outside **NOTES:** Parking 70 **ROOMS:** 5 bedrooms 5 en
suite from s£65 d£75

Dominoes
Dominoes came to Britain from the Continent at
the end of the 18th century, perhaps brought
back by British soldiers serving in the Napoleonic
Wars. French prisoners-of-war made sets of
dominoes, not only for their own amusement but
to sell to the British. Many different varieties are
played in pubs besides the standard block game,
and some pubs belong to dominoe leagues.

OPEN: 12–3 7–11
(All day wknds in summer)
BAR MEALS: L served all week.
D served all week. 12–2.30 7–9.30
Av main course £7.50
RESTAURANT: L served Wed–Sun.
D served Wed–Sat. 12–2.30 7–9.30
Av cost 3 course £25
BREWERY/COMPANY: FREE
HOUSE
PRINCIPAL BEERS: Butts
Traditional, Hook Norton Mild &
Bitter, Caledonian Golden Promise
FACILITIES: Children welcome.
Garden: Beer garden, patio, food
served outdoors
NOTES: Parking 50
ROOMS: 10 en suite Double room
from £70 Single room from £40.

The Swan Inn

Close to the historic Wayfarers Way, this heavily-beamed 17th-century inn stands mid-way between the Berkshire towns of Newbury and Hungerford. Combe Gibbet and Walbury Hill, the highest points in this corner of the south, are a short step away in a wonderful area for exploring on foot.

◆◆◆◆
Craven Road, Lower Green, Inkpen
RG17 9DX
☎ 01488 668326 ▤ 01488 668306
e-mail:
enquiries@theswaninn-organics.co.uk
Dir: S down Hungerford High St, L to common, R on common, pub 3m.

The striking frontage of terracing with its picnic tables and summer umbrellas is a natural draw, nor will visitors be disappointed by the much-extended interior that stays true to the pub's real character. Within are to be found exposed original beams, open fires and old photographic prints of the village and surrounding countryside that lend a lived-in homely feel and a cosy, welcoming atmosphere. Of special interest are unusual stained glass panels on several interior doors that are well worth a look while sampling a pint

of Hook Norton or Butts ale. Owned by local organic beef farmers, it comes as no surprise that organically produced supplies take pride of place on both bar and restaurant menus including beef from their own farm. In the farm shop attached to the Swan their renowned home-cured bacon, gammons and a range of country sausages make a visit doubly worthwhile. Typical of bar meals are home-made steak and kidney pies and puddings, organic beefburgers, sausage and mash, and boiled beef and carrots. Fishcakes, cod in beer batter and vegetarian options exhibit similar attention to detail. The restaurant's 4-course menu highlights fillet of turbot, Mozzarella, tomatoes and olives in puff pastry and beef tournedos Rossini, followed by classic crème brûlée.

KNOWL HILL
Map 04 SU87

Pick of the Pubs

Bird In Hand Country Inn
Bath Rd RG10 9UP
☎ 01628 826622 & 822781 ▤ 01628 826748
Dir: On A4, 5 Miles W of Maidenhead, 7 Miles E of Reading

A fascinating old inn that has remained in the same family for three generations. Dating back to the 14th century, its features include a main bar whose oak panelling came from a Scottish castle and the adjoining farriers, now The Forge Bar, where George III stopped in the late 1700s. He granted a royal charter to the landlord in gratitude for the hospitality shown him. This tradition of warm welcome and friendly service lives on to this day. Bar snacks and main dishes run from croque monsieur to salmon fish cakes on spinach and wine sauce or a lunchtime cold buffet. More serious restaurant food lists asparagus and wild mushroom open ravioli followed by monkfish medallions wrapped in pancetta and roast rack of spring lamb with a mustard and herb crust. Residents beware of the phantom coach and horses that can be heard at night in the inn's oldest part!
OPEN: 11–3 (Sun 12-4) 6-11 (Sun 7-10:30)
BAR MEALS: Lunch served: all week Dinner served: all week 12–2.30 6.30–10 Av main course £7.95 **RESTAURANT:** Lunch served: all week Dinner served: all week 12-2.30 7-10 Av 3 course à la carte £25 Av 3 course fixed price £18.50
BREWERY/COMPANY: Free House
PRINCIPAL BEERS: Brakspear Bitter, Fuller's London Pride.
FACILITIES: Children welcome Garden: Lawn, courtyard, food served outside **NOTES:** Parking 86 **ROOMS:** 15 bedrooms 15 en suite from s£60 d£80

LAMBOURN
Map 04 SU37

The Hare & Hounds
Ermin St RG17 7SD ☎ 01488 71386 ▤ 01488 72329
Dir: On B4000 at Lambourn Woodlands. From motorway: Junction 14 or 15.
Notable for its individual decor and good food, this 17th-century coaching inn in the beautiful Lambourn Valley is a favourite with the horseracing fraternity. Dishes on offer include salmon and cod fishcakes, Aberdeen Angus steaks, pan-fried Pollock steak on a bed of Julienne vegetables, rösti of carrots, parsnips and potato served with a rocket salad, and hot green Thai curry.

OPEN: 11–3.30 6–11 (closed Sun evenings) **BAR MEALS:** Lunch served: all week Dinner served: Mon–Sat 12-2 7-9.30 Av main course £10 **RESTAURANT:** Lunch served: all week Dinner served: Mon-Sat 12–2 7-9.30 Av 3 course à la carte £23 Av 3 course fixed price £25
BREWERY/COMPANY: Free House
PRINCIPAL BEERS: Wadworth 6X, Interbrew Flowers IPA & Boddingtons. **FACILITIES:** Children welcome Garden: Food served outdoors Dogs allowed (water) **NOTES:** Parking 35

LITTLEWICK GREEN
Map 04 SU87

The Cricketers
Coronation Rd SL6 3RA ☎ 01628 822888 ▤ 01628 822888
Dir: 5m W of Maidenhead on A4 toward Reading. From M4 J8/9 take A404(M) to A4 junction
Standing in the shadow of a lovely walnut tree and overlooking the vast village cricket ground spread out opposite, this late-19th-century inn has an intriguing clocking-in-clock inside, possibly once owned by the Great Western Railway.

MAIDENHEAD
Map 04 SU88

The Belgian Arms
Holyport SL6 2JR ☎ 01628 634468
Dir: 0.75m from Maidenhead
The former "Eagle" - unusually renamed to salute our World War I allies - sports a 200-year-old wisteria and a long, colourful history. A selection of meals from the menu may include various curries, poached salmon fillets, lamb noisettes, and a variety of chicken dishes.
OPEN: 11–3 (Fri All day) 5.30–11 (Sat 12-3, 6-11 Sun 12-3, 7-10.30)
BAR MEALS: Lunch served: all week 12–2 Dinner served: Mon-Sat 7-9.30 Av main course £7.95 **BREWERY/COMPANY:** Brakspear
PRINCIPAL BEERS: Brakspear Best. **FACILITIES:** Children welcome Garden: outdoor eating, pond with ducks Dogs allowed **NOTES:** Parking 45

MARSH BENHAM
Map 04 SU46

Pick of the Pubs

The Red House
RG20 8LY ☎ 01635 582017 ▤ 01635 581621
e-mail: redhouse@ukonline.co.uk
Dir: 5m from Hungerford, 3m from Newbury & 400yds off the A4
Formerly known as The Water Rat - yes, this is the same place - a handsome brick-and-thatch pub on the Kennet and Avon Canal, deep in 'Wind in the Willows' Country. With its name change has come a fresh approach to 21st-century innkeeping that is entirely welcome. The canalside patio is a sun-trap of a spot in which to down a pint of ale

continued   *continued*

MARSH BENHAM continued

or dine in fine weather. Describing itself as 'modern British with a French twist' the single menu is full of brio and bright ideas. Served in starter or main dish sizes are wild mushroom risotto in a Parmesan basket and creamed spinach vol-au-vent with poached egg and hollandaise. A vibrant fish list offers salmon fillet with horseradish mousse and brill with ratatouille and pesto sauce. Alternative meaty selections include shank of lamb on honey-roasted parsnip purée and chargrilled beef rib-eye with pancetta, mushrooms and 'café de Paris' butter.

The Red House

OPEN: 11.30-3 6-11 **BAR MEALS:** Lunch served: Tue-Sun 12-2.30 Dinner served: Tue-Sat 7-10 Av main course £13.50 **RESTAURANT:** Lunch served: Tue-Sun 12-2.30 Dinner served: Tue-Sat 7-10 Av 3 course à la carte £25 **BREWERY/COMPANY:** Free House **PRINCIPAL BEERS:** Fuller's London Pride, Greene King Ruddles County Ale. **FACILITIES:** Children welcome Garden: Beer garden, patio, food served outdoors **NOTES:** Parking 40

NEWBURY   Map 04 SU46

The Blackbird Inn
Bagnor RG20 8AQ ☎ 01635 40638
Unpretentious country pub close to Virginia Water. A good range of ales and a pre-theatre menu. Handy for the Watermill Theatre. Large landscaped garden with children's play area.

The White Hart Inn
Kintbury Rd, Hamstead Marshall RG20 0HW
☎ 01488 658201 ▤ 01488 657192
e-mail: whitehartmarsh@waitrose.com
Dir: A4, 2m after Speen, L at x-roads, cross railway & canal, L at jct, R at next jct, inn 300yds on R

A 16th-century coaching inn where tenants of the nearby Craven estate came to pay their rent. Decorating the specials board are unusual chalk drawings, a charming feature in the bar. Examples of the enterprising Italian-based blackboard specials and restaurant menu include scallops wrapped in bacon and sage, wild mushroom stuffed ravioli, chicken escalope with ham, tomato and mozzarella, and pan-fried calves' liver with onions, sage and red wine. The pudding menu also has a delicious Italian tone.
OPEN: 12-2.30 6-11 (closed Sun) Closed: 25-26 Dec, 1 Jan, 2 weeks in summer **BAR MEALS:** Lunch served: Mon-Sat Dinner served: Mon-Sat 12-2 6.30-9 Av main course £10.50 **RESTAURANT:** Lunch served: Mon-Sat Dinner served: Mon-Sat 12-2 6.30-9 Av 3 course à la carte £20 **BREWERY/COMPANY:** Free House **PRINCIPAL BEERS:** Wadworth 6X, Ringwood Best. **FACILITIES:** Garden: patio, Beer garden, food served outdoors **NOTES:** Parking 30 **ROOMS:** 6 bedrooms 6 en suite

Pick of the Pubs

The Yew Tree Inn
Hollington Cross, Andover Rd, Highclere RG20 9SE
☎ 01635 253360 ▤ 01635 255035
Dir: A34 toward Southampton, 2nd exit bypass Highclere, onto A343 at rdbt, thru village, pub on R
Oak-framed inn of local brick and tile, dating back some 350 years and set in rolling countryside close to Highclere Castle. Scrubbed pine tables, low beams and an inglenook fireplace characterise the main bar, while a rambling series of interconnected rooms make up the restaurant area, where log fires and candlelit tables make for an inviting atmosphere. An imaginative menu and daily blackboard specials are served throughout the inn along with a range of fine wines and traditional beers. Representing the fish dishes might be roasted whole Test Valley trout with thyme, lemon and garlic, or whole sea bass stuffed with julienne of vegetables. You can also expect the likes of slow roasted lamb on parsnip mash and red wine jus, or pork stuffed with sage, pistachio and sausage. Accommodation is also available in the cosy rooms upstairs.
OPEN: 11-3 5.30-11 (Sun 9.30-3, 2.30-11)
BAR MEALS: Lunch served: all week 12-2.30 Dinner served: Mon-Sat 6.30-10 Av main course £9 **RESTAURANT:** Lunch served: all week Dinner served: Mon-Sat 12-2.30 6.30-10 Av 3 course à la carte £25 Av 3 course fixed price £25 **BREWERY/COMPANY:** Free House **PRINCIPAL BEERS:** Hampshire King Alfred, Brakspear Bitter. **FACILITIES:** Children welcome Garden: patio/terrace, food served outdoors Dogs allowed **NOTES:** Parking 40 **ROOMS:** 6 bedrooms 6 en suite

---

PEASEMORE   Map 04 SU47

Fox & Hounds
Pleasmore RG20 7JN ☎ 01635 248252
e-mail: lori.fox.hound@tinyworld.co.uk
Next to the village cricket ground, these old buildings were converted into a pub some 100 years ago. At the edge of a pretty village dotted with thatched cottages with stunning views over the Berkshire Downs. The main bar has comfy leather sofas and a double aspect log burner that faces both bar and games room. Popular home-made bar food including basket meals while in the dining room try speciality sausages

continued

continued

in onion gravy, Punjabi butter chicken curry and salmon fillet with black pepper sauce.

OPEN: 11.30–3 6.30–11 (weekdays open 5.30) **BAR MEALS:** Lunch served: Sat–Sun 11.30–2 Dinner served: Tue–Sun 6.30–10 Av main course £7.50 **RESTAURANT:** Lunch served: Sat–Sun 11.30–2 Dinner served: Tue–Sun 6.30–10 Av 3 course à la carte £12 **PRINCIPAL BEERS:** Wadworth 6X, Fuller's London Pride, Greene King IPA. **FACILITIES:** Children welcome Garden: Food served outside Dogs allowed (water) **NOTES:** Parking 40

READING   Map 04 SU77

Fishermans Cottage 🏠 🍸
224 Kennet Side RG1 3DW ☎ 0118 9571553 📠 0118 9571553
Dir: L from Kings Rd into Orts Rd then Canal Way
Listed building with a bar shaped like a canal barge, a conservatory extension and frontage on the Kennet and Avon Canal. Barge moorings at Blake's Lock and easy accessibility from the tow path are a significant summer draw for outdoor types. Quick and easy meals include all-day breakfast and burgers, while batter-fried cod, chicken balti, spicy tomato pasta and standard fare for Junior strike a strictly unchallenging balance. Monthly music nights.
OPEN: 11.30–3 5.30–11 (Fri–Sun & summer 11.30–11)
BAR MEALS: Lunch served: all week Dinner served: all week 12–2.30 6–9 Av main course £5.50 **BREWERY/COMPANY:** Fullers
PRINCIPAL BEERS: Fuller's London Pride, ESB.
FACILITIES: Children welcome Garden: BBQ, large patio, food served outdoors Dogs allowed (water) **NOTES:** Parking 10

The New Inn 🏠 **NEW**
Chalkhouse Green Rd, Kidmore End RG4 9AU
☎ 0118 9723115 & 9724733 📠 0118 9724733
It's not unusual to see horses tethered outside this 16th-century inn, whose lovely garden and good food make it a popular resting place on a country ride. The interior includes real oak studded floorboards, oak beams and a blackboard menu offering a frequently changing selection of home cooked food: perhaps cod in beer batter, freshly made soup, curry or beef and ale pie.
OPEN: 12–3 6–11 (Sat all day, Sun 12–10.30) **BAR MEALS:** Lunch served: all week 12–2.30 Dinner served: Mon–Sat 6.30–9 Av main course £6.95 **RESTAURANT:** Lunch served: all week Dinner served: Mon–Sat 6.30–9 Av 3 course à la carte £25 Av 3 course fixed price £17.25 **BREWERY/COMPANY:** Brakspear
PRINCIPAL BEERS: Brakspear Bitter & Old Ale.
FACILITIES: Garden: Food served outside **NOTES:** Parking 20

★ **Indicates AA inspected hotel accommodation**

Sweeney & Todd
10 Castle St RG1 7RD ☎ 0118 9586466
Town centre pie shop with well-stocked bar. The selection of pies is excellent, as are the pies themselves. A great stop after a hard day's shopping.

SONNING   Map 04 SU77

Bull Inn 🏠 🍸
High St RG4 6UP ☎ 01189 693901 📠 01189 691057
e-mail: dennis1925@aol.com

Enjoying a picture-postcard setting next to the village church, this 16th-century timbered inn boasts sturdy old beams, tiled floors, winter log fires and a recommendation from Jerome K. Jerome, who mentions the pub in his comic novel Three Men in a Boat. Today's menu may feature red snapper, seafood kebabs, Thai green curry, or lamb tagine on pine nut and fresh coriander couscous. The patio at the back of the pub is an ideal place to enjoy a drink.
OPEN: 11–3 5.30–11 **BAR MEALS:** Lunch served: all week Dinner served: all week 12–2 6.30–9 Av main course £9.50
RESTAURANT: Lunch served: all week Dinner served: all week 12–2 6.30–9.30 Av 3 course à la carte £25 **BREWERY/COMPANY:** Gales
PRINCIPAL BEERS: Gale's HSB, Best, Buster Bitter.
FACILITIES: Children welcome Garden: Patio, food served outside Dogs allowed (dog Bowls) **NOTES:** Parking 20 **ROOMS:** 7 bedrooms 6 en suite from s£85 d£85

STANFORD DINGLEY   Map 04 SU57

The Bull Inn 🏠 🍸
RG7 6LS ☎ 0118 9744409 📠 0118 974 4409
e-mail: robert.archard@btinternet.com
Dir: A4/A340 to Pangbourne. 1st L to Bradfield.Thru Bradfield, 0.3m L into Back Lane. At end L, pub 0.25m on L

Traditional 15th-century inn featuring a wealth of timbers and even the remains of an original wattle and daub wall. Don't be surprised to see locals behind the Bull's bar. They liked the

continued

STANFORD DINGLEY continued

pub so much, they bought it! Classic cars, Jaguars in particular, are the landlords' lifetime hobby and passion, and one of the bars reflects this deep interest. An ancient pub game known as 'ring-the-bull' is sometimes played in the next door tap room. Among the interesting food selections are seafood chowder, escalope of veal with wild mushrooms, and grilled salmon with lime and caper butter sauce.
OPEN: 12–3 Mar–Oct 11–3 6–11 Sun 7–10.30 **BAR MEALS:** Lunch served: all week Dinner served: all week 12–2.30 6.30–9.30 Av main course £10 **RESTAURANT:** 12.30–2.30 6.30–9.30 Av 3 course à la carte £18 **BREWERY/COMPANY:** Free House
PRINCIPAL BEERS: West Berkshire Brewery Ales, Brakspear Bitter.
FACILITIES: Children welcome Garden: Beer garden, food served outdoors, patio Dogs allowed (on a lead) **NOTES:** Parking 32
ROOMS: 6 bedrooms 6 en suite from s£45 d£60

The Old Boot Inn
RG7 6LT ☎ 01189 744292 ▤ 01189 744292
Dir: M4 J12, A4/A340 to Pangbourne. 1st L to Bradfield. Through Bradfield & follow signs for Stanford Dingley
In a village of Outstanding Natural Beauty in the glorious Pang Valley, the original 18th-century Old Boot has been extended to include a popular conservatory. Fresh fish is announced daily on the blackboard while further dining options may include freshly-prepared dishes such as Thai fishcakes with a chilli salsa or field mushrooms stuffed with spinach and smoked cheese starters, followed by calves' liver and bacon or roast pheasant with garlic sauce and celeriac chips.
OPEN: 11–3 (Sun 12–3) 6–11 (Sun 7–10.30) **BAR MEALS:** Lunch served: all week Dinner served: all week 12–2.15 7–9.30 Av main course £7.95 **RESTAURANT:** Lunch served: all week Dinner served: all week 12–2.15 7–9.30 Av 3 course à la carte £25
BREWERY/COMPANY: Free House
PRINCIPAL BEERS: Brakspear Bitter, Interbrew Bass, West Berkshire Dr Hexters, Archers Best. **FACILITIES:** Children welcome Garden: Food served outside Dogs allowed **NOTES:** Parking 40

SWALLOWFIELD   Map 04 SU76

Pick of the Pubs

The George & Dragon
Church Rd RG7 1TJ ☎ 0118 9884 432 ▤ 0118 9886474
Behind the unassuming façade of this old inn, set close to the River Blackwater on the village edge, is a smart and cosy interior featuring stripped low beams, terracotta-painted walls, log fires and rug-strewn floors. Very much a dining pub - booking essential. Look for Club sandwiches (goats' cheese, roasted pepper and rocket leaves), seafood bouillabaise, salmon on vegetable noodles with citrus butter sauce, and Cumberland sausage on bubble-and-squeak on the lunch menu; imaginative evening specials may feature seared Thai scallops with marinated cucumber, smoked salmon and pesto linguini, roast rack of lamb with whole garlic cloves and burnt onion mash, and pan-fried sea bream with Puy lentil purée with salsa verde. Round off with caramelised apple tart tatin, chocolate and roast hazelnut terrine with coffee sauce, or cheese with home-made chutney. Seasonal fish and game specials; interesting wines.
OPEN: 12–11 (Sat 12–4, 6–11, Sun 12–4, 7–10.30)
BAR MEALS: 12–2 Av main course £5.50
RESTAURANT: Lunch served: all week Dinner served: all week 12–2 6.30–9.30 Av 3 course à la carte £22

BREWERY/COMPANY: Free House
PRINCIPAL BEERS: Fullers London Pride, Wadworth 6X & guest ale. **FACILITIES:** Garden: Food served outside Dogs allowed **NOTES:** Parking 50

THATCHAM   Map 04 SU56

Pick of the Pubs

The Bladebone Inn
Chapel Row, Bucklebury RG7 6PD
☎ 0118 9712326 ▤ 0118 9712326
e-mail: bladebone@berkshirerestaurants.co.uk
Dir: 5m from Newbury and the A4, 2m from the A4 at Thatcham
Within earshot of the M4 at the southern edge of the North Wessex Downs, but more easily accessed from the A4 east of Thatcham, this historic inn stands at the end of a stately avenue of oak trees planted to commemorate a visit by Elizabeth I. Over the entrance hangs a bladebone which, according to local legend, came from a mammoth that once stalked the Down. It is more likely that it was used to indicate that whale oil was sold here for use in oil-burning lamps and probably of 17th-century origin. What once was a traditional village local has been transformed into a dining venue with emphasis on modern pub food, comfortable furnishings and a relaxed atmosphere. Starters typically consist of crispy tempura prawns and warm Roquefort cheesecake, followed by chicken fillet stuffed with Toulouse sausage, roast halibut on spinach with baby onions and bacon and Tallegio cheese and Mediterranean vegetables on ciabatta bread.
OPEN: 12–3 6.30–11 **BAR MEALS:** Lunch served: Tue-Sun 12–3 Dinner served: Tue-Sat 7–9 Av main course £10
RESTAURANT: Tue-Sun 12–3 7–9 Av 3 course à la carte £25
BREWERY/COMPANY: Whitbread
PRINCIPAL BEERS: Fuller's London Pride, Interbrew Flowers IPA, West Berks Dr Hexters Healer, Brakspear Bitter.
FACILITIES: Garden: Food served outdoors **NOTES:** Parking 20

THEALE   Map 04 SU67

Thatchers Arms ☺ ♀ NEW
North St RG7 5EX ☎ 0118 930 2070 ▤ 0118 930 2070

You'll find a warm welcome and good, home-cooked food at this classic country pub. Despite its location in a small village surrounded by open countryside, the Thatchers Arms is just five minutes drive from the centre of Theale and junction 12 of the M4. The menu changes regularly, but steak and kidney pie, wild boar sausages, and seafood kebabs are typical

continued

continued

precursors to bread and butter pudding, apple crumble, or caramelised plums.
OPEN: 12–2.30 5.30–11 **BAR MEALS:** Lunch served: all week Dinner served: all week 12–2 7–9.30 Av main course £6.95
RESTAURANT: Lunch served: all week Dinner served: all week 12–2 7–9.30 Av 3 course à la carte £15
PRINCIPAL BEERS: Fuller's London Pride, Brakspear Bitter.
FACILITIES: Children welcome Dogs allowed (water)
NOTES: Parking 15

UPPER BASILDON   Map 04 SU57

The Red Lion 🏚
Aldworth Rd RG8 8NG ☎ 01491 671234 📠 01491 671390
Dir: from M4 follow signs to Pangbourne, then L at 1st main jct signed Upper Basildon, thru village, pub on R
Friendly, welcoming and always sporting an open fire when the weather warrants, the oldest pub in the area is handy for the Ridgeway and Thames Path. Widely ranging menus served throughout offer single dishes like pork and leek sausages and smoked salmon omelette, while from a fixed-price menu choices include panache of fish with black linguine and lamb steak with spicy sweet potatoes, followed perhaps by treacle tart with crème fraîche or cheesecake of winter fruits.
OPEN: 12–11 (Sun 12–10.30) **BAR MEALS:** Lunch served: all week Dinner served: all week 12–2.30 6–10 Av main course £8
RESTAURANT: Lunch served: all week Dinner served: all week 12–2.30 6–10 Av 3 course à la carte £17.50 Av 3 course fixed price £17.50 **PRINCIPAL BEERS:** Brakspear Bitter, Scottish Courage Courage Best, Young's Special,. **FACILITIES:** Children's licence Garden: Large with seating, food served outside Dogs allowed
NOTES: Parking 25

WALTHAM ST LAWRENCE   Map 04 SU87

The Bell
The Street RG10 0JJ ☎ 0118 9341788
e-mail: wslbell@fsnet.com
Dir: on B3024 E of Twyford (from A4 turn at Hare Hatch)
Since 1608, when it was left to the village in trust, the rent from this 14th-century inn has been donated to local charities. The same menu operates throughout, offering a variety of meat pies and puddings, chilli, enchiladas, lamb and pork shanks, chicken tikka, and fresh fish on Fridays.
OPEN: 11.30–3 5–11 (Sun 12–7) **BAR MEALS:** Lunch served: all week 12–2 Dinner served: Mon–Sat 7–9.30 Av main course £7
RESTAURANT: Lunch served: all week 12–2 Dinner served: Mon–Sat 7–9.30 **BREWERY/COMPANY:** Free House
PRINCIPAL BEERS: Waltham St Lawrence No.1 Ale, West Berkshire, Brakspear, plus two guest ales. **FACILITIES:** Children welcome Garden: Food served outside Dogs allowed (water bowls provided)
NOTES: Parking 5

WEST ILSLEY   Map 04 SU48

Pick of the Pubs

Harrow Inn ♀
RG20 7AR ☎ 01635 281260 📠 01635 281139
e-mail: theharrowilsley@aol.com
Lying in a peaceful settlement on the edge of the Berkshire Downs, close to the Ridgeway Path and surrounded by horse-racing country, this is a historic inn where Morlands Brewery was founded in 1711. Thoroughbred English food is served in the open plan bar, with its creamy yellow décor and distinctive wall hangings. For

lunch the choice includes filled French rolls (Somerset Brie and mango chutney, roast pork and warm apple sauce), pies and burgers, as well as a more elaborate selection from the regularly-changing carte (same for dinner). Expect confit of rabbit on vanilla risotto, goats' cheese with black pudding to start, followed perhaps by home-made pork and leek sausages on bubble and squeak, chicken supreme wrapped in Parma ham, and fillet of pork stuffed with apricots and prunes. Try some of the award-winning cheeses, or go for puddings like rich lemon tart and cream, or chocolate brownie with caramel sauce.
OPEN: 11–3 6–11 (open Sun eve, Mon in summer)
BAR MEALS: Lunch served: Tue–Sun Dinner served: Tue–Sun 12–2 7–9 Av main course £11
BREWERY/COMPANY: Greene King
PRINCIPAL BEERS: Morland Original, Greene King & Abbot Ale. **FACILITIES:** Children welcome Garden: Food served outside Dogs allowed **NOTES:** Parking 10

WINKFIELD   Map 04 SU97

Pick of the Pubs

Rose & Crown 🏚
Woodside, Windsor Forest SL4 2DP
☎ 01344 882051 📠 01344 885346
Dir: M3 J3 from Ascot racecourse on A332 take 2nd exit from Heatherwood Hosp r'about,then 2nd L
A family-run, 200-year-old traditional pub hidden down a country lane, complete with old beams and low ceilings and a garden overlooking open fields where you can see both horses and llamas at pasture. The recently refurbished interior provides comfortable seating in both bar and restaurant areas, in which a broad cross-section of clientele enjoys real ales, good wines and home-cooked food prepared with due care and attention, cooked in a confident and robust style. To follow pan-fried mushroom salad with crispy bacon, dressed crab salad or wild mushroom carbonara, tuck into red mullet fillets on minted pea purée, magret duck breast with caramelised apples and poached or Scotch beef fillet laid over sweet fried onions with a port jus. Greene King ales take pride of place at the bar: if intending to stay over book into one of the two en suite bedrooms to enjoy hospitality at its best.
OPEN: 11–11 (Sun 12–7) **BAR MEALS:** Lunch served: all week 12–2.30 Dinner served: Tue–Sat 7–9.30 Av main course £5.95
RESTAURANT: Lunch served: all week 12–2.30 Dinner served: Tue–Sat 7–9.30 Av 3 course à la carte £25
BREWERY/COMPANY: Greene King
PRINCIPAL BEERS: Greene King Abbot Ale, Wadworth 6X, Interbrew Bass. **FACILITIES:** Children welcome Garden: Large, Food served outdoors **NOTES:** Parking 24
ROOMS: 2 bedrooms from s£35 d£45

> **Room prices show the minimum double and single rates charged. Room rates in hotels and B&B's often vary depending on the facilities, so be sure to check prices with the establishment before booking.**

continued

England

Pick of the Pubs

The Winterbourne Arms 🛏 ♀
RG20 8BB ☎ 01635 248200 ▤ 01635 248824
Dir: From M4 S on A34, 1st slip road

Originally known as the New Inn, a straightforward village local, this black and white timber-framed free house nestles below the tree-lined slopes of Snelsmore Common, West Berkshire's only country park, which is a wonderful area for walking. There are picnic sets on the pub's tree-shaded lawn from which there are attractive views across rolling countryside. Inside, you'll find well-kept ales, winter fires, dried flowers, and a collection of old fire extinguishers. Evenings bring mellow candlelight to the intimate restaurant, where the owners are continuing the pub's tradition of presenting imaginative dishes created from fresh ingredients. Try, perhaps, one of the game dishes - pheasant, partridge or venison. Alternatively, sample the locally produced sausages or rack of lamb with dauphinoise potatoes and french beans in smoked bacon. Fresh fish dishes include whole grilled sea bass with lemon and parsley butter and stir-fried tiger prawns with vegetables and noodles.
OPEN: 11.30-3 6-11 **BAR MEALS:** Lunch served: Tue-Sun 12-2.30 Dinner served: Tue-Sat 6-9.30 Av main course £12.50
RESTAURANT: Lunch served: Tue-Sun 12-2 Dinner served: Tue-Sat 6-9.30 Av 3 course à la carte £22.50
BREWERY/COMPANY: Free House
PRINCIPAL BEERS: Fuller's London Pride, West Berkshire Good Old Boy, Interbrew Bass. **FACILITIES:** Garden: Food served outside **NOTES:** Parking 40

The Crooked Billet ♀
Honey Hill ☎ 0118 978 0438 ▤ 0118 9789256

An old white weather-boarded pub, reputed to have been moved piece by piece from the other side of the road! Inside there is an open fireplace, traditional decorations and a friendly atmosphere which draws in a strong local following. Most of the food is home made, including specials like calves' liver and bacon, honey-glazed duck, bangers and mash, and, from the menu, chilli con carni, mushroom and stilton tagliatelle.
OPEN: 11-11.40 Closed: Dec 26 **BAR MEALS:** Lunch served: all week 12-2.30 Dinner served: Mon-Sat 7-9.30 Av main course £7.95
RESTAURANT: Lunch served: all week Dinner served: all week 12-2.30 7-9.30 **PRINCIPAL BEERS:** Breakspear Special, Original.
FACILITIES: Children welcome Garden: Food served outside Dogs allowed (water) **NOTES:** Parking 300

The Angel 🛏 ♀
Bath Rd RG7 5RT ☎ 0118 9713307
e-mail: mail@a4angel.com
An impressive Virginia creeper covered building, dating from around 1752, with a large front terrace. Many original features remain: within, a splendid Regency board room with chandeliers and to the rear a Japanese water garden. In an atmosphere that is both informal and relaxing, a wine list of more than 20 selections by the glass augments such fairly serious food as pan-fried lemon sole with spinach potato cake, leek and smoked pancetta tartlet and beef tournedos with horseradish crust and charred asparagus.
OPEN: 12-3 6-11 **BAR MEALS:** Lunch served: all week 12-2.30 Dinner served: Mon-Sat 6-9.30 Av main course £15
RESTAURANT: Lunch served: all week Dinner served: all week 12-2.30 6-10 Av 3 course à la carte £25
BREWERY/COMPANY: Free House
PRINCIPAL BEERS: Interbrew Flowers Original, Boddingtons.
FACILITIES: Garden: Japanese water garden **NOTES:** Parking 40

Pick of the Pubs

The Royal Oak Hotel ★ ★ 🍴🍴 🛏
The Square RG18 0UG ☎ 01635 201325 ▤ 01635 201926
e-mail: theroyaloak@hotmail.com
Dir: From M4 J12, A4 to Newbury, R at 2nd rndbt to Pangbourne then 1st L. From J13, A34 N 1st L, R at T-jnct. L then 2nd R to Yattendon

A 16th-century timber-framed coaching inn on the village square, later re-faced in the red brick that you will encounter today, The Oak - as it was then known - played host to such luminaries as King Charles I and Oliver

continued

continued

Cromwell. A quintessentially English country inn rarely interrupted by more than the footfall of passing horse-riders. While the popular village bar remains, emphasis is based on a brasserie-style menu rooted in local ingredients and sound cooking. Confit of duck leg with pineapple and Thai fishcakes with sweet-and-sour pickle satisfy as a snack or as precursors to roast monkfish tails in goats' cheese and Parma ham or classic-style steak béarnaise. Cap it off with rich chocolate bread and butter pudding or the selection of French and English cheeses. Wonderful bedrooms – at a price – and cossetting service.
OPEN: 11-3 6-11 **BAR MEALS:** Lunch served: all week Dinner served: all week 12-2.30 7-10 Av main course £14.75
RESTAURANT: Lunch served: Sun 12-2.30 Dinner served: Mon-Sat 7-9.30 Av 3 course à la carte £26 **BREWERY/COMPANY:** Regal
PRINCIPAL BEERS: Fuller's London Pride. **FACILITIES:** Garden: Food served outside **NOTES:** Parking 15 **ROOMS:** 5 bedrooms 5 en suite from s£105 d£130

BRISTOL

BRISTOL   Map 03 ST57

Brewery Tap ♀
Upper Maudlin St BS1 5BD ☎ 0117 921 3668 🖺 0117 925 8235
e-mail: brewerytap@smiles.co.uk

Pub adjacent to Smiles Brewery so all the ales are freshly brewed next door. It's a traditional English pub with an emphasis on real beer, though lagers, Guinness, cider, wines and spirits are also served. A menu of pub favourites is offered – fish and chips, chilli, curry and burgers – all home made. You can get Sunday lunch for £4.25, while steak and chips at £5 is the most expensive dish.
OPEN: 11-11 (Sun 11-4, 7-11) Closed: 25-26 Dec, 1 Jan
BAR MEALS: Lunch served: Mon-Sun 12-3 Av main course £4.50
BREWERY/COMPANY: Smiles **PRINCIPAL BEERS:** Smiles, Best, Original, Heritage. **FACILITIES:** Children welcome Dogs allowed

Highbury Vaults
164 St Michaels Hill, Cotham BS2 8DE
☎ 0117 9733203 🖺 0117 9744828
e-mail: highburyvaults@hotmail.com
Dir: Take main road to Cotham from inner ring dual carriageway
All atmosphere at this 1840s pub, once a turnpike station, retaining a Victorian atmosphere and seating in its many nooks and crannies. In days when hangings took place on nearby St Michael's Hill, many victims partook of their last meal in the vaults. Today, its a business crowd by day and students at night feasting on chilli, meat and vegetable

curries, casseroles and hot pots. Young's beers, no music or fruit machines and a heated garden terrace in which to chill out.
OPEN: 12-11 (Sun 12-10.30) **BAR MEALS:** Lunch served: all week 12-3 Dinner served: Mon-Fri 5.30-8.30 Av main course £3.20
BREWERY/COMPANY: Young & Co **PRINCIPAL BEERS:** Smiles Best & Heritage, Brains SA, Young's Special & Bitter.
FACILITIES: Children welcome Garden: Patio, Food served outside No credit cards

BUCKINGHAMSHIRE

AMERSHAM   Map 04 SU99

The Hit or Miss ♀
Penn St Village HP7 0PX ☎ 01494 713109 🖺 01494 718010
A lovely 14th-century country inn opposite the village cricket pitch, with a cricket-themed no smoking dining area. One menu operates throughout offering freshly prepared dishes running from snacks, pies and fish and chips, through to rack of lamb with wild berry jus, and fillet of salmon on crushed new potatoes with fine beans and tarragon sauce.
OPEN: 11-3 5.30-11 (All day Wknd in summer)
BAR MEALS: Lunch served: all week Dinner served: all week 12-2.30 6-9.30 Av main course £9.95 **RESTAURANT:** Lunch served: all week Dinner served: all week 12-2.30 6-9.30 Av 3 course à la carte £20 **BREWERY/COMPANY:** Hall & Woodhouse
PRINCIPAL BEERS: Badger Tanglefoot, Best & IPA.
FACILITIES: Garden: Lawn & Patio Area, food served outside
NOTES: Parking 40

The Kings Arms ♀
30 The High St, Old Amersham HP7 0DJ
☎ 01494 726333 🖺 01494 433480

Historic atmosphere fills the bars of this 15th-century, black and white timbered inn. There are always four real ales on offer, two drawn directly from the cask behind the counter. The bar snack menu lists sandwiches, pies, pasta and chicken tikka, while the restaurant offers a three-month carte and four/five-week fixed price menu. The house speciality is fruits de mer, with oysters, crab, langoustine, mussels, clams, whelks, winkles, prawns and shrimps, available on advertised dates.
OPEN: 11-11 (Sun 12-10.30) **BAR MEALS:** Lunch served: all week 12-2.30 Av main course £6.50 **RESTAURANT:** Lunch served: Tue-Sun 12-2 Dinner served: Tue-Sat 7-9.30 Av 3 course à la carte £27 Av 3 course fixed price £15.50 **BREWERY/COMPANY:** Free House **PRINCIPAL BEERS:** Rebellion IPA, Burton Ale, Benskins Best.
FACILITIES: Children welcome Children's licence Garden: Patio/terrace, food served outside **NOTES:** Parking 25

England

ASTON CLINTON
Map 06 SP81

The Oak ♀
119 Green End St HP22 5EU ☎ 01296 630466 📠 01296 631796
e-mail: theoak@tesco.net
Dir: entry via Brook St, off the A41
Thatched, 500-year-old coaching inn with flagstone floors, inglenook fireplace and bags of old-world charm. Set in the old part of the village, it offers a good family garden and a wide-ranging menu. Summer events include a beer festival and a charity fete. Expect traditional pub favourites, alongside beef Stroganoff, pan-fried salmon, and sweet and sour chicken with sweet peppers.
OPEN: 11.30–2.30 6–11 (open all day Sat-Sun in summer)
BAR MEALS: Lunch served: all week Dinner served: all week 12–2 6–9.30 Av main course £5.25 **RESTAURANT:** Lunch served: all week Dinner served: all week 12–2 6–9.30 Av 3 course à la carte £14.75
BREWERY/COMPANY: Fullers **PRINCIPAL BEERS:** Fullers London Pride, Fullers ESB. **FACILITIES:** Garden: Food served outside Dogs allowed (water) **NOTES:** Parking 30

AYLESBURY
Map 06 SP81

Pick of the Pubs

Bottle & Glass ♀
Gibraltar, Nr Dinton HP17 8TY
☎ 01296 748488 📠 01296 747673
Dir: On A418 between Thame & Aylesbury

In a peaceful rural setting close to the Chiltern Hills, this 17th-century thatched inn with low ceilings, flagstone floors, intimate alcoves, open fires and an appealing decor has an immediately warm and welcoming ambience. Fresh fish and seafood, delivered daily, is a real strength: simply cooked to enhance their best flavours may be tuna on garlic mash with thyme cream and vinaigrette, chargrilled cod with sweet pepper coulis and balsamic reduction, and salmon on Asian noodles with orange dressing, basil oil and mango salsa. Meat dishes cover duck breast with wild mushroom sauce, beef fillet on rösti with Dijon mustard and tarragon sauce, and steak and kidney pie; excellent Sunday roasts with all the trimmings. With lunch in mind are open ciabatta sandwiches or a bowl of mussels served with fresh bread; follow with a home-made pudding, perhaps a tangy citron tart. Superb front terrace seating festooned with flowering hanging baskets and tubs.
OPEN: 11–3 6–11 (closed Sun eve) **BAR MEALS:** Lunch served: all week 12–2.30 Dinner served: Mon-Sat 7–9.30 Av main course £6 **RESTAURANT:** Lunch served: all week 12–2 Dinner served: Mon-Sat 7–9.30 Av 3 course à la carte £25

BREWERY/COMPANY: Morrells
PRINCIPAL BEERS: Morrells Oxford, Varsity & Mild.
FACILITIES: Children welcome **NOTES:** Parking 50

BEACONSFIELD
Map 04 SU99

The Greyhound 🛏
33 Windsor End HP9 2JN ☎ 01494 673823 📠 01494 673379
e-mail: greyhound.windsorend@eldridge-pope.co.uk
Dir: Follow signs to Beaconsfield Old Town, left at central roundabout
Comfortable 16th-century drovers' tavern enjoying a secluded location opposite the parish church. Traditional, home-cooked pub food is served, including garlic chicken breast, poached salmon with a dill sauce, tuna à la Maltese, vegetable Wellington, whole seabass with red pepper sauce, or quarter of lamb shoulder with red wine and mint sauce. Choice of sandwiches, baked potatoes and salads also available.
OPEN: 11–3 5–11 Closed: May 10 **BAR MEALS:** Lunch served: all week 12–2 Dinner served: Tue-Sat 7–9.45 Av main course £8 **RESTAURANT:** Lunch served: all week 12–2 Dinner served: Tue-Sat 7–9.45 Av 3 course à la carte £15 **BREWERY/COMPANY:** Free House **PRINCIPAL BEERS:** Courage Best, Fullers London Pride, Rebellion Beers, Guest Ales. **FACILITIES:** Garden: Food served outside. Dogs allowed **NOTES:** Parking 100

Pick of the Pubs

The Royal Standard of England 🛏
Brindle Ln, Forty Green HP9 1XT
☎ 01494 673382 📠 01494 523332
Dir: A40 to Beaconsfield. R at Church roundabout onto B474 towards Penn. L onto Forty Green Rd, then 1m
Country inn dating from the 12th century with striking stained glass windows, beams, flagstone floors, and a large inglenook fireplace. Situated in a part of the world renowned for Civil War battles and skirmishes, the inn became a Royalist headquarters, and it was this that led to its splendid and impressive name. The inn is a perfect base for walking and here you can rest after a long hike, licking your wounds and stoking up with beef and Owd Rodger ale pie, local speciality sausages, a trio of seafood, traditional beer and herb battered haddock or fillet of chicken, leek and mushroom pie. Mediterranean fresh tuna stir-fry with buttered noodles, shank of lamb slow-cooked with cider and Guinness and baked goats' cheese with toasted walnuts salad are typical examples of the specials board. A range of real ales including Marston's powerful Owd Roger – not suitable for drivers!
OPEN: 11–3 5.30–11 **BAR MEALS:** Lunch served: all week Dinner served: all week 12–2.15 6.30–9.30 Av main course £10 **BREWERY/COMPANY:** Free House **PRINCIPAL BEERS:** Marston's Pedigree, Brakspear Bitter, Greene King Old Speckled Hen, Fuller's London Pride. **FACILITIES:** Children welcome Children's licence Garden: Food served outside **NOTES:** Parking 90

♦ **Indicates AA inspected bed & breakfast accommodation**

continued

PUB WALK

Dorney
Palmer Arms

Combine an easy riverside walk with a visit to Dorney Court, where, apparently, the pineapple was first introduced to this country. The River Thames stretch offers close-up views of Bray film studios and Oakley Court Hotel, used in a number of horror films.

Turn right on leaving the pub, bear left into Court Lane passing the entrance to Dorney Court. Follow the path parallel to the road past the entrance to St James the Less. Continue on the path and when the road bends right, go straight ahead at the sign for Dorney Lake, Park and Nature Reserve. Cross to the right hand side of the drive and follow the parallel path. Later it sweeps to the right by a plaque and a grove of trees. At the Thames Path, bear left and head downstream, with Bray Marina on the opposite bank. Further on, is the imposing facade of Bray film studios, with its sweeping riverside lawns and weeping willows. Further on you catch sight of Oakley Court across the water on the Berkshire

bank. Beyond the hotel can be seen the gin palaces of Windsor Marina and caravans and mobile homes overlooking the river. The trees on this side of the Thames partly screen Eton College's new boathouse and its superb rowing lake. For a closer view, briefly follow a path beside the boathouse, towards the lake and then retrace your steps to the Thames Path. On the opposite (Berkshire) bank of the river is Windsor Racecourse Yacht Basin and ahead the 12th-century chapel of St Mary Magdalen. It may have been used by bargees and boatmen when nearby Boveney Lock was a bustling wharf transporting timber from Windsor Forest. Take the path beside the chapel to a kissing gate and shortly after you reach a lane. With the Old Place opposite and an avenue of chestnut trees on the right, turn left and follow the road across Dorney Common. To the right you can see Windsor Castle and its Round Tower. Keep left at the T junction, walk into Dorney and return to the pub.

PALMER ARMS
Village Road DORNEY nr
Windsor SL4 6QW
Tel: 01628 666612
Directions: From A4 take
B3026, over M4 to Dorney
An 18th-century pub in a
rural location close to
Dorney Court and the
Thames. After a riverside
stroll enjoy a pint of
Rebellion IPA and your
choice from a wide-ranging
menu served in both the bar
and the restaurant.
Open: 12-3 6-11
Bar meals: 12-2.30 6-9.30
Children welcome and dogs
allowed. Garden and
parking available.

Distance: 4 1/2 miles (7.2km)
Map: OS Landranger 175
Terrain: Lowland Thames Valley -
meadows and common
Paths: Roads, paths and stretch of
the Thames Path
Gradient: Level ground, no hills

*Walk submitted and checked
by Nick Channer*

BLEDLOW — Map 06 SP70

The Lions of Bledlow ♀
Church End HP27 9PE ☎ 01844 343345 📠 01844 343345
Dir: *M40 J6 take B4009 to Princes Risborough, through Chinnor into Bledlow*
Unchanged since the early 20th century, this Grade II listed building nestles beneath the Chiltern escarpment and still retains the atmosphere of an old style country pub. The rambling low-beamed bar has a wealth of character, and the patio and large garden are popular for summer drinking. Whole brill with lemon, pork fillet in cream and mushroom sauce, or sun-dried tomato and Portobello mushroom risotto supplement the ever-popular roast beef and Yorkshire pudding.
OPEN: 11.30-3 6-11 (Sun 12-3, 7-10.30) **BAR MEALS:** Lunch served: all week Dinner served: all week 12-2.30 7-9.30 Av main course £7 **RESTAURANT:** Lunch served: all week Dinner served: all week 12-2.30 7-9.30 Av 3 course à la carte £16
BREWERY/COMPANY: Free House
PRINCIPAL BEERS: Wadworth 6X, Scottish Courage Courage Best, Marston's Pedigree, Brakspear Bitter & guest ales.
FACILITIES: Garden: Patio, food served outside Dogs allowed (water, biscuits, toys) **NOTES:** Parking 60

BLETCHLEY — Map 06 SP83

Pick of the Pubs

Crooked Billet ♀
2 Westbrook End, Newton Longville MK17 0DF
☎ 01908 373936 📠 01908 631979
e-mail: john@thebillet.co.uk
See Pick of the Pubs on page 43

BOLTER END — Map 04 SU79

The Peacock ♀
HP14 3LU ☎ 01494 881417
Dir: *A40 through Stokenchurch, then B482*
The oldest part of this pub dates from 1620, featuring original beams and a fireplace dating from the early 1800s. It is situated on top of the Chiltern Hills overlooking the common. A typical menu features Lincolnshire pork sausages, Aberdeen Angus steaks, cheesy mushroom pancakes, and spicy beef and bean chilli. Don't forget the daily specials.
OPEN: 11.45-2.30 6-11 (closed Sun eve) Closed: 26 Dec
BAR MEALS: Lunch served: all week 12-2 Dinner served: Mon-Sat 6-9.30 Av main course £7.25 **BREWERY/COMPANY:** Punch Taverns **PRINCIPAL BEERS:** Tetley, Brakspear Bitter, Fullers London Pride. **FACILITIES:** Children welcome Garden: Beer Garden: Food served outside **NOTES:** Parking 30

BRILL — Map 06 SP61

The Pheasant Inn ♀
Windmill St HP18 9TG ☎ 01844 237104
e-mail: mrcarr@btinternet.com
The large garden and veranda at this 17th-century, beamed inn make the most of its fine hilltop position, with impressive views over seven counties. The pub used to be a village shop, and the en suite bedrooms are housed in the village bakehouse - no doubt supplied with flour from Brill windmill, which is right next door! There are winter fires, and the

popular blackboard menu offers fresh salmon, plus local steaks and pheasant in season.
OPEN: 11-3 5.30-11 (Sun 12-10.30) Closed: Dec 25-26
BAR MEALS: Lunch served: all week Dinner served: all week 12-2 7-9 Av main course £10 **RESTAURANT:** Lunch served: all week Dinner served: all week 12-2 7-9 Av 3 course à la carte £17
BREWERY/COMPANY: Free House
PRINCIPAL BEERS: Carlsberg-Tetley Tetley Bitter, Young's Special.
FACILITIES: Children welcome Garden: food served outside, beautiful views **ROOMS:** 3 bedrooms 3 en suite from s£35 d£65

BUCKINGHAM — Map 06 SP63

The Old Thatched Inn ♀
Adstock MK18 2JN ☎ 01296 712584 📠 01296 715375
Thatched and beamed 17th-century inn which has come through a refurbishment with the traditional beams and inglenook fireplace intact. A modern conservatory and the timbered lounge provide a choice of eating place where the menu plus specials and light bites is offered. Oven-baked cod with Parmesan and bacon crust, trio of sausages on olive mash, pan-fried red snapper, or for something quick, jacket potatoes, tortilla wraps, and sandwiches.
OPEN: 12-3 Open all day bank holidays & weekends Closed: 25 Dec & 1 Jan **BAR MEALS:** Lunch served: all week Dinner served: all week 12-2.30 6-9.30 Av main course £9.15 **RESTAURANT:** Lunch served: all week Dinner served: all week 12-2.30 6-9.30 Av 3 course à la carte £17.90 **PRINCIPAL BEERS:** Hook Norton Best, Old Hooky, Bass. **FACILITIES:** Children welcome Garden: Food served outside. Grass area & benches Dogs allowed (water provided) **NOTES:** Parking 20

The Wheatsheaf ♀
Main St, Maids Moreton MK18 1QR
☎ 01280 815433 📠 01280 814631
Dir: *From M1 J13 take A421 to Buckingham, then take A413*
Old world village pub serving real ales, quality bar snacks and an à la carte menu in the spacious conservatory overlooking the secluded beer garden. Options range from home-made burgers or battered cod and chips at lunchtime, to chicken with lemon and garlic or 16oz T-bone steak from the evening menu. Fish specialities include smoked haddock topped with prawns and cheese, and hickory smoked tuna steak.
OPEN: 12-3 6-11 (Sun 7-10.30) **BAR MEALS:** Lunch served: Mon-Sat 12-2.15 Dinner served: Tue-Sat 7-9.30 Av main course £6 **RESTAURANT:** Lunch served: Mon-Sat 12-2.15 Dinner served: Tue-Sat 7-9.30 Av 3 course à la carte £20
BREWERY/COMPANY: Free House **PRINCIPAL BEERS:** Hook Norton Best & regularly changing ales. **FACILITIES:** Children welcome Garden: beer garden, swings, patio, outside eating **NOTES:** Parking 15

Bar Billiards
The ingenious blend of billiards and skittles is a relative newcomer to the pub scene. It was introduced here from Belgium in the 1930s, with support from billiard table manufacturers. The game caught on rapidly, especially in the South and Midlands, and leagues had been organised by the time the Second World War began. Its much more recent rival is pool, which came here from America in the 1960s in the wake of the Paul Newman film The Hustler.

continued

OPEN: 12–2.30 5.30–11
(Sun 12–4, 7–10.30)
BAR MEALS: L served Tue–Sun.
D served Tues–Sun 12–2 7–10
Av main course £7
RESTAURANT: L served Sun 12–2.
D served Tues–Sun 7–10
Av cost 3 courses £25
BREWERY/COMPANY:
GREENE KING
PRINCIPAL BEERS: Greene King
Abbot Ale, Triumph, Old Speckled
Hen, Badger Tanglefoot
FACILITIES: Garden: Food served
outside
NOTES: Parking 25

Crooked Billet

2 Westbrook End, Newton Longville
MK17 0DF
☎ 01908 373936 📠 01908 631979
e-mail: john@thebillet.co.uk
Dir: Junct 13 on M1, take the A421 head
towards Buckingham until you reach
Bottleaimp Rdbt turn L into the village of
Newton Longville, pub is on the L.

Possibly the best gastro-pub in the area, this 17th-century establishment is all you can dream of in a village local – thatched roof, original oak beams, open log fires. But that's not all; the Crooked Billet also offers a wine-themed restaurant and the input of a talented London chef and an experienced sommelier.

So what you get is innovative modern British food served in informal pub surroundings and a sublime wine list with all 400 wines available by the glass. The place is so popular now that booking is essential, with at least six weeks' notice required for weekends. The weekly changing menus are based on local ingredients where possible, and the suppliers are credited on the menu, so assured is the quality, including the butcher, fishmonger, apiarist, greengrocer, wine merchant, florist, dairy, and cleaner (!) – plus Dr Illy from Italy who supplies the 100% Arabica coffee beans. Local produce is to the fore in fillet of venison with prune stuffing, breaded caramelised white onion, Puy lentil purée and buttered baby carrots, or smoked trout with celeriac remoulade and toasted ciabatta. A seasonally available dish of local provenance is a pudding of rhubarb, raisin and pine nut strudel with Newton Longville honey and pine nut parfait, or you might try the chef's proudly named 'My Trifle', a concoction of Muscat-soaked sponge, blood orange, mango and lychee with pistachio custard. The produce offered from the cheese trolley comes from Neal's Yard and Longman Dairies and is served with quince paste.

England

CHALFONT ST GILES

Map 04 SU99

Pick of the Pubs

Ivy House
London Rd HP8 4RS ☎ 01494 872184 📠 01494 872840
Dir: On A413 2m S of Amersham & 1.5m N of Chalfont St Giles

Owned and run by Jane and Anthony Mears, this lovely free house in the heart of the Chilterns has flint and brick walls, a warm atmosphere of old beams and open fires, and a colourful 200 years of local history. As chef, Jane Mears, and her team have created an interestingly eclectic menu that is, as they say 'Not Just Food for Thought'. A typically imaginative menu may feature green lip mussels with fresh herb and ginger butter, or exotic mushrooms with bacon in red wine for starters. Perhaps followed by chargrilled duck with spiced plum and port sauce, or pan-fried ostrich with mango sauce, finished off with some classic bread and butter pudding or creamy lemon and stem ginger cheesecake for dessert. Anthony Mears provides top-rated real ales and house wines of firm pedigree served by the glass. Special children's and slimline menus are available, along with traditional country afternoon teas between 3pm and 5.30pm at weekends.

OPEN: 12-3.30 6-11.30 (Sat 12-11, Sun 12-10.30) Closed: 25-26 Dec **BAR MEALS:** Lunch served: all week Dinner served: all week 12-2.30 6.30-9.30 Av main course £12.95
RESTAURANT: Lunch served: all week Dinner served: all week 12-2.30 6.30-9.30 Av 3 course à la carte £22
BREWERY/COMPANY: Free House
PRINCIPAL BEERS: Fuller's London Pride, Brakspear Bitter, Wadworth 6X, Hook Norton Old Hooky. **FACILITIES:** Children welcome Garden: Beer garden, patio, food served outdoors Dogs allowed (not in restaurant) **NOTES:** Parking 35

The White Hart

Three Households HP8 4LP
☎ 01494 872441 📠 01494 876375
e-mail: thewhitehartinn@supanet.com
Dir: Off A413 (Denham/Amersham)
High standards and attention to detail are the hallmarks of this prettily located 100 year-old pub. Open fireplaces, comfy sofas and fresh flowers characterise the quiet, relaxed atmosphere in the bar, with its wide choice of cask ales. Book ahead for the popular lodge-style bedrooms and non-smoking restaurant, where four dedicated chefs deliver a varied menu that ranges from a simple sandwich to loin of pork with griddled aubergines, or linguine with salmon, cod and prawns.
OPEN: 11.30-2.30 6-11 (Sun 12-3, 7-10.30) Closed: 26-27 Dec

BAR MEALS: Lunch served: all week Dinner served: all week 12-2 6.30-9.30 Av main course £11 **RESTAURANT:** Lunch served: all week Dinner served: Mon-Sat 12-2 6.30-9.30 Av 3 course à la carte £18 **BREWERY/COMPANY:** Greene King
PRINCIPAL BEERS: Greene King Morland Original, IPA & Old Speckled Hen, Wadworth 6X. **FACILITIES:** Children welcome Garden: Food served outside **NOTES:** Parking 40 **ROOMS:** 11 bedrooms 11 en suite from s£67.50 d£87.50

CHENIES

Map 06 TQ09

Pick of the Pubs

The Red Lion
WD3 6ED ☎ 01923 282722 📠 01923 283797
Dir: Between Rickmansworth & Amersham on A404, Sign posted to Chenies and Latimer

Country free house located near to Chenies Manor and the River Chess. The menu is renowned for its freshly prepared, home-made dishes, particularly the range of popular pies, but some newly introduced dishes run along the lines of roasted red pepper with green pea guacamole, tortilla chips and balsamic dressing, or chicken breast stuffed with bacon and mushrooms and coated with a honey crust.
OPEN: 11-2.30 5.30-11 Closed: 25 Dec **BAR MEALS:** Lunch served: all week Dinner served: all week 12-2 7-10 Av main course £7.50 **BREWERY/COMPANY:** Free House
PRINCIPAL BEERS: Wadworth 6X, Rebellion Lion Pride & guest beers changing weekly. **FACILITIES:** Garden: Food served outside Dogs allowed (water) **NOTES:** Parking 14

CHESHAM

Map 06 SP90

The Black Horse Inn
Chesham Vale HP5 3NS ☎ 01494 784656
Dir: A41 from Berkhamstead, A416 through Ashley Green, 0.75m before Chesham R to Vale Rd, btm of Mashleigh Hill follow rd for 1m, inn on L

continued

continued

Set in some beautiful valley countryside, this 500-year old pub is ideal for enjoying a cosy, traditional environment without electronic games or music. During the winter there are roaring log fires to take the chill off those who may spot one of the resident ghosts. An ever-changing menu includes an extensive range of snacks, while the main menu may feature steak and Stallion Ale pie, lamb shank in red wine and rosemary, or cod topped with avocado, cheese and prawns.
OPEN: 12–3 5.30–11 (summer 12–11) **BAR MEALS:** Lunch served: all week Dinner served: all week 12–2.30 6–9.30 Av main course £8.50 **RESTAURANT:** Lunch served: all week Dinner served: all week 12–2.30 6–9.30 Av 3 course à la carte £12 **PRINCIPAL BEERS:** Adnams Bitter, Fuller's London Pride, Greene King Old Speckled Hen. **FACILITIES:** Garden: Food served outdoors, patio, pond Dogs allowed **NOTES:** Parking 80

The Swan 🏨 ♀
Ley Hill HP5 1UT ☎ 01494 783075
e-mail: swan@putland.com
Dir: E of Chesham by golf course
Well-known locally for real ales, good food and conversation, this 500 year-old pub boasts a large inglenook fireplace, leaded lights and original ship's timbers. The pub overlooks Ley Hill Common, and is handy for walks on the nearby Chiltern Hills. Freshly cooked local ingredients feature on the menu, which includes pot-roasted pheasant in red wine, beef and mushrooms in Guinness, as well as a blackboard of regularly changing fish dishes.
OPEN: 12–3 5.30–11 (Sun 12–3, 7–10.30) **BAR MEALS:** Lunch served: all week Dinner served: all week 12–2.15 Av main course £5.95 **RESTAURANT:** Lunch served: all week Dinner served: all week 12–2 7–9 Av 3 course à la carte £16.50 **BREWERY/COMPANY:** Free House **PRINCIPAL BEERS:** Adnams Bitter, Fuller's London Pride, Timothy Taylor Landlord, Marston's Pedigree. **FACILITIES:** Garden: Patio, lawn, food served outside

CHICHELEY   Map 06 SP94

The Chester Arms
MK16 9JE ☎ 01234 391214 🖷 01234 391214
Dir: On A422, 2m NE of Newport Pagnell. 4m from M1 J14

A philosophy of buying well and keeping it simple pays dividends at this comfortable roadside pub near Chicheley Hall (NT). From a shopping list of Angus beef, spring lamb, poultry and fresh fish chalkboards are written up daily and presented at your table. On a typical day, choices might include avocado with lightly curried prawn starter, grilled cod fillet with garlic butter, English duck breast with orange sauce and steak and kidney pie 'like Mum makes'.
OPEN: 11–3 6–11 **BAR MEALS:** Lunch served: Tues–Sun 12–2 Dinner served: Tues–Sat 6.30–9.30 Av main course £5 **RESTAURANT:** Lunch served: Tues–Sun 12–2 Dinner served:

Tues–Sat 6.30–9.30 Av 3 course à la carte £20
BREWERY/COMPANY: Greene King **PRINCIPAL BEERS:** Greene King IPA & Ruddles County. **FACILITIES:** Garden: Food served outside **NOTES:** Parking 25

CHOLESBURY   Map 06 SP90

The Full Moon 🏨 ♀
Hawridge Common HP5 2UH ☎ 01494 758959 🖷 01494 758797
Dir: At Tring on A41 take turn for Wiggington & Cholesbury

A windmill behind the pub sets the scene for this 16th-century coaching inn, beautifully situated opposite Cholesbury Common. Inside, you'll find beamed ceilings, flagstone floors and winter fires. Six cask ales and an international wine list support the extensive menu, with organic meat and poultry supplied by Eastwoods of Berkhamstead. A range of fish dishes might include breaded plaice, blue marlin or sea bass, and there are daily chef's specials, too.
OPEN: 12–3 5.30–11 (Sat all day, Sun 12–10.30) **BAR MEALS:** Lunch served: all week 12–2 Dinner served: Mon–Sat 6.15–9 Av main course £7 **RESTAURANT:** Lunch served: all week 12–2 Dinner served: Mon–Sat 6.15–9 Av 3 course à la carte £16 **BREWERY/COMPANY:** Enterprise Inns **PRINCIPAL BEERS:** Interbrew Bass & Boddingtons Bitter, Fuller's London Pride, Brakspear Special. **FACILITIES:** Children welcome Garden: Patio, food served outside Dogs allowed (water) **NOTES:** Parking 28

CUDDINGTON   Map 06 SP71

Pick of the Pubs

The Crown 🏨 ♀
Spurt St HP18 0BB ☎ 01844 292222
e-mail: david@thecrowncuddington.co.uk

Having successfully run Annie Bailey's bar-cum-brasserie in Cuddington for a number of years, the Berrys have turned their attention to improving the Crown, a delightful

continued

continued

England

CUDDINGTON continued

Grade II listed pub nearby. Customers are pleasantly surprised to find plenty of character inside, with a popular locals' bar and several low-beamed dining areas filled with charming prints and the glow of evening candlelight. A choice of Fullers' beers on tap, an extensive wine list and an eclectic menu add to the enjoyment of a visit here. A short menu may list various snacks, salads and sandwiches with starters including winter broth with leeks and pearl barley and white crab meat with prawns on mixed leaf with Marie Rose dressing. Main dishes may feature game casserole with mushroom croûton, cabbage and celery, breast of chicken with almonds, wild rice and Amaretto glaze, rib-eye steak, smoked haddock on a Cheddar and smoked bacon rösti and chargrilled Mediterranean vegetables with grilled goats' cheese.
OPEN: 12–3 6–11 **BAR MEALS:** Lunch served: all week Dinner served: all week 12–2.30 6.30–10 Av main course £9.50 **RESTAURANT:** Lunch served: all week Dinner served: all week 12–2.30 6.30–10 Av 3 course à la carte £20 Av 3 course fixed price £20 **BREWERY/COMPANY:** Fullers **PRINCIPAL BEERS:** Fullers London Pride, Adnams. **FACILITIES:** Children welcome Garden: Patio, food served outside **NOTES:** Parking 12

DINTON
Map 04 SU71

Seven Stars
Stars Ln HP17 8UL ☎ 01296 748241
e-mail: secretpub.company@virgin.net
Built around 1640, this picturesque country pub is made from a material known as 'witchert', peculiar to a small area of Buckinghamshire and Oxfordshire. Inside are inglenook fireplaces, wooden settles, and a snug. Restuarant menu includes the likes of potato and red cabbage layer cake, rump steak, twin garlic and mint marinated lamb shanks, poached supreme of lime and coriander marinated salmon, and vegetable bourginon. Sandwiches, light bites, grills, burgers, and specials available in the bar.
OPEN: 12–3 (Sun 12–3) 6–11 (Sun 7–10.30) **BAR MEALS:** Lunch served: all week 12–2.30 Dinner served: Mon–Sat 6.30–9 Av main course £5 **RESTAURANT:** Dinner served: Tues–Sat 6.30–9 **PRINCIPAL BEERS:** London Pride, Greene King IPA. **FACILITIES:** Garden: Food served outside. Lawned area Dogs allowed (in the garden only, water provided) **NOTES:** Parking 20

DORNEY
Map 04 SU97

The Palmer Arms
Village Rd SL4 6QW ☎ 01628 666612
Dir: From A4 take B3026, over M4 to Dorney
An 18th-century pub in a rural location close to Dorney Court and the River Thames. After a riverside stroll enjoy a pint and your choice from a wide ranging menu. Coming under new management at time of going to press.
OPEN: 12–3 6–11 (Sun 12–3, 7–10.30) **BAR MEALS:** Lunch served: all week 12–2.30 Dinner served: Mon–Sat 6–9.30 Av main course £8 **RESTAURANT:** Lunch served: all week 12–2.30 Dinner served: Mon–Sat 6–9.30 Av 3 course à la carte £20 **BREWERY/COMPANY:** Old English Pub Co **PRINCIPAL BEERS:** Rebellion IPA, Theakston Old Peculier, Courage Best. **FACILITIES:** Children welcome Garden: Dogs allowed **NOTES:** Parking 50

See Pub Walk on page 41

FARNHAM COMMON
Map 04 SU98

The Foresters NEW
The Broadway SL2 3QQ ☎ 01753 643340 📠 01753 647524
e-mail: barforesters@aol.com
The combination of a good drinking ambience in the bar and a busy restaurant, renowned for the quality of its food, creates a real buzz at the Foresters - formerly the Foresters Arms. The pub was built in the 1930s, replacing a Victorian building, and is located close to Burnham Beeches, a large woodland area famous for its coppiced trees. The daily menu might include kangaroo steak, fillet of parrot fish, and falafel with pitta bread.
OPEN: 11–11 Mon–Sat 12–10.30 Sun **BAR MEALS:** Lunch served: all week Dinner served: all week 12–3 6.30–10 Av main course £9 **RESTAURANT:** Lunch served: all week Dinner served: all week 12–2.30 6.30–10 Av 3 course à la carte £20 **PRINCIPAL BEERS:** Fullers London Pride, Draught Bass, Youngs Special Bitter. **FACILITIES:** Children welcome Food served outside Dogs allowed (water provided)

FAWLEY
Map 04 SU78

Pick of the Pubs

The Walnut Tree
RG9 6JE ☎ 01491 638360 📠 01491 639508
Dir: From Henley on A4155 towards Marlow, L at 2nd sign for Fawley. R at village green
Set in the Chiltern Hills with wonderful views some 400ft above Henley-on-Thames, the pub retains two gnarled walnut trees in a fine garden that boasts a barbecue, rustic swings and an original hitching-post: there is also walnut furniture in the restaurant reputedly made from a tree felled on the site. An up-to-date feel on the latest menus produces lunchtime fare such as seared sea bass fillets on smoked bacon mash, turkey escalope in a brioche crumb with red onion and celery sauce, Tuscan chicken wrapped in charred leeks with Parma ham, and grilled king scallops in cucumber and lemon butter. Also watch the blackboard menus for daily specials.
OPEN: 12–3 6–11 (Sat-Sun & Bhs 11–11) **BAR MEALS:** Lunch served: all week Dinner served: all week 12–3 7–9.30 Av main course £7 **RESTAURANT:** Lunch served: all week Dinner served: all week 12–3 7–9.30 Av 3 course à la carte £25 **BREWERY/COMPANY:** Brakspear **PRINCIPAL BEERS:** Brakspear. **FACILITIES:** Children welcome Garden: beer garden, patio, outdoor eating, BBQ Dogs allowed **NOTES:** Parking 50

FINGEST
Map 04 SU79

The Chequers Inn
RG9 6QD ☎ 01491 638335
Dir: From M40 L towards Ibstone, L at T junc at end of rd, stay L, pub on R
Set deep in the Chiltern Hills, opposite a splendid Norman church, the Chequers is a 15th-century redbrick pub with log fires in the winter, and a delightful sun-trap garden with rural views for summer imbibing.

England

FORD

Map 06 SP70

Pick of the Pubs

The Dinton Hermit ♀
Water Ln HP17 8XH ☎ 01296 747473 🖨 01296 748316
Dir: Off A418 between Aylesbury & Thame
Set back from the lane in an isolated hamlet, this 15th-century stone-built pub is named after John Biggs, clerk to one of the judges who condemned Charles I to death. So ashamed was he of his part in the execution that he became a hermit, and subsequently a local legend. Another John – John Bingham Chick – runs the pub these days, and offers a good range of beers – Hook Norton, Adnams, Morrells and Marstons – along with hearty, freshly prepared food in both of the beamed and warmly decorated bars. Half a crisp roast Barbary duck (boneless except for the leg bone), served with ginger, chilli and papaya salsa, is a signature dish, and another favourite is seared fillet of Angus beef with pak choy, fresh lime and ginger. The pub has an acre of garden looking out over the countryside, and accommodation is provided in nine letting rooms. Children are made welcome.
OPEN: 11–2.30 6–11 **BAR MEALS:** Lunch served: all week
Dinner served: all week 12–2 7–9.30 Av main course £10
RESTAURANT: Lunch served: all week Dinner served: all week
12–2 7–9.30 Av 3 course à la carte £22
BREWERY/COMPANY: Free House
PRINCIPAL BEERS: Hook Norton Best, Adnams Bitter, Marston's Bitter, Morrells. **FACILITIES:** Children welcome
Garden: Food served outside **NOTES:** Parking 30 **ROOMS:** 9
bedrooms 9 en suite from s£70 d£80

FRIETH

Map 04 SU79

The Prince Albert
RG9 6PY ☎ 01494 881683
An old-fashioned country local, very much a community pub but also ideal for a stop-off when walking in the Chilterns. The customers are a mixed bunch, vehicles in the car park ranging from battered four-wheel drives to Porsches and Rolls Royces, but they all mix well and there are no airs and graces. Brakspear beers are served alongside pub food ranging from sandwiches and jacket potatoes to salmon and rib of beef.
OPEN: 12–3 5.30–11 **BAR MEALS:** Lunch served: all week Dinner served: all week 12–3 6–9.30 Av main course £8
BREWERY/COMPANY: Brakspear **PRINCIPAL BEERS:** Barkspear Bitter, Special. **FACILITIES:** Children welcome Garden: Food served outside Dogs allowed **NOTES:** Parking 20 No credit cards

The Yew Tree
RG9 6PJ ☎ 01494 882330 🖨 01494 882927
e-mail: theyewtree@hotmail.com
Dir: from M40 towards Stokenchurch, thru Cadmore End, Lane End R to Frieth
A huge yew tree spirals majestically outside this 16th-century red-brick pub in this truly rural Chilterns village. Sit in the pretty flower garden, or in the original-beamed bar with its inglenook and tip-top ales, and enjoy a hot chicken sandwich, traditional fish and chips, smoked salmon tagliatelle, or grilled plaice. New restaurant operation sounds interesting.
OPEN: 11–3 (Sun 12–4) 6–11 (Sun 7–10.30) **BAR MEALS:** Lunch served: all week Dinner served: all week 11–2.30 6.30–10 Av main course £9.95 **RESTAURANT:** Lunch served: all week Dinner served: all week 11–2.30 6.30–10 Av 3 course à la carte £18.50

BREWERY/COMPANY: Free House
PRINCIPAL BEERS: Brakspear Bitter, Fullers London Pride, Oakham JBH. **FACILITIES:** Children welcome Garden: Dogs allowed **NOTES:** Parking 60

GREAT BRICKHILL

Map 06 SP93

The Old Red Lion ♀
Ivy Ln MK17 9AH ☎ 01525 261715 🖨 01525 261716
e-mail: fineale@oldredlion.co.uk
Dir: Signposted off A5, 10m S of Milton Keynes

This friendly local was first established as a pub in 1771. The garden overlooks the Aylesbury Vale, and is reckoned to have the best view in Buckinghamshire. Here you'll find fine ales and varied menus, freshly prepared with local ingredients where possible. Lunchtime dishes include warm baguettes, beef or vegetable lasagne, and a daily curry. In the evening, choose from sausage and mushroom casserole, Jamaican jerk chicken, or oven baked salmon.
OPEN: 11–1 5.30–11 (Sun 12–10.30) **BAR MEALS:** Lunch served: all week 12–2 Dinner served: Tue–Sat 7–9 Av main course £9.50
RESTAURANT: Lunch served: all week 12–2 Dinner served: Tue–Sat 7–9 Av 3 course à la carte £20 **BREWERY/COMPANY:** Whitbread
PRINCIPAL BEERS: Interbrew Flowers Original, Greene King IPA & guest beer. **FACILITIES:** Garden: Food served outdoors
NOTES: Parking 6

GREAT HAMPDEN

Map 06 SP70

The Hampden Arms 🍴
HP16 9RQ ☎ 01494 488255 🖨 01494 488255
e-mail: tezy@pubham.fsnet.co.uk
Dir: From M40 take A4010, R before Princes Risborough, Great Hampden signposted
Whether you're celebrating a special occasion or just want a quiet pint of real ale, you'll find a warm and friendly welcome at this mock Tudor pub restaurant in the heart of the beautifully wooded Hampden Estate. The menu features light lunches and a fixed-price range of traditional home-cooked meals, as well as dishes like chicken Somerset, Dover sole or rib-eye steak. There's a nice selection of hot puddings to finish off.
OPEN: 12–3 6.30–11 (Sun 6.30–10.30) **BAR MEALS:** Lunch served: all week Dinner served: all week 12–2 6.30–9.30 Av main course £6.95
RESTAURANT: Lunch served: all week Dinner served: all week 12–2 6.30–9.30 Av 3 course à la carte £17.50 **BREWERY/COMPANY:** Free House **PRINCIPAL BEERS:** Adnams Bitter, Brakspear Bitter, Interbrew Boddingtons Bitter. **FACILITIES:** Children welcome Garden: Beer garden, food served outdoors **NOTES:** Parking 30

continued

The George Inn 🛏 🍸
94 High St HP16 0BG ☎ 01494 862084 ▤ 01494 865622
Dir: off A413 between Aylesbury & Amersham
Established as a coaching inn in 1483, the George has always
had strong ties with nearby Missenden Abbey. The small, cosy
bars boast a wealth of old beams and fireplaces, whilst a tithe
barn in the grounds houses the original stables. The
restaurant offers a relaxed, non-smoking environment for
lunchtime snacks, plus hot dishes like ham, egg and chips,
salmon fishcakes and spicy tomato pasta. Evenings bring a
range of authentic Thai seafood and specials.
OPEN: 11-11 (Sun 12-3, 7-10.30) **BAR MEALS:** Lunch served: all
week 12.30-2.30 Av main course £5.50 **RESTAURANT:** Dinner
served: Tue-Sat 12.30-2.30 Av 3 course à la carte £17.50 Av 3 course
fixed price £12 **BREWERY/COMPANY:** Inn Partnership
PRINCIPAL BEERS: Adnams Bitter, Young's Special, Interbrew
Flowers Original. **FACILITIES:** Children welcome Garden: Food
served outside Dogs allowed (water) **NOTES:** Parking 25
ROOMS: 6 bedrooms 6 en suite from s£65 d£65

Pick of the Pubs

The Polecat Inn 🛏 🍸
170 Wycombe Rd, Prestwood HP16 0HJ
☎ 01494 862253 ▤ 01494 868393
e-mail: polecatinn@btinternet.com
Dir: On the A4128 between Great Missenden and High Wycombe
A three-acre garden, with plenty of tables for alfresco
summer eating, is the setting for this charming 17th-
century inn situated in the heart of the Chiltern Hills. A
rambling series of small, low-beamed rooms with rug-
strewn floors radiate from the central bar, and the
comfortable mix of furnishings includes cabinets full of
stuffed birds. There are good open fires in the winter
months. Local ingredients and herbs from the garden are
the foundation of the wide-ranging menu and interesting
specials boards, and food is freshly prepared on the
premises. Lunchtime brings sandwiches, ploughman's and
hot roast beef in stotty bread, whilst the main menu
includes plenty of choice. Expect starters like salmon crab
and avocado terrine, or leek and potato soufflé, with
smoked haddock bake, lamb cobbler, or roulade of pesto
vegetables and Ricotta cheese to follow. Coconut
meringues or raspberry shortcake if you've room.
OPEN: 11.30-2.30 6-11 Closed: Dec 25-26, Jan 1
BAR MEALS: Lunch served: all week 12-2 Dinner served:
Mon-Sat 6.30-9 Av main course £8 **BREWERY/COMPANY:** Free
House **PRINCIPAL BEERS:** Marston's Pedigree, Wadworth 6X,
Greene King Old Speckled Hen, Interbrew Flowers IPA.
FACILITIES: Children welcome Garden: Food served outside
Dogs allowed **NOTES:** Parking 40 No credit cards

Pick of the Pubs

The Rising Sun 🛏 🍸
Little Hampden HP16 9PS
☎ 01494 488393 & 488360 ▤ 01494 488788
e-mail: sunrising@rising-sun.demon.co.uk
Dir: From A413 N of Gt Missenden take Rignall Rd on L (signed
Princes Risborough) 2.5m turn R signed 'Little Hampden only'
You'll find this 250-year-old country inn tucked away in
the Chiltern Hills surrounded by beech woods and
glorious scenery in an area of outstanding natural beauty

– a network of footpaths beginning from outside the front
door. The pub is a rarity these days, offering a welcome
pause in a fast-moving world. It is situated at the end of a
single track – a no through road seemingly miles from
anywhere – yet London is only 40 minutes away by train
from nearby Great Missenden. The proprietor prides
himself on a well-run, clean and welcoming
establishment, which offers an interesting snack menu, a
popular Sunday lunch and a carte for lunch and dinner. A
good choice of seafood includes poached sea bass with
mushroom and white wine sauce, while other regulars are
roast shoulder of lamb joint with rosemary and honey
sauce, or warm smoked chicken and bacon salad.
OPEN: 11.30-2.30 6.30-11 **BAR MEALS:** Lunch served:
Tue-Sun 12-2 Dinner served: Tue-Sat 7-9 Av main course £8.95
RESTAURANT: Lunch served: Tue-Sun 12-2 Dinner served:
Tue-Sat 7-9 Av 3 course à la carte £18
BREWERY/COMPANY: Free House
PRINCIPAL BEERS: Adnams, Brakspear Bitter, Marstons
Pedigree. **FACILITIES:** Children welcome Garden: Food served
outside Dogs allowed (water) **NOTES:** Parking 20
ROOMS: 2 bedrooms 2 en suite from s£30 d£58

Pick of the Pubs

The Green Dragon 🍴🍴 🛏 🍸
8 Churchway HP17 8AA ☎ 01844 291403
e-mail: paul@eatatthedragon.co.uk
See Pick of the Pubs on page 49

Pick of the Pubs

The Stag & Huntsman Inn
RG9 6RP ☎ 01491 571227 ▤ 01491 413810
Dir: 5m from Henley-on-Thames on A4155 toward Marlow, L at Mill
End towards Hambleden
This warm and welcoming 400 year-old brick and flint inn
lies close to the glorious beech-clad Chilterns. In addition
to its local trade, customers range from walkers and
cyclists to business people and tourists. The charming
building has featured in many films and TV productions,
including *101 Dalmatians*, *Midsomer Murders*, *As Time
Goes By*, *Poirot* and *A Band of Brothers*. After an
exhilarating ramble in the hills, relax in the cosy snug, or
choose the public bar for a traditional game of darts or
dominoes. Alternatively, savour the bustling atmosphere
of the L-shaped, half-panelled lounge, with its low ceilings,
open fire, and upholstered seating. There's also a dining
room, where you can sample home-made chilli,
chargrilled chicken and chips, steaks and seasonal game.
OPEN: 11-2.30 6-11 (Sun 12-3, 7-10.30, Sat 11-3, 6-11) Closed:
Dec 25 **BAR MEALS:** Lunch served: all week 12-2 Dinner
served: Mon-Sat 7-9.30 Av main course £8.25
BREWERY/COMPANY: Free House
PRINCIPAL BEERS: Brakspear Bitter, Wadworth 6X, guest ales.
FACILITIES: Children welcome Garden: Food served outside
NOTES: Parking 60 **ROOMS:** 3 bedrooms 3 en suite from
s£58 d£68

continued

OPEN: 11.30–3 6.30–11
BAR MEALS: L served all week.
D served all week. 12–2 7–9.30
RESTAURANT: L served all week.
D served all week. 12–2 7–9.30 Av
cost 3 course £23
BREWERY/COMPANY:
WHITBREAD
PRINCIPAL BEERS: Vale Notley
Ale, Fullers London Pride, Timothy
Taylor
FACILITIES: Children welcome.
Garden: Food served outside.
NOTES: Parking 18

The Green Dragon

★ ◉◉ ♀
8 Churchway HP17 8AA
☎ 01844 291403
e-mail: paul@eatatthedragon.co.uk
Dir: From M40 A329 to Thame, then
A418, 1st R after entering Haddenham

The Green Dragon enjoys a pretty location in the old part of Haddenham close to the 12th-century church and village green. Head chef Paul Berry has taken this manorial 17th-century former courthouse by the horns, with gratifying results for an ever-increasing following of discerning diners.

Most of the character interior is given over to a food operation that services a pair of stylish dining areas, with an enclosed gravel terrace handling the summer overflow. Do not, however, count on a private chat at the closely spaced tables, a failing possibly rectified by his late evening appearances to check how things have gone - a nice touch. Fine ingredients and execution shine throughout a wide-ranging selection of daily menus that give precious little cause for complaint. Start off perhaps with real ale in the bar, turn off the mobile and then enjoy a compendium of options that begins with the day's soup and toasted snippets, duck liver parfait with orange dressing and a brochette of scallops, langoustine, halibut and salmon on a lime and pine-nut dressing. Main dishes, inclusively served with potato and fresh vegetables, encompass Cornish sea bass with vanilla and Chablis beurre blanc, Gressingham duck on green cabbage with marjoram and Scottish sirloin steak with a sauce of Cashel Blue and walnuts. Dictated by careful daily shopping, specials might include a trio of local pork sausage with mash, gravy and crispy fried onions, pan-seared lambs' liver with onion marmalade and fillet steak flamed in brandy with wild mushroom sauce. A varied selection of puddings is likely to include lemon tart and citrus sorbet, chocolate parfait with cappuccino sabayon and fruit rum toft with home-made Agen ice cream.

England

HIGH WYCOMBE — Map 04 SU89

The Chequers

Bullocks Farm Ln, Wheeler End HP14 3NH ☎ 01494 883070
e-mail: thechequers.inn@virgin.net
Dir: From M4 J5, B482 towards Marlow, L to Wheeler End. Or M4 J5 A40 towards H Wycombe, R to Wheeler End
The Chequers, situated on the edge of Wheeler End Common, dates back 300 years and retains many original features including low beams and open fires. It is known locally for its real ale and freshly produced food. The menu changes regularly and features local game and seasonal fish and meat dishes, such as warm pigeon and apple salad, Chequered venison, and baked sea bass on a sun-dried tomato and potato confit with watercress and rocket dressing.
OPEN: 12–3 5.30–11 (Sat-Sun all day) **BAR MEALS:** Lunch served: all week 12–2 7–9 Av main course £9 **RESTAURANT:** Lunch served: all week Dinner served: all week 12–2.30 7–10 Av 3 course à la carte £17 **BREWERY/COMPANY:** Fullers **PRINCIPAL BEERS:** Fuller's ESB, London Pride. **FACILITIES:** Children welcome Garden: Food served outside Dogs allowed (water & biscuits) **NOTES:** Parking 18

KINGSWOOD — Map 06 SP61

Crooked Billet

Ham Green HP18 0QJ ☎ 01296 770239 ▤ 01296 770094
Dir: On A41 between Aylesbury & Bicester
Located in peaceful Buckinghamshire countryside, The Crooked Billet has been a pub for about 200 years and is believed to be haunted by Fair Rosamund, a girlfriend of Charles I.

LACEY GREEN — Map 06 SP80

Pink & Lily

Pink Rd HP27 0RJ ☎ 01494 488308 ▤ 01494 488013
Dir: Off A4010 S of Princes Risborough
The pub is named after a local butler (Mr Lily), who had a liaison with a chambermaid (Miss Pink). On being dismissed from service they set themselves up as inkeepers. The inn has several refurbished eating and drinking areas serving the likes of home-made pies, fresh cod in beer batter, and favourite sweets such as apple pie and sticky toffee pudding.
OPEN: 11.30–11 (Sat 11–11, Sun 12–10.30) **BAR MEALS:** Lunch served: all week 12–2 Dinner served: Mon-Sat 7–9.30 Av main course £8 **BREWERY/COMPANY:** Free House
PRINCIPAL BEERS: Brakspear Bitter & Special, Fullers London Pride, Vale Notley Ale, Courage Best. **FACILITIES:** Children welcome Garden: beer garden with seating, patio Dogs allowed (garden only) **NOTES:** Parking 40

LONG CRENDON — Map 06 SP60

Pick of the Pubs

The Angel Inn

47 Bicester Rd HP18 9EE ☎ 01844 208268 ▤ 018... 202497
Dir: A418 to Thame, B4011 to L Crendon, Inn on B4011
Wattle and daub walls, a warm yellow interior and an inglenook fireplace testify to the age of this upgraded 16th-century coaching inn. Inside it's an assorted mix of scrubbed pine and sturdy oak tables on light wooden floors, and comfy Chesterfields fronting the bar. Real ales are served, but the commitment is to first-class pub dining, with food provided in the air-conditioned conservatory, as well as the patio and sun terrace. There's

a broad range of modern dishes with a Mediterranean tang, plus daily blackboards listing imaginative fish and seafood dishes. For lunch it's a choice of light bites – pan-fried Highland black pudding, or various crostini breads – and the more substantial chargrilled lambs' liver and bacon, and seafood and saffron risotto. In the evening consider saltimbocca of wild boar, or roast pheasant on a crispy bacon and potato rösti. For dessert try cranberry toffee tart with caramel sauce and vanilla ice cream.
OPEN: 12–3 7–10 **BAR MEALS:** Lunch served: all week 12–3 Dinner served: Mon-Sat 7–10 Av main course £12
RESTAURANT: Lunch served: all week 12–3 Dinner served: Mon-Sat 7–10 Av 3 course à la carte £30 **BREWERY/COMPANY:** Free House
PRINCIPAL BEERS: Hook Norton Best, Adnams Broadside, Ridleys Rumpus. **FACILITIES:** Children welcome Garden: Patio, food served outside **NOTES:** Parking 25 **ROOMS:** 3 bedrooms 3 en suite from s£55 d£65

Pick of the Pubs

Mole & Chicken

Easington Ter HP18 9EY ☎ 01844 208387 ▤ 01844 208250
e-mail: themoleandchicken@hotmail.com
Dir: Off B4011 N of Thame

Built in 1831 in a fold of the Chiltern Hills as a beer and cider house and formerly known as The Rising Sun, this fashionable dining pub was re-named after two latter day proprietors, Mr Mole and Mr Chicken: of such stuff are legends made. A tastefully decorated interior features cosy fireplaces, rag-washed walls and flagstone floors in the oak beamed bar, while the tiered and terraced garden enjoys outstanding views across three counties. Suggested menu specialities, posted on boards over the fireplace's oak lintel, include secret recipe fishcakes with mild curry sauce and skewers of satay chicken and shell-on prawns enticingly entitled Horses Douvay. Follow then with marinated and slow roast rack of pork ribs, salmon filled with prawn and dill mousse in filo pastry or penne pasta tossed in sun-dried tomato pesto. Roast lamb shoulder with honey and rosemary sauce and local pheasant with shallots, red wine, bacon and sage provide further variations on traditional themes.
OPEN: 12–3.30 6–12 Closed: 25 Dec **BAR MEALS:** Lunch served: all week Dinner served: all week 12–2 6–10 Av main course £11 **RESTAURANT:** Lunch served: all week Dinner served: all week 12–2 6–10 Av 3 course à la carte £22
BREWERY/COMPANY: Free House
PRINCIPAL BEERS: Hook Norton, Ruddles Best, Greene King IPA & Old Speckled Hen. **FACILITIES:** Children welcome Garden: Food served outside. **NOTES:** Parking 40
ROOMS: 5 bedrooms 5 en suite from s£50 d£65

continued

MARLOW
Map 04 SU88

The Kings Head 🍴 🍷
Church Rd, Little Marlow SL7 3RZ
☎ 01628 484407 📠 01628 484407
Dir: M40 J4 take A4040 S 1st A4155
This flower-adorned pub, only 10 minutes from the Thames Footpath, dates back to 1654. It has a cosy, open-plan interior with original beams and open fires. From sandwiches and jacket potatoes, the menu extends to the likes of sea bass with ginger, sherry and spring onions; lamb shank with rich minty gravy, mash and fresh vegetables, and a pheasant and chestnut casserole.
OPEN: 11–3 5–11 (Sat-Sun 11–11) **BAR MEALS:** Lunch served: all week Dinner served: all week 12–2.15 6.30–9.30 Av main course £7.95
RESTAURANT: Lunch served: all week Dinner served: all week 12–2.15 6.30–9.30 Av 3 course à la carte £12.50
BREWERY/COMPANY: Whitbread **PRINCIPAL BEERS:** Brakspear Bitter, Fuller's London Pride, Wadworth 6X, Morrells Varsity.
FACILITIES: Children welcome Garden: Food served outside
NOTES: Parking 50

MOULSOE
Map 06 SP94

The Carrington Arms 🍴 🍷
Cranfield Rd MK16 0HB ☎ 01908 218050 📠 01908 217850
Dir: M1 J14 take rd signed 'Cranfield & Moulsoe'. Pub 1m on R
Before becoming a pub, this Grade II listed building was the home of Lord Carrington's estate manager. Orders are taken directly by the chef who cooks on a range in full view of his expectant customers. Food includes excellent steaks and fish, various Thai dishes, beef and ale cobbler and smoked chicken salad.
OPEN: 11–3 6–11 (Sun 12–3, 7–10.30) **BAR MEALS:** Lunch served: all week Dinner served: all week 12–2 6.30–10 Av main course £15
RESTAURANT: Lunch served: all week Dinner served: all week 12–2 6.30–10 Av 3 course à la carte £20 **BREWERY/COMPANY:** Free House **PRINCIPAL BEERS:** Brakspear Special & Best, Brakspear Bitter & seasonal ale. **FACILITIES:** Children welcome Garden: Food served outside. Patio & lawned areas. Dogs allowed (in the garden only) **NOTES:** Parking 100 **ROOMS:** 8 bedrooms 8 en suite from s£40.50 d£40.50

PRINCES RISBOROUGH
Map 06 SP80

Red Lion 🍴
Upper Icknield Way, Whiteleaf HP27 0LL
☎ 01844 344476 📠 01844 273124
e-mail: tim.hibbert@lineone.net
Dir: A4010 thru Princes Risbro', then R into 'Holloway', go to end of road, R, pub on L
Family-owned 17th-century inn in the heart of the Chilterns, surrounded by National Trust land and situated close to the Ridgeway national trail. Plenty of good local walks with wonderful views. A cosy fire in winter and a secluded summer beer garden add to the appeal. Hearty pub fare includes steaks, stir fries and home-made curries, as well as haddock and chips garlic and herb chicken, and various pies.
OPEN: 11.30–3 5.30–11 (Sun 12–9, 7–10.30) (All day Wkds May-Sept)
BAR MEALS: Lunch served: all week 12–2 Dinner served: Mon-Sat 7–9 Av main course £7.25 **RESTAURANT:** Lunch served: all week 12–2 Dinner served: Mon-Sat 7–9 Av 3 course à la carte £20
BREWERY/COMPANY: Free House
PRINCIPAL BEERS: Brakspear Bitter, Hook Norton Best, Tetleys.
FACILITIES: Children welcome Garden: Food served outside. Plenty of benches Dogs allowed (water provided) **NOTES:** Parking 10
ROOMS: 4 bedrooms 4 en suite from s£40 d£50

SKIRMETT
Map 04 SU79

The Frog 🍷
RG9 6TG ☎ 01491 638996 📠 01491 638045

From its pretty, clay-tiled dormer windows to its overflowing flower tubs, this eye-catching whitewashed free house exudes warmth and tranquillity. Set deep in one of the loveliest valleys in the Chiltern Hills, The Frog lies close to the heart of 'Vicar of Dibley' country. There are attractive rural views from the delightful, tree-shaded garden, and you may be tempted to enjoy one of the recommended local walks. Once inside, this family-run pub does not disappoint though in wintertime you may have to queue for a place on the unusual wooden bench that encircles the fireplace. There are five comfortably furnished en suite bedrooms, and a reassuringly civilised non-smoking restaurant. The wide ranging international menu is changed monthly, and daily specials are featured on the blackboard. Fresh ingredients and confident cooking produce home-made soups, Irish fry-up, and braised lamb shank. There's always a good selection of fish, too; expect haddock in beer batter, red mullet, sea bass, or bream.
OPEN: 11–3 6–11 **BAR MEALS:** Lunch served: all week Dinner served: all week 12–2.30 6.30–9.30 Av main course £8.50
RESTAURANT: Lunch served: all week Dinner served: all week 12–2.30 6.30–9.30 Av 3 course à la carte £17.95
BREWERY/COMPANY: Free House
PRINCIPAL BEERS: Adnams Best, Brakspear Bitter, Fullers London Pride. **FACILITIES:** Children welcome Garden: beer garden, patio, outdoor eating Dogs allowed **NOTES:** Parking 15
ROOMS: 5 bedrooms 5 en suite from s£55 d£65

SPEEN
Map 04 SU89

King William IV
Hampden Rd HP27 0RU ☎ 01494 488329 📠 01494 488301
Dir: Through Hughenden Valley, off A4128 N of High Wycombe
Nestling in the Chiltern Hills, this 17th-century, family run pub and restaurant boasts log fires in winter and a popular terrace and garden ideal for summer drinking. Choose from an interesting range of blackboard specials that might include Thai green chicken curry, grilled red snapper and trio of Welsh lamb cutlets.
OPEN: 12–3 6–11 **RESTAURANT:** Lunch served: Tue-Sun 12–2 Dinner served: Tue-Sat 7–9 Av 3 course à la carte £22.50
BREWERY/COMPANY: Free House
PRINCIPAL BEERS: Brakspear, Old Speckled Hen, plus guest ales.
FACILITIES: Children welcome Garden: lawned area with cast iron feature, patio **NOTES:** Parking 50

England

THORNBOROUGH   Map 06 SP73

The Lone Tree
Bletchley Rd MK18 2DZ ☎ 01280 812334
This rather isolated pub sits beside the A421 east of Birmingham, and is reknowned locally for its cheeses and chutneys as well as its choice of real ale. Interesting menu.

TURVILLE   Map 04 SU79

Pick of the Pubs

The Bull & Butcher ♀
RG9 6QU ☎ 01491 638283 📠 01491 638283
e-mail: nick@bull&butcher.com
Dir: M40 J5 follow signs for Ibstone. Turn R T-junc. Pub 0.25m on L
Lovely, black and white timbered 16th-century pub tucked away in a secluded valley in a classic Chiltern village that is regularly used as a film set, including The Vicar of Dibley. Two unspoilt, low-ceilinged bars with open fires, a welcoming atmosphere, and good restaurant-style food in a traditional pub setting. Daily menus, served throughout, show imagination and flair and make good use of fresh local produce, including local estate game and fish bought direct from Billingsgate. Don't expect traditional pub food, light meals include salads – grilled goats' cheese salad with tapenade, warm salad of king scallops and wild mushrooms – or starters like hot home-smoked beef pastrami on rye and smoked haddock, spinach and potato terrine. Hearty, rustic main dishes may feature Toulouse sausages with mash, roast shallots and gravy and calves' liver with peccorino mash and smoked bacon. Tip-top Brakspear ales on tap, 37 wines by the glass and excellent local walks; delightful summer garden.
OPEN: 11–3 (Sun 12–5, 7–10.30) 6–11 (Sat 6.30–11)
BAR MEALS: Lunch served: Mon-Sun 12–2 Dinner served: Mon-Sat 6–11 Av main course £10.95 **RESTAURANT:** Lunch served: Mon-Sun 12–2 Dinner served: Mon-Sat 6–11 Av 3 course à la carte £17 **BREWERY/COMPANY:** Brakspear
PRINCIPAL BEERS: Brakspear Mild, Bitter, Special, Old & Choice. **FACILITIES:** Garden: BBQ, outdoor eating, beer garden Dogs allowed **NOTES:** Parking 20

WENDOVER   Map 06 SP80

Red Lion Hotel ♀
High St HP22 6DU ☎ 01296 622266 📠 01296 625077
e-mail: redlion@regentinns.plc.uk
A 17th-century coaching inn located in the heart of the Chilterns, popular with regulars and providing a welcome break for cyclists and walkers. One menu is served throughout offering the likes of grilled fillet of sea bass with lime, ginger and coriander marinade on linguine pasta, or slow cooked shoulder of lamb with cheddar mash and redcurrant, rosemary and red wine gravy.
OPEN: 7–11 (Sun 8–11) **BAR MEALS:** Lunch served: all week Dinner served: all week 12–2 5–9.30 Av main course £7.50 **RESTAURANT:** Lunch served: all week Dinner served: all week 12–2 5–9.30 Av 3 course à la carte £19 **BREWERY/COMPANY:** Free House **PRINCIPAL BEERS:** Youngs, Adnams, Brakspears and Red Lion, plus guest ales. **FACILITIES:** Children welcome Garden: Food served outside **NOTES:** Parking 60 **ROOMS:** 24 bedrooms 24 en suite from s£55 d£65

WEST WYCOMBE   Map 04 SU89

Pick of the Pubs

The George and Dragon Hotel ♀
High St HP14 3AB ☎ 01494 464414 📠 01494 462432
e-mail: enq@george-and-dragon.co.uk
Dir: M40 North, J5, L onto A40, 4m into village. M40 South, J4, A4010 to T-jct, L onto A40, village 0.5m

Reached through a cobbled archway, this 18th-century coaching inn has seen generations of visitors, one of whom is rumoured to still haunt its corridors. It's a characterful jumble of whitewashed, timber-framed buildings whose comfortable and interesting bedrooms have the uneven floorboards and quirky angles that come with age. The varied menu should keep everybody happy. Dishes range from starters or snacks such as home made soup, grilled goats' cheese or hot crab pot, through to a wide selection of home-made main courses. Typical examples include Cumberland sweet lamb pie, steak and kidney pudding, beef Wellington and chicken Copenhagen (breast stuffed with cream cheese and wrapped in bacon). As well as a good choice of well-kept real ales, don't miss the opportunity to sample wines imported by the hotel and for sale in the wine shop across the courtyard. Outside you'll also find a large garden complete with children's play area.
OPEN: 11–2.30 5.30–11 **BAR MEALS:** Lunch served: all week Dinner served: all week 12–2 6–9.30 Av main course £7.50
BREWERY/COMPANY: Inntrepreneur
PRINCIPAL BEERS: Fuller's London Pride, Wells Bombardier, Greene King Abbot Ale, Wadworth 6X. **FACILITIES:** Children welcome Garden: beer garden, BBQ, food served outdoors Dogs allowed (water) **NOTES:** Parking 35 **ROOMS:** 11 bedrooms 11 en suite from d£72

WHITCHURCH   Map 06 SP82

The White Horse Inn 🛏 ♀
60 High St HP22 4JS ☎ 01296 641377 📠 01296 640454
e-mail: whitchurchhorse@aol.com
Dir: A413 4 M N of Aylesbury
In a picturesque village setting, this 16th-century inn boasts an open fire and a resident ghost. The kitchen uses best local produce and has a good local reputation. Choose from more than twenty steak dishes (all Aberdeen Angus), or maybe sea bass or grilled mackerel.
OPEN: 12–3 6–11 (Sun 12–4.30) **BAR MEALS:** Lunch served: Tues-Sun 12–2 Dinner served: Mon-Sat 7–9 Av main course £7.50 **RESTAURANT:** Lunch served: Tues-Sun 12–2 Dinner served: Mon-Sat 7–9 Av 3 course à la carte £15

continued

BREWERY/COMPANY: Punch Taverns
PRINCIPAL BEERS: Brakspear Bitter, Young's Bitter, Batemans Bitter, Adnams Bitter. **FACILITIES:** Children welcome Garden: Patio, food served outside Dogs allowed (water) **NOTES:** Parking 20
ROOMS: 2 bedrooms 2 en suite from s£30 d£45

WOOBURN COMMON   Map 04 SU98

Pick of the Pubs

Chequers Inn ★ ★
Kiln Ln HP10 0JQ ☎ 01628 529575 ▤ 01628 850124
e-mail: info@chequers-inn.com
Dir: M40 J2 through Beaconsfield towards H Wycombe.1m turn L into Broad Lane. Inn 2.5m
Just two miles from the M40 at Junction 2, it's hard to believe that this deeply rural inn is only 24 miles by road from central London. Built in the 17th century, with a massive oak post and beam bar, it's a splendidly snug spot on a cold winter's night and delightful when sitting out with a drink on balmy summer evenings. Bedroom accommodation is convenient, up-to-date and thoroughly comfortable. Choose the brasserie or bar for relaxed, well-priced meals along the lines of chicken curry or a home made beefburger with bacon, cheese, chips and salad. If you're after something more formal, try the atmospheric dining room, which is prettily decorated with palms and greenery. Here, the award-winning French and English cuisine might include seared salmon with Puy lentil salad and mustard dressing or pot-roast Barbary duck with braised baby beets and deep-fried foie gras.
OPEN: 10-11 **BAR MEALS:** Lunch served: all week Dinner served: all week 12-2.30 6.30-9.30 Av main course £9.95
RESTAURANT: Lunch served: all week Dinner served: all week 12-2.30 7-9.30 Av 3 course à la carte £30
BREWERY/COMPANY: Free House
PRINCIPAL BEERS: Ruddles, IPA, Abbot, Moorlands.
FACILITIES: Children welcome Children's licence Garden: Food served outside Dogs allowed (in the garden only, water)
NOTES: Parking 60 **ROOMS:** 17 bedrooms 17 en suite from s£72.50 d£77.50

CAMBRIDGESHIRE

BARRINGTON   Map 07 TL34

The Royal Oak
West Green CB2 5RZ ☎ 01223 870791 ▤ 01223 871845
Rambling timbered and thatched 14th-century pub. Overlooks village green and provides a wide range of fish and Italian dishes.

BYTHORN   Map 06 TL07

Pick of the Pubs

The White Hart
PE28 0QN ☎ 01832 710226 ▤ 01832 710226
Dir: 0.5m off A14 (Kettering/Huntingdon rd)
In a peaceful, by-passed village just off the A1/M1 link, the White Hart plays host to the chef/patron's eponymous bistro and restaurant, Bennett's. Though the local pub trade is not ignored, it is in a succession of dining areas that one can expect to find the crowds, drawn by bar meals that encompass steak and mushroom pie, game

and Guinness casserole, crispy loin of pork and grilled haddock in cheese sauce, with side orders that include proper chips. Restaurant menus include Thai fish soup, Gressingham duck with apple and herb stuffing, and burnt Cambridgeshire cream with toffee bananas. Three-course, fixed-price Sunday lunches.
OPEN: 11-11 (Sun 12-2.30) Closed: 26 Dec, 1 Jan
BAR MEALS: Lunch served: Tue-Sat 11-2 Dinner served: Tue-Fri 6-10 Av main course £8.50 **RESTAURANT:** Lunch served: Tue-Sun 12-2 Dinner served: Tue-Sat 7-10 Av 3 course à la carte £23.50 **BREWERY/COMPANY:** Free House
PRINCIPAL BEERS: Greene King IPA & Abbott Ale.
FACILITIES: Children welcome Garden: beer garden, patio Dogs allowed (garden only) **NOTES:** Parking 50

CAMBRIDGE   Map 07 TL45

The Anchor
Silver St CB3 9EL ☎ 01223 353554 ▤ 01223 327275
e-mail: staff@theanchorpub.s9.co.uk
Waterside pub frequented by students from Queen's College opposite. There's a good selection of real ale, and the opportunity to hire a punt to go on the River Cam. Lots of bric-a-brac and a good atmosphere.

The Cambridge Blue
85 Gwydir St CB1 2LG ☎ 01223 361382 ▤ 01223 505110
e-mail: cambridgeblue@fsbdial.co.uk
Dir: Town centre
A purpose-built Victorian pub constructed as part of a development to house railway workers. It has fascinating University Boat Race memorabilia, including the bow of the 1984 boat that hit a barge and sank, and for cricket fans a bat used and signed by the legendary Jack Hobbs. Toasted ciabatta rolls, sausage and mash, filled Yorkshire puddings, and pies are typical of the meals available. The garden has a playhouse and rabbit enclosure for younger customers.
OPEN: 12-2.30 6-11 (Sun till 10.30) **BAR MEALS:** Lunch served: all week Dinner served: all week 12-2.30 6-9.30 Av main course £5
BREWERY/COMPANY: Free House
PRINCIPAL BEERS: Woodforde's Wherry, Nethergate IPA, Milton Pegasus. **FACILITIES:** Children welcome Children's licence Garden: Patio, food served outside, rabbits Dogs allowed (water)

The Eagle
Benet St CB2 3QN ☎ 01223 505020
Splendidly atmospheric city-centre pub with a fascinating history, first recorded in 1667, and retaining many original features - mullioned windows, fireplaces, wall paintings and pine panelling. Good Greene King ales and a wide-ranging pub menu.

Free Press
Prospect Row CB1 1DU ☎ 01223 368337
e-mail: freepresspub@hotmail.com
Students, academics, locals and visitors rub shoulders - quite literally - in an atmospheric and picturesque back-street pub near the city centre: normally half a dozen customers can sit comfortably in the Snug, said on one occasion to have accommodated over 60! Non-smoking for a decade and without music or gaming machines, punters are attracted by first-rate real ales and nourishing home-

continued

continued

CAMBRIDGE continued

made soups, raised pies, liver and bacon, and salmon and cod fish cakes.
OPEN: 12-2.30 6-11 Closed: 25-26 Dec, 1 Jan **BAR MEALS:** Lunch served: all week Dinner served: Mon-Sat 12-2 6-9 Av main course £5 **BREWERY/COMPANY:** Greene King **PRINCIPAL BEERS:** Greene King IPA, Abbot Ale, Dark Mild & guest ales. **FACILITIES:** Children welcome Garden: Patio, food served outside

Live & Let Live
40 Mawson Rd CB1 2EA ☎ 01223 460261 🖹 01223 460261
e-mail: liveandletliveph@aol.com
A backstreet traditional pub with no electronic entertainment, only a few minutes from the bus and train stations. Theme nights are a regular event, as are performances by Dave, a local solo singer-guitarist. A hearty menu includes giant Yorkshire pudding with a variety of fillings, bangers and mash, suet puddings and casseroles.
OPEN: 11.30-2.30 5.30-11 Closed: 1 Jan **BAR MEALS:** Lunch served: all week 12-2 Dinner served: Mon-Sat 6-9 Av main course £4.50 **BREWERY/COMPANY:** Free House
PRINCIPAL BEERS: Everards Tiger, Adnams Bitter, Nethergates Umbel, Oakham JHB. **FACILITIES:** Children welcome Dogs allowed

The Tram Depot
5 The Tram Yard, Dover St CB7 4JF
A range of vegetarian meals is a feature of this unusual pub located in an old tramway stable building. The large terrace is the ideal place to relax and enjoy a pint.

CHITTERING   Map 07 TL46

The Travellers Rest
Ely Rd CB5 9PH ☎ 01223 860751 🖹 01223 863362
A friendly welcome and a good choice of wholesome, appetising dishes await the traveller at this pub/restaurant whose owners also run the George & Dragon at Elsworth (qv). Regular theme evenings feature international cuisine and perennial favourites. Prime beef from Scotland is a feature of the menu, and the fish is bought at Lowestoft. Expect lunchtime curries, pies and pasta dishes, as well as lamb cutlets, swordfish steak and vegetable Stroganoff.
OPEN: 11-2.30 6-11 **BAR MEALS:** Lunch served: all week 12-2 Dinner served: Mon-Sat 6-9.30 Av main course £6
RESTAURANT: Lunch served: all week 12-2 Dinner served: Mon-Sat 6-9.30 Av 3 course à la carte £15 **BREWERY/COMPANY:** Free House **PRINCIPAL BEERS:** Greene King IPA, Morland Old Speckled Hen. **FACILITIES:** Children welcome Garden: Food served outside **NOTES:** Parking 30

COTTENHAM   Map 07 TL46

The White Horse
215 High St CB4 5QG ☎ 01954 250257 🖹 01954 206180
Dir: Exit A14 at Histon, on to Cottenham
Friendly old family-run pub with large open bar areas and a restaurant.

DRY DRAYTON   Map 07 TL36

The Black Horse ♀
Park St CB3 8DA ☎ 01954 781055 🖹 01954 782628
Dir: Just outside Cambridge between A14 & A428
Exposed wooden beams and open fires characterise this welcoming 350-year-old village inn, where an extensive menu of traditional pub dishes is served. Expect fresh battered cod, chilli con carne, home-made steak and kidney pie, chicken curry, and

lasagne, as well as filled baguettes, ploughman's, steaks and burgers. Booking is recommended at weekends, especially when there is live music on the first Saturday of the month.
OPEN: 11.30-3 6.30-11 (Sun 12-3, 7-10.30) Closed: Dec 25/26 **BAR MEALS:** Lunch served: all week 12-2 Dinner served: Mon-Sat 6.30-9 Av main course £6.75 **RESTAURANT:** Lunch served: all week 12-2 Dinner served: Mon-Sat 6.30-9 Av 3 course à la carte £16 **BREWERY/COMPANY:** Free House **PRINCIPAL BEERS:** Greene King IPA, Adnams, Bass & Guests. **FACILITIES:** Children welcome Garden: Dogs allowed (not in bedrooms) **NOTES:** Parking 40

DUXFORD   Map 07 TL44

The John Barleycorn
3 Moorfield Rd CB2 4PP ☎ 01223 832699 🖹 01223 832699
Dir: Turn off A505 into Duxford
Traditional thatched and beamed English country pub situated close to Cambridge. The same menu is served throughout and ranges from a cheese sandwich to tournedos Rossini. Typical dishes are large leg of lamb in mint gravy and chicken breast with garlic and herbs.
OPEN: 11-11 (Sun 12-10.30) **BAR MEALS:** Lunch served: all week Dinner served: all week 12-11 Av main course £6.50 **BREWERY/COMPANY:** Greene King **PRINCIPAL BEERS:** Greene King IPA & Abbot Ale. **FACILITIES:** Children welcome Garden: BBQ, garden tables **NOTES:** Parking 25

ELSWORTH   Map 06 TL36

The George & Dragon
41 Boxworth Rd CB3 8JQ ☎ 01954 267236 🖹 01954 267080
Dir: SE of A14 between Cambridge & Huntingdon
Set in a pretty village just outside Cambridge, this pub, originally a row of shops, has one menu and three separate dining areas, each with its own appeal. Dishes feature smoked peppered mackerel, mushroom and spinach lasagne, a variety of steaks, sandwiches, ploughman's and steak and kidney pudding.
OPEN: 11-3 6-11 (Sun 12-3) **BAR MEALS:** Lunch served: all week Dinner served: Mon-Sat 12-2 6-9.30 Av main course £8.50 **RESTAURANT:** Lunch served: all week 12-2 Dinner served: Mon-Sat 6-9.30 Av 3 course à la carte £15 Av 3 course fixed price £13 **BREWERY/COMPANY:** Free House **PRINCIPAL BEERS:** Greene King IPA, Ruddles County, Greene King Old Speckled Hen. **FACILITIES:** Children welcome Garden: Food served outside **NOTES:** Parking 40

ELTISLEY   Map 06 TL25

The Leeds Arms 🛏
The Green PE19 6TG ☎ 01480 880283 🖹 01480 880379
Dir: On A428 between Cambridge & St Neots
Village free house and motel, built towards the end of the 18th century and named after the local landowners. It is situated opposite the village green where the cricket team plays in season. Friday fish and chips and Sunday roasts are popular, as are steak and kidney pie and fillet steaks with various sauces. Sizzling dishes are also a feature - maybe a seafood medley served on a sizzling platter with rice.
OPEN: 11.30-2.30 6.30-11 Closed: Xmas/New Year week **BAR MEALS:** Lunch served: all week Dinner served: all week 12-2 7-9.45 Av main course £8 **RESTAURANT:** Lunch served: all week Dinner served: all week 12-2 7-9.45 **BREWERY/COMPANY:** Free House **PRINCIPAL BEERS:** Greene King IPA, Adnams Broadside, Scottage Courage John Smith's Smooth. **FACILITIES:** Garden: Seating, food served outside **NOTES:** Parking 30 **ROOMS:** 9 bedrooms 9 en suite from s£40 d£55

continued

England

ELTON   Map 06 TL09

Pick of the Pubs

The Black Horse 🐷 ♀
14 Overend PE8 6RU ☎ 01832 280240 🖹 01832 280875
Dir: Off A605 (Peterborough to Northampton rd)
Harry Kirk, the landlord here in the 1950s, was an
assistant to Albert Pierrepoint, Britain's most famous
hangman. Harry's son is now said to haunt the bar. Once
the village jail, the building later became a morgue, but
today's rustic interior is a lot more agreeable. Pop in for a
pint of Deuchars IPA, or a seasonal Nethergate brew, and
a decent bar snack (lunchtime only), and perhaps a rare
roast beef and horseradish sandwich, or home-baked
gammon, egg and chips. Full meals include medallions of
fillet steak in a crème fraîche, with prosciutto and
Roquefort sauce, on a spinach tagliatelle, and daily fish
specials such as fresh wild sea bass, with a trio of king
prawns in garlic, finished with a hollandaise sauce.
Traditional set Sunday lunch menu. Good puddings.
Delightful rear garden overlooking Elton's famous church
and rolling open countryside.

OPEN: 12–3 6–11 (Sun 12–3, 6–11) **BAR MEALS:** Lunch
served: all week 12–2 Dinner served: Mon–Sat 6–9 Av main
course £14 **RESTAURANT:** Lunch served: all week 12–2 Dinner
served: Mon–Sat 6–9.30 Av 3 course à la carte £24
BREWERY/COMPANY: Free House
PRINCIPAL BEERS: Bass, Deuchars IPA, Nethergate, Archers.
FACILITIES: Children welcome Children's licence Garden:
Food served outside. Patio area Dogs allowed (in the garden
only, water provided) **NOTES:** Parking 30

ELY   Map 07 TL58

Pick of the Pubs

The Anchor Inn ♦♦♦♦ 🏵 🐷 ♀
Sutton Gault CB6 2BD ☎ 01353 778537 🖹 01353 776180
e-mail: anchorinnsg@aol.com
*Dir: From A14, B1050 to Earith, take B1381 to Sutton. Sutton Gault on
L*
Situated on the banks of the New Bedford river, the
Anchor was built in 1650 to house men conscripted to
clear the diseased and crime-ridden fens, now changed
into a fine agricultural landscape still attractive to wild
fowl and other wildlife. The inn is fully modernised yet
retains much of its original character, including scrubbed
pine tables, gently undulating floors, gas lighting,
welcoming log fires, and some first class cooking. The
daily-changing menu relies in large part on local produce.
This is put to good use in dishes such as ox liver and

bacon with creamed leeks, roast loin of Denham Estate
venison with celeriac mash, wild boar sausages with
mashed potatoes and braised cabbage or steamed steak
and kidney pudding in a wild mushroom sauce. A good
selection of desserts include organic ice creams and
Armagnac parfait with Agen prunes. There is also an
excellent cheese board, and an extensive wine list.
Accommodation is spacious and charming.
OPEN: 12–3 7–11 (Sat 6.30–11) Closed: Dec 25–26
BAR MEALS: Lunch served: all week Dinner served: all week
12–2 7–9 Av main course £7.95 **RESTAURANT:** Lunch served:
all week Dinner served: all week 12–2 7–9 Av 3 course à la carte
£25 Av 2 course fixed price £7.95 **BREWERY/COMPANY:** Free
House **PRINCIPAL BEERS:** Nethergate IPA, Wolf Bitter,
Batemans XB, Adnams Bitter. **FACILITIES:** Children welcome
Garden: Riverside terrace, food served outdoors
NOTES: Parking 16 **ROOMS:** 2 bedrooms 2 en suite from s£50
d£66.50

The Fountain
1 Silver St CB7 4JF ☎ 01353 663122
Town centre pub close to the Cathedral. Open lunchtimes at
weekends only, but no food served. Lots of bric-a-brac and
memorabilia from the next door King's School..

FEN DITTON   Map 07 TL46

Ancient Shepherds 🐷
High St CB5 8ST ☎ 01223 293280 🖹 01223 293280
Dir: From A14 take B1047 signed Cambridge/Airport
Named after the ancient order of Shepherders who used to
meet here, the pub was originally three cottages built in 1504.
The building is heavily beamed, and has two bars, a lounge
and a dining room. All rooms have inglenook fireplaces. A
typical menu includes rack of lamb, beef and ale pie, half a
duck in orange sauce, smoked haddock, fillet of salmon, and
fillet of seabass on a bed of mashed potato and spinach.
OPEN: 12–3 6–11 (Fri-Sat 11–3, 6.30–11) Closed: 25–26 Dec
BAR MEALS: Lunch served: all week 12–2 Dinner served: Mon–Sat
Av main course £8.95 **RESTAURANT:** Lunch served: all week 12–2
Dinner served: Mon–Sat 6.30–9 Av 3 course à la carte £20
BREWERY/COMPANY: Pubmaster **PRINCIPAL BEERS:** Interbrew
Flowers Original, Adnams Bitter, Greene King IPA.
FACILITIES: Garden: Food served outside **NOTES:** Parking 18

FEN DRAYTON   Map 06 TL36

The Three Tuns
High St CB4 5SJ ☎ 01954 230242 🖹 01954 230242
e-mail: mail@timspubs.com
Dir: between Cambridge and Huntingdon
Originally the Guildhall of Fen Drayton, this thatched building
dates back over 400 years and there are some wonderfully
ornate details on the original oak beams. Recent renovation
work has restored the bar to its original layout, exposed old
flagstones in front of the bar and incorporated a wooden floor
in the lounge area. The pub offers a good choice of beers,
lunchtime bar snacks and a carte menu in the restaurant.
OPEN: 12–2.30 6–11 **BAR MEALS:** Lunch served: all week Dinner
served: all week 12–2 7–9 Av main course £8.50
RESTAURANT: Lunch served: all week Dinner served: all week 12–2
7–9 Av 3 course à la carte £15 **BREWERY/COMPANY:** Greene King
PRINCIPAL BEERS: Greene King IPA, Abbott Ale, Wadworth 6X,
Interbrew Bass. **FACILITIES:** Children welcome Garden: Covered
eating area, well planted **NOTES:** Parking 20

continued

FENSTANTON — Map 07 TL36

King William IV ♀
High St PE28 9JF ☎ 01480 462467 🖹 01480 498205
e-mail: jerry@kingbill.co.uk
Dir: Off A14 between Cambridge & Huntingdon
Originally three 17th-century cottages, this rambling, cream-painted inn occupies a village centre location adjacent to the old clock tower. The low-beamed rooms, including a lively bar area and plant-festooned Garden Room, attract many travellers passing by on the A14, as well as local diners and business people. Choices range from pub favourites such as sandwiches, light meals and jacket potatoes (lunchtime only), to duck liver parfait, French onion tart, steak and kidney pudding and roulade of chicken.
OPEN: 11–3.30 6–11 (Sun 12–11) BAR MEALS: Lunch served: all week 12–2.15 Dinner served: Mon–Sat 7–10 Av main course £4
RESTAURANT: Lunch served: all week 12–2.15 Dinner served: Mon–Sat 7–10 Av 3 course à la carte £16
BREWERY/COMPANY: Greene King PRINCIPAL BEERS: Greene King Abbot Ale, IPA, Ruddles County, Badger Tanglefoot.
FACILITIES: Children welcome Dogs allowed (water)
NOTES: Parking 14 ROOMS: 5 bedrooms 5 en suite

FORDHAM — Map 07 TL67

White Pheasant 🍴 ♀
CB7 5LQ ☎ 01638 720414 🖹 01638 720447
Set beside the A43 in a Fenland village between Newmarket and Ely, this attractive, white-painted 17th-century inn is named after a protected white pheasant that was killed by a previous landlord. Rug-strewn wooden floors, tartan check fabrics, soft wall lighting, interesting paintings and candle-topped scrubbed tables. Sample menu includes calves liver and bacon with red onion gravy, lamb cutlets on creamed leeks and shallots, wild mushroom tortellini, and smoked haddock topped with Welsh rarebit.
OPEN: 12–3 6–11 (Sun 7–10.30) BAR MEALS: Lunch served: all week Dinner served: all week 12–2.30 6–10.30 Av main course £12.95
RESTAURANT: Lunch served: all week Dinner served: all week 12–2.30 6–10.30 Av 3 course à la carte £20
BREWERY/COMPANY: Free House PRINCIPAL BEERS: Greene King Abbot Ale, Interbrew Flowers IPA. FACILITIES: Children welcome Garden: Food served outside NOTES: Parking 30

FOWLMERE — Map 07 TL44

Pick of the Pubs

The Chequers 🍴 ♀
High St SG8 7SR ☎ 01763 208369 🖹 01763 208944
Dir: From M11 A505, 2nd R to Fowlmere
There's a strong sense of history at this bustling inn with its smart gallery restaurant. William Thrist renovated the building in 1675 after a fire had devastated much of the village, and you can still see his initials over the main door. Samuel Pepys once stayed here, but the pub's sign betrays its more recent past with intriguing blue and red chequers in honour of the British and American squadrons based at Fowlmere during World War II. Nowadays, the pub's Mediterranean-style menu and decent wine list are popular with business people, tourists and locals. Eat beside crackling log fires in winter or, on warmer days, sit out in the attractive garden. The extensive seasonal menus might include pan-fried scallops or sweet potato and cumin soup, followed by venison pie,

grilled lamb cutlets or roast Barbary duck. Finish with fresh strawberries, pannacotta with raspberries, or hot date sponge.

OPEN: 12–2.30 6–11 Closed: 25 Dec BAR MEALS: Lunch served: all week Dinner served: all week 12–2 7–10 Av main course £10.60 RESTAURANT: Lunch served: all week Dinner served: all week 12–2 7–10 Av 3 course à la carte £19.20
BREWERY/COMPANY: Free House
PRINCIPAL BEERS: Adnams Bitter. FACILITIES: Garden: Beer garden, patio, food served outdoors NOTES: Parking 30

GODMANCHESTER — Map 06 TL27

The Black Bull Coaching Inn 🍴 ♀
32 Post St PE29 2AQ ☎ 01480 453310 🖹 01480 435623
e-mail: theblackbullpub@aol.com
Dir: Off St Huntington
Five minutes' walk from the Great Ouse River, this 17th-century inn sports beams and a large inglenook fireplace. Examples of fish main courses include sea bass, baked sardines, monkfish and poached salmon. Steak and ale pie and chips, braised knuckle of lamb, tournedos Rossini and baked leek and Stilton crêpes provide meat and vegetarian balance.
OPEN: 11–11 Closed: 25 Dec BAR MEALS: Lunch served: all week Dinner served: all week 12–2.30 6–9.30 Av main course £9
RESTAURANT: Lunch served: all week Dinner served: all week 12–2.30 6–9.30 PRINCIPAL BEERS: Black Bull, Old Speckled Hen, Hobsons Choice, Tetleys. FACILITIES: Garden: Patio area Dogs allowed (in the garden only) NOTES: Parking 30 ROOMS: 8 bedrooms 8 en suite from s£69 d£70

GOREFIELD — Map 07 TF41

Woodmans Cottage 🍴 ♀
90 High Rd PE13 4NB ☎ 01945 870669 🖹 01945 870631
e-mail: magtuck@aol.com
Dir: A47 to Peterborough, ring road to A1M
The brother and sister team who run this popular pub have worked hard to make it a success. Their efforts have paid off and Woodmans Cottage remains a popular local with live entertainment, well-kept beers and a good choice of bar food. Mixed grill, lasagne, Chinese rack of ribs and lobster tails feature among other dishes. Cajun chicken in a pepper sauce, macaroni cheese and grilled salmon fillets are also well-established favourites.
OPEN: 11–2.30 7–11 Closed: 25 Dec BAR MEALS: Lunch served: all week Dinner served: all week 12–2.30 7–10 Av main course £6.75
RESTAURANT: Lunch served: all week Dinner served: all week 12–2.30 7–10 Av 3 course à la carte £18
BREWERY/COMPANY: Free House PRINCIPAL BEERS: Greene

continued

continued

King IPA & Abbot Ale, Interbrew Worthington Bitter.
FACILITIES: Children welcome Garden: Patio, food served outside
NOTES: Parking 40

GRANTCHESTER   Map 07 TL45

The Green Man 🐾 🍷
High St, Grantchester CB3 9NF
☎ 01223 841178 📠 01223 847940
A delightful old pub retaining many original features,
including low ceiling beams (beware!). In winter roaring log
fires burn in the re-opened fireplaces, and in summer
customers can sit out in the restored gardens. Real ales, lagers
and fresh coffees are served, plus a list of 23 wines available
by the glass. The menu is augmented by frequently changing
blackboard specials. Bubble and squeak, home-made curry,
Thai fishcakes, and lamb in Dijon mustard are typical of the
range.
OPEN: 11-3 5.30-11 (Summer open all day) **BAR MEALS:** Lunch
served: all week Dinner served: all week 12-2.30 6-9 Av main course
£7.50 **BREWERY/COMPANY:** Punch Taverns
PRINCIPAL BEERS: Adnams Bitter, Broadside
FACILITIES: Garden: Patio, food served outside **NOTES:** Parking 10

HEYDON   Map 05 TL43

The King William IV 🐾 🍷 NEW
SG8 8PN ☎ 01763 838773 📠 01763 837179
A 16th-century countryside inn with an old world interior. It
has beams an inglenook fireplace and is full of antiques and
farming implements. Unusual oak tables suspended from the
ceiling by chains. A good range of freshly prepared food and
especially strong on vegetarian dishes. On the menu there
may be grilled swordfish steak with and avocado and mango
salad, confit leg of duck marinated in Rioja and oriental spices
or spinach and spring onion cakes with Dijon mustard cream
sauce.
OPEN: 12-2.30 6-11 **BAR MEALS:** Lunch served: all week Dinner
served: all week 12-2 6.30-10 Av main course £9.50
BREWERY/COMPANY: Free House **PRINCIPAL BEERS:** IPA
Greene King, Adnams, Abbot Ale, Fullers London Pride.
FACILITIES: Garden: Food served outside Dogs allowed (in the
garden only) **NOTES:** Parking 50

HILDERSHAM   Map 07 TL54

The Pear Tree
CB1 6BU ☎ 01223 891680 📠 01223 891970
e-mail: dgj-@lycos.com
Dir: Just off A1307
Traditional village pub facing the green, with an unspoilt
atmosphere enhanced by oak beams and a stone floor. It
enjoys a good local trade, and is particularly well known for
its home-cooked food. Bar meals include various grills,
Lincolnshire sausages, battered haddock and chips, and
ploughman's, with good old-fashioned puddings like
blackberry and apple crumble, lemon layer pudding, and
chocolate fudge cake.
OPEN: 11.45-2 6.30-11(Sun 12-2, 7-10.30) **BAR MEALS:** Lunch
served: all week Dinner served: all week 12-2 6.30-9.30 Av main
course £5 **BREWERY/COMPANY:** Greene King
PRINCIPAL BEERS: Greene King IPA & Abbot Ale.
FACILITIES: Garden: Beer garden, food served outdoors Dogs
allowed **NOTES:** Parking 6

HILTON   Map 06 TL26

The Prince of Wales ◆◆◆◆
Potton Rd PE28 9NG ☎ 01480 830257 📠 01480 830257
e-mail: Princeofwales.hilton@talk21.com
Dir: on B1040 between A14 and A428 S of St Ives

Traditional two-bar village inn at the heart of rural
Cambridgeshire, just a short drive from Cambridge,
Peterborough and Huntingdon. Options range from bar
snacks to full meals - Hilton 2 in 1 pies (a meal in themselves)
are a speciality, alongside a choice of grills, fish, curry and
daily specials prepared from local produce. Home-made
puddings include crème brûlée and sherry trifle.
OPEN: 11-2.30 6-11 (Sat 12-3, 7-11) (Sun 12-3, 7-10.30) Closed: 1
Jan **BAR MEALS:** Lunch served: Tue-Sun 12-2 Dinner served: all
week 7-9 Av main course £6 **BREWERY/COMPANY:** Free House
PRINCIPAL BEERS: Adnams Southwold, Elgoods Black Dog Mild,
Timothy Taylor Landlord. **FACILITIES:** Children's licence Garden:
Patio, food served outside **NOTES:** Parking 9 **ROOMS:** 4
bedrooms 4 en suite from s£45 d£65

HINXTON   Map 07 TL44

The Red Lion
High St CB10 1QY ☎ 01799 530601 📠 01799 531201
e-mail: lynjim@lineone.net
Dir: 1m from M11 J9, 2m from M11 J10
Sympathetically extended 16th-century inn with lots of clocks
and other memorabilia. Fresh local produce is featured in an
extensive menu, including light meals available at lunchtime
only. Malaysian chicken curry, Moroccan lamb tagine, and
oven-roasted sea bass are examples of the range.
OPEN: 11-2.30 6-11 (Sun 12-2.30, 7-10.30) Closed: Dec 25-26
BAR MEALS: Lunch served: all week Dinner served: all week 12-2
7-9.30 **RESTAURANT:** Lunch served: all week Dinner served: all
week 12-2 7-9.30 **BREWERY/COMPANY:** Free House
PRINCIPAL BEERS: Adnams, Greene King IPA, Woodforde's Wherry,
plus guest ales including Nethergates & Ridleys.
FACILITIES: Garden: Food served outside. Terrace & lawns
NOTES: Parking 40

HOLYWELL   Map 06 TL37

The Old Ferryboat Inn 🐾 🍷
PE27 4TG ☎ 01480 463227 📠 01480 463245
e-mail: theoldferryboatinn@hotmail.com
Dir: A14 then R onto A1096 then A1123 R to Holywell
Renowned as England's oldest inn, built long before the last
millennium, with immaculately maintained thatch, white stone
walls, and cosy interior. A pleasant atmosphere - despite
resident ghost - in which to enjoy hot chicken curry, roast rack
of lamb, steak and ale pie, fish and chips, and Greene King

continued

England

HOLYWELL continued

ales. Well-furnished riverside rooms offer a comfortable stay for business or pleasure.

The Old Ferryboat Inn

OPEN: 11.30-11 **BAR MEALS:** Lunch served: all week Dinner served: all week 12-2.30 6-9.30 Av main course £8
BREWERY/COMPANY: Greene King
PRINCIPAL BEERS: Greene King Abbot Ale/IPA, Old Speckled Hen, Ruddles County. **FACILITIES:** Children welcome Garden: Food served outside. River views Dogs allowed (in the garden only, water provided) **NOTES:** Parking 100 **ROOMS:** 7 bedrooms 7 en suite from s£50 d£60

HORNINGSEA   Map 07 TL46

Pick of the Pubs

Crown & Punchbowl
CB5 9JG ☎ 01223 860643 📠 01223 441814
e-mail: lizard2020@supanet.com
A 17th-century inn located in beautiful countryside in the village of Horningsea, on the banks of the River Cam, it offers bar food and candlelit dinners in the beamed dining room, lent character by classical music, rugs and antique pieces. Fresh local produce is used and the carte menu in the restaurant has a choice of 15-20 fresh fish options. Maybe fillet of Arctic cod with cheesy mornay sauce, or fresh sardines on a bed of pasta with tomato and garlic sauce. Other options include roast chicken fillet with coconut rice and Thai-style cream sauce, and English lamb shank on a hillock of Irish boxty potato (mash with crispy bacon, spring onion and cheese) with a fruity apricot sauce. The bar menu is served in the conservatory and both bar areas. One of these features a church pulpit and an original stained glass window. Accommodation is provided in five well-equipped bedrooms, all with views over the village and river.
OPEN: 12-2.30 6-10 Closed: 25 Dec **BAR MEALS:** Lunch served: all week Dinner served: all week 12-2.30 6-10 Av main course £9 **RESTAURANT:** Lunch served: all week Dinner served: all week 12-2.30 6-10 Av 3 course à la carte £19
BREWERY/COMPANY: Free House
PRINCIPAL BEERS: Adnams Broadside. **FACILITIES:** Children welcome Garden: beer garden, food served outdoors, patio
NOTES: Parking 50 **ROOMS:** 5 bedrooms 5 en suite from s£45 d£70

For a list of pubs with AA Accommodation
♦ Awards see pages 649-653 ★

The Plough & Fleece
High St CB5 9JG ☎ 01223 860795 📠 01223 860795
Dir: E from A14 take B1047. Top of slip rd turn L Pub opp garden centre
Extended late 18th-century building, in the Dutch style so popular at that time. The bar features ancient settles, a tiled floor and an unusual open fire. Menus offer good regional cooking including a comforting hotpot of Suffolk ham, Welsh fish pie, and home-made steak, kidney and mushroom pie.
OPEN: 11.30-2.30 7-11 (Sun 12-2) **BAR MEALS:** Lunch served: all week 12-2 Dinner served: Tue-Sat 7-9.30 Av main course £6.95
RESTAURANT: Lunch served: all week 12-2 Dinner served: Tue-Sat 7-9.30 Av 3 course à la carte £15 **BREWERY/COMPANY:** Greene King **PRINCIPAL BEERS:** Greene King IPA & Abbott Ale.
FACILITIES: Children welcome Garden: beer garden, outdoor eating, patio **NOTES:** Parking 20

HUNTINGDON   Map 06 TL27

Pick of the Pubs

The Old Bridge House ★ ★ ★ ◎◎ ♀
1 High St PE29 3TQ ☎ 01480 424300 📠 01480 411017
e-mail: oldbridge@huntsbridge.co.uk
Dir: Signposted from A1 & A14

One of a well-known local partnership of chef-managed dining pubs, this handsome 18th-century house stands overlooking the River Ouse on the edge of the town centre. Once a private bank, the building has been much extended to offer 24 stylish bedrooms with modern facilities that include air conditioning, satellite TV and CD players. Meals are served in either the restaurant or the more informal terrace, with menus that strike the upper end of the market in both style and price. Simpler dishes such as oak-smoked salmon with lemon and capers, or wild boar sausages with black cabbage, mashed potato and onion gravy, contrast with more adventurous fare like osso buco alla Milanese, or roast squab pigeon with wild mushroom and liver boudin. Round things off with a mouth-watering desert; cold poached pear in red wine and blackcurrant, or caramel soufflé with prune and Armagnac ice cream are typical.
OPEN: 11-11 (Sun 12-10.30) **BAR MEALS:** Lunch served: all week Dinner served: all week 12-2.30 6.30-10.30 Av main course £9 **RESTAURANT:** Lunch served: all week Dinner served: all week 12-2.30 6.30-10.30 Av 3 course à la carte £25 Av 2 course fixed price £15 **BREWERY/COMPANY:** Huntsbridge Inns **PRINCIPAL BEERS:** Adnams Best, Hobsons Choice, Bateman XXXB. **FACILITIES:** Children welcome Garden: Patio
NOTES: Parking 60 **ROOMS:** 24 bedrooms 24 en suite from s£80 d£100

KEYSTON   Map 06 TL07

Pick of the Pubs

The Pheasant Inn ♀
Village Loop Rd PE28 0RE
☎ 01832 710241 🗎 01832 710340
Dir: Signposted from A14, W of Huntingdon
Yet another of a small group of chef-managed dining pubs
in the area with an admirably egalitarian attitude to eating
out and continuing dedication to the provision of fine
wines and East Anglian ales. Housed in a fine 15th-century
thatched building of oak beams, open fires and simple
wooden furniture, The Pheasant offers a single menu
throughout in a modern eclectic style that recognises the
quality and value of freshly available local produce.
Imaginative and unfussy snacks and simple dishes include
warm goats' cheese or classic Caesar salads, Gloucester
Old Spot sausages and mash in grain mustard sauce and
tagliatelle with wild mushrooms, Jerusalem artichokes and
truffle oil. Main dishes are exemplified by rare char-grilled
tuna loin with Moroccan spiced quinoa, slow-braised
Aberdeenshire beef blade with foie gras sauce and pan-
roast duck breast on spiced barley with braised bok choi.
Caramelised apple tart with Calvados ice cream and
unpasteurised farmhouse cheeses; traditional roast beef
on Sunday and fixed-price mid-week lunches are models
of consistency.
OPEN: 12–2 6–11 **BAR MEALS:** Lunch served: all week Dinner
served: all week 12–2 6.30–10 Av main course £9
RESTAURANT: Lunch served: all week Dinner served: all week
12–2 6.30–10 Av 3 course à la carte £27.50
BREWERY/COMPANY: Huntsbridge
PRINCIPAL BEERS: Adnams. **FACILITIES:** Children welcome
herb garden, patio **NOTES:** Parking 40

KIMBOLTON   Map 06 TL16

The New Sun Inn 🐾 ♀
20–22 High St PE28 0HA ☎ 01480 860052 🗎 01480 869353
*Dir: From A1 N, B645 for 7m, From A1 S B661 for 7m, From A14 B660 for
5m*

An impressive array of flowers greets visitors to this 16th-
century inn near Kimbolton Castle. As well as being a real ale
pub, it has recently won a wine award – for range, quality and
knowledge – and offers a good choice of wines by the glass.
Dishes from the bar and restaurant menus range from
doorstep sandwiches to the likes of crab cakes on wilted
spinach, and home-made steak and kidney pudding.
OPEN: 11–2.30 6–11 **BAR MEALS:** Lunch served: all week Dinner
served: Tues-Sat 12–2.15 7–9.30 **RESTAURANT:** Lunch served:
Tues-Sun Dinner served: Tues-Sat 12–2 7–9.30 Av 3 course à la carte

continued

£18 **BREWERY/COMPANY:** Charles Wells
PRINCIPAL BEERS: Wells Bombardier, Greene King Old Speckled
Hen, Wells Eagle IPA. **FACILITIES:** Children welcome Garden: Patio,
food served outside Dogs allowed

MADINGLEY   Map 07 TL36

Pick of the Pubs

The Three Horseshoes ◉ ♀
High St CB3 8AB ☎ 01954 210221 🗎 01954 212043
Dir: M11 J13. 1.5m from A14
This picturesque old thatched inn is one of the well known
group of Huntsbridge Inns that dot the Cambridge,
Huntingdon and Northamptonshire borders. Beside the
small, bustling bar you'll find a pretty conservatory dining
room, and the large garden extends towards the local
cricket pitch. The menu, which is served throughout the
pub, is little short of sinfully seductive – but you may
choose as much or as little as you wish. The dishes are
imaginative without being outrageous, and washed down
with a range of real ales and outstanding wines that are
hard to resist. Starters range from Arabic chicken, almond
and honey soup to pan-fried foie gras with avocado and
rice. The innovative style continues with extensively
specified dishes like chargrilled beef with ginger roasted
carrots, Thai grass saltimbocca and spiced potato fondant,
or roast sea bass with spinach, pine nuts, raisins, anchovy
and new potatoes with Romesco sauce.
OPEN: 12–2 6–11 **BAR MEALS:** Lunch served: all week Dinner
served: Mon-Sat 12–2 6.30–9.30 Av main course £13
RESTAURANT: Lunch served: all week Dinner served: Mon-Sat
12–2 6.30–9.30 Av 3 course à la carte £25 Av 5 course fixed price
£35 **BREWERY/COMPANY:** Huntsbridge Inns
PRINCIPAL BEERS: Adnams Bitter, Hook Norton Old Hooky,
Smile's Best. **FACILITIES:** Garden: large, Food served outside
NOTES: Parking 70

NEWTON   Map 07 TL44

Pick of the Pubs

The Queen's Head
CB2 5PG ☎ 01223 870436
*Dir: 6m S of Cambridge on B1368, 1.5m off A10 at Harston, 4m from
A505*
This quintessentially English pub, dating back to 1680
(though the cellar is much older), stands in the heart of
the village by the green. There are no fruit machines or
piped music to interrupt the lively conversation in the two
small bars; nor for 40 years has there been a menu – or
specials 'whatever they might be'. The daily home-made
soup is best described by its colour, while the cut-to-order
sandwiches – roast beef, smoked ham, salmon, and
cheese with pickle or salad – are made with the freshest
brown bread and butter. You could also try a Humphry
(banana sandwich with lemon and sugar). Hot alternatives
are limited to Aga-baked potatoes and toast with beef
dripping. Adnams' ales are dispensed direct from the
barrel in studious avoidance of modernisation.
OPEN: 11.30–2.30 6–11 (Sun 12–2.30, 7–10.30) Closed: 25 Dec
BAR MEALS: Lunch served: all week Dinner served: all week
11.30–2.15 6–9.30 Av main course £4
BREWERY/COMPANY: Free House
PRINCIPAL BEERS: Adnams Southwold, Broadside, Fisherman,
Bitter & Regatta. **FACILITIES:** Children welcome Dogs allowed
NOTES: Parking 15 No credit cards

England

PETERBOROUGH
Map 06 TL19

The Brewery Tap ♀
80 Westgate PE1 2AA ☎ 01733 358500 ▤ 01733 310022
Visitors to this unusual American-style pub can view the
operations of the Oakham brewery through a glass wall. The
Tap has a capacity of over 500, specialises in real Thai food,
and runs a nightclub Friday and Saturday.
OPEN: 12–11 Closed: Dec 25–26, Jan 1 **BAR MEALS:** Lunch
served: all week Dinner served: all week 12–2.30 6–9.30 Av main
course £5.50 **RESTAURANT:** Lunch served: all week Dinner served:
all week 12–2.30 6–9.30 **BREWERY/COMPANY:** Free House
PRINCIPAL BEERS: Oakham, Jeffery Hudson Bitter, Bishops
Farewell, White Dwarf. **FACILITIES:** Dogs allowed (water)

Charters Cafe Bar
Town Bridge PE1 1FP ☎ 01733 315700 ▤ 01733 315700
e-mail: manager@charters-bar.fsnet.co.uk
Dir: A1/A47 Wisbech, 2m for city centre & town bridge (River Nene). Barge
is moored at Town Bridge
Charters is a 176ft long barge which proprietor Paul Robert
sailed over from Holland in 1991 and moored right in the
heart of the city, on the River Nene. The East part of the name
applies to the upper deck, which is an oriental restaurant with
dishes from Vietnam, Japan, Thailand, Malaysia and
elsewhere. Twelve hand pumps dispense a continually
changing repertoire of real ales.
OPEN: 12–11.30 Mon–Thu 12–late Fri–Sat Closed: 25–26 Dec, 1 Jan
BAR MEALS: Lunch served: all week 12–2.30 Av main course £3.95
RESTAURANT: Lunch served: all week Dinner served: all week
12–2.30 6–10.30 Av 3 course à la carte £15
BREWERY/COMPANY: Free House **PRINCIPAL BEERS:** Fullers
London Pride, Oakham JHB, Oakham White Dwarf, Bishops Farewell.
FACILITIES: Garden: Food served outside Dogs allowed
NOTES: Parking 15

ST IVES
Map 06 TL37

Pike & Eel Hotel ♀
Overcote Ln, Needingworth PE27 4TW
☎ 01480 463336 ▤ 01480 465467
e-mail: pikeandeelinn@btinternet.com
17th-century listed inn with marina moorings on the River
Ouse where the ferry once crossed: formerly well-known also
for its fine pike fishing. Good fish includes crevettes flambees
and seafood platter. In the bar enjoy Welsh rarebit and steak
and kidney pudding. Restaurant carte and Sunday lunch.
OPEN: 11–11 (Sun 12–10.30) **BAR MEALS:** Lunch served: all week
Dinner served: all week 12–2.30 7–10.30 Av main course £5.75
RESTAURANT: Lunch served: all week Dinner served: all week
12–2.30 7–10.30 Av 3 course à la carte £19.95
BREWERY/COMPANY: Free House **PRINCIPAL BEERS:** Greene
King IPA, Ruddles, Greene King Old Speckled Hen.
FACILITIES: Children welcome Garden: outdoor eating, BBQ,
Marina adjacent **NOTES:** Parking 75 **ROOMS:** 11 bedrooms 11 en
suite from s£35 d£50

Use the AA Hotel Booking Service on
0870 5050505
to book at AA recognised hotels and
B&B's in the UK and Ireland
or through our internet site at
www.theAA.com

STILTON
Map 06 TL18

Pick of the Pubs

The Bell Inn ★ ★ ★ ◎◎ 🐾
Great North Rd PE7 3RA ☎ 01733 241066 ▤ 01733 245173
e-mail: reception@thebellstilton.co.uk
Dir: from A1 follow signs for Stilton, hotel is situated on the main
road in the centre of the village.

The Bell is known as the birthplace of Stilton, and stories
of the famous cheese, first sold to travellers around
1720, abound. It is also associated with famous
highwaymen (Dick Turpin hid here for nine weeks) and
numerous other historic visitors from the Duke of
Marlborough to Lord Byron. Restoration work in the late
1990s added high quality bedrooms and conference
facilities that have been blended into the ageless inn's
stonework around the central courtyard. Beamed
ceilings, a stone floor and open fires imbue the Village
Bar with great character, which is enhanced by fine real
ales and an extensive monthly menu and daily specials.
The ubiquitous cheese appears in dishes as diverse as
braised beef and ale with Stilton dumplings, and
ratatouille, Stilton and polenta sausage served on fine
pasta frittata with tomato. The fixed-price restaurant
menus offer modern British cooking using the best of
Fen country produce.
OPEN: 12–2.30 6–11 (Sun 12–3, 7–10.30) Closed: Dec 25
BAR MEALS: Lunch served: all week 12–2 Dinner served: all
week 6.30–9.30 Av main course £9 **RESTAURANT:** Lunch
served: Sun–Fri 12–2 Dinner served: all week 7–9.30 Av 3 course
fixed price £23.95 **BREWERY/COMPANY:** Free House
PRINCIPAL BEERS: Marston's Pedigree, Greene King Abbot
Ale, Oakham JHB, Interbrew Boddingtons.
FACILITIES: Garden: Courtyard, food served outside
NOTES: Parking 30 **ROOMS:** 19 bedrooms 19 en suite from
s£69.50 d£89.50

STRETHAM
Map 07 TL57

The Lazy Otter 🐾 ♀
Cambridge Rd CB6 3LU ☎ 01353 649780 ▤ 01442 876893
With its large beer garden and riverside restaurant
overlooking the marina, the 'Lazy Otter' lies just off the A10
between Ely and Cambridge. The pub's location beside the
Great Ouse river makes it very popular in summer. Typical
dishes include jumbo cod or fisherman's medley, as well as a
selection of steaks and grills. The marina holds thirty
permanent boats, as well as up to ten day boats.
OPEN: 11–11 Children welcome

CHESHIRE

ALDFORD — Map 08 SJ45

Pick of the Pubs

The Grosvenor Arms ♀
Chester Rd CH3 6HJ ☎ 01244 620228 ▤ 01244 620247
e-mail: grosvenor.arms@brunningandprice.co.uk
Dir: *on B5130 S of Chester*
A relaxing Victorian inn with a bustling atmosphere in its
comfortably refurbished bars. The spacious, open-plan
interior includes an airy conservatory decorated with
hanging baskets, a panelled library filled with books, and
a suntrap terrace for summer eating and drinking. Decent
wines accompany the interesting bistro-style food, and
there's a range of cognacs, ports and good real ales. Daily
menus may offer leek and goats' cheese tart to start, or
corned beef and black pudding hash cake, followed by
deep-fried cod goujons on provençale vegetables, pork
chop with sauté potatoes, mushrooms in a rich Stroganoff
and goulash sauce, and salmon and smoked haddock
fishcake. Appetising desserts range over chocolate tart
with raspberry sauce, apple, almond and sultana flan, and
various sorbets and ice creams. Lighter bites like open
sandwiches also available.
OPEN: 11–11 (Sun 12–10.30) **BAR MEALS:** Lunch served: all
week Dinner served: all week 12–10 Av main course £8.95
BREWERY/COMPANY: Free House
PRINCIPAL BEERS: Interbrew Boddingtons, Flowers IPA,
Beartown Bearskinful, Hanby. **FACILITIES:** Children welcome
Garden: Patio, food served outside Dogs allowed
NOTES: Parking 150

ALSAGER — Map 08 SJ75

Wilbraham Arms
Sandbach Rd North ST7 2AX ☎ 01270 877970 ▤ 01270 877970
e-mail: wilbrahamarms@freeserve.co.uk
Set in well-manicured grounds on the edge of town, this busy
dining pub is opposite an equestrian centre, and offers a
friendly welcome and appetising food. It has a conservatory
restaurant, and has been home to Willy's Jazz Club for 20
years. Expect such fine dishes as steak and kidney pie, lamb
Henry, farmhouse chicken with leek and cheddar mash,
stuffed ducks legs with red wine and fresh thyme gravy, and
ham hock in honey and mustard sauce.

OPEN: 12–3 6–11 (Sun 7–10.30) **BAR MEALS:** Lunch served: all
week Dinner served: all week 12–2 6.30–9.30 Av main course £6.95
RESTAURANT: Lunch served: Wed–Sun Dinner served: Wed–Sun
12–2 6.30–9.30 Av 3 course à la carte £13

PRINCIPAL BEERS: Robinsons Best, Robinsons Frederics, Hartleys
XB, plus guest ales. **FACILITIES:** Children welcome Children's
licence Garden: beer garden, patio, outdoor eating
NOTES: Parking 76

ASTON — Map 08 SJ64

Pick of the Pubs

The Bhurtpore Inn ♀
Wrenbury Rd CW5 0DQ ☎ 01270 780917 ▤ 01270 780170
e-mail: simonbhurtpore@yahoo.co.uk
See Pick of the Pubs on page 62

AUDLEM — Map 08 SJ76

The Shroppie Fly
The Wharf CW3 0DX ☎ 01270 811772 ▤ 01270 811334
Originally built as a canal warehouse for the Shropshire Union
Canal, this interesting building was converted to a pub in
1974. The name comes from the salvaged horse-drawn barge
that now serves as the bar and is a major feature. The main
menu includes broccoli and cream cheese bake, mixed grill,
Goan chicken curry, spinach and ricotta cannelloni, and a
selection of sandwiches and ploughman's. There is a separate
specials board usually offering some 20 or 30 extra dishes.
OPEN: 11.30–11 **BAR MEALS:** Lunch served: all week Dinner
served: all week 12–2.30 6–9 Av main course £5.25
PRINCIPAL BEERS: Interbrew Boddingtons Bitter, Flowers Original,
Wadworth 6X. **FACILITIES:** Children welcome Garden: Food served
outdoors Dogs allowed **NOTES:** Parking 60

BARTHOMLEY — Map 08 SJ75

The White Lion Inn
CW2 5PG ☎ 01270 882242 ▤ 01270 873348
Historic half-timbered and thatched inn with character bars
and a lovely rural setting. It offers bar food ranging from hot
beef "banjo", tuna mayonnaise, and paté with toast, to more
substantial dishes such as pie with peas, mash and gravy, and
a daily roast with creamed potatoes and vegetables.
OPEN: 11.30–11 (Thurs 5–11, Sun 12–10.30) **BAR MEALS:** Lunch
served: Fri–Wed 12–2 Av main course £4
BREWERY/COMPANY: Burtonwood
PRINCIPAL BEERS: Burtonwood Bitter, Top Hat & Guest ale.
FACILITIES: Children welcome Garden: beer garden, patio, outdoor
eating, BBQ Dogs allowed **NOTES:** Parking 20

BOLLINGTON — Map 09 SJ97

The Church House Inn
Church St SK10 5PY ☎ 01625 574014 ▤ 01625 576424
Dir: *Macclesfield turnoff on A34, thru Prestbury, follow Bollington signs.*
Convenient for both the natural landscape of the Peak District
National Park and the bright lights of Manchester, this village
inn has a varied menu. Diners may enjoy lunchtime specials
such as casseroles and home-made pies. Fresh fish dishes
feature on the evening menu.
OPEN: 12–3 5.30–11 **BAR MEALS:** Lunch served: all week
Dinner served: all week 12–2 6.30–9.30 Av main course £6
BREWERY/COMPANY: Free House
PRINCIPAL BEERS: Greene King IPA, Abbot, Old Speckled Hen.
FACILITIES: Children welcome **NOTES:** Parking 4
ROOMS: 5 bedrooms 5 en suite from s£35 d£48

continued

OPEN: 12–2.30 6.30–11
BAR MEALS: L served all week.
D served all week. 12–2 7–9.30
Av main course £7.95
RESTAURANT: L served all week.
D served all week. 12–2 7–9.30
Av cost 3 courses £14.95
BREWERY/COMPANY:
FREE HOUSE
PRINCIPAL BEERS: Hanbys
Drawwell, Salopian Shropshire
Golden Thread, Abbeydale
Absolution
FACILITIES: Dogs welcome.
Garden: Food served outside
NOTES: Parking 40
ROOMS: 2 en suite.

The Bhurtpore Inn

This unassuming village pub offers an unusual combination of a really exceptional range of real ales and an Indian cuisine menu. It is very popular and lively at the weekends. Located not far from the Shropshire Union canal this unpretentious brick-built village pub takes its unusual name from a city in central northern India.

Wrenbury Road CW5 8DQ
☎ 01270 780917 📠 01270 780170
e-mail: simonbhurtpore@yahoo.co.uk
Dir: between Nantwich & Whitchurch on the A530.

It was here that a local landowner, Lord Combermere, was involved in a fierce battle in 1825. The earliest reference to the pub is 1778, when it was known as the Queen's Head, and later it became the Bhurtpore Inn, reflecting Lord Combermere's victory. Re-opened after major refurbishment in 1992 and once again in the ownership of the George family (who had been publicans many years previously), the emphasis here is very much on traditional ales, freshly prepared home-made food and a comfortable village pub atmosphere. The interior is generally quite simple but

there are Indian rugs and pictures as well as local photographs. There is a really extensive choice of beers with a constantly changing range of ten real ales produced by small independent 'craft' brewers on the hand pumps. Many of Europe's finest beers are also available and there are pump-drawn German and Belgian beers as well as about 80 bottled beers from all over the world. The home-cooked food provides a combination of traditional English pub food and a good range of Indian dishes. You can chose from toasties, hot baguettes and jacket potatoes as well as a choice of about six curries and baltis, or dishes like grilled sea bass with lemon and parsley butter, quarter lamb shoulder braised in a mint and sherry gravy and grilled duck breast with a blackcurrant and sloe wine sauce. There is a celebrated annual beer festival.

BROXTON
Map 08 SJ45

The Copper Mine 🐘
Nantwich Rd CH3 9JH ☎ 01829 782293 📠 01829 782183
Dir: A41 from Chester, L at rdbt onto A534, pub 0.5m on R
Convenient for the Candle Factory at Cheshire Workshops, Cheshire Ice Cream Farm, and the 14th-century Beeston Castle, this pub has a conservatory with fine views of the surrounding countryside. Favourite dishes include steak and kidney pie, chicken, duck or lamb with fresh sauces, monkfish, or the 16oz T-bone steak.
OPEN: 12–3 6–11 **BAR MEALS:** Lunch served: all week Dinner served: all week 12–2.30 6–9 Av main course £8
RESTAURANT: Lunch served: all week Dinner served: all week 12–2.30 6–9 Av 3 course à la carte £15 Av 3 course fixed price £12.95
BREWERY/COMPANY: Free House
PRINCIPAL BEERS: Interbrew Bass & Flowers IPA.
FACILITIES: Children welcome Garden: beer garden, patio, outdoor eating, BBQ **NOTES:** Parking 80

BUNBURY
Map 08 SJ55

Pick of the Pubs

The Dysart Arms 🐘 ♈
Bowes Gate Rd CW6 9PH
☎ 01829 260183 📠 01829 261286
e-mail: dysart.arms@brunningandprice.co.uk
Dir: Between A49 & A51, by Shropshire Union Canal, and opposite church
At the top end of a rural Cheshire village this Grade II listed farmhouse, converted into a pub in Victorian times, underwent major extensions in the 1990s. Within is a treasure trove of antique furniture and old prints, in a succession of airy rooms with open fires, set around a central bar. From the terrace tables and attractive garden, visitors can enjoy fine views of Peckforton and Beeston castles as well as the nearby parish church. Careful attention to culinary details includes the use of home-grown herbs in an enticing menu that is served throughout the pub. A selection of dishes includes Bunbury bangers with mash and onion gravy, coconut king prawns with chilli jam and mango salad, braised shoulder of lamb with Madeira and thyme sauce, tuna steak on coriander mash with Cajun onion rings, and grilled seabass fillet on braised chicory. As well as changing guest ales and a dozen house wines, there is also a selection of guest cheeses.
OPEN: 11.30–11 (Sun 12–10.30) **BAR MEALS:** Lunch served: all week Dinner served: all week 12–2.15 6–9.30 Av main course £9.50 **BREWERY/COMPANY:** Free House
PRINCIPAL BEERS: Timothy Taylor Landlord, Weetwood Eastgate, Thwaites Bitter, Coach House Dick Turpin.
FACILITIES: Children welcome Garden: Food served outside, lovely views Dogs allowed (water) **NOTES:** Parking 30

BURWARDSLEY
Map 08 SJ55

Pick of the Pubs

The Pheasant Inn ★ ★
CH3 9PF ☎ 01829 770434 📠 01829 771097
e-mail: reception@thepheasant-burwardsley.com
Dir: From Chester A41 to Whitchurch, after 4m L to Burwardsley. Follow signs 'Cheshire Workshops'
A traditional country inn tucked away in a beautiful rural setting with lofty views of the Cheshire plain. Outside the delightful old sandstone building is a flower-filled courtyard ideal for summer evening drinks. The old outbuildings have been tastefully converted to provide a range of comfortable, modern en suite bedrooms, each one individually decorated and furnished in contemporary styles. The half-timbered former farmhouse makes a great setting for a bar that boasts the largest log fire in the county. The proudest boast of all is the food, however: home-cooked specialities feature on the bar menu, like crab and ginger potato cake, roasted nut and feta cheese risotto, and braised lamb shank. From the quality carte with a strong fish flavour expect starters like carpaccio of tuna, and consommé of pheasant, followed perhaps by baked paupiette of monkfish, and steamed sea bass, plus roast loin of lamb, and chargrilled fillet of beef.
OPEN: 11–11 **BAR MEALS:** Lunch served: all week Dinner served: all week 12–2.30 6.30–9.30 Av main course £8
RESTAURANT: All week 12–2.30 7–9.30 Av 3 course à la carte £25 **BREWERY/COMPANY:** Free House
PRINCIPAL BEERS: Interbrew Bass, Weetwood Old Dog, Timothy Taylor Landlord. **FACILITIES:** Children welcome Garden: Patio, food served outside **NOTES:** Parking 40
ROOMS: 10 bedrooms 10 en suite from s£55 d£80

CHESTER
Map 08 SJ46

Albion Inn
Park St CH1 1RN ☎ 01244 340345
Dir: In Chester City centre adjacent to Citywalls and Newgate overlooking the River Dee
The home fires still burn on cold winter nights at this living memorial to the 1914-18 war. It is a traditional Victorian street corner pub, comprising three rooms (vault, snug and lounge bar) with a splendid cast-iron fireplace, enamelled advertisements and World War I memorabilia adding to the period atmosphere. The menu ranges through the 'Great British Buttie', shepherd's pie and corned beef hash. Home-made puddings are offered from the specials board.
OPEN: 11.30–3 5–11 Closed: 25 Dec, 1 Jan **BAR MEALS:** Lunch served: all week Dinner served: all week 12–2 5–8 Av main course £6
BREWERY/COMPANY: Inn Partnership
PRINCIPAL BEERS: Timothy Taylor Landlord, Cains.
FACILITIES: Dogs allowed (water)

Old Harkers Arms 🐘 ♈
1 Russell St CH1 5AL ☎ 01244 344525 📠 01244 344526
This canal side, Victorian former warehouse is one of Chester's more unusual pubs, with its high windows, lofty ceilings and a bar created from salvaged doors. Six guest beers are offered in addition to the regulars and every wine on the list is available by the glass. There's a good selection of sandwiches and paninis at lunchtime, and an interesting range of dishes that might include Caribbean-style chicken, salmon and smoked haddock fishcakes, and leek and apricot sausages.
OPEN: 11–11 Closed: Dec 26 & Jan 1 **BAR MEALS:** Lunch served: all week 11.30-2.30 Dinner served: Sat-Thur 5.30–9.30 Av main course £7.95 **RESTAURANT:** Lunch served: all week 11.30–2.30 Dinner served: Sat-Thur 5.30–9.30 Av 3 course à la carte £18 **PRINCIPAL BEERS:** Thwaites Bitter, Interbrew Boddingtons, Exmoor Gold, Fuller's London Pride.

continued

CHOLMONDELEY   Map 08 SJ55

Pick of the Pubs

The Cholmondeley Arms ◆◆◆ 🛏 ♀
SY14 8HN ☎ 01829 720300 🖹 01829 720123
e-mail: guy@cholmondeleyarms.co.uk
See Pick of the Pubs on page 65

CHURCH MINSHULL   Map 08 SJ66

The Badger Inn
Over Rd CW5 6DY ☎ 01270 522607 🖹 01270 522607
Originally known as the Brookes Arms, the inn later changed
its name to the Badger Inn and became a coach stop on the
route between Nantwich and Middlewich. The badger was
part of the Brookes's family crest and has been used as the
inn sign for many years. The menu here concentrates on steak
dishes, as well as grills and curries. Baguettes, bar snacks, and
burgers also available. Open for breakfast.
OPEN: 12–12 (Sun 12–11) **BAR MEALS:** Lunch served: all week
Dinner served: all week 12–9 12–9 Av main course £8.95
RESTAURANT: Lunch served: all week Dinner served: all week 12–9
12–9 **PRINCIPAL BEERS:** Mansfield Bitters. **FACILITIES:** Children
welcome Children's licence Garden: Food served outside. Seated
garden area Dogs allowed (water bowls provided) **NOTES:** Parking
30

CONGLETON   Map 08 SJ86

The Egerton Arms Hotel ◆◆◆ ♀
Astbury Village CW12 4RQ ☎ 01260 273946 🖹 01260 277273
e-mail: egertonastbury@totalise.co.uk
Named after Lord Egerton of Tatton, the local lord of the
manor, this 16th-century village inn is situated in the
picturesque village of Astbury, adjacent to the 11th-century
church. A typical menu includes dishes such as liver and
onion, sweet 'n' sour vegetables, spaghetti carbonara, leek
bacon and onion hot pot, seafood macaroni bake and
breaded plaice. Bedrooms are attractive and well equipped.
OPEN: 11.15–11 (Sun 11–3, 7–10.30) **BAR MEALS:** Lunch served:
all week Dinner served: all week 11.30–2 6.30–9 Av main course £5.95
RESTAURANT: Lunch served: all week Dinner served: all week
11.30–2 7–9 Av 3 course à la carte £14 Av 3 course fixed price £9.50
BREWERY/COMPANY: Robinson's
PRINCIPAL BEERS: Robinsons Old Stockport & Fredericks.
FACILITIES: Children welcome Garden: Food served outside
NOTES: Parking 100 **ROOMS:** 6 bedrooms 2 en suite from s£25
d£35

Plough Inn Hotel 🛏 ♀
Macclesfield Rd, Eaton CW12 2NH
☎ 01260 280207 🖹 01260 280207
e-mail: plough@eatonpaddockinns.fsnet.co.uk
Dir: on A536 (Congleton to Macclesfield road)
A combination of small alcoves, comfortable corners and
blazing open hearth fires makes this nicely restored 17th-
century coaching inn an attractive place to meet. The menu
changes regularly and is served in the bar and the Old Barn
restaurant with its high beamed roof, intimate gallery and
wealth of gnarled old timbers. Tuna steak and bean salad or
pasta with a selection of sauces, spare ribs or Feta cheese and
herb salad starters and main courses of pork stincotta or
apricot pork fillet are typical.

OPEN: 11.30–11 (Sun 12–10.30) Closed: 26 Dec, 1 Jan
BAR MEALS: Lunch served: all week Dinner served: all week
12–2.30 6–9.30 Av main course £10.50 **RESTAURANT:** Lunch
served: all week Dinner served: all week 12–2.30 6–9.30 Av 3 course
fixed price £9.95 **BREWERY/COMPANY:** Free House
PRINCIPAL BEERS: Greene King IPA, Bombardier, Taylors Landlord.
FACILITIES: Garden: Food served outside. Secret garden
NOTES: Parking 50 **ROOMS:** 8 bedrooms 8 en suite from s£40
d£50

COTEBROOK   Map 08 SJ56

Alvanley Arms Hotel ◆◆◆◆ 🛏
Forest Rd CW6 9DS ☎ 01829 760200 🖹 01829 760696
Dir: On the A49, 10m from Chester, 18m from M6 J16

Friendly, family-run inn which dates back to the 17th century
or even earlier, when the then landlord was fined for
permitting rogues, whores and general undesirables to lodge
on the premises. Ruth Ellis, the last woman to be hanged in
England, once stayed at the inn with her lover. The pub
utilises local produce and fresh fish is a speciality here,
delivered directly from coastal ports up to five times a week.
Non fish dish options include liver and onions, Farmhouse
grill, cheese, onion and potato pie, hot crusty baguettes,
sandwich platters, and the Shire Horseman's Harvest Hamper.
OPEN: 11.30–3 5.30–11 **BAR MEALS:** Lunch served: all week
Dinner served: all week 12–2 6–9 Av main course £8.95
RESTAURANT: Lunch served: all week Dinner served: all week
12–2.15 6–9.30 Av 3 course à la carte £17.95
PRINCIPAL BEERS: Robinsons Best, Hatter Mild.
FACILITIES: Children welcome Garden: Food served outside, beer
garden & pond **NOTES:** Parking 75 **ROOMS:** 7 bedrooms 7 en
suite from s£35 d£60

continued

OPEN: 11–3 7–11
BAR MEALS: L served all week. D served all week. 12–2.30 7–10 Av main course £10
RESTAURANT: L served all week. D served all week. 12–2.30 7–10 Av cost 3 course £17
BREWERY/COMPANY: FREE HOUSE
PRINCIPAL BEERS: Marston's Bitter, Adnams Bitter, Weetwood Old Dod
FACILITIES: Children and dogs welcome.
NOTES: Parking 60
ROOMS: 6 en suite

The Cholmondeley Arms

◆◆◆ ♀
Cholmondeley SY14 8HN
☎ 01829 720300 📠 01829 720123
e-mail: guy@cholmondeleyarms.co.uk
Dir: on A49, between Whitchurch & Tarporley

The village school in Cholmondeley, set in countryside close to the grounds of Cholmondeley Castle, closed in 1984: re-opening four years later as the Cholmondeley Arms. Once again the community had a centre – albeit a school for drinkers rather than scholars.

The locals were happy with the change of use because of an accident of history that had left them high and dry. In the 1890s the Marquis of Cholmondeley, a passionate teetotaller, had closed all the licensed premises on his estate – in those days a considerable area of some 25,000 acres. So the Cholmondeley Arms was the first pub on the estate for 100 years. Since then it has received a number of awards in recognition of its quality as a pub, with its fine ales and wines, and also for its excellent home-made food. Specialities of the house are Cholmondeley salmon fishcakes with hollandaise sauce, oxtail with haricot beans, rib-eye steak and devilled kidneys. Fresh fish is well represented with dishes such as monkfish gratin, grilled Dover sole and king prawn brochette. A snack menu of sandwiches, pancakes and grills is available at lunchtime, including the Headmaster's Lunch – sliced and rare rib-eye steak in a baguette with chopped lettuce, mustard and mayonnaise. Home-made puddings are also a draw, with the likes of Bakewell tart, meringues and cream, and spotted dick with custard. The pub goes from strength to strength, entertaining both duke and dustman, yet still the owner sometimes senses the disapproving presence of the old headmaster and the teetotal marquis glowering in the corner.

HANDLEY
Map 08 SJ45

The Calveley Arms 🏮 ♀
Whitchurch Rd CH3 9DT ☎ 01829 770619 📠 01829 770619
Dir: *5m S of Chester, sign posted from A41*
First licensed in 1636, this coaching inn has plenty of old
world charm, with beamed ceilings, open fires, and a choice
of classic pub games, including cribbage, dominoes and bar
skittles. A broad spectrum of food is offered, from sandwiches
and a choice of pasta dishes to home-made steak and kidney
pie. Fresh fish and game feature on the specials board, with
options such as whole baked sea bass with fennel and white
wine.
OPEN: 12-3 6-11 (Sun eve 7-10.30) Closed: 25 Dec
BAR MEALS: Lunch served: all week Dinner served: all week 12-2.15
6-9.30 Av main course £6.95 **RESTAURANT:** Dinner served: Same
as bar **BREWERY/COMPANY:** Enterprise Inns
PRINCIPAL BEERS: Interbrew Boddingtons Bitter & Bass, Castle
Eden Ale, Wadworth 6X, Marston's Pedigree. **FACILITIES:** Garden:
Food served outside, Beer garden Dogs allowed (water)
NOTES: Parking 20

KNUTSFORD
Map 08 SJ77

Pick of the Pubs

The Dog Inn ♦♦♦♦ 🏮
Well Bank Ln, Over Peover WA16 8UP
☎ 01625 861421 📠 01625 864800
Dir: *From Knutsford take A50 S. Turn L at 'The Whipping Stocks'. Pub
in 2m*
Originally a row of cottages, built in 1804 in Over Peover
(pronounced Peever), it later became an inn called The
Hen, and was then renamed The Gay Dog until the word
'gay' was dropped 20 years ago. The traditional timbered
building is located in the heart of the Cheshire
countryside between Knutsford and Holmes Chapel, and
in summer it is bedecked with dazzling flowerbeds, tubs
and hanging baskets. A wide use of fresh local produce –
and guest ales from local micro-breweries – attracts a
faithful following for its interesting cooking. Rack of lamb
with apricot and ginger, ham shank with parsley sauce,
braised steak in red wine, and rabbit in herb and mustard
sauce, along with fish dishes like halibut with spinach,
haddock and prawn au gratin, and smoked salmon and
prawn pancakes. **OPEN:** 11.30-3 5.30-11.30 **BAR MEALS:** Lunch served: all
week Dinner served: all week 12-2.30 7-9.30 Av main course
£9.95 **RESTAURANT:** Lunch served: all week Dinner served: all
week 12-2.30 7-9.30 Av 3 course à la carte £17.50
BREWERY/COMPANY: Free House
PRINCIPAL BEERS: Moorhouses Black Cat, Weetwood Old
Dog, Best Bitter, Hydes Traditional Bitter. **FACILITIES:** Garden:
Large patio, food served outside **NOTES:** Parking 100
ROOMS: 6 bedrooms 6 en suite from s£55 d£75

LANGLEY
Map 08 SJ97

Leathers Smithy 🏮
Clarke Ln SK11 0NE ☎ 01260 252313 📠 01260 252313
The landlord claims the views are 'the most stunning of any
pub known!' It's certainly a wonderful location, at the foot of
Macclesfield Forest, and overlooking Ridgegate Reservoir. The
name commemorates William Leather, a licensee in the early
1800s, and the building's one-time use as a forge. Main

courses include chicken Kiev, Cumberland sausage with mash
and onion gravy, and beef tips with Hoisin sauce. Hot
baguettes, light dishes and vegetarian choices too.

OPEN: 12-3 7-11 **BAR MEALS:** Lunch served: all week Dinner
served: all week 12-2 7-10 Av main course £7.25
RESTAURANT: Lunch served: all week Dinner served: all week 12-2
7-10 **PRINCIPAL BEERS:** Theakstons Best, Pedigree, Directors,
Guest cask ale. **FACILITIES:** Garden: Food served outside. Dogs
allowed (in the garden only) **NOTES:** Parking 25

LOWER WHITLEY
Map 08 SJ67

Chetwoode Arms 🏮 ♀
St Lane WA4 4EN ☎ 01925 730203
e-mail: gfidler6@netscapeonline.co.uk
Dir: *Chetwode Arms is on the A49 2 M S from J 10 M56, 6M S of
Warrington*
A country inn comprising a series of small and intimate rooms
and believed to be over 300 years old. It has one of the best
crown green bowling greens in the country, and is the focal
point of the village – a recent best-kept village award winner.
Freshly cooked food is prepared from produce supplied by
small local businesses, and is offered alongside a
comprehensive wine list and a selection of lagers and real
ales.
OPEN: 12-11 **BAR MEALS:** Lunch served: all week Dinner served:
all week 12-3 6-9 Av main course £9.50 **RESTAURANT:** Lunch
served: all week Dinner served: all week 12-3 6-9 Av 3 course à la
carte £18 **BREWERY/COMPANY:** Inn Partnership
PRINCIPAL BEERS: Greenalls Bitter, Cains Bitter, Marston's
Pedigree. **FACILITIES:** Garden: Food served outside Dogs allowed
NOTES: Parking 60

MACCLESFIELD
Map 09 SJ97

The Windmill Inn ♀
Holehouse Ln, Whitely Green, Adlington SK10 5SJ
☎ 01625 574222
Dir: *A523 to Adlington turn off to Holehouse Lane*
On the fringe of the Peak District – just by the Macclesfield
Canal – stands this heavily-beamed former farmhouse that
dates back to 1684. Rustic specials boards promise pepper-pot
mushrooms, monkfish in Pernod, duck breast in wild berry
sauce. More traditional roast middle leg of lamb and fish in
Speckled Hen batter happily co-exist.
OPEN: 12-11 **BAR MEALS:** Lunch served: all week Dinner served:
all week 12-3 6-9.30 Av main course £6 **RESTAURANT:** Lunch
served: all week Dinner served: all week 12-3 6-9.30 Av 3 course à la
carte £12 **PRINCIPAL BEERS:** Worthington, Old Speckled Hen,
Tetley. **FACILITIES:** Children welcome Garden: Patio/terrace,
outdoor eating. Dogs allowed (water) **NOTES:** Parking 100

continued

England

MARBURY
Map 08 SJ54

The Swan Inn
SY13 4LS ☎ 01948 663715 📠 01948 663715
e-mail: pbhalfpenny@aol.com

A country inn with a friendly atmosphere and a reputation locally for good food. Sitting amidst Tudor houses overlooking a small mere, it boasts a large rural beer garden, and plenty of good walks, as well as cycle and bridle paths. Snacks or full meals are served, including giant hot dog and chips, roast rack of lamb, beer-battered salmon, prawns and cod with chips, monkfish with oriental stir-fry, and sea bass with mushroom risotto.
OPEN: 11–3.30 7–11 **BAR MEALS:** Lunch served: Tue–Sun Dinner served: Tue–Sun 12–2.30 7–9 Av main course £9.50
RESTAURANT: Lunch served: Tue–Sun Dinner served: Tue–Sun 12–2.30 7–9 Av 3 course à la carte £16.99
PRINCIPAL BEERS: Tetley Smooth, Timothy Taylors Landlords, Castle Eden, Various other real ales. **FACILITIES:** Children welcome Garden: Food served outside. Beer garden Dogs allowed (water provided) **NOTES:** Parking 40

MOBBERLEY
Map 08 SJ77

Plough & Flail
Paddock Hill WA16 7DB ☎ 01565 873537 📠 01565 873902
Quaint, white-painted stone cottages with plenty of floral decoration. Became a pub after the inhabitants of the cottages found themselves locally famous for their home brew.

NANTWICH
Map 08 SJ65

The Thatch Inn
Wrexham Rd, Faddiley CW5 8JE ☎ 01270 524223
Dir: follow signs for Wrexham from Nantwich, inn is 4m from Nantwich
Homely comfort and good food are the hallmarks of this black and white, 15th-century, thatched inn. There is a lovely garden for summer use, and inside you'll find oak beams, traditional games and open fires in winter. Favourite dishes include Thatcher's Pie (potato-topped mince and vegetables served with pickled beetroot), steaks from the grill, battered cod with chips and mushy peas, and vegetable lasagne.
OPEN: 12–3 6–10 (Sun all day) **BAR MEALS:** Lunch served: all week Dinner served: all week 12–2 6.30–9.30 Av main course £8
RESTAURANT: Lunch served: all week Dinner served: all week 12–2 6.30–9.30 Av 3 course à la carte £10.95 Av 2 course fixed price £7.95
BREWERY/COMPANY: Free House
PRINCIPAL BEERS: Theakstons Best, Scottish Courage Courage Directors & Websters Yorkshire Bitter. **FACILITIES:** Children welcome Garden: Food served outdoors, patio/terrace Dogs allowed
NOTES: Parking 60

OVER PEOVER
Map 08 SJ77

Ye Olde Parkgate Inn
Stocks Ln WA16 8TU ☎ 01625 861455
Dir: A50 from Knutsford. Inn 3m on L after Radbroke Hall
Ivy-covered village pub surrounded by fields and woodland. Attractively furnished beamed bars and comfortable lounge where meals are served. Recent change of hands. All food home-made, with a menu that includes at least 5 starters, three roasts of the day, and a variety of hearty pies.
OPEN: 11.30–11 **BAR MEALS:** Lunch served: all week Dinner served: Tue–Sun 12–2 6.30–9 **BREWERY/COMPANY:** Samuel Smith
PRINCIPAL BEERS: Samuel Smith Old Brewery Bitter.
FACILITIES: Dogs allowed (water provided) **NOTES:** Parking 45

PENKETH
Map 08 SJ58

The Ferry Tavern
Station Rd WA5 2UJ ☎ 01925 791117 📠 01925 791116
e-mail: ferrytavern@talk21.com
Dir: A57 - A562, Fiddler's Ferry signposted

Set on its own island, this 12th-century ale house welcomes walkers and cyclists from the trans-Pennine Way. Beneath the low beams in the stone-flagged bar you'll find a range of unusual guest beers and over 300 different whiskies. There is a bar snack menu at lunchtime and in the evening, and a dining menu from six till nine. Options range from burgers to steaks, with daily curries, cod and chips, and vegetarian alternatives.
OPEN: 12–3 5.30–11 (open all day wknd) **BAR MEALS:** 12–2 6–7.30 **RESTAURANT:** 12–2 6–9 **BREWERY/COMPANY:** Free House **PRINCIPAL BEERS:** Scottish Courage Courage Directors, Interbrew Boddingtons Bitter, Greene King Abbot Ale & Old Speckled Hen. **FACILITIES:** Children welcome Garden: Dogs allowed (toys, water) **NOTES:** Parking 46

The Birds of the Air
Pride of place among bird signs is taken by the Swan, often adopted by inns close to a river. The eccentric Swan with Two Necks probably began as a swan with two nicks in its beak. The Cock may be related to cock-fighting or to St Peter. Geese and chickens appear alone or keeping dangerous company with the Fox. The Bird in Hand comes from falconry and the Dog and Duck either from fowling or from the amusement of setting a dog on a pinioned duck. The Eagle is from Heraldry and the Magpie and Stump from the countryside, while rarities include the Parrot and the Peahen.

PLUMLEY
Map 08 SJ77

The Golden Pheasant Hotel ☺ ♀ NEW
Plumley Moor Rd WA16 9RX ☎ 01565 722261 ▤ 01565 722125
Dir: From M6 J19, take A556 signed Chester. 2m turn L at signs for Plumley/Peover. Through Plumley, after 1m pub opposite rail station.
Set in the heart of the north Cheshire countryside, this century-old pub stands opposite Plumley railway station, enabling customers to enjoy well-kept J W Lees cask ales without driving home! The building has been refurbished to make the most of its nooks and crannies, open fires and traditional hospitality. Extensive menus offer quality home-cooked food, and traditional meals like Brewer's pie or battered cod contrast with salads, saddle of lamb, and oven-baked halibut.
OPEN: 11-11 (Sun 12-10.30) **BAR MEALS:** Lunch served: all week Dinner served: all week 12-2.30 6-9.30 Av main course £5.95
RESTAURANT: Lunch served: all week Dinner served: all week 12-2.30 6-9.30 Av 3 course à la carte £16.50 Av 2 course fixed price £10 **BREWERY/COMPANY:** J W Lees **PRINCIPAL BEERS:** J W Lees Bitter, Mild, Moonraker. **FACILITIES:** Children welcome Garden: 2 patio areas, bowling green. **NOTES:** Parking 80
ROOMS: 8 bedrooms 8 en suite from s£29 d£35

The Smoker ☺ ♀
WA16 0TY ☎ 01565 722338 ▤ 01565 722093
e-mail: smoker@plumley.fsword.co.uk
Dir: from M6 J19 take A556 W. Pub is 1.75m on L
Thought to be Elizabethan, this thatched coaching inn is named after an 18th-century horse owned by local landowner, Lord de Tabley. The white charger called Smoker was bred as a racehorse by the Prince Regent and won twelve races. Within the wood panelled interior are welcoming log fires and a good choice of fish dishes, while specialities of the house include fillet steak de Tabley, steak and kidney pie, and pork fillet in Calvados.
OPEN: 11-3 6-11 (all day Sun) **BAR MEALS:** Lunch served: all week Dinner served: all week 11.30-2.30 6.30-9.30 Av main course £7.95 **RESTAURANT:** Lunch served: all week Dinner served: all week 11.30-2.30 6.30-9.30 Av 3 course à la carte £15.95
PRINCIPAL BEERS: Robinsons Best, Hatters Mild.
FACILITIES: Children welcome Garden: Food served outside
NOTES: Parking 100

PRESTBURY
Map 09 SJ87

The Legh Arms & Black Boy Restaurant ☺ ♀
SK10 4DG ☎ 01625 829130 ▤ 01625 827833
Dir: From M6 thru Knutsford to Macclesfield, turn to Prestbury at Broken Cross. Pub in village centre
15th-century pub, centrally located in historic Prestbury village. An imaginative and varied menu includes fillet of seabass with cucumber spaghetti, lobster thermidor, confit of Gressingham duck with sage, shallot and Bramley apple gateau, venison steak Rossini, sirloin steak with Burgundy and shallot confit sauce, and lamb cutlets with honey and mint glaze. Bar menu offers fish and chips, roast duck, bacon blue cheese burger, and steak and mushroom pudding.
OPEN: 11.30-3.30 5.30-11 **BAR MEALS:** Lunch served: all week Dinner served: all week 12-9.30 Av main course £10
RESTAURANT: Lunch served: all week Dinner served: all week 12-2 7-10 Av 3 course à la carte £25 Av 3 course fixed price £16.95
BREWERY/COMPANY: Frederic Robinson
PRINCIPAL BEERS: Robinsons. **FACILITIES:** Children welcome Garden: Food served outside **NOTES:** Parking 40

SWETTENHAM
Map 08 SJ86

Pick of the Pubs

The Swettenham Arms ☺ ♀
Swettenham Ln CW12 2LF ☎ 01477 571284 ▤ 01477 571284
Dir: M6 J18 to Holmes Chapel, then A535 towards Jodrell Bank. 3m take rd on R (Forty Acre Lane) to Swettenham
In many ways a typical country pub, set in a beautiful area and serving food throughout. This charming white-painted village inn is tucked away behind a 13th-century church in the lovely Dane Valley. It used to be a convent, and once boasted an underground passage where bodies were kept prior to burial. Despite the ghost stories, there's nothing spooky about the heavily-beamed interior, and the large open fireplaces that warm it. Walkers and country lovers flock to the place in summer, drawn in part by the two-acre wild flower meadow, and the adjoining arboretum that is owned by Sir Bernard Lovell of Jodrell Bank fame. Excellent food is cooked to order from fresh local produce, including tried and tested favourites like various roasts, steak and mushroom pie, and venison casserole, with more adventurous choices like sautéed monkfish, and beef Wellington. Unusual real ales and draught cider, and good wine list.
OPEN: 12-3 6.30-11 (Sun 12-4, 7-11) **BAR MEALS:** Lunch served: all week Dinner served: all week 12-2.30 7-9.30 Av main course £10 **RESTAURANT:** 12-2.30 7-9.30 Av 3 course à la carte £20 **BREWERY/COMPANY:** Free House
PRINCIPAL BEERS: Jennings Bitter, Carlsberg-Tetley Tetley Bitter. **FACILITIES:** Children welcome Garden: Large patio, food served outdoors **NOTES:** Parking 150

TARPORLEY
Map 08 SJ56

The Boot Inn ☺
Boothsdale, Willington CW6 0NH ☎ 01829 751375
Dir: off the A54 Kelsall By-pass or off the A51 Chester-Nantwich, follow signs to Willington
Originally a small beer house, the pub has expanded into a charming row of red brick and sandstone cottages, where quarry-tiled floors, old beams and open fires give the interior a character of its own. Local walks prepare you for well-kept ales and freshly prepared food ranging from real sandwiches and hot paninis to specials of pan-seared scallops on tomato sauce with citrus-scented rice, and shoulder of local lamb braised with root vegetables and red wine.
OPEN: 11-3 6-11 (All day Sat-Sun & BHs) Closed: Dec 25
BAR MEALS: Lunch served: all week Dinner served: all week 11-2.30 6-9.30 Av main course £10.50 **RESTAURANT:** Lunch served: all week Dinner served: all week 11-2.30 6-9.30 Av 3 course à la carte £10.50 **BREWERY/COMPANY:** Inn Partnership
PRINCIPAL BEERS: Weetwood Oasthouse Gold, Ambush Old Dog & Eastgate, Cains, Interbrew Flowers Original. **FACILITIES:** Children welcome Garden: Beer garden, food served outdoors Dogs allowed (garden only, water) **NOTES:** Parking 60

Do you have a favourite pub that we have overlooked? Please use the Reader's Report forms at the back of this guide to tell us all about it.

England

The Fox & Barrel
Forest Rd, Cotebrook CW6 9DZ
☎ 01829 760529 📠 01829 760529
e-mail: info@thefoxandbarrel.co.uk
Dir: *On the A49 just outside Tarporley, very close to Oulton Park Race Circuit*

Award-winning pub with an open fire, wooden floors, old tables and odd chairs, set in the heart of the Cheshire countryside. There's a cosy bar offering cask ales and a good choice of wine by the glass, and a no-smoking restaurant extending onto an enclosed patio area. The food is home made and the produce locally sourced to create seasonal dishes. Specialities include bouillabaisse (fish stew from the South of France), and the chef's daily pie.
OPEN: 12–3 5.30–11 Closed: 25 Dec **BAR MEALS:** Lunch served: all week Dinner served: all week 12–2.30 6.30–9.30 Av main course £12 **RESTAURANT:** Lunch served: all week Dinner served: all week 12–2.30 6.30–9 Av 3 course à la carte £20
BREWERY/COMPANY: Pubmaster **PRINCIPAL BEERS:** Interbrew Boddingtons, Marston's Pedigree, Guest Beers. **FACILITIES:** Garden: Patio, food served outside **NOTES:** Parking 40

TUSHINGHAM CUM GRINDLEY   Map 08 SJ54

Blue Bell Inn
SY13 4QS ☎ 01948 662172
e-mail: pagage@aol.com
Dir: *On the A41 N of Whitchurch*
An unknown but friendly spirit is said to inhabit this 17th-century, black and white magpie building that oozes character with its abundance of beams, open fires and horse brasses. The same spirit may influence the warmth of welcome from the landlord. Nonetheless it remains a basic, though characterful pub with well-kept ales. Bar meals include fish bake, whole plaice with various sauces and large, locally-farmed trout: soup, sandwiches, home-baked pies and steaks of similar ilk balance out the variety of choices.
OPEN: 12–3 6–11 (Sun 12–3, 7–11) **BAR MEALS:** 12–3 6–9 **RESTAURANT:** 12–3 6–9 **BREWERY/COMPANY:** Free House **PRINCIPAL BEERS:** Hanby Ales. **FACILITIES:** Children welcome Garden: Food served outside Dogs allowed (water, buscuits) No credit cards

WARMINGHAM   Map 08 SJ76

The Bears Paw Hotel NEW
School Ln CW11 3QN ☎ 01270 526317 📠 01270 526465
Dir: *From M6 J18 take A54 then A533 towards Sandbach. Follow signs for village*
Country hotel close to the River Wheelock. A la carte and specials menus offer the likes of king scallop sizzler, Bear's

Paw combo (chicken tandoori, Creole prawns, pork ribs, Cajun chicken, onion rings) and hot crab cakes with parsley sauce. Traditional favourites include whole Dover sole, rump steak Diane and lamb cutlets with a mint and redcurrant sauce. There is a Carvery lunch on Sundays.
OPEN: 11–11 (Sun 12–10.30) **BAR MEALS:** Lunch served: all week Dinner served: all week 12–2 6–9.30 Av main course £6 **RESTAURANT:** Lunch served: all week Dinner served: all week 12–2 7–9.30 Av 3 course à la carte £20 **BREWERY/COMPANY:** Free House **PRINCIPAL BEERS:** Interbrew Bass, Boddingtons Bitter & Flowers IPA, Marston's Pedigree. **FACILITIES:** Children welcome Garden: Food served outside **NOTES:** Parking 100
ROOMS: 6 bedrooms 6 en suite from s£50 d£60

WARRINGTON   Map 08 SJ68

Ring O Bells NEW
Old Chester Rd, Daresbury WA4 4AJ
☎ 01925 740256 📠 01925 740972
The village of Daresbury is where the author Lewis Carroll was born. The pub was formerly a large farmhouse plus an old courthouse. There is a good choice of handpulled ales and wines and freshly prepared food. The daily changing chalkboards display the dishes of the day. Fresh fish is always available such as swordfish, whole sea bass and red mullet. Other popular dishes are beef and Theakston ale pie and chicken breast stuffed with cream cheese.
OPEN: 11–11 (Sun 12–10.30) Closed: 25 Dec
BAR MEALS: Lunch served: all week Dinner served: all week 12–10 Av main course £6.50 **RESTAURANT:** Lunch served: all week Dinner served: all week 12–10 **PRINCIPAL BEERS:** Greenalls, Theakstons, Courage Directors, Theakstons Mild. **FACILITIES:** Children welcome Garden: Food served outside. Terraced garden **NOTES:** Parking 100

WINCLE   Map 09 SJ96

The Ship Inn
SK11 0QE ☎ 01260 227217
Dir: *Leave A54 at Fourways Motel x-rds, towards Danebridge, Inn 0.5m before bridge on L*
Quaint, 16th-century red-sandstone pub with fascinating historical associations. Reputedly the oldest inn in Cheshire, the Ship is in the lower Pennines, close to some of the finest walking country in the north-west of England. An interesting choice of real ales is complemented by a frequently changing blackboard menu. Typical examples include grilled Danebridge trout, venison fillet in port and cranberry sauce, Brie and leek parcels in mustard cream sauce, and fillet of monkfish in cumin sauce.
OPEN: 12–3 7–11 (Sun 12–3, 7–10.30) **BAR MEALS:** 12–2 7–9 **RESTAURANT:** 12–2 7–9 **BREWERY/COMPANY:** Free House **PRINCIPAL BEERS:** Wye Valley, Timothy Taylor Landlord, York, Beartown. **FACILITIES:** Children welcome Children's licence Garden: **NOTES:** Parking 15

WRENBURY   Map 08 SJ54

The Dusty Miller
CW5 8HG ☎ 01270 780537
e-mail: admin@dustymiller-wrenbury
A black and white lift bridge, designed by Thomas Telford completes the picture postcard setting for this beautifully converted 16th-century mill building beside the Shropshire Union canal. The current landlord is the great grandson of

continued   *continued*

WRENBURY continued

Arthur Summer, who ran the mill up until WWII. The menu features freshly cooked dishes like chargrilled chicken with buttery peppered cabbage and Stilton sauce, or blackened salmon with fried new potatoes and tomato dressing. Watch the blackboard for daily vegetarian and fish dishes.
OPEN: 11.30–3.00 6.30–11 Closed: 2nd 2 wks in Jan
BAR MEALS: Lunch served: Tues–Sun 12–2 Dinner served: all week 6.30–9.30 Av main course £9.25 **RESTAURANT:** Lunch served: all week 12–2 Dinner served: all week 6.30–9.30
PRINCIPAL BEERS: Robinsons: Best, Frederics, Old Tom, Hatters Mild; Hartleys XB. **FACILITIES:** Children welcome Garden: Food served outside Dogs allowed (water, kennel)
NOTES: Parking 60

WYBUNBURY   Map 08 SJ64

The Swan 🍵 ♀
Main Rd CW5 7NA ☎ 01270 841280
e-mail: richard@theswan77.freeserve.co.uk
Dir: M6 J16 towards Chester / Nantwich. Turn L at traffic lights in Wybunbury
The Swan, registered as an alehouse in 1580, is situated next to the church in the village centre. All the food is freshly prepared on the premises and includes prime steaks, grilled lamb cutlets, Tuscan vegetable roulade, steak burger with pear chutney, tuna fish and spring onion fishcakes, and steak, mushroom and Jennings ale pie. Hot sandwiches, ploughmans, sandwiches and salads also available.
OPEN: 12–11 **BAR MEALS:** 12–2 6.30–9.30
RESTAURANT: Dinner served: all week
BREWERY/COMPANY: Jennings **PRINCIPAL BEERS:** Jennings Bitter, Cumberland Ale plus two guest beers. **FACILITIES:** Children welcome Children's licence Garden: **NOTES:** Parking 40
ROOMS: 7 bedrooms 7 en suite

CORNWALL & ISLES OF SCILLY

BODINNICK   Map 02 SX15

Old Ferry Inn 🍵
PL23 1LX ☎ 01726 870237 📠 01726 870116

Astonishingly, this 16th-century former merchant's house, just fifty yards from Bodinnick ferry, once stood on the main route from Plymouth to the west. Now a friendly family inn, the Old Ferry is perfectly situated for walking, sailing or touring - the Eden Project and Heligan Gardens are both nearby. The comprehensive menus feature daily specials and popular pub favourites like ploughman's, jacket potatoes, home-cooked

continued

ham egg and chips, fisherman's bake and, of course, Cornish pasties.
OPEN: 11–11 (Sun 12–10.30) Closed: 25 Dec **BAR MEALS:** Lunch served: all week Dinner served: all week 12–12.30 6–9 Av cost main course £6.50 **RESTAURANT:** Lunch served: Sun Dinner served: all week 12–2.30 7–9 Av cost 3 course à la carte: £15
PRINCIPAL BEERS: Sharps Doom Bar. **FACILITIES:** Garden: Paved terrace, food served outside **NOTES:** Parking 10
ROOMS: 12 bedrooms 8 en suite from d££45

BOSCASTLE   Map 02 SX09

The Wellington Hotel ★ ★ 🍵
The Harbour PL35 0AQ ☎ 01840 250202 📠 01840 250621
e-mail: vtobutt@enterprise.net
Dir: A30 onto A395, then A39, R onto B3314, R onto B3266

Handsome 16th-century coaching inn located in glorious National Trust countryside, within easy reach of the Elizabethan harbour and heritage coastal footpath. The 'Welly Longbar' is a cosy retreat with its log fires and original beams. Real ales and malts are served and traditional folk music is a regular feature. Home-made soups and pudding are popular, and main meals range from burgers, salads and pasties to lamb tagine, Cornish mackerel, and lentil bake.
OPEN: 11–3 5.30–11 (Easter–Oct & BHs all day)
BAR MEALS: Lunch served: all week Dinner served: all week 12–2 6–9.30 Av main course £5.35 **RESTAURANT:** Dinner served: all week 7–9.30 Av 3 course à la carte £17.50
BREWERY/COMPANY: Free House
PRINCIPAL BEERS: Interbrew Flowers IPA, St Austell HSD & Daylight Robbery, Wadworth 6X, Greene King Abbot Ale.
FACILITIES: Children welcome Garden: Terrace, beer garden, food served outdoors Dogs allowed **NOTES:** Parking 20 **ROOMS:** 17 bedrooms 16 en suite from s£34 d£58

> ## SOUTH WEST COAST PATH
> The Cornish coastline has some of the most stunning coastal scenery in Europe passing wide river estuaries, busy seaside resorts and secret coves. Your walk along the South West Coast Path will pass by many pubs and inns, most of them too tempting to resist! Heading east to west you will find the Ship Inn at Fowey and the Rising Sun at Mevagissey before moving on to St Mawes where you'll find the Rising Sun and the Victory Inn. Continue along the coast to the Ferryboat Inn at Helford Passage and the Shipwrights Arms at Helford, then follow the trail further still to the Cadgwith Cove Inn, the Top House at the Lizard and the Halzephron Inn at Gunwalloe. The Ship at Portleven and the Victoria Inn at Perranuthnoe are worth a visit, as are the Old Coastguard Hotel and the Ship Inn at Mousehole. By the time you reach Treen, near Zennor, you may feel in need of a little sustenance. Try the Gurnards Head Hotel. St Ives is the setting for the historic Sloop, and nearby is Lelant where you'll find the Badger and the Watermill. Heading along the county's northern coast brings you to the Port William at Tintagel and the 16th-century Wellington Hotel at Boscastle.

PUB WALK

Dunmere
The Borough Arms

Level and undemanding, disused railway tracks make ideal walking trails. The popular Camel Trail, offering panoramic views and woodland scenery, is no exception, as this very pleasant walk demonstrates.

From the car park behind the pub, go down the slope and turn right. Walk along the Camel Trail for about 1 mile (1.6km) heading towards Bodmin, leave at Scalletts Well car park at the end of the trail and follow the path for about quarter of a mile (400m) where you will reach historic Bodmin Gaol. Turn left up the hill and follow the road around to the right. Continue for about half a mile

(800m) to a small gravel turning circle. Take the track to the left and follow it gradually downhill for about quarter of a mile (400m) to a gate and stile. Take the right-hand track just beyond the gate and descend the hill. Keep ahead for another half mile (800m) and on reaching an open area of ground, take the path leading away to the right. Follow the path for a few hundred yards (metres) and soon it rejoins the Camel Trail. Turn left and follow the riverbank downstream for about half a mile (800m) until you reach a waymarker stone. Take the left fork and then right at the next stone, soon returning to the pub car park.

THE BOROUGH ARMS,
DUNMERE Bodmin PL31 2RD
Tel: 01208 73118
Directions: From A30 take A389 to Wadebridge, pub approx 1m from Bodmin
Set in stunning countryside, the pub is directly on the Camel Trail, for off-road cycling, horse-riding and walking. Trout and salmon fishing available close by. There is a carvery every evening and Sunday lunchtime.
Open: 11–11
Bar meals: 12–2.15 6.30–9.15
Children welcome and dogs allowed. Garden and parking available.

Distance: 4 miles (6.4km)
Map: OS Landranger 200
Terrain: Forestry and riverbank
Paths: Broad tracks and tarmac roads
Gradient: One steep gradient

Walk submitted and checked by The Borough Arms, Dunmere

CADGWITH
Map 02 SW71

Cadgwith Cove Inn
TR12 7JX ☎ 01326 290513 📠 01326 291018
e-mail: enquiries@cadgwithcoveinn.com

Prominently situated overlooking a lovely cove on the Lizard peninsula, the inn is right at the physical and social centre of this fishing and farming community. As might be expected, seafood is a speciality, with popular options of lobster thermidor, fish and chips, cajun salmon, and grilled mackerel. The inn lies on the Lizard Coastal walk, so is an ideal meeting place for walkers. The pub is also host to many local groups and societies, as well as wedding receptions and christenings.
OPEN: 12–3 7–11 (Sat-Sun all day) **BAR MEALS:** Lunch served: all week Dinner served: all week 12–2.30 6–9.30 Av main course £7.95
RESTAURANT: Lunch served: all week Dinner served: all week 12–2.30 6–9.30 **BREWERY/COMPANY:** Inn Partnership
PRINCIPAL BEERS: Interbrew Flowers IPA, Wadworth 6X, Marston's Pedigree, Sharp's. **FACILITIES:** Garden: patio area Dogs allowed (biscuits) **NOTES:** Parking 4 **ROOMS:** 7 bedrooms 7 en suite from d£37.50

CALLINGTON
Map 02 SX36

The Coachmakers Arms
6 Newport Square PL17 7AS ☎ 01579 382567 📠 01579 384679
A wide range of customers - families, old and young - enjoy a drink or meal in comfortable surroundings at this traditional stone-built pub. Antique furniture, clocks, horse brasses and displays of foreign currency all contribute to the atmosphere. Home-made fare, from open sandwiches, through fisherman's crunch, to sirloin or rump steaks, is offered and there's a popular Sunday roast. Convenient for the Cornish coast, the Eden Project, Dartmoor and the Tamar Valley.
OPEN: 11–3 6–11 (Sun 12–3, 7–10.30) **BAR MEALS:** Lunch served: all week Dinner served: all week 12–2 7–9.30 Av main course £6.50
RESTAURANT: Lunch served: all week Dinner served: all week 12–2 7–9.30 Av 3 course à la carte £15 **BREWERY/COMPANY:** Free House **PRINCIPAL BEERS:** Sharps, Doombar.
FACILITIES: Children welcome Dogs allowed (water)
NOTES: Parking 10 **ROOMS:** 4 bedrooms 4 en suite from s£30 d£45

Manor House Inn
Rilla Mill PL17 7NT ☎ 01579 362354
Dir: leave A30 and join B3254, L onto B3257 for 3m. R signed Rilla Mill
At the heart of a designated Cornish conservation area, the pub stands in its own mature gardens and orchard on the banks of the River Lynher. An extensive menu of daily home-made dishes and grills operates throughout; the steak and kidney pie, meat curry and vegetable lasagnes all prepared to the landlady's own recipes.

OPEN: 11–3 6–11 **BAR MEALS:** Lunch served: all week Dinner served: all week 12–2 7–9.30 Av main course £6.50
RESTAURANT: Lunch served: all week Dinner served: all week 12–2 7–9.30 Av 3 course à la carte £17 **BREWERY/COMPANY:** Free House **PRINCIPAL BEERS:** Bass, Whitbread.
FACILITIES: Children welcome Children's licence Garden: beer garden, patio, outdoor eating, BBQ Dogs allowed **NOTES:** Parking 41 **ROOMS:** 12 bedrooms 12 en suite from s£27.50 d£50

CHAPEL AMBLE
Map 02 SW97

The Maltsters Arms
PL27 6EU ☎ 01208 812473
Dir: From Wadebridge take A39 then 1st L, B3314.Village on R

A whitewashed 16th-century village pub a little inland from Cornwall's Atlantic roller-lashed coast. The main bar has heavy oak beams, half-panelled walls and a large log fire. This pub has recently changed hands but among the Cornish fish and seafood dishes expect scallops in wine and cream, fillet of turbot steamed in lemon saffron sauce, or rainbow trout baked with garlic and prawns. For meat eaters, steak and ale pie, or stir-fried duck with ginger and spring onion.
OPEN: 11–2.30 6–11 (Sun 12–2.30, 7–10.30) **BAR MEALS:** Lunch served: all week Dinner served: all week 12–2 6.30–9 Av main course £6 **RESTAURANT:** Lunch served: all week Dinner served: all week 12–2 6.30–9 Av 3 course à la carte £15 **BREWERY/COMPANY:** Free House **PRINCIPAL BEERS:** Sharp's Cornish Coaster & Eden Ale, Interbrew Bass, Greene King Ruddles County & Abbot Ale.
FACILITIES: Garden: patio, food served outdoors
NOTES: Parking 9

CONSTANTINE
Map 02 SW72

Pick of the Pubs

Trengilly Wartha Inn ★ ★
Nancenoy TR11 5RP ☎ 01326 340332 📠 01326 340332
e-mail: trengilly@compuserve.com
Dir: SW of Falmouth
In a peaceful wooded valley - the name means settlement above the trees - near the Helford River, this popular family-run pub appeals to a variety of customers and has its own cricket team and pitch. The pub offers an interesting range of eclectic wines from their own retail range. There is an attractive terraced garden leading down to a small lake where ducks and moorhens nestle in the fringes. Bedroom accommodation is divided between six bedrooms in the main house and newer garden rooms suitable for families. The bar menu includes both traditional and more unusual dishes with the emphasis on the use of produce sought by a chef/patron who founded the Food in Cornwall Association. Expect local smoked

continued

continued

ham and crab open sandwich and ploughman's lunches with home-made breads, pickles and chutneys. Popular classics include crab cakes and Trengilly sausages with mash and onion gravy, while restaurant dishes range from loin of vension to Swiss chard ravioli and John Dory.

OPEN: 11-3 6.30-11 **BAR MEALS:** Lunch served: all week Dinner served: all week 12-2.15 6.30-9.30 Av main course £9
RESTAURANT: Dinner served: all week 7.30-9.30 Av 3 course à la carte £27 Av 3 course fixed price £27
BREWERY/COMPANY: Free House
PRINCIPAL BEERS: Sharps Cornish Coaster, St Austell HSD, Skinners, Exmoor Gold. **FACILITIES:** Children welcome Garden: Beer garden, patio, food served outdoors Dogs allowed **NOTES:** Parking 50 **ROOMS:** 8 bedrooms 8 en suite from s£48 d£70

CRACKINGTON HAVEN   Map 02 SX19

Coombe Barton Inn ◆◆◆ 🍴 ♀

EX23 0JG ☎ 01840 230345 📠 01840 230788
Dir: *S from Bude on A39, turn off at Wainhouse Corner, then down lane to beach*

Originally built for the 'Captain' of the local slate quarry, the Coombe Barton (it means 'valley farm' in Cornish) is over 200 years old and sits in a small cove surrounded by spectacular rock formations. Local seafood is a feature of the menu and includes crab, lemon sole, steaks, turbot, shark and plaice. Curries, pies, carvery, casseroles, pasta and vegetarian dishes are all available. Bedrooms are comfortable and one suite is suitable for families.

OPEN: 11-11 (Winter weekdays closed 3-6) **BAR MEALS:** Lunch served: all week Dinner served: all week 11-2.30 6-10 Av main course £7 **RESTAURANT:** Lunch served: all week Dinner served: all week 11-2.30 6-10 Av 3 course à la carte £12
BREWERY/COMPANY: Free House **PRINCIPAL BEERS:** St Austell Dartmoor Best & Hick's special Draught, Sharp's Doom Bar Bitter **FACILITIES:** Children welcome Garden: Patio, food served outdoors **NOTES:** Parking 40 **ROOMS:** 6 bedrooms 3 en suite from s£30 d£40

CRIPPLESEASE   Map 02 SW53

The Engine Inn 🍴 NEW

TR20 8NF ☎ 01736 740204
Dir: *Pub is on B3311 between St Ives and Penzance*
A homely inn high on the moor offering spectacular views and a quirky, cosy interior furnished with mining memorabilia, books, games and musical instruments which customers frequently take down and play. Outside a paddock provides parking for the horse-riders who regularly stop here. Food includes doorstep sandwiches, ploughman's

continued

lunches, some good vegetarian options and plenty of meat and chips combinations including steak, gammon and scampi.

OPEN: 11-2.30 5-11 **BAR MEALS:** Lunch served: all week Dinner served: all week 12-2 6-10 Av main course £5.50
PRINCIPAL BEERS: Sharp's Doom Bar Bitter, Marston's Pedigree, Greene King Old Speckled Hen. **FACILITIES:** Children welcome Garden: Food served outdoors Dogs allowed (water) **NOTES:** Parking 30

CUBERT   Map 02 SW75

The Smuggler's Den Inn ♀

Trebellan TR8 5PY ☎ 01637 830209 📠 01637 830580
e-mail: hankers@aol.com
Dir: *From Newquay take A3075 to Cubert crossroads, then R, then L signed Trebellan, 0.5m*
An attractive 16th-century stone and thatch pub set in a beautiful valley. Features of the interior are the long bar, barrel seats and inglenook wood-burner. A family room, beer garden and well-kept ales tapped from the cask are among the many other attractions. Specialities of the house are the fresh fish dishes and prime quality steaks. Favourites are fresh Newlyn cod in beer batter and trio of butcher's sausages with mustard, mash and gravy.

OPEN: 11-3 (Winter 12-2) 6-11 **BAR MEALS:** Lunch served: all week Dinner served: all week 12-2 6-9.30 Av main course £10
RESTAURANT: Lunch served: all week Dinner served: all week 12-2 6-9.30 Av 3 course à la carte £20 **BREWERY/COMPANY:** Free House **PRINCIPAL BEERS:** Skinners Cornish Knocker & Betty Stogs Bitter, Sharp's Doom Bar, St Austell Tribute & HSD.
FACILITIES: Children welcome Garden: Beer garden, patio, food served outdoors Dogs allowed (water) **NOTES:** Parking 50

England

DULOE   Map 02 SX25

Ye Olde Plough House Inn 🏠 ⌂
PL14 4PN ☎ 01503 262050 📠 01503 264089
e-mail: alison@theploughinn.freeserve.co.uk
Dir: *A38 to Dobwalls, take turning signed Looe*
A welcoming 18th-century inn with slate floors, wood-burning
stoves, settles and old pews. It is located in a lovely village,
handy for visiting the coast and exploring the Cornish
countryside. Two Jack Russell dogs offer a friendly greeting
and four chefs produce a tempting choice of freshly prepared
dishes. These include beef Wellington, steak on hot stones and
guinea fowl with bacon and tomato in a thyme-scented gravy.
OPEN: 12–2.30 6.30–11 (Sun 7.00–10.30) Closed: Dec 25–26
BAR MEALS: Lunch served: all week Dinner served: all week 12–2
6.30–9.30 Av main course £5.65 **RESTAURANT:** Lunch served: all
week Dinner served: all week 12–2 6.30–9.30 Av 3 course à la carte £15
BREWERY/COMPANY: Free House **PRINCIPAL BEERS:** Sharp's
Doom Bar, Interbrew Bass, Worthington. **FACILITIES:** Children
welcome Garden: Food served outside Dogs allowed (water if
requested) **NOTES:** Parking 20

DUNMERE   Map 02 SX06

The Borough Arms
PL31 2RD ☎ 01208 73118 📠 01208 76788
e-mail: Borougharms@aol.com
Dir: *From A30 take A389 to Wadebridge, pub approx 1m from Bodmin*

Situated in glorious Cornish countryside, this popular pub lies
on the edge of the Camel Trail, a 19-mile traffic-free walking,
horse-riding and cycling route following the Camel between
Padstow and Bodmin Moor. The pub has been extended over
the last 30 years or so. Food options range from jacket
potatoes, ploughman's lunches and hot rolls to pies and grills.
Other options include smoked salmon fillet, spinach and
mushroom lasagne, curry and Stilton bake. Popular carvery
served every evening and Sunday lunchtime.
OPEN: 11–11 (Sun 12–10.30) **BAR MEALS:** Lunch served: all week
Dinner served: all week 12–2.15 6.30–9.15 Av main course £5
RESTAURANT: Lunch served: all week Dinner served: all week
12–2.15 6.30–9.15 **BREWERY/COMPANY:** Scottish & Newcastle
PRINCIPAL BEERS: Sharp's Bitter, Skinner's, Scottish Courage
Courage Best. **FACILITIES:** Children welcome Garden: Food served
outside Dogs allowed (water) **NOTES:** Parking 150
See Pub Walk on page 71

EGLOSHAYLE   Map 02 SX07

The Earl of St Vincent
PL27 6HT ☎ 01208 814807 📠 01208 814445
Originally built to house the masons who built the nearby
church, this pub dates from the Middle Ages, and has

colourful floral displays and a collection of old clocks. The
current name comes from Sir John Jervis, the Earl of St
Vincent and Nelsons superior officer.

FALMOUTH   Map 02 SW83

Quayside Inn & Old Ale House
Fore St TR11 3JQ ☎ 01326 312113
Offering more than thirty real ales and hosting regular beer
festivals, this is a real drinkers pub. Fresh-baked hot rolls in
the bar.

FEOCK   Map 02 SW83

The Punch Bowl & Ladle
Penelewey TR3 6QY ☎ 01872 862237
Thatched roadside inn, handy for Trelissik Gardens. Children
welcome in restaurant. Open all day in summer.

FOWEY   Map 02 SX15

The Ship Inn 🏠 ⌂
Trafalgar Square PL23 1AZ ☎ 01726 834931 📠 01726 834931
Dir: *From A30, take B3269 & A390.*
A traditional old inn, dating back to 1570, in the centre of this
lovely old sea-port – handy for the Eden Project and the Lost
Gardens of Heligan. Modest accommodation and authentic St
Austell ales uphold its long tradition of genuine hospitality.
Lashings of local fish and fresh market produce are prepared
to order such as beer-battered cod, scallops in garlic butter
and Fowey Coddle – local sausages and mash in leek and
mushroom gravy. No bookings, so arrive early to avoid
disappointment.
OPEN: 11–11 Winter times vary please telephone
BAR MEALS: Lunch served: all week Dinner served: all week 12–2
6–8.30 Av main course £5.35 **RESTAURANT:** Lunch served: all week
Dinner served: all week 12–2 6–8.30 **BREWERY/COMPANY:** St
Austell Brewery **PRINCIPAL BEERS:** St Austell Tinners Ale, Daylight
Robbery. **FACILITIES:** Children welcome Dogs allowed (water)
ROOMS: 6 bedrooms 1 en suite from s£17.25 d£17.25

GUNNISLAKE   Map 02 SX47

The Rising Sun Inn
Calstock Rd PL18 9BX ☎ 01822 832201 📠 01822 832201
Dir: *From Tavistock take A390 to Gunnislake, pub is through village and
quarter mile on L. Left at traffic lights and quarter mile on right.*
Quaint 17th-century pub with glorious gardens and fine views
over the Tamar Valley. Cottagey interior featuring a fascinating
collection of china, a wide range of real ales, and home-
cooked food.

GUNWALLOE   Map 02 SW62

Pick of the Pubs

The Halzephron Inn 🏠
TR12 7QB ☎ 01326 240406 📠 01326 241442
e-mail: halzephroninn@bandbcornwall.net
Dir: *3m S of Helston on A3083, R to Gunwalloe. Then through village,
inn is on L overlooking Mount's Bay.*
Quintessentially Cornish, this 500-year old free house is
spectacularly situated on the South-West Coastal Footpath
overlooking Mount's Bay. Formerly known as The Ship,
the pub was 'dry' for half a century until 1956, when its
licence was restored. Its unusual name comes from the

continued   *continued*

old Cornish Als Yfferin, or 'Cliffs of Hell', a name borne out by the numerous wrecks along this rugged coast. A shaft still connects the pub to an underground tunnel, which was used by smugglers such as the Victorian local hero Henry Cuttance, who was also a landlord and wrestler. Modern visitors will find a warm welcome, with real ales and a fine selection of malt whiskies. The menu changes twice daily and may include caramelised Gressingham duck breast on butternut squash purée, whole grilled lobster with garlic butter and rocket and potato salad, pan-fried John Dory on seafood risotto, and peppered venison fillet on pommes fondant and celeriac purée. Desserts feature a lot of both clotted and ice creams. Overnight accommodation is in two cosy en suite rooms.

OPEN: 11-2.30 6.30-11 Closed: 25 Dec **BAR MEALS:** Lunch served: all week Dinner served: all week 12-2 7-9 Av main course £11 **RESTAURANT:** Lunch served: all week Dinner served: all week 12-2 7-9 Av 3 course à la carte £20
BREWERY/COMPANY: Free House
PRINCIPAL BEERS: Sharp's Own, Doom Bar & Coaster, St Austell Tribute, Carlsberg-Tetley Bitter. **FACILITIES:** Garden: Courtyard, food served outside **NOTES:** Parking 14 **ROOMS:** 2 bedrooms 2 en suite from s£40 d£70

GWEEK   Map 02 SW72

The Gweek Inn 🐾
TR12 6TU ☎ 01326 221502 📠 01326 221502
e-mail: gweek.inn@tesco.net
Dir: 2m E of Helston near Seal Sanctuary
Traditional family-run village pub and restaurant set at the mouth of the Helford River close to the National Seal Sanctuary. Plenty of other tourist attractions nearby, including Goonhilly Earth Station and the Lizard peninsula. A very extensive menu offers blackboard specials including a fish choice, grills, vegetarian dishes, traditional roasts, and favourites like cod and chips, seafood pie, lasagne and chicken and mushroom pie. Wadsworth 6X on tap, and two weekly guest ales.
OPEN: 12-3 6.30-11 **BAR MEALS:** Lunch served: all week Dinner served: all week 12-2 6.30-9 Av main course £6.50 **RESTAURANT:** Lunch served: all week Dinner served: all week 12-2.15 6.30-9 Av 3 course à la carte £12.50
BREWERY/COMPANY: Inn Partnership
PRINCIPAL BEERS: Interbrew Flowers IPA & Bass, Greene King Old Speckled Hen, Carlsberg-Tetleys Greenall's Original, Wadsworth 6X. **FACILITIES:** Children welcome Garden: BBQ, food served outdoors Dogs allowed **NOTES:** Parking 70

HAYLE   Map 02 SW53

The Watermill Inn 🐾 ♀
Old Coach Rd, Lelant Downs TR27 6LQ ☎ 01736 757912
e-mail: robandnikki@watermill1999.freeserve.co.uk
Dir: From the A30 take the A3074 towards St Ives take L turns at the next two mini Rdbts
The old water mill here was in constant use as late as the 1970s. Converted from a restaurant into a classic 'local' just four years ago, recent extensions to bar and restaurant allow for speciality sausages and locally caught fish in the one and duck cassoulet and Prime Cornish beef fillet in the upper dining-room. Look also for Thai pork, coconut curry prawns and smoked chicken strudel. Decent real ales, wines and malt whiskies.
OPEN: 11-3 6.30-11 (Jul-Aug 11-11) **BAR MEALS:** Lunch served: all week Dinner served: all week 12-2.15 6.30-9.30 Av main course £6
RESTAURANT: Lunch served: all week Dinner served: all week 12-2.15 6.30-9.30 Av 3 course à la carte £15
BREWERY/COMPANY: Free House **PRINCIPAL BEERS:** Sharp's Doombar Bitter, Eden Ale, Skinner's Figgys Brew, Cornish Blonde. **FACILITIES:** Children welcome Garden: Food served outside Dogs allowed (water) **NOTES:** Parking 35

HELFORD   Map 02 SW72

Pick of the Pubs

Shipwright Arms
TR12 6JX ☎ 01326 231235
Dir: A390 through Truro, A394 to Helston, before Goonhilly Down L for Helford/Manaccan
Superbly situated on the banks of the Helford River in an idyllic village, this small thatched pub is especially popular in summer when customers relax on the three delightful terraces, complete with palm trees and glorious flowers, which lead down to the water's edge. Heavy nautical theme inside. Summer buffet offers crab and lobster subject to availablity, alongside various ploughman's lunches, salads, home-made pies, steaks and a wide range of international dishes. Barbecues in summer on the terrace.
OPEN: 11-2.30 6-11 **BAR MEALS:** Lunch served: all week Dinner served: all week 12-2 7-9 Av main course £4.75
RESTAURANT: Lunch served: Sun Dinner served: Tue-Sat 12-2 7-9 Av 3 course à la carte £14.50 **BREWERY/COMPANY:** Free House **PRINCIPAL BEERS:** Castle Eden, Greene King IPA, Sharps Doombar. **FACILITIES:** Children welcome Garden: barbecue Dogs allowed

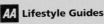

England

HELFORD PASSAGE · Map 02 SW72

Ferryboat Inn
TR11 5LB ☎ 01326 250625 📠 01326 250916
e-mail: gav13@tinyworld.co.uk
Dir: From A39 at Falmouth, head toward River Helford

Beautifully positioned on the north bank of the Helford River, the pub dates back at least 300 years. There's a nautical feel to the main bar, with its unrivalled views and French windows opening onto a spacious terrace. Well kept St Austell ales are backed by a good range of wines, available by the glass. Separate lunchtime and evening menus feature plenty of fresh fish, salads and grills, plus daily specials, too
OPEN: 11-2.30 6.30-11 (Summer 11-11) **BAR MEALS:** Lunch served: all week Dinner served: all week 12-2.30 6.30-9 Av main course £5.95 **RESTAURANT:** Lunch served: all week Dinner served: all week 12-2.30 6.30-9 Av 3 course à la carte £10.95
BREWERY/COMPANY: St Austell Brewery **PRINCIPAL BEERS:** St Austell HSD, Tinners & IPA. **FACILITIES:** Children welcome Garden: Patio, food served outdoors Dogs allowed **NOTES:** Parking 80

HELSTON · Map 02 SW62

Blue Anchor Inn
50 Coinagehall St TR13 8EX
☎ 01326 562821 📠 01326 565765
Dir: A30 to Penzance, then Helston signposted
One of the oldest pubs in Britain to brew its own beer, this unpretentious, thatched pub dates from the 15th century when it was a monks' rest home. The inn has also been the haunt of Victorian tin miners, who collected their wages here. Sample excellent 'Spingo' ales in the low-ceilinged bars, tour the brewery, and tuck into stew and dumplings, fish pie, beef in Spingo, lamb hotpot, or a crusty filled roll.
OPEN: 10.30-11 **BAR MEALS:** Lunch served: all week 12-4 Av main course £4.75 **BREWERY/COMPANY:** Free House
PRINCIPAL BEERS: Blue Anchor Middle, Best, Special & Extra Special, Braggit. **FACILITIES:** Children welcome Garden: Food served outside. Secluded, sunny garden Dogs allowed (water provided)
ROOMS: 4 bedrooms 4 en suite from s£27 d£44 No credit cards

KINGSAND · Map 02 SX45

Pick of the Pubs

The Halfway House Inn
Fore St PL10 1NA ☎ 01752 822279 📠 01752 823146
e-mail: halfway@eggconnect.net
Dir: from either Torpoint Ferry or Tamar Bridge follow signs to Mount Edgcombe
Situated on the coast path and tucked among the narrow lanes and colour-washed houses of this quaint fishing

village is the family-run Halfway House Inn. It was so named because it used to represent the border between Devon and Cornwall and now signifies the dividing line between the conservation villages of Kingsand and Cawsand. The inn, licensed since 1850, has a pleasant stone-walled bar, low-beamed ceilings and a large central fireplace. Locally caught seafood is a speciality in the informal restaurant, and daily blackboard menus might feature grilled cod with Puy lentils, green Thai monkfish and salmon with a sweet pepper and tomato salsa. Alternatives may include grilled duck breast with parsnip purée and mango sauce, sautéed pork tenderloin with red onion gravy and steak and kidney pudding. The modern en suite bedrooms are furnished in pine.

OPEN: 12-3 7-11 **BAR MEALS:** Lunch served: all week Dinner served: all week 12-2 7-9 Av main course £5
RESTAURANT: Lunch served: all week Dinner served: all week 12-2 7-9 Av 3 course à la carte £17
BREWERY/COMPANY: Free House
PRINCIPAL BEERS: Sharp's Doom Bar Bitter, Timothy Taylor Landlord, Scottish Courage Courage Best, Interbrew Boddingtons Bitter. **FACILITIES:** Children welcome Dogs allowed (water, dog chews) **NOTES:** Parking 120 **ROOMS:** 6 bedrooms 6 en suite from s£27.50 d£55

LAMORNA · Map 02 SW42

Lamorna Wink
TR19 6XH ☎ 01736 731566
Dir: 4m along B3315 towards Lands End, then 0.5m to turning on L
This oddly named pub was one of the original Kiddlywinks, a product of the 1830 Beer Act that enabled any householder to buy a liquor license. Popular with walkers and not far from the Merry Maidens standing stones, the Wink provides a selection of local beers and a simple menu that includes sandwiches, jacket potatoes and fresh local crab.
OPEN: 11-11 (Winter 11-4, 6-11) **BAR MEALS:** Lunch served: all week Dinner served: all week 11-3 6-9 Av main course £5.50
BREWERY/COMPANY: Free House **PRINCIPAL BEERS:** Sharp's Doom Bar, Skinners, Cornish Knocker Ale. **FACILITIES:** Children welcome Garden: beer garden, Dogs allowed (in garden only)
NOTES: Parking 40 No credit cards

LANLIVERY · Map 02 SX05

The Crown Inn
PL30 5BT ☎ 01208 872707 📠 01208 871208
Dir: From Bodmin take A30 S,follow signs 'Lanhydrock',L at mini r'about. 3m take A390, Lanlivery 2nd R
An inn built to accommodate the masons who were building the church opposite, which in turn was frequented by the Black Prince. It is a 12th-century longhouse with three-foot

continued

continued

thick exterior walls, a large inglenook fireplace and a priest hole. The pub has an acre of land, incorporating a pretty cottage garden, and is within 10 minutes' of the Eden Project and Lanhydrock House. Fresh fish from the quay is a feature of the menu.
OPEN: 11-3 6-11 **BAR MEALS:** Lunch served: all week Dinner served: all week 12-2.15 7-9.15 Av main course £7.50
RESTAURANT: Lunch served: all week Dinner served: all week 12-2.15 7-9.15 Av 3 course à la carte £15
BREWERY/COMPANY: Free House **PRINCIPAL BEERS:** Sharp's Doom Bar & Eden Ale, Interbrew Worthington Bitter.
FACILITIES: Children welcome Garden: Food served outside Dogs allowed (water, treats) **NOTES:** Parking 40 **ROOMS:** 2 bedrooms 2 en suite from s£30 d£50

LELANT
Map 02 SW53

The Badger Inn ♦♦♦♦
Fore St TR26 3JT ☎ 01736 752181 📠 01736 759398
e-mail: marybadgerinn@aol.com
Dir: from rdbt at end of Hayle Bypass take A3074 to St Ives & Carbis Bay

Devotees of Virginia Woolf come from all over the world to visit this village inn where the author used to stay. Situated in landscaped gardens close to the Hayle Estuary and St Ives Bay, the building has recently been brought up to date without sacrificing its charm. Fresh Cornish produce features strongly on a menu that includes crab Florentine, baked sole, and locally reared pork and lamb; there are daily casseroles and vegetarian dishes, too.
OPEN: 11-2.30 6-11 **BAR MEALS:** Lunch served: all week Dinner served: all week 12-2 6.30-10 Av main course £8.95
RESTAURANT: Lunch served: all week Dinner served: all week 12-2.00 6.30-10 Av 3 course à la carte £17.50
BREWERY/COMPANY: Free House **PRINCIPAL BEERS:** St Austell Hicks & Tribute. **FACILITIES:** Garden: Food served outdoors **NOTES:** Parking 30 **ROOMS:** 5 bedrooms 5 en suite from s£30 d£50

LIZARD
Map 02 SW71

The Top House ☕ ♀
TR12 7NQ ☎ 01326 290974 📠 01326 290089
Dir: From Helston take A3083 to the Lizard
Close to the spectacular granite cliffs bordering Britain's most southerly village, this traditional Cornish local has been run by the Greenslade family for half a century. A collection of lifeboat and shipwreck ephemera reflects the area's maritime heritage, and there's a display of 19th-century watercolours and prints of the Lizard and Kynance. The menu offers home-made pies, steaks, local crab and seafood platter.

continued

OPEN: 11-11 (Sun 12-10.30) **BAR MEALS:** Lunch served: all week Dinner served: all week 12-2.30 6.30-9 Av main course £6.75
BREWERY/COMPANY: Inn Partnership
PRINCIPAL BEERS: Interbrew Flowers IPA, Sharp's Doom Bar.
FACILITIES: Children welcome Garden: Food served outside Dogs allowed (water) **NOTES:** Parking 20

LOSTWITHIEL
Map 02 SX15

Pick of the Pubs

Royal Oak Inn ♀
Duke St PL22 0AQ ☎ 01208 872552 📠 01208 872552
Dir: From Exeter take A30 to Bodmin then onto Lostwithiel or from Plymouth take A38 towards Bodmin then L onto A390 to Lostwithiel

An atmospheric 13th-century inn with an underground tunnel which reputedly connects it to the dungeons in the courtyard of nearby Restormel Castle. The River Fowey is close by, one of the focal points in Cornwall's old capital of Lostwithiel where part of the Civil War was fought out. Inside the locals' saloon bar you can savour the inn's friendly character in front of the open log fire. Alternatively the lounge bar serves as a venue for a quiet drink, as well as offering a full à la carte service with a wide selection of wines and real ales. From a list of specials dishes select pork Dijonnaise, old-style Barbary duck in orange and ginger sauce, or sea bass fillet with hollandaise sauce, while the menu features various salads, vegetarian choices, steaks, and seafood such as scallops, trout and salmon.
OPEN: 11-11 (Sun 12-10.30) **BAR MEALS:** Lunch served: all week Dinner served: all week 12-2 6.30-9.15
RESTAURANT: Lunch served: all week Dinner served: all week 12-2 6.30-9.15 **BREWERY/COMPANY:** Free House
PRINCIPAL BEERS: Interbrew Bass, Fuller's London Pride, Marston's Pedigree, Sharp's Own. **FACILITIES:** Children welcome Garden: Food served outdoors Dogs allowed **NOTES:** Parking 15 **ROOMS:** 6 bedrooms 5 en suite from s£38 d£65

LOSTWITHIEL continued

Ship Inn ♦ ♦ ♦ ♦ ♀
Lerryn PL22 0PT ☎ 01208 872374 📠 01208 872614
e-mail: shiplerryn@aol.com
Dir: *3m S of A390 at Lostwithiel*

Dating back to the early 17th century, the Ship occupies a
delightful riverside setting in the centre of a charming village.
Close by lies woodland ideal for walkers. Handy for golf at
nearby Lostwithiel and Lanhydrock. A sample menu includes
a variety of fish dishes, ranging from steamed salmon with
pink peppercorn sauce to Cornish baked mullet. Steak and
Guinness pie and fresh local meat are an integral part of the
daily fare. Rooms are tastefully furnished.
OPEN: 11.30-3 6-11 (Sun 12-3, 7-10.30) **BAR MEALS:** Lunch
served: all week Dinner served: all week 12-2 6.30-9 Av main course
£8 **RESTAURANT:** Lunch served: all week Dinner served: all week
12-2 6.30-9 Av 3 course à la carte £15 **BREWERY/COMPANY:** Free
House **PRINCIPAL BEERS:** Interbrew Bass, Sharp's, Skinner's, Otter
Ale. **FACILITIES:** Children welcome Garden: Food served outside
Dogs allowed **NOTES:** Parking 36 **ROOMS:** 4 bedrooms 4 en suite
from s£35 d£60

LUDGVAN
Map 02 SW53

White Hart 🐕
Churchtown TR20 8EY ☎ 01736 740574
Dir: *From A30 take B3309 at Crowlas*
An early 14th-century pub with splendid views across St
Michael's Mount and Bay. An old-fashioned atmosphere
means no fruit machines or jukeboxes to disturb the peace.
Cornish pasties made in the village, toad-in-the-hole, and
fresh fish on Thursday and Friday are features of the menu,
along with omelettes, pasta dishes and steaks. Tempting
home-made puddings include apple pie, spotted dick, treacle
tart and crumble, all served with clotted cream.
OPEN: 11-2.30 6-11 **BAR MEALS:** Lunch served: all week 12-2
Dinner served: Tues-Sun(all summer) 7-9 Av main course £5.50
RESTAURANT: Lunch served: all week 12-2 Dinner served: Tues-Sun
(all summer) 7-9 Av 3 course à la carte £10
BREWERY/COMPANY: Inn Partnership
PRINCIPAL BEERS: Marston's Pedigree, Interbrew Flowers, Bass.
FACILITIES: Garden: Food served outside Dogs allowed
NOTES: Parking 12 No credit cards

MANACCAN
Map 02 SW72

The New Inn ♀
TR12 6HA ☎ 01326 231323
Thatched, cottagey pub deep in Daphne du Maurier country
(the original Frenchman's Creek is nearby) that dates back to
Cromwellian times when it was known to be 'out of bounds'
to his soldiers. Enjoy the peaceful village setting, the large,

continued

flower-filled garden, and the homely and traditional bars.
Worth finding for fresh fish - monkfish with creamy Pernod
sauce, crab cakes with tomato sauce, cod and chips - the
wide-ranging sandwich menu and evening favourites like pot-
roasted oxtail, lasagne and fillet steak au poivre.
OPEN: 12-3 6-11 (Sat-Sun all day in summer) **BAR MEALS:** Lunch
served: all week Dinner served: all week 12-2.30 6-9.30 Av main
course £9 **BREWERY/COMPANY:** Pubmaster
PRINCIPAL BEERS: Wadsworth 6X, Flowers IPA.
FACILITIES: Children welcome Garden: Food served outside Dogs
allowed (very welcome, water) **NOTES:** Parking 14

MARAZION
Map 02 SW53

Pick of the Pubs

Godolphin Arms ★ ★ 🐕 NEW
TR17 0EN ☎ 01736 710202 📠 01736 710171
e-mail: enquiries@godolphinsarms.co.uk

Few pubs can boast views this good: the Godolphin Arms
sits directly opposite St Michael's Mount - so close, in fact,
that the sea splashes at the windows in the winter. From
the traditional style bar and beer terrace to the more
homely restaurant and most of the bedrooms, the mount
is visible. It's a family run affair, with an emphasis on a
friendly welcome and good service. The restaurant offers
plenty of seafood - perhaps whitebait, moules marinère
or fish pie - alongside other pub favourites such as
chargrilled steaks, chicken curry or beef Wellington. Less
familiar options might include half a roasted duck with a
cranberry and orange sauce or vegetarian dishes such as
roasted avocado and goats' cheese served with apple and
a tomato and basil sauce. A pared down menu is available
in the bar, along with some imaginative light snacks.
OPEN: 10.30-11 **BAR MEALS:** Lunch served: all week Dinner
served: all week 12-2.30 5.30-9.30 Av main course £5
RESTAURANT: Lunch served: all week Dinner served: all week
12-2.30 5.30-9.30 Av 3 course à la carte £15
BREWERY/COMPANY: Free House
PRINCIPAL BEERS: Sharp's Eden Ale, Skinner's Cornish
Knocker Ale, Interbrew Worthington Bitter, Scottish Courage John
Smith's. **FACILITIES:** Children welcome Garden: Terrace, food
served outside Dogs allowed **NOTES:** Parking 48 **ROOMS:** 10
bedrooms 10 en suite from s£32.50 d£60

METHERELL
Map 02 SX46

Carpenters Arms
PL17 8BJ ☎ 01579 350242
Dir: *From Saltash take A338 to Callington, then A390 to Tavistock, follow
signs to pub*
A 15th-century building, originally the carpenter's workshop
for Cotehele House, with slate floors, an internal well, original
beams and fireplace.

MEVAGISSEY
Map 02 SX04

Rising Sun Inn 🕮 ⏶
Portmellon Cove PL26 6PL ☎ 01726 843235 🖷 01726 843235
e-mail: cliffnsheila@tiscali.co.uk

Superbly situated next to the beach and overlooking the sea, this Grade II listed building is partly built of shipwreck timbers. Cosy beamed bar with snug for children and non-smokers and a new cellar bar serving popular real ales and continental beers. Expect local seafood specialities in addition to spicy pasta provençale, vegetable stir-fry, rack of lamb, Mediterranean chicken and a selection of chargrilled steaks.
OPEN: 11–3 6–11 Closed: 1 Nov–28 Feb **BAR MEALS:** Lunch served: all week Dinner served: all week 12–2 7-9.45 Av main course £5 **RESTAURANT:** Lunch served: all week Dinner served: all week 12–2 7-9.45 Av 3 course à la carte £12 **BREWERY/COMPANY:** Free House **PRINCIPAL BEERS:** Adnams Bitter, St Austells HSD, Fuller's London Pride, Timothy Taylor Landlord. **FACILITIES:** Children welcome patio, food served outdoors Dogs allowed
NOTES: Parking 60 **ROOMS:** 7 bedrooms 7 en suite from s£40 d£30

The Ship Inn ♦♦♦ NEW
Fore St PL26 6UQ ☎ 01726 843324 🖷 01726 844368
Only one minutes' walk from the harbour at Mevagissy, the Ship Inn offers plenty of fresh fish. Accomodation is en suite, and the area is convenient for attractions such as the Eden Project and the Gardens of Heligan.

MITHIAN
Map 02 SW75

Miners Arms 🕮
TR5 0QF ☎ 01872 552375 🖷 01872 552375
e-mail: minersarms@mithian.fsbusiness.co.uk
Dir: From A30 take B3277 to St Agnes. Take 1st R to Mithian
Character pub with slate floors, wall paintings, a cobbled courtyard, exposed beams and ornate plasterwork ceilings that were made for a visit by Edward VII in 1896. Previously used as a courtroom and a pay house for local miners. Interesting bar food includes steak, kidney and oyster pie, monkfish and prawns in pernod, seafood pie, Sunday roasts, butternut squash and barley bake, and hake with herb and horseradish crust.
OPEN: 12–3 6–11 **BAR MEALS:** Lunch served: all week Dinner served: all week 12–2.30 7-9.30 Av main course £7.50 **BREWERY/COMPANY:** Pubmaster **PRINCIPAL BEERS:** Sharp's Doom Bar & Special, Bass, Courage. **FACILITIES:** Children welcome Garden: Food served outside. Patio area Dogs allowed (water provided) **NOTES:** Parking 40

★ **Indicates AA inspected hotel accommodation**

MORWENSTOW
Map 02 SS21

The Bush Inn
EX23 9SR ☎ 01288 331242
A historic country inn set in an isolated cliff-top hamlet close to bracing coastal path walks, the Bush is reputedly one of Britain's oldest pubs. It was originally built as a chapel in 950 for pilgrims from Wales en route to Spain, only becoming a pub some 700 years later. The unspoilt traditional interior, with stone-flagged floors and old stone fireplaces, has a Celtic piscina carved from serpentine and set into a wall behind the bar. Hearty lunchtime food includes generously filled sandwiches, pasties and pasta dishes, and thick soup and home-made stews in winter.
OPEN: 12–3 7–11 (closed Mon) **BAR MEALS:** 12–2
BREWERY/COMPANY: Free House **PRINCIPAL BEERS:** St Austell HSD. **NOTES:** Parking 30 No credit cards

MOUSEHOLE
Map 02 SW42

Pick of the Pubs

The Old Coastguard Hotel ★ ★ ⊛ 🕮 ⏶
The Parade TR19 6PR ☎ 01736 731222 🖷 01736 731720
e-mail: bookings@oldcoastguardhotel.co.uk
Dir: A30 to Penzance, take coast road through Newlyn to Mousehole, pub is 1st building on L

With its stylish bar, brasserie and sun lounge, this is the perfect base to discover the stunning landscape and legends of this delightful part of west Cornwall. Mousehole is a thriving and largely unspoilt village where the harbour, which dates back to 400AD, was once the embarkation point for pilgrims to Rome. Above the village, the hotel is set in subtropical gardens leading down to the sea, and each of the en suite bedrooms enjoys spectacular views over Mounts Bay. Those in the know come to the brasserie to enjoy fresh regional produce, meats and cheeses prepared and presented in a variety of contemporary and traditional ways, with plenty of vegetarian and seafood options. Expect ceviche of mixed fish, or grilled Cornish goats' cheese, followed perhaps by Newlyn crab salad, grilled salmon, rib-eye steak or pan-fried duck. Round off your meal with Cornish ices, or chilled ginger and orange pudding.
OPEN: 12–11 (closed 3–6 in winter) **BAR MEALS:** Lunch served: all week Dinner served: all week 12–3 6-9.30 Av main course £7 **RESTAURANT:** Lunch served: all week Dinner served: all week 12–3 3–6 Av 3 course à la carte £17.50 **BREWERY/COMPANY:** Free House
PRINCIPAL BEERS: Sharp's Doom Bar, Interbrew Bass.
FACILITIES: Children welcome Garden: Beer garden, food served outdoors Dogs allowed **NOTES:** Parking 15
ROOMS: 23 bedrooms 22 en suite from s£35 d£70

England

MOUSEHOLE continued

Ship Inn ◆◆◆
TR19 6QX ☎ 01736 731234
An old-world inn, with low beams and granite floors, overlooking the harbour. Seafood landed at nearby Newlyn figures prominently, with dishes such as crab bisque, seafood platter and fisherman's lunch (smoked mackerel with salad and brown bread). Other options might be monkfish, John Dory, or traditional meat specials.
OPEN: 11-11 (Sun 12-10.30) **BAR MEALS:** Lunch served: all week Dinner served: all week 12-2.15 6-9 Av main course £6.50
RESTAURANT: Dinner served: all week 6-9 Av 3 course à la carte £16 **BREWERY/COMPANY:** St Austell Brewery
PRINCIPAL BEERS: St Austell's HSD & Tinners Ale, Tribute, IPA.
FACILITIES: Children welcome Dogs allowed **ROOMS:** 8 bedrooms 8 en suite from s£42.50 d£50

MYLOR BRIDGE   Map 02 SW83

Pick of the Pubs

Pandora Inn 🐷 ⓨ
Restronguet Creek TR11 5ST
☎ 01326 372678 📄 01326 372678
Dir: North of Falmouth off the A39
This medieval thatched pub on the shore of Restronguet Creek is especially popular with visiting yachtsmen who call here at high tide. The idyllic location is handy for Truro, Falmouth and the Lizard, and within easy reach of some of Britain's most beautiful coastal scenery. Low wooden ceilings and flagstone floors add to the charm of the pub's quaint old interconnecting rooms, and intimate alcoves are just the place for a quiet game of dominoes or crib. Solid fuel stoves and open log fires drive out the winter cold, and in summer you can sit out on the attractive riverside patio or floating pontoon. You'll find plenty of good home cooking; expect Club sandwiches, as well as soups, pâté, and beef, pork or game pies. Other dishes include filled savoury pancakes, Mediterranean fish stew, plus fresh local crab and mussels. Finish off with Bakewell tart, apple and raspberry pie or bread-and-butter pudding.
OPEN: 11-11 (Sun 12-10.30) Winter 11.30-2.30, 7-11
BAR MEALS: Lunch served: all week Dinner served: all week 12-2 7-9 Av main course £6 **RESTAURANT:** Lunch served: Sun only 12-2.30 Dinner served: all week 7-9 Av 3 course à la carte £18 **BREWERY/COMPANY:** St Austell Brewery
PRINCIPAL BEERS: St Austell Tinners Ale, HSD, Bass.
FACILITIES: Children welcome Patio, Food served outside Dogs allowed (water) **NOTES:** Parking 30

PELYNT   Map 02 SX25

Jubilee Inn ★ ★ 🐷
PL13 2JZ ☎ 01503 220312 📄 01503 220920
e-mail: rickard@jubileeinn.freeserve.co.uk
Dir: take A390 signpsted St Austell at village of East Taphouse, turn L onto B3359 signposted Looe & Polperro. Jubilee Inn on left on leaving Pelynt
The name commemorates Queen Victoria's Golden Jubilee in 1887, though the inn actually dates from the 16th century and was formerly known as The Axe. The interior has a homely, welcoming feel, with its oak-beamed ceilings, blazing winter fires, and Staffordshire figurines of the queen and her consort. Accommodation is also provided, comprising 11 en suite bedrooms and a bridal suite. Local seafood features, along with home-made ribs, curries and pies.

OPEN: 12-3 6-11 **BAR MEALS:** Lunch served: all week Dinner served: all week 12-2.30 6-9.30 Av main course £6.90
RESTAURANT: Lunch served: all week Dinner served: all week 12-2.30 7-9.30 Av 3 course à la carte £15
BREWERY/COMPANY: Free House
PRINCIPAL BEERS: Interbrew Bass, Sharp's Doom Bar, Skinner's Betty Stogs Bitter. **FACILITIES:** Children welcome Garden: Food served outside Dogs allowed **NOTES:** Parking 70
ROOMS: 11 bedrooms 11 en suite from s£32 d£52

PENDOGGETT   Map 02 SX07

The Cornish Arms 🐷 ⓨ
PL30 3HH ☎ 01208 880263 📄 01208 880335
e-mail: cornisharms@yahoo.co.uk
Dir: From A30 Launceston, R onto A395, then L on to A39, then R onto B3314. pub 7m along this road.
Atmospheric 16th-century coaching inn a mile or so from the beautiful and unspoiled Cornish coast. Hidden beaches and secret coves are just a short walk away and nearby is the fishing village of Port Isaac where you can watch the catch being landed. Solid beams and stone-flagged floors characterise the pub's interior and bar food might include sirloin steak, prime beef-burger and butterfly chicken. Expect chargrilled monkfish, medallions of pork tenderloin, penne pasta with sausage, or mushroom Stroganoff on the daily-changing restaurant menu.
OPEN: 11-11 (Sun 12-10.30) **BAR MEALS:** Lunch served: all week Dinner served: all week 12-2 6.30-9.00 Av main course £8
RESTAURANT: Lunch served: Sun Dinner served: all week 12-2 7-9 Av 3 course à la carte £16 **BREWERY/COMPANY:** Free House
PRINCIPAL BEERS: Bass, Sharp's Doom Bar, Sharp's Eden, St Austell seasonal ales. **FACILITIES:** Children welcome Garden: Food served outside. Overlooking Port Isaac Dogs allowed (water provided)
NOTES: Parking 50 **ROOMS:** 7 bedrooms 7 en suite from s£39 d£59

PENZANCE   Map 02 SW43

Dolphin Tavern 🐷 ⓨ NEW
Quay St TR18 4BD ☎ 01736 364106 📄 01736 364194
This ancient pub overlooks the harbour and Mounts Bay towards St Michael's Mount. In a history spanning 600 years, the Tavern has seen Sir Walter Raleigh take his first smoke on English soil, and Judge Jeffreys hold court within its walls – not surprisingly it's reputed to be haunted. Part of it also used to be the harbour office. Seafood is a speciality, and the local pilchards and mackerel are popular, as is the range of steaks.
OPEN: 11-11 **BAR MEALS:** Lunch served: all week Dinner served: all week 11-2.30 6.30-9.30 Av main course £5
BREWERY/COMPANY: St Austell Brewery
PRINCIPAL BEERS: HSD, Tinners, Celtic Smooth.
FACILITIES: Children welcome Garden: Food served outside, patio area Dogs allowed (water provided)

continued

The Turks Head Inn ♀

Chapel St TR18 4AF ☎ 01736 363093 📠 01736 360215
e-mail: veronica@turkspz.freeserve.co.uk
The oldest pub in Penzance dating from the 13th century, if
not before, though much of the original building was
destroyed by a Spanish raiding party in the 16th century. Old
flat irons, jugs and beams characterise the interior, and there
is a sunny flower-filled garden at the rear. Typical dishes
include a selection of steaks, fillet of John Dory with mustard,
cider and cream, and local pheasant with port and cranberry
sauce.
OPEN: 11–3 (Sun 12-3) 5.30–11 (Sun 5.30-10.30) Closed: Dec 25
BAR MEALS: Lunch served: all week Dinner served: all week
11–2.30 6–10 Av main course £5.95 **RESTAURANT:** Lunch served:
all week Dinner served: all week 11–2.30 6–10 Av 3 course à la carte
£13 Av 2 course fixed price £6.50 **BREWERY/COMPANY:** Inn
Partnership **PRINCIPAL BEERS:** Marston's Pedigree, Greene King
IPA, Sharp's Doombar Bitter. **FACILITIES:** Children welcome
Garden: Beer garden, food served outside

PERRANUTHNOE   Map 02 SW52

The Victoria Inn ♦♦♦ 🛏 ♀

TR20 9NP ☎ 01736 710309 📠 01736 710309
Dir: *Take the A394 Helston- Penzance road and turn down to the village
following all the signs for Perranuthnoe*

Mentioned in the Domesday Book and reputed to be the
oldest hostelry in Cornwall, this 12th-century inn is idyllically
close to a sandy beach and coastal footpath. With its en suite
accommodation, pretty heated patio, and good food it makes
a pleasant stopover for a pint of Courage Best, and dishes like
panache of shellfish, pan-fried supreme of red snapper, and
meaty choices like seared calves' liver on leek mash, and chilli
con carne.
OPEN: 12–3 (Aug open all day-12-11) 7-11 (From Mar open from
6.30) **BAR MEALS:** Lunch served: all week Dinner served: all week
12-2 7–9 Av main course £11 **RESTAURANT:** Lunch served: all week
Dinner served: all week 12-2 7-9 Av 3 course à la carte £18.95
PRINCIPAL BEERS: Courage Best, Bass, Doom Bar.
FACILITIES: Children welcome Garden: Food served outside.
Mediterranean garden Dogs allowed (water provided)
NOTES: Parking 10 **ROOMS:** 3 bedrooms 2 en suite from s£35
d£50

PHILLEIGH   Map 02 SW83

Pick of the Pubs

The Roseland Inn 🛏 ♀

TR2 5NB ☎ 01872 580254 📠 01872 501528
A tiny village in rural surroundings provides the delightful
setting for this 16th-century cob-built inn, on the old

pilgrim route to Penzance. It's a real gem of a place,
peacefully positioned by the parish church just two miles
from the King Harry Ferry that crosses the River Fal. In
summer, roses bloom on the splendid front terrace,
creating the perfect spot for outdoor eating, while inside
the worn slate floors, old settles, low beams and log fire
make for a cosy atmosphere. Children and dogs are
welcome (especially springer spaniels), and cyclists drop
in regularly as the inn is on the New Cycle Trail. A good
range of food is served including decent sandwiches and
ploughman's lunches. Fresh oven-baked sea bass, steak
and Stilton, and classic shank of lamb braised to the inn's
own recipe are typical of the dishes offered. Well worth
the drive from St Mawes or Truro.
OPEN: 11–3 6-11 **BAR MEALS:** 12-2.15 6–9.30
RESTAURANT: 12-2.15 6-9 **BREWERY/COMPANY:** Greenalls
PRINCIPAL BEERS: Sharp's Doom Bar, Ringwood Best,
Interbrew Bass, Marston's Pedigree. **FACILITIES:** Children
welcome Garden Dogs allowed **NOTES:** Parking 15

POLKERRIS   Map 02 SX05

The Rashleigh Inn ♀

PL24 2TL ☎ 01726 813991
Dir: *off the A3082 outside Fowey*

Set in the harbour of a charming old pilchard fishing village,
the Rashleigh is over 250 years old and is on the coastal path
known as 'The Saint's Way'. The bar specialises in real ales,
and may offer over 300 in one year. Food-wise, the emphasis
is on local produce, especially fish, and dishes include pan-
fried scallops in garlic butter, smoked fish platter with
horseradish cream and sea bass with cream and herb sauce.
OPEN: 11–3 6-11 (Summer 11-11) **BAR MEALS:** Lunch served: all
week Dinner served: all week 11–2.30 6–10 Av main course £6
RESTAURANT: Lunch served: all week Dinner served: all week
11-2.30 6.30-10 Av 3 course à la carte £15
BREWERY/COMPANY: Free House **PRINCIPAL BEERS:** Sharp's
Doom Bar, St Austell HSD, Timothy Taylor Landlord, Exmoor Gold.
FACILITIES: Children welcome Garden: Food served outside
NOTES: Parking 22

POLPERRO   Map 02 SX25

Old Mill House 🛏

Mill Hill PL13 2RP ☎ 01503 272362 📠 01503 272058
e-mail: info@old-millhouse.co.uk
Stroll through the picturesque streets of Polperro and take a
look at the colourful harbour before relaxing at this delightful
old inn, where log fires and a riverside garden enhance the
character of the place. Well-kept ales and good home-cooked
food attract drinkers and diners alike. The emphasis is on

continued

continued

England

POLPERRO continued

seafood, including local scallops, lemon sole, and smoked mackerel. Other options are Cornish pasties, lasagne or spicy chicken.
OPEN: 11-11 (Winter open at 12) **BAR MEALS:** Lunch served: all week Dinner served: all week 12-2 7-9 Av main course £6.20
PRINCIPAL BEERS: Sharp's Eden Ale, Special, Cornish Coaster.
FACILITIES: Children welcome Garden: On riverside, seating, food served outside Dogs allowed (water & Bonio) **NOTES:** Parking 8
ROOMS: 8 bedrooms 8 en suite from s£37.50 d£55

POLRUAN
Map 02 SX15

The Lugger
PL12 6QS ☎ 01726 870007
Waterside pub by Fowey foot-ferry. Great for walkers. St Austell Ales. Open all day.

PORT GAVERNE
Map 02 SX08

Pick of the Pubs

Port Gaverne Hotel ★ ★ 🛏
PL29 3SQ ☎ 01208 880244 📠 01208 880151
e-mail: pghotel@telinco.co.uk
Dir: Signed from B3314, S of Delabole via B3267 on E of Port Isaac
With the sea and a beautiful little cove just down the road, this 17th-century inn is a magnet for holidaymakers as well as locals. The winding old building is a delight with its flagged floors, steep staircases and plenty of nooks and crannies that evoke its fishing origins. Smuggling might have been rife here once, but nowadays it is the day's fishing that forms part of the inn's raison d'être. Local produce is used wherever possible, and all bread is home made. Expect fruits de mer including Cornish crab, and half pint pots of prawns, as well as home-baked steak and ale pie, and ploughman's with local cheeses. Passing walkers on the Heritage Coast Path can sit in the small beer garden, or at one of the tables in front of the hotel, to enjoy Greene King and Bass real ales.
OPEN: 11-2.30 6.00-11 (Summer 11-11) Closed: Early Jan - Mid Feb **BAR MEALS:** Lunch served: all week Dinner served: all week 12-2.30 6.30-9.30 Av main course £6.50
RESTAURANT: Dinner served: all week 7-9.30 Av 3 course fixed price £20 **BREWERY/COMPANY:** Free House
PRINCIPAL BEERS: Sharp's Doom Bar, Bass, Greene King Abbot Ale. **FACILITIES:** Children welcome Children's licence Garden: Food served outside. beer garden Dogs allowed (water provided) **NOTES:** Parking 15 **ROOMS:** 15 bedrooms 15 en suite from s£40 d£40

PORTHLEVEN
Map 02 SW62

The Ship Inn 🛏
TR13 9JS ☎ 01326 564204
Built into steep cliffs and approached by a flight of stone steps, this 17th-century inn has wonderful views over the harbour, especially at night when it is floodlit. Inside is a knocked through bar with log fires, and a family room converted from an old smithy. Four real ales are properly served and a good choice of food includes local crab, fresh fish and the likes of home-cooked lamb shank in red wine and rosemary.

OPEN: 11.30-3 6.30-11 (all day mid Jul-mid Sept)
BAR MEALS: Lunch served: all week Dinner served: all week 12-2 7-9 Av main course £7.95 **BREWERY/COMPANY:** Free House
PRINCIPAL BEERS: Scottish Courage Courage Best, Greene King Abbot Ale, Sharp's Doom Bar & Sharp's Own. **FACILITIES:** Children welcome Garden: Food served outside Dogs allowed (water)

PORTREATH
Map 02 SW64

Basset Arms
Tregea Ter TR16 4NG ☎ 01209 842077 📠 01209 843936
Dir: From Redruth take B3300 to Portreath
Typical Cornish stone cottage, built as a pub in the early 19th century to serve the harbour workers, with plenty of tin mining and shipwreck memorabilia adorning the low-beamed interior.

RUAN LANIHORNE
Map 02 SW84

The Kings Head ♀
TR2 5NX ☎ 01872 501263
Dir: 3m from Tregony Bridge on A3078

With its pretty sun-trap sunken garden overlooking the tidal River Fal, this popular Victorian summer pub enjoys a rural location in the heart of the Roseland Peninsula. Straightforward pub fare is supplemented by daily specials and more imaginative dishes such as chicken lemon couscous, Chinese pork hock and salmon and asparagus tart.
OPEN: 12-2.30 6.30-11 (closed Mon Sep-Etr) **BAR MEALS:** Lunch served: Tue-Sun 12-1.45 Dinner served: Tue-Sun 6.30-9 Av main course £6.50 **BREWERY/COMPANY:** Free House
PRINCIPAL BEERS: Sharp's Special & Doom Bar, Skinners Kings Ruan. **FACILITIES:** Children welcome Garden: Food served outside Dogs allowed **NOTES:** Parking 12

ST AGNES
Map 02 SW75

Driftwood Spars Hotel ♦ ♦ ♦ 🛏
Trevaunance Cove TR5 0RT
☎ 01872 552428 📠 01872 553701
e-mail: driftwoodspars@hotmail.co.uk
Dir: A30 onto B3285, thru St Agnes, down steep hill, L at Peterville Inn, onto rd signed Trevaunance Cove
This atmospheric 17th-century smugglers' inn is situated a stone's throw from a superb beach. Stone walls, shipwreck photographs and granite fireplaces characterise the bars, which have ceiling beams made from the spars of ships wrecked in the Cove. Dishes on offer include fish platter, with four kinds of fresh fish, spicy Mexican nachos, lamb and mint casserole, and roast dinner from the carvery (every night in summer and Sunday lunch off season).

continued

continued

OPEN: 11-11 (Fri-Sat 11-12, Sun 12-10.30) **BAR MEALS:** Lunch served: all week Dinner served: all week 12-2.30 6.30-9.30 Av main course £5.50 **RESTAURANT:** Lunch served: all week Dinner served: all week 12-2.30 6.30-9.30 **BREWERY/COMPANY:** Free House **PRINCIPAL BEERS:** Carlsberg-Tetley Bitter, Interbrew Bass, Sharp's Own, St Austell HSD. **FACILITIES:** Children welcome Garden: Sea views, food served outside Dogs allowed **NOTES:** Parking 80 **ROOMS:** 15 bedrooms 15 en suite from s£32 d£64

ST AGNES (ISLES OF SCILLY)　　Map 02 SW17

Turks Head
TR22 0PL ☎ 01720 422434 🖷 01720 423331
e-mail: johndartatturkshead@ukonline.com
Dir: By boat or helicopter to St Mary's and boat on to St Agnes

Former coastguard boathouse overlooking the cove and island quay, this gem of a pub, Britain's most southwesterly inn, is noted for its atmosphere and superb location. Inside are fascinating model ships and maritime photographs – among other features. Name comes from the Turkish pirates who came here from the Barbary Coast in the 16th century. Sample home-made quiche, mixed seafood, cold roast beef, vegetable pasta bake and breaded scampi from the straightforward but wholesome menu.
OPEN: 11-11 **BAR MEALS:** Lunch served: all week Dinner served: all week 12-2.30 6.30-9.30 Av main course £6.25
BREWERY/COMPANY: Free House **PRINCIPAL BEERS:** St Austell Dartmoor Best &, Carlsberg-Tetley Ind Coope Burton Ale.
FACILITIES: Children welcome Garden: Beer Garden, patio, food served outdoors Dogs allowed **ROOMS:** 1 bedrooms 1 en suite from d£53

⊚ **For a list of pubs with
AA Rosette Awards for food see pages 12 & 13.**

ST BREWARD　　Map 02 SX07

The Old Inn 🐾
Church Town, Bodmin Moor PL30 4PP
☎ 01208 850711 🖷 01208 851671
e-mail: darren@theoldinn.fsnet.co.uk
Dir: 4 miles from A30 near Bodmin, or signed from B3266. Pub next to landmark St Breward church
At 700ft above sea level, the Old Inn is the highest in Cornwall, and having been founded in the 11th century, among the oldest. The pub has slate floors, wooden beams and log fires, along with fine ales and a varying menu served in three main bars and an à la carte restaurant. Fillet of smoked salmon with dill sauce, moorland grill or home-made pies may be featured. One bar is family friendly, and the large beer garden has a pets corner.
OPEN: 11-3 6-11 (Summer open all day) **BAR MEALS:** Lunch served: all week Dinner served: all week 11-2.30 6-9.30 Av main course £5.95 **RESTAURANT:** Lunch served: all week Dinner served: all week 11-2.30 6-9.30 Av 3 course à la carte £19.95 Av 3 course fixed price £20 **BREWERY/COMPANY:** Free House
PRINCIPAL BEERS: Interbrew Bass & John Smiths, Sharp's Doom Bar Bitter, Special. **FACILITIES:** Children welcome Garden: Food served outdoors Dogs allowed (water) **NOTES:** Parking 35

ST EWE　　Map 02 SW94

The Crown Inn
PL26 6EY ☎ 01726 843322
Dir: From St Austell take B3273. At Tregiskey x-rds turn R. St Ewe is signposted on R
Hanging baskets decorate the massive cob walls of this delightful 16th-century village inn, just a mile from the famous 'Lost gardens of Heligan'. Original features include the well behind the bar, and the spit roasting mechanism above the fireplace still used on special occasions. Well kept St Austell ales complement an extensive menu and daily specials; local steaks, Cajun cod, or chicken with leeks and bacon are typical.
OPEN: 12-3 6-11 **BAR MEALS:** Lunch served: all week Dinner served: all week 12-2 6-9 Av main course £7.95
RESTAURANT: Lunch served: all week Dinner served: all week 12-2 6-9 Av 3 course à la carte £15 **BREWERY/COMPANY:** St Austell Brewery **PRINCIPAL BEERS:** Tribute, Hicks Special, Tinners, plus guest ale. **FACILITIES:** Children welcome Garden: Food served outside Dogs allowed (water) **NOTES:** Parking 20

ST IVES　　Map 02 SW54

Pick of the Pubs

The Sloop Inn ◆◆◆◆ ♀
The Wharf TR26 1LP ☎ 01736 796584 🖷 01736 793322
e-mail: sloop@btinternet.com
Dir: On harbour front
Believed to date from around 1312AD, one of Cornwall's oldest and most famous inns is right on the harbour, separated from the sea only by a cobbled courtyard and The Wharf. A favourite haunt of local fishermen, artists and visitors alike, it offers a distinctly fishy slant to menus on display in the panelled Cellar Bar and low-beamed Lounge Bar, both adorned with colourful paintings by the St Ives School. Seafood chowder, home-made salmon and Cornish crab fishcakes, a trio of monkfish and St Ives Bay mackerel fillets are perennial favourites. Alternative main meals include pasta dishes, sirloin steak, ham, egg and

continued

England

ST IVES continued

chips and chicken and bacon and bacon lasagne, while additional specials might be fish pie, chicken curry and crab, prawn and mussel salad. Bedrooms differ in size but all exude an historic charm and contain the modern facilities expected by guests today. Well placed for the Tate Gallery and the Barbara Hepworth Museum and Gallery.

The Sloop Inn

OPEN: 10.30–11 (Sun 12–10.30) **BAR MEALS:** Lunch served: all week Dinner served: all week 12–3 5–8.45 Av main course £5 **BREWERY/COMPANY:** Unique Pub Co **PRINCIPAL BEERS:** John Smiths, Sharp's Doom Bar. **FACILITIES:** Children welcome **ROOMS:** 14 bedrooms 11 en suite from s£47.50 d£65

ST JUST (NEAR LAND'S END)   Map 02 SW33

Star Inn
TR19 7LL ☎ 01736 788767
The Star is reputed to have been built to house workmen constructing the local church. It is very old, with lots of tin mining memories and fishing stories. There's folk music on Monday; live music Thursday, singing Friday, and usually Saturday, too. Food is good, reasonably priced and there's always something to hand if you're in for a pint - fresh crab sandwich, hot soup, pasties (including a veggie alternative), casseroles and hogs' pudding.

The Wellington Hotel ♦♦♦ 🐾
Market Square TR19 7HD ☎ 01736 787319 ▤ 01736 787906
e-mail: hotrod@thewellington.freeserve.co.uk
Named after the Iron Duke, who stayed here, the hotel is an imposing granite-fronted building overlooking St Just's market square. The town is on the scenic coastal road between St Ives and Lands End, close to some of Cornwall's finest cliffs, coves and beaches. Not surprising then that local fish and crab are in great demand. Meat dishes are locally sourced too. Large beer garden.
OPEN: 10.30–11 **BAR MEALS:** Lunch served: all week Dinner served: all week 12–2 6–9 Av main course £5 **RESTAURANT:** Lunch served: all week Dinner served: all week 12–2 6–9 Av 3 course à la carte £12.50 **BREWERY/COMPANY:** St Austell Brewery **PRINCIPAL BEERS:** St Austell Tinners, St Austell HSD, St Austell Cornish Cream Mild. **FACILITIES:** Children welcome Garden: Food served outside. Secluded garden Dogs allowed (must provide own bedding) **NOTES:** Parking 20 **ROOMS:** 11 bedrooms 11 en suite from s£27 d£45

ST KEVERNE   Map 02 SW72

The White Hart ♦♦♦
The Square TR12 6ND ☎ 01326 280325 ▤ 01326 280325
e-mail: whitehart@easynet.co.uk
Opposite the 15th-century church, the White Hart is known for the 300-year-old ghost of a 19th-century landlady, who turns off the gas to the beer pumps and knocks things off the shelves if customers get too rowdy. The lunchtime bar menu offers ploughman's platter, huntsman's platter, various baguettes and jacket potatoes. Good choice of dishes, too, for children. The varied bistro menu includes seared sea bass, chargrilled chicken breast, and chargrilled mature aged fillet steak.
OPEN: 11–2.30 6–11 (July-Aug all day Wkds) **BAR MEALS:** Lunch served: all week Dinner served: all week 12–2 6.30–9.30 Av main course £7.50 **RESTAURANT:** Dinner served: Wed–Sun 7–9.30 Av 3 course à la carte £17.50 **BREWERY/COMPANY:** Inn Partnership **PRINCIPAL BEERS:** Interbrew Flowers Original, Greene King Old Speckled Hen, Sharp's Doom Bar. **FACILITIES:** Children welcome Garden: Food served outside, Patio Dogs allowed (water, Bonios) **NOTES:** Parking 15 **ROOMS:** 2 bedrooms 2 en suite from s£35 d£50

ST KEW   Map 02 SX07

St Kew Inn
PL30 3HB ☎ 01208 841259
e-mail: des@stkewinn.fsnet.co.uk
Dir: *village signed 3m NE of Wadebridge on A39*
Attractive stone-built 15th-century inn near the parish church in a secluded valley. Retains much of its original character, notably its large kitchen range and slate floors. One menu is offered throughout, with dishes ranging from fish pie, and beef in Guinness with herb dumplings, to specialities such as lobster and game pie.
OPEN: 11–2.30 6–11 (Sun 12–3, 7–10.30, all day Jun-Aug) **BAR MEALS:** Lunch served: all week Dinner served: all week 12–2 7–9.30 Av main course £7.50 **RESTAURANT:** Lunch served: all week Dinner served: all week 12–2 7–9.30 Av 3 course à la carte £17 **BREWERY/COMPANY:** St Austell Brewery **PRINCIPAL BEERS:** St Austell HSD & Tinners Ale. **FACILITIES:** Children welcome Garden: barbecue **NOTES:** Parking 80

ST MAWES   Map 02 SW83

Pick of the Pubs

The Rising Sun ★★ 🏵 🐾 ♀
The Square TR2 5DJ ☎ 01326 270233 ▤ 01209 270198
e-mail: therisingsun@bt.click.com
St Mawes's central pub on the square is a deservedly popular meeting-place for yachtsmen - who can moor by the 19th-century harbour opposite - and locals for whom it is the focus of village life. The charming hotel has a convivial atmosphere, the bars are open all day and the up-to-date bedrooms enjoy lovely views across the harbour and Fal estuary.
OPEN: 11–11 (Sun 12–10.30) **BAR MEALS:** Lunch served: all week Dinner served: all week 12–2.30 6.30–9.30 Av main course £7 **RESTAURANT:** Lunch served: Sun Dinner served: All 12–2 7–9.30 Av 3 course à la carte £27 **BREWERY/COMPANY:** St Austell Brewery **PRINCIPAL BEERS:** Hicks Special Draught, St Austell Tinners Ale. **FACILITIES:** Children welcome Garden: Patio, BBQ, food served outdoors Dogs allowed (water) **NOTES:** Parking 6 **ROOMS:** 8 bedrooms 8 en suite from s£30 d£69

Pick of the Pubs

The Victory Inn ♀
Victory Hill TR2 5PQ ☎ 01326 270324 🖹 01326 270238
Dir: In centre of village close to the harbour

'Keep it fresh, keep it simple' is chef Rob Dawson's motto at this friendly fishermen's local, situated a stone's throw from St Mawes's bustling harbour, which successfully combines the traditional virtues of a lively village inn with those of a modern dining pub offering the freshest of local seafood. Quality produce is sourced from the best suppliers; scallops, crabs and mackerel come straight from the boats in the harbour, oyster from beds on the Helford River, smoked fish cured in Penryn, samphire and seaweed is gathered from around the coast, and vegetable and cheeses come from Cornish producers. In the bar, tuck into crab bisque with clotted cream and chive, Spanish-style cod with chorizo, potatoes and peppers, grilled sand soles with roasted cumin and lemon butter, and red Thai curry of monkfish and tiger prawns with lime-scented rice. Alternatively, try the treacle-glazed ham with bubble-and-squeak. Good puddings; fixed-price 3-course seafood menu in the upstairs restaurant.

OPEN: 11-11 (Sun 12-10.30) **BAR MEALS:** Lunch served: all week Dinner served: all week 12-2 6.30-9 Av main course £7.50
RESTAURANT: Dinner served: all week 6.30-9 Av 3 course à la carte £17 **PRINCIPAL BEERS:** Sharps, Bass, Ringwood.
FACILITIES: Children welcome Garden: Food served outside Dogs allowed

The Falcon Inn ♦♦♦♦ 🛏 ♀
TR8 4EP ☎ 01637 860225 🖹 01637 860884
e-mail: enquiries@falconinn.net
Dir: From A30 8m W of Bodmin, follow signs to Newquay St Mawgan Airport. After 2m turn R into village, pub at bottom of hill

Taking its name from a falcon which, at the time of the Reformation, flew over the village to indicate a secret Catholic church service was being held, this 15th-century pub lies in the sheltered Vale of Lanherne. The dazzling gardens have won many awards and there are attractive terraces and wisteria-covered walls. Comprehensive menu and daily specials range from lemon sole and chilli con carne to lamb steak cooked in its own juices and venison medallions with a port and mushroom sauce. Well equipped bedrooms are individual in style and size.

OPEN: 11-3 6-11 **BAR MEALS:** Lunch served: all week Dinner served: all week 12-2 6.30-9.30 Av main course £6
RESTAURANT: Lunch served: all week Dinner served: all week 12-2 6.30-9.30 Av 3 course à la carte £12 **BREWERY/COMPANY:** St

Austell Brewery **PRINCIPAL BEERS:** St Austell HSD, Tinners Ale, Tribute. **FACILITIES:** Children welcome Garden: Food served outside Dogs allowed (water) **NOTES:** Parking 25
ROOMS: 3 bedrooms 2 en suite from s£20 d£30

The Farmers Arms ♦♦♦
PL28 8NP ☎ 01841 520303 🖹 01841 520643

A lively and vibrant community pub dating from the 17th century. Nearby is the fishing port of Padstow and the 'seven bays for seven days' and some of Britain's most beautiful beaches. Excellent golf courses and stunning coastal walks are also close by. One menu is available throughout, offering such dishes as beef in ale pie, lasagne, ham, egg and chips and rack of ribs in barbecue sauce. Accommodation is available in four en suite bedrooms.

OPEN: 11-11 (Apr-Oct 11-3, 5-11) **BAR MEALS:** Lunch served: all week Dinner served: all week 12-2.30 6-8.30 Av main course £6
RESTAURANT: Lunch served: all week Dinner served: all week 12-2.30 6-9.30 Av 3 course à la carte £9 **BREWERY/COMPANY:** St Austell Brewery **PRINCIPAL BEERS:** St Austell HSD, Tinners Ale & Guest Ales. **FACILITIES:** Children welcome Children's licence Dogs allowed (water) **NOTES:** Parking 80 **ROOMS:** 4 bedrooms 4 en suite from d£50

The Crooked Inn ♦♦♦♦ 🛏 ♀
Stoketon Cottage, Trematon PL12 4RZ
☎ 01752 848177 🖹 01752 843203
e-mail: crookedinn@hotmail.com

Originally two cottages, providing accommodation for the cooks and gardeners of Stoketon Manor (the remains of which are still evident across the coutyard), the building was converted into an inn some 15 years ago, now with adjacent bedroom blocks. It is set in 20 acres of grounds overlooking the Lynher Valley. The range of home cooked meals includes locally caught fish, traditional pies, steaks and curries.

OPEN: 11-3 6-11 (Sat 11-11, Sun 11-10.30) **BAR MEALS:** Lunch served: all week Dinner served: all week 12-2.30 6-10
RESTAURANT: Lunch served: all week Dinner served: all week 12-2.30 6-10 **BREWERY/COMPANY:** Free House
PRINCIPAL BEERS: Hicks, Sharp's Eden Ale. **FACILITIES:** Children welcome Garden: Food served outside Dogs allowed
NOTES: Parking 60 **ROOMS:** 15 bedrooms 15 en suite from s£45 d£65

♀ **Pubs offering six or more wines by the glass**

---

continued

SALTASH continued

The Weary Friar Inn ♦♦♦♦ 🛏
Pillaton PL12 6QS ☎ 01579 350238 📠 01579 350238
Dir: 2m W of A388 between Callington & Saltash

This whitewashed 12th-century inn with oak-beamed ceilings, an abundance of brass, and blazing fires lies next to the Church of St Adolphus, tucked away in a small Cornish village. A typical selection from the menu includes grilled haddock fillets, chicken Maryland, vegetarian nut roast, mushroom Stroganoff, Thai green chicken curry, and seafood platter. Salads, sandwiches, afternoon cream teas and ploughman's are also available. Curry and other themed nights are popular. **OPEN:** 11.30-3 6.30-11 (Sun 12-3, 6-10.30) **BAR MEALS:** Lunch served: all week Dinner served: all week 12-2 7-9.30 Av main course £7.50 **RESTAURANT:** Lunch served: all week Dinner served: all week 12-2 7-9 Av 3 course à la carte £15 **BREWERY/COMPANY:** Free House **PRINCIPAL BEERS:** Wadworth 6X, Greene King Abbot Ale, Sharp's Doom Bar. **FACILITIES:** Garden: patio, food served outside **NOTES:** Parking 30 **ROOMS:** 12 bedrooms 12 en suite from s£40 d£50

Who'd Have Thought It Inn 🍺
St Dominic PL12 6TG ☎ 01579 350214
Village free house with beams, open fire, antique furnishings, and lovely views across the Tamar Valley to Plymouth. Handy for Cotehele House (NT). The village of St Dominic is well-known for its strawberries and daffodils.

SENNEN
Map 02 SW32

The Old Success Inn ★ ★ 🛏
Sennen Cove TR19 7DG ☎ 01736 871232 📠 01736 871232
e-mail: oldsuccess@fsbusiness.co.uk
A good catch of fish, especially mackerel, pilchards and grey mullet, explains the name of this late 17th-century inn. Once a rendezvous for smugglers and wreckers, Charlie's Bar is now a focal point for the local lifeboat crew, whose territory includes nearby Land's End. In a glorious location with expansive views over England's only cape - Cape Cornwall. Fresh local fish, including seafood paella and sea bass, as well as 'continental style' specials are popular. **OPEN:** 11-11 Closed: 25 Dec **BAR MEALS:** Lunch served: all week Dinner served: all week 12-2.30 7-9.30 Av main course £5 **RESTAURANT:** Lunch served: Sun Dinner served: all week 12-2.15 7-9.30 Av 3 course à la carte £20 **BREWERY/COMPANY:** Free House **PRINCIPAL BEERS:** Doom Bar, Sharps Special. **FACILITIES:** Children welcome Garden: Food served outside. Beer terrace Dogs allowed **NOTES:** Parking 16 **ROOMS:** s£28 d£60

TINTAGEL
Map 02 SX08

Pick of the Pubs

The Port William ♦♦♦♦ 🛏
Trebarwith Strand PL34 0HB
☎ 01840 770230 📠 01840 770936
Dir: Off B3263 between Camelford & Tintagel

Occupying one of the best locations in Cornwall, this former harbourmaster's house lies directly on the coastal path. Overlooking the beach and cliffs, the inn is 50 yards from the sea and the building dates back about 300 years to a time when coal was brought ashore and slate was shipped from Port William, an adjacent cove. Smuggling was also a regular activity in these parts. There is an entrance to a tunnel at the rear of the ladies' toilet! Focus on the daily-changing specials board for such dishes as seafood tagliatelle with crab, prawns, mussels and halibut, or local fresh cod in the Port William's own beer batter, shank of lamb with a honey balsamic sauce served with herb mashed potatoes and parsnips, and smoked duck platter with cranberry sauce and stuffed whole peppers served with wild rice. There is also and extensive selection of snacks and cold platters. **OPEN:** 11-11 (Sun 12-10.30) 12 opening in winter **BAR MEALS:** Lunch served: all week Dinner served: all week 12-2.30 6-9.30 Av main course £8 **RESTAURANT:** Lunch served: all week Dinner served: all week 12-2.30 6-9.30 Av 3 course à la carte £15.20 **BREWERY/COMPANY:** Free House **PRINCIPAL BEERS:** St Austell Tinners Ale & Hicks, Interbrew Bass & Boddingtons Bitter. **FACILITIES:** Children welcome Garden: Patio overlooking sea, food served outside Dogs allowed (water) **NOTES:** Parking 75 **ROOMS:** 6 bedrooms 6 en suite from s£56 d£73

Tintagel Arms Hotel ♦♦♦♦ 🛏
Fore St PL34 0DB ☎ 01840 770780
Dir: From M5 take A30-by pass Okehampton & Launceston turn L onto dual Rdbt B395 for North Cornwall follow signs Camelford, hotel opposite Lloyd's Bank
This 250-year-old stone-built inn, with its quaint beamed bedrooms and Cornish slate roof, is located in one of Britain's most famous villages, close to the remains of the legendary castle associated with King Arthur. The menu in Zorba's Taverna obviously has a Greek influence, with the expected moussaka, kebabs, stuffed vine leaves and Greek salad. Fresh fish dishes might include swordfish, tuna, cod, salmon and bass, and there is a choice for vegetarians. **OPEN:** 6-11 (Sun 7-10.30) Closed: Nov-Jan **BAR MEALS:** Dinner served: all week 6-9.30 Av main course £6 **RESTAURANT:** Dinner served: all week 6-9.30 Av 3 course à la carte £12.50

continued

BREWERY/COMPANY: Free House
PRINCIPAL BEERS: Interbrew Bass, Sharp's Doom Bar, Scottish Courage John Smiths, Courage Directors. **NOTES:** Parking 7
ROOMS: 7 bedrooms 7 en suite from s£29.50 d£45

TORPOINT   Map 02 SX45

The Edgcumbe Arms ♦♦♦ 🐾 ♀
Cremyll PL10 1HX ☎ 01752 822294 📠 01752 822014
e-mail: edgcumbearms1@btopenworld.com
Dir: *Please phone for directions*
Right on the Tamar estuary and close to the foot ferry from Plymouth, the views from the bow window seats and waterside terrace are glorious. Real ales from St Austell and quality home-cooked food are added attractions for those staying in one of the Laura Ashley-style bedrooms. American oak-panelled bars and stone flagged floors are the setting for fresh scallops, cod stuffed with crab, steak and ale pie and fresh Cornish beef steaks.
OPEN: 11-11 **BAR MEALS:** Lunch served: all week Dinner served: all week 12-2.30 7-9 Av main course £5.95 **RESTAURANT:** Lunch served: all week Dinner served: all week 12-2.30 7-9 Av 3 course à la carte £20 **BREWERY/COMPANY:** St Austell Brewery
PRINCIPAL BEERS: St Austell HSD, Tinners Ale & Tribute.
FACILITIES: Children welcome Garden: Food served outside Dogs allowed (water) **NOTES:** Parking 12 **ROOMS:** 6 bedrooms 6 en suite from s£35 d£60

TREBURLEY   Map 02 SX37

Pick of the Pubs

The Springer Spaniel 🐾 ♀
PL15 9NS ☎ 01579 370424 📠 01579 370113
Dir: *On the A388 halfway between Launceston & Callington*
This unassuming roadside hostelry, dating from the 18th century and formerly part of a farm, remains a warm, comfortable and friendly pub, but is these days particularly popular for its food. The neat parquet-floored main bar has a high-backed settle, farmhouse-style chairs set by the wood-burning stove, rustic tables and a relaxing atmosphere where conversation flows naturally. There is also a separate beamed dining room for a slightly more formal setting. Blackboards in the bar list the lighter snack options - freshly filled sandwiches and rolls, decent soups and daily specials. Main menu options include imaginatively conceived and attractively presented dishes of pheasant breast on gingerbread sauce, West Country chicken with caramelised onions and balsamic vinegar, and cod fillet on provençale sauce. Children's meals are offered, a vegetarian selection (wild mushroom and cashew nut risotto), and tempting puddings like treacle and lemon tart with clotted cream or custard.
OPEN: 11-3 5.30-11 **BAR MEALS:** Lunch served: all week Dinner served: all week 12-2 6.30-9 Av main course £8.95 **RESTAURANT:** Lunch served: all week Dinner served: all week 12-2 6.30-9 Av 3 course à la carte £18
BREWERY/COMPANY: Free House
PRINCIPAL BEERS: Sharp's Doom Bar, Springer Ale.
FACILITIES: Children welcome Garden: Landscaped with seating, food served outside Dogs allowed (water & biscuits)
NOTES: Parking 30

TREEN   Map 02 SW32

The Logan Rock Inn NEW
Treen, St Levan TR19 6LG ☎ 01736 810495 📠 01736 810177
e-mail: anitageorge@loganrockinn.com
Logan Rock itself weighs some 60 tons and, so it's said, rocked at the slightest touch. The pub is solid though and open fires, ancient beams and a host of memorabilia make it assuredly worth a holiday visit. Home-made dishes include the Seafarer with a fish base and the Minack Melody - a vegetarian concoction with lentils, tomato and nuts. Alternative options run a gamut of steaks, various salads, basket meals and pretty standard fare for youngsters.
OPEN: 10.30-2.30 (Sun 12-3, 7-10.30) 5-11 (Summer All day)
BAR MEALS: Lunch served: all week Dinner served: all week 12-2.30 6.30-9 Av main course £6 **RESTAURANT:** Lunch served: all week Dinner served: all week 12-2.30 6.30-9 Av 3 course fixed price £12.50 **BREWERY/COMPANY:** St Austell Brewery
PRINCIPAL BEERS: St Austell Hicks, Tinners. **FACILITIES:** Children welcome Garden: Patio area with seating Dogs allowed (water)
NOTES: Parking 20

TREGADILLETT   Map 02 SX38

Eliot Arms (Square & Compass) 🐾 ♀
PL15 7EU ☎ 01566 772051
Dir: *Turn of A30 for Tregadillett, Bodmin side of Launceston*
Interesting old coaching inn built from Cornish stone, with a huge collection of clocks, horse brasses, pictures and documents, plus 26 ghosts. Was believed to have been a Masonic lodge for Napoleonic prisoners, and boasts two real fires in winter and lovely hanging baskets in summer. Now known for its food, including steak and Stilton pie, lasagne, grilled tuna, Caribbean chicken, plus a wide range of wines and champagnes by the glass.
OPEN: 11-3.00 6-11 (Sat-Sun all day) **BAR MEALS:** Lunch served: all week Dinner served: all week 12-2 7-9 Av main course £7.50
RESTAURANT: Lunch served: all week Dinner served: all week 12-2 7-9 Av 3 course à la carte £15 **BREWERY/COMPANY:** Free House
PRINCIPAL BEERS: Sharp's Eden Ale & Doom Bar, Scottish Courage Courage Best. **FACILITIES:** Children welcome Dogs allowed
NOTES: Parking 20 **ROOMS:** 2 bedrooms 2 en suite from d£50

TRESCO   Map 02 SW17

Pick of the Pubs

The New Inn ★★ 🏵 🐾 ♀
New Grimsby TR24 0QQ ☎ 01720 422844 📠 01720 423200
e-mail: newinn@tresco.co.uk
Dir: *By New Grimsby Quay*
With its beer gardens and slate-roofed pavilion overlooking New Grimsby harbour, the New Inn is popular with islanders and summer visitors alike. The inn draws much of its character from Tresco's exposed location in the Western Approaches, and the main bar is fitted out with timber jettisoned from a passing cargo ship. Five Scillonian or Cornish ales are served across the bar counter, itself made from a 1960s shipwreck. There's also a wide selection of wines and malt whiskies. Lunchtime brings sandwiches, salads, and locally baked pasties. Evening bookings are advisable in the restaurant, where fresh local fish is prominent on the daily changing menus. Expect potted shrimps, home-made pâté, chargrilled chicken with roasted vegetables, or local sea bass on paella with saffron oil. A home-made tart, or

continued

TRESCO continued

crème brûlée with fruit and nut infusions are typical desserts. Half of the beautifully appointed bedrooms have fine ocean views.

The New Inn

OPEN: 11–11 **BAR MEALS:** Lunch served: all week Dinner served: all week 12–2 6–9 Av main course £9
RESTAURANT: Dinner served: all week 7–9 Av 3 course à la carte £27 Av 3 course fixed price £26.50
BREWERY/COMPANY: Free House
PRINCIPAL BEERS: Skinner's Betty Stogs Bitter, Tresco Tipple, Ales of Scilly Maiden Voyage, St Austell IPA.
FACILITIES: Children welcome Garden: Patio area with sub-tropical plants, **ROOMS:** 14 bedrooms 14 en suite from s£96 d£128

TRURO
Map 02 SW84

Old Ale House ♀
7 Quay St TR1 2HD ☎ 01872 271122 🗎 01872 223257
Dir: A30, Truro City centre
Olde-worlde establishment with a large selection of real ales on display, as well as more than twenty flavours of fruit wine. Lots of attractions, including live music and various quiz and games nights. Food includes 'huge hands of hot bread', oven-baked jacket potatoes, ploughman's lunches and daily specials. Vegetable stir fry, five spice chicken and sizzling beef feature among the sizzling skillets.
OPEN: 11–11 (Sun 12–10.30) Closed: Dec 25 **BAR MEALS:** Lunch served: all week Dinner served: Mon–Fri 12–3 7–9 Av main course £4.50 **BREWERY/COMPANY:** Enterprise Inns
PRINCIPAL BEERS: Skinners Kiddlywink, Courage Directors, Bass, Wychwood The Dog's Bollocks. **FACILITIES:** Children welcome

The Wig & Pen Inn & Olivers Restaurant ♀
Frances St TR1 3DP ☎ 01872 273028 🗎 01872 273028
Dir: City centre nr Law Courts
A listed city centre pub, originally known as the Star. It became the Wig & Pen when the county court moved to Truro. Good quality food is offered, with dishes ranging from cream of mushroom and asparagus soup and pan-fried red mullet on a vegetable linguine to rack of English lamb on red onion confit with mint cream. Desserts may include bread and butter pudding on a butterscotch sauce or pear Condé with seasonal fruits
OPEN: 11–11 (Sun 12–10.30) **BAR MEALS:** 12–2.30 6–9
RESTAURANT: 12–2 7–9 **BREWERY/COMPANY:** St Austell Brewery **PRINCIPAL BEERS:** St Austell Tinners Ale & HSD plus guest ales. **FACILITIES:** Children welcome Garden

VERYAN
Map 02 SW93

The New Inn ⌂ ♀
TR2 5QA ☎ 01872 501362 🗎 01872 501078
e-mail: jgayton@btclick.com
Dir: Off A3078 towards Portloe

Unspoilt village pub based on a pair of 16th-century cottages, with a single bar, open fires and a beamed ceiling. The emphasis is on home cooking, with favourites like whole megrim sole on the bone with parsley butter, or duck braised slowly in red wine with forest mushrooms. There's also a range of large home-made pizzas, with toppings as exotic as pilchard and celery, seafood, and bacon and sausage.
OPEN: 12–3 (Winter 12–2.30) 6.30–11 **BAR MEALS:** Lunch served: all week 12–2 Dinner served: Mon–Sat 7–9 Av main course £8
BREWERY/COMPANY: St Austell Brewery **PRINCIPAL BEERS:** St Austell HSD, Tinners Ale & Tribute. **FACILITIES:** Children's licence Garden: Beer garden, patio, food served outdoors
ROOMS: 3 bedrooms 2 en suite from s£25 d£50

WADEBRIDGE
Map 02 SW97

The Quarryman Inn ⌂
Edmonton PL27 7JA ☎ 01208 816444 🗎 01208 815674
Dir: off A39 opp Royal Cornwall Showground
Friendly 18th-century inn that evolved from a courtyard of quarrymen's cottages. Handy for the Royal Cornwall Showground and the Camel Trail. Among the many features at this unusual pub are a small health club and several bow windows, one of which includes a delightful stained-glass quarryman panel. Expect prime Aberdeen Angus steaks, fresh locally-caught fish, home-made pies, curries and pasta on the menu.

OPEN: 12–11 **BAR MEALS:** 12–2.30 6–9 **RESTAURANT:** 12–2.30 6–9 **BREWERY/COMPANY:** Free House
PRINCIPAL BEERS: Sharps, Skinners, Timothy Taylor Landlord.
FACILITIES: Garden: Dogs allowed (water provided)
NOTES: Parking 100

England

Swan Hotel ◆◆◆◆
9 Molesworth St PL27 7DD ☎ 01208 812526 🖹 01208 812526
Town centre hotel, under new management. Family friendly,
St Austell ales on tap.
OPEN: 11–11 **BAR MEALS:** Lunch served: all week Dinner served:
all week 12–9 6.30–9 Av main course £5 **BREWERY/COMPANY:** St
Austell Brewery **PRINCIPAL BEERS:** St Austell: Hicks, Tinners,
Tribute & guest ale. **FACILITIES:** Children welcome Garden: Food
served outside. Patio garden Dogs allowed (in the garden only)
ROOMS: 6 bedrooms 6 en suite from s£30 d£25

ZENNOR   Map 02 SW43

Pick of the Pubs

The Gurnards Head Hotel 🐾 ♀
Treen, Zennor TR26 3DE ☎ 01736 796928 🖹 01736 795313
e-mail: enquiries@gurnardshead.free-online.co.uk

An imposing colour-washed building that dominates the
coastal landscape above Gurnard's Head, this traditional
Cornish pub with its stone-flagged bar and open fires is
just the place to get stranded on a wind-swept winter's
night! Here you can see Cornwall at its most brutal, but
on warmer days there are some great walks along the
coastal path or the rugged Penwith Moors, strewn with
wild flowers and studded with ancient Celtic remains. The
menu is based on wholesome local produce, so as you'd
expect there's plenty of seafood – Cornish seafood broth,
grilled gurnard, and lobster, brill and sole served
according to season. Other options include chicken in
cider cream sauce, confit of duck and Aberdeen Angus
steak. Gurnards special bread and butter pudding is a
treat, made with free-range eggs, double cream and
sultanas soaked in brandy. Live music and storytelling
evenings are regular events.
OPEN: 12–3 6–11 **BAR MEALS:** Lunch served: all week Dinner
served: all week 12–2.15 6.30–9.15 Av main course £8
RESTAURANT: Lunch served: all week Dinner served: all week
12–2.15 6.30–9.15 Av 3 course à la carte £8
BREWERY/COMPANY: Free House
PRINCIPAL BEERS: Interbrew Flowers Original, Skinners
Cornish Knocker Ale, Fuller's London Pride, Interbrew
Boddingtons. **FACILITIES:** Garden: Food served outside, Sea
views Dogs allowed (water) **NOTES:** Parking 60
ROOMS: 6 bedrooms 6 en suite from d£55

For a list of pubs with AA Accommodation
◆ Awards see pages 649-653 ★

CUMBRIA

AMBLESIDE   Map 11 NY30

Pick of the Pubs

Drunken Duck Inn ◆◆◆◆ ◎ ♀
Barngates LA22 0NG ☎ 015394 36347 🖹 015394 36781
e-mail: info@drunkenduckinn.co.uk
*Dir: A592 from Kendal, after reaching Ambleside, follow signs for
Hawkshead, 2.5m sign for inn on R, 1m up the hill*

In the middle of nothing but magnificent scenery, the 17th-
century Drunken Duck stands high in the hills close to the
famous beauty spot of Tarn Hows. Handy for Ambleside
and Hawkshead, it enjoys some of the best Lakeland
views, with distant Lake Windermere and a backdrop of
craggy fells in its sights. The inn's own brewery –
Barngates Brewery – produces some fine ales, notably
Cracker Ale and the more heady Chester's Strong and
Ugly. The heart of the inn lies in the unspoilt bar, with its
oak settles and log fires. The adjoining restaurant has an
informal atmosphere. At lunchtime the food choice ranges
through interesting sandwiches to guinea fowl with Agen
prune risotto and Cumberland sausage on chilli roast
potatoes. In the evening there are imaginative starters like
lobster and squash ravioli, and twice-baked Pecorino
cheese soufflé, followed by the likes of seared monkfish
on smoked bacon, red pepper and chicory risotto or fillet
of venison marinated in espresso. Stylish bedrooms are
well-appointed and furnished with antiques.
OPEN: 11.30–11 **BAR MEALS:** Lunch served: all week Dinner
served: all week 12–2.30 6–9 Av main course £11
RESTAURANT: Lunch served: all week Dinner served: all week
12–2.30 6–9 Av 3 course à la carte £22
BREWERY/COMPANY: Free House
PRINCIPAL BEERS: Jennings Bitter, Barngates Cracker Ale, Chesters
Strong & Ugly & Tag Lag. **FACILITIES:** Garden: Beer garden, patio,
food served outdoors Dogs allowed (water) **NOTES:** Parking 40
ROOMS: 15 bedrooms 15 en suite from s£48.75 d£65

White Lion Hotel ◆◆◆ ♀
Market Place LA22 9DB ☎ 015394 39901 🖹 015394 39902
Right in the heart of town, this Lakeland inn is superbly placed
for both the tourist and business traveller. Spacious
bedrooms; varied bar menu.
OPEN: 11–11 **BAR MEALS:** Lunch served: all week Dinner served:
all week 12–2.30 6–9 Av main course £7.50
PRINCIPAL BEERS: Bass, Worthington. **FACILITIES:** Children
welcome Garden: beer garden, outdoor eating, BBQ Dogs allowed
NOTES: Parking 9 **ROOMS:** 8 bedrooms 6 en suite from s£25 d£45

England

APPLEBY-IN-WESTMORLAND — Map 11 NY62

The New Inn 🛏️
Brampton Village CA16 6JS ☎ 017683 51231
At the heart of Brampton village with splendid Pennine views, a charming 18th-century inn with oak beams and an original range. One menu serves the bar and dining room with all home-cooked fare, from regulars like steak and ale pie and Cumberland sausage to specials of battered haddock, fisherman's platter and home made mushroom balti.
OPEN: 12–3 7–11 **BAR MEALS:** Lunch served: all week Dinner served: all week 12–2 7–9 Av main course £6.50
RESTAURANT: Lunch served: all week Dinner served: all week 12–2 7–9 **BREWERY/COMPANY:** Free House
PRINCIPAL BEERS: Black Sheep, Charles Wells Bombardier, John Smiths. **FACILITIES:** Children welcome Children's licence Garden: Food served outside Dogs allowed (in the garden only)
NOTES: Parking 16 **ROOMS:** 3 bedrooms No credit cards

Pick of the Pubs

The Royal Oak Inn ★ ★ ♀
Bongate CA16 6UN ☎ 017683 51463 📠 017683 52300
e-mail: royaloakinn@mortalmaninns.fsnet.co.uk
See Pick of the Pubs on page 92

Pick of the Pubs

Tufton Arms Hotel ★ ★ ★ ♀
Market Square CA16 6XA ☎ 017683 51593 📠 017683 52761
e-mail: info@tuftonarmshotel.co.uk

Sturdily-built Victorian coaching inn at the heart of the old county town of Appleby-in-Westmorland – 'the place of the apple tree' – and now an ideal venue for casual visitors, anglers and ramblers. On the doorstep lies an intricate network of paths and tracks running through idyllic countryside. Two of Britain's most popular National Parks, the Lake District and the Yorkshire Dales, are within easy reach. The Tufton Arms is stylishly furnished with a smart conservatory restaurant overlooking a cobbled mews courtyard. Impressive menu uses fresh local produce, including meat, game, fish and seafood. Expect roast rack of Cumbrian fell-bred lamb served with duchesse potatoes and mint jus, loin of Scottish Highland venison and tuna seared supreme on a bed of roasted vegetables or penne pasta with balsamic vinegar dressing. Steamed chocolate pudding, lemon cheesecake and warm pancake feature on the dessert menu. Lighter fare includes baguettes, sandwiches, omelettes and pasta dishes. Smart, well-appointed en suite bedrooms.

OPEN: 11–3 6–11 Closed: 26 Dec **BAR MEALS:** Lunch served: all week Dinner served: all week 12–2 7–9 Av main course £7.50
RESTAURANT: Lunch served: all week Dinner served: all week 12–2 7–9 Av 3 course à la carte £18 Av 3 course fixed price £22
BREWERY/COMPANY: Free House
PRINCIPAL BEERS: Tufton Arms Ale, Worthington Bitter.
FACILITIES: Children welcome Dogs allowed **NOTES:** Parking 15 **ROOMS:** 21 bedrooms 21 en suite

ARMATHWAITE — Map 11 NY54

The Dukes Head Hotel ♀
Front St CA4 9PB ☎ 016974 72226
e-mail: HH@hlynch.freeserve.co.uk
Dir: A6, turn at Armathwaite turning
A pub since the building of the Settle to Carlisle railway, and named after Queen Victoria's dissolute son, the Duke of Clarence. For nearly 15 years, the Lynch family have welcomed walkers, climbers, anglers, and all who appreciate comfort and courtesy. A selection of specials may include potted country ham with Cumberland sauce, roast suckling pig with mashed celeriac, carrots and herb gravy, and baked sea bream in a paper parcel. Cycle hire and fishing are available.
OPEN: 12–3 5.30–11 Closed: 25th dec **BAR MEALS:** Lunch served: all week Dinner served: all week 12–2 6.15–9 Av main course £8.45
RESTAURANT: Lunch served: all week Dinner served: all week 12–2 6.15–9 Av 3 course à la carte £14
BREWERY/COMPANY: Pubmaster **PRINCIPAL BEERS:** Jennings Cumberland Ale, Carlsberg-Tetley Tetley's Bitter, Scottish Courage Courage Directors. **FACILITIES:** Children welcome Garden: Food served outdoors Dogs allowed (back bar only, water)
NOTES: Parking 30 **ROOMS:** 5 bedrooms 3 en suite from s£28.50 d£48.50

ASKHAM — Map 11 NY52

The Queen's Head ♦ ♦ ♦ 🛏️
Lower Green CA10 2PF ☎ 01931 712225 📠 01931 712811
e-mail: d.nicholls@btconnect.com
Dir: From M6 N for 7 miles from Motorway
Built in 1682, this welcoming village inn situated in the heart of the Lake District National Park, has neat lounges, exposed beams, brass and copper memorabilia, and open fires. Facilities include a games room with pool and darts, and three bedrooms named Faith, Hope and Charity. Along with a range of curries, salads, cold and hot baguettes and burgers, the Queen's Head offers Cumberland sausage, steak and onion pie, chicken fajita, and three cheese broccoli bake.
OPEN: 12–3 5.30–11 (open all day wknd & summer)
BAR MEALS: Lunch served: all week Dinner served: all week 12–2 6–9 Av main course £6.95 **RESTAURANT:** 12–2 6–9
BREWERY/COMPANY: Pubmaster
PRINCIPAL BEERS: Carlsberg-Tetley John Smiths & Tetleys Bitter, Marston's Pedigree, Interbrew Flowers IPA. **FACILITIES:** Children welcome Garden: Food served outdoors Dogs allowed (water, food, kennel) **NOTES:** Parking 30 **ROOMS:** 4 bedrooms 4 en suite from s£55 d£27.50

> **Most of the pubs in this guide book pride themselves on the quality of their food. This may take a little time to prepare.**

continued

PUB WALK

Loweswater
Kirkstile Inn

A very enjoyable walk that circumnavigates Loweswater, one of the Lake District's smallest lakes situated in the north-west corner of this spectacular region. The lake is in the care of the National Trust.

From the Kirkstile Inn, and with the church opposite, turn left up the short lane. At the top of the hill look back for a stunning view of Crummock Water. Bear left and continue until you reach the bridleway sign for Loweswater. Turn left here and proceed beyond the car park on the right, go through a gate and then cross the bridge. Head across the fields, pass the National Trust's Watergate Farm and follow the path to the lakeshore. Pass through a gate and enter Holme Wood, a natural English woodland. Follow the path and just before you reach a stone bothy, take the left-hand fork to a gate. Pass through a series of gates and continue on the path to make a gentle ascent before passing a farm on the left. Head downhill for a short distance before negotiating the stile on the right. Cross two fields to reach the road. Turn right and follow it for about a quarter of a mile, then take the lakeshore path. Rejoin the road after some distance and follow it until you reach the turning for the Kirkstile Inn.

KIRKSTILE INN,
LOWESWATER Cockermouth
CA13 0RU
Tel: 01900 85219
Directions: between Loweswater and Crummockwater.
In a beautiful setting, a 16th-century Lakeland inn with low beams, open fires and warm hospitality. Good local ales and substantial dishes for hungry walkers or climbers. Good simple accommodation.
Open: 11–11
Bar Meals: 12–2 6–9
Children welcome and dogs allowed. Garden and parking available.

Distance: 4 miles (6.4km)
Map: OS Outdoor Leisure 4
Terrain: Farmland and woodland
Paths: Field and woodland paths, lanes and bridleways
Gradient: Fairly flat

Walk submitted and checked by Roger and Helen Humphreys of the Kirkstile Inn

OPEN: 11-11 (Sun 12-10.30)
BAR MEALS: L served all week.
D served all week 12-2.30 6-9
Av main course £9
RESTAURANT: L served all week.
D served all week 12-2.30 6-9
BREWERY/COMPANY:
FREE HOUSE
PRINCIPAL BEERS: Black Sheep
ROOMS: 9 bedrooms 7 en suite
from s£39 d£39

The Royal Oak Inn

★★ ♀
Bongate, Appleby-in-Westmorland
CA16 6UN
☎ 017683 51463   ▤ 017683 52300
e-mail:
royaloakinn@mortalmaninns.fsnet.co.uk
Dir: M6 J38 take A66 east. Village on
B6542 on R.

The Royal Oak has a long and venerable history with parts of the building dating back to 1100 and many years as a coaching inn. Today, fully modernised and offering good food and ale it is popular with locals and tourists alike. The pub is especially popular as a touring base for both the Yorkshire Dales and the Lake District as it is situated conveniently between the two.

Its well-maintained character interior comprises a classic tap-room with blackened beams, oak panelling and an open fire, a comfortable beamed lounge and two dining rooms. Ingredients for the wholesome food are sourced locally wherever possible and the menus change on a daily or monthly basis. Dishes include home-made soups and desserts, Sunday lunches and vegetarian options. Specials are served in the bar and dining rooms. Items on the monthly menus are likely to include creamed smoked haddock pancake and Black Isle mussels to start, followed by Mrs Ewbank's secret-recipe sausages, baked cod with pancetta and garlic oil, lentil, red pepper and mushroom lasagne and Bongate beef and ale pie. There are also various steaks from Cumbrian fell-bred animals and their own home-smoked produce. The choice of real ales is good with a number of ales from local brewers. These are augmented by a choice from some 50 malt whiskies. There are nine en suite bedrooms to make the most of the excellent location.

BARBON   Map 08 SD68

The Barbon Inn
LA6 2LJ ☎ 015242 76233 📠 015242 76233
Dir: 3.5m N of Kirkby Lonsdale on A683
A 17th-century coaching inn with oak beams and open fires, situated in a quiet village between the lakes and dales. Popular bar meals are smoked salmon baguette and Morecambe Bay shrimps; more substantial dishes include Lakeland lamb casserole, roast breast of duck, and halibut steak.
OPEN: 12-3 6.30-11 **BAR MEALS:** Lunch served: all week Dinner served: all week 12-2 6.30-9 Av main course £6.25
RESTAURANT: Lunch served: Sun Dinner served: all week 12.30-2 7.30-9 Av 3 course à la carte £16.50 **BREWERY/COMPANY:** Free House **PRINCIPAL BEERS:** Theakston. **FACILITIES:** Children welcome Garden: beer garden, outdoor eating Dogs allowed **NOTES:** Parking 6 **ROOMS:** 10 bedrooms 10 en suite from s£40 d£65

BASSENTHWAITE   Map 11 NY23

The Pheasant ♀
CA13 9YE ☎ 017687 76234 📠 017687 76002
e-mail: Pheasant@easynet.co.uk
Dir: A66 to Cockermouth, 8m N of Keswick on L
Former coaching inn, close to Bassenthwaite Lake, set in its own attractive gardens and woodland. The interior is beautifully decorated, with period furnishings set against polished parquet flooring, fresh floral arrangements and blazing log fires. The mellow bar is richly inviting with its panelled walls and oak settles. There is a light lunch menu available in the lounges or bar, and a lunch and dinner menu in the beamed dining room. Light lunches range from open sandwiches to hot dishes like fillet of smoked haddock on a bed of spinach with a light cheese sauce, topped with a poached egg, or 'our own' shepherd's pie served with braised red cabbage and mushy peas. Fine dining options include seared fillet of fell-bred lamb marinated in garlic, rosemary and thyme, and pomegranate-glazed Gressingham duck breast on a bed of roasted black figs and red onions in port jus.

OPEN: 11.30-2.30 5.30-10.30 Closed: Dec 25 **BAR MEALS:** Lunch served: all week 12-2 Av main course £7.50 **RESTAURANT:** Lunch served: all week Dinner served: all week 12.30-2 7-9 Av 3 course à la carte £29.75 **BREWERY/COMPANY:** Free House **PRINCIPAL BEERS:** Theakston Best, Interbrew Bass, Jennings Cumberland Ale. **FACILITIES:** Garden: Woodland garden, food served outside Dogs allowed (kennels) **NOTES:** Parking 50 **ROOMS:** 16 bedrooms 16 en suite from s£60 d£100

BEETHAM   Map 08 SD47

Pick of the Pubs

The Wheatsheaf Hotel 🏠♀
LA7 7AL ☎ 015395 62123 📠 015395 64840
See Pick of the Pubs on page 95

BLENCOGO   Map 11 NY14

The New Inn
CA7 0BZ ☎ 016973 61091 📠 016973 61091
Dir: From Carlisle, take A596 towards Wigton, then B5302 towards Silloth. After 4M Blencogo signed on L
A late Victorian sandstone pub in a farming hamlet with superb views of the north Cumbrian fells and Solway Plain. Popular dinner menu ranges from roast duckling, grilled Cumberland sausage, rainbow trout with black butter, topside of Cumbrian beef, to scampi and mixed grills.
OPEN: (Sun only 12-3) 7-11 (Wed-Sat 7-11, Sun 6.30-10.30)
BAR MEALS: Lunch served: Sun 12-2 Dinner served: Wed-Sun 7-9 Av main course £8 **RESTAURANT:** Lunch served: Sun Dinner served: Wed-Sun 7-9 **BREWERY/COMPANY:** Free House **PRINCIPAL BEERS:** Yates, Carlisle State Bitter, Hesketh New Market. **FACILITIES:** Children welcome Garden: Beer Garden, patio **NOTES:** Parking 50

BOOT   Map 11 NY10

The Burnmoor Inn ♀
CA19 1TG ☎ 019467 23224 📠 019467 23337
e-mail: stay@burnmoor.co.uk

A traditional 16th-century inn, which, not surprisingly given its position at the foot of Scafell Pike, attracts many hill walkers. It is also handy for the Ravenglass and Eskdale Steam Railway. A fire burns in the beamed bar in cooler weather and there is a sheltered front lawn for summer days. As far as possible the food is home made, with options like gravad lax, game stew, Boot pie, stuffed cabbage (vegetarian) and 8oz rump steak.
OPEN: 11-11 **BAR MEALS:** Lunch served: all week Dinner served: all week 11-5 6-9 Av main course £6 **RESTAURANT:** Dinner served: all week 6-9 Av 3 course à la carte £17.50
BREWERY/COMPANY: Free House **PRINCIPAL BEERS:** Jennings Cumberland, Bitter, Black Sheep Best, Barngates Cracker Ale.
FACILITIES: Children welcome Children's licence Garden: Patio, Food served outside Dogs allowed (dog blankets, water) **NOTES:** Parking 50 **ROOMS:** 9 bedrooms 9 en suite from s£28 d£56

England

BOUTH   Map 08 SD38

The White Hart Inn
LA12 8JB ☎ 01229 861229 ▯ 01229 861229
17th-century former coaching inn located in a quiet village at
the heart of South Lakeland and surrounded by woods, fields
and fells. Look out for plenty of bric-à-brac, including farm
tools and long-stemmed clay pipes. Six cask real ales are
available and the menu offers fresh food made to order. A
typical menu might include Cumberland sausage, rare breed
sirloin steaks, lamb Henry and chicken Balti.
OPEN: 12–2 6–11 **BAR MEALS:** 12–2 6–8.45
RESTAURANT: 12–2 6–8.45 **BREWERY/COMPANY:** Free House
PRINCIPAL BEERS: Black Sheep Best, Jennings Cumberland Ale,
Barnsley, Interbrew Boddingtons. **FACILITIES:** Children welcome
Garden: **NOTES:** Parking 30 **ROOMS:** 4 bedrooms 2 en suite No
credit cards

BRAITHWAITE   Map 11 NY22

Coledale Inn
CA12 5TN ☎ 017687 78272
Dir: From M6 J50 take A66 towards Cockermouth for 18 miles. Turn to
Braithwaite then on towards Whinlatter Pass, follow sign on L, over bridge
leading to hotel
Peacefully set above Braithwaite village, this traditional pub
with its terrace and garden is very popular with walkers. Built
as a woollen mill about 1824, it was converted for pencil
making before becoming an inn. Today it is full of attractive
Victorian prints, furnishings and antiques, with a fine cellar
that includes cask conditioned local ales. Expect grills, salads
and baked potatoes, supported by roast lamb, beef in beer,
haddock, salmon and trout.
OPEN: 11–11 **BAR MEALS:** Lunch served: all week Dinner served:
all week 12–2 6–9 Av main course £6.50 **RESTAURANT:** 12–2 6–9
BREWERY/COMPANY: Free House **PRINCIPAL BEERS:** Yates,
Theakstons Best, Jennings Best. **FACILITIES:** Children welcome
Garden: Food served outside Dogs allowed (water)
NOTES: Parking 20 **ROOMS:** 12 bedrooms 12 en suite

BRAMPTON   Map 11 NY56

Abbey Bridge Inn
Lanercost CA8 2HG ☎ 016977 2224 ▯ 016977 42184
e-mail: tim@abbeybridge.co.uk
The pub is located by the bridge over the River Irthing, 400
metres from Lanercost Priory (1166), a mile from Hadrian's
Wall and half a mile from Naworth Castle. The surrounding
area is rich in wildlife and crisscrossed by footpaths - great for
walkers. The pub has three bar areas, one specifically for
walkers where dogs are welcome, a main bar area and a
restaurant/lounge. The menu offers local and British favourites
using locally supplied produce.
OPEN: 11–11 (Winter 11–2.30, 6–11) **BAR MEALS:** Lunch served:
all week Dinner served: all week 12–2.30 6.30–9.30
PRINCIPAL BEERS: Black Sheep Best. **FACILITIES:** Children
welcome Garden Dogs allowed **NOTES:** Parking 15
ROOMS: 5 bedrooms 5 en suite from s£25 d£45

Blacksmiths Arms ♦♦♦ 🛏 🍷
Talkin Village CA8 1LE ☎ 016977 3452 ▯ 016977 3396
e-mail: blacksmithsarmstalkin@yahoo.co.uk
Dir: from M6 take A69 E, after 7m straightover rdbt, follow signs to Talkin
Tarn then Talkin Village
Originally the local smithy, dating from around 1700, this
attractive village inn is close to Talkin Tarn Country Park and
handy for visiting Hadrian's Wall, the Borders and the Lake

District. The well-balanced menu and blackboard specials offer a
good variety of dishes, including lunchtime snacks and traditional
Sunday roasts. Options include Blacksmith's chicken (breast
stuffed with pork and served with mushroom sauce), local
Cumberland sausage, and haddock in home-made beer batter.

OPEN: 12–3 6–11 (Sun 12–3, 6–10.30) **BAR MEALS:** Lunch served:
all week Dinner served: all week 12–2 6.30–9 Av main course £7.50
RESTAURANT: Lunch served: all week Dinner served: all week 12–2
6.30–9 Av 3 course à la carte £12 **BREWERY/COMPANY:** Free
House **PRINCIPAL BEERS:** Black Sheep Best, Jennings Cumberland
Ale, Carlsberg-Tetley Tetley Bitter, Scottish Courage John Smith's.
FACILITIES: Children welcome Children's licence Garden: Food
served outside **NOTES:** Parking 20 **ROOMS:** 5 bedrooms 5 en
suite from s£35 d£50

BROUGHTON IN FURNESS   Map 08 SD28

Blacksmiths Arms
Broughton Mills LA20 6AX ☎ 01229 716824 ▯ 01229 716824
e-mail: blacksmithsarm@aol.com
Dir: A593 from Ambleside to Coniston then on to B-in-F, minor rd 2.5m
from B-in-F

Originally a farmhouse, dating from before 1688, the inn is set
in a secluded Lakeland valley. The interior remains intact, with
the original farmhouse range, worn slate floors and low
beams. Gaslights in the dining room and bar still work when
the electricity fails. Traditional local dishes, such as
Westmoreland hotpot, are offered alongside the more exotic
such as Cajun salmon - all washed down with ales from
nearby micro-breweries.
OPEN: 12–11 (Sun 12–10.30) (Winter Mon 5–11, Tue–Fri 12–2.30/5–11)
Closed: Dec 25 **BAR MEALS:** Lunch served: Tue–Sun 12–2 Dinner
served: Mon–Sun 12–2 Dinner served: Mon–Sun 6–9 Av 3 course à la
carte £11 **BREWERY/COMPANY:** Free House
PRINCIPAL BEERS: Jennings Cumberland Ale, Dent Aviator,
Barngates Tag Lag. **FACILITIES:** Children welcome Garden: Food
served outdoors Dogs allowed (water) **NOTES:** Parking 30

continued

PICK OF THE PUBS
BEETHAM – CUMBRIA

OPEN: 11–3 6–11 (Sun 12–3, 7–10.30)
BAR MEALS: L served all week. D served all week. 12–2 6–9 Av main course £9
RESTAURANT: L served all week. D served all week. 12–2 6–9 Av cost 3 courses £12
BREWERY/COMPANY: FREE HOUSE
PRINCIPLE BEERS: Jennings Cumberland Ale & Bitter
FACILITIES: Children welcome, dogs allowed
NOTES: Parking 40
ROOMS: 4 en suite Double room from £60 Single room from £45

The Wheatsheaf at Beetham

Civilised dining pub with enthusiastic owners who have brought it up to speed, in a historic village that is handy for visiting the Lake District. This 16th-century coaching inn can be found beside the 12th-century church in the beautiful village of Beetham, known locally as the gateway to the Lakes.

Beetham Cumbria A7 7AL
☎ 015395 62123 📄 015395 64840
Dir: On A6 5m N of J35.

With its accessibility to the motorway it makes an ideal base from which to tour much of Cumbria. The owners have injected new life into the inn by an ambitious refurbishment programme that has left a smart, well-furnished dining room where candle-light burns in the evenings, a welcoming beamed lounge, and a traditional bar with a convivial atmosphere. Despite its upmarket designation, this is still a place where you can just pop in for a pint of Jennings - the bar dispenses a noteworthy range of this real ale. Throughout this family owned and run inn you will find homely touches like fresh flowers and table decorations, as well as local and national newspapers and magazines for residents to peruse. This same attention to detail, along with a commitment to purchasing fresh local produce, marks out the cooking at this hospitable inn. A talented young chef has placed his stamp on the menus that encompass the seafood from Morecambe Bay - try the fresh shrimps, or the ragout of mussels and prawns. For a hearty meat dish there might be rib eye steak with Stilton and pancetta crisps, or perhaps local game and redcurrant pie. New World wines head a strong wine list, and traditional Cumbrian breakfasts are worth rising early for.

BUTTERMERE
Map 11 NY11

Bridge Hotel ★ ★
CA13 9UZ ☎ 017687 70252 ▤ 017687 70215
e-mail: enquiries@bridge-hotel.com
Dir: Take B5289 from Keswick
Spend a weekend at this 18th-century former coaching inn
and enjoy its stunning setting, in an area of outstanding
natural beauty located between Buttermere and Crummock
Water. Miles of spectacular Lakeland walks await discovery,
and guests can return to afternoon tea, excellent ales in the
bar, hearty food and peaceful accommodation. Robust main
courses include Cumberland hotpot, home-made steak and
kidney pie, butterbean casserole and deep-fried haddock in
crisp beer batter.
OPEN: 10.30–11 (open all day in summer) **BAR MEALS:** Lunch
served: all week Dinner served: all week 12–2.30 6–9.30 Av main
course £6.50 **RESTAURANT:** Dinner served: all week 7–8.30 Av 5
course fixed price £21 **BREWERY/COMPANY:** Free House
PRINCIPAL BEERS: Theakston's Old Peculier, Black Sheep Best,
Interbrew Flowers IPA. **FACILITIES:** Children welcome Garden:
Food Served Outside Dogs allowed **NOTES:** Parking 60
ROOMS: 21 bedrooms 21 en suite from s£65 d£105

CARTMEL
Map 08 SD37

Pick of the Pubs

The Cavendish
LA11 6QA ☎ 015395 36240 ▤ 015395 36243
e-mail: thecavendish@compuserve.com
*Dir: M6 J36 take A590 follow signs for Barrow in Furness, Cartmel is
signposted. In village take 1st R.*
Cartmel's oldest hostelry, dating from the 15th century,
with oak beams and log fires creating a cosy atmosphere.
Bar food ranges from soup and sandwiches to lamb
Henry or bangers and mash. Typical restaurant dishes
might be stuffed fillet steak, sea bass and local ostrich.
Top quality real ales and a good selection of wines by
glass or bottle.
OPEN: 11.30–11 **BAR MEALS:** Lunch served: all week Dinner
served: all week 12–2.15 6–9.15 Av main course £6.95
RESTAURANT: Lunch served: all week Dinner served: all week
12–2.15 6–9.15 Av 3 course à la carte £20
BREWERY/COMPANY: Free House
PRINCIPAL BEERS: Marston's Pedigree, Theakston's.
FACILITIES: Children welcome **NOTES:** Parking 25
ROOMS: 10 bedrooms 10 en suite from s£30 d£50

COCKERMOUTH
Map 10 NY13

The Trout Hotel ★ ★ ★
Crown St CA13 0EJ ☎ 01900 823591 ▤ 01900 827514
e-mail: enquiries@trouthotel.co.uk
Dating from about 1670 and originally built as a private house,
the Trout became a hotel in 1934. The hand-carved oak
staircase and marble fireplace are among the many striking
features, and the bedrooms are comfortable and well
equipped. Choose between the bar menu - sandwiches,
baked potatoes, steaks - the fixed price dinner menu or the
carte. Options might include rosette of lamb on a rösti,
steamed halibut with spinach and cheese velouté, and stuffed
oven-baked butternut squash.
OPEN: 11–3 5.30–11 **BAR MEALS:** Lunch served: all week 12–2
Dinner served: Mon–Sat 6.30–8.30 **RESTAURANT:** Lunch served: all

week 12–2 Dinner served: all week 7–9.30 Av 3 course à la carte
£32.40 **BREWERY/COMPANY:** Free House
PRINCIPAL BEERS: Jennings Cumberland Ale, Theakston Bitter,
John Smiths, Marston's Pedigree. **FACILITIES:** Children welcome
Garden: Riverside garden, food served outside **NOTES:** Parking 70
ROOMS: 29 bedrooms 29 en suite

CONISTON
Map 11 SD39

Black Bull Inn & Hotel
1 Yewdale Rd LA21 8DU
☎ 015394 41335 ▤ 015394 41168
e-mail: i.s.bradley@btinternet.com
Turner, Coleridge and Donald Campbell were all visitors to
this 400-year-old coaching inn, the latter while attempting to
break the water speed record on Lake Coniston. The inn has a
lovely village setting, by the beck and in the shadow of the
Old Man. Beers are brewed on the premises, and food is
served in both the bar and restaurant. Esthwaite trout, local
steaks, lamb and traditional roasts are among the dishes
offered.
OPEN: 11–11 (Sun 12–10.30) Closed: Dec 25 **BAR MEALS:** Lunch
served: all week Dinner served: all week 12–9.30 Av main course £7
RESTAURANT: Lunch served: By appointment Dinner served: all
week 6–9 Av 3 course à la carte £18 **BREWERY/COMPANY:** Free
House **PRINCIPAL BEERS:** Coniston Blue Bird, Old Man Ale, &
Opium, Coniston Blacksmith & XB. **FACILITIES:** Children welcome
Garden: Stream Dogs allowed (walker, dog beds and meals)
NOTES: Parking 12 **ROOMS:** 16 bedrooms 16 en suite from s£35
d£60

CROOK
Map 08 SD49

The Sun Inn
LA8 8LA ☎ 01539 821351 ▤ 01539 821351
Dir: off the B5284
Built in 1711, a warmly welcoming pub steeped in tradition,
with winter fires and a summer terrace overlooking rolling
countryside. Pride is taken in providing the best local
ingredients in imaginative guises. Look on the regular menu
for mushrooms with Dijon mustard sauce and rack of lamb
with minted gravy. Specials from a separate board might well
include venison steak in red wine, pheasant breast with wild
berries and halibut steak with shrimp butter.
OPEN: 12–3 6–11 **BAR MEALS:** Lunch served: all week Dinner
served: all week 12–3 6–9 **RESTAURANT:** Lunch served: all week
Dinner served: all week 12–3 6–9 **BREWERY/COMPANY:** Free
House **PRINCIPAL BEERS:** Theakston, Scottish Courage John
Smith's, Courage Directors, Wells Bombardier. **FACILITIES:** Children
welcome Garden: Food served outside Dogs allowed
NOTES: Parking 40

CROSTHWAITE
Map 08 SD49

Pick of the Pubs

The Punch Bowl Inn
LA8 8HR ☎ 015395 68237 ▤ 015395 68875
e-mail: enquiries@punchbowl.fsnet.co.uk
*Dir: From M6 J36 take A590 towards Barrow, then A5074 & follow
signs for Crosthwaite. Pub next to church on L*
A 17th-century Lakeland pub with a warm and friendly
atmosphere, and an excellent reputation for good food.
Walkers and casual visitors are welcomed to the bar with
its original beams, low ceilings and open fires, where
Theakston and Black Sheep ales are on tap and

continued

continued

imaginative sandwiches and light bites are served. But this is also a serious dining destination, and ex-Gavroche chef Steven Doherty demonstrates his exciting cooking skills on the lunch menu and evening carte. From the latter you can choose starters like smooth chicken liver parfait, served with the local speciality of spiced damsons, followed by roast salmon on crushed potatoes, and perhaps Charlie Trotter's chocolate and ginger tart. In fine weather, food from the two lunch menus is also served on a terrace overlooking the Lyth Valley, featuring various seafood options, local meats, and perhaps crispy duck with slow-braised pork belly.

OPEN: 11–11 (Sun 12–10.30) Closed: 1wk Nov, 1wk Dec, 1wk Jan 1wk summer **BAR MEALS:** Lunch served: Mon-Sun Dinner served: Mon-Sun 12–2 6–9 Av main course £12
RESTAURANT: Lunch served: Tues-Sun Dinner served: Tues-Sat 12–2 6–9 Av 3 course à la carte £23
BREWERY/COMPANY: Free House
PRINCIPAL BEERS: Black Sheep Best, Barngates Cracker Ale, Greene King Old Speckled Hen. **FACILITIES:** Children welcome Garden: Patio, food served outside **NOTES:** Parking 60
ROOMS: 3 bedrooms 3 en suite from s£37.50 d£55

DENT   Map 08 SD78

Sun Inn
Main St LA10 5QL ☎ 015396 25208
e-mail: martin@dentbrewery.co.uk
Dir: From M6 through Sedburgh, Dent signed, 4.5m
Serving as a magnet for dale walkers and real ale buffs, the pub stands in picturesque Dentdale, surrounded by quaint whitewashed cottages and narrow cobbled streets. Its cosy bars, with original coin-studded beams, open coal fire and local photographs are entirely in keeping with the setting. Just up the road is the Dent Brewery whose award-winning real ales include T'owd Tup. No nonsense bar food is simple and filling, with local Cumberland sausages and home-made pies of the day dished up in trenchermen's portions.
OPEN: 11–2.30 6.30–11 Closed: Dec 25 **BAR MEALS:** Lunch served: all week Dinner served: all week 12–2 6.30–8.30
BREWERY/COMPANY: Free House **PRINCIPAL BEERS:** Dent Bitter, T'Owd Tup, Aviator, Kamikaze. **FACILITIES:** Children welcome Garden: Food served outisde Dogs allowed (water)
NOTES: Parking 15 **ROOMS:** 4 bedrooms from s£20 d£35

DOCKRAY   Map 11 NY32

The Royal Hotel
CA11 0JY ☎ 017684 82356 ▤ 017684 82033
Dir: A66 towards Keswick for 8m, turn L onto A5091 signposted Dockray
Wordsworth and Mary Queen of Scots both visited this 16th-century inn, a mile from the shores of Ullswater. It's a family-run establishment; cosy with a flagstone floor and blazing log fire. A good selection of real ales, wines and malt whiskies is served in the bar, and the restaurant offers all home-made dishes. Whitby scampi and fresh haddock in batter are available every day, and other specialities are roast Herdwick mutton and royal game pie.
OPEN: 11–11 **BAR MEALS:** Lunch served: all week Dinner served: all week 12–2.30 6–9 Av main course £7.50 **RESTAURANT:** Lunch served: all week Dinner served: all week 12–2.30 6–9 Av 3 course à la carte £14 **BREWERY/COMPANY:** Free House
PRINCIPAL BEERS: Castle Eden Ale, Black Sheep Best, Jennings Cumberland Ale, Greene King Old Speckled Hen.
FACILITIES: Children welcome Children's licence Garden: Beer

garden, Food served outside, Stream Dogs allowed (by arrangement)
NOTES: Parking 30 **ROOMS:** 10 bedrooms 10 en suite from s£37 d£64

ELTERWATER   Map 11 NY30

Pick of the Pubs

The Britannia Inn ★ ♀
LA22 9HP ☎ 015394 37210 ▤ 015394 37311
e-mail: info@britinn.co.uk
Dir: A593 from Ambleside, then B5343 to Elterwater
Overlooking the village green in a famous scenic valley, the Britannia captures the essence of a traditional family-run Lakeland inn. Originally a farmhouse and the premises of a local cobbler, the Britannia really comes to life in summer when colourful hanging baskets dazzle the eye and the garden fills up with customers and Morris dancers. Further away is the opportunity for energetic hikes and leisurely strolls amid Lakeland's glorious scenery. Lunches, afternoon snacks and dinner are served daily, with an extensive range of food and daily specials, and the emphasis is very much on freshly prepared home-made food. Steak and mushroom pie and bacon-wrapped chicken stuffed with cream cheese and asparagus in citrus sauce are typical examples of the interesting dishes. With its thirteen attractively furnished bedrooms, the Britannia is an ideal base for a relaxing holiday or a weekend break.
OPEN: 11–11 (Sun 12–10.30) Closed: 25–26 Dec
BAR MEALS: Lunch served: all week Dinner served: all week 12–2 6.30–9.30 Av main course £8.95 **RESTAURANT:** Lunch served: all week Dinner served: all week 12–2 6.30–9.30
BREWERY/COMPANY: Free House
PRINCIPAL BEERS: Jennings Bitter, Coniston Bluebird, Dent Aviator. **FACILITIES:** Children's licence Dogs allowed (water)
NOTES: Parking 10 **ROOMS:** 9 bedrooms 8 en suite from d£32

Jugs
Toby jugs grin cheerfully from their vantage points in many a pub interior. They were first made in the Staffordshire Potteries in the 18th century and the standard figure wears a black tricorn hat, holds a foaming jug of beer and sits in a chair whose sides are covered by the skirts of his ample topcoat. This is the Ordinary Toby, but connoisseurs distinguish between the Long Face, the Sharp Face and the Roman Nose variations. Numerous variants include the Sailor, the Squire, the Tipsy Man and the Drunken Parson. Other jugs represent famous figures of history or literature, from Nelson and Mr Gladstone to Falstaff and John Bull, while modern examples include Winston Churchill and Clark Gable. There are a few female Tobies, but essentially the jugs depict the jovial male toper, benevolent and beery.

continued

ESKDALE GREEN
Map 10 NY10

Pick of the Pubs

Bower House Inn ★ ★ 🛏
CA19 1TD ☎ 019467 23244 🖹 019467 23308
e-mail: info@bowerhouseinn.freeserve.co.uk
Dir: 4m off A595 0.5m W of Eskdale Green
Fine 17th-century stone-built former farmhouse with welcoming log fire and sheltered, well established gardens overlooking Muncaster Fell. Oak beamed bar and alcoves enhance the character of the place and a charming candlelit restaurant plays host to a varied selection of hearty, imaginative dishes. Cumberland wild duck, local pheasant in whisky, salmon with red pesto crust and spinach and mushroom roulade may feature on the specials board, while the dinner menu may offer goats' cheese with hazelnut dressing and snails in garlic butter, followed by shoulder of lamb with mint sauce, roast duck with red wine and plum sauce, halibut with spring onion and Dijon mustard and ostrich fillet with Stilton sauce. Twenty four en suite rooms, including three family rooms, make the Bower House an ideal holiday retreat throughout the year.
OPEN: 11–11 **BAR MEALS:** Lunch served: all week Dinner served: all week 12–2 6.30–9.30 Av main course £8.50
RESTAURANT: Lunch served: Sun Dinner served: all week 12–2 7–8.30 Av 3 course à la carte £22.50
BREWERY/COMPANY: Free House
PRINCIPAL BEERS: Theakston Bitter, Jennings Bitter, Greene King Old Speckled Hen, Dent Ales. **FACILITIES:** Children welcome Garden: Food served outside Dogs allowed (in the garden only) **NOTES:** Parking 50 **ROOMS:** 25 bedrooms 25 en suite from s£35 d£60

King George IV Inn
CA19 1TS ☎ 019467 23262 🖹 019467 23334
e-mail: kinggeorgeiv@eskdale83.fsnet.co.uk
Dir: A590 to Greenodd, A5092 to Broughton-in-Furness then over Ulpha Fell towards Eskdale
Ancient Lakeland inn located at the heart of one of the region's finest hidden valleys. Close by are picturesque Dalegarth Falls. Inside is plenty of old world charm, with open fires, oak beams, low ceilings and flagged floors. Various antiques, gifts, furniture and furnishings to browse among before eating. Popular real ales and more than 100 malt whiskies. Fresh, home-cooked food includes traditional Cumbrian breakfast, bar snacks and a daily-changing specials board. All diets catered for.
OPEN: 11–3 (Sun 12–3) 6–11 Closed: 25 Dec **BAR MEALS:** Lunch served: all week Dinner served: all week 12–2 6–9 Av main course £6.50 **RESTAURANT:** Lunch served: all week Dinner served: all week 12–2 6–9 Av 3 course à la carte £15
BREWERY/COMPANY: Free House
PRINCIPAL BEERS: Theakston Best, Old Peculier, XB, Jennings Cumberland Ale. **FACILITIES:** Children welcome Garden: Food served outside Dogs allowed **NOTES:** Parking 12
ROOMS: 4 bedrooms 4 en suite from s£28 d£50

> **Restaurant and Bar Meal times indicate
> the times when food is available.
> Last orders may be approximately
> 30 minutes before the times stated.**

GARRIGILL
Map 11 NY74

The George & Dragon
CA9 3DS ☎ 01434 381293 🖹 01434 382839
Once serving the local zinc and lead mining communities, this 17th-century coaching inn is now popular with walkers, who enjoy log fires that stave off that brisk North Pennine weather.
OPEN: 12–3 6.30–11 **BAR MEALS:** Lunch served: all week Dinner served: all week 12–2 7–9 Av main course £6.50
RESTAURANT: Lunch served: all week Dinner served: all week 12–2 7–9 Av 3 course à la carte £12.50 **BREWERY/COMPANY:** Free House **PRINCIPAL BEERS:** Castle Eden, Flowers IPA, Guest beers.
FACILITIES: Children welcome Dogs allowed
ROOMS: 4 bedrooms 1 en suite from s£18 d£40 No credit cards

GRANGE-OVER-SANDS
Map 08 SD47

Hare & Hounds Country Inn
Bowland Bridge LA11 6NN ☎ 015395 68333 🖹 015395 68993
Dir: M6 onto A591, L after 3m onto A590, R after 3m onto A5074, after 4m sharp L & next L after 1m
Wonderfully located in Bowland Bridge in the beautiful Winster Valley, with stunning views over Cartmel Fell, this 17th-century coaching inn is 10 minutes from Lake Windermere. Other Lake District attractions are easily reached. Now under new ownership, its oak beams, cosy niches and log fires remain unchanged, contributing to its traditional atmosphere. Main courses include home-made steak and ale pie, bangers and mash, chicken, leek and Stilton topper, and fish and chips.
OPEN: 11–11 (Sun 12–10.30) **BAR MEALS:** 12–2 6–9 Av main course £7.95 **RESTAURANT:** 12–2 6–9
BREWERY/COMPANY: Free House **PRINCIPAL BEERS:** Black Sheep, John Smiths. **FACILITIES:** Garden: Food served outside
NOTES: Parking 80 **ROOMS:** 15 bedrooms 12 en suite from s£35.50 d£59

GRASMERE
Map 11 NY30

The Travellers Rest Inn 🛏
Keswick Rd LA22 9RR ☎ 015394 35604 🖹 017687 72309
e-mail: travellers@lakelandsheart.demon.co.uk
Dir: From M6 take A591 to Grasmere, pub 0.5m N of Grasmere

Some of the finest scenery in the country surrounds this 16th-century former coaching inn, which offers a good range of beers and an extensive menu of home-cooked traditional fare. Typical dishes are moules marinière, pot-roasted lamb shank, and sticky date pudding.
OPEN: 12–11 (Sun 12–10.30) **BAR MEALS:** Lunch served: all week Dinner served: all week 12–3 6–9.30 Av main course £5.95
RESTAURANT: Lunch served: all week Dinner served: all week 12–3 6–9.30 **BREWERY/COMPANY:** Free House

continued

PRINCIPAL BEERS: Jennings Bitter, Cumberland Ale, & Sneck Lifter, Greene King Abbot Ale. **FACILITIES:** Children welcome Children's licence Garden: beer garden, patio, outdoor eating, BBQ Dogs allowed **NOTES:** Parking 60 **ROOMS:** 9 bedrooms 9 en suite from s£30 d£60

GREAT LANGDALE   Map 11 NY20

The New Dungeon Ghyll Hotel 🐑
LA22 9JY ☎ 015394 37213 🖺 015394 37666
e-mail: enquiries@dungeon-ghyll.com
Dir: *From M6 into Kendal then A591 into Ambleside onto A593 to B5343, hotel 6m on R*

Traditional Cumberland stone hotel dating back to medieval times, and full of character and charm. The hotel stands in its own lawned grounds in a spectacular position beneath the Langdale Pikes and Pavey Ark. Local specialities, expertly cooked, are served in the smart dining room. Haggis fritter on fried potatoes, pan-roast duck breast with a cinnamon and honey sauce, and banana and toffee tart with cream could make up a typical dinner.
OPEN: 11-11 (Sun 11-10.30) **BAR MEALS:** Lunch served: all week Dinner served: all week 11.30-9 Av main course £6.50
RESTAURANT: Dinner served: all week 7-8.30 Av 3 course fixed price £17.50 **BREWERY/COMPANY:** Free House
PRINCIPAL BEERS: Courage Directors, Greene King Ruddles Best.
FACILITIES: Children welcome Garden: Dogs allowed
NOTES: Parking 30 **ROOMS:** 20 bedrooms 20 en suite from s£37.50 d£55

HAVERTHWAITE   Map 08 SD38

Rusland Pool 🐑 ♀
LA12 8AA ☎ 01229 861384 🖺 01229 861425
e-mail: enquires@rusland-pool.ndirect.co.uk
Dir: *M6 J36 take A590 towards Barrow-in-Furness for 17m the hotel is on the R hand side of the A590 Westbound*
A traditional coaching inn set in open countryside in the South Lakes, centrally situated for excellent local walks through woodland, open valleys and estuary. The grounds include a paddock, patio and beer garden for warmer weather, while the bar has a welcoming winter fire. The comprehensive carte menu ranges through baguettes, salads, starters/light snacks and main courses like salmon Orlando, fresh cod fillet, breast of duck with plum sauce, and pork fillet au poivre.
OPEN: 11-11 (food served all day, 12-9.15) **BAR MEALS:** Lunch served: all week Dinner served: all week 12-9 Av main course £7.50
RESTAURANT: Lunch served: all week Dinner served: all week 12-9 Av 3 course à la carte £7.50 **BREWERY/COMPANY:** Free House
PRINCIPAL BEERS: Tetleys, Boddingtons. **FACILITIES:** Children welcome Children's licence Garden: beer garden, outdoor eating
NOTES: Parking 35 **ROOMS:** 18 bedrooms 18 en suite from s£42 d£59

HAWKSHEAD   Map 11 SD39

Kings Arms Hotel
The Square LA22 0NZ ☎ 015394 36372 🖺 015394 36006

Low beamed ceilings and a winter log fire are among the charming features at this 16th-century pub, which overlooks the village square and is especially popular with holidaymakers and visitors in summer. Beatrix Potter lived nearby and Wordsworth went to school here. Good choice of starters, and among the main courses are grilled organic trout, chargrilled rump and sirloin steak and home-made steak and kidney pie with creamy mashed potato and peas. Bedrooms are cosy and traditionally furnished.
OPEN: 11-11 (Sun 12-10.30) **BAR MEALS:** Lunch served: all week Dinner served: all week 12-2.30 6-9.30 Av main course £7.50
RESTAURANT: Lunch served: all week Dinner served: all week 12-2.30 6-9.30 **BREWERY/COMPANY:** Free House
PRINCIPAL BEERS: Carlsberg-Tetley Bitter, Black Sheep Best, Yates, Jennings Cumberland Ale. **FACILITIES:** Children welcome Children's licence Garden: patio/terrace, food served outside Dogs allowed (water) **ROOMS:** 9 bedrooms 8 en suite from s£30 d£25

Pick of the Pubs

Queens Head Hotel ★ ★ 🐑 ♀
Main St LA22 0NS ☎ 015394 36271 🖺 015394 36722
e-mail: enquiries@queensheadhotel.co.uk
Dir: *M6 J36 A590 to Newby Bridge. Take 1st R, 8m to Hawkshead*

In this prettiest of Lakeland villages, the Queen's Head doesn't spoil the show. A characterful 16th-century building, it stands in Hawkshead's traffic free centre, festooned with hanging baskets and window boxes. The interior is as you'd hope - bare beams, a real fire and plenty of curios including the famous Girt Clog, a full 20 inches in length and said to have belonged to one John Waterson, a mole catcher who contracted elephantitis in the 1820s. Bedrooms are prettily decorated in country style. The lunch menu offers sandwiches, salads, light

continued

HAWKSHEAD continued

bites, grills and main meals such as seafood tagliatelle, pan fried mussels, Cumberland sausage and mash or roasted Esthwaite trout. In the evening an equally extensive selection might include a whole roasted pheasant with grilled bacon, roasted tomato and gauffret potatoes or grilled leg of Herdwick lamb steak with grilled tomato, glazed button onions and a sharp pepper and brandy sauce.
OPEN: 11–11 (Sun 12–10.30) **BAR MEALS:** Lunch served: all week Dinner served: all week 12–2.30 6.15–9.30
RESTAURANT: Lunch served: all week Dinner served: all week 12–2.30 6.15–8.45 Av 3 course à la carte £20 Av 3 course fixed price £20 **BREWERY/COMPANY:** Frederic Robinson
PRINCIPAL BEERS: Robinsons Hartleys XB & Frederics, Cumbrian Way. **FACILITIES:** Children welcome Children's licence. **NOTES:** Parking 13 **ROOMS:** 13 bedrooms 10 en suite from s£40 d£58

The Sun Inn ◆◆◆◆
Main St LA22 0NT ☎ 015394 36236 ▤ 015394 36155

Listed 17th-century coaching inn at the heart of the village where Wordsworth went to school. Bar dishes range from baguette with bacon and melted Brie to Cumbrian lamb cutlets seasoned with coriander and chilli and served with a mixed fruit couscous. The monthly changing restaurant carte might have trio of local sausages on a creamed celeriac mash or fishcakes of Esthwaite water trout served with sweet chilli and tomato crème fraîche.
OPEN: 11–11 **BAR MEALS:** Lunch served: all week Dinner served: all week 12–2.30 6.15–9.30 Av main course £6
RESTAURANT: Dinner served: all week Av 3 course à la carte £15
BREWERY/COMPANY: Free House **PRINCIPAL BEERS:** Black Sheep, Barn Gates Cracker, plus two guest ales.
FACILITIES: Children welcome Children's licence Garden: beer garden, outdoor eating, patio Dogs allowed **NOTES:** Parking 8
ROOMS: 8 bedrooms 8 en suite from s£45 d£60

HESKET NEWMARKET   Map 11 NY33

The Old Crown
CA7 8JG ☎ 016974 78288 ▤ 016974 78288
Dir: from M6 take B5305, L after 6m toward Hesket Newmarket
One of very few fell-side pubs that has not been refurbished – relying instead on good 'craic', beer and food to fill a niche market: decidedly part of the 'slow food' movement! Supplied by its own community-owned brewery at the top of the garden, the Old Crown is a one-off. All comers can order with confidence from local, fresh ingredients among a list of steaks, casseroles and curries. No 'towny' credit cards or standing on ceremony here.

OPEN: 12–3 5.30–11 **BAR MEALS:** Lunch served: Wed–Sun 12–2 Dinner served: Wed–Sat Av main course £7
BREWERY/COMPANY: Free House **PRINCIPAL BEERS:** Hesket Newmarket Catbells Pale Ale, Doris's 90th Birthday Ale, Skiddaw Special, Blencathra Bitter. **FACILITIES:** Children welcome Garden

HEVERSHAM   Map 08 SD48

Blue Bell Hotel 🛏 ♀
Princes Way LA7 7EE ☎ 015395 62018 ▤ 015395 62455
e-mail: bluebellhotel@aol.com
Dir: On A6 between Kendal & Milnthorpe

An ideal base for touring the Lake District and the Yorkshire Dales, the Blue Bell offers well-equipped modern bedrooms with pleasant country views. Once a vicarage, the comfortable lounge bar and separate restaurant exude charm and period character with their low beams and log fires. Daily specials on offer in either location include farmhouse pâté with oatcakes, lamb curry with spinach, game casserole and grilled Scottish salmon with prawn sauce.
OPEN: 11–11 **BAR MEALS:** Lunch served: all week Dinner served: all week 11–9 6–9 Av main course £7.95 **RESTAURANT:** Lunch served: all week Dinner served: all week 11–9 Av 3 course à la carte £18.50 Av 5 course fixed price £19.95
BREWERY/COMPANY: Samuel Smith
PRINCIPAL BEERS: Samuel Smith Old Brewery Bitter.
FACILITIES: Children welcome Garden: Patio, BBQ
NOTES: Parking 100 **ROOMS:** 21 bedrooms 21 en suite from s£49.50 d£75

HOWTOWN   Map 11 NY41

Howtown Hotel
CA10 2ND ☎ 01768 486514
Pub and hotel right on the shores of Ullswater, very popular with walkers. Bedrooms

continued

KENDAL
Map 10 SD59

Gateway Inn
Crook Rd LA8 8LX ☎ 01539 720605 & 724187 📄 01539 720581
Dir: From M6 J36 take A590/A591, follow signs for Windermere, pub on L after 9m

Located within the Lake District National Park, this Victorian country inn offers delightful views, attractive gardens and welcoming log fires. A good range of appetising dishes includes chicken casserole with red wine and herb dumplings, grilled fillets of sea bass with ratatouille and mussels, and roasted butternut squash filled with leeks and Stilton. Traditional English favourites of liver and onions or rabbit pie are also a feature.
OPEN: 11–11 (all day wknds) **BAR MEALS:** Lunch served: all week Dinner served: all week 12–2 6–9 Av main course £8.50
RESTAURANT: Lunch served: all week Dinner served: all week 12–2 6–9 Av 3 course à la carte £15 **BREWERY/COMPANY:** Thwaites
PRINCIPAL BEERS: Thwaites Bitter, Thwaites Smooth.
FACILITIES: Children welcome Garden: Terrace, food served outside Dogs allowed (water, dog food) **NOTES:** Parking 50
ROOMS: 6 bedrooms 6 en suite from s£35 d£60

KESWICK
Map 11 NY22

Pick of the Pubs

The Horse & Farrier Inn ⏣
Threlkeld Village CA12 4SQ ☎ 017687 79688
Situated below Blencathra and popular with hosts of fell walkers this 300-year-old stone inn is home to comfortable en suite bedrooms with space for all the family plus the dog, imaginative home cooking and the host brewer, Jennings's, real ales. In traditional style its bars and dining-room are warmly welcoming, hung with hunting prints and cheered by a roaring log fire. Available for lunch are cold and hot open sandwiches, seasonal salads and main dishes such as Lamb Jennings, slowly braised in bitter and served with spinach mash, and poached Scottish salmon on a mussel, leek and bacon ragout. Rather more structured dinner menus begin with feta cheese and black olive salad, moving on to chicken breast with mushroom, bacon and sherry cream sauce on herb risotto, red mullet fillets with Thai green curry sauce and choice cuts of beef steak.
OPEN: 11–11 (Sun 12–10.30) **BAR MEALS:** Lunch served: all week 12–2 Av main course £4.50 **RESTAURANT:** Lunch served: all week Dinner served: all week 12–2 6.30–9.30 Av 3 course à la carte £18 **BREWERY/COMPANY:** Jennings
PRINCIPAL BEERS: Jennings: Bitter, Cocker Hoop, Sneck Lifter & Cumberland Ale. **FACILITIES:** Children welcome, Patio, Food served outside **NOTES:** Parking 60 **ROOMS:** 9 bedrooms 9 en suite from s£30 d£60

Pick of the Pubs

The Kings Head ★ ★ ★
Thirlspot, Thirlmere CA12 4TN
☎ 017687 72393 📄 017687 72309
e-mail: kings@lakelandsheart.demon.co.uk
See Pick of the Pubs on page 102

Pick of the Pubs

Swan Hotel & Country Inn
Thornthwaite CA12 5SQ
☎ 0800 0748071 & 01768 778256 📄 01768 778080
e-mail: bestswan@aol.com
Dir: 3m out of Keswick off A66, through Thornthwaite village

Family-run 17th-century coaching inn situated in Thornthwaite village, 3 miles from Keswick. Surrounded by stunning Lakeland scenery, complete with fell views and nearby lakeside walks. Varied and wholesome menu may list Swiss-style chicken, fillet of trout, T-bone steak, Cumberland sausage, lasagne and deep-fried Brie fritters. Good selection of starters and snacks.
OPEN: 11–11 (Sun 12–10.30) **BAR MEALS:** Lunch served: all week Dinner served: all week 12–2 6–8.45 Av main course £6.50
RESTAURANT: Lunch served: all week Dinner served: all week 12–2 6–8.45 Av 3 course à la carte £15
PRINCIPAL BEERS: Jennings Cumberland Ale, Scottish Courage John Smith's & Courage Directors, John Smiths Smooth, Theakstons Bitter. **FACILITIES:** Children welcome Garden: Large, food served outside Dogs allowed **NOTES:** Parking 30
ROOMS: 7 bedrooms 4 en suite from s£30 d£50

The Swinside Inn
Newlands Valley CA12 5UE ☎ 017687 78253 📄 017687 78253
e-mail: info@theswinsideinn.com
Situated in the quiet Newlands valley, the Swinside Inn is a listed building dating back to about 1642. From the pub there are superb views of Causey Pike and Cat Bells – among other landmarks. Nearby is the market town of Keswick, a good base for visiting the area's many attractions. Inside are two bars, traditional open fires and oak-beamed ceilings. Extensive bar menu may offer lamb Henry, Cumberland sausage, Swinside chicken, and fresh, grilled Borrowdale trout.
OPEN: 11–11 (Sun 12–10.30) **BAR MEALS:** Lunch served: all week Dinner served: all week 12–2 6–8.45 Av main course £6.50
RESTAURANT: Lunch served: all week Dinner served: all week 12–2 6–8.45 Av 3 course à la carte £15 **PRINCIPAL BEERS:** Jennings Cumberland Ale, Scottish Courage John Smith's & Courage Directors, John Smiths Smooth, Theakstons Bitter. **FACILITIES:** Children welcome Garden: Large, food served outside Dogs allowed
NOTES: Parking 30 **ROOMS:** 7 bedrooms 4 en suite from s£30 d£50

OPEN: 12–11 (12–10.30 Sundays)
BAR MEALS: L served all week.
D served all week. 12–3 6–9.30
Av main course £5.95
RESTAURANT: L served Sun.
D served all week. 12–3 7–9
BREWERY/COMPANY: FREE HOUSE
PRINCIPLE BEERS: Theakston Best Bitter & Old Peculier, Jennings Bitter
FACILITIES: Children welcome, dogs allowed. Garden: beer garden, patio, BBQ, outdoor eating
NOTES: Parking 60
ROOMS: 17 en suite Min price double room £64 Min price single room £32

The Kings Head

★ ★ ★

Thirlspot Thirlmere CA12 4TN
☎ 017687 72393 📄 017687 72309
e-mail: kings@lakelandsheart.demon.co.uk
Dir: From M6 take A66 to Keswick then A591, pub 4m S of Keswick

A former 17th-century coaching inn at the foot of Helvellyn the pub surrounded by stunning Lakeland scenery. Good value food of a very high standard is served and served with real ales or fine wine. The location of the King's Head is stunning, surrounded as it is by sweeping pasture and arable land, and with lovely views of the Lakeland peaks of Blencathra and Skiddaw.

Inside, old beams and inglenook fireplaces are traditional features of the bar, there is an elegant, award-winning restaurant, while a separate games room offers pool, snooker and darts. There are seventeen comfortable bedrooms and delightful resident's lounge. In summer the beer gardens are popular locations for a meal or a drink. In the bars popular real ales include beers from Theakstons and from Jennings' brewery in nearby Cockermouth plus a fine selection of wines and malt whiskies. An extensive menu of good value bar food including daily specials is served, along with the daily-changing fixed-price restaurant menu. This offers four excellent courses of high quality, freshly made traditional English dishes and local specialities. Start with fettuccine carbonara, perhaps, or broccoli and almond soup, linger over a refreshing sorbet, then move on to baked fillet of Whitby cod wrapped in prosciutto, or roast loin of Cumbrian pork with spiced apple compote. Complete the meal with traditional apple and pear crumble with creamy vanilla custard sauce, or a choice of local cheeses. There are also facilities for banquets and wedding receptions of up to 100 guests.

England

KIRKBY LONSDALE Map 08 SD67

Pick of the Pubs

Pheasant Inn ★ ★ ♀
Casterton LA6 2RX ☎ 015242 71230 ▤ 015242 71230
e-mail: Pheasant.casterton@eggconnect.net
See Pick of the Pubs on page 104

Pick of the Pubs

Snooty Fox Tavern ♀
Main St LA6 2AH ☎ 015242 71308 ▤ 015242 72642
e-mail: Snootyfox84@freeserve.co.uk
Dir: M6 J36 take A65, tavern 6m

One of a trio of privately-owned, well-run Cumbrian inns (qv. Troutbeck's Mortal Man and the Royal Oak in Appleby), the Snooty Fox is a listed Jacobean coaching inn at the centre of town, the 'capital' of the scenic Lune valley. Inside are roaring fires in rambling bars full of eye-catching artefacts, while adjacent to a quaint cobbled courtyard is the pub's own herb garden, which signals its commitment to good food. There is a fairly serious approach to food with dishes on offer such as duck and pistachio parfait, smoked haddock risotto, breast of pheasant and roasted lamb rump with redcurrant jus to feed hungry fishermen and fell-walkers, who will equally enjoy the prime condition of real ales and guest beers. The English cheese board might include an unpasteurised goat's milk cheese, local Crofton and Cumberland oak smoked. The surroundings are comfortably convivial and well-appointed bedrooms promise a good night's sleep.
OPEN: 11-11 (Sun 12-11) **BAR MEALS:** Lunch served: all week 12-2.30 6-9.30 Av main course £9.25 **RESTAURANT:** Lunch served: all week Dinner served: all week 12-2.30 6-9.30 Av 3 course à la carte £26 **BREWERY/COMPANY:** Free House **PRINCIPAL BEERS:** Theakston Best, Greene King IPA, Timothy Taylor Landlord. **FACILITIES:** Children welcome Children's licence Garden: Food served outdoors, Patio Dogs allowed **NOTES:** Parking 12 **ROOMS:** 9 bedrooms 9 en suite from s£36 d£56

The Sun Inn ♀
Market St LA6 2AU ☎ 015242 71965 ▤ 015242 72489
e-mail: thesunhotel@hotmail.com
Dir: From M6 J36 take A65
A popular 17th-century pub rumoured to have a resident ghost, and with two open log fires to add to the atmosphere. During excavations to the yard, a tunnel was found that connects the pub with the church. Home-made food is available in both the 30s-style restaurant (called Mad Carew's

after the poem by J Milton Hayes), and the bar. Try authentic Cumberland sausage and mash, steak frites, lamb Devonshire or the traditional Sunday lunch.
OPEN: 11-11 (Sun 12-10.30) **BAR MEALS:** Lunch served: all week Dinner served: all week 12.30-2.30 6-9.30 Av main course £7.35 **RESTAURANT:** Dinner served: all week 6-9.30 Av 3 course à la carte £14.50 **BREWERY/COMPANY:** Free House **PRINCIPAL BEERS:** Black Sheep Best, Interbrew Boddingtons Bitter & Flowers IPA, Timothy Taylor Best, Theakston Best. **FACILITIES:** Children welcome Dogs allowed (water, toys) **ROOMS:** 9 bedrooms 5 en suite from s£29.50 d£49

Whoop Hall Inn ♀
Skipton Rd LA6 2HP ☎ 015242 71284 ▤ 015242 72154
e-mail: info@whoophall.co.uk
Dir: A65 from M6, pub 1m SE of Kirkby Lonsdale
Built in 1618, Whoop Hall was once the kennels for local fox hounds, and gets its name from the huntsman's call. In an imaginatively converted barn you can sample Yorkshire ales and a good menu of dishes based on local produce. There are now two eating options: The Gallery Restaurant, which concentrates on fine dining, and the Turners' Dining Room, which specialises in light, continental tastes.
OPEN: 7-11.30 **BAR MEALS:** Lunch served: all week Dinner served: all week 11.30-2.30 6-10 Av main course £6.95 **RESTAURANT:** Lunch served: all week Dinner served: all week 12-2.30 6-10 **BREWERY/COMPANY:** Free House **PRINCIPAL BEERS:** Dent, Black Sheep. **FACILITIES:** Children welcome Garden: Food served outside. Terrace & lawn areas Dogs allowed (water provided) **NOTES:** Parking 120 **ROOMS:** 23 bedrooms 23 en suite from s£60 d£70

KIRKBY STEPHEN Map 11 NY70

The Bay Horse
Winton CA17 4HS ☎ 017683 71451
e-mail: wintonpubks@whsmithnet.co.uk

Standing in a moorland hamlet off the A685, the Bay Horse offers home-cooked food and bedrooms.
OPEN: all week except Tues lunchtime **BAR MEALS:** Lunch served: Wed-Mon Dinner served: all week Av main course £7 **RESTAURANT:** Av 3 course à la carte: £12 **FACILITIES:** Dogs allowed Garden: Food served outside. **ROOMS:** 2 bedrooms 2 en suite from d£40

LITTLE LANGDALE Map 11 NY30

Pick of the Pubs

Three Shires Inn ★ ★
LA22 9NZ ☎ 015394 37215
e-mail: enquiries@threeshiresinn.co.uk
See Pick of the Pubs on page 106

continued

OPEN: 11–3 6–11
BAR MEALS: L served all week.
D served all week. 12–2 6.30–9
Av main course £7.50
RESTAURANT: L served Sun. D
served Tue–Sun. 12–2 6.30–9
Av cost 3 course £18
BREWERY/COMPANY: FREE
HOUSE
PRINCIPAL BEERS: Theakston
Best, Cool Cask, Black Sheep Best,
Marston's Pedigree, Dent Aviator
FACILITIES: Children and dogs
welcome. Garden: Food served
outside
NOTES: Parking 40
ROOMS: 11 en suite. Double
room from £76. Single room from
£40

Pheasant Inn

★ ★ ♀   Casterton
Kirkby Lonsdale LA6 2RX
☎ 015242 71230 📠 015242 71230
e-mail: Pheasant.casterton@eggconnect.net
Dir: From M6 J36 onto A65 for 7m, L
onto A683 at Devils Bridge, 1m to
Casterton. Village centre

A traditional 18th-century inn nestling beneath the Cumbrian fells in an idyllic location on the edge of the Lune valley. Ideal for touring the Lake District, the Forest of Bowland and the Yorkshire Dales by car and on foot, as well as savouring the unique beauty of the North of England.

Casterton School, which was attended by the Brontë sisters, was the model for Lowood School in Charlotte Bronte's *Jane Eyre*. About ten minutes from the M6 and one mile away from the pretty market town of Kirkby Lonsdale, where there are excellent 18-hole and 9-hole golf courses, the inn has had its fair share of distinguished visitors, including Prince Michael of Yugoslavia. Well-chosen wines by the glass and real, hand-pulled ales from breweries as diverse as Dent and the Wye Valley indicate dedication to the house's individuality. Relax over an informal bar meal or dine in the attractive oak panelled dining room, enjoying a good choice of imaginative dishes using the finest locally sourced produce. Roast rack of lamb with apple and mint gravy, rabbit and vegetable casserole and fillet of red snapper grilled with Chinese spices and spring onions sit comfortably alongside chicken breast with a pâté, mushroom and red wine sauce, and spicy lamb curry with basmati rice and poppadoms. For lighter fare there are lunchtime sandwiches of honey roast ham, prawns in a Marie Rose sauce and BLT with warm pitta bread. Alternatively, there is cottage pie, fillet of haddock, beef steak and ale pie, and local Cumberland sausage with apple and sultana chutney and mash potato. Bedrooms are individually furnished and offer a high standard of comfort; a twin bedded room for disabled guests is conveniently located on the ground floor.

LOWESWATER
Map 10 NY12

Kirkstile Inn ◆◆◆◆
CA13 0RU ☎ 01900 85219 📠 01900 85239
e-mail: info@kirkstile.com

Beautifully situated, with Melbeck towering above and superb views across Cumbria's fells, this 16th-century inn is an ideal spot to discuss the day's events over a jar of local real ale. While bedrooms are modest, the updated inn offers a home-cooked bar menu whose specials include Kirkstile lamb cobbler with a herb scone. At dinner, expect to find a fixed-price menu of hot avocado and celery cream in a filo basket, pan-fried duck breast on a raspberry sauce and fondant sponge with toffee sauce.
OPEN: 11-11 **BAR MEALS:** Lunch served: all week Dinner served: all week 12-2 6-9 Av main course £6.50 **RESTAURANT:** Lunch served: Sun 12-2 Dinner served: Thur-Sat 7-8.30 Av 4 course fixed price £22.50 **BREWERY/COMPANY:** Free House
PRINCIPAL BEERS: Jennings Bitter, Cumberland Ale.
FACILITIES: Children welcome Children's licence Garden: Food served outside, terrace Dogs allowed (water) **NOTES:** Parking 40
ROOMS: 11 bedrooms 9 en suite from s£35 d£56
See Pub Walk on page 91

MELMERBY
Map 11 NY63

The Shepherds Inn 🛏 ♀
CA10 1HF ☎ 01768 881217 📠 01768 881977
e-mail: eat@shepardsinn.net
Dir: On A686 NE of Penrith

Well-known in the North Pennines, this unpretentious sandstone pub overlooks the village green towards remote moorland country. Close to miles of spectacular walks. Renowned for its extensive choice of country cheeses, including Lanark Blue (ewe's milk similar to Roquefort), Westmorland Smoked (oak smoked Cheddar) and Tasty Lancashire (double curd cheese with a sharp bite). Diners are drawn from far and wide to sample the interesting lunchtime

snack menu or the daily specials, which might include beef in Guinness, tuna and sweetcorn quiche and beef and mushroom pie. Interesting mix of well-kept real ales.
OPEN: 10.30-3 6-11 (Sun 12-3, 7-10.30) Closed: 25 Dec
BAR MEALS: Lunch served: all week Dinner served: all week 10.30-2.30 6-9.45 Av main course £6 **RESTAURANT:** Lunch served: all week Dinner served: all week 10.30-2.30 6-9.45 Av 3 course à la carte £17 **BREWERY/COMPANY:** Free House
PRINCIPAL BEERS: Jennings Bitter, Black Sheep Riggwelter, Hesket Newmarket Blencathra Bitter, Gale's Best. **FACILITIES:** Children welcome Children's licence Dogs allowed **NOTES:** Parking 20

MUNGRISDALE
Map 11 NY33

The Mill Inn
CA11 0XR ☎ 017687 79632
Dir: From Penrith A66 to Keswick, after 10m R to Mungrisdale, pub 2m on L
Set in a peaceful village, this 16th-century coaching inn is handy for spectacular fell walks. Charles Dickens and John Peel once stayed here. The inn has a cask marque for its beer, and the food is also an attraction, with specials such as game casserole, fresh fish, and fillet steak with haggis and whisky sauce.
OPEN: 12-11 (Sun 12-10.30) **BAR MEALS:** Lunch served: all week Dinner served: all week 12-2.30 6-8.30 Av main course £6.95 **RESTAURANT:** Lunch served: all week Dinner served: all week 12-2.30 6-8.30 Av 3 course à la carte £12 **BREWERY/COMPANY:** Free House **PRINCIPAL BEERS:** Jennings Bitter & Cumberland plus guest ale. **FACILITIES:** Children welcome Garden: Dogs allowed **NOTES:** Parking 40 **ROOMS:** 6 bedrooms 5 en suite from s£35 d£55

NEAR SAWREY
Map 08 SD39

Tower Banks Hotel 🛏 ♀
LA22 0LF ☎ 015394 36334 📠 015394 36334
Dir: On B5285 SW of Windermere
This small 17th-century country inn featured in Beatrix Potter's 'The Tales of Jemima Puddleduck' - it stands next door to Hill Top, her former home. With its cosy bedrooms and good facilities - including a fishing licence for the local tarns - this makes an ideal base for exploring the Lake District. There is a good choice of beers and bar lunches and evening meals are available daily with locally made sausages rubbing shoulders with Morecambe Bay potted shrimps, Lakeland game pie and Esthwaite trout.
OPEN: 11-3 6-11 (Summer 6-10.30) Closed: 25 Dec
BAR MEALS: Lunch served: all week Dinner served: all week 12-2 6.30-9 Av main course £6 **RESTAURANT:** Lunch served: all week Dinner served: all week 12-2 6.30-9 Av 3 course à la carte £12 **BREWERY/COMPANY:** Free House
PRINCIPAL BEERS: Theakston Best & Old Peculier, Wells Bombardier, Barngates Tag Lag. **FACILITIES:** Children welcome Garden: Beer garden, food served outdoors **NOTES:** Parking 8 **ROOMS:** 3 bedrooms 3 en suite from s£37 d£52

NETHER WASDALE
Map 10 NY10

The Screes Hotel
CA20 1ET ☎ 019467 26262 📠 019467 26262
e-mail: info@thescreesinnwasdale.com
Dir: E of A595 between Whitehaven & Ravenglass
A 300-year-old inn nestling in the heart of the Wasdale valley, offering magnificent views of the surrounding fells and only a short walk from Wastwater, England's deepest lake. Large

continued

continued

OPEN: 11-11 (Sun 12-10.30) (Dec-Jan 12-3, 8-10.30)
BAR MEALS: L served all week. D served all week. 12-2 6-8.45 Av main course £8
RESTAURANT: D served all week. 6.30-8
BREWERY/COMPANY: FREE HOUSE
PRINCIPAL BEERS: Jennings Best & Cumberland, Ruddles County
FACILITIES: Children welcome, dogs allowed. Garden: Food served outside
NOTES: Parking 20
ROOMS: 10 en suite Min price double room £59 Min price single room £29.50

Three Shires Inn

LITTLE LANGDALE LA22 9NZ
☎ 015394 37215
e-mail: enquiries@threeshiresinn.co.uk
Dir: Turn off A593, 2.3m from Ambleside at 2nd junct signposted for The Langdales. 1st L 0.5m, Hotel 1m up lane.

This 19th-century hotel is close to the Three Shires Stone, which represents the meeting point for Lancashire and the old counties of Cumberland and Westmoreland. Personally run by the same family since 1983, the inn has been giving a warm welcome for over 100 years.

Since the 1880s when the grey stone, slate roofed traditional Cumbrian building was erected, the inn would have provided a much needed resting place and watering hole for travellers on the journey over the high passes of Hardknott and Wrynose. The Three Shires is still playing host to walkers and weekend break visitors to this majestic mountain country throughout the year. Set in a delightful rural location, there are benches on a terrace by the side of a mountain stream, from which to enjoy the plentiful fresh air, and during the summer months the inn boasts wonderful floral displays. Among the real ales served at the inn are Jennings' Best and Cumberland and Coniston Old Man from nearby breweries, and good, home-made snacks and meals from a carte menu are available in the bar. Typical dishes are marinated venison, pan-fried and served with port and Stilton sauce, and whole breaded Whitby scampi served with tartar sauce, salad and chips or a summer salad of chargrilled chicken. There is also a restaurant offering a four-course, fixed-price evening menu which may offer a starter of salmon and crab parfait with a sweet dill and whisky sauce, then sorbet, pan-fried fillets of sea bass served with pickled cucumber and a cinnamon sauce and a selection of desserts.

NETHER WASDALE continued

comfortable bar inside with a cosy log fire and a large selection of malt whiskies. Wide range of traditional and vegetarian dishes, including Woodhall's Cumberland sausages with apple sauce, grilled halibut with fresh herb butter and hollandaise sauce and half a roast chicken. Nine en suite bedrooms have been recently improved .

OPEN: 12-11 **BAR MEALS:** Lunch served: all week Dinner served: all week 12-2.30 6-9.30 Av main course £6.50
RESTAURANT: Lunch served: all week Dinner served: all week 12-2.30 6-9.30 **BREWERY/COMPANY:** Free House
PRINCIPAL BEERS: Black Sheep Best, Yates Bitter.
FACILITIES: Children welcome Garden: views of the fells, food served outdoors Dogs allowed (water) **NOTES:** Parking 30
ROOMS: 5 bedrooms 4 en suite from s£25 d£50

OUTGATE   Map 11 SD39

Outgate Inn
LA22 0NQ ☎ 015394 36413
Dir: From M6, A684 to Kendal, A591 towards Ambleside. At Plumgarths take B5284 to Hawkshead then Outgate

Once a toll house, this 18th-century Lakeland pub became licensed as the Outgate Mineral Water Manufacturer in 1903. Many of the original features have been retained. Plenty of good walks and stunning scenery on the doorstep. Traditional jazz takes place here most Friday evenings. Food can be enjoyed in the cosy dining room or the bar area and among the popular dishes are steak and kidney pie, lamb balti, grilled gammon and rainbow trout.
OPEN: 11-3 6-11 **BAR MEALS:** Lunch served: all week Dinner served: all week 12-2 6.30-9 Av main course £6.95
RESTAURANT: Lunch served: all week Dinner served: all week 12-2 6.30-9 **BREWERY/COMPANY:** Hartleys
PRINCIPAL BEERS: Robinsons Best, Fredericks & Hartleys XB.
FACILITIES: Children welcome Children's licence Garden: patio and lawned area to the rear of pub Dogs allowed (water) **NOTES:** Parking 30 **ROOMS:** 3 bedrooms 3 en suite from s£37.50 d£27.50

RAVENSTONEDALE   Map 11 NY70

Pick of the Pubs

Black Swan Hotel ♀
CA17 4NG
☎ 015396 23204 & 0800 0741394 📠 015396 23604
e-mail: reservations@blackswanhotel.com
Dir: M6 J38 take A685 E towards Brough
In a peaceful village in the foothills of the Eden Valley, in the old county of Westmorland, this comfortable Lakeland stone hotel dates from 1899. The larger of two bars, with a comfortable air afforded by its bright copper-topped tables is well placed for good value portions of steak pie in shortcrust pastry, Cumberland sausage with caramelised apples and salmon marinated in lime and honey. The owners spend much of their day preparing dinner for their restaurant guests, with an emphasis on delights such as local beef, lamb and game and traditionally made cheeses. Flavours are a strong point in scallops with sweet potato purée and tartare of mussels, grilled sea bass with lobster tail and green pea mousse and chocolate torte with peppermint mousse. A perfect place to escape the pressures of the modern day world, there is tennis and fishing nearby, and a sheltered garden approached by way of a footbridge across the stream.
OPEN: 8.30-3 6-11 (wknds 8-midnight) **BAR MEALS:** Lunch served: all week Dinner served: all week 12-2.15 6-9 Av main course £6.50 **RESTAURANT:** Lunch served: all week Dinner served: all week 12-2.15 7-9 Av 3 course à la carte £18
BREWERY/COMPANY: Free House
PRINCIPAL BEERS: Black Sheep, Timothy Taylor Landlord, Greene King IPA. **FACILITIES:** Children welcome Children's licence Garden: beer garden, outdoor eating Dogs allowed **NOTES:** Parking 40 **ROOMS:** 20 bedrooms 18 en suite from s£45 d£70

Pick of the Pubs

The Fat Lamb Country Inn ★ ★ ♀
Crossbank CA17 4LL ☎ 015396 23242 📠 015396 23285
e-mail: fatlamb@cumbria.com
Dir: On A683 between Sedbergh and Kirkby Stephen

Originally a 17th-century farmhouse, the Fat Lamb lies in magnificent countryside above the old market town of Kirkby Stephen. Located on high ground, the inn has been cut off by snow and once, when the inn was hosting a wedding reception, the bride-to-be sat alone, waiting patiently while her future husband battled in vain to get through the snow. The wedding was rescheduled and the bride went to church aboard a tractor complete with white

continued

England

ribbons. A second wedding breakfast then took place at the Fat Lamb. Adjoining the pub is an 11-acre nature reserve, home to many species of wildfowl. Chefs use local produce whenever possible and the varied bar snack menu may offer home-made lasagne, best Whitby scampi, mixed sausage platter and a selection of cold platters. Breaded escalope of pork Holstein, ragout of duck with pears and ginger and seared supreme of salmon with roast vegetables feature among the restaurant main courses.
OPEN: 11-2 6-11 **BAR MEALS:** Lunch served: all week Dinner served: all week 12-2 6-10 Av main course £7
RESTAURANT: Lunch served: all week Dinner served: all week 12-2 6-9 Av 3 course à la carte £15 Av 4 course fixed price £19
BREWERY/COMPANY: Free House
PRINCIPAL BEERS: Interbrew Boddington Bitter.
FACILITIES: Children welcome Children's licence Garden: Food served outside Dogs allowed **NOTES:** Parking 60
ROOMS: 12 bedrooms 12 en suite from s£41 d£66

See Pub Walk on page 109

SCALES   Map 11 NY32

White Horse Inn 🐑
CA12 4SY ☎ 017687 79241 📠 017687 79241
Dir: Off A66 between Keswick & Penrith

Situated on the slopes of Blencathra, this traditional Lakeland inn overlooks outstanding mountain scenery and makes an ideal base for walkers. The building dates from 1610 and is full of character, with beamed ceilings, an open fire and antique furnishings. Favourite dishes include lamb Henry with minted gravy, venison haunch with port and wild mushroom sauce, and Barbary duck breast with cranberries and Stilton.
OPEN: 12-2.30 (Summer open until 4pm) 6.30-10.30
BAR MEALS: Lunch served: all week Dinner served: all week 12-2 6.45-9 Av main course £8 **RESTAURANT:** Lunch served: all week Dinner served: all week 12-2 6.45-9 Av 3 course à la carte £14
BREWERY/COMPANY: Free House
PRINCIPAL BEERS: Interbrew Bass, Jennings Bitter, Black Sheep Best, Worthington Bitter. **FACILITIES:** Children welcome
NOTES: Parking 6

SEATHWAITE   Map 08 SD29

Newfield Inn 🍷
LA20 6ED ☎ 01229 716208
e-mail: paul@seathwaite.freeserve.co.uk
Dir: A590 toward Barrow, then R onto A5092, becomes A595, follow for 1m, R at Duddon Bri, 6m to Seathwaite
Located in Wordsworth's favourite Duddon Valley, six miles from the market town of Broughton-in-Furness, this early 17th-century inn is understandably popular with walkers and climbers, with many good walks (long and short) starting close to its door. The bar has a rare slate floor, a real fire and a small collection of historic photographs. The menu encompasses home-made steak pie, Cumberland sausage, spicy bean casserole, steaks and falafel.
OPEN: 11-11 **BAR MEALS:** Lunch served: all week Dinner served: all week 12-9 12-9 Av main course £6 **RESTAURANT:** Lunch served: all week Dinner served: all week 12-9 12-9
BREWERY/COMPANY: Free House
PRINCIPAL BEERS: Theakston Old Peculier & Black Bull, Jennings Cumberland Ale, J W Lees Bitter, Coniston Bluebird.
FACILITIES: Children welcome Garden: Food served outside, stunning views Dogs allowed (water) **NOTES:** Parking 30

SEDBERGH   Map 08 SD69

The Dalesman Country Inn 🐑
Main St LA10 5BN ☎ 015396 21183 📠 015396 21311
Dir: J37 on M6, follow signs to Sedbergh, 1st pub in town on L.
A 16th-century coaching inn, renowned for its floral displays and handy for walks along the River Dee or up on Howgill Fells. The lunchtime menu concentrates on home-made pies, Angus beefburgers and Dalesman club sandwiches. The evening choice extends to roast dinners, finest quality steaks and fresh home-made beer battered cod. There is a patio and garden, ideal for summer meals.

OPEN: 11-11 **BAR MEALS:** Lunch served: all week Dinner served: all week 12-2.30 6-9.30 Av main course £9 **RESTAURANT:** Lunch served: all week Dinner served: all week 12-2.30 6-9.30
BREWERY/COMPANY: Free House
PRINCIPAL BEERS: Carlsberg-Tetley, Theakston Best Bitter.
FACILITIES: Children welcome Children's licence Garden: Patio, food served outside **NOTES:** Parking 8 **ROOMS:** 7 bedrooms 7 en suite from s£25 d£50

PUB WALK

Ravenstonedale
The Fat Lamb

Enjoy this pastoral walk to the south-west of Kirkby Stephen. The route runs through Cumbria's wild Pennine country, close to the River Eden and the Settle-Carlisle railway. The nature reserve on the walk – where over 80 species of bird have been identified – is owned by the Fat Lamb and managed under a Countryside Stewardship agreement.

From the inn car park walk towards Kirkby Stephen, crossing over both the cattle-grid and Scandal Beck at the foot of the hill. Take the tarmac road to the right immediately beyond the bridge and follow it up over the fell to the farmhouse. Keeping the fields on your right, bear left, follow the path behind the house and continue across the fell, parallel with a wall. Look for a copse and head to the right of the trees. This is Jubilee Wood, planted to mark Queen Victoria's Jubilee. Cross the old packhorse bridge on the far

side of the wood to reach a road. This was once the main route between Sedbergh and Kirkby Stephen. Follow the tarmac road and bear right at a junction by some gates. Leave the road when it bears left and continue ahead down a track to the main road at the bottom. Cross it and turn right for about 200 yards (183m) to a stile in the wall. Cross over and cut straight across the field, veering slightly to the right. Keep to the left of a small fenced enclosure and head diagonally across the far slope, bearing to the right, to the stile in the wall at the top. Walk straight ahead across the next field, crossing the stream by the bridge, and veer towards the right side of the farmhouse ahead. Pass through the stile in the far corner and turn right, keeping by the wall until you reach a gate leading over the bridge. Cross it and bear right by the side of the nature reserve to follow the waymarked route back to the inn.

THE FAT LAMB,
Crossbank RAVENSTONEDALE
Kirkby Stephen CA17 4LL
Tel: 015396 23242
Directions: On A683 between Sedbergh and Kirkby Stephen
Expect a friendly welcome at this historic pub with solid stone walls and open fires, dating back to the 1600s. A useful base for exploring some of the finest scenery in the North of England. Fresh local produce is the mainstay of menus.
Open: 11–2 6–11
Barmeals: 12–2 6–10
Children welcome and dogs allowed. Garden and parking available.

Distance: 3 1/2 miles (5.7km)
Map: OS Landranger 91
Terrain: Fields, fell and wood
Paths: Roads, tracks and paths
Gradient: Undulating

Walk submitted and checked by The Fat Lamb, Ravenstonedale

England

SHAP
Map 11 NY51

Greyhound Hotel 🐑 ⚲
Main St CA10 3PW ☎ 01931 716474 📠 01931 716305
e-mail: postmaster@greyhoundshap.demon.co.uk
Built as a coaching inn in 1684, the Greyhound is recognised
as the first inn travellers and tourists reach after crossing
notorious Shap Fell. Bonnie Prince Charlie once stayed here
overnight on the march south with his Highlanders in 1745.
Appetising menu characterised by dishes such as steak and
kidney pudding, haunch of venison, pot roast brisket of beef,
Dublin Bay prawns, grilled gammon with pineapple or egg,
deep-fried fillet of fresh cod and Westmorland sirloin steak
garni. Good choice of ales.
OPEN: 11-11 **BAR MEALS:** Lunch served: all week Dinner served:
all week 12-2.30 6-9 Av main course £7.50 **RESTAURANT:** Lunch
served: all week Dinner served: all week 12-2.30 6-9 Av 3 course à la
carte £15.50 **BREWERY/COMPANY:** Free House
PRINCIPAL BEERS: Carlsberg-Tetley Bitter, Young's Bitter, Greene
King Old Speckled Hen, Jennings Bitter plus Guest Ales.
FACILITIES: Children welcome Children's licence Garden: Food
served outside Dogs allowed **NOTES:** Parking 30
ROOMS: 11 bedrooms 11 en suite

TIRRIL
Map 11 NY52

Pick of the Pubs

Queens Head Inn 🐑 ⚲
CA10 2JF ☎ 01768 863219 📠 01768 863243
e-mail: bookings@queensheadinn.co.uk
*Dir: A66 towards Penrith then A6 S toward Shap. In Eamont Bridge
take R just after Crown Hotel. Tirril 1m on B5320.*
This typical stone-built Cumbrian pub dates from about
1719, and the Grade II listed building has a long and
colourful history. Formerly owned by the Wordsworth
family in the early 1800s, there's a signed proof in the bar
to establish the link with the great William himself. The
pub produced its own beers until 1899, and the current
owners revived the Tirril brew exactly a century later.
Award-winning Tirril ales are now on tap in the beamed
and flagstoned front bar, which is also renowned for
blazing log fires in a spectacular inglenook. Modest, good-
value accommodation and traditional English pub food
are a bonus for appreciative locals, visiting tourists and
walkers alike. Salmon mousse or pâté maison precede
bacon-wrapped chicken with leeks, parsnip crumble, or
Szechuan beef stir-fry, whilst the extensive pudding menu
features poached pear in rum and honey, or hot lemon
sponge.
OPEN: 12-3 6-11 (Sat-Sun all day) **BAR MEALS:** Lunch
served: all week Dinner served: all week 12-2 6-9.30 Av main
course £9.50 **RESTAURANT:** Lunch served: all week Dinner
served: all week 12-2 6-9.30 Av 3 course à la carte £15
BREWERY/COMPANY: Free House
PRINCIPAL BEERS: Tirril Bewshers Best, Thomas Slee's
Academy Ale & Charles Gough's Old Faithful, Dent Aviator.
FACILITIES: Children welcome Children's licence Dogs allowed
(water) **NOTES:** Parking 60 **ROOMS:** 7 bedrooms 4 en suite
from s£30 d£45

♦ **Indicates AA inspected
bed & breakfast accommodation**

TROUTBECK
Map 11 NY40

Mortal Man Hotel ★ ★ ⚲
Upper Rd LA23 1PL ☎ 015394 33193 📠 015394 31261
e-mail: the-mortalman@btinternet.com
*Dir: 2 1/2m N of jct between A591 & A592, L at Troutbeck sign the R at T
jct, Hotel 800yrds on R*
The 400-year-old inn is famous for its sign that reads: 'O
mortal man that lives by bread, what is it makes thy nose so
red? Thou silly fool that look'st so pale, tis drinking Sally
Birkett's ale.' (Sally Birkett being the original landlady.)
Bounded on three sides by fells, and blessed with wonderful
views, the inn is widely recognised as a ramblers' paradise.
Home-cooked dishes include lamb shank, mussels in white
wine and fillet steak.

OPEN: 12-11 **BAR MEALS:** Lunch served: all week Dinner served:
all week 12-3 Av main course £4.95 **RESTAURANT:** Lunch served:
all week Dinner served: all week 12-3 7-9.30 Av 3 course à la carte
£12.95 **BREWERY/COMPANY:** Free House
PRINCIPAL BEERS: Theakston Best. **FACILITIES:** Garden: Food
served outside Dogs allowed (water) **NOTES:** Parking 15
ROOMS: 12 bedrooms 12 en suite from s£40 d£60

Pick of the Pubs

Queens Head Hotel ♦♦♦♦ 🏵 ⚲
Townhead LA23 1PW ☎ 015394 32174 📠 015394 31938
e-mail: enquiries@queensheadhotel.com
*Dir: M6 J36, A590/591 westbound towards Windermere, R at mini-
rdbt onto A592 signed Penrith/Ullswater, pub 2m on R*

In the shelter of the Troutbeck Valley with stunning views
across the Garburn Pass and Applethwaite Moors, a
classic Lakeland hostelry that has changed little since its
time as a thriving 17th-century coaching inn. Its rambling
rooms are full of character, featuring beams, open fires,
ancient carved settles and stone-flagged floors. Old prints
adorn the walls of a bar servery created from an

continued

Elizabethan four-poster bed. Accomplished cooking is unfussy, with a variety of dishes based on local produce served in both the bar and restaurant. Half-a-dozen good house wines and local Cumberland ales can accompany freshly prepared soup with home-made bread, crab, salmon and coriander fish cakes and braised steak with ale and mushrooms under a savoury cobbler topping. The set menu might feature home-cured salmon with capers and olives, seared ox liver on garlic mash and red wine jus, and traditional sticky toffee pudding. Comfortable, tasteful en suite bedrooms enjoy breathtaking Lakeland views.
OPEN: 11–11 (Sun 12–10.30) Closed: 25 Dec
BAR MEALS: Lunch served: all week Dinner served: all week 12–2 6.30–9 Av main course £9 **RESTAURANT:** Lunch served: all week Dinner served: all week 12–2 6.30–9 Av 4 course fixed price £15.50 **BREWERY/COMPANY:** Free House
PRINCIPAL BEERS: Interbrew Boddingtons Bitter, Coniston Bluebird, Old Man Bitter, Jennings Cumberland Ale.
FACILITIES: Children welcome Children's licence Garden Dogs allowed **NOTES:** Parking 100 **ROOMS:** 15 bedrooms 15 en suite from s£46.50 d£60

ULVERSTON   Map 08 SD27

Pick of the Pubs

Farmers Arms 🛏 ♀ NEW
Market Place LA12 7BA ☎ 01229 584469
e-mail: roger@farmersrestaurant-thelakes.co.uk
A lively 16th-century inn at the centre of the market town overlooking the market cross. The inn offers a warm welcome to locals and visitors alike, with its relaxed atmosphere and cosy front bar with open fire and traditional old beams. A patio area at the front of the inn provides a flower-filled spot to enjoy a drink or a meal, and watch the world, and the many local festivals, go by. The beamed rear dining area is decorated with a collection of old and new mirrors, and landlord Roger Chattaway takes pride in the quality food. The lunchtime menu extends to hot and cold sandwiches on baguette or ciabatta, various salads, and pasta carbonara, or gammon jamboree. In the evening expect stir-fry duck in a spicy Satay sauce, and sea bass fillets with a garlic prawn and saffron risotto.
OPEN: 10–11 **BAR MEALS:** Lunch served: all week Dinner served: all week 11.30–3 5.30–8.30 Av main course £6.50
RESTAURANT: Lunch served: all week Dinner served: all week 11.30–3 5.30–8.30 Av 3 course à la carte £9.95
BREWERY/COMPANY: Free House
PRINCIPAL BEERS: Scottish Courage Courage Directors.
FACILITIES: Children welcome Garden: Food served outside

Royal Oak
Spark Bridge LA12 8BS ☎ 01229 861006
Dir: From Ulverston take A590 N.Village off A5092
Set in a small village, this large, 18th-century pub offers a varied menu. Dishes include breaded sole filled with crab and prawn sauce, fillet steak stuffed with Stilton cheese and wrapped in bacon served on a port wine sauce, steak and mushroom pie, Cumberland sausage and chips, roasted sea bass served on creamy mashed potatoes, chicken and ham pie, or seared scallops on salad. Try the enormous Royal Grill (steak, sausage, porkloin, black pudding, gammon and eggs).

continued

OPEN: 12–3 6–11 **BAR MEALS:** Lunch served: all week Dinner served: all week 12–2 6–9 **BREWERY/COMPANY:** Enterprise Inns
PRINCIPAL BEERS: Tetley, Boddingtons, Marston Pedigree, Black Sheep Best. **FACILITIES:** Children welcome Garden: Food served outside Dogs allowed (water) **NOTES:** Parking 30 **ROOMS:** 2 bedrooms 2 en suite from s£30 d£45

WASDALE HEAD   Map 11 NY10

Wasdale Head Inn 🛏 ♀
CA20 1EX ☎ 019467 26229 📠 019467 26334
e-mail: wasdaleheadinn@msn.com
Dir: Follow signs 'Wasdale' from A595, the inn is at the head of the valley
Dramatically situated at the foot of England's highest mountains and beside her deepest lake, this Lakeland inn is a perfect base for walking and climbing. Slate floors and oak-panelled walls are characteristic of its rustic interior, and the walls are hung with photographs reflecting a passion for climbing. Real ale is made exclusively for the inn, and local Herdwick lamb is a speciality, along with traditional bangers - Cumberland, pork and leek, and venison and herb.
OPEN: 11–11 (Sun 12–10.30) **BAR MEALS:** Lunch served: all week Dinner served: all week 11–9 Av main course £6.50
RESTAURANT: Dinner served: most 7–8 Av 3 course à la carte £22 Av 4 course fixed price £22 **BREWERY/COMPANY:** Free House
PRINCIPAL BEERS: Heskett Newmarket Kern Knott's Cracking Stout, Great Gable Wasd Ale, Yates Bitter. **FACILITIES:** Garden: View of mountains, food served outside Dogs allowed (water)
NOTES: Parking 50 **ROOMS:** 15 bedrooms 15 en suite from s£40 d£80

WATERMILLOCK   Map 11 NY42

Pick of the Pubs

Brackenrigg Inn ♦♦♦ 🛏 ♀
CA11 0LP ☎ 017684 86206 📠 017684 86945
e-mail: enquiries@brackenrigginn.co.uk
See Pick of the Pubs on page 112

> **Room prices show the minimum double and single rates charged.**
> **Room rates in hotels and B&B's often vary depending on the facilities, so be sure to check prices with the establishment before booking.**

OPEN: 12-11 (Sun 12-10.30 Nov-Mar closed 3-5pm)
BAR MEALS: L served all week. D served all week. 12-2.30 6.30-9 Av main courses £8.50
RESTAURANT: L served all week. D served all week. 12-2.30 6.30-9 Av cost 3 course £14.95
BREWERY/COMPANY: FREE HOUSE
PRINCIPAL BEERS: Theakstons Best, Jennings Cumberland, Black Sheep Special
FACILITIES: Dogs allowed. Garden: Food served outside. Lake view terrace
NOTES: Parking 40
ROOMS: 11 en suite Double room from £54 Single room from £32

Brackenrigg Inn

Enjoying sweeping views across Lake Ullswater and surrounding fells from its elevated terrace and fine gardens, this traditional 18th-century coaching inn majors on good quality food and comfortable modern accommodation in en suite bedrooms and self-catering in converted stable cottages.

♦♦♦ ♀🐾
Watermillock, Cumbria CA11 0LP
☎ 017684 86206 🗎 017684 86945
e-mail: enquiries@brackenrigginn.co.uk
Dir: A66 to Keswick, A592 for 6m to Watermillock.

The Brackenrigg Inn is an unpretentious, white-painted roadside hostelry that makes the most of elevated position, offering casual visitors and overnight guests stunnings views of Ullswater and distant peaks, including Helvellyn, from its traditional bar lounge and, no-smoking dining room. Add Black Sheep and Jennings ales, and imaginative choice of modern pub food and varied styles of accommodation to suite all needs and you have the ideal base from which to explore the delights of the Northern Lakes, whether it be walking, climbing, watersports, golfing, or just touring this area. Tuck into a traditional bar snack (hearty soups, filled baguettes) in the

homely bar or out on the terrace of warm summer days, or sample modern British dishes in the restaurant. In the latter a weekly-changing menu may offer jumbo shrimps deep-fried in chilli and lime batter with avocado salad and sweet chilli dressing and warm mussel and leek tart infused with saffron with a lemon butter sauce to start, followed by salmon and crab risotto with Parmesan shavings and a white wine, mussel and dill sauce, oven-baked halibut with tomato, olive and herb crust, roast breast of duck with leg confit, grilled sweet potatoes and a cassis sauce, or Cumberland sausage braised with Puy lentils, smoked bacon and thyme and served with red cabbage. Round off with caramelised rice pudding. Retire to one of the eleven, practically furnished en suite bedrooms, each with breathtaking lake and fell views.

WIGTON　　　　　　　　　　　Map 11 NY24

Oddfellows Arms

Caldbeck CA7 8EA ☎ 016974 78227 📠 016974 78134
Situated in a scenic conservation village in the northern fells,
this 17th-century former coaching inn is in a stunning location
and is popular with walkers on the Cumbrian Way and coast-
to-coast cyclists. Lunchtime snacks and a specials board
supplement the regular menu, and favourite fare includes
roast beef, steak and ale pie, roast duck, lamb Jennings,
curries and steaks. Fresh fish, salads and vegetarian dishes are
listed on the board.
OPEN: 12-3 6-11 (Fri-Sun all day) **BAR MEALS:** Lunch served: all
week Dinner served: all week 12-2 6-8.30 Av main course £7.25
RESTAURANT: Lunch served: all week Dinner served: all week 12-2
6.30-8.30 Av 3 course à la carte £14.50
BREWERY/COMPANY: Jennings **PRINCIPAL BEERS:** Jennings
Bitter, Cumberland Ale. **FACILITIES:** Children welcome Garden:
Food served outside Dogs allowed (water) **NOTES:** Parking 10
ROOMS: 8 bedrooms 8 en suite from s£28 d£48

WINDERMERE　　　　　　　　　Map 08 SD49

Eagle & Child Inn ♦♦♦

Kendal Rd, Staveley LA8 9LP ☎ 01539 821320
e-mail: info@eaglechildinn.co.uk
Dir: Follow M6 to Jct 36 then A590 towards Kendal join A591 towards
Windermere. Staveley approx 2m

Recently refurbished, the name of this inn, in Staveley village
at the foot of the Kentmere valley, refers to the crest of arms
of the Lonsdale family who were local landowners. Excellent
walking, cycling and fishing country on the doorstep. Opposite
the inn, the River Kent rushes past the beer garden.
Appetising range of dishes might include local Kentmere lamb
shank on mustard mash and grilled sea bass with a sweet
lemon dressing. Well-kept local beers also feature.
OPEN: 11-11 **BAR MEALS:** Lunch served: all week Dinner served: all
week 12-3 6-9 Av main course £6.95 **RESTAURANT:** Lunch served: all
week Dinner served: all week 12-3 6-9 Av 3 course à la carte £17
PRINCIPAL BEERS: Black Sheep Best, Coniston Blue Bird, Dent Ales,
Jennings. **FACILITIES:** Children welcome Garden: Food served
outside **NOTES:** Parking 16 **ROOMS:** 5 bedrooms 5 en suite from
s£30 d£40

See Pub Walk on page 114

New Hall Inn NEW

Lowside, Bowness LA23 3DH ☎ 015394 43488
Complete with flagged-floors, exposed beams and open fires,
this historic pub was built in 1612, and was then used as a
blacksmiths. One of its best-known visitors was Charles
Dickens. Typical menu includes pheasant, fish pie, and crab
claws.
OPEN: 11-11 Closed: 25 Dec **BAR MEALS:** Lunch served: all week
Dinner served: all week 12-2.30 6-8.30 Av main course £6.50
PRINCIPAL BEERS: Hartleys XB, Robinsons Best, Red Robin.
FACILITIES: Children welcome Garden: Food served outdoors

The Watermill

Ings LA8 9PY ☎ 01539 821309 📠 01539 822309
e-mail: all@watermillinn.co.uk
This traditional, creeper-clad inn is very popular with walkers,
not least because it is locally renowned for its impressive
selection of real ales. The inn is a former woodmill that once
crafted cart wheels, shuttles and bobbins for the Lancashire
cotton mills. Menu includes a good selection of pies, lamb
steaks marinated in honey and mustard, casseroles, seafood
pancakes, and the Wrynose mixed grill. Sunday roast dinners.
OPEN: 12-11 (Sun 12-10.30) Closed: 25 Dec **BAR MEALS:** Lunch
served: all week Dinner served: all week 12-4.30 5-9 Av main course
£8.25 **BREWERY/COMPANY:** Free House
PRINCIPAL BEERS: Coniston Blue Bird, Black Sheep Special,
Jennings Cumberland Ale. **FACILITIES:** Garden: Food served
outside. Patio area Dogs allowed (biscuits & water provided)
ROOMS: 7 bedrooms 7 en suite from s£28 d£50

YANWATH　　　　　　　　　　Map 11 NY52

Pick of the Pubs

The Yanwath Gate Inn

CA10 2LF ☎ 01768 862386 📠 01768 864006
e-mail: ian.rhind@virgin.net
An unassuming 17th-century village pub popular with
walkers and visitors to the Lake District, as it is not far
from scenic Ullswater but only a couple of miles from J40
of the M6. A charming stone inglenook fireplace tends to
draw both regulars and newcomers. This is the place to
enjoy a pint of Hesket Newmarket Skiddaw Special while
you choose something from the appetising menu. If you
prefer, relax in the congenial surroundings of the inn's
separate restaurant with its pleasant views over the
garden. Good range of bar snacks, including haddock fish
pie, lamb and apricot tagine, salmon fish cakes, and sweet
potato pie layered with apple and Wensleydale cheese
and topped with cheddar cheese pastry. Main courses
range from chicken breast stuffed with leeks and served
with Stilton cream sauce to vegetarian butternut squash
and spinach lasagne. Try squidgy chocolate roulade or
sticky ginger pudding from the dessert menu.
OPEN: 12-2.30 6.30-11 (Summer 12-3, 6-11) Closed: 2nd
2 weeks of Jan **BAR MEALS:** Lunch served: all week Dinner
served: all week 12-2 6-9.30 Av main course £6.50
RESTAURANT: Lunch served: all week Dinner served: all week
12-2 6-9.30 Av 3 course à la carte £16
BREWERY/COMPANY: Free House
PRINCIPAL BEERS: Theakston Best, Hesket Newmarket
Skiddaw Special, Scottish Courage John Smith's Smooth.
FACILITIES: Children welcome Children's licence Garden:
Food served outside, terrace **NOTES:** Parking 20

PUB WALK

Staveley
The Eagle & Child

This walk follows part of the Dales Way, an 84-mile/135km long-distance trail linking two of Britain's most beautiful National Parks – the Yorkshire Dales and the Lake District. The trail crosses pleasant pastoral landscapes, with views to the Lakeland foothills.

From the pub turn right and join the footpath, heading towards Kendal. Follow it for about a quarter of a mile (0.4km) until a signpost for the Dales Way on your left, just before the railway crossing. Take the path and go left across the fields through a kissing gate. Follow the track towards the wall on your left and through the gate to a farm road leading towards the River Kent. This area can be boggy in very wet weather. The path opens out into fields, following the course of the river until you reach a coppice and a stile. This stretch of the walk is known for its excellent fishing. Cross the stile, cut through the woods and across a field to a gap in the wall. The track rises slightly at this point and you are treated to a fine view of the river. Continue across the field to an old barn and gate. Pass through it and carry on to a bridge on your left. Further on is a weir renowned for leaping salmon. Cross the bridge and turn sharp left immediately, following the path through the woods and along the river. Veer left at the first fork and go down over a small footbridge. This area has plenty of wildlife – keep an eye out for heron. In spring and early summer drifts of daffodils and bluebells cover the ground. Eventually you arrive at a quiet back road to Burneside. Turn left along the road and follow it uphill to a superb viewpoint across the river. Staveley lies to your right and far to the left are remote fells. The road levels out; keep walking until you see a sign to your left. Go through the gate and down to 17th-century Staveley Park Farm. Pass through two gates and head back towards the river, over the bridge. On your right is the old wood mill, now housing local crafts. Exit to Staveley high street, turn left and return to the inn.

THE EAGLE & CHILD
Kendal Road, Staveley,
WINDERMERE, LA8 9LP
Tel: 01539 821320
Directions: Follow M6 to Jct 36 then A590 towards Kendal join A591 towards Windermere Stavely approx 2 miles
Recently undergone a major refurbishment, the inn's name refers to the crest of arms of the Lonsdale family, local landowners. Excellent walking country and scope for cycling and fishing. Appetising range of dishes. Well-kept local beers.
Open: 11–11
Bar Meals: 12–3 6–9
Children welcome. Garden and parking available.

Distance: 4 miles (6.4km)
Map: OS Landranger 97
Terrain: Rolling Cumbrian countryside bisected by the River Kent
Paths: Dales Way, roads, tracks and paths.
Gradient: Some climbing

Walk submitted and checked by Eagle & Child, Staveley

DERBYSHIRE

ALFRETON
Map 09 SK45

White Horse Inn ♀
Badger Ln, Woolley Moor DE55 6FG ☎ 01246 590319
Dir: From A632 (Matlock/Chesterfield rd) take B6036. Pub 1m after Ashover. From A61 take B6036 to Woolley Moor
Situated on an old toll road, close to Ogston Reservoir, this 18th-century inn has outstanding views over the Amber Valley. Dishes from the bar menu or restaurant carte can be taken anywhere in the pub, and options range from sandwiches, paninis and traditional fish and chips to pan-fried tuna on niçoise salad, steak on tomato and mushroom ragout with watercress butter.
OPEN: 12-2 6-11 (Sun 12-10.30, all day summer wknds) Closed: 26 Dec
BAR MEALS: Lunch served: all week Dinner served: all week 12-2 6-9 Av main course £5.50 **RESTAURANT:** Lunch served: all week Dinner served: all week 12-2 6-9 Av 3 course à la carte £13
BREWERY/COMPANY: Free House **PRINCIPAL BEERS:** five regularly changing guest ales. **FACILITIES:** Children welcome Garden: beer garden, patio, BBQ, outdoor eating Dogs allowed **NOTES:** Parking 50

ASHBOURNE
Map 09 SK14

Barley Mow Inn
Kirk Ireton DE6 3JP ☎ 01335 370306
On the edge of the Peak District National Park, this imposing inn at the head of the village street dates from 1683, and has remained largely unchanged over the years. Close to Carsington Water, ideal for sailing, fishing and bird watching. Ales from the cask and traditional cider; fresh granary rolls at lunchtime and evening meals for residents only.
OPEN: 12-2 7-11 Closed: Dec 25 & Dec 31
BREWERY/COMPANY: Free House **PRINCIPAL BEERS:** Marston's Pedigree, Hook Norton, Burton Bridge, Whim Hartington.
FACILITIES: Children welcome Garden: beer garden, Dogs allowed **ROOMS:** 5 bedrooms 5 en suite from s£25 d£45 No credit cards

Dog & Partridge Country Inn ★ ★ ◷ ♀
Swinscoe DE6 2HS ☎ 01335 343183 🖷 01335 342742
e-mail: dogpart@fsbdial.co.uk
Within easy reach of Alton Towers, sporting and show business links distinguish this 17th-century coaching inn. Chalets were added in 1966 for the Brazilian World Cup team, who practised in a nearby field. The inn has expanded over the years with a restaurant and stage area, supposedly for visiting celebrities. Very extensive bar and restaurant menus feature fish, grills, curries, pasta and salads, and vegetarians are well catered for.
OPEN: 11-11 **BAR MEALS:** Lunch served: all week Dinner served: all week 11-11 Av main course £7 **RESTAURANT:** Lunch served: all week Dinner served: all week 11-11 Av cost 3 course à la carte £20
BREWERY/COMPANY: Free House **PRINCIPAL BEERS:** Greene King Old Speckled Hen & Ruddles County, Hartington Best, Wells Bombardier, Scottish Courage Directors **FACILITIES:** Children welcome Garden: Food served outdoors, patio, BBQ Dogs allowed **NOTES:** Parking 50 **ROOMS:** 30 bedrooms 30 en suite from s£40 d£60

The Green Man ♦♦♦♦
St Johns St DE6 1GH ☎ 01335 345783 🖷 01335 346613
Dir: In town centre off A52
Located in the heart of Ashbourne, this 17th-century coaching inn has two bars, the Johnson and the Boswell. On the specials board you'll find fresh fish and shellfish, local game, and traditional favourites like beef in Guinness and home made pies. The comfortable en suite bedrooms are attractively decorated.
OPEN: 11-11 (Sun 12-10.30) Closed: Dec 25 **BAR MEALS:** Lunch served: all week Dinner served: all week 12-2.30 6-8.30 Av main course

£5 **BREWERY/COMPANY:** Free House
PRINCIPAL BEERS: Marston's Pedigree, Bass. **FACILITIES:** Children welcome Dogs allowed (not during meal times) **NOTES:** Parking 12 **ROOMS:** 18 bedrooms 18 en suite from s£40 d£60

BAKEWELL
Map 09 SK26

George Hotel ◷
Church St, Youlgreave DE45 1VW ☎ 01629 636292
e-mail: j.m.bather-tyncelyn@talk21.com

Family-run pub close to many popular attractions, including Haddon Hall and Chatsworth House, and a handy base for walking and rock climbing in the Peak District and Derbyshire Dales. Try one of the game dishes - pheasant, rabbit or hare - or a good choice of vegetarian meals. Alternatively, go for salmon steak, home-made pies, or fresh trout.
OPEN: all day **BAR MEALS:** Lunch served: all week Dinner served: all week 12-2 6.30-9 Av main course £6.50
PRINCIPAL BEERS: Scottish Courage Courage Directors, Bateman XB, John Smiths, Theakston. **FACILITIES:** Children welcome Dogs allowed (water) **NOTES:** Parking 20 **ROOMS:** 3 bedrooms 3 en suite No credit cards

Pick of the Pubs

The Lathkil Hotel
Over Haddon DE45 1JE ☎ 01629 812501 🖷 01629 812501
e-mail: info@lathkil.co.uk
Dir: 2m E of Bakewell
Formerly 'The Miners Arms', named from the old lead mines that date back to Roman times, an overnight stay here remains in the memory for its panoramic views from the Victorian-style bar of the hills and dales of the Peak District. Home-cooked food has an enviable reputation locally with a lunchtime hot and cold buffet in summer and more extensive evening choices supplemented by cooked-to-order pizzas. Following onion bhajis with cucumber raita or tiger prawns in filo, indulge perhaps in a fruit sorbet before tackling sea bass with garlic and rosemary, Wootton Farm venison steak with Stilton sauce or Barbary duck breast with blackcurrant coulis. More conventional steaks with optional sauces and steak, kidney and oyster pie, along with a daily vegetarian dish, are regular alternatives. To follow perhaps treacle tart or toffee and apple crumble from the home-made puddings list or cheese with biscuits.
OPEN: 11.30-3 7-11 (Summer open all day Sat-Sun)
BAR MEALS: Lunch served: all week 12-2 Av main course £6.50 **RESTAURANT:** Dinner served: all week 7-9 Av 3 course à la carte £13.50 9 **PRINCIPAL BEERS:** Whim Hartington, Timothy Taylor Landlord, Wells Bombardier, Marston's Pedigree.
FACILITIES: Children welcome Garden: beer garden, outdoor eating Dogs allowed (water) **NOTES:** Parking 28 **ROOMS:** 4 bedrooms 4 en suite from s£37.50 d£55

BAKEWELL continued

Pick of the Pubs

The Monsal Head Hotel ★ ★ 🛏 ♈
Monsal Head DE45 1NL ☎ 01629 640250 📠 01629 640815
e-mail: Christine@monsalhead.com
*Dir: A6 from Bakewell towards Buxton. 1.5m to Ashford. Follow
Monsal Head signs, B6465 for 1m*

Set against a spectacular backdrop of hills and dales, the
disused viaduct at Monsal Head has long been a familiar
landmark in the Peak District. It even crops up on
television from time to time, most notably in the drama
series *Peak Practice*, which is filmed locally. Long before
the era of TV, horses pulled guests and their luggage from
the railway station up the steep incline to the hotel. The
old stable is now a cosy bar and part of the hotel. One
menu operates throughout the restaurant, bar and eating
area, with such dishes as cod in beer batter, gamekeepers
pie, The Monsal Stilton burger, and tagliatelle of oyster
mushrooms, as well as small plates, grills, salads,
omelettes and jacket potatoes. Eight real ales are always
available.
OPEN: 11.30-11 (Sun 12-10.30) Closed: 25 Dec
BAR MEALS: Lunch served: all week Dinner served: all week
12–9 Av main course £8 **RESTAURANT:** Lunch served: all week
Dinner served: all week 12–9 7–9.30 Av 3 course à la carte £16
BREWERY/COMPANY: Free House
PRINCIPAL BEERS: Theakston Old Peculier, Timothy Taylor
Landlord, Scottish Courage Courage Directors, Whim Hartington.
FACILITIES: Children welcome Garden: Food served outdoors
Dogs allowed **NOTES:** Parking 20 **ROOMS:** 7 bedrooms 7 en
suite from s£40 d£40

The Rutland Arms Hotel ★ ★ ★ 🏅 ♈
The Square DE45 1BT ☎ 01629 812812 📠 01629 812309
e-mail: rutland@bakewell.demon.co.uk
Dir: Town centre
The Duke of Rutland planned to create a spa town to rival the
Duke of Devonshire's nearby Buxton. So he built this grand
coaching inn that dominates Bakewell's main street. Byron,
Turner, and Wordsworth all stayed at the inn and Jane Austen
wrote Pride and Prejudice here. Popular dishes include Thai
green curry, Rutland fish cakes, meat balls, grilled beef rump
steak and roasted trout. There are also lighter meals,
baguettes, cold salads and floured baps.
OPEN: 11-11 **BAR MEALS:** Lunch served: all week Dinner served:

continued

all week 12–2 6.30–9 **RESTAURANT:** Lunch served: all week Dinner
served: all week 12–2 7–9 Av 2 course fixed price £19.50
BREWERY/COMPANY: Free House **PRINCIPAL BEERS:** Greene
King Abbot Ale, Carlsberg-Tetley Bitter, Smooth flow.
FACILITIES: Children welcome Dogs allowed **NOTES:** Parking 35
ROOMS: 35 bedrooms 35 en suite from s£47 d£79

BAMFORD — Map 09 SK28

Pick of the Pubs

Yorkshire Bridge Inn ★ ★ 🛏
Ashopton Rd S33 0AZ ☎ 01433 651361 📠 01433 651361
e-mail: mr@ybridge.force9.co.uk
Dir: A57 from M1, L onto A6013, pub 1m on R

A classic 19th-century inn surrounded by majestic Peak
District scenery and immortalised by the Dambusters'
wartime training over the nearby Ladybower reservoir. Its
smart accommodation is particularly useful to know in the
area, with a slightly up-market feel also pervading the
bars and dining room. Meals in the bars and restaurant
are popular. Dishes may include roasted sea bass with
lobster, white wine and tarragon sauce, pork and leek
sausages and Italian proscuitto ravioli cooked in a creamy
mushroom, Parmesan and red pepper sauce among the
daily specials. Regular main dishes may be steak and
kidney pie, chicken Italiano, barbecued English lamb
chops, breaded fried scampi and Mediterranean vegetable
tart. Grills, jacket potatoes, sandwiches and salad platters
make up the snack numbers.
OPEN: 11-11 **BAR MEALS:** Lunch served: all week Dinner
served: all week 12–2 6–9 Av main course £7
RESTAURANT: Lunch served: all week Dinner served: all week
12–2 6–9 **BREWERY/COMPANY:** Free House
PRINCIPAL BEERS: Scottish Courage Theakston Best & Old
Peculier, Interbrew Stones Bitter, Bass, Carlsberg-Tetley Bitter.
FACILITIES: Children welcome Garden: Food served outside
NOTES: Parking 40 **ROOMS:** 14 bedrooms 14 en suite from
s£45 d£60

BEELEY — Map 09 SK26

Pick of the Pubs

The Devonshire Arms 🛏 ♈
The Square DE4 2NR ☎ 01629 733259 📠 01629 733259
See Pick of the Pubs on page 117

OPEN: 11-11
BAR MEALS: L served all week.
D served all week. 12-9.30 Av main
course £5.95
RESTAURANT: L served all week.
D served all week. 12-9.30
Av cost 3 courses £10
BREWERY/COMPANY:
FREE HOUSE
PRINCIPAL BEERS: Black Sheep
Best & Special, Theakston Old
Peculier & XB, Interbrew Bass
FACILITIES: Children welcome.
Garden: Patio area, Food served
outside
NOTES: Parking 120

The Devonshire Arms

This civilised dining pub nestles in a picturesque village at the gateway to Chatsworth House, one of Britain's most palatial stately homes. Beeley's twisting lanes lie within the Peak District National Park, and the village itself is a designated conservation area.

The Square DE4 2NR
☎ 01629 733259 📠 01629 733259
Dir: From A6 onto B6012 at Rowsley.

The Devonshire Arms has a long history, having been built as three honey-coloured stone cottages in 1726 and converted into a popular coaching inn in 1747. John Grosvenor, the present owner, keeps a list of all the innkeepers since that date. In July 1872 a tremendous thunderstorm made the road here quite impassable. History was repeated in August 1997, and a marked beam in the bar records the water level of the second flood. Charles Dickens was a frequent visitor, and it's rumoured that King Edward VII often came here to meet his mistress, Alice Keppel. Today, you'll be greeted by oak beams, stone flagged floors and winter fires. Families, walkers and cyclists are always

welcome, and motorists will appreciate the large car park. Meals are freshly cooked to order, and the extensive menu is also served on the patio in warm weather. Come for home-made soup and a baguette if you must, but starters like seafood hors d'oeuvre, duck and fig terrine or melon with summer fruits, herald a fine selection of main courses. Choose from venison in plum sauce, Barnsley chop with mint jelly, traditional haggis and neeps, or three cheese broccoli and pasta bake. The weekend begins on Friday evenings with an extensive choice of fish - trout with spinach and almond stuffing, deep fried cod in beer batter, or grilled halibut are typical - and continues with a leisurely Victorian breakfast menu between 10.00 and 12.00 on Sundays.

England

BIRCHOVER — Map 09 SK26

Pick of the Pubs

The Druid Inn
Main St DE4 2BL ☎ 01629 650302 📠 01629 650559
Dir: From A6 between Matlock & Bakewell take B5056, signed Ashbourne.Take 2nd L to Birchover
This ivy-covered free house stands in a quiet village above Darley Dale, close to the edge of the Peak District National Park. The nearby caves, canopies and terracing at Row Tor Rocks were supposedly once inhabited by druids. In fact, most of these curious carvings were carried out in the 19th century by a delightfully eccentric local vicar, the Rev Thomas Eyres. A large two storey extension supplements the narrow bar with its open fire and blackboard menus, and there's a terrace garden for alfresco summer dining. The eclectic menu has long been popular with the pub's faithful clientele. You might start with spicy lamb meatballs, deep-fried Brie with redcurrant dip or salmon, cod and prawn fishcakes. Follow these with dishes such as roast Barbary duck breast with orange, honey and grape sauce, chicken tikka masala or Derbyshire beef and vegetable stew with herb dumplings. Puddings include warm Bakewell pudding and apple and marzipan torte.
OPEN: 12-3 7-11 Closed: 25/26 Dec **BAR MEALS:** Lunch served: all week Dinner served: all week 12-2 7-9 Av main course £10 **RESTAURANT:** Lunch served: all week Dinner served: all week 12-2 7-9 Av 3 course à la carte £17.50
BREWERY/COMPANY: Free House
PRINCIPAL BEERS: Marstons Pedigree, Druid Bitter.
FACILITIES: Children welcome Garden: Food served outside. Terrace area Dogs allowed (guide dogs only inside, water & biscuits) **NOTES:** Parking 36

BIRCH VALE — Map 09 SK08

Pick of the Pubs

The Waltzing Weasel Inn
New Mills Rd SK22 1BT ☎ 01663 743402 📠 01663 743402
e-mail: w-weazel@zen.co.uk
Dir: W from M1 at Chesterfield
Set within the heart of the Peak District Hills, a popular traditional English country inn beloved of walkers and business people alike – no music nor machines and no mobile phones permitted. Country antiques are a feature of the bedrooms and bar, while from the garden and mullion-windowed restaurant there are dramatic views of Kinder Scout, one of the region's most famous natural landmarks. Solidly English bar menus are supplemented by specialities from the owners' love of Italy. Thus duck and cherry pie and pork loin rub shoulders with Fantasia Italiana – a confection of Italian delights which vary daily and might include tarta peperonata, roast fennel, black olive crostini, aubergine with chilli sauce and prosciutto. Other options range from casserole of the day to vegetable crêpe. Pizzas are a regular feature and there is à la carte dining nightly in the restaurant. On Sunday only, traditional roast beef with Yorkshire pudding.
OPEN: 12-3 6-11 (Sun 12-3, 6-10.30) **BAR MEALS:** 12-2 7-9.30 **RESTAURANT:** 12-2 7-9
BREWERY/COMPANY: Free House
PRINCIPAL BEERS: Marston's Best & Pedigree, Timothy Taylor

Landlord, Camerons Strongarm. **FACILITIES:** Garden: Food served outside, patio Dogs allowed **NOTES:** Parking 42 **ROOMS:** 8 bedrooms 8 en suite from s£45 d£75

BRADWELL — Map 09 SK18

The Bowling Green
Smalldale S33 9JQ ☎ 01433 620450 📠 01433 620280
The Bowling Green is an attractive 16th-century, white village inn decorated with colourful hanging baskets. Bedrooms.

BRASSINGTON — Map 09 SK25

Ye Olde Gate Inne
Well St DE4 4HJ ☎ 01629 540448 📠 01629 540448
e-mail: p.s.burlinson@amserve.net
Dir: 3m NW of Carsington Water
The inn was built in 1616 of local stone and salvaged Armada timbers, and has one or two supernatural residents. There is a huge inglenook fireplace with a range, and a smaller one in the snug. Connections are claimed with Bonnie Prince Charlie's rebellion. Menu includes cod and prawn crumble, BBQ chicken with Parma ham and cheese, cod and mussels provençale, or monkfish kebabs.
OPEN: 12-2.30 6-11 (Sun 7-10.30) **BAR MEALS:** Lunch served: Tue-Sun Dinner served: Tue-Sun 12-1.45 7-8.45 Av main course £6
BREWERY/COMPANY: W'hampton & Dudley
PRINCIPAL BEERS: Marstons Pedigree & Head Brewer's Choice.
FACILITIES: Garden: Food served outside. Quaint garden Dogs allowed (water provided) **NOTES:** Parking 20

BUXTON — Map 09 SK07

Bull i' th' Horn
Flagg SK17 9QQ ☎ 01298 83348
Part medieval hall and part roadhouse in the heart of the Dales, this charming pub dates back to 1472 and has oak panelled walls setting off a display of armour, swords and pikes. Medieval banquets are served in full period dress, and jesters, jugglers and knights in battle can be provided for larger events. Dishes range from paneer curry to haunch of lamb in red wine and rosemary sauce.
OPEN: 12-2.30 6-11 **BAR MEALS:** Lunch served: all week Dinner served: all week 12-2.30 6-9 Av main course £6.50
RESTAURANT: Lunch served: all week Dinner served: all week Av 3 course à la carte £17 **PRINCIPAL BEERS:** Robinsons Best Bitter, Fredericks, XB, Cumbria Way. **FACILITIES:** Children welcome Garden: Food served outside Dogs allowed (water)
NOTES: Parking 70 **ROOMS:** 3 bedrooms 3 en suite from d£50

The Queen Anne ♦♦♦
Great Hucklow, nr Tideswell SK17 8RF ☎ 01298 871246
e-mail: malcom_hutton@bigfoot.com
Dir: A623 turn off at Anchor pub toward Bradwell, 2nd R to Great Hucklow
A traditional country inn with log fires and cosy atmosphere, serving as an ideal base for touring and exploring the spectacular Peak District National Park. Reputedly haunted by the friendly ghost of a previous licensee. Try the Lincolnshire sausages or perhaps one of the fish dishes - haddock, scampi, tuna steak or salmon with hollandaise sauce.
OPEN: 12-3 (except Mon & Wed) 6-11 (Sat 11.30-11, Sun 12-10.30)
BAR MEALS: Lunch served: Wed-Sun Dinner served: Wed-Sun 12-2 7-9 Av main course £6 **BREWERY/COMPANY:** Free House
PRINCIPAL BEERS: Mansfield Cask Ale, Oakwell Barnsley Bitter, Storm Ale Force. **FACILITIES:** Children welcome Garden:

continued

continued

patio/terrace, food served outdoors, BBQ Dogs allowed
NOTES: Parking 30 **ROOMS:** 2 bedrooms 2 en suite from s£25
d£50

The Sun Inn
33 High St SK17 6HA ☎ 01298 23452
Traditional town pub full of beams, boards, open fires and a
wealth of memorabilia. New management now offers an
extensive and improved menu. Reports please.

CASTLETON   Map 09 SK18

The George
Castle St S33 8QG ☎ 01433 620238 ▤ 01433 620886
The earliest known reference to this pub comes from the
Domesday Book, and the building has been used as an
alehouse since at least 1557. This distinguished heritage is
guarded and extended by the current team who serve an
imaginative international menu. Typical menu includes pan-
fried seared salmon fillet, beer-battered cod, steak and kidney
pie, lamb curry, and chicken breast with a julienne of leeks.
OPEN: 12–3 6–11 **BAR MEALS:** Lunch served: all week Dinner
served: all week 12–2 12–2 Av main course £6.95
RESTAURANT: Lunch served: all week Dinner served: all week 12–2
7–9 **BREWERY/COMPANY:** Free House
PRINCIPAL BEERS: John Smiths, Wadworths 6x, Flowers IPA.
FACILITIES: Children welcome Garden: Food served outside Dogs
allowed

The Olde Nag's Head
Cross St S33 8WH ☎ 01433 620248 ▤ 01433 621501
Grey-stone 17th-century coaching inn situated in the heart of
the Peak District National Park, close to Chatsworth House,
Haddon Hall and miles of wonderful walks. Cosy lounge bar
with open fire and antiques and a Victorian restaurant. Tea
room, weekend lunchtime carvery. New owners.

DARLEY ABBEY   Map 09 SK33

The Abbey 🐑
Darley St DE22 1DX ☎ 01332 558297
Dir: *A38 onto A6 to Duffield Rd*
The Abbey was built in 1147 as part of an enormous
monastery, most of which was destroyed in the dissolution.
What is now the pub was probably the bakehouse or brewery
originally, and has served as cottages and shops in its time. It
still has a spiral stone staircase, beehive bread oven and,
apparently, some ghostly visitations. Church pews and
tapestries retain the period feel, and pub food includes
sandwiches, home-cooked ham, and chicken curry.
OPEN: 11.30–2.30 6–11 (all day Sat-Sun) Closed: Dec 25
BAR MEALS: Lunch served: all week 12–2 Av main course £5.50
BREWERY/COMPANY: Samuel Smith
PRINCIPAL BEERS: Samuel Smith Old Brewery Bitter.
FACILITIES: Children welcome Dogs allowed (water)
NOTES: Parking 20 No credit cards

DERBY   Map 09 SK33

The Alexandra Hotel
203 Siddals Rd DE1 2QE ☎ 01332 293993 ▤ 01332 293993
Two-roomed hotel filled with railway memorabilia. Noted for
its real ale (450 different brews on tap each year), range of
malt whiskies, and friendly atmosphere. Traditional pub food.

DOE LEA   Map 09 SK46

Hardwick Inn 🐑 ♀
Hardwick Park S44 5QJ ☎ 01246 850245 ▤ 01246 856365
e-mail: Batty@hardwickinn.co.uk
Dir: *M1 J29 take A6175. 0.5m L (signed Stainsby/Hardwick Hall). After
Stainsby, 2m L at staggered jnctn*

Dating from 1607 and built of locally quarried sandstone, this
historic inn has been in the same family since 1928. Extensive
gardens surround the pub and all food is home-cooked.
Home-made pies feature on the menu and the specials board
includes fresh fish delivered daily. Also available are the likes
of rabbit and cider casserole, Hardwick mixed grill and
ploughman's. Various salads and sandwiches are also
available. A very popular location near Hardwick Hall and the
M1.
OPEN: 11.30–11 **BAR MEALS:** Lunch served: all week Dinner
served: all week 11.30–9.30 Av main course £6
RESTAURANT: Lunch served: Tues-Sun 12–2 Dinner served:
Tues-Sat 7–9 Av 3 course à la carte £15 Av 3 course fixed price £12
BREWERY/COMPANY: Free House
PRINCIPAL BEERS: Theakston Old Peculier, XB & Black Bull, Greene
King Old Speckled Hen & Ruddles County. **FACILITIES:** Children
welcome Children's licence Garden: Patio, food served outside
Dogs allowed

DRONFIELD   Map 09 SK37

The Old Sidings
91 Chesterfield Rd S18 2XE ☎ 01246 410023 ▤ 01246 292202
Unpretentious, stone-built tavern, situated just 30 feet from
the main Sheffield railway line. A must for railway buffs, it's
full of railway paraphernalia.

The Trout Inn NEW
33 Valley Rd, Barlow S18 7SL ☎ 0114 2890893 ▤ 0114 2891284
A few miles outside Chesterfield this quaint country pub is
located at the gateway to the superb Peak District, renowned
for its walking and splendid scenery. There is a pleasant, cosy
atmosphere inside where you can dine by candlelight,
sampling the inn's extensive menu. Among the main courses
are halibut in white wine sauce, whole grilled sea bass, duck
breast in a port and berry sauce and chicken stuffed with
Stilton.
OPEN: 12–3 6–11 **BAR MEALS:** Lunch served: all week Dinner
served: all week 12–2.30 6.30–9 Av main course £7
RESTAURANT: Lunch served: all week Dinner served: all week
12–2.30 6.30–9 Av 3 course à la carte £15
BREWERY/COMPANY: Free House
PRINCIPAL BEERS: Wadworth 6X, Scottish Courage John Smith's,
Worthington. **FACILITIES:** Children welcome Garden: Paved patio,
food served outside **NOTES:** Parking 20

England

EYAM   Map 09 SK27

Miners Arms ♦♦♦ ⚲
Water Ln S32 5RG ☎ 01433 630853 📠 01433 639050
Dir: Off B6521, 5m S of Bakewell

Expect a warm welcome at this 17th-century inn and restaurant in the famous plague village of Eyam. During Roman times the village was an important centre for lead mining – hence the name. Supposedly, the inn is haunted by the ghosts of two girls who died in a fire on this site. Food is freshly prepared with the use of local produce and the seasonally changing dining room menu is traditionally English in style with some French influences. Good bar meals include lamb casserole, salmon in white wine and cream sauce, breast of chicken and gammon with egg or pineapple.
OPEN: 12–11 **BAR MEALS:** Lunch served: all week Dinner served: Mon–Sat 12–6.30 Av main course £7 **RESTAURANT:** Dinner served: Tue–Sat 7–9 Av 3 course à la carte £20 **BREWERY/COMPANY:** Free House **PRINCIPAL BEERS:** Interbrew Bass, Stones Bitter, Scottish Courage John Smith's. **FACILITIES:** Garden: seating at front and rear of pub Dogs allowed **NOTES:** Parking 50
ROOMS: 7 bedrooms 7 en suite from s£30 d£60

FENNY BENTLEY   Map 09 SK14

The Coach and Horses Inn ⚲
DE6 1LB ☎ 01335 350246

Beautifully located on the edge of the Peak District National Park, this family-run former coaching inn is handy for Dovedale and the Tissington Trail. It's a 17th-century building providing an inviting setting for well-kept ales and good home cooking. The blackboard menu offers a choice of firm favourites and new dishes based on fresh seasonal produce – maybe poached Mayfield trout, venison, port and thyme casserole, or vegetable rogan josh.
OPEN: 11–11 **BAR MEALS:** Lunch served: all week Dinner served: all week 12–2.30 6.30–9 Av main course £6.50
RESTAURANT: Lunch served: all week Dinner served: all week

12–2.30 6.30–9 Av 3 course à la carte £13
BREWERY/COMPANY: Free House
PRINCIPAL BEERS: Marston's Pedigree, Timothy Taylor Landlord, Black Sheep Best. **FACILITIES:** Children welcome Garden: Food served outside **NOTES:** Parking 24

FOOLOW   Map 09 SK17

The Bulls Head Inn ♦♦♦♦ 🐑
S32 5QR ☎ 01433 630873 📠 01433 631738
Dir: Just off A623, N of Stoney Middleton

Typically English, family-owned inn with flagged floors, roaring fires and an inglenook fireplace in the oak-panelled dining room. Set in a tiny conservation village in the heart of the Peak National Park it's a welcoming venue for 'walkers and their boots and dogs'. Fresh fish such as sea bass and monkfish tails – perhaps with lime and ginger cream – are seasonally supplemented by the likes of rabbit and prune casserole and beef fillet in brandied gravy.
OPEN: 12–3 5.30–11 **BAR MEALS:** Lunch served: Tue–Sun 12–2 Dinner served: Tue–Sat 7–9 Av main course £9 **RESTAURANT:** Lunch served: Tue–Sun Dinner served: Tue–Sat 12–2 7–9
BREWERY/COMPANY: Free House **PRINCIPAL BEERS:** Black Sheep Best, Marston's Pedigree, Carlsberg-Tetley Bitter, Fuller's London Pride. **FACILITIES:** Children welcome Garden: Patio, food served outdoors Dogs allowed (water) **NOTES:** Parking 20
ROOMS: 3 bedrooms 3 en suite from s£40 d£60

FROGGATT

Pick of the Pubs

The Chequers Inn 🐑 ⚲
Froggatt Edge, Calver, Hope Valley S32 3ZJ
☎ 01433 630231 📠 01433 631072
On the steep banks of Froggatt Edge high above Calver Bridge and close to many Peak District attractions, this Grade II listed building was converted from 18th-century cottages and now offers imaginative food and comfortable en suite accommodation. The smart interior has a distinct bistro feel with rag-washed yellow walls, bare board floors, attractive prints and comfortable furnishings. The Chequers dinner menu is characterised by a wide variety of European and British dishes, including game in season, and the daily changing blackboard menu might offer Thai fish cakes, speciality local sausages, grilled marinated shark steak and game casserole. Other options may include whole grilled plaice, mackerel fillets and grilled cod steak, as well as a range of hearty sandwiches. Behind the pub, a landscaped beer garden gives way to some ten acres of steep, wild woodland.

continued   *continued*

OPEN: 12–3 6–11 Closed: 25 Dec **BAR MEALS:** Lunch served: all week Dinner served: all week 12–2 6–9.30 Av main course £9 **BREWERY/COMPANY:** Free House **PRINCIPAL BEERS:** Theakstons Best Bitter, Marston's Pedigree, Scottish Courage John Smiths. **FACILITIES:** Garden: Food served outside **NOTES:** Parking 45 **ROOMS:** 5 bedrooms 5 en suite from s£54 d£64

GRINDLEFORD   Map 09 SK27

Pick of the Pubs

The Maynard Arms ★ ★ ★ 🛏 ♀
Main Rd S32 2HE ☎ 01433 630321 📠 01433 630445
e-mail: info@maynardarms.co.uk
Dir: From M1 take A619 into Chesterfield, then onto Baslow. A623 to Calver, R into Grindleford
This fine 1898 coaching inn overlooks the village and the Derwent Valley beyond and is situated at the heart of the Peak District National Park. During the 1950s and 60s it frequently accommodated touring Australian cricket teams. The interior design is thoroughly up-to-date and the Longshore Bar and Padley Restaurant menus have a confidently contemporary approach. Fishy dishes include fillet of salmon dressed on mange-tout, with fine beans, cut asparagus and a light tarragon sauce, and grilled halibut steak with sautéed courgettes and a prawn and caper butter. Local produce is a feature of two favourite dishes: roast rack of Derbyshire pork glazed with Mozzarella and served with sautéed greens and charcuterie sauce, and rabbit casserole cooked with herbs and winter vegetables. For a traditional finish, go for the original Bakewell pudding and custard, or a platter of Yorkshire and Derbyshire cheeses.
OPEN: 11–3 5.30–11 (Sun 12–10.30) **BAR MEALS:** Lunch served: all week Dinner served: all week 12–2 6–9.30 Av main course £8 **RESTAURANT:** Lunch served: Sun–Fri 12–2 Dinner served: all week 7–9.30 Av 4 course fixed price £23.50 **BREWERY/COMPANY:** Free House **PRINCIPAL BEERS:** Interbrew Boddingtons Bitter, Greene King Old Speckled Hen, Marston's Pedigree, Timothy Taylor Landlord. **FACILITIES:** Children's licence **NOTES:** Parking 60 **ROOMS:** 10 bedrooms 10 en suite from s£69 d£79

HASSOP   Map 09 SK27

Eyre Arms 🛏 ♀
DE45 1NS ☎ 01629 640390
Dir: Take the A6 to Bakewell, then the A619 towards Sheffield, after 0.5m turn onto the B6001 to Hathersage & Hassop
This 17th-century coaching inn, just a short drive north of Bakewell, is associated with the Civil War and has its own Cavalier ghost. Unaltered since the 1950s, it's a traditional pub with oak pews, beams, old photographs and maps creating a cosy atmosphere. The garden, with eight tables around the fountain, overlooks rolling Peak District countryside and there are some lovely local walks. Typical dishes are rabbit pie, minted lamb banquet and chicken Hartington.
OPEN: 11.30–3 6.30–11 (Nov–March eve open from 7pm) Closed: 25 Dec **BAR MEALS:** Lunch served: all week Dinner served: all week 12–2 6.30–9 Av main course £6.95 **BREWERY/COMPANY:** Free House **PRINCIPAL BEERS:** Marston Pedigree, John Smiths, Black Sheep Special. **FACILITIES:** Garden: beer garden, outdoor eating **NOTES:** Parking 20

HATHERSAGE   Map 09 SK28

Millstone Inn ◆◆◆◆ ♀
Sheffield Rd S32 1DA ☎ 01433 650258 📠 01433 651664
e-mail: jerry@millstone.fsbusiness.co.uk
With its superb views over the unspoiled Hope Valley, this tastefully furnished former coaching inn has been reinvented for the twenty-first century. There's an open fire in the bar, and the relaxed, civilised restaurant makes extensive use of fresh local produce. Start with mussel and saffron risotto or chilled gazpacho soup, before moving on to lamb and asparagus with couscous, baked gnocchi with Wensleydale, or monkfish and pernod. Comfortable well equipped bedrooms are suitable for both the business and leisure guest.
OPEN: 11.30–3 6–11 (Sat 11–11, Sun 12–10.30) **BAR MEALS:** Lunch served: all week Dinner served: all week 12–2 6–9 Av main course £7 **RESTAURANT:** Dinner served: all week 6.30–9.30 Av 3 course à la carte £18 **BREWERY/COMPANY:** Free House **PRINCIPAL BEERS:** Taylor Landlord, Black Sheep, Stones plus guest beers. **FACILITIES:** Children welcome Children's licence Garden: outdoor eating, patio, historic well **NOTES:** Parking 50 **ROOMS:** 7 bedrooms 7 en suite from s£35 d£55

The Plough Inn ◆◆◆◆ 🛏 ♀
Leadmill Bridge S32 1BA
☎ 01433 650319 & 650180 📠 01433 651049
e-mail: theploughinn@leadmillbridge.co.uk

Situated in nine acres of its own grounds by the meandering River Derwent, this 17th-century stone-built inn was originally a farmstead. The public rooms are charming, with exposed beams and brickwork. Food is prepared using the finest quality produce and the menu is an eclectic mix of modern European and traditional English. The garden is a popular sun-trap, the perfect place to relax over a meal, a glass of wine or afternoon tea.
OPEN: 11–11 Closed: Dec 25 **BAR MEALS:** Lunch served: all week Dinner served: all week 11.30–2.30 6.30–9.30 Av main course £10 **RESTAURANT:** Lunch served: all week Dinner served: all week 11.30–2.30 6.30–9.30 Av 3 course à la carte £20 **BREWERY/COMPANY:** Free House **PRINCIPAL BEERS:** Theakstons Old Peculier, Carlsberg-Tetley, Adnams Bitter, Smiles Best. **FACILITIES:** Children welcome Garden: **NOTES:** Parking 50 **ROOMS:** 5 bedrooms 5 en suite from s£49.50 d£69.50

HAYFIELD   Map 09 SK08

The Sportsman
Kinder Rd SK22 2LE ☎ 01663 741565
Dir: Hayfield is 5m S of Glossop on A624
Standing in the glorious Peak District, this comfortable, family-run inn is an obvious watering hole for those tackling the

continued

England

HAYFIELD continued

popular Kinder Scout Trail, which runs out of Hayfield village centre towards Kinder Scout. Wholesome home-cooked food and hand-pulled beers are available in the traditional bar, with its warming log fires and welcoming atmosphere. Expect Somerset pork casseroled in cider, pan-fried Thai chicken in Oriental sauce, fresh Scottish plaice and spinach pancake topped with cheese among the range of blackboard dishes.
OPEN: 12–3 7–11 Closed: 1Wk Mar/Oct **BAR MEALS:** Lunch served: Tue–Sun 12–2 Dinner served: Mon–Sat 7–9 Av main course £8.75 **RESTAURANT:** Lunch served: Tue–Sun 12–2 Dinner served: Mon–Sat 7–9 Av 3 course à la carte £16.25
BREWERY/COMPANY: Thwaites **PRINCIPAL BEERS:** Thwaites Bitter & Reward, Daniels Hammer. **FACILITIES:** Garden: Food served outside Dogs allowed (water bowl) **NOTES:** Parking 3
ROOMS: 6 bedrooms 4 en suite from s£30 d£40

HOGNASTON
Map 09 SK25

Pick of the Pubs

The Red Lion Inn
Main St DE6 1PR ☎ 01335 370396 ▤ 01335 370961
e-mail: lionrouge@msn.com
Dir: M1 J25 take A52 towards Derby & Ashbourne. Hognaston on B5035

A traditional 17th-century country inn, with quaint beamed ceilings and open fireplaces, where the owners have been at pains to maintain a pub atmosphere and a value for money philosophy while serving the kind of food you'd expect in a restaurant. House specialities include a starter of warm smoked chicken set on a bed of seasonal leaves and croûtons, topped with a Dijon and honey dressing, and a main course of lamb shank set on a basil mash with a rich port and mint gravy. The Red Lion is located in the main street of a small village, surrounded by attractive countryside, so it is popular with walkers who stop off for lunch or use the inn as a base for exploring the nearby Peak District National Park. With three well-appointed letting rooms available, customers often decide to make a night of it and stay for breakfast in the conservatory.
OPEN: 12–3 6–11 **BAR MEALS:** Lunch served: Tue–Sun 12–2 Dinner served: Tue–Sat 6.30–9 Av main course £8.95
RESTAURANT: Lunch served: Tue–Sun 12–2 Dinner served: Tue–Sat 6.30–9 Av 3 course à la carte £16.85
BREWERY/COMPANY: Free House
PRINCIPAL BEERS: Greene King Old Speckled Hen, Interbrew Bass. **NOTES:** Parking 30 **ROOMS:** 3 bedrooms 3 en suite from s£45 d£75

HOPE
Map 09 SK18

Cheshire Cheese Inn ♀
Edale Rd S33 6ZF ☎ 01433 620381 ▤ 01433 620411
e-mail: cheshire.cheese@barbox.net
Dir: On A6187 between Sheffield & Chapel-en-le-Frith
In heart of the Peak District, close to the Pennine Way, this 16th-century inn offers a traditional pub experience in wonderful surroundings. It's on the old salt route, and payment for lodging in those days was made in cheese, hence the name. Real ales and home-cooked food are further attractions, including the Cheshire Cheese Mammoth Mixed Grill, chicken jalfrezi, poached salmon in prawn and mushroom sauce, liver and bacon on a bed of mash, and Cumberland sausage. Sandwiches, ploughmans' and jacket potatoes also available.
OPEN: 12–3 6.30–11 (all day Sat) **BAR MEALS:** Lunch served: all week Dinner served: all week 12–2 6.30–9 **RESTAURANT:** Lunch served: all week Dinner served: all week 12–2 6.30–9 Av 3 course à la carte £13.50 **BREWERY/COMPANY:** Free House
PRINCIPAL BEERS: Barnsley Bitter, Wentworthy Pale Ale, Black Sheep Best, Timothy Taylor Landlord. **FACILITIES:** Garden: Food served outside, patio Dogs allowed (water) **NOTES:** Parking 8
ROOMS: 1 bedrooms 1 en suite from d£60

ILKESTON
Map 09 SK44

Stanhope Arms
Stanhope St DE7 4QA ☎ 0115 9322603
Handy for the M1, yet set in an unspoilt village, this friendly local serves excellent home-made pies.

LITTON
Map 09 SK17

Red Lion Inn
SK17 8QU ☎ 01298 871458 ▤ 01298 871458
e-mail: redlioninn@littonvillage.fsnet.co.uk
Dir: just off the A623 Chesterfield to Stockport rd 1m E of Tideswell
Overlooking the village green, a 17th-century pub where in summer visitors can enjoy a meal under the trees. Many local walks begin and end here, and it is therefore very popular with hikers. Indoors it's all beams and log fires in cosy rooms, where favourite dishes include braised steak in real ale, duck in whisky, and steak, ale and mushroom pie.
OPEN: 11–3 6–11 (Sat–Sun 11–11) **BAR MEALS:** Lunch served: all week Dinner served: Mon–Sat 12–2 6–8.30 Av main course £6.50
BREWERY/COMPANY: Free House **PRINCIPAL BEERS:** Jennings Bitter, Barnsley Bitter, Shepherd Neame Spitfire, Black Sheep Best.
FACILITIES: Dogs allowed

MATLOCK
Map 09 SK35

The White Lion Inn
195 Starkholmes Rd DE4 5JA ☎ 01629 582511 ▤ 01629 582511
e-mail: info@whitelion-matlock.com
Right in the heart of the Peak District, with spectacular views over Matlock Bath, this 18th-century inn is the ideal venue for a relaxing break. Close to many beautiful dales and valleys, and historic buildings it makes a good starting point. Typical dishes are Aberdeen Angus beef, medallions of ostrich fillet, wild Bodmin boar, supreme of chicken and hot smoked salmon. Ragout of mushrooms and baked goats' cheese feature among the appetising starters.

continued

OPEN: 12–3 5–11 (All day Sat-Sun) **BAR MEALS:** Lunch served: all week 12–2 Dinner served: Mon-Sat 7–9.30 Av main course £6 **RESTAURANT:** Lunch served: all week 12–2 Dinner served: Tue-Sat 7–9.30 Av 3 course à la carte £20 **BREWERY/COMPANY:** Burtonwood **PRINCIPAL BEERS:** Scottish Courage John Smiths, Marston's Pedigree plus guest ales. **FACILITIES:** Garden: Food served outside, Boules pitch Dogs allowed (water) **NOTES:** Parking 50 **ROOMS:** 3 bedrooms 3 en suite from s£35 d£48

MELBOURNE   Map 09 SK32

Hardinge Arms
54-56 Main St, Kings Newton DE73 1BX
☎ 01332 863808 📠 01332 865892
Handy for Donnington and Midlands Airports. Smart lounge area, children welcome, chalet-style bedrooms.

RIPLEY   Map 09 SK35

The Moss Cottage
Nottingham Rd DE5 3JT ☎ 01773 742555 📠 01773 741063
Specialising in carvery dishes, and offering four roast joints each day, the Moss Cottage also offers blackboard specials, and a selection of home-made puddings. Look out for the likes of chicken princess, 10oz gammon with egg and pineapple, wild mushroom pasta, salmon linguini, lamb chops with Rosemary, fillet of pork Calvados, tuna pasta bake, mushroom Stroganoff, vegetable dim sum, or cod mornay. **OPEN:** 12–3 6–11 **BAR MEALS:** Lunch served: all week 12–3 Dinner served: Mon-Sat 6–9 Av main course £10 **RESTAURANT:** Lunch served: all week 12–3 Dinner served: Mon-Sat 6–9 Av 3 course à la carte £15 **BREWERY/COMPANY:** Free House **PRINCIPAL BEERS:** Interbrew Bass & Worthingtons.

ROWSLEY   Map 09 SK26

The Grouse & Claret
Station Rd DE4 2EB ☎ 01629 733233 📠 01629 733010
Dir: On A6 between Matlock & Bakewell
Situated in the heart of the Peak District, this refurbished pub is handy for touring the area. Several historic towns are close by and Haddon Hall and Chatsworth House are only a few minutes' drive away. The name of the pub is taken from a kind of fishing fly, and the pub is very popular with local fly fishermen. Appetising menu features such perennial favourites as liver and sausage sizzler, Thai prawns, various pies and traditional Sunday roast. **OPEN:** 11–11 (Sun 12–10.30) **BAR MEALS:** Lunch served: all week Dinner served: all week 12–9 Av main course £6 **RESTAURANT:** Lunch served: all week Dinner served: all week 12–9 Av 3 course à la carte £10 **BREWERY/COMPANY:** W'hampton & Dudley **PRINCIPAL BEERS:** Marston's Pedigree, Mansfield Cask,

continued

Original, Smooth. **FACILITIES:** Children welcome Children's licence Garden: Food served outside, great views **NOTES:** Parking 60 **ROOMS:** 5 bedrooms from s£25 d£40

SHARDLOW   Map 09 SK43

The Old Crown
Cavendish Bridge DE72 2HL ☎ 01332 792392
Dir: M1 J24 take A6 towards Derby turn L before river bridge into Shardlow
This bustling 17th-century village pub was once a staging post for convicts en route to the Assizes. The pub is sited on the old A6 next to the River Trent, where the former toll bridge was washed away during the 1947 floods. Besides an impressive choice of Shardlow's real ales, customers can tuck into a good range of starters and light meals; expect calves' liver with bacon and onions, game pie, or Cumberland lamb. **OPEN:** 11.30–3 5–11 (Sun 12–10.30) **BAR MEALS:** Lunch served: all week 12–2 Av main course £6.50 **BREWERY/COMPANY:** Free House **PRINCIPAL BEERS:** Marston's Pedigree, Interbrew Bass, Batemans XXXB, Fuller's London Pride. **FACILITIES:** Children welcome Garden: Beer garden, patio, food served outdoors, BBQ Dogs allowed (water) **NOTES:** Parking 25 **ROOMS:** 1 bedroom from s£25 d£40

TIDESWELL   Map 09 SK17

Three Stags' Heads
Wardlow Mires SK17 8RW ☎ 01298 872268
Dir: Junct of the A623 & B6465 on the Chesterfield/Stockport road
Unspoilt 300-year-old Derbyshire longhouse located in the limestone uplands of the northern Peak District. Grade II listed and designated by English Heritage as one of over 200 heritage pubs throughout the UK. Award-winning for their well-kept real ales and hearty, home-cooked food for ramblers, cyclists and locals includes liver in red wine, chicken and pepper curry, pigeon breasts and game in season. No children under 8. **OPEN:** Open Fri 7–11, Sat-Sun and public holidays 12–11 Closed Mon-Thurs, Fri Till 7pm, except public holidays **BAR MEALS:** Lunch served: Sat-Sun Dinner served: Sat-Sun 12.30–3 7.30–9.30 Av main course £8.50 **BREWERY/COMPANY:** Free House **PRINCIPAL BEERS:** Broadstone Charter Ale, Abbeydale Matins, Absolution, Black Lurcher. **FACILITIES:** Dogs allowed **NOTES:** Parking 14 No credit cards

WARDLOW   Map 09 SK35

The Bull's Head at Wardlow
SK17 8RP ☎ 01298 871431
For over 300 years this pub has stood in the heart of the Peak National Park, adjacent to one of the country's oldest drovers' routes dating back to the Iron Age. Largely unaltered within, it is adorned with antique prints, clocks, coach lamps, brass and copperware. Locally famous for its chargrilled steaks which share a menu with steak and kidney and cottage pies, seafood mornay and large fillets of cod and halibut. **OPEN:** 11.30–3 6.30–11 **BAR MEALS:** Lunch served: Sat-Sun 11.30–3 Dinner served: all week 6.30–9.30 Av main course £6.50 **RESTAURANT:** Lunch served: Sat-Sun 11.30–3 Dinner served: all week 6.30–9.30 Av 3 course à la carte £12 **BREWERY/COMPANY:** Free House **PRINCIPAL BEERS:** Scottish Courage John Smith's. **FACILITIES:** Children welcome Garden: Food served outdoors **NOTES:** Parking 50 **ROOMS:** 3 bedrooms 3 en suite from s£30 d£35 No credit cards

DEVON

ASHBURTON   Map 03 SX77

Pick of the Pubs

The Rising Sun ◆◆◆◆ 🛏 🍷
Woodland TQ13 7JT
☎ 01364 652544 📠 01364 654202 & 653628
e-mail: mail@risingsunwoodland.co.uk
Dir: E of Ashburton from the A38 take lane signed to Woodland and Denbury pub is on the L approx 1.5m

Originally a drovers' inn on the road from Dartmoor to Newton Abbot market standing in an isolated spot overlooking the beautiful Devon countryside. The name comes from the sun rising directly opposite the main building, and the sunny south-facing terrace is a delightful place for summer eating and drinking. Following a fire which gutted the inn, it was rebuilt in keeping with its past, including rough plaster walls and exposed beams. Two cosy en suite bedrooms provide the accommodation. Landlady Heather Humphries is dedicated to providing good food from fresh market produce, and her menus are updated on a daily basis. Her commitment to quality shines through blackboard starters like leek and Devon blue cheese tart, Thai fishcakes, and home-made country pâté, and such mains as gurnard fillet with Denhay ham and a herb crust, courgettes and hazelnut bake, and breast of Gressingham duck with pomegranate and molasses jus. Speciality evenings often held.
OPEN: 11–3 6–11 Closed: Dec 25 **BAR MEALS:** Lunch served: Tue–Sun Dinner served: Tue–Sun 12-2.15 6-9.15 Av main course £6.95 **RESTAURANT:** Lunch served: Tue–Sun Dinner served: Tue–Sun 12-2.15 6-9.15 Av 3 course à la carte £15
BREWERY/COMPANY: Free House
PRINCIPAL BEERS: Princetown Jail Ale, IPA, Teignworthy Reel Ale & Changing guest ales. **FACILITIES:** Children welcome Garden: Food served outside, patio, pond and fountain Dogs allowed (water) **NOTES:** Parking 30 **ROOMS:** 2 bedrooms 2 en suite from s£28 d£53

AVONWICK   Map 03 SX75

The Avon Inn
TQ10 9NB ☎ 01364 73475
Dir: From A38 take South Brent turning, Avonwick signed on B3210
Unassuming, cream-painted pub beside the River Avon, with a popular locals bar and a restaurant with a strong Italian theme influenced by the chef/owner. From authentic pasta dishes - maybe penne with broccoli, sun-dried tomatoes and anchovies - the menu extends to crab risotto, swordfish with

hot salsa, and turbot in lobster bisque with prawns and asparagus.
OPEN: 11.30-2.30 6-11 (Sun 7-10.30) **BAR MEALS:** Lunch served: Mon-Sat Dinner served: Mon-Sat 12-2 6.30-9.30 Av main course £5.95 **RESTAURANT:** Lunch served: Mon-Sat Dinner served: Mon-Sat 12-2 6.45-9.30 Av 3 course à la carte £20
BREWERY/COMPANY: Free House **PRINCIPAL BEERS:** Bass, Badger Best. **FACILITIES:** Children welcome Garden: outdoor eating **NOTES:** Parking 30

AXMOUTH   Map 03 SY29

The Ship Inn 🛏 🍷
EX12 4AF ☎ 01297 21838
e-mail: theshipinn@axmouth.com
Dir: From Lyme Regis take A3052 W towards Seaton/Sidmouth, then L onto B3172 to Axmouth
Built soon after the original Ship burnt down on Christmas Day 1879, this creeper-clad inn can trace its landlords back to 1769. The pub is currently run by Christopher Chapman - the son of TV's first super-cook, Fanny Craddock - and his family, and boasts a huge collection of Guinness memorabilia, and a large doll collection. A selection of specials includes whole local plaice, smoked salmon, asparagus and cheese on toast, fiery Cajun fishcakes, and broccoli and tomato pasta bake.
OPEN: 11-2.30 6-11 (open all day Sunday) **BAR MEALS:** Lunch served: all week Dinner served: all week 12-2 7-9 Av main course £5.50 **RESTAURANT:** Lunch served: all week Dinner served: all week 12-2 7-9 Av 3 course à la carte £12 Av 4 course fixed price £12
BREWERY/COMPANY: Inn Partnership
PRINCIPAL BEERS: Interbrew Bass, Otter Ale & Bitter.
FACILITIES: Children welcome Garden: Beer garden, food served outdoors Dogs allowed (on leads, water) **NOTES:** Parking 20
See Pub Walk on page 125

Strange Games
Competition and ingenuity have thrown up a rich variety of pub games besides the best-known ones, from lawn billiards to maggot racing to clay pipe smoking contests, where the object is to keep a pipeful of tobacco alight longest. Cribbage and other once popular card games are not seen so often nowadays, but bagatelle is alive and well in Chester and Coventry. In Knur and Spell up North the players hit a small ball (the knur) as far as possible with a bat. Bat and Trap, an odd variety of cricket, has a long history going back at least to the 16th century in Kent. In Sussex the game of Toad in the Hole involves pitching flat discs into a hole in a table and in Lincolnshire they throw pennies into a hole and call it gnurdling. For all the video games and one-arm bandits, older and more convivial pastimes are still alive in British pubs.

---

continued

PUB WALK

Axmouth
The Ship

Explore the pretty countryside around Axmouth by following green lanes and roads winding through the Devon landscape

Turn right on leaving the inn and follow Church Street for a short distance, passing the church and the Harbour Inn to reach Coronation Corner and the River Axe. Follow Axmouth Road downstream and the next turning on the left takes you uphill to Axe Cliff golf course. Continue straight ahead across the fairways, following a green lane (Barn Close Lane). Avoid the path on the right, part of the South West Way leading to Lyme Regis, continue straight ahead, at the junction with Stepps Lane bear right and follow the tarmac road for half a mile (800m). Take the first left turning, signposted Axmouth. After about a quarter of

mile (400m) the lane turns sharply to the left. However, avoid this by continuing ahead, following Leggs or Leggets Lane. Keep ahead to the other side of the valley, making for the junction with Bushes Lane. Turn left here to head back to the village. The road turns sharply to the left and at this point, go straight ahead, following Green Lane. Green Lane joins up with Bushes Lane at Pit Orchard. Turn right into Higher Lane and continue down towards the village, passing Mack's Barn. Chapel Street is below on your left, running parallel with Higher Lane. If you wish to descend to the street, follow any one of three short, steep paths or continue along to Kemps Lane. Follow the lane, turn right and walk along the main street, returning to the Ship.

THE SHIP,
AXMOUTH EX12 4AF
Tel: 01297 21838
Directions: From Lyme Regis takeA3052 W towards Seaton/Sidmouth, then L onto B3172 to Axmouth
A creeper-clad inn, run by son of TV cook Fanny Craddock and his family, the pub boasts over 700 items of Guinness memorabilia, and a fine collection of international dolls. Home-cooked food and good fresh fish dishes.
Open: 11–2.30 6–11
Bar Meals: 12–2 7–9
Children welcome and dogs allowed. Garden and parking available.

Distance: 5 miles (8km)
Map: OS Landranger 192 & 193
Terrain: Undulating countryside and valley walking around Axmouth
Paths: Tracks and lanes
Gradient: Easy walking, with an altitude difference of 300ft (91.44m)

Walk submitted and checked by Paul Chapman

England

BANTHAM   Map 03 SX64

Sloop Inn ♦♦♦ ♀
TQ7 3AJ ☎ 01548 560489 & 560215 ▤ 01548 561940
Dir: *From Kingsbridge take A379. At roundabout after Churchstow follow*
signs for Bantham

Just a short stroll from the beach, this 16th-century smugglers'
inn features oak beams, a flagstone floor, and a bar made
from half a rowing boat. Fresh local produce is to the fore in a
comprehensive choice of dishes from the regular menu
(basket meals, salads, steaks and sandwiches) while the
blackboard offers the likes of deep-fried squat lobster with
lemon and tarragon mayonnaise, and grilled Devon lamb with
rosemary sauce. **OPEN:** 11-2.30 6-11 (Sun 12-2.30, 7-10.30) **BAR MEALS:** Lunch
served: all week Dinner served: all week 12-2 7-10 Av main course
£8.50 **RESTAURANT:** Lunch served: all week Dinner served: all
week 12-2 7-10 Av 3 course à la carte £14.50
BREWERY/COMPANY: Free House **PRINCIPAL BEERS:** Palmers
IPA, Bass, Palmers Copper Ale. **FACILITIES:** Children welcome
Garden: Food served outside Dogs allowed **NOTES:** Parking 10
ROOMS: 5 bedrooms 5 en suite from d£66

BEER   Map 03 SY28

The Anchor Inn
Fore St EX12 3ET ☎ 01297 20386 ▤ 01297 24474
Dir: *Turn off A3052 following signs for Beer, continue through the village*
to slip road for Beach Anchor Inn on the R.
One of Britain's best sited inns, the Anchor overlooks the tiny
working harbour and beach in this popular little resort. Good
summer cliff-top garden and an open-plan bar where you can
enjoy pub snacks and excellent fresh fish. From mussels and
oysters, the choice extends to red mullet with crab and herb
crust and white wine sauce, and sea bass with creamy
tarragon and orange sauce. **OPEN:** 11-11 **BAR MEALS:** Lunch served: all week Dinner served:
all week 12-2 7-9.30 Av main course £7 **RESTAURANT:** Lunch
served: all week Dinner served: all week 12-2 7-9.30 Av 3 course à la
carte £20 **BREWERY/COMPANY:** Old English Inns
PRINCIPAL BEERS: Otter Bitter, Greene King IPA, and Abbot.
FACILITIES: Children welcome Garden: **ROOMS:** 8 bedrooms 5
en suite from s£55 d£75

BERE FERRERS   Map 02 SX46

Old Plough Inn 🏠
PL20 7JL ☎ 01822 840358
e-mail: paul.nikki@oldeplough.freeserve.co.uk
Dir: *A386 from Plymouth, A390 from Tavistock*
Originally three cottages, dating from the 16th century, this
inn has bags of character, with its old timbers and flagstones,

which on closer inspection are revealed to be headstones. To
the rear is a fine patio overlooking the River Tavey, and there
are lovely walks in the Bere Valley on the doorstep. Dishes on
offer range through fresh fish, crab, local pies, curries and stir-
fries.

OPEN: 12-3 7-11 **BAR MEALS:** Lunch served: all week Dinner
served: all week 12-2 7-9 Av main course £6 **RESTAURANT:** Lunch
served: all week Dinner served: all week 12-2 7-9
BREWERY/COMPANY: Free House **PRINCIPAL BEERS:** Sharp's
Doom Bar & Sharp's Own, Interbrew Flowers. **FACILITIES:** Children
welcome Garden: Safe beer garden with river views Dogs allowed
(water)

BICKLEIGH   Map 03 SS90

Fisherman's Cot ♀
EX16 8RW ☎ 01884 855237 ▤ 01884 855241
e-mail: fishermanscot.bickleigh@eldridge-pope.co.uk

Well-appointed inn by Bickleigh Bridge over the River Exe with
food all day and large beer garden: just a short drive from
Tiverton and Exmoor. The Waterside Bar is the place for
snacks and afternoon tea; restaurant incorporates carvery and
à la carte menus: Sunday lunch: champagne and smoked
salmon breakfast optional. The cosy bedrooms are
comfortable and well equipped. **OPEN:** 11-11 (Sun 12-10.30) **BAR MEALS:** Lunch served: all week
Dinner served: all week 12-10 Av main course £7.55
RESTAURANT: Lunch served: all week Dinner served: all week 12-10
PRINCIPAL BEERS: Courage Best, Tetley Cask, John Smiths.
FACILITIES: Children welcome Children's licence Garden: Food
served outside. Dogs allowed **NOTES:** Parking 100
ROOMS: 21 bedrooms 21 en suite from s£59 d£74

★ **Indicates AA inspected hotel accommodation**

continued

BIGBURY-ON-SEA Map 02 SX46

Pilchard Inn

Burgh Island TQ7 4BG ☎ 01548 810514 🖹 01548 810514
e-mail: reception@burghisland.ndirect.co.uk
Dir: *From A38 turn off to Modbury then follow signs to Bigbury & Burgh Island*

Atmospheric 14th-century white-walled pub located on a tiny tidal island reached only by giant sea tractor when the tide is in. The island was frequently used as a base by pirates and smugglers, the most notorious of which – Tom Crocker – is said to still haunt the island. An effigy of the pirate can be seen on the fireplace. The main catch off the island was pilchard – hence the name. Unsurprisingly, seafood figures large on the menu.
OPEN: 11.30–11 (Sun 12-10.30) **BAR MEALS:** Lunch served: all week Dinner served: all week 12-2.30 7-9
BREWERY/COMPANY: Free House
PRINCIPAL BEERS: Interbrew Bass, Greene King Abbot Ale, Black Sheep Best, Wells Bombardier. **FACILITIES:** Children welcome Garden: on edge of beach, food served outside Dogs allowed
NOTES: Parking 100

BLACKAWTON Map 03 SX85

Normandy Arms

Chapel St TQ9 7BN ☎ 01803 712316 🖹 01803 712191
Dir: *A381 from Totnes, L onto A3122, 1st R to Blackawton after Kingsbridge turning*
Venture off the beaten track to find this 15th-century inn, re-named in honour of the Normandy Landings, for which training exercises took place on nearby Slapton Beach. The pub has interesting memorabilia from that period. Mussels and Torbay sole feature along with grilled steaks and meat pies.
OPEN: 12-2.30 7-11 **BAR MEALS:** Lunch served: all week Dinner served: all week 12-1.45 7-9 Av main course £3.95
RESTAURANT: Lunch served: all week Dinner served: all week 12-1.45 7-9 Av 3 course à la carte £12 **BREWERY/COMPANY:** Free House **PRINCIPAL BEERS:** Blackawton Bitter,Youngs Special.
FACILITIES: Children welcome Garden: beer garden, outdoor eating Dogs allowed **NOTES:** Parking 10 **ROOMS:** 5 bedrooms 5 en suite from s£38 d£42

BRANSCOMBE Map 03 SY18

The Fountain Head NEW

EX12 3BG ☎ 01297 680359
Approximately 500 years old, and set among some of the oldest dated houses in Branscombe. Its small interior has flagstone floors and wood-panelling; outside are stools made from tree trunks, and a stream. The dining area was once the village forge and retains its central chimney. Representative dishes include no-nonsense steak and kidney pie and fresh battered cod. Beer comes from the local Branscombe Vale micro-brewery. Popular with hikers and their dogs.
OPEN: 11.30-3 6-11 **BAR MEALS:** Lunch served: all week Dinner served: all week 12-2 7-9 Av main course £5.95
BREWERY/COMPANY: Free House
PRINCIPAL BEERS: Preyman's, Hell's Belles. **FACILITIES:** Food served outside. Dogs allowed (water & biscuits provided)
NOTES: Parking 12

Pick of the Pubs

The Masons Arms ★ ★ 🛏 ♀

EX12 3DJ ☎ 01297 680300 🖹 01297 680500
e-mail: reception@masonsarms.co.uk
Dir: *Turn off A3052 towards Branscombe, head down hill, hotel in the valley at the bottom of the hill*
Picturesque Branscombe lies in a steep valley, deep in National Trust land and only a ten-minute stroll from the sea. In the centre of the village is this delightful 14th-century, creeper-clad inn, formerly a cider house and well known smugglers' haunt. Beyond the pretty front terrace lies a charming bar with stone walls, ancient ships beams, slate floors and a splendid open fireplace, used for spit-roasts on a weekly basis and including Sunday lunch. Popular bar food ranges from a tried-and-tested selection of sandwiches, ploughman's lunches and hot filled baguettes to beer-battered cod, duck and bacon pie, pasta with pesto, and interesting daily dishes like Mediterranean fish soup, chargrilled red mullet with fennel compote and a coriander and cream sauce, and braised pork with root vegetables, Calvados and prunes. Separate fixed-price restaurant menu. Newly refurbished bedrooms are split between the main building and neighbouring terraces of cottages; all are attractive and tastefully decorated. Conference/function room.
OPEN: 11-11 (winter 11-3, 6-11) Times vary please phone
BAR MEALS: Lunch served: all week Dinner served: all week 12-2 7-9 Av main course £9.50 **RESTAURANT:** Dinner served: all week 7-8.45 Av 3 course à la carte £24 Av 3 course fixed price £24 **BREWERY/COMPANY:** Free House
PRINCIPAL BEERS: Otter Ale, Masons Ale, Interbrew Bass plus guest ales. **FACILITIES:** Children welcome Garden: Patio, food served outside Dogs allowed (water) **NOTES:** Parking 30
ROOMS: 22 bedrooms 19 en suite from s£22 d£44

BRENDON Map 03 SS74

Rockford Inn 🛏 ♀

EX35 6PT ☎ 01598 741214 🖹 01598 741265
e-mail: enquiries@therockfordinn.com

continued

continued

BRENDON continued

Situated within the spectacular Exmoor National Park, on the banks of the East Lyn River at Brendon, this traditional West Country pub is ideally placed for touring Devon and Somerset on foot or by car. Nearby is the spectacular Doone Valley, made famous by R D Blackmore's classic 19th-century novel *Lorna Doone*. Sample battered cod, home-made cottage pie or Lancashire hotpot at lunchtime. Alternatively, choose local trout, 8oz (225gm) rump steak or chicken tikka masala from the evening menu.

OPEN: 12–3 6–11 **BAR MEALS:** Lunch served: all week Dinner served: all week 12–2.30 7–9 Av main course £5.50 **BREWERY/COMPANY:** Free House **PRINCIPAL BEERS:** Cotleigh Barn Owl, Tawny, Greene King Old Speckled Hen. **FACILITIES:** Garden: Food served outside Dogs allowed (water) **NOTES:** Parking 12 **ROOMS:** 6 bedrooms from s£20 d£40

BROADHEMBURY   Map 03 ST10

Pick of the Pubs

Drewe Arms

EX14 3NF ☎ 01404 841267
e-mail: nigleburge@btconnect.co.uk
Dir: A373 halfway between Cullompton and Honiton

Set in an archetypal thatched Devon village in sprawling unspoiled countryside handy for Dartmoor and the spectacular Devon coast, its striking mullioned windows and quaint old furniture lend the Drewe Arms its particular tasteful character. The best available West Country produce form the basis of the daily menus that major in fresh fish. Expect on any one day to feast on pollack baked with Cheddar and cream or sea bream with orange and chilli. Steamed mussels with garlic and herbs, griddled sardines and smoked haddock and Stilton rarebit are all offered in two portion sizes – large and very large. Alongside seared scallops with rouille and turbot fillet with hollandaise, on the fixed-price dining menu might be venison tenderloin with wild mushroom sauce, followed by chocolate St Emilion. For more dedicated meat-eaters are rare beef and hot chicken baguettes and a Bookmaker's fillet steak with anchovy butter. Good house wines from around the world are all offered by the glass.

OPEN: 11–3 6–11 (Sun 12–3 only) Closed: Dec 25 & Dec 31 **BAR MEALS:** Lunch served: all week 12–2 Dinner served: Mon–Sat 7–10 Av main course £10.50 **RESTAURANT:** Lunch served: all week 12–2 Dinner served: Mon–Sat 7–10 Av 3 course à la carte £27 **BREWERY/COMPANY:** Free House **PRINCIPAL BEERS:** Otter Ale, Otter Bitter, Otter Head, Otter Bright. **FACILITIES:** Children welcome Garden: outdoor eating, patio Dogs allowed (water)

BUCKFASTLEIGH   Map 03 SX76

Dartbridge Inn 🗺 ♀

Totnes Rd TQ11 0JR ☎ 01364 642214 📠 01364 643839
Dir: Turn off A38 onto A384, the Dartbridge Inn is 200yrds on the L

This beamed inn, renowned for its colourful floral displays, is situated on the banks of the River Dart, and is convenient for the Buckfastleigh to Totnes steam railway as well as Buckfast Abbey. A good range of food is available, from sandwiches to steaks, and local fish and seafood, perhaps scallops, rainbow trout, salmon and lemon sole.

OPEN: all day **BAR MEALS:** Lunch served: all week Dinner served:

all week 12–2 6.30–9 Av main course £8 **RESTAURANT:** Lunch served: all week Dinner served: all week 12–2 7–9.30 Av 3 course à la carte £15 **BREWERY/COMPANY:** Old English Inns **PRINCIPAL BEERS:** Scottish Courage Courage Best & Directors, Wadworth 6X. **FACILITIES:** Children welcome **NOTES:** Parking 100 **ROOMS:** 11 bedrooms 11 en suite from s£40 d£50

BUCKLAND BREWER   Map 03 SS42

The Coach & Horses 🗺

EX39 5LU ☎ 01237 451395

A popular, thatched free house dating from the 13th century, and once the village courthouse. Set in lovely countryside close to the Tarka Trail. Beneath its heavily beamed ceilings, locals and tourists gather around the inglenook fireplaces, or spill out onto the terrace and garden. Fresh food cooked to order has a good local reputation, including pan-fried skate wing, beef fillets in port and mushroom sauce, spinach and stilton filo parcels, and lamb in red wine.

OPEN: 12–3 6–11 (Sun 7–10.30) **BAR MEALS:** Lunch served: all week Dinner served: all week 12–2 7–9.30 Av main course £8 **RESTAURANT:** Lunch served: all week Dinner served: all week 12–2 7–9.30 Av 3 course à la carte £18 **BREWERY/COMPANY:** Free House **PRINCIPAL BEERS:** Fuller's London Pride, Interbrew Flowers Original, Flowers IPA, Whitbread Bitter. **FACILITIES:** Children welcome Garden: Dogs allowed (not overnight in bedrooms) **NOTES:** Parking 12 **ROOMS:** 2 bedrooms

BUCKLAND MONACHORUM   Map 02 SX46

Drake Manor Inn 🗺

The Village PL20 7NA ☎ 01822 853892 📠 01822 853892
Dir: Off A386 near Yelverton

A mainly 16th-century inn nestling between the church and the stream, named after nearby resident Sir Francis Drake. Old fireplaces with wood-burning stoves and heavy beams are still in evidence, and the pub is renowned for its pretty gardens and colourful, award-winning floral displays. At lunchtime there are baguettes, ploughman's, and other bar snacks like sausage and chips, or spicy chicken goujons, and in the evening, home-made lasagne, steak and kidney pie, beef chilli, and breaded plaice.

OPEN: 11.30–2.30 6.30–11 (Sun 12–3, 7–10.30) **BAR MEALS:** Lunch served: all week Dinner served: all week 12–2 7–10 Av main course £6.50 **RESTAURANT:** Lunch served: all week Dinner served: all week 12–2 7–10 Av 3 course à la carte £14 **PRINCIPAL BEERS:** Scottish Courage John Smiths & Courage Best, Interbrew Bass, Wadworth's 6X, Greene King Abbott Ale. **FACILITIES:** Children welcome Garden: Beer garden, food served outdoors Dogs allowed **NOTES:** Parking 4

continued

BUTTERLEIGH   Map 03 SS90

The Butterleigh Inn
EX15 1PN ☎ 01884 855407 📠 01884 855600
Dir: 3m from J 28 on the M5 turn R by The Manor Hotel in Cullompton and follow Butterleigh signs
Tucked away in a sleepy village amid glorious countryside south of Tiverton, this 400-year-old pub remains delightfully unpretentious and worth seeking out for its relaxed, traditional atmosphere and excellent Cotleigh Brewery ales. Homely and comfortably furnished bars with open fires and time-honoured pub games. Menu ranges from Cumberland sausage with a cucumber and mint raita, leek, mushroom and Brie tartlet, or Thai spiced tiger prawns, to filled rolls, ploughmans', or the famous Buttleigh Burger.
OPEN: 12–2.30 6–11 **BAR MEALS:** Lunch served: all week Dinner served: all week 12–2 7–9.45 Av main course £6
BREWERY/COMPANY: Free House **PRINCIPAL BEERS:** Cotleigh Tawny Ale, Barn Owl Bitter, Old Buzzard. **FACILITIES:** Children welcome Garden: Food served outside Dogs allowed
NOTES: Parking 30

CADELEIGH   Map 02 SS90

Cadeleigh Arms 🐾
Cadeleigh EX16 8HP ☎ 01884 855238 📠 01884 855385
Known as the New Inn, till it burnt down in 1892, the Cadeleigh Arms is part of a small community in the hills above the Exe valley. It is reputedly haunted, and what is now the skittle alley was once a stable for racehorses. The bar snack menu offers hot filled baguettes, home-made soup and the Cadeleigh burger, while favourites from the full menu are Cajun chicken, sirloin steak and mussels in garlic and white wine.
OPEN: 11–2.30 6–11 (Sat 12–11, Sun 12–10.30)
BAR MEALS: Lunch served: all week Dinner served: Tues–Sat 12–2.30 7–9.30 Av main course £8 **RESTAURANT:** Lunch served: all week Dinner served: Tues–Sat 12–2.30 7–9.30 Av 3 course à la carte £18 **BREWERY/COMPANY:** Free House
PRINCIPAL BEERS: Cotleigh Tawny Bitter, Scottish Courage John Smith's, Whitbread Best Bitter. **FACILITIES:** Children welcome Garden: Food served outside Dogs allowed **NOTES:** Parking 30

CHAGFORD   Map 03 SX78

Ring O'Bells 🐾 🍷
44 The Square TQ13 8AH ☎ 01647 432466 📠 01647 432466
Dir: From Exeter take A30 to Whiddon Down Rdbt, take 1st L onto A382 to Mortonhampstead. After 3.5m to Easton Cross Turn R Signed to Chagford
A traditional West Country inn in one of the prettiest old stannary towns. The area is also especially popular as a base for walking expeditions and tours of Dartmoor. Daily changing menus use local produce as often as possible, including fresh fish and seafood. Expect pork cooked in West Country cider with honey, game dishes and home-made curry. Traditional bar menu offers jacket potatoes, home-cooked ham, ploughman's lunches and butcher's sausages.
OPEN: 9–3 5–11 (Sun 12–3, 5–10.30) **BAR MEALS:** Lunch served: all week 12–2 Dinner served: Wed–Mon 6–9 Av main course £7.95
RESTAURANT: Lunch served: all week 12–2 Dinner served: Wed–Mon 6–9 **BREWERY/COMPANY:** Free House
PRINCIPAL BEERS: Butcombe Bitter & Gold, Exmoor Ale, Devon Cream. **FACILITIES:** Children welcome Garden: Food served outdoors, patio Dogs allowed (very dog friendly, water and biscuits provided) **ROOMS:** 4 bedrooms 2 en suite from s£20 d£40

The Sandy Park Inn 🐾 🍷
Sandy Park TQ13 8JW ☎ 01647 432236 📠 01647 432236
Dir: on A382 between Moretonhampstead and Whiddon Down

A 16th-century thatched inn set in a small, picturesque Teign Valley hamlet, and quite unspoilt by progress. No jukeboxes, loud music or gambling machines disturb the peace, and only the chatter of locals and visitors can be heard. Local fresh ingredients widely used in dishes like wild boar and apple sausages, or chicken liver and bacon salad at lunchtime, and in the evening, sea bass with a creamy seafood sauce, rack of lamb, and a choice of steaks.
OPEN: 12–2.30 6.30–11 **BAR MEALS:** Lunch served: Wed–Sun 12–2 Dinner served: Tue–Sun 7–9.30 Av main course £8
RESTAURANT: Lunch served: Wed–Sun 12–2 Dinner served: Tue–Sun 7–9.30 Av 3 course à la carte £8
BREWERY/COMPANY: Free House **PRINCIPAL BEERS:** Otter Bitter, Butcombe Bitter, Wadworth 6X. **FACILITIES:** Garden: Patio, food served outside Dogs allowed **NOTES:** Parking 6

Three Crowns Hotel ★ ★ NEW
High St TQ13 8AJ ☎ 01647 433444 & 433441 📠 01647 433117
e-mail: three.crowns@msn.com
This 13th-century inn is a fine example of Chagford's striking architecture. A shooting in the nearby churchyard of the 15th-century church is said to have given RD Blackmore inspiration for part of his classic novel Lorna Doone. Sturdy oak beams and a wonderful open fireplace enhance the inn's delightful surroundings. Expect rack of lamb, pork Dijonnaise, salmon steak, red mullet and mushroom and pepper Stroganoff among a wide-ranging choice of favourite dishes.
OPEN: all day **BAR MEALS:** Lunch served: all week Dinner served: all week 12–12.30 6–9.30 Av cost main £5.50 **RESTAURANT:** Lunch served: all week (Booking essential) Dinner served: all week 6–9.30 Av 3 course à la carte £22.50 **BREWERY/COMPANY:** Free House
PRINCIPAL BEERS: Flowers Original, Boddingtons
FACILITIES: Children welcome Dogs allowed **NOTES:** Parking 20
ROOMS: 20 bedrooms 17 en suite from s£55 d£55

Nine Men's Morris
A certain eeriness clings to one of the world's oldest games, which was played in Ancient Egypt 3,000 years ago and in Ireland in prehistoric times. It involves moving pegs or counters to form rows of three on a board or playing surface with 24 holes marked on it in an intricate pattern.

CHARDSTOCK   Map 03 ST30

The George Inn 🏨 ⚲
EX13 7BX ☎ 01460 220241 📠 01460 221291
e-mail: info@tytherleighcot.co.uk
Dir: A358 to Chard, then A358 toward Axminster, R at Tytherleigh
The George is over 700 years old, has graffiti from 1648 and
was once the church school. Underneath is a sealed-off crypt.
Two resident ghosts, one a parson, haunt the main entrance
and restaurant. On offer are likely to be 15 daily specials,
including 'legendary' fillet steak gateau with Stilton, wrapped
in smoked bacon, and served with red wine jus, Chinese stir
fry, vegetable kebabs and moules marinière. Also pasta, fish,
vegetarian and ploughman's.
OPEN: 11.30-3 12-2.30 (winter 6-11) **BAR MEALS:** Lunch served:
all week Dinner served: all week 12-2.30 6.30-9.30 Av main course
£6.95 **RESTAURANT:** Lunch served: all week Dinner served: all
week 12-2.30 6.30-9.30 Av 3 course à la carte £17
BREWERY/COMPANY: Free House
PRINCIPAL BEERS: Guinness, Wells Bombardier, Otter Ale, Otter
Bitter. **FACILITIES:** Children welcome Garden: Food served outside,
courtyard Dogs allowed (water provided) **NOTES:** Parking 50
ROOMS: 4 bedrooms 4 en suite from s£40 d£40

CHERITON BISHOP   Map 03 SX79

The Old Thatch Inn
EX6 6HJ ☎ 01647 24204 📠 01647 24584
e-mail: theoldthatchinn@aol.com
Dir: Take A30 from M5, about 10m turning on L signed Cheriton Bishop
Old world charm and modern comforts are effectively
combined at this listed inn, originally built as a coaching
house and licensed as a public house as recently as 1974.
Close by is Fingle Bridge, described by R D Blackmore as 'the
finest scene in all England.' Meals range from baked chicken
breast to breaded scampi, and there are also various grills,
toasted sandwiches and Old Thatch ploughman's lunches.
OPEN: 11.30-3 6-11 Closed: 25 Dec **BAR MEALS:** Lunch served:
all week Dinner served: all week 12-2 7-9.30 Av main course £7.95
RESTAURANT: Lunch served: all week Dinner served: all week 12-2
7-9.30 Av 3 course à la carte £17 **BREWERY/COMPANY:** Free
House **PRINCIPAL BEERS:** Branscombe Vale Branoc, Sharp's Own,
Otter Ale, Skinners Figgy's Brew plus guest beers.
FACILITIES: Children welcome Garden: Food served outdoors
NOTES: Parking 30 **ROOMS:** 3 bedrooms 3 en suite from s£35
d£49

CHUDLEIGH KNIGHTON   Map 03 SX87

The Claycutters Arms
TQ13 0EY ☎ 01626 853345
Dir: Turn off the Devon Expressway at Chudleigh Knighton
Thatched village pub, originally three Quaker cottages, on the
flanks of Dartmoor, complete with beams, an open fire and an
abundance of hanging baskets in summer. Dishes range from
home-made pigeon pie, wild boar sausages and cider apple
sauce, to duck with leeks and port, and venison with honey
and juniper.
OPEN: 11-3 6-11 **BAR MEALS:** Lunch served: all week Dinner
served: all week 12-2.30 6-9.30 Av main course £5.95
RESTAURANT: Lunch served: all week Dinner served: all week
12-2.30 6-9.30 Av 3 course à la carte £15
BREWERY/COMPANY: Heavitree **PRINCIPAL BEERS:** Bass,
Greene King Old Speckled Hen, Otter, Abbot. **FACILITIES:** Children
welcome Garden: Dogs allowed **NOTES:** Parking 60

CLYST HYDON   Map 03 ST00

Pick of the Pubs

The Five Bells Inn 🏨 ⚲
EX15 2NT ☎ 01884 277288 📠 01884 277693
*Dir: B3181 3m out of Cullompton, L to Clyst Hydon then R to Clyst St
Lawrence. Pub on R*
So called because of its close proximity to the village
church, this inn was moved lock, stock and literally barrel
to its present position - in a 16th-century Devon
longhouse - after the vicar objected to its presence a
century ago. Many of the old outbuildings have been
incorporated into the thatched inn, and its careful
modernisation has left the old world atmosphere intact.
Far-reaching country views can be enjoyed from the front
terrace and raised side garden, and a warm welcome
awaits inside. Main menu and specials board meals are
available in the carpeted open-plan bar, including fresh
fish like monkfish, bream, and whole plaice, plus
fisherman's bake, various salads and ploughman's, and a
children's choice. An à la carte menu served in the
restaurant offers home-cooked choices like fresh mussels
in cider, pan-fried venison fillet with red wine, whole sea
bass stuffed with ginger and orange, and the
enigmatically-named 'chocolate mint torment'.
OPEN: 11.30-3 6.30-11 (winter 7-11, expt Sat 6.30 open) Closed:
Dec 26 & Jan 1 **BAR MEALS:** Lunch served: all week Dinner
served: all week 12-2 7-10 Av main course £8.95
RESTAURANT: Lunch served: all week Dinner served: all week
12-2 7-10 Av 3 course à la carte £25
BREWERY/COMPANY: Free House
PRINCIPAL BEERS: Cotleigh Tawny Ale, Otter Bitter, O'Hanlon's
Blakeley's. **FACILITIES:** Garden: Beer garden, patio, food
served outdoors Dogs allowed (water) **NOTES:** Parking 40

COCKWOOD   Map 03 SX98

The Anchor Inn 🏨 ⚲
EX6 8RA ☎ 01626 890203 📠 01626 890355
Dir: Off A379 between Dawlish & Starcross
With its splendid setting on the broad estuary of the River Exe,
overlooking a landlocked harbour, it's hardly surprising this
historic inn attracts a wide-ranging mix of smart diners, local
fishermen, birdwatchers and walkers. Unspoilt main bar with
low ceilings, black panelling and intimate little alcoves, one
with an open fire. Seemingly endless fish and seafood menu.
Expect oysters with smoked ham or scallops with spinach and
Boursin among other imaginative dishes. Non-fish fanciers
can choose from a good range of bar snacks.
OPEN: 11-11 (Sun 12-10.30) **BAR MEALS:** Lunch served: all week
Dinner served: all week 12-3 6.30-10 Av main course £5.95
RESTAURANT: Lunch served: all week Dinner served: all week 12-3
6.30-10 Av 3 course à la carte £25
BREWERY/COMPANY: Heavitree **PRINCIPAL BEERS:** Interbrew
Bass & Flowers Original, Wadworth 6X, Fuller's London Pride,
Marston's Pedigree. **FACILITIES:** Garden: Food served outside
Dogs allowed (water) **NOTES:** Parking 15

⚲ **Pubs offering six or more wines by the glass**

OPEN: 12–3 6–11
BAR MEALS: L served all week.
D served all week. 12–2 7–10
Av main course £9.95
RESTAURANT: L served all week.
D served all week. 12–2 7–10
Av cost 3 course £16.95
BREWERY/COMPANY:
FREE HOUSE
PRINCIPAL BEERS: Wadworth 6X,
Otter Ale, Badger Bitter, Shepherd
Neame Spitfire
FACILITIES: Children welcome,
dogs allowed. Garden: Patio, food
served outside
NOTES: Parking 50
ROOMS: 6 en suite Double room
from £68 Single room from £53

The New Inn

Original beams under an historic cob-and-thatch roof are particular features of this 13th-century listed building in a conservation village alongside Cole Brook, a tributary of the River Yeo, with comfortable en suite accommodation in an interesting variety of styles. The ancient bar blends successfully with extensions created from the old barns, with the latter accommodating dining areas that enjoy a rare balance of local and tourist clientele.

Coleford EX17 5BZ
☎ 01363 84242 🖹 01363 85044
e-mail: new-inn@reallyreal-group.com
Dir: from Exeter take A377, 1.5m after Crediton turn L for Coleford. Pub in 1.5m.

Customers are attracted by conservative food choices that score highly in freshness and value. Best choices will be found on daily blackboards offering West Country dishes from local suppliers, in particular fresh fish from Brixham. Cheeses for ploughman's lunches are made in Devon, with clotted cream produced by a local farm. Eggs, too, come

from a local farm, are free range and reared completely on natural feeds. The restaurant menu offers an impressive choice. Perhaps start with Brie, spinach and nutmeg bake, then choose chicken and mushroom crumble, bangers and mash, Mediterranean lamb or salmon fish cakes. To round off, try pine nut, pecan and honey tart or chocolate cup with Amaretto mousse and berry sauce. There is an extensive list of malt whiskies and ports, and four traditional ales in a cooled cellar decent wine by the glass, and the stream-side patio is perfect for alfresco summer drinking. There's accommodation in six spacious, light and airy bedrooms. But, to add a frisson of apprehension, the inn is reputed to be haunted by a ghost called Sebastian, who appears in one of the bedrooms and sometimes along adjacent corridors.

CORNWORTHY — Map 03 SX85

Hunters Lodge Inn ☺ ♀
TQ9 7ES ☎ 01803 732204 📠 01803 732056
e-mail: rog.lij@hunterslodgeinn.com
Dir: Off A381 S of Totnes

Dating from the early 18th century, this country local is tucked away in quiet village close to the River Dart. The interior is simply furnished and a real fire burns in the gorgeous fireplace. Fresh local produce is used in the cooking, and the water sold originates from a spring in the village. Grilled cod with herb and cheese topping and roast rack of lamb in red wine sauce are typical dishes.
OPEN: 11.30-2.30 6.30-11 **BAR MEALS:** Lunch served: all week Dinner served: all week 12-2 7-9 Av main course £10.25
RESTAURANT: Lunch served: all week Dinner served: all week 12-2 7-9 Av 3 course à la carte £16.50 **BREWERY/COMPANY:** Free House **PRINCIPAL BEERS:** Teignworthy Reel Ale & Beach Comber.
FACILITIES: Children welcome Garden: Patio, food served outdoors Dogs allowed **NOTES:** Parking 18

CREDITON — Map 03 SS80

Pick of the Pubs

The New Inn ☺ ♀
Coleford EX17 5BZ ☎ 01363 84242 📠 01363 85044
e-mail: new-inn@reallyreal-group.com
See Pick of the Pubs on page 131

CULMSTOCK — Map 03 ST11

Culm Valley Inn ☺ ♀ NEW
EX15 3JJ ☎ 01884 840354
With up to six real ales and a wine for every week of the year, this traditional 300-year-old village inn stands by the River Culm where it emerges from the Blackdown Hills. Tuck into good plates of fresh, home-made food; free-range gingered chicken, duck breast with port and redcurrant sauce, and boat-loads of seafood dishes precede crème brûlée, prune and Armagnac tart, or apple and almond pudding.
OPEN: 12-3 6-11 Closed: 25 Dec **BAR MEALS:** Lunch served: all week Dinner served: Mon-Sat 12-2 7-9 Av main course £10
RESTAURANT: Lunch served: all week Dinner served: Mon-Sat 12-2 7-9 Av 3 course à la carte £25 **BREWERY/COMPANY:** Free House **PRINCIPAL BEERS:** Cotleigh Tawney, Bath Ales Rare Hare,.
FACILITIES: Garden: Overlooking The River Culm Dogs allowed (water) **NOTES:** Parking 40 **ROOMS:** 2 bedrooms 2 en suite from d£60 No credit cards

DALWOOD — Map 03 ST20

Pick of the Pubs

The Tuckers Arms ☺ ♀
EX13 7EG ☎ 01404 881342 📠 01404 881802
e-mail: tuckers.arms@cwcom.net
See Pub Walk on page 133
See Pick of the Pubs on page 134

DARTINGTON — Map 03 SX76

Cott Inn ♀
TQ9 6HE ☎ 01803 863777 📠 01803 866629
Dir: On A384 between Totnes & Buckfastleigh
Picture-postcard pretty, 14th-century stone and cob-built inn, continuously licensed since 1320, with a wonderful 183ft thatched roof - one of the longest in England. Carpeted bar with open fires, a wealth of beams and a comfortable collection of antique and older-style furnishings. Popular buffet-style lunchtime menu; more elaborate evening dishes like wild sea bass dressed with dill and sweet pepper, and beef filler stuffed with pâté with a rich game jus. Pine-furnished upstairs bedrooms. Old English Pub Company.
OPEN: 11-11 **BAR MEALS:** Lunch served: all week Dinner served: all week 12-2.30 6.30-9.30 Av main course £9
RESTAURANT: Lunch served: all week Dinner served: all week 12-2.30 6.30-9.30 Av 3 course à la carte £20
BREWERY/COMPANY: Old English Inns
PRINCIPAL BEERS: Greene King IPA, Abbot Ale, Otter Ale.
FACILITIES: Children welcome Garden: Food served outside Dogs allowed **NOTES:** Parking 40 **ROOMS:** 6 bedrooms 6 en suite from s£55 d£65

DARTMOUTH — Map 03 SX85

The Cherub Inn ♦♦♦♦ ☺ ♀
13 Higher St TQ6 9RB ☎ 01803 832571 📠 01803 832762
e-mail: enquiries@the-cherub.co.uk
The Cherub Inn is Dartmouth's oldest building. It dates from about 1380 and survived the threats of fire during World War II bombing and demolition in 1958 to be finally restored and Grade II listed. Bar meals are available lunchtime and evenings, and the restaurant serves dinner every night, offering a selection of steak, poultry, game and fish dishes. Expect seafood salad, curry and steak, mushroom and Guinness pie among many popular favourites.
OPEN: 11-11 (Sun 12-10.30) **BAR MEALS:** Lunch served: all week Dinner served: all week 12-2 7-9.30 Av main course £7
RESTAURANT: Dinner served: all week 7-9.30 Av 3 course à la carte £20 **BREWERY/COMPANY:** Free House
PRINCIPAL BEERS: Cherub Best Bitter, Brakspear Bitter, Shepherd Neame Best, Exmoor Ale. **FACILITIES:** Children welcome Dogs allowed

Pick of the Pubs

Royal Castle Hotel ★★★ ☺ ♀
11 The Quay TQ6 9PS ☎ 01803 833033 📠 01803 835445
e-mail: enquiry@royalcastle.co.uk
See Pick of the Pubs on page 137

PUB WALK

Dalwood
The Tuckers Arms

Enjoy a varied walk from the centre of Dalwood which nestles in the Corry Vale. Before starting, you may like to visit the National Trust's Loughwood Meeting House nearby. It was built by the early Baptist congregation who attended services here at the risk of transportation or imprisonment.

From the inn, cross the river and keep straight ahead, passing to the right of a telephone box. Go up the farm track, past a few houses and through a gate. Cross the field to the crossing point in the top corner. Walk ahead to a gap in the hedge, turn right and follow the drive to a lane. Turn left to a crossroads, then bear right down past the house and veer left at the first gate into the field. Continue down to a finger post, cross a stile and descend to a gate at the bottom. Bear left to the lane and go towards Membury. Cross the River Yarty, pass through a gate into a field on your left and follow the path beside the river until it bears right at a hedge. Continue to the gate and follow the path to the next stile, keeping straight on to a gate leading out to the lane. Walk ahead towards the farm and just before it, turn right to join a footpath running up through the trees. At the top, cross the farm track and keep straight on. Pass through a farm gate, cross the field exiting by the gate on the far side. Continue along the rough road and then bear left down to the river. Cross the ford or take the bridges in the field to the left. Head up the slope and turn right along the lane. Bear to your left further up and then fork right to follow the bridleway. Take the right-hand track further up the hill, go up over the higher ground and then down to some houses. Follow the track to the left between them, down to the hamlet of Heathstock. Bear left at the junction along a pretty lane until just before some power lines. Look for a stile on the right to a path across a small pasture to the next stile, passing below some buildings on your left. With the Corry Brook on your right, cross two more stiles to a bridge, turn left and follow the track to a gate. Turn right at the road and return to the pub.

THE TUCKER ARMS
DALWOOD Axminster EX13 7EG
Tel: 01404 881342
Directions: Off A35 between Honiton & Axminster
Historic, part-thatched 13th-century pub, with colourful hanging baskets in summer, The classic, low-ceilinged bar, with flagstone floor and inglenook fireplace, is the pleasantly rustic setting for sampling reliable bar food.
Open: 12-3 6.30-11
Bar meals: 12-2 6.30-8
Dogs allowed. Garden and parking available.

Distance: 5 miles (8km)
Map: OS Landranger 192
Terrain: Undulating farmland and woodland
Paths: Mainly bridleways, farm tracks and field paths.
After heavy rain sections can become wet and slippery
Gradient: Some climbing

Walk submitted and checked by David Beck of The Tucker Arms, Dalwood

OPEN: 12–3 6.30–11
BAR MEALS: L served all week.
D served all week. 12–2 6.30–8
Av main course £5
RESTAURANT: L served all week.
D served all week. 12–2 6.30–8
Av cost 3 courses £18.95
BREWERY/COMPANY:
FREE HOUSE
PRINCIPAL BEERS: Otter Bitter,
Otter Ale, Scottish Courage
Courage Directors, Courage Best
FACILITIES: Dogs allowed.
Garden: Food served outside
NOTES: Parking 5
ROOMS: 5 en suite

The Tuckers Arms

Dalwood, Devon EX13 7EG
☎ 01404 881342 📠 01404 881802
e-mail: tuckers.arms@cwcom.net
Dir: off A35 between Honiton &
Axminster

The Tuckers Arms is a pretty thatched inn, decked with colourful hanging baskets in summer, set in a delightful Axe valley village in a quiet corner of East Devon. Although it has seen many changes through the centuries, for all its life the inn has been involved in the provision of hospitality, food and drink.

Parts of the building date back to the 12th century, and it was originally a hunting lodge built on the banks of what was once a much wider river. Inside there are low beams, flagstone floors and inglenook fireplaces and a cosy atmosphere. Overnight accommodation is offered in comfortable en suite bedrooms. Fresh fish and game are specialities of the menu, which changes daily being dependent on market availability. There are at least three 'fish of the day' dishes - maybe fillets of lemon sole with spicy Greek capers and butter, fresh halibut and prawns with parsley and lemon butter, or fillet of cod with banana, chilli and spice. Locally caught lobster and crab are available in season. Examples of alternative options are sautéed kidneys with tarragon, mustard and sherry, or fillet steak du chef served with a topping of home-made pâté in a sauce of soft green peppercorns, cream and brandy. Home-made puddings, local cheeses and clotted cream also feature daily. Country pursuits, including walks, golfing and fishing are available nearby. Also within easy striking distance are the coastal resorts of Sidmouth and Lyme Regis, the city of Exeter and the antiques capital of Honiton.

DENBURY   Map 03 SX86

The Union Inn 🍴 ⚲ NEW
Denbury Green TQ12 6DQ ☎ 01803 812595 🖹 01803 814206
This pretty country inn lies just outside Newton Abbot, right next door to the village green and very much the hub of the local community. Inside are rustic stone walls, a traditional log fire with an adjacent settle, plus snugs and a cosy restaurant. Varied menu ranges from whole lemon sole and half a duck with port and leek, to homity pie and Devon fire chicken. Appetising bar snacks and a good choice of local Devon dishes, including rabbit pie and home-made pasty.
OPEN: 11-3 6-11 (Sat 11-11, Sun 12-3, 6-10.30)
BAR MEALS: Lunch served: all week Dinner served: all week 12-2.30 6.30-10 Av main course £5.95 **RESTAURANT:** Lunch served: all week Dinner served: all week 12-2.30 6.30-10 Av 3 course à la carte £25 **PRINCIPAL BEERS:** Interbrew Bass, Flowers IPA, Black Sheep Special, Greene KIng Abbot Ale. **FACILITIES:** Dogs allowed (water) **NOTES:** Parking 10

DITTISHAM   Map 03 SX85

The Ferry Boat
Manor St TQ6 0EX ☎ 01803 722368
Picture windows make the most of the charming waterside location at this homely pub. Popular with walkers and Dart boatmen.

DODDISCOMBSLEIGH   Map 03 SX88

Pick of the Pubs

The Nobody Inn ⚲
EX6 7PS ☎ 01647 252394 🖹 01647 252978
e-mail: info@nobodyinn.co.uk
Dir: *From A38 follow signs for Dunchideock and Doddiscombeleigh*
A relaxed 16th-century inn with a wealth of old beams, plus ancient settles, antique tables and a huge inglenook fireplace. This charming inn is just off the old Plymouth to Exeter road where refreshment-seeking travellers were reputedly greeted from behind the door with calls of 'Nobody in'! Nowadays visitors, weary or otherwise, are given a warm welcome, and offered imaginative meals sourced from fresh local ingredients including herbs from the vegetable garden. In the bar expect dishes such as seafood pasta, Cumberland sausage with mashed potatoes, and steak and kidney pudding, plus filled ciabatta bread and a countryman's lunch. A typical meal in the more formal restaurant might be warm kiln-roasted salmon on brioche with citrus sauce and roasted peppers, breast of pheasant in a rich red wine sauce, and raspberry and frangipane tart with cream. Also offered are some unusual ales, wines and whiskies. There is accommodation upstairs and in a nearby small manor house.
OPEN: 12-2.30 6-11 Closed: 25/26 & 31 Dec
BAR MEALS: Lunch served: all week Dinner served: all week 12-2 7-10 Av main course £7.99 **RESTAURANT:** Dinner served: Tue-Sat 7.30-9 Av 3 course à la carte £16
BREWERY/COMPANY: Free House
PRINCIPAL BEERS: Bass, Nobody's Bitter, Teign Valley Tipple.
FACILITIES: Garden: Food served outside, patio area Dogs allowed (in the garden only) **NOTES:** Parking 50
ROOMS: 7 bedrooms 5 en suite from s£23 d£33

DOLTON   Map 02 SS51

Pick of the Pubs

The Union Inn ♦♦♦♦ 🍴
Fore St EX19 8QH ☎ 01805 804633 🖹 01805 804633
e-mail: union.inn@eclipse.co.uk
Dir: *From A361 take B3227 to S Moulton, then Atherington. L onto B3217 then 6m to Dalton. Pub on R*
Built as a Devon longhouse in the 17th century, it became a hotel 200 years later to serve the local cattle markets. The conversion resulted in a combination of large Georgian rooms with sash windows, and a traditional pub interior complete with homely beamed bar, oak settles and sturdy wooden tables. Visitors are guaranteed a warm welcome and a choice of good bar food plus a specials menu served in the restaurant. Fresh Scottish langoustine grilled with garlic and olive oil, and Devon mussels steamed with shallots, wine and cream might start a meal, followed by whole black bream, venison steak with red wine and orange sauce, or pork fillet and tiger prawns in a black bean sauce. Other freshly made dishes might include lamb shanks braised with red wine and rosemary, and pan-fried lambs' liver with cassis and blackcurrant sauce. West Country ales are served, and there is comfortable accommodation.
OPEN: 12-2 6-11 (closed Wed & 1st 2wks Feb)
BAR MEALS: Lunch served: Thu-Tue Dinner served: Thu-Tue 12-2 7-9 Av main course £5 **RESTAURANT:** Lunch served: Sun Dinner served: Thu-Tue 12-2 7-9 Av 3 course à la carte £15.50
BREWERY/COMPANY: Free House
PRINCIPAL BEERS: Sharp's Doom Bar, St Austell HSD, Barum Original, Jollyboat Freebooter. **FACILITIES:** Garden: Beer garden, food served outdoors Dogs allowed **NOTES:** Parking 15
ROOMS: 3 bedrooms 3 en suite from s£30 d£50

DREWSTEIGNTON   Map 03 SX79

Pick of the Pubs

The Drewe Arms ⚲
The Square EX6 6QN ☎ 01647 281224
Dir: *W of Exeter on A30 for 12 Miles L at Woodleigh junction follow signs for 3 Miles to Drewsteignton*
Picture-postcard, long and low thatched inn tucked away in a sleepy village square high above the wooded slopes of the Teign Valley, close to Castle Drogo (NT), Dartmoor and beautiful walks. A rural gem, once totally in a time warp when Britain's longest-serving landlady Mabel Mudge (75 years) was at the helm until she officially retired in 1996 aged 99. Although sympathetically refurbished by Whitbread, beers are still drawn from the cask and served through two hatchways, one in a classic, unspoilt and simply adorned bar, and a pine-furnished room with roaring log can also be found off the flagged passageway. 'Mabels Kitchen', now the dining-room, retains her old black range and original dresser. Good food, listed on a short blackboard menu, ranges from decent ploughman's lunches, crispy belly pork with neeps and tatties, home-made steak pudding, hock of ham with mash and cabbage and Devonshire junket, to scallops with pesto, trio of grilled fish and grilled bass on gratin leeks.
OPEN: 11-3 6-11 **BAR MEALS:** Lunch served: all week Dinner served: all week 12-2 6.30-9.30 Av main course £6.95

continued

England

DREWSTEIGNTON continued

RESTAURANT: Dinner served: all week 6.30-9.30 Av 3 course à la carte £20 **BREWERY/COMPANY:** Whitbread
PRINCIPAL BEERS: Flowers IPA, Bass ,Greene King, Greene King Old Speckled Hen. **FACILITIES:** Children welcome beer garden, patio, outdoor eating, Dogs allowed **NOTES:** Parking 12 **ROOMS:** 3 bedrooms 1 en suite from d£60

EXETER   Map 03 EX99

Double Locks Hotel
Canal Bank EX2 6LT ☎ 01392 256947 📠 01392 250247
Dir: From M5 follow signs for Marsh Barton Trading Est, R at 2nd rdbt, then onto slip rd to L of incinerator, R after bridge across canal
Not the easiest to find, but well worth the effort involved for real ale enthusiasts – and families in summer – the pub enjoys a peaceful setting on the old ship canal within sight of Exeter Cathedral. Alongside everything from garlic bread with blue cheese through filled granary rolls to ploughman's, jacket potatoes and salads in multifarious guises, house specialities include bangers and mash and feta cheese and spinach pie. Fine weather adds to the enjoyment with a huge barbecue menu.
OPEN: 11-11 (Sun 12-10.30) **BAR MEALS:** Lunch served: all week Dinner served: all week 11-10.30 (Sun 12-10) Av main course £5.45
RESTAURANT: Lunch served: all week Dinner served: all week 11-10.30 **BREWERY/COMPANY:** Smiles
PRINCIPAL BEERS: Adnams Broadside, Everard's Original, Branscombe Vale Branoc, Young's PA. **FACILITIES:** Children welcome Garden: Food served outdoors Dogs allowed
NOTES: Parking 100

Red Lion Inn 🍽 🍷
Broadclyst EX5 3EL ☎ 01392 461271
e-mail: redlion@broadclyst.fsbusiness.co.uk
Dir: on the B3181 Exeter to Culompton.
Situated at the centre of a National Trust village, close to Killerton House and Gardens, this renowned 15th-century inn features original beams and antique furniture inside and a cobbled courtyard outside. Plans are underway for an extension of the restaurant, and the new owners are enthusiastic about food. Among the kitchen's dishes you may find double lamb chops, saddle of venison, roasted polenta, wild mushroom and pea risotto, or pan-fried brill.
OPEN: 11-2.30 5.30-11 (Sun 12-3, 7-10.30) **BAR MEALS:** Lunch served: all week Dinner served: all week 12-2 6-9.30 Av main course £5 **RESTAURANT:** Lunch served: all week Dinner served: Mon-Sat 12-2 6-9.30 Av 3 course à la carte £17 **BREWERY/COMPANY:** Free House **PRINCIPAL BEERS:** Bass, Fullers London Pride, Hardy Royal Oak, Worthington Best. **FACILITIES:** Children welcome Garden: Food served outside Dogs allowed (in garden only, water & biscuits provided) **NOTES:** Parking 70 **ROOMS:** s£18 d£22

EXMINSTER   Map 03 SX98

Swans Nest 🍷
Station Rd EX6 8DZ ☎ 01392 832371
Dir: From M5 follow A379 Dawlish Rd
A much extended pub in a pleasant rural location whose facilities, unusually, extend to a ballroom, dance floor and stage. The carvery is a popular option for diners, with a choice of meats served with freshly prepared vegetables, though the salad bar is a tempting alternative, with over 39 items, including quiches, pies and home-smoked chicken. A carte of home-cooked fare ranges through Asian, Oriental, European and African cuisine.

OPEN: 10.30-2.30 6-11 Closed: Dec 26 **BAR MEALS:** Lunch served: all week Dinner served: all week 12-2 6-10 Av main course £7
BREWERY/COMPANY: Free House **PRINCIPAL BEERS:** Otter Bitter, Princetown Jail Ale. **FACILITIES:** Children welcome Garden
NOTES: Parking 102

Turf Hotel 🍷
Turf Lock EX6 8EE ☎ 01392 833128 📠 01392 832545
Dir: Off A379 turn L at end of Exminster by-pass/over rail bridge. Park by canal (pub is 0.75m on foot)
Built around 1830, and remotely situated on the Exeter Canal, this is one of only a few pubs in the country that cannot be reached by car. Follow the paths or travel there on the inn's own boat. The beautifully hand-drawn menu includes toasties, jacket potatoes, platters, sandwiches, snacks, and 'yummy specials'. Vegetarian dishes and daily specials are on the blackboard, and there is also a 'cook-your-own' BBQ menu.
OPEN: 11-3 6-11 (Jul-Aug 11-11) Closed: Nov-Feb
BAR MEALS: Lunch served: all week Dinner served: Mon-Sat 12-2.30 6.30-9 Av main course £7.50 **BREWERY/COMPANY:** Free House **PRINCIPAL BEERS:** Otter Bitter, Otter Ale, Otter Bright.
FACILITIES: Children welcome Garden: Food served outside. Overlooks Estuary Dogs allowed (water & dog chews)
ROOMS: 2 bedrooms from s£30 d£60

HARBERTON   Map 03 SX75

The Church House Inn 🍽 🍷
TQ9 7SF ☎ 01803 863707
Dir: From Totnes take A381 S. Take turn for Harberton on R, adjacent to church in centre of village

Originally built to house the stonemasons working on the church next door around 1100, this charming inn has also been used as a chantry house for monks. Inside there are a medieval oak screen, the original oak beams, and a latticed window containing 13th-century glass. The specials board changes regularly, but may include mixed mushroom and spinach lasagne, Portuguese steak picado, chicken wrapped in

continued

continued

OPEN: 11–11
BAR MEALS: L served all week.
D served all week. 11.30–6.30
6.30–10 Av main course £6
RESTAURANT: L served all week.
D served all week. 12–2 7–9.30
Av cost 3 courses £20
BREWERY/COMPANY: FREE
HOUSE
PRINCIPLE BEERS: Exe Valley
Dob's Bitter, Wadworth 6X, Scottish
Courage Directors, Interbrew
Flowers IPA
FACILITIES: Children and dogs
welcome
NOTES: Parking 14
ROOMS: 25 en suite

Royal Castle Hotel

The imposing quay front façade of the Royal Castle Hotel
masks the considerable age of the building behind. With a
commanding position overlooking the stunning estuary of
the river Dart, the hotel offers lively bars and good food.

★ ★ ♀ 🏠
The Quay TQ6 9PS
☎ 01803 833033 📠 01803 835445
e-mail: enquiry@royalcastle.co.uk

The hotel was developed from two private residences dating from the 1630s. One became the New Inn a century
later, frequented by thirsty seamen coming ashore. By 1782 the two houses were combined to become the Castle
Inn, with the addition of a brew house and stables at the rear. In the 1800s, with the coming of the turnpike, the inn
was extensively developed to provide a proper coaching house, with a third floor, the new façade topped by a
castellated cornice, and two Doric columns at the entrance. Thus the Castle Hotel was established. The large oak
beams in the Galleon Lounge are reputed to come from the wreckage of Spanish men o'war, and the Lydstone

range, opposite the bar, was forged in Dartmouth over 300 years
ago (joints are still roasted on it during the winter months). Tudor
fireplaces, spiral staircases, priest holes and period furniture
contribute to the sense of history, as does the bell board in the
courtyard, with each room's bell pitched to a different note. The
lively Harbour Bar, with its nautical décor, retains a traditional pub
atmosphere. Here you'll find local farm cider, cask ales,
numerous malt whiskies and a good choice of wines by the glass.
Morning coffee and decent pub food are also served in the
Galleon Lounge, while imaginative food is available in the
upstairs Adam Room Restaurant overlooking the river. Seafood
specialities include lobster, crab, Dover sole, and oven-roasted
sea bass with almond butter.

HARBERTON continued

bacon and filled with Brie, almonds and apricots, and chicken and spinach balti. Light bites are also available.
OPEN: 12–3 6–11 (Sat 12–4, 6–11 Sun 12–3, 7–10.30)
BAR MEALS: Lunch served: all week Dinner served: all week 12–1.45 7–9.30 Av main course £6.95 **RESTAURANT:** Lunch served: all week Dinner served: all week 12–1.45 7–9.30 Av 3 course à la carte £16.75
BREWERY/COMPANY: Free House **PRINCIPAL BEERS:** Bass, Wells Bombardier, Palmers IPA. **FACILITIES:** Children welcome Dogs allowed (water, dog biscuits) **NOTES:** Parking 20 **ROOMS:** 3 bedrooms from s£30 d£40

HATHERLEIGH — Map 02 SS50

Tally Ho Inn & Brewery ♀
14 Market St EX20 3JN ☎ 01837 810306 📠 01837 811079
e-mail: tally.ho@virgin.net
Great food, good beer, and a welcoming atmosphere are promised at this 15th-century pub located in the heart of the historic town. With its beamed bar and open fires, own ales brewed on site, and prize-winning home-made dishes, it clearly succeeds in its philosophy. In the cosy dining room and beamed bar expect crispy duck breast served with a roasted pepper and red onion chutney, plus Tally Ho sausages made with the house beer.
OPEN: 11–3 6–11.30 Closed: 25th Dec **BAR MEALS:** Lunch served: all week Dinner served: all week 11–2.30 6–9.30 Av main course £9
RESTAURANT: Lunch served: all week Dinner served: all week 11–2.30 6–9.30 Av 3 course à la carte £20
BREWERY/COMPANY: Free House **PRINCIPAL BEERS:** Tally Ho Tarka's Tipple, Nutters Ale. **FACILITIES:** Children welcome Children's licence Garden: Food served outside Dogs allowed
ROOMS: 3 bedrooms 3 en suite

HAYTOR VALE — Map 03 SX77

Pick of the Pubs

The Rock Inn ★ ★ ☺ ☜ ♀
TQ13 9XP ☎ 01364 661305 📠 01364 661242
e-mail: inn@rock-inn.co.uk
Dir: A38 from Exeter, at Drum Bridges rdbt take A382 for Bovey Tracey, 1st ex at 2nd rdbt (B3387), 3m L to Haytor Vale.
A coaching inn from around 1750, with much evidence of an earlier past, the Rock stands at the heart of a pretty village in the Dartmoor National Park. The open fires, antique tables and study furnishings lend a traditional feel to the rambling bars where menu options can include wild boar and apple sausages, Teign river mussels in mustard sauce and vegetarian linguini pasta. The kitchen's pride in West Country produce shines through in the roasted ostrich steaks, chargrilled rib-eye steaks and halibut fillets on pea purée, which typify the larger restaurant menu. Start here perhaps with goats' cheese roulade and herb pesto, and round off – if you've room – with treacle and walnut tart with lashings of clotted cream. Residents are offered champagne and roses in the four-poster or garden view bedrooms, which are named after former Grand National winners.
OPEN: 11–11 Closed: Dec 25–26 **BAR MEALS:** Lunch served: all week Dinner served: all week 12–2.30 6.30–9.30 Av main course £10 **RESTAURANT:** Lunch served: all week Dinner served: all week 12–2.30 7–9 Av 3 course à la carte £21.95
BREWERY/COMPANY: Free House
PRINCIPAL BEERS: Hardy Royal Oak, St Austell Dartmoor Best,

Interbrew Bass. **FACILITIES:** Children welcome Garden: Food served outside **NOTES:** Parking 35 **ROOMS:** 9 bedrooms 9 en suite from s£65.50 d£71.50

HOLBETON — Map 03 SX65

Mildmay Colours Inn ☜
PL8 1NA ☎ 01752 830248 📠 01752 830432
e-mail: louise@mildmaycolours.fsnet.co.uk
Dir: S from Exeter on A38, Yealmpton/Ermington, S past Ugborough & Ermington R onto A379. After 1.5m, turn L, signposted Mildmay Colours/Holbeton
A 17th-century pub with bedrooms, which derives its unusual name from a famous jockey, Lord Anthony Mildmay, whose portrait and silks are hung in the pub. Surrounded by thatched cottages and rolling hills, the inn has a well-equipped family room.There are simple bar snacks and children's meals, along with daily specials such as Dartmouth smoked chicken. or locally-caught mackerel, Modbury home-made stilton sausages and organic local farm lamb racks as further proof of an up-to-date approach.
OPEN: 11–3 6–11 (Sun 12–3, 7–10.30) **BAR MEALS:** Lunch served: all week Dinner served: all week 12–2 6–9 Av main course £6
RESTAURANT: Lunch served: Sun 12–2 Av 3 course à la carte £11.95 Av 3 course fixed price £10.95 **BREWERY/COMPANY:** Free House
PRINCIPAL BEERS: Mildmay Colours Bitter & Mildmay SP, Sharps Eden Ale. **FACILITIES:** Children welcome Garden: Picnic tables, food served outside Dogs allowed (water) **NOTES:** Parking 20
ROOMS: 8 bedrooms 8 en suite from s£32.50 d£50

HOLNE — Map 03 SX76

Church House Inn ♀
TQ13 7SJ ☎ 01364 631208 📠 01364 631525
Dir: From A38 at Ashburton (Peartree Junction) take road to Dartmoor. Follow road over Holne bridge, up hill and take L turn, signed to Holne.

Tucked away in the tranquil south Devon countryside, this traditional 14th-century free house offers a warm welcome and old-fashioned service. This is a paradise for outdoor enthusiasts, and the new owners are building a reputation for quality local fare. Bar lunches include sandwiches, salads and Dartmoor rabbit pie, whilst evening brings good fresh soups, scallops, venison casserole, or West Country fish pie.
OPEN: 12–2.30 7–11 (Summer 12–3) **BAR MEALS:** Lunch served: all week Dinner served: all week 12–2.15 7–9.15 Av main course £8
RESTAURANT: Lunch served: Sun Dinner served: all week 12.00–2.15 7–9.15 Av 3 course à la carte £20
BREWERY/COMPANY: Free House **PRINCIPAL BEERS:** Butcome Gold, Badger Tanglefoot, Palmer IPA. **FACILITIES:** Children welcome Garden: Food served outside Dogs allowed **NOTES:** Parking 6
ROOMS: 6 bedrooms 5 en suite from s£27.50 d£50

continued

Pick of the Pubs

The Otter Inn ♀
Weston EX14 3NZ ☎ 01404 42594
Dir: *Just off A30 W of Honiton*
On the banks of the idyllic River Otter, this ancient 14th-century inn is set in over two acres of grounds and was once a cider house. Enjoy one of the traditional real ales, try your hand at scrabble, dominoes or cards, or peruse the inn's extensive book collection. A wide-ranging menu caters for all tastes and includes fresh fish, game, steak, vegetarian dishes, bar meals and Sunday lunch.
OPEN: 11–11 (Fri-Sun 12–3) **BAR MEALS:** Lunch served: all week Dinner served: all week 12–2 6–9 Av main course £5.95
RESTAURANT: Lunch served: all week Dinner served: all week 12–2 6–9 Av 3 course à la carte £15.95
BREWERY/COMPANY: Free House
PRINCIPAL BEERS: Bass, Otter Ale. **FACILITIES:** Children welcome Garden: Food served outside Dogs allowed (water)
NOTES: Parking 60

The Elephant's Nest Inn 🍴
PL19 9NQ ☎ 01822 810273
e-mail: elephant@globalnet.co.uk
Dir: *Off A386 N of Tavistock*

An isolated inn on the flanks of Dartmoor reached via narrow lanes from Mary Tavy. The 16th-century buildings retain their real fires, slate floors and low beamed ceilings, decorated with loads of elephant memorabilia, including 'Elephant's Nest' written on the beams in over 80 languages. From a fairly safe menu using much local produce come a Trawlerman's Lunch of fresh fish, nine different ploughman's, numerous steaks and vegetarian alternatives, and up to a dozen home-made puds to follow.
OPEN: 11.30-2.30 6.30–11 (Sun 12-2.30, 7-10.30)
BAR MEALS: Lunch served: all week Dinner served: all week 11.30-2 6.30-10 **BREWERY/COMPANY:** Free House
PRINCIPAL BEERS: Interbrew Boddingtons Bitter, Palmers IPA, St Austells HSD plus changing guest ales. **FACILITIES:** Children welcome Garden: Food served outside Dogs allowed
NOTES: Parking 30

For a list of pubs with AA Accommodation
♦ Awards see pages 649-653 ★

Pick of the Pubs

Hoops Country Inn & Hotel 🍴♀
'Hoops', nr Clovelly EX39 5DL
☎ 01237 451222 📠 01237 451247
e-mail: sales@hoopsinn.co.uk
Dir: *Hoops in on the A39 between Bideford & Clovelly*

Set in 16 acres of garden and meadow close to the National Trust coastal path, the thatch-roofed, cob-walled 13th-century smugglers' inn combines olde worlde charm with up-to-date fine cuisine. Throughout the bar and dining-rooms potted herring roes with cognac and chicken livers grilled in pancetta precede main dishes such as Hoops crackly pork knuckle, seasonal game pie and goose breast with apple tempura and onion mash. Pride of place goes to the fish blackboards with daily-changing offers of Clovelly mackerel with mustard mash and monkfish collops with raspberry vinaigrette. Round off with deep treacle tart or Chocolate Ectasy with Cointreau cream.
OPEN: 8–11 (Sun 8.30-10.30) Closed: Dec 25
BAR MEALS: Lunch served: all week Dinner served: all week 12–3 5.30-9.30 Av main course £8.50 **RESTAURANT:** Lunch served: all week Dinner served: all week 12–3 7-9.30 Av 3 course à la carte £16.50 **BREWERY/COMPANY:** Free House
PRINCIPAL BEERS: Jollyboat Mainbrace, Cottage, Exe Valley, Cotleigh Barn Owl. **FACILITIES:** Children welcome Children's licence Garden: outdoor eating, BBQ Dogs allowed
NOTES: Parking 150 **ROOMS:** 12 bedrooms 12 en suite from s£55 d£90

The Royal Inn
PL19 8PJ ☎ 01822 870214
e-mail: paul@royalinn.co.uk
Dir: *South of B3362 Launceston/Tavistock road*
Originally a nunnery, pub is situated on the banks of the Tamar in a wooded river valley. Its name comes from a visit, verified by his seal in the granite doorstep, of King Charles I. It remains today a cosy old 'proper' pub, without jukebox or amusement machines. Locally raised beef is used in the steaks, casseroles and stews (beef in ale, perhaps), that rub shoulders with mussels Royale, chilli cheese tortillas, and chicken in bacon and mushroom sauce.
OPEN: 12–3 7-11 **BAR MEALS:** Lunch served: all week Dinner served: all week 12-2 7-9 Av main course £6 **RESTAURANT:** Lunch served: all week Dinner served: all week 12-2 7-9
BREWERY/COMPANY: Free House **PRINCIPAL BEERS:** Sharp's Doom Bar & Special, Interbrew Bass, Ring O'Bells Tipsy Trotter.
FACILITIES: Garden: Patio, food served outside Dogs allowed
NOTES: Parking 30

England

IVYBRIDGE
Map 03 SX65

Anchor Inn
Lutterburn St, Ugborough PL21 0NG ☎ 01752 892283
Although it has a nautical name, this pub is nowhere near the
sea. It seems that it may be named after a local community of
anchorite monks from the 14th century. The menu has a
definite international feel, complete with flags and maps.
Britain, North America, France, Australia, and Italy are all
represented with a variety of dishes. Vegetarians also have
their own menu, which also has a cosmopolitan theme.
Regularly changing specials.
OPEN: 11-11 **BAR MEALS:** Lunch served: all week Dinner served:
all week 12-2.30 7-9 Av main course £7 **RESTAURANT:** Lunch
served: all week Dinner served: all week 12-3 7-10 Av 3 course à la
carte £25 **BREWERY/COMPANY:** Free House
PRINCIPAL BEERS: TSB, Spitfire, Interbrew Bass.
FACILITIES: Children welcome Garden: Food served outside. Dogs
allowed (water & biscuits provided) **NOTES:** Parking 15 **ROOMS:** 5
bedrooms 5 en suite from s£35 d£50

KENTON
Map 03 SX98

Devon Arms ♦♦♦
Fore St EX6 8LD ☎ 01626 890213 ▤ 01626 891678
e-mail: devon.arms@ukgateway.net
Dir: *on A379 between Exeter & Dawlish 7m from Exeter, 5m from Dawlish,
adjacent to Powderham Castle*
A comfortable, family-run free house this old coaching house
dates back to 1592 and its 1846 lease described an inn,
posting house and brewery producing 'forty hogsheads per
week'. Today's modern comforts comprise a garden with
patio, barbecue, pets' corner and children's play area, and
comfortably furnished bedrooms. The bar menu encompasses
steak and ale pie, cod in beer batter, ploughman's and salads,
supplemented by steak grills.
OPEN: 11-2.30 5.30-11 (Sun 12-3, 7-10.30) **BAR MEALS:** Lunch
served: all week Dinner served: all week 12-2 6.30-9.30
RESTAURANT: Lunch served: all week Dinner served: all week 12-2
6.30-9 **BREWERY/COMPANY:** Free House
PRINCIPAL BEERS: Teign Valley Tipple, Wadworth 6X, Marston's
Pedigree. **FACILITIES:** Children welcome Garden: Food served
outside Dogs allowed **NOTES:** Parking 20 **ROOMS:** 6 bedrooms 6
en suite from s£30 d£45

KINGSBRIDGE
Map 03 SX74

Church House Inn
Churchstow TQ7 3QW ☎ 01548 852237
Dir: *On A379 1.5m W of Kingsbridge*
Set in some lovely Devon countryside on the way to
Salcombe, this historic 15th-century inn was originally the site
of a rest house for Cistercian monks during the 13th century.
Look out for sea bass, steak and kidney pie, devilled chicken,
or smoked salmon. There is also a very popular hot carvery.

The Crabshell Inn
Embankment Rd TQ7 1JZ ☎ 01548 852345 ▤ 01548 825262
You can fish for crab from the quay of this family-run
waterside inn that boasts 240 feet of free mooring for
customers. There are panoramic views of the Kingsbridge
estuary and occasionally seals playing right by the sea wall.
Fresh local fish is, of course, the highlight of a menu with
pride of place going to the lobster and crab platters for two if
ordered a day ahead. Additionally there are numerous grills,

vegetarian choices and an imaginative selection for (well-
behaved) children.
OPEN: 11-11 (Sun 12-10.30) **BAR MEALS:** Lunch served: all week
Dinner served: all week 12-2.30 6-9.30 Av main course £5
RESTAURANT: Lunch served: all week Dinner served: all week
12-2.30 6-9.30 Av 3 course à la carte £10
BREWERY/COMPANY: Free House **PRINCIPAL BEERS:** Bass
Bitter, Crabshell Bitter, Wadworth 6X. **FACILITIES:** Children welcome
Garden: Patio area Dogs allowed (water) **NOTES:** Parking 40

KINGSKERSWELL
Map 03 SX86

Barn Owl Inn ♀
Aller Mills TQ12 5AN ☎ 01803 872130
Located at the heart of an area of sleepy Devon hamlets, this
16th-century longhouse boasts many charming features,
including flagged floors, a black leaded range and oak beams
in a high-vaulted converted barn with a minstrel's gallery.
Handy for Dartmoor and the English Riviera towns of Torquay,
Brixham and Paignton. The menu offers hearty wholesome
fare such as hog roast, mixed grill, half-shoulder of lamb and
steak and kidney pie with Guinness.
OPEN: 11-11 (Sun 12-10.30) **BAR MEALS:** Lunch served: all week
Dinner served: all week 12-2.30 6-9.30 Av main course £4.75
RESTAURANT: Lunch served: all week Dinner served: all week
12-2.30 6-9.30 Av 3 course à la carte £15
BREWERY/COMPANY: Eldridge Pope **PRINCIPAL BEERS:** Bass,
Courage Best. **FACILITIES:** Children welcome Garden: Food
served outside **NOTES:** Parking 30 **ROOMS:** 6 bedrooms from
s£49 d£64

KINGSTEIGNTON
Map 03 SX87

Old Rydon Inn ♀
Rydon Rd TQ12 3QG ☎ 01626 354626 ▤ 01626 356980
Dir: *From A380 take B3193 into Kingsteignton*
A feature of this Grade II listed former farmhouse is its large
family dining conservatory filled with flowering tropical plants
and grape vines. Adjacent, the pub area is housed in the old
stables with a cider apple loft above it. A typical menu
features Old Rydon seafood salad, grilled salmon on vegetable
spaghetti, venison and wild boar steaks, and Nasi Goreng.
Light bites include salads, jacket potatoes, toasted muffins,
and ploughmans.
OPEN: 11-3 6-11 Closed: 25 Dec **BAR MEALS:** Lunch served: all
week Dinner served: all week 12-2 6.30-9.30 Av main course £7.95
RESTAURANT: Dinner served: Mon-Sat 7-9.30 Av 3 course à la carte
£25 **BREWERY/COMPANY:** Heavitree **PRINCIPAL BEERS:** Bass,
Fullers London Pride. **FACILITIES:** Children welcome Garden: beer
garden, patio, outdoor eating **NOTES:** Parking 40

KINGSTON
Map 03 SX64

The Dolphin Inn
TQ7 4QE ☎ 01548 810314 ▤ 01548 810314
Historic 16th-century beamed inn situated in a delightful South
Hams village. Bigbury Bay and Burgh Island are nearby and
the pub is handy for rambling by the tranquil River Erme or
strolling to the coast. Relax by the inglenook fireplace and
enjoy a pint of real ale or perhaps something from the
appetising menu which uses locally-grown produce. Typical
dishes include Welsh chicken casserole, salmon with lemon
and ginger sauce, venison and Guinness casserole, or scallops
pan-fried with garlic and bacon.
OPEN: 11-2.30 (Summer 3) 6-11 (Sun 12-3, 7-10.30)
BAR MEALS: Lunch served: all week Dinner served: all week 12-2

continued

continued

6–9.30 Av main course £6.95 **PRINCIPAL BEERS:** Ushers - Founders & Four Seasons Ale, Courage Best. **FACILITIES:** Children welcome Garden: Food served outside. Dogs allowed (in the garden only, water provided) **NOTES:** Parking 40 **ROOMS:** 3 bedrooms 3 en suite from s£39.50 d£55

KINGSWEAR   Map 03 SX85

The Ship
Higher St TQ6 0AG ☎ 01803 752348
Historic village pub overlooking the scenic River Dart towards Dartmouth and Dittisham. Located in one of South Devon's most picturesque corners, this tall, character inn is very much a village local with a friendly, welcoming atmosphere inside. Well-prepared fresh food is the hallmark of the menu. Sandwiches, baguettes and pies are available in the bar, while the restaurant menu offers duck, venison, sea bass, and crab wrapped in a salmon parcel.
OPEN: 12–3 6–11 **BAR MEALS:** Lunch served: all week Dinner served: all week 12.30–2 7–9.30 Av main course £4.95
RESTAURANT: Dinner served: all week 7–9.30 Av 3 course à la carte £13.95 **BREWERY/COMPANY:** Heavitree
PRINCIPAL BEERS: Flowers IPA, Bass, Otter. **FACILITIES:** Children welcome Garden: outdoor eating, patio/terrace Dogs allowed (water) No credit cards

KNOWSTONE   Map 03 SS82

Pick of the Pubs

Masons Arms Inn ♀
EX36 4RY ☎ 01398 341231
e-mail: masonsarmsinn@aol.com
Dir: M5 J27 Off A361 between Tiverton & S Molton

Nestling in a sleepy thatched village and surrounded by farmland in the foothills of Exmoor, this 13th-century inn is a classic medieval hostelry. Unspoilt and still complete with inglenook fireplaces, bread ovens, heavy black oak beams and beers from the cask, it is enthusiastically run by owners Jo and Paul Stretton-Downes. A new dining extension has offered much scope for developing the food side of the business. In this cosy, atmospheric area there are polished dark wood dining tables, tasteful prints and warming log fires, plus excellent views of Exmoor. For a light lunch you can try filled baguettes (bacon and Brie), jacket potatoes, and salads, while the carte offers seafood pancake, game and red wine pie, garlic and rosemary-crusted rack of lamb, with malted bread and butter pudding for an unusual dessert. There's a snug cottage for two just a short stroll away.
OPEN: 12–3 6–11 (Sun 12–3, 7–10.30) Closed: Dec 25

BAR MEALS: Lunch served: all week Dinner served: all week 12–2 7–9 Av main course £8 **BREWERY/COMPANY:** Free House **PRINCIPAL BEERS:** Cotleigh Tawny.
FACILITIES: Garden: Food served outside. Dogs allowed (on lead) **NOTES:** Parking 10 **ROOMS:** 1 bedrooms 1 en suite from s£40 d£60

LEWDOWN   Map 02 SX48

The Harris Arms ♀
Portgate EX20 4PZ ☎ 01566 783331 ▤ 01566 783161
e-mail: peterdgrant@hotmail.com
Dir: From A30 take Lifton turning, halfway between Lifton and Lewdown
A former corn merchants and church brewery, this 16th-century building stands on a Roman ridge road providing spectacular country views. Growing in popularity with locals and visitors alike, the pub offers an informal atmosphere, prompt service and good food. The emphasis is on home-made sauces and a weekly changing specials board reflecting the excellence of local produce. Typical dishes are Devon steaks, fresh haddock fillet with lemon and butter, and pork Calvados.
OPEN: 11–3 5.30–11 (Sun 12–3, 7–10.30) (winter 12–3, 5.30–11)
BAR MEALS: Lunch served: all week Dinner served: all week 12–2.30 6.30–9.15 Av main course £7.75 **RESTAURANT:** Lunch served: all week Dinner served: all week 12–2.30 6.30–9.15 Av 3 course à la carte £15.85 **BREWERY/COMPANY:** Free House
PRINCIPAL BEERS: Interbrew Bass, St Austell Tinners, Ring O' Bells Bodmin Boar. **FACILITIES:** Garden: Food served outside **NOTES:** Parking 30

LIFTON   Map 02 SX38

Pick of the Pubs

The Arundell Arms ★ ★ ★ ◎◎◎◎ ♀
PL16 0AA ☎ 01566 784666 ▤ 01566 784494
e-mail: reservations@arundellarms.com
Dir: 2/3m off the A30 dual carriageway, 3m E of Launceston
Some forty years in the same ownership, this creeper-clad 18th-century coaching inn at the heart of a delightful Devon village draws discerning guests to its comfortable rooms and relaxing atmosphere, spurred on by 20 miles of private fishing and numerous country pursuits. The Courthouse Bar (originally the magistrates' court) has a year-round local appeal, while the Arundell Bar is a focal point of the hotel proper. Starters and light meals run from baked goats' cheese salad with avocado, through toasted fillet steak with Dijon mustard to sweet pepper salad with pickled anchovies, pesto and Parmesan shavings. There are salads of smoked salmon, home-cured gammon and roast Devon beef with horseradish cream. Daily hot dishes might be Spanish omelette with deep-fried onions or sole fritters in beer batter with curried mayonnaise. A la carte dining of considerable class features locally-sourced meat, fish, vegetables and cheeses.
OPEN: 11.30–3 6–11 **BAR MEALS:** Lunch served: all week Dinner served: all week 12–2.30 6–9.30 Av main course £10
RESTAURANT: Lunch served: all week Dinner served: all week 12.30–2 7.30–9.30 Av 5 course fixed price £38.25
BREWERY/COMPANY: Free House
PRINCIPAL BEERS: Guest beers. **FACILITIES:** Children welcome Garden: Food served outside Dogs allowed **NOTES:** Parking 70 **ROOMS:** 27 bedrooms 27 en suite from s£48 d£96

continued

LITTLEHEMPSTON
Map 03 SX86

Tally Ho Inn
TQ9 6NF ☎ 01803 862316 📠 01803 862316
Dir: Off the A38 at Buckfastleigh

A traditional 14th-century inn very much at the centre of the community, and catering for visitors and locals alike. In summer the hanging baskets and flower-filled patios are a gardener's delight, while roaring log fires and cosy corners have their own charm in winter. An ever-changing specials board supplements dishes such as tournedos Rossini, whole plaice stuffed with prawns and crab, and escalope of turkey with Camembert. Well-kept real ales, and excellent overnight accommodation.

OPEN: 12–3 6–11 Closed: Dec 25 **BAR MEALS:** Lunch served: all week Dinner served: all week 12–2 7–9 Av main course £5.95
BREWERY/COMPANY: Free House
PRINCIPAL BEERS: Interbrew Bass plus guest ales.
FACILITIES: Children welcome Garden: Patio, food served outdoors Dogs allowed **NOTES:** Parking 20 **ROOMS:** 4 bedrooms 4 en suite from s£50 d£60

LOWER ASHTON
Map 03 SX88

Manor Inn
EX6 7QL ☎ 01647 252304
e-mail: manorinn@aol.com
Dir: A38, Teign Valley turning, follow signs for B3193, pub 5m on R, Just over the stone bridge

A traditional and authentic country inn set in a small village surrounded by trees and hills at the heart of the Teign Valley. Completely unspoilt within, it boasts traditional furnishings and plenty of atmosphere in the homely bars, warmed in winter by blazing log fires, while in summer the peaceful garden is an added attraction. Menus scarcely stray from the tried-and-tested ploughman's, baked potatoes and grilled steaks supplemented by a specials board that might include ragout of lamb, tuna and prawn bake and vegetable and nut curry.

OPEN: 12–2 6.30–11 **BAR MEALS:** Lunch served: Tues-Sun Dinner served: Tues-Sun 12–1.30 7–9.30 Av main course £6.95
BREWERY/COMPANY: Free House
PRINCIPAL BEERS: Teignworthy Reel Ale, Wadworth 6X, Princetown Jail Ale, RCH Pitchfork. **FACILITIES:** Garden: Food Served outside Dogs allowed (water) **NOTES:** Parking 20

LUSTLEIGH
Map 03 SX78

The Cleave
TQ13 9TJ ☎ 01647 277223 📠 01647 277223
e-mail: alisonperring@supanet.com
Dir: Off A382 between Bovey Tracy and Moretonhampstead

Originally a Devon longhouse, this 15th-century thatched inn is set in a beautiful village on the flanks of Dartmoor, a perfect stop for walkers. Once used as an unofficial waiting room for the now long-gone railway station. There is a cosy lounge bar with granite walls and a vast inglenook fireplace, and a bigger Victorian bar with an impressive array of musical instruments. Menu includes Cleave steak and kidney pie, breast of chicken stuffed with Stilton and wrapped in bacon, poached salmon steak, and local butcher's sausages with mash and onion gravy.

continued

OPEN: 11–3 6.30–11 (summer 11–11) Closed: Mon Nov–Feb
BAR MEALS: Lunch served: all week Dinner served: all week 12–2.30 6.30–9 Av main course £7.50 **RESTAURANT:** Lunch served: all week Dinner served: all week 12–2 6.30 Av 3 course à la carte £16
BREWERY/COMPANY: Heavitree **PRINCIPAL BEERS:** Flowers Original, Bass, Wadworth 6X. **FACILITIES:** Children welcome Garden: Food served outside. Pretty garden Dogs allowed
NOTES: Parking 10

LYDFORD
Map 02 SX58

Pick of the Pubs

Castle Inn & Hotel
EX20 4BH ☎ 01822 820242 & 820241 📠 01822 820454
e-mail: castle1lyd@aol.com
Dir: Off A386 S of Okehampton

Located beside the medieval castle and within walking distance of Lydford Gorge (NT), this pretty, wisteria-clad inn dates from the 16th-century. The interior oozes atmosphere and period charm, with its slate floors, low, lamp-lit beams, decorative plates and huge Norman fireplace. A change of hands has inevitably resulted in some changes but there is plenty of enthusiasm for the task in hand. Freshly prepared dishes are the mainstay of the short menu. Fresh fish appears daily such as fillet of salmon with coriander dressed noodles and lemon-butter sauce. Among starters chicken liver and green peppercorn pâté or warm Stilton and plum tartlet with a redcurrant and port sauce are typical. Main courses may include several vegetarian dishes such as mixed bean curry with Canadian wild rice and long grain rice or wild mushroom and nut risotto with pimento sauce. Comfortable accommodation; shrub-filled garden for summer alfresco eating. Close to Dartmoor and miles of beautiful walks.
OPEN: 11–11 **BAR MEALS:** Lunch served: all week Dinner served: all week 12–2.15 7–9.15 Av main course £8
RESTAURANT: Lunch served: all week Dinner served: all week 12–2.15 7–9.15 Av 3 course à la carte £17 Av 3 course fixed price £17 **BREWERY/COMPANY:** Heavitree
PRINCIPAL BEERS: Fullers London Pride, Flowers IPA, Greene King Old Speckled Hen. **FACILITIES:** Children welcome Garden: Food served outside. Dogs allowed (allowed in bar, patio & bedrooms) **NOTES:** Parking 10 **ROOMS:** 9 bedrooms 9 en suite from s£40 d£68

Pick of the Pubs

Dartmoor Inn ◉◉ ⓘ ♀
EX20 4AY ☎ 01822 820221 📄 01822 820494
Dir: On A386 S of Okehampton

A 16th-century coaching house, the Dartmoor Inn is set in the pretty village of Lydford on the western side of Dartmoor National Park. It is almost certainly the inn described by Charles Kingsley in Westward Ho! as the place where Roger Rowe, King of Gubbinses was slain. The bar with its welcoming log fire and fresh fires is augmented by intimate dining areas where candlelit dinners are served. British classics form the basis of the menus, with potted ox tongue, Cornish fish casserole and liver, bacon and onions on the bar selection, along with a two-course PDQ lunch for those on the move. There's a set lunch from the main menu too. House specialities include a mixed grill of sea fishes (for two), double rib of Devon beef, slowly cooked confit of Gressingham duck leg with spiced sauce, and hot kumquat pudding with clotted cream.
OPEN: 11.30–3 6.30–11 (6–11 in Summer) Closed: BHs
BAR MEALS: Lunch served: Tue-Sun 12–2.15 Dinner served: Tue-Sat 6.30–10 Av main course £11.50 **RESTAURANT:** Lunch served: Tue-Sun 12–2.15 Dinner served: Tue-Sat 6.30–10 Av 3 course à la carte £23.75 **BREWERY/COMPANY:** Free House
PRINCIPAL BEERS: Interbrew Bass, Greene King Old Speckled Hen, St Austell Hicks Special & Dartmoor Best.
FACILITIES: Children welcome Garden: Food served outside, patio Dogs allowed **NOTES:** Parking 35 **ROOMS:** 3 bedrooms 3 en suite

---

LYMPSTONE — Map 03 SX98

The Globe Inn ⓘ ♀
The Strand EX8 5EY ☎ 01395 263166
Set in the estuary village of Lympstone, this traditional beamed inn has a good local reputation for seafood. The separate restaurant area serves as a coffee bar during the day. Look out for seafood platter, Thai grilled haddock, bass with plum and ginger sauce, crab sandwiches, and battered fish and chips on Thursdays. Weekend music nights. Quiz night weekly.
OPEN: 11–3 5.30–11 **BAR MEALS:** Lunch served: all week 12–2 Dinner served: Mon-Sat 6.30–9.30 Av main course £5
RESTAURANT: Dinner served: Mon-Sat 7–9.30 Av 3 course à la carte £15 **BREWERY/COMPANY:** Heavitree
PRINCIPAL BEERS: Flowers IPA, Otter, Bass, Whitbread Best.
FACILITIES: Children welcome Dogs allowed (water & treats provided) **ROOMS:** 2 bedrooms 1 en suite from d£19

LYNMOUTH — Map 03 SS74

Pick of the Pubs

Rising Sun Hotel ⓘ ♀
Harbourside EX35 6EG ☎ 01598 753223 📄 01598 753480
e-mail: risingsunlynmouth@easynet.co.uk
Dir: From M5 J25 to Minehead, A39 to Lynmouth

The Rising Sun is a 14th-century thatched smugglers inn. It overlooks the tiny harbour and Lynmouth Bay, set against the highest cliffs in England. Uneven floors, thick walls and crooked ceilings speak volumes of the hotel's history, and the wild romance of Lorna Doone is captured here, where R D Blackmore wrote several chapters of his classic book. The poet Shelley is believed to have honeymooned in the garden cottage, which now bears his name. Lynmouth is on the edge of Exmoor National Park, where herds of red deer, wild ponies and birds of prey roam free. Exmoor game and seafood are house specialities, with dishes such as saddle of roast venison with root vegetable tatin and apple dauphinoise, and grilled Lynmouth Bay lobster with béarnaise sauce. At night the oak-panelled, candlelit dining room exemplifies the best of romantic British inn-keeping. Bedrooms are individually designed and offer modern facilities and harbour views.
OPEN: 11–3 6.30–11 **BAR MEALS:** Lunch served: all week Dinner served: all week 12–2 7–9 Av main course £7.50
RESTAURANT: Lunch served: all week Dinner served: all week 12–2 7–9 Av 3 course à la carte £27.50
BREWERY/COMPANY: Free House
PRINCIPAL BEERS: Exmoor Gold, Fox & Exmoor Ale, Cotleigh Tawny Ale. **FACILITIES:** Garden: Patio, sea views, food served outside **ROOMS:** 16 bedrooms 16 en suite

---

MEAVY — Map 02 SX56

The Royal Oak Inn
PL20 6PJ ☎ 01822 852944
e-mail: royaloakinn.meavy@barbox.net
Dir: Off A386 between Tavistock & Plymouth
Standing on the edge of Dartmoor, between Tavistock and Plymouth, this 12th-century brew house is a popular watering hole for those touring and exploring the National Park. Good quality fare is prepared from produce bought locally and much of the meat is free-range. A local fishmonger delivers fresh fish from Plymouth. Expect filled baguettes, local pasties and salads at lunchtime, while the evening menu consists of stuffed plaice, lemon butterfly chicken, gammon steak and salsa sardines.
OPEN: 11.30–3 6.30–11 (Sun 12–3, 6.30–10.30)
BAR MEALS: Lunch served: all week Dinner served: all week 11.30–2.00 7–9.00 Av main course £5 **BREWERY/COMPANY:** Free House **PRINCIPAL BEERS:** Bass, Courage Best, Princetown Jail Ale, IPA. **FACILITIES:** Dogs allowed

England

NEWTON ABBOT   Map 03 SX87

The Court Farm Inn
Wilton Way, Abbotskerswell TQ12 5NY ☎ 01626 361866

Former Devon longhouse, rebuilt in 1721 as a farmhouse and converted to a pub in the early 1970s. The character, listed building has a cosy, relaxed atmosphere, a delightful lawned beer garden, and good home-cooked food. There's a plentiful choice of traditional bar snacks, including filled baguettes, jacket potatoes and various ploughman's. Light meals and more robust dishes like chicken stir-fry, moules marinière, and pan-fried breast of duck with orange and Grand Marnier sauce.
OPEN: 11-11 (Sun 12-10.30) **BAR MEALS:** Lunch served: all week Dinner served: all week 11.30-2.30 5-10 Av main course £5.95
RESTAURANT: 11.30-2.30 5-10 10
BREWERY/COMPANY: Heavitree **PRINCIPAL BEERS:** Interbrew Bass, Flowers IPA, Fuller's London Pride, Wadworth 6X.
FACILITIES: Children welcome Garden: Food served outdoors, flower beds, bird table Dogs allowed **NOTES:** Parking 70

The Linny Inn & Hayloft Dining Area
Coffinswell TQ12 4SR ☎ 01803 873192 ▤ 01803 873395
e-mail: alexatex@aol.com
Dir: follow signs from A380

Dating from the 14th century, this family-run inn stands in a charming, picture-postcard village full of thatched cottages near Torquay. The Linny Inn is well kept and a new state-of-the-art kitchen was installed in 2002. Popular restaurant with a large patio leading out to the sun-trap garden and numerous delightful walks on the doorstep. Same menu throughout offers everything from sandwiches, salad platters, pasta and seafood specials to trio of lamb chops and beef curry.
OPEN: 11.30-3 6.30-11 **BAR MEALS:** Lunch served: all week Dinner served: all week 12-2 6.30-9.30 Av main course £9
RESTAURANT: 12-2 6.30-9.30 **BREWERY/COMPANY:** Free House **PRINCIPAL BEERS:** Carlsberg-Tetley Bitter, Interbrew Bass.
FACILITIES: Children welcome Garden: patio/terrace, food served outside **NOTES:** Parking 34

The Wild Goose Inn
Combeinteignhead TQ12 4RA ☎ 01626 872241
Dir: from A380 at the Newton Abbot rdbt, take the B3195 Shaldon rd, signed Milber, for 2.5m into village then R at signpost
Originally known as the Country House Inn, this Devon longhouse was renamed after the local geese who leapt from a high field onto passing customers. Virtually unchanged since first licensed in 1840, it boasts a peaceful beer garden overlooking a 14th-century church and a stream winding its way through the valley. Real ales from West Country micro-breweries, and a good choice of chef's specials including fresh pasta, home-made pies, whole rack of pork ribs, game sausages and fresh fish.
OPEN: 11.30-2.30 6.30-11 (Sun 12-2.30, 7-10.30)
BAR MEALS: Lunch served: all week Dinner served: all week 12-2 7-10 Av main course £6 **RESTAURANT:** Lunch served: all week Dinner served: all week 12-2 7-10 Av 3 course à la carte £14
BREWERY/COMPANY: Free House **PRINCIPAL BEERS:** Otter Ale, Cotleigh, Sharps Bitter, Skinner's Bitter. **FACILITIES:** Garden: Food served outside, patio **NOTES:** Parking 40

NEWTON ST CYRES   Map 03 SX89

The Beer Engine
EX5 5AX ☎ 01392 851282 ▤ 01392 851876
e-mail: enquiries@thebeerengine.co.uk
Dir: from Exeter take A377 towards Crediton, pub is opp train station in Newton St Cyres

A white-painted local with a straightforward appearance, formerly a railway hotel. It has been brewing its own beer for nearly 20 years, mainly for the consumption of customers. Expect a good choice of fish dishes - grilled sea bass, haddock mornay, salmon fillet, and monkfish - along with steak and ale pie, chicken supreme, aubergines bake, and steak and ale pie. Occasional live music in the cellar bar.
OPEN: 11-11 (Sun 12-10.30) **BAR MEALS:** Lunch served: all week Dinner served: all week 12-2 6.30-9.30 Av main course £6.50
BREWERY/COMPANY: Free House **PRINCIPAL BEERS:** Beer Engine, Piston Bitter, Rail Ale, Sleeper Heavy. **FACILITIES:** Children welcome Garden: Food served outside Dogs allowed **NOTES:** Parking 30

Crown and Sceptre
EX5 5DA ☎ 01392 851278
Dir: 2m NW of Exeter on A377
Twice razed by fire (the last time in 1962), today's pub has still managed to keep original character with oak beams and open fires, while summer barbecues and children's play areas feature among its added attractions. From straightforward bar meals of pies of the day, curries and 'big plate specials' (such as the 24oz mixed grill), the dining menu extends to duck

continued

breast with plum sauce, Mexican chilli and grilled steaks with saucy options such as chasseur and Diane.

OPEN: 11.30 -11 **BAR MEALS:** Lunch served: all week Dinner served: all week 12-9 Av main course £8.95 **RESTAURANT:** Lunch served: all week Dinner served: all week 12-2 6-9 Av 3 course à la carte £15 **BREWERY/COMPANY:** Heavitree
PRINCIPAL BEERS: Interbrew Bass, Wadworth 6X, Otter Ale plus guest beers. **FACILITIES:** Children welcome Garden: Patio area, food served outside **NOTES:** Parking 30

NOSS MAYO   Map 02 SX54

Pick of the Pubs

The Ship Inn 🐾 ♀
PL8 1EW ☎ 01752 872387 📄 01752 873294
e-mail: ship@nossmayo.com
Dir: 3m S of Yealmpton, on the S side of the Yealm estuary
The Ship is a traditional 16th-century waterside inn attracting walkers, tourists and yachtsmen alike (you can tie your boat up outside). It's fun to reach the pub at high tide and relax at one of the terrace tables overlooking the scenic estuary. A refit three years ago returned the pub to its roots, with good local and regional beers, home-made food, and comfortable surroundings – wood floors, log fires, old furniture, people, papers and books. The daily menu is based on local produce, and there's a choice of granary bread sandwiches ranging from cheese and tomato to aromatic duck with spring onions. Favourite dishes, earning a regular slot on the carte, include classic prawn cocktail with Marie Rose dressing, braised shoulder of Devon lamb served with herb mash and mixed vegetables, and salmon fishcakes with chive mayonnaise and mixed salad.
OPEN: 11-11 **BAR MEALS:** Lunch served: all week Dinner served: all week 12-9.30 Av main course £10
BREWERY/COMPANY: Free House
PRINCIPAL BEERS: Tamar, Exmoor Gold, Shepherd Neame Spitfire Premium Ale, St Austell Dartmoor Best.
FACILITIES: Children welcome Garden: Food served outdoors Dogs allowed (downstairs only) **NOTES:** Parking 100

OTTERY ST MARY   Map 03 SY19

The Talaton Inn
Talaton EX5 2RQ ☎ 01404 822214
Timber-framed, well-maintained 16th-century inn. Popular with the locals. Themed food nights.

PARRACOMBE   Map 03 SS64

Pick of the Pubs

The Fox & Goose 🐾 ♀ NEW
EX31 4PE ☎ 01598 763239 📄 01598 763621
e-mail: foxandgoose@mrexcessive.net
Dir: The Fox is 1m from the A39 between Blackmoor Gate (2m) and Lynton (6m). Signposted to Parracombe (With a 'Fox & Goose' sign on approach)

Photographs in the bar show this pub to have been two farm cottages until around 1900 when the landlord decided to make it a bit grander. His extensions have not spoilt the atmosphere, and despite a sound reputation for good food this remains a relaxing place where drinkers are welcome. Set in the heart of a pretty, unspoilt village with a narrow street, the Fox takes pride in offering a wide selection of dishes to suit all tastes, based on produce from the surrounding farms and the Devon coast. The blackboard menus keep up with the daily changes, which include the popular venison steak with cognac and redcurrant gravy, and a prize-winning steak and kidney pie. Fish choices might be turbot fillet with saffron risotto, and red bream with prawns, with perhaps pina colada cheesecake with raspberry sauce to round things off.
OPEN: 12-3 6-11 **BAR MEALS:** Lunch served: all week Dinner served: all week 12-2 6-9.30 Av main course £10
BREWERY/COMPANY: Free House
PRINCIPAL BEERS: Cotleigh Barn Owl, Carlsberg, Dartmoor Best, Exmoor Gold. **FACILITIES:** Garden: Food served outside Dogs allowed (water) **NOTES:** Parking 30

PETER TAVY   Map 02 SX57

Pick of the Pubs

The Peter Tavy Inn ♀
PL19 9NN ☎ 01822 810348 📄 01822 810835
e-mail: Peter.tavy@virgin.net
Dir: Off A386 NE of Tavistock
A true pub in the best English tradition, this 15th-century inn retains its character with slate floors, low beams and large fireplaces filled with blazing logs in cold weather. In summer the beautiful garden is popular, surrounded as it is by moorland on the edge of Dartmoor. Food is at the centre of the operation, with a regularly changing blackboard menu listing home-made dishes based on fresh local produce. At lunchtime the choice ranges around traditional bar meals and the likes of game casserole with a Stilton dumpling, chicken balti with rice,

continued

England

PETER TAVY continued

and breaded lamb cutlets with minted gooseberry sauce. In the evening the tone is raised a few notches to include roast lamb shank with garlic mashed potatoes, salmon and asparagus mornay, beef fillet tail with chasseur sauce, and medallions of pork tenderloin. Known for its real ales, with at least eight wines by the glass.

The Peter Tavy Inn

OPEN: 12–2.30 6.30–11 Closed: 25 Dec **BAR MEALS:** Lunch served: all week Dinner served: all week 12–2 7–9 Av main course £8 **RESTAURANT:** Lunch served: all week Dinner served: all week 12–2 7–9 Av 3 course à la carte £18
BREWERY/COMPANY: Free House
PRINCIPAL BEERS: Princetown Jail Ale, Interbrew Bass, Summerskills Tamar, Badger Dorset Best. **FACILITIES:** Children welcome Children's licence Garden: Patio, food served outside Dogs allowed (water) **NOTES:** Parking 40

See Pub Walk on page 147

PLYMOUTH   Map 02 SX45

The China House ⚲
Marrowbone Slip, Sutton Harbour PL4 0DW
☎ 01752 661592 📠 01752 661593
Dir: A38 to Plymouth centre, follow Exeter St to Sutton Rd, follow signs for Queen Anns Battery
Built as a warehouse in the mid-17th century, this waterfront pub has also been used as a gun wharf, a bakehouse, a wool warehouse and even a prison. The current name comes from the short-lived local manufacture of porcelain by William Cookworthy in the 1770s. Expect dishes such as chargrilled tuna with warm potato salad, Cumberland sausage with cheese mash and onion gravy, or Bantry Bay mussels, on a typical menu. Fresh baguettes and doorstops served all day.
OPEN: 12–11 **BAR MEALS:** Lunch served: all week Dinner served: all week 12–10 Av main course £5.50 **RESTAURANT:** Lunch served: all week Dinner served: all week 12–10 7–10.30 Av 3 course à la carte £17 **BREWERY/COMPANY:** Vintage Inns
PRINCIPAL BEERS: Bass, Tetley's. **FACILITIES:** Children welcome Garden: Food served outside **NOTES:** Parking 120

Langdon Court Hotel ★ ★ 🏠 ⚲
Down Thomas PL9 0DY ☎ 01752 862358 📠 01752 863428
e-mail: langdon@eurobell.co.uk
Dir: On A379 from Elburton follow brown tourist signs, also HMS Cambridge signs
Once owned by Henry VIII, this historic, picturesque manor became the home of his last wife Catherine Parr. The Elizabethan walled garden is Grade II listed. Close to outstanding coastal scenery. Primarily a hotel, Langdon Court offers a comfortable bar with freshly cooked meals and real

ale. Menu includes whole roasted John Dory with shellfish risotto, rack of Devon lamb, steak and kidney pudding, and baked cod with saffron mash and brown shrimp salsa.
OPEN: 12–2.30 6.30–11 **BAR MEALS:** Lunch served: all week Dinner served: all week 12–2.30 6.30–9.30 Av main course £10
RESTAURANT: Lunch served: all week Dinner served: all week 12–2.30 7–9.30 Av 3 course à la carte £25
BREWERY/COMPANY: Free House
PRINCIPAL BEERS: Wadworth 6X, Bass, Flowers Original.
FACILITIES: Children welcome Garden: Food served outside, Elizabethan gardens Dogs allowed **NOTES:** Parking 50
ROOMS: 17 bedrooms 17 en suite from s£45 d£75

POSTBRIDGE   Map 03 SX67

Warren House Inn
PL20 6TA ☎ 01822 880208
Dir: Take B3212 through Morehamptonstead on for 5m
High up on Dartmoor, this old tin miners' inn was cut off during the harsh winter of 1963 and supplies were delivered by helicopter. A peat fire has burned here continuously since 1845. Home-made cauliflower cheese, seafood platter, mushroom Stroganoff, rabbit pie and venison steak in a port and cranberry sauce feature among the popular dishes. Good choice of snacks and sandwiches.
OPEN: 11–3 6–11 (May–Oct all day) (Sun til 10:30)
BAR MEALS: Lunch served: all week Dinner served: all week 12–2 6–9.30 Av main course £6 **BREWERY/COMPANY:** Free House
PRINCIPAL BEERS: Sharps Special, Butcombe Bitter, Badger Tanglefoot. **FACILITIES:** Children welcome Garden: Food served outside Dogs allowed (water) **NOTES:** Parking 30

RACKENFORD   Map 03 SS81

The 12th Century Stag Inn ⚲ NEW
EX16 8DT ☎ 01884 881369
It's hard to imagine a more traditional inn than the Stag, which as its name proclaims dates from the 12th century and has a thatched roof and all original features, including the beams and open fireplace. It is located opposite a 12th-century church, and is ideal for families and dog lovers who enjoy walking. Dishes include home-made pasties, steaks, sticky ribs and freshly made curries.
OPEN: 11–3.30 6–11 **BAR MEALS:** Lunch served: all week 12–3 Dinner served: Mon–Sat 7–10 Av main course £7
RESTAURANT: Lunch served: all week 12–3 Dinner served: Mon–Sat 7–10 Av 3 course à la carte £15.95 **PRINCIPAL BEERS:** Barn Owl, Tawny, John Smith Smooth. **FACILITIES:** Children welcome Garden: Food served outside. Beer garden Dogs allowed (water & toys provided) **NOTES:** Parking 20 **ROOMS:** 3 bedrooms 1 en suite from d£20

RATTERY   Map 03 SX76

Church House Inn ⚲
TQ10 9LD ☎ 01364 642220
One of Britain's oldest pubs, parts of which date from about 1028. Previously a rest home for monks, and lodgings for the craftsmen who built the Norman church. Large fireplaces, solid oak beams and an original spiral staircase. Expect steak and kidney, chicken and cranberry curry, Moroccan lamb, rump steak and stilton pie.
OPEN: 11–3 6–11 (Winter 11–2.30, 6.30–10.30)
BAR MEALS: Lunch served: all week Dinner served: all week 12–2 7–9 **RESTAURANT:** Lunch served: all week Dinner served: all week 12 7–9 **BREWERY/COMPANY:** Free House
PRINCIPAL BEERS: St Austell Dartmoor Best, Marston's Pedigree, Greene King Abbot Ale. **FACILITIES:** Children welcome Garden: Patio, Food served outside Dogs allowed (water) **NOTES:** Parking 30 No credit cards

continued

PUB WALK

Peter Tavy
The Peter Tavy Inn

This attractive walk serves as an introduction to the wild and varied beauty of Dartmoor, one of Britain's most popular national parks. Further information on the route, including a map and notes on features to look out out for, is available at the Peter Tavy Inn.

Leave the inn and follow the lane back towards the centre of the village. Look for a path on the left, running along beside the churchyard wall. After passing the village cross, go along the short track in front of two cottages to join the road. Turn left up the hill and then take the first lane on the right, leading out to Dartmoor. On reaching the foot of Smeardon Down, take a broad, green path to the left, just beyond the moor gate, and keep to the upper path at a fork. Continue ahead and, with a drystone wall ahead, turn right and begin a fairly long and gradual climb, all the way to Boulter's Tor. Keep following the line of the wall until a wooden,

five-barred gate and turn right. Cross open ground between a wall on the left and stone markers on the right to reach a rough track. Follow it downhill for about 200 yards (183m) and turn left at the wall corner. Cross the road to Lower Godsworthy Farm and aim for a finger post and wooden, five-barred gate below. Enter a field, keeping a line of trees and a hedgerow on the left before crossing open ground to a marker post and a wall stile. A twisty and uneven path descends through Peter Tavy Combe to reach a junction of paths. Take the path ahead, passing through a metal gate. The path broadens out and passes alongside a row of cottages, dropping downhill to reach Higher Mill. Cross the bridge over the Colly Brook and veer right at the fork, following the rough path beside the brook. Reaching the village 'square' take the road round to the right for a short distance before turning left. Return to the inn.

THE PETER TAVY INN
PETER TAVY Tavistock PL19 9NN
Tel: 01822 810348
Directions: Off A386 NE of Tavistock
Surrounded by moorland on the very edge of Dartmoor, this 15th-century inn is directly adjacent to the national cycle route. A true pub in the best English tradition with freshly cooked food and carefully selected real ales.
Open: 12-2.30 6.30-11
Bar Meals: 12-2 7-9
Children welcome and dogs allowed. Garden and parking available.

Distance: 3 miles (5km)
Map: OS Outdoor Leisure 28
Terrain: Moorland
Paths: Moorland paths, tracks and lanes
Gradient: A steady ascent to the moor, with a fairly steep section to follow

Walk submitted and checked by Patrick Cashell

ROCKBEARE   Map 03 SY09

Pick of the Pubs

Jack in the Green Inn ◉ 🐑 ⛾
London Rd EX5 2EE ☎ 01404 822240 📠 01404 823445
e-mail: info@jackinthegreen.uk.com
Dir: *from M5 take A30 towards Honiton signed Rockbeare*
A very popular dining pub, peaceful now thanks to the
opening of the A30 trunk road into Exeter. Consistency,
attention to detail and use of fresh local produce are
central to the philosophy of the kitchen, and the young
staff show confidence and a delightful willingness to
please. Several eating areas indoors are extended in
summer to include the garden with lovely views across
the Devon countryside. The food, designed for 'those who
live to eat!', ranges through bar food like hot chilli con
carne, braised faggot with onion gravy, and smoked
haddock pasta and parsley bake, plus various interesting
ploughman's. For a serious meal try smoked eel salad, or
fresh linguine tossed with sautéed wild mushrooms,
followed by pavé of monkfish with a mild curry and
coriander sauce, or roast rack of lamb.
OPEN: 11-2.30 6-11 (Sun 12-10.30) Closed: Dec 25 - Jan 2
inclusive **BAR MEALS:** Lunch served: all week Dinner served: all
week 11-2 6-9.30 Av main course £8 **RESTAURANT:** Lunch
served: all week Dinner served: all week 11-2 6-9.30 Av 3 course
fixed price £19.75 **BREWERY/COMPANY:** Free House
PRINCIPAL BEERS: Interbrew Bass, Cotleigh Tawny Ale, Thomas
Hardy Hardy Country, Otter Ale. **FACILITIES:** Children welcome
Garden: Courtyard, Food served outside **NOTES:** Parking 120

SHEEPWASH   Map 02 SS40

Half Moon Inn
EX21 5NE ☎ 01409 231376 📠 01409 231673
e-mail: lee@halfmoon.demon.co.uk
Dir: *from M5 take A30 to Okehampton then A386, at Hatheleigh, L onto
A3072, after 4m R for Sheepwash*

This white-painted village inn overlooking the village square in
a remote Devon village is a Grade II listed building with fishing
rights for ten miles of the River Torridge (very popular with
anglers). Inside you'll find slate floors and a huge inglenook
fireplace where a log fire burns in cooler weather. Bar snacks
are available at lunchtime and a set menu of traditional fare at
dinner. Typical dishes are prawn cocktail and roast beef.
OPEN: 11-2.30 6-11 Closed: 20-27 Dec **BAR MEALS:** Lunch
served: all week 12-1.45 **RESTAURANT:** Dinner served: all week Av
5 course fixed price £20.50 **BREWERY/COMPANY:** Free House
PRINCIPAL BEERS: Scottish Courage Courage Best, Marston's
Pedigree, Ruddles Best Bitter. **FACILITIES:** Dogs allowed
NOTES: Parking 30 **ROOMS:** 14 bedrooms 12 en suite from d£80

SIDMOUTH   Map 03 SY18

The Blue Ball 🐑 ⛾
Stevens Cross, Sidford EX10 9QL
☎ 01395 514062 📠 01395 514062
e-mail: rogernewton@blueballinn.net

Smart thatched inn built of cob and flint, dating back to the
late 14th century and run by the same family for 90 years.
Converted from its farmhouse origins, with the bar occupying
the old dairy. Beams and log fires indoors, terrace, gardens
and playhouse outside, and food centred around fresh fish
and other local produce. Steak and kidney suet pudding, chilli
con carne, chicken and mushroom pie served alongside
salads, ploughman's and sandwiches.
OPEN: 11-11 (Closed 25 Dec evening) **BAR MEALS:** Lunch
served: all week Dinner served: all week 12-2 6-9.30 Av main course
£5 **BREWERY/COMPANY:** Inn Partnership
PRINCIPAL BEERS: Bass, Otter Bitter, Flowers IPA, Greene King Old
Speckled Hen, plus guest ale each week **FACILITIES:** Children
welcome Garden: Food served outside. Colourful gardens Dogs
allowed (not overnight in rooms, water provided) **NOTES:** Parking
100 **ROOMS:** 6 bedrooms 4 en suite from s£28 d£45

SLAPTON   Map 03 SX84

Pick of the Pubs

The Tower Inn 🐑 ⛾
Church Rd TQ7 2PN ☎ 01548 580216 📠 01548 580140
e-mail: towerinn@slapton.org
Dir: *Off A379 south of Dartmouth, turn L at Slapton Sands*

A charming 14th-century inn in the centre of a delightful
and historic village. Originally part of the Collegiate
Chantry of St Mary, founded by King Edward III's standard
bearer, the inn was built to house the men working on the
chantry and it may have started life as the College's
guesthouse for dispensing alms and hospitality. Much of the
adjoining chantry tower, which gives the pub its name,

continued

remains. Inside is a fascinating series of interconnecting rooms with stone walls, low ceilings and open fires. Typical dishes include beef fillet pesto served on a beetroot and courgette salad, pigeon breast with apricot and onion relish, braised lamb shank with mashed potatoes and harissa, and plaice fillets with tomato, chilli jam and spinach. To follow, try warm lemon and almond pudding with raspberries and clotted cream or frozen white chocolate and orange terrine with honeycomb and cherries.

OPEN: 12–3 6–11 (Sun 7–10.30) Closed: 2wks Nov
BAR MEALS: Lunch served: all week Dinner served: all week 12–2.30 6–9.30 **RESTAURANT:** Lunch served: all week Dinner served: all week 12–2.30 6–9.30 **BREWERY/COMPANY:** Free House **PRINCIPAL BEERS:** Adnams Southwold, Badger Tanglefoot, St Austell Dartmoor Best, Exmoor Ale.
FACILITIES: Children welcome Garden: Food served outside Dogs allowed (water, biscuits) **NOTES:** Parking 6 **ROOMS:** 3 bedrooms 3 en suite from s£35 d£50

SOURTON
Map 02 SX59

The Highwayman Inn
EX20 4HN ☎ 01837 861243 📠 01837 861196
e-mail: info@thehighwaymaninn.net
Dir: Situated on the A386 Okehampton to Tavistock Rd come off main A30 following directions for Tavistock. We are 4m from Okehampton and 12 from Tavistock

A fascinating old inn full of eccentric furniture, eerie architectural designs, and creepy bric-a-brac. The vision of Buster Jones, and now run by his daughter Sally, it is made from parts of sailing ships, wood hauled from Dartmoor's bogs, and Gothic church arches. Popular with tourists, but only pasties are served, so if you fancy a more extensive menu, make sure you eat first.
OPEN: 11–2 6–10.30 (Sun 12–2, 7–10.30) **BAR MEALS:** Lunch served: all week Dinner served: all week 11–10.15 Av main course £5 **BREWERY/COMPANY:** Free House **PRINCIPAL BEERS:** Whitbread Best, Flowers Best. **FACILITIES:** Garden: Food served outside Dogs allowed **NOTES:** Parking 150 **ROOMS:** 3 bedrooms 3 en suite from s£20 d£50

See Pub Walk on page 150

SOUTH POOL
Map 03 SX74

Millbrook Inn ⌾
TQ7 2RW ☎ 01548 531581 📠 01548 531868
Dir: Take A379 from Kingsbridge to Frogmore then E
Customers can arrive at this quaint 16th-century village pub close to Salcombe estuary by boat when the tide is high. Inside, it is small, cosy and unspoilt, with open fires, fresh flowers cushioned wheelback chairs, and original beams adorned with old banknotes and clay pipes. Good local reputation for simple, wholesome bar food, notably the

selection of fresh crab dishes, especially the heavenly crab sandwiches, bouillabaisse, kiln-roasted salmon, roasted cod, halibut au poivre, and prime Scottish fillet steaks. Peaceful sunny rear terrace overlooking a stream with resident ducks.
OPEN: 11.30–2.30 5.15–11 (Sun 12–3, 7–10.30)
BAR MEALS: Lunch served: all week Dinner served: all week 12–2 7–9 Av main course £5.95 **BREWERY/COMPANY:** Free House **PRINCIPAL BEERS:** Interbrew Bass, Wadworth 6X, Fuller's London Pride. **FACILITIES:** Children welcome Garden: Terrace, Food served outside **ROOMS:** 2 bedrooms 2 en suite No credit cards

---

SOUTH ZEAL
Map 03 SX69

Oxenham Arms ★ ★
EX20 2JT ☎ 01837 840244 📠 01837 840791
e-mail: jhenry1928@aol.com
Dir: just off A30 4m E of Okehampton in the centre of the village
Historic inn believed to date from the 12th century and first licensed in 1477. Of particular interest are the large granite fireplace in the lounge and the granite pillar supporting the beam in the dining room. Local produce figures in the choice of dishes, including a daily curry and local pork sausages from the bar selection, and seafood thermidor, or roast topside of Devon beef chasseur from the daily dinner menu.
OPEN: 11–2.30 6–11 **BAR MEALS:** Lunch served: all week Dinner served: all week 12–2 7–9.15 Av main course £6.25
RESTAURANT: Lunch served: all week Dinner served: all week 12–2 7–9 Av 3 course à la carte £15 Av 3 course fixed price £15
BREWERY/COMPANY: Free House
PRINCIPAL BEERS: Princetown Dartmoor IPA, Sharp's Doom Bar Bitter. **FACILITIES:** Garden: Beer garden, food served outdoors Dogs allowed (water) **NOTES:** Parking 8 **ROOMS:** 8 bedrooms 7 en suite from s£40 d£50

SPREYTON
Map 03 SX69

The Tom Cobley Tavern
EX17 5AL ☎ 01647 231314
e-mail: fjwfilor@tomcobley.fsnet.co.uk
Dir: From Merrymeet roundabout take A3124 north

According to legend, this is the pub that 'Uncle Tom Cobley and all' set off from en route to Widecombe Fair. Thomas Cobley was a wealthy man who owned eight properties in Spreyton and nearby parishes. Expect a welcoming atmosphere at this traditional village local. Food is home-made and the menu ranges from fillet steak and venison and wild mushroom pie to baked cod and spinach pancakes. There is also a good selection of bar snacks and lighter fare.
OPEN: 12–2 6–11 **BAR MEALS:** Lunch served: Tue–Sun Dinner served: Tue–Sun 12–1.45 7–8.45 Av main course £6 **RESTAURANT:** Lunch served: Sun 12–1.45 Dinner served: Wed–Sat 7–8.45 Av 3 course à la carte £15 **BREWERY/COMPANY:** Free House **PRINCIPAL BEERS:** Cotleigh Tawny Ale, Interbrew Bass. **FACILITIES:** Garden: Food served outside Dogs allowed **NOTES:** Parking 8 **ROOMS:** 4 bedrooms from s£22.50 d£45 No credit cards

continued

PUB WALK

Sourton
The Highwayman Inn

Take a stroll on to Dartmoor, which, when the weather is fine, is ideal for walking. Dramatic and exhilarating and offering something new and unexpected at every turn, the 368 square miles (953 sq km) of Dartmoor National Park, represent some of the most beautiful country in Britain.

From the Highwayman cross over to the village green, with its pre-Norman standing stone, and take the path to the right of the church. Go through the gate and follow the track towards the base of Sourton Tor. According to legend, the Devil has been seen hereabouts more often than any other tor on Dartmoor. Take the path on your right and follow it as it meanders up the eastern side of the tor. This stretch of the walk is steep.

As the tor levels out, glance to your right for a view of a stone circle, but look carefully as the stones are flat as opposed to upstanding. If you glance slightly to your left now you will see the remains of a stone split in two. Continue to a boggy area on your right and follow the track in a semi-circular fashion past two granite posts. In the 19th century Sourton's excellent spring water and cold winters conspired to produce large quantities of ice which were then transported for use in the fish market at Plymouth. Begin the descent now and from this high ground you can see Meldon Reservoir in the distance and an old copper mine to your right. Follow what is known as 'the Stroll' between ditches and take the path to Sourton Church and return to the inn.

THE HIGHWAYMAN INN, SOURTON Okehampton EX20 4HN Tel: 01837 861243
Directions: Situated on the A386 Okehampton to Tavistock Rd Come off main A30 following directions for Tavistock. We are 4m from Okehampton and 12m from Tavistock.
The interior is made from old sailing ships, gnarled wood from Dartmoor bogs, and Gothic church arches. Packed with bric-a-brac and peculiar antiques. Popular with tourists, this startling pub is well worth a visit.
Open: 11–2 6–10.30 11–10.15
Dogs allowed. Garden and parking available.

Distance: 2 1/2 miles (4km)
Map: OS Landranger 191
Terrain: Craggy tors and exposed ground
Paths: Dartmoor paths and tracks
Gradient: Steep in places

Walk submitted and checked by The Highwayman Inn, Sourton

STAVERTON   Map 03 SX76

Pick of the Pubs

The Sea Trout ★ ★ ◎ 🛏 ♀
TQ9 6PA ☎ 01803 762274 📠 01803 762506
e-mail: enquiries@seatroutinn.com
Dir: M5/A38

Set in the heart of a quiet Devon village, this attractive
15th-century inn is a firm favourite with both locals and
visitors. Inside the rambling, whitewashed building you'll
find an easy combination of comfortable hotel, elegant
restaurant, and village pub. Eleven comfortably furnished
en suite bedrooms make this an ideal base for touring
Dartmoor and the South Devon coast; Dartington Hall is
on the doorstep, and Dart Valley steam trains cover the
short journey to Buckfast Abbey. An interesting bar menu
features steaks, plenty of fresh local fish, and daily
specials like game pie or chargrilled venison. The
attractive conservatory style restaurant overlooks pretty
gardens; starters here include vegetable soup with home-
made bread, or melon and citrus salad, with chargrilled
venison medallions with game jus and cranberry
compote, braised brill, chicken and leek pie or home-
baked gammon to follow. Home-made desserts like apple
and cinnamon strudel, crème brûlée or Salcombe Dairy
ice creams round off the meal.
OPEN: 11-3 6-11 (Sun 12-3, 7-10.30) **BAR MEALS:** Lunch
served: all week Dinner served: all week 12-2 7-9 Av main course
£7 **RESTAURANT:** Lunch served: Sun Dinner served: all week
12-2 7-9 Av 3 course à la carte £20
BREWERY/COMPANY: Palmers
PRINCIPAL BEERS: Palmers IPA, Dorset Gold, Palmers Bi-
Centenary '200'. **FACILITIES:** Children welcome Garden: Food
served outside. Patio area Dogs allowed (bowls & water
provided) **NOTES:** Parking 80 **ROOMS:** 11 bedrooms 11 en
suite from s£42.50 d£50

STOCKLAND   Map 03 ST20

Pick of the Pubs

Kings Arms ♦ ♦ ♦ 🛏 ♀
EX14 9BS ☎ 01404 881361 📠 01404 881732
e-mail: info@kingsarms.net
By the Great West Way, at the heart of the Blackdown
Hills, stands this long Grade II, thatched and whitewashed
16th-century inn. It has an impressive flag-stoned walkway
entrance and a medieval oak screen and an original bread
oven as well as an old grey-painted phone box. The
atmospheric Farmers bar is a lively and popular meeting

place, while the Cotley restaurant bar offers a wide range
of blackboard specials such as breast of Quantock duck,
venison pie, lamb Siciliano, Membury trout meunière,
king prawn madras, and mushroom thermidor. The British
and classic cooking is complemented by well-kept real
ales and an outstanding collection of cheeses. According
to the management, the 'wine list and selection of
liqueurs, malts and cigars is unashamedly self-indulgent'.

OPEN: 12-3 6.30-11.30 Closed: Dec 25 **BAR MEALS:** Lunch
served: Mon-Sat 12-2 Av main course £6.50
RESTAURANT: Lunch served: all week Dinner served: all week
12-2 6.30-9 Av 3 course à la carte £16.50
BREWERY/COMPANY: Free House
PRINCIPAL BEERS: Otter Ale, Exmoor Ale, Scottish Courage
John Smiths, Courage Directors. **FACILITIES:** Children welcome
Garden: Food served outside Dogs allowed **NOTES:** Parking
45 **ROOMS:** 3 bedrooms 3 en suite from s£30 d£50

STOKE FLEMING   Map 03 SK84

The Green Dragon Inn NEW
Church Rd TQ6 0PX ☎ 01803 770238 📠 01803 770238
e-mail: pcrowther@btconnect.com
Originally built for the stonemasons who constructed the
church opposite, this 12th-century pub near the historic port
of Dartmouth supposedly has a smugglers' tunnel connecting
it to Blackpool Sands just below the village. The present
landlord is an intrepid seafarer who sets off every four years
to sail across the Atlantic. Warm and welcoming atmosphere
inside and appetising menu offers dishes such as Californian-
style cod, game pie, battered squid and Thai chicken curry.
OPEN: 11-3 5.30-11 (Sun 12-3 6.30-10.30) **BAR MEALS:** Lunch
served: all week Dinner served: all week 12-2.30 6.30-9 Av main
course £6.20 **RESTAURANT:** Lunch served: all week Dinner served:
all week 12-2.30 6.30-9 **BREWERY/COMPANY:** Heavitree
PRINCIPAL BEERS: Wadworth 6X, Otter Ale, Flowers IPA, Bass
FACILITIES: Children welcome Garden: Two paved areas with pots of
flowers, children's climbing frame. Dogs allowed **NOTES:** Parking 4
No credit cards

STOKENHAM   Map 03 SX84

Pick of the Pubs

Tradesman's Arms 🛏
TQ7 2SZ ☎ 01548 580313 📠 01548 580313
e-mail: elizabethsharman@hotmail.com
Dir: just off A379 between Kingsbridge & Dartmouth
This part-thatched free house dates from 1390 and forms
the centre-piece of a picturesque old village that was
given to Anne of Cleves by Henry VIII in 1539.

continued   *continued*

England

STOKENHAM continued

Incorporating a former brew-house and three cottages, the pub takes its name from the tradesmen who used to call at the brew-house while working in the area. Unpretentious and simply furnished, the interior has a stone fireplace and enjoys fine views of the parish church. Chef/proprietor John Sharman is a keen angler and hunter, which gives the menu a strong emphasis on fish and game. This is shown in dishes such as braised pheasant and smoked bacon in a red wine sauce, poached turbot with citrus sauce, wild pigeon breast with cream and chorizo, collops of monkfish flamed with anise and served with saffron and ginger sauce, and sauté of rabbit with horseradish. Interesting puddings, real ales, local cider and a fine range of malt whiskies round off the package.
OPEN: 12–2 6.30–11 Closed: 2wks Nov or Mar
BAR MEALS: Lunch served: Sun 12–1.45 Dinner served: Tues-Sat 6.30–9 Av main course £9 **RESTAURANT:** Lunch served: Sun 12–1.45 Dinner served: Tues-Sat 6.30–9
BREWERY/COMPANY: Free House
PRINCIPAL BEERS: Adnams Bitter, Adnams Broadside, Otter Ale, Exmoor Gold. **FACILITIES:** Garden: Raised garden overlooking the valley Dogs allowed (water) **NOTES:** Parking 14
See Pub Walk on page 153

TEDBURN ST MARY　　　　Map 03 SX89

Kings Arms Inn ♀
EX6 6EG ☎ 01647 61224 📠 01647 61324
e-mail: reception@kingsarmsinn.co.uk
Dir: A30 W to Okehampton, 1st exit R signed Tedburn St Mary

Log fires and exposed beams are features of this charming village centre inn, which is conveniently located for exploration of Dartmoor's rugged beauty. Expect a good range of traditional bar meals, daily fish specials, perhaps monkfish in garlic, skate in Pernod sauce, or freshly battered cod. Comfortable overnight accommodation in simply decorated bedrooms.
OPEN: 11–3 6–11 **BAR MEALS:** Lunch served: all week Dinner served: all week 11.30–2 6–9.30 Av main course £7.50
RESTAURANT: Lunch served: all week Dinner served: all week 11.30–2 6–9.30 Av 3 course à la carte £15
BREWERY/COMPANY: Free House
PRINCIPAL BEERS: Interbrew Bass & Worthington Best, Sharps Cornish Coaster, Whitbread Best,. **FACILITIES:** Garden: Food served outdoors, patio, **NOTES:** Parking 40 **ROOMS:** 8 bedrooms 1 en suite from s£24 d£48

THURLESTONE　　　　Map 03 SX64

The Village Inn 🐷 ♀
TQ7 3NN ☎ 01548 563525 📠 01548 561069
e-mail: enquires@thurlestone.co.uk
Dir: Take A379 from Plymouth towards Kingsbridge at Bantham Rdbt go straight over on to the B3197, then right onto a lane signed Thurlestone 2.5m

In the same family ownership for over a century, a friendly village local that draws seasonal trade from the nearby coastal path to Bigbury Bay. Once a farmhouse B&B, the 16th-century free house today prides itself on good service, well-kept ales and decent food. Blackboards offer daily choices such as shell-on prawns with garlic mayonnaise, seared scallops with Parma ham, smoked chicken tagliatelle and ostrich medallions with pink peppercorn sauce.
OPEN: 11.30–3 6–11 (July-Aug all day) **BAR MEALS:** Lunch served: all week Dinner served: all week 12–2 6.30–9.30 Av main course £6 **BREWERY/COMPANY:** Free House
PRINCIPAL BEERS: Palmers IPA, Interbrew Bass, Sharp's Doom Bar, Wadworth 6X. **FACILITIES:** Children welcome Garden: Patio, food served outside Dogs allowed (water) **NOTES:** Parking 50

TOPSHAM　　　　Map 03 SX98

The Lighter Inn ♀
The Quay EX3 0HZ ☎ 01392 875439 📠 01392 876013

The imposing 17th-century customs house on Topsham Quay has been transformed into a popular waterside inn. A strong nautical atmosphere is reinforced with pictures, ship's instruments and oars beneath the pub's wooden ceilings, and the attractive quayside sitting area is popular in summer. Dishes may include whole sea bass or plaice, steaks, curries and salads, or steak, ale and mushroom pie.
OPEN: 11–11 (12–9 in summer) **BAR MEALS:** Lunch served: all week Dinner served: all week 12–2.30 6–9 Av main course £7
BREWERY/COMPANY: Woodhouse Inns
PRINCIPAL BEERS: Badger Best, Badger Tanglefoot, Sussex.
FACILITIES: Children welcome Children's licence Public Quay Dogs allowed (water provided) **NOTES:** Parking 40

PUB WALK

Stokenham
The Tradesman's Arms

This varied and scenic coastal walk in South Devon visits Slapton Ley, a freshwater lake and nature reserve. An important winter roost for wildfowl, the lake is also the haunt of coots and great crested grebes. The village of Torcross has a shingle beach backed by a sea wall completed in 1980 after the village's defences were badly eroded by a storm in the winter of 1978-79. It was in this area that practice for the D-Day landings of June 1944 took place.

From the pub, bear left to join a narrow winding lane running uphill. At the end of the lane turn sharp right and then sharp left at a bungalow called Kiln Lodge. Go uphill again, passing Quarry Farm and France Farm and continue until you reach Frittiscombe. Look for the Slapton sign and descend a steep hill, crossing a stream at the bottom. Keep an eye out for a footpath on the right, part of a nature trail, and follow it to Slapton Ley. The path runs alongside a marsh and stream before reaching the A379 Dartmouth to Kingsbridge road. Turn right and follow the path parallel to the road and the sea. This takes you the full length of Slapton Ley, noted for its abundance of flora, fauna and wildlife. On reaching the village of Torcross, take the lane by the side of the hotel, signposted Widewell, and walk up the steep hill, to a viewpoint with spectacular views of Slapton Ley and the sea. Pass through the hamlet of Widewell, take the first right turning and walk downhill beside a lovely woodland on your right. The private wood is open to the public and worth a spring visit for its glorious bluebells. Continue to the main A379 and cross over, passing the Church House Inn and Stokenham's parish church of St Michael and All Angels. Go up the narrow lane, turn left to return to the pub.

THE TRADESMAN'S ARMS
STOKENHAM Kingsbridge
TQ7 2SZ
Tel:1548 580313
Directions: Just off A379 between Kingsbridge & Dartmouth
Dating from 1390, the centrepiece of a picturesque old village. Unpretentious and simply furnished. The owner is a keen angler and hunter, so the menu is strong on fish and game. Real ales, local cider and a fine range of malt whiskies.
Open: 12–2 6.30-11
Bar meals: 12–1.45 6.30-9
Dogs allowed. Garden and parking available.

Distance: 5 1/2 miles (8.8km)
Map: OS Landranger 202
Terrain: Woodland, country lanes, freshwater nature reserve
Paths: Mainly footpaths and country lanes
Gradient: Several moderate ascents

Walk submitted and checked by The Tradesman's Arms, Stokenham

TORCROSS Map 03 SX84

Pick of the Pubs

Start Bay Inn 🍷
TQ7 2TQ ☎ 01548 580553 📠 01548 580941
e-mail: cstubbs@freeuk.com
Dir: between Dartmouth & Kingsbridge on the A379
For the best 'fish and chips' in Devon, head to this 14th-century thatched pub situated between Slapton Ley and the panoramic sweep of Start Bay in the beautiful South Hams. Fish could not be fresher as it is delivered from a local trawler, while the landlord dives for plaice and scallops and catches sea bass by rod and line. Expect to find whole bass, skate, lemon sole, whole Dover sole, along with cod, haddock and plaice, deep-fried in a light and crispy batter and served in small, medium and large portions. Arrive soon after opening, especially in the summer. Crab and seafood platters are also available, as are sandwiches, ploughman's lunches, Devon ham and chips, and sirloin steak with pepper sauce for carnivores. The bar and dining areas are simply furnished and decorated with photographs of the storm-ravaged pub.
OPEN: 11.30-2.30 6-11.30 (Summer 11.30-11.30)
BAR MEALS: Lunch served: all week Dinner served: all week 11.30-2 6-10 Av main course £5.50
BREWERY/COMPANY: Heavitree
PRINCIPAL BEERS: Flowers Original, Interbrew Bass, Otter Ale.
FACILITIES: Children welcome Patio, food served outdoors Dogs allowed (on leads, water) **NOTES:** Parking 18

TOTNES Map 03 SX86

Pick of the Pubs

Durant Arms ♦♦♦♦ 🏵 🍷
Ashprington TQ9 7UP ☎ 01803 732240
e-mail: info@thedurantarms.com
See Pick of the Pubs on page 155

The Steam Packet Inn 🍷
St Peter's Quay TQ9 5EW ☎ 01803 863880 📠 01803 862754
e-mail: esther@thesteampacketinn.co.uk
Dir: Leave A38 at Totnes Junct, proceed to Dartington & Totnes. Straight across lights & rdbt following signs for town centre with river on L, follow The Plains in town centre for 100yds. Pub on river

The Steam Packet's inn sign depicts the Amelia, a regular steam packet to this historic, stone-built inn during the 19th century. With the coming of the railway era, she became redundant. One of the pub's most popular attractions is the

myriad of wildlife inhabiting the banks and waters of the River Dart. Varied and tempting dishes on the menu and fresh, locally caught fish features daily. Poultry and meat menu varies according to the seasons, as does local fresh produce. Try breast of chicken wrapped in bacon, grilled cod fillet, tenderloin of pork or warm salad of lemon-cooked salmon, prawns and garlic potatoes.
OPEN: 11-11 (Sun 12-10.30) **BAR MEALS:** Lunch served: all week Dinner served: all week 12-2.30 6.30-9.30 Av main course £5.95
RESTAURANT: Lunch served: all week Dinner served: all week 12-2.30 7-9.30 Av 3 course à la carte £15
BREWERY/COMPANY: Free House **PRINCIPAL BEERS:** Scottish Courage Courage Directors, Courage Best, Interbrew Bass.
FACILITIES: Garden: Food served outside Dogs allowed (water)
NOTES: Parking 16 **ROOMS:** 4 bedrooms 4 en suite from s£40 d£60

Pick of the Pubs

The Watermans Arms 🍷
Bow Bridge, Ashprington TQ9 7EG
☎ 01803 732214 📠 01803 732314
Dir: A38, A381, follow signs for Kingsbridge out of Totnes, at top of hill turn L for Ashprington and Bow Bridge
This charming old free house is located in a wildlife paradise at the head of Bow Creek, close to the ancient Bow Bridge. Robert Ashwick was using the building as a smithy in 1850, when he was also listed in the parish directory as a publican and brewer. At one time the inn was a favourite haunt of the hated press-gangs, who 'spirited away' their victims for military service. Nothing could be further from the tranquil nature of the pub today, with its delightful riverside garden and 15 beautifully furnished en suite bedrooms. As well as bar snacks, the full menu offers honey glazed ham platter, three cheese lasagne, Waterman's pure beef burger, half shoulder of lamb roasted in red wine and garlic, chicken, ham and leek pie, and salmon fillet with pesto.
OPEN: 11-11 (Sun 12-10.30) **BAR MEALS:** Lunch served: all week Dinner served: all week 12-2.30 6.30-9.30
RESTAURANT: 12-2.30 6.30-9.30
BREWERY/COMPANY: Eldridge Pope
PRINCIPAL BEERS: Interbrew Bass, Bow Bridge Bitter, Theakston XB. **FACILITIES:** Children welcome Garden: Food served outside Dogs allowed **NOTES:** Parking 100
ROOMS: 15 bedrooms 15 en suite

The Green Man
The most uncanny and enigmatic of inn signs represents a figure of folk custom from the distant past, the Jack in the Green who appeared at May Day revels. He was a man covered with green leaves and branches, who probably stood for the rebirth of plants, trees and greenery in the spring. Virile and wild, part human and part tree, he is often found carved eerily in churches. A connection grew up between him and Robin Hood, the forest outlaw, and this is perpetuated in some Green Man pub signs, which show an archer or a forester in Lincoln green.

continued

OPEN: 11.30–2.30 6.30–11
(Sun 12–2.30, 7–10.30).
BAR MEALS: 12–2.30 7–9.15.
RESTAURANT: 12–2.30 7–9.15.
BREWERY/COMPANY:
Free House.
PRINCIPAL BEERS: Flowers
Original, Wadworth 6X.
FACILITIES: Children Welcome.
NOTES: Parking 6.
ROOMS: 6 en suite

The Durant Arms

◆◆◆◆ ◎ ♀
Ashprington TQ9 7UP
☎ 01803 732240
e-mail: info@thedurantarms.com
Dir: Leave A38 at Totnes Jct, proceed to
Dartington & Totnes, at 1st set of traffic
lights R for Knightsbridge on A381, after
1m L for Ashprington

The 18th-century Durant Arms is located in a beautiful South Hams village close to the River Dart and the Dart Valley, and just a few miles from the Elizabethan town of Totnes. As such, it is ideally placed for touring this popular area.

The comfortable bar is fitted out in traditional style, and serves a good choice of real ales and bottle lagers. Taking its name from the owners of the original village estate, this award-winning inn is renowned for its cuisine, with all food freshly cooked to order and based on a wide variety of locally-sourced meat, fish and vegetables. There are three separate dining rooms to choose from, all supervised by owners Eileen and Graham Ellis who pride themselves on the quality of service and hospitality. Fish is prominent on the blackboard menu, including grilled turbot garni, monkfish with tiger prawns in cream and garlic, poached salmon with dill and cucumber sauce, and halibut steak with a cheese and prawn sauce. For lovers of meat and game there is venison fillet steak with red wine and mushroom sauce, wild boar steak with mushrooms, bacon and sherry sauce, casseroled mixed game in red wine, sliced Banbury duck breast with brandy and orange sauce, crispy-coated rack of lamb, and turkey escalope with tomato and basil sauce. The six tasteful en suite bedrooms offer visitors a chance to extend their stay. Each room is individually designed and furnished, with charming exposed beams a feature in some.

England

TOTNES continued

Pick of the Pubs

The White Hart Bar 🐑 ⅋
Dartington Hall TQ9 6EL ☎ 01803 866051 & 866303
e-mail: dhcc.reservations@btinternet.com
Dir: Totnes turning on A38 to Plymouth, approx 4m

Dartington Hall is set in 1200 beautiful acres of farmland, ancient deer parkland and woodland as well as lovely landscaped gardens surrounding the house. In this stunning location beside the great hall, in a 14th-century medieval courtyard, is the bar and restaurant. It was opened as a private club in 1934 and is now a stylish dining venue. With its flagstoned floors, limed oak settles, roughcast walls and historic photographs, its exudes a warm and welcoming atmosphere that is hard to beat. West Country ales are served and organic produce features at lunchtime and in the evenings on the interesting menus. Try dishes such as roast best end of lamb with a herb butter sauce which might appear along with seafood chowder, confit of duck mash on hazelnut and thyme mash, and pan-fried John Dory fillets with asparagus and fricassée of wild mushrooms. Also filled baguettes, Greek salad, and smoked salmon bagel.
OPEN: 11-11 Closed: 24 Dec-6 Jan **BAR MEALS:** Lunch served: all week Dinner served: all week 12-2.30 6-9 Av main course £9.50 **RESTAURANT:** Lunch served: all week Dinner served: all week 12-2.30 6-9 Av 3 course à la carte £17
BREWERY/COMPANY: Free House
PRINCIPAL BEERS: Princetown Jail Ale, Butcombe Bitter, Blackawton Bitter, White Hart Ale. **FACILITIES:** Garden: Food served outside **NOTES:** Parking 250 **ROOMS:** 52 bedrooms 30 en suite from s£30 d£40

TRUSHAM   Map 03 SX88

Cridford Inn 🐑
TQ13 0NR ☎ 01626 853694 ▤ 01626 853694
e-mail: cridford@eclipse.co.uk
Built in 1081, and originally a Devon longhouse, this historic inn was also a farm at one time, owned by the same family for generations. The transept window in the bar is said to be the oldest domestic window in Britain. The present proprietor's wife is a Malaysian culinary expert from Kuala Lumpur, so Malaysian specialities are offered alongside traditional pub dishes like sausage and mash, steak and kidney pudding, and duck breast in orange sauce.
OPEN: 12-3 7-11 Closed: 8 Jan-31 Mar **BAR MEALS:** Lunch served: all week Dinner served: all week 12-3 7-10.30 Av main course £6.50 **RESTAURANT:** Dinner served: all week 7-9.30 Av 3 course à

la carte £10 **BREWERY/COMPANY:** Free House
PRINCIPAL BEERS: Teign Valley Tipple, Greene King Ruddles County, Trusham Ale, Tinners. **FACILITIES:** Children welcome Garden: Food served outside Dogs allowed (water & toys provided)
NOTES: Parking 35 **ROOMS:** 4 bedrooms 4 en suite from s£40 d£50

TUCKENHAY   Map 03 SX85

Pick of the Pubs

The Maltsters Arms 🐑 ⅋
TQ9 7EQ ☎ 01803 732350 ▤ 01803 732823
e-mail: pub@tuckenhay.demon.co.uk
Beautifully located by the wooded and tidal Bow Creek, this splendid 18th-century pub has overcome many former dramas and reinvented itself as a classy residential inn and dining venue. You can snack from the lunch menu or go for a blow out. It is quite flexible, with ploughman's and sandwiches, or starters doubling as light bites – maybe a smoked fish platter, or mussels in white wine. Both the lunchtime and evening menu offer a good choice for vegetarians - fennel, polenta and Mozzarella bake, and lentil and vegetable biriyani among them. Dishes change daily and mains have included casserole of hare with blackberries, redcurrants and shag cider, and baked cod fillet with tomato and Sharpham Rustic. Puddings from winter berry crumble to warm chocolate fudge cake are designed to tempt, though you can finish with cheese, biscuits and optional port. Children really appreciate their own menu of real food.
OPEN: 11-11 (Sun 12-10.30) **BAR MEALS:** Lunch served: all week Dinner served: all week 12-2.30 7-9.30 Av main course £8
RESTAURANT: Lunch served: all week Dinner served: all week 12-2.30 7-9.30 Av 3 course à la carte £15
BREWERY/COMPANY: Free House
PRINCIPAL BEERS: Princetown Dartmoor IPA, Young's Bitter, Otter Ale, Exe Valley Devon Glory. **FACILITIES:** Children welcome Garden: Food served outside Dogs allowed (dog bowl, biscuits, lots of pals) **NOTES:** Parking 50 **ROOMS:** 7 bedrooms 5 en suite from d£50

TYTHERLEIGH   Map 03 ST30

Tytherleigh Arms Hotel 🐑 ⅋ NEW
EX13 7BE ☎ 01460 220400 & 220214 ▤ 01460 220406
e-mail: tytherleigharms@aol.com
Notable features of this 17th-century former coaching inn are the beamed ceilings, huge roaring fire and the lovely lady's loo. It is a family-run, food-led establishment, situated on the Devon, Somerset and Dorset borders, with accommodation also provided in the old stable block. Fresh home-cooked dishes using local ingredients include lamb shank with cider and honey glaze, West Country cod in beer batter, and seafood pancakes.
OPEN: 11-2.30 6.30-11 **BAR MEALS:** Lunch served: all week Dinner served: all week 12-2.30 6.30-9 Av main course £8.95
RESTAURANT: Lunch served: all week Dinner served: all week 12-2.30 6.30-9 Av 3 course à la carte £18.95
BREWERY/COMPANY: Free House
PRINCIPAL BEERS: Butcombe Bitter. **FACILITIES:** Children welcome Garden: large terraced patio with hanging baskets
NOTES: Parking 60 **ROOMS:** 5 bedrooms 5 en suite from s£36 d£60

continued

PUB WALK

Umberleigh
Rising Sun

With its glorious views, wild flowers and high banks, this attractive country walk reveals some of Devon's prettiest scenery. You might even glimpse a deer, that most graceful of animals, skipping swiftly through the woods and sunny glades.

From the inn walk across the bridge spanning the river and follow the road round to the left. Umberleigh railway station is seen on the right. Continue along the road and over the railway bridge. Once across it, turn right to the village school, walk past it and follow the lane along to the farm. At this stage the lane dwindles to a path. Begin to climb the hill at a medium gradient, following the lane to a footpath sign. Go through the right-hand gate and follow the left edge of the field to a stile.   Take the path into the wood and join the main track running left to a gateway.

Continue uphill to the next gate and look back here to admire spectacular views. Make for Pitt Farm and from here you keep ahead, following the lane uphill. At the top turn right, still on the lane. Note the large stone cross on the roadside on the left. This was once a marker for pilgrims on their way to the church at nearby Chittlehampton, indicating to them that they were on the right route. Follow the lane downhill now, heading back to Umberleigh. The road passes through Brightly Barton, with its beautifully maintained farmhouse visible from the lane. Look out, too, for its coat-of-arms. The lane drops down to the valley bottom; turn right at the junction and head back to the centre of the village. Beyond the Post Office, you can see the Antiques Emporium ahead. Turn left, back across the river and return to the Rising Sun.

RISING SUN,
UMBERLEIGH EX37 9DU
Tel: 01769 560447
Directions: Situated at Umberleigh Bridge on the A377, Exeter/Barnstaple road, at the junc of the B3227 Overlooking the River Taw and a haven for anglers and visitors to North Devon. Comfortable accommodation and good home-cooked food in traditional flagstoned interior, with its open fire, daily papers, sofas and wood-burning fire.
Open: 11-3 6-11
Bar Meals: 12-2 7-9
Children welcome and dogs allowed. Garden and parking available.

Distance: 3 miles (4.8km)
Map: OS Landranger 180
Terrain: Typical rolling Devon landscapes
Paths: Mainly footpaths and country lanes
Gradient: Some climbing

Walk submitted and checked by the Rising Sun, Umberleigh

PUB WALK

Widecombe-in-the-Moor
Rugglestone Inn

A pleasant Dartmoor walk around the delightful village of Widecombe-in-the-Moor, famous for its song Widecombe Fair and its 14th-century church. In 1638, during a service, a bolt of fire demolished a tower pinnacle killing four people. The thunderbolt was thought to be the work of the Devil.

From the pub car park, turn left along the lane, back towards Widecombe village. The 120ft tower of the church is on your right as you climb the hill. Beside the church is Church House which has craft fairs on Thursdays. Dating from 1537, Church House now in the care of the National Trust. Adjacent Sexton's Cottage is a National Trust shop and Dartmoor National Park information point. Turn right towards the green, and then bear left towards Natsworthy and Wooder Manor. This lane takes you away from the village, passing tennis courts on your right. Follow the lane passing Wooder Manor and Farm on your left. Further up, cross the East Webburn River and enter a stretch of woodland. The gentle climb to the top twill reveal a lovely view of Devon countryside. Just over half a mile (1km) from the river, take a track off to the right, just before a cattle-grid. Climb to a gate and veer right just beyond it, following the track through the bracken to the foot of Honeybag Tor. If you are energetic, climb to the top for a magnificent view. Keeping to the track will lead to the base of Chinkwell Tor, with a view of Widecombe. The track now veers to the left around Bell Tor. A short distance to the lane, across the road with Bonehill Rocks on your left. Bear right to follow the lane downhill, past some pretty stone houses. At the bottom cross the river again to the road into the village. At the T junction is a stile and footpath sign almost opposite. Keep to the footpath beside the river and go through a meadow which can become very wet. At the far end another stile and a low fence back to the lane. Turn left for the inn.

RUGGLESTONE INN,
WIDECOMBE-IN-THE-MOOR
TQ13 7TF
Tel: 01364 621327
Directions: A38 Drumbridges exit towards Bovey Tracey, L at 2nd rdbt, L at sign Haytor 8 Widecombe, village is 5m
Open: 11–2.30 6–11
Bar Meals: 12–2 7–9
Dogs allowed. Garden and parking available.

Distance: 4 miles (6.4km)
Map: OS Landranger 191
Terrain: Devon lanes and woodland and typical Dartmoor landscape
Paths: Tracks, lanes and paths
Gradient: Some climbing

Walk submitted and checked by the Rugglestone Inn, Widecombe-in-the-Moor

UMBERLEIGH
Map 02 SS62

Pick of the Pubs

The Rising Sun Inn ★ ★ 🏠 ♇
EX37 9DU ☎ 01769 560447 📠 01769 564764
e-mail: risingsuninn@btinternet.com
Dir: Situated at Umberleigh Bridge on the A377, Exeter/Barnstaple road, at the junc of the B3227
Idyllically set beside the River Taw and with a very strong fly fishing tradition, the Rising Sun dates back in part to the 13th century. The traditional flagstoned bar is strewn with fishing memorabilia, comfortable chairs and daily papers and magazines for a very relaxing visit. Outside is a sunny raised terrace with beautiful rural views of the valley, and the riverside walk is equally enjoyable before or after a meal. The quality of food has put this friendly inn firmly on the map, with the daily blackboard offering a choice of specials alongside the carte and bar menu. For a quick snack you could try salmon and ginger fishcakes, or tagliatelle with mushroom and pesto sauce. From the carte expect fillet of sea bass on truffle mash with citrus cream, roast breast of duck with kirsch cherries, and fresh fish ragout. Devon micro-brewery ales served, plus several wines by the glass.
OPEN: 11–3 6–11 **BAR MEALS:** Lunch served: all week Dinner served: all week 12-2 7–9 Av main course £7.50
RESTAURANT: Lunch served: all week Dinner served: all week 12–2 7–9 Av 3 course à la carte £20 Av 3 course fixed price £19.95
BREWERY/COMPANY: Free House
PRINCIPAL BEERS: Bass, Clearwater Cavalier, Cotleigh Tawny Bitter, Barn Owl. **FACILITIES:** Children welcome Garden: Food served outside Dogs allowed **NOTES:** Parking 30 **ROOMS:** 9 bedrooms 9 en suite from s£40 d£68
See Pub Walk on page 157

WIDECOMBE-IN-THE-MOOR
Map 03 SX77

The Old Inn 🏠 NEW
TQ13 7TA ☎ 01364 621207 📠 01364 621407
e-mail: oldinn.wid@virgin.net
An old stone inn dating from the 15th century which was partly ruined by fire but rebuilt around the old fireplaces. Two main bars and no fewer than five eating areas offer plenty of scope for visitors to enjoy the home-cooked food. From several menus plus blackboard specials expect mixed grill, supreme of chicken, steak and kidney pie, lamb in gin sauce, barbecued chicken, and various grills including spicy pork chops, and gammon steaks.
OPEN: 11-3 7-11 (Summer 6.30-11) Closed: 25 Dec
BAR MEALS: Lunch served: all week Dinner served: all week 11-2 7-10 Av main course £7.25 **RESTAURANT:** Lunch served: all week Dinner served: all week 11-4 7-10 Av 3 course à la carte £15.75
BREWERY/COMPANY: Free House
PRINCIPAL BEERS: Interbrew Flowers IPA & Boddingtons.
FACILITIES: Children welcome Garden: Food served outdoors, pond, stream Dogs allowed (water) **NOTES:** Parking 55

Rugglestone Inn
TQ13 7TF ☎ 01364 621327 📠 01364 621224
Dir: A38 Drumbridges exit towards Bovey Tracey, L at 2nd rdbt, L at sign Haytor & Widecombe, village is 5m
Converted from a farm cottage in 1832, a pretty Dartmoor inn surrounded by peaceful moorland. Open fires, stone floors and a good local following give the pub its special

atmosphere, and the attractive garden offers stunning views. Real ales straight from the barrel and local farm cider are served alongside home-cooked pies and pot meals, like beef casserole with dumplings, using local produce wherever possible. Old-fashioned puddings include treacle tart and fruit crumble.
OPEN: 11–2.30 (Sat 11–3, Sun 12–3) 6–11 (7–11 in winter, Sun 10.30 in winter) **BAR MEALS:** Lunch served: all week Dinner served: all week 12–2 7–9 Av main course £5 **BREWERY/COMPANY:** Free House **PRINCIPAL BEERS:** Butcombe Bitter, St Austells Dartmoor Best. **FACILITIES:** Garden: Food served outside, stream Dogs allowed (water and biscuits) **NOTES:** Parking 40
See Pub Walk on page 158

WINKLEIGH
Map 03 SS60

Pick of the Pubs

The Duke of York ♇
Iddesleigh EX19 8BG ☎ 01837 810253 📠 01837 810253
Thatched 15th-century inn set in a sleepy village in the heart of rural mid-Devon, Originally three cottages, built to house workers restoring the parish church, it has all the timeless features of a classic country pub - heavy old beams, a huge inglenook fireplace with winter log fires, old scrubbed tables and farmhouse chairs, and an unspoilt atmosphere free from electronic games. Popular with local farmers, business people and visitors alike, it offers great real ale and hearty home cooking, with all dishes displayed on the large blackboard menu being freshly prepared in the pub kitchen using local produce, including meat reared on nearby farms. From starters or light meals like port and Stilton pâté, smoked trout fillet with dill, and home-made soups, the menu choice extends to freshly battered cod and chips, beef and Guinness casserole, lamb and mint pie, Thai green chicken curry, and liver and bacon with mash and onion gravy. Delightful hosts and excellent value overnight accommodation.
OPEN: 11-11 Closed: Dec 25 **BAR MEALS:** Lunch served: all week Dinner served: all week 12–10 Av main course £7
RESTAURANT: Dinner served: all week 7–10 Av 3 course à la carte £19 Av 3 course fixed price £19
BREWERY/COMPANY: Free House
PRINCIPAL BEERS: Adnams Broadside, Cotleigh Tawny, Guest beers. **FACILITIES:** Children welcome Garden: patio/terrace, outdoor eating Dogs allowed (water provided)
ROOMS: 7 bedrooms 7 en suite from s£25 d£50

The Kings Arms 🏠 ♇ NEW
Fore St EX19 8HQ ☎ 01837 83384
An ancient thatched country inn in this hilltop village set between the rivers Taw and Torridge. Three wood-burning stoves keep the beamed bar and dining room warm in chilly weather, and help to maintain a traditional atmosphere. Typical pub snacks like baked potato, baguettes and ploughman's are supported by a decent choice including lamb and mint pastry parcels, chicken breast wrapped in bacon, mixed grills, and all-day breakfast.
OPEN: 11-11 (Sun 12-10.30) **BAR MEALS:** Lunch served: all week Dinner served: all week 11-9.30 Av main course £6.50
BREWERY/COMPANY: Enterprise Inns **PRINCIPAL BEERS:** Wells Bombardier, Butcombe Bitter, Interbrew Bass. **FACILITIES:** Children welcome Garden: Small courtyard to side of property Dogs allowed

continued

YARCOMBE   Map 03 ST20

The Yarcombe Angel
EX14 9BD ☎ 01404 861676
Dir: On A30 between Chard and Honiton, 1m from A303
Once owned by Sir Francis Drake, this historic pub offers a
range of imaginatively devised chef's specials. Expect home-
made steak and kidney pie, warm onion and potato tart,
lobster and tiger prawn ravioli, stuffed guinea fowl with port
jus, and farmhouse mixed grill on the menu. Ploughman's and
open sandwiches are always available.
OPEN: 12–3 6–11 **BAR MEALS:** Lunch served: all week 12–2
Dinner served: Tues–Sun 7–9.30 Av main course £4.95
BREWERY/COMPANY: Free House
PRINCIPAL BEERS: Interbrew Bass, Black Sheep Best, Timothy
Taylor Landlord, Fuller's London Pride. **FACILITIES:** Children
welcome Garden: Food served outside Dogs allowed
NOTES: Parking 20 **ROOMS:** 2 bedrooms 2 en suite from s£30
d£60

YELVERTON   Map 02 SX50

The Skylark Inn
PL20 6JD ☎ 01822 853258
e-mail: sueandroger@skylarkinn.fsnet.co.uk
Dir: 5m North of Plymouth, just off the A386 to Tavistock Road
Attractive village inn set in Dartmoor National Park, with a
beamed bar and large fireplace with wood-burning stove. A
good area for cyclists and walkers, yet only 10 minutes from
Plymouth. Good wholesome food is served from an extensive
menu, with specials like beef bourguignon, pork loin
forestière, seafood platter and lamb tagine. There are also
snacks including pasties and Cumberland sausage, plus
various vegetarian choices.
OPEN: 11.30–2.30 (Summer 11.30–3) 6–11
BAR MEALS: 11.30–2.30 6.30–9.30 Av main course £7.50
PRINCIPAL BEERS: Interbrew Bass, Greene King Old Speckled Hen,
Scottish Courage Courage Best. **FACILITIES:** Garden: Food served
outdoors, patio Dogs allowed **NOTES:** Parking 16

The George and Dragon
As England's patron saint, St George figures
frequently on inn signs, often with the dragon
whose defeat was his most celebrated exploit.
According to the legend, he killed it to save a
beautiful princess who would otherwise have
been given to the monster. Alternatively, the
George is the jewel of the Order of the Garter,
England's premier order of knighthood, which
was founded by King Edward III in the 14th
century. An allied name is the Star and Garter,
which also refers to the order's insignia. Or
again, the George can mean any of the six kings
of that name since the Hanoverian dynasty
succeeded to the throne.

DORSET

ASKERSWELL   Map 03 SY59

The Spyway Inn
DT2 9EP ☎ 01308 485250
Dir: On A35 between Dorchester & Bridport
There are outstanding views of the Dorset countryside from
this quiet country pub, possibly an old smugglers look-out.
Straightforward menu and interesting specialities.

BLANDFORD FORUM   Map 03 ST80

The Crown Hotel ★ ★ ★ ♀
West St DT11 7AJ ☎ 01258 456626 ▤ 01258 451084
e-mail: thecrownhotel@blandforddorset.freeserve.co.uk
*Dir: M27 W onto A31 to junction with A350 W to Blandford. 100 metres
from town bridge*
Classic Georgian coaching inn on the banks of the River Stour
overlooking Blandford's handsome redbrick-and-stone town
centre, with plenty of period atmosphere. Bar fare ranges
from ploughman's and hot baguettes to spicy chorizo pasta,
pan-fried lambs' liver, and baked gammon hock, while the
restaurant menu may feature escalopes of pork loin,
chargrilled lamb cutlets, and steak, kidney and mushroom pie.
To finish perhaps try Dutch apple pie, bread and butter
pudding, and chocolate caramel gateau.
OPEN: 10–2.30 6–11 Closed: 25–28 Dec **BAR MEALS:** Lunch
served: all week Dinner served: all week 12–2 7–9 Av main course £9
RESTAURANT: Lunch served: all week 12.30–2 Dinner served:
Mon–Sat 7.15–9.15 Av 3 course à la carte £17 Av 3 course fixed price
£15 **BREWERY/COMPANY:** Hall & Woodhouse
PRINCIPAL BEERS: Badger Tanglefoot & Best.
FACILITIES: Children welcome Garden: Food served outside Dogs
allowed **NOTES:** Parking 70 **ROOMS:** 32 bedrooms 32 en suite
from s£68 d£82

BOURTON   Map 03 ST73

The White Lion Inn
High St SP8 5AT ☎ 01747 840866 ▤ 01747 841529
Dir: Off A303, opposite B3092 to Gillingham
The epitomy of an English pub, this stone-built village inn
features old beams, flagstones, and real fires. Good range of
English home-cooked food and traditional pub favourites. Two
comfortable Bedrooms.

BRIDPORT   Map 03 SY49

The George Hotel ♀
4 South St DT6 3NQ ☎ 01308 423187
Dir: Town centre
Handsome Georgian town house, with a Victorian-style bar
and a mellow atmosphere, bustles all day, and offers a
traditional English breakfast, decent morning coffee and a
good menu featuring fish and crab from West Bay, home-
made rabbit pie, Welsh rarebit, and lambs' kidneys in
Madeira.
OPEN: 9–11 (Sun 9.30–10.30) **BAR MEALS:** Lunch served:
Mon–Sat Dinner served: Mon–Sat (seasonal please ring) 12–2.30
6.30–9 Av main course £7.50 **BREWERY/COMPANY:** Palmers
PRINCIPAL BEERS: Palmers - IPA, Copper & 200.
FACILITIES: Children welcome Dogs allowed

PUB WALK

Evershot
The Acorn Inn

A gentle walk from Evershot to the small village of Melbury Osmond, returning via the grounds of Melbury Park. Along the way are impressive views of Melbury House, and here and there you may catch sight of deer in the park.

From the inn head left down Fore Street to the village green. Bear left here and make your way along the tarmac road through the Melbury estate. Keep dogs on a lead along here. Take the first right turning and follow the gravel track uphill and down the far side, passing a conifer woodland. Keep left where another route branches off to the right and pass a small pond on the left. Further on, look for a large private lake on the right. Turn right just beyond it to a gate, cross a bridge and go through a second gate. Head straight across the field, keeping the fence on your right. Look for a small concealed gate in the far right-hand corner, leading into an

oak copse. Once through the gate, veer left along the track and down to a cottage by the road. Follow the tree-lined track to the right of the property and enter a field when it terminates at a gate. Make for a small waymarked gate over to the right and follow the often wet and muddy path beside a stream to a bridge. Cross it and pass under a stone bridge, bearing left. Soon you pass several thatched cottages before reaching the road. Bear left and keep on the road as it runs through the Melbury estate and back to Evershot. Dogs should be on a lead again along this stretch. Begin a gentle climb and soon the outline of Melbury House looms into view. Pass right round the house and through the deer park on the other side. Now the road climbs quite steeply before descending to Evershot village green. To avoid the main street, turn right along Back Lane to a left-hand foot-path which leads to the pub car park.

THE ACORN
EVERSHOT Dorchester
DT2 0JW
Tel: 01935 83228
Directions: A303 to Yeovil, Dorchester Rd, on A37 R to Evershot
A fine stone building painstakingly restored.
Open: 11.30–3 6–11
Bar Meals: 12–2 6.30–9
Children welcome and dogs allowed. Garden and parking available.

Distance: 4 1/2 miles (7.2km)
Map: OS Explorer 117
Terrain: Farmland and parkland
Paths: Tracks, paths and estate roads
Gradient: Two moderate climbs with long descents

Walk submitted and checked by The Acorn, Evershot

England

BRIDPORT continued

Pick of the Pubs

Shave Cross Inn ♀
Shave Cross, Marshwood Vale DT6 6HW ☎ 01308 868358
Dir: From Bridport take B3162 2m turn L signed 'Broadoak/Shave Cross' then Marshwood

Thatched, 14th-century cob and flint inn tucked away down narrow lanes in the heart of the beautiful Marshwood Vale. Once a resting place for pilgrims and travelling monks, it is worth the short drive from the coast for its delightful sun-trap garden and the imaginative food prepared by chef patron Nic Tipping. Eat outside in summer and in the tastefully refurbished interior on cooler days; classic flagstone-floored bar with warming log fire in a huge inglenook. Lunchtime fare changes daily and the short blackboard list may highlight spicy seafood soup, corned beef hash, a delicious warm salad of chorizo, and salmon fishcakes. Civilised evening dining in warm yellow and terracotta-painted rooms may take in sautéed chicken liver and king prawns sautéed with sweet chilli and fresh ginger for starters. Main course options may include confit of fresh tuna with roasted garlic and red wine sauce or beef fillet with peppercorn and port jus. Excellent Otter Ale, a changing local guest ale and farmhouse cider on tap.
OPEN: 11–3 7–10 **BAR MEALS:** Lunch served: Tue–Sun Dinner served: Tue–Sun 12–2 7–9 Av main course £7
RESTAURANT: Lunch served: Tue–Sun Dinner served: Tue–Sun 12–2 7–9 Av 3 course à la carte £25
BREWERY/COMPANY: Free House
PRINCIPAL BEERS: Otter Ale, Local guest beers.
FACILITIES: Children welcome Garden: Dogs allowed
NOTES: Parking 30 No credit cards

BROADWINDSOR   Map 03 ST40

The White Lion 🛏
The Square DT8 3QD ☎ 01308 867070 🖹 01308 867740
e-mail: johnandsuebei@aol.com
Close to Marshwood Vale and the Dorset coast is this 17th-century village inn. The modernised interior has an open fire, and serves Palmer's ales on tap. A varied menu offers traditional home-made pub food with a specials board that changes daily. Look out for whole trout with prawns and mushrooms, tuna steaks in garlic, haddock Florentine, butterfish on a bed of bloody Mary, and hake fillets on a fisherman's sauce.
OPEN: 11.30–2.30 6–11 (Sun 12–2.30, 7–10.30)
BAR MEALS: Lunch served: all week Dinner served: all week 12–2 6.30–9 Av main course £6 **RESTAURANT:** Lunch served: all week Dinner served: all week 12–2 6.30–9 Av 3 course à la carte £14.50
BREWERY/COMPANY: Palmers **PRINCIPAL BEERS:** Palmer IPA, Bridport Bitter. **FACILITIES:** Children welcome Garden: Food served outdoors, patio Dogs allowed (water, biscuits)

BUCKLAND NEWTON   Map 03 ST60

Gaggle of Geese ♀
DT2 7BS ☎ 01300 345249
e-mail: Gaggle@bucklandnewton.freeserve.co.uk
Dir: On B3143 N of Dorchester
When the former landlord started keeping geese 20 years ago, this pub changed its name from the Royal Oak. Built as a village shop in 1834, it has a modern approach to food that includes plenty of traditional dishes. The specials blackboard offers curries, pasta and fishy choices to supplement regulars like chicken Kiev, grilled gammon steak, and pizza. Special children's menu, and a good choice of ploughman's.
OPEN: 12–2.30 6.30–11 **BAR MEALS:** Lunch served: all week Dinner served: all week 12–2 7–10 Av main course £5.95
RESTAURANT: Lunch served: all week Dinner served: all week 12–2 7–10 Av 3 course à la carte £12 **BREWERY/COMPANY:** Free House
PRINCIPAL BEERS: Badger Dorset Best, Ringwood Best & Fourtyniner. **FACILITIES:** Children welcome Garden: Food served outside, patio/terrace Dogs allowed **NOTES:** Parking 30

BURTON BRADSTOCK   Map 03 SY48

Pick of the Pubs

The Anchor Inn 🛏 ♀
High St DT6 4QF ☎ 01308 897228 🖹 01308 897228
e-mail: sleepingsat@hotmail.com
Dir: 2m SE of Bridport on B3157 in the centre of the village of Burton Bradstock

A 300-year-old coaching inn just a few steps from the beach at the centre of the village. This cosy inn lives up to its maritime name, with fishing nets draped across the ceilings, old fishing tools and shellfish art on the walls, created by the chef after cooking the contents. As you might expect, seafood is the house speciality, with lobster brought in daily from Lyme Bay, and scallops hand-picked by local divers. Villagers also bring in their own garden produce so that much of the menu is fresh and sourced nearby. Seafood choices include monkfish and Parma ham, cod and crab baked in the oven, steamed brill fillet stuffed with crab, and Cornish mackerel with a crab and cheese sauce. Those preferring meat can choose from lamb noisette, Barbary duck, chicken and Stilton mango, and stir-fry pork. Several real ales are on sale, and over 50 different Scottish whiskies.
OPEN: 11–3 6–11.30 **BAR MEALS:** Lunch served: all week Dinner served: all week 12–2 6.30–9 Av main course £15
RESTAURANT: Lunch served: all week Dinner served: all week 12–2 6.30–9 Av 3 course à la carte £24
PRINCIPAL BEERS: Ushers Best, Bass, Wadworth 6X, Flowers IPA. **FACILITIES:** Dogs allowed (water) **NOTES:** Parking 24

CERNE ABBAS   Map 03 ST60

The Red Lion
24 Long St DT2 7JF ☎ 01300 341441
Victorian pub built to replace the original inn which burnt down in the 1890s, and therefore far more modern than most of this picturesque village. The impressive fireplace was believed to have originated from the old abbey, and the Victorian windows are Grade II listed. Locals and tourists enjoy the food served in the separate eating area: lamb cutlets, three shire sausages and mash, or sandwiches and baked potatoes.
OPEN: 11.30–2.30 6.30–11 **BAR MEALS:** Lunch served: all week Dinner served: all week 12–2.30 6.30–9.30 Av main course £6.50
RESTAURANT: Lunch served: all week Dinner served: all week 11.30–2.30 6.30–11 **BREWERY/COMPANY:** Free House
PRINCIPAL BEERS: Palmer IPA. **FACILITIES:** Garden: Food served outdoors Dogs allowed (water, biscuits)

continued

The Royal Oak
23 Long St DT2 7JG ☎ 01300 341797 ▤ 01300 341797
e-mail: royal.oak@cerne.abbas.fsnet.co.uk
Dir: On A352 N of Dorchester
Thatched, creeper-clad, 16th-century inn, formerly a coaching
inn and blacksmiths, situated in a picturesque village below
the Dorset Downs. A previous owner of the pub also owned
land in America. In 1791 this land was given to the US
government, and became the site of Capitol Hill. Home-
cooked food is served in the cosy, traditional interior. An
imaginative menu includes pan fried black bream fillets,
seafood chowder, poached salmon salad, venison sausages,
and wild mushroom strüdel. Attractive courtyard garden.
OPEN: 11-3 6-11 **BAR MEALS:** Lunch served: all week Dinner
served: all week 12-2 7-9 **BREWERY/COMPANY:** Free House
PRINCIPAL BEERS: Greene King Old Speckled Hen, Butcombe,
Wadworths IPA, Quay Brewery Weymouth. **FACILITIES:** Children
welcome Garden: Food served outside. Dogs allowed (water bowl in
garden)

CHIDEOCK   Map 03 SY49

Pick of the Pubs

The Anchor Inn
Seatown DT6 6JU ☎ 01297 489215
e-mail: david@theanchorinn.co.uk
*Dir: On A35 turn S in Chideock opp church & follow single track rd for
0.75m to beach*

A spectacular location in the middle of a little cove
surrounded by National Trust land, and nestling under the
Golden Cap, the highest point on the south coast. The
Anchor Inn is blessed with its setting smack on the Dorset
coastal path to the west of the bustling market town of
Bridport, and makes the most of its position with a large
sun terrace and Cliffside beer garden overlooking the
beach. On winter weekdays it is blissfully quiet, while the
summer sees it thronging with holidaymakers. The menu
offers something for everyone, and what is not shown
there is likely to be found on the special blackboard.
Plenty of sea food subject to the daily catch: lobster, crab,
fish pie, king prawn stir fry, monkfish kebabs, and squid in
garlic mayonnaise, plus burgers, beef curry, ploughman's
and jacket potatoes. Palmers ales on tap.
OPEN: 11-2.30 6-11 (Summer 11-11) **BAR MEALS:** Lunch
served: all week Dinner served: all week 12-2 6.30-9.30 Av main
course £5 **BREWERY/COMPANY:** Palmers
PRINCIPAL BEERS: Palmers200 Premium Ale, IPA.
FACILITIES: Children welcome Garden: Food served outside
Dogs allowed (water, dog treats) **NOTES:** Parking 20
ROOMS: 2 bedrooms from s£25 d£45

The George Inn
Main St DT6 6JD ☎ 01297 489419 ▤ 01297 489411
e-mail: george.inn@virgin.net
Dir: On A35

Traditional Dorset thatched inn located close to the famous
and spectacular sandstone-scarred cliff-top known as Golden
Cap, the highest cliff in southern England. Under new
management and including a patio garden and a popular
choice of real ales, the George offers an impressive range of
snacks, home-made pies and light lunches, plus more
substantial dishes – fillet steak Rossini, steamed salmon
supreme and moules marinière among them.
OPEN: 11-2.30 6-11 **BAR MEALS:** Lunch served: all week Dinner
served: all week 12-2 6-9 Av main course £6.95
RESTAURANT: Lunch served: all week Dinner served: all week 12-2
6-9 Av 3 course à la carte £15.95 Av 3 course fixed price £12.95
BREWERY/COMPANY: Palmers **PRINCIPAL BEERS:** Palmers IPA
& 200, Dorset Gold. **FACILITIES:** Children welcome Garden: Patio,
food served outside Dogs allowed **NOTES:** Parking 40

CHRISTCHURCH   Map 03 SZ19

Fishermans Haunt Hotel
Salisbury Rd, Winkton BH23 7AS
☎ 01202 477283 484071 ▤ 01202 478883
Dir: 2.5m north on B3347(Christchurch/Ringwood rd)
A popular place with those who enjoy angling and walking,
this old world inn, which dates from 1673, overlooks the River
Avon. Winkton has its own fishery and there are many others
locally. The area is also well endowed with golf courses. The
menu offers a daily fish selection, including trout and whole
plaice, and pub staples such as the roast of the day, steak and
kidney pie and lasagne.
OPEN: 10.30-2.30 5-11 (Sat-Sun open all day)
BAR MEALS: Lunch served: all week Dinner served: all week 12-2
6.30-9 Av main course £7.50 **RESTAURANT:** Lunch served: Sat-Sun
Dinner served: Sat-Sun 12-2 7-9 Av 3 course à la carte £14.95 Av 3
course fixed price £14.50 **BREWERY/COMPANY:** Gales
PRINCIPAL BEERS: Gales GB & HSB, Ringwood Fortyniner,
Interbrew Bass. **FACILITIES:** Children welcome Children's licence
Garden: Beer garden, food served outdoors Dogs allowed (water)
NOTES: Parking 80 **ROOMS:** 18 bedrooms 18 en suite from
s£49.50 d£66

The Ship In Distress
66 Stanpit BH23 3NA ☎ 01202 485123
e-mail: seafood@shipindistress.co.uk
A 200-year-old smugglers' pub close to Mudeford Quay,
specialising in seafood mainly caught by local fishermen. The
name derives from a smuggling vessel rescued by regulars from a nearby
creek. Legend says that the pub's owners, Mother Sellers, warned
smugglers of the coastgards' presence by wearing a red dress.

continued

England

CHRISTCHURCH continued

The Ship in Distress

Nowadays the food provides the excitement: expect roasted monkfish tails, baked fillet of pollock, and stir-fried tiger prawns, plus braised duck breast.
OPEN: 11–11 Closed: Dec 25 & Jan 1 **BAR MEALS:** Lunch served: all week Dinner served: all week 12–2 7–9 Av main course £13.50 **RESTAURANT:** Lunch served: all week Dinner served: all week 12–2 7–9 Av 3 course à la carte £23.50 **BREWERY/COMPANY:** Inn Partnership **PRINCIPAL BEERS:** Ringwood Best, Fourtyniner, Interbrew Bass. **FACILITIES:** Garden: Patio, food served outside Dogs allowed (water) **NOTES:** Parking 40

CHURCH KNOWLE  Map 03 SY98

The New Inn 🍴 ⛱
BH20 5NQ ☎ 01929 480357 🖃 01929 480357
In a charming village in the Purbeck hills, this partly thatched 16th-century inn has been run by the same family for nearly 20 years. All dishes are freshly made and fresh fish is delivered daily, with at least 12 fish dishes always available. These may include grilled trout topped with roasted almonds or salmon steak in lobster cream and brandy sauce. Special recommendations are the Dorset Blue Vinney soup, the good selection of ports, and an extensive wine list.
OPEN: 11–3 6.30–11 (closed Mon Jan–Mar) **BAR MEALS:** Lunch served: all week Dinner served: all week 12–2.15 6–9.15 Av main course £10 **RESTAURANT:** Lunch served: all week Dinner served: all week 12–2.15 6–9.15 Av 3 course à la carte £18.70
BREWERY/COMPANY: Inn Partnership
PRINCIPAL BEERS: Wadworth 6X, Greene King Old Speckled Hen, Interbrew Flowers Original. **FACILITIES:** Garden: Beer garden, food served outdoors Dogs allowed (only on lead) **NOTES:** Parking 100

CORFE CASTLE Map 03 SY98

The Greyhound Inn 🍴
The Square BH20 5EZ ☎ 01929 480205
Dir: *W from Bournemouth, take A35, after 5m L onto A351, 10m to Corfe*
On National Trust land and probably one of Britain's most photographed pubs, this coaching inn thought to be Tudor, when Corfe Castle was one of England's five royal castles. The inn's name changed to the Greyhound during the coaching era. Traditional pub fare includes bangers and mash and steak and Guinness pie, while 8oz Aberdeen sirloin steak is available from the charcoal grill. Daily vegetarian specials, home-made cakes and Dorset cream teas.
OPEN: 11–3 6–11.30 Summer open all day **BAR MEALS:** Lunch served: all week Dinner served: all week 12–2.30 6–9 Av main course £8.95 **RESTAURANT:** Lunch served: all week Dinner served: all week 12–2.30 6–9 Av 3 course à la carte £11.95
BREWERY/COMPANY: Free House
PRINCIPAL BEERS: Interbrew Flowers IPA, Ringwood Best,

Whitbread Best. **FACILITIES:** Children welcome Garden: Food served outdoors, patio, BBQ Dogs allowed (water) **NOTES:** Parking 10 **ROOMS:** 2 bedrooms d£50

Scott Arms 🍴 ⛱
West St, Kingston BH20 5LH ☎ 01929 480270
The Scott Arms is a large creeper-clad stone-built inn with excellent views of the Purbeck Hills and Corfe Castle from its attractive garden. It's a family pub with excellent facilities including en suite accommodation. Staff are cheerful, and welcoming fires are lit in the winter months. Home-made pies, curries and fresh fish and seafood feature among the popular dishes.
OPEN: 11.30–3 6–11 (Summer open all day) **BAR MEALS:** Lunch served: all week Dinner served: all week 12–2.30 6–9 Av main course £11 **RESTAURANT:** Lunch served: all week Dinner served: all week 12–2.30 6–9.30 **PRINCIPAL BEERS:** Ringwood Best, Marston's Pedigree, Scottish Courage John Smith's. **FACILITIES:** Children welcome Garden: Views of Corfe Castle, food served outside Dogs allowed **NOTES:** Parking 40 **ROOMS:** 2 bedrooms 2 en suite from d£45

CORSCOMBE Map 03 ST50

Pick of the Pubs

The Fox Inn ♦♦♦♦ 🏵 🍴 ⛱
DT2 0NS ☎ 01935 891330 🖃 01935 891330
e-mail: dine@fox-inn.co.uk
See Pick of the Pubs on page 165

EAST CHALDON Map 03 SY78

The Sailors Return 🍴
DT2 8DN ☎ 01305 853847 🖃 01305 851677
Dir: *1m S of A352 between Dorchester & Wool*

Tucked away in rolling downland, this splendid 17th-century thatched country inn is close to Lulworth Cove and miles of cliff walks. The comfortable beamed and flagstoned bar is where a blackboard lists available dishes, which may include wok black tiger prawns, halibut steaks, whole gammon hock, saddle of rabbit or red mullet.
OPEN: 11–3 6–11 (all day open from Easter–end Sept)
BAR MEALS: Lunch served: all week Dinner served: all week 12–2 6.30–9.30 Av main course £6.95 **RESTAURANT:** Lunch served: all week Dinner served: all week 12–2 6.30–9.30 Av 3 course à la carte £14.50 **BREWERY/COMPANY:** Free House
PRINCIPAL BEERS: Ringwood Best, Hampshire Strongs Best Bitter, Badger Tanglefoot. **FACILITIES:** Children welcome Children's licence Garden: Beer garden, food served outdoors, patio, Dogs allowed **NOTES:** Parking 100

OPEN: 12–2.30 7–11
BAR MEALS: L served all week.
D served all week. 12–2 7–9
Av main course £11
RESTAURANT: L served all week.
D served all week. 12–2 7–9 Av cost
3 course £21.50
BREWERY/COMPANY: FREE
HOUSE
PRINCIPLE BEERS: Exmoor Ale &
Fox, Fuller's London Pride
FACILITIES: Children welcome.
Garden: Lawned seating area
NOTES: Parking 50
ROOMS: 4 en suite Double room
from £80 Single room from £55

The Fox Inn

Built in 1620 as a cider house, The Fox is gem of a country pub standing on the old droving route to Yeovil, opposite the stream where the sheep used to be dipped. Hollyhocks and roses climb the cream-painted exterior walls and beyond the tiny entrance lobby lie two unspoilt beamed bars but the excellent food and real ales pull in the customers too.

◆◆◆◆ ◎ ♀
CORSCOMBE DT2 0NS
☎ 01935 891330 🖨 01935 891330
e-mail: dine@fox-inn.co.uk
Dir: From A37, between Yeovil & Dorchester, follow signs for Halstock/Corscombe on R.

The attractive thatched inn has hunting prints, old pine furniture and chatty locals in one bar, and the other prettily furnished with sturdy tables topped with blue gingham tablecloths in front of a huge stone fireplace where a log fire burns in winter. There's a long wooden table in the rear conservatory, surrounded by plants; it seats 20 and is ideal for parties. In addition to a cracking pint of Exmoor ale, local farm cider, home-made damson vodka and sloe gin, the attraction of Martyn and Susie Lee's are the meals prepared from

quality ingredients, including fish from Bridport and local game. In addition to the regular menu, the daily blackboard always offers at least seven starters, and seven fish and four meat main courses. Favourite dishes include gratin of crab, brill and prawns, roast rack of Dorset lamb, and local estate venison braised in red wine and juniper berries. Comforting puddings like treacle tart or meringues with clotted cream are hard to resist. Each of the letting bedrooms has individual character, furnished with personally collected antique pieces. The Fox is close to the World Heritage coastal site, and information on a number of excellent local walks is available on a printed sheet free from the bar.

EAST KNIGHTON Map 03 SY88

The Countryman Inn ♀
Blacknoll Ln DT2 8LL ☎ 01305 852666 📠 01305 854125
Dir: On A352 between Warmwell Cross & Wool
There's a comfortable, farmhouse atmosphere at this
attractive whitewashed free house, tucked away just off the
A352 in the heart of Hardy country. There are open fires in
the bars, plus a family room, garden and play area. The
menus cater for all tastes; everything from sandwiches,
ploughman's and jacket potatoes to pan-fried chicken, lemon
sole, or tomato and lentil lasagne. Daily carvery roasts and
specials include old-fashioned home-made puddings.
OPEN: 11-2.30 6-11 Closed: 25 Dec **BAR MEALS:** Lunch served:
all week Dinner served: all week 12-2 6.30-9.30 Av main course £7.95
RESTAURANT: Lunch served: all week Dinner served: all week 12-2
6.30-9.30 Av 3 course à la carte £18 **BREWERY/COMPANY:** Free
House **PRINCIPAL BEERS:** Greene King Old Speckled Hen,
Courage Directors & Best, Ringwood Best & Old Thumper.
FACILITIES: Children welcome Garden: Food Served outside Dogs
allowed **NOTES:** Parking 200 **ROOMS:** 6 bedrooms 6 en suite
from s£49 d£65

EAST MORDEN Map 03 SY99

Pick of the Pubs

The Cock & Bottle 🕮 ♀
BH20 7DL ☎ 01929 459238
Dir: From A35 W of Poole take B3075. Pub 2m on R

Originally a cob-walled Dorset longhouse, dating back
some 400 years, this delightful pub was given a brick skin
around 1800. From the modern rear extension there are
lovely pastoral views and inside it is comfortably rustic with
quaint, low-beamed ceilings, attractive paintings and lots of
nooks and crannies around its log fires. Outside, a large
field occasionally hosts vintage car and motorcycle rallies
during the summer. Alongside its popular locals' bar are a
lounge bar and a restaurant with the accent on fresh
produce, including fish and game. Typical starters might
include wild mushroom tartlet with a seed mustard
hollandaise sauce, grilled goats' cheese or duck spring rolls
served with a chilli jam. Main courses may feature loin of
cod topped with a crab, cheese and herb crust and served
with a tomato coulis, and lamb rump set on a bubble and
squeak potato cake with a rosemary and redcurrant sauce.
OPEN: 11-3 6-11 (Sun 12-3, 7-10.30) **BAR MEALS:** Lunch
served: all week Dinner served: all week 12-2 6-9 Av main course
£9 **RESTAURANT:** Lunch served: all week Dinner served: all
week 12-2 6-9 **BREWERY/COMPANY:** Hall & Woodhouse
PRINCIPAL BEERS: Badger Dorset Best & Tanglefoot & Sussex.
FACILITIES: Children welcome Garden: Patio, food served
outside Dogs allowed (water) **NOTES:** Parking 40

EVERSHOT Map 03 ST50

Pick of the Pubs

The Acorn Inn ♦♦♦♦ 🕮 🕮 ♀
DT2 0JW ☎ 01935 83228 📠 01935 83707
e-mail: stay@acorn-inn.co.uk
See Pub Walk on page 161
See Pick of the Pubs on page 167

FARNHAM Map 03 ST91

Pick of the Pubs

The Museum Arms 🕮 🕮 ♀
DT11 8DE ☎ 01725 516261
e-mail: themuseuminn@supernet.co.uk
See Pick of the Pubs on page 168

GILLINGHAM Map 03 ST82

The Kings Arms Inn 🕮
East Stour Common SP8 5NB ☎ 01747 838325
e-mail: jenny@kings-arms.fsnet.co.uk
Dir: 4m W of Shaftesbury on A30

A 200-year-old country inn set in the beautiful Blackmore
Vale, where the visitor can spend days exploring the maze of
small roads, footpaths and bridle-ways in a lush pastoral
landscape. Alongside a warm welcome and three cosily
furnished bedrooms, the inn sports an extensive beer garden
and a wide selection of real ales. Traditional pub food
encompasses ploughman's lunches, tempting pizzas and
house specials such as orchard pork, home-made steak and
kidney pie and assorted grills.
OPEN: 12-2.30 5-11 Closed: 25 Dec **BAR MEALS:** Lunch served:
all week Dinner served: all week 12-2 6-9 Av main course £5.50
RESTAURANT: Lunch served: all week Dinner served: all week 12-2
6-9 Av 3 course à la carte £12.50 Av 3 course fixed price £10
BREWERY/COMPANY: Free House
PRINCIPAL BEERS: Interbrew Worthington Bitter.
FACILITIES: Children welcome Garden: Food served outdoors,
patio/terrace. Dogs allowed (water) **NOTES:** Parking 40
ROOMS: 3 bedrooms 3 en suite from s£25.50 d£45

> **Most of the pubs in this guide book
> pride themselves on the quality of their food.
> This may take a little time to prepare.**

OPEN: 11.30–3 6–11
BAR MEALS: L served all week.
D served all week. 12–2 6.30–9
Av main course £11
RESTAURANT: L served all week.
D served all week. 12–2 7–9
Av cost 3 courses £19.50
BREWERY/COMPANY:
FREE HOUSE
PRINCIPAL BEERS: Fuller's
London Pride, Butcombe, Palmer
FACILITIES: Children and dogs
welcome. Garden: Patio, food
served outdoors
NOTES: Parking 30
ROOMS: 9 en suite. Double room
from £75. Single room from £55

The Acorn Inn

◆◆◆◆ ⊛ ⏆ 🐾
Evershot, Dorset DT2 0JW
☎ 01935 83228 🖷 01935 83707
e-mail: stay@acorn-inn.co.uk
Dir: A303 to Yeovil, Dorchester Rd, on
A37 R to Evershot

A fine stone building, under the same ownership as the Fox Inn at Corscombe, the Acorn Inn has been carefully restored to create the perfect rural base from which to explore Hardy Country and the beautiful Dorset coastline.

Thomas Hardy wrote about this 16th century inn as 'the Sow and Acorn' in *Tess of the D'Urbervilles*, and is believed to have stayed here when writing *Jude the Obscure*. The pub still has a sleepy village setting surrounded by fabulous countryside and some great walks. The dining room used to be a grand hall, thought to have been used by Judge Jeffreys as a court-house, and the old stables have been converted into a skittle alley. There are two oak-panelled bars with flagstone floors and log fires in caved Hamstone fireplaces. The bars serve traditional ales and a selection of wines, and in addition to the choice of bar food, such as hearty soups and substantial sandwiches, a full menu is offered in the Hardy Dining Room or the no-smoking restaurant. Fresh fish from nearby Bridport and local game are specialities frequently featured on the short menu. Fish options may range from cod in beer batter with mushy peas to grilled red snapper on crushed potato with pesto. Other options include local estate game casserole with port and juniper berries, or loin of pork with wild mushroom sauce. A tempting array of puddings takes in a traditional apple crumble and a white chocolate parfait with dark chocolate sauce. Accommodation is provided in individually styled rooms, two with four-poster beds, and mid-week special breaks are available all year.

OPEN: 12–3 6–11
BAR MEALS: L served all week.
D served all week. 12–2 7–9.30
Av main course £9.50
RESTAURANT: L served Sun 12–3.
D served all week. 7–9.30
Av cost 3 courses £25
BREWERY/COMPANY: FREE
HOUSE
PRINCIPLE BEERS: Ringwood Best
Bitter, Hopback Glory, Quay Best
Bitter, Timothy Taylor Landlord
FACILITIES: Dogs allowed. Garden:
Food served outside
NOTES: Parking 12
ROOMS: 8 en suite Double room
from £65 Single room from £5

The Museum Arms

A 17th-century part-thatched country inn which was built by the famous archaeologist Augustus Pitt Rivers to provide accommodation and refreshments for visitors to his nearby museum. A recent renovation by owners Vicky Eliot and Mark Stephenson has left all of the original features intact, with flagged stone floors, inglenook fireplace, bread oven and antique furniture adding up to a warm and cosy atmosphere that attracts a well-heeled clientele.

Farnham, Dorset DT11 8DE
☎ 01725 516261
e-mail: themuseuminn@supernet.co.uk
Dir: From Salisbury take the A354 to Blandford Forum. After approx 12 m, Farnham is signposted to the R, the pub is in the centre of the village.

The addition of eight smart en suite bedrooms allows visitors to extend their stay in this idyllic little Dorset village in the heart of Cranborne Chase where thatched cottages almost outnumber their modern counterparts. Most exciting is the opening of a separate restaurant along with the bar, where the modern cooking is well worth sampling. The

freshest of seasonal produce is sourced locally for traditionally-reared stock, free-range poultry, south-coast fish and game from neighbouring estates. Organic ingredients are used whenever possible, and everything from bread to jams and chutneys is home made. The results of this obvious commitment to good food can be sampled from the Shed Restaurant's short carte: Scottish salmon tortellini with lobster, basil and fennel, perhaps followed by pot-roasted squab pigeon with pancetta and wild mushrooms, and brought to a satisfying conclusion with lemon curd tart and orange sorbet. From the bar expect the likes of grilled yellow fin tuna, confit leg of chicken with chorizo, sautÈ potatoes and caramelised onions and, for a lighter bite, roast beef sandwich. Local real ales always on tap, and a sound range of global wines.

GODMANSTONE   Map 03 SY69

Smiths Arms
DT2 7AQ ☎ 01300 341236
With only around six tables, this is one of the smallest pubs in
Britain. 15th-century and thatched in a riverside setting, the
Smiths Arms offers hearty meals including home-cooked ham
off the bone, curried prawn lasagne, ham and broccoli au
gratin, and haddock and mushroom bake.
OPEN: 11–5.30 **BAR MEALS:** Lunch served: all week 12–3 Av main
course £4.95 **BREWERY/COMPANY:** Free House
PRINCIPAL BEERS: Wadworth 6X, Kronenbourg, Stowford Press
Cider. **FACILITIES:** Garden: Food served outside Dogs allowed (in
the garden only) No credit cards

GUSSAGE ALL SAINTS   Map 03 SU01

The Drovers Inn
BH21 5ET ☎ 01258 840084
Dir: A31 Ashley Heath rdbt, R onto B3081

Recently re-opened after total refurbishment, this 16th-century
pub with a fine terrace has retained its traditional appeal with
flagstone floors and oak furniture. All food is home-made and
includes such dishes as slow roasted shank of lamb with
redcurrant and rosemary, Drover's steak and Guinness pie,
seafood bake, salmon fillet, pork Valentine steak with creamy
mushroom and cider sauce, and seafood platter.
OPEN: 11.45–2.30 6–11 (Sat 11–3 6–11 Sun 12–3 6–11)
BAR MEALS: Lunch served: all week Dinner served: Tue–Sun 12–2
7–9 Av main course £6.95 **PRINCIPAL BEERS:** Ringwood Best, Old
Thumpe & Fortyniner. **FACILITIES:** Children welcome Garden:
Food served outdoors Dogs allowed (water) **NOTES:** Parking 35

LODERS   Map 03 SY49

Loders Arms
DT6 3SA ☎ 01308 422431
Dir: off the A3066, 2m NE of Bridport
Unassuming stone-built local tucked away in a pretty thatched
village close to the Dorset coast. Arrive early to bag a seat in
the bar or in the homely (and tiny) dining room. Interesting
blackboard menus may list fish soup, smoked haddock
fishcakes and filled baguettes for bar diners, with the likes of
scallops in Pernod, rack of lamb, and sea bass with salsa
verde available throughout. Lovely summer garden.
OPEN: 11.30–3 6–11 (Sun 11.30–11) **BAR MEALS:** Lunch served: all
week Dinner served: all week 12.30–2 7.15–9 Av main course £6.95
RESTAURANT: Lunch served: all week Dinner served: all week
12.30–2 7.15–9 Av 3 course à la carte £18
BREWERY/COMPANY: Palmers Brewery
PRINCIPAL BEERS: Palmers Bridport Bitter, Palmers IPA, Palmers
200. **FACILITIES:** Children welcome Garden: Dogs allowed
ROOMS: 2 bedrooms 2 en suite from s£40 d£40

LOWER ANSTY   Map 03 ST70

The Fox Inn ★ ★ ◎ ♀
DT2 7PN ☎ 01258 880328 ▤ 01258 881440
e-mail: hotel@fox-inn-ansty.co.uk
Dir: A35 from Dorchester towards Poole, onto B3142, 1st R for
Cheselbourne, keep to road for 4 miles.
This reassuringly civilised brick and flint dining pub with its
delightful en suite bedrooms makes a perfect base for touring
Hardy's Wessex. The Hall and Woodhouse brewing families
were both linked with The Fox, and old family photos
decorate the bar. Varied menus serve the bar and restaurants;
choices range from hot filled baguettes, or cod in beer batter,
to lamb shank on olive oil mash, aromatic duck leg, or
mushroom and red onion tart. Finish with meringue basket
and fresh strawberries, or tangy lemon tart.
OPEN: 11–11 (Sun 12–10) **BAR MEALS:** Lunch served: all week
Dinner served: all week 12–3 6.30–9.30 Av main course £9
RESTAURANT: Lunch served: all week Dinner served: all week 12–3
6.30–9.30 Av 3 course à la carte £27.50 Av 5 course fixed price £29.50
BREWERY/COMPANY: Free House **PRINCIPAL BEERS:** Badger
Tanglefoot, Badger Best. **FACILITIES:** Children welcome Garden:
Food served outside **NOTES:** Parking 40 **ROOMS:** 14 bedrooms 14
en suite from s£45 d£70

LYME REGIS   Map 03 SY39

Pilot Boat Inn ♀
Bridge St DT7 3QA ☎ 01297 443157
This busy town centre pub is close to the sea front and has a
number of old smuggling and sea rescue connections, but it's
biggest claim to fame would seem to be as the possible
birthplace of the inspiration for Hollywood's favourite super-
collie, Lassie. Meals include a wide range of fish dishes, steaks
and grills, ploughman's, salads, sandwiches and a full page of
vegetarian options. An interesting wine list.
OPEN: 11–11 (Sun 12–10.30) Closed: Dec 25 **BAR MEALS:** Lunch
served: all week Dinner served: all week 12–10 Av main course £7
RESTAURANT: 12–10 **BREWERY/COMPANY:** Palmers
PRINCIPAL BEERS: Palmers Dorset Gold, IPA, Palmers 200 &
Bridport Bitter. **FACILITIES:** Children welcome Children's licence
Garden: Patio, food served outside Dogs allowed

MARSHWOOD   Map 03 SY39

Pick of the Pubs

The Bottle Inn
DT6 5QJ ☎ 01297 678254 ▤ 01297 678739
e-mail: thebottleinn@msn.com
Dir: 4m inland from the A35 on the B3165
Standing beside the B3165 on the edge of the glorious
Marshwood Vale, the thatched Bottle Inn was first
mentioned as an ale house back in the 17th century. It
was the first pub in the area during the 18th century to
serve bottled beer rather than beer from the jug – hence
the name. Present day landlords, Shane and Chloe, lead
the way in local organic food and drink, including organic
Caledonian Golden Promise on handpump. The rustic
interior has simple wooden settles, scrubbed tables and a
blazing fire. Diners will find pan-fried wild boar steak with
honey, plums and balsamic vinegar, whole chicken breast
wrapped in pancetta and served on a Caesar salad,
kumara and lemongrass bake, and traditional beef and
Guinness pie on the menu. Taking the organic food theme

continued

MARSHWOOD continued

to its furthest reaches, the pub is home to the annual World Stinging-Nettle Eating Championships.
OPEN: 12-3 6.30-11 **BAR MEALS:** Lunch served: all week Dinner served: all week 12-2 7.30-9 Av main course £8.50
RESTAURANT: Lunch served: all week Dinner served: all week Av 3 course à la carte £25 **BREWERY/COMPANY:** Free House
PRINCIPAL BEERS: Otter Ale, Greene King Old Speckled Hen.
FACILITIES: Children welcome Garden: Food served outside
NOTES: Parking 40

MILTON ABBAS   Map 03 ST80

The Hambro Arms 🐑 ♀
DT11 0BP ☎ 01258 880233
Traditional whitewashed 18th-century thatched pub located in a picturesque landscaped village. Enjoy an appetising bar snack or, perhaps, half shoulder of lamb with minted redcurrant sauce, liver and bacon, duck with orange sauce, venison sausages, or grilled sea bass, in the comfortable lounge bar or on the popular patio.
OPEN: 11-3 6.30-11 **BAR MEALS:** Lunch served: all week Dinner served: all week 12-2 7-9 Av main course £10 **RESTAURANT:** Lunch served: all week Dinner served: all week 12-2 7-9
BREWERY/COMPANY: Pubmaster **PRINCIPAL BEERS:** Bass, Greene King Old Speckled Hen. **FACILITIES:** Dogs allowed (in the garden only) **NOTES:** Parking 20 **ROOMS:** 2 bedrooms 2 en suite from d£60

MOTCOMBE   Map 03 ST82

The Coppleridge Inn 🐑 ♀
SP7 9HW ☎ 01747 851980 🖀 01747 851858
e-mail: thecoppleridgeinn@btinternet.com
Set in 15 acres with beautiful views across the Blackmore Vale, this tastefully converted farm complex offers spacious bedrooms in refurbished barns and wide-ranging menus in the old farmhouse, complete with flagstone floors, stripped pine and country views. Choose from a list of specials that may include confit of duck in a rich plum sauce, haggis, neeps and stovies, or sauté of calves' liver with champagne and cream sauce, in the light and airy restaurant. Tennis court, cricket pitch and other facilities are available.
OPEN: 11-3 5-11 All day Sat & Sun **BAR MEALS:** Lunch served: all week Dinner served: all week 12-2.30 6-9.30 Av main course £7.50
RESTAURANT: Lunch served: all week Dinner served: all week 12-2.30 6-9.30 Av 3 course à la carte £15 Av 3 course fixed price £11.50 **BREWERY/COMPANY:** Free House
PRINCIPAL BEERS: Butcombe Bitter, Adnams Southwold, Wadworth 6X, Fullers London Pride. **FACILITIES:** Children welcome Garden: Food served outside, playground Dogs allowed (garden only, water provided) **NOTES:** Parking 60 **ROOMS:** 10 bedrooms 10 en suite from s£42.50 d£75

NETTLECOMBE   Map 03 SY59

Marquis of Lorne ♦♦♦♦ 🐑 ♀
DT6 3SY ☎ 01308 485236 🖀 01308 485666
e-mail: julie.woodroffe@btinternet.com
Dir: 3m E of A3066 Bridport-Beaminster rd, after Mangerton Mill & West Milton
The Marquis is a 16th-century farmhouse, converted to a pub in 1870, and set amid lovely countryside in the hamlet of

Nettlescombe, with its quaint yellow-stone cottages. The daily changing blackboard menus offer dishes based on fresh local produce, whether you choose a light snack or à la carte dinner - though be warned, the portions are generous. The proprietors have joined the Campaign for Real Food, and even the children's menu provides proper wholesome cooking.

OPEN: 11-2.30 6.30-11 (Sun 12-2.30, 7-10.30)
BAR MEALS: Lunch served: all week Dinner served: all week 12-2 6.30-9 Av main course £7.95 **RESTAURANT:** Lunch served: all week Dinner served: all week 12-2 6.30-9 Av 3 course à la carte £15
BREWERY/COMPANY: Palmers **PRINCIPAL BEERS:** Palmers Bridport, IPA, 200 Premium Ale. **FACILITIES:** Children welcome Garden: Large, food served outside Dogs allowed (water)
NOTES: Parking 50 **ROOMS:** 7 bedrooms 7 en suite from s£35 d£63

NORTH WOOTTON   Map 03 ST61

The Three Elms 🐑 ♀
DT9 5JW ☎ 01935 812881 🖀 01935 812881
e-mail: threeelms@talk21.com
Dir: From Sherborne take A352 towards Dorchester then A3030. Pub 1m on R
An interesting choice of real ales and locally produced ciders awaits you at this family-run free house overlooking Blackmore Vale. There are stunning views from the pub's garden, and the landlord boasts a collection of around 1,300 model cars. The wide-ranging menu includes dishes like shark and bacon cassoulet, royal ocean platter (a mixture of hot and cold fish and seafood), lamb and mango casserole, and Thai-style salmon supreme with noodles and stir-fried vegetables.
OPEN: 11-2.30 6.30-11 (Sun 12-3, 7-10.30) Closed: 25-26 Dec
BAR MEALS: 12-2 6.30-10 **RESTAURANT:** 12-2 6.30-10
BREWERY/COMPANY: Free House **PRINCIPAL BEERS:** Fuller's London Pride, Butcombe Bitter, Shepherd Neame Spitfire, Otter Ale.
FACILITIES: Children welcome Garden: Food served outside Dogs allowed **NOTES:** Parking 50 **ROOMS:** 1 bedroom from s£25 d£45

OSMINGTON MILLS   Map 03 SY78

The Smugglers 🐑
DT3 6HF ☎ 01305 833125 🖀 01305 832219
The inn has a unique position in a hollow on the Dorset coastal path, a convenient landing place for smugglers in the 18th and 19th centuries. It was the headquarters of notorious French smuggler Pierre Latour who later married the landlord's daughter. Inside there are black beams and flagstone floors and outside there's a play area and a brook running through the garden. Seafood is a speciality, including local lobster, crab cakes, and seafood platter.

continued

PUB WALK

Piddletrenthide
The Piddle Inn

This circular walk around Piddletrenthide offers the chance to savour the peace and beauty of the renowned Piddle Valley. The 15th-century village church has one of Dorset's best towers and nearby is a fine 18th-century manor house.

From the Piddle Inn take the footpath behind the pub, cross the river and head round to the right by the farm outbuildings. On reaching the Cerne Abbas road, turn left and then right after a few paces. Keep straight on along a wide track and when you reach a sign for Kiddles Farm, turn right and follow Church Lane to the junction with the B3143. Turn left and walk towards Alton Pancras for about 160 yards (146m), heading up the track on the right which climbs to Hollery Down. Make for a stile at the top of the track, then walk across the down towards a clump of trees. Draw level with a

drinking trough and continue to the north-east corner of Hollery Down. Follow the hedge on the right to the north-east corner of the next field. Negotiate a sometimes overgrown section of fencing and enter a pretty hilltop meadow known as Watcombe Plain. Exit by the first field gate on the left, beside a small round copse. Stay on the bridleway across the next field and continue to a fork. Veer right down the side of Burnt House Bottom to a concrete drinking trough. Fork left off the track into a sunken area, go through a gate and keep ahead between houses to the B3143. Turn left and follow the road back into the centre of the village, passing Church Lane on your right and the Poachers Inn beyond. Look out for the manor house also on the right. There is a hidden bend here, so take care and stay close to the wall for safety. Pass turnings on the left and right and return to the inn.

THE PIDDLE INN,
PIDDLETRENTHIDE Dorchester DT2 7QF
Tel: 01300 348468
Directions: in middle of village
This friendly village local stands in an unspoilt valley on the banks of the River Piddle. Good food, open fires and traditional pub games make this a favourite spot with visitors, and the riverside patio is popular in summer.
Open: 11-3 6-11
Bar meals: 12-2 6.30-9.30
Children welcome and dogs allowed. Garden and parking available.

Distance: 6 miles (9.7km)
Map: OS Landranger 194
Terrain: Rolling fields, farmland and woodland
Paths: Bridleways, paths and tracks
Gradient: Gently undulating

Walk submitted and checked by The Piddle Inn, Piddletrenthide

England

PIDDLEHINTON
Map 03 SY79

The Thimble Inn
DT2 7TD ☎ 01300 348270
Dir: *A35 westbound, R onto B3143, Piddlehinton 4m*
Good food, open fires and traditional pub games make this friendly village local a favourite spot with visitors. The pub stands in an unspoilt valley on the banks of the River Piddle, and the riverside patio is popular in summer. The extensive menu caters for all tastes, from sandwiches, jacket potatoes and children's meals, to grilled Torbay sole, steak and oyster pudding, or spinach and ricotta cannelloni. Warm sticky puddings, too, if you've room!
OPEN: 12–2.30 7–11 (Sun 12–2.30 7–10.30) Closed: 25 Dec
BAR MEALS: Lunch served: all week Dinner served: all week 12–2 7–9 Av main course £6 **RESTAURANT:** Lunch served: all week Dinner served: all week 12–2 7–9 **BREWERY/COMPANY:** Free House **PRINCIPAL BEERS:** Badger Best & Tanglefoot, Thomas Hardy Hardy Country, Ringwood Old Thumper, Palmer IPA.
FACILITIES: Children welcome Garden: Beer garden, food served outdoors, patio, Dogs allowed **NOTES:** Parking 50

PIDDLETRENTHIDE
Map 03 SY79

Piddle Inn
DT2 7QF ☎ 01300 348468 🗎 01300 348102
e-mail: inn.piddle@btinternet.co.uk
Friendly village local set in a deep valley of great natural beauty. A pub since the 1760s, it was once a staging post for the exchange of prisoners from Sherborne and Dorchester and has many a tale to tell of drunken prisoners and their escorts. Seafood is a speciality - seafood platter, John Dory with roasted artichokes, mushrooms and a sun-dried tomato salsa, and seared scallops with garlic, bacon and fragrant rice. The riverside patio is popular in summer.
OPEN: 11–3 6–11 **BAR MEALS:** Lunch served: Tues-Sun Dinner served: Tues-Sun 12–2 6.30-9.30 **RESTAURANT:** Lunch served: Tues-Sun Dinner served: Tues-Sun 12–2 6.30-9.30 Av 3 course à la carte £18 Av 3 course fixed price £11.50
BREWERY/COMPANY: Free House **PRINCIPAL BEERS:** Greene King Old Speckled Hen, IPA, Abbot Ale, Wadworth 6X.
FACILITIES: Children welcome Garden: Patio, food served outside Dogs allowed **NOTES:** Parking 20

See Pub Walk on page 171

The Poachers Inn ♦♦♦♦
DT2 7QX ☎ 01300 348358 🗎 01300 348153
e-mail: thepoachers@piddletrenthide.fsbusiness.co.uk
Dir: *8m from Dorchester on B3143*

At the heart of Thomas Hardy country, this family-run free house is in a small village by the River Piddle. Open fires and traditional pub games reflect its identity as a genuine English

local, whose riverside patio is especially popular in summer. Home-made soups, steak and ale pie and vegetarian options such as mushroom Stroganoff and an impressive array of beef steaks and grills. Leave room for a treat to follow - hot, home-made Dorset apple cake.
OPEN: 12–11 Closed: 24-26 Dec **BAR MEALS:** Lunch served: all week 12–6.30 Dinner served: all week 6.30-9 Av main course £6 **RESTAURANT:** Lunch served: all week 12–6.30 Dinner served: all week 6.30-9 Av 3 course à la carte £10
BREWERY/COMPANY: Free House
PRINCIPAL BEERS: Interbrew Bass & Worthington Bitter, Carlsberg-Tetley Tetley Bitter, Poachers Ale,. **FACILITIES:** Children welcome Garden: Food served outside Dogs allowed **NOTES:** Parking 40 **ROOMS:** 18 bedrooms 18 en suite from s£35 d£60

PLUSH
Map 03 ST70

Pick of the Pubs

Brace of Pheasants
DT2 7RQ ☎ 01300 348357
e-mail: geoffreyknights@braceofpheasants.freeserve.co.uk
Dir: *A35 onto B3143,5m to Piddletrenthide, then R to Mappowder & Plush*

Tucked away in a fold of the hills, east of Cerne Abbas, is one of Dorset's prettiest 16th-century thatched village inns, hidden at the heart of Hardy's beloved county. He is believed to have used Plush as the model for Flintcomb-Ash in *Tess of the d'Urbervilles*. Beginning life as two cottages, the Brace of Pheasants then became a village smithy. Over the years it has been transformed into one of the area's most popular pubs. Inside the ambience is warm and welcoming, with an open fire, oak beams and fresh flowers. Lunch, dinner and bar meals are available, and the choice of menu reflects the changing of the seasons. Game dishes include loin of venison with grain mustard and brandy, and roast partridge with Madeira and mushrooms. Crusty pies and warming soups also form part of the menu, together with roast monkfish, baked salmon herb crust, medallions of pork tenderloin and breast of chicken. Various snacks and starters.
OPEN: 12–2.30 7–11 (Sun 12–3 7–10.30) Closed: Dec 25
BAR MEALS: Lunch served: all week Dinner served: all week 12–1.45 7–9.30 Av main course £8.50 **RESTAURANT:** Lunch served: all week Dinner served: all week 12–1.30 7–9.30 Av 3 course à la carte £17.50 **BREWERY/COMPANY:** Free House
PRINCIPAL BEERS: Fuller's London Pride, Butcombe Bitter, Hop Back Summer Lightning, Ringwood Best.
FACILITIES: Garden: Large, food served outside Dogs allowed (water) **NOTES:** Parking 30

See Pub Walk on page 173

continued

PUB WALK

Plush
The Brace of Pheasants

Discover a peaceful Dorset landscape that has changed little since novelist Thomas Hardy was inspired by its beauty and tranquillity. This is good walking country, with a large network of remote tracks and ancient paths to explore and enjoy.

Take the road opposite the pub, past the Old Schoolhouse towards Mappowder. Pass several cottages and head up the hill until a waymaked path on your right. Pass through a metal gate to follow the well-defined path to the stile at the top of the hill and glance back for a view of Plush and Plush Manor. Head slightly left across the next field to the stile in the opposite hedgerow. Walk straight across this field to a gate and then turn immediately left, following the fence until a the bridleway sign on your left. Pass through the gate and into the next field. Follow the ridge, keeping close to the fence, and head gently uphill to the wood ahead. As you pass the wood on your right see the views across the Blackmore Vale towards Shaftesbury. On reaching a gate on the right, bear slightly left and go downhill along the shallow track. Continue along the ever-deepening right of way to the stile at the bottom. Turn left to join a broad track running through a copse. Make for Folly Farm and the road. To cut short the walk, turn left here and return directly to the inn. To continue, cross the road and follow the deep track, signposted Alton Pancras, as it climbs the hill up to a gate at the top. Pass through it, continue to the next gate and then keep the hedgerow on your right. Make for a wood and a gate in the right-hand corner of the field. Follow the track through the woods to a gate out to Watcombe Plain. Aim slightly left now, keeping the hedge on the right, you will see a metal gate far ahead. Go through the gap in the hedge to the left which runs at right angles to the gate. Keep straight ahead,and then veer a little left towards the metal gate in the distance. The ground drops away steeply to the left. Pass through the gate, and a second, descend to the road and turn left, back to the inn.

THE BRACE OF PHEASANTS,
PLUSH Dorchester DT2 7RQ
Tel: 01300 348357
Directions: A35 onto B3143, 5m to Piddletrenthide, then R to Mappowder & Plush
Tucked in the hills east of Cerne Abbas, a delightful 16th-century thatched inn with beams, an inglenook, log fires, and a big garden for the summer. A welcome refreshment stop with a good selection of cask ales, and reviving pub food.
Open: 12–2.30 7–11
Bar meals: 12–1.45 7–9.30
Dogs allowed. Garden and parking available.

Distance: 4 1/2 miles (7.2km)
Map: OS Landranger 194
Terrain: Undulating landscape overlooking the Blackmore Vale. Soft and muddy in places
Paths: Mainly paths and tracks
Gradient: Some climbing

Walk submitted and checked by The Brace of Pheasants, Plush

POOLE
Map 03 SZ09

The Guildhall Tavern ☺ NEW
15 Market St BH15 1NB ☎ 01202 671717 📠 01202 242346
e-mail: sewerynsevfred@aol.com
Dir: *2 minutes from Poole Quay*
In a prime location, just two minutes' walk from Poole Quay, these historic premises are enjoying a new life. Formerly a cider house, today's re-incarnation is decidedly French, from the staff to its food and smart nautical decor. Herring roes on toast and a home-made tart of crab and scallops are typical starters, followed by real bouillabaisse or braised shank of lamb set on Puy lentils. Don't expect a quick snack – nor much change from a 'monkey'!
OPEN: 11–3.30 6.30–11 **BAR MEALS:** Lunch served: all week Dinner served: all week 11–2.30 6.30–10 Av main course £12
RESTAURANT: Lunch served: all week Dinner served: all week 12–2.30 6.30–10 Av 3 course à la carte £25
BREWERY/COMPANY: Inn Partnership
PRINCIPAL BEERS: Ringwood Best, Interbrew Flowers IPA,.
FACILITIES: Children welcome **NOTES:** Parking 10

POWERSTOCK
Map 03 SY59

Pick of the Pubs

Three Horseshoes Inn ☺ ♀
DT6 3TF ☎ 01308 485328 📠 01308 485328
Dir: *E of A3066 (Bridport/Beaminster rd)*

Visitors can enjoy lovely coastal views from the steeply rising lawns rising above this picturesque stone-and-thatch pub in a tiny Dorset village. The pub fits in perfectly with its idyllic setting in the village of Powerstock, which has featured in several films – *A Murder is Announced*, based on one of Agatha Christie's murder mysteries, and *Far from the Madding Crowd*, adapted from Thomas Hardy's novel. Reached down winding country lanes and an ideal stop for walkers and cyclists, the Three Horseshoes once housed the old blacksmith's shop. The extensive menu has an emphasis on fish dishes and traditional English food cooked with fresh ingredients. Expect steak and kidney pie, whole Lyme Bay plaice, prawn and haddock pie and medallions of Scottish fillet steak with peppercorn and cream sauce. The blackboard menu changes continuously and the food can be accompanied by wine from a wide-ranging list and several draught beers.
OPEN: 12–3 6–11 **BAR MEALS:** Lunch served: all week Dinner served: all week 12–2 7–9 Av main course £10.50
RESTAURANT: Lunch served: all week Dinner served: all week 12–2 7–9 Av 3 course à la carte £18.50
BREWERY/COMPANY: Palmers **PRINCIPAL BEERS:** Palmer

Bridport Bitter & IPA. **FACILITIES:** Children welcome Garden: Patio, food served outside **NOTES:** Parking 30 **ROOMS:** 3 bedrooms 2 en suite from d£50

PUNCKNOWLE
Map 03 SY58

The Crown Inn
Church St DT2 9BN ☎ 01308 897711 📠 01308 898282
e-mail: thecrowninn@puncknowle48.fsnet.co.uk
Dir: *From A35, into Bridevally, thru Litton Cheney. From B3157, inland at Swyre.*
Picturesque 16th-century thatched inn, once a haunt of smugglers en route from nearby Chesil Beach to visit prosperous customers in Bath. There is a traditional atmosphere within its rambling, low-beamed bars. Food ranges from light snacks to hearty home-made dishes like beef, mushroom and horseradish casserole cooked in Palmers beer, or salmon and broccoli casserole cooked in white wine. A good choice of vegetarian dishes is offered (bean and ratatouille hotpot), and a children's menu.
OPEN: 11–3 (Sun 12–3, 7–10.30) 7–11 (Summer 6.30 opening) Closed: 25 Dec **BAR MEALS:** Lunch served: all week Dinner served: all week 12–2 7–9 Av main course £7
BREWERY/COMPANY: Palmers **PRINCIPAL BEERS:** Palmers IPA, 200 Premium Ale. **FACILITIES:** Children welcome Garden: Food served outdoors, patio Dogs allowed (water) **NOTES:** Parking 12 **ROOMS:** 3 bedrooms 1 en suite from s£25 d£42 No credit cards

SHERBORNE
Map 03 ST61

The Digby Tap
Cooks Ln DT9 3NS ☎ 01935 813148
e-mail: peter@lefevrefslife.co.uk
Old-fashioned town pub with stone-flagged floors, old beams and a wide-ranging choice of real ale. Simple pub food. Close to Sherborne Abbey.
OPEN: 11–2.30 5.30–11 Closed 1 Jan **BAR MEALS:** Lunch Mon–Sat 12–1.45 Av main course £3.45 **BREWERY/COMPANY:** Free House
PRINCIPAL BEERS: Ringwood Best, Otter Ale, Teignworthy Reel Ale, Sharp's Own **FACILITIES:** Dogs welcome **NOTES:** No credit cards

Half Moon ☺ ♀
Half Moon St DT9 3LN ☎ 01935 812017 📠 01935 815295
Standing close to Sherborne Abbey, this half-timbered Cotswold stone inn stands in the centre of town. The Half Moon is one of an expanding group of character accommodation inns, offering 16 comfortable en suite bedrooms. Eat in the restaurant or the warm and inviting bar: daily specials might include chicken pomodoro, and Thai salmon supreme, while the main menu offers a choice of steaks, plus old favourites like steak and ale pie, lasagne, and chicken tikka masala.
OPEN: 11–11 (Sun 12–10.30) **BAR MEALS:** Lunch served: all week Dinner served: all week 12–2 6–9.30 Av main course £5
RESTAURANT: Lunch served: all week Dinner served: all week 12–2 6–9.30 **BREWERY/COMPANY:** Eldridge Pope
PRINCIPAL BEERS: Scottish Courage Courage Best & Courage Directors. **FACILITIES:** Children welcome Garden: **NOTES:** Parking 40 **ROOMS:** 16 bedrooms 16 en suite from s£49 d£69

Queen's Head ☺
High St, Milborne Port DT9 5DQ
☎ 01963 250314 📠 01963 250339
e-mail: queensmp@ftech.co.uk
A Grade II listed building, parts of it dating back to Elizabethan times, the pub has charm, character and a very friendly

continued

continued

atmosphere in two comfortable bars and dining-room. Enthusiastic licensees oversee a wide-ranging menu in which they take great pride. The most accomplished dishes include beef Stroganoff, warm lemon chicken salad, swordfish steaks with lime and ginger sauce and vegetarian Mexican mixed-bean chilli. There are home-made beefburgers in adult and junior portions and an ice cream menu amongst the desserts.
OPEN: 11–3 5.30–11 **BAR MEALS:** Lunch served: all week Dinner served: all week 12–2 7–9.30 Av main course £8
RESTAURANT: Lunch served: all week Dinner served: all week 12–2 7–9.30 **BREWERY/COMPANY:** Enterprise Inns
PRINCIPAL BEERS: Fuller's London Pride, Butcombe Bitter, Interbrew Flowers Original, Wells Bombardier. **FACILITIES:** Children welcome Garden: Patio/terrace, food served outside Dogs allowed (water)
NOTES: Parking 15 **ROOMS:** 3 bedrooms from s£27.50 d£37.50

Skippers Inn
Horsecastles DT9 3HE ☎ 01935 812753
e-mail: chrisfrowde@lineone.net
Dir: From Yeovil A30 to Sherborne
End-of-terrace converted cider house that is much larger inside that it looks from the outside. All meals are cooked to order, and the inn is well-known locally for its large selection of fish dishes that use freshly caught local produce wherever possible. Seafood includes plaice, bass, trout, scallops, hake, cod and various soles. Other choices include beef strips in Dijon mustard, duck in plum sauce, and pork tenderloin in brandy cream. Bookings for Sunday lunch are recommended.
OPEN: 11–2.30 5.30–11 (Oct–Jan 6–11) **BAR MEALS:** Lunch served: all week Dinner served: all week 11.15–2 6.30–9.30 Av main course £7
RESTAURANT: Lunch served: all week Dinner served: all week 11.15–2 6.30–9.30 Av 3 course à la carte £17.90
BREWERY/COMPANY: Wadworth **PRINCIPAL BEERS:** Wadworth 6X & Henrys IPA, Butcombe Butter. **FACILITIES:** Garden: Beer garden, food served outdoors **NOTES:** Parking 30

White Hart
Bishops Caundle DT9 5ND
☎ 01963 23301 ✉ 01963 23301 (by arrangement)
Dir: On A3030 between Sherborne & Sturminster Newton
The walkers who come to pretty Bishops Caundle owe a big thank you to whoever waymarked the route that starts here - it ends here too. Once a monks' brewhouse, this 16th-century pub was later used by the notorious Judge Jeffreys. On the menu, poached salmon with lemon and dill sauce, home-made chicken korma, spicy sizzling pork, and spinach and mushroom tagliatelle. For children there are trampolines, a playhouse and a skittle alley if wet.
OPEN: 11.30–3 6.30–11 **BAR MEALS:** Lunch served: all week Dinner served: all week 12–2 6.45–9.30 Av main course £13
RESTAURANT: Lunch served: all week Dinner served: all week 12–2 6.30–9.30 **BREWERY/COMPANY:** Hall & Woodhouse
PRINCIPAL BEERS: Badger Best, Tanglefoot, Golden Champion, Sussex Golden Glory. **FACILITIES:** Children welcome Garden: Food served outside. Patio area Dogs allowed (water provided) **NOTES:** Parking 32

SHROTON — Map 03 ST82

Pick of the Pubs

The Cricketers
Shroton, Iwerne Courtney DT11 8QD
☎ 01258 860421 ✉ 01258 861800
Dir: Off the A350 Shaftesbury to Blandford
An oh-so-English country pub, nestling between the village green and the cricket pitch. The new landlords

have brought fresh enthusiasm, adding furniture, patio heaters and flowers outside and new decor in the restaurant. It continues to be a welcoming local, luring hikers from the Wessex Way which runs through the garden, as well as members of the local cricket team who gather in the homely bar during the summer months. An extensive menu reveals that the owners' enthusiasm has not been limited to decorating. Light meals might include Cajun chicken tortilla wrap, casseroled rabbit in red wine or lambs' kidneys wrapped in bacon, grilled en brochette and served with a devilled Gubbins sauce. Main meals could include long-lost favourites such as coq au vin, traditional pub fare including gammon steak with egg and chips, or imaginative spicy dishes ranging from Moroccan lamb tagine to chicken deep fried with a ham and banana filling and a mild curry cream sauce.

OPEN: 11.30–2.30 7–11 **BAR MEALS:** Lunch served: all week Dinner served: all week 12–2 7–9.30 Av main course £8
RESTAURANT: Lunch served: all week Dinner served: all week 12–2 7–9.30 Av 3 course à la carte £15
BREWERY/COMPANY: Free House
PRINCIPAL BEERS: Fuller's London Pride, Ringwood True Glory, Interbrew Bass, Young's Spesial. **FACILITIES:** Children welcome Garden: Patio with heaters, food served outside
NOTES: Parking 19 **ROOMS:** 1 bedroom 1 en suite from d£65

STOKE ABBOTT — Map 03 ST40

The New Inn
DT8 3JW ☎ 01308 868333
e-mail: webbs@newinnstokeabbott.fsnet.co.uk
Expect a traditional welcome at this 17th-century thatched village inn. An attractive large garden is among the features, and inside is a cosy beamed bar with a roaring log fire. The Sunday roast is particularly memorable. Specials may include pan-fried duck breast with gooseberry sauce, grilled salmon, and lamb noisettes. Wide range of vegetarian dishes.
OPEN: 11.30–3 7–11 (Sun 12–3, 7–10.30) **BAR MEALS:** Lunch served: all week Dinner served: all week 12–2 6–9.30 Av main course £8 **RESTAURANT:** Lunch served: all week Dinner served: all week 12–2 7–9.30 **BREWERY/COMPANY:** Palmers
PRINCIPAL BEERS: Palmers IPA, 200 Premium Ale.
FACILITIES: Children welcome Garden: Food served outside Dogs allowed **NOTES:** Parking 25

We endeavour to be as accurate as possible but changes to times and other information can occur after we have gone to press

continued

STRATTON
Map 03 SY69

Saxon Arms ⌂ ♀
DT2 9WG ☎ 01305 260020 🖳 01305 264225
e-mail: saxonarms@btinternet.com
Dir: 3 M NW of Dorchester on A37 Saxon arms is at the back of the village Green between the church and new village hall

This flint and brick pub has a massive thatched roof, with a patio overlooking the village green. Solid oak beams inside, flagstone floors and the log-burning stove lend a great atmosphere. Since re-opening some three years ago experienced licensees, Ian and Anne Barrett, have aimed to provide a high quality village inn. Menus offer the best local 'catch' of Portland crab and battered cod with chips or grilled black pudding and apple, rib-eye steaks and home-made pies.
OPEN: 11–2.30 5.30–11 **BAR MEALS:** Lunch served: all week Dinner served: all week 11.30–2 6.30–9 Av main course £7.25
BREWERY/COMPANY: Free House **PRINCIPAL BEERS:** Fuller's London Pride, Palmers IPA,. **FACILITIES:** Garden: Food served outside, Patio **NOTES:** Parking 35

STUDLAND
Map 03 SZ08

The Bankes Arms Hotel ⌂
Watery Ln BH19 3AU
☎ 01929 450225 & 450310 🖳 01929 450307
Dir: B3369 from Poole, across on Sandbanks chain ferry, or A35 from Poole, A351 then B3351

Set close to sweeping Studland Bay, this old, creeper-clad, smugglers' inn is popular in summer months, and is a peaceful retreat on winter weekdays. Eight changing real ales are always on offer, and a varied menu specialises in fresh fish and seafood. Plaice fillets rolled around asparagus spears, seafood provençale and smoked haddock in mornay sauce are among the seafood options. Other choices include game casserole, leek and mushroom Stroganoff or calves' liver.
OPEN: 11–11 Closed: Dec 25 **BAR MEALS:** Lunch served: all week Dinner served: all week 12–3.00 7–9.30 Av main course £7.95

BREWERY/COMPANY: Free House **PRINCIPAL BEERS:** Badger Best, Hampshire King Alfred's,. **FACILITIES:** Garden: Patio, food served outdoors Dogs allowed **NOTES:** Parking 10 **ROOMS:** 9 bedrooms 7 en suite from d£50

SYDLING ST NICHOLAS
Map 03 SY69

The Greyhound Inn ♀
DT2 9PD ☎ 01300 341303 🖳 01300 341303
Dir: Off A37 Yeovil to Dorchester Road, turn off at Cerne Abbas/Sydling St Nicholas
Located in one of Dorset's loveliest villages and surrounded by picturesque countryside, this traditional, brightly painted inn is characterised by its relaxed, welcoming atmosphere and delightful walled garden. Fresh home-cooked food served daily includes rib-eye steak, rack of lamb with a herb crust and port jus, pan-fried King scallops in a ginger butter, and goats' cheese topped with pesto and grilled on salad.
OPEN: 11–3.30 6–11 **BAR MEALS:** Lunch served: all week Dinner served: all week Av main course £10 **RESTAURANT:** Lunch served: all week Dinner served: all week Av 3 course à la carte £22
BREWERY/COMPANY: Free House **PRINCIPAL BEERS:** Youngs Special, Greene King IPA,. **FACILITIES:** Garden: Food served outside Dogs allowed **NOTES:** Parking 24 **ROOMS:** 6 bedrooms 6 en suite from s£40 d£70

TARRANT MONKTON
Map 03 ST90

Pick of the Pubs

The Langton Arms ♦♦♦♦ ♀
DT11 8RX ☎ 01258 830225 🖳 01258 830053
e-mail: info@thelangtonarms.co.uk
Dir: A31 from Ringwood, or A357 from Shaftesbury, or A35 from Bournemouth
A 17th-century thatched free house, in the same capable hands for a decade, offering guest accommodation in rustic brick outhouses around an attractive courtyard. Good real ales, on tap in the beamed bar, can be accompanied by home-made steak and ale pie. In The Stables an evening bistro menu conjures up smoked seafood terrine and breast of guinea fowl, followed by lemon tart with rhubarb confit perhaps, at an inclusive price. With its skittle alley and function room, this beautifully situated country inn offers something for everyone.
OPEN: 11.30–11 (Sun 12–10.30) **BAR MEALS:** Lunch served: all week Dinner served: all week 11.30–2.30 6–9.30 Av main course £6.95 **RESTAURANT:** Lunch served: Sun 12–2 Dinner served: Wed–Sat 7–9 Av 3 course à la carte £25 Av 3 course fixed price £14.95 **BREWERY/COMPANY:** Free House
PRINCIPAL BEERS: Hop Back Best & 4 changing guest beers.
FACILITIES: Children welcome Garden: Food served outdoors Dogs allowed (overnight only) **NOTES:** Parking 100
ROOMS: 6 bedrooms 6 en suite from s£50 d£70

TOLPUDDLE
Map 03 SY79

The Martyrs Inn ⌂ ♀
DT2 7ES ☎ 01305 848249 🖳 01305 848977
Dir: Off A35 between Bere Regis (A31/A35 Junction)
Tolpuddle is the somewhat unlikely birthplace of the Trades Union Congress. Its seeds were sown in 1834 by six impoverished farm labourers who tried to bargain with local landowners for better conditions. Martyrs' memorabilia

continued

continued

abounds. Home-made starters include chicken liver and wild mushroom pâté, and garlic mushrooms en croûte; main courses include Tolpuddle sausages with mash and onion gravy, country vegetable pasta bake, and spicy chicken curry with rice and naan bread.

OPEN: all day **BAR MEALS:** Lunch served: all week Dinner served: all week Av main course £7 **RESTAURANT:** Lunch served: all week Dinner served: all week Av 3 course à la carte £20 Av 3 course fixed price £7 **BREWERY/COMPANY:** Hall & Woodhouse
PRINCIPAL BEERS: Badger Dorset Best & Tanglefoot.
FACILITIES: Children welcome Garden Food served outside. Dogs allowed **NOTES:** Parking 25 **ROOMS:** 14 bedrooms 14 en suite from s£45 d£70

TRENT   Map 03 ST51

Rose & Crown Inn ♓

DT9 4SL ☎ 01935 850776
Dir: W on A30 towards Yeovil. 3m from Sherborne R to Over Compton/Trent, 1.5m downhill, then R. Pub opp church
Stone-built thatched pub, with beams and flagstones, converted from two cottages in 1720. It reputedly hid the France-bound Charles II. Today's visitors come for the bistro-style food, in particular fresh fish and local game. Typical dishes are lemon peppered chicken, and Louisiana blackened swordfish.
OPEN: 12-2.30 7-11 Closed: Dec 25 **BAR MEALS:** Lunch served: all week Dinner served: Fri & Sat 12-1.45 7-9.30 Av main course £8 **RESTAURANT:** Lunch served: all week Dinner served: Tue-Sat 12-1.45 7-9 Av 3 course à la carte £15 **BREWERY/COMPANY:** Free House **PRINCIPAL BEERS:** Shepherd Neame Spitfire, Butcombe Bitter. **FACILITIES:** Children welcome Garden: Beer garden, outdoor eating, BBQ, play area Dogs allowed (on lead only) **NOTES:** Parking 30

WEST BEXINGTON   Map 03 SY58

The Manor Hotel ★ ★ 🐷

DT2 9DF ☎ 01308 897616 📠 01308 897035
e-mail: themanorhotel@btconnect.com
Just 500 yards from spectacular Chesil Beach and the clear waters of Lyme Bay lies this 16th-century manor house, featuring Jacobean oak panelling and flagstone floors. A handy base for exploring Dorset's numerous delights and enjoying stunning coastal walks. Imaginative cooking and freshly prepared specialities, with dishes such as Murphy's steak and kidney pudding, game pie, lamb shank and chicken stir-fry. Fish options include whole local plaice and sea bass with scallops and king prawns.
OPEN: 11-11 **BAR MEALS:** Lunch served: all week Dinner served: all week 12-2 6.30-10 **RESTAURANT:** Lunch served: all week Dinner served: all week 12-1.30 7-9.30 **BREWERY/COMPANY:** Free House **PRINCIPAL BEERS:** Hardy Royal Oak, County, Wadworth 6X. **FACILITIES:** Children welcome Garden: Food served outside **NOTES:** Parking 25 **ROOMS:** 13 bedrooms 13 en suite

---

WEST KNIGHTON   Map 03 SY78

The New Inn

DT2 8PE ☎ 01305 852349
A 200-year-old pub with listed archway, formerly a row of farm cottages. Good base for walks and exploring the surrounding countryside.

WEST LULWORTH   Map 03 SY88

The Castle Inn 🐷

Main Rd BH20 5RN ☎ 01929 400311 📠 01929 400415
Dir: on the Wareham to Dorchester Rd, L approx 1m from Wareham
A picturesque, beamed and thatched 17th-century inn occupying a delightful setting near Lulworth Cove. Plenty of good walks nearby and a host of popular attractions within easy reach. Prize-winning gardens add plenty of dazzling colour during the summer months. Extensive menus throughout offer a varied choice of dishes. In the bar expect chilli con carne, curry, steak and kidney pie and various grills, while the restaurant main courses range from guinea fowl breast and sesame chicken with ginger and onion sauce, to seafood stew and fillet Stilton beefsteak.
OPEN: 11-2.30 (Winter 12-2.30, 7-11) 6-11 Closed: 25 Dec **BAR MEALS:** Lunch served: all week Dinner served: all week 11-2.30 6-10.30 Av main course £5 **RESTAURANT:** Dinner served: Fri & Sat 7-9.30 Av 3 course à la carte £15
BREWERY/COMPANY: Free House
PRINCIPAL BEERS: Interbrew Bass, Ringwood Best, Gales, Websters. **FACILITIES:** Children welcome Children's licence Garden: Food served outside Dogs allowed **NOTES:** Parking 30 **ROOMS:** 15 bedrooms 12 en suite from s£25 d£35

WEST STAFFORD   Map 03 SY78

The Wise Man Inn 🐷 ♓

DT2 8AG ☎ 01305 263694 📠 01305 751660
e-mail: ray3bears@supanet.com
Dir: 2m from A35

Set in the heart of Thomas Hardy country, this thatched 16th-century pub is a regular stopping off point for those on the Hardy trail, and is proud to use local produce on its menu. Alongside light bar meals, expect the likes of gamekeeper venison sausages, trio of lamb chops, Elizabethan chicken, pan-fried scallops, battered cod or haddock, lamb's liver with mustard mash potatoes, and whole plaice on the bone.
OPEN: 11-3 6-11 **BAR MEALS:** Lunch served: all week Dinner served: Mon-Sat 12-2.30 7-9.30 Av main course £6.50 **RESTAURANT:** Lunch served: all week Dinner served: Mon-Sat 12-2.30 7-9.30 Av 3 course à la carte £14
BREWERY/COMPANY: Pubmaster
PRINCIPAL BEERS: Ringwood, 3 casked ales each week.
FACILITIES: Children welcome Garden: Food served outside. Lawned area Dogs allowed (water & biscuits provided)
NOTES: Parking 25

England

WEYMOUTH   Map 03 SY67

The Old Ship NEW 🐾 ♀
7 The Ridgeway DT3 5QQ ☎ 01305 831822
One of his regular watering holes, Thomas Hardy refers to this historic pub in his novels *Under the Greenwood Tree* and *The Trumpet Major*. The terrace offers views over Weymouth, while inside there are copper pans, old clocks and a beamed open fire. Wholesome menu ranges from home-made beef and ale pie, chicken topped with goats' cheese and basil pesto, lamb's liver and bacon, pan-fried crab cakes with a light chilli mayonnaise and supreme of guinea fowl with cider apples and shallots.
OPEN: 12–3 6–11 **BAR MEALS:** Lunch served: all week Dinner served: all week 12–2 6–9.30 **RESTAURANT:** Lunch served: all week Dinner served: all week 12–2 6–9.30 Av 3 course à la carte £17 **BREWERY/COMPANY:** Inn Partnership
PRINCIPAL BEERS: Greene King Old Speckled Hen, Ringwood Best, Scottish Courage Courage Directors. **FACILITIES:** Children welcome Garden: Views of Weymouth, food served outside, patio Dogs allowed (water) **NOTES:** Parking 12

WORTH MATRAVERS   Map 03 SY97

The Square & Compass
BH19 3LF ☎ 01929 439229
Classic, unspoilt ale house run by the Newman family for the last ninety years. Simple interior, ales from the cask, limited food options, but lovely views and superb coastal walks along Purbeck.

CO DURHAM

AYCLIFFE   Map 11 NZ22

The County 🐾 ♀
13 The Green, Aycliffe Village DL5 6LX
☎ 01325 312273 📠 01325 308780
e-mail: enquiries@the-county.co.uk
Dir: Off the A167 into Aycliffe Village
Overlooking pretty Aycliffe village green, this historic pub has been sympathetically restored. Within Tony Blair's Sedgefield constituency, this is where the PM entertained France's President Jacques Chirac. The emphasis is firmly on appetising, well-presented modern pub food. Extensive wine list, good range of guest and local ales and a daily-changing specials board. Expect grilled goats' cheese and wild mushroom risotto among the starters, while Harry Coats' prize-winning sausages and casserole of caramelised root vegetables are typical examples of main courses.
OPEN: 12–3 5.30–11 Closed: 25 Dec 1 Jan **BAR MEALS:** Lunch served: all week Dinner served: Mon–Fri 12–2 6–7 Av main course £12 **RESTAURANT:** Lunch served: all week Dinner served: Mon–Sat 12–2 6–9.30 Av 3 course à la carte £22 **BREWERY/COMPANY:** Scottish & Newcastle **PRINCIPAL BEERS:** Changing ales.
FACILITIES: Children welcome **NOTES:** Parking 30

BARNARD CASTLE   Map 11 NZ24

Pick of the Pubs

The Morritt Arms Hotel ★ ★ ★ 🐾 ♀
Greta Bridge DL12 9SE ☎ 01833 627232 📠 01833 627392
e-mail: relax@themorritt.co.uk
Dir: At Scotch Corner take A66 towards Penrith, after 9m turn at Greta Bridge. Hotel over bridge on L
The present building dates back to the 17th century when there was farm on the site. Over the years the outbuildings were incorporated into the hotel to create the stylish inn you will find today. Log fires warm the building in winter and you can eat out in the handsomely landscaped gardens on balmy summer days. Through the 19th century, Greta Bridge became the second overnight stop of the London-Carlisle coaches. Food is served in the commemorative Dickens Bar (he stayed here in 1839) as well as in an informal bistro, Pallat's, and the more formal Copperfield restaurant. Representative dishes include leek and pork sausages on a Yorkshire pudding topped with onion gravy, braised lamb shank with minted jus and a broad fresh fish selection that might include smoked haddock with grain mustard hollandaise or hake with grape and cherry tomato compote.
OPEN: 11–11 **BAR MEALS:** Lunch served: all week Dinner served: all week 12–3 6–9.30 Av main course £6.50 **RESTAURANT:** Lunch served: all week Dinner served: all week 12–3 7–9 Av 3 course à la carte £22.50 Av 4 course fixed price £18.95 **BREWERY/COMPANY:** Free House
PRINCIPAL BEERS: Scottish Courage John Smith's, Theakston Best Bitter, Timothy Taylor Landlord, Black Sheep Best.
FACILITIES: Children welcome Children's licence Garden: Food served outdoors Dogs allowed (water) **NOTES:** Parking 100 **ROOMS:** 23 bedrooms 23 en suite from s£59.50 d£83.50
See Pub Walk on page 179

BOLAM   Map 11 NZ12

Countryman Inn ♀
DL2 2UP ☎ 01388 834577 📠 01388 834577
Fresh, wholesome ingredients are the foundation of The Countryman's innovative home-cooked menu. Quietly situated near the Roman Dere Street, this award-winning village local is handy for the surrounding urban centres. Starters like black pudding layered with braised leeks, topped with grain mustard and crispy leeks and a port jus complement main courses such as pan-fried duck breast with red onion marmalade, Toulouse sausage and red wine sauce. Finish with warm frangipane tart, with fresh blackcurrants and home-made vanilla ice cream.
OPEN: 12–3 6–12 **BAR MEALS:** Lunch served: Sat–Sun 12–2 Dinner served: Tues–Sat 7–10 Av main course £9.50 **RESTAURANT:** Lunch served: Sat–Sun 12–2 Dinner served: Tues–Sat 7–10 Av 3 course à la carte £17.50 **BREWERY/COMPANY:** Free House **PRINCIPAL BEERS:** Black Sheep Best, Rudgate Battleaxe, Mordue Workie Ticket, Northumberland Secret Kingdom.
FACILITIES: Garden: Food served outside **NOTES:** Parking 60

The Birds of the Air
Pride of place among bird signs is taken by the Swan, often adopted by inns close to a river. The eccentric Swan with Two Necks probably began as a swan with two nicks in its beak. The Cock may be related to cock-fighting or to St Peter. Geese and chickens appear alone or keeping dangerous company with the Fox. The Bird in Hand comes from falconry and the Dog and Duck either from fowling or from the amusement of setting a dog on a pinioned duck. The Eagle is from Heraldry and the Magpie and Stump from the countryside, while rarities include the Parrot and the Peahen.

PUB WALK

Greta Bridge
The Morritt Arms

MORRITT ARMS,
Greta Bridge BARNARD
CASTLE DL12 9SE
Tel: 01833 627232
Directions: At Scotch Corner
take A66 towards Penrith, after
9m turn at Greta Bridge. Hotel
over bridge on L
In large mature gardens this
substantial, 17th-century hotel
continues the tradition of
coaching inn hospitality. Log
fires, alfresco summer dining
and good food in the bar,
bistro or formal restaurant.
Four-poster and brass beds.
Open: 11–11 Bar meals: 12–3
6–9.30 Children welcome and
dogs allowed. Garden and
parking available.

Distance: 5 miles (8km)
Map: OS Landranger 92
Terrain: Banks of the River Greta,
fields and woodland
Paths: Roads, lanes, field paths
and riverside trails
Gradient: Some climbing

*Walk submitted and checked by The
Morritt Arms, Greta Bridge*

Enjoy a very attractive walk beside the sparkling River Greta, in landscape that inspired Charles Dickens and Sir Walter Scott.

Turn right out of the hotel and just before the bridge cross the stile to go along the banks of the River Greta, then by a field side and a descent back to the river. A little over a mile (1.6km) along, through a wall opening, your path is to the right signed to Brignall Village. (The ruins of St Mary's church are a short detour straight ahead.) The path ascends from the river to join a grassy path past the vicarage and on to Brignall Church. (For a short walk, turn right here to go back down the road to the hotel.) Otherwise, turn left and then right along the drive of 'Brookside'. The path goes through a gate and left of the farm building. Follow the yellow markers along the edge of two fields and then left to cross two streams running through a wooded dell. Straight across the next field into woodland, then through another field to the A66. Cross with care to another church. Go through the churchyard and cross a stile keeping the fence to your left. The path meets the main road by a stream. Cross the road and follow the stream, turning right to join the Teesdale Way. After emerging on to a private road, turn left. Follow the River Tees to the 'Meeting of the Waters' where it is joined by the River Greta. Cross the Dairy Bridge, follow the drive up to Mortham Tower and then follow the wall round to the left. After two stiles, head for a barn in the middle of the field. Turn right at the barn to rejoin the park wall and descend to an underpass by the river. Cross the field and then turn right to cross the arched bridge and return to the Morritt.

COTHERSTONE Map 11 NZ01

The Fox and Hounds 🛏
DL12 9PF ☎ 01833 650241 📠 01833 650518
Dir: *4m W of Barnard Castle, from A66 turn onto B6277, Cotherstone signposted*

Characterised by heavy beams and original features, this traditional coaching inn dates back to the 1700s. Close to the Rivers Tees and Balder and overlooking the village green, the pub is ideally placed for local walks and touring. Home-made bar food is available at lunchtime and in the evening and the dinner menu provides an imaginative and varied range of dishes to suit all tastes. Expect rack of Teesdale lamb, ratatouille-filled crêpe baked with Cotherstone cheese, fresh salmon parcel and pan-fried pork tenderloin.
OPEN: 12–3 6.30–11 Closed: 25–26 Dec **BAR MEALS:** Lunch served: all week Dinner served: all week 12–2 6–9.30 Av main course £7.50 **RESTAURANT:** Lunch served: all week Dinner served: all week 12–2 6–9.30 Av 3 course à la carte £16.50
BREWERY/COMPANY: Free House **PRINCIPAL BEERS:** Black Sheep Best, Scottish Courage John Smith's Smooth.
FACILITIES: Children's licence Garden: Beer garden, food served outside **NOTES:** Parking 20 **ROOMS:** 3 bedrooms 3 en suite from s£40 d£60

CROOK Map 11 NZ13

Duke of York Residential Country Inn ♦♦♦♦
Fir Tree DL15 8DG ☎ 01388 762848 📠 01388 767055
e-mail: suggett@firtree-crook.fsnet.co.uk
Dir: *on A68 trunk road to Scotland, 12m W of Durham City*

Former drovers' and coaching inn on the old York to Edinburgh coach route, this 18th-century white-painted inn is noted for its furniture which contains the famous carved mouse trademark of Robert Thompson, a renowned Yorkshire woodcarver. There is also a collection of flint arrowheads, axes and Africana. Relax inside and choose from varied blackboard menus characterised by fresh food, including

home-made steak and kidney pie, Aberdeen cod, pork in ginger and gammon in sherry and peaches. Large, landscaped beer garden.
OPEN: 11–2.30 6.30–10.30 **BAR MEALS:** Lunch served: all week Dinner served: all week 12–2 6.30–9 Av main course £6.95
RESTAURANT: Lunch served: all week Dinner served: all week 12–2 6.30–9 Av 3 course à la carte £20
BREWERY/COMPANY: Free House
PRINCIPAL BEERS: Black Sheep,. **FACILITIES:** Children welcome Children's licence Garden: Food served outside. Large garden
NOTES: Parking 65 **ROOMS:** 5 bedrooms 5 en suite from s£52 d£69

DURHAM Map 11 NZ24

Pick of the Pubs

Seven Stars Inn 🛏
High St North, Shincliffe Village DH1 2NU
☎ 0191 3848454 📠 0191 3860640
e-mail: enquiries@sevenstarsinn.co.uk

A little gem tucked away on the edge of picturesque Shincliffe, this quaint and cosy inn remains virtually unaltered since 1724, although tasteful decoration and the addition of antique furniture have improved levels of comfort for discerning local diners. Pretty in summer with its tubs and window boxes and cosily lit within in winter, it offers a fine setting for imaginative British cuisine with exotic influences. Typically, goats' cheese wonton or fresh local crab and avocado salad with gazpacho dressing; followed by Parma ham-wrapped salmon on herb mash with tomato fondue, open ravioli of monkfish, pan-fried calves' liver with bacon and red wine jus, and mixed vegetable ratatouille. Round off with mixed summer fruit crumble or French apple tart. Individually furnished bedrooms.
OPEN: 11.30–11 **BAR MEALS:** Lunch served: all week Dinner served: all week 12–2.30 6–9.30 Av main course £12
RESTAURANT: Lunch served: all week Dinner served: all week 12–2.30 6–9.30 Av 3 course à la carte £22
BREWERY/COMPANY: Free House
PRINCIPAL BEERS: Marston's Pedigree, Scottish Courage Courage Directors, Black Sheep Best, Daleside Bitter.
FACILITIES: Garden: Patio **NOTES:** Parking 20
ROOMS: 8 bedrooms 8 en suite from s£40 d£60

 Pubs offering a good choice of fish on their menu

continued

OPEN: 11.30–3 5.30–11
BAR MEALS: L served all week.
D served all week. 12–1.30
6.30–9.30 Av main course £9.50
RESTAURANT: L served all week.
D served all week. 12–1.30 7.30–9
BREWERY/COMPANY: FREE
HOUSE
PRINCIPAL BEERS: Theakston
Best, Black Sheep Best
FACILITIES: Children and dogs
welcome.
NOTES: Parking 24
ROOMS: 12 en suite. Double room
from £90.

Rose and Crown
AA Pub of the Year for England 2003

The Rose & Crown is a classic old English coaching inn, built in 1733, and set on the middle green of a typical English village, next to the church – the Cathedral of the Dale – and opposite the old stocks and water pump. It is a fine establishment – a pub for locals, a hotel for residents, a restaurant for diners, but an inn above all else.

★ ★ ◎◎ ♇
Romaldkirk DL12 9EB
☎ 01833 650213 📄 01833 650828
e-mail: hotel@rose-and-crown.co.uk
Dir: 6m NW from Barnard Castle on B6277

The wood-panelled bar has old oak beams, a large dog grate with a roaring fire in the stone fireplace, and lots of brass, copper and old sepia photographs to complete its rustic charm. You can eat lunch in the old bar and Crown Room, where good quality bar meals are popular with all comers. These range from filled baps through creamed scrambled egg with ribbons of smoked salmon and buttered toast, to beefsteak, kidney and mushroom pie with

Theakstons' ale. More elaborate bar suppers include pan-fried pink trout with sesame seed crust, wilted spinach and lemon butter sauce, or slow roast confit of lamb with vegetable couscous and red wine jus. Desserts like hot sticky toffee pudding are not to be trifled with either. Overnighters will more likely opt for a set-price four-course dinner in the restaurant, with choices such as Loch Fyne smoked salmon, trout bisque, and slow roast loin of British pork with black pudding farce, caramelised apple and sage and onion gravy. The fourth option is between pudding (maybe warm baked chocolate cheesecake with marmalade ice cream) and a plate of Swaledale, Dunsyre Blue and Appleby Cheshire cheeses. The bedrooms, decorated in vibrant colours and rich fabrics, have luxurious modern bathrooms, and residents have use of the lounge, with its exposed stone walls and period furniture.

England

MIDDLETON-IN-TEESDALE — Map 11 NY92

The Teesdale Hotel
Market Square DL12 0QG
☎ 01833 640264 & 640537 ▪ 01833 640651
A tastefully-modernised 17th-century coaching inn in the heart of the High Pennines. The friendly bars, one with a log fire, are convivial places to relax over a meal. From the bar menu expect chicken curry, and poached salmon plus toasted sandwiches, and specials including venison sausages in coarse grain mustard sauce, steak and kidney pie, and baked egg and asparagus gratinée.
OPEN: 11-11 **BAR MEALS:** Lunch served: all week Dinner served: all week 12-2 7-9 Av main course £7 **RESTAURANT:** Lunch served: Sun Dinner served: all week 12-1.30 7.30-8.30 Av 3 course à la carte £19.95 **BREWERY/COMPANY:** Free House
PRINCIPAL BEERS: Guinness, Tetley, Smooth.
FACILITIES: Children welcome Garden: Food served outside. Courtyard terrace Dogs allowed **ROOMS:** 12 bedrooms 10 en suite from s£42.50 d£65

NEWTON AYCLIFFE — Map 11 NZ22

Blacksmiths Arms NEW
Preston le Skerne, (off Ricknall Lane) DL5 6JH
☎ 01325 314873 ▪ 01325 307417
e-mail: pub@blacksmithsarms.co.uk
Built into a disused railway embankment, the pub dates from around 1800 and was originally a blacksmith's shop. It is set in isolated farmland a mile or two from the new town of Newton Aycliffe. Now a family business, the emphasis is on good value home-cooked food and a weekly changing range of real ales, as many as 150 each year, supporting micro-breweries wherever possible. The beer garden is a great summer attraction.
OPEN: 12-3 6-11 (Sun- 10.30) Closed: 25 Dec 1 Jan
BAR MEALS: Lunch served: Tue-Sun Dinner served: Tue-Sat 12-2 6.30-9 **BREWERY/COMPANY:** Free House **FACILITIES:** Children welcome Garden: Food served outside. Large beer garden **NOTES:** Parking 25 No credit cards

ROMALDKIRK — Map 11 NY92

Pick of the Pubs
AA Pub of the Year for England 2003.
Rose and Crown ★★
DL12 9EB ☎ 01833 650213 ▪ 01833 650828
e-mail: hotel@rose-and-crown.co.uk
See Pick of the Pubs on page 181

ESSEX

ARKESDEN — Map 07 TL43
Pick of the Pubs
Axe & Compasses
High St CB11 4EX ☎ 01799 550272 ▪ 01799 550906
See Pick of the Pubs on page 184

BLACKMORE END — Map 07 TL73
Pick of the Pubs
The Bull Inn
CM7 4DD ☎ 01371 851037 ▪ 851037
Off-the-beaten-track at the heart of tranquil north Essex countryside, two 17th-century cottages and an adjoining barn form this traditional village pub, full of original beams and open hearths, that looks out over open farmland little changed over 300 years. An attractive garden also produces herbs for kitchen staff full of enthusiasm and up-to-date ideas. In the beginning are potted brown shrimps, chicken and sun-dried tomato terrine and grilled goats' cheese with raspberry vinaigrette. In the middle come beef tournedos rossini with Marsala jus, monkfish in bacon garnished with queen scallops and game and oyster suet pudding in rich gravy with creamed mash. Vegetarians at this point have their own menu - wild mushroom Stroganoff or aubergine and Stilton polenta gateau perhaps - before all join in at the end for apple and forest fruits crumble, chocolate and hazelnut roulade and ice cream sundae. Only on a Sunday is there a set-price lunch with similar starters, traditional roasts and nursery puddings.
OPEN: 12-3 6-11 (Summer open 12-3 5-11)
BAR MEALS: Lunch served: all week Dinner served: all week 12-3 6.30-9.45 Av main course £5.60 **RESTAURANT:** Lunch served: all week Dinner served: all week 12-3 6.30-9.30 Av 3 course à la carte £22 **BREWERY/COMPANY:** Free House
PRINCIPAL BEERS: Greene King IPA, Abbot Ale, Adnams Best.
FACILITIES: Children welcome Garden: beer garden, outdoor eating, BBQ Dogs allowed (guide dogs) **NOTES:** Parking 36

BRADWELL — Map 07 TL82
The Swan Inn
CM7 8ED ☎ 01376 562111
Dir: On A120 between Braintree & Coggeshall
Sympathically extended and refurbished old pub, with exposed beams and brickwork, open fires, and cricketing memorabilia in the character bars.

Skittles
Skittles is a far older game than darts or dominoes, on record in London since the 15th century, when it was banned. Henry VIII enjoyed it and had his own skittle alley, but governments kept vainly trying to stop ordinary people playing, because they ought to have been practising their archery and because they gambled so heavily. Even so, the game became popular enough to make 'beer and skittles' proverbial. Basically, three wooden balls are propelled at nine pins to knock them down, but there are sharp variations in the rules between different areas and pubs. Varieties include London or Old English Skittles, West Country Skittles, Long Alley and Aunt Sally, as well as several types of table skittles.

PUB WALK

Dedham
Marlborough Head Hotel

MARLBOROUGH HEAD HOTEL,
Mill Lane DEDHAM Colchester
CO7 6DH
Tel: 01206 323250
Directions: E of A12, N of
Colchester
In a delightgtful village close to
Flatford Mill and peaceful walks,
this former wool merchants house
dates from 1455. An inn since
1704, it is heavily timbered with
beautiful wood carving in the
lounge. An extensive menu.
Open: 11–11
Bar Meals: 12–2.30 7–9.
Children welcome. Garden and
parking available.

Distance: 6 miles (10km)
Map: OS Landranger 168
Terrain: Meadows and farmland by
the River Stour
Paths: Footpaths, tracks, pasture and
wood. Some road walking
Gradient: No steep hills

*Walk submitted and checked
by Nick Channer*

A country ramble, reflecting the tranquil scenes of Constable's famous paintings of Flatford Mill and Willy Lott's cottage. The cottage is now National Trust, can only be viewed from the outside.

Left out of the hotel and follow the High Street into Brook Street. Where it curves right, veer left into the drive of Muniment House. Cross a stile on the left to a track, signposted Flatford. Beyond another stile, follow the track right to a further stile, then continue through three gates before crossing meadows to the riverbank. Cross the sluice, then follow the river for nearly a mile (1.5km) to Flatford. Cross a stile and turn right along the the track beside the river. (To visit NT properties and the Constable Exhibition cross bridge ahead and turn right.) Keep to the riverbank, pass Flatford Lock and behind Flatford Mill. Cross a concrete water barrier and go immediately left by the Lower Barn Farm sign. Cross two stiles, pass under power lines and turn right just beyond another stile. The Judas Gap Weir is on the left. Climb the next stile, follow the path between bushes, under a railway bridge and turn left. Just before Manningtree Station turn right, opposite the car park, and follow the footpath. Enter Lawson churchyard and go through the gate opposite main gates. Cross two stiles iover to the right. Climb another stile, go left along the track to the road and turn left. Bear right after about 100 yards (91m) into a field. Veer diagonally right, under power lines to a ladder stile in the corner. Keep ahead to a stile and track, turn left and follow the path to the right. Descend to the left of a house to a choice of tracks. Take the waymaeked permitted route for a short way, then go right, through the woods to a footbridge and stile. Keep straight ahead, cross a railway line and over several stiles to join a road. Climb the stile almost opposite and veer diagonally left across the field to a stile and lane. Turn right on to the B1029 at Castle House. Bear right, then left (Coopers Lane) and then right along a metalled drive between cottages. Through a gate and stile behind a farmhouse, then keep to left side of a paddock to cross a stile and footbridge into a field. Turn right to another stile and footbridge in the far right-hand corner. Keep ahead, cross into a playing field, turn right to pass behind the pavilion and bear left down The Drift, back into Dedham.

OPEN: 11.30-2.30 6-11
BAR MEALS: L served all week.
week. D served all week. week. 12-2
6.45-9.30 Av main course £9.95
RESTAURANT: L served all week.
D served all week. 12-2 6.45-9.30
Av cost 3 course £20
BREWERY/COMPANY:
GREENE KING
PRINCIPAL BEERS: Greene King
IPA, Abbot Ale & Old Speckled Hen
FACILITIES: Garden: Patio, food
served outdoors
NOTES: Parking 12

Axe & Compasses

High St ARKESDEN CB11 4EX
☎ 01799 550272 📄 01799 550906
Dir: From Buntingford B1038 towards
Newport.Then L for Arkesden

Arguably one of the country's prettiest and unspoilt villages whose narrow main street runs alongside the village stream, spanned by a succession of footbridges that give access to white, cream and pink-washed cottages. At its heart stands this thatched jewel whose long-standing motto is 'Relax at the Axe'.

Not without cause, as at its centre the Axe's thatched section, dating from around 1650, leads to the former stabling and a 19th-century extension housing today's convivial bar and a laid-back lounge featuring easy chairs, settees, antique furniture and brass reflecting the glow of an open fire. Floral tubs and hanging baskets adorn the front in summer when the crowds are tempted by the comprehensive sandwich selection and bar meals that draw exclusively on home-produced dishes - soup, smoked fish roulade and sausage-and-mash with onion gravy - that are its stock in trade. Here Greene King's ales predominate alongside a fair wine selection, including up to ten by the glass, and a notable collection of up to two dozen malt whiskies. In the separate dining-room the clientele can expect to find fresh fish selections encompassing suitably-sauced monkfish, halibut and skate wings and a selection of grilled steaks, all with a hint of the Mediterranean in their composition. For a full meal, start perhaps with home-made soup or chicken liver p‚tÈ, and round off with popular desserts from the trolley such as tiramis and raspberry and hazelnut Pavlova. Friendly service amid the constant bustle, and a safe summer retreat on the side terrace for quieter moments of reflection, add to the Axe's unfailing charm.

BRAINTREE   Map 07 TL73

Pick of the Pubs

The Green Dragon at Young's End
Upper London Rd, Young's End CM7 8QN
☎ 01245 361030 📠 01245 362575
e-mail: green.dragon@virgin.net
*Dir: M11 J8 take A120 towards Colchester. At Braintree b'pass take
A131 S towards Chelmsford*

Close to the Essex County Showground, this former
private house and stables is a comfortable dining venue
these days with a garden and play area for families in fair
weather and a choice of dining options within. Cosy bars
lead through to the 'Barn' and non-smoking, first-floor
'Hayloft' with their plain brick walls and wealth of old
beams. Available throughout are pub dishes such as
chicken liver pâté, beefsteak, mushroom and kidney pie
and steaks from the Buccleuch Scotch beef company. A
fixed-price menu weighs in with deep-fried Camembert,
turkey escalopes with bacon and mushroom cream sauce
and hot home-made nursery puddings. From the specials
board look for such seafood offerings as dressed crab
salad and smoked haddock with bacon mornay, curries of
the day and assorted pasta dishes with cherry tomato
salad and garlic bread. Sunday lunch served from noon
through to 6pm appears rather less easy on the pocket.

OPEN: 12–3 5.30–11 (Sat-Sun & BHs 12–11)
BAR MEALS: Lunch served: all week Dinner served: all week
12–2.15 6–9.30 Av main course £8 **RESTAURANT:** Lunch
served: all week Dinner served: all week 12–2.15 6–9.30 Av 3
course à la carte £15.50 Av 3 course fixed price £13.50
BREWERY/COMPANY: Greene King
PRINCIPAL BEERS: Greene King IPA, Abbot Ale, Ruddles
County & Old Speckled Hen. **FACILITIES:** Garden: Beer garden,
patio, food served outdoors **NOTES:** Parking 40

BURNHAM-ON-CROUCH   Map 05 TQ99

Ye Olde White Harte Hotel
The Quay CM0 8AS ☎ 01621 782106 📠 01621 782106
Directly overlooking the River Crouch, the hotel dates from
the 17th century and retains many original features, including
exposed beams. The pub has her own private jetty. The food
is mainly English-style with such dishes as boiled ham, steak
and kidney pie, baked lamb chops, and Old English roast
forerib of beef and Yorkshire pudding. Fish is well represented
on the menu and much of it is locally caught.

continued

OPEN: 11–11 **BAR MEALS:** Lunch served: all week Dinner served:
all week 12–2 7–9 Av main course £6 **RESTAURANT:** Lunch served:
all week Dinner served: all week 12–2 7–9 Av 3 course à la carte £18
Av 3 course fixed price £12.80 **BREWERY/COMPANY:** Free House
PRINCIPAL BEERS: Adnams Bitter, Crouch Vale Best.
FACILITIES: Children welcome Dogs allowed **NOTES:** Parking 15
ROOMS: 19 bedrooms 11 en suite from d£37

CASTLE HEDINGHAM   Map 07 TL73

The Bell Inn
St James St CO9 3EJ ☎ 01787 460350
e-mail: bell-inn@ic24.net
Dir: On A1124(A604) N of Halstead, R to Castle Hedingham

In a charming medieval village with a colourful history the
15th-century Bell has been owned by a local Chelmsford
brewery since 1897. Upstairs is a splendid barrel-vaulted
function room that has been a theatre, courthouse and
assembly room: today it plays host to live jazz on Sunday
lunchtimes. The majority of the menu is home-made using
local produce; typical examples include roast vegetable
kebabs, Thai chicken curry and steak and Guinness pie.
Monday is fish night – maybe with barbecued pink sea bream
or Mediterranean fish stew.
OPEN: 11.30–3 (Sun 12–3) 6–11 (Sun 7–10.30) Closed: 25 Dec
BAR MEALS: Lunch served: all week Dinner served: all week 12–2
7–9.30 Av main course £7 **BREWERY/COMPANY:** Grays
PRINCIPAL BEERS: Shepherd Neame Spitfire, Greene King IPA ,
Adnams Bitter. **FACILITIES:** Children welcome Garden: Red brick
walled orchard garden Dogs allowed **NOTES:** Parking 15

CHAPPEL   Map 07 TL82

The Swan Inn
CO6 2DD ☎ 01787 222353 📠 01787 220012
*Dir: Pub visible just off A1124 Colchester-Halstead road, from Colchester
1st L after viaduct*

Set in the shadow of a magnificent Victorian viaduct, this
rambling, low-beamed old free house boasts a charming

continued

England

CHAPPEL continued

riverside garden, cobbled courtyard and overflowing flower tubs. Fresh market meat and fish arrives daily: expect scallops grilled with bacon, butterfish Florentine, Swan seafood special, plus calves' liver, chicken Kiev, gammon steak, and various lunchtime snacks such as filled rolls and sandwiches, and beef burgers with chips.
OPEN: 11-3 6-11 (Sat 11-11, Sun 12-10.30) **BAR MEALS:** Lunch served: all week Dinner served: all week 12-2.30 7-10.30 Av main course £10 **RESTAURANT:** Lunch served: all week Dinner served: all week 12-2.15 7-10 Av 3 course à la carte £16
BREWERY/COMPANY: Free House **PRINCIPAL BEERS:** Greene King IPA, Abbot Ale. **FACILITIES:** Children welcome Garden: Food served outside Dogs allowed (water) **NOTES:** Parking 55

CHELMSFORD   Map 07 TL70

Prince of Wales
Woodham Rd, Stow Maries CM3 6SA ☎ 01621 828971
Simple, friendly marshland pub specialising in real ale - six on handpump - and unusual continental beers. Barbecues every Sunday in summer. Pub incorporates old bakery with bread oven.

CHIPPING ONGAR   Map 07 TL50

The Black Bull
Dunmow Rd, Fyfield CM5 0NN ☎ 01277 899225
Vine-covered pub which offers a wide range of bar meals in its 15th-century black-beamed rooms. Aviary with budgies and cockateels in car park.

CLAVERING   Map 07 TL43

Pick of the Pubs

The Cricketers 🛏 ♀
CB11 4QT ☎ 01799 550442 📠 01799 550882
e-mail: info@thecricketers.co.uk
Dir: From M11 J10 take A505 E. Then A1301, B1383. At Newport take B1038

A celebrated family-owned inn at the heart of a beautiful and unspoilt Essex village, opposite the local cricket pitch and just a step from Saffron Walden and Audley End House. Cricketing memorabilia dots the bars and restaurant with their beamed ceilings and log fires that serve to create a friendly, relaxed atmosphere. Bar menus are priced individually on an eat-what-you-like basis from the English and celebrated Italian versions. Seasonal options thus include pasta parcels of ricotta and crabmeat, shank of lamb with Mediterranean vegetables and

pappardelle with porcini mushroom sauce. Plainer choices add home-made soda bread with grilled goats' cheese and Parma ham, guinea fowl with apricot stuffing and home-made steak, kidney and Guinness pie. Multi-choice dinner menus in the restaurant come at a fixed price from a kitchen where Mr & Mrs Oliver's son took his first steps to celebrity.
OPEN: 10.30-3 6-11 Closed: 25-26 Dec **BAR MEALS:** Lunch served: all week Dinner served: all week 12-2 7-10 Av main course £9 **RESTAURANT:** Lunch served: all week Dinner served: all week 12-2 7-10 Av 3 course à la carte £25 Av 3 course fixed price £23 **BREWERY/COMPANY:** Free House
PRINCIPAL BEERS: Adnams Bitter, Carlsberg-Tetley Tetley Bitter.
FACILITIES: Children welcome Garden: Patio, food served outdoors **NOTES:** Parking 100 **ROOMS:** 8 bedrooms 8 en suite from s£70 d£100

COLCHESTER   Map 07 TL92

Rose & Crown Hotel 🛏
East St CO1 2TZ ☎ 01206 866677 📠 01206 866616
e-mail: 101711.2201@compuserve.com
Dir: From M25 J28 take A12 N & follow signs for Colchester
Situated in the heart of Britain's oldest town, this splendid 14th-century posting house retains much of its Tudor character. With ancient timbers, smartly decorated bedrooms, and wide-ranging menus, it is a popular destination. Part of the bar is made of cell doors from the old jail that was once on the site. The focus is on fresh seafood, with other options such as rack of lamb, calves' liver and bacon, breast of duck with orange sauce, or seared venison fillet.
OPEN: 12-2 7-11 **BAR MEALS:** Lunch served: all week Dinner served: Mon-Sat 12-2 7-10 Av main course £7.95
RESTAURANT: Lunch served: all week Dinner served: Mon-Sat 12-2 7-11 Av 3 course à la carte £25 Av 3 course fixed price £19.95
BREWERY/COMPANY: Free House
PRINCIPAL BEERS: Carlsberg-Tetley Tetley Bitter, Rose & Crown Bitter, Adnams Broadside. **FACILITIES:** Children welcome
NOTES: Parking 50 **ROOMS:** 29 bedrooms 29 en suite from s£65 d£75

The Rose & Crown ♀
Nayland Rd, Great Horkesley CO6 4AH ☎ 01206 271251
e-mail: petitfour@dlingley.freeserve.co.uk

Dating from the 17th century, the pub maintains tradition with a welcoming log fire and a choice of well-kept real ales. The licensees have a wealth of experience, and by cooking everything on the premises, and using fresh local produce, they are able to offer an imaginative, regularly changing menu in the bars and timbered restaurant. Special themed events

continued

continued

include Bangers & Booze Night, Curry Weekend, Veggie Night, Italian Night and more.
OPEN: 12–3 6–11 **BAR MEALS:** Lunch served: all week Dinner served: all week 12-2 6-9.30 Av main course £8.95
RESTAURANT: Lunch served: Sun 12-2 Dinner served: Tue-Sat 7-9.30 Av 3 course à la carte £19 **BREWERY/COMPANY:** Greene King **PRINCIPAL BEERS:** Greene King Ipa, Abbot Ale.
FACILITIES: Children welcome Garden: Food served outside. Country garden Dogs allowed (water provided) **NOTES:** Parking 32

DANBURY   Map 07 TL70

The Anchor 🐾 ♀ NEW
Runsell Green CM3 4QZ ☎ 01245 222457 📠 01245 222457
A popular 16th-century timbered pub close to the estuary of the River Blackwater and handy for exploring the desolate landscape of the Essex marshes. The conservatory and dining area offer a wide-ranging menu. Cumberland sausage, lamb rosemary, cheesy cottage pie and gammon, ham and eggs feature among the more traditional dishes, while for something more spicy, try vegetable curry, chilli con carne or chicken balti. Daily specials, plenty of starters and sizzler and fish dishes.
OPEN: 12–3 6–11 **BAR MEALS:** Lunch served: all week Dinner served: all week 12-2.30 6-9.30 Av main course £8.95
RESTAURANT: Lunch served: all week Dinner served: all week 12-2.30 6-9.30 Av 3 course à la carte £16.50
BREWERY/COMPANY: Ridley & Sons
PRINCIPAL BEERS: Ridleys IPA, Rumpus, Old Bob.
FACILITIES: Children welcome Garden: Food served outside Dogs allowed (water) **NOTES:** Parking 50

DEDHAM   Map 07 TM03

Marlborough Head Hotel ♀
Mill Ln CO7 6DH ☎ 01206 323250 📠 01206 322331
Dir: E of A12, N of Colchester
Set in glorious Constable country, close to Flatford Mill and peaceful walks, this former wool merchants house dates from 1455. Became an inn in 1704, the year of the Duke of Marlborough's famous victory over the French at the Battle of Blenheim. Extensive menu might feature fisherman's pie, king cod, hot cross bunny, or duck delight.
OPEN: 11–11 **BAR MEALS:** Lunch served: all week Dinner served: all week 12-2.30 7-9.30 Av main course £8 **RESTAURANT:** Lunch served: all week Dinner served: all week 12-2.30 7-9.30 Av 3 course à la carte £16 **PRINCIPAL BEERS:** Adnams Southwold, Greene King IPA, Adnams Broadside. **FACILITIES:** Children welcome Children's licence Garden: Beer garden outdoor eating, Dogs allowed (garden only) **NOTES:** Parking 28 **ROOMS:** 3 bedrooms 3 en suite from s£45 d£55

See Pub Walk on page 183

ELSENHAM   Map 07 TL52

The Crown
The Cross, High St CM22 6DG ☎ 01279 812827
Dir: M11 J8 towards Takeley L at traffic lights
A pub for 300 years, with oak beams, open fireplaces and Essex pargetting at the front. The menu, which has a large selection of fresh fish, might offer seafood mixed grill or pork fillet with Calvados.
OPEN: 11–3 6–11 (Sun 12–3, 7-10.30) **BAR MEALS:** Lunch served: all week 12-2 Dinner served: Tue-Sat 7.30-9 Av main course £7.95 **RESTAURANT:** Lunch served: all week Dinner served: Tue-Sat 12-2 7-9 Av 3 course à la carte £20 Av 2 course fixed price £10

continued

PRINCIPAL BEERS: Youngs PA, Adnams Broadside.
FACILITIES: Garden: Beer garden, outdoor eating **NOTES:** Parking 28

FEERING   Map 07 TL82

The Sun Inn
Feering Hill CO5 9NH ☎ 01376 570442
Dir: On A12 between Colchester and Witham
Thought to date from 1525 and originally part of a gentleman's residence, this lively pub offers between 20 and 30 different beers a week and is home to the Feering Beer Festival. An ever-changing menu board of home-cooked dishes includes some Maltese specialities, courtesy of the landlord. Braised liver and bacon cooked in Adnams Best Bitter, jugged hare, and sweet and sour pork casserole are fairly typical.
OPEN: 12–3 6–11 (Sun 12-3 6-9.30) **BAR MEALS:** Lunch served: all week Dinner served: all week 12-2 6-9.30 Av main course £7 **BREWERY/COMPANY:** Free House **FACILITIES:** Children welcome Garden: Food served outside. Continental patio Dogs allowed (water provided) **NOTES:** Parking 19 No credit cards

---

FINGRINGHOE   Map 07 TM02

The Whalebone
Chapel Rd CO5 7BG ☎ 01206 729307 📠 01206 729307
e-mail: whale.bone@virgin.net
In the shadow of the oldest tree in Essex, the 250-year-old Whalebone is situated next to the village green and pond, close to Colchester, the Fingrinhoe Nature Reserve, and the foot ferry that crosses the River Colne from Wivenhoe. The new management has instigated considerable refurbishment. A current menu includes fillet of cod on a bed of ribbon vegetables with herb potato and coriander lime butter, monkfish on herb potato bake, roast vegetable risotto with red pepper and tomato compote, and Moroccan braised lamb fillet.
OPEN: 10–3 5.30–11 (all day Sat-Sun) **BAR MEALS:** Lunch served: all week Dinner served: all week 12-2.30 6.30-9.30 Av main course £9 **RESTAURANT:** Lunch served: all week Dinner served: all week 12-2.30 6.30-9.30 Av 3 course fixed price £10.95 **BREWERY/COMPANY:** Free House
PRINCIPAL BEERS: Greene King IPA, Old Speckled Hen & Abbot Ale, Mauldon Moletrap. **FACILITIES:** Garden: Patio/terrace, food served outdoors Dogs allowed **NOTES:** Parking 25

GOSFIELD   Map 07 TL72

The Green Man 🐾 ♀
The Street CO9 1TP ☎ 01787 472746
Dir: Braintree A131 then A1017
Smart yet traditional village dining pub with old beams, named after a pagan symbol of fertility. Popular for the relaxing atmosphere, Greene King ales and decent bar food. Blackboard menus may list steak and kidney pudding, lamb casserole with dumplings, pork chops marinated in mustard and dill, lasagne, pheasant in red wine, or tuna steak with herb and tomato. Cold buffet table available at lunch time.
OPEN: 11–3 6.15–11 (Sun 12-3, 7-10.30) **BAR MEALS:** Lunch served: all week 12-2 Dinner served: Mon-Sat 12-2 Av main course £6.95 **RESTAURANT:** Lunch served: all week 12-2 Dinner served: Mon-Sat 6.45-9 **BREWERY/COMPANY:** Greene King **PRINCIPAL BEERS:** Greene King IPA & Abbot Ale.
FACILITIES: Children welcome Garden: Patio, food served outside Dogs allowed **NOTES:** Parking 25

GREAT BRAXTED | Map 07 TL81

Du Cane Arms
The Village CM8 3EJ ☎ 01621 891697
Dir: *Great Braxted signed between Witham and Kelvedon on A12*

Walkers and cyclists mingle with the locals at this friendly pub, built in 1935 at the heart of a leafy village: handy for the A12 today, it is a popular spot and comes up with a variety of lively real ales and daily fresh fish. Adnams bitter boosts the beer batter for fresh cod or haddock, while the steak and kidney pie is livened up with a splash of Guinness. Seared tuna on a bed of crushed rosemary potatoes and linguine of salmon and prawns with tomato and cream sauce are more accomplished dishes.
OPEN: 11.30–3 6.30–11 **BAR MEALS:** Lunch served: Tues-Sun
Dinner served: Tues-Sun 12–2 7–9.30 Av main course £7.95
RESTAURANT: Lunch served: Tues-Sun Dinner served: Tues-Sun
12–2 7–9.30 Av 3 course à la carte £16.95
BREWERY/COMPANY: Free House **PRINCIPAL BEERS:** Adnams
Bitter, Greene King IPA,. **FACILITIES:** Garden: Food served outside
NOTES: Parking 25

GREAT YELDHAM | Map 07 TL73

Pick of the Pubs

The White Hart
Poole St CO9 4HJ ☎ 01787 237250 📠 01787 238044
e-mail: reservations@whitehartyeldham.co.uk
See Pick of the Pubs on page 189

HARLOW | Map 07 TL41

Rainbow & Dove
Hastingwood Rd CM17 9JX ☎ 01279 415419 📠 01279 415419
Dir: *M11 J7 take A414 towards Chipping Ongar. Then L into Hastingwood Rd*
Quaint listed inn with many charming features, originally a farmhouse and staging post. Became a pub when Oliver Cromwell stationed his new model army on the common here in 1645. Relaxed atmosphere inside and good quality bar food.

HORDON ON THE HILL | Map 05 TQ68

Pick of the Pubs

Bell Inn & Hill House
High Rd SS17 8LD ☎ 01375 642463 📠 01375 361611
e-mail: info@bell-inn.co.uk
Dir: *Off M25 J30/31 signed Thurrock. Lakeside A13 then B1007 to Horndon*

A former coaching inn dating from the 15th century with many original features intact, including a courtyard balcony where luggage was taken from the coach roof. Since being bought in 1938 with no running water or electricity by the present family, it has been transformed into a comfortable inn with stylish accommodation in an adjoining property. The two bars offer real ales and guest beers, and an imaginative daily-changing menu that supplements some interesting bar food. Rillette of salmon with a celeriac and Parmesan fondue, and parsnip and goats' cheese wun tun with plum sauce might be followed on the carte by roast pigeon with red cabbage velouté, or pan-fried haddock with an anchovy and Parmesan crust. Fixed price dishes include spiced bean soup, and roast pork chop with mustard jus, pan-fried kidneys, and chicken Caesar salad on the bar menu.
OPEN: 11–2.30 (Wkds times vary) 5.30–11 Closed: 25–26 Dec
BAR MEALS: Lunch served: all week Dinner served: all week
12–1.45 6.45–9.45 Av main course £11.95 **RESTAURANT:** Lunch
served: all week Dinner served: all week 12–1.45 6.45–9.45 Av 3
course à la carte £15.95 **BREWERY/COMPANY:** Free House
PRINCIPAL BEERS: Greene King IPA, Interbrew Bass, Young's
Special. **FACILITIES:** Children welcome Garden: Courtyard,
food served outside Dogs allowed **NOTES:** Parking 50
ROOMS: 15 bedrooms 15 en suite from s£50 d£50

Hops in Ale
The introduction of hops was stoutly resisted. Henry VIII would drink only hopless ale and the brewers were castigated for ruining the traditional drink. Beer brewed with hops kept better for longer, however, which stimulated the development of large-scale breweries and both inns and alehouses gradually gave up brewing their own.

OPEN: 11-3 6-11 Closed: Dec 25-26 & Jan 1 evenings
BAR MEALS: Lunch served: all week Dinner served: all week 12-2 6.30-9.30
RESTAURANT: Lunch served: all week Dinner served: all week 12-2 6.30-9.30 Av cost 2 course fixed price £8.50 Av 3 course à la carte £23
BREWERY/COMPANY: FREE HOUSE
PRINCIPAL BEERS: Guest ales
FACILITIES: Children welcome Garden: 4.5 acres, patio, food served outside.
NOTES: Parking 40

The White Hart

Set in acres of garden, this stunning timberframed building offers wide choice of excellent dishes and both real ales and an interesting range of bottled beers. A Grade I star listed building, the White Hart dates back to 1505 and still has its own jail (a legacy of the days of the highwayman).

★ ⚛ ♟
Poole Street CO9 4HJ
☎ 01787 237250 📄 01787 238044
e-mail: reservations@whitehartyeldham.co.uk
Dir: On A1017 between Haverhill & Halstead.

It is timber framed with oak beams and traditional Norfolk pammets; the magnificent chimney stacks have gabled buttresses and octagonal shafts, and the impressive whole is set in four acres of recently landscaped gardens with a riverside walk. There is a roaring log fire in the winter, while the garden and patio are ideal for lunch or evening drinks when the weather is fine and the spring apple blossom or autumn leaves can be appreciated both from here

or by the river. Popular with drinkers, real ales are a speciality, with an ever-changing selection from micro-breweries across the country, plus a range of Belgian and international bottled beers. There are a dozen wines by the glass, organic fruit juices, natural ginger beer and a superb choice of malt whiskies and Cognacs. The inn has had a good reputation for the standard of its cooking for many years. Food is served in the main restaurant, the Garden Room, or the bar. There is always a selection of fish dishes and a wide-ranging menu. Typical dishes are seared scallops on bok choy and oyster mushroom stir-fry; loin of venison on red cabbage with herb fettucine, roasted quince and poivrade sauce or osso buco with lemon gremolata, creamy polenta and braised toasted fennel. Desserts might include warm pear tatin with cardamom ice cream or meringue vacherin with a stewed-fruit compote.

LANGHAM
Map 07 TM03

The Shepherd and Dog 🐾 ♀
Moor Rd CO4 5NR ☎ 01206 272711 📄 01206 273136
Dir: A12 toward Ipswich, 1st turning on L out of Colchester, marked Langham
Deep in Dedham Vale, a friendly and popular local much loved by an increasing range of regulars. Amongst its claims to fame is the succession of foodie events: a Moroccan week, French fortnight, fish'n'chip suppers. Good wine and good beer accompany locally sourced ingredients in dishes that encompass fresh market sardines, plaice and skate along with lasagne, various curries, grilled chump of lamb and Sunday lunch of up to four roasts.
OPEN: 11-3 5.30-11 **BAR MEALS:** Lunch served: all week Dinner served: all week 12-2.15 6-10 Av main course £7.95
RESTAURANT: Lunch served: all week Dinner served: all week 12-2.15 6-10 Av 3 course à la carte £12.50 **BREWERY/COMPANY:** Free House **PRINCIPAL BEERS:** Greene King IPA, Abbot Ale & Ruddles County. **FACILITIES:** Children welcome Garden: Food served outside Dogs allowed **NOTES:** Parking 40

LEIGH-ON-SEA
Map 05 TQ88

Crooked Billet
51 High St, Old Town SS9 2EP ☎ 01702 480289
Dir: A13 towards Southend, follow signs for Old Leigh
Fine 16th-century timbered ale house, with open fires, original beams and local fishing pictures, set in the picturesque fishing village of Old Leigh. Enjoy views of cockle boats and the estuary from the terrace.

LITTLE CANFIELD
Map 07 TL52

The Lion & Lamb 🐾 ♀
CM6 1SR ☎ 01279 870257 📄 01279 870423
e-mail: info@lionandlambtakeley.co.uk
Dir: M11 J8 A120 towards Braintree

There's a friendly welcome at this traditional country pub restaurant, with its soft red bricks, oak beams and winter log fires. Although handy for Stansted airport and the M11, the pub's charm and individuality makes it a favourite for business or leisure. The full menu is served throughout; typical dishes include sausages and mash with Ridley's ale and onion gravy, pan-fried calves' liver and bacon, and monkfish with scallops in saffron and champagne sauce.
OPEN: 11-11 (Sun 12-10.30) **BAR MEALS:** Lunch served: all week Dinner served: all week 12-10 Av main course £5
RESTAURANT: Lunch served: all week Dinner served: all week 12-10 Av 3 course à la carte £20 **BREWERY/COMPANY:** Ridley & Sons **PRINCIPAL BEERS:** Ridleys IPA, Old Bob & Rumpus and Ridleys seasonal beers.. **FACILITIES:** Children welcome Garden: Patio area overlooking farm land **NOTES:** Parking 50

LITTLE DUNMOW
Map 07 TL62

Flitch of Bacon 🐾 ♀
The Street CM6 3HT ☎ 01371 820323 📄 01371 820338
Dir: A120 to Braintree for 10m, turn off at Little Dunmow, 1/2m pub on R
The name of this 15th-century country inn refers to the ancient award of half a salted pig, or 'flitch', to couples who have been married for a year and a day, and 'who have not had a cross word'. Sit down to sausage, egg and chips, steak and kidney pie, smoked haddock and spinach bake, lamb with redcurrant and rosemary, 8oz sirloin steak with trimmings, or scampi and chips.
OPEN: 12-3 6-11 **BAR MEALS:** Lunch served: all week Dinner served: Mon-Sat 12-2 7-9 Av main course £6.50
BREWERY/COMPANY: Free House **PRINCIPAL BEERS:** Greene King IPA plus regular changing ales. **FACILITIES:** Children welcome Garden: Patio, food served outside Dogs allowed **NOTES:** Parking 6 **ROOMS:** 3 bedrooms 3 en suite from s£40 d£55 No credit cards

MANNINGTREE
Map 07 TM13

Thorn Hotel
High St, Mistley CO11 1HE ☎ 01206 392821 📄 01206 392133
Historic pub in the centre of Mistley, which stands on the estuary of the River Stour near Colchester and is the only surviving Georgian port in England today. Wide choice of freshly cooked food is available, with dishes such as chicken curry, home-made cottage pie, beef and ale pie, seafood platter and mixed grill.
OPEN: 11-11 **BAR MEALS:** Lunch served: all week 12-2.30 7-9 Av main course £4 **RESTAURANT:** Lunch served: all week Dinner served: Mon-Sat 12-2.30 7-9 Av 3 course à la carte £10.50
BREWERY/COMPANY: Free House **PRINCIPAL BEERS:** Greene King IPA, Adnams. **FACILITIES:** Children welcome Dogs allowed (except in garden) **NOTES:** Parking 6 **ROOMS:** 4 bedrooms 4 en suite from s£42.50 d£60

NORTH FAMBRIDGE
Map 05 TQ89

The Ferry Boat Inn
Ferry Ln CM3 6LR ☎ 01621 740208
e-mail: Sylviaferryboat@aol.com
Dir: From Chelmsford take A130 S then A132 to South Woodham Ferrers, then B1012. R to village
The 500-year-old Ferry Boat Inn is located on the River Crouch, close to the well-known yachting centre and the Essex Wildlife Trust's 600-acre sanctuary. Low beams and log fires characterise the interior, and there is reputed to be a poltergeist in residence. Typical pub fare includes dishes such as steak and kidney pie and ham, egg and chips.
OPEN: 11.30-3 (Sun 12-4) 7-11 (Sun 7-10.30)
BAR MEALS: Lunch served: all week Dinner served: all week 12-2 7-9.30 Av main course £9 **RESTAURANT:** Lunch served: all week Dinner served: all week 12-1.30 7-9.30 Av 3 course à la carte £15
BREWERY/COMPANY: Free House
PRINCIPAL BEERS: Shepherd Neame Bishops Finger, Spitfire & Best Bitter. **FACILITIES:** Children welcome Garden: Food served outside Dogs allowed **NOTES:** Parking 30 **ROOMS:** 6 bedrooms 6 en suite from s£30 d£40

PAGLESHAM
Map 05 TQ99

Plough & Sail 🐾 ♀
East End SS4 2EQ ☎ 01702 258242 📄 01702 258242
Charming weatherboarded 17th-century dining pub on the bracing Essex marshes, within easy reach of the rivers Crouch and Roach. Inside are pine tables, brasses and low beams,

continued

giving the place a quaint, traditional feel. The attractive, well-kept garden is a popular spot during the summer months. Renowned for its good quality food and fresh fish dishes, including sea bass, smoked haddock and chargrilled tuna steak with pepper and lime chilli salsa.
OPEN: 11.30-3 6.45-11 **BAR MEALS:** Lunch served: all week Dinner served: all week 12-2.15 7-9.30 **RESTAURANT:** Lunch served: all week Dinner served: all week 12-2.15 7-9.30 **BREWERY/COMPANY:** Free House **PRINCIPAL BEERS:** Greene King IPA, Ridley's.
FACILITIES: Children welcome Garden: Patio **NOTES:** Parking 30

The Punchbowl
Church End SS4 2DP ☎ 01702 258376
Weatherboarded pub with rural views and a small garden. Bar food and dining room. Changing guest ale.

PATTISWICK   Map 07 TL82

The Compasses Inn ♀
CM77 8BG ☎ 01376 561322 📠 01376 561780
Dir: off A120 between Braintree & Coggeshall
Set in idyllic Essex countryside surrounded by woodland and rolling fields and much extended from the original, this inn dates back to the 13th century. Lighter bar bites are supplemented on the bistro menu by local favourites such as Trucker's Platter, liver and bacon, toad-in-the-hole, braised Scottish steak and kidney pie, and spinach and goats' cheese cannelloni. Multi-choice Sunday lunch.
OPEN: 11-3 6-11 (open all day wknds and summer)
BAR MEALS: Lunch served: all week Dinner served: all week 12-2.30 6-9.30 Av main course £7.95 **RESTAURANT:** Lunch served: all week Dinner served: all week 12-2.30 6-9.30 Av 3 course à la carte £20 Av 4 course fixed price £12.95 **BREWERY/COMPANY:** Free House **PRINCIPAL BEERS:** Greene King - IPA, Abbot Ale, Adnams. **FACILITIES:** Children welcome Garden: Beer garden, patio, outdoor eating **NOTES:** Parking 40

RADWINTER   Map 07 TL63

The Plough Inn 🐶 ♀
CB10 2TL ☎ 01799 599222 📠 01799 599161
Dir: 4m E of Saffron Walden, at Jct of B2153 & B2154
A Essex woodland exterior, old beams and a thatched roof characterise this listed inn, once frequented by farm workers. The menu extends from lunchtime snacks to three course meals, with fresh fish from Lowestoft Tuesday to Saturday - maybe cod or haddock fillet in beer batter or plaice fillet au gratin with prawns. Other favourites are 8oz fillet steak au poivre, Radwinter pie and veggie Wellington.
OPEN: 12-3 6.30-11 Closed: Dec 25 **BAR MEALS:** Lunch served: all week Dinner served: all week 12-2.15 7-9 Av main course £6.95 **RESTAURANT:** Lunch served: all week Dinner served: Mon-Sat 12-2.15 7-9 Av 3 course à la carte £10 **BREWERY/COMPANY:** Free House **PRINCIPAL BEERS:** Adnams Best, Youngs Best, Brakspear Special, Greene King IPA. **FACILITIES:** Children welcome Garden: Food served outside Dogs allowed (water) **NOTES:** Parking 28 **ROOMS:** 3 bedrooms 3 en suite from s£50 d£50

SAFFRON WALDEN   Map 07 TL53

The Cricketers' Arms ♦♦♦ ♀
Rickling Green CB11 3YG ☎ 01799 543210 📠 01799 543512
e-mail: reservations@cricketers.demon.co.uk
Dir: exit B1383 at Quendon. Pub 300yds on L opp cricket ground
Historic inn originally built as a terrace of timber-framed cottages, now offering accommodation in 10 en suite

bedrooms. The cricketing connection began in the 1880's when Rickling Green became the venue for London society cricket matches. One menu serves all three dining areas with choices including leek and feta cheese parcels, liver and bacon, chilli con carne, Chinese style duck on a bed of noodles, or veal saltimbocca.

OPEN: 11-11 Sun 12-22.30 **BAR MEALS:** Lunch served: all week Dinner served: all week 12-2.30 7-9.30 **RESTAURANT:** Lunch served: all week Dinner served: all week 12-2.30 7-9.30 Av 3 course fixed price £10.50 **BREWERY/COMPANY:** Free House **PRINCIPAL BEERS:** Interbrew Flowers IPA, Wadworth 6X, Fuller's ESB. **FACILITIES:** Children welcome Garden: Food served outdoors, patio/terrace Dogs allowed (on lead) **NOTES:** Parking 40 **ROOMS:** 10 bedrooms 10 en suite from s£55 d£70

Queen's Head ♀
Littlebury CB11 4TD ☎ 01799 522251 📠 01799 522251
Only a short drive from the Duxford Air Museum, a 16th-century inn with quarry-tiled floors, rustic furniture, beams and open fires. French regional cuisine influences dishes that might include corn-fed chicken with saffron risotto, smoked haddock on creamed spinach with a rarebit crust and slow roast lamb shank with flageolet beans. Speciality of the house is a daube de boeuf à la provençale with garlic roast potatoes. In summer the walled garden is an added attraction and hosts regular barbecues.
OPEN: 12-3 5.30-11 (All day Fri-Sat) **BAR MEALS:** Lunch served: Tues-Sun Dinner served: Mon-Sat 12-2.30 6.30-9.30 Av main course £8 **RESTAURANT:** Lunch served: Wed-Sun 12-2.30 Dinner served: Thur-Sat 6.30-9.30 Av 3 course à la carte £20
BREWERY/COMPANY: Greene King **PRINCIPAL BEERS:** Greene King IPA, Ruddles Best, Batemans XXXB. **FACILITIES:** Children welcome Garden: Large open plan, food served outside, Dogs allowed **NOTES:** Parking 25 **ROOMS:** 6 bedrooms 6 en suite from s£40 d£55

STOCK   Map 05 TQ69

The Hoop 🐶
21 High St CM4 9BD ☎ 01277 841137
Dir: On B1007 between Chelmsford & Billericay
Built as weavers' cottages in the 15th-century, The Hoop became an alehouse inthe 17th-century and has been serving good ale ever since. An annual beer festival is held at the end of May. The homely little bar offers a good selection of snacks and light meals. Expect sandwiches, steak and kidney pie, fish pie, and ploughmans', and don't forget to check the blackboards for today's specials.
OPEN: 11-11 (Sun 12-10.30) **BAR MEALS:** Lunch served: all week from 11 Dinner served: all week 5-9 Av main course £5.50
BREWERY/COMPANY: Free House **PRINCIPAL BEERS:** Fuller's London Pride, Hop Back, Crouch Vale, Adnams Bitter.
FACILITIES: Garden: Outdoor heaters, food served outside, BBQ

continued

England

TILLINGHAM
Map 07 TL90

Cap & Feathers Inn
South St CM0 7TH ☎ 01621 779212 📠 01621 779212
Dir: From Chelmsford take A414, follow signs for Burnham-on-Crouch, then for Tillingham

Originally built in 1500 by Dutch labourers working on land drainage, the classic white-painted, weather-boarded frontage is delightfully unspoiled, as is its timeless old-fashioned, quiet interior, traditional furnishings and unassuming pub food that attracts its fair share of hikers, cyclists, bird-watchers and fishermen. Locally smoked fish and meats and fresh fish such as sole, dab and cod are main-stays of the menu supported by a host of meat pies, hand-made sausages and game in winter. Commendable real ales.
OPEN: 12-3 5.30-11 (Sat 12-11, Sun 12-10.30)
BAR MEALS: Lunch served: all week Dinner served: all week 12-2.30 7-9.30 Av main course £7.50 **RESTAURANT:** Lunch served: all week Dinner served: all week 12-2.30 7-9.30 Av 3 course à la carte £15 **BREWERY/COMPANY:** Crouch Vale
PRINCIPAL BEERS: Crouch Vale Best. **FACILITIES:** Children welcome Garden: Food served outside Dogs allowed
NOTES: Parking 20 **ROOMS:** 3 bedrooms from s£35 d£45

WENDENS AMBO
Map 07 TL53

The Bell
Royston Rd CB11 4JY ☎ 01799 540382
e-mail: sthorp31@aol.com
Dir: Near Audley End train station
Formerly a farmhouse and brewery, this 16th-century timber-framed building is set in a pretty Essex village close to Audley End House. The pub is surrounded by extensive gardens, and the cottage-style rooms have low ceilings and open fires in winter. An allegedly friendly ghost, Mrs Goddard, is also in residence. Food on offer includes light snacks, six daily specials and a big steak menu. Favourites are seafood platter and home-made steak and kidney pie.
OPEN: 11.30-2.30 6-11 (Summer all day Sat-Sun)
BAR MEALS: Lunch served: all week 12-2 Dinner served: Tue-Sun 7-9 Av main course £6.95 **RESTAURANT:** Lunch served: all week Dinner served: Tue-Sun 12-2 7-9 Av 3 course fixed price £14
BREWERY/COMPANY: Free House **PRINCIPAL BEERS:** Adnams Bitter, Carlsberg-Tetley Ansells Mild, Greene King Old Speckled Hen.
FACILITIES: Garden: 3.5 acres, food served outside Dogs allowed (water) **NOTES:** Parking 40

WICKHAM BISHOPS
Map 07 TL81

The Mitre
2 The Street CM8 3NN ☎ 01621 891378 📠 01621 891378
Dir: Off B1018 between Witham and Maldon
The Bishops of London used to stay at this 19th-century pub – hence the name. Noted for its friendly atmosphere and character.

WIVENHOE
Map 07 TM02

The Black Buoy Inn
Black Buoy Hill CO7 9BS
☎ 01206 822425 📠 01206 827834
e-mail: enquiries@blackbuoy.com
Dir: From Colchester take A133 towards Clacton, then B1027, B1028. In Wivenhoe turn L after church into East St

Wivenhoe's oldest inn has a smugglers' tunnel running from the quay - though we are reliably informed that it is no longer in use. The landlord has a passion for food, particularly Far Eastern and Asian cooking, examples of which can be found on the extensive menu. Produce is locally sourced, and the daily blackboard menu depends on the day's catch and the chef's mood.
OPEN: 11.30-2.30 6.30-11 (Sun 12-3.30 7-10.30)
BAR MEALS: Lunch served: all week 12-2 Dinner served: Mon-Sat 7-9 Av main course £7.95 **RESTAURANT:** Lunch served: all week 12-2 Dinner served: Mon-Sat 7-9.30
BREWERY/COMPANY: Pubmaster **PRINCIPAL BEERS:** Greene King IPA & Old Speckled Hen, Adnams Bitter, Broadside, Marston's Pedigree. **FACILITIES:** Children welcome Garden: small patio area, food served outdoors Dogs allowed (water and biscuits available)
NOTES: Parking 12

GLOUCESTERSHIRE

ALMONDSBURY
Map 03 ST68

The Bowl
Church Rd BS12 4DT ☎ 01454 612757 📠 01454 619910
e-mail: reception@theoldbowlinn.co.uk
A character whitewashed pub on the edge of the Severn Vale, originally home to monks building the adjoining church. The unusual name comes from the bowl-shaped terrain around it, and it's handy for Bristol and the M4 and M5 motorways. Bar menu with pies, roasts, grills, pasta and salads etc, and from the restaurant carte, braised lamb shank, roast fillet of venison, and smoked haddock chowder. Try carrot and coconut steamed pudding to finish.

continued

OPEN: 11–3 5–11 (Sun 7–10.30) **BAR MEALS:** Lunch served: all week Dinner served: all week 12–2.30 6–10 Av main course £7.95 **RESTAURANT:** Lunch served: all week Dinner served: all week 12–2.30 7–10 Av 3 course à la carte £25 **BREWERY/COMPANY:** Free House **PRINCIPAL BEERS:** Scottish Courage Courage Best, Smiles Best. **FACILITIES:** Children welcome Garden: Food served outside Dogs allowed **NOTES:** Parking 50 **ROOMS:** 13 bedrooms 13 en suite from s£39.50 d£64

ANDOVERSFORD   Map 03 SP01

The Frogmill Inn
Shipton GL54 4HT ☎ 01242 820547 ▤ 01242 820237
Just off the A40 this 14th-century inn is set on the banks of the River Coln, and a smaller river runs through the car park. The mill wheel still turns, and can be seen under the restaurant window. Traditional pub food. Bedrooms.

Pick of the Pubs

The Kilkeney Inn ♀
Kilkeney GL54 4LN ☎ 01242 820341 ▤ 01242 820133
Dir: On A436 1m W of Andoversford

Formerly a terrace of six stone cottages, dating from the 1850s, this charming country pub-restaurant has some delightful views from both the mature gardens and the conservatory dining area, which look out over rolling Cotswold landscape. Inside, it is very much a dining venue serving real ales in a cosy atmosphere created by log fires and exposed beams. The menu varies from light lunches of filled ciabattas, to locally made sausages, omelettes and fresh fish. In the evening dishes include slow roast shoulder of lamb, skate wings, salmon en croûte, and the exotic strawberry grouper. It is advisable to book for the popular traditional Sunday lunches ales and there are a number of special events that include monthly jazz sessions
OPEN: 11–3 5–11 (all day Easter-Oct) **BAR MEALS:** Lunch served: all week Dinner served: all week 12–2 7–9.30 Av main

course £8 **RESTAURANT:** Lunch served: all week Dinner served: all week 12–2 7–9.30 Av 3 course à la carte £20 **BREWERY/COMPANY:** Free House **PRINCIPAL BEERS:** Hook Norton Best, Interbrew Bass, Wadworth 6X plus guest ales. **FACILITIES:** Garden: Patio, food served outside **NOTES:** Parking 50

The Royal Oak Inn 🐾 ♀
Old Gloucester Rd GL54 4HR ☎ 01242 820335
e-mail: bleninns@clara.net
Dir: 200metres from A40, 4m E of Cheltenham

One of a small chain of popular food-oriented pubs in the area, the Royal Oak stands on the banks of the River Coln. Originally a coaching inn, its main dining room, galleried on two levels, occupies the converted former stables. At lunchtime bar fare offers filled ciabatta baguettes and home-made steak and kidney pie. By night the menu extends to specials such as chicken supreme with stir-fry vegetables, skate wings with bacon lardons and nut butter and home-made bubble and squeak in a rich red wine sauce.
OPEN: 11–2.30 5.30–11 **BAR MEALS:** Lunch served: all week Dinner served: all week 12–2.30 7–9.30 Av main course £7.50 **RESTAURANT:** Lunch served: all week Dinner served: all week 12–2.30 7–9.30 Av 3 course à la carte £14 **BREWERY/COMPANY:** Free House **PRINCIPAL BEERS:** Marston's Pedigree, Fuller's London Pride, Hook Norton Best. **FACILITIES:** Children welcome Garden: Patio area with tables on banks of the river Dogs allowed (water) **NOTES:** Parking 44

ARLINGHAM   Map 03 SO71

The Old Passage Inn ♦♦♦♦ 🐾 ♀ NEW
Passage Rd GL2 7JR ☎ 01452 740547 ▤ 01452 741871
e-mail: oldpassageinn@ukonline.co.uk
This bright green pub is unmissable in its remote riverside location. Marking the point of an ancient ford across the Severn, it's been transformed into a renowned eating place. The stylish interior is a far cry from your traditional pub, but still feels relaxed and inviting. Two seawater tanks house much of what's on the menu, from oysters to lobsters, but posh versions of pub favourites are also available. More exotic offerings might include assiette of walnut smoked salmon with Avruga caviar.
OPEN: 12–3 6.30–11.30 Closed: Dec 24–Dec 30
BAR MEALS: Lunch served: Tue–Sun 12–2.15 Dinner served: Tue–Sat 7–9.30 Av main course £13 **RESTAURANT:** Lunch served: Tue–Sun 12–2.15 Dinner served: Tue–Sat 7–9.30 Av 3 course à la carte £25 **BREWERY/COMPANY:** Free House **PRINCIPAL BEERS:** Bass, John Smiths. **FACILITIES:** Children welcome Garden: Food served outside. Grass area with terrace Dogs allowed **NOTES:** Parking 60 **ROOMS:** 3 bedrooms 3 en suite from s£50 d£80

continued

ASHLEWORTH   Map 03 SO82

Boat Inn
The Quay GL19 4HZ ☎ 01452 700272 📠 01452 700272
Turn off the A417 at Hartpury, to come across the Boat, standing beside Ashleworth quay and close by the medieval Tithe Barn and former Court House. In the same family for 300 years, it's a gem of a pub with its tiny front parlour, flagstone floors and ancient kitchen range; a magnet to the many walkers exploring the nearby Severn or the village itself (leaflets available from the bar). Interesting real ales from Wye Valley and Church End breweries, dispensed direct from the cask, are ideal to accompany perhaps a generously filled roll or ploughman's lunch with pickle. There is plenty of seating outside to enjoy the location.
OPEN: 11–2.30 6–11 (Oct-Apr 11–2.30, 7–11)
BREWERY/COMPANY: Free House **PRINCIPAL BEERS:** Wye Valley, Churchend, Arkells. **FACILITIES:** Children welcome Garden: **NOTES:** Parking 10 No credit cards

Pick of the Pubs

The Queens Arms 🐑 ⚲
The Village GL19 4HT ☎ 01452 700395

Signed off the A417 north of Gloucester, Ashleworth is a pretty village close to the banks of the Severn: at its heart, this brick-fronted 18th-century inn with Victorian additions. An immaculate interior has original beams, lovely iron fireplaces and comfy chairs in the homely bar and dining room, with their ever-growing collection of antiques. The latter has been divided into two intimate rooms for more flexibility without detracting from the warm, pubby atmosphere. With an accent on the use of fresh local ingredients combined with the philosophy that consistency is the secret to good dining, results certainly live up to their promise. Prominently placed chalkboards list lunchtime baguettes, Greek salad and South African bobotie, a house favourite. Similarly posted evening specials list fresh salmon fillet with English asparagus and hollandaise, pork tenderloin with brandy and apricot sauce and, to follow such home-made treats as orange and Cointreau trifle and chocolate Kahlua tart.
OPEN: 12–2.30 7–11 Closed: Dec 25 **BAR MEALS:** Lunch served: all week Dinner served: all week 12–2 7–9 Av main course £10 **RESTAURANT:** Lunch served: all week Dinner served: all week 12–2 7–9 Av 3 course à la carte £20
BREWERY/COMPANY: Free House
PRINCIPAL BEERS: Shepherd Neame Spitfire, Donnington BB, Interbrew Bass, Young's Special. **FACILITIES:** Children welcome Garden: Patio, food served outside **NOTES:** Parking 80

AUST   Map 03 ST58

The Boar's Head 🐑 ⚲
Main Rd BS35 4AX ☎ 01454 632278 📠 01454 632570
e-mail: boarshead.aust@eldridge-pope.co.uk
Dir: Off the M48 just before the first built Seven Bridge, A403 to Avonmouth about 60 yds from Rdbt L into Aust Village. 1/2 mile ion L the house
For those in the know, this popular 16th-century pub close to the M48 Severn Road Bridge offers a fine alternative to the nearby motorway service area. Seasonal log fires and a large stone-walled garden still enhance the hospitality offered to travellers, as they did in the days of the old Aust ferry. Expect home-made lasagne, Cajun chicken, peppered fresh tuna steaks, vegetable nut roast, and steak and ale pie.
OPEN: 11.30–3 6–11.30 (Sun 12–3, 6–10.30) **BAR MEALS:** Lunch served: all week 12–2.30 Dinner served: Tue–Sat 6–9.30 Av main course £7 **RESTAURANT:** Lunch served: all week 12–2.30 Dinner served: Tue–Sat 6.30–9.30 Av 3 course fixed price £15 **BREWERY/COMPANY:** Eldridge Pope **PRINCIPAL BEERS:** Scottish Courage Courage Best & Courage Directors, Greene King Ruddles County. **FACILITIES:** Children welcome Garden: Food served outside **NOTES:** Parking 30

AWRE   Map 03 SO70

The Red Hart Inn 🐑
GL14 1EW ☎ 01594 510220 📠 01594 517249
Dir: E of A48 between Gloucester & Chepstow, access is from Blakeney or Newnham villages

A cosy traditional pub with a history that predates 1640. It was formerly a drovers' inn for farmers on the ancient road to London. Close to the River Severn, with poor access for cars but ideal for hikers. Plenty of attractive features, including a glass-covered, illuminated well. Specials menu changes constantly, with local produce (pheasant, hare, venison) as well as oriental duck, fillet steak Rossini, and roast rack of lamb. Good real ales and several malts.
OPEN: 12–3 6.30–11 Closed: Jan 1–2 **BAR MEALS:** Lunch served: Tue–Sun 12–2 Dinner served: all week 7–9 Av main course £16 **RESTAURANT:** Lunch served: Tue–Sun 12–2 Dinner served: all week 7–9 Av 3 course à la carte £22 **BREWERY/COMPANY:** Free House **PRINCIPAL BEERS:** Fuller's London Pride, Freeminer Speculation Ale, Goff's Jouster, Wickwar BOB. **FACILITIES:** Children welcome **NOTES:** Parking 30

BARNSLEY   Map 03 SP00

Pick of the Pubs

The Village Pub ◎◎ ⚲
GL7 5EF ☎ 01285 740421 📠 01285 740142
e-mail: reservations@thevillagepub.co.uk
Dir: On B4425 3m NE of Cirencester
Light years away from being your average 'local', this mellow-stoned pub has earned its place amongst the best

continued

of the new breed of successful pub-restaurants. The keynote is innovative, modern British food, served in a traditional country pub with the emphasis on atmosphere. The beautifully restored dining rooms with flagstoned floors, exposed beams and open fires are the stylish setting for menus that change twice a day, and offer the best of local and traceable produce. For lunch, perhaps, feta, green bean and artichoke salad, pan-fried monkfish with fennel and black bean salad, and sunken chocolate cake with marinated cherries. The evening choice might be steamed mussels and clams followed by spiced duck breast, and pannacotta and poached rhubarb. This distinctly dining destination with its warm terracotta walls, rugs and eclectic mix of furniture is still very much the village pub, and attracts both local drinkers and well-heeled 'foodies'.

OPEN: 11-3.30 6-11 Closed: 25 Dec **BAR MEALS:** Lunch served: all week Dinner served: all week 12.00-2.30 7-9.30 Av main course £11 **RESTAURANT:** Lunch served: all week Dinner served: all week 12-2.30 7-9.30 Av 3 course fixed price £20 **BREWERY/COMPANY:** Free House **PRINCIPAL BEERS:** Hook Norton Bitter, Wadworth 6X, Donnington BB & SBA. **FACILITIES:** Children welcome Garden: Food served outside. Paved courtyard Dogs allowed **NOTES:** Parking 35 **ROOMS:** 6 bedrooms 6 en suite from s£65 d£65

BERKELEY   Map 03 ST69

The Malthouse 🛏
Marybrook St GL13 9BA ☎ 01453 511177 📠 01453 810257
Dir: From A38 towards Bristol from exit 13 of M5, Aprox 8 M Berkeley is signposted, the Malthouse is situated on the main road of Berkeley heading towards Sharpness
Close by the Severn Way is this century-old former slaughterhouse. Over the years it has been turned into comfortable inn with en suite bedrooms and a range of menus to suit all tastes and pockets. A warm greeting is extended to all, be it for a refreshing pint (guest ales change regularly), a snack or a full meal. Malthouse steak and ale pie and Cajun chicken in cream and pepper sauce are favourites. Home-made soup and liver and onions at a give-away price for Mature Students (60 years plus)!
OPEN: 12-3.30 6-11 **BAR MEALS:** Lunch served: Tues-Sun 12-2.30 Dinner served: Mon-Sat 6.30-10 Av main course £5.95 **RESTAURANT:** Lunch served: Tues-Sat 12-2.30 Dinner served: Mon-Sat 6.30-10 Av 3 course à la carte £17 **BREWERY/COMPANY:** Free House **PRINCIPAL BEERS:** Scottish Courage Courage Best, Greene King Ruddles Best, Marston's Pedigree, Wickwar BOB. **FACILITIES:** Children welcome Garden: Food served outside **NOTES:** Parking 40 **ROOMS:** 9 bedrooms 9 en suite from s£45 d£65

BIBURY   Map 03 SP10

Catherine Wheel 🛏
Arlington GL7 5ND ☎ 01285 740250 📠 01285 740779
e-mail: Catherinewheel.bibury@eldridge-pope.co.uk
Low-beamed 15th-century pub situated in a classic Cotswold village, close to Arlington Row (NT) - a group of ancient cottages - and the River Coln. An ideal area for walking. Traditional home-made pub food includes grilled Bibury trout, medallions of pork with a blackberry and mint sauce, Jamaican chicken, leek and Gruyère crown, roast shoulder of lamb, and peppered beef casserole.

continued

OPEN: 11-11 (Sun 12-10.30) **BAR MEALS:** Lunch served: all week Dinner served: all week 12-2 6-9 Av main course £8 **RESTAURANT:** Lunch served: all week Dinner served: all week 12-2 6-9 **BREWERY/COMPANY:** Eldridge Pope. **PRINCIPAL BEERS:** Courage Best, Wadworth 6X, Bass. **FACILITIES:** Garden: Food served outside. Vintage orchard Dogs allowed (water provided) **NOTES:** Parking 20 **ROOMS:** 4 bedrooms 4 en suite from s£60 d£60

BIRDLIP   Map 03 SO91

The Golden Heart ♀
Nettleton Bottom GL4 8LA ☎ 01242 870261 📠 01242 870599
Dir: on the main road A417 Gloucester to Cirencester
In glorious Cotswold countryside, with memorable views from terraced gardens. Look to the blackboards for daily specials that use prize-winning stock from local markets to offer wild boar terrine with Armagnac, or goose breast in orange and Cognac and exotic items including ostrich and crocodile. For the more conservative: pork tenderloin in crab-apple sauce and vegetarian mushroom pasta in wild mushroom sauce, followed by traditional nursery puddings. All supported by an extensive list of award-winning wines and decent real ales.
OPEN: 11-3 5.30-11 (Fri-Sat 11-11, Sun 12-10.30) **BAR MEALS:** Lunch served: all week Dinner served: all week 12-3 6-10 Av main course £8.25 **RESTAURANT:** Lunch served: all week Dinner served: all week 12-3 6-10 **BREWERY/COMPANY:** Free House **PRINCIPAL BEERS:** Interbrew Bass, Timothy Taylor Landlord, Archers Bitter, Golden Best. **FACILITIES:** Children welcome Garden: Food served outside, patio Dogs allowed (kennel, water) **NOTES:** Parking 60 **ROOMS:** 3 bedrooms 3 en suite from s£35 d£55

BISLEY   Map 03 SO90

The Bear Inn
George St GL6 7BD ☎ 01452 770265
e-mail: thebear@cyberphile.co.uk
Dir: E of Stroud off B4070
A former courthouse, The Bear opened as a village inn around 1766, its outstanding features including a huge inglenook fireplace, a bread oven and an old priest hole; though the rock-hewn cellars (including a 60ft well) are more likely Tudor. Menu items include 'bear burgers', 'bear necessities' and 'bear essentials' that include rabbit and vegetable pie, casserole of prawns and white fish in cider and vegetable pasty in white wine sauce.
OPEN: 11-3 6-11 **BAR MEALS:** Lunch served: all week 12-2.30 Dinner served: Mon-Sat 7-9 Av main course £10 **BREWERY/COMPANY:** Pubmaster **PRINCIPAL BEERS:** Tetley, Flowers IPA, Charles Wells Bombardier, Courage Directors. **FACILITIES:** Children welcome Garden: Food served outside Dogs allowed **NOTES:** Parking 20 **ROOMS:** 2 bedrooms d£20

BLEDINGTON
Aug. 2006   Map 06 SP22

Pick of the Pubs

Kings Head Inn & Restaurant♦♦ ♀
The Green OX7 6XQ ☎ 01608 658365 ▤ 01608 658902
e-mail: kingshead@orr-ewing.com
See Pick of the Pubs on page 197

BLOCKLEY   Map 03 SP13

The Crown Inn & Hotel
High St GL56 9EX ☎ 01386 700245 ▤ 01386 700247
e-mail: info@crown-inn-blockley.co.uk
A sleepy, attractive village houses this mellow, 16th-century
coaching inn. The charming interior is filled with old beams,
log fires and exposed stone walls to create a warm and
welcoming atmosphere. Fine home-made country dishes and
specialities of the Cotswolds are served in the bar, including
moules marinière, Thai crab cakes, and fish and chips. The
Rafters Restaurant offers an interesting choice of food in a
smart setting.
OPEN: 11-11 **BAR MEALS:** Lunch served: all week Dinner served:
all week 12-2.30 6.30-9.30 Av main course £8
RESTAURANT: Lunch served: all week Dinner served: all week
12-2.30 7-9.30 Av 3 course à la carte £25
BREWERY/COMPANY: Free House **PRINCIPAL BEERS:** Hook
Norton Best, Scottish Courage John Smith's, Wadworth 6X.
FACILITIES: Garden: Food served outdoors Dogs allowed (water)
NOTES: Parking 40 **ROOMS:** 24 bedrooms 24 en suite from s£60
d£39.95

BOURTON-ON-THE-WATER   Map 03 SP12

The Duke of Wellington 🐾
Sherborne St GL54 2BY ☎ 01451 820539 ▤ 01451 810919
e-mail: mail@dukeofwellingtonbourton.co.uk
Standing right by the River Windrush, a pleasantly presented,
16th-century former coaching inn with large gardens that are
a tourist trap in summer. The open-plan bar leads to a dining
area where the pick of dishes is at night with tempura chicken
and Hoisin sauce, honey glazed ham and Cotswold sausages
with mash and onion gravy. A bonus is the Early Bird menu
until 7pm with faggots and mushy peas or beef stew and
dumplings at a set price. Only snacks at lunch.
OPEN: 12-3 5-11 (Summer all day) **BAR MEALS:** Lunch served:
all week Dinner served: all week 12-2.30 6-9.30 Av main course £7
RESTAURANT: Lunch served: all week Dinner served: all week
12-2.30 6-9.30 Av 3 course à la carte £15
BREWERY/COMPANY: Free House **FACILITIES:** Children
welcome Garden: River setting, seating, food served outside
NOTES: Parking 15 **ROOMS:** 4 bedrooms 4 en suite from s£40
d£45

Kingsbridge Inn ♀
Riverside GL54 2BS ☎ 01451 820371 ▤ 01451 810179
Village-centre inn with waterside bar, garden and patios by
the Windrush, and a childrens' play area. Diverse menu
choices include cod in home-made beer batter, guinea fowl
with chicken and cranberry mousse, daily pies, curries and
roast lunches: variously filled baguettes; childrens' menu and
Sunday lunch.

OPEN: 11-11 (Sun 12-10.30) **BAR MEALS:** Lunch served: all week
Dinner served: all week 11-3 6-9 Av main course £4.50
BREWERY/COMPANY: Eldridge Pope
PRINCIPAL BEERS: Deuchars IPA, Bass, Courage Best.
FACILITIES: Children welcome Garden: Outdoor eating, patio
Dogs allowed **NOTES:** Parking 5 **ROOMS:** 3 bedrooms 3 en suite
from s£39 d£54

BROCKWEIR   Map 03 SO50

Brockweir Country Inn 🐾
NP16 7NG ☎ 01291 689548
A 400-year-old inn, with a small garden and covered
courtyard, close to the River Wye in the old village of
Brockweir. It is popular with locals and retains many
characteristics of a traditional alehouse. Ideal for walkers
enjoying the unspoilt Wye Valley. Menu includes naturally
smoked haddock, home-cooked ham, Welsh steak, salmon in
butter with chilli, lime and coriander, and Cajun chicken.
OPEN: 12-3 6-11.30 (Sun 7-11.30) **BAR MEALS:** Lunch served: all
week Dinner served: all week 12-2.30 6-9 Av main course £5
RESTAURANT: 12-2.30 6-9 **BREWERY/COMPANY:** Free House
PRINCIPAL BEERS: Butcombe Bitter, Interbrew Bass, Hook Norton
Bitter. **FACILITIES:** Children welcome Garden: Food served outside
Dogs allowed **ROOMS:** 3 bedrooms d£35 No credit cards

CHALFORD   Map 03 SO80

Pick of the Pubs

The Crown Inn 🐾 ♀
Frampton Mansell GL6 8JG ☎ 01285 760601 ▤ 01285
760681
e-mail: crowninn@eldridge-pope.co.uk
A 17th-century coaching inn gloriously situated in the
heart of Stroud's Golden Valley. With its tastefully
furnished bedrooms the Crown makes an excellent base
for touring the Cotswolds, while nearby are the Royal
residences of Highgrove and Gatcombe Park. Honey-
coloured stone walls, old beams and an open fire from
September to May make for a warm atmosphere in the
bar, while the pub garden is a perfect summer spot, with
superb views of the surrounding countryside and, if
you're lucky, buzzards soaring overhead. Entirely home-
produced, seasonal menus featuring English lamb and
kiln-smoked salmon are supplemented by specials from
the chalkboard, such as hog roast with crispy crackling
and wild mushroom risotto with Parmesan shavings.
There is a selection of imaginative puds and a very decent
cheeseboard.
OPEN: 11-3 5.30-11 **BAR MEALS:** Lunch served: all week
Dinner served: all week 12-2.30 6.30-9.30 Av main course £8
RESTAURANT: Lunch served: all week Dinner served: all week
12-2.30 6.30-9.30 Av 3 course à la carte £25
BREWERY/COMPANY: Eldridge Pope
PRINCIPAL BEERS: Scottish Courage Courage Best, John
Smith's, Wadworth 6X. **FACILITIES:** Children welcome Garden:
Patio, food served outside Dogs allowed **NOTES:** Parking 100
ROOMS: 12 bedrooms 12 en suite from s£39 d£69

continued

OPEN: 11–2.30 6–11
BAR MEALS: L served all week.
D served all week. 12–2 7–9.30
RESTAURANT: L served all week.
D served all week. 12–2 7–9.30
Av cost 3 course £20
BREWERY/COMPANY:
FREE HOUSE
PRINCIPAL BEERS: Hook Norton
Bitter, Wadworth 6X, Shepherd
Neame Spitfire, Timothy Taylor
Landlord, Breakspear Bitter
FACILITIES: Garden: Food served
outside
NOTES: Parking 60
ROOMS: 12 en suite. Min price
double room £70. Min price single
room £50

Kings Head Inn

◆◆◆◆ ♀
The Green BLEDINGTON OX7 6XQ
☎ 01608 658365 📠 01608 658902
e-mail: kingshead@orr-ewing.com
Dir: On B4450 4m from Stow-on-the-Wold

Occupying a delightful setting on Gloucestershire's border with Oxfordshire, this 16th-century honey-coloured stone building represents the best of Cotswold inns. It offers excellent food, wines and ales plus re-vamped, comfortable accommodation.

The pub is located by the idyllic village green with its brook, stone bridge and patrolling ducks. Since the summer of 2000, when enthusiastic new owners Archie and Nicola Orr-Ewing took over the Kings Head, there have been significant and continuing improvements. Parts of the original cider house have survived, adding character to an interior of low ceilings, ancient beams, open fires, exposed stone walls and sturdy wooden furnishings. High-backed wooden settles, gate-leg or pedestal tables and a large black kettle hanging in the stone inglenook also enhance the surroundings. Real ales and an extensive wine list complement the menu which utilises seasonal produce, notably local game and fresh fish, and the impressive choice of dishes earned the pub a Country Dining Pub of the Year award for 2001. After a relaxing drink in the bar perhaps begin with game terrine set on a red onion marmalade and seasonal leaves before moving on to fresh linguine with baby leek, feta cheese, sun-dried tomato and a pesto dressing or medallions of fillet of pork, braised leek and chive-flavoured mashed potato. Alternative options might include oven roasted fillet of salmon, potato, garlic and saffron broth, and herb crusted rack of lamb with roast fennel, braised potato and red wine jus.

England

CHEDWORTH

Map 03 SP01

Hare & Hounds 🛏 ⛄
Foss Cross GL54 4NN ☎ 01285 720288 📠 01285 720488
Dir: *On A429(Fosse Way), 6m from Cirencester*
Situated on a remote stretch of the ancient Fosse Way and
surrounded by beautiful Cotswold countryside, this rustic stone
pub features flagged floors, splendid open fires, spiral
staircase, and working bread oven. A sample menu includes
pan-fried chicken supreme on ratatouille, baked pork fillet on
sage and celeriac purée, steak and ale suet pudding, swordfish
steak Cajun style, and calves' liver with bacon and mash.
OPEN: 11-3 6-11 **BAR MEALS:** Lunch served: all week Dinner
served: all week 12-2.30 7-9.45 Av main course £16.95
RESTAURANT: Lunch served: all week Dinner served: all week
11-2.30 6.30-9.45 Av 3 course à la carte £15
PRINCIPAL BEERS: Arkells 3B JRA. **FACILITIES:** Children welcome
Garden: Food served outside Dogs allowed (water)
NOTES: Parking 40

Seven Tuns 🛏 ⛄
Queen St GL54 4AE ☎ 01285 720242 📠 01285 720242
e-mail: seventuns@yahoo.com
Dir: *A40 then A429 towards Cirencester, after 5m R for Chedworth, 3m
then 3rd turning on R*

Traditional village inn dating back to 1610 and the ideal place
to relax in after an exhilarating walk in the Cotswolds. Handy
also for visiting nearby Chedworth Roman villa which can be
reached on foot. Directly opposite the inn, which takes its
name from seven chimney pots, are a waterwheel, a spring
and a raised terrace for summer drinking. The freshly
prepared daily-changing menu might feature braised rabbit,
cheese and walnuts with a Stilton sauce, steak and kidney pie
and ravioli. Well-kept real ales.
OPEN: 11-11 (Sun 12-10.30) (Nov-Mar 11-3, 6-11)
BAR MEALS: Lunch served: all week 12-3 Dinner served: Mon-Sat
6-10 Av main course £7 **RESTAURANT:** Lunch served: all week
Dinner served: all week 12-3 6-10 **BREWERY/COMPANY:** Free
House **PRINCIPAL BEERS:** Young's Bitter, Everards, Greene King
Abbot Ale. **FACILITIES:** Children welcome Garden: Beer garden,
patio, food served outdoors Dogs allowed (water, biscuits)
NOTES: Parking 30 **ROOMS:** 2 bedrooms 2 en suite from s£45 d£60

CHELTENHAM

Map 03 SO92

The Little Owl 🛏 ⛄
Cirencester Rd, Charlton Kings GL53 8EB
☎ 01242 529404 📠 01242 252523
e-mail: alan@littleowl.totalserve.co.uk
Dir: *on A435 Cirencester Rd, 2.5m from Cheltenham Spa*
This substantial double-fronted pub is handy for the popular
Cotswold Way and Cheltenham Racecourse, its unusual name

commemorates the Gold Cup winner of 1981. Its latest
addition is a luxurious function suite. Bar food includes many
traditional favourites supplemented with more up-to-date
renditions of green Thai chicken curry. Fresh fish delivered
daily might include gilt head bream and whole sea bass.
OPEN: 11.30-2.30 5.30-11.30 **BAR MEALS:** Lunch served: all week
Dinner served: all week 12-2 6.30-10 Av main course £8.50
RESTAURANT: Lunch served: all week Dinner served: all week 12-2
6.30-10 Av 3 course à la carte £18
BREWERY/COMPANY: Whitbread
PRINCIPAL BEERS: Wadworth 6X, Carlsberg-Tetley Tetley Bitter,
Fuller's London Pride, Goff's Jouster. **FACILITIES:** Children welcome
Garden: Food served outdoors, plum and apple trees Dogs allowed
(water) **NOTES:** Parking 40

CHIPPING CAMPDEN

Map 03 SP13

The Bakers Arms
Broad Campden GL55 6UR ☎ 01386 840515

Small Cotswold inn with a great atmosphere - visitors are
welcomed and regulars are involved with the quiz, darts and
crib teams. The traditional look of the place is reflected in its
time-honoured values, with good meals at reasonable prices
and a choice of four to five real ales. Typical specials are
marinated duck breast, cottage pie, smoked haddock bake,
chicken curry, mariners pie, and leek and mushroom crumble.
OPEN: 11.30-2.30 6-11 Mon-Sat 11.30-11, Summer open all day Sun
12-10.30 Closed: 25 Dec **BAR MEALS:** Lunch served: all week
Dinner served: all week 12-2 6-9 **RESTAURANT:** 6-9
BREWERY/COMPANY: Free House **PRINCIPAL BEERS:** Hook
Norton, Donnington, Stanway Bitter, Bombardier.
FACILITIES: Children welcome Garden: Food served outside. Grass
area Dogs allowed (garden only, water provided) **NOTES:** Parking
30 No credit cards

Pick of the Pubs

The Churchill Arms ◎ 🛏 ⛄
Paxford GL55 6XH ☎ 01386 594000 📠 01386 594005
e-mail: the-churchill-arms@hotmail.com
Dir: *2m E of Chipping Campden, 4m N of Moreton-in-Marsh*
Part of the ever-growing Sonya Kidney stable of food
lovers' pubs and. located in the heart of one of the most
sought-after villages in the north Cotswolds, the pub
enjoys magnificent views over the rolling countryside,
popular with walkers and lovers of outdoor pursuits.
Those lucky enough to stay overnight in the four cosy
bedrooms can be confident of a warm welcome and
cultured, modern-style pub food. Example from menus
that change daily are spiced tomato and herb soup and
duck salad with grapefruit and fennel salad, followed by
organic salmon with crisp bacon, rabbit loin with spiced

continued

continued

England

aubergine lentils and vegetarian options compiled in a trice. To these, add saffron-marinated mackerel with cucumber sauce, pork fillet with prunes and ginger, followed by sticky toffee pudding or pistachio and orange parfait fully to appreciate the range of treats on offer. The Churchill Arms deservedly continues to attract discerning custom.

OPEN: 11.30–3 6–11 **BAR MEALS:** Lunch served: all week Dinner served: all week 12-2 7-9 Av main course £10
RESTAURANT: Lunch served: all week Dinner served: all week 12-2 7-9 Av 3 course à la carte £20
BREWERY/COMPANY: Free House
PRINCIPAL BEERS: Hook Norton Bitter, Arkells 3B.
FACILITIES: Children welcome Garden: Beer garden, food served, patio **ROOMS:** 4 bedrooms 4 en suite from s£40 d£70

Pick of the Pubs

Eight Bells Inn
Church St GL55 6JG ☎ 01386 840371 📄 01386 841669
e-mail: neilhargreaves@bellinn.fsnet.co.uk
See Pick of the Pubs on page 200

The Noel Arms Hotel ★ ★ ★
High St GL55 6AT ☎ 01386 840317 📄 01386 841136
e-mail: bookings@cotswold-inns-hotels.co.uk
Civil War buffs will enjoy this 14th-century inn on the main street of perhaps the Cotswold's most attractive town. Charles II rested here in 1651 after his defeat by Cromwell at Worcester, and contemporary weaponry festoons its grand stone hall. Light meals are served in both the historic beamed bar and the modern conservatory and will include home-made pâté and delicious puddings. On offer in the restaurant could be marinated lamb chump with thyme and rosemary borlotti bean cassoulet, Parma ham-wrapped pork fillet with roasted new potatoes, apple and cider sauce, or a choice of two seafood main courses.
OPEN: 11–11 (Sun 12-10.30) **BAR MEALS:** Lunch served: all week Dinner served: Sat 12-2 7-9 Av main course £6.50
RESTAURANT: Lunch served: Sun Dinner served: all week 12-2 7-9.30 Av 3 course à la carte £21.95 **BREWERY/COMPANY:** Free House **PRINCIPAL BEERS:** Hook Norton, Interbrew Bass, Scottish Courage John Smith's. **FACILITIES:** Children welcome Food served outdoors Dogs allowed **NOTES:** Parking 25 **ROOMS:** 26 bedrooms 26 en suite from s£80 d£115

The Volunteer
Lower High St GL55 6DY ☎ 01386 840688 📄 01386 840543
e-mail: saravol@aol.com
A 300-year-old inn where in the mid-19th century the able-bodied used to sign up for the militia - hence its name. In the same family hands for over 17 years, its unspoilt local charm attracts many visitors, particularly to the 'olde worlde' rear garden by the River Cam where Aunt Sally is played in summer. Ramblers set off from here to walk the Cotswold Way refreshed by a pint from the six real ales. Food choices include home-made pies and casseroles, honey-roast ham and delicious summer salads.
OPEN: 11.30–3 5–11 (Sun 12-3, 7-10.30) **BAR MEALS:** Lunch served: all week Dinner served: all week 12-2 7-9 Av main course £7.50 **BREWERY/COMPANY:** Free House
PRINCIPAL BEERS: Hook Norton Best, North Cotswold Genesis, Stanway Bitter, Fuller's London Pride. **FACILITIES:** Garden: Food served outside **ROOMS:** 5 bedrooms 5 en suite from s£30 d£55

CIRENCESTER   Map 03 SP00

Bathurst Arms ♀
North Cerney GL7 7BZ ☎ 01285 831281 📄 01285 831155
Dir: *The Bathurst Arms is set back from the Cheltenham Rd (A435)*
Former coaching inn with bags of period charm - antique settles on flagstone floors, stone fireplaces, beams and panelled walls. The pretty garden stretches down to the River Churn, and a large barbecue is in use most summer weekends. Local delicacies include grilled Cerney goats' cheese with mixed leaves and walnuts, and trio of organic sausages with garlic mash and red onion gravy.
OPEN: 11–3 6–11 (Sun 12-2.30, 7-10.30) **BAR MEALS:** Lunch served: all week Dinner served: all week 12-2 7-9 Av main course £9.50 **RESTAURANT:** Lunch served: all week Dinner served: all week 12-2 7-9 Av 3 course à la carte £15
BREWERY/COMPANY: Free House **PRINCIPAL BEERS:** Hook Norton, Wadworth 6X,. **FACILITIES:** Children welcome Garden: Food served outside Dogs allowed **NOTES:** Parking 30 **ROOMS:** 5 bedrooms 5 en suite from s£45 d£65

Pick of the Pubs

The Crown of Crucis ★ ★ ★ ◎ ♀
Ampney Crucis GL7 5RS ☎ 01285 851806 📄 01285 851735
e-mail: info@thecrownofcrucis.co.uk
Dir: *On A417 to Lechlade, 2m E of Cirencester*

The unusual name of this stylish Cotswold hotel derives from the old cross that stands in the churchyard nearby. In a lovely setting, where swans meander along the river, assorted tables and chairs look out over the local cricket pitch. Built in two parts, the bar and dining areas are housed in the original 16th-century inn, while bedrooms are housed in a modern block that surrounds the courtyard. The casual, bubbling atmosphere attracts a broad church of clientele. Bar menus are similarly varied, with daily specials such as minced beef cobbler, cod Veronique and chicken chasseur prominently displayed. The regular Crown selection includes a 22oz mixed grill, cod in beer batter, chicken korma and spinach pancakes with cream cheese filling, followed by home-made desserts or a board of local cheeses.
OPEN: 10.30–11 (Sun 12–11) Closed: Dec 25
BAR MEALS: Lunch served: all week Dinner served: all week 12-2.30 6-10 Av main course £7 **RESTAURANT:** Lunch served: all week Dinner served: all week 12-2.30 7-9.30 Av 3 course fixed price £25.50 **BREWERY/COMPANY:** Free House
PRINCIPAL BEERS: Wadworth 6X, Archers Village, Scottish Courage John Smith's. **FACILITIES:** Children welcome Garden Food served outside, patio, riverside setting Dogs allowed **NOTES:** Parking 70 **ROOMS:** 25 bedrooms 25 en suite from s£64 d£92

OPEN: 11–3 5.30–11 (all day Jul-Aug)

BAR MEALS: L served all week. D served all week. 12–2.30 6.30–9.30 Av main course £9

RESTAURANT: L served all week. D served all week. 12–2.30 6.30–9.30

BREWERY/COMPANY: FREE HOUSE

PRINCIPAL BEERS: Hook Norton Best, Goff's Jouster, Hook Norton, guest beers

FACILITIES: Children welcome, dogs allowed. Garden: Courtyard, food served outside

ROOMS: 4 en suite Double room from £70 Single room from £40

The Eight Bells Inn

Church Street GL55 6JG
☎ 01386 840371 📠 01386 841669
e-mail: neilhargreaves@bellinn.fsnet.co.uk

A tiny, low Cotswold stone frontage conceals two atmospheric, cosy bars where both good ales and good food are taken quite seriously. Originally built in the 14th century to house the stonemasons and store the bells during construction of the nearby church, the original oak beams, open fireplaces and even a priest's hole still survive.

The pub continues to play a role as supplier of refreshment to this historic wool and silversmith town although many customers are now tourists. During the summer the pub is hung with attractive flower baskets. The pub can be entered through a cobbled entranceway where the two bars lead on through to the newly added dining room and an enclosed courtyard for drinking and dining - weather permitting. In these unspoilt surroundings, freshly prepared local food is offered on a daily changing menu. The good range of starters or light meals may seared scallops on balsamic marinated hot new potatoes, pheasant, pine kernel and mushroom terrine or fricassÈe of woodland mushrooms with venison sausage and caramelised shallot and garlic Tatin. Among the main courses are dishes such as baked red mullet niçoise or breast of pigeon with bitter chocolate shavings. Round off the meal with a pudding of treacle and hazelnut sponge or apple and sultana pancakes, or for those without a sweet-tooth a good selection of Continental and English cheeses with Scottish oat-cakes. Sunday roast lunch is served with nary a quick sandwich to be seen. A barn has been converted to house en suite accommodation.

England

CLEARWELL
Map 03 SO50

Pick of the Pubs

Wyndham Arms ★ ★ ★ 🛏 ♀
GL16 8JT ☎ 01594 833666 📠 01594 836450
Dir: In centre of village on the B4231
This highly civilised small hotel is at the heart of an
enchanting village on the fringe of the Royal Forest of
Dean. It has discernible origins back in the 14th century,
with additions in the 16th and a relatively new bedroom
block to meet guests' expectations of the 21st. The
Stanford family's ownership and love of the setting lives
on with style and enthusiasm. A bustling bar offering
hand-pulled real ales, good wines and a notable malt
whisky collection attracts a well-heeled clientele. In the
bar, snacks may include pear with Stilton and orange
mayonnaise, a mermaid's seafood salad or chicken liver
pâté, leading on to numerous grills, chicken breast with
barbecue sauce, and spinach and cheese roulade with
walnuts and spring onions. Tempting desserts include
tiramisù and a chocoholic sundae. In the restaurant, fixed-
price lunches and dinner are backed up with items from
the carte such as Wyndham tournedos and poached
salmon steak with fish velouté.
OPEN: 11–11 (Sun 12–10.30) Closed: 23 Dec
BAR MEALS: Lunch served: all week Dinner served: all week 12–2
6.45–9 Av main course £10 **RESTAURANT:** Lunch served: all
week Dinner served: all week 12–2 6.45–9.30 Av 3 course à la carte
£20 Av 3 course fixed price £20 **BREWERY/COMPANY:** Free
House **PRINCIPAL BEERS:** Interbrew Bass.
FACILITIES: Children welcome Garden: Food served outside,
patio Dogs allowed **NOTES:** Parking 50 **ROOMS:** 18 bedrooms
18 en suite from s£55 d£75

COLD ASTON
Map 03 SP11

The Plough Inn
GL54 3BN ☎ 01451 821459 📠 01451 824000
Dir: village signed from A436 & A429 SW of Stow-on-the-Wold

A delightful 17th-century pub standing at the heart of this
lovely Cotswold village close to Stow-on-the-Wold, at a
convergence point of four major Cotswold walks. Full of old
beams, flagstone floors, cottagey windows and open log fires
in winter. Typical menu includes steak and kidney pie, chicken
and leek pie, shank of lamb, red Thai curry, and salmon
fishcakes. Patio and garden for summer alfresco drinking.
Under new management.
OPEN: 11.30–2.30 6.30–11 (Sun 12–3, 7–10.30)
BAR MEALS: Lunch served: all week Dinner served: all week 12–2
6.30–9 Av main course £6.95 **BREWERY/COMPANY:** Free House

continued

PRINCIPAL BEERS: Hook Norton, Donningtons, Adnams.
FACILITIES: Children welcome Garden: Food served outside Dogs
allowed (garden only) **NOTES:** Parking 30

COLESBOURNE
Map 03 SP01

The Colesbourne Inn ♀
GL53 9NP ☎ 01242 870376 📠 01242 870397
e-mail: info@colesbourneinn.com
Dir: On A435 (Cirencester to Cheltenham road)
Large log fires, beams, cosy bedrooms in the converted
stables and a large garden overlooking wooded hills are all
features of this 18th-century coaching inn. The interior is
decorated with a wealth of bric-a-brac, and there are cask ales
to sup and traditional food in both lounge bar and dining
room. Lunch might offer boiled gammon and wild boar
sausages with favourites at night that take in pan-fried king
prawns and scallops and lamb or beef sizzlers.
OPEN: 11.30–3 6.30–11 **BAR MEALS:** Lunch served: all week Dinner
served: all week 12–2.30 7–9.30 Av main course £11
RESTAURANT: Lunch served: all week Dinner served: all week
12–2.30 7–9.30 Av 3 course à la carte £21
BREWERY/COMPANY: Wadworth **PRINCIPAL BEERS:** Wadworth
6X, Henrys IPA, Badger Tanglefoot. **FACILITIES:** Children welcome
Garden: Food served outside Dogs allowed (water, toys)
NOTES: Parking 40 **ROOMS:** 9 bedrooms 9 en suite from s£45 d£65

COLN ST-ALDWYNS
Map 03 SP10

Pick of the Pubs

The New Inn At Coln ★ ★ 🏮🏮 🛏 ♀
GL7 5AN ☎ 01285 750651 📠 01285 750657
e-mail: stay@new-inn.co.uk
See Pick of the Pubs on page 203

COWLEY
Map 03 SO91

Pick of the Pubs

The Green Dragon Inn 🛏
Cockleford GL53 9NW ☎ 01242 870271 📠 01242 870171
A 17th-century building set slightly back from the A435 in
the hamlet of Cockleford - a tranquil, picturesque setting.
Refitted some three years ago with purpose-built furniture
by Yorkshire craftsman, Robert Thompson, his unique
moniker lends its name to the popular Mouse Bar, whose
stone-flagged floors, beamed ceilings and crackling log
fires add to its cosy individuality. Light meals from warm
salad of grilled Brie and bacon and salmon and dill
fishcakes with lemon mayonnaise come in two sizes, with
main dishes listing Gloucester Old Spot sausages on leek
mash and roast duck breast with plum sauce. Look too for
the daily specials such as seafood thermidor or chicken
breast stuffed with avocado and cream cheese, with
banoffee pie or English cheeses to follow. Also on offer
are good real ales, a heated dining terrace and some
comfortable courtyard bedrooms.
OPEN: 11–11 **BAR MEALS:** Lunch served: all week Dinner
served: all week 12–2.30 6.30–10.30 Av main course £7.95
BREWERY/COMPANY: Free House
PRINCIPAL BEERS: Hook Norton, Wadsworth 6X, Courage Best
Bitter, Smiles Best Bitter. **FACILITIES:** Children welcome
Garden: Food served outside Dogs allowed (water)
NOTES: Parking 100 **ROOMS:** 9 bedrooms 9 en suite from
s£40 d£55

CRANHAM   Map 03 SO81

The Black Horse Inn 🛏
GL4 8HP ☎ 01452 812217
Dir: A46 towards Stroud, follow signs for Cranham
Situated in a small village surrounded by woodland and
commons, a mile from the Cotswold Way and Prinknash
Abbey, this is a traditional inn with two open fires, a stone-
tiled floor and two dining rooms upstairs. On the menu you
may find beef and Guinness pie, toad-in-the-hole, lamb and
apricot casserole, or Mediterranean cod fishcakes. Any eggs
used have probably come from the pub's own chickens. A
wide range of fresh fish is also served. Quite a bit of Morris
dancing throughout the season.
OPEN: 11.30–2.30 6.30–11 (Sun 12–3, 7–10.30) Closed: 25 Dec
BAR MEALS: Lunch served: all week 12–2 Dinner served: Mon–Sat
6.45–9 Av main course £7.50 **RESTAURANT:** Lunch served: all week
Dinner served: Mon–Sat **BREWERY/COMPANY:** Free House
PRINCIPAL BEERS: Wickwar Brand Oak, Hook Norton, Marstons
Pedigree, Flowers Original. **FACILITIES:** Children welcome Garden:
Dogs allowed **NOTES:** Parking 25

DIDMARTON   Map 03 ST88

Pick of the Pubs

The Kings Arms ♦♦♦♦ ♀
The Street GL9 1DT ☎ 01454 238245 📠 01454 238249
e-mail: info@kadidmarton.com
*Dir: M4 Junct 18 take A46 N signed Stroud, after 8m take A433
signed Didmarton 2m*

An attractive 17th-century coaching inn on the fringe of
the Badminton Estate, the pub was originally leased from
the Beaufort family for 1,000 years at six (old) pence per
year. An ideal base for exploring the area, being near
Westonbirt Arboretum and horse trials at Badminton and
Gatcombe Park. Accommodation includes four en suite
bedrooms and self-catering holiday cottages in the former
stable block and barn. A selection of guest real ales is
offered in the two beamed bars, which retain their
original character and are busy with tourists and locals.
On offer here might be game terrine, haddock in beer
batter and pork and hop sausages with champ and onion
gravy. Though the restaurant is a tad more formal, dishes
from the monthly dining menu may also be ordered in
the bar. Typical dishes include baked goats' cheese with
sautéed leeks or casseroled venison with buttered
noodles. Home-made desserts include treacle tart and
poached pears with pecan toffee sauce.
OPEN: 12–3 6–11 (Sun 12–3, 7–10.30) **BAR MEALS:** Lunch
served: all week Dinner served: all week 12–1.45 7–9.30 Av main
course £10.95 **RESTAURANT:** Lunch served: all week 12–1.45

continued

Dinner served: Mon–Sat 7–9.30 Av 3 course à la carte £20
BREWERY/COMPANY: Free House **PRINCIPAL BEERS:** Uley
Bitter, Scottish Courage John Smiths. **FACILITIES:** Garden: Food
served outside, picnic benches Dogs allowed **NOTES:** Parking
28 **ROOMS:** 4 bedrooms 4 en suite from s£45 d£70

DURSLEY   Map 03 ST79

Pickwick Inn 🛏
Lower Wick GL11 6DD ☎ 01453 810259 📠 01453 810259
e-mail: gerryrichard@amserve.co.uk
Built in 1762, this has always been an inn, but has also
doubled as a barber's and a slaughterhouse. The restaurant
was built on in the mid-1980s, and the bar has an Old Codger
Corner especially reserved for elderly regulars. Log burners
warm the building in cooler months. Typical menu includes
duck in black cherry sauce, Pickwick special mixed grill, steak
and ale pie, and plenty of fish options.
OPEN: 11–11 (Sun 12–10.30) **BAR MEALS:** Lunch served: all week
Dinner served: all week 12–2.30 6.30–10 Av main course £5
RESTAURANT: Lunch served: all week Dinner served: all week
12–2.30 6.30–10 Av 3 course à la carte £15
BREWERY/COMPANY: Youngs **PRINCIPAL BEERS:** Youngs
Bitter, Youngs Special, Wagale Dance. **FACILITIES:** Children welcome
Garden: Food served outside. Lawn & flower beds
NOTES: Parking 80

EBRINGTON   Map 03 SP14

Ebrington Arms 🛏
Ebrington GL55 6NH ☎ 01386 593223
A charmingly down-to-earth village pub dating from the mid-
18th century, with plenty of beams to go with traditional
flagstone floors and large inglenook fireplaces. Walkers
frequent the pub for its locally-brewed ales and good home-
cooked food, including gammon with eggs or pineapple, filled
crêpes, and lasagne at lunchtime, and lamb shanks in
redcurrant sauce or medallions of pork in cider in the
evening. New owners are planning a complete upgrade to be
completed for 2003.
OPEN: 11–2.30 6–11 **BAR MEALS:** Lunch served: Tues–Sun Dinner
served: Tues–Sat 12–2 6–9 Av main course £7 **RESTAURANT:** Lunch
served: Tues–Sun Dinner served: Tues–Sat 12–2 6–9 Av 3 course à la
carte £15 **BREWERY/COMPANY:** Free House
PRINCIPAL BEERS: Hook Norton Best, Donnington SBA Carlsberg-
Tetely Tetely Smooth. **FACILITIES:** Children welcome Garden: Food
served outside Dogs allowed (water) **NOTES:** Parking 12
ROOMS: 2 bedrooms 2 en suite from d£50

EWEN   Map 03 SU09

Pick of the Pubs

The Wild Duck ★ ★ 🏨 🛏 ♀
Drakes Island GL7 6BY ☎ 01285 770310 📠 01285 770924
e-mail: wduckinn@aol.com
See Pick of the Pubs on page 204

♦ **Indicates AA inspected
bed & breakfast accommodation**

OPEN: 11-11 (Sun 12-10.30)
BAR MEALS: L served all week.
D served all week. 12-2 7-9
Av main course £10
RESTAURANT: L served all week.
D served all week. 12-2 7-9
BREWERY/COMPANY
FREE HOUSE
PRINCIPAL BEERS: Hook Norton
Best Bitter, Wadworth 6X,
Butcombe Bitter
FACILITIES: Dogs allowed. Garden:
Food served outside. Terrace area
NOTES: Parking 24
ROOMS: 14 en suite Double room
from £110 Single room from £80

The New Inn At Coln

Entering its tenth year since rescue from near-dereliction, this is a remarkable tale of an inn that was old when Christopher Wren was building St Paul's, for over the intervening centuries little of the inn's fabric has changed, but how times have.

★ ★ ◉◉ ♀
COLN ST-ALDWYNS GL7 5AN
☎ 01285 750651 📠 01285 750657
e-mail: stay@new-inn.co.uk
Dir: Between Bibury (B4425) & Fairford
(A417), 8m E of Cirencester.

The bedrooms offer every modern comfort yet the bars with flagstone floors, exposed beams and open fires, as well as the flower-filled summer courtyard, show that the 16th century has ceded gracefully to the 21st. Freshly prepared dishes such as gratin of whiting and macaroni, satay chicken with roasted peanuts and Caesar salad with poached egg may be taken in small or large portions, while ambitious choices from an ever-changing main menu may likely include traditional fish and chips with mushy peas alongside ribeye

steak, field mushrooms and tomato. More adventurously, go for salmon omelette with crème fraiche, sweet and sour pork stir-fry with pineapple or daube of beef with smoked bacon and mushrooms; following with an envious choice between apple and cinnamon crumble and pannacotta with a thyme-roasted plum. Real ales and quality wines are legion, appealing equally to partakers of the imaginative fixed-price menus offered in the restaurant. Remarkable indeed.

OPEN: 11-11 (Sun 12-10.30)
BAR MEALS: L served all week.
D served all week. 12-2 7-10
Av main course £6.95
RESTAURANT: L served all week.
D served all week. 12-2 7-10
Av cost 3 course £20
BREWERY/COMPANY: FREE
HOUSE
PRINCIPAL BEERS: Theakston Old
Peculier, Wells Bombardier, Greene
King, Old Speckled Hen, Smiles Best
FACILITIES: Children welcome,
dogs allowed
GARDEN Food served outside
NOTES: Parking 50
ROOMS: 11 en suite Double room
from £80 Single room from £60

The Wild Duck

The Wild Duck is a mellow Cotswold stone Elizabethan inn, which was converted over the years from a collection of barns, goat sheds and a farm cottage and is steeped in character. The unusual clock on the outside wall is surrounded by a series of ducks in flight which light up in sequence.

★ ★ ⊚ ♀
Drakes Island, Ewen GL7 6BY
☎ 01285 770310 📄 01285 770924
e-mail: wduckinn@aol.com
Dir: From Cirencester take A429, at Kemble take L turn to Ewen, pub in village centre

In many ways a typical local inn, it boasts a great many exposed beams, plenty of oak panelling and open fires, with old portraits of English ancestors adorning the walls. Well-equipped bedrooms, all en suite, feature several four poster beds and fully up-to-date facilities. The delightful garden is secluded, and makes an ideal place for summer dining. The country-style dining room offers fresh seasonal food, including game in winter and fresh fish from Brixham delivered overnight.

The food is traditionally British with a hint of European and Oriental influences, and vegetarian choices are always available. A daily board highlights snacks served throughout the day to supplement light lunches such as wild boar and apple sausages with crushed potatoes and mustard sauce, fettuccini pasta with Rocquefort cheese, walnuts and parsley, and Italian bean broth with basil dumplings. In the evening, the choice ranges around wok-fried monkfish and tiger prawns with a coconut and chilli sauce, pan-fried lamb chump on a feta cheese and black olive salad, and goats' cheese and asparagus with a red pepper salad. Exotic fare such as parrot fish and tilapia is also sometimes served. Real ales are kept in tip-top condition, and there's an eclectic choice of wines from an extensive list. A wide range of cigars is also kept.

FORD   Map 03 SP02

Plough Inn ♀
GL54 5RU ☎ 01386 584215 🖷 01386 584215
e-mail: Plough.ford.glos@ukonline.co.uk
Dir: *4m from Stow-on-the-Wold on the Tewkesbury road*
Long a favourite of Cotswold ramblers and lovers of the
traditional English pub everywhere, the interior of the idyllic
little 13th-century Plough Inn, with its flagstone floors,
warming open fires, sturdy pine furnishings and lively
conversation, has all the atmosphere you could wish for.
Blackboards list the day's menu, the interesting choice may
include home-made soups and pâtés, steak and Guinness pie,
home-baked gammon and eggs, beef and mushrooms in red
wine, pork tenderloin in mustard sauce and fresh Donnington
trout. A notable event is the traditional spring asparagus feasts
(April-June). Excellent Donnington ales and accommodation in
simple en suite bedrooms.
OPEN: 11-11 (Sun 12-10.30) Closed: Dec 25 **BAR MEALS:** Lunch
served: all week Dinner served: Mon-Sat 12-2 6.30-9 Av main course
£6.95 **PRINCIPAL BEERS:** Donnington BB & SBA.
FACILITIES: Children welcome Garden: Food served outside
NOTES: Parking 50 **ROOMS:** 3 bedrooms 3 en suite from s£35
d£48

FOSSEBRIDGE   Map 03 SP01

Pick of the Pubs

Fossebridge Inn 🐾 ♀
GL54 3JS ☎ 01285 720721 🖷 01285 720793
e-mail: fossebridgeinn@aol.com
Dir: *From M4 J15, take A419 towards Cirencester, then take A429*
towards Stow, pub approx 7m on L
A long-standing favourite, the creeper-clad Fossebridge
makes an ideal base for touring the Cotswolds and for
visits to Bibury, Northleach and Chedworth. A Roman
settlement stood here at the spot where the Fosse Way
once crossed the River Coln: the gardens that run
alongside the river are a picture in summer. Inside, the
beamed Bridge Bar with its flagstone floors and open fires
is Tudor and the main hotel building looking out on the
gardens is certainly Regency. Typical of favourite bar
snacks are the smoked salmon with scrambled eggs,
home-made cheese and bacon beefburgers with chunky
chips and Mediterranean roast vegetables on ciabatta
topped with grilled goats' cheese. Set-price and à la carte
menus change daily, offering a commendably wide
choice. From the former, select warm bacon and cherry
tomato salad, slow roast lamb with root vegetables
and tangy lemon tartlets. At the top of the range, dinner
runs to chilli tiger prawns on coriander noodles, venison
steak with sorrel cream sauce and Parma ham potatoes
and vanilla poached pear with chocolate sauce.
OPEN: 11-3 6-11 **BAR MEALS:** Lunch served: all week Dinner
served: all week 12-2.30 6.30-9.30 Av main course £8
RESTAURANT: Lunch served: all week Dinner served: all week
12-2.30 6.30-9.30 Av 3 course à la carte £18 Av 3 course fixed price
£11.95 **BREWERY/COMPANY:** Free House
PRINCIPAL BEERS: Hook Norton Best, Greene King Old Speckled
Hen, Black Sheep Best. **FACILITIES:** Children welcome Garden:
3.5 acres, food served outside Dogs allowed **NOTES:** Parking 34
ROOMS: 10 bedrooms 10 en suite from s£49.50 d£49.50

GLOUCESTER   Map 03 SO81

Queens Head 🐾 ♀
Tewkesbury Rd, Longford GL2 9EJ
☎ 01422 301882 🖷 01422 524 368
e-mail: finefoodpub@aol.com
Dir: *On the A38 Tewkesbury to Gloucester road in the village of Longford*

Just out of town, this 250 year-old pub/restaurant, which is
festooned with hanging baskets in summer, looks back
towards the city and cathedral. There's a lovely old locals' bar
with flagstoned floor and two dining areas. The pub is popular
so booking is essential at weekends. In addition to the
renowned slow-roasted Longford lamb, evening specials may
list fresh calamari with teriyaki sauce, sea bream fillets and
classic osso buco in herb and root vegetable sauce.
OPEN: 11-3 5.30-11 **BAR MEALS:** Lunch served: all week Dinner
served: all week 12-2 6.30-9.30 Av main course £9.50
RESTAURANT: Lunch served: all week Dinner served: all week 12-2
6.30-9.30 Av 3 course à la carte £12.50
BREWERY/COMPANY: Free House
PRINCIPAL BEERS: Interbrew Bass, Greene King Old Seckled Hen,
Hook Norton Best. **NOTES:** Parking 40

GREAT BARRINGTON   Map 06 SP21

The Fox ♀
OX18 4TB ☎ 01451 844385
Few pubs in this area offer a more picturesque setting than
the Fox. On warm days the delightful patio and large beer
garden overlooking the River Windrush attract drinkers and
alfresco diners, making it a perfect summer watering hole.
Built of mellow Cotswold stone and characterised by low
ceilings and log fires, the inn offers a range of well-kept
Donnington beers and a choice of food which might include
beef and ale pie, sea bass, Thai curry and various home-made
chillies and casseroles.
OPEN: 11-11 **BAR MEALS:** Lunch served: all week Dinner served: all
week 12-2.30 6.30-9.30 Av main course £8.50 **RESTAURANT:** Lunch
served: all week Dinner served: all week 12-2.30 6.30-9.30 Av 3 course à
la carte £16.50 **PRINCIPAL BEERS:** Donnington BB, SBA.
FACILITIES: Children welcome Garden: Food served outside Dogs
allowed **NOTES:** Parking 60 **ROOMS:** 4 bedrooms 4 en suite from
s£37.50 d£64

♀ **Pubs offering six or more wines by the glass**

GREAT RISSINGTON · Map 03 SP11

The Lamb Inn 🛏 🍷
GL54 2LP ☎ 01451 820388 📠 01451 820724
Dir: Between Oxford & Cheltenham off A40
Make this delightful former farmhouse your base for exploring the picturesque Cotswold countryside on foot and touring the region's famous old towns by car. Many other popular attractions lie within easy reach of this busy inn, parts of which date back 300 years. Among the more unusual features here is part of a Wellington bomber which crashed in the garden in 1943. Home-cooked pub food might include shoulder of Cotswold lamb with redcurrant and red wine gravy, roast fillet of salmon, or a choice of casseroles.
OPEN: 11.30–2.30 6.30–11 **BAR MEALS:** Lunch served: all week Dinner served: all week 12-2 7–9 Av main course £8.95 **RESTAURANT:** Lunch served: all week Dinner served: all week 12–2 7–9 Av 3 course à la carte £16 **BREWERY/COMPANY:** Free House **PRINCIPAL BEERS:** Hook Norton, John Smiths, Wychwood, Greene King. **FACILITIES:** Children welcome Children's licence Garden: Food served outside.Overlooks Windrush Valley Dogs allowed (In the garden. Water & toys provided) **NOTES:** Parking 15 **ROOMS:** 14 bedrooms 14 en suite from s£40 d£50

GREET · Map 03 SP03

The Harvest Home 🛏 🍷
Evesham Rd GL54 5BH ☎ 01242 602430
e-mail: steveandsarah@theharvesthome.freeserve.co.uk
Dir: M5 J9 take A435 towards Evesham, then B4077 & B4078 towards Winchcombe. 200 yds from Winchcombe station.
Traditional country inn built in the early 1900s to serve the Great Western Railway, which is now run past the end of the garden by steam enthusiasts. Surrounded by pretty Cotswold villages, and handy for Cheltenham Racecourse and Sudeley Castle. Expect a good range of snacks including baguettes and burgers, plus various specials and five fish and five steak dishes. Separate kids' menu of standard fare.
OPEN: 11–3 (12–3 in Winter) 6–11 (Sun 6–10.30) **BAR MEALS:** Lunch served: all week Dinner served: all week 12-2.30 6–9.30 Av main course £8.50 **RESTAURANT:** Lunch served: all week Dinner served: all week 12-2.30 6–9.30 Av 3 course à la carte £16 **BREWERY/COMPANY:** Whitbread **PRINCIPAL BEERS:** Fuller's London Pride, Greene King IPA & Old Speckled Hen. **FACILITIES:** Children welcome Children's licence Garden: Patio/terrace, BBQ, food served outdoors Dogs allowed **NOTES:** Parking 30

GUITING POWER · Map 03 SP02

The Hollow Bottom ♦♦♦ 🛏
GL54 5UX ☎ 01451 850392 📠 01451 850392
e-mail: hollow.bottom@virgin.net
Dir: From Stow-on-the-Wold take B4068 (approx 5m) past golf course, 2nd R signed Guiltings, at T-junc, R again, next left signed Guiting Power
An 18th-century, Cotswold stone pub with a horse-racing theme, and frequent visits from the racing fraternity associated with Cheltenham. A number of nooks and crannies for an intimate drink or meal, and there's a separate dining room plus tables outside for fine weather. Freshly made dishes like grilled marlin with warm butter sauce, crocodile tail cooked in wine with a mustard sauce, and pan-fried lamb cutlets, with a carvery on Sundays. Three smart bedrooms available.

OPEN: 11-11 **BAR MEALS:** Lunch served: all week Dinner served: all week 9.30 Av main course £8 **RESTAURANT:** Lunch served: all week Dinner served: all week to 9.30 Av 3 course à la carte £16 **BREWERY/COMPANY:** Free House **PRINCIPAL BEERS:** Hook Norton Bitter, Wadworth 6X, Goff's Jouster. **FACILITIES:** Children welcome Garden: Food served outdoors Dogs allowed **NOTES:** Parking 15 **ROOMS:** 3 bedrooms 2 en suite from s£30 d£50

HINTON · Map 03 ST77

The Bull Inn
SN14 8HG ☎ 0117 9372332 📠 0117 9372332
Dir: From M4 Junc 18, A46 to Bath for 1m then R, 1m down hill, Bull on R
15th-century farmhouse off the old London to Bath road, converted to an inn about 100 years ago. Traditional pub atmosphere, with bars and non-smoking area candlelit in the evening. Food is freshly prepared on the premises, and the varied menu is offered throughout. Expect beef, ale and mushroom pie, shark and monkfish curry, and Moroccan spiced lamb with apricots, almonds and prunes.
OPEN: 11.30–3 6–11 (Sun 6.30-10.30) **BAR MEALS:** Lunch served: all week Dinner served: all week 11.30-2 6-9.00 Av main course £8.95 **RESTAURANT:** Lunch served: all week Dinner served: all week 11.30-2 6–9 Av 3 course à la carte £20 **BREWERY/COMPANY:** Wadworth **PRINCIPAL BEERS:** Wadworth 6X & Henrys IPA, Interbrew Bass. **FACILITIES:** Children welcome Garden: Food served outside Dogs allowed **NOTES:** Parking 30

HYDE · Map 03 SO80

Ragged Cot Inn 🍷
Cirencester Rd GL6 8PE ☎ 01453 884643 📠 01453 731166
e-mail: davidsauagk-@oasisholdings-.com
Dir: From M5 take A429 for Cirencester, Hyde 2m after Stroud on R
Set high up on Minchinhampton Common, this 17th-century Cotswold free house is the perfect base for a weekend break. Set within easy reach of Stratford, Bath and Cheltenham, it epitomises the coaching inn, with a real inglenook log fires, oak beams and exposed stonework. The bar is the focal point, with its comfortable settles and traditional pub games. Home-made bar snacks include lasagne, chicken curry, and steak, ale and mushroom pie. Separate restaurant menu.
OPEN: 11-3.00 5-11 (open all day Sat-Sun) Closed: 25 Dec **BAR MEALS:** Lunch served: all week Dinner served: all week 12-2.30 6.30-9.30 Av main course £5.95 **RESTAURANT:** Lunch served: all week Dinner served: all week 12-2.30 6.30-9.30 Av 3 course à la carte £15 **BREWERY/COMPANY:** Free House **PRINCIPAL BEERS:** Interbrew Bass, Theakston Best Bitter, Uley Old Spot Prize Ale, Badger Tanglefoot. **FACILITIES:** Children welcome Garden: Food served outside Dogs allowed (manager's discretion) **NOTES:** Parking 55 **ROOMS:** 10 bedrooms 10 en suite from s£40 d£60

continued

LECHLADE   Map 04 SU29

The Five Alls ♀
Filkins GL7 3JQ ☎ 01367 860306 📠 01367 860776
Dir: *A40 exit Burford, Filkins 4m, A361 to Lechlade*
New landlords have recently moved into this 17th-century inn,
set in a peaceful Cotswold village just outside Lechlade.
Comfortable, traditionally styled bedrooms are a perennial
draw, as are the popular Sunday lunches. The new food
operation is offering home-made pies such as steak and
kidney and chicken and mushroom, with a range of grilled
sirloin and fillet steaks. The lawned garden has an over-sized
chess set and a patio for a summer snack outdoors. A clear
case of 'watch this space!'.
OPEN: 11–3 6–11 **BAR MEALS:** Lunch served: all week Dinner served:
all week 11.30–2 7–9.30 Av main course £8 **RESTAURANT:** Lunch
served: all week Dinner served: all week 11.30–2 7–9.30
BREWERY/COMPANY: Free House **PRINCIPAL BEERS:** Hook
Norton Best, Old Hooky. **FACILITIES:** Children welcome Garden:
Patio, food served outside Dogs allowed **NOTES:** Parking 100
ROOMS: 6 bedrooms 6 en suite from s£40 d£55

The Five Bells Broadwell ♦♦♦
Broadwell GL7 3QS ☎ 01367 860076
e-mail: trevorcooper@skynow.net
Dir: *A361 from Lechlade to Burford, after 2m R to Kencot Broadwell, then
R after 200m, then R at crossrds*

Attractive 16th-century Cotswold stone inn overlooking the
manor and parish church. The bars are full of character with
beams and flagstones, and the conservatory leads to a pretty
garden. An extensive choice of dishes includes salmon and
prawn gratin, pheasant in red wine, and steak and kidney pie.
Accommodation comes in the shape of five luxury chalets.
OPEN: 11.30–2.30 7–11 (Sun 12–3, 7–10.30) Closed: Mon except BHs
25 & 26 Dec **BAR MEALS:** 12–1.45 7–9 **RESTAURANT:** Lunch
served: Tue–Sun 12–1.45 Dinner served: Tue–Sat 7–9
BREWERY/COMPANY: Free House
PRINCIPAL BEERS: Interbrew Bass Bitter, Archers Village.
FACILITIES: Children welcome Garden: Dogs allowed
NOTES: Parking 30 **ROOMS:** 5 bedrooms 5 en suite from d£50

The Trout Inn 🍴 ♀
St Johns Bridge GL7 3HA ☎ 01367 252313
Dir: *From A40 take A361 then A417. From M4 to Lechlade then A417 to Trout*
Dating from around 1220, a former almshouse with a large
garden on the banks of the Thames. Things are generally
humming here, with tractor and steam events, jazz and folk
festivals and sustenance for all, right down to baby food. The
interior is all flagstone floors and beams in a bar that
overflows into the old boat house. Soups, pizza and burgers
graduate to grilled local trout, sausage and cider hotpot and
mushrooms à la king in creamy pepper sauce.

OPEN: 10–3 6–11 **BAR MEALS:** Lunch served: all week Dinner
served: all week 12–2 7–10 Av main course £10
PRINCIPAL BEERS: Wadworth 6X, Scottish Courage Courage
Directors & Courage Best. **FACILITIES:** Children welcome
Garden: Food served outside, overlooking Weir Pool Dogs
allowed (water)

LITTLE WASHBOURNE   Map 03 SO93

Hobnail's Inn ♀
GL20 8NQ ☎ 01242 620237 📠 01242 620458
e-mail: finefoodpub@aol.com
Dir: *From J9 of the M5 take A46 towards Evesham then B4077 to Stow on
Wold. Hobnails is1 1/2 m on the L*
15th century exposed beams, a log fire and various other
character features complement this charming old inn which,
until recently, was owned by the same family for about 250
years. Well-known in the area, the pub is within easy reach
of the region's many attractions, including the scenic
Cotswolds, Beckford Silk Mill and Sudeley Castle. Food
ranges from filled baps to marinated lamb, beef cooked in
beer and herbs with creamed horseradish potato, and
scampi.
OPEN: 11–3 6–11 (May–Sept 11–11) **BAR MEALS:** Lunch served: all
week Dinner served: all week 11–2 6.30–9.30 Av main course £6.25
RESTAURANT: Dinner served: all week 6.30–9.30 Av 3 course à la
carte £12 **BREWERY/COMPANY:** Free House
PRINCIPAL BEERS: Jousters, Fullers London Pride,.
FACILITIES: Children welcome Garden: Food served outside Dogs
allowed **NOTES:** Parking 80

LOWER APPERLEY   Map 03 SO82

The Farmers Arms 🍴
Ledbury Rd GL19 4DR ☎ 01452 780307 📠 780307
Dir: *On B4213 SE of Tewkesbury (off A38)*
This traditional country pub is in a lovely setting between the
Cotswolds and the Malverns, with extensive views towards
Cheltenham. A warm welcome in the traditional bar, with its
low beams, open fire, and real ales to go with the extensive
menu including fresh fish. Expect monkfish with an orange
and brandy sauce, Stilton chicken, mushroom Stroganoff,
kidneys in red wine with shallots, and saddle of lamb in a rich
red wine sauce.
OPEN: 11–2.30 6–11 **BAR MEALS:** Lunch served: all week Dinner
served: Mon–Sat 12–2 6–9 Av main course £8.95
RESTAURANT: Lunch served: all week 12–2 Dinner served:
Mon–Sun 6–9 Av 3 course à la carte £15
BREWERY/COMPANY: Wadworth
PRINCIPAL BEERS: Wadworth 6X, Henry's Original IPA plus guest
beers. **FACILITIES:** Children welcome Garden: Patio, food served
outside **NOTES:** Parking 60

continued

LOWER ODDINGTON
Map 06 SP22

Pick of the Pubs

The Fox 🛏 ♀
GL56 0UR ☎ 01451 870555 📠 01451 870669
e-mail: info@foxinn.net

See Pick of the Pubs on page 209

LYDNEY
Map 03 SO60

The George Inn 🛏 ♀
St Briavels GL15 6TA ☎ 01594 530228 📠 01594 530260

In a quiet village high above the Wye Valley and close to the Forest of Dean, the pub overlooks a moody 12th-century castle ruin. The pub possesses an interior of great character. Local produce features high on grills and specials menus. Ever-popular are the traditional steak and kidney and beef and Guinness pies, fresh fish such as fresh prawns, plaice and sea bass alongside daily specials assorted curries. Comfortable bedrooms and a flagstone terrace: walkers welcome - but no muddy boots.
OPEN: 11–2.30 6.30–11 **BAR MEALS:** Lunch served: all week Dinner served: all week 11–2.30 6.30–9.30 Av main course £7.50 **RESTAURANT:** 6.30–9.30 **BREWERY/COMPANY:** Free House **PRINCIPAL BEERS:** Marston's Pedigree, Interbrew Bass, RCH Pitchfork, Greene King IPA. **FACILITIES:** Children welcome Garden: Patio, Food served outside Dogs allowed (water) **NOTES:** Parking 20 **ROOMS:** 4 bedrooms 4 en suite from s£35 d£45

MARSHFIELD
Map 03 ST77

The Catherine Wheel 🛏
39 High St ☎ 01225 892220

A friendly country pub that appeals equally to locals and visitors from further afield. The old-style inn serves a good range of food such as fresh fish dishes like sea bass with

salmon mousse, and luxury fish stew, as well as chicken stuffed with smoked cheese served with mango coulis, lamb shanks with mint and redcurrant gravy, and duck breast with plum sauce. Roasted Mediterranean tartlet in a smoked cheese sauce is one of several vegetarian choices.
OPEN: 11–3 6–11 **BAR MEALS:** Lunch served: Tue-Sun 12–2 Dinner served: Mon–Sat 7–10 Av main course £10.95
RESTAURANT: Lunch served: Tue-Sun 12–2 Dinner served: Mon–Sat 7–10 Av 3 course à la carte £17 **BREWERY/COMPANY:** Free House **PRINCIPAL BEERS:** Scottish Courage Courage Best, Abbey Ales Bellringer, Brains Reverend James, Scottish Courage John Smith's.
FACILITIES: Children welcome Garden: Food served outside Dogs allowed **NOTES:** Parking 10 **ROOMS:** 5 bedrooms 5 en suite from s£40 d£60

MEYSEY HAMPTON
Map 03 SP10

The Masons Arms ♦♦♦ 🛏
28 High St GL7 5JT ☎ 01285 850164 📠 01285 850164
e-mail: jane@themasonsarms.freeserve.co.uk
Dir: A417 from Cirencester toward Fairford, after 6m R into village, pub on R by village green
An ideal touring base for the southern Cotswolds with comfortable bedrooms. This 17th-century stone inn has home-cooked food served throughout the bar and separate dining room. Light bites of salad bowls, and filled jacket potatoes graduate to Stilton, bacon and mushroom starters, plum duck flamed with cassis and haddock with prawns and dill. The gargantuan mixed grill is a must for meat lovers and fish specials feature ling and shark, while spinach and mushroom filo parcels appeals to vegetarians.
OPEN: 11.30–2.45 6–11 **BAR MEALS:** Lunch served: all week 12–2 Dinner served: Mon–Sat 7–9.30 Av main course £6.45
RESTAURANT: Lunch served: all week 12–2 Dinner served: Mon–Sat 7–9.30 Av 3 course à la carte £12.50
BREWERY/COMPANY: Free House
PRINCIPAL BEERS: Interbrew Bass, Hook Norton Best.
FACILITIES: Garden: Food served outside Dogs allowed (water) **NOTES:** Parking 5 **ROOMS:** 9 bedrooms 9 en suite from s£45 d£60

MINCHINHAMPTON
Map 03 SO80

The Old Lodge Inn 🛏 ♀
Minchinhampton Common GL6 9AQ ☎ 01453 832047
Former 16th-century hunting lodge set in the middle of a 600 acre common. Pleasing rural outlook from pine-furnished rooms, good real ales and an imaginative choice of food. From sandwiches and jacket potatoes, the menu may also feature steak and ale pie, sausage and mash, halibut, and mixed grills. Watch out for cows and horses in the garden and car park!
OPEN: 12–3 6–11 **BAR MEALS:** Lunch served: all week 12–3 Dinner served: Mon–Sat 6.30–9 Av main course £6
RESTAURANT: Lunch served: all week 12–2 Dinner served: Mon–Sat 6–9.30 **BREWERY/COMPANY:** Youngs
PRINCIPAL BEERS: Smiles, Youngs. **FACILITIES:** Children welcome Garden: Food served outside. Dogs allowed

continued

OPEN: 11.30-3 6.30-11
BAR MEALS: L served
Tue-Sun 12-2.
D served Mon-Sat. 6.30-9.
Av main course £7.50
RESTAURANT: L served
Tue-Sun 12-2. D served Mon-Sat.
6.30-9 Av cost 3 course £20
BREWERY/COMPANY: FREE
HOUSE
PRINCIPLE BEERS: Black Sheep
Best, Carlsberg-Tetley Bitter
FACILITIES: Children welcome.
Garden: Patio area
NOTES: Parking 30
ROOMS: 3 en suite. Double room
from £80

The Fox

LOWER ODDINGTON, GL56 0UR
☎ 01451 870555 📠 01451 870669
e-mail: info@foxinn.net
Dir: A436 from Stow-on-the-Wold then
R to Lower Oddington

A rare commitment to all things good; food, wines, real ales, accommodation and engaging company adds a refreshing dimension to the Fox - located within another rarity - a virtually unspoilt of Cotswold villages.

Top professionals, Kirk and Sally Ritchie are just the right people to have carried out the subtle improvements that have steadily lifted the Fox to an ever higher plane. Behind the creeper-clad, 16th-century, mellow Cotswold stone façade lies an interior that has been rejuvenated with style and flair. Polished slate floors, rustic pine tables topped with fresh flowers and candles, rag-washed walls adorned with tasteful prints, subdued classical music, daily papers and a blazing log fire in the convivial bar: these are ingredients that encourage a meal-time detour from Stow-on-the-Wold or Chipping Camden with high expectations. Food asserts itself in imaginative and colourful dishes that will spoil one for choice from an up-to-date menu of favourites, supplemented by daily specials that quite likely will include tiger prawns in chilli, garlic and coriander, scallops with ginger and smoked chicken Caesar salad with marinated anchovies.

Speciality fish dishes may then include baked whole sea bass with creamed leeks and saffron, whilst in season look for wild boar sausages with sweet potato mash and for vegetarian tastes perhaps goats' cheese and roasted pepper tart. For pudding try the cherry and almond tart or iced orange and Cointreau terrine. There are hearty French bread sandwiches on weekdays at lunchtime, but on Wednesday evenings you would be advised to book for the Hunt Supper and on Sunday lunch when the beef sirloin is rare and succulent. An immaculately kept, walled cottage garden has heat lamps for alfresco eating followed, for those so lucky, by a peaceful night's sleep in one of the three tasteful bedrooms.

MISERDEN
Map 03 SO90

The Carpenters Arms ♀
GL6 7JA ☎ 01285 821283
e-mail: Bleninns@clara.net
Dir: *Leave A417 at Birdlip, take B4010 toward Stroud, after 3m Miserden signed*

Built around 1700 and named after the old carpenter's workshop, this inn on the Miserden Park Estate, retains its inglenook fireplaces and original stone floors. Old benches still carry the nameplates used by the locals a century ago to reserve their seats at the bar. Popular menu includes Barnsley lamb chop, oven roast vegetables with pilau rice, and beef and Stilton pie. The village is very popular with film crews as it so untouched by modern times.
OPEN: 11.30–2.30 6.30–11 (Sun 12–3, 7–10.30) **BAR MEALS:** Lunch served: all week Dinner served: all week 12–2.30 7–9.30 Av main course £6.50 **RESTAURANT:** Lunch served: all week Dinner served: all week 12–2.30 7–9.30 Av 3 course à la carte £12.50
BREWERY/COMPANY: Free House **PRINCIPAL BEERS:** Fuller's London Pride, Goff's Jouster, Greene King IPA. **FACILITIES:** Children welcome Children's licence Garden: Beer garden, food served outdoors, patio, Dogs allowed (water) **NOTES:** Parking 22

NAILSWORTH
Map 03 ST89

The Britannia ♀
Cossack Square GL6 0DG ☎ 01453 832501 📠 01453 872228

Impressive 17th-century former manor house occupying a prominent position on the south side of Nailsworth's Cossack Square. Refurbished several years ago, the interior is bright and uncluttered with an open plan design and a blue slate floor. Modern works of art separate the restaurant from the bar, which is heated a large open fire. Spiral staircases and glass-topped wells are also among the more interesting features inside. The Britannia's menu is a mix of modern British and continental food with an extensive choice of dishes for vegetarians.
OPEN: 11–11 Closed: 25 Dec **BAR MEALS:** Lunch served: all week Dinner served: all week 11–2.45 5.30–10 Av main course £7.25

RESTAURANT: Lunch served: all week Dinner served: all week 11–2.45 5.30–10 Av 3 course à la carte £18
BREWERY/COMPANY: Free House **PRINCIPAL BEERS:** Greene King Abbot Ale, Fuller's London pride. **FACILITIES:** Garden: Terrace, food served outside Dogs allowed (water) **NOTES:** Parking 100

Pick of the Pubs

Egypt Mill ★ ★ ◎ 🕲 ♀
GL6 0AE ☎ 01453 833449 📠 01453 836098
Formerly a corn and woollen mill, and many original features of the mill are from the 16th century at this delightful riverside hotel. The old millstones and lifting gear remain in place in the lounge bar, which looks out over water-gardens. The newly refurbished ground floor bar and bistro enjoy a similarly picturesque setting. There is a choice of eating in the bistro or restaurant and in both there is a good selection of wines by the glass. The tempting bistro menu might offer creamed chicken mousse, haddock fillets in beer batter or crispy confit duck leg. Fresh daily fish specials such as roast monkfish wrapped in Parma ham are worth seeking out from the blackboard menu. Restaurant dishes include field mushrooms topped with Stilton rarebit, Cornish cod with chive butter and pot-roast beef brisket in rich red wine gravy. Round off with chocolate parfait with pistachio ice cream, tropical fruit brûlée or a selection of well-chosen British cheeses.
OPEN: 10–3 6.30–11 **BAR MEALS:** Lunch served: all week Dinner served: all week 12–2 7–10 Av main course £10
RESTAURANT: Lunch served: all week Dinner served: all week 12–2 7–10 Av 3 course à la carte £20 **BREWERY/COMPANY:** Free House **FACILITIES:** Children welcome Garden: Waterside garden, food served outside **NOTES:** Parking 100 **ROOMS:** 17 bedrooms 17 en suite from s£49.50 d£75

NAUNTON
Map 03 SP12

The Black Horse
GL54 3AD ☎ 01454 850565

Renowned for its home-cooked food, Donnington real ales and utterly peaceful bed and breakfast, this friendly inn enjoys a typical Cotswold village setting beloved of ramblers and locals alike. Dishes range from ploughman's and jacket potatoes to some accomplished main dishes: steak and kidney pudding, grilled trout, chicken breasts with Stilton and bacon and salmon fillet in saffron sauce. Plus the day's selection of 'sinful sweets'!
OPEN: 11.30–3 6–11 **BAR MEALS:** 12–2 6.30–9.30 Av meal £6.95
RESTAURANT: 12–2 6.30–9.30 Av 3 courses £14.95
BREWERY/COMPANY: Donnington
PRINCIPAL BEERS: Donnington BB, SBA **FACILITIES:** Garden: Food served outside **NOTES:** Parking 12

continued

NEWENT — Map 03 SO72

The Yew Tree
Clifford Mesne GL18 1JS ☎ 01531 820719
Dir: Follow A40 to Ross on Wye, 2 M, pass Huntley turn R sign
Mayhill/Cliffords Mesne, pass Glass House, turn L Yew Tree 50 Yds
The Yew Tree Inn is in glorious countryside overlooking
the Malvern Hills. The 18th-century former cider press is
in five acres of grounds, with a patio which is a blaze of
floral colour in summer. Both the open-plan bar and
Hacketts restaurant have been refurbished. Under the
direction of chef/patron Paul Hackett, the kitchen's
philosophy revolves around top quality produce from
local suppliers. The kitchen butchers and prepares all its
own meats and fish. Chickens, ducks and geese are kept
for their eggs, and herbs, salads and various fruits are
home grown. There is a bar menu with simple blackboard
options, and also a more complex fixed-price five-course
dinner menu. Typical dishes are wild sea bass with risotto
and champagne chive butter, or roasted saddle of local
venison with caramelised cranberries. Real ales are served
– Wye Valley and Shepherd Neame on hand pump – and
there's an extensive choice of wines. Two en suite
bedrooms.
OPEN: 12-3 6.30-11 Closed: 1-14 Jan **BAR MEALS:** Lunch
served: Tue-Sun Dinner served: Tue-Sun 12-3 6.30-10.30 Av main
course £10.50 **RESTAURANT:** Lunch served: Tue-Sun Dinner
served: Tue-Sun 12-3 6.30-10.30 Av 3 course à la carte £24.50 Av
3 course fixed price £18.50 **BREWERY/COMPANY:** Free House
PRINCIPAL BEERS: Shepherds Neame Spitfire, Wye Valley
Butty Bach, Fuller's London Pride. **FACILITIES:** Children
welcome Garden: Food served outside Dogs allowed (toys,
water) **NOTES:** Parking 30 **ROOMS:** 2 bedrooms 2 en suite
from s£40 d£60

NEWLAND — Map 03 SO50

The Ostrich Inn
GL16 8NP ☎ 01594 833260 📠 01594 833260
e-mail: kathryn@theostrich.freeserve.co.uk
Dir: Follow Monmouth signs from Chepstow (A466), Newland is signed
from Redbrook
A late 13th-century inn situated opposite the fine church
known as the 'Cathedral of the Forest'. Huge open fireplace,
old furniture, and friendly pub dog. A good choice of food is
offered, from red brill with chilli and lime vinaigrette, or
fishcakes with parsley sauce, to wild boar and apple
sausages, ostrich fillet with plums and Marsala, or pork
tenderloin with Calvados cream sauce. Specials board
changes weekly. Eight constantly changing ales always
available.
OPEN: 12-2.30 6.30-11 **BAR MEALS:** Lunch served: all week
Dinner served: all week 12-2.30 6.30-9.30 Av main course £6.50
RESTAURANT: Lunch served: all week Dinner served: all week
12-2.30 6-9.30 Av 3 course à la carte £20
BREWERY/COMPANY: Free House
PRINCIPAL BEERS: Timothy Taylor Landlord, Pitchfork, Butty
Bach, Exmoor Gold. **FACILITIES:** Children welcome Garden:
Food served outside. Lawn & patio areas Dogs allowed (water &
companions to play with)

NORTHLEACH — Map 03 SP11

Wheatsheaf Inn
GL54 3EZ ☎ 01451 860244 📠 01451 861037
e-mail: pint@wheatsheafinn.org.uk

Under new ownership this 16th-century Cotswold stone
coaching inn has undergone extensive refurbishment with
simple, comfortable bedrooms, a civilised real ale bar and
dining areas with an adventurous new menu. There are plenty
of choices from market fresh produce right down to
marinated olives or garlic and Parmesan bread. Typically, start
with seared tuna with rocket and coriander salsa or lentil and
goats' cheese salad before tackling breast of local pheasant or
grilled sea bass with creamed leeks.
OPEN: 12-3 6-11 (Fri-Sun 12-11) Closed: 25 Dec
BAR MEALS: Lunch served: all week Dinner served: all week
12-2.30 7-10 Av main course £8.95 **RESTAURANT:** Lunch served:
all week Dinner served: all week 12-2.30 7-10 Av 3 course à la carte
£20 **BREWERY/COMPANY:** Free House
PRINCIPAL BEERS: Wadsworth 6X, Fuller's London Pride, Hook
Norton Best Bitter, Greene King. **FACILITIES:** Garden: Food served
outside **NOTES:** Parking 15 **ROOMS:** 8 bedrooms 8 en suite from
s£45 d£55

OAKRIDGE — Map 03 SO90

The Butcher's Arms
GL6 7NZ ☎ 01285 760371 📠 01285 760602
Dir: From Stroud take A419 turn L for Eastcombe. Then follow signs for
Bisley. Just before Bisley turn R to Oakridge
Traditional Cotswold country pub with stone walls, beams and
log fires in the renowned Golden Valley. Once a
slaughterhouse and butchers shop. A full and varied
restaurant menu offers steak, fish and chicken dishes, while
the bar menu ranges from ploughman's lunches to home-
cooked daily specials.
OPEN: 11-3 6-11 Closed: 25-26 Dec, 1 Jan **BAR MEALS:** 12-2
6.30-9 **RESTAURANT:** Lunch served: Tue-Sun 12-3 Dinner served:
Tue-Sat 7.30-9 Av 3 course à la carte £17.50
BREWERY/COMPANY: Free House **PRINCIPAL BEERS:** Greene
King Abbot Ale, Tetleys, Wickwar BOB, Archers Best.
FACILITIES: Children welcome Garden: Food served outside.
Overlooks Golden Valley Dogs allowed **NOTES:** Parking 50

OLDBURY-ON-SEVERN — Map 03 ST69

The Anchor Inn
Church Rd BS35 1QA ☎ 01454 413331
Dir: From N A38 towards Bristol, 1.5m then R, village signed. From S A38
through Thornbury
17th-century pub built from traditional Cotswold stone on the
site of an old mill near the River Severn. There's a friendly

continued

OLDBURY-ON-SEVERN continued

atmosphere in the bar with its log fire and oak furniture, while summer dining in the garden overlooking a large boules area is increasingly popular. Choose to eat from an interesting light meals menu including various salads, and beef, ham or smoked salmon with bread. Traditional dishes include kedgeree, fettucini pescatore, and beef Madras. Real ales served.
OPEN: 11.30-2.30 6.30-11 (Sat 11.30-11, Sun 12-10.30) Closed: Dec 25 **BAR MEALS:** Lunch served: all week Dinner served: all week 11.30-2.30 6.30-9.30 Av main course £6.95
RESTAURANT: Lunch served: all week Dinner served: all week 11.30-2.30 6.30-9.30 Av 3 course à la carte £12 Av 3 course fixed price £13.95 **BREWERY/COMPANY:** Free House
PRINCIPAL BEERS: Interbrew Bass, Theakston Best & Old Peculier, Butcombe Best. **FACILITIES:** Children welcome Garden: Beer garden, food served outdoors, patio Dogs allowed
NOTES: Parking 15

PAINSWICK   *August 2006*   Map 03 SO80

The Falcon Inn 🏠 ♀
New St GL6 6UN ☎ 01452 814222 📠 01452 813377
e-mail: bleninns@clara.net
Dir: On A46 in centre of Painswick

Boasting the world's oldest known bowling green in the grounds, the Falcon stands at the heart of this conservation village. Dating from 1554, for three centuries it was the Courthouse. Today, its comfy accommodation and friendly service even includes a drying room for walkers' gear. Menus move with the seasons: Welsh salt-land lamb in spring, grilled lobster in summer and pheasant and spatchcock partridge in the winter months. Try tiger prawns in filo, chicken fricassée and home-made desserts.
OPEN: 11-4 5.30-11 (Sun 12-4, 6-10.30) **BAR MEALS:** Lunch served: all week Dinner served: all week 12.30-2.30 7-9.30 Av main course £8 **RESTAURANT:** Lunch served: all week Dinner served: all week 12-2.30 7-9.30 Av 3 course à la carte £15
BREWERY/COMPANY: Free House **PRINCIPAL BEERS:** Hook Norton Best, Old Hooky, Wadworth 6X, Boddingtons.
FACILITIES: Children welcome Children's licence Garden: Courtyard and large bowling green to rear **NOTES:** Parking 35
ROOMS: 12 bedrooms 12 en suite from s£42.50 d£63

The Royal Oak Inn 🏠 ♀ NEW
St Mary's St GL6 6QG ☎ 01452 813129
e-mail: bleninns@clara.net
Dir: In the centre of Painswick on the A46 between Stroud & Cheltenham
The Royal Oak is truly a part of Old England. Tucked away behind the church of this conservation village, it features two main rooms and a huge, open fire. Very low ceilings, old paintings and artefacts and a sun-trap rear courtyard contribute to its atmosphere. A solidly Old English approach:

for lunch maybe cauliflower cheese with grilled bacon or a rare beef topside salad; in the evenings, liver, bacon and fried onions, or grilled lamb cutlets. Daily specials might be home-made fishcakes or steak and kidney pie.

OPEN: 11-2.30 5.30-11 **BAR MEALS:** Lunch served: all week Dinner served: all week 12-2.30 7-9.30 Av main course £6
RESTAURANT: Lunch served: all week Dinner served: all week 12-2.30 7-9.30 Av 3 course à la carte £13
BREWERY/COMPANY: Free House **PRINCIPAL BEERS:** Hook Norton Best, Wadworth 6X, Interbrew Flowers Original, plus Guest Ales. **FACILITIES:** Children welcome Garden: Patio/Courtyard, food served outside Dogs allowed

REDMARLEY D'ABITOT   Map 03 SO73

Rose & Crown 🏠
Playley Green GL19 3NB ☎ 01531 650234
Dir: on the A417 Gloucester to Ledbury, 1M from exit 2 of the M50
This pretty old roadside building, dating from the 1720s with numerous later additions, is a blaze of summer colour from hanging baskets and flower troughs, and an array of daffodils in spring. The dishes on the main menu change very little, but the daily specials may offer fresh sea bream with lime butter, Moroccan spiced lamb with couscous or beef and ale casserole. The prime Herefordshire beef steaks are a further plus, as are the Sunday roast lunches, that make booking advisable.
OPEN: 11-2.30 6-11 (Sun 12-3, 7-10.30) Closed: Dec 25
BAR MEALS: Lunch served: all week 12-2 Dinner served: Mon-Sat 6.30-9 Av main course £8 **RESTAURANT:** Lunch served: all week 12-2 Dinner served: Mon-Sat 6.30-9 Av 3 course à la carte £14.95
BREWERY/COMPANY: Pubmaster **PRINCIPAL BEERS:** Interbrew Flowers Original IPA, Young's Special, Wadworth 6X, Greene King Old Speckled Hen & Ruddles County Ale. **FACILITIES:** Children welcome Garden: Food served outdoors, patio Dogs allowed (water)
NOTES: Parking 50

SHEEPSCOMBE   Map 03 SO81

The Butchers Arms 🏠 ♀
GL6 7RH ☎ 01452 812113 📠 01452 814358
e-mail: bleninns@clara.net
Dir: 1.5m south of A46 (Cheltenham to Stroud road), N of Painswick
Originally built to hang and butcher deer hunted by Henry VIII from his Royal deer park, this friendly hostelry on a beautiful hillside has a long established reputation for good food. The pub was a particular favourite of writer Laurie Lee, author of *Cider with Rosie*. A wide and varied menu includes whole oven-baked sea bass, pork escalope with mustard mashed potato, the Butchers Arms' mixed grill, carrot and coriander goujons, and skate wings marinated in ginger and olive oil.

continued

continued

OPEN: 11.30–2.30 (Sun 12–3, 7–10.30) 6–11.30
BAR MEALS: Lunch served: all week Dinner served: all week
12–2.30 7–9.30 Av main course £6.75 **RESTAURANT:** Lunch served:
all week Dinner served: all week 12–2.30 7–9.30 Av 3 course à la carte
£14.50 **BREWERY/COMPANY:** Free House
PRINCIPAL BEERS: Hook Norton Best & Old Hooky, Timothy Taylor
Landlord, Wychwood Hobgoblin. **FACILITIES:** Children welcome
Children's licence Garden: Beer garden, food served outdoors, patio,
Dogs allowed (in garden and on terrace only, water)
NOTES: Parking 16

SHURDINGTON · Map 03 SO91

The Bell Inn 🕯 NEW
Main Rd, Shurdington GL51 4XQ
☎ 01242 862245 📠 01242 862245
Late 18th-century pub which combined the roles of alehouse
and bakery until 1949. Set in a lovely spot overlooking the
village green where cricket is played, and well placed for
interesting walks on Cheltenham Ring and the Cotswold Way.
Serves good food including tournedos Rossini, root vegetable
truffle pie with watercress sauce, smoked haddock fishcake
with mild curry sauce, and tuna steak with tomato, basil and
cream sauce. **OPEN:** 11–12.15 5–11 (Fri–Sun all day) **BAR MEALS:** Lunch served:
all week Dinner served: all week 12–2.30 6–10 Av main course £6
RESTAURANT: Lunch served: all week Dinner served: all week
12–2.30 6–9.30 **PRINCIPAL BEERS:** Timothy Taylor Best, Greene
King IPA, Fuller's London Pride Interbrew Boddingtons.
FACILITIES: Garden: Shelterd garden, food served outside
NOTES: Parking 25

SIDDINGTON · Map 03 SU09

The Greyhound
Ashton Rd GL7 6HR ☎ 01285 653573 📠 650054
*Dir: A419 from Swindon, turn at sign for industrial estate, L at main rdbt,
follow Siddington signs, pub at far end of village on R*
Village pub, formally a coach house, built of Cotswold stone
with flagstone floors inside. Friendly, relaxed atmosphere.

SOUTHROP · Map 03 SP10

The Swan
GL7 3NU ☎ 01367 850205 📠 01367 860331
Dir: Off A361 between Lechlade and Burford
Creeper-clad Cotswold pub, refurbished under new
ownership. Emphasis on good quality pub food and classic
country pub atmosphere. Expect crab risotto with spring
onions and chilli oil, and pan-fried calves' liver with mashed
potato and red onion marmalade. **OPEN:** 12–3 7–11 Closed Mon **BAR MEALS:** Lunch served:
Tue–Sun Dinner served: Tue–Sun 12–2.30 7–9.30 Av main course £7.95

continued

RESTAURANT: Lunch served: Tue–Sun Dinner served: Tue–Sun
12–2.30 7–9.30 Av 3 course à la carte £19
BREWERY/COMPANY: Free House **PRINCIPAL BEERS:** Hook
Norton, Greene King IPA, guest ale. **FACILITIES:** Children welcome
Dogs allowed

STONEHOUSE · Map 03 SO80

The George Inn ♦♦♦ 🕯
Bath Rd, Frocester GL10 3TQ ☎ 01453 822302 📠 01453 791612
e-mail: enquiries@georgeinn.fsnet.co.uk
A village pub in the traditional mould, undisturbed by music
or games machines. A former coaching inn with huge
inglenook fireplaces and the original stables surrounding the
courtyard garden. The food is mainly locally produced and
cooked to order. Look for British roast beef baguettes, chicken
goujons with lemon mayonnaise, and Frocester Fayre faggots
with creamy mash - followed by treacle pudding or Gaelic
whiskey trifle. Sunday lunch carvery, occasional live music and
a warm village welcome. Three bedrooms are imposingly
large.
OPEN: 11.30–2.30 5–11 (Sat–Sun open all day)
BAR MEALS: Lunch served: all week Dinner served: all week 12–2
6.30–9.30 Av main course £6 **RESTAURANT:** Lunch served: all week
Dinner served: all week 12–2 6.30–9.30 Av 3 course à la carte £14
BREWERY/COMPANY: Enterprise Inns
PRINCIPAL BEERS: Wadworth 6X, Greene King Ruddles County,
Scottish Courage John Smith's. **FACILITIES:** Children welcome
Garden: Beer garden, food served outdoors **NOTES:** Parking 25
ROOMS: 8 bedrooms 3 en suite from s£29 d£49

STOW-ON-THE-WOLD · Map 03 SP12

Coach and Horses
Ganborough GL56 0QZ ☎ 01451 830208
Dir: On A424 2.5m from Stow-on-the-Wold
Built of Cotswold stone and set beside an old coach road, this
250-year-old inn boasts a welcoming bar with beams,
flagstones and an open fire. Well-kept Donnington ales.

Pick of the Pubs

The Eagle and Child 🕯 🕯 ♀
C/o The Royalist Hotel, Digbeth St GL54 1BN
☎ 01451 830670 📠 01451 870048
e-mail: info@theroyalisthotel.co.uk
*Dir: From the A40 take the A429 towards Stow on the Wood turn into
town and we are situated by the green on the L handside*

A cracking good pub - rated among England's best pubs -
is a popular watering hole for locals and visitors alike.
Access to the pub is through the reception of the Royalist
Hotel, dating from 947AD and certified as the oldest inn in

continued

STOW-ON-THE-WOLD continued

England. Both hotel and pub have been totally refurbished by Rosette awarded chef/owner Alan Thompson. The name Eagle & Child is said to come from the crest of the Earl of Derby dating back to the 14th century. With the pubs stone walls, polished flagstone floor, rustic wooden furnishings and airy rear conservatory, this is a relaxing venue in which to sample the excellent food that arrives from the hotel kitchen and local real ales. Expect first-class steak and kidney pudding, local sausages with onion gravy and mash, clay-roast corn-fed chicken breast with olive and Feta spaghetti, local roast partridge, fillet of sea bass with avocado risotto and salsa verde, Cotswold lamb hotpot with champ mash and sautéed greens. Good puddings.

OPEN: 11-11 (Winter open at 12) **BAR MEALS:** Lunch served: all week Dinner served: all week 12-2.30 6.30-10 Av main course £7.95 **RESTAURANT:** Lunch served: all week Dinner served: all week 12-2.30 6.30-10 Av 3 course à la carte £16.50 **BREWERY/COMPANY:** Free House **PRINCIPAL BEERS:** Hook Norton Best, Greene King Abbot Ale,. **FACILITIES:** Children welcome Garden: Patio, food served outside Dogs allowed **NOTES:** Parking 10 **ROOMS:** 10 bedrooms 10 en suite from s£50 d£90

STROUD   Map 03 SO80

Pick of the Pubs

Bear of Rodborough Hotel ★ ★ ★ ☼
Rodborough Common GL5 5DE
☎ 01453 878522 ▤ 01453 872523
Dir: From M5 J13 follow signs for Stonehouse then Rodborough
300-year-old imposing former coaching inn situated high above Stroud in acres of National Trust parkland, with magnificent Cotswolds views. Minchinhampton and Rodborough Commons comprise open grassland and woodland which form a steep-sided plateau particularly important for wild flowers. The hotel is worth seeking out for the comfortable accommodation, open log fires, stone walls and solid wooden floors. There is certainly plenty of character here and the elegant Mulberry restaurant epitomises the inherent charm of the building. Appetising menu uses Cotswold produce where possible, including good local cheeses. Try the home-made chicken pie, Cotswold cheese platter, local hot buttered crumpets or the fish of the day.
OPEN: 10.30-11 **BAR MEALS:** Lunch served: all week Dinner served: all week 11.30-2 6-9 Av main course £6.95 **BREWERY/COMPANY:** Free House **PRINCIPAL BEERS:** Bass, Uley Bitter, Wadworth 6x, John Smiths Smooth. **FACILITIES:** Children welcome Children's licence Garden: Food served outside. Patio area Dogs allowed (water provided) **NOTES:** Parking 175 **ROOMS:** 46 bedrooms 46 en suite

> **Do you have a favourite pub
> that we have overlooked?
> Please use the Readers' Report forms at
> the back of this guide to tell us all about it.**

Pick of the Pubs

Halfway Inn ◉ ☼
Box GL6 9AE ☎ 01453 832631 ▤ 01453 835275

Once a wool store for the drovers of Michinhampton common, this building has been stunningly converted to create a pub that manages to feel fresh, modern and rustic. There's plenty of bare wood, pine furniture and brightly painted walls, along with a rejuvenated garden for summer drinks and dining. It's a popular destination after a walk on the common, or perhaps a round of golf, and despite a change of hands the reputation for good food remains. The AA rosette-winning menu has a distinctly modern feel. Dishes range from classic combinations such as pan fried steak with rösti potato, glazed baby vegetables and port wine, through to creative or internationally inspired dishes – perhaps tuna spring roll with a spiced avocado and aïoli salad or a trio of lobster sausage, salmon fishcake and red mullet fillet with saffron.
OPEN: 11-11 **BAR MEALS:** Lunch served: all week Dinner served: Mon-Sat 12-2.30 7-9.30 Av main course £12 **RESTAURANT:** Lunch served: all week 12-2.30 Dinner served: Mon-Sat 7-9.30 Av 3 course à la carte £20 **BREWERY/COMPANY:** Free House **PRINCIPAL BEERS:** Wickwar Brand Oak Bitter, Coopers, Hook Norton. **FACILITIES:** Garden: Food served outside. Landscape garden **NOTES:** Parking 60

The Ram Inn 🐑
South Woodchester GL5 5EL ☎ 01453 873329 ▤ 01453 872880
e-mail: drink@raminn.com
Dir: A46 from Stroud to Nailsworth, R after 2m into S.Woodchester (brown tourist signs)
Something for everyone at The Ram, set in the heart of the Cotswolds with it lovely walks and a cycle track nearby. There is a large patio with splendid country views. Daily up-dated menus list liver and bacon pâté with locally baked bread and Mediterranean prawns with garlic dip, followed by chargrilled tuna steaks or shallot and Stilton lasagne. Top up with apple pie or spotted Dick and wash down with notable regularly changing real ales.
OPEN: 11-11 (Sun 12-10.30) **BAR MEALS:** Lunch served: all week Dinner served: all week 12-2.30 6.00-9.30 Av main course £7 **RESTAURANT:** Lunch served: all week Dinner served: all week 12-2.30 6-9.30 Av 3 course à la carte £12.50 **BREWERY/COMPANY:** Free House **PRINCIPAL BEERS:** Theakston Old Peculiar, Uley Od Spot, Wickwar BOB. **FACILITIES:** Children welcome Garden: Patio, food served outdoors Dogs allowed **NOTES:** Parking 60

Pick of the Pubs

Rose & Crown Inn ♦♦♦ 🛏
The Cross, Nympsfield GL10 3TU
☎ 01453 860240 📠 01453 860900
Dir: M5 J13 off B4066 SW of Stroud

A honey-coloured, 16th-century stone building in the heart of the village close to the Cotswold Way. This welcoming pub is as appealing inside as out, with neat stone-walled bars and warming log fires bringing comfort to the many walkers who seek refreshments. In the evening the informal dining room is romantically lit by candles, making it just the place to enjoy local produce like Gloucestershire spotted pig, and locally-shot game. Dinner might begin with smoked trout mousse with dill cream, or lean braised belly of pork, and continue with slow-roast duck, or cutlet of pork with apple chutney. For a filling bar snack try jacket potato with chicken tikka, or a choice of filled baguettes and sandwiches. Spacious bedrooms with a good range of amenities.
OPEN: 12-11 **BAR MEALS:** Lunch served: all week Dinner served: all week 12-9 Av main course £9.50
RESTAURANT: Lunch served: all week Dinner served: all week 12-9 Av 3 course à la carte £19 **BREWERY/COMPANY:** Free House **PRINCIPAL BEERS:** Greene King IPA, Wickwar Brand Oak Bitter, Archers Best. **FACILITIES:** Children welcome Garden: Food served outside, half football pitch Dogs allowed (water provided) **NOTES:** Parking 20 **ROOMS:** 3 bedrooms 3 en suite from s£42.50 d£70

The Woolpack Inn NEW
Slad Rd, Slad GL6 7QA ☎ 01452 813429 📠 01452 813429
Dir: 2 miles from Stroud, 8 miles from Gloucester
Situated in the Slad valley close to the Cotswold Way, a friendly local that offers good real ales, interesting wine selections and middle-of-the-road food based largely on chargrills and popular daily specials. Tempting starters include smoked mackerel and country pâté, followed by butcher's faggots with mustard mash, beef and ale stew and a mammoth mixed grill. Save room for fruit crumble or treacle sponge. Booking advised for Richard's good-value Sunday roast.
OPEN: 12-3 6-11 **BAR MEALS:** Lunch served: all week 12-2 Dinner served: Tues-Sat 6.30-9 Av main course £6.95
RESTAURANT: Lunch served: all week Dinner served: Tues-Sat 12-2 6.30-9 Av 3 course fixed price £18 **BREWERY/COMPANY:** Free House **PRINCIPAL BEERS:** Uley Pig's Ear Strong Beer, Old Sport Prize Ale,. **FACILITIES:** Garden: Food served outside Dogs allowed (water) **NOTES:** Parking 8 No credit cards

Pick of the Pubs

Gumstool Inn 🛏 ♀
Calcot Manor GL8 8YJ ☎ 01666 890391 📠 01666 890394
e-mail: reception@calcotmanor.co.uk
Dir: In Calcot (on jct of A4135 & A46, 4m W of Tetbury)

The Gumstool Inn is the pub at Calcot Manor Hotel, a lavishly converted farmhouse with outbuildings dating back to the 13th century, when the land was farmed by Cistercian monks. In this setting, by a flower-filled central courtyard, the Gumstool is where the chefs can exhibit their skills in a rustic style that well matches the informal surroundings. Alongside cask ales is an impressive selection of some 18 wines by the glass, including champagne. Classical combinations in new and innovative ways seek to utilise all that is best from Britain and to promote local Cotswold produce wherever it warrants. Sweetcorn and potato fritters with spiced brown shrimps can precede slow roasted duck salad with sweet and sour dressing: while offered in two sizes according to your appetite are penne pasta with prosciutto, Thai-spiced crab cakes and caramelised red onion tart with rocket salad.
OPEN: 11.30-2.30 6-11 (Sat-Sun 11.30-11)
BAR MEALS: Lunch served: all week Dinner served: all week 12-2 7-9.30 Av main course £9 **RESTAURANT:** Lunch served: all week Dinner served: all week 12-2 7-9.30 Av 3 course à la carte £25 **BREWERY/COMPANY:** Free House
PRINCIPAL BEERS: Courage Directors, Courage Best,.
FACILITIES: Children welcome Children's licence Garden: food served outside. **NOTES:** Parking 100 **ROOMS:** 28 bedrooms 28 en suite from s£120 d£150

Pick of the Pubs

Trouble House Inn ◎◎ 🛏 ♀
Cirencester Rd GL8 8SG ☎ 01666 502206 📠 01666 504508
Dir: On A433 between Tetbury & Cirencester
The Trouble House has had a troubled past involving agricultural riots and suicidal landlords, but there's no looking back for chef/proprietor Michael Bedford, who has previously worked for Gary Rhodes and Raymond Blanc and is attracting many accolades for his cooking here. The historic Cotswold inn has just been refurbished and now provides more seating, four open fires, low-beamed rooms, rustic wooden furnishings and a classic pub ambience. Used to heading up a brigade of 15, Michael runs the pub with his wife Sarah, and it's a very informal set up. Diners place their orders at the bar, choosing from options such as moules marinière or foie

continued

TETBURY continued

gras and apple terrine to start. From the main course range are roasted monkfish with creamed haricot beans, lentils and pancetta, and braised shoulder of lamb with button onions, bacon and mushrooms, and you might finish with treacle and walnut tart or a selection of cheeses.
OPEN: 11–3 6.30–11 (Sun 12–3, 7–10.30) Closed: Dec 25
BAR MEALS: Lunch served: Tue–Sun Dinner served: Tue–Sun 12–2 7–9.30 Av main course £12 **RESTAURANT:** Lunch served: Tue–Sun Dinner served: Tue–Sun 12–2 7–9.30 Av 3 course à la carte £25 **BREWERY/COMPANY:** Wadworth
PRINCIPAL BEERS: Wadworth 6X & Henrys IPA.
FACILITIES: Garden: Food served outdoors, patio Dogs allowed **NOTES:** Parking 30

TEWKESBURY   Map 03 SO83

The Fleet Inn
Twyning GL20 6DG ☎ 01684 274310 🖷 01684 291612
e-mail: fleetinn@hotmail.com
Dir: 1/2M Junction 1 – M50
On the banks of the River Avon, this 15th-century pub with restaurant has lawns and patios that can seat up to 350. Fishing, boules, play area, pet's corner, bird garden, craft shop, tea room and a Japanese water garden are all to hand. The olde worlde bars and themed areas provide a wide range of dishes including jumbo cod fillet, Cajun chicken, Norwegian prawn salad, vegetarian cannelloni, traditional Sunday lunch and Atlantic tuna pasta bake.
OPEN: 11–11 **BAR MEALS:** 12–9.30 6–9.30
RESTAURANT: 12–2.30 6.00–9.30
BREWERY/COMPANY: Whitbread
PRINCIPAL BEERS: Boddingtons, Greene King Abbot Ale, Bass, Fullers London Pride. **FACILITIES:** Children welcome Garden: Food served outside. Riverside garden **NOTES:** Parking 50
ROOMS: 3 bedrooms 3 en suite from d£55

TORMARTON   Map 03 ST77

Compass Inn ★ ★ 🛏
GL9 1JB ☎ 01454 218242 🖷 01454 218741
e-mail: info@compass-inn.co.uk
Dir: From M4 take A46 towards Stroud for 100yds then R
Standing in its own six acres of land, the Compass enjoys easy access from the M4 (J18). An extended former coaching inn that offers accommodation, conference facilities and a choice of bar and dining areas. From sandwiches to steaks, Thai-style curries and fresh sea bass and Dover soles there is plenty of choice to suit all tastes and pockets. Special activities that can be arranged include horse riding, hot-air ballooning and clay pigeon shooting.
OPEN: 7–11 Closed: 25–26 Dec **BAR MEALS:** Lunch served: all week Dinner served: all week 11–10 Av main course £6
RESTAURANT: Lunch served: all week Dinner served: all week 7–10 Av 3 course à la carte £20 **BREWERY/COMPANY:** Free House
PRINCIPAL BEERS: Interbrew Bass & Worthington Bitter, Smiles Bitter. **FACILITIES:** Children welcome Garden: Food served outside Dogs allowed (water) **NOTES:** Parking 200 **ROOMS:** 26 bedrooms 26 en suite from s£55 d£65

UPPER ODDINGTON   Map 06 SP22

Horse & Groom Inn NEW
GL56 0XH ☎ 01451 830584 🖷 01451 870494
Dir: Between A436 & B4450 E of Stow-on-the-Wold
Just a mile from Stow-on-the-Wold, in a quiet Cotswold village, stands this 16th-century village inn full of beamed ceilings and open log fires. Up-to-date bedrooms are popular equally with tourists, ramblers and lovers of horseracing, with Cheltenham just a short drive away. Braised lamb shank with celeriac purée and root vegetables, poached salmon on a chive butter sauce and fillet steak with wild mushrooms and port sauce indicate a kitchen of serious intent.
OPEN: 11.30–2.30 6–11 **BAR MEALS:** Lunch served: all week Dinner served: all week 12–2 6.30–9.30 Av main course £4
RESTAURANT: Lunch served: all week Dinner served: all week 12–2 6.30–9.30 Av 3 course à la carte £15 **BREWERY/COMPANY:** Free House **PRINCIPAL BEERS:** Hook Norton, Ruddles, Manchester Gold, Wadworth 6X. **FACILITIES:** Children welcome Garden: Dogs allowed (not allowed in restaurant) **ROOMS:** 7 bedrooms 7 en suite from s£40 d£55

WINCHCOMBE   Map 03 SP02

Royal Oak
Gretton GL54 5EP ☎ 01242 604999 🖷 01242 602387
Lovely views across the Malvern Hills can be enjoyed from the extensive gardens and conservatory at this old Cotswold inn, complete with beamed and flagstoned bars. An unusual attraction is the steam train at the bottom of the garden. Plenty of live music.

WITHINGTON   Map 03 SP01

The Mill Inn ♀
GL54 4BE ☎ 01242 890204 🖷 01242 890195
Dir: 3m from the A40 between Cheltenham & Oxford
The Mill is a gem of a pub that has stood in a deep Cotswold valley beside the River Coln for over 400 years: in summer you can snack at tables on the river bank. Inside are stone-flagged floors, oak panelling and open log fires just as in olden days. Under new management, we are promised steak and ale pie, fish with chips and mushy peas, 'basket meals' (said to have originated here in the late 1950s), ploughman's and Sunday roasts.
OPEN: 11.30–3 6.30–11 (Sun 12–3, 6.30–10.30)
BAR MEALS: Lunch served: all week Dinner served: all week 12–2 6.30–9 Av main course £6 **BREWERY/COMPANY:** Samuel Smith **PRINCIPAL BEERS:** Samuel Smith Old Brewery Bitter.
FACILITIES: Children welcome Garden: Riverside, seating, food served outside Dogs allowed (water, biscuits), **NOTES:** Parking 80
ROOMS: 4 bedrooms 4 en suite from s£45 d£55

WOODCHESTER   Map 03 SO80

The Old Fleece 🛏 ♀
Bath Rd, Rooksmoor GL5 5NB ☎ 01453 872582 🖷 01453 872228
Dir: 2M S of Stroud on the A46
Popular 18th-century coaching inn built of Cotswold stone with a traditional stone roof. Cosy log fires bring a welcome glow to the inn's timeless, open-plan interior, characterised by wooden floors, wood panelling and exposed stone. Fine food cooked daily by the proprietor, with an extensive menu offering modern English and continental dishes. Sample seared scallops wrapped in smoked bacon, tournedos Rossini or filo parcels with ricotta, basil and sun-dried tomatoes.

contir

Wide-ranging choice of starters and light meals, fish dishes and puddings.
OPEN: 11–11 Closed: 25 Dec **BAR MEALS:** Lunch served: all week Dinner served: all week 11–2.45 5.30–10 Av main course £9.85 **RESTAURANT:** Lunch served: all week Dinner served: all week 11–2.45 5.30–10 Av 3 course à la carte £17 **BREWERY/COMPANY:** Pubmaster **PRINCIPAL BEERS:** Bass, Greene King Abbot Ale, Boddington. **FACILITIES:** Garden: Food served outside. Attractive terrace Dogs allowed (water provided) **NOTES:** Parking 40

The Royal Oak
Church Rd GL5 5PQ ☎ 01453 872735 ▤ 01453 873150
Dir: Take A46 south from Stroud, R at N Woodchester sign onto Selsley Road. Church Rd on L
At the start of the popular Five Valleys Walk, in the heart of the glorious Cotswolds, it's not surprising that this welcoming 17th-century inn attracts many walkers and tourists. The rural views are stunning, and there's a popular beer garden. Expect a good range of local real ales, and traditional home cooking using fresh produce. Chicken pie, rib-eye steak, and venison casserole on the bar menu, with breast of duck with apple cider from the restaurant.
OPEN: 11–3 5.30–11 (all day Sat) (Sun 12–4, 7–10.30) Closed: 1 Jan **BAR MEALS:** Lunch served: Tues-Sun 12–2.30 Dinner served: Tues-Sat 6.30–9.30 Av main course £5.50 **RESTAURANT:** Lunch served: Tues-Sun 12–2.30 Dinner served: Tues-Sat 6.30–9.30 Av 3 course à la carte £15 **BREWERY/COMPANY:** Free House **PRINCIPAL BEERS:** Uley Old Spot, Archers Best. **FACILITIES:** Garden: Patio ,food served outside Dogs allowed (water) **NOTES:** Parking 15

GREATER LONDON

COULSDON   Map 07 TQ25

The Fox
Coulsdon Common CR3 5QS ☎ 01883 330401
Dir: Off B2030 between Caterham & Coulsdon
Standing above Happy Valley, - a site of special scientific interest – yet convenient for major roads into London, this Victorian pub is in a tranquil and secluded location. Traditional pub menu.

KESTON   Map 07 TQ46

The Crown
Leaves Green BR2 6DQ ☎ 01959 572920
Dir: A21 onto A232, then L onto A233, pub 4m
An old pub, not far from Biggin Hill, where the food ranges from sandwiches and ploughman's to a filo basket filled with fresh mussels and white wine, garlic and bacon sauce, or fillet of halibut with tarragon mash and fresh broccoli.
OPEN: 11–2.30 5–11 (Sat-Sun, all week in summer 11–11) **BAR MEALS:** Lunch served: all week 12–2 Dinner served: Mon-Sat 6–9 Av main course £5.95 **RESTAURANT:** Lunch served: all week 12–2 Dinner served: Mon-Sat 6–9 Av 3 course à la carte £15 **BREWERY/COMPANY:** Shepherd Neame **PRINCIPAL BEERS:** Shepherd Neame Master Brew, Spitfire & Best. **FACILITIES:** Garden: BBQ **NOTES:** Parking 30

UXBRIDGE   Map 06 TQ08

The Turning Point ♀
Canal Cottages, Packet Boat Ln, Cowley Peachey UB8 2JS
☎ 01895 440550 ▤ 01895 422144
e-mail: bookings@turningpoint.co.uk
Dir: From M4 J4 2m N on A408

Housed in former workers' cottages on the Grand Union Canal, the last point where horse-drawn barges could be turned round. Explorers are rewarded with a waterside bar and restaurant whose daily output runs from sandwiches and salads to house favourites such as steak and vegetable pie and chicken curry. Saturday night menus for dinner and dancing offer liver pâté with red onion jam, calves' liver with mash and crispy bacon and lobster thermidor (given 48 hours' notice and a good supplement).
OPEN: 12–11 Closed: 26 Dec, 1 Jan **BAR MEALS:** Lunch served: all week Dinner served: Mon-Sat 12–9.30 Av main course £10.95 **RESTAURANT:** Lunch served: all week Dinner served: all week 12–2.30 6.30–9.30 **BREWERY/COMPANY:** Free House **PRINCIPAL BEERS:** Fuller's London Pride, Interbrew Boddingtons Bitter. **FACILITIES:** Children welcome Garden: Patio, food served outside Dogs allowed **NOTES:** Parking 60

GREATER MANCHESTER

ALTRINCHAM   Map 08 SJ78

The Old Packet House ♦♦♦♦
Navigation Rd, Broadheath WA14 1LW
☎ 0161 929 1331 ▤ 0161 233 0048
Standing by the Bridgewater Canal, this charming black and white traditional inn takes its name from the horse-drawn post boat that once travelled the canal to Manchester. Colourful floral displays adorn the pub and garden in summer, and make outdoor dining a pleasure. Among the dishes on offer are haddock and prawn au gratin, braised steak casserole in red wine, roast Cheshire turkey, and chargrilled steak with plum tomatoes and mushrooms. The comfortable bedrooms come with many extras.
OPEN: 11–11 (Sun 12–10.30) **BAR MEALS:** Lunch served: all week Dinner served: Tue-Sat 12–2.30 7–9.30 Av main course £7.95 **PRINCIPAL BEERS:** Hydes, Websters. **FACILITIES:** Children welcome Garden: Food served outside. Patio area **NOTES:** Parking 10 **ROOMS:** 4 bedrooms 4 en suite

England

ASHTON-UNDER-LYNE
Map 09 SJ99

The Station
2 Warrington St OL6 6XB ☎ 0161 3306776 & 3437778
Dir: A627
Built in 1845 to serve the railway, the Station has a collection
of 'railwayana'.

BAMFORD
Map 09 SD81

Egerton Arms ♀
Ashworth Rd, Ashworth Valley OL11 5UP
☎ 01706 646183 🖹 01706 715343
e-mail: barry@egertonarms.co.uk
Dir: Bamford on B6222
Old-world pub, next to the ancient chapel, haunted by the
ghost of a tragic woman, killed with her lover while trying to
defend him from crossbow attack. Bar favourites are the pies,
daily roast and fish and chips, while the restaurant may offer
Chateaubriand and sole with asparagus mousse.
OPEN: 12–3 5.30–11 (Restaurant lunch on Sun only)
BAR MEALS: Lunch served: all week Dinner served: all week
12–2.30 5.30–9 Av main course £4 **RESTAURANT:** Lunch served:
Sun 12–2.30 Dinner served: all week 5.30–10.30 Av 3 course à la carte
£14.95 **BREWERY/COMPANY:** Free House
PRINCIPAL BEERS: Theakston Old Peculier, Greene King, Old
Speckled Hen, Ruddles County. **FACILITIES:** Children welcome
Garden: BBQ, beer garden, patio, outdoor eating Dogs allowed
(garden only) **NOTES:** Parking 100

DELPH
Map 09 SD90

Green Ash Hotel 🛏
New Tame, Denshaw Rd OL3 5TS
☎ 01457 871035 🖹 01457 871414
Dir: Just off A670 NE of Oldham

Dating back to about 1800 and once a branch of the Co-op,
this is a listed hotel with thoroughly modern bedrooms stands
in a half-acre garden surrounded by open countryside. An
old-world-style dining room adjoining the bar and
conservatory share the fabulous views. In addition to a
popular lunchtime carvery, specials might be king prawns with
garlic and coriander and lamb cutlets with minted gravy.
Restaurant main courses at night take in lemon sole with
warm green salsa and fillet steak with Roquefort and bacon.
OPEN: 7am–midnight (Sun 8–11) **BAR MEALS:** Lunch served:
Tue–Fri & Sun 12–2 Dinner served: all week 6–10 Av main course
£11.50 **RESTAURANT:** Lunch served: Tue–Fri & Sun 12–2 Dinner
served: all week 7–10 Av 3 course à la carte £19
BREWERY/COMPANY: Free House **PRINCIPAL BEERS:** Black
Sheep Best, Intrbrew Boddington. **FACILITIES:** Garden: Food

served outside, patio **NOTES:** Parking 37 **ROOMS:** 18 bedrooms
18 en suite from s£40 d£70

DIDSBURY
Map 08 SJ89

The Royal Oak
729 Wilmslow Rd M20 6WF ☎ 0161 434 4788
Character town pub gutted by fire in 1995 but now fully
restored. Victorian fireplaces and old theatre memorabilia.
Sources suggest the pub was once run by an ex-zookeeper
who trained a monkey to clear glasses in the bar. Renowned
for cheese and pâté lunches, with a daily choice of about 30
cheeses.
OPEN: 11–11 (Sun 12–10.30) **BAR MEALS:** Lunch served: Mon–Fri
12–2 Av main course £3.70 **BREWERY/COMPANY:** W'hampton &
Dudley **PRINCIPAL BEERS:** Marstons Pedigree, Banks Bitter, Banks
Original, Marstons Bitter.

LITTLEBOROUGH
Map 09 SD91

The White House 🐑 ♀ NEW
Blackstone Edge, Halifax Rd OL15 0LG ☎ 01706 378456
High on the Pennines, 1,300 feet above sea level, with
panoramic views of the moors and Hollingworth Lake far
below, this old coaching house dates from 1671. On the
Pennine Way so popular with walkers and cyclists who sup on
Theakston's and regular guest ales, and on Sundays can
benefit from an all-day menu. Blackboard specials that
regularly include fresh fish: sea bass, marlin and halibut
steaks, a seafood medley. Also various grilled steaks, 'lamb
Henrietta' and steak and kidney pie. Children welcome until
9pm only.
OPEN: 12–3 6–11.30 Closed: 25 Dec **BAR MEALS:** Lunch served:
all week Dinner served: all week 12–2 6.30–9 Av main course £6
BREWERY/COMPANY: Free House **PRINCIPAL BEERS:** Timothy
Taylor Landlord, Theakstons Bitter, Exmoor Gold,.
FACILITIES: Children welcome **NOTES:** Parking 44

MANCHESTER
Map 08 SJ89

Dukes 92
14 Castle St, Castlefield M3 4LZ
☎ 0161 8398646 🖹 0161 832 3592
e-mail: dukes92@freenet.co.uk
Dir: Town centre
Situated with its vast patio beside the 92nd lock of the Duke of
Bridgewater canal, this beautifully restored 19th-century stable
building is full of surprises, with minimalist decor downstairs
and an upper gallery displaying local artistic talent. Bar meals
with choice from 10 pâtés and over 50 cheeses are a great
draw, along with Greek and Caesar salads, dim sum and
seafood platters to share and a carvery Sunday lunch.
OPEN: 11–11 (Fri–Sat 11–12, Sun 12–10.30) Closed: 25–26 Dec, 1 Jan
BAR MEALS: Lunch served: all week 12–3 Dinner served: Sun–Thurs
5–8 Av main course £3.95 **RESTAURANT:** Lunch served: all week
12–3 Dinner served: Mon–Fri 5–8 Av 3 course à la carte £12
BREWERY/COMPANY: Free House
PRINCIPAL BEERS: Interbrew Boddingtons Bitter.
FACILITIES: Children welcome Garden: Food served outside
NOTES: Parking 30

Lass O'Gowrie ♀
36 Charles St, Chorlton-cum-Medlock M1 7DB ☎ 0161 273 6932
Not far from the BBC complex, this is a traditional pub with
wooden floors, 20 constantly changing cask beers, and its own
brewery. Very busy and popular with students, but has its

continued

continued

quieter times. The real gas lamps add to the atmosphere. Straightforward bar menu includes lasagne, chicken tikka masala, steak and mushroom pudding, Glamorgan sausages, and chicken and bacon salad bowl.
OPEN: 11-11 **BAR MEALS:** Lunch served: all week 11-6 Av main course £3.50 **RESTAURANT:** Lunch served: all week 11-6 **PRINCIPAL BEERS:** Marstons Pedigree, Hook Norton Old Hooky, Black Sheep. **FACILITIES:** Dogs allowed

The White Lion
43 Liverpool Rd, Castlefield M3 4NQ
☎ 0161 8327373 🖷 0161 832 9008
One of the oldest licensed premises in Manchester, adjacent to Castlefields historic Roman fort and Granada Studios.

MELLOR   Map 09 SJ98

The Oddfellows Arms 🐾 ♀
73 Moor End Rd Sk 6 5PT ☎ 0161 449 7826
This old pub changed its name after extensions in 1860 were carried out to accommodate the Oddfellows Society, a fore-runner of the Trade Unions. A friendly welcome can be expected in the stone-flagged bars and dining room, where pride of place goes to the selection of real ales and a choice of bar food or imaginative daily specials. Try Thai-spiced prawns or smoked duck breast; followed by good fresh fish, a roast of the day, bangers and champ or mushroom and pepper goulash.
OPEN: 12-3 5-11 (Sun 12-3, 7-10.30) Closed: 25-26 Dec, 31 Dec **BAR MEALS:** Lunch served: Tues-Sun 12-2 Dinner served: Tues-Sat 6.30-9.30 Av main course £9 **RESTAURANT:** Lunch served: Sun 12-2 Dinner served: Tue-Sat 7-9.30 Av 3 course à la carte £19 **BREWERY/COMPANY:** Free House **PRINCIPAL BEERS:** Adnams Southwold, Marston's Pedigree, Interbrew Flowers IPA.
FACILITIES: Dogs allowed **NOTES:** Parking 21

OLDHAM   Map 09 SD90

The Rams Head Inn 🐾 ♀
Denshaw OL3 5UN ☎ 01457 874802 🖷 01457 820978
e-mail: ramshead-denshaw@btconnect.com
Dir: *From M62 towards Oldham, Denshaw 2m on R*
A 400-year-old farmhouse-style pub with panoramic views of Saddleworth Moor, overlooking the former pack-horse route from Huddersfield to Rochdale. With its original beams, furniture and log fires in each room, the otherwise modest interior is a treasure trove of fascinating memorabilia. Menus offer specialities that include oven-baked haddock with cheese sauce, tuna steak with peperonata, roast suckling pig with caramelised apples and fillet steak with creamy sherry sauce.
OPEN: 12-2.30 6-11 Closed: 25 Dec **BAR MEALS:** Lunch served: all week Dinner served: all week 12-2 6-10 Av main course £9.95 **RESTAURANT:** Lunch served: all week Dinner served: all week 12-2 6-10 Av 3 course à la carte £20 **BREWERY/COMPANY:** Free House **PRINCIPAL BEERS:** Carlsberg-Tetley Tetley Bitter, Timothy Taylor Landlord, Golden, Best. **FACILITIES:** Children welcome **NOTES:** Parking 30

The Roebuck Inn 🐾 ♀
Strinesdale OL4 3RB ☎ 0161 6247819 🖷 0161 624 7819
e-mail: smhowarth1@aol.com
Dir: *From Oldham take A62 then A672 towards Ripponden. 1m turn R at Moorside Public House into Turf Pit Lane. Pub 1m.*
An 18th-century inn located on the edge of Saddleworth Moor in the Pennines. An upstairs room was once used for the 'laying out' of bodies - often taken from the reservoirs at

Strinesdale - and the last of these, a young woman, is believed to revisit on occasion. Part of the restaurant once served as a Sunday School. Favourite fare includes steak and ale pudding, roast duck with orange stuffing and Grand Marnier sauce, and fresh deep-fried haddock with mushy peas.
OPEN: 12-2.30 5-12 **BAR MEALS:** Lunch served: all week Dinner served: all week 12-2.15 5-9.30 Av main course £6 **RESTAURANT:** Lunch served: all week Dinner served: all week 12-2.15 5-9.30 Av 3 course à la carte £12.50 Av 3 course fixed price £7.25 **BREWERY/COMPANY:** Free House **PRINCIPAL BEERS:** Boddingtons smoothflow,Wadsworth. **FACILITIES:** Children welcome Garden: Dogs allowed **NOTES:** Parking 40

Pick of the Pubs

The White Hart Inn ◎◎ 🐾 ♀
Stockport Rd, Lydgate OL4 4JJ ☎ 01457 872566 🖷 01457 875190
e-mail: charles@thewhitehart.co.uk
Dir: *From Manchester A62 to Oldham. R onto bypass, A669 through Lees. Inn 500yds past Grotton brow of hill turn R*
A 200-year-old inn that has brought stunning food high up into the rugged moors above Oldham. The traditional inn, which has a colourful history, looks out over the Pennines, and has expanded to include new bedrooms and a varied dining option including a restaurant, brasserie and bar. The quality stamp is on every dish, whether simple or complicated, and cooking is based on the best available local produce. From the brasserie expect speciality sausages, seared calves' liver with pickled red cabbage and black pudding fritters, roast rump of lamb, and fillet of haddock in a beer batter. The short restaurant carte offers seared scallops and curried glazed oysters with coriander salad to start perhaps, followed by pan-fried black beef fillet with sautéed sweetbreads, and toasted coconut bavarois with passion fruit sorbet. There's also a gourmet menu, and a delicious choice of English cheeses.
OPEN: 12-11 (Sun 1-10.30) **BAR MEALS:** Lunch served: all week Dinner served: all week 12-2.30 6-9.30 Av main course £12 **RESTAURANT:** Lunch served: Sun Dinner served: Tue-Sat 1-3.30 6.30-9.30 Av 3 course à la carte £25 Av 5 course fixed price £25 **BREWERY/COMPANY:** Free House **PRINCIPAL BEERS:** Interbrew Boddingtons Bitter, Timothy Taylor Best, J W Lees Bitter. **FACILITIES:** Children welcome Garden: Food served outside **NOTES:** Parking 60 **ROOMS:** 12 bedrooms 12 en suite

SALFORD   Map 08 SJ89

Mark Addy
Stanley St M3 5EJ ☎ 0161 832 4080
On the banks of the River Irwell close to Salford Quays, a former river-ferry landing stage - where Mark Addy saved 50 passengers from drowning in Victorian times. Up to 50 cheeses from eight countries and eight Belgian pâtés are served with granary bread - and soup in winter. Wine tasting notes accompany: free doggy bags.
OPEN: 11.30-11 Closed: 25/26 Dec, Jan 1 **BAR MEALS:** Lunch served: all week Dinner served: all week 11.30-9 **BREWERY/COMPANY:** Free House **PRINCIPAL BEERS:** Boddingtons, three guest beers. **FACILITIES:** Children's licence Garden: Riverside patio

continued

England

STALYBRIDGE
Map 09 SJ99

Stalybridge Station Buffet Bar ♀
The Railway Station SK15 1RF ☎ 0161 303 0007
e-mail: esk@buffetbar.com
Unique Victorian railway station refreshment rooms dating from 1885 and including original bar fittings, open fire and conservatory. Recently extended using the old living accommodation and first class ladies waiting room. There have been over 3600 real ales served here in the last five years, and the bar hosts regular beer festivals. Expect pasta bake, pies and black peas, liver and onions, and sausage and mash on the bar menu.
OPEN: 11-11 Mon-Sat 12-10.30 Sun Closed: Dec 25
BAR MEALS: Lunch served: all week 11-8 Av main course £3.50
BREWERY/COMPANY: Free House
PRINCIPAL BEERS: Boddingtons, Flowers, Wadworth 6X, Guest Ales each week. **FACILITIES:** Children welcome Food served outside Dogs allowed (water provided) **NOTES:** Parking 60 No credit cards

SWINTON
Map 08 SD70

The New Ellesmere ♀
East Lancs Rd M27 3AA ☎ 0161 728 2791 ⊠ 0161 794 8222
Bedrooms. Handy for M6 and M62. Dogs not allowed, except guide dogs. Once was a cinema. Typical menu includes steak and ale pie, gammon, haddock and plaice.

WIGAN
Map 08 SD50

Bird I'th Hand NEW
Gathurst Rd, Orell WN5 0LH ☎ 01942 212006
Not far from Aintree racecourse, Orrell is noted for both its rugby club and this vibrant pub. Set in a large well-maintained garden, it possibly was the home of Dr Beecham of 'powders' fame. Home-made food, freshly prepared from fresh market produce, typically offers plaice in brown butter, capers and prawns, chicken supreme in bacon with white wine sauce and rump steak with wild mushrooms and onions. Large garden and activity centre popular with families. No credit cards

HAMPSHIRE

ALRESFORD
Map 04 SU53

The Fox Inn ♀
Bramdean SO24 0LP ☎ 01962 771363
e-mail: thefoxinn@callnet.com
400-year-old village pub situated in the beautiful Meon Valley surrounded by copper beech trees. Produce is locally sourced and a good choice of fresh fish is featured on blackboard menus written up twice a day. Options might include pan-fried wing of skate, whole sea bass with a chilli salsa, roast rack of lamb, and fillet steak in a mushroom cream sauce. No evening meals Sunday or Mondays from Jan to Mar.
OPEN: 11-3 6-11 (Winter open at 6.30) **BAR MEALS:** Lunch served: all week Dinner served: all week 12-2 7-9 Av main course £9.95 **BREWERY/COMPANY:** Greene King
PRINCIPAL BEERS: Greene King Abbot Ale, Greene King IPA.
FACILITIES: Garden: Food served outside **NOTES:** Parking 25

Pick of the Pubs

The Globe on the Lake ♀
The Soke, Broad St SO24 9DB
☎ 01962 732294 ⊠ 01962 736211
e-mail: duveen-conway@supanet.com
See Pick of the Pubs on page 223

ANDOVER
Map 04 SU34

The Old Bell & Crown ♀ NEW
Hatherden SP11 0HT ☎ 01264 735321 ⊠ 01264 735321
Dir: From Andover follow signs for Charlton, then for Hatherden, pub in 2 miles
Idyllic 15th-century thatched inn with roses around the door, located in the scenic Test Valley. Its farmhouse origins are evident from exposed flint walls and open fires in the bars, and oak beams in the restaurant, where good home-cooked food is served. Dishes on offer included Cajun spiced salmon, pan-fried wild boar steak, home-made lamb, leek and rosemary pie, supreme of chicken with a Stilton cream sauce, and baked fillets of bass with a herb and pesto crust.
OPEN: 12-2.30 6-11 **BAR MEALS:** Lunch served: all week Dinner served: all week 12-2 6.30-9.30 Av main course £8
RESTAURANT: Lunch served: all week Dinner served: all week 12-2 6.30-9.30 Av 3 course à la carte £16.50
BREWERY/COMPANY: Wadworth **PRINCIPAL BEERS:** Wadworth 6X & JCB, Henry's IPA,. **FACILITIES:** Garden: Food served outdoors Dogs allowed (water) **NOTES:** Parking 50

BASINGSTOKE
Map 04 SU65

Hoddington Arms ♀
Upton Grey RG25 2RL ☎ 01256 862371 ⊠ 01256 862371
e-mail: justinhoddy@lineone.net
A traditional 18th-century English pub near the duck pond of a village acclaimed over several years as Hampshire's best kept. Old beams and log fires encourage relaxation in a music and machine-free environment. Home-cooked meals include steak and Guinness pie, game and juniper casserole, or Hoddington fish bake. Special requests are catered for on the principle that 'if we have it, so may you'. A peaceful rear terrace and garden are added draws in summer.
OPEN: 11.30-2.30 6-11 **BAR MEALS:** Lunch all week 12-2 Dinner Mon-Sat 6.30-9.30 Av meal £6.95 **RESTAURANT:** Lunch 12-2 Mon-Sat Dinner 7-9 Av 3 courses £22 **PRINCIPAL BEERS:** Greene King IPA, Abbot Ale **FACILITIES:** Garden: Food served outside Dogs welcome (water) **NOTES:** Parking 30

BEAUWORTH
Map 04 SU52

The Milburys
SO24 0PB ☎ 01962 771248 ⊠ 01962 7771910
Dir: A272 towards Petersfield, after 6m turn R for Beauworth
Rustic hill-top pub dating from the 17th century and named after the Bronze Age Mill-barrow nearby. Noted for its massive, 250-year-old treadmill that used to draw water from the 300ft well in the bar, and for the far-reaching views across Hampshire that can be savoured from the lotfy garden. Menu includes chargrilled venison steak with woodland berry jus, crispy aromatic duck, four cheese pasta, and pan-fried king scallops on crispy bacon salad. Jacket potatoes, potato skins, and sandwiches also available.
OPEN: 11-11 (Sun 12-10.30) **BAR MEALS:** Lunch served: all week Dinner served: all week 12-2 6.30-9.30
BREWERY/COMPANY: Free House **PRINCIPAL BEERS:** Cheriton Best Bitter, Cheriton Diggers Gold, Hopback Best Bitter, Theakstons Old Peculier. **FACILITIES:** Children welcome Garden: Food served outside Dogs allowed (water provided) **NOTES:** Parking 60
ROOMS: 2 bedrooms from s£28.50 d£40

```
⊛ For a list of pubs with
AA Rosette Awards for food see pages 12 & 13.
```

PUB WALK

Sparsholt
The Plough

The middle stages of this varied and scenic walk are under cover of trees. The route passes through a delightful and ancient coppice on the edge of Farley Mount Country Park. Extending to 1,000 acres, the park is a popular amenity area with a wide variety of wildlife. The views over open countryside are some of the most striking in Hampshire.

From the front of the inn turn left and walk up the road towards Lainston House. At the first junction, turn right and drop down narrow Dean Lane between trees and hedgerows. Pass a path in the right-hand bank. Continue down beyond Dean Hill Cottage to the pretty hamlet of Dean. As the road bends left by Barn Cottage, go straight on along a bridleway running between hedges and trees. Head up the chalk slope and avoid turnings on the left and right. Keep left at the fork and now the path runs through a tunnel of yew trees, passing a turning on the right. Continue on the main bridleway all the way to the road. Turn right and pass a remote house

and some barns. Just beyond them the lane becomes enveloped by woodland. Avoid a path running into the trees on the right and make for the second wide entrance to Farley Mount Country Park, also on the right. Follow the winding track through Crab Wood, all the way to the road. Cross over to two barriers. Take the left one and turn right onto a path after about 50 yards (46m). Keep right at the next fork and then turn right at a crossroads. On reaching a straight track after a few paces, turn left and walk along to a junction. Cross over the track and follow the path with fencing on the left. Follow the bridleway as it heads for the north-east boundary of West Wood, passing alongside silver birch trees. Eventually the trees thin and beside you now are fields and paddocks. After about half a mile (800m) on the bridlepath you join a track serving various bungalows. Just before reaching the road junction, look for a path veering off half left into the trees. Follow it down to the lane and turn left. Walk back into Sparsholt and return to the inn.

THE PLOUGH
Main Road SPARSHOLT Nr Winchester SO21 2NW
Tel: 01962 776353
Directions: From Winchester take B3049(A272) W, take L turn to village of Sparsholt. The Plough Inn is 1m down the lane
A 200-year-old cottage with a delightful garden - the perfect spot for a summer evening drink. Inside, a bustling bar, a log fire, Wadworth ales and decent wines. Imaginative home-cooked food.
Open: 11–3 6–11 (Sun 12–3 6–10.30)
Bar Meals: 12–2 6–9
Children welcome and dogs allowed. Garden and parking available.

Distance: 4 miles (6.4km)
Map: OS Landranger 185
Terrain: Remote, unpopulated expanses of woodland and downland
Paths: Bridleways, country roads, woodland tracks and paths
Gradient: Undulating countryside

Walk submitted and checked by Nick Channer

BENTLEY
Map 04 SU74

The Bull Inn
GU10 5JH ☎ 01420 22156 & 23334 📠 01420 520772
Dir: *2m out of Farnham on the A31 towards Winchester*

A handy refuge from the A31 between Alton and Farnham, a recently refurbished 15th-century road house that retains its old-fashioned character with oak beams, inglenook and open fires. Simple bar snacks stray little from the tried and tested baguettes, jacket potatoes and ham, egg and chips. However, monthly changing dinner menus add duck and Grand Marnier parfait, roast chump of lamb and selections from the chargrill. Booking advised.
OPEN: 11-11 (Sun 12-10.30) **BAR MEALS:** Lunch served: all week Dinner served: all week 12-2.30 6.30-10 Av main course £12
RESTAURANT: Lunch served: all week Dinner served: all week 12-2.30 6.30-10 Av 3 course à la carte £25
BREWERY/COMPANY: Free House **PRINCIPAL BEERS:** Scottish Courage Courage Best, Hogs Back TEA, Young's Bitter, Marston's Pedigree. **FACILITIES:** Children welcome Garden: Food served outside Dogs allowed **NOTES:** Parking 40

BENTWORTH
Map 04 SU64

The Star Inn 🍴
GU34 5RD ☎ 01420 561224
e-mail: mk@star-inn.com
Dir: *N of Alton 3 M off A339*
The Star occupies a charming spot opposite the village green; eye-catching with its summer floral displays and handy for visitors to the nearby Woodland Trust. Toasties, bacon, egg and chips and pizzas are on offer in the bar. A separate dining room menu offers pork steaks in brandy and mushroom sauce, or boozy bangers in beer gravy. Salmon in prawn and dill sauce, and vegetable moussaka are among the house specialities. Live music on Fridays, jam sessions on Sunday and Tuesday curry nights.
OPEN: 12-3 5-11 **BAR MEALS:** Lunch served: all week Dinner served: all week 12-2 6.30-9 Av main course £4.95
RESTAURANT: Lunch served: all week Dinner served: all week 12-2 6.30-9 Av 3 course à la carte £16 **BREWERY/COMPANY:** Free House **PRINCIPAL BEERS:** Interbrew Bass, Gale's Butser Bitter.
FACILITIES: Garden: Food served outside **NOTES:** Parking 12

Pick of the Pubs

The Sun Inn 🍷
Sun Hill GU34 5JT ☎ 01420 562338
Located down a narrow lane on the village edge, this delightful, flower-adorned 17th-century pub, originally two cottages, has three interconnecting rooms, each with open log fires, brick or boarded floors, low-beamed ceilings,

and lots of old pews, settles and scrubbed pine tables. A thriving free house it offers eight real ales, including local Hogs Back TEA and Cheriton Brewhouse Pots Ale, on handpump and a traditional pub atmosphere. It is particularly cosy and inviting in the evenings when candles top the tables. Food is equally traditional; expect filled giant Yorkshire puddings, bacon, mushroom and tomato pasta salad, cheesy haddock bake, liver and bacon with creamy mash and braised steak in red wine and mushroom sauce, alongside Mediterranean lamb and venison in Guinness and pickled walnuts.

OPEN: 12-3 6-11 (Sun 12-10.30) **BAR MEALS:** Lunch served: all week Dinner served: all week 12-2 7-9.30 Av main course £6.95 **BREWERY/COMPANY:** Free House
PRINCIPAL BEERS: Cheriton Pots Ale, Ringwood Best & Old Thumper, Brakspear Bitter, Fuller's London Pride.
FACILITIES: Children welcome Garden: Food served outside Dogs allowed

BISHOP'S WALTHAM
Map 04 SU51

The Priory Inn
Winchester Rd SO32 1BE ☎ 01489 891313 📠 01489 896370
Dir: *from M3 take Marwell Zoo turnoff thru Twyford, L at Queens Head pub, follow Winchester Rd into Bishops Waltham*
Traditional, friendly inn, originally known as The Railway, located in one of Hampshire's most famous villages, renowned for its ruined palace, built around 1135. Handy for Winchester and the coast. Real log fire, garden and games bar are among the features.
OPEN: 11.30-11 (Sun 12-10.30) **BAR MEALS:** Lunch served: all week Dinner served: all week 11.30-2 5-9.30 Av main course £5.50
RESTAURANT: 11.30-2 5.00-9.30
BREWERY/COMPANY: Whitbread
PRINCIPAL BEERS: Wadworth 6X, Hampshire Pride of Romsey.
FACILITIES: Children welcome Garden: outdoor eating, patio, BBQ
NOTES: Parking 15 **ROOMS:** 2 bedrooms 2 en suite from s£20 d£40

BOLDRE
Map 04 SZ39

The Red Lion Inn 🍴🍷
Rope Hill SO41 8NE ☎ 01590 673177 📠 01590 676403
Dir: *0.25m E off A337, 1m N of Lymington*
Although it was mentioned as an alehouse in the Domesday Book, today's inn harks back only to the 15th century. The current pub was formed from two cottages and a stable. Outside, an old cart strewn with flowers adds to the eye-catching hanging baskets that are a riot of summer colour. Inside there are interesting collections of old bottles, chamber

continued
continued

OPEN: 11–3 6–11
BAR MEALS: L served all week.
D served all week. 12–2 6.30–9.30
Av main course £8.50
RESTAURANT: L served all week.
D served all week. 12–2 6.30–9.30
Av cost 3 courses £17.25
BREWERY/COMPANY:
UNIQUE PUB CO LTD
PRINCIPAL BEERS: Wadworth 6X,
Scottish Courage Directors,
Brakspear Bitter, Fuller's London
Pride
FACILITIES: Children welcome.
Garden: Food served outside

The Globe on the Lake

In an exceptional location on the banks of a reed-fringed lake and wildfowl sanctuary, The Globe offers a convivial atmosphere in which to enjoy good food, good beer and good wine. In the attractive town of Alresford, this 17th-century inn has one of the most enviable locations beside Alresford Pond, where waterfowl swim amongst the reeds and sunbathe amongst the picnic tables in the lakeside gardens.

The Soke, Broad Street SO24 9DB
☎ 01962 732294 📄 01962 736211
e-mail: duveen-conway@supanet.com

The interior of pub is being refurbished and decorated with objects for Britain and the East, while on the walls are a selection of interesting artworks. Located at the bottom of the superb Georgian main street, it is a popular dining pub where freshly-prepared food is served in the restaurant area or bustling bar with log fires in winter. Summer meals

can be enjoyed in the garden, while the lovely view can be appreciated on cooler days from the restaurant and enclosed and heated rear terrace. The daily changing blackboard menus feature many fresh fish dishes: perhaps halibut Normandy, fillet of cod in beer batter, pan-fried tuna steak with Mediterranean vegetables, and salmon fishcakes with sorrel sauce. Otherwise expect estoufade (rich stew) of beef, sautéed pork tenderloin, Meon Valley pork and leek sausages, roast rump of lamb, or a choice of tapas. Finish with cherries soaked in Kirsch and brandy, or Belgian biscuit cake with cream. A fixed price menu is served on Sunday with a choice of four starters and four main courses including a traditional roast. Real ales and a good selection of wines to accompany the meal.

England

BOLDRE continued

pots and various old farming implements adorning the
rambling series of interconnecting beamed rooms.
OPEN: 11-11 (Sun 12-10.30) **BAR MEALS:** Lunch served: all week
Dinner served: all week 12-2.30 6.30-9.30 Av main course £6
RESTAURANT: Lunch served: all week Dinner served: all week
12-2.30 6.30-9.30 **PRINCIPAL BEERS:** Scottish Courage Courage
Directors & Courage Best. **FACILITIES:** Garden: Food served outside
NOTES: Parking 50

BROCKENHURST   Map 04 SU30

The Filly Inn 🛏️
Lymington Rd, Setley SO42 7UF
☎ 01590 623449 🖷 01590 623449
e-mail: pub@fillyinn.co.uk
One of the most picturesque, cosy traditional pubs in the
heart of the New Forest. Locals attest to frequent sightings of
George, the resident ghost, thought to be a long-dead,
repentant highwayman. The far from spooky menu offers
standard pub snacks of baguettes and filled jacket potatoes, as
well as home-cooked English ham with egg and chips, beef
lasagne and home-baked pies of the day. Daily specials could
include traditional battered cod, seafood platter and lamb
sizzlers. Cream teas in summer.
OPEN: 10-11 **BAR MEALS:** Lunch served: All Dinner served: All
10-2.15 6.30-10 Av main course £5 **RESTAURANT:** Lunch served: all
week Dinner served: all week 10-2.15 6.30-10
BREWERY/COMPANY: Free House
PRINCIPAL BEERS: Ringwood Best, Old Thumper,.
FACILITIES: Children welcome Children's licence Garden: Large
seating area, food served outside Dogs allowed (water)
NOTES: Parking 90 **ROOMS:** 3 bedrooms 1 en suite from s£40
d£40

BROOK   Map 04 SU21

Pick of the Pubs

The Bell Inn ★ ★ ★ 🏵 🛏️
SO43 7HE ☎ 023 80812214 🖷 023 80813958
e-mail: bell@bramshaw.co.uk
Dir: From M27 J1 (Cadnam) take B3078 signed Brook, 0.5m on R

This handsome listed inn is part of the Bramshaw Golf
Club and includes facilities for conferences and golf
societies. It also makes an ideal base for touring the New
Forest and the nearby south coast. The main building,
dating from 1782, contains many period features, notably
in the bar with its imposing inglenook fireplace and in the
beamed bedrooms of the inn's oldest part. Menus incline
towards Anglo-French, with embellishments such as

Indonesian-style turkey bang-bang, roast tuna loin with
guacamole crust and penne carbonara with Parmesan.,
Popular dishes include traditional cottage pie and faggots
in onion gravy, as well as the more sophisticated venison
haunch with pink peppercorn cream sauce and rainbow
trout with almonds and caper butter. Traditional plum
pudding with clotted cream and dark chocolate quenelles
are tempting afters for the sweet-toothed.
OPEN: 11-11 (Sun 12-10.30) **BAR MEALS:** Lunch served: all
week Dinner served: all week 12-2.30 6.30-9.30 Av main course
£8.95 **RESTAURANT:** Lunch served: Sun 12-2 Dinner served:
all week 6.30-9.30 Av 3 course fixed price £26.50
BREWERY/COMPANY: Free House
PRINCIPAL BEERS: Ringwood Best, Scottish Courage Courage
Directors. **FACILITIES:** Children welcome Children's licence
Garden: Food served outside **NOTES:** Parking 60
ROOMS: 25 bedrooms 25 en suite from s£60 d£80

BROUGHTON   Map 04 SU33

The Tally Ho!
High St SO20 8AA ☎ 01794 301280
Dir: Winchester to Stockbridge rd then A30, 1st L to Broughton
Traditional, well restored pub nestling in a pretty village close
to the Test Valley and a popular refreshment stop for walkers
undertaking the Clarendon Way.

BUCKLERS HARD   Map 04 SU40

The Master Builders House Hotel ★ ★ ★ 🏵🏵 ♀
SO42 7XB ☎ 01590 616253 🖷 01590 616297
e-mail: res@themasterbuilders.co.uk
On the banks of the Beaulieu River this former house of the
master shipbuilder Henry Adams has been carefully
refurbished. Grassy areas in front of this fine 18th-century
building run right down to the river - a delightful spot. The
beamed Yachtsman's Bar which is very popular in summer
with tourists. Good light snacks and short menu
offering the likes of fish pie and beef bourguignon.
Imaginative restaurant menu, and stylish bedrooms in the
upmarket hotel side of the operation.
OPEN: 11-11 (Sun 12-10.30) **BAR MEALS:** Lunch served: all week
Dinner served: all week 12-2.30 6.30-9 Av main course £12.50
RESTAURANT: Lunch served: all week Dinner served: all week
12-2.30 6.30-9 Av 3 course à la carte £19.60
BREWERY/COMPANY: Free House **PRINCIPAL BEERS:** Scottish
Courage Courage Directors, Samuel Smith, Ringwood Best.
FACILITIES: Children welcome Garden: Food served outdoors
Dogs allowed (water) **NOTES:** Parking 50 **ROOMS:** 25 bedrooms
25 en suite from s£120 d£165

BURITON   Map 04 SU71

The Five Bells 🛏️ ♀
High St GU31 5RX ☎ 01730 263584 🖷 01730 263584
Dir: village signposted off A3 S of Petersfield
The South Downs Way runs through Buriton on its way to
Winchester, and this characterful 17th-century village inn
makes a welcome refreshment stop. In addition to its quaint
beams, cosy fires and solid stone walls, the Five Bells has a
fascinating history. The restaurant was formerly the farriers,
then a clay pipe factory, and at one point even the village
morgue! A typical menu may feature fresh red bream with
onions and deep-fried prosciutto, steak and kidney pie,
spinach and Brie filo parcels, and grilled whole plaice.

continued   *continued*

OPEN: 11-2.30 5.30-11 **BAR MEALS:** Lunch served: all week Dinner served: all week 12-2 6-10 Av main course £7
RESTAURANT: Lunch served: all week Dinner served: all week 12-2 7-9.30 Av 3 course à la carte £20 **BREWERY/COMPANY:** Hall & Woodhouse **PRINCIPAL BEERS:** Badger Best, Tanglefoot, Champion, K&B Sussex. **FACILITIES:** Children welcome Garden: Food served outside. Secluded garden Dogs allowed (water & biscuits provided) **NOTES:** Parking 12

BURLEY
Map 04 SU20

The Burley Inn 🛏 ♀
BH24 4AB ☎ 01425 403448 ▤ 01425 402058
e-mail: info@theburleyinn.co.uk
Dir: between the A31 & A35

At the centre of a quiet New Forest village, a former doctor's house from Edwardian times, successfully converted into a comfortable country inn and renowned for its tree house where the doctor himself once sold cream teas. The menu offers oak-smoked trout, beef and Stilton pie and Mexican chilli bean pot, with venison listed among the choice of steaks and regular roast joints.
OPEN: 11-3 6-11 (all day Summer) **BAR MEALS:** Lunch served: all week 12-2.15 Dinner served: Mon-Sat 6.30-9.15 Av main course £8
RESTAURANT: Lunch served: all week 12-2.15 Dinner served: Mon-Sat 6-9.15 Av 3 course à la carte £15.50
BREWERY/COMPANY: Wadworth
PRINCIPAL BEERS: Wadworth 6X, Henry's IPA,.
FACILITIES: Garden: Terrace, food served outside **NOTES:** Parking 18 **ROOMS:** 8 bedrooms 8 en suite from s£40 d£45

CADNAM
Map 04 SU31

The White Hart ♀
Old Romsey Rd SO40 2NP ☎ 023 80812277
Dir: M27 J1 Just off rdbt to Lyndhurst
Smartly refurbished old coaching inn located on the edge of the New Forest and a very convenient refreshment for M27/A31 travellers. Rambling series of interconnecting rooms with open fires, a comfortable mix of old and new furniture, tiled floors and traditional decor. Food is the attraction here, the extensive blackboard menu listing home-cooked dishes prepared from fresh local produce, including fish and game. Typical dishes may include lamb noisettes on garlic mash with red wine sauce, pan-fried monkfish with Thai curry sauce, and game casserole; good snacks like open sandwiches and pasta dishes. Large rear garden.
OPEN: 11-3 6-11 **BAR MEALS:** Lunch served: all week Dinner served: all week 12-2 6-9 Av main course £9.25
PRINCIPAL BEERS: Wadworth 6X, Ringwood Best, Boddingtons.
FACILITIES: Children welcome Garden: Food served outside
NOTES: Parking 60

CHALTON
Map 04 SU71

The Red Lion 🛏 ♀
PO8 0BG ☎ 023 92592246 ▤ 023 92596915
e-mail: redlionchalton@aol.com
Dir: Just off A3 between Horndean & Petersfield. Take exit near Queens Elizabeth Country Park

Hampshire's oldest pub, dating back to 1147, was originally a workshop for craftsmen building the Norman church opposite. In addition to real ales, there's a choice of over 20 malts and imaginative dishes from the daily menu. Expect the likes of mahi-mahi fillets poached in coconut milk, guinea fowl in Calvados, and fresh sea bass with roasted macadamia nuts and honey dressing - as well as the usual pub snacks.
OPEN: 11-3 6-11 **BAR MEALS:** Lunch served: all week 12-2 Dinner served: Mon-Sat 6.30-9.30 Av main course £8.50
RESTAURANT: Lunch served: all week 12-2 Dinner served: Mon-Sat 6.30-9.30 Av 3 course à la carte £8.95
BREWERY/COMPANY: Gales **PRINCIPAL BEERS:** Gales Butser, Winter Brew, GB & HSB. **FACILITIES:** Children welcome Garden: beer garden, food served outdoors Dogs allowed Dogs welcome in public bar **NOTES:** Parking 80

CHARTER ALLEY
Map 04 SU55

The White Hart
White Hart Ln RG26 5QA ☎ 01256 850048 ▤ 01256 850524
e-mail: h4howard@aol.com
Dir: From M3 J6 take A339 towards Newbury.Take turning to Ramsdell. Turn R at church, then 1st L into White Hart Lane
Built in 1819, this village pub originally catered for local woodsmen and coaches visiting the farrier's next door. These days it's popular with cyclists and walkers from Basingstoke and Reading and real ale enthusiasts from all over, having sold more than 450 real ales from around the country in the last 10 years and won five CAMRA awards in recent times. Guest ales change weekly and home-made food is served in generous portions.
OPEN: 12-2.30 7-11 Closed: Dec 25-26 **BAR MEALS:** Lunch served: all week 12-2 Dinner served: Tue-Sun 7-9 Av main course £7.50 **RESTAURANT:** Lunch served: all week 12-2 Dinner served: Tue-Sun 7-9 Av 3 course à la carte £18
BREWERY/COMPANY: Free House **PRINCIPAL BEERS:** Timothy Taylor Landlord, Batemans XB, West Berkshire Mild, Adnams Broadside. **FACILITIES:** Garden: Food served outside Dogs allowed
NOTES: Parking 30

CHERITON   Map 04 SU52

Pick of the Pubs

The Flower Pots Inn
SO24 0QQ ☎ 01962 771318 📠 01962 771318
Dir: *A272 toward Petersfield, L onto B3046, pub 0.75m on R*
Originally built as a farmhouse in the 1840s by the head
gardener of nearby Avington House, this unassuming and
homely brick village pub has become a popular place in
which to sample award-winning ales, brewed in the
micro-brewery across the car park, and simple, honest bar
food. Two traditional bars are delightfully music- and
electronic game-free, the rustic public bar being furnished
with pine tables and benches and the cosy saloon having
a relaxing sofa among other chairs; both have warming
winter log fires. A short value-for-money menu offers
home-cooked meals, including jacket potatoes with decent
filling, giant baps (try the home-baked ham), hearty soups
and casseroles and a bowl of delicious chilli served with
garlic bread or rice. Come on a Wednesday night for an
authentic Punjabi curry and wash it down with a first-rate
pint of Pots Ale or Diggers Gold. Neat, pine-furnished
bedrooms are housed in a well-converted outbuilding.
Beer Festival August Bank Holiday.
OPEN: 12–2.30 6–11 (Sun 12–3, 7–10.30) **BAR MEALS:** Lunch
served: all week 12–2 Dinner served: Mon–Sat 7–9 Av main
course £5 **BREWERY/COMPANY:** Free House
PRINCIPAL BEERS: Cheriton Pots Ale, Best Bitter, Diggers Gold.
FACILITIES: Garden: Dogs allowed **NOTES:** Parking 30
ROOMS: 5 bedrooms 5 en suite No credit cards

CRONDALL   Map 04 SU74

Pick of the Pubs

The Hampshire Arms 🛏 NEW
Pankridge St GU10 5QU ☎ 01252 850418 📠 01252 850418
e-mail: paulychef@hantsarms.freeserve.co.uk
Dir: *From M3 junct 5 take A287 South towards Farnham. Follow signs
to Crondall on R*
Since they took over two years ago, chef-proprietor Paul
Morgan and his wife Gillian have struck an award winning
balance between preservation of this pub's traditional
charms and the introduction of a level of food and service
that easily exceeds the norm. It's still good and pubby,
with open fires, bare beams, hop bines and candlelight.
Outside is a lovely garden, complete with river and ducks.
Dine in the bar or the restaurant, where white linen and
sparkling glassware hint that this won't be your average
pub meal: dishes might include roasted sea bass on
aubergine caviar, with a confit of roasted vine tomato,
pesto pomme purée and tomato and butter sauce or
venison on spiced red cabbage with caramelised shallots,
glazed walnuts and fondant potatoes. Still, in the spirit of
the whole operation, they've preserved traditional pub
pluses including value for money and old favourites such
as the mixed grill or steak and kidney pie.
OPEN: 11–3.30 5.30–11 (all day Sat, Sun 12–10.30)
BAR MEALS: Lunch served: all week 12–2.30 Dinner served:
Mon–Sat 7–9 Av main course £13 **RESTAURANT:** Lunch served:
all week Dinner served: Mon–Sat 12–2.30 7–9 Av 3 course à la
carte £22 **BREWERY/COMPANY:** Greene King
PRINCIPAL BEERS: Greene King IPA, Abbot Ale, Ruddles
County,. **FACILITIES:** Children welcome Garden: Food served
outside Dogs allowed (water) **NOTES:** Parking 40

DAMERHAM   Map 03 SU11

The Compasses Inn ◆◆◆ ⊉
SP6 3HQ ☎ 01725 518231 📠 01725 518880
Dir: *From Fordingbridge (A338) follow signs for Sandleheath/Damerham.
Or signs from B3078*

Located in the village centre next to the local cricket pitch this
400-year-old coaching is full of character and atmosphere in
both the cottagey bedrooms and pine-furnished bars. Real
ales, including their own brew and regular guests, and a fine
collection of over 100 malt whiskies. Locally produced fresh
food with offerings of smoked haddock with cheese sauce and
pork chops with coriander and lemon. Notable for its cheeses,
served with home-made pickles, and large garden with superb
views.
OPEN: 11–3 6–11 (all day Sat, Sun 12–4, 7–10.30)
BAR MEALS: Lunch served: all week Dinner served: all week
12–2.30 7–9.30 Av main course £8.50 **RESTAURANT:** Lunch served:
all week Dinner served: all week 12–2.30 7–9.30 Av 3 course à la carte
£20 **BREWERY/COMPANY:** Free House
PRINCIPAL BEERS: Compasses Ale, Ringwood Best, Hop Back
Summer Lightning, Wadworth 6X. **FACILITIES:** Children welcome
Children's licence Garden: Patio area, food served outdoors Dogs
allowed (By arrangement) **NOTES:** Parking 30 **ROOMS:** 6
bedrooms 6 en suite from s£39.50 d£69

DOGMERSFIELD   Map 04 SU75

The Queens Head 🛏 ⊉ NEW
Pilcot Ln RG27 8SY ☎ 01252 613531
A 17th-century coaching inn linked to Catherine of Aragon, set
beside a stream and some pretty thatched cottages with
Dogmersfield Park and lake nearby. An extensive international
menu of over 120 dishes is served by friendly staff, including
honey and ginger chicken, beef Stroganoff, tournados Rossini,
kleftiki, and plenty of fish such as halibut, turbot, whole sea
bass and lemon sole.
OPEN: 11.30–3.30 5.30–11 **BAR MEALS:** Lunch served: Tue–Sun
Dinner served: Tue–Sun 12–2 6–9 Av main course £9
RESTAURANT: Lunch served: Tue–Sun Dinner served: Tue–Sun 12–2
6–9 Av 3 course à la carte £15.95 **BREWERY/COMPANY:** Free
House **PRINCIPAL BEERS:** Fuller's London Pride, Young's Special,
Scottish Courage Courage Best. **FACILITIES:** Children welcome
Garden: Food served outdoors

DUMMER   Map 04 SU54

The Queen Inn
Down St RG25 2AD ☎ 01256 397367 📠 01256 397601
Dir: *M3 J7, turn into Dummer*
You can dine by candlelight at this 16th-century village pub,
with its low beams and huge open log fire. Everything is home

continued

made, from the soup and light bites to the famous fish and chips with beer batter, fresh sea bass, and prime steaks. The steak and kidney pudding is only for the heartier appetite!
OPEN: 11–3 6–11 (Sun 12–3 7–10.30) **BAR MEALS:** Lunch served: all week Dinner served: all week 12–2 6–9.30 Av main course £7.95 **RESTAURANT:** Lunch served: all week Dinner served: all week 12–2 6–9.30 Av 3 course à la carte £17.50 **BREWERY/COMPANY:** Free House **PRINCIPAL BEERS:** Courage Best, Greene King IPA, Fullers London Pride. **FACILITIES:** Children welcome Garden:
NOTES: Parking 20

EAST END   Map 04 SZ39

Pick of the Pubs

The East End Arms
Main Rd SO41 5SY ☎ 01590 626223 📠 01590 626223
e-mail: jennie@eastendarms.co.uk
Dir: From Lymington follow signs for Isle of Wight ferry. Pass ferry terminal on R & continue for 3m
Traditional New Forest pub tucked away down quiet lanes, close to Beaulieu and historic Buckler's Hard. Worth the short diversion off The Solent Way for the short, interesting range of modern, brasserie-style dishes served in the comfortably refurbished lounge bar. Oven-baked ciabatta's, filled baguettes, fish pie and liver and bacon appear on the light snack menu, while the main fortnightly changing menu could list duck and apple terrine, roast glazed duck with North African couscous, slow-roasted lamb shank with forest mushrooms, and pan-fried ribeye steak with roast red pepper butter and fresh-cut chips. Fish specials may include roast haddock with mussels and chorizo or baked red bream with fennel and peppers. Rustic Foresters Bar with stone floor, open fires, Ringwood ales drawn straight from the wood, and gamekeepers with guns!
OPEN: 11.30–3 6–11 (Sun 12–9) Closed: 1 Jan
BAR MEALS: Lunch served: Tue–Sun 12–2 Av main course £6.50 **RESTAURANT:** Lunch served: Tue–Sun 12–2 Dinner served: Tue–Sat 7–9 Av 3 course à la carte £18.50
BREWERY/COMPANY: Free House
PRINCIPAL BEERS: Ringwood Best & Fortyniner.
FACILITIES: Children welcome Garden: Food served outside Dogs allowed (water provided) **NOTES:** Parking 20

EAST MEON   Map 04 SU62

Ye Olde George Inn
Church St GU32 1NH ☎ 01730 823481 📠 01730 823759
Dir: S of A272 (Winchester/Petersfield) turning 1.5m from Petersfield on L opp church

In a lovely village on the River Meon, a charming 15th-century inn close to a magnificent Norman church. Nearby is Queen Elizabeth Country Park. Its open fires, heavy beams and rustic artefacts create an ideal setting for relaxing over a good choice of real ales or enjoying freshly prepared bar food. Fish and seasonal game are the mainstays of the menu, with sea bass, monkfish and salmon regularly featured: for meat-eaters steaks and racks of lamb. Cream teas in summer and comfortable accommodation.
OPEN: 11–3 (Sun 12–3, 7–10.30) 6–11 **BAR MEALS:** Lunch served: all week Dinner served: all week 12–2 7–9 Av main course £8 **RESTAURANT:** Lunch served: all week Dinner served: all week 12–2 7–9 Av 3 course à la carte £20 Av 3 course fixed price £14.95
BREWERY/COMPANY: Hall & Woodhouse
PRINCIPAL BEERS: Badger Best, Tanglefoot & King & Barnes Sussex,.
FACILITIES: Children welcome Dogs allowed (water)
NOTES: Parking 30 **ROOMS:** 6 bedrooms 6 en suite from s£40 d£60

EASTON   Map 04 SU53

The Chestnut Horse ♀
SO21 1EG ☎ 01962 779257 📠 01962 779014
Dir: From M3 J9 take A33 towards Basingstoke, then B3047. Take 2nd R then 1st left

At the heart of the Itchen valley – great for walking – the Three Castles Path passes this delightful 16th-century dining pub. Low-beamed ceilings are festooned with old beer mugs and potties, while intimate dining areas are divided by standing timbers. Substantial lunchtime snacks and specials that catch the eye include salmon fishcakes with red pepper sauce, seared salmon fillet on stir-fried vegetables and pan-fried calves' liver with crispy bacon and olive oil mash. Sunday lunches, good local ales and colourful summer patio.
OPEN: 11–3 5.30–11 **BAR MEALS:** Lunch served: all week Dinner served: all week 12–2.30 6.30–9.30 Av main course £10 **RESTAURANT:** Lunch served: all week Dinner served: all week 12–2.30 6.30–9.30 Av 3 course à la carte £18
BREWERY/COMPANY: Free House **PRINCIPAL BEERS:** Bass, Courage Best, Chestnut Horse Special, Fullers London Pride.
FACILITIES: Children welcome Garden: Beer garden, outdoor eating Dogs allowed (water) **NOTES:** Parking 40

Cricketers Inn
SO21 1EJ ☎ 01962 779353 📠 01962 779010
e-mail: geoffgreen 1382@aol.com
Dir: M3 J9,A33 towards Basingstoke.Turn R at Kingsworthy onto B3047.0.75m turn R
A traditional free house in a pretty village close to the River Itchen. Regularly featuring well-kept real ales from independent brewers to complement extensive home-cooked menus, facilities include a non-smoking dining-room and comfortable en suite accommodation. Bar snacks include

continued   *continued*

England

EASTON continued

crusty doorstep sandwiches and challenging open toasties, while main dishes take in grilled salmon, plaice with prawn and lobster bisque sauce, whole rack of pork ribs, steak and Ringwood ale pie and gargantuan Cricketers' mixed grills.
OPEN: 12-3 6-11 (Sun 12-3 7-10.30) **BAR MEALS:** Lunch served: all week 12-2 Dinner served: Mon-Sat 7-9 Av main course £8
RESTAURANT: Lunch served: all week 12-2 Dinner served: Mon-Sat 7-9 Av 3 course à la carte £15 Av 3 course fixed price £15
BREWERY/COMPANY: Free House
PRINCIPAL BEERS: Changing guest ales. **FACILITIES:** Children welcome Garden: Patio, food served outside Dogs allowed
NOTES: Parking 16 **ROOMS:** 3 bedrooms 3 en suite from s£32 d£55

EAST STRATTON   Map 04 SU54

The Northbrook Arms 🖼
SO21 3DU ☎ 01962 774150
Dir: just off A33, 9m S of Basingstoke, 7m N of Winchester, follow Kingsworthy signs from M3

In an idyllic setting adjoining the green and an assortment of thatched cottages, the pub was formerly known as the Plough. Built around 1847, it was once the village shop and bakery and has a skittle alley in converted stables. Home-produced fare includes steak and kidney pie, breast of Barbary duck, mushroom and watercress lasagne and traditional cod and chips. Handy for Winchester and some of mid-Hampshire's loveliest walks.
OPEN: 12-3 6-11 (Sun 12-3, 7-10.30) **BAR MEALS:** Lunch served: Tues-Sun Dinner served: Tues-Sat 7-9 Av main course £7.95
RESTAURANT: Lunch served: Tues-Sun 12-2 Dinner served: Tues-Sat 7-9.30 Av 3 course à la carte £14.95
BREWERY/COMPANY: Free House **PRINCIPAL BEERS:** Gales HSB, Gales GB, Otter Bitter, Ringwood Best. **FACILITIES:** Garden: patio/terrace, food served outside Dogs allowed (water)
NOTES: Parking 30 **ROOMS:** 4 bedrooms from s£38 d£50

EAST TYTHERLEY   Map 04 SU22

Pick of the Pubs

Star Inn ♦♦♦♦ 😊😊 🖼 ♀
SO51 0LW ☎ 01794 340225
e-mail: info@starinn-uk.com
Dir: 5 M N of Romsey off A3057 take L Turn Dunbridge B3084 left turn for Awbridge & Lockerley follow Rd past Lockerly 1 M
Close to the attractions of the Test Valley, this brick-built 16th-century coaching inn overlooks the village cricket ground on a quiet back lane between Romsey and Salisbury. In new hands, imaginative cooking has brought a contemporary slant to the blackboard menu that hangs over an open fireplace in the modernised bar. Dine where

you like, in the bar or at dark-wood tables in the main dining room, and enjoy the thought of staying overnight in one of the three stylish bedrooms. The menu offers a good selection with a weather eye to available local produce. Representative dishes may be scallops with smoked salmon and creamed leeks or emperor fish with peanut crust and ginger soy sauce. Also meaty alternatives such as venison with red cabbage and blood orange sauce and generous vegetarian options typified by linguine with artichoke and french beans with roasted tomato oil and Parmesan shavings.

OPEN: 11-2.30 6-11 (all day Sat-Sun May-Sept)
BAR MEALS: Lunch served: Tues-Sun Dinner served: Tues-Sun 12-2 7-9. **RESTAURANT:** Lunch served: Tues-Sun Dinner served: Tues-Sun 12-2 7-9 Av 3 course à la carte £25
BREWERY/COMPANY: Free House
PRINCIPAL BEERS: Ringwood Best plus guest beers.
FACILITIES: Children welcome Garden: Food served outside
NOTES: Parking 60 **ROOMS:** 3 bedrooms 3 en suite from s£45 d£60

EMSWORTH   Map 04 SU70

The Sussex Brewery 🖼 ♀
36 Main Rd PO10 8AU ☎ 01243 371533 📠 01243 379684
e-mail: drobbo@aol.com
Dir: On A259 (coast road), between Havant & Chichester
A fresh 'carpet' of sawdust is laid daily in the bars of this traditional 17th-century pub that boasts wooden floors, large open fires and a typically warm welcome. Fully 50 sausage recipes are on offer, ranging from gluten-free Moroccan lamb and vegetarian varieties to the full-blown Feathered Platter, which includes spiced ostrich, chicken piri-piri, Sussex pigeon and pheasant. Daily specials might include pan-fried salmon fillets, Irish Stew and beef Wellington.
OPEN: 11-11 **BAR MEALS:** Lunch served: all week Dinner served: all week 12-2.30 7-10 Av main course £6 **RESTAURANT:** Lunch served: all week Dinner served: all week 12-2.30 7-10 Av 3 course à la carte £12 **BREWERY/COMPANY:** Young & Co
PRINCIPAL BEERS: Smiles Best Bitter, Young's PA, AAA & Special, Timothy Taylor Landlord. **FACILITIES:** Children welcome Garden: Food served outside Dogs allowed (water) **NOTES:** Parking 30

EVERSLEY   Map 04 SU76

The Golden Pot ♀
Reading Rd RG27 0NB ☎ 0118 9732104
e-mail: justin.winstanley@lycos.co.uk
Dir: Between Reading and Camberley on theB3272 about 1/4 M from the Eversley cricket ground
Dating back to the 1700s and located in a famous village where *The Water Babies* author Charles Kinglsey was once

continued

rector, this former standard local went more upmarket in the late 1990s when the pool bar was converted into a full á la carte restaurant. Strong emphasis on style, friendliness and good food cooked from fresh ingredients, as well as two bars with a connecting open fire which is always alight in winter. Live music once a week and an interesting bar and restaurant menu featuring pan-fried fillets of bream, sautéed duck breast, grilled wild venison, or monkfish tail steamed with cardamom and coriander.

OPEN: 11-3 6-11 **BAR MEALS:** Lunch served: all week Dinner served: all week 12-2.15 6.30-9.15 Av main course £7.50 **RESTAURANT:** Lunch served: Sun-Fri Dinner served: Mon-Sat 12-2 7-9.15 Av 3 course à la carte £22 **BREWERY/COMPANY:** Free House **PRINCIPAL BEERS:** Greene King Ruddles Best, Abbot Ale, Wadworth 6X. **FACILITIES:** Garden: **NOTES:** Parking 30

FACCOMBE   Map 04 SU35

The Jack Russell Inn
SP11 0DS ☎ 01264 737315
e-mail: alanjo@jackruss.u-net.com
Situated amongst some 4,500 acres of walking country just a step out of Newbury, an ivy-clad inn with comfortable bedrooms that overlook the village pond and open farmland. Bar and conservatory menus feature ingredients such as fresh fish, game from the Faccombe estate and fresh meats delivered daily by the local butcher. Specials include home-made pies, seafood platter and Louisiana vegetable roast. At the weekends there are often popular theme nights.
OPEN: 12-3 7-11 (Summer all day) **BAR MEALS:** Lunch served: all week Dinner served: all week 12-2 7-9 Av main course £6.50 **RESTAURANT:** Lunch served: all week Dinner served: all week 12-2 7-9 Av 3 course à la carte £9 **BREWERY/COMPANY:** Free House **PRINCIPAL BEERS:** Fuller's London Pride, Brakspear Bitter, Interbrew Boddingtons. **FACILITIES:** Children welcome Garden: Food served outside Dogs allowed **NOTES:** Parking 30 **ROOMS:** 3 bedrooms 3 en suite from s£35 d£40

FORDINGBRIDGE   Map 03 SU11

The Augustus John 🛏 🍷
116 Station Rd SP6 1DG ☎ 01425 652098
e-mail: peter@augustusjohn.com
Named after the renowned British painter who lived in the village (the pub was also his local), this unassuming brick buildings was transformed a few years ago into a smart dining pub with comfortable en suite accommodation – ideal base for exploring the New Forest. Of particular interest is the changing blackboard menu which may offer home-made soups, salmon and herb fishcakes, rack of lamb with redcurrant and mint, liver and bacon with mash and onion

gravy and fresh Poole plaice. Good puddings and short list of good wines; 10 by the glass.
OPEN: 11.30-3.30 6-12 **BAR MEALS:** Lunch served: all week Dinner served: all week 11.30-2 6.30-9 **RESTAURANT:** Lunch served: all week Dinner served: all week 11.30-2 6.30-9 **BREWERY/COMPANY:** Eldridge Pope **PRINCIPAL BEERS:** Burtons Ale, Courage Best, John Smiths. **FACILITIES:** Children welcome Garden: Food served outside Dogs allowed **NOTES:** Parking 40 **ROOMS:** 8 bedrooms 8 en suite from s£35 d£50

FRITHAM   Map 04 SU21

The Royal Oak NEW
SO43 7HJ ☎ 02380 812606 📠 02380 814066
e-mail: royaloakfritham@btopenworld.com

Unaltered for some 100 years, this small thatched 17th-century country pub on a working farm deep in the New Forest maintains its long tradition of preferring conversation to the distractions of juke box and fruit machines. Ideally located for walkers and ramblers, warming open fires are maintained from October to March with ploughman's lunches and home-baked munch on, and home-made evening meals on two nights per week.
OPEN: 11-3 6-11 (Sat 11-11, Sun 12-11) **BAR MEALS:** Lunch served: all week 12-2.30 Dinner served: 2 days a wk winter only 7-9 Av main course £4 **BREWERY/COMPANY:** Free House **PRINCIPAL BEERS:** Ringwood Best, Fourtyniner, Hop Back Summer Lightning, Palmers Dorset Gold. **FACILITIES:** Children welcome Garden: Food served outside Dogs allowed (water) No credit cards

---

FROXFIELD GREEN   Map 04 SU72

The Trooper Inn 🍷
Alton Rd GU32 1BD ☎ 01730 827293 📠 01730 827103
e-mail: bazziebaz@aol.com

Unpretentious roadside inn enjoying an isolated downland position west of Petersfield. There is a relaxed atmosphere

continued   *continued*

England

FROXFIELD GREEN continued

throughout the rustic, pine-furnished interior; evening candlelight enhances the overall ambience. In addition to changing guest ales and decent wines by the glass, expect interesting home-cooked food. From lunchtime snacks like scrambled eggs and smoked salmon and fisherman's pie, freshly prepared evening dishes may include medallions of pork with garlic and honey, apricot, minted couscous and pinenut filo parcel, and hoi sin glazed breast of duck. Visit on a Wednesday evening and experience excellent live jazz.
OPEN: 12–3 6.30–12 Closed: Dec 26, Jan 1 **BAR MEALS:** Lunch served: all week Dinner served: all week 12–2 7–10
RESTAURANT: Lunch served: all week Dinner served: all week 12–2 7–10 **BREWERY/COMPANY:** Free House
PRINCIPAL BEERS: Ringwood Best, Fortyniner, Interbrew Bass, guest ales. **FACILITIES:** Children welcome Garden: Food served outside **ROOMS:** 8 bedrooms 8 en suite from s£55 d£75

HAVANT — Map 04 SU70

The Royal Oak 🛏 ♀
19 Langstone High St, Langstone PO9 1RY
☎ 023 92483125 📠 023 9247 6838
Occupying an outstanding position on Langstone Harbour, this historic 16th-century pub is noted for its rustic, unspoilt interior. Flagstone floors, exposed beams and winter fires contrast with the waterfront benches and secluded rear garden for alfresco summer drinking. Starters such as feta cheese with sun-dried tomatoes, or battered squid and caper dip, precede minted loin of lamb, home-made fish pie, Cajun chicken sizzler or Brie and redcurrant tart.
OPEN: 11–11 (Sun 12–10.30) **BAR MEALS:** Lunch served: all week Dinner served: all week 12–9 Av main course £7.95
RESTAURANT: Lunch served: all week Dinner served: all week 12–2.30 6–9 Av 3 course à la carte £15
BREWERY/COMPANY: Whitbread **PRINCIPAL BEERS:** Gales HSB, Interbrew Flowers. **FACILITIES:** Children welcome Garden: Patio, food served outside Dogs allowed (water)

HAWKLEY — Map 04 SU72

Hawkley Inn
Pococks Ln GU33 6NE ☎ 01730 827205
Tucked away down narrow lanes on the Hangers Way Path, an unpretentious rural local with a fine reputation for quality ale from local micro-breweries and its own cider. Ambitious bar food offers Brie and bacon or spinach and Ricotta tart, duck breast in peppercorn sauce, Mediterranean chicken and green pesto spaghetti: for traditionalists, sausage and mash and faggots with onion gravy. Frequent venue for live jazz and blues.
OPEN: 12–2.30 6–11 **BAR MEALS:** Lunch served: all week 12–2 Dinner served: Mon-Sat 7–9.30 Av main course £7.20
PRINCIPAL BEERS: RCH East Street Cream, Itchen Valley Godfathers, Triple FFF Alton's Pride, Ballards Best Bitter.
FACILITIES: Garden: Food served outdoors Dogs allowed (water)

HOLYBOURNE — Map 04 SU74

White Hart ♦ ♦ ♦ 🛏
GU34 4EY ☎ 01420 87654 📠 01420 543982
Dir: off A31 between Farnham & Winchester
Traditional village inn popular with locals and business guests. Comfortable bedrooms and good selection of bar food.

OPEN: 11–3 5–11 **BAR MEALS:** Lunch served: all week Dinner served: all week 12–2.30 7–10 Av main course £6.50
RESTAURANT: Lunch served: all week Dinner served: all week 12–2.30 7–10 Av 3 course à la carte £13
BREWERY/COMPANY: Greene King **PRINCIPAL BEERS:** Scottish Courage Courage Best, Wadworth 6X, Greene King Abbot Ale.
FACILITIES: Children welcome Children's licence Garden: Lawn, food served outside Dogs allowed **NOTES:** Parking 40
ROOMS: 4 bedrooms from s£25 d£45

HOOK — Map 04 SU75

Crooked Billet ♀
London Rd RG27 9EH ☎ 01256 762118 📠 01256 761011
e-mail: Richardbarwise@aol.com
Dir: From M3 take Hook Ring Road. At third Rdbt turn R on A30 towards London, pub on L 1/2 mile by river.

Standing back from the A30 and with a large garden stretching down to the River Whitewater, there is plenty to amuse all the family at this popular traditional pub with its play area, barbecue, monthly quiz nights and regular meetings of the Morris Men. Well-kept cask ales merit mention to accompany meats, grills and fish from all-day breakfast through avocado and prawn platter to a deep-fried 'Combo' of chicken, mushrooms and scampi with a choice of dips.
OPEN: 11.30–3 6–11 **BAR MEALS:** Lunch served: all week Dinner served: all week 12–2.30 7–9.30 Av main course £10
BREWERY/COMPANY: Free House **PRINCIPAL BEERS:** Scottish Courage Courage Best & Directors & John Smith's, Hogs Back TEA.
FACILITIES: Children welcome Garden: Food served outside Dogs allowed (water) **NOTES:** Parking 60

HORSEBRIDGE — Map 04 SU33

John O'Gaunt Inn 🛏 NEW
SO20 6PU ☎ 01794 388394
Some five miles north of Romsey, a small country inn, popular with walkers from the nearby Test Way footpath, that scores highly for atmosphere, well-kept ales and generously priced food. Frequented also by fishermen and the winter shooting fraternity, diners can expect trenchermen's portions of steak and kidney pudding, local pheasant in red wine and fresh local trout with almonds – 'a great meeting place for dogs, closely followed by their owners'.
OPEN: 11–2.30 6.30–11 **BAR MEALS:** Lunch served: all week Dinner served: all week 12–2 7–9.30 Av main course £7
BREWERY/COMPANY: Free House
PRINCIPAL BEERS: Ringwood Best Bitter, Ringwood Fortyniner, Itchen Valley Fagins. **FACILITIES:** Garden: Small area covered by attractive pergola Dogs allowed **NOTES:** Parking 12 No credit cards

continued

IBSLEY · Map 03 SU10

Olde Beams Inn ♀
Salisbury Rd BH24 3PP ☎ 01425 473387
Dir: On A338 between Ringwood & Salisbury
The cruck beam is clearly visible from the outside of this
thatched, 14th-century building. In addition to the restaurant
there is also a popular buffet counter. Located in the Avon
Valley and handy for the New Forest.
OPEN: 11-3 6-11 **BAR MEALS:** All week 12-2 7-10 Av meal £6.95
BREWERY/COMPANY: Old English Hotels
PRINCIPAL BEERS: Ringwood Beers, Theakston Old Peculier,
Courage Best, Bateman XB **FACILITIES:** Garden: Food served
outside **NOTES:** Parking 120

LINWOOD · Map 03 SU10

Red Shoot Inn
Toms Ln BH24 3QT ☎ 01425 475792
Dir: From M27 take A338, take Salisbury turning and follow brown signs to
the Red Shoot

Set in the heart of the New Forest, with its own micro-
brewery, the bustling Red Shoot Inn offers real ale and real
food in a real country pub.
OPEN: 11-3 6-11 (wknd and summer 11-11) **BAR MEALS:** All
week 12-2 6.30-9.30 Av meal £5.25
BREWERY/COMPANY: Wadworth
PRINCIPAL BEERS: Wadworth 6X, Henrys IPA, Summersault, Tom's
Tipple, Forest Gold **FACILITIES:** Garden: Dogs welcome
NOTES: Parking 30

LONGPARISH · Map 04 SU44

The Plough Inn
SP11 6PB ☎ 01264 720358 ▤ 01264 720377
Dir: Off A303 4m S of Andover
As it is only 100 yards away from the River Test this 400-year
old pub is regularly visited by the local duck population.
Typical menu includes scallops Mornay, lobster thermidor,
shoulder of lamb kleftico, wild boar sausage, and salmon
hollandaise.
OPEN: 11-3.30 6-11 (11-3, 6-11 in winter) **BAR MEALS:** Lunch
served: all week Dinner served: all week 12-2.30 6.30-9.30 Av main
course £5.95 **RESTAURANT:** Lunch served: all week Dinner served:
all week 12-2.30 6.30-9.30 Av 3 course à la carte £15.95 Av 3 course
fixed price £20 **BREWERY/COMPANY:** Enterprise Inns
PRINCIPAL BEERS: Hampshire King Alfred, Greene King Old
Speckled Hen, Wadworth 6X, Boddingtons. **FACILITIES:** Children
welcome Garden: BBQ Dogs allowed **NOTES:** Parking 60
ROOMS: 2 bedrooms from s£20 d£40

LYMINGTON · Map 04 SZ39

The Chequers Inn
Lower Woodside SO41 8AH ☎ 01590 673415
Dir: From Lymington take A337 towards New Milton. Turn L at White Hart
PH

Dating from about 1625, this was reputedly the salt exchange
(or exchequer). A warm and friendly welcome awaits along
with the open fire, antique furniture and old beams. The
menu offers a good choice of traditional bar food: steaks,
pork chops, burgers, and local fish straight from the boats.
OPEN: 11-3 6-11 (all day Sat-Sun) Closed: 25 Dec
BAR MEALS: Lunch served: all week Dinner served: all week 12-2
7-10 Av main course £5 **RESTAURANT:** Lunch served: all week
Dinner served: all week 12-2 7-10 Av 3 course à la carte £12.50 10
BREWERY/COMPANY: Enterprise Inns
PRINCIPAL BEERS: Ringwood Best, Wadworth 6X, Bass.
FACILITIES: Children welcome Garden: Dogs allowed
NOTES: Parking 16

The Kings Arms ♦♦♦ ♀
St Thomas St SO41 9NB ☎ 01590 672594
Dir: Approaching Lymington from N on A337, head L onto St Thomas St.
Kings Arms 50yds on R
King Charles I is reputed to have patronised this historic
coaching inn, which these days enjoys an enviable reputation
for its cask ales, housed on 150-year-old stillages. Local
Ringwood ales as well as national brews are served. It is a real
community pub, with a dartboard and Sky TV, and the open
brick fireplaces are used in winter. Good food includes home-
cooked beefsteak and ale pie, jumbo cod, and sirloin steak.
OPEN: 11-1 **BAR MEALS:** Lunch served: all week Dinner served:
all week 12-2 6.30-9.30 Av main course £5.95
RESTAURANT: Lunch served: all week Dinner served: all week 12-2
6.30 Av 3 course à la carte £12 **BREWERY/COMPANY:** Whitbread
PRINCIPAL BEERS: Fullers London Pride, Greene King Abbot Ale,
Gales HSB, Ringwood. **FACILITIES:** Garden: Beer garden, outdoor
eating Dogs allowed (water) **NOTES:** Parking 8
ROOMS: 2 bedrooms 2 en suite from s£48 d£48 No credit cards

Dominoes
Dominoes came to Britain from the Continent at
the end of the 18th century, perhaps brought
back by British soldiers serving in the Napoleonic
Wars. French prisoners-of-war made sets of
dominoes, not only for their own amusement but
to sell to the British. Many different varieties are
played in pubs besides the standard block game,
and some pubs belong to dominoe leagues.

England

LYMINGTON continued

Mayflower Inn ♀
Kings Saltern Rd SO41 3QD ☎ 01590 672160 📠 01590 679180
Dir: A337 towards New Milton, L at rdbt by White Hart, L to Rookes Ln, R at mini-rdbt, pub 0.75m

Located by the water's edge with views of the Solent and Lymington River, this solid mock-Tudor inn is as inviting as it looks. The cosy log fire is a good place to relax beside on cold days, while the flower-filled patio is popular in summer. A lengthy evening menu offers confit of duck, griddled calves' liver, and braised shank of lamb, while the lunch choice might include salads and panninis, and creamy baked seafood ramekin.
OPEN: 11-11 (Sun 12-10.30) **BAR MEALS:** Lunch served: all week Dinner served: all week 12-3 6.30-9.30 Av main course £7
RESTAURANT: 12-3 6.30-9.30 Av 3 course à la carte £8.50
BREWERY/COMPANY: Whitbread
PRINCIPAL BEERS: Ringwood Best, Fuller's London Pride, Young's Special. **FACILITIES:** Children welcome Garden: Food served outdoors **NOTES:** Parking 20 **ROOMS:** 6 bedrooms 6 en suite from s£45 d£65

LYNDHURST   Map 04 SU30

New Forest Inn 🛏 ♀
Emery Down SO43 7DY ☎ 023 8028 2329
Delightfully situated in the scenic New Forest, this rambling inn lies on land claimed from the crown by use of squatters' rights in the early 18th-century. Ale was once sold from a caravan which now forms the front lounge porchway. Lovely summer garden and welcoming bars with open fires and an extensive menu listing local game in season and plenty of fresh fish - whole Dover sole, fresh tuna, monkfish thermidor - alongside traditional pub meals.
OPEN: 11-11 **BAR MEALS:** Lunch served: all week Dinner served: all week 12-2.30 6-9 Av main course £7 **RESTAURANT:** Lunch served: all week Dinner served: all week 11-10 6-10
BREWERY/COMPANY: Enterprise Inns
PRINCIPAL BEERS: Ringwood Best, London Pride, Abbot Ale, Old Hooky. **FACILITIES:** Children welcome Children's licence Garden: Food served outside Dogs allowed **NOTES:** Parking 20 **ROOMS:** 4 bedrooms 4 en suite from s£30 d£50

The Oak Inn 🛏 ♀ NEW
Pinkney Ln, Bank SO43 7FE ☎ 02380 282350
Ponies graze outside this 18th-century New Forest inn, which was once a cider house. Idyllically set in this Heritage Area, and with a beer garden for summer use, it specialises in freshly prepared food including Mexican chilli, chicken Kiev, spicy Thai fish cakes, and vegetable Wellington. Expect also sea bass, cod and chips, moules steamed in onion and garlic.

There are plenty of real ales to try, like Holden's Black Country and Ringwood's Best.
BAR MEALS: Lunch served: all week Dinner served: all week 12-2 6.30-9.30 Av main course £7.95 **BREWERY/COMPANY:** Free House **PRINCIPAL BEERS:** Ringwood Best, Holdens Black Country, Interbrew Bass, Hop Back Summer Lightening. **FACILITIES:** Children welcome Garden Food served outdoors Dogs allowed (water)
NOTES: Parking 40

The Trusty Servant 🛏
Minstead SO43 7FY ☎ 02380 812137

Popular Victorian pub in the picturesque New Forest. An ideal watering hole for walkers just a stone's throw from Sir Arthur Conan Doyle's grave at Minstead Church. The famous pub sign depicts a strange mythical beast and is a copy of a picture belonging to Winchester College. Menu choices include medallions of Scotch beef, Thai roasted duck breast, mushroom and pimento Stroganoff, and a variety of ploughmans, jacket potatoes, omelettes, and giant Yorkshire puddings. Bedrooms are named after English kings and Sherlock Holmes characters.
OPEN: 11-11 (Sun 12-10.30) **BAR MEALS:** Lunch served: all week Dinner served: all week 12-2.30 7-10 Av main course £6.95
RESTAURANT: Lunch served: all week Dinner served: all week 12-2.30 7-10 **BREWERY/COMPANY:** Whitbread
PRINCIPAL BEERS: Ringwood Best, Fuller's London Pride, Wadworth 6X, Gale's HSB. **FACILITIES:** Children welcome Garden: Patio, food served outside Dogs allowed (water) **NOTES:** Parking 16
ROOMS: 6 bedrooms 6 en suite from s£27 d£55

MAPLEDURWELL   Map 04 SU65

The Gamekeepers 🛏 NEW
Tunworth Rd RG25 2LU ☎ 01256 322038 📠 01256 357831
e-mail: traceynother@aol.com

Welcoming 19th-century pub with a well in the centre, located in a very rural spot. All food is made on the premises from fresh produce, and the extensive carte includes five fish

continued
continued

dishes, a couple of vegetarian choices like wild mushroom Thai curry, plus pheasant supreme, venison steak marinated in pork, and ostrich medallions with hickory-flavoured gravy. Lunchtime specials include seafood mornay, chilli con carne, and Cumberland sausage.   No credit cards

---

MATTINGLEY   Map 04 SU75

The Leather Bottle
Reading Rd RG27 8JU ☎ 01189 326371 🖷 01189 326547
Dir: From M3 J5 follow signs for Hook then B3349
Established in 1714, the Leather Bottle is a wisteria-clad pub with heavy beams, huge open winter fires and a new dining extension leading to a summer terrace. Standard extensive menu.

MEONSTOKE   Map 04 SU53

The Bucks Head 🐑
Bucks Head Hill SO32 3NA ☎ 01489 877313
Dir: by the jct of A32 & B2150
A beautiful 16th-century inn on the banks of the River Meon, popular with locals as well as visitors. Surrounded by fields and woodland, it is ideal walking country with Winchester Hill and the old Watercress railway line nearby. Two character bars with open fires, and a range of home-cooked meals including sausages and mash, pork steak in blue cheese sauce, liver and bacon, and fish pie.
OPEN: 11–3 6–11 **BAR MEALS:** Lunch served: all week 12–2.15 Dinner served: Mon-Sat 7–9.15 Av main course £5.50
RESTAURANT: Lunch served: all week Dinner served: all week 12–2.15 7–9.15 **BREWERY/COMPANY:** Greene King
PRINCIPAL BEERS: Old Speckled Hen, Ruddles County, IPA.
FACILITIES: Children welcome Garden: Food served outside, beer garden with river Dogs allowed (water provided) **NOTES:** Parking 40 **ROOMS:** 5 bedrooms 5 en suite from s£30 d£50

MICHELDEVER   Map 04 SU53

Half Moon & Spread Eagle 🐑
Winchester Rd SO21 3DG ☎ 01962 774339 🖷 01962 774834
e-mail: rayhalfmoon@aol.com
Dir: Take A33 from Winchester towards Basingstoke. After 5m turn L after petrol station. Pub 0.5m on R
Located in the heart of a quintessential thatched and timbered Hampshire village, this well-maintained 16th-century pub recently reverted back to its old name, having been called the Dever Arms for just eight years. The three neatly furnished and carpeted interconnecting rooms sport a village local atmosphere and an extensive menu offering a range of imaginative salads, fresh mussels, tandoori chicken, half shoulder of lamb with minted gravy, Moon burger, or tuna steak in herb and tomato sauce. Occasional music nights.
OPEN: 12–3 6–11 (Sun 7–10.30) **BAR MEALS:** Lunch served: all week Dinner served: all week 12–2 6–9 Av main course £10
RESTAURANT: Lunch served: all week Dinner served: all week 12–2 6–9 Av 3 course à la carte £19 **BREWERY/COMPANY:** Greene King
PRINCIPAL BEERS: Greene King IPA Abbot Ale, XX Mild and guest ales. **FACILITIES:** Children welcome Garden: Food served outside. Dogs allowed (water provided) **NOTES:** Parking 20

> **Restaurant and Bar Meal times indicate the times when food is available. Last orders may be approximately 30 minutes before the times stated.**

NORTH WALTHAM   Map 04 SU54

The Fox 🐑
RG25 2BE ☎ 01256 397288 🖷 01256 397288
e-mail: info@thefoxinn.tinyworld.co.uk
Dir: From M3 J7 take A30 towards Winchester. Village signposted on R

Built as three farm cottages in 1624, this peacefully situated village pub enjoys splendid views across fields and farmland and has its own award-winning garden. A varied bar menu features basket meals, baguettes and jacket potatoes. In the restaurant, look out for a variety of exotic meats - crocodile, kangaroo, wild boar - as well as plenty of game and fish choices.
OPEN: 11–3 5.30–12 (all day w/end) **BAR MEALS:** Lunch served: all week Dinner served: all week 12–2.30 6.30–10 Av main course £8.50 **RESTAURANT:** Lunch served: all week Dinner served: all week 12–2.30 6.30–10 Av 3 course à la carte £25 Av 3 course fixed price £12 **BREWERY/COMPANY:** Ushers
PRINCIPAL BEERS: Scottish Courage Courage Best, Jennings Cumberland Ale, Greene King Old Speckled Hen.
FACILITIES: Children welcome Children's licence Garden: BBQ, food served outdoors Dogs allowed (water) **NOTES:** Parking 40

OLD BASING   Map 04 SU65

The Millstone
Bartons Mill Ln RG24 8AE ☎ 01256 331153
Dir: From M3 J6 follow brown signs to Basing House
Enjoying a rural location beside the River Loddon, close to a country park and Old Basing House, this attractive old building is a popular lunchtime spot for summer alfresco imbibing.

OVINGTON   Map 04 SU53

The Bush
SO24 0RE ☎ 01962 732764 🖷 01962 735130
Dir: A31 from Winchester, E to Alton & Farnham, approx 6m turn L off dual carriageway to Ovington. 0.5m to pub
Tucked away down a lane on the Pilgrim's Way, this delightful rose-covered pub, is situated by the gently flowing River Itchen. Take a riverside stroll before relaxing over a meal in the character bars, complete with roaring log fires in winter. Tuck into beef and ale pie, pan-fried calves' liver with smoked bacon, mustard mash and onion gravy, leek, mushroom and baby corn vegetarian pie, venison casserole with red wine and juniper, and plenty of seafood choices. Everything is fresh and home-cooked.
OPEN: 11–3 6–11 (Sun 12–2 7–10.30) Closed: Dec 25
BAR MEALS: Lunch served: all week 12–2 Dinner served: Mon-Sat 6.30–9.30 Av main course £10 **BREWERY/COMPANY:** Wadworth
PRINCIPAL BEERS: Wadworth 6X, IPA & Farmers Glory, Badger Tanglefoot, Red Shoot Tom's Tipple. **FACILITIES:** Children welcome Children's licence Garden: beer garden, outdoor eating, Dogs allowed **NOTES:** Parking 40

OWSLEBURY   Map 04 SU52

The Ship Inn 🛏 ♀
Whites Hill SO21 1LT ☎ 01962 777358 📠 01962 777458
e-mail: theshipinn@freeuk.com
Dir: M3 J11 take B3335 follow signs for Owslebury

With ne'er a vessel in sight, the Ship stands high on a chalk ridge with wonderful views of the South Downs: an ideal starting point for country walking. The pub is often very busy, as it is particularly family-friendly with a large garden, animal corner and bouncy castle. Blackboards may offer freshly made sautéed chicken livers and squid stuffed with salmon mousse, followed by wild mushroom Stroganoff and locally-made speciality sausages of lamb, venison and wild boar.
OPEN: 11-3 6-11 (Sun 12-10.30) **BAR MEALS:** Lunch served: all week Dinner served: all week 12-2 6.30-9.30 **RESTAURANT:** Lunch served: all week Dinner served: all week 12-2 6.30-9.30
BREWERY/COMPANY: Greene King **PRINCIPAL BEERS:** Greene King IPA & Triumph, Bateman XXXB, Cheriton Pots Ale.
FACILITIES: Children welcome Garden: Patio area with seating, Childrens area. Dogs allowed **NOTES:** Parking 50

PETERSFIELD   Map 04 SU72

The Good Intent 🛏 ♀
40-46 College St GU31 4AF ☎ 01730 263838 📠 01730 302239
e-mail: pstuart@goodintent.freeserve.co.uk
Candlelit tables, open fires and well-kept ales characterise this 16th-century 'country pub in the town'. In summer, flower tubs and hanging baskets festoon the front patio, and the pub is well known for live music on Sunday evenings. Regular gourmet evenings are also held. Speciality sausages (up to 20 varieties), smoked fish pasta, monkfish with red pepper sauce, fillet steaks with choice of sauce, washed down with award-winning local and other ales.
OPEN: 11-3 5.30-11 **BAR MEALS:** Lunch served: all week Dinner served: all week 12-2.30 6-9.30 Av main course £7.95
RESTAURANT: Lunch served: all week Dinner served: all week 12-2 6-9.30 Av 3 course à la carte £17 **BREWERY/COMPANY:** Gales
PRINCIPAL BEERS: Gale's HSB, GB, Buster. **FACILITIES:** Children welcome Garden: Food served outside Dogs allowed (water)
NOTES: Parking 10 **ROOMS:** 3 bedrooms 2 en suite

The White Horse Inn
Priors Dean GU32 1DA ☎ 01420 588387 📠 01420 588387
Dir: A3/A272 to Winchester/Petersfield. In Petersfield L to Steep, 5m then R at small X-rds to E Tisted, 2nd drive on R
Also known as the 'Pub With No Name' as it has no sign, this splendid 17th-century farmhouse was originally used as a forge for passing coaches. The blacksmith sold beer to the travellers while their horses were attended to. Hearty pub grub includes chargrills, vegetarian lasagne, liver and bacon

with onion gravy, Cumberland sausages with mash and onion gravy, and steak and ale pie made with HSB bitter.
OPEN: 11-2.30 6-11 (Sun 11-2.30, 6-10.30) **BAR MEALS:** Lunch served: all week 12-2 Dinner served: Mon-Sat 7-9 Av main course £7.50 **RESTAURANT:** Lunch served: all week 12-2 Dinner served: Mon-Sat 7-9 **BREWERY/COMPANY:** Gales
PRINCIPAL BEERS: No Name Best, No Name Strong, Fullers London Pride, Bass. **FACILITIES:** Children welcome Garden: Dogs allowed **NOTES:** Parking 60

PILLEY   Map 04 SZ39

The Fleur de Lys ♀
Pilley St SO41 5QG ☎ 01590 672158 📠 01590 672158
Arguably the oldest pub in the New Forest, tracing its origins back to 1096, is this traditional thatched pub with stone flagged hallway, low beamed ceilings and open log fires. Fresh food is prepared daily using local suppliers, and results include Lolly's fish or steak, kidney and Guinness pies, pork hocks and half shoulders of lamb. Fish from the specials board and a variety of inspired dishes with oriental influences keep customers - and the kitchen - on their toes.
OPEN: 11-2.30 6-11 (Sun 12-3, 7-10.30) **BAR MEALS:** Lunch served: all week Dinner served: all week 12-2 6.30-9.30 Av main course £7.95 **RESTAURANT:** All week 12-2 6.30-9.30
PRINCIPAL BEERS: Ringwood Best, Gales HSB.
FACILITIES: Children welcome Garden: Food served outside Dogs allowed (water) **NOTES:** Parking 18

PORTSMOUTH & SOUTHSEA   Map 04 SZ69

The Still & West 🛏 ♀
2 Bath Square, Old Portsmouth PO1 2JL ☎ 023 92821567
Nautically themed pub close to HMS Victory and enjoying excellent views of Portsmouth Harbour and the Isle of Wight. Built in 1504, the main bar ceilings are hand-painted with pictures relating to local shipping history. Plenty of fish on the menu including trout, black beam, seabass on red cabbage and risotto, and the famous Still & West fish grill of fresh fish and mussels.
OPEN: 11-11 **BAR MEALS:** Lunch served: all week 12-3 Av main course £8 **RESTAURANT:** Lunch served: all week Dinner served: all week 12-3 6-10 **BREWERY/COMPANY:** Gales
PRINCIPAL BEERS: HSB, GB, Butsers. **FACILITIES:** Children welcome Garden: Food served outside. Overlooks harbour Dogs allowed (in the garden only)

The Wine Vaults ♀
43-47 Albert Rd, Southsea PO5 2SF
☎ 023 92864712 📠 023 92865544
e-mail: winevaults@freeuk.com
Originally several Victorian shops converted into a Victorian-style alehouse with wooden floors, panelled walls, and old church pew seating. Partly due to the absence of a jukebox or fruit machine, the atmosphere here is relaxed and there is a good range of real ales and good-value food. A typical menu includes oriental stir fry, roast chicken, fresh salmon with prawn and Gruyère fondue, and pork-loin steak marinated in Spanish paprika.
OPEN: 12-11 (12-10.30 Sun) Closed: 1 Jan **BAR MEALS:** Lunch served: all week Dinner served: all week 12-9.30 Av main course £6.25 **RESTAURANT:** Lunch served: all week Dinner served: all week 12-9.30 Av 3 course à la carte £12.50 **BREWERY/COMPANY:** Free House **PRINCIPAL BEERS:** Hop Back Gilbert's First Brew & Summer Lightening, Scottish Courage Courage Best, Interbrew Bass, Fuller's

continued   *continued*

London Pride. **FACILITIES:** Children welcome Children's licence
Garden: Food served outdoors, patio Dogs allowed

PRESTON CANDOVER — Map 04 SU64

The Crown at Axford
near Preston Candover RG25 2DZ ☎ 01256 389694 📄 01256
389149
e-mail: crown@axfordc.fsnet.co.uk
Small country inn set at the northern edge of the pretty
Candover Valley and handy for Basingstoke and the M3
motorway. Completely refurbished early in 2002, and serving
well-kept real ales along with good pub food based on
seasonal produce. Pheasant Rossini, aromatic poussin,
chargrilled pepper, and fillet of pork stuffed with herbed
sausagemeat, plus blackboard specials, all cooked to order.
OPEN: 12–2.30 6–11 **BAR MEALS:** Lunch served: Tues–Sun Dinner
served: Tues–Sun 12–2 6.30–9.30 Av main course £8.95
RESTAURANT: Lunch served: Tues–Sun 12–2 Dinner served:
Tues–Sat 6.30–9.30 **BREWERY/COMPANY:** Free House
PRINCIPAL BEERS: Fuller's London Pride, Young's Bitter, Greene
King Abbot Ale, Tripple FFF Dazed & Confused.
FACILITIES: Children welcome Garden: Terrace, food served
outside Dogs allowed **NOTES:** Parking 25

ROCKBOURNE — Map 03 SU11

Pick of the Pubs

The Rose & Thistle ♀
SP6 3NL ☎ 01725 518236
e-mail: enquiries@roseandthistle.co.uk
See Pick of the Pubs on page 236

ROMSEY — Map 04 SU32

The Dukes Head
Greatbridge Rd SO51 0HB ☎ 01794 514450 📄 01794 518102

This rambling 400-year-old pub, festooned with flowers in
summer, nestles in the Test Valley just a stone's throw
from the famous trout stream. An adventurous menu
offers duck sausages in hoi sin sauce, tian of crab, chicken
breast stuffed with pineapple, and fresh local trout
delivered daily.
OPEN: 11–11 **BAR MEALS:** Lunch served: all week Dinner served:
all week 12–3 6–9.30 Av main course £8.95
BREWERY/COMPANY: Free House
PRINCIPAL BEERS: Theakston Old Peculier, Fullers London Pride.
FACILITIES: Children welcome Garden: Beer garden
NOTES: Parking 50

The Mill Arms ♦♦♦♦ 🛏
Barley Hill, Dunbridge SO51 0LF ☎ 01794 340401 📄 01794
340401
e-mail: info@themillarms.co.uk

Situated in a picturesque village in the heart of the Test Valley,
the Mill is an 18th-century coaching inn with accommodation
of 21st-century quality. An ideal base for exploring the New
Forest, its private fishing on the River Itchen is especially
popular. Catch-of-the-day – though not from the Itchen –
might be baked smoked haddock, along with regular starters
such as roast pepper salad and Feta cheese, followed by fillet
steak with Stilton rarebit, morels and truffle mash.
OPEN: 12–3 6–11 **BAR MEALS:** Lunch served: all week Dinner
served: all week 12–2.30 7–9.30 **RESTAURANT:** Lunch served: all
week Dinner served: all week 12–2.30 7–9.30 Av 3 course à la carte
£25 **BREWERY/COMPANY:** Free House
PRINCIPAL BEERS: Dunbridge Test Tickler, Timothy Taylor
Landlord,. **FACILITIES:** Children welcome Garden: Seating, food
served outside Dogs allowed (water) **NOTES:** Parking 90
ROOMS: 6 bedrooms 6 en suite from s£50 d£55

ROWLANDS CASTLE — Map 04 SU71

Castle Inn
1 Finchdean Rd PO9 6DA ☎ 023 92412494 📄 92412494
*Dir: N of Havant take B2149 to Rowlands Castle. Pass green, under rail
bridge, pub 1st on L opp Stansted Park*
Victorian building directly opposite Stansted Park, part of the
Forest of Bere. Richard the Lionheart supposedly hunted here,
and the house and grounds are open to the public for part of
the year. Traditional atmosphere with wooden floors and fires
in both bars. Recent change of management.
OPEN: 11.30–3 5–11.30 (Winter 12–3, 5–11.30)
BAR MEALS: Lunch: all week 12–2 Dinner Tues–Sat 7–9 Av meal £5
BREWERY/COMPANY: Gales **PRINCIPAL BEERS:** Gales Butser,
HSB & GB **FACILITIES:** Garden Dogs welcome (water & chews)
NOTES: Parking 30

The Fountain Inn ♦♦♦♦
34 The Green PO9 6AB ☎ 023 9241 2291
Lovely Georgian building recently refurbished in a classical
English country style. Beside the village green. Bedrooms.
Children's play area.

**All AA listed accommodation can also be
found on the AA's internet site**

www.theAA.com

OPEN: 11-3 6-11
BAR MEALS: L served all week.
D served all week. 12-2.30
6.30-9.30 Av main course £10
RESTAURANT: L served all week.
D served all week. 12-2.30
6.30-9.30 Av cost 3 course £16
BREWERY/COMPANY: FREE
HOUSE
PRINCIPAL BEERS: Fuller's
London Pride, Marstons Pedigree,
Adnams Broadside, Wadworth 6X,
FACILITIES: Children welcome.
Garden: Beer garden, outdoor
eating
NOTES: Parking 28

The Rose & Thistle

♀
Rockbourne SP6 3NL
☎ 01725 518236
e-mail: enquiries@roseandthistle.co.uk
Dir: Rockbourne is signposted from
B3078 and from A354

Picture-postcard inn in a pretty downland village, with a stunning rose arch outside and beautiful flowers all around the door. This idyllic pub consists of two long and low whitewashed 16th-century cottages, converted nearly 200 years ago and still full of charming original features.

Located at the top of a delightful street filled with thatched cottages and period houses, it is handily placed for visiting the New Forest, Salisbury and Breamore House. Inside there are some tasteful features to add to the unspoilt low-beamed bar and dining area. Country-house fabrics, floral arrangements and magazines bring a civilised touch along with polished oak tables and chairs, cushioned settles and carved benches. Open fires make it a warm and relaxing haven in cool weather, while the summer sun brings visitors into the neat front garden where they can soak up the warmth under smart umbrellas, and watch the doves in the quaint dovecot. Since landlord Tim Norfolk bought the pub from a consortium of locals, he has maintained its tradition of serving fine fresh food, cooked to order, along with good ales and decent wines. Lunchtime sees a choice of light favourites - local sausages with spring onion mashed potatoes and onion gravy, and bacon and mushrooms on toast - plus more robust dishes like medallions of pork fillet with a wild mushroom and Marsala sauce. In the evening you can start a meal with warm goats' cheese and bacon salad, or smoked trout, and move on to grilled fillet steak with port and Stilton sauce, or three lamb cutlets. Both menus are supplemented by blackboard specials including fish choices like fish pie with a crumble nut topping, red mullet on fennel in a dry Vermouth liquor, seafood platter, and cod fillet on bubble and squeak. Puddings like steamed syrup sponge and lemon tart.

ST MARY BOURNE　　　　　　　Map 04 SU45

The Bourne Valley Inn
SP11 6BT ☎ 01264 738361 📠 01264 738126
e-mail: bournevalleyinn@wessexinns.fsnet.co.uk
Situated in the picturesque rural community of St Mary
Bourne, this is the ideal location for conferences, exhibitions,
weddings or other celebrations. The riverside garden abounds
with wildlife, and the children can play safely in the special
play area. Recently refurbished without losing any of its
traditional charm. Typical menu includes lamb shank with pot
roasted vegetables and red wine sauce, chicken Stroganoff,
cauliflower and broccoli bake, poached salmon, and sausage
and mash.
OPEN: 11-11 **BAR MEALS:** Lunch served: all week Dinner served:
all week 12-2.30 6.30-9.30 Av main course £8
RESTAURANT: Lunch served: all week Dinner served: all week 12-2
7-9.30 Av 3 course fixed price £16 **BREWERY/COMPANY:** Free
House **PRINCIPAL BEERS:** Draught Bass, Flowers, Brakspeare.
FACILITIES: Children welcome Garden: Food served outside.
Riverside, secluded garden Dogs allowed (water & biscuits provided)
NOTES: Parking 50 **ROOMS:** 9 bedrooms 9 en suite from s£45
d£55

The George Inn
SP11 6BG ☎ 01264 738340 📠 01264 738877
Dir: M3 J8/A303, then A34 towards Newbury. Turn at Whitchurch & follow
signs for St Mary Bourne
Listed village inn in the picturesque Tarrant valley, with a bar
full of cricket memorabilia, one dining room decorated with
regimental battle scenes, and another one with a mural of the
River Test. Bedrooms.

SOUTHAMPTON　　　　　　　Map 04 SU41

The Jolly Sailor ♀
Lands End Rd, Bursledon SO31 8DN
☎ 023 8040 5557 📠 023 80402050
e-mail: jollysailor@freshnet.co.uk

Occupying one of the south coast's most picturesque
settings overlooking the River Hamble marina in
Bursledon, this famous village local will be familiar to
former fans of BBC TV's *Howard's Way*. Approached by a
steep path down from the road, a treasure-trove of
maritime memorabilia packs the interior, where menus of
Torbay sole with crispy prawns and fresh beer-battered
cod, in keeping with its nautical theme, accompany a
diversity of good real ales.
OPEN: 11-11 (Sun 12-10.30) Closed: 25 Dec **BAR MEALS:** Lunch
served: all week Dinner served: all week 12-9.30 Av main course £9.95
BREWERY/COMPANY: Woodhouse Inns

PRINCIPAL BEERS: Badger Best, IPA, Tanglefoot, King & Barnes
Sussex. **FACILITIES:** Children welcome Garden: Terrace, Food
served outside Dogs allowed (water, biscuits)

St Jacques Bar & Restaurant ♀ NEW
Romsey Rd, Copythorne SO40 2PE
☎ 023 80812321 80812800 📠 023 80812158
Dir: On A31 between Cadnam & Ower, south of M27 between junctions 1
& 2
Once called The Old Well, this large pub and restaurant has
recently been refurbished to cater for visitors to the New
Forest. Set in attractive surroundings, it offers comfortable
seating and a wide choice of well-cooked food. Light bites
might include sausages and mash, cottage pie, and ham with
eggs and chips, while the restaurant carte offers braised oxtail
in a red wine sauce, breast of duckling with orange sauce, and
Thai-style baked red snapper.
OPEN: 11-3 5.30-11 (Sun 12-10.30) **BAR MEALS:** Lunch served:
all week Dinner served: all week 12-2.15 6-9 Av main course £10.50
RESTAURANT: Lunch served: all week Dinner served: all week
1-2.15 6-9 Av 3 course à la carte £16.50
BREWERY/COMPANY: Free House **FACILITIES:** Garden: Patio
NOTES: Parking 100 **ROOMS:** 4 bedrooms 4 en suite from s£35
d£50

SPARSHOLT　　　　　　　Map 04 SU43

Pick of the Pubs

The Plough Inn ♀
Main Rd SO21 2NW ☎ 01962 776353 📠 01962 776400
Dir: From Winchester take B3049(A272) W, take L turn to village of
Sparsholt. tthe Plough Inn is 1M down the lane

Just two miles from Winchester, this extended 200-year-
old cottage located on the village edge overlooks open
fields from its delightful flower- and shrub-filled garden.
Inside you will find a bustling bar with pine tables, its
beams garlanded with dried hops, an open log fire and
a decent selection of wines and real ales from
Wadworths. Original cottage front rooms are
particularly conducive to intimate dining from extensive
blackboard menus offering imaginative home-cooked
food. At lunchtime expect 'doorstep' sandwiches and
locally made speciality sausages, served in a
comfortable atmosphere devoid of juke-box or fruit
machines. If planning to dine at leisure, booking is
advised for the evening session when representative
dishes might include pan-fried monkfish with king
prawn and saffron sauce and beef fillet medallions
glazed with Mozzarella and red wine jus. Nursery
puddings include fruit crumbles, with British cheeses as

continued

continued

SPARSHOLT continued

a popular alternative. There is good walking country just on the doorstep. **OPEN:** 11-3 6-11 (Sun 12-3, 6-10.30) Closed: 25 Dec **BAR MEALS:** Lunch served: all week Dinner served: all week 12-2 6-9 Av main course £8.50 **RESTAURANT:** Lunch served: all week Dinner served: all week 12-2 6-9 Av 3 course à la carte £13 **BREWERY/COMPANY:** Wadworth **PRINCIPAL BEERS:** Wadworth Henry's IPA, 6X, Farmers Glory & Old Timer. **FACILITIES:** Children welcome Garden: Food served outside, patio Dogs allowed on leads **NOTES:** Parking 90

See Pub Walk on page 221

STEEP   Map 04 SU72

Pick of the Pubs

Harrow Inn
GU32 2DA ☎ 01730 262685
Dir: Off A3 to A272, L through Sheet, take road opp church (school lane) then over A3 by-pass bridge
A gem of a rustic pub, run by the McCutchen family since 1929, that is totally unspoilt and tucked away down a sleepy lane that was once the drovers' route from Liss to Petersfield. Today the tile-hung 500-year-old building is a popular watering hole with hikers following the Hanger's Way, who stop to enjoy the delightful cottage garden. The two character bars, each with scrubbed wooden tables, boarded walls and seasonal flower arrangements, are the perfect environment to relax over a decent pint of local ale. This give an opportunity to contemplate choices of smoked salmon sandwiches, ploughman's lunches and maybe Stilton and broccoli quiche, followed by treacle tart or chocolate nut biscuits, all cooked in the long-serving Rayburn. Little has changed over the years - and why should it? A true survivor, the Harrow remains, as ever, resistant to change.
OPEN: 12-2.30 6-11 (Sat 11-3, 6-11, Sun 12-3, 7-10.30) **BAR MEALS:** Lunch served: all week Dinner served: all week 12-2 7-9 Av main course £7.50 **BREWERY/COMPANY:** Free House **PRINCIPAL BEERS:** Ringwood Best, Cheriton Diggers Gold & Pots Ale, Ballards Trotton. **FACILITIES:** Garden: Seating, food served outside Dogs allowed (water) **NOTES:** Parking 15

STOCKBRIDGE   Map 04 SU33

Mayfly
Testcombe SO20 6AZ ☎ 01264 860283
Dir: Between A303 & A30, on A3057
One of the county's most famous riverside pubs, this former farmhouse evolved into a watering hole in the early 1900s. It is a wonderful location for a summertime pint and lunch in the delightful garden beside the River Test. Winchester, Stockbridge and Romsey are within easy reach, and for walkers the long-distance Test Way runs close by. Up to 40 cheeses and a selection of cold meats and pies is laid out buffet-style along with a few hot daily specials.

continued

OPEN: 10-11 **BAR MEALS:** Lunch served: all week Dinner served: all week 11.30-9 Av main course £8 **PRINCIPAL BEERS:** Wadworth 6X, Interbrew Flowers Original, Ringwood Best. **FACILITIES:** Children welcome Garden: Next to riverside Dogs allowed **NOTES:** Parking 48

The Peat Spade
Longstock SO20 6DR ☎ 01264 810612
e-mail: peat.spade@virgin.net

A red-brick and gabled Victorian pub with unusual paned windows, tucked away in in the Test Valley, just 100 metres from Hampshire's finest chalk stream. It offers an informal atmosphere in which to enjoy a decent pint of Hampshire ale and a satisfying meal chosen from the short, daily-changing blackboard menu. Pork and red pepper terrine or smoked mackerel and horseradish pâté may precede Moroccan lamb with cumin lemon and couscous or beef and vegetable cottage pie. Small rear garden for the summer.
OPEN: 11.30-3 6.30-11 Closed: Dec 25-26 & 31Dec-1 Jan **BAR MEALS:** Lunch served: Tue-Sun Dinner served: Tue-Sun 12-2.30 7-9.30 Av main course £10.50 **RESTAURANT:** Lunch served: Tue-Sun Dinner served: Tue-Sun 12-2 7-9.30 Av 3 course à la carte £18.50 **BREWERY/COMPANY:** Free House **PRINCIPAL BEERS:** Ringwood Best, Ringwood 49er & guest ales. **FACILITIES:** Children welcome Garden: Food served outside, Paved terrace Dogs allowed on a lead **NOTES:** Parking 22 **ROOMS:** 4 bedrooms 4 en suite from s£58.75 d£58.75 No credit cards

STRATFIELD TURGIS   Map 04 SU65

The Wellington Arms ★ ★ ★
RG27 0AS ☎ 01256 882214 ☐ 01256 882934
e-mail: wellington.arms@virgin.net
Dir: on A33 between Basingstoke & Reading
Former farmhouse, dating from the 17th century, situated at one of the entrances to the ancestral home of the Duke of Wellington. There is a monthly restaurant carte, and lounge

continued

bar favourites such as Wellington chicken liver pâté, home-made pie, and sirloin steak. Most of the bedrooms are located in the modern Garden Wing, though rooms in the original house with a more period feel are available.
OPEN: 11–11 (Sun 12–10.30) **BAR MEALS:** Lunch served: all week Dinner served: all week 12–2.30 6–10 Av main course £12
RESTAURANT: Lunch served: Sun-Fri 12–2 Dinner served: Mon–Sat 6.30–9.30 Av 3 course à la carte £25
BREWERY/COMPANY: Woodhouse Inns
PRINCIPAL BEERS: Badger Best Bitter & Tanglefoot.
FACILITIES: Children welcome Garden: Beer garden, food served outdoors Dogs allowed **NOTES:** Parking 60
ROOMS: 30 bedrooms 30 en suite from s£65 d£75

TANGLEY
Map 04 SU35

The Fox Inn
SP11 0RY ☎ 01264 730276 ▤ 01264 730478
e-mail: foxinn@wessexinns.fsbusiness.co.uk
Dir: 4m N of Andover

Well worth the detour off the A343, the 300-year-old Fox is a remote brick and flint cottage with a friendly atmosphere. In the bar, choose from steak and kidney pie, moussaka, or chicken tikka. The restaurant might offer fresh crab cakes, salmon en croûte, monkfish, or tenderloin of pork in Calvados.
OPEN: 12–3 6–11 **BAR MEALS:** Lunch served: all week Dinner served: all week 12–3 6–11 Av main course £8.95
RESTAURANT: Lunch served: all week Dinner served: all week 12–3 6–11 Av 3 course à la carte £20 **PRINCIPAL BEERS:** Flowers IPA, London Pride, Bass. **FACILITIES:** Children welcome Children's licence Dogs allowed (water provided) **NOTES:** Parking 50

TICHBORNE
Map 04 SU53

Pick of the Pubs

The Tichborne Arms
SO24 0NA ☎ 01962 733760 ▤ 01962 733760
e-mail: kjday@btinternet.com
Dir: off A31 towards Alresford, after 200yds R at sign for Tichborne
A heavily thatched free house in the heart of the Itchen Valley, dating from 1423 but destroyed by fire and rebuilt three times; the present red-brick building was erected in 1939. An interesting history is attached to this idyllic rural hamlet, which was dramatised in the feature film *The Tichborne Claimant*. The pub displays much memorabilia connected with the film's subject, the impersonation and unsuccessful claim to the title and estates of Tichborne. Real ales straight from the cask are served in the comfortable, atmospheric bars, and all food is home made. Traditional choices range from steak, ale and Stilton pie, venison in Guinness with pickled walnuts,

chicken, tarragon and mushroom pie, and fish pie to toasted sandwiches and filled jacket potatoes. Expect hearty old-fashioned puddings. A large, well-stocked garden is ideal for summer eating and drinking.

OPEN: 11.30–2.30 6–11 **BAR MEALS:** Lunch served: all week Dinner served: all week 12–1.45 6.30–9.45 Av main course £7
BREWERY/COMPANY: Free House
PRINCIPAL BEERS: Ringwood Best & True Glory, Triple FFF Moondance, Wadworth 6X, Otter Ale. **FACILITIES:** Garden: Food served outside Dogs allowed (water, biscuits)
NOTES: Parking 30

UPPER FROYLE
Map 04 SU74

The Hen & Chicken Inn
GU34 4JH ☎ 01420 22115 ▤ 01420 23021
Dir: 6m from Farnham on A31 on R

Situated on the old Winchester to Canterbury road, this 16th-century inn was once the haunt of highwaymen. It retains its traditional atmosphere with large open fires, panelling and beams. Now owned by Hall & Woodhouse.
OPEN: 11–11 (Sun 12–10.30) **BAR MEALS:** All week 12–10 Av meal £9 **RESTAURANT:** All week 12–9 Av 3-course meal £25
BREWERY/COMPANY: Free House **PRINCIPAL BEERS:** Badger Best, IPA, Tanglefoot, Old Ale, Sussex Bitter **FACILITIES:** Children welcome (play equipment) Garden: Large, food served outside Dogs welcome **NOTES:** Parking 36

> **Room prices show the minimum double and single rates charged.**
> **Room rates in hotels and B&B's often vary depending on the facilities, so be sure to check prices with the establishment before booking.**

continued

WARSASH Map 04 SU40

The Jolly Farmer Country Inn 🐾 ♀
29 Fleet End Rd SO31 9JH ☎ 01489 572500 🖷 01489 885847
Dir: Exit M27 Juct 9, head towards A27 Fareham, turn R onto Warsash Rd
Follow for 2 M then L onto Fleet end Rd
Look out for the multi-coloured classic car outside this white-painted pub with its abundance of hanging baskets. The bars are furnished in rustic style with plenty of farming equipment on walls and ceilings, and there's a patio for summer eating. An interesting menu focuses on dishes such as fisherman's pie, Isle of Wight crab salad, Dover sole, mixed grill, and steak Murphy pie.
OPEN: 11–11 **BAR MEALS:** Lunch served: all week Dinner served: all week 12–2.30 6–10 Av main course £8.95 **RESTAURANT:** Lunch served: all week Dinner served: all week 12–2.30 6–10 Av 3 course à la carte £15.95 **BREWERY/COMPANY:** Whitbread
PRINCIPAL BEERS: Gale's HSB, Fuller's London Pride, Interbrew Flowers IPA. **FACILITIES:** Children welcome Garden: Food served outside Dogs allowed (water) **NOTES:** Parking 50
ROOMS: 4 bedrooms 4 en suite from s£42.50 d£55

WELL Map 04 SU74

The Chequers Inn
RG29 1TL ☎ 01256 862605 🖷 01256 862133
e-mail: chequers.odiham.wi@freshnet.com
Dir: from Odiham High St turn R into Long Lane, follow for 3m, L at T jct, pub 0.25m on top of hill

A charming, old-world 17th-century pub with a rustic, low-beamed bar, replete with log fire, scrubbed tables, and vine-covered front terrace, set deep in the heart of the Hampshire countryside. Choose from a menu including spinach and Feta cheese parcel, spicy Thai chicken, duck breast topped with red wine and plum sauce, Cumberland sausage wheel, grilled cod, or trout stuffed with Feta cheese and apricots.
OPEN: 11–3 6–11 (Sat 11–11, Sun 12–10.30) **BAR MEALS:** Lunch served: all week Dinner served: all week 12–2.30 6–9.30 Av main course £9 **RESTAURANT:** Lunch served: all week Dinner served: all week 12–2.30 6–10 Av 3 course à la carte £15
BREWERY/COMPANY: Hall & Woodhouse
PRINCIPAL BEERS: Gribble Inn Fursty Ferret, Badger Tanglefoot & Best. **FACILITIES:** Garden: Food served outside Dogs allowed
NOTES: Parking 30

WHERWELL Map 04 SU34

The White Lion 🐾
Fullerton Rd SP11 7JF ☎ 01264 860317 🖷 01264 860317
Dir: Off A303 onto B3048, pub on B3420
Former coaching inn at the centre of one of Hampshire's most unspoilt villages, just a few minutes' walk from the River Test.

The inn came under fire during the Civil War, when one of Oliver Cromwell's cannon balls reputedly dropped down the chimney. A lengthy daily specials menu lists the likes of spinach, pasta and cheese bake, lamb shank, pheasant casserole, and sweet and sour pork.
OPEN: 10–2.30 (Sat 10–3 Sun 12–3) 6–11 (Sun 7–10.30, Mon–Tue 7–11) **BAR MEALS:** Lunch served: all week Dinner served: all week 12–2 7–9.30 Av main course £7 **RESTAURANT:** Lunch served: all week Dinner served: all week 12–2 7–9.30 Av 3 course à la carte £15
BREWERY/COMPANY: Inn Partnership
PRINCIPAL BEERS: Interbrew Flowers Original, Adnams Bitter, Ringwood Best Bitter. **FACILITIES:** Children welcome Garden: Enclosed courtyard, food served outside Dogs allowed
NOTES: Parking 40 **ROOMS:** 3 bedrooms from s£32.50 d£45

WHITCHURCH Map 04 SU44

Pick of the Pubs

The Red House Inn ◉ 🐾 ♀
21 London St RG28 7LH ☎ 01256 895558
Dir: From M3 or M4 take A34 to Whitchurch
In the centre of a small Hampshire town, only a few minutes' walk from southern England's only working silk mill, this is a busy 16th-century coaching inn with quaint flagstones and gnarled beams. Counted among the fraternity of chef-owned free houses, here diners can expect to find modern cooking of first-rate fresh local produce offered in imaginative guises. There are two bars, one very much a locals' bar and the other, with its stripped pine floor, large mirror and old fireplace is for eating. Specials on any one day might be fresh halibut with smoked salmon crust, roast Cajun scallops with saffron dressing and rack of lamb with mushrooms and spinach, accompanied by carefully chosen house wines and regularly changing cask ales. At night try roasted langoustines with herb and Parmesan crust and teriyaki venison steak on Savoy cabbage and red mullet with Caesar salad and saffron potatoes. Fixed-price dinners may offer crab and watercress soup, duck breast with honey-glazed apples and an accomplished chocolate terrine.
OPEN: 11.30–3 6–11 (Sun 12–3, 7–10.30) **BAR MEALS:** Lunch served: all week Dinner served: all week 12–2 6.30–9.30 Av main course £11 **RESTAURANT:** Lunch served: all week Dinner served: all week 12–2 6.30–9.30 Av 3 course à la carte £25 Av 3 course fixed price £25 **BREWERY/COMPANY:** Free House
PRINCIPAL BEERS: Cheriton Diggers Gold & Pots Ale, Itchen Valley Fagins, Hop Back Summer Lightning.
FACILITIES: Children welcome Garden: Food served outside, patio Dogs allowed **NOTES:** Parking 25

Watership Down Inn 🐾
Freefolk Priors RG28 7NJ ☎ 01256 892254
e-mail: mark@watershipdowninn.co.uk
Dir: On B3400 between Basingstoke & Andover
Enjoy an exhilarating walk on Watership Down itself before relaxing with a welcome pint at this homely 19th-century inn named after Richard Adams' classic tale of rabbit life. A popular beer garden, a conservatory and plenty of character are among the attractions, and the pub is renowned for its eclectic choice of beers. The same menu is offered throughout, including seafood platter, sausage and mash, ham, egg and chips and T-bone steak.
OPEN: 11.30–3.30 6–11 **BAR MEALS:** Lunch served: all week Dinner served: all week 12–2.30 6–9.30 Av main course £5.50

continued
continued

BREWERY/COMPANY: Free House
PRINCIPAL BEERS: Brakspear Bitter, Butts Barbus Barbus, Triple FFF Pressed Rat & Warthog, Hogs Back TEA. **FACILITIES:** Children welcome Garden: Beer garden, food served outdoors, patio
NOTES: Parking 18

WHITSBURY   Map 03 SU11

The Cartwheel Inn ♀
Whitsbury Rd SP6 3PZ ☎ 01725 518362 📠 01725 518886
e-mail: thecartwheelinn@lineone.net
Dir: Off A338 between Salisbury & Fordingbridge
Handy for exploring the New Forest, visiting Breamore House and discovering the remote Mizmaze on the nearby downs, this extended, turn-of-the-century one-time wheelwright's and shop has been a pub since the 1920s. Venue for a beer festival held annually in August, with spit-roast pigs, barbecues, Morris dancing and a range of 30 real ales. Popular choice of well kept beers in the bar too. Home-made food on daily specials boards - steak and kidney pudding, fisherman's pie and chicken curry.
OPEN: 11–2.30 6–11 **BAR MEALS:** Lunch served: all week Dinner served: all week 12–2 7–9.30 Av main course £6
RESTAURANT: Lunch served: all week Dinner served: all week 12–2 7–9.30 Av 3 course à la carte £13.50 **BREWERY/COMPANY:** Free House **PRINCIPAL BEERS:** Adnams Broadside, Ringwood Best, Smiles, Hop Back Summer Lightning. **FACILITIES:** Children welcome Garden: Food served outside Dogs allowed (water)
NOTES: Parking 25

WINCHESTER   Map 04 SU52

Pick of the Pubs

Wykeham Arms ♦♦♦♦ ◉ 🐾 ♀
75 Kingsgate St SO23 9PE ☎ 01962 853834 📠 01962 854411
Dir: Near Winchester College & Winchester Cathedral
Buzzy, atmospheric inn filled with old school desks, photographs and other Winchester College memorabilia, with a great sense of history and a strong identity as a 'local' pub. Tucked away in the back streets in the oldest part of the city between the college and the cathedral, it offers blazing log fires in winter and a series of interconnecting rooms. Menus are updated daily, sourced from local produce, and full of interesting choices: from the specials list expect pork and duck rillette, lamb and rosemary casserole, and chocolate roulade. The dinner carte suggests starters like game and green peppercorn terrine, pan-fried calves' liver or grilled halibut steak to follow, and iced walnut parfait, or lemon tart. An evolving list of some 40 wines, with up to 20 sold by the glass or carafe. Generously-furnished bedrooms offer all modern comforts.
OPEN: 11–11 (Sun 12–10.30) Closed: 25 Dec
BAR MEALS: Lunch served: Mon–Sat Dinner served: Mon–Sat 12–2.30 6.30–8.45 Av main course £6.25 **RESTAURANT:** Lunch served: all week Dinner served: Mon–Sat 6.30–8.45 Av 3 course à la carte £22 Av 3 course fixed price £22.95
BREWERY/COMPANY: Gales **PRINCIPAL BEERS:** Interbrew Bass, Gales Butser Bitter, Special, HSB. **FACILITIES:** Garden: Terrace, food served outside Dogs allowed **NOTES:** Parking 12
ROOMS: 14 bedrooms 14 en suite from s£50 d£79.50

WOODLANDS   Map 04 SU31

The Game Keeper
268 Woodlands Rd SO40 7GH ☎ 023 80293093
Dir: M27 J2 follow signs for Beaulieu/Fawley(A326). At 1st rndbt after the Safeway rndbt turn R, then next L. 1m on L
Backing onto open fields on the very edge of the New Forest, this 150-year-old extended cottage is the perfect resting place after a long forest walk. Comfortable modernised interior and traditional pub food.
OPEN: 11–2.30 5–11 (open all day Fri-Sun) **BAR MEALS:** All week 12–2 6.30–9.30 **RESTAURANT:** All week 12–2 6.30–9.30
BREWERY/COMPANY: Wadworth
PRINCIPAL BEERS: Wadworth 6X, IPA & Farmers Glory, Rockingham Forest Gold, Fuggles **FACILITIES:** Children welcome (bouncy castle) Garden: Patio Dogs welcome **NOTES:** Parking 40

HEREFORDSHIRE

AYMESTREY   Map 03 SO46

Pick of the Pubs

Riverside Inn & Restaurant ♀
HR6 9ST ☎ 01568 708440 📠 01568 709058
e-mail: richard.gresko@btinternet.com
Dir: Situated on A4110 between Hereford & Knighton

Originally a Welsh longhouse dating from 1580, this riverside inn is an attractive black and white building with many original features including beams and log fires. Set on the banks of the River Lugg, with a mile of private fishing rights, and also on the Mortimer Way which is popular with walkers. The inn has a serious approach to food, and wherever possible, locally grown or farmed produce is used, including vegetables, salads and herbs from the garden. The chef has developed some special menus, like the popular steak, kidney and Red Kite (local beer) pie. Expect dishes such as carpaccio of beef with fresh Parmesan, or tartlette of kedgeree with poached egg and vierge dressing, followed by sea bass fillets on cumin-flavoured leeks, or vegetarian choices like plum tomato tarte Tatin with herb Mascarpone.
OPEN: 11–3 6–11 (Open All day in summer) Closed: Dec 25
BAR MEALS: Lunch served: all week Dinner served: all week 12–2.30 7–9.30 Av main course £11 **RESTAURANT:** Lunch served: all week Dinner served: all week 12–2.30 7–9.30 Av 3 course à la carte £21 Av 3 course fixed price £19
BREWERY/COMPANY: Free House
PRINCIPAL BEERS: Woodhampton. **FACILITIES:** Children welcome Garden: 3 acres/woodland, Food served outside Dogs allowed (water, food bowls) **NOTES:** Parking 40
ROOMS: 5 bedrooms 5 en suite from s£35 d£55

England

BODENHAM
Map 03 SO55

England's Gate Inn NEW
HR1 3HU ☎ 01568 797286 🖥 01568 797768

A pretty black and white coaching inn dating from around
1540, with atmospheric beamed bars and blazing log fires in
winter. A picturesque garden attracts a good summer
following, and so does the food. Chef's specials like mixed grill,
and pan-fried loin of pork steak glazed in red Leicester and
herbs might be offered along with steak and ale pie, breast of
duck in a port and redcurrant jus, and baked fillet of cod.
OPEN: 11-11 (Sunday 12-10.30) **BAR MEALS:** Lunch served: all
week 12-2.30 Dinner served: Mon-Sat 6-9.30 Av main course £8.95
RESTAURANT: Lunch served: all week 12-2.30 Dinner served:
Mon-Sat 6-9.30 Av 3 course à la carte £15
BREWERY/COMPANY: Free House
PRINCIPAL BEERS: Marston's Pedigree, Wye Valley Bitter & Butty
Bach. **FACILITIES:** Children welcome Garden: Food served
outdoors, patio Dogs allowed (water) **NOTES:** Parking 100

CANON PYON
Map 03 SO44

The Nags Head Inn 🏠
HR4 8NY ☎ 01432 830252

Dating back some 400 years, a listed building containing
flagstone floors, open fires and beams. The bedrooms are
housed in an adjacent former brewery. Simple pub food
ranges from filled baguettes to grilled steaks, fish dishes and
vegetarian options. Specials might be garlic mushrooms and
baked golden trout. The large garden features a children's
adventure playground.
OPEN: 11-3 6-11 **BAR MEALS:** Lunch served: Tue-Sun 12-2.30
Dinner served: all week 6.30-9.30 Av main course £5.50
RESTAURANT: Lunch served: Tue-Sun 12-2.30 Dinner served: all
week 6.30-9.30 Av 3 course à la carte £15
BREWERY/COMPANY: Free House
PRINCIPAL BEERS: Wadworth 6X, Fuller's London Pride.
FACILITIES: Children welcome Garden: Beer garden, patio, food
served outdoors, BBQ **NOTES:** Parking 50 **ROOMS:** 6 bedrooms 6
en suite from s£35 d£45

CAREY
Map 03 SO53

Cottage of Content
HR2 6NG ☎ 01432 840242 🖥 01432 840208
Dir: From A40 W of Ross-on-Wye take A49 towards Hereford.Follow signs
for Hoarworthy, then Carey

A 500-year-old building, formerly three cottages, situated
beside a stream. The specials board is likely to feature chargrilled chicken with apricot, mango and green pepper sauce,
salmon with saffron and herb butter sauce, fillet of beef with
wild mushrooms and port sauce, and vegetarian options.
OPEN: 12-2.30 7-11 Closed: 25 Dec **BAR MEALS:** Lunch served:
all week Dinner served: all week 12-2 **BREWERY/COMPANY:** Free
House **PRINCIPAL BEERS:** Hook Norton. **FACILITIES:** Children
welcome Garden: Dogs allowed **NOTES:** Parking 30
ROOMS: 4 bedrooms 3 en suite

CRASWALL
Map 03 SO23

Bulls Head 🏠
HR2 0PN ☎ 01981 510616 🖥 01981 510383

In the heart of some great walking country, this isolated 200
year-old drover's inn offers rough camping as well as bed and
breakfast. Recent refurbishments have retained the traditional
atmosphere, with flagstone floors, a farmhouse range and

butler sink. Local ingredients drive the menu; try the huge
home-baked wholemeal sandwiches, Craswall pie, or Ledbury
lamb chops. Lots of authentic curries, plus vegetarian options
and sticky puddings, too.
OPEN: 11-3 6-11 **BAR MEALS:** Lunch served: all week Dinner
served: all week 12-3 6-9.30 Av main course £7.95
RESTAURANT: Lunch served: all week Dinner served: all week 12-3
6-9.30 **BREWERY/COMPANY:** Free House
PRINCIPAL BEERS: Wye Valley Butty Bach,. **FACILITIES:** Children
welcome Garden: Food served outside Dogs allowed
NOTES: Parking 6 **ROOMS:** 3 bedrooms 1 en suite from s£30 d£40

DORMINGTON
Map 03 SO54

Yew Tree Inn 🏠
Len Gee's Restaurant, Priors Frome HR1 4EH
☎ 01432 850467 🖥 01432 850467
Dir: A438 Hereford to Ledbury, turn at Dormington towards Mordiford, 1/2
mile on L.

Len Gee uses only the finest ingredients in his dining pub;
local game and vegetables, butcher's meats plus an extensive
selection of fresh fish. His weekend carvery is arguably the
best for miles around. Imaginative bar snacks include smoked
wild boar with raspberry vinaigrette and main dishes such as
seafood penne pasta and sirloin steak with Stilton sauce.
Leave room for the wild greengage ice cream. Panoramic
views over the Lugg and Wye valleys toward Hereford and the
Black Mountains from the terrace.
OPEN: 12-2 7-11 **BAR MEALS:** Lunch served: all week Dinner
served: all week 12-2 7-9 Av main course £5.95
RESTAURANT: Lunch served: all week Dinner served: all week 12-2
7-9 Av 3 course à la carte £14 Av 3 course fixed price £11.50
BREWERY/COMPANY: Free House **PRINCIPAL BEERS:** Tetley,
Wye Valley, Red Kite. **FACILITIES:** Children welcome Garden:
3 terraces, food served outside Dogs allowed **NOTES:** Parking 25

DORSTONE
Map 03 SO34

The Pandy Inn ♀
HR3 6AN ☎ 01981 550273 🖥 01981 550277
Dir: Off B4348 W of Hereford

The oldest inn in Herefordshire, the Pandy was built in 1185,
originally to house workers building Dorstone Church. Oliver
Cromwell was a frequent visitor in the 17th-century. Alongside
the usual pub favourites, the South African owners offer
traditional dishes from back home, bobotie and tomato
bredie, along with English dishes such as lamb and apricot
casserole, broccoli and cream cheese bake, and fillet of
salmon poached in white wine.
OPEN: 12-3 7-11 (Mon 6-11 only, Sat 12-11, Sun 12-10.30)
BAR MEALS: Lunch served: Tue-Sun 12-2.30 Dinner served: all
week 7-9.30 Av main course £8 **RESTAURANT:** Lunch served:
Tue-Sun 12-2.30 Dinner served: all week 7-9.30 Av 3 course à la carte
£15 **BREWERY/COMPANY:** Free House
PRINCIPAL BEERS: Wye Valley Butty Bach & Dorothy Goodbody.
FACILITIES: Children welcome Children's licence Garden: Beer
garden, patio, BBQ, food served outdoors Dogs allowed
NOTES: Parking 30

FOWNHOPE
Map 03 SO53

The Green Man Inn ★ ★ 🏠
HR1 4PE ☎ 01432 860243 🖥 01432 860207
Dir: From M50 take A449 then B4224 to Fownhope

Set in a charming garden close to the River Wye, this 15th-
century country inn is white painted with a host of black

continued

continued

PUB WALK

Little Cowarne
The Three Horseshoes

THE THREE HORSESHOES
LITTLE COWARNE nr Bromyard
HR7 4RQ
Tel: 01885 400276
Directions: Off A456
(Hereford/Bromyard). At
Stokes Cross, take turning
signed Little
Cowarne/Pencombe
Formerly a blacksmith's shop
and alehouse, this country inn
offers home-made food using
fresh local produce, and the
Garden Room conservatory is a
pleasant place to eat at
lunchtime.
Open:11–3 6.30–11
Bar meals: 12–2 6.30–10
Garden and parking available.

Distance: 4 1/2miles (7.2km)
Map: OS Landranger 149 or
Explorer 202
Terrain: Picturesque, rolling
country of the Welsh Borders
Paths: Bridleways, footpaths and
country roads
Gradient: Undulating

Walk submitted and checked
by Roy Johnson

This peaceful walk explores the delightful landscapes of the Welsh Borders - a perfect area for anyone who likes country walking in undisturbed surroundings.

From the pub car park, turn left up the lane. At the top swing right, down the road to Little Cowarne church. Just past the church turn left along a track down to a stream. Follow the track uphill to a road. Turn right and then veer left opposite Pencombe Hall. Walk down the road to Pencombe. As you enter the village at the road junction, look for a narrow entrance to a footpath running alongside the stream. Bear right down this footpath and follow the stream, ignoring paths to the right and left until you come to a crossing track by the wall of a bungalow. Take the path a few paces to the left. Continue between the dwellings to enter a field and keep ahead on the same line across two more fields and round the front of some barns. At the road turn right, go down the road a short way and cross a stile in the hedge on the right. Walk up the field with the boundary hedge on your right, cross a stile and continue until the next stile. Cross over and continue with the hedge still on the right, until you come to a track at the front of the house on your left. Bear left and follow the track round between the house and Glebe Farm. Keep ahead until you reach a waymarked bridleway on your right. Follow it, cross a stream and then a field to a gate leading into the drive to Meadow Court. Cross over the drive, enter the field opposite, continuing ahead on the same line across two fields to pass through a bridle-gate. Turn right and downhill to the gate in the bottom right corner of the field. Follow the sunken track into Little Cowarne and go left at the road. At the right-hand bend, cross the stile ahead and follow the hedge on your left to a further stile, leading out to the road. Turn left and return to the inn.

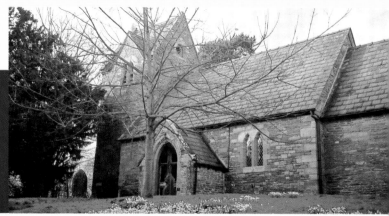

England

FOWNHOPE continued

beams inside and out. The former coaching inn is in picturesque countryside amidst wooded hills, an ideal base for walking, touring and local salmon fishing. The Petty Sessional Court was once held here, and a bare-fist fighter was a notorious former owner. Expect steak sandwich, steak and ale pie, swordfish, salmon and trout.
OPEN: 11-11 **BAR MEALS:** Lunch served: all week Dinner served: all week 12-10 Av main course £7.95 **RESTAURANT:** Lunch served: Sun 12-2 Dinner served: all week 7-9 Av 3 course à la carte £15.95 **BREWERY/COMPANY:** Free House **PRINCIPAL BEERS:** Scottish Courage Courage Directors, Hook Norton Best **FACILITIES:** Children welcome Garden: Beer garden, patio, food served outdoors Dogs allowed **NOTES:** Parking 80 **ROOMS:** 20 bedrooms 20 en suite from s£38.50 d£65

GLADESTRY Map 03 SO25

Royal Oak Inn
HR5 3NR ☎ 01544 370669 ▧ 01544 370669
e-mail: iris@theroyaloak.junglelink.co.uk
Dir: 2m off A44

Comfortable 17th-century pub, one of the few actually on Offa's Dyke footpath and therefore popular with walkers. A friendly, inviting atmosphere greets visitors, with cosy coal fires in winter and Welsh cream teas and home-made cakes in summer. Good choice of food, from toasted sandwiches to home-made chicken curry, broccoli cheese bake, and grilled Welsh lamb chops, plus such fresh fish as plaice, cod and haddock.
OPEN: 11.30-2 7-11 (summer all day) Closed: Dec 25
BAR MEALS: Lunch served: all week Dinner served: all week 12-2 7-9.30 Av main course £5.50 **RESTAURANT:** Lunch served: all week Dinner served: all week 12-2 7-9.30 **BREWERY/COMPANY:** Free House **PRINCIPAL BEERS:** Hancocks HB, Albright,Interbrew Bass,. **FACILITIES:** Children welcome Children's licence Garden: Food served outside, seating Dogs allowed (water, food) **NOTES:** Parking 20 **ROOMS:** 4 bedrooms from s£20 d£40 No credit cards

HAMPTON BISHOP Map 03 SO53

The Bunch of Carrots
HR1 4JR ☎ 01432 870237 ▧ 01432 870237
Dir: From Hereford take A4103, A438, then B4224
Friendly pub with real fires, old beams and flagstones. Its name comes from a rock formation in the River Wye which runs alongside the pub. There is an extensive menu (steaks, salmon fillet and Cajun chicken) plus a daily specials board, a carvery, salad buffet and simple bar snacks.
OPEN: 11-3 6-11 **BAR MEALS:** Lunch served: all week Dinner served: all week 12-2 6-10 **RESTAURANT:** Lunch served: all week

Dinner served: all week 12-2 6-10 **BREWERY/COMPANY:** Free House **PRINCIPAL BEERS:** Bass, Hook Norton, Wye Valley. **FACILITIES:** Children welcome Garden: Food served outside Dogs allowed **NOTES:** Parking 100

HEREFORD Map 03 SO54

The Ancient Camp Inn ★ ★
Ruckhall HR2 9QX ☎ 01981 250449 ▧ 01981 251581
e-mail: enquiries@theancientcamp.co.uk
Dir: Take A465 from Hereford, then B4349.Follow signs 'Belmont Abbey/Ruckhall'
From its elevated position some 70 feet above the winding River Wye the views across the river and Golden Valley from the terrace are stunning. The low-beamed interior with its stone-flagged floors and simple furnishings is typical of a country inn. A change of hands as we go to press will no doubt lead to changes. The style of the food has been to use local ingredients with venison and partridge as the basis of popular dishes. Reports please.
OPEN: 12-3 7-11 (Sun 12-3 only) Closed: 2 weeks Jan
BAR MEALS: Lunch served: Sat-Sun 12-2.30 Av main course £6.50 **RESTAURANT:** Lunch served: Sat-Sun 12-2 Av 4 course fixed price £19.50 **BREWERY/COMPANY:** Free House **FACILITIES:** Garden: Terrace overlooking the River Wye **NOTES:** Parking 30 **ROOMS:** 5 bedrooms 5 en suite from s£50 d£60

The Crown & Anchor
Cotts Ln, Lugwardine HR1 4AB
☎ 01432 851303 ▧ 01432 851637
e-mail: jscrownandanchor@care4free.net
Dir: 2 miles from Hereford city centre on A438, turn left into Lugwardine down Cotts Lane
Attractive old black-and-white pub on the Lugg flats, with quarry tile floors and a large log fire. An extensive list of sandwiches includes smoked trout, apple and horseradish, and Cambazola, cucumber and kiwi. Interesting main courses offer an imaginative vegetarian choice, and the likes of pan-fried Herefordshire sirloin steak, supreme of escolar with ginger, coriander and lime, fillets of Torbay sole with mussels and white wine sauce, and pan-fried Gressingham duck breast with pomegranate molasses.
OPEN: 12-11 Closed: 25 Dec **BAR MEALS:** Lunch served: all week Dinner served: all week 12-2 7-10 Av main course £7
BREWERY/COMPANY: Free House
PRINCIPAL BEERS: Worthington Bitter, Hobsons Best, Theakstons XB. **FACILITIES:** Children welcome Garden: Food served outdoors, patio **NOTES:** Parking 30

KIMBOLTON Map 03 SO56

Pick of the Pubs

Stockton Cross Inn
HR6 0HD ☎ 01568 612509
e-mail: stocktoncross@aol.com
Dir: On the A4112 off A49 between Leominster and Ludlow
A 17th-century drovers' inn set by the side of a crossroads where hangings are reputed to have taken place. The atmosphere outside the picturesque black and white inn is peaceful nowadays, and the scene so beautiful that it is regularly photographed by tourists, and featured on calendars and chocolate boxes. The food is equally desirable, and good home cooking appears on a variety of menus offering starters and light bites, main dishes and specials. Expect 'Good Old Percy's Rabbit', proper cod and

continued

continued

chips, poached salmon with lemon, and various steaks from the main menu, and specials like cottage pie, hearty lamb casserole, steak and kidney pie, and ham, egg and chips. Puddings have their own menu, with old favourites like treacle tart, fresh fruit Pavlova, and jam roly poly, and luxury caramel ice cream for a sublime finish.

OPEN: 12–3 7–11 **BAR MEALS:** Lunch served: all week 12-2.15 Dinner served: Tues-Sun 7-9 Av main course £7
RESTAURANT: Lunch served: all week 12-2.15 Dinner served: Tues-Sun 7-9 Av 3 course à la carte £20 Av 3 course fixed price £25 **BREWERY/COMPANY:** Free House
PRINCIPAL BEERS: Castle Eden Ale, Whitbread OB Mild, Wye Valley Butty Bach, Interbrew Bass. **FACILITIES:** Garden: Food served outside Dogs allowed **NOTES:** Parking 30

KINGTON   Map 03 SO25

Pick of the Pubs

The Stagg Inn & Restaurant ◎◎ ♀
Titley HR5 3RL ☎ 01544 230221
e-mail: reservations@thestagg.co.uk

Situated at the meeting point of two drovers' roads, the Mortimer Trail and Offa's Dyke Path, the pub retains many original features from its often colourful past. Fireplaces with real fires, a bread oven, and antique furniture all add to the convivial atmosphere, and make this a welcoming spot for a drink or a meal. The Stagg's Roux-trained chef/proprietor Steve Reynolds makes excellent use of the abundant quality produce for which the Marches area is renowned. Menus served throughout the homely, pine-furnished bar with wood burner and visiting local farmers, and the separate informal dining room show the breadth of his imagination and skill. Seasonal cartes may start with pan-fried foie gras with Pembridge apple jelly, or mussel and saffron risotto, move on to saddle of venison with roast shallots, or fillet of Herefordshire beef with sautéed mushrooms, and rise to a climax with whole roasted baby pineapple with vanilla ice cream. Local Hobson Brewery ales, Dunkerton's organic cider, and a well-chosen wine list, with eight choices by the glass.

OPEN: 12–3 6.30–11 (Sun 12–3, 7-10.30) Closed: 1st 2wks Nov **BAR MEALS:** Lunch served: Tue-Sun Dinner served: Tue-Sun 12-2 6.30-10 Av main course £7.50 **RESTAURANT:** Lunch served: Tue-Sun Dinner served: Tue-Sun 12-2 6.30-10 Av 3 course à la carte £22 **BREWERY/COMPANY:** Free House **PRINCIPAL BEERS:** Hobsons Town Crier, Hobsons Old Henry, Hobsons Best Bitter, Brains Reverand James.
FACILITIES: Children welcome Garden: Food served outside Dogs allowed **NOTES:** Parking 40 **ROOMS:** 2 bedrooms 2 en suite from s£40 d£60

LEDBURY   Map 03 SO73

The Farmers Arms ♀
Horse Rd, Wellington Heath HR8 1LS ☎ 01531 632010
Handy for the breathtaking high ground of the Malvern Hills and the seductive charms of Ross and the Wye Valley, this popular country inn offers a varied menu, with dishes cooked daily on the premises. Extensive specials board with perennial favourites such as fresh fish and game. Hog roast, steak and mushroom pie, red Thai curry, half a shoulder of lamb and salmon Wellington are typical examples of what to expect.
OPEN: 12–3 6–11 **BAR MEALS:** Lunch served: all week Dinner served: all week 12-2 7-10 Av main course £9.95
RESTAURANT: Lunch served: all week Dinner served: all week 12-2 7-10 Av 3 course à la carte £15.95 **BREWERY/COMPANY:** Free House **PRINCIPAL BEERS:** Fuller's London Pride, Hancocks HB plus guest ales. **FACILITIES:** Children welcome Garden: Food served outside **NOTES:** Parking 40

Pick of the Pubs

The Feathers Hotel ★ ★ ★ ◎ ♀
High St HR8 1DS ☎ 01531 635266 ▤ 01531 638955
e-mail: mary@feathers-ledbury.co.uk
Dir: S from Worcester A449, E from Hereford A438, N from Gloucester A417.

With its striking black-and-white timbered frontage that dominates the High Street, this fine old coaching inn has been a haven for travellers since Elizabethan times (the first one!). Its character is enhanced by an interior full of oak beams, panelled walls and open log fires. Fuggles Brasserie is adorned with dried Herefordshire hops of the same name, while local produce is a major feature of daily menus posted on large blackboards. Fresh pheasant breasts are served on wilted greens with a mustard crust; Hereford beef tournedos come with thyme, wild mushrooms and glazed shallots. Fresh Cornish fish features strongly, as in hake fillet with garlic, lemon and capers and crispy-skinned sea bass with sesame, chilli and oyster glaze. An adjacent real ale bar also offers world-famous Herefordshire ciders and a selection of lunchtime sandwiches while across the foyer the restaurant provides a more formal dining atmosphere. Upstairs, and in modern extensions, bedrooms are individually styled and well equipped.

OPEN: 11–11 (Sun 12–10.30) **BAR MEALS:** Lunch served: all week Dinner served: all week 12-2 7–9.30 **RESTAURANT:** Lunch served: all week Dinner served: all week 12-2 7–9.30 Av 3 course à la carte £19.50 **BREWERY/COMPANY:** Free House
PRINCIPAL BEERS: Worthington Bitter, Interbrew Bass, Fuller's London Pride, Greene King Old Speckled Hen.
FACILITIES: Children welcome Garden: **NOTES:** Parking 30 **ROOMS:** 19 bedrooms 19 en suite from s£75 d£95

continued

LEDBURY continued

The Talbot ♀
14 New St HR8 2DX ☎ 01531 632963 🖷 01531 633796
e-mail: talbot.ledbury@wadworth.co.uk
Dir: *follow Ledbury signs, turn into Bye St, 2nd L into Woodley Rd, over bridge to jct, L into New St. Talbot on R*
Take a step back in time at this historic black-and-white coaching inn dating from 1596. The oak-panelled dining room, with its fine carved overmantel, was once the scene of fighting between Roundheads and Cavaliers – the musket-holes are still visible today. A good choice of local ales and wines by the glass accompanies port, apricot and cider pâté or mushroom and red pepper vol au vent, followed by steak and ale pie, game casserole and Herefordshire steaks.
OPEN: 11.30–3 5–11 **BAR MEALS:** Lunch served: all week Dinner served: all week 12–2.30 6.30–9.30 Av main course £7.95
RESTAURANT: Lunch served: all week Dinner served: all week 12–2.30 6.30–9.30 Av 3 course à la carte £17.22
PRINCIPAL BEERS: Wadworth 6X & Henrys Original IPA, Wye Valley Butty Bach,. **FACILITIES:** Children welcome Dogs allowed
NOTES: Parking 10 **ROOMS:** 7 bedrooms 6 en suite from s£27.50 d£49.50

Trumpet Inn NEW
The Trumpet Inn, Trumpet HR8 2RA
☎ 01531 670277 🖷 01531 670277
e-mail: aa@trumpetinn.com
Dir: *4 miles from Ledbury on the Hereford Road, Pub on the X-Roads of the A438 and A417*
Historic coaching inn and post house dating from the late 1400s, called after the horn blown as the coach approached a crossroads. The traditional black and white building with many exposed beams has cosy bars with open fireplaces and a separate dining area. Specials on the blackboard include Thai fishcakes, cottage pie, pasta with mushrooms, and cannelloni, with the menu offering steaks, pork escalope, and vegetable Stroganoff.
OPEN: 11.30–2.30 6–11 **BAR MEALS:** Lunch served: all week Dinner served: all week 12–2 6–9 Av main course £6.50
RESTAURANT: Lunch served: all week Dinner served: all week 12–2 6–9 Av 3 course à la carte £12 **BREWERY/COMPANY:** Free House
PRINCIPAL BEERS: Interbrew Flowers IPA, Scottish Courage John Smith's, Castle Eden Ale,. **FACILITIES:** Children welcome Garden: Large, overlooking the From Valley Dogs allowed **NOTES:** Parking 60 **ROOMS:** 3 bedrooms

---

Ploughman's Lunch - a pub classic
Only comparatively recently has pub grub become a important feature of the license trade. Without it, most hostelries would simply go out of business. Food trends come and go and new, imaginatively prepared dishes crop up every day on the specials board. However, there is one favourite item on the menu that remains constant and unchanging and that is the good old ploughman's lunch. The simple but appetising ploughman's is based on the medieval farm labourer's lunchtime snack of bread and cheese and is available in just about every pub in the country. It has changed little down the years, though today most pubs complement the ploughman's lunch with a pickled onion and a garnish of salad or a variety of exotic cheeses and cold meats. Home-made pickle is also a popular favourite.

LEOMINSTER
Map 03 SO45

The Royal Oak Hotel ★ ★
South St HR6 8JA ☎ 01568 612610 🖷 01568 612710
Dir: *Junc A44/A49*

Coaching inn dating from before 1700, with log fires, antiques and a minstrels' gallery in the original ballroom.
OPEN: 10–2.30 6–9 (Sun 10.30–7) **BAR MEALS:** All week 12–2 6.30–9 Av main course £4.25 **RESTAURANT:** All week 12–2 6.30–9 Av 3-course £14 **BREWERY/COMPANY:** Free House
PRINCIPAL BEERS: Brains SA Best, Woods Special Bitter
FACILITIES: Children welcome Patio Dogs welcome (not in restaurant) **ROOMS:** 18 bedrooms 18 en suite from s£35 d£48

LITTLE COWARNE
Map 03 SO65

The Three Horseshoes Inn 🛏
HR7 4RQ ☎ 01885 400276 🖷 01885 400276
Dir: *Off A456 (Hereford/Bromyard). At Stokes Cross, take turning signed Little Cowarne/Pencombe*

Named after the horses brought for shoeing at the next-door blacksmiths', and an alehouse for nearly 200 years. This country inn offers home-made food using local produce, and served in the Garden Room conservatory at lunchtime. Expect fresh fish, vegetarian tomato tart Tatin, and the likes of wild duck with orange sauce, rabbit in the orchard, pork in damson sauce, and sticky ginger cake pudding.
OPEN: 11–3 6.30–11 Closed: Dec 25 **BAR MEALS:** Lunch served: all week Dinner served: all week 12–2 6.30–10 Av main course £5.50
RESTAURANT: Lunch served: all week Dinner served: all week 12–2 6.30–10 Av 3 course à la carte £15 **BREWERY/COMPANY:** Free House **PRINCIPAL BEERS:** Marston's Pedigree, Greene King Old Speckled Hen, Websters Yorkshire Bitter, Wye Valley Bitter.
FACILITIES: Garden: Patio and lawned area, food served outside
NOTES: Parking 50 **ROOMS:** 2 bedrooms 2 en suite from s£27.50 d£23

See Pub Walk on page 243

MADLEY
Map 03 SO43

The Comet Inn
Stoney St HR2 9NJ ☎ 01981 250600 ▤ 01981 250643
Dir: approx 6m from Hereford on the B4352
Located on a prominent corner position and set in two and a half acres, this black and white 19th-century inn has beamed walls and ceilings, and a large open fire.

MICHAELCHURCH ESCLEY
Map 03 SO33

The Bridge Inn
HR2 0JW ☎ 01981 510646 ▤ 01981 510646
Dir: from Hereford take A465 towards Abergavenny, then B4348 towards Peterchurch. Turn L at Vowchurch for village
By Escley Brook, at the foot of the Black Mountains and close to Offa's Dyke, there are 14th-century parts to this oak-beamed family pub: the dining-room overlooks the river and garden, abundant in rose and begonias. Under new management.

MUCH COWARNE
Map 03 SO64

Fir Tree Inn
HR7 4JN ☎ 01531 640619 640725 ▤ 01531 640663
Dir: off the A4103 Hereford to Worcester
Set in three acres of grounds with fishing lake and small caravan site, this part 16th-century modernised inn is a versatile establishment situated in unspoilt countryside. Dishes may include home-made steak and ale pie, toad in the hole, lamb and apricot casserole, mixed grill, Dover sole, lasagne, and sirloin steak.
OPEN: 11–11 **BAR MEALS:** Lunch served: Tue–Sun 12–3 Dinner served: all week 7–9.30 Av main course £6 **RESTAURANT:** Lunch served: Tue–Sun 12–2.30 Dinner served: all week 7–9.30 Av 3 course à la carte £11 Av 1 course fixed price £10
BREWERY/COMPANY: Free House
PRINCIPAL BEERS: Carlsberg-Tetley Tetley Bitter, Ansells Best Bitter.
FACILITIES: Children welcome Garden: Food served outdoors, Orchard **NOTES:** Parking 80 **ROOMS:** 3 bedrooms 3 en suite from s£40 d£35

MUCH MARCLE
Map 03 SO63

The Scrumpy House Bar & Restaurant
The Bounds HR8 2NQ ☎ 01531 660626
e-mail: matt@scrumpyhouse.co.uk
Dir: approx 5 miles from Ledbury & Ross-on-Wye on A449, follow signs to Cidermill
A renovated hay barn on the site of a family-run cider mill with a bar and restaurant separated by a woodburner in the fireplace. Over 20 different ciders are offered alongside local bitters and a varied wine list. All food is prepared on the premises, including 16 kinds of ice cream, and fresh fish on Friday from Grimsby. Favourite dishes include award-winning local bangers and oven-baked sea bass stuffed with home-grown herbs.
OPEN: 12–2.30 7–12 (Fri-Sat 12–2.30, 6.30–12) Closed: 25-26 Dec
RESTAURANT: Lunch served: all week 12–2.30 Dinner served: Wed-Sat 7–11 Av 3 course à la carte £22
BREWERY/COMPANY: Free House **PRINCIPAL BEERS:** Guest ales. **FACILITIES:** Children welcome Children's licence Garden: Patio, Food served outside **NOTES:** Parking 30

The Slip Tavern ♀
Watery Ln HR8 2NG ☎ 01531 660246
Dir: Follow the signs off the A449 at the Much Marcle junction
This country pub, surrounded by cider apple orchards, is named after the landslip of 1575. Sit in the cosy bar or the attractive conservatory overlooking the award-winning garden. A comprehensive menu ranges through steaks, salads, pork and pears, crispy lemon chicken, and faggots with mushy peas and chips.
OPEN: 11.30–2.30 6.30–11 (Sun 12–2.30, 6.30–10.30)
BAR MEALS: Lunch served: all week Dinner served: all week 12–2 7–9.30 Av main course £6.45 **RESTAURANT:** Lunch served: all week Dinner served: all week 12–2 7–9.30 Av 3 course à la carte £12
BREWERY/COMPANY: Free House **PRINCIPAL BEERS:** Hook Norton, Wadworth 6X, Scottish Courage John Smith's.
FACILITIES: Children welcome Garden: Beer garden, patio, food served outside Dogs allowed **NOTES:** Parking 45

PEMBRIDGE
Map 03 SO35

The Cider House Restaurant
Dunkerton's Cider Mill, Luntley HR6 9ED
☎ 01544 388161 ▤ 01544 388654
Dir: W on A44 from Leominster, L in Pembridge centre by New Inn, 1m on L
A converted, half-timbered 16th-century barn with natural oak beams, and beautiful view over rolling countryside. Susie and Ivor Dunkerton started the restaurant after years of cidermaking on the farm, and are dedicated to fresh local produce and home cooking. Expect chicken, chive and pearl barley soup, and marinaded monkfish tails in basil, lemon and shallot sauce. Breads, cakes and desserts all made on the premises.
OPEN: 10–5 Closed: 1 Oct - Easter **BAR MEALS:** Lunch served: Mon–Sat 12–2.30 Av main course £10.20 **RESTAURANT:** Lunch served: Mon–Sat 12–2.30 Av 3 course à la carte £17
BREWERY/COMPANY: Free House
PRINCIPAL BEERS: Dunkertons Ciders, Caledonian Golden Promise. **FACILITIES:** Children welcome **NOTES:** Parking 30

New Inn
Market Square HR6 9DZ ☎ 01544 388427 ▤ 01544 388427
Dir: From M5 J7 take A44 W through Leominster towards Llandrindod Wells
A black and white timbered inn at the centre of a picture-postcard village full of quaint cottages. It dates from the early 14th century, and is one of the oldest pubs in England, once used as the local courthouse and reputedly haunted. Full of old beams, wonky walls and worn flagstones. The menu lists home cooked dishes such as salmon steak, fish chowder, lamb fillet in elderberry wine, pork steak in mustard and cream sauce, and beef casserole.
OPEN: 11–2.30 6–11 **BAR MEALS:** 12–2 7–9.30
RESTAURANT: 12–2 7–9.30 **BREWERY/COMPANY:** Free House
PRINCIPAL BEERS: Fuller's London Pride, Interbrew Bass, Wood Shropshire Lad, Black Sheep Best. **FACILITIES:** Children welcome Garden: **NOTES:** Parking 25 **ROOMS:** 6 bedrooms d£40

ROSS-ON-WYE
Map 03 SO52

Pick of the Pubs

The Moody Cow ♀
Upton Bishop HR9 7TT ☎ 01989 780470
See Pick of the Pubs on page 248

OPEN: 12–2.30 6.30–11
BAR MEALS: L served all week.
D served all week. 12–2 6.30–9.30
Av main course £8.95
RESTAURANT: L served all week.
D served all week. 12–2 6.30–9.30
Av cost 3 courses £16
BREWERY/COMPANY:
FREE HOUSE
PRINCIPAL BEERS: Wadworth 6X,
Flowers IPA, Hook Norton Best
FACILITIES: Children welcome,
dogs allowed. Garden: Food served
outside, patio area
NOTES: Parking 40

The Moody Cow

One of two Moody Cow pubs (the other is at the Wykeham Arms at Sibford Gower in Oxfordshire), this old stone inn has found a winning formula that attracts people from a wide local area. The philosophy is simple: produce good home-baked food at sensible prices, present it attractively in pleasant, convivial surroundings, and enjoy the sight of satisfied customers.

Upton Bishop Ross-on-Wye HR9 7TT
☎ 01989 780470

The buildings has been carefully and tastefully converted to create a choice of comfortable eating and drinking outlets in which to relax. The restaurant used to be a barn, and is now a smart room on two levels with exposed beams, while the Fresco dining room has displays of crockery and plenty of cow-themed ornaments. The farmhouse-style bar

is a friendly place in which to enjoy real ales or a meal under the exposed beams, and the Snug – wood-burning fire, cosy settees and armchairs – is for drinks only. The long menu of imaginative dishes shows why this has been a successful dining destination since the early 1990s. For a light snack or starter, choose from pasta carbonara, tempura-battered king prawns, or wedge of deep-fried Brie with cranberry and red wine sauce. The menu moves on to casserole of guinea fowl, breast of chicken stuffed with Stilton, chicken or prawn jalfrezi, slow-roasted half shoulder of lamb, wild mushroom cassoulet, and pan-fried duck breast with a sweet raspberry compote. Kids choices include perennial favourites, and there are desserts like lavender créme brûlée, summer pudding, and hot gooey chocolate pudding. A blackboard list of specials is changed daily.

ST OWEN'S CROSS
Map 03 SO52

The New Inn 🍴
HR2 8LQ ☎ 01989 730274 📠 01989 730547
e-mail: newinn@stowencross.fsnet.co.uk
Dir: Off A4137 W of Ross-on-Wye

Heavily beamed 16th-century coaching inn on the Chepstow to Hereford route, with three Dobermans, several ghosts and many colourful hanging baskets in summer. It is probably the oldest site of refreshment in the county - as far back as the 6th century. St Owen, a pilgrim saint, is known to have stopped here. Lunch menu offers carved ham, egg and chips, Cumberland sausage, steak and kidney pie, and mushroom and asparagus pancake.
OPEN: 12–2.30 6–11 **BAR MEALS:** Lunch served: all week Dinner served: all week 12–2.30 6.30–9.30 Av main course £7
RESTAURANT: Lunch served: all week Dinner served: all week 12–2.30 6.30–9.30 Av 3 course à la carte £13
BREWERY/COMPANY: Free House
PRINCIPAL BEERS: Wadworth 6X, Carlsberg-Tetley Tetley Bitter, Interbrew Bass. **FACILITIES:** Children welcome Garden: Food served outside Dogs allowed (water, food) **NOTES:** Parking 45
ROOMS: 2 bedrooms 2 en suite from s£35 d£70

SELLACK
Map 03 SO52

Pick of the Pubs

The Lough Pool Inn ◎◎ ♀
HR9 6LX ☎ 01989 730236 📠 01989 730462
Dir: A49 from Ross-on-Wye toward Hereford, side rd signed Sellack/Hoarwithy, pub 2m from R-on-W

Situated in a fold of low hills opposite a large pond with waterfowl and weeping willows, a black and white half-timbered pub with flagstones, beams and open fires. Respected London chef/restaurateur Stephen Bull has extended the kitchen, begun refurbishing the traditional bar and intimate dining room, and brought the focus

firmly onto the excellent food. The Lough Pool will not become a country restaurant, however, and real ales as well as an improved wine list will be served with bar and restaurant meals. The daily carte, using quality ingredients from local suppliers, might feature modern starters like haggis fritters with beetroot chutney, or chargrilled squid, to be followed by linguine with tomatoes and olives, chicken and chorizo ballotine, or traditional steak and kidney with Guinness. There's plenty of choice on the dessert menu, like rich chocolate and brandy cake, upside-down pear and ginger cake, or mango parfait.
OPEN: 11.30–2.30 6.30–11 Closed: 25 Dec **BAR MEALS:** 12–2 7–9.30 **RESTAURANT:** 12–2 7–9.30
BREWERY/COMPANY: Free House **PRINCIPAL BEERS:** Wye Valley, Scottish Courage John Smiths, Greene King Ruddles Country & Old Speckled Hen. **FACILITIES:** Children welcome Garden: Food served outside **NOTES:** Parking 40

SHOBDON
Map 03 SO46

The Bateman Arms
HR6 9LX ☎ 01568 708374
Dir: On B4362 off A4110 NW of Leominster

Black and white 18th-century coaching inn. Traditional interior with open fire, wooden settles and a welcoming atmosphere. Under new management. A great area for walking. The village also has an outstanding old church.
OPEN: 12–2.30 7–11 (Sun 10.30–7) **BAR MEALS:** All week 12–2 7–10 Av main course £7.50 **RESTAURANT:** Lunch Sun 12–2 Dinner Fri-Sun 7–10 Av 3 course £18 **BREWERY/COMPANY:** Free House **PRINCIPAL BEERS:** Wood Ales, Bass **FACILITIES:** Garden: Dogs allowed **NOTES:** Parking 35

SYMONDS YAT (EAST)
Map 03 SO51

The Saracens Head Inn ★ ★ 🍴 ♀
HR9 6JL ☎ 01600 890435 📠 01600 890034
e-mail: email@saracensheadinn.co.uk

continued

continued

England

SYMONDS YAT (EAST) continued

Riverside inn on the east bank of the glorious Wye, situated by the ancient hand ferry which has been in use for 250 years. Handy for exploring the Wye Valley and Forest of Dean. Wide range of home-made bar food and restaurant dishes includes beef in Guinness pie, French leek flan, Middlewhite pork sausages, baked sea bass, chicken in port and Stilton, tuna steak, liver and onions, and grilled trout.
OPEN: 11-11 (Sun 12-10.30) **BAR MEALS:** Lunch served: all week Dinner served: all week 12-2.30 7-9.15 Av main course £6.50
RESTAURANT: Dinner served: all week 7-9.15 Av 3 course à la carte £20 **BREWERY/COMPANY:** Free House
PRINCIPAL BEERS: Theakstons,Greene King Old Speckled Hen, Wells Bombardier, Wye Valley HPA. **FACILITIES:** Children welcome Garden: Beer garden, patio, outdoor eating Dogs allowed **NOTES:** Parking 38 **ROOMS:** 9 bedrooms 9 en suite from s£35 d£60

ULLINGSWICK   Map 03 SO54

Pick of the Pubs

Three Crowns Inn @@ 🐾 🍷
HR1 3JQ ☎ 01432 820279 📠 01432 820279
e-mail: info@threecrownsinn.com
Dir: From Burley Gate rdbt take A465 toward Bromyard, after 2m L to Ullingswick, L after 0.5m, pub 0.5m on R
Unspoilt country pub in deepest rural Herefordshire with a solid reputation for showcasing the best ingredients and drink from the county. They do it well with organically grown produce, rare breed livestock and artisans' cheeses to accompany beers from nearby breweries and famous Hereford cider. Home-grown varieties of old herbs, fruit and vegetables that are not commercially available go into the food, all of which is made on the premises in the inn's own distinctive style of cooking. Meals from the daily-changing menus are served in an informal environment of simple sophistication, including perhaps loin of old spot pork with confit belly, rack of Marches lamb with a little sausage cassoulette, and turbot with marinated cucumber and Pommery mustard. Regular food festivals are held promoting local foods, producers and chefs.
OPEN: 12-2.30 7-11 (May-Aug 12-3, 6-11) Closed: 2wks from Dec 25 **BAR MEALS:** Lunch served: all week Dinner served: all week 12-3 7-10.30 Av main course £13 **RESTAURANT:** Lunch served: all week Dinner served: all week 12-2.30 7-10.30 Av 3 course à la carte £22.25 **BREWERY/COMPANY:** Free House
PRINCIPAL BEERS: Hobsons Best, Wye Valley Butty Bach.
FACILITIES: Children welcome Garden: Food served outdoors, heated patio Dogs allowed except when food is being served in bar **NOTES:** Parking 20

WALTERSTONE   Map 03 SO32

Carpenters Arms 🍷
HR2 0DX ☎ 01873 890353
Dir: Off the A465 between Hereford & Abergavenny at Pandy
Dating back over 300 years, this popular country pub is located on the edge of the Black Mountains, and the owner Mrs Watkins was born here. It has plenty of character, with beams, antique settles and a leaded range where open fires burn all winter. Options range from smoked salmon and scrambled egg to 10oz sirloin steak, with home-made dishes such as cod and prawn pie, lasagne and chicken curry.

OPEN: 11-3 7-11 **BAR MEALS:** 12-3 7-9.30
RESTAURANT: 12-3 7-9.30 **BREWERY/COMPANY:** Free House
PRINCIPAL BEERS: Wadworth 6X, Worthington Best.
FACILITIES: Children welcome Garden: Dogs allowed (only by arrangement) **NOTES:** Parking 15 No credit cards

WEOBLEY   Map 03 SO45

Pick of the Pubs

Ye Olde Salutation Inn ♦♦♦♦ 🍷
Market Pitch HR4 8SJ ☎ 01544 318443 📠 01544 318216
e-mail: info@salutationinn.com
            See Pick of the Pubs on page 251

See Pick of the Pubs on page 251

WHITNEY-ON-WYE   Map 03 SO24

Rhydspence Inn ★ ★ 🐾
HR3 6EU ☎ 01497 831262 📠 01497 831751
Dir: N side of A438 1m W of Whitney-on-Wye

Converted 14th-century manor house on the English side of the Welsh Borders, with a spacious dining room overlooking the Wye Valley. For many years it was a meeting place for drovers on the Black Ox Trail, taking livestock as far as London. Imaginative menus ranging from panache of Cornish fish, and fillet of venison with a brandy sauce to bar bites like chicken liver pâté, and scallop mornay.
OPEN: 11-2.30 7-11 (closed 2wks Jan) Closed: 2 wks in Jan
BAR MEALS: Lunch served: all week Dinner served: all week 11-2 7-9.30 Av main course £6.50 **RESTAURANT:** Lunch served: all week Dinner served: all week 11-2 7-9.30 Av 3 course à la carte £22.50
BREWERY/COMPANY: Free House
PRINCIPAL BEERS: Robinsons Best, Interbrew Bass.
FACILITIES: Children welcome Garden: Beer Garden:, Food served outside **NOTES:** Parking 30 **ROOMS:** 7 bedrooms 7 en suite from s£32.50 d£65

continued

OPEN: 11–11 (Sun 12–10.30)
BAR MEALS: L served all week.
D served all week. 12–2 7–9.30
Av main course £6.95
RESTAURANT: L served Tue-Sun.
D served Tue-Sat. 12–2 7–9 Av cost
3 course £25
BREWERY/COMPANY: FREE
HOUSE
PRINCIPAL BEERS: Hook Norton
Best, Fuller's London Pride,
Interbrew Flowers IPA, Wye Valley
Butty Bach
FACILITIES: Children welcome.
Garden: food served outside
NOTES: Parking 14
ROOMS: 4 en suite Double room
from £69 Single room from £45

The Salutation Inn

One of the area's most popular watering holes, where good food is part of the enduring appeal, and the historic building in an idyllic setting is the icing on the cake. The Salutation Inn can be found in one of the prettiest villages in the heart of the Herefordshire countryside.

◆◆◆◆ ♀
Market Pitch Weobley HR4 8SJ
☎ 01544 318443 📠 01544 318216
e-mail: info@salutationinn.com
Dir: In the village centre facing Broad st.

The 500-year-old black and white timber-framed building has been tastefully converted from an old ale house into today's inn and restaurant. With food at the forefront of the operation, it is not surprising that there are two separate areas for dining. Less formal meals are served in the traditional lounge bar, which is full of charm and character. Here the favourite dishes are steak and stout pie, supreme of pheasant, and venison sausages, all washed down with a selection of quality real ales or acceptable wines by the glass. The stylish restaurant, known as the Oak Room, is a

comfortable place to dine with its large open fireplace and partly exposed stone walls. In here, guests can enjoy modern English dishes cooked by a talented young chef using only the finest local ingredients to guarantee freshness and quality. The á la carte menu offers, perhaps, medallions of beef fillet, cannon of lamb, and wild mushroom risotto, and there is a decent selection of wines from the cellar to accompany a meal. The inn also offers delightful bedrooms for guests wanting to enjoy the Herefordshire countryside and its many activities.

England

WINFORTON   Map 03 SO24

Pick of the Pubs

The Sun Inn 🛏️
HR3 6EA ☎ 01544 327677 📠 01544 327677
Set in the heart of a typical black and white Herefordshire village, the Sun's long-standing success lies with its dedicated licensees, Brian and Wendy Hibbard. Whilst Brian takes care of guests at the bar, Wendy and her brigade are busy preparing the best local ingredients in an upbeat mix of modern and traditional guises. They'll reward you with starters like woodpigeon, bacon and mushroom salad, or Camembert filo parcels with elderflower and cranberry sauce. Main courses include tuna fishcakes with tomato, basil and chilli; venison in sloe gin sauce; or a wild mushroom and spinach strudel. Summer berries sorbet, or tipsy bread and butter pudding with hot fruit compote, are typical deserts. The delightful en suite bedrooms are cosy and comfortable, and make a good touring base. In summer relax in the orchard, or let the proprietors put you in touch with more adventurous activities like canoeing, hang-gliding or pony trekking.
OPEN: 11.30–3 6.15–11 (closed Tue) **BAR MEALS:** Lunch served: Wed-Mon Dinner served: Wed-Mon 12–2 6.45–9.30 Av main course £8 **RESTAURANT:** Lunch served: Wed-Mon Dinner served: Wed-Mon 12–2 6.45–9.30 Av 3 course à la carte £17 **BREWERY/COMPANY:** Free House
PRINCIPAL BEERS: Jennings, Hook Norton, Woods.
FACILITIES: Children welcome Garden: Beer garden, patio, food served outdoors Dogs allowed (guide dogs only)
NOTES: Parking 40 **ROOMS:** 3 bedrooms 3 en suite from s£32 d£52 No credit cards

WOOLHOPE   Map 03 SO63

The Butchers Arms 🛏️
HR1 4RF ☎ 01432 860281
e-mail: mark-vallely@lineone.net
Dir: Off B4224 between Hereford & Ross-on-Wye
Set in glorious walking country close to the Marcle Ridge, this 14th-century pub welcomes you with low beams, comfortable old settles, and roaring log fires. Well-kept ales complement substantial dishes like rack of lamb with wild berry sauce, mushroom biryani or Woolhope pie (rabbit in local cider). There's plenty of seafood, too; baked trout or ocean pie, as well as cod, plaice, scampi or salmon.
OPEN: 11.30–2.30 6.30–11 **BAR MEALS:** Lunch served: all week Dinner served: all week 12–2 6.30–9.30 Av main course £7 **RESTAURANT:** Lunch served: Sat-Sun Dinner served: Sat-Sun 12–2.30 6.30–9.30 Av 3 course à la carte £15
BREWERY/COMPANY: Free House **PRINCIPAL BEERS:** Hook Norton Best & Old Hooky. Wye Valley Bitter, Shepherd Neame Spitfire.
FACILITIES: Children welcome Garden: Patio, Food served outdoors **NOTES:** Parking 50 **ROOMS:** 2 bedrooms 2 en suite from s£30 d£39

The Crown Inn 🛏️ 🍷
HR1 4QP ☎ 01432 860468 📠 01432 860633
Dir: from Hereford take B4224 to Mordiford, L immediately after Moon Inn. Crown Inn is in village centre
A mainly 18th-century stone and rendered pub in the centre of a tiny village, part of a beautiful conservation area. A stone mounting block outside is dated 1520, and parts of the building go back 500 years. The extensive menu offers herb

and mushroom stuffed tomatoes, and grilled sardines with garlic to start, perhaps, with lamb and cranberry casserole, spaghetti Bolognaise, and sweet and sour chicken. Good vegetarian choice, and excellent Wye Valley ales on tap.
OPEN: 12–2.30 6.30–11 Closed: 25 Dec **BAR MEALS:** Lunch served: all week Dinner served: all week 12–2 6.30/7–10 Av main course £7.20 **RESTAURANT:** Lunch served: all week Dinner served: all week 12–2 6.30/7–10 Av 3 course à la carte £15
BREWERY/COMPANY: Free House **PRINCIPAL BEERS:** Smiles Best, Wye Valley Best plus guest beers. **FACILITIES:** Children welcome Garden: Food served outside **NOTES:** Parking 30

HERTFORDSHIRE

ALDBURY   Map 06 SP91

The Greyhound Inn 🛏️
19 Stocks Rd HP23 5RT ☎ 01442 851228 📠 01442 851495
The Chiltern Hills begin at this peaceful village pub overlooking a duck pond and old stocks, making it popular with walkers. In winter visitors gravitate towards the blazing inglenook fireplace to enjoy a bar snack like steak and Tanglefoot pie or a filled baked potato, while in the evening the carte lists dishes such as halibut with prawns and cream sauce, rack of lamb, and duck breast.
OPEN: 11–11 Closed: 25 Dec **BAR MEALS:** Lunch served: all week 12–2.30 Dinner served: Mon-Sat 7–10 Av main course £10 **RESTAURANT:** Lunch served: all week 12–2.30 Dinner served: Mon-Sat 7–10 Av 3 course à la carte £18
BREWERY/COMPANY: Hall & Woodhouse
PRINCIPAL BEERS: Badger Best, Tanglefoot, Champion, IPA.
FACILITIES: Children welcome Garden: Courtyard, Food served outside Dogs allowed (water) **NOTES:** Parking 9
ROOMS: 10 bedrooms 10 en suite from s£45 d£60

The Valiant Trooper 🛏️ 🍷
Trooper Rd HP23 5RW ☎ 01442 851203 📠 01442 851071
Dir: A41 Tring jct, follow signs for railway station, go past for about 1/2m, once at village green turn R then 200yds on L
Family-run free house in a pretty village surrounded by the Chiltern Hills, where hikers, cyclists and dogs are all made welcome. Local and guest beers feature, and interesting daily specials from the blackboard are hot and spicy chicken stir fry, beef fillet Stroganoff, steak, kidney and ale pie, and shark and tuna Breton. The Duke of Wellington is rumoured to have held a tactical conference at the pub - hence the name.
OPEN: 11–11 (Sun 12–10.30) **BAR MEALS:** Lunch served: all week 12–2.30 Dinner served: Tue-Sat 6.30–9.15 Av main course £9 **RESTAURANT:** Lunch served: Tue-Sun Dinner served: Tue-Sun 12–2 6.30–9.15 Av 3 course à la carte £16 **BREWERY/COMPANY:** Free House **PRINCIPAL BEERS:** Fuller's London Pride, Scottish Courage John Smith's, Marston's Pedigree, Greene King Ruddles Best.
FACILITIES: Children welcome Garden: Beer garden, food served outdoors Dogs allowed **NOTES:** Parking 36

ARDELEY   Map 06 TL32

The Jolly Waggoner 🛏️
SG2 7AH ☎ 01438 861350
Dating back 500 years, this pink-washed village pub is characterised by original beams and antique furniture. In winter there are roaring log fires and in summer a beautiful garden to enjoy. Favourite dishes range through omelette Arnold Bennett, filled with smoked haddock and served with a light béchamel sauce, home-made burgers topped with

continued

continued

cheddar and bacon, local sausages, and fillet of sea bass with mash and fresh asparagus.
OPEN: 12–2.30 6.30–11 (open BH Mon, closed Tue after BH)
BAR MEALS: Lunch served: Tue–Sun 12–2 Dinner served: Tue–Sat 6.30–9.00 Av main course £11 **RESTAURANT:** Dinner served: Tue–Sat 12.30–2 6.30–9 Av 3 course à la carte £32.50
BREWERY/COMPANY: Greene King **PRINCIPAL BEERS:** Greene King IPA & Abbot Ale. **FACILITIES:** Children welcome Garden: Beer garden, food served outdoors **NOTES:** Parking 15

ASHWELL   Map 06 TL23

Bushel & Strike ♀
Mill St SG7 5LY ☎ 01462 742394 📄 01462 742300
Popular inn located in a pretty village with ancient springs and lovely local walks. The main bar has wooden floors, leather chesterfields and open fires in winter, while the conservatory restaurant is a conversion of the old school hall. Food based on fresh, locally sourced ingredients is served in both areas, with options such as cracker of pork fillet, knuckle of lamb, and chicken balti.
OPEN: 11.30–3 6–11 (all day Sun) **BAR MEALS:** Lunch served: all week Dinner served: all week 12–2.30 7–9.30 Av main course £8
RESTAURANT: Lunch served: all week Dinner served: all week 12–2.30 7–9.30 Av 3 course à la carte £18
BREWERY/COMPANY: Charles Wells
PRINCIPAL BEERS: Greene King Old Speckled Hen, Wells Bombadier/Eagle, Adnams Broadside. **FACILITIES:** Children welcome Garden: beer garden, outdoor eating, Dogs allowed
NOTES: Parking 40

The Three Tuns 🛏
High St SG7 5NL ☎ 01462 742107 📄 01462 743662
e-mail: claire@tuns.co.uk
This 19th-century inn has a lot of original features, and is next to an ancient natural spring. Parts of the building date back to the 18th century. The village itself has the Ashwell Springs, and its own museum. Old world atmosphere, and locally renowned home-made food. Typical menu includes grilled lamb chops, dressed crab, steak and kidney pie, and chicken supreme stuffed with pâté.
OPEN: 11–11 Closed: 25 Dec, Bank holiday **BAR MEALS:** Lunch served: all week Dinner served: all week 12–2.30 6.30–9.30 Av main course £6.95 **RESTAURANT:** Lunch served: all week Dinner served: all week 12–2.30 6.30–9.30 Av 3 course à la carte £15
BREWERY/COMPANY: Greene King **PRINCIPAL BEERS:** IPA Ruddles, Abbot, Carling, Stella. **FACILITIES:** Children welcome Garden: Food served outside, lovely garden Dogs allowed
ROOMS: s£39 d£49

AYOT ST LAWRENCE   Map 06 TL11

Pick of the Pubs

The Brocket Arms ♦♦♦ 🛏 ♀
AL6 9BT ☎ 01438 820250 📄 01438 820068
This delightful 14th-century inn is located in the village where George Bernard Shaw lived for 40 years until his death in 1950. The inn was originally the monastic quarters for the Norman church until the Reformation. Henry VIII supposedly wooed his sixth wife, Catherine Parr, in the nearby manor house. There are many charming features inside the pub, including oak-beamed, low-ceilinged bars and restaurant and outside the extensive walled garden is a glorious sun-trap in summer.

The accommodation is in idiosyncratic bedrooms varying in shape and size. Some of the bedrooms are furnished with four-poster beds, which are especially popular. Traditional English game and home-cooked dishes characterise the menu, with game pie, marinated venison and salmon cutlet among them. Other options include vegetarian Stroganoff, grilled sirloin steak, sea bass and pheasant Rossini.

OPEN: 11–11 **BAR MEALS:** 12–2.30 7.30–10
RESTAURANT: 12–2.30 7.30–10 **BREWERY/COMPANY:** Free House **PRINCIPAL BEERS:** Greene King Abbot Ale & IPA, Adnams Broadside, Fullers London Pride, Youngs IPA.
FACILITIES: Children welcome Garden: Dogs allowed (garden only) **NOTES:** Parking 7 **ROOMS:** 7 bedrooms 3 en suite from s£70 d£80

BARLEY   Map 07 TL43

The Fox & Hounds
High St SG8 8HU ☎ 01763 848459 📄 01763 849274
Dir: A505 onto B1368 at Flint Cross, pub 4m
Enjoying a pretty thatched village setting, this former 17th-century hunting lodge is notable for its pub sign which extends across the lane. Real fires and a warm welcome. The garden has a pétanque court, and boules are available for those interested in this fine Gallic pastime. Typical menu includes Thai vegetable schnitzel, steak and Guinness pie, lamb and mint pudding, and harvest vegetable and leek crumble. Watch the daily changing blackboard menus for today's specials.
OPEN: 12–3 6–11 **BAR MEALS:** Lunch served: all week Dinner served: all week 12–2 6–9.30 **RESTAURANT:** 12–2 6–9.30
BREWERY/COMPANY: Free House **PRINCIPAL BEERS:** Adnams Broadside, Greene King Old Speckled Hen, IPA, Marston's Pedigree.
FACILITIES: Children welcome Garden: Food served outside Dogs allowed **NOTES:** Parking 25

BERKHAMSTED   Map 06 SP90

The Boat ♀
Gravel Path HP4 2EF ☎ 01422 877152
Very modern canalside pub that has a lot of character despite its relative youth. A summer terrace overlooks the canal.

BUNTINGFORD   Map 06 TL32

The Sword in Hand 🛏 ♀
Westmill SG9 9LQ ☎ 01763 271356
Dir: Off A10 1.5m S of Buntingford
Early 15th-century inn, once the home of the Scottish noble family, Gregs. The pub's name taken from a motif within their

continued

continued

BUNTINGFORD continued

family crest. The dining room looks out over open coutryside, and offers a regularly changing menu that may include the likes of sausage and mash with red onion gravy, escalope of veal topped with Mozzarella, pan-fried swordfish with a caper salsa and basil dressing, and salmon steak with a light curry and prawn sauce.
OPEN: 12-3 5.30-11 **BAR MEALS:** Lunch served: Tues-Sun Dinner served: Tues-Sun 12-2.30 6.30-9.30 Av main course £8
RESTAURANT: Lunch served: Tues-Sun Dinner served: Tues-Sun 12-2.30 6.30-9.30 Av 3 course à la carte £18
BREWERY/COMPANY: Free House **PRINCIPAL BEERS:** Greene King IPA, Abbot Ale & Old Speckled Hen, Young's Bitter,.
FACILITIES: Children welcome Garden: Large, beautiful view, food served outside Dogs allowed **NOTES:** Parking 25

COTTERED
Map 06 TL32

The Bull at Cottered
Cottered ☎ 01763 281243
Attractively situated in a pretty village, this traditional local boasts low-beamed ceilings, an open log fire and pub games like cribbage and dominoes. A good-sized garden, well kept ales and interesting, good quality meals makes this a pub worth visiting. Popular dishes include steak, Guinnes and Stilton pie, prime Scottish sirloin, chicken with cheese, mushroom and garlic sauce, and a variety of burgers, jacket potatoes, sandwiches, soups, and salads.
OPEN: 12-2.30 6.30-11 **BAR MEALS:** Lunch served: all week Dinner served: Wed-Mon 12-2 6.30-9 Av main course £9
RESTAURANT: Lunch served: all week Dinner served: Wed-Mon 12-2 6.30-9 Av 3 course à la carte £20 Av 3 course fixed price £21.50
BREWERY/COMPANY: Greene King **PRINCIPAL BEERS:** Greene king IPA & Abbot Ale. **FACILITIES:** Children welcome Garden: Food served outside **NOTES:** Parking 30

FLAUNDEN
Map 06 TL00

The Bricklayers Arms
Hogpits Bottom HP3 0PH ☎ 01442 833322
e-mail: brickies-flaunden@talk21.com
Dir: M1 J8 through H Hempstead to Bovington then follow Flaunden sign. M25 J18 through Chorleywood to Chenies/Latimer then Flaunden
A traditional country pub clad with Virginia creeper, with a low-beamed bar and wooden wall seats within and dazzling floral baskets without. Popular with walkers and locals and those who enjoy relaxing in the delightfully old-fashioned garden in the summer months. Once inside, the inn offers a friendly, informal ambience enhanced by good quality, freshly prepared dishes such as grilled lamb cutlets, seared halibut, stuffed chicken and spinach and Ricotta roll.
OPEN: 11.30-3 6-11 **BAR MEALS:** Lunch served: all week Dinner served: all week 12-2 7-9 **RESTAURANT:** Lunch served: all week Dinner served: all week 12-2 7-9 Av 3 course à la carte £20
BREWERY/COMPANY: Free House **PRINCIPAL BEERS:** Fuller's London Pride, Brakspear Bitter, Ringwood Old Thumper, Marston's Pedigree. **FACILITIES:** Garden: Food served outside Dogs allowed (water) **NOTES:** Parking 40

The Green Dragon
HP3 0PP ☎ 01442 832269
Dir: B4505 from Hemel Hempstead to Bovington then S to Flaunden
Walkers and cyclists visiting the Chilterns find this a welcome watering hole, as did some other, rather more unlikely guests. Both Hitler's ambassador Von Ribbentrop, and British spy Guy

Burgess, have visited this historic village inn. Food comes in large portions, and children are very welcome.

HARPENDEN
Map 06 TL11

Gibraltar Castle
70 Lower Luton Rd AL5 5AH ☎ 01582 460005
Bustling Fuller's pub located opposite a common in Batford. The comfortable carpeted bar is decorated with a collection of militaria. Traditional pub food is available including potato, leek and cheese bake, grilled Cajun chicken breast, steak and ale pie, club sandwiches and steak with all the trimmings. Live Irish music is popular on Tuesdays.
OPEN: 11-3 5-11 (Sun 12-4, 6-10.30) **BAR MEALS:** Lunch served: all week Dinner served: Mon-Sat 12-2.30 6-9 Av main course £8.95
RESTAURANT: Lunch served: all week Dinner served: Mon-Sat
BREWERY/COMPANY: Fullers **PRINCIPAL BEERS:** Fuller's London Pride, ESB, Chiswick Bitter, Honey Dew & Red Fox.
FACILITIES: Children welcome Patio, food served outdoors Dogs allowed (water) **NOTES:** Parking 25

The Old Bell NEW
177 Luton Rd AL5 3BN ☎ 01582 712484 📠 01582 715015
A historic 18th-century pub which began selling beer to local straw-plaiters and farm workers, and later the railway navvies who built a branch line from Luton to Harpenden. It still serves full-bodied ales along with freshly-prepared food - fish is the house speciality. Expect Mediterranean swordfish, grilled plaice stuffed with prawn mousse, paella, and perhaps roast shoulder of lamb, beef and Theakston pie, and lemon-basted chicken.
OPEN: 11-11 (Sun 12-10.30) **BAR MEALS:** Lunch served: all week Dinner served: all week 11-10 Av main course £6.95
RESTAURANT: Lunch served: all week Dinner served: all week 11-10
BREWERY/COMPANY: Chef & Brewer
PRINCIPAL BEERS: Scottish Courage Courage Best, Theakston OP, Greene King Old Speckled Hen. **FACILITIES:** Children welcome Garden: Food served outside **NOTES:** Parking 100

HEMEL HEMPSTEAD
Map 06 TL00

Pick of the Pubs

Alford Arms
Frithsden HP1 3DD ☎ 01442 864480 📠 01422 876893
A pretty place, surrounded by National Trust woodland, the Alford Arms is typically Victorian, full of traditional finishes - log fires, old furniture and pictures, quarry tiles and reclaimed wooden floors - though the feel is still light and modern. The atmosphere is very relaxed - this is very much a pub that just happens to do great food. The same menu is served throughout, and whether you're after a pint and a sandwich or a slap up feed, there is some serious eating to be done. Local, free-range and organic ingredients are used wherever possible, in dishes like bubble and squeak with smoked bacon, poached egg and hollandaise sauce, or calves' liver with dauphinoise potatoes and thyme gravy. A vegetarian option might be roast pumpkin, sage and toasted pine nut risotto. On warm days the sunny terrace is always packed.
OPEN: 11-11 (Sun 12-10.30) Closed: 25-26 Dec
BAR MEALS: Lunch served: all week Dinner served: all week 12-2.30 7-10 Av main course £11 **RESTAURANT:** Lunch served: all week Dinner served: all week 12-2.30 7-10 Av 3 course à la carte £20 **BREWERY/COMPANY:** Free House
PRINCIPAL BEERS: Marstons Pedigree, Wadworth 6X,

continued

continued

Flowers, Tetley. **FACILITIES:** Children welcome Garden: Food served outside, terrace area Dogs allowed (water provided)
NOTES: Parking 25

HEXTON
Map 06 TL13

The Raven 🛏 🍷
SG5 3JB ☎ 01582 881209 📠 01582 881610
e-mail: jack@ravenathexton-fg.co.uk

Named after Ravenborough Castle in the Chiltern Hills above attractive Hexton, this neat 1920s pub has a large garden with terrace and play area, comfortable bars, and an extensive menu highlighting traditional pub food. Expect scrumpy pork, Mediterranean pasta bake, Cajun chicken, Whitby Bay scampi, traditional roast beef, and plenty of steaks from the grill. Various salads, ploughman's lunches and daily specials.
OPEN: 11-3 6-11 (Sun 12-10.30) **BAR MEALS:** Lunch served: all week Dinner served: all week 12-2 6-10 Av main course £7.95
RESTAURANT: Lunch served: all week Dinner served: all week 12-2 6-10 Av 3 course à la carte £15 **PRINCIPAL BEERS:** Greene King Old Speckled Hen, Fullers London Pride. **FACILITIES:** Children welcome Garden: Food served outside. Patio & grass area Dogs allowed (in the garden only, water provided) **NOTES:** Parking 40

HINXWORTH
Map 06 TL24

Three Horseshoes 🛏
High St SG7 5HQ ☎ 01462 742280
Dir: E of A1 between Biggleswade and Baldock
Thatched 18th-century country pub with a dining extension into the garden. Parts of the building date back 500 years, and the walls are adorned with pictures and photos of the village's history. Samples from a typical menu include chicken of the wood, lamb cutlets with champ, rainbow trout with almonds, sea bass provençale, steak and Guinness pie, bacon and cheese pasta bake, and roasted Tuscan red peppers.
OPEN: 11.30-2.30 6-11 **BAR MEALS:** Lunch served: all week 12-2 Dinner served: Mon-Sat 7-9 Av main course £10
RESTAURANT: Lunch served: all week 12-2 Dinner served: Mon-Sat 7-9 Av 3 course à la carte £20 **BREWERY/COMPANY:** Greene King **PRINCIPAL BEERS:** Greene King IPA, Abbot Ale.
FACILITIES: Garden: Food served outside. Lawn area Dogs allowed (in the garden only) **NOTES:** Parking 16

HITCHIN
Map 06 TL12

The Greyhound ♦♦♦ 🛏 🍷
London Rd, St Ippolyts SG4 7NL ☎ 01462 440989
Friendly family-run inn surrounded by farmland yet conveniently located for the M1 and Luton Airport. People

who eat here drop in like drinkers in the old days, some dressed up and meeting friends, and others straight from doing the garden because they don't want to cook. The food is good, fresh and unpretentious, offering the likes of rabbit pie, grilled haddock fillet, and venison in red wine sauce.
OPEN: 11.30-2.30 5-11 Closed: Dec 25-26 **BAR MEALS:** Lunch served: all week Dinner served: all week 12-2 7-10 Av main course £7
RESTAURANT: Lunch served: all week 12-2 Dinner served: all week 7-10 Av 3 course à la carte £13.50 **BREWERY/COMPANY:** Free House **PRINCIPAL BEERS:** Adnams, Greene King IPA.
FACILITIES: Garden: Patio, outdoor eating **NOTES:** Parking 25
ROOMS: 4 bedrooms 4 en suite

The Red Lion 🛏
The Green SG4 7UD ☎ 01462 459585 📠 01462 442284
e-mail: janebaerlein@hotmail.com
The first village-owned pub in Britain was purchased in 1982 from Whitbreads. The driving force behind the venture was to ensure a continuing social focal point for the village when the pub was under threat of closure. The venture has been successful and the pub won awards for the quality of its beer and offers a regularly changing menu board with options such as pheasant in red wine, salmon kedgeree, home-made lasagne, quiche and fillet of trout.
OPEN: 12-2.30 5.30-11 **BAR MEALS:** Lunch served: all week 12-2 Dinner served: Wed-Sat, Mon 7-9 Av main course £5.95
BREWERY/COMPANY: Free House **PRINCIPAL BEERS:** Greene King IPA & Changing real ales. **FACILITIES:** Children welcome Garden: Food served outside, seating Dogs allowed (water)
NOTES: Parking 60 No credit cards

KIMPTON
Map 06 TL11

The White Horse 🍷 NEW
22 High St SG4 8RJ ☎ 01438 832307 📠 01438 833842
e-mail: thewhitehorsepub@aol.com
In a delightful village surrounded by picturesque countryside, this popular low-roofed pub dates from the mid-1500s and there is a priest hole behind the bar. First licensed as an alehouse in the 1820s, the building has been used as a local bank and a laundry. Cosy bar and welcoming ambience inside, with background music likely to be jazz or swing. Good, varied menu with the likes of Highland steak, pork and leek sausage with mustard mash, and whole plaice with prawn and mushroom butter.
OPEN: 12-2.30 6-11 **BAR MEALS:** Lunch served: Tues-Sun 12-2
RESTAURANT: Lunch served: all week 12-2 Dinner served: all week 7-9 Av 3 course à la carte £16.50 **PRINCIPAL BEERS:** Scottish Courage Courage Directors, Interbrew Bass,. **FACILITIES:** Garden: Sun deck with seating **NOTES:** Parking 10

KNEBWORTH
Map 06 TL22

The Lytton Arms 🍷
Park Ln SG3 6QB ☎ 01438 812312 📠 01438 815289
e-mail: thelyttonarms@btinternet.com
Dir: From A1(M)take A602.At Knebworth turn R at rail station.Follow signs 'Codicote'. Pub 1.5m on R
Popular with ramblers, horse-riders and cyclists in picturesque north Hertfordshire countryside, this 1877 Lutyens-designed inn claims to have served over 4,000 real ales in 14 years. Without pool tables, video games or juke box, the pub offers a relaxing atmosphere in which to enjoy carefully prepared pub food. Speciality sausages with English ale chutney, Thai

continued

continued

England

KNEBWORTH continued

chicken and banana curry, and treacle sponge with custard create a blend of traditional and exotic choices.
OPEN: 11-3 5-11 (Sun 12-10.30, Fri-Sat open all day)
BAR MEALS: Lunch served: Mon-Sun 12-2 Dinner served: Mon-Sat 6.30-9.30 Av main course £6.95 **RESTAURANT:** Lunch served: Mon-Sun 12-2 Dinner served: Mon-Sat 6.30-9.30
BREWERY/COMPANY: Free House **PRINCIPAL BEERS:** Fuller's London Pride, Adnams Best Bitter & Broadside, Interbrew Bass.
FACILITIES: Children welcome Garden: Food served outside Dogs allowed (water) **NOTES:** Parking 40

LITTLE HADHAM
Map 07 TL42

The Nags Head 🐑 🍷
The Ford SG11 2AX ☎ 01279 771555 📠 01279 771555
Dir: *M11 J8 take A120 towards Puckeridge & A10. At lights in Little Hadnam turn L. Pub 0.75m on R*
16th-century, former coaching inn that has in its time been a brewery, a bakery and an arsenal for the Home Guard during WWII. It has an oak-beamed bar and a restaurant area with open brickwork and an old bakery oven (now seating two people). Popular and wide-ranging menu includes vegetarian moussaka, Swiss lamb joint, spaghetti bolognese, sirloin steak chasseur, fresh rainbow trout Grenobloise, Louisiana roast with mango and lime sauce, and deep fried skate wing in Abbot batter.
OPEN: 11-2.30 6-11 (Sun 12-3.30 7-10.30) **BAR MEALS:** Lunch served: all week Dinner served: all week 12-2 6-9.00 Av main course £7.95 **RESTAURANT:** Lunch served: all week Dinner served: all week 12-2 6-9.00 Av 3 course à la carte £14.50
BREWERY/COMPANY: Greene King **PRINCIPAL BEERS:** Greene King Abbot Ale, IPA, Old Speckled Hen, Ruddles County.
FACILITIES: Children welcome Garden: beer garden, food served outside Dogs allowed Garden: Only, Water

---

MUCH HADHAM
Map 07 TL41

Jolly Waggoners 🐑
Widford Rd SG10 6EZ ☎ 01279 842102
Dir: *On B1004 between Bishops Stortford & Ware*
Daily fresh fish features on the evening menu at this Victorian pub built from two older cottages. A large open fire and beamed interior lend character to the non-smoking bar, and there are no noisy games machines to disturb the convivial atmosphere. From the specials board expect several choices of fish, plus roast meats and grills, and the likes of chicken Kiev, curries, lamb cutlets and vegetarian dishes, all home made.
OPEN: 12-2.30 6.30-11 (Sun 12-3, 7-10.30) **BAR MEALS:** Lunch served: all week Dinner served: all week 12-2 6.30-9 Av main course £5.95 **RESTAURANT:** Lunch served: all week Dinner served: all week 12-2.30 6.30-9.30 Av 3 course à la carte £12 Av 2 course fixed price £5.95 **BREWERY/COMPANY:** McMullens
PRINCIPAL BEERS: McMullen Original AK & Country Best Bitter, Scottish Courage Courage Directors. **FACILITIES:** Children welcome Garden: Food served outdoors Dogs allowed (water)
NOTES: Parking 40

POTTERS CROUCH
Map 06 TL10

The Hollybush
AL2 3NN ☎ 01727 851792 📠 01727 851792
Dir: *Ragged Ln off A405 or Bedmond Ln off A4147*
Picturesque, attractively furnished country pub with quaint, white-painted exterior and large, enclosed garden. Close to St

Albans and there are good local walks. An antique dresser, a large fireplace and various prints and paintings help give the inn a delightfully welcoming atmosphere. Food is simple and unfussy, with a range of jacket potatoes, burgers, platters and sandwiches. Smoked mackerel fillet, Cornish pasty and home-made chilli con carne also feature.
OPEN: 11.30-2.30 6-11 (Sun 12-3.30, 7-10.30)
BAR MEALS: Lunch served: Mon-Sun 12-2
BREWERY/COMPANY: Fullers **PRINCIPAL BEERS:** Fuller's Chiswick Bitter, London Pride, ESB. **FACILITIES:** Garden: Food served outside **NOTES:** Parking 50

ROYSTON
Map 06 TL34

The Green Man
Lower St, Thriplow SG8 7RJ ☎ 01763 208855 📠 01763 208431
e-mail: greenmanthriplow@ntlworld.com
Dir: *1M W of junction 10 on M11*

A step north east of Royston and handy for the M11 (J10), this rejuvenated early 19th-century pub stands at the heart of a quaint rural village. Fixed-price menus offer twice-baked goats' cheese soufflé, roasted stuffed chicken ballotine and caramelised bananas and pineapple in rum syrup. Both menus and ales change frequently: wines are more limited. Picnic tables out in the large landscaped garden.
OPEN: 12-2.30 6-11 **BAR MEALS:** Lunch served: Mon-Sun Dinner served: Wed-Mon 12-2.30 7-9.30 Av main course £8
RESTAURANT: Lunch served: Mon-Sun Dinner served: Mon-Sun 12-2.30 7-9.30 Av 3 course à la carte £22
BREWERY/COMPANY: Free House
PRINCIPAL BEERS: Eccleshall Slaters Original, Hop Back Summer Lightning, Batemans XXXB. **FACILITIES:** Children welcome Garden: patio Dogs allowed (guide dogs only) **NOTES:** Parking 12

ST ALBANS
Map 06 TL10

Rose & Crown 🍷
10 St Michael St AL3 4SG ☎ 01727 851903 📠 01727 766450
e-mail: dekker.rosecrown@faxvia.net
Traditional 16th-century pub situated in a beautiful part of St Michael's 'village', opposite the entrance to Verulamium Park and Roman Museum. Classic beamed main bar with huge inglenook, and lovely flower-decked summer patio. Noted for excellent American deli-style 'royalty' sandwiches served with potato salad, kettle crisps and pickled cucumber. Try the 'Porky Pig' – bacon, wholegrain mustard, ham, American cheese, tomato and lettuce!
OPEN: 11.30-3 5.30-11 **BAR MEALS:** Lunch served: Mon-Sat 12-2 Av main course £5 **BREWERY/COMPANY:** Inn Partnership
PRINCIPAL BEERS: Adnams Bitter, Carlsberg-Tetley Tetley Bitter, Scottish Courage Courage Directors + Guest beers.
FACILITIES: Children welcome Garden: Patio, food served outside Dogs allowed (water) **NOTES:** Parking 6

continued

SARRATT — Map 04 TQ09

The Cock Inn ♀
Church End, Church Ln WD3 6HH
☎ 01923 282908 ▤ 01923 286224
Dir: Between M25 J18 & A404 opposite St Clement Danes School
Cream-painted 17th-century pub opposite the 12th century church and overlooking open countryside at the rear. The pub takes its name from the cockhorse that pulled carts up the hill from the nearby mill. Character interior includes a cosy snug with a vaulted ceiling and original bread oven. The restaurant is a converted barn with exposed beams and high-pitched roof. Good quality menu and daily specials feature the likes of lamb shank, steak and ale pie, seafood pasta, wild boar sausages, red snapper and roasted vegetable kebabs.
OPEN: 11–3 (all day wknds) 5.30–11 **BAR MEALS:** Lunch served: all week Dinner served: all week 12–2.30 6–9.30 Av main course £6
RESTAURANT: Lunch served: all week Dinner served: all week 12–2.30 6–9.30 Av 3 course à la carte £25
BREWERY/COMPANY: Hall & Woodhouse
PRINCIPAL BEERS: Badger Tanglefoot, Dorset Best & IPA King and Barnes Sussex Bitter. **FACILITIES:** Children welcome Garden: beer garden, outdoor eating Dogs allowed **NOTES:** Parking 40

STOTFOLD — Map 06 TL23

The Fox & Duck ♀
149 Arlesey Raod SG5 4HE ☎ 01462 732434 ▤ 01462 835962
e-mail: foxandduck@cragg-inns.co.uk
Set on a large site, this picturesque family pub has a big garden, a children's playground, a caravan site, weekly football matches, and regular barbecues. Children's birthday parties catered for. A sample menu selection includes 8oz fillet steak with Stilton and Madeira, sizzling black bean chicken, medallions of pork with honey and ginger, and a wide range of home-made soups and pâtés.
OPEN: 12–3 6–11 **BAR MEALS:** Lunch served: all week Dinner served: all week 12–2 6–9 **RESTAURANT:** Lunch served: all week Dinner served: all week 12–2 6–9 Av 3 course à la carte £21
BREWERY/COMPANY: Greene King **PRINCIPAL BEERS:** Greene King Old Speckled Hen & IPA. **FACILITIES:** Children welcome Garden: Food served outdoors **NOTES:** Parking 40

IRISH ELIXIR
'Guinness is Good For You'

was the slogan of one of the most successful campaigns in advertising history. Launched in 1928, with pictures and words by Rex Whistler and Dorothy L Sayers among others, it made a brew of black from Ireland into a household name. The firm originated with Arthur Guinness, who started brewing in Dublin in 1759. Besides fathering some 21 children, he sired Ireland's most famous commercial product and one of the great dynasties of the annals of brewing.

TEWIN — Map 06 TL21

The Plume of Feathers 🐦
Upper Green Rd AL6 0LX ☎ 01438 717265
Dir: E from A1 J6 toward WGC, follow B1000 toward Hertford, Tewin signed on L

Built in 1596, this historic inn, a former hunting lodge of Elizabeth I and later the haunt of highwaymen, now boasts several ghosts including a 'lady in grey'. Interesting food.

WALKERN — Map 06 TL22

The White Lion ♀
31 The High St SG2 7PA ☎ 01438 861251 ▤ 01438 861160
Dir: B1037 from Stevenage
Late 16th-century timber-framed building, originally a coaching inn on the Nottingham to London route.

WELLPOND GREEN — Map 07 TL42

Nag's Head ♦♦♦♦ 🐦 NEW
SG11 1NL
Situated in a sleepy hamlet in pretty rolling countryside, the Nag's Head offers Ruddles County ales and comfortable overnight accommodation.

WESTON — Map 06 TL23

The Rising Sun 🐦
21 Halls Green SG4 7DR ☎ 01462 790487
e-mail: mike@therisingsun-hallsgreen.co.uk
Dir: A1(M)J9 take A6141(dual carriageway)towards Baldock(take outside lane) & turn R towards Graveley. 100yds take 1st L
Set in picturesque Hertfordshire countryside, the Rising Sun welcomes those with children in tow, providing an appropriate menu, play equipment, and tuck shop in summer. For adults, the regularly changing menu offers starters such as Stilton mushrooms and salmon fishcakes with dill sauce. Main courses include chargrilled steaks, lamb tagine, chicken balti, and wild boar, venison and cranberry en croûte. For fish lovers, there's roast cod with a herb crust, or pan-fried skate in wine.
OPEN: 11–2.30 6–11 **BAR MEALS:** Lunch served: all week Dinner served: all week 12–2 6–9 Av main course £6.95
RESTAURANT: Lunch served: all week Dinner served: all week 12–2 6–9 Av 3 course à la carte £14 **BREWERY/COMPANY:** McMullens
PRINCIPAL BEERS: McMullen Original AK Ale, Gladstone,Interbrew Bass,Scottish Courage Courage Directors. **FACILITIES:** Garden: Food served outside Dogs allowed **NOTES:** Parking 40

KENT

APPLEDORE
Map 05 TQ92

The Red Lion
Snargate TN29 9UQ ☎ 01797 344648
Few pubs invite you to picnic in their garden but then, they don't serve food at this one. Doris Jemison's family has run this unspoilt free house since 1911, and little has changed here in fifty years. Well kept local ales and Double Vision cider are served over the original marble counter and, for entertainment, there's the piano, and traditional games like shove ha'penny or toad-in-the-hole.
OPEN: 12–3 7–11 Sun 12–3, 7–10.30) **BREWERY/COMPANY:** Free House **PRINCIPAL BEERS:** Goachers Fine Light, Goachers Mild, Hop Daemon Golden Braid, Goachers Gold Star.
FACILITIES: Children welcome Garden: Large garden with chickens
NOTES: Parking 15 No credit cards

BENENDEN
Map 05 TQ83

The Bull at Benenden ♀
The Street TN17 4DE ☎ 01580 240054
e-mail: thebull@thebullatbenenden.co.uk
Dir: Benenden is on the B2086 between Cranbrook and Tenterden
Adjoining the village green, this listed family-run pub is thought to date back to 1608. The subject of recent renovation work, it lies in a picturesque Kentish village and is also the headquarters of the local cricket club. Varied home-cooked fare might include lamb chops with redcurrant and mint sauce, fish brochette, whiskey steak, roast beef and Yorkshire pudding, fresh poached salmon in prawn and cucumber sauce, or vegetable chilli.
OPEN: 11.30–3 6–11 **BAR MEALS:** Lunch served: all week Dinner served: all week 12–2.30 7–9.30 Av main course £6.95
RESTAURANT: Lunch served: all week Dinner served: all week 12–2.30 7–9.30 Av 3 course à la carte £18
BREWERY/COMPANY: Free House **FACILITIES:** Garden: Food served outside **NOTES:** Parking 12 **ROOMS:** 3 bedrooms 3 en suite from s£45 d£65

See Pub Walk on page 259

BIDDENDEN
Map 05 TQ83

Pick of the Pubs

The Three Chimneys
Biddenden Rd TN27 8LW ☎ 01580 291472
Dir: On A262 between Biddenden and Sissinghurst
Unspoilt 15th-century country pub in the Kentish Weald, complete original, small room layout with old settles, low beams, wood-panelled walls, flagstone floors and warming fires. Evening candlelight enhances the atmosphere. Everything is cooked to order here, the daily-changing menu may feature dishes such as chargrilled fish, rack of lamb, roast loin of venison, and tomato, red pepper and goats' cheese tartlet. Meat is supplied by a local farmer and the menu aims to reflect the changing seasons. A classic country pub.
OPEN: 11.30–3 6–11 Closed: 25 Dec **BAR MEALS:** Lunch served: all week Dinner served: all week 12–2 6–10 Av main course £8 **RESTAURANT:** Lunch served: all week Dinner served: all week 12–2 6–10 Av 3 course à la carte £25
BREWERY/COMPANY: Free House
PRINCIPAL BEERS: Shepherd Neame, Adnams.
FACILITIES: Garden: Dogs allowed **NOTES:** Parking 70

BOYDEN GATE
Map 05 TR26

Pick of the Pubs

The Gate Inn ♀
Boyden Gate CT3 4EB ☎ 01227 860498
Dir: From Canterbury on A28 turn L at Upstreet
Just off the A28 and surrounded by marshland and pasture, as rustic a rural retreat – popular with walkers and cyclists – as you'll find anywhere. The garden is a picture in summer, bounded by a stream and resident ducks on the pond. Quarry-tiled floors and pine furnishings feature in the family-friendly interconnecting bars, while no-nonsense food includes Gate burgers, torpedo sandwiches and spicy home-made hot pots.
OPEN: 11–2.30 6–11 (Sun 12–4, 7–10.30) **BAR MEALS:** Lunch served: all week Dinner served: all week 12–2 6–9 Av main course £4 **BREWERY/COMPANY:** Shepherd Neame
PRINCIPAL BEERS: Shepherd Neame Master Brew, Spitfire & Bishops Finger. **FACILITIES:** Children welcome Garden: Beer garden, food served outdoors Dogs allowed (water & dog biscuits) **NOTES:** Parking 14 No credit cards

BRABOURNE
Map 05 TR14

The Five Bells ♀
The Street TN25 5LP ☎ 01303 813334 📠 01303 814667
e-mail: five.bells@lineone.net
Dir: 5m E of Ashford
Named after the village church which boasted five bells, this 17th-century inn nestles at the foot of the North Downs. Its beamed interior with inglenook fireplace and traditional upholstery is a welcoming and hospitable place, and in summer the delightful garden is the ideal setting for a meal or a drink. Extensive menus include home-made specialities like spaghetti carbonara, steak and kidney pie, and butterfly chicken, plus various snacks, salads and a children's menu.
OPEN: 11.30–3 6.30–11 **BAR MEALS:** Lunch served: all week Dinner served: all week 12–2 7–10 Av main course £10
RESTAURANT: Lunch served: all week Dinner served: all week 12–2 7–12 Av 3 course à la carte £18 **BREWERY/COMPANY:** Free House
PRINCIPAL BEERS: Shepherd Neame Master Brew, Wells Bombardier, Interbrew Bass & Flowers IPA. **FACILITIES:** Children welcome Garden: Beer garden, food served outdoors Dogs allowed (water) **NOTES:** Parking 65

BROOKLAND
Map 05 TQ92

Woolpack Inn
TN29 9TJ ☎ 01797 344321
Partly built from old ship timbers and set in Kentish marshland, this 15th-century cottage inn was originally a beacon keeper's house, and has a large collection of waterjugs. One of the long Victorian tables has penny games carved into the top. Homemade wholesome pub food includes pork chops, mixed grill, cod and chips, vegetable lasagne, ploughmans, sandwiches, jacket potatoes, and salads.
OPEN: 11–3 6–11 **BAR MEALS:** Lunch served: all week Dinner served: all week 12–2 6–9 Av main course £4.95
BREWERY/COMPANY: Shepherd Neame
PRINCIPAL BEERS: Shepherd Neame Spitfire Premium Ale, Master Brew. **FACILITIES:** Children welcome Garden: Food served outdoors Dogs allowed (water) **NOTES:** Parking 30

PUB WALK

Benenden
The Bull at Benenden

A walk at the heart of rural Kent, exploring a fine mix of farmland and woodland on Benenden's doorstep.

Leave the pub and take Walkhurst Road opposite, passing a striking World War I memorial and passing Walkhurst Cottages on your right. The road dips down a hill and then bends sharply to the left. At this point cross a stile on your right marked WP 350. Pass some derelict farm buildings, then cross another stile, again marked WP 350. Walk through a field with a waste disposal unit seen to your left, cross another stile and follow the path down to a delightful stream. Over a small wooden bridge, go up and diagonally to the right to join a path at the top of Nine Acre Wood. The stream is visible to your right. Follow the path, pass two signs for WP 349 and ascend a slight incline. Take the righthand fork at the top and pass several ponds. The path now graduates to a hedged farm track. Look for delightful views in the gaps. Keep on the track, passing Mount Le Hoe, a farm oast house, and Mount Hall Farm on your right. Continue on the undulating farm lane to a T junction. Bear right and follow the road down and over Stepneyford Bridge. Pass Little Maplesden on your left and Green Lane Cottages on your right. Soon after reaching Green Lane Farmhouse, look for a waymarked path to the right. Climb the stile into the field and over the gate marked FP352. In this field keep to your left and cross the first stile on the left into a field fenced off to grow Christmas trees. Still keeping to the left look for a charming apple orchard on your right. Follow the path to a stile, again marked FP352. Climb over and walk through the field to the road. Turn right along the B2086, passing Beacon Hall House on your right. Walk back into Benenden to the pub.

THE BULL
The Street BENENDEN
TN17 4DE
Tel: 01580 240054
Directions: Benenden is on the B2086 between Cranbrook and Tenterden
By the village green, a listed family-run pub thought to date back to 1608. Recently renovated, it lies in a picturesque Kentish village and is also the headquarters of the local cricket club. Varied home-cooked fare.
Open: 11.30–3 6–11
Bar Meals: 12–2.30 7–9.30
Garden and parking available.

Distance: 6 miles (9.6km)
Map: OS Explorer 125
Terrain: Farmland and woodland
Paths: Country lanes, farm tracks, footpaths and road
Gradient: Slightly undulating

Walk submitted and checked by The Bull at Benenden

BOUGHTON ALUPH — Map 05 TR04

The Flying Horse Inn
TN25 4ET ☎ 01233 620914
15th-century inn with oak beams and open log fires.
Comfortable minstrel bar with sunken wells. Regular cricket
matches in summer on the spacious village green opposite.
Good selection of real ales and a varied menu which might
include roast rack of lamb, poached salmon, monkfish with
mushroom, lemon and butter sauce, baked avocado with
spinach, or braised lamb shank.
OPEN: 12-11 **BAR MEALS:** Lunch served: all week Dinner served: all
week 12-2 7-9 Av main course £8.50 **RESTAURANT:** Lunch served: all
week Dinner served: all week 12-2 7-9 Av 3 course à la carte £25
BREWERY/COMPANY: Unique Pub Co **PRINCIPAL BEERS:** Fullers
London Pride,Courage Best, Youngs Special, Greene King IPA.
FACILITIES: Garden: Outdoor eating, patio/terrace, BBQ
NOTES: Parking 40 **ROOMS:** 3 bedrooms from s£25 d£40

BURHAM — Map 05 TQ76

The Golden Eagle 🏚️
80 Church St ME1 3SD ☎ 01634 668975 📠 01634 668975
Dir: South from M2 J3 or North M20 J6 on A229, signs to Burham

Situated on the North Downs with fine views of the Medway
Valley, this traditional free house has a friendly and informal
atmosphere. The appearance of an old-fashioned English inn
is belied by the fact that the kitchen specialises in oriental
cooking, with an extensive menu that includes dishes from
China, Malaysia, Thailand and Singapore. House specials
include pork babibangang, king prawn sambal, wor-tip
chicken, vegetarian mee goreng, and chicken tom yam.
OPEN: 11.30-2.30 6.15-11 Closed: Dec 25-26 **BAR MEALS:** Lunch
served: all week Dinner served: all week 12-2 7-10 Av main course
£7.90 **RESTAURANT:** Lunch served: all week Dinner served: all week
12-2 7-10 Av 3 course à la carte £17.50 Av 3 course fixed price £17.50
BREWERY/COMPANY: Free House
PRINCIPAL BEERS: Wadworth 6X, Marston's Pedigree.
NOTES: Parking 45

CANTERBURY — Map 05 TR15

The Chapter Arms 🏚️ ♀ NEW
New Town St, Chartham Hatch CT4 7LT ☎ 01227 738340
Dir: 3 miles from Canerbury Off A28 in the village of Chartham Hatch
A charmingly picturesque free house on a hill just three miles
from the centre of Canterbury. Home grown vegetables and
fruit or from local sources play a large part on daily menus
that also offer plenty of fresh fish. Dressed baby crab and king
prawns with chilli and ginger cream precede main dishes such
as teriyaki tuna steak and a steamy pot of Spanish fish stew
simmered in white wine. House specials list beef suet pudding
and home-made banoffee pie with Tia Maria cream.

continued

OPEN: 11-3 6.30-11 Closed: 25 Dec **BAR MEALS:** Lunch served: all
week Dinner served: all week 12-2 7-9 **RESTAURANT:** Lunch
served: all week Dinner served: all week 12-2 7-9 Av 3 course à la
carte £17.50 **BREWERY/COMPANY:** Free House
PRINCIPAL BEERS: Shepherd Neame Master Brew, Cambrinus
Herald, Harveys Sussex best. **FACILITIES:** Children welcome Garden:
1 acre overlooking apple & plum orchards **NOTES:** Parking 40

Pick of the Pubs

The Dove Inn 🏅🏅 🏚️ ♀
Plum Pudding Ln, Dargate ME13 9HB ☎ 01227 751360
e-mail: thedoveinn@hotmail.com
Tucked away in a sleepy hamlet on the delightfully named
Plum Pudding Lane, the Dove is the sort of pub you
dream of as your local. Roses round the door, a simple
interior with stripped wooden floors, plain tables, a hop-
garlanded bar, tip-top Shepherd Neame ales, a relaxing
atmosphere, and astonishingly good food sum up this
charming rural pub. Food is simply described on a series
of blackboard menus that feature fresh fish from Hythe
and local game expertly prepared by talented
chef/proprietor Nigel Morris. For a lunchtime snack order
a starter, perhaps grilled local herrings flavoured with
virgin olive oil and garlic or pan-fried crevettes with fresh
garden herbs and pickled ginger. Main courses range
from confit duck leg with braised red cabbage and braised
shank of lamb on chive potato purée, to roast monkfish
wrapped in Bayonne ham and basil and wild sea bass on
crushed new potatoes with tapenade. Desserts such as
lemon tart and classics. Good Sunday lunch choices.
Splendid sheltered garden for summer meals.
OPEN: 11-3 6-11 **BAR MEALS:** Lunch served: Tue-Sun 12-2
Dinner served: Wed-Sat 7-9 **RESTAURANT:** Lunch served:
Tue-Sun 12-2 Dinner served: Wed-Sat 7-9 Av 3 course à la carte
£25 **BREWERY/COMPANY:** Shepherd Neame
PRINCIPAL BEERS: Shepherd Neame Master Brew.
FACILITIES: Children welcome **NOTES:** Parking 14

The Duke William 🏚️ ♀
Ickham CT3 1QP ☎ 01227 721308 📠 01227 722042
Built in 1611, this is a family-run free house in a picturesque
village between Canterbury and Sandwich. There's an open
fire in the comfortable bar, with a summer garden and rural
views. The extensive menu in the conservatory-style
restaurant features home-cooked dishes like stuffed quail with
noisette of lamb, 1lb poussin grandmère with bacon,
mushrooms and button onions, aubergine, Brie and wild
mushroom stack, and roasted cod on a mussel, prawn and
squid seacake.
OPEN: 11-11 **BAR MEALS:** Lunch served: all week Dinner served:
all week 11-2 6-10 **RESTAURANT:** Lunch served: all week Dinner
served: all week 11-2 6-10 Av 3 course à la carte £20

continued

BREWERY/COMPANY: Free House
PRINCIPAL BEERS: Shepherd Neame Master Brew, Young's Special, Adnams Bitter, Fuller's London Pride. **FACILITIES:** Children welcome Garden: Food served outside Dogs allowed (water)

The Old Coach House 🛏 🍷
A2 Barnham Downs CT4 6SA ☎ 01227 831218 📠 01227 831932
Dir: 7M Sof Canterbury, on the A2 Turn at Jet Petrol Station.
A former stop on the original London-Dover coaching route, and listed in the 1740 timetable, this inn stands some 300 metres from the Roman Way. Noteworthy gardens with home-grown herbs and vegetables, weekend spit-roasts, and unabashed continental cuisine mark it as an auberge in the finest Gallic tradition. Food options include game in season, venison, wild duck, lobster, sea bass and seafood.
OPEN: 11-11 **BAR MEALS:** Lunch served: all week Dinner served: all week 12-2.30 6.30-9 Av main course £10 **RESTAURANT:** Lunch served: all week Dinner served: all week 12-2.30 6.30-9 Av 3 course à la carte £18 **BREWERY/COMPANY:** Free House
PRINCIPAL BEERS: Whitbread Best Bitter. **FACILITIES:** Children welcome Garden: 2 1/2 acres, food served outside Dogs allowed
NOTES: Parking 60 **ROOMS:** 10 bedrooms 10 en suite from s£42 d£48

CHIDDINGSTONE   Map 05 TQ54

Pick of the Pubs

Castle Inn 🛏
TN8 7AH ☎ 01892 870247 📠 01892 870808
e-mail: info@castleinn.co.uk
See Pick of the Pubs on page 262

CHILHAM   Map 05 TR05

The White Horse 🍷
The Square CT4 8BY ☎ 01227 730355
Dir: Take A28 from Canterbury then A252, 1m turn L
Built in 1422, the White Horse is located in the picturesque Tudor square of Chilham, opposite the entrance to Chilham Castle.

CHILLENDEN   Map 05 TR25

Griffins Head 🛏
CT3 1PS ☎ 01304 840325 📠 01304 841290
Dir: A2 from Canterbury towards Dover,then B2046.Village on R

A Wealden hall house, dating from 1286, with a lovely garden. Once occupied by monks who farmed the surrounding land, it features inglenook fireplaces, beamed bars, fine Kentish ales and home-made food. Typical dishes include game in season,

continued

lasagne, Aberdeen Angus steaks, marinated half shoulder of lamb, stuffed chicken breast, cottage pie, and fisherman's pie. Vintage car club meets here first Sunday every month.
OPEN: 10.30am-11pm **BAR MEALS:** Lunch served: all week 12-2 Dinner served: Mon-Sat 7-9.30 Av main course £7.50
RESTAURANT: Lunch served: Sun-Fri 12-2 Dinner served: Mon-Sat 7-9.30 Av 3 course à la carte £17 **BREWERY/COMPANY:** Shepherd Neame **PRINCIPAL BEERS:** Shepherd Neame.
FACILITIES: Garden: Large garden with BBQs in summer
NOTES: Parking 25

CLIFFE   Map 05 TQ77

The Black Bull
186 Church St ME3 7QD ☎ 01634 220893 📠 01634 221382
e-mail: the_black_bull@msn.com
Dir: On B2000 N of Rochester
Pip's meeting place with Magwitch in Dickens's *Great Expectations* is within easy reach of this distinctive free house situated near the Thames estuary. The Tapestries restaurant has a 50ft ancient well. Authentic Malaysian, Thai and Chinese cuisine includes mixed seafood, sweet and sour pork and orange chicken.
OPEN: 12-2.30 7-11 (Mon 12-2.30 only) **BAR MEALS:** Lunch served: all week 12-2.30 Dinner served: Tue-Sat 7-11 Av main course £6.50 **RESTAURANT:** Lunch served: all week 12-2.30 Dinner served: Tue-Sat 7-10 Av 3 course à la carte £17
BREWERY/COMPANY: Free House **PRINCIPAL BEERS:** Flagship Destroyer, Shepherd Neame, Courage Directors, Black Bull.
FACILITIES: Children welcome Garden: patio, outdoor eating, BBQ, Dogs allowed (water) **NOTES:** Parking 16

DARTFORD   Map 05 TQ57

The Rising Sun Inn ♦ ♦ ♦ 🛏
Fawkham Green, Fawkham DA3 8NL
☎ 01474 872291 📠 01474 872291

16th-century inn set in a peaceful picturesque village not far from the Thames and Medway estuaries. The Rising Sun has been a pub since 1702. Friendly atmosphere inside, inglenook log fire and cosy restaurant. Convenient for Brands Hatch racing circuit. Traditional fish 'n' chips, t-bone steak, steak and kidney pudding, oven baked trout, and tournados royale are among the popular dishes. Barbecues, special events and jazz on the first Wednesday of each month.
OPEN: 12-3 6-11 Closed: 1 Jan **BAR MEALS:** Lunch served: all week Dinner served: all week 12-2.30 6.30-9.30 Av main course £7
RESTAURANT: Lunch served: all week Dinner served: all week 12-2.15 6.30-9.30 Av 3 course à la carte £20
BREWERY/COMPANY: Free House **PRINCIPAL BEERS:** Scottish Courage Courage Best, Courage Directors. **FACILITIES:** Garden: Food served outside **NOTES:** Parking 30 **ROOMS:** 5 bedrooms 5 en suite from s£40 d£65

OPEN: 11–11
BAR MEALS: L served all week. D served all week.
RESTAURANT: L served Wed-Mon. D served all week. 12–2 7.30–9.30 Av cost 3 course £28
BREWERY/COMPANY: FREE HOUSE
PRINCIPAL BEERS: Larkins Traditional, Harveys Sussex, Young's Ordinary
FACILITIES: Children and dogs welcome. Garden: food served outside.

Castle Inn

CHIDDINGSTONE Kent TN8 7AH
☎ 01892 870247 📠 01892 870808
e-mail: info@castleinn.co.uk
Dir: S of B2027 between Tonbridge & Edenbridge

The Castle Inn is reputed to have been named in honour of Anne Boleyn who lived at nearby Hever Castle, but its roots go back much farther than that. Nowadays its picturesque mellow brick exterior is a much-used film set - *The Wicked Lady* and *Room with a View* were shot here.

In 1420 the inn was known as Waterslip House, and it was licensed to sell ale in about 1730 when it was known as The Five Bells. Inside it is full of nooks and crannies, period furniture and evocative curios, with the rambling beamed bar having been remodelled carefully to preserve its unique character. The same family owners have dispensed traditional ales for nearly 40 years including Larkins and Porter which are brewed nearby at Larkins Farm. The inn is also well known for its food, around which the chef brothers Philip and David Lamb have built a strong reputation. Typical pub food is available, including open sandwiches, ploughman's, filled baguettes, and more substantial dishes like chilli con carne, chicken curry, and three cheese tortellini. Moving up a few notches comes the Fireside Menu, dispensing the likes of ham hock and foie gras terrine, sole and leek mousse, and tomato and goats' cheese tartlet, followed by pavé of salmon on saffron mash, roast pheasant on braised red cabbage, and seared calves' liver. The carte menu including some of these dishes can be sampled in the small restaurant, where a meal might consist of salad of crispy tamarind-marinated quail, wild duck breast followed by and iced coconut terrine, or plate of award-winning British cheeses. Serious wines to match, including fine clarets.

DEAL
Map 05 TR35

The King's Head
9 Beach St CT14 7AH ☎ 01304 368194 📠 01304 364182
e-mail: booking@kingsheaddeal.co.uk

Traditional 18th-century seaside pub, overlooking the seafront and situated in one of the south-east's most picturesque coastal towns. Deal's famous Timeball Tower is a few yards away and the pub is within easy reach of Canterbury, Walmer Castle and the Channel Tunnel. Bar meals include steaks, sandwiches and seafood, and there is a daily-changing specials board.
OPEN: 10–11 (Sun 12–10.30) **BAR MEALS:** Dinner served: all week 11–3 6–9.30 Av main course £5.95 **BREWERY/COMPANY:** Free House **PRINCIPAL BEERS:** Shephard Neame Master Brew, Courage Best, Spitfire. **FACILITIES:** Children welcome Garden: Food served outside. Seafront terrace Dogs allowed **NOTES:** Parking 3 **ROOMS:** 14 bedrooms 13 en suite from s£40 d£50

DOVER
Map 05 TR34

The Cliffe Tavern ♀
High St, St Margaret's at Cliffe CT15 6AT
☎ 01304 852400 📠 01304 851880
Dir: 3m NE of Dover
Located opposite the parish church and just half a mile from the white cliffs north of Dover, this 16th-century Kentish clapboard building, formerly an 'academy for young gentlemen', has undergone major refurbishment since new owners took over in February 2000. Convivial main bar and neatly furnished lounge leading out to the delightful walled rose garden. Food now includes fresh local fish, traditional dishes like toad-in-the-hole, steak and pie and calves' liver and bacon, and mushroom and herb tagliatelle, Thai curries, and home-made ice creams among the puddings.
OPEN: 11–3 5–11 (Sun 12–10.30) **BAR MEALS:** Lunch served: all week Dinner served: all week 11.30–2.30 7–9 Av main course £8 **RESTAURANT:** Lunch served: all week Dinner served: all week 12–2.30 7–9 Av 3 course à la carte £25 **BREWERY/COMPANY:** Free House **PRINCIPAL BEERS:** Shepherd Neame Spitfire, Masterbrew, Pickled Porter. **FACILITIES:** Children welcome Garden: Food served outside Dogs allowed **NOTES:** Parking 35 **ROOMS:** 15 bedrooms 15 en suite from s£40 d£50

EASTLING
Map 05 TQ95

Carpenters Arms ♦♦♦
The Street ME13 0AZ ☎ 01795 890234 📠 01795 890654
e-mail: carpenters-arms@lineone.net
Dir: A251 towards Faversham, then A2, 1st L Brogdale Rd, 4m to Eastling
An early Kentish hall house, built in 1380, this listed building soon became an ale house serving carpenters working in the nearby sawmill. It features oak beams, an inglenook fireplace, a brick-tiled floor, and a profusion of local bygones. The bar offers home-cooked pub fare, snacks and daily specials, while restaurant dishes include steaks, salmon en croûte, and slow cooked lamb shank.
OPEN: 11–4 6–11 (Sun 12–6) **BAR MEALS:** Lunch served: all week 12–2.30 Dinner served: Mon–Sat 7–10 Av main course £6 **RESTAURANT:** Lunch served: all week 12–2.30 Dinner served: Mon–Sat 7–10 Av 3 course à la carte £20 **BREWERY/COMPANY:** Shepherd Neame **PRINCIPAL BEERS:** Shepherd Neame Master Brew, Bishops Finger & Spitfire. **FACILITIES:** Children welcome Garden: Beer garden, food served outdoors Dogs allowed on lead only, Water **NOTES:** Parking 20 **ROOMS:** 3 bedrooms 3 en suite from s£41.50 d£49.50

EDENBRIDGE
Map 05 TQ44

The Kentish Horse
Cow Ln, Markbeech TN8 5NT ☎ 01342 850493
A recent extension at this white-painted inn has provided a new dining area, while the original part - dating from 1340 with a smuggling history - remains unchanged. The inn is popular in summer with families using the gardens, and all year round for food like traditional cod and chips, pies, puddings and casseroles, plus salads, ploughman's and sandwiches. Look out for the unique street-bridging Kentish sign.
OPEN: 12–11 **BAR MEALS:** Lunch served: all week Dinner served: all week 12–2.30 7–9.30 Av main course £5.95 **RESTAURANT:** Lunch served: all week Dinner served: all week 12–2.30 7–9.30 **PRINCIPAL BEERS:** Fuller's London Pride plus Guest Ales. **FACILITIES:** Children welcome Garden: Food served outside Dogs allowed (water, biscuits) **NOTES:** Parking 40

Ye Old Crown ♦♦♦♦
74-76 High St TN8 5AR ☎ 01732 867896 📠 01732 868316
e-mail: yeold@lionheartinns.co.uk

An unmissable landmark on account of its unusual street-bridging Kentish inn sign, this has been an inn since the mid-14th century, and a concealed passage from the 1630s confirms its history as a smugglers' den. Today it dispenses local Larkins' ale, traditional English bar and restaurant food, and offers comfortable tourist accommodation. Simple menu includes baguettes, lasagne, jacket potatoes, sandwiches, and ploughman's.
OPEN: 11–11 (Sun 12–10.30) **BAR MEALS:** Lunch served: all week Dinner served: all week 12–3 6–10 Av main course £5.95 **RESTAURANT:** Lunch served: all week Dinner served: all week 12–3 6–10 **PRINCIPAL BEERS:** Courage Directors & Best, Shepherd Neame, Larkins, Master Brew. **FACILITIES:** Children welcome Garden: Food served outside. Courtyard Dogs allowed **NOTES:** Parking 20 **ROOMS:** 6 bedrooms 6 en suite

continued

EDENBRIDGE continued

The Wheatsheaf
Hever Rd, Bough Beech TN8 7NU
☎ 01732 700254 📠 01732 700141

Merrie England comes to life beneath the lofty timbered ceilings of this splendid medieval pub, originally built as a hunting lodge for Henry V. You'll find massive stone fireplaces, roasting chestnuts and mulled wine in winter, plus lovely summer gardens with swings for the children. The Wheatsheaf also has a well-deserved reputation for good food; expect ciabatta open sandwiches, liver and bacon, Welsh fillet steaks and home-made curries.
OPEN: 11–11 **BAR MEALS:** Lunch served: all week Dinner served: all week 12–10 Av main course £5.95 **RESTAURANT:** Lunch served: all week Dinner served: all week 12–10 Av 3 course à la carte £15
BREWERY/COMPANY: Free House **PRINCIPAL BEERS:** Harveys Sussex Bitter, Shepherds Neame, Fullers London Pride, Old Speckled Hen. **FACILITIES:** Children welcome Garden: Food served outside Dogs allowed (water) **NOTES:** Parking 30

EYNSFORD
Map 05 TQ56

Swallows' Malt Shovel Inn 🐾 🍷
Station Rd DA4 0ER ☎ 01322 862164 📠 01322 864132
Dir: A20 to Brands Hatch, then A225, 1m to pub

Close to the Darenth River, this charming village pub is very popular with walkers and those visiting the Roman villa in Eynsford, or Lullingstone Castle. Fish is very well represented on the menu, and dishes may include grilled monkfish, best smoked Scotch salmon, whole lobster, sea bass, tiger prawns, tuna, plaice, trout, skate or dressed baby crab. Rack of ribs, venison pie, leek and lentil lasagne and vegetable curry also turn up on a typical menu.
OPEN: 11–3 7–11 Closed: 25–26 Dec **BAR MEALS:** Lunch served: all week Dinner served: all week 12–2.30 7–10 Av main course £8
RESTAURANT: Lunch served: all week Dinner served: all week 12–2.30 7–10 **BREWERY/COMPANY:** Free House
PRINCIPAL BEERS: Morland Old Speckled Hen, Harveys Armarda, Fullers London Pride, Taylor Landlord. **FACILITIES:** Children welcome **NOTES:** Parking 26

FAVERSHAM
Map 05 TR06

The Albion Tavern 🐾
Front Brents, Faversham Creek ME13 7DH
☎ 01795 591411 📠 01795 591587
Dir: From Faversham take A2 W. In Ospringe turn R just before Ship inn, at Shepherd Neame Brewery 1m turn L over creek bridge

Popular 18th-century white weatherboarded pub overlooking Faversham Creek and just a stone's throw from the owning brewery - Shepherd Neame. The open-plan bar is adorned with nautical artefacts, including oars, a hammock and photographs of old boats. Picture windows look out across the creek, and a tiny, vine-festooned rear conservatory leads out to a pretty garden. Menu includes chicken, mushroom and tarragon crêpes, pan-fried calves' liver with lime, sage and butter sauce, slow cooked lamb shank on lentils, and steak and kidney with onions and button mushrooms.
OPEN: 11.30–3 6.30–11 **BAR MEALS:** Lunch served: all week Dinner served: all week 12–2 6.30–9.30 Av main course £7
RESTAURANT: Lunch served: all week Dinner served: all week 12–2 6.30–9.30 **BREWERY/COMPANY:** Shepherd Neame
PRINCIPAL BEERS: Shepherd Neame Spitfire, Master Brew, Bishops Finger & Porter. **FACILITIES:** Children welcome Garden
NOTES: Parking 50

Shipwrights Arms
Hollowshore ME13 7TU ☎ 01795 590088
Dir: A2 through Osprince then R at rdbt. Turn R at T-junct then L opp Davington School & follow signs
Find this classic pub on the Kent marshes on foot and savour its wonderful atmosphere. First licensed in 1738, this was once a haunt of pirates and smugglers. There are numerous nooks and crannies inside and beer is served traditionally by gravity straight from the cask. Frequently changing range of Kent-brewed real ales. Self-sufficient landlord generates his own electricity and draws water from a well. Home-cooked food might include mushroom Stroganoff and sausage and mash. Emphasis on English pies and puddings during the winter.
OPEN: 12–3 7–11 (Sun 12–3,6–10.30) Summer Open all day
BAR MEALS: Lunch served: Tue–Sun 12–3 Dinner served: Tue–Sat 7–9 Av main course £5.50 **BREWERY/COMPANY:** Free House
FACILITIES: Children welcome Garden: Food served outdoors Dogs allowed **NOTES:** Parking 30 No credit cards

FORDCOMBE
Map 05 TQ54

Chafford Arms 🐾 🍷
TN3 0SA ☎ 01892 740267
e-mail: bazzer@chafford-armsfsnet.co.uk
Dir: On B2188 (off A264) between Tunbridge Wells & E Grinstead
Creeper-clad village pub with an award-winning garden, situated between Penshurst Place and Groombridge Place. Originally built in 1851 for the local paper works that made

continued

paper for the Royal Mint. One menu serves all in the homely bars and dining room. The main emphasis is on fish with the likes of fresh Dover sole from Hastings grilled with butter, prawn provençale or local Weald smoked trout served cold with horseradish sauce. There is also a good range of snacks, salads, vegetarian and meat dishes. Ask about the skate-boarding dog.

OPEN: 11.45–3 6.30–11 **BAR MEALS:** Lunch served: all week 12.30–2 Dinner served: Tue–Sat 7.30–9 Av main course £6.95 **RESTAURANT:** Lunch served: all week 12.30–2 Dinner served: Tue–Sat 7.30–9 Av 3 course à la carte £16 **PRINCIPAL BEERS:** Larkins Bitter, Fuller's London Pride. **FACILITIES:** Children welcome Garden: Food served outside Dogs allowed (water) **NOTES:** Parking 16

FORDWICH   Map 05 TR15

Fordwich Arms ♀
King St CT2 0DB ☎ 01227 710444 🖹 01227 712811
Dir: *From A2 take A28, on approaching Sturry turn R at 'Welsh Harp' pub into Fordwich Rd*
Solid Tudor-style village pub situated opposite the tiny, half-timbered 16th-century town hall, a reminder of the days when Fordwich was a Borough. Large bar with log-burning fires, an oak-panelled dining room and delightful riverside patio and garden for summer sipping. Modern, daily-changing menus encompass pork fillet with Savoy cabbage and bacon, duck breast on noodles with plum and hoi sin sauce, garlic and herb ravioli, and rabbit in ale with dumplings. Good Sunday lunch menu.
OPEN: 11–11 (Sun 12–3, 7–10.30) **BAR MEALS:** Lunch served: all week 12–2.30 Dinner served: Mon–Sat 6.30–9.30 Av main course £9 **RESTAURANT:** 12–2.30 6.30–9.30 **BREWERY/COMPANY:** Whitbread **PRINCIPAL BEERS:** Interbrew Flowers Original & Boddingtons Bitter, Shepherd Neame Masterbrew, Wadworth 6X,. **FACILITIES:** Garden: Dogs allowed **NOTES:** Parking 12

GOUDHURST   Map 05 TQ73

Pick of the Pubs

Green Cross Inn
TN17 1HA ☎ 01580 211200 🖹 01580 212905
Dir: *Tonbridge A21 toward Hastings turn L A262 leading to Ashford 2 M from the turning on the A262 Station road Goudhurst on the R hand side*
Food orientated pub in a delightful unspoiled corner of Kent, ideally placed for visiting Tunbridge Wells, the Ashdown Forest and the remote fenland country of Pevensey Levels. The dining-room is prettily decorated with fresh flowers and white linen table cloths and, with a new chef/proprietor at the helm, the whole pub is undergoing a gradual but extensive makeover. Fresh seafood is the house speciality here, with all dishes

cooked to order and incorporating the freshest ingredients. Main courses in the bar range from home-made steak, kidney and mushroom pie with shortcrust pastry, to calves' liver and bacon Lyonnaise. Restaurant fish dishes might include fillet of turbot with spinach and a creamy cheese sauce, grilled lemon sole with home-made tartare sauce, and Cornish cock crab with fresh dressed leaves.
OPEN: 11–3 6–11 **BAR MEALS:** Lunch served: all week 12–2.30 Dinner served: Mon–Sat 7–9.45 Av main course £6.50 **RESTAURANT:** Lunch served: all week 12–2.30 Dinner served: Mon–Sat 7–9.45 Av 3 course à la carte £23 **BREWERY/COMPANY:** Free House **PRINCIPAL BEERS:** Harveys Best, Shepherd Neame Master Brew, Larkins. **FACILITIES:** Garden: Food served outside Dogs allowed **NOTES:** Parking 26

Pick of the Pubs

The Star & Eagle ♀
High St TN17 1AL ☎ 01580 211512 🖹 01580 212589
e-mail: StarandEagle@btconnect.com
Dir: *On A262 E of Tunbridge Wells*
This fine 14th-century timbered and gabled hostelry is reputed to have been an ancient monastery, and relics of vaulted stonework are still visible in the building. A tunnel used to run from the cellars to a point underneath the parish church next door. In the 18th-century the inn was the headquarters of a group of desperados known as the Goudhurst Gang. Around 1749 these smugglers and robbers terrorised the district until the village raised a militia and defeated them in battle. Situated at the highest point of the village, 400ft above sea level, the inn commands outstanding views across the Kentish Weald. The carte menu is supported by daily specials, including medley of monkfish, salmon and king prawns, whole roasted pheasant with rich port wine sauce, and a leek, roasted aubergine, pepper and chestnut bake.
OPEN: 11–11 (Sun 12–10.30) **BAR MEALS:** Lunch served: all week Dinner served: all week 12–2.30 7–9.30 Av main course £8.95 **RESTAURANT:** Lunch served: all week Dinner served: all week 12–2.30 7–9.30 Av 3 course à la carte £20 **PRINCIPAL BEERS:** Interbrew Flowers Original & Boddingtons Bitter, Adnams Bitter. **FACILITIES:** Garden: Patio, food served outside **NOTES:** Parking 25 **ROOMS:** 10 bedrooms 8 en suite from d£60

GRAVESEND   Map 05 TQ67

The Cock Inn
Henley St, Luddesdowne DA13 0XB
☎ 01474 814208 🖹 01474 812850
e-mail: cockinn@amserve.net
No jukeboxes and no children permitted at this traditional English alehouse. Set in the beautiful Luddesdowne Valley, this is an ideal watering hole for walkers, with its constantly changing range of ales and good bar food. Typical dishes include ham, eggs and chips, breaded scampi, Thai green chicken curry, Cumberland sausages, cod and chips, and a selection of sandwiches and toasties.
OPEN: 12–11 (Sun 12–10.30) **BAR MEALS:** Lunch served: Mon–Sat Dinner served: Mon–Sat 12–2.30 6–8 Av main course £6 **BREWERY/COMPANY:** Free House **PRINCIPAL BEERS:** Adnams Southwold, Adnams Broadside Shepherd Neame Masterbrew, Goacher's Real Mild Ale. **FACILITIES:** Garden: Enclosed patio area Dogs allowed **NOTES:** Parking 60

continued

England

HADLOW — Map 05 TQ65

The Artichoke Inn
Park Rd, Hamptons TN11 9SR ☎ 01732 810763
Dir: *From Tonbridge take A26. In Hadlow turn L into Carpenters Lane. L at junction, 2nd on R*
Built as a farmworker's cottage, and licensed in 1585 as a pub, with large inglenook fireplace, and masses of brass and old farm implements. A front terrace with awning is ideal for summer dining, and it's handy for walking the Weald Way. Bar food ranges through plaice stuffed with asparagus, salmon and cream cheese, Mediterranean king prawns in garlic butter, chargrilled steak, and steak and kidney pie.
OPEN: 12–3 7–11 Closed: 25/26 Dec **BAR MEALS:** Lunch served: Tue–Sun 12–2 Dinner served: Tue–Sat 7–9 Av main course £7.95
BREWERY/COMPANY: Free House **PRINCIPAL BEERS:** Young's PA, Fuller's London Pride. **FACILITIES:** terrace **NOTES:** Parking 30

HARRIETSHAM — Map 05 TQ85

The Pepper Box Inn
ME17 1LP ☎ 01622 842558 ▤ 01622 844218
e-mail: pbbox@nascr.net
Dir: *Take the Fairbourne Heath turning from A20 in Harrietsham and follow for 2M to crossroads straight over follow for 200 yds pub is on the L*

Delightful 15th-century country pub situated on the Greensand Ridge, with stunning views of the Weald of Kent. The pub takes its name from an early type of pistol, a replica of which hangs behind the bar. Inglenook fireplaces, a separate non-smoking dining area and a terrace attract a good mix of customers. Typical dishes might include sweet figs, Mozzarella and Parma ham salad, roast sea bass with crab mashed potatoes or Portuguese sizzling steak.
OPEN: 11–3 6.30–11 **BAR MEALS:** Lunch served: all week 12–2.15 Dinner served: Tue–Sat 7–9.45 Av main course £10
RESTAURANT: Lunch served: Tue–Sat 12–2 Dinner served: Tue–Sat 7–9.45 Av 3 course à la carte £18 **BREWERY/COMPANY:** Shepherd Neame **PRINCIPAL BEERS:** Shepherd Neame Master Brew, Bishops Finger, Spitfire. **FACILITIES:** Garden: Food served outside, patio Dogs allowed **NOTES:** Parking 30

HERNHILL — Map 05 TR06

Pick of the Pubs

Red Lion ☺ ♀
The Green ME13 9JR ☎ 01227 751207 ▤ 01227 752990
e-mail: theredlion@lineone.net
Dir: *S of A299 between Faversham & Whitstable*
Beams and flagstones, rustic pine tables and roaring winter log fires are all part of the charm at this handsome, half-timbered 14th-century hall house, which overlooks

---

the village green to the historic church. Now privately owned, visitors will find local Shepherd Neame ales on tap, a monthly-changing carte and a blackboard listing a good range of daily specials. Sample from a menu that includes Thai chicken, liver and bacon, fresh sea bass, seafood pancake, beef Wellington, or braised beef in ale. Traditional puddings include chocolate fudge cake, fruit crumble and apple pie. Fully-equipped two bedroom cottage with garden and patio to rent.

OPEN: 11–3.30 6–11 Closed: 25 Dec **BAR MEALS:** Lunch served: all week Dinner served: all week 12–2.30 6–9.30 Av main course £7.95 **RESTAURANT:** Lunch served: (Sun only) Dinner served: all week 6–9.30 Av 3 course à la carte £25
BREWERY/COMPANY: Free House
PRINCIPAL BEERS: Shepherd Neame Master Brew, Spitfire, Wadworth 6X. **FACILITIES:** Children welcome Garden: Food served outside, attractive garden **NOTES:** Parking 40

HOLLINGBOURNE — Map 05 TQ85

The Dirty Habit ☺
Upper St ME17 1UW ☎ 01622 880880 ▤ 01622 880773
Historic pub on the old Pilgrim's Way to Canterbury, where travellers could change their dusty clothes, and imbibe the wine and ale introduced by monks as refreshments. The tradition is upheld in a more sophisticated way today, where visitors can dine on roast breast of duckling, poached salmon fillets, and loin of beef along with various grilled dishes including veal, spatchcock and swordfish, sizzling platters like chilli prawns, and pasta choices.
OPEN: 11.30–3 6.30–11 (Sun 12–4, 7–10.30) **BAR MEALS:** Lunch served: all week Dinner served: all week 12–2.45 7–10 Av main course £12 **RESTAURANT:** Lunch served: all week Dinner served: all week 12–2.45 7–10.30 Av 3 course à la carte £22
BREWERY/COMPANY: Enterprise Inns
PRINCIPAL BEERS: Shepherd Neame Spitfire, Bass, Wadworth 6X, Harveys Sussex Best. **FACILITIES:** Children welcome Garden: Large Patio, food served outside **NOTES:** Parking 30

IDEN GREEN — Map 05 TQ73

The Peacock ☺
Goudhurst Rd TN17 2PB ☎ 01580 211233
Dir: *A21 from Tunbridge Wells to Hastings, onto A262, pub 1.5m past Goudhurst*
Grade II listed building dating from the 12th century with low beams, an inglenook fireplace, old oak doors, real ales on tap, and a wide range of traditional pub food. Look out for grilled salmon with dill mayonnaise, omelettes, steak and ale pie, tagliatelle with salmon and prawns, and stuffed trout with almonds. Under new management.

continued

continued

OPEN: 12–11 (Sun 12–10.30) **BAR MEALS:** Lunch served: all week 12–2 Dinner served: Thur-Sun 7–9 Av main course £7.95 **RESTAURANT:** Lunch served: all week Dinner served: all week 12–2 7–9 Av 3 course à la carte £14.45
BREWERY/COMPANY: Shepherd Neame
PRINCIPAL BEERS: Shepherd Neame Master Brew, Spitfire & Best plus seasonal ales. **FACILITIES:** Children welcome Garden: Food served outside Dogs allowed (water) **NOTES:** Parking 50

IGHTHAM — Map 05 TQ55

Pick of the Pubs

George & Dragon
The Street TN15 9HH ☎ 01732 882440 📠 01732 883209
Dir: From M20, A20 then A227 towards Tonbridge
This historic pub dating from 1515 is a fine example of Tudor architecture with exposed beams inside and out. Set in a striking Kentish village, local folklore claims that Guy Fawkes stayed here the night before he attempted to blow up Parliament. It is also believed that the Duke of Northumberland was imprisoned in the old restaurant after the discovery of his part in the Gunpowder Plot. Some years ago a neighbouring barn was converted into a large restaurant, and there is also a cosy bar and a patio for summer weather. A varied menu is which changes with the seasons might offer smoked Dutch eel, clam chowder, and blue swimmer crab for starters. Main choices may be shrimp and leek pasta, marinated lamb skewers, seafood platter, coq au vin, and steamed steak and suet pudding, padded out with specials such as beef Wellington, rib-eye steak, and Gressingham duck. The inn is not far from Ightham Mote, one of the oldest continuously inhabited houses in England.
OPEN: 11–11 (Sun 12–10.30) Closed: 25–26 Dec eve, 1 Jan eve
BAR MEALS: Lunch served: Mon-Sat 12–3 Dinner served: all week 6.30–9.30 Av main course £4.10 **RESTAURANT:** Lunch served: all week 12–3 Dinner served: Mon-Sat 6.30–9.30
BREWERY/COMPANY: Shepherd Neame
PRINCIPAL BEERS: Shepherd Neame Master Brew, Spitfire & Seasonal Ale. **FACILITIES:** Children welcome Garden: Food served outside, patio Dogs allowed **NOTES:** Parking 20

Pick of the Pubs

The Harrow Inn
Common Rd TN15 9EB ☎ 01732 885912
Dir: Off A25 between Sevenoaks & Borough Green. Signposted to Ightham common
Within easy reach of both M20 and M26 motorways, yet tucked away down country lanes close to the National Trust's Knole Park and Igtham Mote, this Virginia creeper-hung stone inn clearly dates back to the 17th century and beyond. The bar area comprises two rooms with a great brick fireplace, open to both sides, piled high with blazing logs: meanwhile the restaurant boasts a vine-clad conservatory that opens to a terrace that is ideal for summer dining. Food options display imaginative use of fresh produce, with salmon and chive fishcakes with citrus sauce catching the eye in the bar; while wild venison terrine with cranberry compote before roasted shank of lamb with garlic mash, shallots and red wine jus are particularly tempting. Amongst popular house specialities, expect to find hot Kent

smoked haddock pie, smoked salmon and halibut with creamed horseradish, wild mushroom and saffron risotto and beef Wellington with Marsala sauce, followed by home-made apple tart or crispy roulade flavoured with lemon and lime.
OPEN: 12–3 6–11 (Sun 12–3 only) Closed: Dec 26 Jan 1, BHs
BAR MEALS: 12–2.30 6–9.30 **RESTAURANT:** Lunch served: Tue-Sat Dinner served: Tue-Sat 12–2.30 6–9.30 Av 3 course à la carte £22 **BREWERY/COMPANY:** Free House
PRINCIPAL BEERS: Greene King Abbot Ale, IPA,.
FACILITIES: Garden: Patio, food served outside
NOTES: Parking 20

IVY HATCH — Map 05 TQ55

Pick of the Pubs

The Plough
High Cross Rd TN15 0NL ☎ 01732 810268 📠 01732 811287
e-mail: alisonhumbert@btconnect.com
Dir: M25 J5 take A25 towards Borough Green follow signs for Ivy Hatch

Long-established owners here have little to say except that they perennially produce more of the same – and if it ain't broke they don't fix it! Deep in Kent countryside and close to the National Trust's 14th-century Ightham Mote, this decidedly food-faceted dining pub whose special draw remains the variety of fish and sea-foods dished up daily according to market availability. Warm home-potted shrimps, fresh Irish oysters and sweet marinated anchovies with lemon dressing are precursors to steamed skate, grilled fillets of haddock and grilled or cold-dressed lobster as available. At lunch only there may be wild boar sausages with apricot and redcurrant jus, as alternatives to spicy fishcakes laid on a calypso sauce. Salads of smoked chicken and Stilton, or beef tomato with Mozzarella, followed by honey-roast poussin and braised game casserole en croûte extend choices for the less fishy-minded. More than a dozen wines by the glass and some perfectly acceptable Larkin's ales ensure none shall go thirsty, even if not eating.
OPEN: 12–3 6–11 **BAR MEALS:** Lunch served: all week Dinner served: all week 12–3 7–11 Av main course £12.95
RESTAURANT: Lunch served: all week Dinner served: all week 12–3 7–11 Av 3 course à la carte £25
BREWERY/COMPANY: Free House
PRINCIPAL BEERS: Larkins. **FACILITIES:** Children welcome Garden: Food served outside. Patio area Dogs allowed (in the garden only) **NOTES:** Parking 30

continued

England

LINTON
Map 05 TQ75

The Bull Inn
Linton Hill ME17 4AW ☎ 01622 743612 ▤ 01622 749513
Dir: *A229 through Maidstone to Linton*
Traditional 17th-century coaching inn in the heart of the Weald with stunning views from the glorious garden. Popular with walkers and very handy for the Greensand Way. Large inglenook fireplace and a wealth of beams inside. Bar snacks and freshly prepared restaurant meals are available, ranging from Barnsley lamb chops with mint gravy and grilled salmon fillet to home-made lamb and apricot pie with Mediterranean vegetables and roast duck with Cumberland sauce.
OPEN: 12–3 6–11 (Sat-Sun 12–11) **BAR MEALS:** Lunch served: Tues-Sun 12-2.30 Dinner served: Tues-Sat 7-9 Av main course £6.95
RESTAURANT: Lunch served: Tue-Sun 12-2.30 Dinner served: Tue-Sat 7-9 Av 3 course à la carte £16
BREWERY/COMPANY: Shepherd Neame
PRINCIPAL BEERS: Shepherd Neame Master Brew, Spitfire & Bishop's Finger. **FACILITIES:** Children welcome Garden: beer garden, outdoor eating, patio Dogs allowed **NOTES:** Parking 50

LITTLEBOURNE
Map 05 TR25

Pick of the Pubs

King William IV 🍴
4 High St CT3 1UN ☎ 01227 721244 ▤ 01227 721244
Dir: *From A2 follow signs to Howletts Zoo. After zoo & at end of road, pub is straight ahead*
Located just outside the city of Canterbury is this thriving country inn overlooking the village green, and well placed for Sandwich and Herne Bay. Dawn and Dave Reed generate a friendly, welcoming atmosphere, helped by open log fires and exposed oak beams, and they offer a popular range of food including fish specials. From the ocean expect the likes of charred fillet of salmon with steamed asparagus and hollandaise, milk-poached smoked haddock with prawns and scrambled egg, and baked whole sea bass with a tomato, bacon and basil sauce. The carte extends to starters like moules marinière or king prawn green curry, followed by roast half pheasant with a wild mushroom and chestnut sauce, and chicken Wellington. From the dessert menu try caramelised lemon tart with sorbet, and mixed berry Pavlova. En suite accommodation is also available.
OPEN: 11–11 **BAR MEALS:** Lunch served: all week Dinner served: all week 12-2.30 7-9.30 Av main course £5
RESTAURANT: Lunch served: all week Dinner served: all week 12-2.30 7-9.30 Av 3 course à la carte £18 Av 2 course fixed-price £11.95 **BREWERY/COMPANY:** Free House
PRINCIPAL BEERS: Shepherd Neame Master Brew, Scottish Courage John Smith's. **FACILITIES:** Children welcome Garden: Terrace, food served outside **NOTES:** Parking 15
ROOMS: 7 bedrooms 7 en suite from s£30 d£45

MAIDSTONE
Map 05 TQ75

Pick of the Pubs

The Ringlestone Inn ◆◆◆◆◆ 🍷
Ringlestone Hamlet, Nr Harrietsham ME17 1NX
☎ 01622 859900 ▤ 01622 859966
e-mail: bookings@ringlestone.com
See Pick of the Pubs on page 269

NEWNHAM
Map 05 TQ95

Pick of the Pubs

The George Inn 🍴 🍷
44 The Street ME9 0LL ☎ 01795 890237 ▤ 01795 890726
Dir: *5m SW of Faversham*

The George, in the ancient parish of Newnham, was built in the year 1540 and was used as a farm dwelling until it was licensed in 1718, during the reign of George I, and subsequently became a coaching inn. Despite the many changes it has seen, the inn retains much of its historic character, with beams festooned with hop bines, polished wooden floors, open fires and candlelit tables. It also has the advantage of a large garden. A good range of beer includes Shepherd Neame's Master Brew, Spitfire and Bishops Finger, plus a winter/summer ale. Bar snacks range from sandwiches to sausage and mash, while typical chef's specials are pan-fried fillet of sea bass with fresh asparagus and hollandaise sauce, or large half shoulder of lamb served with a thyme, redcurrant and port sauce.
OPEN: 11–3 6.30–11 **BAR MEALS:** Lunch served: all week Dinner served: all week 12-2..30 7-9.45 Av main course £9
RESTAURANT: Lunch served: all week Dinner served: all week 12-2.30 7-9.45 Av 3 course à la carte £19
BREWERY/COMPANY: Shepherd Neame
PRINCIPAL BEERS: Shepherds Neame Master Brew, Spitfire, Bishops Finger, Winter Ale. **FACILITIES:** Children welcome Garden: Food served outside Dogs allowed **NOTES:** Parking 25

The Making of Beer

The traditional ingredients of beer are water, barley malt, hops, yeats and ripe judgement. One traditional brewery's products will taste different from another's because of variations in the blending of the ingredients and the timing of process. It all starts with barley, malted in a kiln at the malting: the higher the temperature, the darker the beer. The powdered malt is mixed with hot water to make a mash. How the hot mash is and how long it is allowed to stand will affect the taste and in the old days local spring water gave beer a distinctive local flavour. Burton upon Trent's eminent reputation for bitter rested on the gypsum in the town's water.
The liquid from the mash is boiled up with hops - the more hops, the bitterer - and sugar is often added. Next the liquid is cooled and yeast is stirred in to make it ferment. The 'green beer' is eventually run into casks to mature. Keg beer is filtered, sterilised, carbonated and stored in sealed containers. It tastes more like bottled beers, which are put through the same process.

OPEN: 12-3 6-11 (Sat-Sun 12-11)
BAR MEALS: L served all week.
D served all week. 12-2 7-9.30
Av main course £8
RESTAURANT: L served all week.
D served all week. 12-2 7-9.30
Av cost 3 course £22
BREWERY/COMPANY:
FREE HOUSE
PRINCIPAL BEERS: Shepherd
Neame Bishops Finger & Spitfire,
Greene King Abbot Ale, Theakston
Old Peculiar
FACILITIES: Children welcome.
Garden: Beer garden, food served
outdoors, patio
NOTES: Parking 50
ROOMS: 3 en suite. Min price
double room £96 Min price single
room £85

The Ringlestone Inn

◆◆◆◆◆ ♀
Ringlestone Hamlet Nr Harrietsham
Maidstone ME17 1NX
☎ 01622 859900 📄 01622 859966
e-mail: bookings@ringlestone.com
Dir: Take A20 E from Maidstone/at rndbt
opp Great Danes Hotel turn to
Hollingbourne. Through village, R at
crossroads at top of hill

It started out as a hospice for monks in 1533 on the ancient Pilgrim's Way, but less than a hundred years later Ringlestone found its present identity as an ale house. Very little has changed in the fabric of the building since those days, and the original brick and flint walls and floors, inglenooks and centuries-old furniture still fulfill their original functions today.

The Domesday Book mentions the 'ring stone' for tethering mounts which can still be seen in the brickwork. The warm welcome awaiting visitors reflects the old promise of a 'ryghte joyeuse greetynge', and along with a mind-boggling selection of country fruit wines, ciders and real ales, there is a range of home-cooked food to bring cheer. A hot and cold buffet is a popular lunchtime feature, with its seasonal choice of traditional country dishes. Expect chilli beef goulash, lamb, and coconut and banana curry, or cold pork and apple lattice pie with salad. For dinner it's a more formal candle-lit affair, with starters like garlic prawns, and local trout pâté, followed by cidered chicken casserole, beef bacon and spinach lasagne, or mushroom Stroganoff. A separate list of home-made pies such as game with redcurrant wine, or fish with elderflower, promises to evoke a typically English way of eating. Puddings continue in the same satisfying vein, with chocolate fudge cake, and home-made fruit crumble probably appearing on the menu. A nearby converted farmhouse contains smart modern bedrooms, furnished with individual touches such as CD players and fresh milk in the fridge.

England

PLUCKLEY
Map 05 TQ94

Pick of the Pubs

The Dering Arms 🐾 ♀
Station Rd TN27 0RR ☎ 01233 840371 ▤ 01233 840498
e-mail: jimo@deringarms.com
Dir: M20 J8 take A20 to Ashford. Then R onto B2077 at Charing to
Pluckley

Located a mile from the village beside Pluckley Station, this impressive building with curved Dutch gables and uniquely arched windows was formerly a family hunting lodge for the Dering Estate. Splendid interior to match, with high ceilings, wood or stone floors, simple antique furniture and winter log fires. Expect a relaxing atmosphere, ale from Goacher's micro-brewery in Maidstone and good food using fresh vegetables from the family farm and herbs from the pub garden. Chef/patron James Buss has a real passion for fresh fish and seafood as is evident across the interesting menu, with starters like fish soup, Irish oysters with shallot and red wine vinegar, and herring roes pan-fried with smoked bacon. Follow with pan-fried scallops with basil spaghetti and saffron sauce, monkfish with bacon, orange and cream sauce, salmon fishcakes with sorrel sauce, or – given notice – Jim's massive seafood special. Pies of the day, sirloin steaks and confit of duck redress the balance. Impressive list of wines and regular gourmet evenings.
OPEN: 11–3 6–11 Closed: 26–29 Dec **BAR MEALS:** Lunch served: all week Dinner served: all week 12-2 7–9.30 Av main course £13.95 **RESTAURANT:** Lunch served: all week Dinner served: all week 12-2 7–9.30 Av 3 course à la carte £23
BREWERY/COMPANY: Free House
PRINCIPAL BEERS: Goacher's Dering Ale, Maidstone Dark, Gold Star, Old Ale. **FACILITIES:** Children welcome Garden: Beer garden, food served outdoors Dogs allowed (water)
NOTES: Parking 20 **ROOMS:** 3 bedrooms from s£30 d£40

The Rose and Crown ♀
Munday Bois TN27 0ST ☎ 01233 840393 ▤ 01233 756530
An ale house since 1780, the Rose and Crown is set in a remote hamlet - allegedly part of England's most haunted parish. The bar menu offers local sausages, steak and kidney pie and hearty brunches. Specials might include chicken and Boursin en croûte and lamb 'Shrewsbury'. Children's and Sunday lunch menus.
OPEN: 11.30–3 6–11 (Sun 12–3, 7–11) **BAR MEALS:** Lunch served: all week Dinner served: all week 12-2 6.30–9.30 Av main course £7.95
RESTAURANT: Lunch served: all week Dinner served: all week 12-2 6.30–9.30 Av 3 course à la carte £16 **BREWERY/COMPANY:** Free

House **PRINCIPAL BEERS:** Master Brew, Hook Norton, Shepherd Neame Bishops Finger. **FACILITIES:** Children welcome Garden: Food served outside. Picnic tables Dogs allowed Garden: only ,Water provided **NOTES:** Parking 30

SANDWICH
Map 05 TR35

St Crispin Inn ♀
The Street, Worth CT14 0DF ☎ 01304 612081 ▤ 01304 614838
e-mail: job.tob@virgin.net
Set at the end of a dead-end village lane, this delightful inn has a carvery and chargrill, as well as summer barbeques. Close to Royal links courses. En suite bedrooms.

SELLING
Map 05 TR05

The Rose and Crown
Perry Wood ME13 9RY ☎ 01227 752214
Dir: A28 to Chilham R at Shottenden turning. R at Old Plough x roads, next R signed Perry Wood. Pub at top of hill
Set against 150 acres of natural woodland, this traditional 16th-century pub is decorated with local hop garlands and a unique corn dolly collection. Log fires in winter and a very attractive pub garden. Wide-ranging menu offers homemade steak and kidney pie, steak and mushroom suet pudding, curry, cod and smoked haddock mornay, and a variety of Chinese and Mexican specials. Try your hand at Bat and Trap in the garden.
OPEN: 11–3 6.30–11 **BAR MEALS:** Lunch served: all week 12-2 Dinner served: Tue–Sat 7–9.30 Av main course £6
RESTAURANT: Lunch served: Sun 12-2 Dinner served: Tue–Sat 7–9.30 Av 3 course à la carte £13 **BREWERY/COMPANY:** Free House **PRINCIPAL BEERS:** Adnams Southwold, Harvey's Best, Goacher's Real Mild Ale. **FACILITIES:** Children welcome Garden: Food served outside Dogs allowed (water, biscuit on welcome)
NOTES: Parking 25

SMARDEN
Map 05 TQ84

The Bell ♀
Bell Ln TN27 8PW ☎ 01233 770283 ▤ 01233 770726

Built in the year 1536, the Bell was originally a farm building on a large estate. It was used as a blacksmiths forge right up until 1907, but it had also been an alehouse since 1630. A typical menu includes seared king scallops with spinach and a crab sauce, chargrilled chicken breast with Mozzarella, basil and wild mushroom sauce, gammon steak with beetroot mash and parsley sauce, and tournedos of monkfish Rossini.
OPEN: 11.30–3 5.30–11 (Sun all day) **BAR MEALS:** Lunch served: all week Dinner served: all week 12-2 6.30–10 Av main course £11
RESTAURANT: Lunch served: all week Dinner served: all week 12-2

continued

continued

6.30–10 Av 3 course à la carte £20 **BREWERY/COMPANY:** Free House **PRINCIPAL BEERS:** Shepherd Neame Master Brew Bitterm Spitfire, Interbrew Flowers IPA, Fuller's London Pride.
FACILITIES: Garden: Food served outside **NOTES:** Parking 20

Pick of the Pubs

The Chequers Inn ♦♦♦♦ 🛏 ♀
The Street TN27 8QA ☎ 01233 770217 📠 01233 770623
e-mail: charliebullock@lineone.net
Dir: Through Leeds village, L to Sutton Valence/Headcorn then L for Smarden. Pub in village centre

An atmospheric 14th-century village inn clad in unusual rounded weatherboarding. A recent refurbishment has not detracted from the building's charm, and there are now two separate restaurants.
OPEN: 11–3 6–11 (Sat & Sun all day) **BAR MEALS:** Lunch served: all week Dinner served: all week 12–2.30 6–9 Av main course £7 **RESTAURANT:** Lunch served: all week Dinner served: all week 12–2.30 6–9 Av 3 course à la carte £20
BREWERY/COMPANY: Free House
PRINCIPAL BEERS: Harveys, Interbrew Bass, Fuller's London Pride. **FACILITIES:** Children welcome Garden: Courtyard, food served outside Dogs allowed **NOTES:** Parking 15
ROOMS: 4 bedrooms 4 en suite from s£40 d£70

SMARTS HILL   Map 05 TQ54

Pick of the Pubs

The Bottle House Inn 🛏 ♀
Coldharbour Rd TN11 8ET
☎ 01892 870306 📠 01892 871094
e-mail: gordonmeer@aol.com
See Pick of the Pubs on page 272

Pick of the Pubs

The Spotted Dog ♀
TN11 8EP ☎ 01892 870253 📠 870107
Dir: Off B2188 between Penshurst & Fordcombe
Relax and enjoy far-reaching views over the Weald from the terraced gardens of this 15th-century weatherboarded pub, situated within easy reach of Penshurst Place and Hever Castle. Rambling interior with a wealth of beams, open log fires, tiled and oak floors and intimate nooks and crannies. Blackboards list the day's interesting choice of food, perhaps including Indian ocean butter fish, Dublin Bay crayfish, chicken tagine, crispy aromatic duck,

or spinach and ricotta filo parcels. Wide range of salads and light bites available.
OPEN: 12–3 6–11 (Seasonal times vary, ring for details) Closed: 25 & 26 Dec **BAR MEALS:** Lunch served: all week Dinner served: all week 12–2.30 6–9.30 Av main course £10
RESTAURANT: Lunch served: all week Dinner served: all week 12–2 6–9.30 Av 3 course à la carte £20
BREWERY/COMPANY: Free House
PRINCIPAL BEERS: Greene King Abbot Ale, Adnams, Harveys.
FACILITIES: Children welcome Garden: Beer garden with seating, patio **NOTES:** Parking 60

SPELDHURST   Map 05 TQ54

The George and Dragon
Speldhurst Hill TN3 0NN ☎ 01892 863125
Dating from 1213, this is one of the oldest three pubs in England. It was used as a stopping going point by knights off to the Crusades.

STALISFIELD GREEN   Map 05 TQ95

The Plough 🛏 ♀
ME13 0HY ☎ 01795 890256
Dir: A20 to Charing, on dual carriageway turn L for Stalisfield
Originally a farmhouse, this 15th-century free house inn has been unspoilt by time, and boasts a lady ghost among its original beams and log fires. Set in a pretty village on top of the North Downs, it is run by Italian owners who hold regular theme evenings from their homeland. Interesting menus are supplemented by the specials, which might include lamb fillets with flageolet beans, pan-fried chicken supreme, duck brochettes with honey and orange sauce, and spicy vegetable roast.
OPEN: 12–3 7–11 **BAR MEALS:** Lunch served: Tue–Sun Dinner served: Tue–Sun 12–3 7–11 Av main course £12.95
RESTAURANT: Lunch served: Tue–Sun Dinner served: Tue–Sun 12–3 7–11 Av 3 course à la carte £15 Av 2 course fixed price £15.75
BREWERY/COMPANY: Free House **PRINCIPAL BEERS:** Adnams Bitter, Wadworth 6X, Interbrew Flowers IPA. **FACILITIES:** Children welcome Garden: Food served outdoors Dogs allowed
NOTES: Parking 100

STOWTING   Map 05 TR14

The Tiger Inn ♀ NEW
TN25 6BA ☎ 01303 862130 📠 01303 862990
e-mail: willetttiger@aol.com
Dir: From M20 J11 take B2068 towards Canterbury. After 3m turn R to Stowting. Pub 2m on R
A lively pub with a good atmosphere, hosting regular jazz and Irish evenings and a popular annual beer festival. Renowned locally for good food, there is a separate restaurant (and in summer a large terrace) where dishes are listed on a daily-changing blackboard. Expect starters like tempura king prawns, and duck liver and Grand Marnier pâté, followed by Thai chicken stir-fry, calves' liver with bacon, and poached salmon with fennel and lime hollandaise.
OPEN: 12–2.30 6.30–11 **BAR MEALS:** Lunch served: all week Dinner served: all week 12–2 6.30–9 Av main course £9.95
RESTAURANT: Lunch served: all week Dinner served: all week 12–2 6.30–9 Av 3 course à la carte £20 **PRINCIPAL BEERS:** Fuller's London Pride, Shepherd Neame Master Brew Bitter, Spitfire, Theakston Old Peculier. **FACILITIES:** Children welcome Garden: Food served outside Dogs allowed (water) **NOTES:** Parking 50

continued

OPEN: 11–3 6–11 (Sat-Sun all day)
BAR MEALS: L served all week.
D served all week. 12–2 6–10
Av main course £18
RESTAURANT: L served all week.
D served all week. 12–2 6–10
Av cost 3 course £18
BREWERY/COMPANY: FREE
HOUSE
PRINCIPAL BEERS: Larkins Ale,
Harveys Best
FACILITIES: Children and dogs
welcome.
GARDEN: Patio,and lawned area,
food served outside
NOTES: Parking 36

The Bottle House Inn

A very attractive inn of great character, now a dining pub of some repute but first licensed around the end of the 19th century when cider was produced on the premises. In those days the Bottle House was a barn belonging to a local estate, but a smart conversion has left it with quaint beams, low ceilings, a copper-topped bar and open fires to create a cosy atmosphere.

♀
Coldharbour Road, Smarts Hill
TN11 8ET
☎ 01892 870306 📄 01892 871094
e-mail: gordonmeer@aol.com
Dir: From Tunbridge Wells take A264 W then B2188 N

Run by the same friendly family for seventeen years, it is a handy stopover place for visiting the famous houses and castles of Kent, including Penshurst Place, Hever Castle and Chartwell. There are also plenty of good walks and striking views to be enjoyed in the vicinity. A considerable range of dishes is offered on the daily-changing menu, all made from locally supplied fresh produce. A long list of starters includes dressed crab, duck and port terrine with plum and apple chutney, spinach, Roquefort and baby onion tartlet, and Thai-spiced fishcake with chilli jam. Meat and fish are listed separately: carnivores can expect breast of pheasant stuffed with wild boar, pork loin steak with apple, date and cranberry sauce, fillet of beef Wellington with a mushroom and Madeira sauce, calves' liver and bacon with garlic mash, and the famous Speldhurst sausages with mashed potatoes or chips. For lovers of seafood there is roasted wing of skate, grilled red snapper, moules mariniére, seared fillet of sea bass, and smoked salmon and dill omelette. The same high standard of cooking goes into desserts like treacle tart with Calvados créme frèiche, pannacotta with raspberry coulis, and such old favourites as spotted dick with custard, and lemon meringue pie. Local Larkins bitter is on tap, and there's a separate children's menu.

TENTERDEN
Map 05 TQ83

White Lion Inn ♦♦♦♦ 🛏 ⚲
57 High St TN30 6BD ☎ 01580 765077 📠 01580 764157
e-mail: whitelion@lionheartinns.co.uk
Dir: on the A28 Ashford/Hastings road

A 16th-century coaching inn on a tree-lined street of this old Cinque Port, with many original features retained. The area is known for its cricket connections, and the first recorded county match between Kent and London was played here in 1719. The menu offers plenty of choice, from calves' liver and bacon, shoulder of lamb, and Cumberland cottage pie to tuna pasta bake and various ploughman's.
OPEN: 11–11 (Sun 12–10.30) **BAR MEALS:** Lunch served: all week Dinner served: all week 12–2.30 6–10 Av main course £7.25
RESTAURANT: Lunch served: all week Dinner served: all week 12–2.30 6–10 Av 3 course à la carte £14.25 Av 2 course fixed price £7.75 **BREWERY/COMPANY:** Lionheart
PRINCIPAL BEERS: Shepherd Neame, Interbrew Bass, Boddingtons Bitter, Wadworth 6X. **FACILITIES:** Children welcome Garden: Patio, food served outside Dogs allowed (water) **NOTES:** Parking 30
ROOMS: 15 bedrooms 15 en suite from s£40 d£50

TUNBRIDGE WELLS (ROYAL)
Map 05 TQ53

The Beacon 🛏 ⚲
Tea Garden Ln, Rusthall TN3 9JH
☎ 01892 534288 📠 01892 534288
Dir: From Tunbridge Wells take A264 towards East Grinstead. Pub 1m on L

The Beacon was built in 1895 as the elegant country home of a former Lord Lieutenant of the City of London. Set in sixteen acres of grounds with lakes, woodland, and its own chalybeate spring, there's also a dining terrace with lovely rural views. Fresh local ingredients drive interesting menus, including confit of duck on bubble and squeak, roast cod fillet with crispy fried noodles, baked smoked haddock fillet on mustard mash, canon of lamb with herb crust and spiced couscous, and Thai chicken and cashew nut curry.

OPEN: 11–11 (Sun 12–10.30) **BAR MEALS:** Lunch served: all week Dinner served: all week 12–2.30 6.30–9.30 Av main course £7.50
RESTAURANT: Lunch served: all week Dinner served: all week 12–2.30 6–9.30 Av 3 course à la carte £23
BREWERY/COMPANY: Free House **PRINCIPAL BEERS:** Harveys Best, Timothy Taylor Landlord, Breakspear Bitter.
FACILITIES: Children welcome Children's licence Garden: 17 acres of land, food served outside Dogs allowed (water, biscuits)
NOTES: Parking 40

The Crown Inn ⚲
The Green, Groombridge TN3 9QH ☎ 01892 864742
e-mail: www.crowninngroombridge@aol.com
Dir: Take A264 W of Tunbridge Wells, then B2110 S
A cosy and inviting 16th-century inn once frequented by smugglers and now peacefully situated by the village green. In winter there's a huge open fire in the beamed bar, and in summer a popular garden. Traditional bar food plus various salads with chips, filled bagels and steak and mushroom pie washed down with local real ales from Harveys or Larkins. Evening fare in the restaurant may offer diced curried lamb, seared salmon, or sirloin steak.
OPEN: 11–3 6–11 (Summer Fri-Sun open all day)
BAR MEALS: Lunch served: all week 12–3 Dinner served: Mon–Sat 7–9 Av main course £6.50 **RESTAURANT:** Lunch served: all week 12–3 Dinner served: Mon–Sat 7–9 Av 3 course à la carte £16
BREWERY/COMPANY: Free House **PRINCIPAL BEERS:** Harveys IPA, Greene King IPA & Abbot Ale, Larkins. **FACILITIES:** Children welcome Garden: Beer garden, patio, food served outside Dogs allowed **NOTES:** Parking 12 **ROOMS:** 4 bedrooms from s£35 d£40

The Hare on Langton Green 🛏 ⚲
Langton Rd TN3 0JA ☎ 01892 862419 📠 01892 861275
Dir: On A264 W of Tunbridge Wells
Rebuilt in 1901 following a fire, the pub has big windows, wooden floors and plenty of space for a collection of old books and bric-a-brac. In addition to real ales, there's an impressive range of malt whiskies and wines by the glass. Fish is well represented on the menu - roasted monkfish with spicy Mexican salsa and whole plaice grilled with Pernod and lemon butter - but the biggest sellers are fishcakes and shoulder of lamb.
OPEN: 12–11 (Sun 12–10.30) **BAR MEALS:** Lunch served: all week Dinner served: all week 12–9.30 Av main course £10
RESTAURANT: Lunch served: all week Dinner served: all week 12–9.30 Av 3 course à la carte £18 **PRINCIPAL BEERS:** Greene King IPA & Abbot Ale. **FACILITIES:** Children's licence Garden: Terrace, food served outside Dogs allowed **NOTES:** Parking 15

Pick of the Pubs

Royal Wells Inn ★ ★ ★ 🍴🍴 🛏 ⚲
Mount Ephraim TN4 8BE ☎ 01892 511188 📠 01892 511908
e-mail: info@royalwells.co.uk
Dir: 75 yds from junction of A26 & A264
A handsome white-painted hotel in a commanding position overlooking the common, with its first-floor conservatory restaurant being something of a landmark. The award-winning food is also available in the informal brasserie and bar, where a classic and vintage car theme decorates the clean modern lines. At lunchtime the choice includes twice-baked cheese soufflé, pork and brandy pâté, and warm crispy duck salad followed by flash-fried calves' liver, pheasant casserole, and stuffed aubergines with wild mushroom risotto. In the evening the range extends to crab Andalouse, fried sprats in smoked paprika with lemon, and avocado and bacon salad, with mains

continued

continued

TUNBRIDGE WELLS (ROYAL) continued

such as crispy leg of duck confit, fillet of beef Stroganoff, and braised shank of lamb. For pudding look no farther than apple and almond pie with cream, rhubarb and ginger tart, and gooseberry and elderflower mousse. Fine Kentish real ales, and wine by the glass.

Royal Wells Inn

OPEN: 11–11 (Sun 12–10.30) **BAR MEALS:** Lunch served: all week 12.30–2.15 **RESTAURANT:** Lunch served: all week Dinner served: all week 12.15–2.15 6.30–10.15 Av 3 course à la carte £17.50 **BREWERY/COMPANY:** Free House
PRINCIPAL BEERS: Harveys Best, Shepherd Neame Master Brew, Bishop's Finger & Spitfire. **FACILITIES:** Children welcome Garden: Food served outdoors, patio Dogs allowed
NOTES: Parking 28 **ROOMS:** 18 bedrooms 18 en suite from s£65 d£85

Pick of the Pubs

Sankey's Cellar Wine Bar 🐖 ♀
39 Mount Ephraim TN4 8AA
☎ 01892 511422 🖹 01892 511450
e-mail: seafood@sankeys.co.uk
Dir: on A26
Seafood restaurant, oyster bar, cellar wine bar and pub supporting small local and international brewers, Sankeys is something of a Tunbridge institution. The atmosphere is uniquely bustling and the place is cluttered with bric-a-brac. Steps lead from the street down to the old cellars that open onto a sheltered garden protected from the weather by huge umbrellas and patio heaters. One sensibly priced menu applies throughout, bringing diners the best of British seafood, with oysters from nearby Whitstable, Loch Fyne langoustines, and lobster and crab from Cornwall. Dishes range from bouillabaisse and paella to fresh cod and chips, and a house speciality is cock crab with huge claws, hand dressed and served with salad. The wine list aims to offer quality wines at reasonable prices, and by public demand this side of the business has recently been developed so that most of the wines are now available to take home.
OPEN: 11–3.30 6–12 (Open all day in summer) Closed: 25–26 Dec **BAR MEALS:** Lunch served: all week Dinner served: all week 12–2.30 7–10 Av main course £10 **RESTAURANT:** Lunch served: all week Dinner served: all week 12–2.30 7–10 Av 3 course à la carte £20 **BREWERY/COMPANY:** Free House
PRINCIPAL BEERS: Timothy Taylor Landlord, Larkins Traditional Bitter, Harveys Sussex Best. **FACILITIES:** Children welcome Garden: Patio, food served outside

WARREN STREET
Map 05 TQ95

The Harrow Hill Hotel ♦♦♦
Hubbards Hill ME17 2ED ☎ 01622 858727 🖹 01622 850026
Dir: A20 to Lenham, follow sign for Warren St on L, pub on R
Situated high up on the North Downs, this country inn was once a forge and rest house for travellers heading for Canterbury on the Pilgrim's Way. Good food is served in the cosy bar, including sizzling platter, pasta silvana, lasagne, and vegetarian gateau. In the relaxed restaurant expect starters such as smoked duck and ginger salad or smoked seafood tower, followed by confit of guinea fowl, fan of lamb fillet, and chicken Hiawatha.
OPEN: 12–3 7–11 (Sun 7–10.30) Closed: 25–26 Dec
BAR MEALS: Lunch served: all week Dinner served: all week 12–2 7–10 **RESTAURANT:** Lunch served: all week Dinner served: all week 12–1.30 7–9 Av 3 course à la carte £25 **BREWERY/COMPANY:** Free House
PRINCIPAL BEERS: Greene King IPA, Adnams Bitter, Fuller's London Pride, Marston's Pedigree. **FACILITIES:** Children welcome Garden: Patio, food served outside **NOTES:** Parking 80 **ROOMS:** 14 bedrooms 14 en suite from s£45 d£70

WESTERHAM
Map 05 TQ45

The Fox & Hounds
Toys Hill TN16 1QG ☎ 01732 750328
A traditional family-run country pub in the heart of National Trust land, with no music or gaming machines to disturb the convivial atmosphere. Beautiful gardens, and open fires and comfortable old furniture inside, add to its unspoilt character, and the cask ales, good wines and delicious food are recommended. Expect beef and Stilton pie, country cottage pie, tarragon chicken, and home-made soups. Plenty of good walks locally.
OPEN: 11.30–2.30 (Winter 12–2.30) 6–11 (Sun 12–3, 7–11) Closed: Dec 25 **BAR MEALS:** Dinner served: Snacks 12–2 Av main course £4 **BREWERY/COMPANY:** Greene King
PRINCIPAL BEERS: Greene King IPA Abbot Ale.
FACILITIES: Children welcome Garden: Dogs allowed at discretion of innkeeper **NOTES:** Parking 15 No credit cards

WHITSTABLE
Map 05 TR16

Pick of the Pubs

The Sportsman 🐖
Faversham Rd CT5 4BP ☎ 01227 273370 🖹 01227 262314
Reached via a winding lane across open marshland from Whitstable, and tucked beneath the sea wall, the Sportsman seems an unlikely place to find such astonishingly good food. The rustic, yet comfortable, interior is fuss free with wooden floors, sturdy tables and an interesting collection of prints. A first rate pint of Shepherd Neame Master Brew is served and a decent glass of wine. Similar care is taken over the quality of the food, and the daily menu is based on local produce, mostly sourced from within a five-mile radius. There are usually three or four fresh fish dishes, depending on what's available - one day's offerings were Dover sole, brill, cod and smoked haddock. Speciality dishes are crispy duck with smoked chilli salsa, local brill fillet braised in vin jeune, and whole grilled Dover sole with a tartare of mussels. The pub is ideally positioned for walkers on the Saxon Shore Way.
OPEN: 12–3 6–11 (all day Sun) Closed: 25 Dec **BAR MEALS:** Lunch served: Tues-Sun 12–2 Av main course £11.95 **RESTAURANT:** Lunch served: Tues-Sun 12–2 Dinner served: Tues-Sat 7–9 Av 3 course à la carte £22.50 **BREWERY/COMPANY:** Shepherd Neame
PRINCIPAL BEERS: Shepherd Neame Bishops Finger, Spitfire, Masterbrew. **FACILITIES:** Garden: Dogs allowed **NOTES:** Parking 25

WROTHAM
Map 05 TQ65

The Green Man 🐾 🍷
Hodsoll St, Ash-cum-Ridley TN15 7LE ☎ 01732 823575
Dir: Off A227 between Wrotham & Meopham
Once the home of Fred Kempster, the Wiltshire Giant, this
early 19th-century brick and timber building has impressive
floral displays in summer. The interior is warmly decorated
with hops, horse brasses and local pictures. Look out for
regular Morris dancing. Menu features roast duck with onion
marmalade, skate wing with black butter and capers, pork
fillet with black pudding, and saddle of rabbit with wild boar.
OPEN: 11–2.30 6.30–11 (Sat 11–3, 6.30–11/Sun 12–3, 7–10.30)
BAR MEALS: Lunch served: all week Dinner served: all week 12–2
6.30–9.30 Av main course £9 **RESTAURANT:** 12–2 6.30–9.30 Av 3
course à la carte £17 **BREWERY/COMPANY:** Whitbread
PRINCIPAL BEERS: Marstons Pedigree, Youngs Bitter, Fuller's London
Pride, Larkins Chiddingstone. **FACILITIES:** Children welcome Garden:
Large garden with seating Dogs allowed **NOTES:** Parking 35

WYE
Map 05 TR04

The New Flying Horse
Upper Bridge St TN25 5AN ☎ 01233 812297
400-year-old Shepherd Neame inn, characterised by low
ceilings, black beams and open fire. Tucked away in pretty
village beneath the North Downs. Bedrooms.

LANCASHIRE

BELMONT
Map 08 SD61

Black Dog
2/4 Church St BL7 8AB ☎ 01204 811218
Dir: M65 J3 onto A675
Traditional moorland pub adorned with antiques and bric-a-brac
and noted for classical music with occasional live orchestras.
Good value bar food includes everything from toasted
sandwiches, ploughman's and barm cakes, to lamb cutlets,
grilled gammon, tandoori vegetable masala, and jumbo sausage.
OPEN: 12–11 **BAR MEALS:** Lunch served: all week Dinner served:
all week 12–3 7–9 Av main course £5 **BREWERY/COMPANY:** Holts
PRINCIPAL BEERS: Holt-Bitter, Diamond, Mild.
FACILITIES: Children welcome Garden: Small courtyard garden for
residents only Dogs allowed (guide dogs only) **NOTES:** Parking 28
ROOMS: 3 bedrooms 3 en suite from s£32 d£42 No credit cards

BILSBORROW
Map 08 SD52

Owd Nell's Tavern 🍷
Guy's Thatched Hamlet, Canal Side PR3 0RS
☎ 01995 640010 🖺 01995 640141
e-mail: guyshamlet@aol.com

Busy thatched pub tucked away in a large thatched tourist
hamlet beside the Lancaster Canal. Always a wide selection of
guest ales from all over the country. Great for families, specials
include steak and kidney pie, giant Fleetwood fish and chips,
mssel hot pot, scallop provençale, and swordfish Americana.
OPEN: 11–11 Closed: 25 Dec **BAR MEALS:** Lunch served: all week
Dinner served: all week 11–10.30 Av main course £5
RESTAURANT: Lunch served: all week Dinner served: all week
12–2.30 5.30–10.30 **BREWERY/COMPANY:** Free House
PRINCIPAL BEERS: Interbrew Boddingtons Bitter & Flowers, Jennings
Bitter, Castle Eden Ale. **FACILITIES:** Children welcome Garden:
Canal side patio, food served outside Dogs allowed **NOTES:** Parking
300 **ROOMS:** 53 bedrooms 53 en suite from s£41.50 d£41.50
See Pub Walk on page 276

BLACKBURN
Map 08 SD62

Pick of the Pubs

Millstone Hotel ★ ★ 🛇 🍷
Church Ln, Mellor BB2 7JR ☎ 01254 813333 🖺 01254
812628
e-mail: millstone.reception@shirehotels.co.uk
*Dir: From M6 J31 take A59 towards Clitheroe, past British Aerospace. R at
rndbt signed Blackburn/Mellor. Next rndbt 2nd L. Hotel- top of hill on R*
This fine inn, the original flagship of Daniel Thwaites'
Brewery, was developed from a 17th-century tithe barn,
retaining many of its original features such as oak beams,
linen-fold panelling and the circular grinding-stone,
incorporated in the façade, from which the hotel derives
its name. Equally well preserved is the ambience of a
traditional country inn with the options of bar food and
restaurant dining. Bistro-style food, with its awareness of
fresh produce, offers good value in the likes of casserole
of beef in stout, pan-fried supreme of chicken and Loch
Fyne scallops baked with garlic and Gruyère. A la carte
dinners and Sunday lunch.
OPEN: 11–11 (Sun 12–10.30) **BAR MEALS:** Lunch served: all
week Dinner served: all week 12–2 6.30–9.15 Av main course
£7.75 **RESTAURANT:** Lunch served: all week Dinner served: all
week 12–2 6.30–9.30 Av 3 course à la carte £23.50
BREWERY/COMPANY: Shire Hotels
PRINCIPAL BEERS: Thwaites, Guinness, Carlsberg.
FACILITIES: Children welcome **NOTES:** Parking 45
ROOMS: 23 bedrooms 23 en suite

BLACKO
Map 08 SD84

Moorcock Inn 🐾
Gisburn Rd BB9 6NG ☎ 01282 614186 🖺 01282 614186
Dir: M65 J13, A682 for Kendal
Family-run country inn ideally placed for non-motorway travel
to the Lakes and the Yorkshire Dales. Specialises in home-
cooked meals, with a wide choice including grilled trout with
lemon and herb butter, Cajun chicken, pork in orange and
cider, vegetarian dishes like blue cheese and broccoli pasta
bake, and stuffed sweet peppers, and some tasty
Scandinavian-style desserts. Also enhanced by traditional log
fires and good views towards the Pendle Way.
OPEN: 12–2.30 6–9.30 **BAR MEALS:** Lunch served: all week
Dinner served: Tues-Sun 12–2 6–9.30 Av main course £5.95
RESTAURANT: Lunch served: all week Dinner served: Tues-Sun
12–2.30 6–9.30 **BREWERY/COMPANY:** Thwaites
PRINCIPAL BEERS: Thwaites, Best Bitter, Smooth, Murphys.
FACILITIES: Children welcome Garden: Food served outside. Picnic
benches Dogs allowed (in the garden only, water and food)
NOTES: Parking 80

continued

PUB WALK

Bilsborrow
Owd Nell's Tavern

An interesting waterside walk along a stretch of the Lancaster Canal, one of Britain's historic inland waterways.

From the pub car park take the footbridge over the Bacchus Brook, go up the cobbled street (Spout Lane) and into the flagged School House Square. Turn left to join the towpath and wind along the Lancaster Canal under bridge 45 to Brock Aqueduct, completed in 1797 by John Rennie. The Lancaster Canal dates back to 1792. Continue along the towpath, passing a mile post indicating that Preston is 13 miles (20.9km) away. At bridge 47, go up the steps and turn right along the pavement beside the A6 to a post box and a finger post. Turn left and follow the track to the railway crossing with gates and lights. Cross the main line – this used to be Brock station. Keep ahead along the track to the River Brock, pass under the bridge to reach an aluminium footbridge. Cross the river, which rises high on Snape Fell and feeds into the Wyre, and look for the finger post and the path running through the ruins of the old Matshead Paper Mill.

Cross the cobbled courtyard and go through a gap to the left of the old paper mill garage. Pass through a gate and cross several stiles. Take the footpath around the edge of the field and through a metal gate, crossing a footbridge at Bull Brook. Take the concrete footpath to 17th century Bilsborrow Hall Farm. Go through the farmyard, taking care to shut all the gates, and out to Bilsborrow Lane. Turn right and go down over the bridge. Pause for views over Beacon Fell, Fairsnape and Bleasdale Moors. Continue along the pavement, passing an old Wesleyan Methodist Chapel. It is claimed that earthenware pots were once made here and land by the chapel was quarried for clay to produce the pots. Keep ahead over Bilsborrow Lane Bridge, crossing the Preston to Lancaster railway. Turn right into Church Lane and go past St Hilda's Church to the A6. Turn right, cross over and continue for a short distance. Turn left into Myerscough Hall Drive and cross the canal bridge (number 45). Go down the steps and follow the towpath back along the Lancaster Canal to the pub.

OWD NELL'S TAVERN, Guy's Thatched Hamlet, Canal Side BILSBORROW Nr Garstang PR3 0RS
Tel: 01995 640010
Directions: On A6 between Barton Bilsborrow follow brown tourist sign into St Michaels Road.
A busy, thatched pub tucked away in a hamlet beside the Lancaster Canal. A wide selection of guest ales and good foodinternational foof suitable for the whole family.
Open: 11-11
Bar Meals: 11-10.30
Children welcome and dogs allowed. Garden and parking available.

Distance: 4 miles (6.4km)
Map: OS Landranger 102
Terrain: Attractive stretches of canal and river. Pleasant farmland and an historic village
Paths: Towpath, pavement, field paths, roads and tracks
Gradient: No steep hills

Walk submitted and checked by Owd Nell's Tavern, Bilsborrow

BROOKHOUSE
Map 08 SD56

Black Bull Inn
LA2 9JP ☎ 01524 770329
Dir: Leave M6 at Juct 34, take A683 to Kirby Lonsdale for 2.5 M, at mini Rdbt turn R for 0.75 M pub is located on R
16th-century coaching inn situated in a picture postcard village. Originally made up of three cottages, the inn was also used as a local courthouse in the 1820s. Lots of old beams and local atmosphere.
OPEN: 12-3 6-11 **BAR MEALS:** Lunch served: all week Dinner served: all week 12-2 6-9 Av main course £5 **RESTAURANT:** Lunch served: all week Dinner served: all week 12-2 6-9 Av 3 course à la carte £12.50 **FACILITIES:** Children welcome Dogs allowed No credit cards

BURNLEY
Map 08 SD83

The Ram 🌾 ♀ NEW
399 Burnley Rd, Cliviger ☎ 01282 418921
In the shadow of Thievely Peak, the pub dates back to 1630. The food is best described as leaning towards traditional home-style cooking with a contemporary twist. Best illustrated by its Vintage Collection platter of assorted salmon, cheese and salad tasters or baby leek and Caerphilly sausage plate with onion gravy and deep-fried parsnips. Also traditional Sunday roasts and lemon chicken with parsley butter from the main menu.
OPEN: 11-11 **BAR MEALS:** Lunch served: all week Dinner served: all week 12-10 Av main course £6.95
BREWERY/COMPANY: Vintage Inns **FACILITIES:** Garden: Large patio area with amazing views

CARNFORTH
Map 08 SD47

Dutton Arms ♀
Station Ln, Burton LA6 1HR ☎ 01524 781225 ▯ 01524 782662
Dir: from M6 take A6 signed Milnthorpe (Kendal), 3m before Milnthorpe turn R signed Burton/Holme
Close to a host of tourist attractions, including Morecambe Bay, the Lancashire Canal and the Northern Yorkshire Dales, the Dutton Arms boasts a conservatory area that provides access to the pub's colourful gardens. Food is expertly prepared from fresh ingredients, with confit of duck, mussels marinière, and paupiette of turkey, plus specials like boozy beef in beer, and crispy duck legs in black bean sauce.
OPEN: 10-3.30 6-11 **BAR MEALS:** Lunch served: all week Dinner served: all week 11-2.30 6-9.30 Av main course £8
RESTAURANT: Lunch served: all week Dinner served: all week 11-2.30 6-9.30 Av 3 course à la carte £8 **BREWERY/COMPANY:** Free House
PRINCIPAL BEERS: Interbrew Boddingtons, Greene King Old Speckled Hen, Dent, Black Sheep Best. **FACILITIES:** Children welcome Garden: Food served outside Dogs allowed (water) **NOTES:** Parking 30
ROOMS: 4 bedrooms 4 en suite from s£19.80 d£19.80

CHIPPING
Map 08 SD64

Dog & Partridge
Hesketh Ln PR3 2TH ☎ 01995 61201 ▯ 01995 61446
Dating back to 1515, this comfortably modernised rural inn in the Ribble Valley enjoys wonderful views of the surrounding fells. The next door barn has been converted into an additional dining area, and the emphasis is on home-made food using local produce. Many dishes on the dinner carte and fixed-price lunch menu are available as bar snacks: roast duckling, steak and kidney pie, grilled pork chops, and leek and mushroom crumble.
OPEN: 11.45-3 6.45-11 **BAR MEALS:** Lunch served: all week 12-1.45 Av main course £9 **RESTAURANT:** Lunch served: all week Dinner served: all week 12-1.30 7-9 Av 3 course à la carte £17
BREWERY/COMPANY: Free House **PRINCIPAL BEERS:** Tetleys.
FACILITIES: Children welcome **NOTES:** Parking 30

CLITHEROE
Map 08 SO74

Pick of the Pubs

Assheton Arms 🌾 ♀
Downham BB7 4BJ ☎ 01200 441227 ▯ 01200 440581
e-mail: asshetonarms@aol.com
Dir: From A59 take Chatburn turn. In Chatburn follow signs for Downham
Standing at the head of the village by the Norman church and surrounded by picturesque cottages, the Assheton Arms retains a cheerfully warm traditional air. It is named after Lord Clitheroe's family who own the whole village. A single bar and sectioned rooms house an array of solid oak tables, wing-back settees, window seats, an original stone fireplace, and a large blackboard listing the interesting range of daily dishes available. Typical choices may include English lobster thermidor, pan-fried monkfish, grilled red sea bream with caper sauce or Espetada, a Portuguese kebab of beef, pork and mutton. A long menu of traditional pub favourites includes grills, peppered fillet steak, chicken and mushroom pie, and cauliflower and mushroom provençale. Well placed for a wild moorland walk up Pendle Hill which looms high above the village.
OPEN: 12-3 7-11 (summer Sun open all day) Closed: 1st wk in Jan **BAR MEALS:** Lunch served: all week Dinner served: all week 12-2 7-10 Av main course £9.50
BREWERY/COMPANY: Whitbread
PRINCIPAL BEERS: Castle Eden Ale, Interbrew Boddingtons Bitter. **FACILITIES:** Children welcome Patio, food served outside Dogs allowed **NOTES:** Parking 12

The Shireburn Arms ★ ★ ♀ NEW
Whalley Rd, Hurst Green BB7 9QJ
☎ 01254 826518 ▯ 01254 826208
e-mail: sales@shireburn-hotel.co.uk
Dir: Telephone for directions

Once frequented by J R R Tolkien, the Shireburn stands in the heart of the village which some say was the inspiration for Tolkien's Hobbiton. Certainly the blazing fires, low beams and real ales of this 17th-century inn do little to dispel the rumour. The menu offers all the usual favourites (soup, ploughman's and things with chips) alongside a few less familiar dishes such as supreme of chicken oriental or salmon cummerbach.
OPEN: 11-11 **BAR MEALS:** Lunch served: all week Dinner served: all week 12-2 5.30-9.30 Av main course £6 **RESTAURANT:** Lunch served: all week Dinner served: all week 12-2 5.30-9.30 Av 3 course à la carte £15 Av 4 course fixed price £13.50
BREWERY/COMPANY: Free House **PRINCIPAL BEERS:** Scottish Courage Theakstons Best Bitter, Mild & Guest Cask Ales.
FACILITIES: Children welcome Garden: Landscaped with view across the Ribble Valley Dogs allowed **NOTES:** Parking 100
ROOMS: 18 bedrooms 18 en suite from s£45 d£70

England

DARWEN
Map 08 SD62

Old Rosins Inn ★ ★ 🌑
Treacle Row, Pickup Bank, Hoddlesden BB3 3QD
☎ 01254 771264
Dir: M65 J5, follow signs for Haslingdon then R after 2m signed Egworth. 0.5m R & continue for 0.5m
The original inn, set in the heart of the Lancashire Moors, has been extended to provide a variety of facilities. A typical menu includes halibut in lemon sauce, steak and ale pie, spinach tortellini, salmon with a herb crust, lasagne, lamb Jennings, cod in lemon and prawn butter, and mussels in cream and white wine.
OPEN: 11–11 (Sun 12–10.30) **BAR MEALS:** Lunch served: all week Dinner served: all week 11.30–10 5.30–9.30 Av main course £5.95
RESTAURANT: Lunch served: all week Dinner served: all week 6.30–10.30 Av 3 course à la carte £14.95 Av 4 course fixed price £15
BREWERY/COMPANY: Jennings **PRINCIPAL BEERS:** Jennings Bitter & Cumberland Ale , Sneck Lifter. **FACILITIES:** Children welcome Garden: Lawns and shrubbery, food served outdoors Dogs allowed (manager's discretion only) **NOTES:** Parking 200
ROOMS: 15 bedrooms 15 en suite from s£52.50 d£52.50

EDGWORTH
Map 08 SD71

Strawberry Duck Hotel 🌑 NEW
Overshores Rd, Turton BL7 0LU ☎ 01204 512013
Surrounded by reservoirs and beautiful countryside, this cosy country pub is a favourite haunt of real ale lovers. The traditional bar also serves decent food, from platters of salad with choice of topping (beef, ham, cheese) to various grills and lamb Devonshire, chicken Stilton with asparagus, and Drunken Bullock (beef cooked slowly in Taylor's Landlord). There are also a few bedrooms with four-poster beds.
OPEN: 12–11 (Sun 12–10.30, 12pm bank holidays)
BAR MEALS: Lunch served: all week Dinner served: all week 12–9.30 Av main course £6 **RESTAURANT:** Lunch served: all week Dinner served: all week 12–9.30 Av 3 course à la carte £15
BREWERY/COMPANY: Free House **PRINCIPAL BEERS:** Taylors Landlord, Pendle Witches Brew, Black Sheep, Bank Top various.
FACILITIES: Children welcome Garden: Food served outside. Patio area Dogs allowed In the garden & overnight rooms
NOTES: Parking 30 **ROOMS:** 4 bedrooms 4 en suite

FENCE
Map 08 SD83

Fence Gate Inn & Banqueting Centre
Wheatley Lane Rd BB12 9EE ☎ 01282 618101 📠 01282 615432
Dir: From M65 L 1.5m, set back on R opposite T-junction for Burnley

This substantial inn was originally a collection point for cotton delivered by barge and distributed to surrounding cottages to be spun into cloth. Wide-ranging menus are offered in the Topiary Brasserie.

continued

OPEN: 12–11 **BAR MEALS:** All week 12–2.30 6.30–9.30 Av main course £5 **RESTAURANT:** All week 12–2.30 6.30–9.30 Av 3 course £19 **BREWERY/COMPANY:** Free House
PRINCIPAL BEERS: Theakston, Directors **FACILITIES:** Children welcome Garden: Food served outside Dogs allowed
NOTES: Parking 100

FORTON
Map 08 SD45

Pick of the Pubs

The Bay Horse Inn 🌑 ♀
LA2 0HR ☎ 01524 791204 📠 01524 791204
e-mail: cwilki5769@aol.com
Dir: 1 M S off Junct 33 of M6
Bay Horse is a name given to this picturesque area to the south of Lancaster, which stretches to Cockerham Sands and the Lune estuary. The building dates back to the early 17th century and was originally a farmhouse, and the old barn has been converted to provide a function room. It is a traditional local with roughcast walls, bay windows and a small dining room, but these days serves food to lords, sirs and famous footballers. The inn specialises in simple, fresh and imaginative food from a chef who is wholly self-taught (now a member of the Master Chefs of Great Britain), and whose shopping policy reveals his total commitment. Start with a local delicacy, potted Morecambe Bay shrimps, and move on to grilled fillets of brill with sun-blush tomatoes, potato purée and dill butter, or shank of lamb with goats' cheese mash and ale and thyme sauce.
OPEN: 12–3 6.30–11 (Sun 12–5, 8–10.30) **BAR MEALS:** Lunch served: Tue-Sun 12–2 Dinner served: Tue-Sat 7–9.30 Av main course £11.95 **RESTAURANT:** Lunch served: Tue-Sun 12–2 Dinner served: Tue-Sat 7–9.30 Av 3 course à la carte £23 Av 3 course fixed price £25 **PRINCIPAL BEERS:** Wadworth 6X, Everards Tiger. **FACILITIES:** Children welcome Garden: Food served outdoors **NOTES:** Parking 30

GALGATE
Map 08 SD45

The Stork Hotel
Conder Green LA2 0AN ☎ 01524 751234 📠 01524 752660
Dir: M6 J33 take A6 north. At Galgate turn L & next L to Conder Green
Sprawling white-painted coaching inn on the banks of the Conder Estuary, distinguished by its colourful window boxes. The quaint sea port of Glasson Dock, and the Lancashire Coastal Way are close by, and the Lake District is easily accessible. A lengthy menu covers bar snacks like toasted sandwiches, grills and seafood dishes, and there's a daily-changing specials list including game casserole, halibut steak, Barbary duck breast, and beef Stroganoff. En suite bedrooms.
OPEN: 11–11 (Sun 12–10.30) Closed: 25 Dec **BAR MEALS:** Lunch served: all week Dinner served: all week 12–2.30 6.30–9 Av main course £6 **RESTAURANT:** Lunch served: all week Dinner served: all week 12–2.30 6.30–9 Av 3 course à la carte £12
BREWERY/COMPANY: Free House **PRINCIPAL BEERS:** Interbrew Boddingtons Bitter. **FACILITIES:** Children welcome Garden: Patio, food served outside Dogs allowed **NOTES:** Parking 30 **ROOMS:** 9 bedrooms 9 en suite from s£27 d£44

GARSTANG
Map 08 SD44

Th'Owd Tithebarn
Church St PR3 1PA ☎ 01995 604486
Set on the canal bank and adorned inside with antique farming memorabilia. Open all day.

GOOSNARGH
Map 08 SD53

The Bushell's Arms 🛏
Church Ln PR3 2BH ☎ 01772 865235 📠 01772 865235
A major refurbishment has made this Georgian village pub
more family friendly. The new owners have separated the
restaurant from the bar area, and regular themed nights, eg
Chinese banquet or Indian curry night, focus on the good
home cooking. Create your own stir-fry from a 'rock the wok'
blackboard, plus duck in hoi sin sauce, Cajun chicken, lasagne,
and home-made pies (steak and kidney, chicken and
mushroom), with typical bar snacks.
OPEN: 12-3 6-11 **BAR MEALS:** Lunch served: all week Dinner
served: all week 12-2 6-9.30 Av main course £6.50
RESTAURANT: Lunch served: all week Dinner served: all week 12-2
6-9.30 **BREWERY/COMPANY:** Whitbread
PRINCIPAL BEERS: Timothy Taylor Landlord, Interbrew
Boddingtons Bitter. **FACILITIES:** Children welcome Garden: lawned
with childrens play area **NOTES:** Parking 10

Ye Horns Inn 🛏
Horns Ln PR3 2FJ ☎ 01772 865230 📠 01772 864299
e-mail: info@yehornsinn.co.uk
Dir: *From M6 J32 take A6 N. At traffic lights turn R onto B5269. In
Goosnargh follow Inn signs*
An 18th-century, black and white coaching inn with a patio
and outdoor seating area. Located in a peaceful country
setting it has retained much of its original character. The
family of the present owners have been here for 50 years, and
are in their third generation of ownership. The food on offer
includes fillet of fresh salmon, steak and kidney pie,
mushroom Stroganoff, roast Goosnargh duckling, grilled
gammon steak, and fresh battered cod.
OPEN: 11.30-3 (ex Mon) 6-11 **BAR MEALS:** Lunch served:
Tue-Sun Dinner served: all week 12-2 7-9.15 Av main course £8
RESTAURANT: Lunch served: Tue-Sun Dinner served: all week 12-2
7-9.15 Av 3 course à la carte £16 **BREWERY/COMPANY:** Free
House **PRINCIPAL BEERS:** No real ale. **FACILITIES:** Children
welcome Garden: Food served outside. Large patio area Dogs
allowed (in the garden only) **NOTES:** Parking 70
ROOMS: 6 bedrooms 6 en suite from s£55 d£75

HASLINGDEN
Map 08 SD72

Farmers Glory 🛏
Roundhill Rd BB4 5TU ☎ 01706 215748 📠 01706 215748
Dir: *7 miles equidistant from Blackburn, Burnley and Bury, 1/2m from M66*
Stone-built 350-year-old pub situated high above Haslingden
on the edge of the Pennines. Formerly a coaching inn on the
ancient route to Whalley Abbey, it now offers locals and
modern A667 travellers a wide-ranging traditional pub menu
of steaks, roasts, seafood, pizzas, pasta and sandwiches. Live
folk music every Wednesday and a large beer garden.
OPEN: 12-3 7-11.30 **BAR MEALS:** 12-2.30 7-9.30
RESTAURANT: 12-2.30 7-9.30 **BREWERY/COMPANY:** Pubmaster
PRINCIPAL BEERS: Carlsberg-Tetley Tetley Bitter, Marston's Pedigree,
Greene King IPA. **FACILITIES:** Children welcome Garden:
NOTES: Parking 60

HESKIN GREEN
Map 08 SD51

Farmers Arms 🛏
85 Wood Ln PR7 5NP ☎ 01257 451276 📠 01257 453958
e-mail: andy@farmersarms.co.uk
Dir: *On B5250 between M6 & Eccleston*
Long, creeper-covered country inn with two cosy bars decorated
in old pictures and farming memorabilia. Once known as the
Pleasant Retreat, this is a family-run pub proud to offer a warm

continued

welcome. Typical dishes include steak pie, fresh salmon with
prawns and mushroom, halibut, rack of lamb and chicken curry.
OPEN: 12-11 **BAR MEALS:** Lunch served: all week Dinner served:
all week 12-9.30 **RESTAURANT:** Lunch served: all week Dinner
served: all week 12-9.30 **PRINCIPAL BEERS:** Timothy Taylor
Landlord, Castle Eden Ale, Interbrew Flowers IPA & Boddingtons,
Carlsberg-Tetley Tetely Bitter. **FACILITIES:** Children welcome Garden:
Dogs allowed **NOTES:** Parking 50 **ROOMS:** 5 bedrooms 5 en suite

HEST BANK
Map 08 SD46

Hest Bank Hotel 🛏
2 Hest Bank Ln LA2 6DN ☎ 01524 824339 📠 01524 824948
e-mail: hestbankhotel@hotmail.com
Dir: *From Lancaster take A6 N, after 2m L to Hest Bank*
Beside the Lancaster Canal, this fine old inn was originally a
staging post for coaches traversing Morecambe Bay. Freshly
produced food relies wherever possible on local meat and fish
suppliers, who receive honourable mention on the menu. Seasonal
specials list the likes of Jalapeño peppers with tomato relish and
marinated herrings, followed by chargrilled sea bass with garlic
prawns and lamb steak with cranberry and orange glaze.
OPEN: 11.30-11 (Sun 12-10.30) **BAR MEALS:** Lunch served: all
week Dinner served: all week 12-9 Av main course £5.50
BREWERY/COMPANY: Inn Partnership
PRINCIPAL BEERS: Interbrew Boddingtons,Cains Bitter, Timothy
Taylor Landlord. **FACILITIES:** Garden: Patio, food served outside
NOTES: Parking 20

MERECLOUGH
Map 09 SD83

Kettledrum Inn & Restaurant
302 Red Lees Rd BB10 4RG ☎ 01282 424591 📠 01282 424591
Dir: *from Burnley town centre, past Burnley FC, 2 1/2m, 1st pub on L*
Inviting well-kept country inn with superb views of the famous
Pendle Hills. Good range of traditional pub food.

PARBOLD
Map 08 SD41

Pick of the Pubs

The Eagle & Child 🛏 ♇
Maltkiln Ln L40 3SG ☎ 01257 462297 📠 01257 464718
Dir: *From M6 J27 to Parbold. At bottom of Parbold Hill turn R on
B5246 to Hilldale. Then 1st L to Bispham Green*

A dining-pub where the emphasis is firmly placed on
good ales and cider, a daily-changing menu of freshly
cooked food, and a peaceful atmosphere conducive to
conversation (no juke boxes or fruit machines). The
interior is characterised by flagged floors, coir matting,
oak settles, antique furniture and old prints, and includes
a no-smoking room. Seven ever-changing real ales are
served, and an interesting selection of wines. Options

continued

PARBOLD continued

from the daily menu range from salads and snacks – chargrilled tuna niçoise, chicken pannini – to full meals with dishes like baked halibut troncetta with saffron potatoes and sun-dried tomato sauce, and mini fillet of beef Wellington with caramelised shallots and bordelaise sauce. Perennially popular special events include an annual beer festival in May. The pub also has its own bowling green.
OPEN: 12–3 5.30–11 **BAR MEALS:** Lunch served: all week Dinner served: all week 12–2 6–8.30 Av main course £9
RESTAURANT: Lunch served: all week Dinner served: all week 12–2 6–8.30 Av 3 course à la carte £16 **BREWERY/COMPANY:** Free House **PRINCIPAL BEERS:** Moorhouses Black Cat, Thwaites Bitter, 5 changing guest beers. **FACILITIES:** Children welcome Garden: Food served outside **NOTES:** Parking 50

PRESTON   Map 08 SD52

Pick of the Pubs

Cartford Country Inn & Hotel 🐾 ♀
Little Eccleston PR3 0YP ☎ 01995 670166 📠 01995 671785
In a picturesque area, this pleasantly rambling old inn sits beside a toll bridge over the tidal River Wyle. The inn is laid out on three levels, with dining in two areas enhanced by plenty of oak beams and dried flowers. An open log fire adds to the convivial atmosphere, and visitors can play pool, darts and dominoes whilst enjoying one of seven guest ales, or a pint of the home-brewed Harts. There's a good range of food on the bar menu, from sandwiches to pizzas, and from jacket potatoes to dishes like Cumberland sausage with egg, chilli con carne, and lasagne; various specials might include Caribbean chicken, and lamb Henry. Meals can also be taken outside overlooking the river, and there is direct access to some lovely country and riverside walks, as well as a mile and a half of fishing rights.
OPEN: 12–3 7–11 (Open 6.30 in summer) (Sun 12–10.30)
BAR MEALS: Lunch served: all week Dinner served: all week 12–2 6.30–9.30 Av main course £5.50 **BREWERY/COMPANY:** Free House **PRINCIPAL BEERS:** Hart Beers, London Pride, Moorhouse, Guest ales. **FACILITIES:** Children welcome Food served outside. Benches overlook river Dogs allowed **NOTES:** Parking 60
ROOMS: 6 bedrooms 6 en suite from s£36.95 d£48.95

RIBCHESTER   Map 08 SD63

The White Bull 🐾
Church St PR3 3XP ☎ 01254 878303
Partly on the site of an old Roman town, a 17th-century, Grade II listed courthouse abounding in antiquity; the former Roman bathhouse can be seen from the beer garden. Cask beers in the lounge and bars accompany a comprehensive selection of traditional pub food and grills supplemented by regularly changed specials. Look here for filo parcels of black pudding and onion, salmon supreme with black bream and sherry sauce and home-made cheesecake.
OPEN: 11.30–3 6.30–11 (Sun 12–10.30; food 12–8)
BAR MEALS: Lunch served: all week 11.30–2 Dinner served: Tue–Sun 6.30–9.30 Av main course £6.50 **RESTAURANT:** Lunch served: all week 11.30–2 Dinner served: Tue–Sun 6.30–9.30 Av 3 course à la carte £9.50 **PRINCIPAL BEERS:** Interbrew Boddingtons Bitter, Timothy Taylor Landlord, Black Sheep Best, Coach House Honeypot Bitter. **FACILITIES:** Children welcome Garden: Food served outdoors **NOTES:** Parking 14 **ROOMS:** 3 bedrooms 3 en suite from s£25 d£30

SAWLEY   Map 08 SD74

The Spread Eagle ♀
BB7 4NH ☎ 01200 441202 📠 01200 441973
Dir: N on A59 to Skipton, 3m N of Clitheroe
Charting its history back to a mention in records of the 16th century, this inn at the heart of the Forest of Bowland has a long history. Large picture windows in the smart, split-level riverside restaurant give sweeping views over the River Ribble and the Ribble Valley. Special events include dinner dances and regular wine tastings enlivened by the presence of their local wine merchant.
OPEN: 11–11 (Sun 12–3 only) **BAR MEALS:** 12–2 6–9
RESTAURANT: Lunch served: Tue–Sun Dinner served: Tue–Sun 12–2 6–9 Av 3 course à la carte £19.25 Av 3 course fixed price £10.95
BREWERY/COMPANY: Free House **FACILITIES:** Children welcome Garden: Beer garden, patio, food served outdoors **NOTES:** Parking 50

SLAIDBURN   Map 08 SD75

Hark to Bounty Inn
Townend BB7 3EP ☎ 01200 446246 📠 01200 446361
e-mail: manager@hark-to-bounty.co.uk
Dir: From M6 J31 take A59 to Clitheroe then B6478, through Waddington and Newton and on to Slaidburn
In the Trough of Bowland, a 13th-century stone-built inn, named after a long-past village squire's dog, Bounty, whose loud bark could be heard above the baying of the local pack. The inn also contains a remarkable courtroom, still in use up to 1937. Today's kitchen output remains mostly traditional, with bread baked daily on the premises along with up-to-date versions of Lancashire black pudding with grain mustard sauce, gargantuan steak and kidney pie or home-made fishcakes with tomato and basil sauce.
OPEN: 11–11 **BAR MEALS:** Lunch served: all week Dinner served: all week 12–2 6–9 Av main course £7.50 **RESTAURANT:** Lunch served: all week Dinner served: all week 12–2 6–9 Av 3 course à la carte £15
BREWERY/COMPANY: Scottish Courage
PRINCIPAL BEERS: Theakston Old Peculier, Mild & Bitter, Scottish Courage Courage Directors. **FACILITIES:** Children welcome Children's licence Garden: Food served outside Dogs allowed **NOTES:** Parking 25 **ROOMS:** 9 bedrooms 9 en suite from s£29.50 d£54.50

WHALLEY   Map 08 SD73

Freemasons Arms 🐾 ♀
8 Vicarage Fold, Wiswell BB7 9DF ☎ 01254 822218
e-mail: freemasons@wiswell.co.uk
A traditional country dining pub in the quiet village of Wiswell. Numerous walks in the area take in some stunning views at the heart of the Ribble Valley. Formerly housing the monks from nearby Whalley Abbey, it was converted into a pub some four centuries ago and hosted secret freemasons' meetings – hence its 'new' name. The Livesey family have enhanced its fine reputation for good ales and food both in the spacious bar area, the old tap room and in a more refined upstairs dining room.
OPEN: 12–3 6.30–12 (closed Mon–Tue) Closed: 25–26 Dec, 1–2 Jan
BAR MEALS: 12–2 6.30–9.30 **RESTAURANT:** Lunch served: Wed–Sun Dinner served: Wed–Sun 12–2 6.30–9.30 Av 3 course à la carte £16.95
BREWERY/COMPANY: Free House **PRINCIPAL BEERS:** Jennings Bitter & Cumberland Ale, Black Sheep Best.

WHITEWELL   Map 08 SD64

Pick of the Pubs

The Inn At Whitewell ♦♦♦♦ ♀
Forest of Bowland BB7 3AT ☎ 01200 448222 📠 01200 448298
Dir: Take B6243 and follow signs for Whitewell
A slightly eccentric inn, packed with a haphazard arrangement of furnishings and bric-a-brac, that stands on

continued

the east bank of the River Hodder at the heart of the Forest of Bowland. Parts of the building date back to the 1300s, when it would have been the forest keeper's house; nonetheless today's bedroom accommodation is bang up-to-date. The comprehensive bar lunch and supper menus are supplemented by daily specials that might include the ever-popular fisherman's pie, grilled black pudding with poached pear and Cumberland sausages with champ. There are also substantial sandwiches at lunchtime, traditional home-made puddings and fine hand-made cheeses at any time. A la carte dining at night in a relaxing atmosphere where no-one stands on ceremony - a fine old inn.

OPEN: 11–3 6–11 **BAR MEALS:** Lunch served: all week Dinner served: all week 12–2 7.30–9.30 Av main course £9
RESTAURANT: Dinner served: all week 7.30–9.30 Av 3 course à la carte £24.50 **BREWERY/COMPANY:** Free House
PRINCIPAL BEERS: Marston's Pedigree, Interbrew Boddingtons Bitter. **FACILITIES:** Children welcome Garden: Overlooking the river Dogs allowed **NOTES:** Parking 50
ROOMS: 17 bedrooms 17 en suite from s£59 d£83

WREA GREEN   Map 08 SD33

The Grapes Hotel
Station Rd PR4 2PH ☎ 01772 682927 📠 01772 687304
Dir: From M55 J3 follow signs for Kirkham then Wrea Green
Situated in the centre of the village opposite the green and duck pond. One menu caters for everybody, offering a selection of snacks and traditional pub meals.

WRIGHTINGTON   Map 08 SD51

Pick of the Pubs

The Mulberry Tree ⊛⊛ 🐑 ♈
WN6 9SE ☎ 01257 451400 📠 01257 451400
Dir: Juct 27 off M6 turn into Mossy Lea Road 2 M on the right
Under the tutelage of former Roux Brothers' head chef, Mark Prescott, the former Scarisbrick Arms continues to go from strength to strength. A growing number of locals and discerning diners feel much at home in its clean, airy ambience whilst choosing from a veritable feast of options. Starters on the bar menu include, perhaps, curried parsnip soup and chicken liver parfait with fig chutney, followed by seared salmon with teriyaki, penne pasta with asparagus and pesto and rib-eye steak with hand-cut chips. More complex dishes feature on the specials list, such as warm terrine of foie gras and confit duck, followed by lobster with cream champagne sauce, pan-fried skate wing with capers and brown shrimps or slow-roasted belly pork. These are accompanied by a good selection of house wines. In addition there are popular multi-choice Sunday lunches at fixed prices.
OPEN: 12–3 6–11 Closed: 26 Dec, 1 Jan **BAR MEALS:** Lunch served: Tue–Sun Dinner served: Tue–Sun 12–2 6–9 Av main course £10 **RESTAURANT:** Lunch served: all week Dinner served: all week 12–2 6–10 Av 3 course à la carte £20
BREWERY/COMPANY: Free House
PRINCIPAL BEERS: Interbrew Flowers IPA,.
FACILITIES: Children welcome Tables outside, patio, food served outdoors **NOTES:** Parking 100

YEALAND CONYERS   Map 08 SD57

The New Inn
40 Yealand Rd LA5 9SJ ☎ 01524 732938
e-mail: newinn.yealand@virgin.net
Dir: Join A6 between Carnforth & Milnthorpe, 3m then L after Yealand Conyers sign, .25m to pub

Built in the 1600s, this ivy-clad building is situated in an Area of Outstanding Natural Beauty close to Leighton Moss Nature Reserve. A wide range of home-cooked food is offered either in the oak-beamed bar or non-smoking dining room. Seasonal local produce features in leek, sweetcorn, mushroom and Parmesan risotto and garlic mushrooms topped with Lancashire cheese; followed by beef in red wine and cask ale, bacon and shallot stuffing and sirloin or fillet steaks with classical sauces of choice.
OPEN: 11–11 (Sun 12–10.30) **BAR MEALS:** Lunch served: all week Dinner served: all week 11.30–9.30 Av main course £8
RESTAURANT: Lunch served: all week Dinner served: all week 11.30–9.30 Av 3 course à la carte £16
BREWERY/COMPANY: Frederic Robinson
PRINCIPAL BEERS: Hartleys XB,. **FACILITIES:** Children welcome Garden: Food served outside Dogs allowed (water)
NOTES: Parking 50

Strange Games
Competitive and ingenuity have thrown up a rich variety of pub games besides the best-known ones, from lawn billiards to maggot racing to clay pipe smoking contests, where the object is to keep a pipeful of tobacco alight longest. Cribbage and other once popular card games are not seen so often nowadays, but bagatelle is alive and well in Chester and Coventry. In Knur and Spell up North the players hit a small ball (the knur) as far as possible with a bat. Bat and Trap, an odd variety of cricket, has a long history going back at least to the 16th century in Kent. In Sussex the game of Toad in the Hole involves pitching flat discs into a hole in a table and in Lincolnshire they throw pennies into a hole and call it gnurdling. For all the video games and one-arm bandits, older and more convivial pastimes are still alive in British pubs.

England

LEICESTERSHIRE

CASTLE DONINGTON   Map 09 SK42

Pick of the Pubs

The Nag's Head 🐾 ♀
Hilltop DE74 2PR ☎ 01332 850652

Originally four cottages, the Nag's Head spread out from the middle cottage until it had taken over all four after World War II. Inside the plain, whitewashed building are low beamed ceilings, open coal fires and a friendly atmosphere. The pub is ideal for those visiting the East Midlands airport or the nearby motor racing circuit. There's a bistro feel to the large, well-decorated dining room, with its colour-washed walls and plain scrubbed tables. The extensive menu features an upmarket range of starters and snacks, including grilled goats' cheese, seared scallops with balsamic vinegar, and bacon and poached egg salad. Unusual and inventive dishes like blackened swordfish with crème fraîche and lime, sliced beef fillet in Cajun sauce with tsatziki dressing, or aubergine, black olive and polenta layer with sun-dried tomato dressing. Traditional home made puddings round off the menu.
OPEN: 11.30-2.30 5.30-11 (Sun 12-3, 7-10.30)
BAR MEALS: Lunch served: Mon-Sat Dinner served: Mon-Sat 12-2 5.30-9.30 Av main course £14 **RESTAURANT:** Lunch served: Mon-Sat Dinner served: Mon-Sat 12-2 5.30-9.30 Av 3 course à la carte £25 **PRINCIPAL BEERS:** Bank's Bitter, Marston's Pedigree, Mansfield Riding Bitter.
FACILITIES: Garden: Food served outdoors, patio Dogs allowed **NOTES:** Parking 20

CROXTON KERRIAL   Map 09 SK82

Peacock Inn 🐾 ♀
1 School Ln NG32 1QR ☎ 01476 870324 🖷 01476 870171
e-mail: peacockcroxton@globalnet.co.uk
Dir: Situated on A607, 3M from Junct with A1
A 300-year-old inn, set on the edge of the Vale of Belvoir with its famous castle just a mile away. Noted for its beautiful garden and views, the pub is popular with walkers, anglers and equestrians, and sports eight luxury bedrooms. Everything is prepared on the premises from fresh, local ingredients providing trendy bar food and speciality dishes such as mushroom goulash, butter-glazed Dover sole and Scottish sirloin steak. Celebrated Sunday roasts.

continued

OPEN: 12-3.30 6-11 **BAR MEALS:** Lunch served: all week Dinner served: all week 12-3.30 6.30-10 Av main course £7.50
RESTAURANT: Lunch served: all week Dinner served: all week 12-3.30 6.30-10 Av 3 course à la carte £22 Av 3 course fixed price £22
BREWERY/COMPANY: Free House **PRINCIPAL BEERS:** Scottish Courage John Smith's, Timothy Taylor Landlord plus guest beers.
FACILITIES: Children welcome Garden: Beautiful views, food served outside Dogs allowed (water) **NOTES:** Parking 40
ROOMS: 8 bedrooms 8 en suite from s£45 d£60

EAST LANGTON   Map 06 SP79

Pick of the Pubs

The Bell Inn ♀
Main St LE16 7TW ☎ 01858 545278 🖷 01858 545748
e-mail: achapman@thebellinn.co.uk

Tucked away in the a quiet village, this listed inn was built in the 16th century, and boasts a pretty walled garden, low beams and an open log fire. The attractive creeper-clad inn has a cosy atmosphere, and comfy en suite accommodation for those wishing to extend their stay. The Langton micro-brewery operates from outbuildings, and produces two regular brews as well as seasonal ales; the wine cellar also offers some notable wines by the bottle or glass. To match these fine alcoholic beverages is a wide range of food from starters and light bites to more hearty fare: warm pigeon and smoked bacon salad, vegetable samosas, and tortilla chicken wraps are good on their own or followed by faggots in onion gravy, seasonal sausages, boeuf bourguignon, or fish and sweetcorn pie.
OPEN: 11.30-2.30 7-11 Closed: Dec 25 **BAR MEALS:** Lunch served: all week Dinner served: all week 12-2 7-10 Av main course £9.10 **BREWERY/COMPANY:** Free House
PRINCIPAL BEERS: Greene King IPA & Abbot Ale, Langton Bowler Strong Ale & Caudle Bitter. **FACILITIES:** Children welcome Garden: Beer garden, food served outdoors Dogs allowed **NOTES:** Parking 20 **ROOMS:** 2 bedrooms 2 en suite from s£39.50 d£55

PUB WALK

Somerby
The Stilton Cheese Inn

THE STILTON CHEESE INN
High Street SOMERBY
LE14 2QB
Tel: 01664 454394
Directions: On main road through Somerby village. At the heart of a working village in beautiful countryside, this sandstone building dates from the 16th century. The same menus service both bar and restaurant, with good selections to be found on the specials boards.
Open: 12–3 6–11
Bar Meals: 12–2 6–9
Children welcome. Garden and parking available.

A very pleasant ramble exploring unspoiled countryside around the village of Somerby.

On leaving the pub turn right down the High Street, taking the first right into Manor Lane. At the bottom of the lane go through the gate ahead and cross the field to the far side. Go through the gate and head down the next field, keeping the hedge on your left. Make for a small gate at the bottom still keeping the hedge on your left. Pass through the next gate and follow the well-used path to the next gate, looking out for a footbridge crossing a stream. Cross it and go through a gate, following the path to the right. Look for a large gap in the hedge, pass through it and veer left. Keep along the left boundary of three fields until you reach the lane. Turn right and follow it through two gates. Turn right after the second gate and follow the lane uphill, back towards Somerby. Pass through an avenue of chestnut trees and at the junction,

turn right and return to the Stilton Cheese which will be found about 150 yards (137m) along the road. If time allows, you may like to look around the village of Somerby. During World War II paratroopers were billeted here prior to 'Operation Market Garden,' the disastrous parachute drop into the Netherlands in 1944. It was an overly-ambitious attempt to end the war swiftly by invading eastern Holland with 35,000 airborne troops in a desperate bid to push the Nazis back into Germany. For the plan to succeed, the Allies needed to capture five vital bridges and the roads linking them then Allied tanks could have penetrated Germany's industrial Ruhr. Field Marshal Montgomery correctly called it 'a bridge too far'. Bad-timing and poor planning resulted in thousands of men paying the ultimate price. Part of Arnhem Bridge is seen in the village hall and the operation is commemorated in a stained glass window in the church.

Distance: 4 miles (6.4km)
Map: OS Landranger 129 & 141
Terrain: Typical English farmland and pasture
Paths: Mainly waymarked paths and country lanes
Gradient: Some gentle climbing

Walk submitted and checked by The Stilton Cheese Inn, Somerby

England

FLECKNEY
Map 06 SP69

The Old Crown ♀
High St LE8 8AJ ☎ 0116 2402223
e-mail: old-crown-inn@fleckney7.freeserve.co.uk

Close to the Grand Union Canal and Saddington Tunnel, a traditional village pub that is especially welcoming to hiking groups and families. Noted for good real ales and generous opening times (evening meals from 5pm) offering a wide choice of popular food. Indian-style curries of the day and boozy beef casserole with dumplings alongside baguettes, burgers, baked potatoes and children's options: home-made soup to start and 'Spotted Richard' to follow.
OPEN: 11–11 (Sun 12–10.30) **BAR MEALS:** Lunch served: all week 12–2 Dinner served: Tues-Sat 5–9 Av main course £4
RESTAURANT: Lunch served: all week 12–2 Dinner served: Tues-Sat 5–9 Av 3 course à la carte £10 **BREWERY/COMPANY:** Everards Brewery **PRINCIPAL BEERS:** Everards Tiger, Beacon,Scottish Courage Courage Directors, Adnams Bitter. **FACILITIES:** Children welcome Garden: Food served outside Dogs allowed (water) **NOTES:** Parking 60 No credit cards

GLOOSTON
Map 06 SP79

Pick of the Pubs

The Old Barn Inn & Restaurant 🐾 ♀
Andrew's Ln LE16 7ST ☎ 01858 545215 ▤ 01858 545215
e-mail: theoldbarninn@yahoo.co.uk
Dir: A6 from Market Harborough. At Kibworth follow signs to Langtons/Hallaton. Glooston signposted

Well off the beaten track, yet within easy reach of Rutland Water and Rockingham Castle, the stylish old inn is opposite a row of charming stone cottages at a dead end of the original Roman road. Peaceful sleep is promised in two cottagey bedrooms without fear of traffic noise. Generally local produce is cooked by chef/patron John Buswell with enthusiasm and flair, the freshest fish

showing the way in seafood crêpes, perhaps, and tuna fish Italienne with melted Mozzarella. Meanwhile from the bar menu are steak and kidney ale pie and fusilli carbonara with smoked ham and mushrooms. A la carte, expect to find whole grilled Dover sole, beef fillet with mushroom compote and home-made vegetable pie. Popular Gourmet Seafood Evenings are held every six weeks. Bar snacks include baguettes, ploughman's and soufflé omelettes and there will be four prime-condition real ales on offer on any one day.
OPEN: 12–3.00 6.30–11 **BAR MEALS:** Lunch served: all week Dinner served: all week 12–2 7–9.30 Av main course £12
RESTAURANT: Lunch served: all week Dinner served: all week 12–2 7–9.30 Av 3 course à la carte £22
BREWERY/COMPANY: Free House
PRINCIPAL BEERS: Adnams Bitter, Fuller's London Pride, Shepherd Neame Spitfire,. **FACILITIES:** Garden: Small but attractive with seating **NOTES:** Parking 8
ROOMS: 2 bedrooms 2 en suite from s£42.50 d£55

GRIMSTON
Map 09 Sk 62

The Black Horse ♀
3 Main St LE14 3BZ ☎ 01664 812358 ▤ 01664 813138
e-mail: joe.blackhorsepub@virgin.net
A traditional 400-year-old country inn set in a quiet village with views over the Vale of Belvoir. Close by the old Saxon church and next to the old Roman road, it was formerly the local smithy. Lunchtime bar snacks can be chicken baguettes, bacon chops with scrumpy apple cider sauce and vegetarian and pasta specials, all home prepared. Evening choices may include redcurrant glazed lamb steaks, fresh fish of the day and Belvoir ale steak pie.
OPEN: 12–3 6–11 **BAR MEALS:** Lunch served: all week 12–2 Dinner served: Mon-Sat 6.30–9 Av main course £5
RESTAURANT: Lunch served: all week 12–2 Dinner served: Mon-Sat 6.30–9 Av 3 course à la carte £14 **BREWERY/COMPANY:** Free House **PRINCIPAL BEERS:** Belvoir, Interbrew Bass, Marstons Pedigree. **FACILITIES:** Children welcome Children's licence Garden: Patio, food served outside **NOTES:** Parking 30

HALLATON
Map 06 SP49

Pick of the Pubs

The Bewicke Arms 🐾
1 Eastgate LE16 8UB ☎ 01858 555217 ▤ 01858 555598
Dir: S of A47 between Leicester & junction of A47/A6003

A 400-year-old thatched country inn on picturesque Hallaton's village green. The village is famous for its vigorous Easter Monday hare-pie (beef these days)

continued

continued

scramble and no-holds barred bottle-kicking contest with neighbouring Medbourne. The bottles are actually small wooden barrels containing ale which, naturally, the winners drink. Inside this historic inn, modern design and colours blend well with its traditional features, while imaginative menus give pub favourites a contemporary twist. Representative examples of evening dishes, prepared from fresh ingredients, include homemade soup, hot Cajun prawn salad, mussels in white wine, cream and garlic, chargrilled sirloin with Brie and bacon, chicken Boursin, sausages with Dijon mash and onion marmalade, fish of the day and home-made casserole with pie-crust. Desserts are home-made too. Good global wine list. Play area and miniature farm with animals to keep children amused.
OPEN: 12–3 6–11 (Sun 12–3 7–10.30) **BAR MEALS:** Lunch served: Sun–Sat 12–2 Dinner served: Mon–Sat 7–9.30 Av main course £7.95 **RESTAURANT:** Lunch served: Sun–Sat 12–2 Dinner served: Mon–Sat 7–9.30 Av 3 course à la carte £17.65 **BREWERY/COMPANY:** Free House **PRINCIPAL BEERS:** Caudle Bitter, IPA Flowers, Grainstore Triple B. **FACILITIES:** Garden: Patio area **NOTES:** Parking 20

HOSE
Map 09 SK72

Rose & Crown
43 Bolton Ln LE14 4JE ☎ 01949 860424
e-mail: brian@rosehose.freeserve.co.uk
Dir: Off A606 N of Melton Mowbray
Renowned for its real ales and good food, a 200-year-old pub in the picturesque Vale of Belvoir. There is a large lounge bar with open fires, a heavily beamed restaurant and, weather permitting, alfresco eating on the patio. Daily menus encompass smoked salmon fishcakes with hollandaise, chicken balti and plain ham and egg, followed by treacle sponge and banana split. For lighter appetites, filled jacket potatoes and baguettes.
OPEN: 12–2.30 7–11 (Sun 12–3, 7.30–10.30) **BAR MEALS:** Lunch served: Thur–Sun 12–2.30 Dinner served: Wed–Sat 7–9 Av main course £5.50 **RESTAURANT:** Lunch served: Thu–Sun 12–2.30 Dinner served: Thu–Sat 7–8.30 Av 3 course à la carte £5.50
BREWERY/COMPANY: Free House **PRINCIPAL BEERS:** Greene King IPA & Abbot Ale, Carlsberg-Tetley Ansells Mild.
FACILITIES: Garden: Food served outside **NOTES:** Parking 30

KEGWORTH
Map 09 SK42

Cap & Stocking
20 Borough St DE74 2FF ☎ 01509 674814
Dir: Village centre (chemist on LHS. Turn left & left again to Borough St)
A traditional, unspoilt country pub with authentic features and a very attractive garden. Comfortable, old-fashioned rooms where Bass is still served from the jug and appetising, home-cooked meals are provided. Food options range from hot rolls and ploughman's lunches to specials such as beef in brandy, minty lamb, Thai chicken and chilli con carne.
OPEN: 11.30–2.30 6.30–11 **BAR MEALS:** Lunch served: all week Dinner served: all week 11.30–2.15 6.30–8.45 Av main course £6.50
BREWERY/COMPANY: Punch Taverns
PRINCIPAL BEERS: Interbrew Hancocks HB & Bass.
FACILITIES: Children welcome Garden: Food served outside Dogs allowed **NOTES:** Parking 4 No credit cards

LOUGHBOROUGH
Map 09 SK51

The Swan in the Rushes ♀
21 The Rushes LE11 5BE ☎ 01509 217014
e-mail: tynemill@tynemill.co.uk
Dir: On A6 (Derby road)
A 1930s tile-fronted real ale pub with two drinking rooms, a cosmopolitan atmosphere and no frills. Ten ales always
continued

available, including six guests. Two annual beer festivals, acoustic open-mic nights, folk club, and skittle alley. Simple menu lists dishes like chilli, cottage pie, spinach and Feta pie, and curry.
OPEN: 11–11 (Sun 12–10.30) **BAR MEALS:** Lunch served: all week 12–2.30 Dinner served: Mon–Fri 6–8.30 Av main course £5
BREWERY/COMPANY: Tynemill Ltd **PRINCIPAL BEERS:** Archers Golden, Carlsberg-Tetley Tetley Bitter plus guest ales.
FACILITIES: Children welcome Dogs allowed (water) if required **NOTES:** Parking 16 **ROOMS:** 4 bedrooms 2 en suite from d£40

MARKET HARBOROUGH
Map 06 SP78

The Queens Head Inn ♀
Main St, Sutton Bassett LE16 8HP ☎ 01858 463530
Traditional English pub with real ale, bar meals and an upstairs restaurant specialising in regional Italian cuisine. Full range of pasta, pizza, fish, steak and chicken dishes, while the bar menu features chef's special grills, fresh Whitby scampi, beef Stroganoff, Harborough gammon and potato skins supreme. Well-kept real ales.
OPEN: 11–3 6.30–11 Closed: 25 Dec **BAR MEALS:** Lunch served: all week 12–2 Dinner served: Mon–Sat 7–9.30 Av main course £6
RESTAURANT: Dinner served: Tue–Sat 7–11 Av 3 course à la carte £17 **BREWERY/COMPANY:** Free House
PRINCIPAL BEERS: Adnams, Taylor Landlord, Marstons Pedigree, Fullers London Pride. **FACILITIES:** Children welcome Garden: patio, BBQ, food served outside Dogs allowed (garden only)
NOTES: Parking 15

Pick of the Pubs

The Sun Inn ★ ★ ◉ ♀
Main St, Marston Trussel LE16 9TY
☎ 01858 465531 🖺 01858 433155
e-mail: Manager@suninn.com
Dir: S of A4304 between Market Harborough & Lutterworth
Head for Marston Trussell, in the heart of the Leicestershire countryside some three miles southwest of Market Harborough, to find this late 17th-century coaching inn offering cosy, up-to-date accommodation and modern amenities subtly combined with historic charm. Three separate dining areas include a popular locals' bar and an informal restaurant. Expect roaring fires, a friendly welcome, well-kept ales and a fair selection of wines by the glass. Fresh local produce plays a major part in the regularly updated menus. These offer a winning combination of traditional favourites such as roast rack of lamb or deep-fried monkfish with French fries, and dishes with a modern, international appeal – perhaps Indonesian chicken and prawn laksa or fillets of sea bass with a saffron risotto and fine ratatouille. Charming waitress service and equally good breakfasts create a feeling of all round quality.
OPEN: 12–6 6–10 Closed: Dec 25, Jan 1 **BAR MEALS:** Lunch served: Sat–Sun 12–2.30 Dinner served: all week 7–10 Av main course £5.95 **RESTAURANT:** Lunch served: Sat–Sun 12–2.30 Dinner served: all week 7–10 Av 3 course à la carte £23.95
BREWERY/COMPANY: Free House
PRINCIPAL BEERS: Bass, Hook Norton Best, Marstons Pedigree, Charles wells Bombardier. **FACILITIES:** Children welcome **NOTES:** Parking 60 **ROOMS:** 20 bedrooms 20 en suite from s£69 d£69

MEDBOURNE — Map 06 SP89

The Nevill Arms
12 Waterfall Way LE16 8EE ☎ 01858 565288 ▤ 01858 565509
e-mail: nevillarms@hotmail.com
Dir: *From Northampton take A508 to Market Harborough then B664 for 5m.L for Medbourne*
Warm golden stone and mullioned windows make this traditional old coaching inn, in its riverside setting by the village green, truly picturesque. Popular pub garden has its own dovecote and is a great attraction for children who like to feed the ducks. Handy for visiting Rutland Water, Burghley House, Bosworth Field and Stamford. A choice of appetising home-made soups, lamb in mint and redcurrant and deep fried goats' cheese are typical examples of the varied menu.
OPEN: 12–2.30 (Sun 12–3) 6–11 (Sun 7–10.30)
BAR MEALS: Lunch served: all week Dinner served: all week 12–2 7–9 Av main course £5.75 **BREWERY/COMPANY:** Free House
PRINCIPAL BEERS: Fuller's London Pride, Adnams Bitter, Greene King Abbot Ale. **FACILITIES:** Children welcome **NOTES:** Parking 30
ROOMS: 8 bedrooms 8 en suite from s£45 d£55

MELTON MOWBRAY — Map 09 SK71

Anne of Cleves House ♀
12 Burton St LE13 1AE ☎ 01664 481336
Fine old 14th-century building once used to house chantry priests. After Henry VIII dissolved the monasteries it was given to Anne of Cleves as part of her divorce settlement. The building is under a local heritage protection order, as many of the features are original. Log fires in winter and a picturesque garden for summer enjoyment. Make a selection from a menu that includes warm bacon and Stilton salad, lasagne, roast of the day, sausage and mash, and battered cod and chips. More main courses on the blackboard.
OPEN: 11–11 **BAR MEALS:** Lunch served: all week Dinner served: all week 11.30–2.30 6–9 **BREWERY/COMPANY:** Everards Brewery
PRINCIPAL BEERS: Everards Tiger Best. **FACILITIES:** Garden: Food served outside Dogs allowed **NOTES:** Parking 20

MOUNTSORREL — Map 09 SK51

The Swan Inn
10 Loughborough Rd LE12 7AT
☎ 0116 2302340 ▤ 0116 2376115
e-mail: dmw@jvf.co.uk
Dir: *On main road between Leicester & Loughborough*
Privately-owned former coaching inn between Loughborough and Leicester. Among the attractive interior features are various exposed beams, granite walls, flagstone floors and comfortable seating. Food is freshly cooked on the premises and the varied menu includes game and vegetarian dishes. Expect crostini of mushroom, chicken gumbo, leek with Feta and thyme, beef casseroled in Old Peculier, duck Reine-Claude, and game pie. Good quality cask conditioned ales and an extensive wine list.
OPEN: 12–2 5.30–11 (all day Sat) (Sun 12–3, 7–10.30)
BAR MEALS: Lunch served: all week 12–2 Dinner served: Mon–Sat 7–9.30 Av main course £7 **RESTAURANT:** Lunch served: all week 12–2 Dinner served: Mon–Sat 7–9.30 Av 3 course à la carte £14
BREWERY/COMPANY: Free House
PRINCIPAL BEERS: Theakston Best, XB, Old Peculier, Ruddles County. **FACILITIES:** Garden: Food served outside. Waterside garden Dogs allowed manager's discretion **NOTES:** Parking 12
ROOMS: 3 bedrooms

OLD DALBY — Map 09 Sk 62

Pick of the Pubs

The Crown Inn ☺
Debdale Hill LE14 3LF ☎ 01664 823134 ▤ 01664 822638
e-mail: lynn@phoenixcons.demon.co.uk
Dir: *Newark A46 R at Upper Broughton, from A46 towards Leicester take turn to Broughton 100Mtrs turn L, 0.3Miles L again. 1 Mile take rd to Old Dalby*
Dating back to 1590 and set in extensive gardens and orchards, this traditional pub has remained unchanged for centuries. Open fires warm several small rooms and the two restaurants, and you can play a quiet game of solitaire or dominoes undisturbed by background music or fruit machines. Local ingredients feature extensively on the menus, which include bar meals like filled ciabattas and sandwiches, lamb shanks, and various pasta dishes like seafood medley, plus salmon and crab fishcake, and steak and real ale pie. From the restaurant come starters like wild mushroom mille feuille, and panade of pigeon and rabbit, followed by jugged hare, and classic daube of beef. The Crown is proud of its real ales served straight from the cask, which can also be enjoyed in the large garden.
OPEN: 12–3 6–11 (Winter 12–2.30, 6.30–11)
BAR MEALS: Lunch served: Tues–Sun 12–2.30 Dinner served: Mon–Sat 7–9.30 Av main course £7 **RESTAURANT:** Lunch served: Tues–Sun 12–2.30 Dinner served: Tue–Sat 7–9.30 Av 3 course à la carte £12 Av 3 course fixed price £12.95
BREWERY/COMPANY: Free House
PRINCIPAL BEERS: Wells Bombardier, Wadworth 6X, Morrells Varsity, Castle Rock Hemlock. **FACILITIES:** Garden: Beer garden, patio, outdoor eating Dogs allowed (water)
NOTES: Parking 32

REDMILE — Map 09 SK73

Pick of the Pubs

Peacock Inn ☺
Church Corner NG13 0GB
☎ 01949 842554 ▤ 01949 843746
e-mail: peacock@redmile.fsbusiness.co.uk
Dir: *From A1 take A52 towards Nottingham*
The Peacock is a 16th-century country inn set in the pretty village of Redmile, beside the Grantham Canal, in the heart of the Vale of Belvoir. It offers a relaxed and informal setting for wining, dining and socialising against a background of beamed ceilings and roaring log fires. Accommodation is provided in 10 en suite bedrooms, each individually decorated and named after an animal - The Rabbit, The Pig and the Fox, to name a few. The range of menus - snack, lunch and dinner - offer a good choice, from a prawn and apple sandwich to pan-fried sea bass on new potato salad with Chablis cream sauce, or magret of Goosenargh duck with hoi sin and stir-fry vegetables. Vegetarians might opt for aubergine thins flavoured with pesto, wrapped around buffalo Mozzarella and baked with white truffle oil.
OPEN: 11–11 **BAR MEALS:** Lunch served: all week Dinner served: all week 12–2.30 7–9.30 Av main course £14.95
RESTAURANT: Lunch served: all week Dinner served: all week 12–2.30 7–9.30 Av 3 course à la carte £25
BREWERY/COMPANY: Free House

continued

PRINCIPAL BEERS: Marston's Pedigree, Timothy Taylor Landlord, Whitbread IPA, Wadworth 6X. **FACILITIES:** Children welcome Garden: Food served outside **NOTES:** Parking 50 **ROOMS:** 10 bedrooms 10 en suite from s£55 d£65

England

SADDINGTON   Map 06 SP69

The Queens Head 🍺
Main St LE8 0QH ☎ 0116 2402536
e-mail: bebbingtonb@aol.com
Dir: *Between A50 & A6 S of Leicester, NW of Market Harborough*
Traditional English pub with terrific views from the restaurant and garden over the Saddington Reservoir. Specialises in real ale and very good food, with four specials boards to supplement the evening menu. Foil-cooked cod fillet, roast Banbury duck, lamb shank with garlic mash, steak and ale pie, salmon in watercress sauce, and pan-fried tuna steak with sweet pepper and oyster sauce means something for everyone. **OPEN:** 11–3 5.30–11 **BAR MEALS:** Lunch served: all week Dinner served: Mon–Sat 12–2 6.30–9.30 Av main course £7 **RESTAURANT:** Lunch served: all week Dinner served: Mon–Sat 12–2 6.30–9.30 Av 3 course à la carte £16 Av 2 course fixed price £3.50 **BREWERY/COMPANY:** Everards Brewery **PRINCIPAL BEERS:** Everards Tiger Best & Beacon Bitter, Adnams. **FACILITIES:** Garden: Food served outdoors, over looking reservoir **NOTES:** Parking 50

SIBSON   Map 09 SK30

Pick of the Pubs

The Cock Inn 🍺 🍷
Twycross Rd CV13 6LB ☎ 01827 880357 📠 01827 880976
e-mail: cockinnsibson@aol.com
Dir: *On A444 between Nuneaton & M42 J11*

Dick Turpin reputedly returned to this thatched inn after a day of highway robbery, hiding in the bar chimney and stabling his horse in the cellar, and the rear lawn was used for cockfighting until about 1870 - hence the name. The Cock Inn is one of the oldest in the country, dating back to about 1250, and was a witness to the Battle of Bosworth in the late 15th century. Ancient timbers and low beams are testament to its history, and the former stables have been converted into an atmospheric restaurant. In here the good value fixed-price menu offers perhaps blue cheese and walnut pâté, and fillet of pork farcie or catch of the day. Otherwise the choice extends to oriental duck breast, medallions of veal Marsala, and various grills, with bar meals providing steak and kidney pie, chilli con carne, and a selection of salads and sandwiches.

continued

OPEN: 11.30–2.30 6.30–11 (Sun 12–3, 7–10.30) **BAR MEALS:** Lunch served: Mon–Sat 11.30–2 Dinner served: all week 6.30–9.45 Av main course £8.50 **RESTAURANT:** Lunch served: all week 11.30–2 Dinner served: Mon–Sat 6.30–9.45 Av 3 course à la carte £18 **BREWERY/COMPANY:** Punch Taverns **PRINCIPAL BEERS:** Interbrew Bass, Greene King Old Speckled Hen, Adnams Bitter, Young's Special. **FACILITIES:** Children welcome Garden: Courtyard, food served outside **NOTES:** Parking 60

SILEBY   Map 09 Sk 61

The White Swan 🍺
Swan St LE12 7NW ☎ 01509 814832 📠 01509 815995
Beyond the unassuming exterior of this 1930s pub lies a homely bar, an open fire and a book-lined restaurant. Regularly-changing menu and specials might include baked pheasant breasts wrapped in bacon with a chestnut and apple stuffing, beef cobbler in Guinness with Stilton scone topping, deep-fried lemon sole in breadcrumbs, pan-fried sirloin steak in red wine topped with garlic prawns. Good range of starters. **OPEN:** 11.45–3 7–11 Closed: 1–7 Jan **BAR MEALS:** 12–2 7–10 **RESTAURANT:** 12–2 7–10 **BREWERY/COMPANY:** Free House **PRINCIPAL BEERS:** Marstons Pedigree, Shipstones, Ansells. **FACILITIES:** Children welcome Garden: **NOTES:** Parking 10

SOMERBY   Map 06 SK71

The Old Brewery 🍺
High St LE14 2PZ ☎ 01664 454777 📠 01664 454777
Dir: *Between Melton Mowbray & Oakham off the A606 at Leesthorpe*
Holder of the record for brewing the strongest beer in the world, (a mind pummelling 23% ABV!) this 15th-century coaching inn offers eight traditional cask ales. In addition to fine ale, the pub is also known for its food. Typical menu includes lemon sole, breaded haddock, and battered cod. Lots of good walking country around. Live music every Saturday night. **OPEN:** 12–2 7–9 (Fri–Sat 9.30) **BAR MEALS:** Lunch served: Tues–Sun 12–2 Dinner served: all week 7–9 Av main course £5 **RESTAURANT:** Lunch served: all week Dinner served: all week Av 3 course à la carte £6 **BREWERY/COMPANY:** Free House **PRINCIPAL BEERS:** Parish, Bass, Carling, Grolsh. **FACILITIES:** Children welcome Garden: Food served outside Dogs allowed On lead only **NOTES:** Parking 50 **ROOMS:** s£20 d£30

The Wool Business

The trade in wool and cloth, which was the backbone of England's economy all through the Middle Ages and on into modern times, has left its mark behind it in such names as the Woolpack, the Ram, the Lamb (sometimes religious), the Shears, the Weavers Arms and the Fleece, often with sign of a dangling ram or sheep. The Golden Fleece is a neat reference to both the wealth derived from the wool business and the classical legend of Jason and the Argonauts.

SOMERBY continued

Stilton Cheese Inn
High St LE14 2QB ☎ 01664 454394

At the heart of a working village in beautiful countryside, this sandstone building dates from the 16th century. The same menus service both bar and restaurant areas, with good selections to be found on the Specials boards. Try salmon fillet wrapped in pastry with avocado and béarnaise sauce, rib-eye steak with a Stilton crust, rack of lamb in mint and redcurrant glaze, monkfish in chopped tomato and garlic sauce, or Rutland water trout with honey and almond glaze.
OPEN: 12–3 6–11 **BAR MEALS:** Lunch served: all week Dinner served: all week 12–2 6–9 Av main course £6.50
RESTAURANT: Lunch served: all week Dinner served: all week 12–2 6–9 Av 3 course à la carte £6.50 **BREWERY/COMPANY:** Free House **PRINCIPAL BEERS:** Marston's Pedigree, Black Sheep Best, Carlsberg-Tetley Bitter. **FACILITIES:** Children welcome Garden: patio, food served outside **NOTES:** Parking 14

See Pub Walk on page 283

THORPE LANGTON
Map 06 SP79

Pick of the Pubs

The Bakers Arms
Main St LE16 7TS ☎ 01858 545201
Dir: Take A6 S from Leicester then L signed 'The Langtons'
A charming thatched pub set in a pretty village, with plenty of period charm and an enthusiastic following locally and further afield. The first class modern pub food is one of the key attractions, though this remains an informal pub rather than a serious dining pub or restaurant. The Bakers Arms is located close to a popular walk, the Leicestershire Round, which cuts across the Candle Hills at the rear of the pub. The area is popular with walkers, riders and mountain bikers. An intimate and welcoming atmosphere prevails throughout, helped by low beams, rug-strewn quarry-tiled floors and open fires. The inn is furnished in character with large pine tables and antique pews, and the walls are painted in a warm terracotta. In this relaxing and cosy setting, the food is well worth sampling. There is a good choice of fish dishes including whole baked sea bass with mushrooms and spinach, cod fillet with Welsh rarebit crust and pesto mash, supreme of salmon with creamed leeks and prawn jus, and monkfish with peppers, rocket and tapenade. Meat eaters are not ignored either, with a selection that might include breast of chicken filled with salmon and Ricotta cheese, or roast shank of lamb with colcannon. Vegetarians might try filo parcel filled with goats' cheese

and roasted vegetables. Puddings like hot chocolate fudge cake with vanilla ice cream are a tempting option, and there's an extensive list of wines, including six by the glass, and Tetley Bitter from the handpump. Expect quick and efficient service from friendly staff.
OPEN: 12–3 6.30–11 (closed all Mon, Tue-Fri lunch, Sun eve)
BAR MEALS: Lunch served: Sat-Sun 12–2.15 Dinner served: Tue–Sat 6.30–9.30 Av main course £12 **RESTAURANT:** Lunch served: Sat-Sun 12–2.15 Dinner served: Tue–Sat 6.30–9.30 Av 3 course à la carte £22 **BREWERY/COMPANY:** Free House
PRINCIPAL BEERS: Carlsberg-Tetley Bitter.
FACILITIES: Garden: beer garden, food served outdoors
NOTES: Parking 12

WOODHOUSE EAVES
Map 09 SK51

The Pear Tree Inn
Church Hill LE12 8RT ☎ 01509 890243 ▤ 01509 891362
Dir: Village centre
Well refurbished, family-run inn at the centre of a lovely village in the beauty spot known as Charnwood Forest. Noted for freshly cooked food. Excellent local walks.

The Wheatsheaf Inn
Brand Hill LE12 8SS ☎ 01509 890320 ▤ 01509 890891
Dir: M1 Jct 22 follow directions for Quorn

A charming 18th-century pub accessed through an archway, with a solid character imposed by the local slate quarrymen who built it for their own use. Set in rural Charnwood Forest, close to the ruins of Lady Jane Gray's house. The competent menu has something for everyone: pork noisettes in a Calvados and cream sauce, cod and chips, beef stroganoff, various salads and vegetarian dishes, and tasty snacks.
OPEN: 12–2.30 6–11 **BAR MEALS:** Lunch served: all week Dinner served: Mon-Sat 12–2 7–9.30 Av main course £8
RESTAURANT: 12–2 7–9.30 **BREWERY/COMPANY:** Free House
PRINCIPAL BEERS: Greene King Abbot Ale, Interbrew Bass, Timothy Taylor Landlord, Marston's Pedigree. **FACILITIES:** Children welcome Garden: Food served outside, patio Dogs allowed (water)
NOTES: Parking 70

continued

WYMONDHAM   Map 09 SK81

Pick of the Pubs

The Berkeley Arms
59 Main St LE14 2AG ☎ 01572 787587 📠 01572 787587
e-mail: nick-cathy@mcgeown.fslife.co.uk
Equidistant from Oakham and Melton Mowbray in the
heart of the county's largely unsung countryside, this
chef-managed country inn has become a favoured dining
destination since refurbishment some three years ago. Its
interior comprises a village bar of exposed stonework and
original beams hung with dried hops, a carpeted, non-
smoking dining-room with well-spaced pine tables and a
garden that is popular with families and walkers in
summer. The landlord prides himself on utilising the best
available locally produced meats, poultry and fresh herbs
on monthly menus that are a modern mix of traditional
and trendy. Typically, bar lunches might include garlic
chicken and chorizo sausage with roast tomato and basil
ciabatta and cornbeef hash with fired egg and herb butter
sauce. At night, begin perhaps with pancetta with honey-
glazed baby pears, herb and walnut dressing before
seared calves' liver on a truffle spinach with horseradish
mash and truffle oil. For dessert, chocolate cappucino
mousse or sticky toffee sponge.
OPEN: 12-3 6-11 **BAR MEALS:** Lunch served: Thu-Sun 12-2
Dinner served: Tue-Sat 6-7.30 Av main course £5.95
RESTAURANT: Lunch served: Thu-Sun Dinner served: Tue-Sat
12-2 7-9 Av 3 course à la carte £21
BREWERY/COMPANY: Pubmaster
PRINCIPAL BEERS: Marstons Pedigree, Greene King Old
Speckled Hen, Batemans XXXB. **FACILITIES:** Children welcome
Garden: Food served outside Dogs allowed (garden only)
NOTES: Parking 40

LINCOLNSHIRE

ALLINGTON   Map 09 SK84

The Welby Arms ♀
The Green NG32 2EA ☎ 01400 281361 📠 01400 281361
Dir: From Grantham take either A1 north, or A52 west. Allington is 1.5m
Village pub in the time-honoured style with no loud music
or pinball machines, providing a welcoming retreat for
travellers on the A1. Dishes are prepared from fresh
ingredients and include a daily home-made soup and
comforting puddings like treacle sponge. Sunday lunch is a
traditional meal with freshly cooked joints of locally
produced meat.
OPEN: 12-2.30 6-11 (Sun 12-2.30 6-10.30) **BAR MEALS:** Lunch
served: all week Dinner served: all week 12-2 6.30-9.30 Av main
course £8.50 **RESTAURANT:** Lunch served: all week Dinner served:
all week 12-2 6.30-9.30 **BREWERY/COMPANY:** Free House
PRINCIPAL BEERS: Scottish Courage John Smith's, Interbrew Bass,
Timothy Taylor Landlord, Fuller's London pride.
FACILITIES: Children welcome Garden: Food served outdoors
Dogs allowed (garden only) **NOTES:** Parking 35 **ROOMS:** 3
bedrooms 3 en suite from s£48 d£60

⎕ **Pubs offering six or more wines by the glass**

ASWARBY   Map 09 TF03

The Tally Ho Inn ♦♦♦
NG34 8SA ☎ 01529 455205 📠 01529 455773
*Dir: From A1 take Grantham exit onto A52 towards Boston. Take A15
towards Sleaford.*
Part of the Aswarby Estate in deepest rural Lincolnshire, this
17th-century coaching inn has exposed stone walls, oak beams
and open log fires: tables outside, under the fruit trees,
overlook sheep-grazing meadows. A selection of
representative dishes includes salmon and spinach fishcakes,
beef and ale pie, sausage with cheese and onion mash, and
halibut with spicy salsa.

OPEN: 12-3 6-11 Closed: Dec 26 **BAR MEALS:** Lunch served: all
week Dinner served: all week 12-2.30 6.30-10 Av main course £6.75
RESTAURANT: Lunch served: Sun 12-2.30 Dinner served: Mon-Sat
7-10 Av 3 course à la carte £18 **BREWERY/COMPANY:** Free House
PRINCIPAL BEERS: Batemans, Interbrew Bass.
FACILITIES: Garden: Lovely open views, food served outside Dogs
allowed **NOTES:** Parking 40 **ROOMS:** 6 bedrooms 6 en suite from
s£35 d£60

BARNOLDBY LE BECK   Map 09 TA20

The Ship Inn ♀
Main Rd DN37 0BG ☎ 01472 822308
Dir: Off A46/A18 SW of Grimsby
Situated on the edge of the Lincolnshire Wolds, this 200-year-
old inn is filled with interesting bric-a-brac, and has a beautiful
garden. Award-winning cooking includes specials such as
lobster thermidor, crab and prawn cakes, pan-fried breast of
duck with fig and brandy sauce, and Mediterranean
Wellington - seasonal vegetables with tomato, garlic and
mozzarella in puff pastry with saffron sauce.
OPEN: 11-3 5-11 **BAR MEALS:** Lunch served: all week Dinner
served: all week 12-2 7-9.30 Av main course £6.95
RESTAURANT: Lunch served: all week Dinner served: all week 12-2
7-9.30 Av 3 course à la carte £15 **BREWERY/COMPANY:** Punch
Taverns **PRINCIPAL BEERS:** Batemans XB, Black Sheep Best.
FACILITIES: Children welcome Garden: Food served outside
NOTES: Parking 30

BOURNE   Map 09 TF02

Pick of the Pubs

The Black Horse Inn ♀
Grimsthorpe PE10 0LY ☎ 01778 591247 📠 01778 591373
e-mail: dine@blackhorseinn.co.uk
See Pick of the Pubs on page 291

BOURNE continued

The Wishing Well Inn
Main St, Dyke PE10 0AF ☎ 01778 422970 📠 01778 394508
Dir: Inn 1.5m from the A15, 12m from A1 Colsterworth rdbt
Modernised country inn with old oak beams and an inglenook
fireplace with roaring open fires in winter, and named after the
wishing well in the smaller of the two restaurants. An annual
family fun day is held in the nearby paddock every August, but
families are welcome all year. Typical menu features Village
grill, homemade pies, battered jumbo cod, and seafood platter.
OPEN: 11–3 6–11 **BAR MEALS:** Lunch served: all week Dinner served:
all week 12–2 6.30–9 Av main course £7 **BREWERY/COMPANY:** Free
House **PRINCIPAL BEERS:** Abbot Ale, Tiger Bitter.
FACILITIES: Children welcome Children's licence Garden: Food
served outside Dogs allowed (in the garden only) **NOTES:** Parking 100
ROOMS: 12 bedrooms 12 en suite from s£35 d£60

BRIGG   Map 09 TA00

The Jolly Miller
Brigg Rd, Wrawby DN20 8RH ☎ 01652 655658 📠 01652 652048
Dir: 1.5m E of Brigg on the A18, on L
Popular country inn situated a few miles south of the Humber
estuary. Pleasant bar and dining area fitted out in traditional
pub style. Saturday night entertainment and facilities for
christenings, weddings and other functions. As well as
comfortable B&B accommodation, a five-van caravan site is
also available. Straightforward menu offers the likes of
haddock, gammon, shepherd's pie and curry.
OPEN: 12–3 5–11 **BAR MEALS:** Lunch served: all week Dinner served:
all week 12–2 6.30–9 Av main course £3.95 **BREWERY/COMPANY:** Free
House **PRINCIPAL BEERS:** Two changing guest ales.
FACILITIES: Children welcome Garden: outdoor eating, patio
NOTES: Parking 40 **ROOMS:** 3 bedrooms 3 en suite from s£21 d£42

COLEBY   Map 09 SK96

The Bell Inn
3 Far Ln LN5 0AH ☎ 01522 810240 📠 01522 811800
Dir: 8m S of Lincoln on A607. In Coleby village turn right at church.
There is a cosy atmosphere at this 18th-century inn, with its
low beamed ceilings, log fire and a barrel-shaped bar. Decking
area for outside eating. Menu includes king prawns and sweet
chilli sauce, braised shoulder of lamb with Greek style
potatoes, chicken with mushroom sauce, Aberdeen Angus
fillet steak stuffed with mushrooms. Bedrooms.
OPEN: 11.30–3 5.30–11 Closed: 2–4 Jan **BAR MEALS:** Lunch
served: all week Dinner served: all week 12–2.30 5.30–9 Av main
course £9.95 **RESTAURANT:** Lunch served: all week Dinner served:
all week 12–2.30 5.30–9.30 Av 3 course à la carte £25
BREWERY/COMPANY: Pubmaster **PRINCIPAL BEERS:** Interbrew
Bass, Carlsberg-Tetley Bitter, Batemans XB. **FACILITIES:** Garden:
Dogs allowed **NOTES:** Parking 40 **ROOMS:** 3 bedrooms 2 en suite
from s£34.50 d£34.50

CONINGSBY   Map 09 TF25

The Old Lea Gate Inn
Leagate Rd LN4 4RS ☎ 01526 342370
e-mail: enquiries@theleagateinn.co.uk
Dir: Off B1192 just outside Coningsby
The oldest licensed premises in the county, dating from 1542,
this was the last of the Fen Guide Houses that provided shelter
before the treacherous marshes were drained. The oak-beamed
pub has a priest's hole and a very old inglenook fireplace among
its features. The gardens have a koi carp pond and play area.
Typical bar menus list stuffed lemon sole and seafood parcels.

The Inn at Lea Gate

OPEN: 11.30–2.30 6.30–11 (Sun 12–2.30, 6.30–10.30) Closed: Oct
19–Oct 26 **BAR MEALS:** 12–2 6.30–9.30 **RESTAURANT:** Lunch
served: all week Dinner served: all week 6.30–9.15 Av 3 course à la
carte £14.50 **BREWERY/COMPANY:** Free House
PRINCIPAL BEERS: Theakstons XB, Marston's Pedigree.
FACILITIES: Children welcome Garden: seated area, patio, food
served outside **NOTES:** Parking 60 **ROOMS:** 8 bedrooms 8 en
suite from s£49.50 d£60

CORBY GLEN   Map 09 TF02

The Coachman Inn
NG33 4NS ☎ 01476 550316
e-mail: mikep-j@btconnect.com
Dir: 4m E of A1 Colsterworth roundabout on the A151

Late Georgian country inn with an imaginative range of freshly
prepared dishes and a daily-changing menu. Recent changes
have included the introduction of cabaret nights, a larger
kitchen, and a more spacious dining room. Menu includes
baked seabass with lime butter, rack of lamb with herb crust,
grilled ribeye steak with pink peppercorn sauce, fillet of
salmon with punjabi spices, and wild mushroom risotto with
balsamic dressing.
OPEN: 12–2.30 6.30–11 (All day bank holidays) **BAR MEALS:** Lunch
served: all week Dinner served: all week 12–2.30 7–9.30 Av main course
£8.75 **RESTAURANT:** Lunch served: all week Dinner served: all week
12–2.30 7–9.30 Av 3 course à la carte £21 Av 3 course fixed price £17.50
BREWERY/COMPANY: Free House **PRINCIPAL BEERS:** Theakston
- Best, XB, Abbott Ale, IPA. **FACILITIES:** Children welcome Garden:
Food served outside **NOTES:** Parking 30 **ROOMS:** 3 bedrooms 3 en
suite from s£37.50 d£45

> **We endeavour to be as accurate as possible
> but changes to times and other information
> can occur after we have gone to press**

continued

OPEN: 11.30–2.30 6.30–11
BAR MEALS: L served all week.
D served all week. 12–2 7–9.30
Av main course £9.25
RESTAURANT: L served all week.
D served all week. 12–2 7–9 Av
cost 3 courses £18
BREWERY/COMPANY: FREE
HOUSE
PRINCIPAL BEERS: Black Horse
Bitter, Grimsthorpe Caste Bitter
FACILITIES: Children welcome.
Garden: Food served outside
NOTES: Parking 40
ROOMS: 6 en suite

The Black Horse Inn

♀
Grimsthorpe Lincolnshire PE10 0LY
☎ 01778 591247 📠 01778 591373
e-mail: dine@blackhorseinn.co.uk

Built in the early 18th century as a coaching inn, renovated and modernised to tasteful effect, and today, with stylish bedrooms for a comfortable stay, serving quality food that inspires a growing following.

Nestling in idyllic countryside on the Lincolnshire/Rutland border, and almost in the shadows of Grimsthorpe Castle, this is very much a dining destination for a discerning clientele. There's a small bar and a cosy lounge for a pre-dinner drink and a chance to study the menu perhaps, before entering the recent extension with exposed stone walls that houses the Buttery restaurant. The choice reflects chef/owner Brian Wey's love of getting the best from fresh local produce, with some of Lincolnshire's finest ingredients finding their way into his kitchen. Starters (and light snacks) might include pan-fried Haloumi cheese, sautéed lambs' kidneys with wild mushrooms on roasted brioche, and oak-smoked salmon with avocado and chive cream. The list of main dishes could contain, from the deep, black halibut with creamed leeks and roasted onions, pan-fried mackerel fillets, and roast salmon niçoise, and hearty meat offerings along the lines of lamb casserole in coriander, glazed duck breast, and Barnsley chop. A separate menu is a game lover's delight: kick off with roast snipe, or pheasant and mushroom sausages before tackling hare casseroled in a rich wine sauce, or roast mallard with pear sauce. Rave about Turkish delight pannacotta, and Eton Mess, and finish with speciality teas and coffees. 'Black Horse' and 'Grimsthorpe Castle' are good real ales, and there is a well-chosen wine list. To cap it all you can spend the night in a four-poster.

England

DONINGTON ON BAIN
Map 09 TF28

The Black Horse ★ ♀
Main Rd LN11 9TJ ☎ 01507 343640 📠 01507 343640
Ideal for walkers, this old-fashioned country pub is set in the heart of the Lincolnshire Wolds on the Viking Way. The specials are chalked up on a blackboard and include the likes of fresh Grimsby haddock, Viking grill, many varieties of sausage and mash, and seafood platter.

OPEN: 11.30–3 6.30–11 Closed: 25 Dec **BAR MEALS:** Lunch served: all week Dinner served: all week 12–2 7–9.30 Av main course £5.95 **RESTAURANT:** Lunch served: all week Dinner served: all week 12–2 7–9.30 Av 3 course à la carte £12.50
BREWERY/COMPANY: Free House **PRINCIPAL BEERS:** John Smiths, Ruddles, Tom Woods, Boddingtons. **FACILITIES:** Children welcome Garden: Food served outside Dogs allowed (water provided) **NOTES:** Parking 50 **ROOMS:** 8 bedrooms 8 en suite from s£25 d£40

EAST BARKWITH
Map 09 TF18

The Crossroads Inn ★
Lincoln Rd LN8 5RW ☎ 01673 858363
e-mail: xroads@skynow.net

Reputed to be the old crossroads toll house, the original building has been a pub for 200 years with later additions. This homely village inn has a welcoming atmosphere, and there's a good choice of food including fresh fish twice a week. A choice of Mexican dishes includes tacos, enchilada (cheese and onion, spicy mince, or chicken), burritos, chilli Relleno, and fajitas, plus the likes of lasagne, lemon chicken breast, and salmon Balmoral.
OPEN: 12–2.30 7–11 (Sun 12–3, 7–10.30) **BAR MEALS:** Lunch served: Tues-Sun 12–2 Dinner served: all week 7–9.30 Av main course £5.20 **RESTAURANT:** Lunch served: Tues-Sat 12–2 Dinner served: all week 7–9.30 **BREWERY/COMPANY:** Free House
PRINCIPAL BEERS: Carlsberg-Tetley, Greene King Abbot Ale, Batemans XB. **FACILITIES:** Children welcome Garden: Patio, food served outside Dogs allowed (water) **NOTES:** Parking 20

EWERBY
Map 09 TF14

Finch Hatton Arms ★
43 Main St NG34 9PH ☎ 01529 460363 📠 01529 461703
e-mail: bookings@finchhatton.fsnet.co.uk
Dir: from A17 to Kirkby-la-Thorne, then 2m NE. Also 2m E of A153 between Sleaford & Anwick
Originally known as the Angel Inn, this 19th-century pub was given the family name of Lord Winchelsea who bought it in 1875. After a short period of closure, it reopened as a new-style pub/restaurant in the 1980s. Extensive, varied menu includes salmon, sweet and sour chicken, steak and kidney pie, and sea bass.
OPEN: 11.30–2.30 6.30–11 Closed: 25/26 Dec **BAR MEALS:** Lunch served: all week Dinner served: all week 11.30–2.30 6.30–11 Av main course £8 **RESTAURANT:** Lunch served: all week Dinner served: all week 11.30–2.30 6.30–11 Av 3 course à la carte £13.50
BREWERY/COMPANY: Free House **PRINCIPAL BEERS:** Everards Tiger Best, Greene King Abbot Ale, Scottish Courage Courage Directors. **FACILITIES:** Children welcome Garden: Beer garden, patio, food served outdoors **NOTES:** Parking 60
ROOMS: 8 bedrooms 8 en suite from s£36 d£54

FREISTON
Map 09 TF34

Kings Head
Church Rd PE22 0NT ☎ 01205 760368
Dir: from Boston take A52 towards Skegness. 3m turn R at Haltoft End to Freiston
Originally two cottages, this village pub is renowned for its prize-winning hanging baskets and colourful window boxes. Inside, you can relax by an open fire and enjoy straightforward wholesome bar food. Home-made pies are a speciality and include steak and kidney, chicken and mushroom, sausage, and apple. The blackboard specials change on a weekly basis.
OPEN: 11–2.30 (Sun 12–3) 7–11 (Sun 7.30–10.30)
BAR MEALS: Lunch served: Tues-Sun 12–2 Dinner served: Wed-Sat 7–9 **RESTAURANT:** Lunch served: Tues-Sun 12–2 Dinner served 7–9 Av 3 course à la carte £15 **BREWERY/COMPANY:** Batemans
PRINCIPAL BEERS: Batemans XB & Dark Mild. **FACILITIES:** Children welcome **NOTES:** Parking 30 No credit cards

FROGNALL
Map 06 TF11

The Goat ★
155 Spalding Rd PE6 8SA ☎ 01778 347629
e-mail: goat.frognall@virgin.net
Dir: A1 to Peterborough, A15 to Market Deeping, old A16 to Spalding, pub about 1.5m from jct of A15 & A16

Welcoming country pub dating back to the 17th century, with a large beer garden and plenty to amuse the kids. A straightforward but comprehensive menu ranges through fish, grills and chicken dishes, while the chef's home-made

continued

selection includes sweet and sour pork, steak and kidney pie, spaghetti bolognaise, and leek and mushroom crumble.
OPEN: 11-2.30 6-11 (Sun 12-3, 7-10.30) Closed: 25 Dec
BAR MEALS: Lunch served: all week Dinner served: all week 12-2 6.30-9.30 Av main course £8 **RESTAURANT:** Lunch served: all week Dinner served: all week 12-2 6.30-9.30 Av 3 course à la carte £19
BREWERY/COMPANY: Free House **PRINCIPAL BEERS:** Adnams Bitter, Batemans XB. **FACILITIES:** Children welcome Garden: Covered patio, food served outside **NOTES:** Parking 50

FULBECK   Map 09 SK95

Hare & Hounds Country Inn ♦♦♦ ♀
The Green NG32 3JJ ☎ 01400 272090 ▤ 01400 273663
Family-owned inn dating from 1648, facing the church, vicarage and green of one of Lincolnshire's prettiest villages. The emphasis is on top quality, hand prepared food in both the bar and restaurant. Steak and Stilton pie is a speciality, alongside dishes of roast rump of lamb with redcurrant and Rosemary sauce, seabass on crispy bacon with wilted spinach and bubble and squeak, and wild mushroom risotto Milan style.
OPEN: 12-2 6-11 (Sun 7-10.30) (Open all day Easter-Oct)
BAR MEALS: Lunch served: all week Dinner served: all week 12-2 6.30-9.30 Av main course £6.50 **RESTAURANT:** Lunch served: all week Dinner served: all week 12-2 7-9.30 Av 3 course à la carte £17 Av 2 course fixed price £10 **BREWERY/COMPANY:** Free House
PRINCIPAL BEERS: Fuller's London Pride, Hook Norton, Greene King Ruddles County & Old Speckled Hen, Interbrew John Smith's.
FACILITIES: Children welcome Garden: Food served outdoors, patio **NOTES:** Parking 32 **ROOMS:** 8 bedrooms 8 en suite from s£30 d£45

GEDNEY DYKE   Map 09 TF42

The Chequers 🐾 ♀
PE12 0AJ ☎ 01406 362666 ▤ 01406 362666
e-mail: chequerspub@bllmember.net
Dir: From King's Lynn take A17, 1st roundabout after Long Sutton take B1359
Located in a remote fen-land village close to The Wash wildlife sanctuaries, an 18th-century country inn with an undimmed reputation for its food. Pan-fried scallops on crispy cabbage, baked cod with Welsh Rarebit crust and tuna with black spaghetti feature on a heady fish list. Gloucester Old Spot pork, Lincoln Red beef and seasonal winter game are carefully sourced and imaginatively cooked for both bar and dining-room clientele. Well-chosen ales, patio garden and outdoor eating in summer.
OPEN: 12-2 7-11 (Sun 12-2 7-10.30) Closed: 26 Dec
BAR MEALS: Lunch served: all week Dinner served: all week 12-2 7-9 Av main course £11 **RESTAURANT:** Lunch served: all week Dinner served: all week 12-2 7-9 Av 3 course à la carte £19.50 Av 3 course fixed price £19.95 **BREWERY/COMPANY:** Free House
PRINCIPAL BEERS: Adnams, Greene King Abbot Ale.
FACILITIES: Garden: Beer garden, patio, food served outside
NOTES: Parking 20

GRANTHAM   Map 09 SK93

The Beehive Inn
10/11 Castlegate NG31 6SE ☎ 01476 404554
Dir: A52 to town centre, L at Finkin st, pub at end
Grantham's oldest inn (1550) is notable for having England's only living pub sign - a working beehive high up in a lime tree. Otherwise, this simple town hostelry offers a good pint of Batemans XB and good-value, yet basic bar food.

HECKINGTON   Map 09 TF14

The Nags Head
34 High St NG34 9QZ ☎ 01529 460218
Dir: 5m E of Sleaford on A17
Overlooking the green of a village boasting the only eight-sailed windmill in the country, this white-painted 17th-century coaching inn reputedly once played host to Dick Turpin. Garden and play area. Bedrooms.

HOLDINGHAM   Map 09 TF04

Jolly Scotchman
NG34 8NP ☎ 01529 304864
Dir: 200yds S of A15/A17 rdbt, 1m from Sleaford
With an indoor play room and a garden featuring an adventure playground, aviary and pets' corner, this friendly old pub is the perfect family destination. Victorian-style conservatory restaurant and homely bars where traditional pub food is served.

HOUGH-ON-THE-HILL

The Brownlow Arms ♦♦♦♦ ♀
Grantham Rd NG32 2AZ ☎ 01400 250234 ▤ 01400 250772
Dir: Take A607 Grantham to Sleaford Rd, Hough on the Hill is signposted from Barkston
Quaint 16th-century inn, originally the game keepers house for the Brownlow Estate of Belton House, situated in a tranquil village. Features include stone mullioned windows, open fires and tastefully decorated bedrooms. Daily-changing menus highlight freshly prepared dishes. The restaurant carte changes weekly and includes plenty of fresh fish.
OPEN: 12-3 (Sun 12-4 only) 7-11 (closed Mon-Fri lunch and Sun eve) **BAR MEALS:** Lunch served: Mon-Sat Dinner served: Mon-Sat 12-2 7-9.30 Av main course £6.50 **RESTAURANT:** Lunch served: Mon-Sat Dinner served: Mon-Sat 12-2 7-9.30 Av 3 course à la carte £14.95 **BREWERY/COMPANY:** Free House
PRINCIPAL BEERS: Timothy Taylor Landlord, Marstons Pedigree, Greene King Old Speckled Hen, Fullers London Pride.
FACILITIES: Children welcome Garden: beer garden, patio, outdoor eating **NOTES:** Parking 45 **ROOMS:** 7 bedrooms 7 en suite from s£40 d£52

LINCOLN   Map 09 SK97

Pyewipe Inn 🐾
Fossebank, Saxilby Rd LN1 2BG
☎ 01522 528708 ▤ 01522 525009
e-mail: robert@pyewipeinn.co.uk
Dir: Out of Lincoln on A57 past Lincoln A46 Bypass, pub signed after 0.5m
The Pyewipe is an 18th-century alehouse on the Roman Fossedyke Canal, set in four acres with great views of the city and the cathedral - a 25-minute walk along the Fossedyke. A two-storey lodge housing 21 en suite bedrooms is a recent addition to the grounds. All food from pâté to ice cream is freshly prepared and offered from a daily board in the bar or seasonal carte in the restaurant. Look out for steak and kidney pudding, drunken pig pie, shank of lamb with a mint glaze, and plaice fillet with mushrooms and capers.
OPEN: 11-11 (Sun 12-10.30) **BAR MEALS:** Lunch served: all week Dinner served: all week 12-9.30 **RESTAURANT:** Lunch served: all week Dinner served: all week 12-3 7-9.30
BREWERY/COMPANY: Free House **PRINCIPAL BEERS:** Timothy Taylor Landlord, Greene King Abbot Ale, Interbrew Bass, Carlsberg-Tetley. **FACILITIES:** Garden: Food served outside **NOTES:** Parking 100 **ROOMS:** 20 bedrooms 20 en suite from d£50

England

LINCOLN continued

The Victoria
6 Union Rd LN1 3BJ ☎ 01522 536048 📠 01522 536048
Situated right next to the Westgate entrance of the Castle and within a stone's throw of Lincoln Cathedral, a long-standing drinkers' pub with a range of real ales and a terrace for imbibing. Nonetheless it also offers splendid meals with exclusively home-prepared food including hot baguettes and filled bacon rolls, Saturday breakfast and Sunday lunches. House specials include sausage and mash, various pies, chilli con carne and home-made lasagne.
OPEN: 11–11 (Sun 12–10.30) **BAR MEALS:** Lunch served: all week 12–2.30 Av main course £3.75 **RESTAURANT:** Lunch served: Sun 12–2 Av 3 course à la carte £8.50 **BREWERY/COMPANY:** Tynemill Ltd **PRINCIPAL BEERS:** Timothy Taylor Landlord, Batemans XB, Everards Original, Castle Rock Union Gold. **FACILITIES:** Garden: Patio, food served outside Dogs allowed

Pick of the Pubs

Wig & Mitre 🌐 🍽 🍷
30/32 Steep Hill LN2 1TL ☎ 01522 535190 📠 01522 532402
Dir: Town centre adjacent to cathedral & castle and Lincoln Castle car park, at the top of Steep Hill
A reassuringly civilised place toward the top of historic Steep Hill, the Wig & Mitre makes a perfect refreshment stop for those following Lincoln's fascinating city trail. Many 14th-century timbers have happily survived its numerous re-incarnations to provide a wonderful, evocative interior. With continuous service from 8am to midnight, in an ambience free of music and amusement machines, it is justifiably popular for its food, served every day of the week, all year round. There is simply something for everyone: sandwiches, set meals of two or three courses, breakfast and main menus, home-made puddings and commendable wine selection by the glass, champagne included. Among the noteworthy dishes are spiced crab risotto, sea bass fillet with crispy fried leeks, baked cheese soufflé with roasted red onion, rack of lamb with celeriac dauphinoise and steamed plum jam sponge. Fine real ales and many decent wines by the glass.
OPEN: 8–12 **BAR MEALS:** Lunch served: all week Dinner served: all week 8–12 Av main course £9.50
RESTAURANT: Lunch served: all week Dinner served: all week 8–12 Av 3 course à la carte £22.50 Av 3 course fixed price £12.75
BREWERY/COMPANY: Free House
PRINCIPAL BEERS: Greene King Ruddles County & Ruddles Best. **FACILITIES:** Children welcome Dogs allowed

LONG BENNINGTON   Map 09 SK84

The Reindeer
Main Rd NG23 5EH ☎ 01400 281382
e-mail: terry@reindeerinn.co.uk
Dir: 7m North of Grantham on the A1
Welcoming pub, with exposed beams and open fireplaces, in a pretty village setting. A varied menu may include mushroom and celery Stroganoff, chicken with sherry cream and mushroom, steak and kidney pie, or salmon on mixed leaves with lemon mayonnaise.
OPEN: 12–3 7–11 (Sat/Sun 12–4, Sun 7–10.30) **BAR MEALS:** Lunch served: all week 12–2 Dinner served: Mon–Sat 7–10 Av main course £8.95 **RESTAURANT:** Lunch served: all week Dinner served: Mon–Sat 12–2 7–10 Av 3 course à la carte £20 **BREWERY/COMPANY:** Free House **PRINCIPAL BEERS:** John Smiths, Greene King Old Speckled Hen, Ruddles County, Wells Bombadier. **FACILITIES:** Children welcome Children's licence Garden

LOUTH   Map 09 TF38

Masons Arms ♦♦♦ 🍽 🍷
Cornmarket LN11 9PY ☎ 01507 609525 📠 0870 7066450
e-mail: justin@themasons.co.uk

A former coaching inn dating from 1714, known as the Bricklayers Arms until 1801, and located in the busy Cornmarket in the centre of town. Renowned locally for its quality food and the six well-kept real ales on tap, the comfortable bars are open throughout the day for tea and coffee, as well as lunch. The lofty restaurant - Upstairs at the Masons - offers an award-winning menu of interesting dishes made from fresh local produce. The choice varies from week to week, with plenty of daily specials and extras on the blackboard. Expect fish dishes like moules marinière, monkfish, and lemon sole, along with perhaps loin of local pork, chargrilled chicken breast, and pan-fried pigeon. Comfortable, well-equipped bedrooms make this an ideal base for touring the Lincolnshire Wolds and their capital Louth.
OPEN: 10–11 (Sun 12–10.30) **BAR MEALS:** Lunch served: all week 12–2 Dinner served: Mon–Sat 6–9 Av main course £6 **RESTAURANT:** Lunch served: Sun 12–2 Dinner served: Fri–Sat 7–9.30 Av 3 course à la carte £18 **BREWERY/COMPANY:** Free House **PRINCIPAL BEERS:** Batemans XB, Timothy Taylor Landlord, Marston's Pedigree, Sam Smiths. **FACILITIES:** Children welcome Children's licence **NOTES:** Parking 20 **ROOMS:** 10 bedrooms 5 en suite from s£23 d£38

MARSTON   Map 09 SK84

Thorold Arms
Main St NG32 2HH ☎ 01400 250899 📠 01400 251057
Dir: Off A1 N of Grantham
A typical country pub, this large Victorian building is situated in the centre of the village on the Viking Way. Good range of regularly changing real ales. Bar snacks and restaurant meals are available.

NEWTON   Map 09 TF03

The Red Lion 🍽
NG34 0EE ☎ 01529 497256
e-mail: redlionnewton@aol.com
Dir: 10m E of Grantham on A52
A haven for walkers and cyclists, the only pub in a tiny hamlet of around 20 houses. Dating back to the 17th century, it abounds in low beams, exposed stone walls and an open fire in the bar. Top sellers include home-made steak and ale pie and haddock in beer batter. The carvery dispenses cold meats and salads through the week and a hot buffet on weekend evenings and Sunday lunch. Look, too, for grilled steaks, pan-fried trout and curries in various guises.

continued

OPEN: 12–2.30 6–11 (Sun 12–4, 7–10.30) Closed: 26 Dec, 1 Jan
BAR MEALS: Lunch served: all week 12–2 Dinner served: Tues–Sat
7–9 Av main course £7.95 **RESTAURANT:** Lunch served: all week
12–2 Dinner served: Fri–Sat 7–9 Av 3 course à la carte £15
BREWERY/COMPANY: Free House
PRINCIPAL BEERS: Batemans XB. **FACILITIES:** Children welcome
Garden: Patio, Food served outside Dogs allowed (water)
NOTES: Parking 40

PARTNEY   Map 09 TF46

Red Lion Inn
PE23 4PG ☎ 01790 752271 ⧉ 01790 753360
Dir: On A16 from Boston, or A158 from Horncastle
Parts of this Lincolnshire inn may date back 400 years, but
reports of a ghost seem to be unsubstantiated, although the
new management may be lucky enough to see something!
The large menu lists some fifty homemade dishes, including
steaks and grills, and a special Sunday roast.
OPEN: 11–3 7–11 (Sun 12–2.30, 7–10.30, closed Mon–Tue) Closed: 25
Dec **BAR MEALS:** Lunch served: Wed–Sun Dinner served: Mon–Sun
12–2 7–9.30 Av main course £7 **RESTAURANT:** Lunch served:
Wed–Sun Dinner served: Mon–Sun 12–2 7–9.30
BREWERY/COMPANY: Free House
PRINCIPAL BEERS: Marstons Pedigree, Bateman, Tomwoods.
FACILITIES: Garden: Dogs allowed **NOTES:** Parking 40
ROOMS: 3 bedrooms 3 en suite from s£30 d£40

RAITHBY   Map 09 TF36

Red Lion Inn
PE23 4DS ☎ 01790 753727
Dir: Take A158 from Horncastle, R at Sausthorpe, keep L into Raithby

Traditional beamed black-and-white village pub, parts of
which date back 300 years. Log fires provide a warm welcome
in winter. A varied menu of home-made dishes includes
seabass with lime stir fry vegetables, roast guinea fowl with
tomato, garlic and bacon, and medallions of beef with
peppercorn sauce.
OPEN: 12–3 7–11 **BAR MEALS:** Lunch served: Sat–Sun Dinner
served: Wed–Mon 12–2.30 7–10 Av main course £7
RESTAURANT: Lunch served: Sat–Sun Dinner served: Wed–Mon
12–2.30 7–10 Av 3 course à la carte £15
BREWERY/COMPANY: Free House **PRINCIPAL BEERS:** Raithby,
Marstons Pedigree, Mansfield IPA. **FACILITIES:** Children welcome
Children's licence Food served outside. Terrace patio Dogs allowed
NOTES: Parking 20 **ROOMS:** 3 bedrooms 3 en suite from s£28
d£38 No credit cards

SAXILBY   Map 09 SK87

The Bridge Inn
Gainsborough Rd LN1 2LX ☎ 01522 702266
Dir: On A57 W of Lincoln
For some 14 years the landlady of the Bridge Inn has kept a
tidy pub with traditional furnishings. Perching on the canalside with its own moorings, it has safe areas for children and
plenty of dining space. Two guest ales on offer to accompany
bar snacks and more extensive menus taking in Grimsby fish,
poached or pan-fried halibut and home-made fishcakes.
Freshly cooked pies and grilled steaks; two roasts on Sundays
with free soup or salad starters.
OPEN: 11–2.30 5.30–11 (open all day Sun, closed Mon) Closed: 25
Dec, Jan 1 **BAR MEALS:** Lunch served: Tue–Sun 11.30–2 Dinner
served: Tue–Sat 7–10 Av cost main course £5.95 **RESTAURANT:** Lunch
served: Tue–Sun 11.30–2 Dinner served: Tue–Sun 7.30–10
BREWERY/COMPANY: LincInns **PRINCIPAL BEERS:** John Smiths
FACILITIES: Children welcome **NOTES:** Parking 60

SKEGNESS   Map 09 TF56

The Vine ★ ★ ★
Vine Rd, Seacroft PE25 3DB ☎ 01754 763018 ⧉ 01754 769845
e-mail: info@vinehotel.com

Ivy-covered Victorian hotel, converted from a farmhouse and
bought by Harry Bateman in 1928. Now this charming
hostelry offers a fine selection of ales, silver service in the
restaurant and comfortable accommodation. Weddings a
speciality. Once a haunt of poet Alfred Lord Tennyson, who
has given his name to The Tennyson Lounge.
BAR MEALS: Lunch served: all week Dinner served: all week
12.15–2.15 7–9.15 Av cost main course £5.50 **RESTAURANT:** Lunch
served: all week Dinner served: all week 12.30–2.15 7–9.45 Av 3 course
à la carte £25 **BREWERY/COMPANY:** Batemans
PRINCIPAL BEERS: Batemans XXB & XXXB **FACILITIES:** Children
welcome Dogs allowed Garden: Food served outside **NOTES:** Parking
50 **ROOMS:** 25 bedrooms 25 en suite from s£55 d£75

SOUTH WITHAM   Map 09 SK91

Blue Cow Inn & Brewery
High St NG33 5QB ☎ 01572 768432 ⧉ 01572 768432
e-mail: richard@thirlwell.fslife.co.uk
Dir: Between Stamford & Grantham on the A1
Situated on the borders of Lincolnshire and Rutland, a once
derelict local inn standing close to the source of the River
Witham, which flows down to Lincoln. Named after the
landlord, Thirwell's real ales are brewed on the premises – with
guided tours of the micro-brewery an added attraction. Eclectic
menus embrace Thai seafood curry and Malaysian chicken

continued

SOUTH WITHAM continued

satay along with home-made pub pie, fresh Grimsby fish and British steak grills that culminate in a king-size mixed grill. **OPEN:** 12–11 **BAR MEALS:** Lunch served: all week Dinner served: all week 12–2.30 6–9.30 Av main course £7 **RESTAURANT:** Lunch served: all week Dinner served: all week 12–2.30 6–9.30 Av 3 course à la carte £11 **BREWERY/COMPANY:** Free House **PRINCIPAL BEERS:** Own beers. **FACILITIES:** Children welcome Garden: Food served outside Dogs allowed (water) **NOTES:** Parking 45 **ROOMS:** 6 bedrooms 6 en suite from s£40 d£45

SPILSBY   Map 09 TF46

Blacksmiths Arms
Skendelby PE23 4QE ☎ 01754 890662 📄 01754 890030
Old fashioned bar with 17th-century cellar and indoor wishing well. Open fire. Batemans beers. Standard pub food.

STAMFORD   Map 06 TF00

The Blue Bell Inn ♀
Shepherds Walk Belmesthorpe PE9 4JG ☎ 01780 763859
Dir: 2 m N of Stamford on the A6121 Bourn Road, turn R for Belmesthorpe and pub is on the L
After four years at the Blue Bell, a 350-year-old, partly thatched village pub, enthusiastic owners, Andrew Cunningham and Susan Bailey, are still deeply enthusiastic about innovative pub food using fresh local produce. Served throughout the homely, cottagey bars, both featuring impressive inglenook fireplaces, are a reliable range of traditional pub meals and interesting daily specials. Some of Andrew's most popular dishes include calves' liver with a red wine and jus accompanied by bubble and squeak, smoked haddock and tomato hotpot, seafood risotto with saffron and spring onions, and noisettes of venison with red wine and pickled walnut sauce.
OPEN: 12–2.30 6–11 **BAR MEALS:** Lunch served: all week Dinner served: Mon–Sat 12–2 7–9.30 Av main course £10 **RESTAURANT:** Lunch served: all week Dinner served: Mon–Sat 12–2 7–9.30 Av 3 course à la carte £18 **BREWERY/COMPANY:** Free House **PRINCIPAL BEERS:** Interbrew Bass, Greene King Ruddles County, Badger Best. **FACILITIES:** Children welcome Garden: Food served outside, Patio, Lawn **NOTES:** Parking 30 **ROOMS:** 3 bedrooms 3 en suite

Pick of the Pubs

The George of Stamford ★ ★ ★ ◎ 🍴 ♀
71 St Martins PE9 2LB ☎ 01780 750750 📄 01780 750701
e-mail: reservations@georgehotelofstamford.com
Dir: take A1 N from Peterborough. From A1 roundabout signposted B1081 Stamford, down hill to lights. Hotel on L
A beautiful 16th-century coaching inn in the centre of the old stone-built town of Stamford. History lovers will be interested to know that the monastery gardens were the burial ground of a church built on the site around 800 years ago. A medieval crypt remains beneath the cocktail bar, and Charles I was a visitor. Just inside the entrance are two bars called the York and the London, which were once the waiting rooms for the 40 or so coaches which plied between these cities every day. Nowadays they offer

continued

high levels of comfort in tasteful surroundings, with the York bar serving light snacks like filled ciabatta (Stilton and celery, smoked salmon, beef), sausage and mash, plus soups and pâtés along with Adnams real ales. In the Garden lounge and restaurant expect Brittany seafood platter, dressed crab, risotto con funghi (wild mushrooms), and tagliatelle al salmone.
OPEN: 11–2.30 6–11 (Sat–Sun open all day from 11) **BAR MEALS:** Lunch served: all week Dinner served: all week 7–11 Av main course £8.95 **RESTAURANT:** Lunch served: all week Dinner served: all week 12–2.30 7–10 Av 3 course à la carte £34 Av 2 course fixed price £16.50 **PRINCIPAL BEERS:** Adnams Broadside, Fuller's London Pride. **FACILITIES:** Children welcome Garden: Dogs allowed Dog Pack, Towel, Blanket, feeding mat **NOTES:** Parking 120 **ROOMS:** 47 bedrooms 47 en suite from s£78 d£105

WOOLSTHORPE   Map 09 SK83

Rutland Arms
NG32 1NY ☎ 01476 870111
Known to locals as the 'Dirty Duck', this family pub sits at the side of the Grantham canal, in the shadow of Belvoir Castle.

LONDON

E1

Prospect of Whitby 🍴 ♀   Map GtL C3
57 Wapping Wall E1W 3SH ☎ 020 7481 1095 📄 020 7481 9537
Originally known as The Devil's Tavern, this famous 16th century inn has been a meeting place for sailors and was also a gruesome setting for public executions. Samuel Pepys was a regular here before the tavern was renamed in 1777. Today, old ships timbers retain the seafaring traditions of this venerable riverside inn, which also boasts a rare pewter bar counter. Expect beef Wellington, minted lamb loins, and a good selection of fish dishes.
OPEN: 11.30–11 **BAR MEALS:** Lunch served: all week Dinner served: all week 11.30–9 Av main course £6 **RESTAURANT:** Lunch served: Sun–Fri Dinner served: Mon–Sat Av 3 course à la carte £20 **BREWERY/COMPANY:** Scottish & Newcastle **FACILITIES:** Children welcome Garden: Overlooking the River Thames Dogs allowed

Town of Ramsgate   Map GtL C3
62 Wapping High St E1W 2NP ☎ 020 7481 8000
Old pub close to The City. Plenty of bric-a-brac and old prints. Value for money bar food.

Darts
Although darts is now regarded as the archetypal pub game, its history is shrouded in almost total mystery and it may not have entered the pub scene until well into the 19th century. The original board may have been the end of a barrel, with the doubles ring as its outer ring. The accepted arrangement of numbers round the rim dates from the 1890s, but there are variant types of board in different areas of the country. The Yorkshire board, for instance, has no trebles ring. Nor does the Lancashire or Manchester board, which has a very narrow doubles ring and is customarily kept soaked in beer when not in use.

PUB WALK

Central London
Pub Crawl

Visit five of London's most historic taverns on this fascinating heritage trail from High Holborn to Blackfriars.

From Holborn Underground Station turn right into High Holborn and pass Chancery Court Hotel, with its distinctive domed tower and wrought iron gates. Left is Warwick Court and to the right is Chancery Lane. Keep ahead along High Holborn and look for the **Cittie of York** *(see page 314)* pub on the left. In summer the pub is decorated with a dazzling floral display of brightly-coloured hanging baskets. Pass Chancery Lane Underground Station and Grays Inn Road and look for the sign indicating the entrance to the City of London. Cross Furnival Street, turn left at Holborn Circus into Hatton Garden. After about 50 yards (46m) look for a doorway on the right with '**Ye Olde Mitre** - established 1546' above it *(see page 299)*. Walk through Ely Court to the inn and continue for a few paces to admire the Georgian architecture of Ely Place. Return to Hatton Garden

and Holborn Circus, cross at the lights and go down New Fetter Lane. At the statue of John Wilks, 1727-97, MP and Lord Mayor of London, turn sharp right into Bream's Buildings and along to Chancery Lane. Turn left, pass the Knights' Templar pub and the Law Society to Fleet Street. On the right is the **Old Bank of England** *(see page 299)*. Cross the road, veer left and walk back along the street. Pass Prince Henry's Room and the Samuel Pepys exhibition at 17 Fleet Street. The AA opened its first office next door in 1905. Keep ahead to reach Whitefriars Street. Opposite is Hind Court leading to Dr Johnson's House. Take a look, then return to Fleet Street, turn left and left again for **Ye Olde Cheshire Cheese** *(see page 300)*. Continue down Fleet Street, past the distinctive black and silver frontage of the old *Express* building. Make for Ludgate Circus, turn right into New Bridge Street and walk along to **The Black Friar** *(see page 299)*. Take the subway beside it to Blackfriars Underground Station.

PUB CRAWL, LONDON
Nearest Underground Station:
start, Holborn (Piccadilly & Central lines)
finish, Blackfriars (Circle & District lines)

(see pages 299, 300 & 314 for full entry of individual pubs)

Distance: 1 1/2 miles (2.4km)
Map: Any good street map of London
Terrain: Mostly pavements
Gradient: Easy street walking

Walk submitted and checked by Nick Channer

England

E3

Pick of the Pubs

The Crown ♀ Map GtL C3
223 Grove Rd E3 5SW ☎ 020 8981 9998 ▤ 020 8980 2336
e-mail: crown@singhboulton.co.uk
Dir: Nearest tube: Mile End Central Line & District line. Buses 277 to Victoria Park
A carefully-restored Grade II listed building whose smart, upmarket image is based on sound environmental practices. Only reclaimed building materials were used in the upgrade, and everything from the secondhand furniture to the organic menu and wine list reinforces the 'green' message. Upstairs, a series of dining rooms with balconies over Victoria Park, while the open-plan bar downstairs encourages lively conversation, or offers the perfect ambience for some peaceful newspaper reading on quiet afternoons. The seasonal menus with their emphasis on European cuisine change twice daily. Dine simply on leek and parsnip soup, slow-roast shoulder of lamb stuffed with anchovies, garlic and rosemary, and bitter chocolate mousse. Or push the boat out, and go for pan-fried chicken livers with sage, walnuts and noodles, venison and juniper stew with potato gnocchi, and queen of puddings with cream.
OPEN: 10.30-11 (Sat-Sun 10.30-3.30, 6.30-10) Closed: 25-26 Dec, 1 Jan **BAR MEALS:** Lunch served: Tue-Sun 12-3.30 Dinner served: Mon-Sun 6.30-10.30 **RESTAURANT:** Lunch served: Tue-Sun 10.30-3.30 Dinner served: Mon-Sun 6.30-10.30 Av 3 course à la carte £20 **BREWERY/COMPANY:** Free House **PRINCIPAL BEERS:** St Peter's Organic Ale, Best Bitter, Pitfield Eco Warrior, East Kent Goldings. **FACILITIES:** Children welcome Garden: Food served outside Dogs allowed

E14

Pick of the Pubs

The Grapes 🐾 ♀ Map GtL C3
76 Narrow St, Limehouse E14 8BP
☎ 020 7987 4396 ▤ 020 7987 3137
Dir: Docklands Light Railway stations: Limehouse or West Ferry
The pub has been standing on its narrow riverside site since 1720, and was used by Charles Dickens as the model for The Six Jolly Fellowship Porters in his novel *Our Mutual Friend*. The Grapes has been carefully renovated since Dickens' day, and whilst the novelist might still recognise many of its features; it's questionable what he would have made of nearby Canary Wharf or the handy Docklands Light Railway! There are no fruit machines here; mobile phones are frowned on, and the pub is proud of its traditional image as a place for grown-ups who like good food, wine and cask-conditioned real ales. Bar meals include home-made soups, salads, or bangers and mash, whilst the tiny upstairs restaurant offers a wide selection of seafood. Starters include lobster bisque, crab cocktail or avocado vinaigrette. Dover sole, halibut or grilled King scallops and bacon are typical main course dishes.
OPEN: 12-3 5.30-11 Sat 12-11, Sun 12-10.30 Closed: BHs **BAR MEALS:** Lunch served: all week 12-2 Dinner served: Mon-Sat 7-9 Av main course £6.50 **RESTAURANT:** Lunch served: Mon-Fri 12-2.15 Dinner served: Mon-Sat 7.30-9.15 Av 3 course à la carte £28 **BREWERY/COMPANY:** Allied Domecq **PRINCIPAL BEERS:** Adnams, Burton Ale, Carlsberg-Tetley Bitter, Interbrew Bass. **FACILITIES:** Dogs allowed (water)

EC1

Bishop's Finger Map F4
9-10 West Smithfield EC1A 9JR ☎ 020 7248 2341
Close to Smithfield Market, this relaxed bar offers interesting food from an open kitchen. Plenty of real ales on tap.

Pick of the Pubs

The Bleeding Heart Tavern 🍷 ♀ Map E4
19 Greville St EC1N 8SQ ☎ 0207 4040333 ▤ 0207 4040333
e-mail: enquiries@bleedingheart.co.uk
The original Tavern opened in 1746, given its name in memory of Elizabeth Hatton, brutally murdered in nearby Hatton Garden a century earlier. Recently restored, it has plenty of glass, original stone and rustic scrubbed tables on wooden floors give the place an authentic yet contemporary atmosphere. Supplementing the full range of tip-top ales from Adnam's Brewery and an impressive list of wines is the menu of traditional pub food with a contemporary twist. Spit-roast game and Suffolk pork from the unusual French rotisserie are of particular note, as are pork and plum terrine, ale-battered haddock with fat chips and rib-eye steak with béarnaise sauce. Look, too, for warm Norfolk pigeon salad, spit-roast duck with red cabbage and a sinful-sounding Pink Gin sorbet to round off this novel experience.
OPEN: 11-11 Closed: Sat/Sun BHs, 10 days at Christmas **BAR MEALS:** Lunch served: Mon-Fri 11-10.30 Dinner served: Mon-Fri 6-10.30 Av main course £7.25 **RESTAURANT:** Lunch served: Mon-Fri Dinner served: Mon-Fri 12-3 6-10.30 Av 3 course à la carte £12.50 Av 3 course fixed price £9.95 **BREWERY/COMPANY:** Free House **PRINCIPAL BEERS:** Adnams Southwold Bitter, Broadside, Fisherman **NOTES:** Parking 20

Pick of the Pubs

The Eagle 🍷 🐾 ♀ Map E4
159 Farringdon Rd EC1R 3AL ☎ 020 7837 1353
Dir: Angel/Farringdon Stn. North end Farringdon Road
Successful, popular pub which has been at the heart of local community affairs for well over ten years. Despite a serious interest in food (it has published a cookbook called *Big Flavours and Rough Edges*), the Eagle remains faithful to its major role as a pub. The single dining area is filled with simple, random furniture from school chairs to bare tables, and food is served from an open kitchen that is an extension of the bar. Carefully-constructed Mediterranean dishes like carabaccia (Florentine pea soup), polenta with field mushrooms, Swiss chard and tomatoes, and bife Ana - a marinated rumpsteak sandwich, might be followed by linguine with crab, shoulder of lamb en sofrito (couscous with dried nuts and fruit), and grilled tuna with salmoriglio (Italian herb and oil sauce). Try pecorino for afters - a Sardinian ewes' milk cheese with flatbread and marmalade.
OPEN: 12-11 Closed: 1Wk Xmas, BHs **BAR MEALS:** Lunch served: all week 12.30-2.30 Dinner served: Mon-Sat 6.30-10.30 Av main course £9.50 **RESTAURANT:** Lunch served: all week Dinner served: Mon-Sat Av 3 course à la carte £9.50 **BREWERY/COMPANY:** Free House **PRINCIPAL BEERS:** Wells Eagle IPA & Bombardier. **FACILITIES:** Children welcome Dogs allowed

Pick of the Pubs

The Jerusalem Tavern
Map F4

55 Britton St, Clerkenwell EC1M 5NA
☎ 020 7490 4281 📠 020 7490 4281
e-mail: beers@stpetersbrewery.co.uk
Dir: *100m NE of Farringdon tube, 300m N of Smithfield*

Named after the Priory of St John of Jerusalem, this historic tavern has occupied several sites in the area since the 14th century. The current building dates from 1720 when it was a merchant's house, and lies in a fascinating and wonderfully atmospheric corner of London. The likes of Samuel Johnson, David Garrick and the young Handel were visitors and the inn has been used as a film set on many occasions. Owned by St Peter's Brewery, it features a dimly-lit bar with bare boards, rustic wooden tables, old tiles, magazines and daily papers, and candles, open fires and cosy corners add to the unspoilt charm of the place. Renowned as one of the finest pubs in the capital, it is open every weekday and offers the full range of St Peter's ales, as well as simple bar fare, including speciality sandwiches, sausage baguettes, and beef casserole.
OPEN: 11-11 (Mon–Fri only) Closed: Sat/Sun, 25 Dec, Etr, BH Mon's **BAR MEALS:** Lunch served: Mon–Fri Dinner served: Mon–Fri 12–3 Av main course £6 **BREWERY/COMPANY:** St Peters Brewery **PRINCIPAL BEERS:** St Peters (complete range).

Pick of the Pubs

The Peasant 🐾 🍷
Map D3

240 St John St EC1V 4PH
☎ 020 7336 7736 📠 020 7490 1089
Dir: *Angel& Faringdon Rd Tube Station. On the corner of St John Street and Percival Street.*
Founded in 1993 as one of London's original gastro pubs, with a reputation based as much on consistently good bar mezze food as the restaurant carte. Once a Victorian pub, its original features have been restored to their former glory, including an inlaid mosaic floor, horseshoe bar and lovely conservatory. The upstairs restaurant has also been transformed, and beneath period chandeliers the inventive modern menu makes good reading. Peasant-style food with a Mediterranean leaning is the main thrust: pan-fried chorizo with sherry, pears and walnuts, fried calamari with sweet chilli sauce, and to follow perhaps, roast monkfish with spring greens and mussels, or marinated beef fillet with potato gratin and rosemary jus. Passion fruit crème brûlée brings up the rear, while the acclaimed wine list is joined by real ales and cocktails.
OPEN: 12.30-12.30 **BAR MEALS:** Lunch served: Mon–Fri Dinner served: Mon–Sat 12.30–3 6.30–11 Av main course £10

RESTAURANT: Lunch served: Mon–Fri Dinner served: Mon–Sat 12.30-3.30 6.30–11 Av 3 course à la carte £22.50
BREWERY/COMPANY: Free House
PRINCIPAL BEERS: Bombardier, Watt Tyler.
FACILITIES: Garden: terrace Dogs allowed

Ye Olde Mitre
Map E4

13 Ely Place, Hatton Garden EC1N 6SJ ☎ 020 7405 4751
Just off Holborn Circus, this pub has been here since 1546, and retains its historic atmosphere. It is also a Heritage Inn, which means its preservation is bound to continue. In the bar is part of a cherry tree that Elizabeth I is thought to have danced around. Very busy at lunchtimes. Real ales from hand-pumps. Bar snacks.
OPEN: 11-11 Closed Sat-Sun, BHs **BAR MEALS:** Snacks only 11-9.30 **BREWERY/COMPANY:** Punch Retail

EC2

Old Dr Butler's Head
Map F4

Mason's Av, Coleman St, Moorgate EC2V 5BY
☎ 020 7606 3504 📠 020 7600 0417
Traditional, gas-lit pub that dates back to the 17th century. Split over three floors, the bars offer up to six cask ales at any one time. Straighforward pub food.

EC4

The Black Friar
Map F3

174 Queen Victoria St EC4V 4EG ☎ 020 7236 5474
Boasting a fine collection of Edwardian art nouveau decorations, this deceptively large pub is very busy with after-work drinkers. Close to Blackfriars Bridge.

The Centre Page 🍷
Map F3

29 Knightrider St EC4V 5BH ☎ 020 7236 3614
Situated in the shadow of St Paul's Cathedral, this historic pub used to be known as the Horn Tavern and was mentioned by Charles Dickens in *The Pickwick Papers*, and in Samuel Pepys' diary. Varied menu offers the likes of baby spinach salad with grilled goats' cheese, pan-fried tuna on a Niçoise salad, and Cumberland sausages with colcannon and onion gravy.
OPEN: 11-11 (for hire at weekends) Closed: all BHs
BAR MEALS: Lunch served: all week 12–3 Av main course £8.50
BREWERY/COMPANY: Front Page Pubs Ltd
PRINCIPAL BEERS: Wells Bombardier, Brakspear, Shepherd Neame Spitfire. **FACILITIES:** Children welcome Dogs allowed

The Old Bank of England 🍷
Map E4

194 Fleet St EC4A 2LT ☎ 020 7430 2255 📠 020 7242 3092
e-mail: oldbankofengland@fullers.co.uk
This magnificent building was formerly the Law Courts branch of the Bank of England, and it lies between the site of Sweeney Todd's barbershop and his mistress' pie shop. It was in the tunnels and vaults below the present building that their unfortunate victims were butchered before being cooked and sold in Mrs Lovett's pies. The bar menu ranges from light snacks to the likes of lamb casserole with dumplings and jam sponge pudding with custard.
OPEN: 11-11 (closed wknds, BHs) **BAR MEALS:** Lunch served: Mon–Fri Dinner served: Mon–Thurs 12–8 12–8 Av main course £6.50 **BREWERY/COMPANY:** Fullers **PRINCIPAL BEERS:** Fuller's London Pride, ESB, Chiswick Bitter.

continued

England

EC4 continued

Ye Olde Cheshire Cheese
Map F4

Wine Office Court, 145 Fleet St EC4A 2BU
☎ 020 7353 6170 ▤ 020 7353 0845
e-mail: cheshirecheese@compuserve.com

17th-century pub with a long history of entertaining literary greats such as Arthur Conan Doyle, Yeats and Dickens. One of the few remaining Chop houses rebuilt after the Great Fire of London in 1666. Plenty of nooks and crannies, traditional pub food and quiet at weekends.

N1

The Albion ♀
Map GtL C3

10 Thornhill Rd, Barnsbury N1 1HW
☎ 020 7607 7450 ▤ 020 7607 8969
e-mail: keithinwood@aol.com

An ivy-clad pub of uncertain antiquity with a warren of homely rooms. The pub often plays host to local TV celebrities. Baguettes, burgers and jacket potatoes of choice clutter the chalkboards. Starters and 'lite bites' include breaded lobster tails and asparagus and Gruyère tart, with main dishes represented by ham and eggs, herb roasted salmon and penne pasta with wild mushroom sauce. Grilled steaks with multifarious side orders: outdoor eating in fine weather.
OPEN: 12–10 (Sun 12–10.30) **BAR MEALS:** Lunch served: all week Dinner served: all week 12–3 6–9.30 Av main course £7.95
RESTAURANT: Lunch served: all week Dinner served: all week 12–3 6–9.30 Av 3 course à la carte £15 **BREWERY/COMPANY:** Scottish & Newcastle **PRINCIPAL BEERS:** Fuller's London Pride, Theakstons Best Bitter. **FACILITIES:** Garden

The Compton Arms ♀
Map GtL C3

4 Compton Av, Off Canonbury Rd N1 2XD ☎ 0207 359 6883
A country pub in the middle of town with a peaceful, rural feel. Real ales from the hand pump, and good value steaks, mixed grill, big breakfast and Sunday roast.

The Crown ♀
Map GtL C3

116 Cloudsley Rd, Islington N1 0EB
☎ 020 7837 7107 ▤ 020 7833 1084
Bustling, Grade II listed pleasantly situated in an upmarket and peaceful residential area in the heart of Islington. Wealth of period features, including Victorian etched glass, stylish furnishings, tip-top Fuller's ales, and a modern pub menu. Alongside traditional sausage and mash look out for caramelised salmon steak, chargrilled lamb, Mediterranean vegetables with goats' cheese, and various casseroles.
OPEN: 12–11 Closed: 25/26 Dec **BAR MEALS:** Lunch served: all week 12–3 Dinner served: Mon–Sat 6.30–10 Av main course £8
RESTAURANT: Lunch served: all week Dinner served: all week 12–3

6.30–10 Av 3 course à la carte £15 **BREWERY/COMPANY:** Fullers
PRINCIPAL BEERS: Fullers full range. **FACILITIES:** Children welcome Garden: beer garden, outdoor eating Dogs allowed

Pick of the Pubs

The Duke of Cambridge 🛏 ♀
Map GtL C3

30 St Peter's St N1 8JT ☎ 020 7359 3066 ▤ 020 7359 1877
e-mail: duke@singhboulton.co.uk
Owners Geetie Singh and Esther Boulton have established an impressive pedigree since opening The Duke in 1998. Their stylishly modernised building can be found in a residential street close to the heart of Islington. Now certified by the Soil Association, this was arguably London's first gastro-pub specialising in organic food, wines and beers. Its owners combine a passion for good food with a sound business ethic; there is no music or TV, juke boxes or pinball machines. The blackboard menus, which feature uncomplicated seasonal recipes in a modern European style, are changed twice a day. Genuine care goes into dishes like pumpkin and sage soup; grilled asparagus with anchovies, capers and poached egg; pan-fried sea trout; slow roast pork belly; or baked aubergine with tomato, onion and parsley. Leave space for rhubarb fool with shortbread, or citrus pudding and cream. Children's portions are always available.
OPEN: 12–11 (Mon 5–11) Closed: Dec 25–26, Jan 1
BAR MEALS: Lunch served: Tue–Sun 12.30–3 Dinner served: Mon–Sun 6.30–10.30 Av main course £10 **RESTAURANT:** Lunch served: Tue–Sun 12.30–3 Dinner served: Mon–Sun 6.30–10.30 Av 3 course à la carte £15 **BREWERY/COMPANY:** Free House
PRINCIPAL BEERS: Pitfield Singhboulton, Eco Warrior, St Peter's Best Bitter, East Kent Golding. **FACILITIES:** Children welcome Children's licence Garden: patio, food served outside Dogs allowed

The Northgate 🛏 ♀ NEW
Map GtL C3

113 Southgate Rd, Islington NW1 3JS
☎ 020 7359 7392 ▤ 020 7359 7393
This thriving gastro-pub has recently been transformed from a run-down community local into a friendly modern establishment serving excellent food. A regular guest beer supplements the two resident real ales, and there's also a good mix of draught lagers and imported bottled beers. The blackboard menu features fresh, seasonal dishes: chargrilled barbecue pork with cornbread and spring greens; pan-fried wild salmon; or roast red pepper tortilla with olive and tomato salad are typical choices.
OPEN: 5–11 (Sat 12–11, Sun 12–10.30) Closed: 24–26 Dec, 1 Jan
BAR MEALS: Lunch served: Sun 12–4 Dinner served: all week 6.30–10.30 Av main course £10.50 **RESTAURANT:** Lunch served: Sun 12–4 Dinner served: all week 6.30–10.30 Av 3 course à la carte £22 **BREWERY/COMPANY:** Punch Taverns
PRINCIPAL BEERS: Adnams Bitter, Fuller's London Pride & Guest ales. **FACILITIES:** Garden: Patio with seating Dogs allowed (water, biscuits)

N16

The Fox Reformed ◉
Map GtL C4

176 Stoke Newington Church Str N16 0JL
☎ 020 7254 5975 ▤ 020 7254 5975
Wine bar at the heart of community life, with its own reading circle, backgammon club and wine tastings. Good food comes from regular and specials menus.

continued

N19

Pick of the Pubs

St Johns
Map GtL B4
91 Junction Rd, Archway N19 5QU
☎ 020 7272 1587 ▤ 020 7272 8023
e-mail: st.johnarchway@virgin.net

The exterior of this Victorian street corner pub is pure Albert Square. Yet, inside, the airy bar and spectacular dining room attract trendy North London thirty-somethings. Beyond the long, attractively converted bar, owner Nic Sharpe has transformed the adjoining snooker hall into a vast, comfortable restaurant. Idiosyncratic decor, solid oak and pine tables, deep red walls hung with modern works of art and comfy settees around the fire. You'll need to book - and be sure to come hungry. St John's portions are lavish, the food's very good, and the happy staff generate a relaxed atmosphere. Starters like terrine of Serrano ham, chorizo, chicken and rabbit or chargrilled mackerel fillets are chalked up on huge, daily-changing blackboards. Main courses might be caramelised duck breast with celeriac rösti, apples and prunes, or beetroot risotto with goats' cheese pesto. If you've space, dark chocolate and Amaretto tart will round things off nicely.
OPEN: 11-11 Closed: Dec 25-26, Jan 1 **BAR MEALS:** Lunch served: Tue-Sun 12-3 Dinner served: Mon-Sun 6.30-11 Av main course £11 **RESTAURANT:** Lunch served: Tue-Sun 12-3 Dinner served: Mon-Sun 6.30-11 Av 3 course à la carte £22 **PRINCIPAL BEERS:** Greene King Abbot Ale, Marston's Pedigree. **FACILITIES:** Children welcome Food served outdoors Dogs allowed

NW1

Pick of the Pubs

The Chapel
Map B4
48 Chapel St NW1 5DP ☎ 020 7402 9220 ▤ 020 7723 2337
e-mail: thechapel@btconnect.com
Dir: By A40 Marylebone Rd & Old Marylebone Rd junc. Off Edgware Rd by tube station
A modern, open-plan gastro-pub, the Chapel derives its name from nothing more than its location: bright and airy within, its stripped floors and pine furniture create a relaxed, informal atmosphere. Menus posted daily on the chalk-boards have a trendy Anglo-Mediterranean feel. On any given day expect starters such as chilled watercress soup, fish croquette salad with roast vegetables, and goats' cheese terrine with braised chicory. Follow with

continued

wild mushroom tart, marlin steak with anchovy dressing, and pan-fried bison with roast parsnips (for the less adventurous, chicken breast with roquette and rice), rounding off with tarte tatin or banoffee pie.
OPEN: 12-11 (Sun 12-3.30, 7-10.30) Closed: Dec 24-Jan 2 **BAR MEALS:** Lunch served: all week Dinner served: all week 12-2.30 7-10 Av main course £13 **RESTAURANT:** Lunch served: all week Dinner served: all week 12-2.30 7-10 Av 3 course à la carte £20 **BREWERY/COMPANY:** Punch Taverns **PRINCIPAL BEERS:** Greene King IPA, Adnams, Stella, Grolsch. **FACILITIES:** Children welcome Garden: Food served outside. Paved terrace Dogs allowed

Crown & Goose
Map GtL B3
100 Arlington Rd NW1 7HP ☎ 020 7485 2342 ▤ 020 7485 2342
Dir: Nearest tube: Camden Town
One of the original gastro-pubs with a relaxed atmosphere attracting a fashionable media crowd. The food has an Anglo-Mediterranean flavour with bar snacks like potato skins and ciabatta rolls, and daily specials often feature fish. A typical menu includes chargrilled tuna with mixed pepper salsa, pork chop with apple sauce, red cabbage and mash, gigot lamb with Greek salad and new potatoes, beer battered cod and chips, and fragrant Thai fish or chicken stew with coconut and rice.
OPEN: 11-11 (Sun 12-10.30) Closed: 25 Dec **BAR MEALS:** Lunch served: all week Dinner served: all week 12-3 6-10 Av main course £7 **RESTAURANT:** Lunch served: all week Dinner served: all week 12-3 6-10 Av 3 course à la carte £15 **BREWERY/COMPANY:** Scottish Courage **PRINCIPAL BEERS:** Fuller's London Pride, Scottish Courage Courage Directors. **FACILITIES:** Children welcome

Pick of the Pubs

The Engineer
Map GtL B3
65 Gloucester Av, Primrose Hill NW1 8JH
☎ 020 7722 0950 ▤ 020 7483 0592
e-mail: info@the-engineer.com
Dir: Nearest tube: Camden Town/Chalk Farm, on the corner of Princess Rd and Gloucester Ave
Situated in a very residential part of Primrose Hill close to Camden Market, this unassuming corner street pub, surprisingly built by Isambard Kingdom Brunel in 1841, attracts a discerning dining crowd for imaginative and well prepared food and its friendly, laid-back atmosphere. Fashionably rustic interior with a spacious bar area, sturdy wooden tables with candles, simple decor and changing art exhibitions in the restaurant area. A walled, paved and heated garden to the rear is extremely popular in fine weather. A first-class, fortnightly-changing menu features an eclectic mix of home-made, Mediterranean inspired dishes and uses organic or free-range meats. Start, perhaps, with split pea and ham soup with truffle oil and home-made bread or Mozzarella with figs and Parma ham with honey and grain mustard dressing, following on with salmon fishcakes with coriander, chilli and ginger served with roast garlic aïoli, whole roasted sea bass with coarse chopped tapenade, or chargrilled organic sirloin steak with herb butter. Excellent Sunday brunch.
OPEN: 9-11 Closed: 25-26 Dec, 1 Jan **BAR MEALS:** Lunch served: all week Dinner served: all week 12.30-3 7-10.30 Av main course £7.50 **RESTAURANT:** Lunch served: all week Dinner served: all week 12-3 7-11 **BREWERY/COMPANY:** Bass **PRINCIPAL BEERS:** Fullers London Pride, Greene King Old Speckled Hen. **FACILITIES:** Children welcome Garden: Food served outside, paved garden Dogs allowed (in the garden only)

NW1 continued

The Globe 🍷   Map B4
43-47 Marylebone Rd NW1 5JY
☎ 020 7935 6368 ▤ 020 7224 0154
Dir: Nr Baker St tube
Consisting of wine bar, main bar and restaurant, this 18th-century, three-storey pub, opposite Baker Street tube station, was once frequented by such luminaries as Charles Dickens, Sir Arthur Conan Doyle, and Alfred Lord Tennyson. Typical menu includes steak and Stilton pie, pork escalope with wild mushroom sauce, light snacks, and the Globe's speciality: fish and chips. Due to undergo major refurbishment programme at time of going to press. Convenient for the Planetarium and Madame Tussaud's.
OPEN: 11-11 (Sun 12-10.30) Closed: 25 Dec **BAR MEALS:** Lunch served: all week Dinner served: all week 11-10 Av main course £5
RESTAURANT: Lunch served: all week Dinner served: all week 11-10 Av 3 course à la carte £9 **PRINCIPAL BEERS:** Scottish Courage Courage Best & Directors, Theakston Best. **FACILITIES:** Children welcome

Pick of the Pubs

The Lansdowne 🍷   Map GtL B4
90 Gloucester Av, Primrose Hill NW1 8HX
☎ 020 7483 0409 ▤ 0207 5861723
Dir: Nearest tube: Chalk Farm. From station turn L, cross road, first L over bridge, L again along Gloucester Ave, pub on L
One of the earlier dining pubs in Primrose Hill, The Lansdowne blends a light, spacious bar and outdoor seating area with a slightly more formal upper dining room. Here you'll find waiter service, and it's worth reserving your table. There's no music or other distractions, so this is an ideal venue for simply eating, drinking and talking with friends. All food is freshly prepared on the premises, using organic or free-range ingredients wherever possible. The seasonal menu offers such dishes as home-made pizzas and sausages, chicken and chorizo stew, roast cod with Seville orange sauce, grilled sea bass with purple-sprouting broccoli, and pan-fried scallops.
OPEN: 12-11 (Sun 12-4, 7-10.30) **BAR MEALS:** Lunch served: Tue-Sun 12.30-2.30 Dinner served: Mon-Sun 7-10 Av main course £9 **RESTAURANT:** Lunch served: Sun 1-4 Dinner served: Tue-Sat 7-11 Av 3 course à la carte £20 Av 3 course fixed price £16.50 **BREWERY/COMPANY:** Bass
PRINCIPAL BEERS: Staropramen, Fuller's London Pride.
FACILITIES: Children welcome

The Lord Stanley 🍷   Map GtL B4
51 Camden Park Rd NW1 9BH
☎ 0207 428 9488 ▤ 020 7209 1347
e-mail: winras@aol.com
In the mid-1990s, Lord Stanley was stripped and re-kitted in a gastro-pub garb that has served the pub well. At an open grill, food is produced in full view - a typically modern idiom producing, perhaps, chicken with mango salsa. Other dishes include seasonal soups, steaks, pasta or sausages with various accompaniments. Monday night jazz.
OPEN: 12-11 Closed: 26 Dec & 1 Jan **BAR MEALS:** Lunch served: Tue-Sun 12.30-3 Dinner served: all week 7-10 Av main course £7.50 **RESTAURANT:** Lunch served: Tue-Sun 12.30-3 Dinner served: all week 7-10 **BREWERY/COMPANY:** Free House

PRINCIPAL BEERS: Young's Special, Adnams Broadside, Greene King Old Speckled Hen. **FACILITIES:** Children welcome Garden: Food served outside Dogs allowed

The Queens 🍷   Map GtL B3
49 Regents Park Rd, Primrose Hill NW1 8XD
☎ 020 7586 0408 ▤ 020 7586 5677
Dir: Nearest tube station - Chalk Farm
With a balcony overlooking Primrose Hill, this Victorian pub is five minutes from Regents Park and the zoo. The management claim to focus their style on a 'shabby chic' image. Specials may feature seared swordfish, rack of lamb, or steamed mussels, while other main courses often include pork and ginger sausages, steamed salmon trout, potato gnocchi, and salmon and smoked haddock cakes.
OPEN: 11-11 **BAR MEALS:** Lunch served: all week Dinner served: all week 12-2.30 7-9.45 Av main course £10 **RESTAURANT:** Lunch served: all week Dinner served: all week 12-2.30 7-9.45 Av 3 course à la carte £30 **BREWERY/COMPANY:** Youngs
PRINCIPAL BEERS: Youngs, guest ales. **FACILITIES:** Drinks may be taken onto Primrose Hill Dogs allowed (water provided)

NW3

The Flask 🍷   Map GtL B4
14 Flask Walk, Hampstead NW3 1HE ☎ 020 7435 4580
Dir: Nearest tube: Hampstead
Friendly local with a new landlord and a fascinating clientele - writers, poets, actors, tourists, locals, workmen, shopkeepers, office-workers, professors and medics. The name reflects the time when flasks were made on site for the healing waters of the Hampstead spa. Dishes range through home-made soup, pies and burgers, fish and chips, sausage and mash and various pastas.
OPEN: 11-11 (Sun 12-11) **BAR MEALS:** Lunch served: all week 12-3 Dinner served: Tue-Sat 6-8.30 Av main course £5
BREWERY/COMPANY: Young & Co **PRINCIPAL BEERS:** Young's: Special, Winter Warmer, WaggleDance. **FACILITIES:** Children welcome Dogs allowed (on lead)

The Holly Bush   Map GtL B4
Holly Mount, Hampstead NW3 6SG ☎ 020 7435 2892
Old-fashioned pub with lots of Edwardian fixtures and fittings. Set in the heart of Hampstead village. Guest ales.

Spaniards Inn 🍷   Map GtL B4
Spaniards Rd, Hampstead NW3 7JJ
☎ 020 8731 6571 ▤ 020 8731 6572
Notorious highwayman Dick Turpin was supposedly born here, the son of landlord John Turpin. The Turpin Bar is where Dick may have sat to watch passing coaches, observing his next victim. The inn, a former tollhouse, was mentioned in Bram Stoker's *Dracula* and the poet Keats frequented the Spaniards when he lived in Hampstead. Traditional pub fare includes fish and chips, pan-fried calves' liver with bacon and sausages with a red onion gravy. Sandwiches and vegetarian dishes are also available.
OPEN: 11-11 (Sun 12-10.30) **BAR MEALS:** Lunch served: all week Dinner served: Mon-Sat 12-10 Av main course £7.50
RESTAURANT: Dinner served: Mon-Sat 5-9 Av 3 course à la carte £15 **BREWERY/COMPANY:** Bass
PRINCIPAL BEERS: Bass, Fullers London Pride, Adnams Broadside, Coachhouse Dick Turpin. **FACILITIES:** Children welcome Children's licence Garden: beer garden, outdoor eating, patio Dogs allowed **NOTES:** Parking 50

continued

England

Ye Olde White Bear ♈   Map GtL B4
Well Rd, Hampstead NW3 1LJ ☎ 0207 4353758
Victorian pub with a Hampstead village feel and varied
clientele. Friendly and traditional. There has been a pub on
this site since 1704. 'A country pub in the heart of London.'
Lots of theatrical memorabilia. Patio at rear. All day bar food
includes steak and Guinness pie, home-made cheeseburger,
and tuna steak.
OPEN: 11–11 **BAR MEALS:** Lunch served: all week Dinner served:
all week Av main course £6 **RESTAURANT:** Lunch served: all week
Dinner served: all week Av 3 course à la carte £13
PRINCIPAL BEERS: Stella, Abbot, Youngs, Carlsberg.
FACILITIES: Children welcome Garden: Food served outside, patio
area Dogs allowed (water provided)

NW5

Pick of the Pubs

The Vine ⌂   Map GtL B4
86 Highgate Rd NW5 1PB
☎ 020 7209 0038 📠 020 7209 3161
What looks like a Victorian pub on the outside has a very
contemporary feel on the inside, with its copper bar,
wooden floors, huge mirrors and funky art. The Vine is
billed as a bar, restaurant and garden, and the latter is a
great asset – fully covered in winter. Rooms are also
available upstairs for private meetings or dinner parties.
The pub is run by James and Paula Myers, and the head
chef is Joel Gottlieb who has recently spent four years in
Australia. Lunch, dinner and weekend brunch menus are
offered, the latter including eggs Benedict, burgers and
roast cod. Bar snack favourites include fish cakes, chicken
satay and tempura sweetcorn, while restaurant fare
features crispy duck pancakes with watercress, ginger and
mango salsa, cassoulet, risottos and classic dishes like
calves liver with dried prosciutto, potato rösti and Madeira
jus.
OPEN: 12.30–3.30 6.30–10.30 Closed: 25/26 Dec
BAR MEALS: Lunch served: all week Dinner served: all week
12.30–3.30 6.30–10.30 Av main course £10
RESTAURANT: Lunch served: all week Dinner served: all week
12.30–3.30 6.30–10.30 Av 3 course à la carte £22
BREWERY/COMPANY: Punch Taverns **FACILITIES:** Children
welcome Garden: patio/terrace, food served outdoors

NW6

The Flask ♈   Map GtL B4
Highgate West Hill N6 6BU ☎ 020 83487346
17th-century former school in one of London's loveliest
villages. Dick Turpin hid from his pursuers in the cellars, and
TS Elliot and Sir John Betjeman enjoyed a glass or two of ale
here. The interior is listed and includes the original bar with
sash windows which lift up come opening time. Enjoy a glass
of mulled wine or a malt whisky while you peruse the menu.
Beer-battered cod, beef and horseradish burger, spaghetti and
hand-made speciality sausages and mash are among the
favourites.
OPEN: 11–11 Closed: Dec 25 **BAR MEALS:** Lunch served: all week
Dinner served: all week 12–3 6–10 Av main course £6.50
PRINCIPAL BEERS: Rooster's Rooster, Adnams, Harveys, Landlord.
FACILITIES: Children welcome Garden: Food served outside Dogs
allowed (water, doggie snacks)

NW8

Pick of the Pubs

The Salt House ◉ ♈   Map GtL B3
63 Abbey Rd NW8 0AE ☎ 020 7328 6626 📠 020 7625 9168
Situated in a leafy area of St Johns Wood, a compact and
informal dining pub with a tiny open-plan kitchen that
takes its food, though not itself, seriously. Expect nothing
short of well-prepared fresh ingredients along with decent
pints of real ale and numerous house wines served by the
glass. A sample menu features Thai fishcakes with sweet
chilli dressing, spiny artichoke, rocket and lentil salad with
olive dressing or potato gnocchi with butternut squash,
sage and Parmesan. For more substantial dishes try roast
free range chicken with flageolet beans and roast garlic,
duck breast with smashed celeriac, or fillet of sea bass
with beetroot, mizuna and horseradish. For afters try the
wonderfully named Rhubarb Eton mess from a tempting
selection.
OPEN: 12–11 Closed: Dec 25–26 & Jan 1 **BAR MEALS:** Lunch
served: all week Dinner served: all week 12.30–3 6.30–10.30 Av
main course £10.50 **RESTAURANT:** Lunch served: all week
Dinner served: all week 12–3 6.30–10.30 Av 3 course à la carte
£20 Av 3 course fixed price £11.75
BREWERY/COMPANY: Greene King
PRINCIPAL BEERS: Greene King IPA, Abbot Ale,.
FACILITIES: Children welcome Garden: Food served outside

NW10

William IV Bar & Restaurant ⌂ ♈   Map GtL B3
786 Harrow Rd NW10 5JX ☎ 020 8969 5944 📠 020 8964 9218
Dir: Nearest tube: Ladbroke Grove or Kensal Green

Located close to lively Ladbroke Grove and Notting Hill, this
popular and tastefully refurbished bar and restaurant is
renowned for live music, art exhibitions and local theatre
productions. The pub also caters for functions and press
launches for its many media and music industry clients. The
daily changing menus might include Middle Eastern lamb
kebabs, roast poussin, pan-fried mackerel, or fettuccine with
roast Mediterranean vegetables.
OPEN: 12–11 (Thu–Sat 12–12, Sun 12–10.30) Closed: Dec 25 & Jan 01
BAR MEALS: Lunch served: all week Dinner served: all week 12–3
6–10.30 Av main course £9 **RESTAURANT:** Lunch served: all week
Dinner served: all week 12–3 6–10.30 Av 3 course à la carte £25
BREWERY/COMPANY: Free House **PRINCIPAL BEERS:** Fuller's
London Pride, Greene King IPA, Interbrew Bass, Brakspear.
FACILITIES: Children welcome Garden: Food served outside

England

SE1

The Anchor 🏠 ♈︎   Map F3
Bankside, 34 Park St SE1 9EF
☎ 020 7407 1577 & 7407 3003 📠 020 7407 0741
e-mail: info@theanchorbankside.co.uk
In the shadow of the Globe Theatre, this historic pub lies on
one of London's most famous tourist trails. Samuel Pepys
supposedly watched the Great Fire of London from here in
1666, and Dr Johnson was a regular, with Oliver Goldsmith,
David Garrick and Sir Joshua Reynolds. The river views are
excellent, and inside are black beams, old faded plasterwork,
and a maze of tiny rooms. A varied menu includes fish and
chips, pan-fried halibut with olives, and cod in crispy bacon
served on wilted spinach.
OPEN: 11-11 (Sun 12-10.30) Closed: Dec 24 **BAR MEALS:** Lunch
served: all week Dinner served: all week 11.30-8.30 Av main course
£12.50 **RESTAURANT:** Lunch served: all week Dinner served: all
week 12-2.30 6-10 Av 3 course à la carte £22.50
PRINCIPAL BEERS: Wadworth 6X, Scottish Courage Courage
Directors, Greene King IPA. **FACILITIES:** Children welcome Garden:
Patio overlooking the River Thames **ROOMS:** 56 bedrooms 56 en
suite from d£69.95

Pick of the Pubs

The Fire Station Restaurant & Bar ◉ 🏠 ♈︎ Map D2
150 Waterloo Rd SE1 8SB
☎ 020 7620 2226 📠 020 7633 9161
e-mail: firestation@regent-inn.plc.uk
Close to Waterloo Station, and handy for the Old Vic
Theatre and the Imperial War Museum, this remarkable
conversion of a genuine early-Edwardian fire station has
kept many of its former trappings intact – possibly the
high point being a rear dining room facing the open
kitchen. An interesting menu includes dishes such as Fire
Station avocado Caesar salad, baked cod with cheese
polenta and pimento and pesto dressing, roast spiced
pork belly with sticky rice and pak choi. Alternatively try
Tandoori seared yellowfin tuna loin, parsley-crusted
calves' liver or traditional bangers and mash. There are
also imaginative midweek and Sunday set-price lunches.
OPEN: 11-11 (Sun 12-10.30) Closed: 25/26 Dec
BAR MEALS: Lunch served: all week Dinner served: all week
12-5.30 Av main course £6 **RESTAURANT:** Lunch served: all
week Dinner served: all week 12-2.45 5-11 Av 3 course à la carte
£18.50 Av 2 course fixed price £16.95
BREWERY/COMPANY: Regent Inns
PRINCIPAL BEERS: Adnams Best Bitter, Brakspear, Youngs Bitter,
Carlsberg-Tetley Bitter. **FACILITIES:** Children welcome patio

---
Pick of the Pubs

The George   Map G3
77 Borough High St SE1 1NH
☎ 020 7407 2056 📠 020 7403 6956
e-mail: info@georgeinn-southwark.co.uk
*Dir: London Bridge tube station, take Borough High Street exit, turn L,
200 yrds on left hand side.*
London's last remaining galleried coaching inn dating
back at least to 1542 when one William Shakespeare
drank here. Now owned by the National Trust, its river
views are breathtaking, while inside there is fading
plasterwork, black beams and a warren of tiny rooms.
Food is almost of secondary importance, offering steak,

ale and Guinness pie and traditional fish 'n' chips along
with some decent real ales- a 'real' olde English pub with
plenty of buzz.
OPEN: 11-11 (Sunday 12-10.30) Closed: 25 Dec
BAR MEALS: Lunch served: all week Dinner served: Mon-Sat
12-4 Av main course £5.50 **RESTAURANT:** Dinner served:
Mon-Sat 5-10 Av 3 course fixed price £12.95
PRINCIPAL BEERS: Fuller's London Pride, Greene King Abbot
Ale, Interbrew Flowers Original. **FACILITIES:** Children welcome
Garden: Food served outdoors

The Market Porter ♈︎   Map F3
9 Stoney St, Borough Market, London Bridge SE1 9AA
☎ 020 7407 2495 📠 020 7403 7697
Dir: Close to London Bridge Station
Traditional tavern serving a market community that has been
flourishing for about 1,000 years. Excellent choice of real ales.
Worth noting is an internal leaded bay window unique in
London. Menu includes beer battered fish and chips, sirloin
steak and Thai and Indian dishes.
OPEN: 6.30-8.30am 11-11 (Sun 12-10.30) **BAR MEALS:** 12-2.30
5-8.30 **RESTAURANT:** 12-2.30 **BREWERY/COMPANY:** Free
House **PRINCIPAL BEERS:** Harveys Best, Scottish Courage Courage
Best, Youngs Bitter, Brakspears Bitter.

The Old Thameside   Map F3
Pickford's Wharf, Clink St SE1 9DG
☎ 020 7403 4243 📠 020 7407 2063
Just two minutes' walk from Tate Modern, the Millennium
Bridge and Shakespeare's Globe, this former spice warehouse
is also close to the site of England's first prison, the Clink. The
pub features a large outdoor seating area that overhangs the
River Thames, and the friendly staff are always happy to point
bewildered tourists in the right direction! Traditional pub fare
includes fish and chips, sausage and mash, curries and
vegetarian pies.
OPEN: 11-11 Closed: 25 Dec **BAR MEALS:** Lunch served: all week
Dinner served: all week 12-3 5-9 Av main course £6.95
PRINCIPAL BEERS: Fuller's London Pride, Adnams Bitter.
FACILITIES: Children welcome

SE5

The Sun and Doves NEW ♈︎   Map GtL C2
61-63 Coldharbour Ln, Camberwell SE5 9NS
☎ 020 7924 9950 📠 020 7924 9330
e-mail: sun.doves@virgin.net
A gastro-pub in recently gentrified Camberwell, known for its
food, drink and art. Free-range produce features, and
specialities are skewers - Haloumi and roast vegetables,
swordfish tikka - prepared on beech skewers, marinated and
grilled to order - and dishes such as moules marinière, bean
and pepper lasagne, and pork and leek bangers. The drinks
range extends to a comprehensive wine list and selection of
cocktails. Bi-monthly art exhibitions include work by Anthony
Gormley, Anish Kapoor, Chris Ofili and Sarah Raphael.
OPEN: 11-11 Closed: 25/26 Dec **BAR MEALS:** Lunch served: all
week Dinner served: all week 12-10 Av main course £9
RESTAURANT: Lunch served: all week Dinner served: all week 11-11
Av 3 course fixed price £17 **BREWERY/COMPANY:** Scottish
Courage **FACILITIES:** Children welcome Garden: Food served
outdoors Dogs allowed

continued

SE10

The Cutty Sark   Map GtL D3
4-7 Ballast Quay, Lassell St SE10 9PD
With commanding views of the Thames and the Millennium Dome, this waterside pub has plenty of atmosphere, well kept beers, wines by the glass and a wide selection of malt whiskies. Busy at weekends.

Pick of the Pubs

North Pole Bar & Restaurant 🐷 ♀   Map GtL D3
131 Greenwich High Rd, Greenwich SE10 8JA
☎ 020 8853 3020 📠 020 8853 3501

This clubby, style-conscious establishment enjoys a prime Greenwich location with views of the Thames and the Millennium Dome. The ground floor bar features a cosmopolitan mix of cocktails and designer leather sofas, whilst the curving wooden staircase leads up to the comfortable restaurant. Here you'll find two calm, dignified rooms, decorated in red and green, with live goldfish swimming in the chandeliers. By contrast, the South Pole champagne and cocktail bar in the basement is themed on an aeroplane cabin, with cool blue and white decor, disco music and air conditioning to maintain the chilled atmosphere. The kitchen exhibits plenty of style, and the menu transcends the overworked gastro-pub image. A reasonably priced lunch menu includes moules marinières or lamb burger on ciabatta bread, with main courses in the restaurant ranging from seafood bouillabaisse or wild mushroom tart to fillet of beef, duck confit, or sautéed monkfish cheeks.
OPEN: 12-12 **BAR MEALS:** Lunch served: all week Dinner served: all week 12-3 Av main course £5 **RESTAURANT:** Lunch served: Sun 12-4 Dinner served: all week 6-11 Av 3 course à la carte £25 Av 3 course fixed price £17
BREWERY/COMPANY: Free House

The Observatory Bar   Map GtL D3
56 Royal Hill, West Greenwich SE10 8RT ☎ 020 8692 6258
Formerly the Observatory Bar, now the first in a chain owned by Charlton micro-brewery, the Meantime Brewing Company. Start with dim sum with chilli dip, or tomato, Mozzarella and basil salad. Then try sirloin steak sandwich with caramelised onions béarnaise and fries, king prawns in filo pastry with plum sauce, or chilli con carne with rice and sour cream. Produces lagers, a cask ale, a chocolate stout and a raspberry beer. Booking essential for Sunday roasts.
OPEN: 11-11 (Sun 12-10.30) **BAR MEALS:** Lunch served: Mon-Sun 12-2 Dinner served: Mon-Sat 6.30-9 Av main course £5.95

FACILITIES: Children welcome Garden: Food served outside. Patio area Dogs allowed (water provided)

SE16

Mayflower Inn ♀   Map GtL C3
117 Rotherhithe St, Rotherhithe SE16 4NF
☎ 020 7237 4088 📠 020 7237 0548
Dir: Exit A2 at Surrey Keys roundabout onto Brunel Rd, 3rd L onto Swan Rd, at T jct L, 200m to pub on R
Before embarking on her historic voyage to the New World, The Mayflower was moored at the jetty you can still see today from the patio of the Mayflower Inn – then known as The Spread Eagle. Links with the voyage have been maintained through the memorabilia now on display. Pub fare includes sausage and mash, liver and bacon, and steak and Abbot Ale pie.
OPEN: Please Phone **BAR MEALS:** 12-3 **RESTAURANT:** 12-4 6.30-9 **BREWERY/COMPANY:** Greene King
PRINCIPAL BEERS: Greene King Abbot Ale, IPA, Old Speckled Hen.
FACILITIES: Jetty over river, Food served outside

SE21

The Crown & Greyhound 🐷 ♀   Map GtL C2
73 Dulwich Village SE21 7BJ ☎ 020 8299 4976 📠 020 8693 8959
Large turn of the century pub which can easily absorb plenty of people, and is very welcoming towards families. The unusual name came from two inns which used to stand here, but it's known locally as The Dog. Meals can be eaten in the conservatory and adjoining restaurant, from daily-changing menus: chicken shitake, lamb shank, speciality sausage and mash, and specials like herb fishcakes, vegetable moussaka, plus a popular Sunday carvery.
OPEN: 11-11 (Sun 12-10.30) **RESTAURANT:** Lunch served: all week Dinner served: all week 12-2.30 6-10
PRINCIPAL BEERS: Adnams Bitter, Fuller's London Pride, Carlsberg Tetley Bitter. **FACILITIES:** Children welcome Garden: Food served outside

SW1

The Albert   Map D2
52 Victoria St SW1H 0NP
☎ 020 7222 5577 & 7222 7606 📠 020 7222 1044
e-mail: thealbert.westminster@snr.co.uk
Dir: Nearest tube - St James Park

Built in 1864, this Grade II Victorian pub is named after Queen Victoria's husband, Prince Albert. The main staircase is decorated with portraits of British Prime Ministers, from Salisbury to Blair, and the pub is often frequented by MPs. The pub was the only building in the area to survive the Blitz

continued

continued

England

of WWII, with even its old cut-glass windows remaining intact. The traditional menu includes a carvery, buffet, a selection of light dishes and other classic fare.
OPEN: 11-11 (Sun 12-10.30) Closed: 25-26 Dec
BAR MEALS: Lunch served: all week Dinner served: all week 11-10.30 Av main course £5 **RESTAURANT:** Lunch served: all week Dinner served: all week 12-9.30 5-9.30 Av 3 course à la carte £14.95 Av 3 course fixed price £14.95 **PRINCIPAL BEERS:** Scottish Courage Courage Directors & Best, Theakston Best, Greene King Abbott Ale.

The Buckingham Arms ♀   Map D2
62 Petty France SW1H 9EU ☎ 020 7222 3386
Dir: St James's Park tube
Known as the Black Horse until 1903, this elegant, busy Young's pub is situated close to Buckingham Palace. Popular with tourists, business people and real ale fans alike, it offers a good range of simple pub food, including the 'mighty' Buckingham burger, nachos with chilli, chicken ciabatta and old favourites like ham, egg and chips in its long bar with etched mirrors.
OPEN: 11-11 (Sat 12-5.30, Sun 12-5.30) **BAR MEALS:** Lunch served: all week 12-2.30 Dinner served: Mon-Fri 6-9 Av main course £4 **BREWERY/COMPANY:** Young & Co
PRINCIPAL BEERS: Youngs Bitter, Special & Winter Warmer.

The Clarence   Map D3
55 Whitehall SW1A 2HP ☎ 020 7930 4808 🖷 020 7321 0859
Dir: Between Big Ben & Trafalgar Sq
Haunted pub, situated five minutes' walk from Big Ben, the Houses of Parliament, Trafalgar Square and Buckingham Palace, with leaded windows and ancient ceiling beams from a Thames pier.

The Grenadier ♀   Map B2
18 Wilton Row, Belgravia SW1X 7NR
☎ 020 7235 3074 🖷 020 7235 3400
Regularly used for films and television series, once the Duke of Wellington's officers' mess and much frequented by King George IV, the ivy-clad Grenadier stands in a cobbled mews behind Hyde Park Corner, largely undiscovered by tourists. Outside is the remaining stone of the Duke's mounting block. Food ranges from traditional fish and chips and beef Wellington to Belgravia salmon and Scottish game pie with oysters.
OPEN: 12-11 (Sun 12-10.30) **BAR MEALS:** Lunch served: all week Dinner served: all week 12-2 6-9.30 Av main course £7
RESTAURANT: Lunch served: all week Dinner served: all week 12-2 6-9.30 Av 3 course à la carte £25 Av 3 course fixed price £20
PRINCIPAL BEERS: Courage Best, Greene King Old Speckled Hen, Fullers London Pride, Bombardier. **FACILITIES:** Children welcome

Nags Head   Map B2
53 Kinnerton St SW1X 8ED ☎ 020 7235 1135
e-mail: bugsmoran@hotmail.com
In a quiet mews near Harrods, this old pub has the feel of a homely local. Once described as the smallest pub in London, it changed hands in 1921 for £11 7s and 6d – the price of a few drinks today! The pub boasts a 'What the Butler Saw' kinescope, used for donations to Queen Charlotte's Hospital. A good choice of decent, home-cooked food and kitchen favourites might include chicken and ham pie, tuna mayonnaise, Mediterranean vegetable quiche and chilli.
OPEN: 11-11 (Sun 12-11) **BAR MEALS:** Lunch served: all week

Dinner served: all week 11-9.30 Av main course £6
BREWERY/COMPANY: Free House **PRINCIPAL BEERS:** Adnams Best, Broadside. **FACILITIES:** Children welcome No credit cards

The Orange Brewery ♀   Map C1
37-39 Pimlico Rd SW1 W8NE ☎ 020 7730 5984
Dir: Nr Sloane Sq or Victoria tube stations
The name comes from local associations with Nell Gwynne, a 17th-century purveyor of oranges and a favourite of Charles II. The building dates from 1790, and fronts onto an appealing square. Beers are brewed in the cellar, including SW1, SW2 and Pimlico Porter, and regulars will find a different guest beer every month. Expect traditional pub food; steak, Guinness and suet pudding, chicken curry, or scampi and chips are favourites.
OPEN: 11-11 (Sun 12-10.30, bar food all day) **BAR MEALS:** Lunch served: all week Dinner served: all week 11-9 Av main course £5.45
PRINCIPAL BEERS: Scottish Courage Courage Directors & Courage Best, Theakston Best, Greene King Ruddles County & Old Speckled Hen. **FACILITIES:** Children welcome Dogs allowed

Westminster Arms   Map D2
Storey's Gate SW1P 3AT ☎ 020 7222 8520
Busy Westminster pub crowded after work with staff from the Houses of Parliament which is just across the square. Wide choice of real ales. Traditional pub food.

SW3

Pick of the Pubs

The Admiral Codrington 🛏 ♀ NEW   Map B2
17 Mossop St SW3 2LY
Affectionately known as The Cod, this old Chelsea pub has been given a make-over to create a smart but homely neighbourhood restaurant. The emphasis is on serving quality food in comfortable surroundings, and the restaurant is bright and warm, with a large skylight to let the sun in on the bare wooden floor. There's a separate bar with its own distinct identity, where you can have a drink or a bar meal: expect home-made linguini with fresh salmon and dill, a grilled chicken, avocado and tomato sandwich, and goats' cheese and roast peppers on ciabatta. In the restaurant the carte might offer starters like wild mushroom tartlet, foie gras and chicken liver parfait, and moules marinière, with such main choices as confit rabbit terrine, green king prawn curry, roast rump of lamb, and crispy salmon fishcake. Virtually all of the well chosen wines are available by the glass.
OPEN: 11.30-11 (Sun 12-10.30) **BAR MEALS:** Lunch served: all week Dinner served: all week 12-2.30 **RESTAURANT:** Lunch served: all week Dinner served: all week 12-2.30 7-10.30 Av 3 course à la carte £33 Av 3 course fixed price £33
BREWERY/COMPANY: Free House **FACILITIES:** Garden: Food served outside. Beer garden

Pick of the Pubs

The Coopers of Flood Street ♀   Map B1
87 Flood St, Chelsea SW3 5TB
☎ 020 7376 3120 🖷 020 7352 9187
A quiet backstreet Chelsea pub close to the Kings Road and the river. Celebrities and the notorious rub shoulders with the aristocracy and the local road sweeper in the bright, vibrant atmosphere, while the stuffed brown bear,

continued

continued

Canadian moose and boar bring a character of their own to the bar. Food is served here and in the quiet upstairs dining room, with a focus on meat from the pub's own organic farm. The fresh, adventurous menu also offers traditional favourites: from a secret recipe there's Aberdeen Angus 'steak les Hooches', along with the likes of seared king scallops with rocket, crème frâiche and sweet chilli sauce, Cooper's Welsh rarebit with crisp prosciutto and Worcestershire sauce, and garlic and chilli prawn linguine in a white wine and cream sauce. Good staff-customer repartee makes for an entertaining atmosphere.
OPEN: 11-11 Closed: 25 Dec **BAR MEALS:** Lunch served: all week 12.30-3 Dinner served: Mon-Sat 6.30-9.30 Av main course £8 **BREWERY/COMPANY:** Young & Co
PRINCIPAL BEERS: Youngs Special, Smiles Bitter, Youngs Bitter.

Pick of the Pubs

The Cross Keys ♀   Map GtL B3
1 Lawrence St, Chelsea SW3 5NB
☎ 0207 3499111 📠 0207 349 9333
A fine Chelsea pub dating from 1765 which has been a famous bolthole for the rich and famous since the 1960s. The stylish interior includes a Bohemian-style banqueting room and open-plan conservatory, plus a restaurant and a first-floor gallery that is adorned with works of modern art. New landlords have introduced a modern European flavour to the menu, although Sunday is mainly traditional with some adventurous forays. The set meals offer good value around dishes likes smoked duck terrine, Toulouse sausages with mash, and date and pecan sponge pudding for lunch. Evening fare differs only in the extra choice on the carte: asparagus and broad bean risotto, or deep-fried Oriental samosas, followed by grilled marinated lamb steak, or baked tranche of cod with seafood linguine.
OPEN: 12-11 (Sun 12-10.30) Closed: Dec 25-26 Jan 1, Easter Mon **BAR MEALS:** Lunch served: all week Dinner served: all week 12-3 6-8 Av main course £12.95 **RESTAURANT:** Lunch served: Mon-Sat Dinner served: Mon-Sat 12-3 7-11 Av 3 course à la carte £23 **PRINCIPAL BEERS:** Theakston Best, Courage Directors. **FACILITIES:** Children welcome

The Front Page   Map A1
35 Old Church St, Chelsea SW3 5BS
☎ 020 7352 0648 & 7352 2908 📠 020 7352 2908
Dir: Nearest tube-Sloane Square & Sth Kensington. (halfway between Albert Bridge & Battersea Bridge)
Backstreet pub nestled between the Thames and Kings Road in Chelsea. Offers a good meal, a chance to catch up on the big screen sporting action, or a quiet pint in front of the fire.

The Phene Arms   Map B1
Phene St, Chelsea SW3 5NY ☎ 020 7352 3294 📠 020 7352 7026
Dir: Nearest tube: Sloane Square & South Kensington
Hidden away down a quiet Chelsea cul-de-sac, a short stroll from The Embankment, this welcoming neighbourhood pub has a charming roof terrace and large garden for summer alfesco eating. Food options range from Jerusalem salad, burgers and Cumberland sausage through to oven-baked cod and fillet steak.
OPEN: 11-11 (Sun 12-10.30) **BAR MEALS:** Lunch served: all week Dinner served: all week 12-3 6-10 Av main course £6.95

RESTAURANT: Lunch served: all week Dinner served: all week 12-3 6-10 Av 3 course à la carte £15 **BREWERY/COMPANY:** Free House
PRINCIPAL BEERS: Adnams Bitter Broadside, Courage Best & Directors, Greene King Old Speckled Hen, Fullers London Pride.
FACILITIES: Children welcome Garden: Dogs allowed

SW4

The Belle Vue   Map GtL B2
1 Clapham Common Southside SW4 7AA
☎ 0207 498 9473 📠 0207 627 0716
Overlooking Clapham Common, the Belle Vue is a popular dining-pub that provides a relaxing atmosphere for enjoyment of its bistro-style food. Comfortable sofas, scrubbed wood panelling and modern art around the walls are the setting for daily dishes posted on chalkboards: lamb shank with winter vegetables, perhaps, or roast cod with scallop gratin. No lunchtime food except at weekends: check for details.
OPEN: 5-11 (Wkds 12-11) Closed: 4-5 days at Xmas
BAR MEALS: Lunch served: Sat-Sun 12.30-4 Dinner served: all week 6.30-10.30 Av main course £8 **BREWERY/COMPANY:** Free House

The Windmill on the Common ★ ★ ★ ♀   Map GtL B2
Clapham Common South Side SW4 9DE
☎ 020 8673 4578 📠 020 8675 1486
Dir: Nearest tube: Clapham Common
There was a windmill on this site in 1655 but it has long gone. In later years the building became a popular watering hole for crowds returning to London from the Epsom Derby and it even appears in the background of a famous painting, now in the Tate Gallery. Inside are two spacious bars, a conservatory and a back room with a roof in the shape of a flattened Byzantine dome. Dishes range from steak and ale pie and sausage and mash, to pasta carbonara and chicken satay with peanut sauce. Separate oak-panelled restaurant and hotel accommodation.
OPEN: 11-11 (Sun 12-10.30) **BAR MEALS:** Lunch served: all week Dinner served: all week 12-2.30 7-10 Av main course £7.95
RESTAURANT: Lunch served: all week Dinner served: all week 12-2.30 7-10 Av 3 course à la carte £16
BREWERY/COMPANY: Young & Co **PRINCIPAL BEERS:** Youngs Bitter, Special, Winter Warmer, Youngs Triple A. **FACILITIES:** Children welcome Children's licence Garden: Food served outside Dogs allowed (water bowl) **NOTES:** Parking 16 **ROOMS:** 29 bedrooms 29 en suite from s£86 d£96

SW6

Pick of the Pubs

The Atlas ♀   Map GtL B3
16 Seagrave Rd, Fulham SW6 1RX
☎ 020 7385 9129 📠 020 7386 9113
e-mail: richardmanners@msn.com
Dir: 2mins walk from West Brompton underground
In a contemporary twist on a old institution, this Victorian pub offers traditional ales along with restaurant quality food and facilities for business meetings, seminars and private dining. The main bar retains its period feel and there's a walled garden for outside eating. The food is Mediterranean inspired with a daily changing menu of 12 dishes ranging from soup, antipasti, risotto and pasta to grilled and roasted fish and meat dishes, as well as casseroles and stews. Favourites among them are wild rocket and saffron risotto with vine tomatoes and Parmesan, and Moroccan lamb tagine with dates, apricots,

continued

continued

SW6 continued

cumin, cinnamon and coriander. Daily deliveries ensure the freshest possible produce available. The wine list is also updated regularly. Ten wines are offered by the glass each month and a further 20 or so by the bottle, representing a good range of varieties and countries.
OPEN: 12–11 (Sun 12–10) Closed: Dec 24–Jan 1, Easter
BAR MEALS: Lunch served: all week Dinner served: all week 12.30–3 7–10.30 Av main course £10
BREWERY/COMPANY: Free House
PRINCIPAL BEERS: Greene King, Charles Wells Bombardier, Wadworth 6X, Fullers London Pride. **FACILITIES:** Children welcome Garden: Food served outside. Heated garden

The Imperial Arms   Map B1
577 Kings Rd SW6 2EH ☎ 020 7736 8549 ▤ 020 7731 3780
e-mail: imperial@fulham.co.uk
Mid 19th-century food pub in one of London's most famous and fashionable streets. Vibrant and spacious inside, with wooden floors, striking features, and a lively and varied clientele. Paved terrace at the back. Wild boar sausages with bubble and squeak and onion gravy, grilled goats' cheese salad, spinach and cheese in puff pastry, various burgers and a selection of snacks feature on the popular menu.
OPEN: 11–11 Closed: BHs **BAR MEALS:** Lunch served: all week 12–2.30 Dinner served: Mon-Fri 7–9.30 Av main course £6.50
BREWERY/COMPANY: Free House **PRINCIPAL BEERS:** Wells Bombardier, Haggard's Imperial Best Bitter. **FACILITIES:** Garden: Food served outdoors, patio Dogs allowed (Garden only)

Pick of the Pubs

The White Horse ♀   Map A1
1–3 Parson's Green, Fulham SW6 4UL
☎ 020 7736 2115 ▤ 020 7610 6091
e-mail: inn@whitehorsesw6.com
Dir: 140 mtrs from Parson's Green tube
The ribald history of the coaching inn that has stood on this site since at least 1688 has been well documented. The inn has advanced a little since then, with an imaginative Sunday brunch menu, popular summer barbecues and beer festivals and a Coach House restaurant serving good value evening meals. Now dubbed the 'Sloaney Pony', the White Horse has the unusual distinction of a cellarman who holds down a day job in the City; nevertheless, his well-kept ales have received the highest accolades. Unusually most of the menu choices include drink suggestions; Highgate Mild with traditional English breakfast, for example, or Schlenkerla Rauchbier with smoked salmon and scrambled eggs on toast. Lunchtime might bring fishcake with tarragon mayonnaise washed down with Forrest Estate Sauvignon Blanc; beer battered cod and chips with Harvey's Sussex Best; or a chargrilled rib-eye steak accompanied by Tim Gramp Grenache.
OPEN: 11–11 (Sun 12–10.30) **BAR MEALS:** Lunch served: all week Dinner served: all week 12–3.30 6–10.30 Av main course £8.25 **RESTAURANT:** Lunch served: all week Dinner served: all week 12–3.30 6–11 Av 3 course à la carte £20
PRINCIPAL BEERS: Adnams Broadside, Interbrew Bass, Harveys Sussex Best, Highgate Mild. **FACILITIES:** Children welcome Garden: Food served outside

SW7

The Anglesea Arms ♀   Map A1
15 Selwood Ter, South Kensington SW7 3QG
☎ 020 7737 7960 ▤ 020 73705611
This South Kensington pub is one of very few privately owned free houses in West London. Its interior is little changed since 1827, though the relatively new dining area has proved a popular addition. The style is clubby with panelled walls and leather-clad chairs. Serving real ales and real food such as grilled sardines, crab fishcakes, honey-roast ham with bubble-and-squeak and pork fillet with celeriac and cider have all proven popular, whilst the Sunday roasts served all day make booking advisable.
OPEN: 11–11 (Sun 12–10.30) Closed: Xmas pm only
BAR MEALS: Lunch served: all week 12–3 Dinner served: all week 6.30–10 Av main course £7.95 **RESTAURANT:** Lunch served: all week Dinner served: all week 12–3 6.30–10 Av 3 course à la carte £17
BREWERY/COMPANY: Free House **PRINCIPAL BEERS:** Fuller's London Pride, Brakspear Bitter, Special, Adnams Bitter.
FACILITIES: Children welcome Garden: Terrace, food served outside Dogs allowed

Pick of the Pubs

Swag and Tails ♀   Map B2
10/11 Fairholt St SW7 1EG
☎ 020 7584 6926 ▤ 020 7581 9935
e-mail: swag&tails@mway.com
See Pick of the Pubs on page 309

SW8

The Artesian Well ♀   Map GtL B2
693 Wandsworth Road, SW8 3JF
☎ 020 7627 3353 ▤ 020 7627 2850
e-mail: max@artesianwell.co.uk
Near Clapham Common, this Italian bar and eatery has a very eccentric interior, with a fireplace as the open mouth of a huge bearded face, and a glass skylight forming part of the floor of the Moody Room and also the ceiling of the bar. Live music is a weekly feature, with open mics on Mondays (acoustic) and Wednesdays (electrified) and a DJ every Friday and Saturday. The menu is wholly Italian, with dishes such as bistecca artesiana, timballo vegetariano, and scaloppine alla principessa.
OPEN: 12–3 6–11 **BAR MEALS:** Lunch served: all week 12–3 Dinner served: Tues-Sat 6–8 Av main course £10.95
RESTAURANT: Lunch served: all week 12–4 Dinner served: Tues-Sat 6–11 Av 3 course à la carte £19.90 Av 2 course fixed price £15.90
PRINCIPAL BEERS: Scottish Courage John Smith's.
FACILITIES: Children welcome

> **Room prices show the minimum double and single rates charged.**
> **Room rates in hotels and B&B's often vary depending on the facilities, so be sure to check prices with the establishment before booking.**

OPEN: 11–11 (Sat 6–11, Sun 12–3)
BAR MEALS: L served Mon–Fri.
D served Mon–Fri. 12–3 6–10
Av main course £10.95
RESTAURANT: L served Mon–Fri.
D served Mon–Fri. 12–3 6–10
Av cost 3 courses £22
BREWERY/COMPANY: FREE HOUSE
PRINCIPAL BEERS: Marston's Pedigree, Wells Bombardier, Scottish Courage John Smiths Smooth
FACILITIES: Children and dogs welcome

Swag and Tails

★ ◎ ♀
10/11 Fairholt Street SW7 1EG
☎ 020 7584 6926 📠 020 7581 9935
e-mail: swag&tails@mway.com
Dir: nearest tube: Knightsbridge tube

Tucked away in a tiny back street in Knightsbridge village, this pretty, flower-decked Victorian pub is just a two-minute stroll from Harrods. Well away from the hustle and bustle, the Swag and Tails is a civilised retreat with warm, friendly service and modern pub food cooked to restaurant standards.

Over the last twelve years, owner Annamarie Boomer-Davies has created a successful and welcoming neighbourhood pub-restaurant with a discerning local trade. Good quality food is served in a warm, relaxing and civilised environment, with high standards of cleanliness and presentation. Pop in for a pint of Wells Bombardier and peruse the daily papers over a decent steak sandwich at the bar, or look to the interesting and constantly changing blackboard menu for something more substantial. Open fires, original panelling and pine tables complement the stripped wooden floors, whilst the windows with their attractive 'swag and tailed' curtains set the scene in which to savour freshly prepared seasonal dishes, inspired by Mediterranean cuisine. A simple dish of marinated olives, or houmous with hot pitta bread head up a list of more adventurous starters like Oriental spring rolls with sweet chilli sauce, or Parma ham and goat's cheese crostini with a wild mushroom salad. There are main courses for every taste, from a roast fillet of peppered salmon with cassoulet of cannellini beans, chorizo, celery and pesto, through pot-roast shoulder of lamb, to serpentini pasta with roasted parsnips, rosemary, pecorino and lemon oil. Round off the meal with Morello cherry sorbet, steamed chocolate and pecan sponge or a selection of English cheeses with pear and date chutney. A decent wine list with tasting notes features a dozen wines by the glass – including champagne.

SW8 continued

The Masons Arms ⟡ ♀
Map GtL B2
169 Battersea Park Rd SW8 4BT
☎ 020 7622 2007 ▤ 020 7622 4662
Dir: *Opposite Battersea Park BR Station*
More a neighbourhood local with tempting food than a
gastro-pub, the worn wooden floors and tables support
refreshingly delightful staff and honest, modern cuisine. Here
you'll find a warm and welcoming atmosphere, equally suited
for a quiet romantic dinner or partying with friends. Open
fires in winter and a summer dining terrace. Daily changing
menus feature wasabi salmon cake, pan-fried blackened tuna,
or spinach and duck spring roll.
OPEN: 12-11 **BAR MEALS:** Lunch served: all week Dinner served:
all week 12-4 6-10 Av main course £8 **RESTAURANT:** 12-4 6-10 Av
3 course à la carte £15 **BREWERY/COMPANY:** Free House
PRINCIPAL BEERS: Brakspear, Wadworth 6X.
FACILITIES: Children welcome Children's licence Garden: Food
served outdoors, patio/terrace Dogs allowed

SW10

Pick of the Pubs

The Chelsea Ram ♀
Map GtL B2
32 Burnaby St SW10 0PL ☎ 020 7351 4008 ▤ 020 73490885
e-mail: chelsearam@establishment.ltd.uk
Dir: *Nearest tube - Earls Court*
Just off the beaten track, this busy neighbourhood gastro-
pub is located close to Chelsea Harbour and Lots Road. It
offers a distinct emphasis on fresh produce, including
market fish and meat from Smithfield. The set monthly
menu has a manifestly modern flavour, exemplified by
interesting and eclectic starters like crispy Thai duck salad,
and ballotine of chicken with pancetta and artichokes.
Main dishes which include special market selections from
the blackboard range from braised lamb shanks with olive
oil mash, Chelsea Ram salad with grilled chicken, bacon
avocado and sour cream dressing, and bangers and mash
with roast field mushrooms and spinach. Wild mushroom
risotto is suitable for vegetarians, while Sunday roasts
might finish with puddings like glazed lemon tart with
lemon sorbet, and caramelised pineapple with raspberry
and mint sorbet. Other pubs in the same ownership are
the Thatched House at Hammersmith, and the Fox and
Hounds off Sloane Square.
OPEN: 11-3 (Fri 11-11, Sun 12-10.30) 5.30-11 Closed: 25-26
Dec, 1 Jan **BAR MEALS:** Lunch served: all week Dinner served:
all week 12-2.30 7-10 Av main course £9 **RESTAURANT:** Lunch
served: all week Dinner served: all week 12-2.30 7-10 Av 3 course
à la carte £18 Av 3 course fixed price £20
BREWERY/COMPANY: Young & Co
PRINCIPAL BEERS: Youngs Bitter, Special & Winter Warmer.

The Sporting Page ♀
Map A1
6 Camera Place SW10 0BH ☎ 020 7349 0455 ▤ 020 7352 8162
e-mail: sportingpage@frontpagepubs.com
Smart Chelsea pub offering good quality food - modern
British and European - with friendly service. Popular with
Chelsea fans meeting up before heading off to Stamford
Bridge. If you don't have a ticket, you can still watch the
action on the large screen TV.
OPEN: 11-11 (Sun 12-10.30) Closed: 25-26 Dec
BAR MEALS: Lunch served: all week 12-2.30 Dinner served:

Mon-Fri 7-10 Av main course £8.50 **BREWERY/COMPANY:** Front
Page Pubs Ltd **PRINCIPAL BEERS:** Shepherd Neame Spitfire
Premium Ale, Charles Wells Bombardier. **FACILITIES:** Children
welcome terrace Dogs allowed

SW11

The Castle
Map GtL B2
115 Battersea High St SW11 3HS ☎ 020 7228 8181
Dir: *Nearest tube - Clapham Junction*
Ivy-covered pub tucked away in 'Battersea Village', with rugs
and rustic furnishings on bare boards inside, and an outside
enclosed patio garden. From home-made soup and cod in
beer batter, the menu extends to beef stew, salmon fishcakes,
Creole fish stew, and organically-reared roast lamb.
OPEN: 12-11 (Sun 12-10.30) Closed: 25-26 Dec
BAR MEALS: Lunch served: all week 12-3 Dinner served: Mon-Sat
7-9.45 Av main course £7.95 **BREWERY/COMPANY:** Young & Co
PRINCIPAL BEERS: Youngs Bitter, Special. **FACILITIES:** Children
welcome Dogs allowed

Duke of Cambridge
Map GtL B2
228 Battersea Bridge Rd SW11 3AA
☎ 020 7223 5662 ▤ 020 7801 9684
e-mail: info@geronimo-inns.co.uk
An award-winning community pub with an eclectic mix of
locals and just a stone's throw from Battersea Park and two of
London's most famous Thames crossings - Battersea Bridge
and Albert Bridge. Popular Saturday brunch menu and
traditional Sunday roasts. The interesting range of dishes
includes chicken and leek pie with Irish champ, confit of duck
on fondant potato jus, asparagus and wild mushroom risotto
and saffron-infused fillet of red mullet with marinated roast
pepper couscous.
OPEN: 11-11 **BAR MEALS:** Lunch served: all week Dinner served:
all week 12-3 7-9.45 Av main course £9.50 **RESTAURANT:** Lunch
served: all week Dinner served: all week 12-2.30 7-9.30 Av 3 course à
la carte £20 **BREWERY/COMPANY:** Young & Co
PRINCIPAL BEERS: Youngs Bitter & Special. **FACILITIES:** Children
welcome Garden: Beer garden, patio, food served outdoors, BBQ

The Fox & Hounds ♀ NEW
Map GtL B2
66 Latchmere Rd, Battersea SW11 2JU
☎ 020 7924 5483 ▤ 020 7738 2678
e-mail: richardmanners@ogh.demon.co.uk
Dir: *Nearest station is Clapham Junction. From the station turn left to go
down St John's Hill then up Lavender Hill. Turn left at the first set of traffic
lights down Latchmere Road. Pub is 200 yards on the left*
A late-19th century pub, restored rather than refurbished by
its latest owners. Fresh, best quality ingredients are delivered
daily from London's markets, so the Mediterranean-style
menu changes accordingly. There are usually two
starters/snacks, half a dozen main dishes, one cheese, one
pudding. For lunch, Moroccan lamb tagine with sultana,
apricots, cinnamon, ginger, cayenne pepper, chickpea salad
and harissa; for dinner, marinated pan-roasted rainbow trout
with coriander, lemon, chilli, roast-garlic mashed potatoes,
tomato and caper salsa.
OPEN: Closed: Easter Day, 24 Dec-01 Jan **BAR MEALS:** Lunch
served: Tue-Sun Dinner served: all week 12.30-3 7-10.30 Av main
course £8 **BREWERY/COMPANY:** Free House
PRINCIPAL BEERS: Bass, Greene King IPA, Fullers London Pride.
FACILITIES: Children welcome Garden: Food served outside. Dogs
allowed

continued

England

SW13

The Bull's Head 🐶 🍷
Map GtL B3
373 Lonsdale Rd, Barnes SW13 9PY
☎ 020 8876 5241 📠 020 8876 1546
e-mail: jazz@thebullshead.com
Established in 1684, overlooking the Thames, the Bull has made its reputation over the last 40 years as a top venue for mainstream, modern jazz and blues. Nightly concerts draw music lovers from miles around encouraged by some fine cask-conditioned ales, more than 200 wines, and over 80 malt whiskies. Traditional, home-cooked meals are on offer in the bar, and from the Nuay Thai Bistro in the converted stable, fine Thai cooking is available throughout the pub in the evening.
OPEN: 11-11 **BAR MEALS:** Lunch served: all week Dinner served: all week 12-3 6-11 Av main course £4.50 **RESTAURANT:** Dinner served: all week 6-11 Av 3 course à la carte £10
BREWERY/COMPANY: Young & Co **PRINCIPAL BEERS:** Young's Special, Bitter, Winter Warmer. **FACILITIES:** Children welcome Garden: Patio, food served outside Dogs allowed

SW18

Pick of the Pubs

The Alma Tavern 🍷
Map GtL B2
499 Old York Rd, Wandsworth SW18 1TF
☎ 020 8870 2537 📠 020 8488 6603
e-mail: drinks@thealma.co.uk
Dir: Wandsworth Town station opposite
Conveniently located across from Wandsworth Station and close to Young's brewery, the Alma is a classic Victorian tavern with a very distinctive green-tiled façade and fine etched-glass windows. The bar's high ceiling, decorative hand-painted mirrors, open fires, simple furnishings, daily papers and lively conversation are all very traditional, but there's a decidedly continental atmosphere to the airy central room and rag-washed rear dining-room. This extends to the imaginative food on offer, which includes organic meats from their own livestock farm in Surrey and home-made breads and pasta. Besides good value sandwiches, moules marinière and chips, warm goats' cheese salad and smoked haddock crostini, the daily-changing menu may list tagliatelle with scallops in a lemon and thyme butter sauce, Moroccan beef with steamed couscous, smoked haddock fishcake with bok choy and poached egg and traditional sausages and mash. Tip-top Young's ales, good house wines (20 by the glass) and excellent coffee.
OPEN: 11-11 Closed: 25-26 Dec **BAR MEALS:** Lunch served: all week Dinner served: all week 12-3 7-10.30 Av main course £8.50 **RESTAURANT:** 12-3 7-10.30
BREWERY/COMPANY: Young & Co
PRINCIPAL BEERS: Youngs PA, SPA, Triple A, Winter Warmer.
FACILITIES: Dogs allowed (water provided)

The Ship Inn 🍷
Map GtL B2
Jew's Row SW18 1TB ☎ 020 8870 9667 📠 020 8874 9055
e-mail: drinks@theship.co.uk
Dir: Wandsworth Town BR station nearby
Situated next to Wandsworth Bridge on the Thames, the Ship exudes a lively, bustling atmosphere. Saloon bar and extended conservatory area lead out to a large beer garden and in the summer months an outside bar is open for business. There is

a popular restaurant, and all-day food is chosen from a single menu, with the emphasis on free-range produce from the landlord's organic farm. Expect the likes of lamb cutlets, chargrilled marlin fillet, shepherds pie, and peppers stuffed with hazelnuts and goats cheese.
OPEN: 11-11 (Sun 12-10.30) **BAR MEALS:** Lunch served: all week Dinner served: all week 12-10.30 7-10.30 Av main course £8.75 **RESTAURANT:** Lunch served: all week Dinner served: all week 12-10.30 Av 3 course à la carte £17 **BREWERY/COMPANY:** Young & Co **PRINCIPAL BEERS:** Youngs: PA, SPA, Triple A, Winter Warmer. **FACILITIES:** Children welcome Garden: Food served outside Dogs allowed (water provided)

W1

The Argyll Arms
Map C4
18 Argyll St, Oxford Circus W1F 7TP ☎ 020 7734 6117
Dir: Nearest tube - Oxford Circus
A tavern has stood on this site since 1740, but the present building is mid-Victorian and is notable for its stunning floral displays. There's a popular range of sandwiches and the hot food menu might offer vegetarian moussaka, beef and Guinness pie, chicken and leek pie, haddock and lasagne.
OPEN: 11-11 (Sun 12-9) Closed 25 Dec **BAR MEALS:** Lunch served: all week 11-3 Dinner served: Mon-Sat Av main course £5.95
BREWERY/COMPANY: Six Continents Retail
PRINCIPAL BEERS: Tetley, Bass, Fullers London Pride, Greene King IPA

French House 🍷
Map D4
49 Dean St, Soho W1D 5BG
☎ 020 7437 2799 📠 020 7287 9109
Notable for its custom of only serving half pints of beer, this small Bohemian bar holds an annual 'Pint Day' in aid of the NSPCC. The bar remains much as it was in the1950s, when it was popular with writers, artists and actors - Brendan Behan, Dylan Thomas and Francis Bacon to name but a few. Weekly changing menus might feature navarin of lamb, roast monkfish with Parma ham, confit of duck with braised lentils and red cabbage, or risotto of roast pumpkin.
OPEN: 12-11 (Sun 12-10.30) Closed: 25 Dec **BAR MEALS:** Lunch served: Mon-Sat 12.30-3 **RESTAURANT:** Lunch served: Mon-Sat Dinner served: Mon-Sat 12-3 5.30-11.30 Av 3 course à la carte £25 **BREWERY/COMPANY:** Free House **PRINCIPAL BEERS:** Scottish Courage John Smith's.

The Glassblower
Map D3
42 Glasshouse St W1V 5JY ☎ 020 7734 8547 📠 020 7494 1049
Ideally placed for visiting the shops and theatres, this wine bar is in the heart of the West End.

The Mortimer NEW
Map D4
40 Berners St W1A 3AA ☎ 020 7436 0451 📠 020 7436 0456
Converted from a former tax office, The Mortimer has become a spacious modern brasserie that's a popular lunchtime venue for local business people. Later on, the mood changes as a wide range of customers flock in for the evening.

Red Lion
Map C3
No 1 Waverton St, Mayfair W1X 5QN
☎ 020 7499 1307 📠 020 7409 7752
e-mail: gregpeck@redlionmayfair.co.uk
Dir: Nearest tube - Green Park
Built in 1752, The Red Lion is one of Mayfair's most historic pubs. Originally used mainly by 18th-century builders, the clientele is now more likely to be the rich and famous of Mayfair, yet the friendly welcome remains.

continued

England

W1 continued

Zebrano
Map C3
14-16 Gantan Street W1V 1LB ☎ 020 72875267 📠 020 72872729
e-mail: info@freedombrew.com
Dir: *5 min walk from Oxford Circus Tube, the micro brew bar is half way down Carnaby Street*
The second of the Fulham-based Freedom Brewing Company's new micro-brew bars, this popular watering hole opened in 1999, taking advantage of the growing demand for fresh, hand-crafted beer. The bar sells a range of six ales made on the premises, as well as offering a varied choice of freshly prepared salads, sandwiches, tortilla wraps and main dishes. Expect fish and chips, baked chicken with steamed greens, Thai spiced mussels, and lamb steak with grilled vegetables.
OPEN: 11-11 Closed: 25-26 Dec, 1 Jan **BAR MEALS:** Lunch served: Mon-Sat Dinner served: Mon-Sat 12-5 6-10 Av main course £6.50 **PRINCIPAL BEERS:** Freedom Beers.

W2

Pick of the Pubs

The Cow Saloon Bar & Dining Rooms
Map GtL B3
89 Westbourne Park Rd W2 5QH
☎ 020 7221 5400 📠 020 7727 8687
e-mail: thecow@thecow.freeserve.co.uk
Dir: *Nearest tubes - Royal Oak & Westbourne Park*
Once known as the Railway Tavern but reputedly renamed after a former landlady of dubious personality, this pub is also close to the 500-year-old drovers' trail leading to Smithfield Market, a fact which might provide a more plausible account of its title. Whatever its genesis, the Cow is well known locally for its enterprising approach to food, promising 'fine dining, oysters, Guinness and cigars'. If Guinness isn't your tipple, there are some good London beers to try as well as a selection of fairly priced wines. Native and rock oysters are on the menu as claimed, along with fish stew, poached hake, grilled mackerel fillet, mussels in Thai yellow sauce, seafood platter and whole crab. Meat lovers can try grilled calves' liver, and sausage and mash from an imaginative menu. Try to arrive early to get the table of your choice - ideally in the upper dining room - as the place can get very busy.
OPEN: 12-11 Closed: 25 Dec **BAR MEALS:** Lunch served: all week Dinner served: all week 12.30-3.30 6.30-10.30 Av main course £10 **RESTAURANT:** Lunch served: Sat-Sun Dinner served: all week 12.30-3.30 6.30-10.30 Av 3 course à la carte £25
BREWERY/COMPANY: Free House
PRINCIPAL BEERS: Fuller's ESB, London Pride.

The Prince Bonaparte
Map GtL B3
80 Chepstow Rd W2 5BE ☎ 020 7313 9491 📠 020 7792 0911
A large Victorian pub, airy and open plan, which has recently come under new management. As the new owners put it, 'A place to enjoy great quality food in a relaxed and very friendly environment.'

Most of the pubs in this guide book pride themselves on the quality of their food. This may take a little time to prepare.

The Westbourne
Map GtL B3
101 Westbourne Park Villas W2 5ED
☎ 020 7221 1332 📠 020 7243 8081
e-mail: ollydna@aol.com
Classic Notting Hill pub/restaurant favoured by bohemian clientele, including a sprinkling of celebrities. Sunny terrace is very popular in summer. Tempting, twice-daily-changing menu is listed on a board behind the bar and might include skate with capers, Morrocan stew, duck breast salad and rabbit with mustard.
OPEN: 11-11 (Mon 5.30-11 only) (Sun 12-10.30) Closed: 24 Dec-5 Jan **BAR MEALS:** Lunch served: Tue-Sun 12.30-3.30 Dinner served: all week 7-9.30 Av main course £8 **RESTAURANT:** Lunch served: all week Dinner served: all week 12.30-3.30 7-9.30 Av 3 course à la carte £20 Av 3 course fixed price £10 **BREWERY/COMPANY:** Free House **PRINCIPAL BEERS:** Boddingtons, Greene King Old Speckled Hen.
FACILITIES: Children's licence Dogs allowed

W5

The Wheatsheaf
Map GtL A3
41 Haven Ln, Ealing W5 2HZ ☎ 020 8997 5240
Dir: *1m from A40 junction with North Circular*
Just a few minutes from Ealing Broadway, this large Victorian pub has a rustic appearance inside. Ideal place to enjoy a big screen sporting event or a warm drink among wooden floors, panelled walls, beams from an old barn, and real fires in winter. Trad pub grub includes cottage pie, beer battered cod and chips, steak, ale and mushroom pie, pork and leek sausage and mash, and vegetable lasagne.
OPEN: 11-11 (Sun 12-10.30) **BAR MEALS:** Lunch served: all week 12-3 Dinner served: Mon-Sat 6-9 Av main course £5
BREWERY/COMPANY: Fullers **PRINCIPAL BEERS:** Fullers London Pride, ESB & Chiswick, Seasonal ales. **FACILITIES:** Children welcome Garden: Food served outside. Dogs allowed

W6

Pick of the Pubs

Anglesea Arms
Map GtL B3
35 Wingate Rd W6 0UR ☎ 020 8749 1291 📠 020 8749 1254
e-mail: Fievans@aol.com
Real fires and a relaxed, smokey atmosphere are all part of the attraction at this traditional corner pub. Behind the Georgian façade the decor is basic but welcoming, and the place positively hums with people eagerly seeking out the highly reputable food. A range of simple, robust dishes might include starters like braised leg of pheasant with caramelised apple and polenta, Anglesea charcuterie platter, or butternut squash and goats' curd risotto. Among main courses could be seared calves' liver with bacon, pot-roast stuffed saddle of lamb, and toasted sea bass with saffron potatoes. Puddings are also exemplary: expect poached pear, brandy snap and pear sorbet, chocolate, pecan and hazelnut 'brownie' cake with vanilla ice cream, or perhaps buttermilk pudding with pineapple and almond biscotti. A savoury alternative might be Cornish yarm with chutney and water biscuits.
OPEN: 11-11 (Sun 12-10.30) Closed: 24-31 Dec
BAR MEALS: Lunch served: all week Dinner served: all week 12.30-2.45 7.30-10.45 Av main course £9.75
RESTAURANT: Lunch served: all week Dinner served: all week 12.30-2.45 7.30-10.45 Av 3 course à la carte £19.50
BREWERY/COMPANY: Free House
PRINCIPAL BEERS: Scottish Courage Courage Best, Greene King Old Speckled Hen, Fuller's London Pride.
FACILITIES: Children welcome

The Stonemasons Arms ♀ NEW   Map GtL B3
54 Cambridge Grove W6 0LA ☎ 020 8748 1397 📠 020 8748 6068
A trendy yet welcoming London gastro-pub with warm
wooden floors and trestle tables, serving 'modern, but honest
British cuisine.' Sample such delights as coriander and corn
pancakes, Cumberland sausages with mash and onion gravy,
grilled blackened tuna on sweet potato and roast garlic ragout,
spinach and duck spring roll on pok choi, and stuffed chicken
breast with goats cheese and beetroot on parsnip mash.
OPEN: 12-11 **BAR MEALS:** Lunch served: all week Dinner served:
all week 12-4 6-10 Av main course £8 **RESTAURANT:** Lunch served:
all week Dinner served: all week 12-4 6-10 Av 3 course à la carte £15
BREWERY/COMPANY: Free House
PRINCIPAL BEERS: Brakspear, Wadworth 6X.
FACILITIES: Children welcome Garden: Food served outdoors
Dogs allowed

Pick of the Pubs

The Thatched House ♀   Map GtL B3
115 Dalling Rd W6 0ET ☎ 020 87486174
e-mail: thatchedhouse@establishment.ltd.uk
This trendy sister pub to the Chelsea Ram (qv), the
Thatched House, in a leafy Hammersmith backwater, is not
thatched at all - nor do the Mediterranean-style features of
a 'modern British' menu evoke the English countryside.
Cosmopolitan gastro-pub fare delivers monthly changing
menus of freshly prepared modern dishes. Expects the
likes of of roasted red pepper soup, seared scallops with
ginger and stir-fried vegetables and American-style
doughnuts with coffee cream and chocolate sauce. The
popular English breakfast salad is borrowed from Gary
Rhodes: grilled black pudding and sausage with bacon and
poached egg on crisp salad leaves. There is a full range of
Youngs' beers on tap plus some 20 wines-by-glass on the
list. The pub also acts as a gallery for artists as the walls
are decorated with paintings that are for sale.
OPEN: 11-3 5.30-11 **BAR MEALS:** Lunch served: all week
Dinner served: all week 12-2.30 7-10 Av main course £9
RESTAURANT: Lunch served: all week Dinner served: all week
12-2.30 7-10 Av 3 course à la carte £20
BREWERY/COMPANY: Young & Co
PRINCIPAL BEERS: Youngs Bitter, Special, AAA.
FACILITIES: Garden: Food served outside Dogs allowed

W8

The Churchill Arms   Map GtL B3
119 Kensington Church St W8 7LN ☎ 020 7727 4242
Dir: Off A40 (Westway). Nearest tube-Notting Hill Gate
Thai food is the speciality at this traditional 200-year-old pub
with strong emphasis on exotic chicken, beef and pork dishes.
Try Thai rice noodles with ground peanuts, spicy sauce and a
choice of pork, chicken or prawns (Kwaitiew Pad Thai), or
special Thai roast duck curry served with rice (Kaeng Ped
Phed Yang). This Oriental feast notwithstanding the Churchill
Arms has many traditional British aspects including oak
beams, log fires and an annual celebration of Winston
Churchill's birthday.
OPEN: 11-11 (Sun 12-10.30) **RESTAURANT:** Lunch served: all
week 12-2.30 Dinner served: Mon-Sat 6-9.30 Av 3 course à la carte £9
Av 1 course fixed price £5.50 **BREWERY/COMPANY:** Fullers
PRINCIPAL BEERS: Fullers London Pride, ESB & Chiswick Bitter.
FACILITIES: Children welcome Garden: Exotic butterflies and plants
Dogs allowed

W10

Goldborne House ♀ NEW   Map GtL B3
36 Goldborne Rd W10 5PR
In an area bristling with the new breed of upmarket dining
pub, this forgotten local as been transformed into a thriving
gastro-pub. Daily dishes are listed on the blackboard menu;
always a seasonal soup, tapas or mezze plate, pasta, risotto
and options such as grilled mullet fillet with caponata, or roast
rack of lamb with roast new potatoes, red onion and balsamic
french beans and red wine jus. Service is exceptional,
provided by helpful and well-informed staff.
OPEN: 12-11 (Sat 12-12, Sun 12-10.30) Closed: 25-26 Dec, 1 Jan
BAR MEALS: Lunch served: all week Dinner served: all week
12.30-3.45 6.30-10.15 Av main course £9 **RESTAURANT:** Lunch
served: all week Dinner served: all week 12.30-3.45 6.30-10.15 Av 3
course à la carte £20 **BREWERY/COMPANY:** Free House
PRINCIPAL BEERS: Fuller's London Pride. **FACILITIES:** Children
welcome Dogs allowed

The North Pole ♀   Map GtL B3
13-15 North Pole Rd W10 6QH
☎ 0208 964 9384 📠 0208 960 3774
A former run-down local transformed by large new windows
and bright decor into a modern 'gastro-pub'. Expect leather
sofas, armchairs, daily papers, a good range of wines by the
glass and a lively atmosphere in the bar. Separate bar and
restaurant menus continue to show real interest, dishes are
modern in style and simply described. 'Small Plates' may
include seared scallops with pineapple salsa, chicken Caesar
salad and rocket and Parmesan salad. 'Main Flavours' include
ribeye steak with roasted potatoes and asparagus risotto.
OPEN: 12-11 (Sun 12-10.30) **BAR MEALS:** Lunch served: all week
Dinner served: all week 12-10 Av main course £7.50
RESTAURANT: Lunch served: all week Dinner served: all week 12-10
Av 3 course à la carte £20 **BREWERY/COMPANY:** Free House
PRINCIPAL BEERS: Fullers London Pride. **FACILITIES:** Children
welcome Food served outside Dogs allowed

Royal State

The Crown is one of the commonest
inn names, for patriotic reasons and
sometimes because the inn stood on royal
land. The Rose and Crown celebrates Henry
VII's achievement in ending civil war by
reconciling the rival roses of York and
Lancaster in the crown. The King's Head, King's
Arms and Queen's Arms are equally familiar,
often with Henry VIII on the sign, roughly after
Holbein. Elizabeth I, the Georges, Queen
Victoria and Prince Albert make their
appearances, too, and many pubs are names
after childen of George III or Queen Victoria
(the Duke of York, Duke of Clarence, Duke of
Edinburgh, etc). Others honour the Prince of
Wales or his badge of the Feathers, while the
Fleur de Lys recalls the fact that down to 1801
the kings of England claimed to be kings of
France as well.

W10 continued

Pick of the Pubs

Paradise by Way of Kensal Green Map GtL B3
19 Kilburn Ln, Kensal Rise W10 4AE
☎ 020 8969 0098 📠 020 8960 9968
e-mail: seeyou@theparadise.co.uk
A truly eclectic pub atmosphere with bare boards, bric-à-brac, oriental tapestries and wrought iron chandeliers creating a Bohemian setting for working artists, musicians and actors. The unusual name derives from the last line of G K Chesterton's poem 'The Rolling English Road', and there are plenty of original Victorian features in keeping with its late 19th-century origins. The food at this lively venue stands up well to the demands placed on it by weekly live jazz and special events like weddings, but don't expect bar snacks or too much flexibility. The self-styled gastro-pub serves classy food from the carte, such as Parma ham with rocket and roasted figs, or crispy fried squid salsa to start, followed by monkfish and mussels in a creamy garlic sauce with linguine, and Moroccan spiced haddock with roast vegetable couscous.
OPEN: 12–11 (Sun 12–10.30) Closed: 25 Dec & Jan 1
BAR MEALS: Lunch served: all week Dinner served: all week 12–4 7.30–11 Av main course £12 **RESTAURANT:** Lunch served: all week Dinner served: all week 12.30–4 7.30–11 Av 3 course à la carte £20 Av 2 course fixed price £15
BREWERY/COMPANY: Free House
PRINCIPAL BEERS: Shepherds Neame Spitfire.
FACILITIES: Children welcome Children's licence Garden: Food served outside. Courtyard Dogs allowed (water provided)

W11

Pick of the Pubs

The Ladbroke Arms Map GtL B3
54 Ladbroke Rd W11 3NW
☎ 020 7727 6648 📠 020 7727 2127
One of London's trendier districts is the location of this pub, close to Holland Park and fashionable Notting Hill, renowned for its street market, chic restaurants and film location image. A broad spectrum of regulars, including the young well-heeled, is drawn to the chatty atmosphere, and seating areas which encompass the popular front courtyard and a split-level dining area to the rear. The menu changes daily, and offers imaginative but not outlandish choices: confit tuna with garlic lentils, soft boiled egg and bottarga, or prawns wrapped in betel leaves (Miang Gung) to start perhaps, then linguini with sweet tomato and basil, or pan-fried salmon with proscuitto, pea and mint risotto. Don't leave without trying banana cake with mascarpone sorbet and custard, or blood orange and chocolate parfait.
OPEN: 11–3 5.30–11 (11–11 Summer months) Closed: Dec 25
BAR MEALS: Lunch served: all week Dinner served: all week 12–7 **RESTAURANT:** Dinner served: Same as bar
BREWERY/COMPANY: Free House
PRINCIPAL BEERS: Wadworth 6X, Everards Tiger, Scottish Courage Courage Directors, Greene King Old Speckled Hen & Abbot Ale.

The Pelican NEW Map GtL B3
45 All Saints Rd W11 1HE ☎ 020 7792 3073 📠 020 7792 1134
e-mail: pelican@singhboulton.co.uk
Built as a pub in 1869, The Pelican organic pub is spread over two floors and has a ground floor bar with outside seating on All Saints Road. There's a wide choice of real ales and over 50 organic wines; upstairs, the dining room is bright, with a view of the working kitchens. The menu changes twice daily. Typical choices include crab and parsley risotto, grilled swordfish, and roast lamb chump.
OPEN: 12–11 **BAR MEALS:** Lunch served: Tues-Sun 12.30–3 Dinner served: all week 6.30–10.30 Av main course £10
RESTAURANT: Lunch served: Tues-Sun Dinner served: all week 12.30–3 6.30–10.30 **BREWERY/COMPANY:** Free House
PRINCIPAL BEERS: Pitfield Eco Warrior, East Kent Goldings, St Peter's Best Bitter. **FACILITIES:** Children welcome Dogs allowed

W14

Pick of the Pubs

The Havelock Tavern Map GtL B3
57 Masbro Rd, Brook Green W14 0LS
☎ 020 7603 5374 📠 020 7602 1163
Dir: Nearest tubes: Shepherd's Bush & Olympia
Renowned as one of the first gastro-pubs, the popular Havelock Tavern occupies a spacious, sunny corner site between Shepherd's Bush and Olympia. The emphasis is very much on an eclectic, ever-changing menu, presented in comfortable informal surroundings; large wooden tables, dark floorboards, and a broadly-based clientele help to give the place its distinctive character and atmosphere. The food is reasonably priced and the menu changes twice daily. The pub is often busy at lunchtime, with working diners who have little time to unwind and savour their meal; but, whilst it's just as crowded in the evening, most of the regulars are much more relaxed and stress-free. Typical dishes might include slow-roast belly of pork with apple and horseradish sauce; grilled scallops with potato purée, spinach, parsley and garlic butter; deep-fried skate cheeks with aïoli and lemon; or smoked haddock with bacon, spring onion and potato mash and a poached egg.
OPEN: 11–11 (Sun 12–10.30) Closed: Xmas 5 days
BAR MEALS: Lunch served: all week Dinner served: all week 12.30–2.30 7–10 Av main course £9.50
BREWERY/COMPANY: Free House
PRINCIPAL BEERS: Brakspear, Marston's Pedigree, Wadworth 6X. **FACILITIES:** Garden: Food served outside No credit cards

WC1

Pick of the Pubs

Cittie of Yorke Map E4
22 High Holborn WC1V 6BS
☎ 020 7242 7670 📠 020 7405 6371
A pub has stood on this site since 1430. In 1695, it was rebuilt as the Gray's Inn Coffee House and the large cellar bar dates from this period. The panelled front bar features an original chandelier and portraits of illustrious locals, including Dickens and Sir Thomas More. In addition to a variety of sandwiches, salads and soups, six hot dishes are freshly prepared each day.
OPEN: 11.30–11 (closed Sun) **BAR MEALS:** Lunch served: all

continued

week Dinner served: all week 12–9 Av main course £5
BREWERY/COMPANY: Samuel Smith
PRINCIPAL BEERS: Samuel Smith Old Brewery Bitter.
FACILITIES: Children welcome

Pick of the Pubs

The Lamb ♀   Map E4
94 Lamb's Conduit St WC1N 3LZ ☎ 020 7405 0713
Dir: Nearest tube: Holborn or Russell Square
Dickens reputedly enjoyed a drink at this traditional
watering hole, with its distinctive green-tiled façade. Built
around 1729, it is an unspoilt Victorian gem of a pub, with
very rare glass snob screens, dark polished wood, and
original sepia photographs of music hall stars who
performed at the old Holborn Engine. The absence of
television, piped music and fruit machines allows the art
of conversation to thrive, although a polyphon in the bar
can be wound up to play a selection of discs by customer
request. A interesting selection of home-cooked bar food
includes a vegetarian corner, a fish choice, light bites, and
from the 'stove', perhaps, lambs' liver and bacon,
traditional shepherd's pie, and sausage and mash. For a
more informal lunch expect also jumbo sausage,
vegetable samosas, and old-fashioned ploughman's.
OPEN: 11–11 (Sun 12–4, 7–10.30) **BAR MEALS:** Lunch served:
all week 12–2.30 Dinner served: Mon–Sat 6–9 Av main course
£5.25 **BREWERY/COMPANY:** Young & Co
PRINCIPAL BEERS: Youngs (full range). **FACILITIES:** Garden:
Small patio, outdoor eating

The Museum Tavern   Map D4
49 Great Russell St WC1B 3BA ☎ 020 7242 8987
Built long before the British Museum, which is just across the
road, this historic inn first opened its doors in 1723. Real ales
from the pump and wines by the glass. Food available all day.

The Perseverance ♀ NEW   Map E4
63 Lambs Conduit St WC1N 3NB
☎ 020 7405 8278 ▯ 020 7831 0031
A Central London haven of good food, fine wine and
abundant conviviality. The elegant, candlelit dining room
upstairs offers six starters: home-made gnocchi, courgettes
and mussels, maybe, while mains might include gilt-head sea
bream with globe artichokes, confit potatoes and red wine
sauce, or daube of pork with cep casserole. Sunday lunch
requires booking.
OPEN: 12–11 Closed: Xmas **BAR MEALS:** Lunch served: 12.30-3
7-10 Av main course £11 **RESTAURANT:** Lunch served: Sun-Fri
12.30-3 7-10 Av 3 course fixed price £22 Av 3 course à la carte £25
BREWERY/COMPANY: Pub Estate Co

PRINCIPAL BEERS: Scottish Courage Courage Directors
FACILITIES: Children welcome

WC2

Freedom Brewing Company   Map D4
41 Earlham St WC2H 9LD ☎ 020 72400606 ▯ 020 72404422
e-mail: info@freedombrew.com
Dir: 5 min walk from Leicester Square or Covent Garden tube station
Launched in 1995, the Freedom Brewing Company is Britain's
first dedicated lager micro-brewery, establishing a reputation
for quality beer and lager among London's more discerning
drinkers. The Earlham Street bar in Covent Garden was
originally part of the Soho Brewing Company and when it
opened, it was the new company's first branded micro-brew
bar. Interesting restaurant and bar menus offering grilled
chicken, rocket salad and bacon, seafood hotpot, calves' liver
with bacon and mash, steak sandwich, fish and chips, and a
daily-changing risotto.
OPEN: 12–11 Closed: 25–26 Dec, 1 Jan **BAR MEALS:** Lunch
served: all week Dinner served: all week 12–10 6–10 Av main course
£7.25 **PRINCIPAL BEERS:** Freedom Beers. **FACILITIES:** Children
welcome

The Lamb and Flag ♀   Map D3
33 Rose St, Covent Garden WC2E 9EB ☎ 020 7497 9504
Opened in 1627 the Lamb and Flag certainly has a long
history, and in 1679 the poet Dryden was almost done to
death in an alley nearby. These days this Covent Garden pub
is well loved by Londoners meeting after work. A typical menu
includes beef and onion pie, roast lamb with Yorkshire
pudding and toad in the hole. No electronic games or music
except jazz on Sunday nights.
OPEN: Mon–Thur 11–11 Fri–Sun 11–10.45 Closed: 25 Dec
BAR MEALS: Lunch served: all week 12–3 Av main course £4.50
PRINCIPAL BEERS: Scottish Courage Courage Best & Directors,
Young's IPA & Special, Charles Wells Bombardier. No credit cards

The Seven Stars   Map E4
53 Carey St WC2A 2JB ☎ 020 7242 8521
e-mail: nathan.silver@htlworld.com
Shakespeare was living in London when the Seven Stars was
constructed in 1602. Nowadays, the pub's clientele is drawn
from the nearby Law Courts, and 'Spy' cartoons of eminent
lawyers decorate the walls. This highly individual free house
serves Adnams ales, and fresh, home-made dishes arrive from
the kitchen in a glass-panelled hoist redolent of an old British
telephone booth. Expect Welsh rarebit, penne in garlic sauce,
or Portuguese pork with clams.
OPEN: 11–11 Closed: 25–26 Dec, 1 Jan, Easter Mon
BAR MEALS: Lunch served: all week Dinner served: all week 11.30–3
5–8 Av main course £7 **BREWERY/COMPANY:** Free House
PRINCIPAL BEERS: Adnams Best, Broadside, Fuller's London Pride,.
FACILITIES: Dogs allowed (water)

Smuggling and Skulduggery

All round Britain's coast an explosion of smuggling was the 18th-century response to high excise
duties on goods imported from abroad. There were villages in Kent where people were said to wash
their windows with smuggled gin, it was so cheap. Inns were often involved, because they had cellars where
casks and bales could conveniently be hidden and they could sell smuggled drink. Smugglers were nothing like
as romantic in real life as they are in fiction. Lawless and violent smuggling gangs could exercise a reign of terror.
Other criminal activities were often associated with some of the rougher pubs, where thieves planned
operations, the landlord fenced stolen goods and the 'gentlemen of the road' dropped in. Many
a pub on the Great North Road claims the famous highwayman Dick Turpin as a habitué.

MERSEYSIDE

BARNSTON   Map 08 SJ28

Fox and Hounds
Barnston Rd CH61 1BW ☎ 0151 6487685
Dir: From M53 J4 take A5137 to Heswell. R to Barnston on B5138

Situated in the conservation area of Barnston, this pub
displays an assortment of 1920s/30s memorabilia, featuring a
collection of policemen's helmets. Traditional pub fare is on
offer, including a range of platters, sausage and mash, hot
pot, lasagne, and chilli, along with daily specials - notably fish
dishes.
OPEN: 11–11 (Sun 12-10.30) **BAR MEALS:** Lunch served: all week
12-2 Av main course £5.95 **BREWERY/COMPANY:** Free House
PRINCIPAL BEERS: Websters Yorkshire Bitter, Theakston XB, Best &
Old Peculier, Marston's Pedigree plus guest beers.
FACILITIES: Children welcome Garden: Food served outside Dogs
allowed **NOTES:** Parking 60 No credit cards

LIVERPOOL   Map 08 SJ39

Everyman Bistro ♀
9–11 Hope St L1 9BH ☎ 0151 708 9545 ▤ 0151 708 9545
e-mail: info@everyman.co.uk
*Dir: Town centre. Bistro in basement of Everyman Theatre, between the
two cathedrals*
The bistro under the Everyman Theatre (which it now owns),
popular with the theatrical and artist communities. Dishes are
made from scratch using prime ingredients; there's a good
vegetarian choice and the sweets are legendary. The menu
changes twice a day, and after 8pm there are 'Small Eats', and
the place becomes more of a candlelit pub, with cask beers
and wines by the bottle or glass. Live music is also a feature.
OPEN: 12-12 (Thur 12-1, Fri-Sat 12-2) Closed: BHs
BAR MEALS: Lunch served: Mon-Sat Dinner served: Mon-Sat 10-2
5-8 Av main course £6.95 **RESTAURANT:** Lunch served: Mon-Sat
Dinner served: Mon-Sat 12-3 4.30-8 Av 3 course à la carte £12
BREWERY/COMPANY: Free House **PRINCIPAL BEERS:** Timothy
Taylor, Castle Eden Ale, Black Sheep Best, Derwents.
FACILITIES: Children welcome Children's licence

Ship & Mitre
133 Dale St L2 2JH ☎ 0151 236 0859 ▤ 0151 236 0855
e-mail: shipandmitre.co.uk
Dir: 5mins from Moorfields underground, 5mins from Lime St Station
Award-winning pub in the heart of bustling Liverpool. Built in
the art deco style of the 1930s and boasting the city's largest
and most varied range of independent or micro-brewery ales;
regular beer festivals. Choose something from the frequently-
changing menu, perhaps chicken and mushroom pie or

cassoulet. There is always a selection of sausages, provided by
a local butcher, as well as at least three vegetarian options.
OPEN: 11.30–11 (Sat 12.30-11, Sun 12.30-10.30) Closed: Dec 25-26,
Jan 1 **BAR MEALS:** Lunch served: Mon-Fri 11.30-2.30 Av main
course £2.75 **BREWERY/COMPANY:** Free House
PRINCIPAL BEERS: Roosters, Salopian, Cottage Pride Old Cottage,
Hyde's Mild. **FACILITIES:** Dogs allowed No credit cards

ST HELENS   Map 08 SJ59

Pick of the Pubs

The Red Cat 🐾 ♀ NEW
8 Red Cat Ln WA11 8RU ☎ 01744 882422 ▤ 01744 886693
Dir: From A580/A570 Junct follow signs for Crank
Reputedly bearing the nickname of a local witch executed
in 1612, the Red Cat is a relaxed, friendly inn dating back
at least 700 years. Whatever it may have seen during that
time, the last few years have been a period of magical
transformation from a bog standard frozen pie and chips
venue into a pub restaurant serving well-sourced, home-
cooked food. Chef/proprietor Ian Martin offers his own
versions of bar classics such as steak and mushroom pie,
curry, fish and chips or ploughman's, whilst the well-
priced set menu has more of a restaurant feel. A meal
could include grilled goat's cheese with olive and tomato
salad followed by braised lamb shank with couscous and
spiced apricot sauce. A seasonally changing blackboard
menu extends the boundaries even further: look out for
dishes such as grilled salmon with mussels, prawn, cream
and parsley sauce or corn-fed Goosenargh chicken with
roast vegetables, garlic and parsley jus. Excellent wine list.
OPEN: 12–11 (Sun 12-10.30) **BAR MEALS:** Lunch served:
Wed-Sun Dinner served: Wed-Sun 12-2 9.30 Av main course £6
RESTAURANT: Lunch served: Wed-Sun Dinner served:
Wed-Sun 12-2 6-9.30 Av 3 course à la carte £18 Av 2 course fixed
price £8.95 **BREWERY/COMPANY:** Inn Partnership
PRINCIPAL BEERS: Carlsberg-Tetley Greenalls Bitter, Scottish
Courage Theakston Best Bitter, Timothy Taylor Landlord,.
FACILITIES: Children welcome **NOTES:** Parking 60

NORFOLK

ATTLEBOROUGH   Map 07 TM09

Griffin Hotel
Church St NR17 2AH ☎ 01953 452149
Town centre inn dating back to the 16th century. Bedrooms.

BAWBURGH   Map 07 TG10

Kings Head 🐾 ♀
Harts Ln NR9 3LS ☎ 01603 744977 ▤ 01603 744990
Dir: From A47 W of Norwich take B1108 W
There are beautiful views of the River Yare and the old mill
from this village pub, which dates from 1602. Log fires make
for a warm welcome in winter and in summer customers
enjoy the pretty garden. The restaurant overlooks the Old Mill,
and the River Yare. A good range of real beer is offered and a
varied menu featuring fresh fish dishes (panfried seabass,
roast cod, seared salmon niçoise, and crayfish and prawn
cocktail), Thai chicken and tiger prawn curry, and steak and
kidney pudding.

continued   *continued*

PUB WALK

Brancaster Staithe
The White Horse

This spectacular walk follows the Norfolk Coast Path. Although know widely as 'Very flat, Norfolk' within its boundaries lies a host of things to see and do. Walking alongside the county's desolate and marshy coastline, one of the finest in Europe, offers a wonderful sense of space and freedom.

Make for the bottom of the garden at the White Horse and turn right to join the Norfolk Coast Path. Walk for 500 yards (457m), enjoying the spectacular views of the wind-blown sand dunes of Scolt Head Island beyond. Numerous species of birds swoop down in search of food as the tide comes in. Turn right to follow a lane known as The Drove (not signposted) towards Burnham Deepdale. Before crossing the A149, the coast road, note 11th-century St Mary's Church, with a rare 11th-century font with figures representing the months of the year. Cross the road at the bus shelter, turn left into Delgate Lane (not signposted) and

walk in a southwards past Valley Farm on the right. Just beyond it you reach The Breaks, a woodland area that sailors at sea used as a navigation point. Continue for another few hundred yards and turn right at a lovely copse and cut through it to a right-hand gated road to Barrow Common. Gorse, ferns and a host of wild flora bring this area to life. Take a path, marked by a finger post, about 20ft (6m) to the left and follow it to where the old Branodunum fort, built to guard the approaches to The Wash, once stood. Retrace your steps to the road where you turn towards the top of Barrow Common. Follow the road downhill, cross the A149 and turn left. Turn right shortly into Harbour Way. During the season you can catch a ferry here to Scolt Head Island. Rejoin the Norfolk Coast Path in front of Brancaster Staithes Sailing Club and head east along the old quayside. Continue for about half a mile (800m) to the marsh-side entrance to the White Horse.

THE WHITE HORSE
Main Road, Brancaster Staithe
KING'S LYNN PE31 8BY
Tel: 01485 210262
Directions: Mid-way between King's Lynn & Wells-next-the-sea on the A149 coastal road. Stunning views across glorious, coastal marshland from conservatory restaurant, sun deck and elegant bedrooms, each with its own terrace, at this stylish dining pub, on the Norfolk Coastal Path. Strong reputation for food with local seafood is a speciality.
Open: 11.30–11 (Sun 12–10.30)
Restaurant : 12–3 7–9
Children welcome and dogs allowed. Garden and parking available.

Distance: 3 1/2 miles (5.7km)
Map: OS Landranger 132
Terrain: Open marshland, gorse and heather common
Paths: Paths, tracks and roads
Gradient: Gentle climbing

Walk submitted and checked by Pamela Farrell

England

BAWBURGH continued

Kings Head

OPEN: 11.30-11 (Sun 12-10.30) **BAR MEALS:** Lunch served: all week Dinner served: all week 12-2.30 6.30-9.30 Av main course £8.50 **RESTAURANT:** Lunch served: all week Dinner served: all week 12-2.30 6.30-9.30 Av 3 course à la carte £25 **BREWERY/COMPANY:** Free House **PRINCIPAL BEERS:** Adnams, Woodforde's Wherry, Green King IPA, Courage Directors. **FACILITIES:** Garden: Food served outside, patio **NOTES:** Parking 100

BINHAM   Map 07 TF93

Chequers Inn ◆◆◆ 🛏
Front St NR21 0AL ☎ 01328 830297
Dir: On B1388 between Wells next the Sea & Walsingham
Located between the picturesque yachting harbour at Blakeney and the village of Walsingham, famous for its shrine, the 17th-century Chequers is ideally placed for exploring North Norfolk's scenic coastline and the famous Stiffkey salt marshes. Popular for good food and real ales, served throughout the beamed bars which feature open fires. Extensive menu highlighting local game, including venison in red wine and the oddly named 'Grunt, Gobble, Zoom & Coo Pie' which contains wild boar, turkey, hare and pigeon. A variety of fish and vegetarian options are also available. Pine-furnished bedrooms are equipped with many useful extras.
OPEN: 11.30-3 5.30-11 (Sun 11.30-3, 7-11) Closed: 25 Dec
BAR MEALS: Lunch served: all week Dinner served: all week 12-2 6-9 Av main course £6.50 **RESTAURANT:** Lunch served: all week Dinner served: all week 12-2 6-9 Av 3 course à la carte £15
BREWERY/COMPANY: Free House **PRINCIPAL BEERS:** Greene King Abbot Ale & IPA, Woodforde's Wherry, Adnams Bitter.
FACILITIES: Garden: Beer garden, food served outdoors
NOTES: Parking 20 **ROOMS:** 2 bedrooms 2 en suite from s£30 d£50

BLAKENEY   Map 07 TG04

The Kings Arms ♀
Westgate St NR25 7NQ ☎ 01263 740341 📠 01328 711733
Grade II listed building on the wonderfully atmospheric North Norfolk coast. An ideal spot for walking and birdwatching. Regular ferry trips to unique seal colony and world-famous bird sanctuaries. Large beer garden with swings for children. Menu offers locally caught fish including cod, haddock, plaice and trout. Other food options include jacket potatoes, sandwiches, steaks and a vegetarian selection.
OPEN: 11-11 **BAR MEALS:** Lunch served: all week Dinner served: all week 12-9.30 Av main course £5 **BREWERY/COMPANY:** Free House **PRINCIPAL BEERS:** Greene King Old Speckled Hen, Woodfordes Wherry, Marston's Pedigree, Adnams Best Bitter.
FACILITIES: Children welcome Garden: Food served outside Dogs allowed (water) **NOTES:** Parking 10 **ROOMS:** 7 bedrooms 7 en suite from s£30 d£60

Pick of the Pubs

White Horse Hotel 🛏 ♀
4 High St NR25 7AL ☎ 01263 740574 📠 01263 741303
e-mail: whitehorse4@lineone.net
Dir: From A148 (Cromer to King's Lynn rd) turn onto A149 signed to Blakeney.

Set in the National Trust marshes with fine views across the harbour, this 17th-century coaching inn, built of traditional brick-and-flint and set around the old courtyard and stables has a deserved reputation for both its accommodation and its food. Comprehensive bar menus have an unsurprisingly strong aquatic bias - herring roes on toast, plaice or cod in beer batter with home-cut chips and home-made fisherman's pie - supplemented by a blackboard of daily specials that embraces salmon fillet with mussel and thyme sauce and sea bass grilled with caramelised onions. Salads, sandwiches and children's items all play their part here. Dinner in the restaurant overlooking a walled garden, by comparison, takes a more serious if well-tried route that offers poached chicken and crayfish salad with sweet pepper mayonnaise and fricassee of monkfish, leeks and wild mushrooms followed by traditional treacle tart. Alternatives include tomato, spinach and Brie flan, roast partridge with bread sauce and bacon and fillet of beef with roasted butternut squash.
OPEN: 11-3 6-11 (Sun 12-3, 7-10.30) Closed: 4-19 Jan
BAR MEALS: Lunch served: all week Dinner served: all week 12-2 6-9 Av main course £6.95 **RESTAURANT:** Dinner served: Tue-Sat 7-9 Av 3 course à la carte £20
BREWERY/COMPANY: Free House
PRINCIPAL BEERS: Adnams Bitter, Interbrew Bass.
FACILITIES: Children welcome Garden: courtyard, food served outside **NOTES:** Parking 14 **ROOMS:** 10 bedrooms 10 en suite from s£40 d£60

Shove Halfpenny
The game is still played with pre-decimal halfpennies, lovingly preserved, but is not as popular and widespread in pubs as it used to be. It is a scaled-down version of shuffleboard, which involved propelling flat metal discs along a smooth wooden table up to 30ft long. Down to the First World War a playing area was often drawn in chalk on the bar or a tabletop, but today a special wooden or slate board is used, 24 inches long by 15 inches wide. As usual, the house rules vary in detail from one pub to another.

BLICKLING   Map 07 TG12

Pick of the Pubs

The Buckinghamshire Arms
Blickling Rd NR11 6NF ☎ 01263 732133
Dir: From Cromer (A140) take exit at Aylsham onto B1354
There is a strongly traditional feel to this late 17th-century
coaching inn, right by the gates of the National Trust's
spectacular Blickling Hall. The inn was originally built for
house guests and their servants, and Anne Boleyn is said to
wander in the adjacent courtyard and charming garden.
There is nothing ethereal about the pub's strong local
following, or the solid furniture and wood-burning stoves in
the lounge bar and restaurant. House guests are still
welcome in the three charming four-poster bedrooms, two
of which have majestic views of Blickling Hall. A dinner carte
is offered in the restaurant, and a bar snack menu for lunch
and supper, supplemented by daily specials such as beef in
ale casserole, baked black bream with avocado salsa, and
red peppers baked with tomatoes, basil and Mozzarella.
OPEN: 11–3.30 6.15–11 Closed: 25 Dec **BAR MEALS:** Lunch
served: all week Dinner served: all week 12.30–2 Av main
course £8 **RESTAURANT:** Lunch served: all week Dinner
served: all week 12.30–2 7.30–9 Av 3 course à la carte £14
BREWERY/COMPANY: Free House
PRINCIPAL BEERS: Adnams, Woodforde's Blickling.
FACILITIES: Garden: Food served outside. Sheltered garden &
lawn Dogs allowed (in the garden only) **NOTES:** Parking 60
ROOMS: 3 bedrooms 1 en suite from s£30 d£40

BRANCASTER   Map 07 TF74

Pick of the Pubs

The White Horse
Main Rd, Brancaster Staithe PE31 8BY
☎ 01485 210262 ▯ 01485 210930
e-mail: reception@whitehorsebrancaster.co.uk
See Pub Walk on page 317
See Pick of the Pubs on page 320

BRISTON   Map 07 TG03

The John H Stracey ♦♦♦
West End NR24 2JA ☎ 01263 860891 ▯ 01263 862984
e-mail: thejohnhstracey@btinternet.com

15th-century inn originally known as the Three Horseshoes.
Renamed after the British boxer who was world welterweight
champion in the mid-1970s. Plenty of character inside, with

log fire and copper features. Norfolk's spectacular coast is
close by. Wide choice of good food includes Trout Van Den
Berg, lasagne verdi, steak and ale pie, seafood platter and
chips, steak Mirabeau, and duck Normandy.
OPEN: 11–2.30 6.30–11 **BAR MEALS:** Lunch served: all week
Dinner served: all week 12–2.30 6.30–10 Av main course £7.50
RESTAURANT: Lunch served: all week Dinner served: all week
12–2.30 6.30–10 **BREWERY/COMPANY:** Free House
PRINCIPAL BEERS: Greene King Old Speckled Hen, Ruddles County,
Greene King IPA. **FACILITIES:** Children welcome Garden: Food
served outside **NOTES:** Parking 30 **ROOMS:** 3 bedrooms 1 en suite

BURNHAM MARKET   Map 07 TF84

Pick of the Pubs

The Hoste Arms ★ ★ ◉◉ ⌂ ♀
The Green PE31 8HD ☎ 01328 738777 ▯ 01328 730103
e-mail: reception@hostearms.co.uk
See Pick of the Pubs on page 323

BURNHAM THORPE   Map 07 TF84

Pick of the Pubs

The Lord Nelson
Walsingham Rd PE31 8HN ☎ 01328 738241
e-mail: lucy@nelsonslocal.co.uk
Step inside this 350-year-old cottage, with its huge high-
backed settles, old brick floors, open fires and traditional
atmosphere. This unspoilt gem was named after England's
most famous seafarer who was born in the rectory of this
sleepy village in 1758. Nelson memorabilia can also be
seen in the pub. Greene King and Woodforde ales are
tapped from the cask in the cellar room, or a dram of the
popular rum concoction called 'Nelson's Blood', made to a
secret recipe, can be sampled here. The food also makes a
visit worthwhile, with its seafood, vegetarian choices, grills
and baguettes: starters like chicken leg terrine with red
onion marmalade, and star anise confit, might be followed
by chicken and wild mushroom pasta bake, and braised
lamb shank with tomato cassoulet. Families are warmly
welcomed, and children will enjoy the garden with its
climbing frame, wooden play area and basketball net.
OPEN: 11–3 6–11 (Sun 12–3, 7–10.30) **BAR MEALS:** Lunch
served: all week 12–2 Dinner served: Mon-Sat 7-9 Av main
course £9.50 **BREWERY/COMPANY:** Greene King
PRINCIPAL BEERS: Greene King Abbot Ale & IPA, Woodforde's
Nelsons Revenge. **FACILITIES:** Children welcome Garden:
Food served outdoors Dogs allowed (on lead, water)
NOTES: Parking 30

continued

OPEN: 11.30–11 (Sun 12–10.30)
RESTAURANT: L served all week.
D served all week. 12-2 7-9
Av cost 3 course £20
BREWERY/COMPANY:
FREE HOUSE
PRINCIPAL BEERS: Greene King
Abbot Ale, IPA, Adnams Regatta
FACILITIES: Children welcome,
dogs allowed. Garden: Terrace,
food served outside
NOTES: Parking 45
ROOMS: 15 en suite Double room
from £68 Single room from £54

The White Horse

Gloriously located dining pub set beside the tidal marshes at Brancaster Staithe, with stunning views across the wildlife-rich coastline. The award-winning seafood can be enjoyed in the airy conservatory restaurant, the scrubbed bar or the summer sun deck.

⚲
Main Road Brancaster Staithe PE31 8BY
☎ 01485 210262 🖷 01485 210930
e-mail:
reception@whitehorsebrancaster.co.uk
Dir: mid-way between King's Lynn & Wells-next-the-sea on the A149 coastal road.

Expect a friendly welcome at this stylish pub which can be found in an unspoilt part of North Norfolk near the coastal path and Scolt Head Island. Scrubbed pine tables, high-backed settles, an open log fire in winter and cream painted walls contribute to the bright, welcoming atmosphere. In summer the sun deck comes into its own, where diners can watch the small sailing boats heading for the harbour entrance, and the sea retreating from the salt marsh. Local seafood is the reason for

the pub's enviable reputation, with freshly-harvested local mussels, oysters and samphires often appearing on the menu. Lunch (daily-changing) might see the menu offering a seafood risotto starter (or larger helping as a main dish) alongside chargrilled red mullet fillets, local mussels steamed in white wine, carpaccio of beef fillet, and a classic Caesar salad. Move on to pan-fried plaice or fillet of black bream, seared loin of tuna, pan-roasted breast of guinea fowl, or mushroom and spinach risotto. Some similar evening dishes including tempura of king prawns, pan-fried pigeon breasts, and to follow, pan-fried monkfish tail or fillet of red snapper, roast cod with linguini, and roasted fillet of salmon. If you can't tear yourself away from this heavenly spot, eight tasteful bedrooms, some with terrace and one on a split level with internal balcony, enjoy the same fantastic views.

CLEY NEXT THE SEA   Map 07 TG04

George & Dragon Hotel 🏨 ♀
High St NR25 7RN ☎ 01263 740652 📠 01263 741275
e-mail: thegeorge@cleynextthesea.com
Dir: *On coast road (A149). Centre of village*
The George and Dragon is a classic Edwardian Inn overlooking the marshes to the sea, and it is here that the first naturalist trust was formed in 1926. Sandwiches, ploughman's and jacket potatoes are available until 6pm, in addition to the main menu. Typical dishes from the latter are mixed seafood salad, Norfolk chicken breast stuffed with Brie and bacon and served with rosemary risotto, and smoked Norfolk ham with egg and chips.
OPEN: 11-3 6-11 (Winter 11.30-2.30 6.30-11) **BAR MEALS:** Lunch served: all week Dinner served: all week 12-2.30 6.30-9 Av main course £6 **RESTAURANT:** Lunch served: all week Dinner served: all week 12-2 6.30-9 Av 3 course à la carte £13
BREWERY/COMPANY: Free House **PRINCIPAL BEERS:** Greene King IPA, Abbot Ale & Old Speckled Hen, Adnams Bitter, Woodforde's Wherry. **FACILITIES:** Children welcome Garden: Beer garden, food served outdoors Dogs allowed **NOTES:** Parking 15 **ROOMS:** 9 bedrooms 9 en suite from s£40 d£44

COLKIRK   Map 07 TF92

The Crown 🏨 ♀
Crown Rd NR21 7AA ☎ 01328 862172 📠 01328 863916
e-mail: exhgrd@paston.co.uk
Dir: *2m from B1146 Fakenham-Dereham rd*

A quietly-located inn in a country village with plenty of enjoyable walks nearby. Open fires in winter, and a sunny terrace on warmer days make this a popular haunt with a lively atmosphere. The menu offers oriental tiger prawns and mushrooms, pan-fried chicken fillet, and various steaks, plus blackboard specials like fruity pork curry, chicken with Stilton sauce, and fillet of salmon with lemon sauce.
OPEN: 11-2.30 6-11 **BAR MEALS:** Lunch served: all week Dinner served: all week 12-1.45 7-9.30 Av main course £7.75
RESTAURANT: Lunch served: all week Dinner served: all week 12-1.45 7-9.30 Av 3 course à la carte £14
BREWERY/COMPANY: Greene King **PRINCIPAL BEERS:** Greene King - IPA, Abbot Ale, Mild, Ruddles County. **FACILITIES:** Children welcome Garden: Food served outside. Lawned area Dogs allowed **NOTES:** Parking 30

♦ **Indicates AA inspected bed & breakfast accommodation**

COLTISHALL   Map 07 TG21

Pick of the Pubs

Kings Head ♦♦♦ ⊛⊛ 🏨 ♀
26 Wroxham Rd NR12 7EA
☎ 01603 737426 📠 01603 736542
Dir: *A47 Norwich ring road onto B1150 to North Walsham at Coltishall. R at petrol station, follow rd to R past church, on R next to car park*

Beamed 17th-century inn located on the banks of the River Bure in the heart of the Norfolk Broads. Bar meals are available at lunchtime, and the evening carte can be served in the bar or no-smoking restaurant. Fish features prominently, and popular starters include pan-fried herring roes served on a bread croûton, or Brancaster mussels with white wine, cream and shallots. Main course options take in cod with bacon lardons and button mushrooms, and half a crispy aromatic duck roasted in sesame seeds and honey. A choice of vegetarian dishes might include vegetable Thai green curry, and other special diets can be catered for. You can finish your meal with traditional vanilla crème brûlée served with a tuile and strawberry Romanoff, or sticky toffee pudding with ice cream and banoffee cream. Accommodation is provided in comfortable bedrooms with en suite or private facilities.
OPEN: 11-3 6-11 (Sun all day) Closed: 25-26 Dec
BAR MEALS: Lunch served: all week Dinner served: all week 12-2 7-9 Av main course £6.95 **RESTAURANT:** Lunch served: all week Dinner served: all week 12-2 7-9 Av 3 course à la carte £22 **BREWERY/COMPANY:** Free House
PRINCIPAL BEERS: Adnams Bitter, Scottish Courgae Courage Best, Marston's Pedigree. **FACILITIES:** Children welcome **NOTES:** Parking 20 **ROOMS:** 4 bedrooms 2 en suite from s£25 d£50

DOCKING   Map 07 TF73

Pilgrims Reach 🏨 ♀
High St PE31 8NH ☎ 01485 518383
Dir: *From Hunstanton take A1495 then B1454 or A149 E then B1153*
Once a resting place for pilgrims journeying to the shrine at Walsingham, parts of this traditional flint and chalk building date from 1580. Now a warm and friendly village inn, the pub is deservedly popular for its excellent food. There's an extensive range of fish, from Blakeney whitebait to salmon, halibut and monkfish, with special seasonal menus, too. Other dishes include pies, steaks and pasta.

continued

England

DOCKING continued

Pilgrims Reach

OPEN: 12–2.30 6–11 Closed: 1st Wk Feb **BAR MEALS:** Lunch served: Wed–Mon Dinner served: Wed–Mon 12–2 6–9 Av main course £7 **RESTAURANT:** Lunch served: Wed–Mon Dinner served: Wed–Mon 12–2 6–9 Av 3 course à la carte £19
BREWERY/COMPANY: Free House **PRINCIPAL BEERS:** Shepherd Neame Spitfire & Bishops Finger, Greene King IPA plus guest ales.
FACILITIES: Children welcome Garden: Food served outside Dogs allowed (water) **NOTES:** Parking 50

EASTGATE   Map 07 TG12

Pick of the Pubs

Ratcatchers Inn
Easton Way NR10 4HA ☎ 01603 871430 🖹 01603 873343
Dir: Off A140, past Norwich Airport take B1149 to Holt, thru Horsford, 6m then pub signed

A white pan-tiled Norfolk country inn that, 'tis said, derives its unusual name from the 'one-penny-per-tail' bounty paid to local rat catchers in the 19th century. Today's home-made, home-cooked policy includes no such delicacy but promises their own bread baked on the premises, home oils, chutneys, purées and stocks. All menu items are cooked to order, with vegetarians especially spoiled for choice, so do not expect to cut and run. Enjoy instead a choice of real ales and a sensible selection of wines by glass or bottle whilst awaiting Cley smoked mackerel, locally-smoked sausage with Norfolk mustard and parcels of deep-fried Camembert and Stilton. Move on to steak and kidney pie, Coxwain's fish pie or vegetable Stroganoff, and for massive appetites steaks with speciality sauces, Continental and Eastern dishes and the best available local or Billingsgate fish listed daily on blackboards. Various choices for youngsters and loads of home-made desserts reward the adventurous.
OPEN: 11.45–3 6–11 Closed: 26 Dec **BAR MEALS:** Lunch served: all week Dinner served: all week 11.45–2 6–10 Av main

course £9 **RESTAURANT:** Lunch served: all week Dinner served: all week 11.45–2 6–10 Av 3 course à la carte £20
BREWERY/COMPANY: Free House
PRINCIPAL BEERS: Adnams, Hancocks, Greene King IPA.
FACILITIES: Children welcome Garden: Food served outside. Lawned area Dogs allowed (in the garden only)
NOTES: Parking 30

See Pub Walk on page 325

EATON   Map 07 TG20

Red Lion
50 Eaton St NR4 7LD ☎ 01603 454787 🖹 01603 456939
Dir: off the A11
17th-century coaching inn retaining original features such as Dutch gables, beams, panelled walls and inglenook fireplaces. Bar food includes home-made soups, freshly-cut sandwiches, and sausages and mash. The restaurant offers Norfolk duck, prime beef ribs and steaks, game in season, Scotch salmon, Dover sole, and Norfolk skate.
OPEN: 11–3 6–11 (Sun 12–3, 7–10.30) **BAR MEALS:** Lunch served: all week Dinner served: all week 12–2.15 7–9 Av main course £6.95
RESTAURANT: Lunch served: all week Dinner served: all week 12–2 7–9 Av 3 course à la carte £16.50 **BREWERY/COMPANY:** Free House **PRINCIPAL BEERS:** Theakston Bitter, Scottish Courage Courage Best, Courage Directors, Greene King IPA.
FACILITIES: Garden: Covered Patio, food served outside
NOTES: Parking 40 **ROOMS:** 7 bedrooms 7 en suite

ERPINGHAM   Map 07 TG13

Pick of the Pubs

Saracen's Head
Wolterton NR11 7LX ☎ 01263 768909 🖹 01263 768993
e-mail: saracenshead@wolterton.freeserve.co.uk
Dir: A140 2.5m N of Aylsham, L through Erpingham, signs 'Calthorpe'. Through Calthorpe 1m on R (in field)

In the same hands for some 13 years, it is known as north Norfolk's 'Lost Inn' and merits both the name and the detour to find it. There is a great sense of fun in its mildly eccentric approach and inventive menus that don't go in for chips or peas. Unexpected pleasures include the possibility of dining alfresco in the garden, and a lack of piped music or amusement machines to disturb the delightful parlour-room atmosphere of the interior, warmed by welcoming open fires on colder days. Seasonally changing blackboard menus reflect the enthusiasm, undimmed over many years, of chef/proprietor Robert Dawson-Smith. Morston mussels cooked in cider and cream, baked Cromer crab with mushrooms and sherry and grilled whole plaice with red

continued   *continued*

OPEN: 11-11
RESTAURANT: L served all week.
D served all week. 12–2 7–9
Av cost 3 course £25
BREWERY/COMPANY: FREE
HOUSE
PRINCIPAL BEERS: Woodforde's
Wherry, Greene King Abbot Ale &
IPA
FACILITIES: Dogs allowed.
Garden: Patio, food served outside
NOTES: Parking 45
ROOMS: 36 en suite

The Hoste Arms

★ ★ ◎◎ ♀
The Green, Burnham Market PE31 8HD
☎ 01328 738777 🖹 01328 730103
e-mail: reception@hostearms.co.uk
Dir: Signposted off B1155, 5m w of
Wells-next-the-Sea

A great transformation over recent years has turned this into one of the truly great inns of Britain. Twelve years of hard work has seen the 16th-century Hoste Arms grow from a fairly run-down village pub which was allowed to run to seed by unsympathetic brewers, into today's classy little hotel.

In its former lives it has been a court assizes, an auction house and a brothel, and now dedicated owners Jeanne and Paul Whittome have pledged themselves to creating a classically egalitarian atmosphere. The non-dining village bar has been restored, and local fishermen may literally drop in for a pint or two with their catch. Several interlinked and air-conditioned dining areas have been added, serviced by a well-run kitchen that copes well with popular demand. Food is in the capable hands of Australian chef Andrew McPherson, and to see his menu is to be unable to resist. Starters or light meals come in the guise of carpaccio of beef, terrine of tuna and monkfish, and grilled goats' cheese with pimento purée. For a main course, consider a pot of Brancaster mussels, tempura monkfish with chorizo risotto, or baked halibut with a watercress and Stilton crust. If meat takes your fancy, try honey-glazed ham hock and green pea purée, chargrilled fillet of beef with horseradish mash, and Thai chicken curry. Pasta dishes also listed along with oriental stir-fry, and there are irresistible puddings like chocolate truffle cake, Christmas pudding parfait, and sticky toffee pudding. Beers, wines, malt whiskies and digestifs are legion, and meticulously chosen to go with the food. To round off a visit here there are comfortable, individually designed bedrooms.

England

ERPINGHAM continued

pesto butter are the stars of the fish list. On a par for meat lovers are medallions of Gunton venison with blackberries and Marsala, roast woodpigeon, and rare roast beef rib for Sunday lunch. Crispy fried aubergine with garlic mayonnaise, followed perhaps by baked avocado and sweet pear with Mozzarella, are equally inspired vegetarian options. To follow, nursery puddings are a house speciality. Delightful en suite bedrooms.
OPEN: 11.30–3 6–11.30 (Sun 12–3, 7–10.30) Closed: 25 Dec
BAR MEALS: Lunch served: all week Dinner served: all week 12.30–2.15 7.30–9.15 Av main course £9.50
RESTAURANT: Lunch served: all week Dinner served: all week 12.30–2 7.30–9 Av 3 course à la carte £17.50
BREWERY/COMPANY: Free House
PRINCIPAL BEERS: Adnams Bitter. **FACILITIES:** Children welcome Garden: courtyard garden, food served outside
NOTES: Parking 50 **ROOMS:** 4 bedrooms 4 en suite from s£30 d£60

FAKENHAM
Map 07 TF92

The Wensum Lodge Hotel 🍴
Bridge St NR21 9AY ☎ 01328 862100 📠 01328 863365
e-mail: enquiries@wensumlodge.fsnet.co.uk
Originally built around 1750 as the grain store to Fakenham Mill, this privately-owned family establishment opened as a restaurant in 1983. It later became the Wensum Lodge Hotel, taking its name from the river it overlooks. The emphasis is on friendly service and quality home-cooked food. Expect mixed seafood, steak, mushroom and Guinness pie, pan-fried peppered fillet of lamb, griddled salmon fillet, roast vegetable lasagne, and a variety of 'Sizzling Combos', savoury pancakes, salads, jacket potatoes, baguettes, and chargrills.
OPEN: 11–11 **BAR MEALS:** Lunch served: all week Dinner served: all week 11.30–3 6.30–10 Av main course £8.50
RESTAURANT: Lunch served: all week Dinner served: all week 11.30–3 6.30–10 Av 3 course à la carte £22 Av 3 course fixed price

£15.50 **BREWERY/COMPANY:** Free House
PRINCIPAL BEERS: Greene King Abbot Ale & IPA, Scottish Courage John Smith's, Norfolk Wherry. **FACILITIES:** Children welcome Garden: Beer garden, food served outdoors, patio **NOTES:** Parking 20 **ROOMS:** 17 bedrooms 17 en suite from s£55 d£70

The White Horse Inn ♦♦♦ 🍴
Fakenham Rd, East Barsham NR21 0LH
☎ 01328 820645 📠 01328 820645
e-mail: rsteele@btinternet.com

Near 10th-century East Barsham Manor, this refurbished 17th-century inn with its log-burning inglenook has lost none of its character. Freshest ingredients are assured in daily specials that may include seafood platter, grilled chicken spiced chicken breast, steak and kidney suet pudding, chargrilled leg of lamb steak, or green leaves with goats cheese and roasted peppers.
OPEN: 11–3 6–11 **BAR MEALS:** Lunch served: all week Dinner served: all week 12–2 7–9.30 Av main course £5.50
RESTAURANT: Lunch served: all week Dinner served: all week 12–2 7–9.30 **BREWERY/COMPANY:** L & J Leisure
PRINCIPAL BEERS: Adnams Best, Greene King, Woodforde's, Wells Eagle IPA. **FACILITIES:** Children welcome Garden: Patio, foood served outside **NOTES:** Parking 50 **ROOMS:** 3 bedrooms 3 en suite from s£27 d£35

National Trust pubs

The National Trust began in 1895 and secured its first property a year later, paying the princely sum of £10 for it. Today, it is the country's biggest landowner, with over 600,000 acres of countryside, 550 miles of coastline, over 300 historic houses and more than 150 gardens. As a rule, we don't associate the National Trust with Britain's pubs, but this long-established independent charity owns a number of notable hostelries around the country. Among the most famous are the ancient Fleece Inn – originally a medieval farmhouse – at Bretforton in the Cotswolds, the 18th-century Castle Inn in the picturesque Kent village of Chiddingstone, and the historic George at Lacock in Wiltshire. The National Trust's George in London's Borough High Street is the only surviving example of the capital's once numerous galleried coaching inns, while the Spread Eagle at Stourhead, close to the Somerset/Wiltshire border, was acquired by the Trust in 1947. A number of distinguished visitors have passed through its doors over the years, including Horace Walpole and David Niven.

PUB WALK

Eastgate
The Ratcatchers Inn

A very pleasant stroll through a rural Norfolk village, visiting the famous Church of St Agnes and providing a hint of the county's classic arable countryside.

Leave the pub and take the lane to the north signposted Cawston. After about half a mile (800m) turn left at a row of conifers and walk through a bluebell wood, turning right at Wood Farm. Head in a northerly direction towards the village of Cawston. Turn left at the crossroads into Back Lane and follow it towards the Church of St Agnes, noted for its hammerbeam roof. The church, once patronised by Michael de la Pole, Earl of Suffolk, is stark but impressive. Inside is a pulpit delicately balanced on a stone base, and nearby is the screen which still has its doors and original paintings. Some of the stalls and benches have carvings. The church is well worth a visit. The walk continues through the churchyard to the lane where you can see the memorial to the Flying Fortress which crashed here in 1944. Walk north towards the High Street and here you have a choice. Turn right to the village centre, then make for the south side of the village and return to the inn; to continue the main walk turn left to the railway bridge where you descend a few steps on the left to the Marriott's Way track, a disused railway line. Pass under the bridge and walk to the next junction where you turn right, back into the village beside Broadland Wineries. Turn left, then take the first right past the garage to bring you back to the crossroads on the south side of the village. Here you can retrace your steps or turn left, taking you directly back to the inn. Another option would be to turn left just beyond the bluebell wood and the conifers, following a track known as Craft Lane. On sunny summer days many butterflies can be seen on this stretch of the walk. Turn right at the road and return to the pub.

THE RATCATCHERS,
Easton Way EASTGATE nr Cawston NR10 4HA
Tel: 01603 871430
Directions: Off A140, past Norwich Airport take B1149 to Holt, thru Horsford, 6m then pub signed 5m.

A pan-tiled Norfolk country inn deriving its name from the bounty once paid to local rat-catchers. Home-made, home-cooked food so do not expect fast food. Enjoy instead a choice of real ales and good wines.
Open: 11.45–3 6–11
Bar meals:11.45–2 6–10
Children welcome and dogs allowed. Garden and parking available

Distance: 3 1/2miles (5.7km)
Map: OS Landranger 133
Terrain: -Arable farmland and village
Paths: - Mostly lanes woodland paths
Gradient: -Virtually flat except optional steps down to Marriott's Way

Walk submitted by Peter McCarter of The Ratcatchers Inn

GREAT BIRCHAM — Map 07 TF73

King's Head Hotel
PE31 6RJ ☎ 01485 578265

Attractive 17th-century inn with a beamed snug, comfortable lounge and a wood-burning stove in the inglenook fireplace. The village has an impressive restored windmill, and is close to Haughton Hall.
OPEN: 11-2.30 7-11 **BAR MEALS:** Lunch served: all week Dinner served: all week 12-2 7-9.30 Av main course £6.50
RESTAURANT: Lunch served: Wed-Mon Dinner served: Mon, Wed-Sat Av 3 course à la carte £18 **BREWERY/COMPANY:** Free house **PRINCIPAL BEERS:** Interbrew Worthington Best & Bass, Adnams Bitter **FACILITIES:** Children welcome Dogs allowed
NOTES: Parking 100 **ROOMS:** 6 bedrooms 6 en suite from s£38 d£59

GREAT RYBURGH — Map 07 TF92

The Boar Inn
NR21 0DX ☎ 01328 829212
e-mail: boarinn@aol.com
Dir: Off A1067 4m S of Fakenham

Deep in rural Norfolk, this 300-year-old inn sits opposite the village's round-towered Saxon church. Its new owners offer a good variety of food, including bar/alfresco snacks and children's meals. Try beef Madras served with rice 'and things', sweet and sour chicken with noodles, plaice fillet with prawns in Mornay sauce, or prime Norfolk steaks. Specials include skate wing with garlic and herb butter, and wild boar steak with cranberry and red wine jus.
OPEN: 11-2.30 6.30-11 **BAR MEALS:** Lunch served: all week Dinner served: all week 12-2 7-9.30 Av main course £5.95
RESTAURANT: 12-2 7-9.30 **BREWERY/COMPANY:** Free House **PRINCIPAL BEERS:** Adnams, Boar Ale. **FACILITIES:** Children welcome Children's licence Garden: Food served outside.
NOTES: Parking 30 **ROOMS:** 5 bedrooms 5 en suite from s£29 d£49

HAPPISBURGH — Map 07 TG33

The Hill House
NR12 0PW ☎ 01692 650004 ⎙ 01692 650004
Dir: 5m from Stalham, 8m from North Walsham
16th-century coaching inn with original timbers situated in an attractive coastal village. Sir Arthur Conan Doyle stayed here and was inspired to write a Sherlock Holmes story called The Dancing Men. One of the bedrooms is in a converted railway signal box. Changing guest ales; good value bar food; large summer garden. Look out for the likes of steaks, chicken breast with leek and Stilton, vegetable tikka masala, or seafood platter. Beer festival each June.
OPEN: 12-3 7-11 (Sat-Sun all day) (Summer all day)
BAR MEALS: Lunch served: all week Dinner served: all week 12-2.30 7-9.30 Av main course £5 **RESTAURANT:** Lunch served: all week Dinner served: all week 12-2.30 7-9.30 Av 3 course à la carte £16 **BREWERY/COMPANY:** Free House
PRINCIPAL BEERS: Shepherd Neame Spitfire, Buffy's, Woodforde's Wherry , Adnams Bitter. **FACILITIES:** Children welcome Garden: Large, Patio, food served outside Dogs allowed (water)
NOTES: Parking 20 **ROOMS:** 3 bedrooms 1 en suite from s£13 d£26

HETHERSETT — Map 07 TG10

Kings Head Public House
36 Norwich Rd NR9 3DD ☎ 01603 810206
Dir: Old Norwich Road just off B1172 Cringleford to Wymondham road. 5m SW of Norwich
Attractive 17th-century roadside inn with a wealth of original beams and a large inglenook fireplace. There is a pleasant enclosed rear garden. In October 1818 following the murder of a local glove-maker Hethersett's police constables arrested one James Johnson at the pub. A good range of food, with typical dishes on the menu including lasagne, steak and kidney pie, all-day brunch, and cod. Daily specials vary from Cajun chicken to fillet of beef.
OPEN: 11-2.30 5.30-11 (Sun 12-3, 7-10.30) **BAR MEALS:** Lunch served: all week 12-2 Dinner served: Mon-Sat 6.30-9 Av main course £6.50 **RESTAURANT:** Lunch served: all week Dinner served: Mon-Sat 12-2 6.30-9.30 Av 3 course à la carte £15
BREWERY/COMPANY: Unique Pub Co
PRINCIPAL BEERS: Adnams Best Bitter, Greene King Abbot Ale, IPA, Scottish Courage John Smith's Smooth. **FACILITIES:** Children welcome Garden: Patio, food served outside **NOTES:** Parking 20

HEVINGHAM — Map 07 TG12

Marsham Arms Freehouse
Holt Rd NR10 5NP ☎ 01603 754268 ⎙ 01603 754839
e-mail: nigelbradley@marshmarms.co.uk
Dir: 4m N of Norwich Airport on B1149 through Horsford

continued

Built by local Victorian landowner and philanthropist Robert Marsham as a hostel for farm labourers, this beamed inn has brick interiors and a large open fire. The addition of a new function facility means that cabaret and live music is now a feature. Traditional English fare is the order of the day, and main dishes include steak and kidney pie, peppered steak, salmon fillet, seafood mornay, cashew nut roast, and a variety of grills.
OPEN: 10–3 6–11 (open All day Summer) Closed: 25 Dec
BAR MEALS: Lunch served: all week Dinner served: all week 11–3 6–9.30 Av main course £8 **RESTAURANT:** Lunch served: all week Dinner served: all week 12–3 6–9.30 Av 3 course à la carte £15
BREWERY/COMPANY: Free House **PRINCIPAL BEERS:** Adnams Best, Woodforde's Wherry Best Bitter, Greene King IPA, Interbrew Bass. **FACILITIES:** Children welcome Garden: Beer garden, food served outdoors, BBQ **NOTES:** Parking 100 **ROOMS:** 10 bedrooms 10 en suite from s£45 d£65

HEYDON — Map 07 TG12

Earle Arms 🐷 ♀
The Street NR11 6AD ☎ 01263 587376
Dir: signed off the main Holt to Norwich rd, between Cawston & Corpusty
The Earle Arms is a 17th-century pub situated opposite the village green in a classic estate village – a great base for exploring the North Norfolk Coast. The interior retains much of this timeless quality, with log fires, attractive wallpapers, prints and a collection of china and other bric-a-brac. It comprises two rooms, one with service through a hatch, and there are more tables outside in the pretty back garden, a blaze of colour in the summer months. You can expect a good pint of Adnams bitter, Woodforde's Wherry or a third guest ale, and proper home-cooked food from the bar menu. Local fish features, and popular dishes include baked crab, Chinese beef stir-fry, chicken and mushroom Stroganoff, and aubergine and pepper au gratin.
OPEN: 12–3 6–11 (Sun 12–3, 7–10.30) **BAR MEALS:** Lunch served: all week 12–2 7–9 Av main course £5.50
BREWERY/COMPANY: Free House **PRINCIPAL BEERS:** Adnams, Woodfordes Wherry, Adnams Broadside, Bass. **FACILITIES:** Children welcome Garden: Food served outside. Cottage garden Dogs allowed **NOTES:** Parking 6 No credit cards

HORSEY — Map 07 TG42

Nelson Head 🐷
The Street NR29 4AD ☎ 01493 393378 📠 01692 670383
Dir: On coast rd (B1159) between West Somerton & Sea Palling
Located on a National Trust estate, just a short walk from the beach and Horsey Mere, this 17th-century inn has a cosy country pub atmosphere with a log fire in the winter. Hearty menu includes cod and plaice in beer batter, cauliflower cheese, cottage pie, fish pancakes, skate with black butter and capers, and a variety of filled baguettes.
OPEN: 11–2.30 7–11 **BAR MEALS:** Lunch served: all week Dinner served: all week 11–2 6–9 Av main course £7.50
RESTAURANT: Lunch served: all week Dinner served: all week 11–2 6–9 Av 3 course à la carte £14 **BREWERY/COMPANY:** Free House
PRINCIPAL BEERS: Woodforde's Wherry, Nelsons Revenge, Greene King IPA. **FACILITIES:** Garden: Food served outside
NOTES: Parking 30 No credit cards

HORSTEAD — Map 07 TG21

Recruiting Sergeant 🐷 ♀
Norwich Rd NR12 7EE ☎ 01603 737077 📠 01603 736905
Dir: on the B1150 between Norwich & North Walsham
Listed in the Domesday Book, this inviting country pub in one of the prettiest areas of Norfolk offers good food, ales and wines in homely surroundings. Its name comes from the tradition of recruiting serviceman by giving them the king's/queen's shilling in a pint of beer. The menu is ever changing, with daily specials reflecting local produce and seasonal variety - fresh wing of Norfolk skate, spicy chicken stir-fry, and fillet steak with Roquefort sauce.
OPEN: 11–11 **BAR MEALS:** Lunch served: all week Dinner served: all week 12–2 6.30–9.30 Av main course £8.95 **RESTAURANT:** Lunch served: all week Dinner served: all week 12–2 6.30–9.30 Av 3 course à la carte £15 **BREWERY/COMPANY:** Free House
PRINCIPAL BEERS: Elgoods, Adnams, Interbrew Boddington, Greene King Abbot Ale. **FACILITIES:** Children welcome Garden: Food served outdoors, patio Dogs allowed (water) **NOTES:** Parking 40

ITTERINGHAM — Map 09 TG13

Walpole Arms ♀
NR11 7AR ☎ 01263 587258

A formidable new team runs this handsome country inn on the edge of the village: a producer from BBC's Master Chef, a respected local wine merchant and a chef dedicated to use of finest seasonal produce. Such produce includes mussels from Morston, venison reared at nearby Gunton Hall and organic meat from the Felbrigg (NT) Estate. Imaginative bar snacks, à la carte dining, a fine selection of cask ales and, naturally, some pretty tidy wines.
OPEN: 12–3 6–11 **BAR MEALS:** Lunch served: all week 12–2.30 Dinner served: Mon–Sat 7–9.30 Av main course £9
RESTAURANT: Lunch served: all week Dinner served: Mon–Sat 12–2.30 7–9.30 Av 3 course à la carte £25
PRINCIPAL BEERS: Adnams Broadside, Woodfordes Wherry Best Bitter. **FACILITIES:** Children welcome Garden: Food served otudoors Dogs allowed **NOTES:** Parking 100

KING'S LYNN — Map 07 TF62

The Tudor Rose Hotel ★ ★
St Nicholas St PE30 1LR ☎ 01553 762824 📠 01553 764894
e-mail: frances@tudorrosehotel.com
Dir: Hotel is off Tuesday Market Place in the centre of Kings Lynn
Built by a local wool merchant and situated in the heart of King's Lynn, the oldest part of this historic inn dates back to 1187 and was originally part of the winter palace of a Norfolk bishop. The Dutch gable extension of 1645 remains one of the best examples of its kind in the town. Cosy snug and medieval-style tapestries inside. Dishes range from steak and kidney pie and ham, egg and chips to Mexican chilli and prawn salad. Various light bites and starters and a good choice of well-kept beers, whiskies and popular wines.
OPEN: 11–11 (Sun 7–10.30) **BAR MEALS:** Lunch served: Mon–Sat Dinner served: Mon–Sat 12–2 7–9 Av main course £5.50
RESTAURANT: Lunch served: Sun 12–3 Dinner served: Mon–Sat 7–9 Av 3 course à la carte £20 9 **BREWERY/COMPANY:** Free House
PRINCIPAL BEERS: Fullers London Pride & 3 guest ales.
FACILITIES: Children welcome Garden: beer garden, outdoor eating, patio **ROOMS:** 13 bedrooms 11 en suite from s£40 d£60

continued

LARLING
Map 07 TL98

Angel Inn 🍴 ♀
NR16 2QU ☎ 01953 717963 📠 01953 718561
In 1983, after a forty year gap, the current landlord resumed the family residency at this traditional and charming roadside pub that was once managed by his great-grandfather. There is a big collection of jugs in the bar, which also houses a woodburner in its brick fireplace. Over a hundred malt whiskies are available. The menu includes steaks, grills, seafood, Indian dishes, a vegetarian selection, burgers, sandwiches and salads. Also a wide choice of reasonably priced ice cream sundaes.
OPEN: 10–11 **BAR MEALS:** Lunch served: Sun–Sat Dinner served: Sun–Sat 12–2 6.30–9.30 Av main course £6.95 **RESTAURANT:** Lunch served: Mon–Sun Dinner served: Mon–Sun 12–2 6.30–9.30 Av 3 course à la carte £14 **BREWERY/COMPANY:** Free House
PRINCIPAL BEERS: Adnams Bitter, Buffy's Bitter, Wolf Bitter.
FACILITIES: Children welcome Garden: Beer garden, food served outdoors **NOTES:** Parking 100 **ROOMS:** 5 bedrooms 5 en suite from s£30 d£50

LITTLE FRANSHAM
Map 07 TF91

The Canary and Linnet 🍴
Main Rd NR19 2JW ☎ 01362 687027 📠 01362 687021
e-mail: canaryandlinnet@btinternet.co.uk
Pretty former blacksmith's cottage with exposed beams, low ceilings, inglenook fireplace and a conservatory dining area overlooking the rear garden. Food is offered in the bar, restaurant or garden from daily specials, a la carte or bar menu. Typical dishes include cod in beer batter, steak and ale pie, salmon fillet with chive butter sauce, panfried liver and bacon, or shark steak. Selection of malt whiskies.
OPEN: 12–3 6–11 (Sun 12–3 7–10) **BAR MEALS:** Lunch served: Mon–Sat 12–2 Dinner served: all week 7–9.30 Av main course £7.20 **RESTAURANT:** Lunch served: all week Dinner served: Mon–Sun 7–9.30 **BREWERY/COMPANY:** Free House
PRINCIPAL BEERS: Greene King IPA, Woodfordes Wherry, Adnams Bitter, Wolf. **FACILITIES:** Children welcome Garden: Food served outside Dogs allowed **NOTES:** Parking 70

LITTLE WALSINGHAM
Map 07 TF93

The Black Lion Hotel 🍴 NEW
Friday Market Place NR22 6DB
☎ 01328 820235 📠 01328 821406
e-mail: blacklionwalsingham@btinternet.com
Dir: From Kings Lynn take A148 and B1105 or from Norwich take A1067 and B1105.
Frequented by Edward III on his numerous pilgrimages to one of England's oldest shrines at Walsingham, it became a coaching inn in the 17th century, and later hosted the Petty Sessions. Nowadays catering for seekers of good food and drink, it offers an interesting bar menu with snacks alongside a medley of seafood, and chicken and leek pie. The à la carte choice includes shredded duck with orange sauce, and Chinese hock of pork.
OPEN: 12–3 6–11 (Easter–Oct 11.30–11) **BAR MEALS:** Lunch served: all week Dinner served: all week 12–2 7–9.30 Av main course £7.50 **RESTAURANT:** Dinner served: all week 7–9.30 Av 3 course à la carte £14.50 **BREWERY/COMPANY:** Free House
PRINCIPAL BEERS: Greene King IPA, Carlsberg-Tetley Bitter.
FACILITIES: Children welcome Garden: Food served outdoors, well Dogs allowed (water) **ROOMS:** 6 bedrooms 4 en suite from s£35 d£55

MARSHAM
Map 07 TG12

The Plough Inn 🍴
Old Norwich Rd NR10 5PS ☎ 01263 735000 📠 01263 735407
e-mail: enquiries@ploughinnmarsham.co.uk
Smart, traditional style country pub and restaurant close to the historic town of Aylsham and ideally placed for the Norfolk Broads. Good base for fishing and walking; 10 en suite bedrooms. A typical menu includes dishes like home-made pies, vegetarian options, and fish choices such as plaice, cod and red snapper.
OPEN: 11–3 6–11 **BAR MEALS:** Lunch served: all week Dinner served: all week 12–2.30 6.30–8.30 Av main course £4 **RESTAURANT:** Lunch served: all week Dinner served: all week 12–2.30 6.30–8.30 Av 3 course à la carte £15 **BREWERY/COMPANY:** Free House **PRINCIPAL BEERS:** Adnams, Greene King IPA, Woodforde's. **FACILITIES:** Children welcome Garden: beer garden, food served outdoors **NOTES:** Parking 80 **ROOMS:** 11 bedrooms 11 en suite from s£43.50 d£60

MUNDFORD
Map 07 TL89

Crown Hotel
Crown Rd IP26 5HQ ☎ 01842 878233 📠 01842 878982
Dir: Take A11 until Barton Mills interception, then A1065 to Brandon & thru to Mundford
Ideal for those who enjoy walking, the Crown is surrounded by the Thetford Forest and was once a hunting inn. Unusually for Norfolk, the property is built on a hill so the garden is on the first floor. The Court Restaurant was once used as a magistrate's court. Today's menu may offer monkfish and lobster tails with savoury citrus butter, or beef roulade with pork forcemeat.
OPEN: 11–11 **BAR MEALS:** Lunch served: all week Dinner served: all week 12–3 7–10 Av main course £6.50 **RESTAURANT:** Lunch served: all week Dinner served: all week 12–3 7–10 Av 3 course à la carte £20 **BREWERY/COMPANY:** Free House
PRINCIPAL BEERS: Woodforde's Wherry, Courage Directors, Marstons Pedigree, Theakston Best. **FACILITIES:** Children welcome Garden: beer garden patio, food served outside Dogs allowed **ROOMS:** 16 bedrooms 16 en suite from s£35 d£55

NORWICH
Map 05 TG20

Adam & Eve ♀
Bishopsgate NR3 1RZ ☎ 01603 667423 📠 01603 667438
e-mail: theadamandeve@hotmail.com
Customers have been quenching their thirst at this historic, award-winning pub in the heart of Norwich for centuries. The Adam & Eve was first recorded as an alehouse in 1249 when it was used by workmen building the nearby cathedral. The building grew in the 14th and 15th centuries when living accommodation and the Flemish gables were added. A varied menu offers dishes like beef and ale pie with mushrooms, battered cod or plaice, Elizabethan pork and salmon goujons.
OPEN: 11–11 Closed: 25–26 Dec, 1 Jan **BAR MEALS:** Food served: all week 12–7 Av main course £4 **BREWERY/COMPANY:** Free House **PRINCIPAL BEERS:** Adnams Bitter, Theakston Old Peculiar, Greene King IPA, Wells Bombadier. **NOTES:** Parking 10 No credit cards

The Fat Cat ♀
49 West End St NR2 4NA ☎ 01603 624364
Back street pub with a wide choice of up to 26 real ales and four Belgian draught beers. Food is limited to filled rolls, and there are tables outside in summer.

Ribs of Beef ♀
24 Wensum St NR3 1HY ☎ 01603 619517 📠 01603 625446
e-mail: roger@cawdron.co.uk
Welcoming riverside pub incorporating remnants of the
original 14th-century building destroyed in the Great Fire in
1507. Once used by the Norfolk wherry skippers, it is still
popular among boat owners cruising the Broads. The pub is
named after one of Henry VIII's favourite dishes. Wide range
of real ales.
OPEN: 10.30-11 **BAR MEALS:** Lunch served: all week 12-2.30
Dinner served: by arrangement Av main course £4.65
BREWERY/COMPANY: Free House
PRINCIPAL BEERS: Woodforde's Wherry, Adnams Bitter, Whitbread
Bitter, Marston's Pedigree. **FACILITIES:** Children welcome

REEDHAM   Map 05 TG40

Pick of the Pubs

Railway Tavern 🐾 ♀
17 The Havaker NR13 3HG ☎ 01493 700340
e-mail: railwaytavern@tiscali.co.uk
See Pick of the Pubs on page 331

The Reedham Ferry Inn
Ferry Rd NR13 3HA ☎ 01493 700429 📠 01493 700999
Dir: 6m S of Acle on B1140 (Acle to Beccles rd)
Quaint 17th-century inn, situated in lovely Norfolk Broads
country and associated with the last working chain ferry in East
Anglia. With the same name over the door for more than fifty
years, this is one of the longest running family inns in East
Anglia. Typical bar food includes sandwiches and baguettes,
prawn submarine and home-made curry, while the restaurant
offers market fresh fish, rack of pork ribs, and home-made pies.
OPEN: 11-3 6.30-11 (Sun 12-10.30) **BAR MEALS:** Lunch served:
Mon-Sat 12-2 Dinner served: all week 7-9 Av main course £6
RESTAURANT: Lunch served: Mon-Sat 12-2 Dinner served: all week
7-9 **BREWERY/COMPANY:** Free House
PRINCIPAL BEERS: Woodforde's Wherry, Adnams - Best &
Broadside, Greene King Abbot Ale. **FACILITIES:** Children welcome
Garden: Food served outside. Riverside with tables Dogs allowed
(water provided) **NOTES:** Parking 50

REEPHAM   Map 07 TG12

The Old Brewery House Hotel ★ ★
Mallet Place NR10 4JJ ☎ 01603 870881 📠 01603 870969
e-mail: enquiries@oldbreweryhousehotel.co.uk
Dir: off the A1067 Norwich to Falenham rd, B1145 signed Aylsham
A grand staircase, highly polished floors and wooden
panelling characterise this fine hotel, originally built as a
private residence in 1729. It became a hotel in the 1970s,
retaining many of its Georgian features. Alongside the real
ales and fine wines, there's a bar menu of freshly produced
dishes. Full hotel facilities are also available, including 23
bedrooms, restaurants, conference rooms and a license to
hold marriage ceremonies.
OPEN: 11-11 (Sun 12-10.30) **BAR MEALS:** Lunch served: all week
Dinner served: all week 12-2 6.30-9.30 Av main course £5.95
RESTAURANT: Lunch served: all week Dinner served: all week 12-2
6.30-9.30 Av 3 course à la carte £18 Av 3 course fixed price £16.95
BREWERY/COMPANY: Free House **PRINCIPAL BEERS:** Adnams
Bitter, Greene King Abbot Ale & Old Speckled Hen.
FACILITIES: Children welcome Children's licence Garden: Food
served outside, Patio Dogs allowed **NOTES:** Parking 80
ROOMS: 23 bedrooms 23 en suite from s£47.50 d£75

RINGSTEAD   Map 09 TF74

Gin Trap Inn
High St PE36 5JU ☎ 01485 525264
e-mail: margaret@gintrap.co.uk
Dir: take A149 from Kings Lynn to Hunstanton, after 15m R at Heacham
Gin traps adorn the beamed interior of this 17th-century
former coaching inn set in a peaceful village on the Peddars
Way, a short drive from the North Norfolk coast. Good range
of traditional pub food on varied menus, including steak and
kidney pie, fresh local sausages, vegetable kiev, lasagne and a
specials board listing fish and chicken options, all served in
the split-level bar. The Brew House Barn is available as self-
catering accommodation.
OPEN: 11.30-2.30 6.30-11 Closed: 25 Dec **BAR MEALS:** Lunch
served: all week Dinner served: all week 12-2 7-9 Av main course
£6.50 **RESTAURANT:** Lunch served: all week Dinner served: all
week 12-2 7-9 **BREWERY/COMPANY:** Free House
PRINCIPAL BEERS: Gin Trap, Adnams Best, Greene King Abbot Ale,
Woodfordes Norfolk Nog. **FACILITIES:** Children welcome Garden:
Patio, food served outside **NOTES:** Parking 50 No credit cards

---

SALTHOUSE   Map 07 TG04

The Dun Cow
NL25 7XG ☎ 01263 740467
*Dir: Situated on A149 main coast road, 3 miles E from Blakeney, 6 miles
West from Sheringham*

The front garden of this attractive pub overlooks a large
swathe of freshwater marsh. The bar area was formerly a
blacksmith's forge, and many of the original 17th-century
beams have been retained. Children are welcome, but there's
also a tranquil rear garden reserved for adults. The bar menu
includes snacks, pub favourites like burgers and jacket
potatoes, as well as home-made daily specials - maybe local
crab salad, halibut in tarragon batter, or cauliflower cheese.
OPEN: 11-11 (Sun 12-10.30) Closed: 25 Dec **BAR MEALS:** Lunch
served: all week Dinner served: all week 12-9 12-9 Av main course
£6.95 **BREWERY/COMPANY:** Pubmaster
PRINCIPAL BEERS: Greene King IPA & Abbot Ale, Adnams
Broadside. **FACILITIES:** Children welcome Garden: Food served
outside Dogs allowed **NOTES:** Parking 12 **ROOMS:** 2 bedrooms
2 en suite from d£55

**Do you have a favourite pub
that we have overlooked?
Please use the Readers' Report forms at
the back of this guide to tell us all about it.**

England

SCOLE   Map 07 TM17

Scole Inn 🛏 🍷
Norwich Rd IP21 4DR ☎ 01379 740481 📠 01379 740762
Just off the Ipswich to Norfolk road, two miles from Diss, this
fine old Grade I listed inn was once the area's prime coaching
inn. It has a striking Dutch façade and a wealth of authentic
features within its comfortable bedrooms, old-fashioned bars
and intimate restaurant. Bar food includes steak and
mushroom pie, fresh Lowestoft plaice and vegetarian options
such as Ricotta and spinach tortellini. Fixed-price restaurant
dinners are rather more formal.
OPEN: 11-11 (Sun 12-10.30) **BAR MEALS:** Lunch served: all week
Dinner served: all week 12-2.30 6.30-9.30 Av main course £5.95
RESTAURANT: Lunch served: Sun-Fri 12-2 Dinner served: all week
7-9.30 Av 3 course à la carte £17.50 **BREWERY/COMPANY:** Greene
King **PRINCIPAL BEERS:** Greene King IPA, Abbot Ale.
FACILITIES: Children welcome Garden: Food served outside
NOTES: Parking 48 **ROOMS:** 23 bedrooms 23 en suite

SCULTHORPE   Map 07 TF83

Sculthorpe Mill ★ ★
Lynn Rd NR21 9QG ☎ 01328 856161 📠 01328 856651
Dir: 0.25m off A148, 2m from Fakenham
Splendid 18th-century listed watermill straddling the River
Wensum, with extensive riverside gardens for summer
alfresco drinking. Character oak-beamed bar and upstairs
restaurant serving reliable food.

SNETTISHAM   Map 07 TF63

Pick of the Pubs

The Rose & Crown ♦♦♦♦ 🏵 🛏 🍷
Old Church Rd PE31 7LX ☎ 01485 541382 📠 01485 543172
e-mail: roseandcrown@btclick.com
*Dir: Head N from Kings Lynn on A149 signed to Hunstanton. Inn in
centre of Snettisham between market square and the church*
Built in the 14th century to house the craftsmen building
Snettisham's famous church, the Rose & Crown is a
family-run inn of great charm. Situated opposite the
village cricket pitch, the pub offers an ideal base from
which to visit Sandringham, the nearby bird reserves, and
the lovely North Norfolk beaches. With a growing
reputation for exciting, good quality food and a regularly
changing menu encompassing both traditional pub
favourites and more exotic dishes, it's hardly surprising
that large numbers of drinkers and diners are drawn here.
Expect home-cooked fish and chips, Teriyaki-style pork
with wok-fried chow mein, green peppers and mange-tout
or crisp confit of duck, apple fritters and parsnip purée.
Starters and lighter meals might include scorched
Haloumi, toasted ciabatta, vine tomatoes, chives and
crème fraîche. Home-made three nut chocolate brownies
with ice cream features among the appetising desserts. A
wide range of real ales and an interesting wine list with
many available by the glass.
OPEN: 11-11 (Sun 12-10.30) **BAR MEALS:** Lunch served: all
week Dinner served: all week 12-2 6.30-9 Av main course £8.50
RESTAURANT: Lunch served: all week Dinner served: all week
12-2 6-9 **BREWERY/COMPANY:** Free House
PRINCIPAL BEERS: Adnams Bitter & Broadside, Interbrew Bass,
Fuller's London Pride, Greene King IPA. **FACILITIES:** Children
welcome Garden: Food served outside Dogs allowed (water)
NOTES: Parking 70 **ROOMS:** 11 bedrooms 11 en suite from
s£70 d£100

STIFFKEY   Map 09 TF94

Pick of the Pubs

Stiffkey Red Lion 🛏 🍷
44 Wells Rd NR23 1AJ ☎ 01328 830552 📠 01328 830882
Dir: Take A149 from Wells toward Sherinham, 4m onL
Rustic 16th-century brick-and-flint cottage nestling in the
Stiffkey Valley amid rolling Norfolk countryside. Fresh fish
from King's Lynn, crab from Cromer, mussels from local
beds, and first-rate ales from East Anglian brewers like
Woodfordes, Elgoods, Adnams and Greene King, draw
coast path walkers, birdwatchers, holidaymakers and
devoted fish fanciers to this welcoming watering-hole.
Charming interior comprising three bare board or quarry-
tiled floored rooms with open fires and a simple mix of
wooden settles, pews and scrubbed tables. Ever-changing
blackboard menus may list deep-fried Blakeney whitebait,
fish pie, local cod, sole, plaice and lobster, alongside
Norfolk game casserole, lambs' liver and bacon in onion
gravy and prime beef steaks from local farms. Lighter
bites include filled baguettes and ploughman's lunches.
After a day on the beach or strolling the Peddars Way this
is a good stop for families, who have use of a large and
airy rear conservatory with access to the terraced garden.
OPEN: 11-3 6-11 **BAR MEALS:** Lunch served: all week Dinner
served: all week 12-2 6-9 Av main course £6.95
BREWERY/COMPANY: Free House
PRINCIPAL BEERS: Woodforde's Wherry, Adnams Bitter,
Greene King Abbot Ale. **FACILITIES:** Children welcome
Garden: Patio, Food served outdoors Dogs allowed (water)
NOTES: Parking 40

STOKE HOLY CROSS   Map 07 TG20

Pick of the Pubs

The Wildebeest Arms 🛏 🍷
82-86 Norwich Rd NR14 8QJ ☎ 01508 492497 📠 01508
494353
e-mail: wildebeest@animalinns.co.uk
A passion for fine food underpins the operation of this
unusually named dining pub, situated just two miles south
of Norwich. Formerly the Red Lion, about eight years ago
the old pub was opened up to create a wonderful space
with low ceilings and beams on one side, and higher
ceilings on the other, working fireplaces at either end and
a horseshoe bar in the middle. The interior is striking and
sophisticated, but the atmosphere casual and relaxed,
attracting a good range of clients from country and city.
Good quality local produce forms the basis of dishes
along the lines of confit guinea fowl leg with warm apple
boudin, roast celeriac and mustard seed jus, and
peppered monkfish with saffron risotto, etuvée leeks and
courgette tagliatelle. There is an extensive wine list and a
good monthly choice by the glass.
OPEN: 12-3 6-11 (Sun 12-3 7-10.30) Closed: Dec 25-26
RESTAURANT: Lunch served: all week Dinner served: all week
12-2 7-10 Av 3 course à la carte £22.50 Av 3 course fixed price
£18 **BREWERY/COMPANY:** Free House
PRINCIPAL BEERS: Adnams, Greene King Old Speckled Hen.
FACILITIES: Children welcome Garden: Beer garden, food
served outdoors **NOTES:** Parking 30

OPEN: 11.30–3 5.30–11
BAR MEALS: L served all week.
D served all week. 12–1.30
6.30–9.30 Av main course £9.50
RESTAURANT: L served all week.
D served all week. 12–1.30 7.30–9
BREWERY/COMPANY:
FREE HOUSE
PRINCIPAL BEERS: Theakston
Best, Black Sheep Best
FACILITIES: Children and dogs
welcome.
NOTES: Parking 24
ROOMS: 12 en suite. Double room
from £90.

Railway Tavern

A quiet country pub in the middle of the Norfolk Broads, where visitors are as likely to arrive by boat as by car. It also makes an ideal meeting place for friends or business colleagues, Whatever the reason for calling in here, you won't be disappointed. Truly a railway tavern as it is next to Reedham Station where trains from Norwich, Lowestoft and Great Yarmouth make frequent stops.

♀
17 The Havaker, Reedham, nr Beccles, NR13 3HG
☎ 01493 700340
e-mail: railwaytavern@tiscali.co.uk

The classic Victorian pub serves its own Humpty Dumpty beers brewed in the village, and organises tours of the brewery with a buffet afterwards. The Tavern also plays host to beer festivals twice a year when over 70 real ales from all around the county can be sampled, and imbibers can take part in a traditional hog roast. Good home-cooked meals are served at other times in the restaurant, bar or beer garden from a varied and innovative menu. Starters run

along the lines of red Thai salmon fishcakes with coriander and lemongrass mayonnaise, baked feta with olives and red peppers, and orange and Cointreau pâté. These can be followed by main courses like Haloumi salad with chargrilled vegetables, home-made fish pie, beer-battered cod with chips and mushy peas, wild mushroom risotto with rocket and shaved Parmesan, and fillet of beef Wellington. Weekly fish specials might include mixed seafood tagliatelle, skate wing, and salmon en crôte. No meal would be complete without one of the tasty sweets, notably poached pears with cinnamon cream, and apple and blackberry crumble. Bed and breakfast accommodation is available in the pleasant courtyard of a converted stable block

STOW BARDOLPH   Map 07 TF60

Pick of the Pubs

The Hare Arms 🐑 ♀
PE34 3HT ☎ 01366 382229 📠 01366 385522
e-mail: info@harearms.freeserve.co.uk
Dir: From King's Lynn take A10 to Downham Market.After 9m village signed on L

An attractive ivy-clad pub in the heart of a Norfolk village, surrounded by the Hare estate from which it got its name over 200 years ago. (Don't miss the creepy wax effigy of Lady Sarah Hare in the nearby church). There's a conservatory and terrace overlooking the garden, where peacocks roam at will. The welcoming atmosphere and excellent food appeals to a wide range of customers. Only fresh produce is used: seasonal game, fish and shellfish from the coast, and local lamb, beef and vegetables. Bar and restaurant menus are offered, plus an abundance of daily specials. Fish dishes are a strength – sea bass with soft parsley crust, chive and white wine sauce, and roast monkfish flavoured with curry spice and served on a bed of creamy curried mussels. Other options include steaks, beef bourguignon, and half a roast guinea fowl with thyme, Madeira sauce and bubble and squeak.
OPEN: 11-2.30 6-11 Closed: 25-26 Dec **BAR MEALS:** Lunch served: all week Dinner served: all week 12-2 7-10 Av main course £8 **RESTAURANT:** Lunch served: Sun 12-2 Dinner served: Mon-Sat 7-9.30 Av 3 course à la carte £28 Av 3 course fixed price £20 **BREWERY/COMPANY:** Greene King
PRINCIPAL BEERS: Greene King, Abbot Ale, IPA & Old Speckled Hen. **FACILITIES:** Garden: Food served outside
NOTES: Parking 50

SWANTON MORLEY   Map 07 TG01

Darbys Freehouse
1&2 Elsing Rd NR20 4NY ☎ 01362 637647 📠 01362 637987
Dir: From A47 (Norwich/King's Lynn) take B1147 to Dereham

Converted from two cottages in 1988 and originally built as a large country house in the 1700s, this popular freehouse opened when the village's last traditional pub closed. Named after the woman who lived here in the 1890s and farmed the adjacent land. Stripped pine tables, exposed beams and inglenook fireplaces enhance the authentic country pub atmosphere. Up to eight real ales are available and home-cooked food includes pigeon breast, steak and mushroom pudding, pesto pasta and salmon fillet. Farmhouse bed and breakfast accommodation at the landlord's farm 2 miles away.
OPEN: 11.30-3 6-11 (Sat 11.30-11, Sun 12-10.30)
BAR MEALS: Lunch served: all week Dinner served: all week 12-2.15

6.30-9.45 Av main course £6.95 **RESTAURANT:** Lunch served: all week Dinner served: all week 12-2.15 6.30-9.45 Av 3 course à la carte £15.50 **BREWERY/COMPANY:** Free House
PRINCIPAL BEERS: Woodforde's Wherry, Badger Tanglefoot, Greene King IPA, Adnams Broadside. **FACILITIES:** Children welcome Garden: Beer garden, outdoor eating, Dogs allowed
NOTES: Parking 75 **ROOMS:** 5 bedrooms 5 en suite from s£24 d£48

THOMPSON   Map 07 TL99

Pick of the Pubs

Chequers Inn ◆◆◆◆ 🐑
Griston Rd IP24 1PX ☎ 01953 483360 📠 01953 488092
e-mail: themcdowalls@barbox.net

The 14th-century Chequers stands in a secluded country garden surrounded by open fields, in a sleepy village close to Thompson Water. Full of wonky timbers and beams - with its Norfolk reed thatch swooping almost to the ground, this is as special place. Once a Manor Court dealing with local petty crime, today it thrives as a popular public house and restaurant. Adjacent purpose-built accommodation offers all the comforts appreciated by today's discerning traveller. Amid an abundance of gleaming horse brasses and bucolic bygones, low ceilings and uneven floors, diners can expect an excellent variety of wholesome, home-prepared food. Favourites among regular diners appear to be the Stilton mushrooms and home-made pâté, followed perhaps by peppered steak or mushroom Stroganoff. The more adventurous could go for Oriental duck with plum sauce or black sea bream with lemon and coriander from the large specials board. Follow then with home-made passion fruit crème brûlée or toffee cream tart.
OPEN: 11.30-2.30 6.30-11 (Sun 12-3, 6.30-10.30)
BAR MEALS: Lunch served: all week Dinner served: all week 12-2 6.30-9.30 Av main course £7 **RESTAURANT:** Lunch served: all week Dinner served: all week 12-2 6.30-9.30 Av 3 course à la carte £16 **BREWERY/COMPANY:** Free House
PRINCIPAL BEERS: Fuller's London pride, Adnams Best, Wolf Best, Greene King IPA. **FACILITIES:** Children welcome Garden: Secluded and quiet, food served outside Dogs allowed (water, sweeties) **NOTES:** Parking 35 **ROOMS:** 3 bedrooms 3 en suite from s£40 d£60

> Most of the pubs in this guide book pride themselves on the quality of their food. This may take a little time to prepare.

continued

THORNHAM | Map 07 TF74

Pick of the Pubs

Lifeboat Inn ★ ★ ◎ ☺
Ship Ln PE36 6LT ☎ 01485 512236 ▤ 01485 512323
e-mail: reception@lifeboatinn.co.uk
Dir: A149 to Hunstanton, follow coast rd to Thornham, pub 1st L

There's a long and colourful history to this much extended
16th-century inn, overlooking the salt marshes and
Thornham Harbour, and its original character has been
retained. There are roaring log fires in winter and fine
summer views across open meadows to a sandy beach.
Beyond the centuries-old Smugglers' Bar, with its hanging
paraffin lamps and creaking oak door, is the conservatory,
renowned for its ancient vine and adjacent walled patio
garden. Traditional country fare is served, featuring the
best available fish and game. Mussels are the Lifeboat
speciality, and fish and chips – fillet of finest fresh cod in a
crisp beer batter. Other options are peppered lemon and
coriander chicken, or spinach and Mozzarella lasagne.
Most bedrooms have a view of the sea, and provision is
made for children and well-behaved dogs.
OPEN: 11-11 **BAR MEALS:** Lunch served: all week Dinner
served: all week 12-2.30 6.30-9.30 Av main course £8.75
RESTAURANT: Dinner served: all week 7-9.30 Av 3 course fixed
price £24 **BREWERY/COMPANY:** Free House
PRINCIPAL BEERS: Adnams, Woodforde's Wherry, Greene
King Abbot Ale. **FACILITIES:** Children welcome Children's
licence Garden: Food served outside. Patio garden Dogs
allowed (water provided) **NOTES:** Parking 100
ROOMS: 22 bedrooms 22 en suite from s£35 d£50

THORPE MARKET | Map 07 TG23

Green Farm Restaurant & Hotel ★ ★
North Walsham Rd NR11 8TH ☎ 01263 833602 ▤ 01263 833163
e-mail: grfarmh@aol.com
Dir: Situated on A149
Conveniently situated for exploring the Norfolk Broads, or the
historic houses at Blickling, Felbrigg and Sandringham, this
16th-century former farmhouse features a pubby bar and an
interesting menu. Typical dishes may include ribeye of beef,
crispy duck leg salad, Cromer crab salad, and lobster in
season. Bedrooms are attractively furnished in pine.
OPEN: 11-2.30 6.30-11 **BAR MEALS:** Lunch served: all week
Dinner served: all week 12-2 7-8.30 Av main course £7.95
RESTAURANT: Lunch served: Sun 12-2.30 Dinner served: all week
7-8.30 Av 3 course à la carte £22.50 **BREWERY/COMPANY:** Free
House **PRINCIPAL BEERS:** Greene King IPA, Abbot.
FACILITIES: Children welcome Garden: Food served outside Dogs

continued

---

allowed manager's discretion **NOTES:** Parking 75
ROOMS: 14 bedrooms 14 en suite from s£55 d£70

TITCHWELL | Map 07 TF74

Pick of the Pubs

Titchwell Manor Hotel ☺
PE31 8BB ☎ 01485 210221 ▤ 01485 210104
e-mail: margaret@titchwellmanor.co.uk
Dir: A149 (coast rd) between Brancaster & Thornham

Titchwell Manor is over 100 years old and retains many of
its Victorian features. With its walled garden, full of
interesting specimen plants, log fires and wonderful views
to the sandy beaches, the hotel has all-round appeal and
is popular with family parties. The hamlet of Titchwell
grew around the manor farm and the charming round-
towered church, but is best known these days for the
important RSPB reserve here, which attracts visitors from
all over the world. There are two championship golf
courses just minutes away, so despite the rural location
there's plenty to do. The seafood bar menu makes no
secret of the house speciality, with dishes ranging from
warm fruits de mer with dill cream to fresh cod in beer
batter. Typical options are locally caught lobster in
thermidor sauce, mussels with garlic and wine, crispy
whitebait and Brancaster oysters served chilled on ice.
OPEN: 11-11 **BAR MEALS:** Lunch served: all week Dinner
served: all week 12-2 6.30-9.30 Av main course £10
RESTAURANT: Lunch served: all week Dinner served: all week
12-2 6.30-9.30 Av 3 course à la carte £24
BREWERY/COMPANY: Free House
PRINCIPAL BEERS: Greene King IPA & Abbot Ale.
FACILITIES: Children welcome Garden: Food served outside,
seating Dogs allowed (water) **NOTES:** Parking 50
ROOMS: 16 bedrooms 16 en suite from s£25 d£25

TIVETSHALL ST MARY | Map 07 TM18

The Old Ram Coaching Inn ★ ★ ☺ ⚲
Ipswich Rd NR15 2DE ☎ 01379 676794 ▤ 01379 608399
e-mail: theoldram@btinternet.com
Dir: On A140 approx 15m S of Norwich
Grade II listed property dating from the 17th century.
Sympathetically refurbished with exposed brickwork and
original beams throughout, the inn features comfortably
furnished bedrooms, including one with a four poster bed.
Generously served food includes an excellent choice at
breakfast (served from 7.30am), good snacks (filled baguettes,
chicken goujons) and daily specials such as Madagascan king
prawns, pan-fried in garlic butter, salmon supreme with ginger,

continued

TIVETSHALL ST MARY continued

coriander and lemon grass, spaghetti bolognaise, and Scottish rib-eye steak. Special menus for children and the over-60s.
OPEN: 07.30-11 Closed: Dec 25-26 **BAR MEALS:** Lunch served: all week Dinner served: all week 11.30-10pm Av main course £9.95
BREWERY/COMPANY: Free House **PRINCIPAL BEERS:** Adnams Bitter, Woodforde's Wherry Best Bitter, Interbrew Bass.
FACILITIES: Children welcome Garden: Beer garden, food served outdoors, patio **NOTES:** Parking 150 **ROOMS:** 11 bedrooms 11 en suite from s£45 d£57

UPPER SHERINGHAM   Map 07 TG14

The Red Lion Inn
The Street NR26 8AD ☎ 01263 825408
Dir: A140(Norwich to Cromer) then A148 to Sheringham/Upper Sheringham
A small village setting for this 17th-century cottage inn, close to the steam railway and North Norfolk's splendidly isolated coast. It's a flint building, with original floors, natural pine furniture and a large wood-burning stove. All food is cooked on the premises, with local produce used whenever possible, including plenty of grilled fish with a variety of fresh sauces. Other options are Drunken Thumper (rabbit in wine and herbs) or Red Thai curry.
OPEN: 11.30-3 6.30-11 **BAR MEALS:** Lunch served: all week Dinner served: all week 12-2 6.30-9 Av main course £8
RESTAURANT: Lunch served: all week Dinner served: all week 12-2 6.30-9 **BREWERY/COMPANY:** Free House
PRINCIPAL BEERS: Woodforde's Wherry, Greene King IPA.
FACILITIES: Children welcome Garden: Food served outside Dogs allowed (water) **NOTES:** Parking 16 **ROOMS:** 3 bedrooms from s£25 d£40 No credit cards

WARHAM ALL SAINTS   Map 07 TF94

Pick of the Pubs

Three Horseshoes
NR23 1NL ☎ 01328 710547
Dir: From Wells A149 to Cromer, then R onto B1105 to Warham
Wellingtons are welcome on the stone floors of the 18th-century brick and flint alehouse, set in a quiet village just a mile from the North Norfolk coast. It has one of the best original interiors in the area, with gas lights in the main bar, scrubbed deal tables and Victorian fireplaces. There's a rare example of a Norfolk 'twister' set into the ceiling - a curious red and green dial for playing village roulette. Memorabilia from all the original Norfolk breweries is displayed in the bar, another room has royal mementos and a third is full of old vacuum cleaners, cooking implements and local artefacts. There's also a museum of wind-up sound (open by appointment). Expect East Anglian ales from the cask and hearty Norfolk cooking using fresh local ingredients - crab, cider mussels, grilled dabs, seafood bake, and a variety of pies including Norfolk turkey and hare and red wine.
OPEN: 11.30-2.30 (Sun 12-3) 6-11 (Sun 6-10.30)
BAR MEALS: Lunch served: all week Dinner served: all week 12-2 6.30-8.30 Av main course £7
BREWERY/COMPANY: Free House
PRINCIPAL BEERS: Greene King IPA, Woodforde's Wherry.
FACILITIES: Children welcome Garden: Food served outside Dogs allowed (water, dog food and biscuits) **ROOMS:** 4 bedrooms 1 en suite from s£22 d£48 No credit cards

WELLS-NEXT-THE-SEA   Map 07 TF94

Pick of the Pubs

Rococo at the Crown
The Buttlands NR23 1EX ☎ 01328 710209 🖷 01328 711432
e-mail: reception@rococoatthecrown.co.uk
Dir: 10m from Fakenham on B1105
Locally born Horatio Nelson brought his wife home from the West Indies to live in the picturesque old fishing port of Wells and may even have called at this 16th-century coaching inn. The building's long history also includes a stint as a girls school. Recent refurbishments have wrought huge changes to the public areas, which have kept the old world charm of bare beams and floorboards whilst acquiring the bright colours and minimalist decor of a stylish, modern venue. Dining options now include the award-winning Rococo restaurant and the Jewel in the Crown bar/brasserie. Choose the former for dishes such as saddle of venison on Jerusalem artichoke purée with liquorice jus, caramelised shallots and garlic confit or breast of guineafowl served with leg confit, dauphinoise potatoes and a morel jus. The bar/brasserie menu includes salads, pasta and familiar main courses such as sausages and mash or battered cod with saffron mayonnaise.
OPEN: 11-11 **BAR MEALS:** Lunch served: all week Dinner served: all week 12-2 6-9 Av main course £7.95
RESTAURANT: Lunch served: Sun 12-2 Dinner served: all week 7-9 Av 2 course fixed price £25.50
BREWERY/COMPANY: Free House
PRINCIPAL BEERS: Adnams Bitter, Fisherman.
FACILITIES: Children welcome Garden: Patio, food served outside Dogs allowed on leads **NOTES:** Parking 8
ROOMS: 11 bedrooms 11 en suite from s£85 d£110

WEST BECKHAM   Map 07 TG13

The Wheatsheaf
Manor Farm, Church Rd NR25 6NX
☎ 01263 822110 🖷 01263 822110
e-mail: wheatsheaf@ukpub.net
Dir: off the A148 (between Holt & Cromer) opp Sheringham Park, signed Baconsthorpe Castle, L at village triangle after 1m
Former manor house converted to a pub in 1984 and retaining many original features. Sample one of the real ales from Woodfordes Brewery and relax in the large garden where a fully restored gypsy caravan is on display. On summer evenings you can even enjoy a game of floodlit petanque. Great pub atmosphere inside and a mix of traditional pub food and more adventurous specials. Expect smoked haddock topped with a Brie sauce, steak and kidney pie, roast duck breast, and cauliflower in Stilton sauce.
OPEN: 11.30-3 (Winter 12-3, 6.30-11) 6.30-11 **BAR MEALS:** Lunch served: all week 12-2 Dinner served: Mon-Sat 7-9 Av main course £6.95 **RESTAURANT:** Lunch served: all week 12-2 Dinner served: Mon-Sat 7-9 Av 3 course à la carte £12.50
BREWERY/COMPANY: Free House
PRINCIPAL BEERS: Woodforde's Wherry Best Bitter, Nelson's Revenge, Norfolk Nog,. **FACILITIES:** Children welcome Garden: beer garden, food served outdoors, patio Dogs allowed (water) **NOTES:** Parking 50

WEST RUDHAM — Map 07 TF82

The Dukes Head
Lynn Rd PE31 8RW ☎ 01485 528540
Dir: *from King's Lynn follow A148 towards Cromer, after 8.5m enter village of W Rudham*

Beamed country inn, once used as the local court and handy for exploring the Norfolk countryside, Houghton Hall, Royal Sandringham, Holkham Hall and Little Walsingham. It's known not only for its good beers but also for Norfolk Nudge Pudding, developed by owners David and John. Other house specialities are gourmet sausages, stuffed duck's leg, and sea bass with ginger and spring onions.
OPEN: 11.30–2 6.30–11 (May vary if quiet) **BAR MEALS:** Lunch served: all week Dinner served: all week 12–2 6.30–9.30 Av main course £7.50 **RESTAURANT:** Lunch served: all week Dinner served: all week 12–2 6.30–9.30 Av 3 course à la carte £15
BREWERY/COMPANY: Free House
PRINCIPAL BEERS: Woodfordes Wherry, Ketts, Great Eastern & Nelsons Revenge. **FACILITIES:** Children welcome Garden: Food served outside Dogs allowed (water) **NOTES:** Parking 14
ROOMS: 2 bedrooms 2 en suite from s£30 d£45

WINTERTON-ON-SEA — Map 07 TG41

Fishermans Return
The Lane NR29 4BN ☎ 01493 393305 📠 01493 393951
e-mail: fishermans_return@btopenworld.com
Dir: *8 miles N of Gt Yarmouth on B1159*

A 300-year-old brick and flint pub just a short distance from the beach (sensible shoes essential for climbing over dunes!). It's popular with walkers, twitchers, landed gentry and young folk on their way to the clubs in Yarmouth and Norwich. Dogs, too, are welcome. In addition to the standard pub fare, there are dishes based on local produce, including fish, veg and salad, offered from the regular menu and the ever-changing specials board.
OPEN: 11–2.30 6.30–11 (Sat 11–11, Sun 12–10.30)
BAR MEALS: Lunch served: all week Dinner served: all week 11.30–2 6.30–9 Av main course £7.50 **BREWERY/COMPANY:** Free House
PRINCIPAL BEERS: Woodforde's Wherry & Norfolk Nog, Wells Bombardier. **FACILITIES:** Children welcome Garden: Beer garden, patio, food seved outdoors Dogs allowed (water, chews)
NOTES: Parking 50 **ROOMS:** 3 bedrooms 3 en suite from s£40 d£60

WIVETON — Map 07 TG04

Wiveton Bell
Blakeney Rd NR25 7TL ☎ 01263 740101
Close to the green and church, this heavily-beamed village pub uses mainly fresh produce. The owner is Danish so expect

some native influence here. Dishes might include venison steak with a cranberry and ginger sauce, chicken stir-fry in noodles, cod fillet in home-made batter and mussels and crab in season.
OPEN: 12–2.30 6.30–11 **BAR MEALS:** Lunch served: all week Dinner served: all week 12–2 7–9 Av main course £7
RESTAURANT: Lunch served: all week Dinner served: all week 12–2 7–9 Av 3 course à la carte £16.50 **BREWERY/COMPANY:** Free House **PRINCIPAL BEERS:** Interbrew Bass, Adnams Bitter.
FACILITIES: Garden: Food served outside Dogs allowed

WOODBASTWICK — Map 07 TG31

The Fur & Feather
Slad Ln NR13 6HQ ☎ 01603 720003 📠 01603 722266
e-mail: penny.ridley@virgin.net
Dir: *1.5m N of B1140, 8m NE of Norwich*

An idyllic country pub in a peaceful location, it was originally two farm cottages and now boasts three cosy bar areas and a smart restaurant. Next door is Woodforde's Brewery, and all eight ales are offered here, served straight from the cask. Two of these ales feature in the inn's signature dishes of Nogin Yorky and bangers and mash. From an interesting menu expect chicken fajitas, barbecued ribs, Bastwick burger, and seafood medley.
OPEN: 11.30–3 6–11 (Summer Mon–Sat 11–11, Sun 11–10.30)
BAR MEALS: Lunch served: all week Dinner served: all week 12–2 6.30–9.30 Av main course £8 **RESTAURANT:** Lunch served: all week Dinner served: all week 12–2 6.30–9.30 Av 3 course à la carte £16
BREWERY/COMPANY: Woodforde's
PRINCIPAL BEERS: Woodforde's Wherry, Great Eastern, Norfolk Nog & Nelsons Revenge. **FACILITIES:** Garden: Pond, beer garden,food served outdoors **NOTES:** Parking 100

WRENINGHAM — Map 07 TM19

Pick of the Pubs

Bird in Hand
Church Rd NR16 1BH ☎ 01508 489438 📠 01508 488004
Dir: *6m S of Norwich on the B1113*
An eclectic mixture of styles characterises this interesting pub-restaurant in the heart of the Norfolk countryside. The quarry tiled bar features an attractive, open beamed roof, whilst diners can choose between the elegant Victorian-style dining room and the more traditional farmhouse restaurant. The pub's reputation for an extensive range of freshly cooked food is more consistent. The bar menu combines traditional pub favourites like chargrilled burgers and filled jacket potatoes with more adventurous offerings which include grilled duck with red cabbage, or vegetarian roulade. In the restaurant, you'll

continued

WRENINGHAM continued

be spoilt for choice; pan-fried venison, marinated chicken supreme, seared red mullet, or tortellini with Gorgonzola and walnuts are typical choices. Award-winning desserts like mulled wine pudding, raspberry pavlova, or white chocolate and Malibu cheesecake round off your visit.

Bird in Hand

OPEN: 11.30-3 6-11 **BAR MEALS:** 12-2 6-9.30 **RESTAURANT:** Lunch served: all week Dinner served: all week 12-2 6-9.30 **BREWERY/COMPANY:** Free House **PRINCIPAL BEERS:** Adnams, Woodforde's Wherry, Fullers London Pride, Greene King IPA. **FACILITIES:** Children welcome Garden: Food served outside. Beer garden Dogs allowed (in the garden only) **NOTES:** Parking 55

NORTHAMPTONSHIRE

ASHBY ST LEDGERS
Map 06 SP56

The Olde Coach House Inn 🛏️ 🍷
CV23 8UN ☎ 01788 890349 📠 01788 891922
e-mail: oldcoachhouse@traditionalfreehouses.com
Dir: M1 J18 follow signs A361/Daventry.Village on L

A late 19th-century farmhouse and outbuildings, skilfully converted into a pub with dining areas, accommodation and meeting rooms, set in a village that dates way back to the Domesday Book of 1086. Beer is taken seriously here with up to eight regularly changing real ales and legendary beer festivals, the pub also serves fresh, high quality food in comfortable surroundings; featuring game casserole, seafood linguine, massive mixed grills and summer barbecues.
OPEN: 12-2.30 6-11 (Sat 12-11, Sun 12-10.30)
BAR MEALS: Lunch served: all week Dinner served: all week 12-2 6-9.30 Av main course £8 **RESTAURANT:** Lunch served: all week Dinner served: all week 12-2 6-9.30 Av 3 course à la carte £16

continued

BREWERY/COMPANY: Free House **PRINCIPAL BEERS:** Everards Original, Interbrew Flowers Original, Fuller's London Pride, Hook Norton Best. **FACILITIES:** Children welcome Garden: Food served outdoors Dogs allowed **NOTES:** Parking 50 **ROOMS:** 6 bedrooms 6 en suite from s£51 d£65

BADBY
Map 06 SP55

The Windmill Inn 🍷
Main St NN11 3AN ☎ 01327 702363 📠 01327 311521
Dir: M1 J16 take A45 to Daventry then A361 S. Village 2m
A relaxing air pervades this traditional 17th-century thatched inn at the centre of a picturesque village. Blenheim Palace, Stratford and Silverstone are nearby. Inside are friendly beamed and flagstoned bars decorated with cricketing, rugby and racing pictures. There are also good hotel facilities with a modern extension discreetly sited at the rear. Varied menu and daily specials might include leg of lamb, vegetarian nut roast, venison burgers, and Whitby battered scampi. Good choice of sandwiches and snacks.
OPEN: 11.30-3.30 5.30-11 **BAR MEALS:** Lunch served: all week Dinner served: all week 12-2 7-9.30 Av main course £9 **RESTAURANT:** Lunch served: all week Dinner served: all week 12-2 7-9.30 Av 3 course à la carte £16 **BREWERY/COMPANY:** Free House **PRINCIPAL BEERS:** Bass , Flowers, Boddingtons, Wadworth 6X. **FACILITIES:** Children welcome Garden: Patio, outdoor eating Dogs allowed **NOTES:** Parking 25 **ROOMS:** 8 bedrooms 8 en suite from s£55 d£69

BULWICK
Map 06 SP99

Pick of the Pubs

The Queen's Head 🛏️ 🍷
High St NN17 3DY ☎ 01780 450272
Dir: Just off the A43 nr Corby, 12m from Peterborough, 2m from Dene Park
New owners but no changes to the charm of this 17th-century inn. Overlooking the village church and open countryside, it's a warren of small rooms with stone floors and log fires - perfect for enjoying a wide selection of ales, wines and modern pub food. Dishes could include roasted duck breast with cassis sauce, chicken breast filled with wild mushroom and smoked bacon or whole steamed sea bass with herbs and a saffron butter sauce.
OPEN: 12-2 6-11 **BAR MEALS:** Lunch served: Tue-Sun 12-2 Dinner served: Tue-Sat 6-10 Av main course £9 **RESTAURANT:** Lunch served: Tue-Sun 12-2 Dinner served: Tue-Sat 6-10 Av 3 course fixed price £16 **BREWERY/COMPANY:** Free House **PRINCIPAL BEERS:** Timothy Taylor Landlord, Greene King Old Speckled Hen, Fullers London Pride, Jennings Sneck Lifter. **FACILITIES:** Garden: Food served outside. Patio area Dogs allowed (water provided) **NOTES:** Parking 40

**Room prices show the minimum double and single rates charged.
Room rates in hotels and B&B's often vary depending on the facilities, so be sure to check prices with the establishment before booking.**

PUB WALK

Grafton Regis
The White Hart

THE WHITE HART
Northampton Road GRAFTON REGIS Nr Towcester NN12 7SR
Tel: 01908 542123
Directions: M1, J15 on A508 between Northampton & Milton Keynes
Small, stone-built thatched pub, licensed since 1750. The historic village of Grafton Regis is where Edward IV married Elizabeth Woodville, a locally-born widow, in 1464. Home-cooked food on the varied menu.
Open:12–2.30
Bar meals: 12–2 6–9.30
Dogs allowed. Garden and parking available.

Aspects of Grafton Regis's colourful and varied history are brought to life on this short, fascinating walk around the village.

On leaving the pub car park, turn left and follow the A508. Look for the post box on the corner of the A508 and Church Lane. From here you have a very good view of Tudor Cottage, a fine example of a 16th-century Northamptonshire building. Proceed down Church Lane and further on is Grove Cottage, probably the oldest cottage in the village. At the small village green, you have a magnificent view of the manor house built for Charles II's son Henry Fitzroy, 1st Duke of Grafton. On this site stood Henry VIII's palace which was destroyed during the Civil War. Continue down the lane towards the church and the impressive gate-house to the manor once part of the palace. Walk on to the church and inside you will see there are many monuments to the Fitzroy family. Pass through the churchyard to a kissing gate and rejoin the road, turn

leftheading towards the site of Bozenham Mill. Walk downhill to bridge number 57 on the canal and turn right along the towpath. Continue for a few paces to a weir and a nature reserve. Retrace your steps via the church to the village green, taking the right-hand fork to the main road. Just before the main road is the Old School, now the village hall. During 2000 the hall was decorated with murals of the many famous people who have been associated with the village over the years, including Elizabeth I and Cardinal Wolsey. Cross the road and look for a stile to the right of the drive to Grafton Lodge. Cross the field, veering to the left of several mounds, and keep an eye out for the Woodville Oak, planted by Prince Charles in 2000 to commemorate the marriage of Edward IV here in 1464. Return to the main road and turn right. Pass a house called 'Rouen' where a portrait of William Shakespeare was found in a secret chamber in the chimney breast. Keep ahead to the pub.

Distance: 2 miles (3.2km)
Map: OS Landranger 152
Terrain: Open farmland and canal bank
Paths: Pavements and footpaths
Gradient: Generally flat but long descent and return ascent

Walk submitted and checked by The White Hart, Grafton Regis

CASTLE ASHBY
Map 06 SP85

Falcon Hotel ★ ★  ⊚ 🍺 ♀
NN7 1LF ☎ 01604 696200 🖹 01604 696673
e-mail: falcon@castleashby.co.uk
Dir: A428 between Bedford & Northampton, Opposite War Memorial

In tranquil village surroundings, the Falcon is perhaps the archetypal Northamptonshire country-cottage hotel. In the 60-seat restaurant everything is prepared from fresh ingredients. The fixed-price lunch menu offers salad of home-cured gravad lax, with artichokes and olives, breast of guinea fowl, with tarragon mousse and Parma ham, and grilled pavé of salmon, topped with a mustard and herb crust. At dinner try spiced mussel broth, followed perhaps by pan-fried fillet of venison, or grilled sea bass.
OPEN: 12-3 6-11 **BAR MEALS:** Lunch served: all week Dinner served: all week 12-2 7-9.30 Av main course £8.50
RESTAURANT: Lunch served: all week Dinner served: all week 12-2 7-10 Av 3 course à la carte £28.50 Av 3 course fixed price £23.50
BREWERY/COMPANY: Old English Inns
PRINCIPAL BEERS: Scottish Courage John Smith's, Greene King Ruddles County & IPA. **FACILITIES:** Children welcome Garden: Food served outdoors, herb garden Dogs allowed **NOTES:** Parking 60 **ROOMS:** 16 bedrooms 16 en suite from s£69.50 d£85

CHACOMBE
Map 06 SP44

Pick of the Pubs

George and Dragon 🍺
Silver St OX17 2JR ☎ 01295 711500 🖹 01295 758827
e-mail: chacombepub@aol.com
Dir: From M40 take A361 to Daventry, 1st R to Chacombe, 2nd L in village
Well placed for M40 travellers (J11 2 miles) and popular with business folk from nearby Banbury, the George & Dragon is an attractive, honey-stoned, 16th-century pub tucked away by the church in a pretty conservation village. Expect a welcoming atmosphere within the three comfortable bars, with low beams, log fires, simple wooden chairs and settles, and a warm terracotta decor enhancing the overall charm of the inn. Blackboards list the interesting choice of food, from sandwiches, filled jacket potatoes and unusual pasta dishes to crispy duck breast with chilli and cranberry sauce, collops of pork with creamy leek and sage sauce, and decent fish specials - roasted monkfish with spring onion and mushroom sauce. Comfortable accommodation in three en suite upstairs bedrooms.
OPEN: 12-11 **BAR MEALS:** Lunch served: all week Dinner served: all week 12-2 6-9.30 Av main course £10
RESTAURANT: Lunch served: all week Dinner served: all week

continued

12-2 6-9.30 Av 3 course à la carte £17
BREWERY/COMPANY: Free House
PRINCIPAL BEERS: Theakston Best ,XB, Scottish Courage Courage Directors.. **FACILITIES:** Children welcome Dogs allowed **NOTES:** Parking 40 **ROOMS:** 3 bedrooms 3 en suite from s£45 d£60

CLIPSTON
Map 06 SP78

The Bulls Head 🍺 ♀
Harborough Rd LE16 9RT ☎ 01858 525268 🖹 01858 525266
Dir: On B4036 S of Market Harborough
A distinguishing characteristic of this village pub is the large number of coins pushed between the beams. This tradition was begun by service men in World War II as a token of good luck. In addition to its good choice of real ales, the pub has a collection of over 450 whiskies. The menu offers a comprehensive range of dishes, including a selection of vegetarian and children's meals, plus fresh fish specials from the board.
OPEN: 11.30-3 5-11 **BAR MEALS:** Lunch served: Tue-Sun 11.30-2 Dinner served: all week 6.30-9.30 Av main course £8
RESTAURANT: Lunch served: Tue-Sun 11.30-2 Dinner served: all week 6.30-9.30 Av 3 course à la carte £15
BREWERY/COMPANY: Free House
PRINCIPAL BEERS: Batemans XB, Timothy Taylor Landlord, Black Sheep Best, Greene King Old Speckled Hen. **FACILITIES:** Children welcome Children's licence Garden: Patio, food served outdoors, BBQ Dogs allowed **NOTES:** Parking 40 **ROOMS:** 3 bedrooms 3 en suite from s£29.50 d£49

COSGROVE
Map 06 SP74

The Navigation Inn
Thrupp Wharf, Castlethorpe Rd MK19 7BE ☎ 01908 543156
Dir: From A5 W of Milton Keynes take A508 N.Take 2nd R, 1st L.Inn 0.5m
Built 200 years ago at the same time as the Grand Union Canal beside which it stands. Home-made specials are available.

CRICK
Map 09 SP57

The Red Lion Inn 🍺
52 Main Rd NN6 7TX ☎ 01788 822342 🖹 01788 822342
Dir: M1 J18 0.75m E on A428
A thatched, stone-built former coaching inn dating from the 1600s, with open fires, beams and horse brasses. Family run for the last 23 years, continuity is the secret of the Red Lion Inn's success. People know just what to expect - a clean and tidy pub, a friendly atmosphere, real ales and traditional food. The daily home-made pie is a lunchtime favourite and steaks are a speciality of the evening menu.
OPEN: 11-2.30 6.15-11 (Sun 12-3 7-10.30) **BAR MEALS:** Lunch served: all week 12-2 Dinner served: Mon-Sat 7-9 Av main course £7
BREWERY/COMPANY: Wellington Pub Co
PRINCIPAL BEERS: Websters, Marston's Pedigree, Theakston Best, Greene King Old Speckled Hen. **FACILITIES:** Garden: Patio, food served outside Dogs allowed (water) **NOTES:** Parking 40

EASTCOTE
Map 06 SP65

Eastcote Arms 🍺 ♀
6 Gayton Rd NN12 8NG ☎ 01327 830731
Brick and stone village inn dating from 1670 with inglenook fireplaces, original beams, a welcoming atmosphere, and a

continued

splendid south-facing garden. Good value lunchtime snacks include filled baguettes, old favourites like ham, egg and chips, and fish and chips, while evening fare features Cumberland sausage in onion gravy, steak and ale pie, and lobster pastry purse.
OPEN: 12–3 6–11 (Sun 12–4, 7–10.30, Mon closed lunch)
BAR MEALS: Lunch served: Tue–Sat 12–2 Dinner served: Wed–Sun 7–9.30 Av main course £3.50 **RESTAURANT:** Lunch served: Tue–Sun 12–2 Dinner served: Wed–Sun 7–9.30 Av 3 course à la carte £20
PRINCIPAL BEERS: Adnams, Greene King IPA, Ansells, Pedigree.
FACILITIES: Children welcome Garden: Food served outside, colourful garden Dogs allowed (in the garden only, water provided)
NOTES: Parking 20

EAST HADDON
Map 06 SP66

Red Lion Hotel 🐷 ♀
NN6 8BU ☎ 01604 770223 📠 01604 770767
e-mail: red_lion_hotel@yahoo.co.uk
Dir: 7m NW of Northampton on A428, 8m from J18 of M1. Midway between Northampton & Rugby.
Handy for visiting nearby Althorp Park, the final resting place of Diana, Princess of Wales, this smart 17th-century inn is built of eye-catching golden stone and thatch with a popular walled side garden where you can relax over coffee or a drink amid lilac, roses and fruit trees. Oak panelled settles, cast-iron framed tables and recessed china cabinets characterise the interior. Wide-ranging menu features the likes of lamb noisettes with redcurrant stuffing, loin of pork with green lentil broth, and chicken wrapped in proscuitto crudo. Extensive wine list and a good selection of real ales.
OPEN: 11–2.30 6–11 Closed: Dec 25–26 **BAR MEALS:** Lunch served: all week 12.15–2 Dinner served: Mon–Sat 7–9.30 Av main course £12 **RESTAURANT:** Lunch served: all week 12.15–2 Dinner served: Mon–Sat 7–9.30 Av 3 course à la carte £30
BREWERY/COMPANY: Charles Wells **PRINCIPAL BEERS:** Wells Eagle IPA, & Bombardier, Adnams Broadside. **FACILITIES:** Children welcome Garden: Food served outside **NOTES:** Parking 40
ROOMS: 5 bedrooms 5 en suite from s£60 d£75

EASTON-ON-THE-HILL
Map 06 TF00

The Exeter Arms ♀
Stamford Rd PE9 3NS ☎ 01780 757503 📠 01780 757503
Dir: A43 & A1 junct
An old, white-painted stone building – dating from 1765 – the inn gets its name from the estates of the Marquis of Exeter on which it once stood. The garden and patio enjoy views of the superb Welland Valley. Favourite dishes include grilled duck breast with an orange and Cointreau sauce, halibut steak on roast vegetables, seafood ragout, medallions of pork with apple compote and sage and cider sauce, and cod and prawns in a mild curry sauce on spinach.
OPEN: 12–3 7–11 (closed Mon) **RESTAURANT:** Lunch served: Tue–Sun 12–2.30 Dinner served: Tue–Sat 6.30–9.30 Av 3 course à la carte £20 **BREWERY/COMPANY:** Enterprise Inns
PRINCIPAL BEERS: Theakstons. **FACILITIES:** Children welcome Garden: Food served outside. Lawn & patio **NOTES:** Parking 100

FARTHINGSTONE
Map 06 SP65

The Kings Arms
Main St NN12 8EZ ☎ 01327 361604 📠 01327 361604
e-mail: paul@kingsarms.fsbusiness.co.uk
Dir: from M1 take A45 W, at Weedon join A5 then R on road signed Farthingstone
Tucked away in unspoilt countryside near canons Ashby (NT), this cosy 18th-century Grade II listed inn is adorned with a collection of stone gargoyles. Excellent real ales are served here. There is basically no food, except ploughman's at weekends, although the landlord does sell cheese!

FOTHERINGHAY
Map 06 TL09

Pick of the Pubs

The Falcon Inn 🍴 ♀
PE8 5HZ ☎ 01832 226254 📠 01832 226046
Dir: N of A605 between Peterborough & Oundle

Attractive 18th-century stone-built inn set in a historic village close to the site of Fotheringhay Castle, where Mary Queen of Scots was beheaded. The garden has just been redesigned by landscape architect Bunny Guinness, with an extensive lawn overlooking Fotheringhay Church. The Falcon and chef/patron Ray Smikle are members of the select Huntsbridge Inns group, each member producing innovative food in a relaxing pub environment. Eat what you like where you like, and accompany your meal with excellent wines or a pint of good ale – Adnams, Greene King, and a range of guest beers. The choice is between the locals' tap bar, the smart rear dining room, or the conservatory extension, where you can then choose from the seasonal carte or blackboard snack selection. Onion bhaji, spicy fishcake, Jamaican jerk chicken, and slow braised daube of beef give some idea of the variety of dishes on offer.
OPEN: 11.30–3 6–11 (Sun 12–3,7–10.30) **BAR MEALS:** Lunch served: all week Dinner served: all week 12–2.15 7–9.30 Av main course £9 **RESTAURANT:** Lunch served: all week Dinner served: all week 12–2.15 7–9.30 Av 3 course à la carte £24 Av 2 course fixed price £11.50 **BREWERY/COMPANY:** Free House
PRINCIPAL BEERS: Adnams Bitter, Greene King IPA, Scottish Courage John Smith's, Nethergate. **FACILITIES:** Children welcome Children's licence Garden: Beer garden, patio, food served outdoors **NOTES:** Parking 30

Nine Men's Morris
A certain eeriness clings to one of the world's oldest games, which was played in Ancient Egypt 3,000 years ago and in Ireland in prehistoric times. It involves moving pegs or counters to form rows of three on a board or playing surface with 24 holes marked on it in an intricate pattern.

England

GRAFTON REGIS · Map 06 SP74

The White Hart ⓘ ♀
Northampton Rd NN12 7SR ☎ 01908 542123
Dir: M1 J15 on A508 between Northampton & Milton Keynes

Small, stone-built thatched pub, licensed since 1750. The historic village of Grafton Regis is where Edward IV married Elizabeth Woodville, a locally-born widow, in 1464. Expect Mexican chicken grilled in dry Cajun rices, steak and mushroom pie, lasagne, fillet steak Diane, chicken leek and Stilton, garlic mushroom tagliatelle, and fresh fillet of plaice Italian style on the menu.
OPEN: 12–2.30 6–11 (Sun 12–2.30, 7–10.30) **BAR MEALS:** Lunch served: Tue–Sun 12–2 Dinner served: Tue–Sat 6–9.30 Av main course £6.95 **RESTAURANT:** Lunch served: Tue–Sun 12–1.30 Dinner served: Tue–Sat 6.30–9 Av 3 course à la carte £20
BREWERY/COMPANY: Free House **PRINCIPAL BEERS:** Greene King Abbot Ale & IPA. **FACILITIES:** Garden: Patio, food served outside Dogs allowed Toys, water **NOTES:** Parking 40
See Pub Walk on page 337

GREAT OXENDON · Map 06 SE48

The George Inn ♀
LE16 8NA ☎ 01858 465205 🖹 01858 465205
Country inn where you can enjoy a pint, a snack or a full-scale meal, including a traditional Sunday lunch. Full service is provided in the restaurant, but food is also available in the bar or the attractive conservatory overlooking the flower garden. Dishes based on fresh local produce are cooked to order: typically honey roast shank of lamb, roast cod and butterbean casserole, sauté pigeon breast, and crispy oriental duck breast.
OPEN: 11.30–3 6–11 **BAR MEALS:** Lunch served: all week 12–2.30 Dinner served: Mon–Sat 7–10 Av main course £7.95
RESTAURANT: Lunch served: Tues–Sun 12–2.30 Dinner served: Mon–Sat 7–10 Av 3 course à la carte £22.50 Av 3 course fixed price £13.75 **BREWERY/COMPANY:** Free House
PRINCIPAL BEERS: Interbrew Bass, Adnams Bitter.
FACILITIES: Children welcome Garden: Food served outside Dogs allowed (water) **NOTES:** Parking 34 **ROOMS:** 3 bedrooms 3 en suite from d£55.50

HARRINGTON · Map 06 SP78

The Tollemache Arms
High St NN6 9NU ☎ 01536 710469
Dir: 6M from Kettering directly off the A14 both E & W bound signposted as Harrington
New licensees have recently taken over this pretty, thatched 16th-century village inn, situated near to Harrington Airfield and Museums. In addition to ales from Wells and Greene

Kings breweries, freshly prepared food from local produce is served throughout the character bars and restaurant. Typical dishes include smoked haddock and horseradish parfait, roast rack of lamb with red wine jus and good fish options like whole sea bass with sweet and sour sauce. Popular Sunday lunch menu.
OPEN: 12–3 6–11 **BAR MEALS:** Lunch served: all week Dinner served: all week 12–2.30 6.30–9 Av main course £8
RESTAURANT: Lunch served: all week Dinner served: all week 12–2.30 6.30–9 Av 3 course à la carte £20
BREWERY/COMPANY: Charles Wells **PRINCIPAL BEERS:** Wells Eagle IPA & Bombardier, Adnams Broadside, Greene King Triumph & Old Speckled Hen. **FACILITIES:** Garden: Food served outisde **NOTES:** Parking 60

HARRINGWORTH · Map 06 SP99

The White Swan
Seaton Rd NN17 3AF ☎ 01572 747543 🖹 01572 747323
e-mail: white.swan 1@virgin.net
Dir: Off B672 NE of Corby

Photographs recalling the nearby World War II airbase decorate the bar of this stone-built 15th century coaching inn. The prettily-situated free house also displays an old collection of craftsman's tools and memorabilia. There's a nice selection of well-kept real ales, and the constantly changing blackboard menu offers dishes like braised lamb knuckle, beef Wellington, duck with plum sauce, grilled salmon, or parsnip, ginger and mushroom bake.
OPEN: 11.30–2.30 6.30–11 (Sun 12–3, 7–10.30) Closed: 25 Dec, 1 Jan **BAR MEALS:** Lunch served: all week Dinner served: all week 12–2 7–10 Av main course £7.50 **RESTAURANT:** Lunch served: all week Dinner served: all week 12–2 7–10 Av 3 course à la carte £15
BREWERY/COMPANY: Free House **PRINCIPAL BEERS:** Greene King IPA & Abbot Ale, Marston's Pedigree. **FACILITIES:** Children welcome Garden: Patio, food served outside **NOTES:** Parking 10
ROOMS: 6 bedrooms 6 en suite from s£30 d£42

KETTERING · Map 06 SP87

The Overstone Arms ⓘ ♀
Stringers Hill, Pytchley NN14 1EU
☎ 01536 790215 🖹 01536 791098
Dir: village situated 1m from Kettering, 5m from Wellingborough
The 18th-century coaching inn is at the heart of the village and has been home to the Pytchley Hunt, which over the years has attracted many royal visitors. Years ago guests would travel up from London, staying here or at Althorpe Hall, mainly for the hunting. Despite its rural location, the pub is just a mile from the busy A1-M1 link road (A14). Home-made pies, grilled trout, steaks, lasagne and curry are typical dishes.
OPEN: 12–2.30 7–11 Closed 1 Jan **BAR MEALS:** All week 12–2

continued

continued

7-10 Av main course £6.50 **RESTAURANT:** All week 12-2 7-10 Av 3 course meal £14 **BREWERY/COMPANY:** Unique
PRINCIPAL BEERS: Greene King, Marston's Pedigree, Interbrew Bass, Adnams Bitter **FACILITIES:** Garden: Orchard, food served outside **NOTES:** Parking 50

LITTLE ADDINGTON
Map 06 SP97

The Bell Inn ☺
High St NN14 4BD ☎ 01933 651700 ▤ 01933 653209
e-mail: thebellinnaddington@btopenworld.com
Dir: From A14, S of Kettering, follow signs for The Addingtons
A country pub and separate à la carte restaurant, where the service and atmosphere is friendly. There's plenty going on, with quiz nights, live bands and happy hours during the week in the pub, as well as theme nights and a two-courses-for-a-tenner deal on Wednesday nights. Friday night is fish night with a choice of six to eight main course fish dishes. The pub also caters for parties, functions and weddings.
OPEN: 12-2.30 6.30-11 (Fri-Sat all day) **BAR MEALS:** 12-2.30 7-9.30 **RESTAURANT:** 12-2 7-10 **BREWERY/COMPANY:** Free House **PRINCIPAL BEERS:** Greene King IPA, Interbrew Bass, Fuller's London Pride, Wadworth 6X. **FACILITIES:** Children welcome Food served outside **NOTES:** Parking 40

LITTLE HARROWDEN
Map 06 SP87

The Lamb
Orlingbury Rd NN9 5BH ☎ 01933 673300 ▤ 01933 403131
Tucked away in a delightful village, this neatly refurbished 17th-century pub offers a friendly welcome in its comfortable lounge bar and adjoining public bar with games area. Just coming under new management at time of going to press.

LOWICK
Map 06 SP98

The Snooty Fox
NN14 3BS ☎ 01832 733434
Dir: off the A14 5 m E of Kettering on A6116. Straight over at 1st roundabout and L into Lowick
Exquisite carved beams are among the more unusual features at this 16th-century pub. Originally the manor house, it is supposedly haunted by a horse and its rider killed at the Battle of Naseby. Varied bar food includes steaks, chicken and pork; a good vegetarian selection, and fresh fish delivered daily.
OPEN: 12-3 6.30-11 **BAR MEALS:** Lunch served: all week Dinner served: all week 12-2 7-10 Av main course £6.95
RESTAURANT: Lunch served: all week Dinner served: all week 12-2 7-10 **PRINCIPAL BEERS:** Greene King, Hook Norton Best, Batemans XB. **FACILITIES:** Children welcome Garden: Dogs allowed **NOTES:** Parking 100

MARSTON ST LAWRENCE
Map 06 SP54

The Marston Inn
OX17 2DB ☎ 01295 711906
Dir: 5m from M40 J11
Originally three cottages, this 15th-century inn was seized by Cromwell prior to the Battle of Edgehill and sold to raise money for his cause. Used to be known as 'The Case is Altered'. Just coming under change of management at time of going to press. Ring for details.
OPEN: 12-2.30 7-11 (Sun eve winter) **RESTAURANT:** Lunch served: Tue-Sun Dinner served: Tue-Sat 12-2 7-9.30 Av 3 course à la carte £15 **BREWERY/COMPANY:** Hook Norton

continued

PRINCIPAL BEERS: Hook Norton Best, Old Hooky & Generation.
FACILITIES: Garden: Outdoor eating, patio **NOTES:** Parking 12 No credit cards

---

OUNDLE
Map 06 TL08

The Mill at Oundle ☺ ♀
Barnwell Mill PE8 5PB ☎ 01832 272621 ▤ 01832 272221
e-mail: reservations@millatoundle.com
Dir: A14 Thrapston exit, A605 toward Peterborough, 8m Oundle turning, 1m to pub
Set on the banks of the River Nene, this converted watermill dates back to the Domesday Book and the mill was in use until 1947. It has a bar at the waterside and two restaurants. The menu ranges through a choice of grills, Tex Mex dishes, fish and pasta to specials such as blushed lamb, Somerset pork, and Thai sizzler (vegetarian). The Granary Restaurant on the top floor is ideal for wedding receptions and other private functions.
OPEN: 11-3 6.30-11 (Summer all day Sat-Sun) Closed: Dec 26/27
BAR MEALS: Lunch served: all week Dinner served: all week 12-2 6.30-9 Av main course £9.95 **RESTAURANT:** Lunch served: all week Dinner served: all week 12-2 6.30-9 Av 3 course à la carte £20
BREWERY/COMPANY: Free House
PRINCIPAL BEERS: Interbrew Bass, Greene King Old Speckled Hen, Fuller's London Pride, Wadworth 6X. **FACILITIES:** Children welcome Garden: Food served outside, river, patio **NOTES:** Parking 80

The Montagu Arms ☺
Barnwell PE8 5PH ☎ 01832 273726 ▤ 01832 275555
Dir: off A605 opposite Oundle slip Rd, access to A605 via A14 or A1
One of Northamptonshire's oldest inns, set beside a babbling brook, the Montagu Arms was originally three cottages built for workmen constructing the manor house. It is named after Edward Montagu, one-time lord of the manor and chief justice to the court of the King's bench during the reign of Henry VIII. Beef and ale pie, pheasant and monkfish feature alongside salsa crevettes, nachos and fajitas.
OPEN: 12-3 6-11 (Sat-Sun all day) **BAR MEALS:** Lunch served: all week Dinner served: all week 12-2.30 7-10 Av main course £7
RESTAURANT: Lunch served: all week Dinner served: all week 12-2.30 7-10 Av 3 course à la carte £12.50
BREWERY/COMPANY: Free House **PRINCIPAL BEERS:** Adnams Broadside, Southwold Bitter, Interbrew Flowers IPA, Original.
FACILITIES: Children welcome Garden: Large with patio, food served ouside **NOTES:** Parking 25 **ROOMS:** 3 bedrooms 3 en suite from s£27.50 d£45

Horse-brasses
Delightful and attractive as they are, horse-brasses are nothing like as old as is generally believed. The working horse in a harness gleaming with ornamental hanging brasses is a creature of the period since 1850. The brasses were mass-produced folk art, following the earlier precedent of the heraldic badges worn by the carriage horses of aristocratic families. Favourite symbols include the sun, the moon, the stars and such heraldic creatures as the lion, the stag, the unicorn and the eagle, as well as railway locomotives and ships.

SIBBERTOFT
Map 06 SP68

The Red Lion 🍸
43 Welland Rise LE16 9UD ☎ 01858 880011 🖷 01858 880011
e-mail: redlion@sibbertoft.demon.co.uk
Dir: From Market Harborough take A4304, then A50. After 1m turn L
Friendly and civilised village pub, believed to be 300 years old,
with a cottage-like frontage. The same menu is offered in both
the beamed restaurant and the comfortably furnished bar,
ranging from baguettes filled with hot Brie and bacon, or
steak and onion, through to roast nut Wellington, lambs' liver
and onions, Thai green curry, and a daily pasta dish from the
specials board.
OPEN: 12–2 6.30–11 **BAR MEALS:** Lunch served: Wed–Sun 12–2
Dinner served: all week 7–9.45 Av main course £8.50
RESTAURANT: Lunch served: Wed–Sun 12–2 Dinner served: all
week 7–9.45 Av 3 course à la carte £15
BREWERY/COMPANY: Free House **PRINCIPAL BEERS:** Everards
Tiger, Adnams Bitter, Interbrew Bass. **NOTES:** Parking 15
ROOMS: 2 bedrooms 2 en suite from s£30 d£50

STOKE BRUERNE
Map 06 SP74

The Boat Inn 🍸
NN12 7SB ☎ 01604 862428 🖷 01604 864314
e-mail: info@boatinn.co.uk
Dir: just off A508

Thatched canalside inn by working locks and opposite the
canal museum, where narrowboat trips on the 40-seater
Indian Chief are a feature. The bar menu offers the likes of
home-made steak and ale pie, salads and jacket potatoes,
while restaurant dishes might include whole lobster with black
bean salsa or beef Wellington. Good vegetarian choice.
OPEN: 9–11 (3–6 closed Mon–Thu in winter) **BAR MEALS:** Lunch
served: all week Dinner served: all week 9.30–9 Av main course £6
RESTAURANT: Lunch served: Tue–Sun 12–2 Dinner served: all week
7–9 **BREWERY/COMPANY:** Free House
PRINCIPAL BEERS: Banks Bitter, Marstons Pedigree, Adnams
Southwold, Thwaites. **FACILITIES:** Children welcome Children's
licence Garden: Food served outside, Canalside & locks Dogs
allowed **NOTES:** Parking 50

SULGRAVE
Map 06 SP54

The Star Inn 🍸
Manor Rd OX17 2SA ☎ 01295 760389 🖷 01295 760991
e-mail: repose@starinnsulgrave.co.uk
*Dir: M1 J15A follow signs for Silverstone race circuit or M40 J11 follow
brown signs for golf course, then for Sulgrave Manor*
The Star, located on the Oxfordshire/Northamptonshire
border, is a delightful 300-year-old creeper-clad inn, full of
character. The new landlord is an experienced chef returning

continued

to his family roots in the county. Fishy options include tiger
prawn bruschetta, smoked haddock fishcakes, and roast cod
with garlic mash and squid ink sauce. Other favourites
encompass four-cheese risotto, game pie, and roast loin of
pork with crackling, apple crisps and black pudding gravy.
OPEN: 11–2.30 6–11 (Sun 12–5 only) Closed: 25 Dec
BAR MEALS: Lunch served: Tue–Sun 12–2 Dinner served: Tue–Sat
6.30–9.30 Av main course £7.95 **RESTAURANT:** Lunch served:
Tue–Sun 12–2 Dinner served: Tue–Sat 6.30–9.30 Av 3 course à la carte
£17 **BREWERY/COMPANY:** Hook Norton
PRINCIPAL BEERS: Hook Norton Best, Old Hooky, Generation, &
Haymaker. **FACILITIES:** Garden: Food served outside
NOTES: Parking 20 **ROOMS:** 3 bedrooms 3 en suite from s£45 d£65

THORPE MANDEVILLE
Map 06 SP54

The Three Conies 🍸
Banbury Ln OX17 2EX ☎ 01295 711025
A uniquely named drovers' inn dating from 1622, with
inglenook fireplaces and herb terracing leading from the
dining room. Renowned for its speciality fish menu, which
includes mahi-mahi in cider and ginger, barracuda with white
wine and mushroom sauce, and orange tilapi with crème
Grand Marnier. A menu entitled 'Strange Food, From Strange
Places' features such delights as squid pathia, ostrich fillet
steak provençal, and crocodile steak, Dundee style!
OPEN: 12–2.30 6–11 **BAR MEALS:** Lunch served: all week 12–2
Dinner served: Mon–Sat 7–9 Av main course £5.95
RESTAURANT: Lunch served: all week 12–2 Dinner served: Mon–Sat
7–11 Av 3 course à la carte £18 **BREWERY/COMPANY:** Hook
Norton **PRINCIPAL BEERS:** Hook Norton Best, Hook Norton Old
Hooky. **FACILITIES:** Children welcome Garden: Food served
outside Dogs allowed **NOTES:** Parking 30

WADENHOE
Map 06 TL08

Pick of the Pubs

The King's Head 🍸
Church St PE8 5ST ☎ 01832 720024
e-mail: thekingshead@wadenhoe.freeserve.co.uk
This part-thatched, 17th-century stone inn, peacefully
situated beside the River Nene, insists that it remains
resolutely a drinkers' pub and boasts a separate bar
featuring real ales. Oak beams, quarry-tiled floors and
open fires characterise the welcoming and neatly
refurbished interior, while a ban on mobile phones is
vigilantly enforced. Popular with local villagers, boating
types, cyclists and walkers who drop by for a pint. Food
though plays an increasingly important part. Lunchtime
runs to soups, sandwiches and real burgers, while in the
evening, the cooking shifts up a notch with the likes of
roast sea bass with Pernod and almonds, monkfish tail
wrapped in bacon, roast duck with port jus and fresh
plums, and home-made puddings. Good value three-
course Sunday lunch. In the summer it its possible to dine
alfresco by the river. Two en suite bedrooms.
OPEN: 12–3 7–11 (Fri–Sat 6–11, Summer all day Sat–Sun)
BAR MEALS: Lunch served: all week 12–2 Dinner served:
Tue–Sat 7–11 Av main course £4 **RESTAURANT:** Lunch served:
all week Dinner served: Tue–Sat 7–11 Av 3 course à la carte £12
BREWERY/COMPANY: Free House
PRINCIPAL BEERS: Adnams Broadside. **FACILITIES:** Children
welcome Garden: Beer garden, patio Dogs allowed (water)
NOTES: Parking 20 **ROOMS:** 2 bedrooms 2 en suite from
s£35 d£55

England

WESTON — Map 06 SP54

The Crown ♀
Helmdon Rd NN12 8PX ☎ 01295 760310 🖷 01295 760310
e-mail: terry@thearty.freeserve.co.uk
This 16th-century listed building has exposed beams and an inglenook fireplace, and is very good for local walks. The beamed function room is also a live music venue. Reputedly this was the last place that Lord Lucan was seen before his mysterious disappearance. A typical menu includes steak and ale pie, marlin in tarragon and white wine sauce, lamb shank with garlic and rosemary, tuna steak with lime and chillies, and Barbary duck in plum and ginger sauce.
OPEN: 6–11 (Fri 12–2, 6–11, Sat 12–3, 6–11) (Sun 12–10.30) Closed: 26 Dec & Easter Sunday **BAR MEALS:** Lunch served: Fri–Sun 12–2 Dinner served: Tue–Sun 6.30–9 Av main course £7
PRINCIPAL BEERS: Greene King IPA & Abbot Ale, Timothy Tailor Landlord, Interbrew Flowers IPA. **FACILITIES:** Children welcome Garden: Food served outdoors Dogs allowed (water)
NOTES: Parking 10 **ROOMS:** 3 bedrooms 3 en suite from s£25 d£50

WOODNEWTON — Map 06 TL09

The White Swan 🍸
22 Main St PE8 5EB ☎ 01780 470381 🖷 01780 470422
Welcoming village local comprising a simple, single oblong room, one end focusing on the bar and wood-burning stove, the other set up as a dining area. The regularly changing blackboard menu may offer home-made soup, fresh cod fillet in beer batter, stuffed chicken, pies, curries and steaks. Finish with a traditional home-made sweet, like fruit crumble or sticky toffee pudding.
OPEN: 12–2.30 7–11 **BAR MEALS:** Lunch served: Tue–Sun Dinner served: Tue–Sun 12–1.45 7–9 Av main course £4.99
RESTAURANT: Lunch served: Tue–Sun Dinner served: Tue–Sun 12–1.45 7–9 Av 3 course à la carte £16 **BREWERY/COMPANY:** Free House **PRINCIPAL BEERS:** Adnams Southwold, Interbrew Bass, Otter Bright, Bitter. **FACILITIES:** Garden: Food served outside
NOTES: Parking 20

NORTHUMBERLAND

ALLENDALE — Map 11 NY85

Kings Head Hotel ♀
Market Place NE47 9BD ☎ 01434 683681
Dir: From Hexham take B6305/B6304/B6295
Dating from 1754, the Kings Head is the oldest inn in Allendale, situated in the centre of the North Dales village. Traditional food. Bedrooms.

ALLENHEADS — Map 11 NY84

The Allenheads Inn
NE47 9HJ ☎ 01434 685200 🖷 01434 685200
Dir: From Hexham take B6305, then B6295 to Allenheads
In a remote village high in the Pennines, the 18th-century Allenheads retains the character and charm of a bygone age, full of unique memorabilia. Accommodation is nonetheless up-to-date with showers and baths en suite and a residents' sitting-room, with television, on the first floor. Both the Antiques Bar and the unusually-named Forces Room provide good food and ales in a cosy, welcoming atmosphere, offering steak pie or cod and chips, plus seasonal specials such as game pie and rabbit casserole.

OPEN: 12–4 7–11 (all day Fri–Sat) **BAR MEALS:** Lunch served: all week Dinner served: all week 12–2.30 7–9 Av main course £5
BREWERY/COMPANY: Free House **PRINCIPAL BEERS:** Greene King Abbott Ale & IPA, Carlsberg-Tetley Tetley Bitter, Timothy Taylor Landlord. **FACILITIES:** Garden: Food served outdoors
NOTES: Parking 10 **ROOMS:** 8 bedrooms 8 en suite from s£26.50 d£23 No credit cards

ALNWICK — Map 11 NU11

Masons Arms ♀
Stamford, Nr Rennington NE66 3RX
☎ 01665 577275 🖷 01665 577894
e-mail: masonarms@lineone.net
Dir: 3.5m from A1 on B1340
Known locally by farmers as the Stamford Cott, and a useful staging post for visitors to Hadrian's Wall and Lindisfarne, this 200-year-old coaching inn has been tastefully modernised. The same substantial home-cooked food is available in the bar and restaurant: beef and wild venison casserole, chicken chasseur, and cannelloni verdi, plus fresh fish (haddock, lemon sole, and scampi) and chef's specials like seafood gratin.
OPEN: 12–2 6.30–11 (Sun 12–2 7–10.30) **BAR MEALS:** Lunch served: all week Dinner served: all week 12–2 7–9 Av main course £6.75 **RESTAURANT:** Lunch served: all week Dinner served: all week 12–2 7–9 Av 3 course à la carte £15 **BREWERY/COMPANY:** Free House **PRINCIPAL BEERS:** Scottish Courage John Smith's, Theakston Best. **FACILITIES:** Children welcome Garden: **NOTES:** Parking 25 **ROOMS:** 6 bedrooms 6 en suite from s£35 d£21

BAMBURGH — Map 11 NU13

Lord Crewe Arms Hotel ★ ★ 🍸
Front St NE69 7BL ☎ 01668 214243 🖷 01668 214273
e-mail: lca@tinyonline.co.uk
Historic coaching inn named after Lord Crewe, who was one of the Prince Bishops of Durham. Perfect base for touring Northumberland, exploring the Cheviot Hills and visiting nearby Holy Island. Good, wholesome pub food ranges from local kipper pâté, wild boar and apple sausages and pan-fried supreme of chicken, to breast of guinea fowl with an apricot, apple and raisin stuffing.
OPEN: 12–3 6–11 Closed: Jan–Feb **BAR MEALS:** Lunch served: all week Dinner served: all week 12–2.30 6–9 Av main course £6.50
RESTAURANT: Lunch served: all week Dinner served: all week 12–2.30 6–9 Av 3 course à la carte £20
BREWERY/COMPANY: Free House
PRINCIPAL BEERS: Interbrew Bass, Black Sheep Best,.
FACILITIES: Children welcome Children's licence Garden: Food served outside **NOTES:** Parking 20 **ROOMS:** 18 bedrooms 17 en suite from s£25 d£40

Pick of the Pubs

Victoria Hotel ★ ★ ◉ 🍸 ♀
Front St NE69 7BP ☎ 01668 214431 🖷 01668 214404
e-mail: enquiries@victoriahotel.net
Dir: In centre of Bamburg village green
Friendly, attentive service is just one feature of this stylishly refurbished hotel, overlooking Bamburgh's historic village green. The exuberant stone building is late 19th century but the welcome is uncompromisingly modern. There's an airy candlelit brasserie, a children's playden and 29 cheerful, well-equipped bedrooms. Two

continued
continued

BAMBURGH continued

real ales are always available in the popular bar. The brasserie has a domed glass ceiling, a white tiled floor and well-spaced tables. Both traditional or adventurous appetites are catered for: starters could include oak-smoked local salmon with a parsley and walnut pesto or black pudding and toasted muffin stack served on a grain mustard honey dressing. For main courses expect the likes of pan-fried Bamburgh sausages with aïoli mash and a carbonnade of onions, or fillet of beef with wild mushrooms and malt whiskey jus followed by appetising sweets or Northumbrian cheeses. Morning coffee and afternoon tea are also available.

Victoria Hotel

OPEN: 11–11 **BAR MEALS:** Lunch served: all week Dinner served: all week 12–3 6–9 Av main course £5.50 **RESTAURANT:** Lunch served: Sun 12–3 Dinner served: all week 7–9 Av 3 course à la carte £20 **BREWERY/COMPANY:** Free House **PRINCIPAL BEERS:** John Smiths, Theakstons Cool Keg, Harp Irish. **FACILITIES:** Children welcome Dogs allowed (water provided) **NOTES:** Parking 6 **ROOMS:** 29 bedrooms 29 en suite from s£42 d£80

BELFORD
Map 11 NU13

Blue Bell Inn ★ ★ ★ 🏵 🐾
Market Place NE70 7NE ☎ 01668 213543 📠 01668 213787
e-mail: bluebell@globalnet.co.uk
A long-established and creeper-clad coaching inn located in the centre of Belford just off the A1 making a convenient base for exploring Northumberland's magnificent coastline and the Cheviot Hills. The inn offers a friendly, relaxed atmosphere, and a good range of real ales. An choice of menus in the elegant restaurant includes pepper pan-fried mignon of beef, and mille feuille of monkfish, while lamb balti, chicken fajitas, and steak and kidney pie with Newcastle brown are typical of the bar and buttery. Individually decorated bedrooms.
OPEN: 11–2.30 6.30–11 **BAR MEALS:** Lunch served: all week Dinner served: all week 11–2.30 6.30–9 Av main course £7.95 **RESTAURANT:** Lunch served: Sun 12–2 Dinner served: all week 7–8.45 Av 3 course à la carte £28 Av 5 course fixed price £23 **BREWERY/COMPANY:** Free House **PRINCIPAL BEERS:** Interbrew Boddingtons Bitter. **FACILITIES:** Children welcome Garden: Food served outside **NOTES:** Parking 17 **ROOMS:** 17 bedrooms 17 en suite from s£44 d£44

BELSAY
Map 11 NZ09

The Highlander
NE20 0DN ☎ 01661 881220
Dir: (On A696, 2m S of Belsay)

Traditional pub meals, interesting home-cooked specials and all-day food are available at this popular, flower-adorned roadside hostelry. Choose from salads, casseroles, pasta meals, and substantial dishes like rack of lamb with minted jus, and pork with apple and cider sauce.
OPEN: 9.30–11 (Sun 12–10.30) **BAR MEALS:** Lunch served: all week Dinner served: all week 12–9.30 Av main course £7 **PRINCIPAL BEERS:** John Smiths, Theakston Best. **FACILITIES:** Children welcome Garden: Heated Dogs allowed

BERWICK-UPON-TWEED
Map 11 NT95

The Rob Roy 🍴 ⨏
Dock Rd, Tweedmouth TD15 2BE
☎ 01289 306428 📠 01289 303629
e-mail: therobroy@btinternet.com
Dir: Exit A1 2m S of Berwick at A1167 signed Scremerston, to rdbt signed Spittal, then R. 1m to Albion PH, L, 1m to pub

Situated on the south bank of the Tweed, one of the world's most famous salmon rivers, the Rob Roy has been capably run by Keith and Julie Wilson for over 20 years. In this time they have transformed the Rob Roy from a small steak house into a cosy pub with a strong fishing theme and an accent very much on seafood. Expect lobster, crab and fresh white fish, with salmon and sea trout in season from the Tweed itself. Comfortable accommodation in two en suite bedrooms.
OPEN: 12–2.30 7–11 Closed: 3wks Feb or Mar. Xmas & New Year **BAR MEALS:** Lunch served: All week Dinner served: All week 12–2 7–9 Av main course £7.50 **RESTAURANT:** Lunch served: Wed–Mon Dinner served: Wed–Mon 12–1.45 7–9.30 Av 3 course à la carte £25 **PRINCIPAL BEERS:** Tennants 70/-. **ROOMS:** 2 bedrooms 2 en suite from s£25 d£42

BLANCHLAND   Map 11 NY95

Lord Crewe Arms ★ ★
DH8 9SP ☎ 01434 675251 🖷 01434 675337
e-mail: lordcrewearms@freeserve.co.uk
Dir: 10m S of Hexham via B6306
Once the abbot's house of Blanchland Abbey, this is one of
England's oldest inns. Antique furniture, blazing log fires and
flagstone floors make for an atmospheric setting. Wide-ranging
bar and restaurant menus, and well equipped period bedrooms
split between the main house hotel and a former estate building.
OPEN: 11-11 **BAR MEALS:** Lunch served: Mon-Sat 12-2 Dinner
served: all week 7-9 Av main course £6 **RESTAURANT:** Lunch
served: Sun 12-2 Dinner served: all week 7-9.15 Av 3 course à la carte
£28 Av 4 course fixed price £28 **BREWERY/COMPANY:** Free House
PRINCIPAL BEERS: Castle Eden Ale. **FACILITIES:** Children
welcome Garden: Dogs allowed **ROOMS:** 19 bedrooms 19 en suite
from s£80 d£110

CARTERWAY HEADS   Map 11 NZ05

▮ Pick of the Pubs ▮

The Manor House Inn 🐾 ♀
DH8 9LX ☎ 01207 255268
Dir: A69 W from Newcastle, L onto A68 then S for 8m. Inn on R
From its lonely position high on the A68, this small family-
run free house enjoys spectacular views across open
moorland and the Derwent Reservoir. The cosy stone-
walled bar, with its log fires, low beamed ceiling and
massive timber support, offers a good range of well-kept
real ales and around 70 malt whiskies. Built circa 1760, the
inn has a succession of dining areas, and a huge collection
of mugs and jugs hangs from the beams in the candlelit
restaurant. Dishes range through Cumberland sausage and
mash, blackened salmon with roasted Italian vegetables,
and pigeon breast with Madeira and braised shallots.
Home-made puddings are a feature, with the likes of
ginger grundy, and fig and almond cake with Baileys and
butterscotch sauce. There's also a selection of up to 16
local cheeses. If you can't face the drive home after dinner,
accommodation is also available in four guest bedrooms.
OPEN: 11-3 5.30-11 **BAR MEALS:** Lunch served: all week
Dinner served: all week 12-2.30 5.30-9.30 Av main course £10
RESTAURANT: Lunch served: all week Dinner served: all week
12-2.30 7-9.30 Av 3 course à la carte £22
BREWERY/COMPANY: Free House
PRINCIPAL BEERS: Theakstons Best, Mordue Workie Ticket,
Greene King Ruddles County, Scottish Courage Courage Directors.
FACILITIES: Children welcome Children's licence Garden:
Patio, food served outside Dogs allowed **NOTES:** Parking 60
ROOMS: 4 bedrooms 4 en suite from s£33 d£55

CHATTON   Map 11 NU02

The Percy Arms Hotel
Main Rd NE66 5PS ☎ 01668 215244
Dir: From Alnwick take A1 N, then B6348 to Chatton
Built in the early 19th-century as a hunting lodge by the Duke
of Northumberland, this ivy-covered pub enjoys a peaceful
village setting in the unspoilt Till Valley. Bar food includes game
and vegetable pie, grilled lamb chops with rosemary and garlic
butter, Aberdeen Angus fillet and fresh Lindisfarne crab salad.
OPEN: 11-3 6-11 (Sun 12-3, 7-10.30) **BAR MEALS:** Lunch served:
all week Dinner served: all week 12-2.30 6.30-9.30 Av main course

£6.95 **RESTAURANT:** Lunch served: all week Dinner served: all week
12-2.30 6.30-9.30 Av 3 course à la carte £13.50
BREWERY/COMPANY: Free House **PRINCIPAL BEERS:** Scottish
& Newcastle Ales. **FACILITIES:** Children welcome Children's licence
Garden: patio/terrace, outdoor eating Dogs allowed **NOTES:** Parking
30 **ROOMS:** 8 bedrooms 5 en suite from s£30 d£60

CORBRIDGE   Map 11 NY96

The Angel of Corbridge ★ ★ 🐾
Main St NE45 5LA ☎ 01434 632119 🖷 01434 633496
e-mail: info@theangelofcorbridge.softnet.co.uk
Dir: 0.5m off A69, signed Corbridge
Stylish 17th-century coaching inn overlooking the River Tyne.
Relax with the daily papers in the wood-panelled lounge or
attractive bars, or enjoy a home-made dish or two from the
extensive menu choice. Options include tempura of sole, oven
baked salmon en croûte with buttered spinach, baked peppered
goats' cheese with spicy turmeric tomatoes, and roasted duck
breast with hotpot potatoes and sautéed Savoy cabbage.
OPEN: 11-11 (Sun 12-10.30) **BAR MEALS:** Lunch served: all week
12-2.30 Dinner served: Mon-Sat 6-9.30 Av main course £8
RESTAURANT: Lunch served: all week Dinner served: all week
12-2.30 6-9.30 Av 3 course à la carte £18 Av 3 course fixed price £16
BREWERY/COMPANY: Free House **PRINCIPAL BEERS:** Black
Sheep Best, Scottish Courage Courage Directors & John Smith's.
FACILITIES: Children's licence Garden: Food served outside
NOTES: Parking 25 **ROOMS:** 5 bedrooms 5 en suite from s£49 d£74

CRASTER   Map 11 NU22

Cottage Inn ♦ ♦ ♦ 🐾 ♀
Dunstan Village NE66 3SZ ☎ 01665 576658 🖷 01665 576788
Dir: NW of Howick to Embleton road
In an area of outstanding natural beauty, easily accessible
from the A1, this 18th-century inn is located in a hamlet close
to the sea. There is a beamed bar, Harry Hotspur Restaurant,
conservatory, loggia and patio. One menu serves all - a
comprehensive choice of snacks, full meals, kids' and
vegetarian options, supplemented by daily specials. Local
ingredients are used wherever possible in dishes such as
Craster fish stew and whole joint of lamb.
OPEN: 11-11 (Sun 12-3, 7-10.30) **BAR MEALS:** Lunch served: all
week Dinner served: all week 12-2.30 6-9.30 Av main course £6.50
RESTAURANT: Lunch served: all week Dinner served: all week
12-2.30 6-9.30 Av 3 course à la carte £14
BREWERY/COMPANY: Free House **PRINCIPAL BEERS:** Belhaven
80/-, Wylam Bitter. **FACILITIES:** Children welcome Garden:
Woodland garden **NOTES:** Parking 60 **ROOMS:** 10 bedrooms 10 en
suite from s£35 d£63

Jolly Fisherman Inn
Haven Hill NE66 3TR ☎ 01665 576461
e-mail: muriel@silk.fsnet.co.uk
Authentic, unpretentious pub situated in a tiny fishing village
famous for its kipper sheds. Handy for local walks, visiting
Dunstanburgh Castle and exploring the scenic delights of
Northumberland and the beautiful Scottish Borders. Delicious
home-made crabmeat soup, kipper paté and crab sandwiches
feature on the menu.
OPEN: 11-3 6-11 (all day from Jun-Aug) **BAR MEALS:** Lunch
served: all week Dinner served: all week 11-2.30 6-8
BREWERY/COMPANY: Pubmaster
PRINCIPAL BEERS: Carlsberg-Tetley Tetley Bitter, Scottish Courage
John Smith's. **FACILITIES:** Children welcome Garden: Dogs
allowed **NOTES:** Parking 10 No credit cards

continued

England

EGLINGHAM
Map 11 NU21

Tankerville Arms 🛏 ♈
NE66 2TX ☎ 01665 578444 🖥 01665 578444
Dir: B6346 from Alnwick

Traditional stone-built pub with a good reputation for its real ales and good food prepared from local produce. The historic village, local castles and wonderful nearby beaches, make the pub a favourite with walkers and cyclists, particularly as there are spectacular views from the beer garden. A menu of snacks, salads and entrees is supplemented by specials like supreme of halibut wrapped in Craster salmon, and collops of venison with roast onion and celeriac confit.
OPEN: 12-2 7-11 Times may vary Closed: 25 Dec
BAR MEALS: Lunch served: all week Dinner served: all week 12-2 6-9 Av main course £9.50 **RESTAURANT:** Lunch served: all week Dinner served: all week 12-2 6-9 Av 3 course à la carte £15
BREWERY/COMPANY: Free House **PRINCIPAL BEERS:** Greene King Ruddles Best, Scottish Courage Courage Directors, Black Sheep Best, Mordue Workie Ticket. **FACILITIES:** Children welcome Garden: Food served outside **NOTES:** Parking 15

ETAL
Map 11 NT93

Black Bull
TD12 4TL ☎ 01890 820200
e-mail: blackbulletal@aol.com
Dir: 10m N of Wooler R off A697, L at Jct for 1m then L into Etal.
This 300-year-old hostelry is the only thatched pub in Northumberland, located by the ruins of Etal Castle. Close to the River Till and a short distance to the grand walking country of the Cheviots. Typical dishes include lamb with fennel, game casserole, haddock with prawn and mushroom sauce, roast duck, and beer, beef and bacon casserole.
OPEN: 11.30-3.30 7-11 (11-11 Summer) **BAR MEALS:** Lunch served: all week Dinner served: all week 12-3 7-10 Av main course £8 **RESTAURANT:** Lunch served: all week Dinner served: all week 12-3 7-10 Av 3 course à la carte £15 **BREWERY/COMPANY:** Pubmaster **PRINCIPAL BEERS:** Tetley, John Smiths. **FACILITIES:** Dogs allowed **NOTES:** Parking 10

FALSTONE
Map 11 NY78

The Blackcock Inn ♦♦♦ 🛏 ♈
NE48 1AA ☎ 01434 240200 🖥 01434 240200
e-mail: enquiries@blackcock.co.uk
Dir: off unclassified rd from Bellingham (accessed from A68 or B6320)
Traditional 18th-century stone-built inn, close to Kielder Reservoir and Forest, with some lovely walks accessible from the village. The pub is also handy for the Rievers Cycle Route. Old beams and open log fires make for a cosy atmosphere, and food is served in the bar, lounge and dining area

alongside a good choice of beers. Dishes are based on the best local produce, ranging from snacks to steaks, with fish and vegetarian options.
OPEN: 11-3 6-11 (Winter 7-11) **BAR MEALS:** Lunch served: all week Dinner served: all week 11-2 7-9 Av main course £6.95 **RESTAURANT:** Dinner served: Fri-Sun 7-9 Av 3 course à la carte £12.50 **BREWERY/COMPANY:** Free House **PRINCIPAL BEERS:** Blackcock Ale, Scottish Courage Courage Directors Marston's Pedigree, Theakston Cool Cask.
FACILITIES: Children welcome Garden: Food served outside Dogs allowed **NOTES:** Parking 20 **ROOMS:** 5 bedrooms 5 en suite from s£22 d£50

Pick of the Pubs

The Pheasant ♦♦♦♦ 🛏
Stannersburn NE48 1DD ☎ 01434 240382 🖥 01434 240382
e-mail: enquiries@thepheasantinn.com
Dir: From A68 onto B6320, or from A69, B6079, B6320, follow signs 'Kielder Water'

Situated close to Kielder Water, this 17th-century building was originally a farmstead with some 250 acres, but even then it included a bar. Its long farming history is evident in the cosy interior, which includes a wealth of beams, exposed stone walls, open fires and farming memorabilia. Nowadays guests who wish to extend their stay can book one of eight attractive en suite bedrooms, arranged around a courtyard. The restaurant is furnished in mellow pine and has warm teracotta walls. It's a relaxing environment in which to enjoy a good selection of traditional home cooked food. Dishes are carefully prepared and make use of the very best local produce wherever possible. Typical examples include roast Northumberland lamb, cider-baked gammon with Cumberland sausage, poached salmon with herbed yogurt and sirloin steak with garlic butter. Finish with desserts such as home-made sticky toffee pudding, crème brûlee or kiwi and passion fruit Pavlova.
OPEN: 11-3 6-11 (opening times vary, ring for details) Closed: Dec 25-26 **BAR MEALS:** Lunch served: all week Dinner served: all week 12-2.30 7-9 Av main course £6.50 **RESTAURANT:** Lunch served: Sun Dinner served: all week 12-2.30 7-9 Av 3 course à la carte £16 **BREWERY/COMPANY:** Free House **PRINCIPAL BEERS:** Theakston Best, Marstons Pedigree, Timothy Taylor Landlord, Greene King Old Speckled Hen.
FACILITIES: Children welcome Garden: Food served outside. Courtyard area Dogs allowed By arrangement only **NOTES:** Parking 30 **ROOMS:** 8 bedrooms 8 en suite from s£30 d£55

continued

England

GREAT WHITTINGTON   Map 11 NZ07

Pick of the Pubs

Queens Head Inn & Restaurant
NE19 2HP ☎ 01434 672267
Dir: *Off A68 & B6318 W of Newcastle upon Tyne*
At the heart of Hadrian's Wall country this old
pub/restaurant, once a coaching inn, radiates a
welcoming atmosphere in comfortable surroundings of
beamed rooms, oak settles and open fires. In addition to
Black Sheep beers there can be found some three dozen
wines of choice and nearly as many malt whiskies. Menus
combine the best of local and international cuisine, taking
in avocado, prawn and apple tian, vegetable tempura with
sweet and sour sauce and venison medallions with celery
and chestnut confit. Speciality dishes include baked cod
fillet with herb and cheese crust, prime sirloin and pork
tenderloin steaks and home-made desserts such as
chocolate mousse with coffee custard. Sunday lunch can
start with home-made soup or chef's game pâté before
traditional butchers' meats and pot-roasted pheasant with
mushroom, bacon and baby onion jus.
OPEN: 12–3 6–11 **BAR MEALS:** Lunch served: Tues–Sun
Dinner served: Tues–Sun 12–2 6.30–9 Av main course £8.95
RESTAURANT: Lunch served: Tues–Sun Dinner served:
Tues–Sun 12–2 6.30–9 Av 3 course à la carte £18.95
BREWERY/COMPANY: Free House
PRINCIPAL BEERS: Black Sheep, Queens Head, Hambleton.
FACILITIES: Children welcome Garden: **NOTES:** Parking 20

HALTWHISTLE   Map 11 NY76

Milecastle Inn
Military Rd, Cawfields NE49 9NN
☎ 01434 321372 & 320682 ☐ 01434 321671
e-mail: milecastleinn@fsbdial.co.uk
Dir: *Leave A69 at Haltwhistle, pub about 2 miles from Haltwhistle at
junction with B6318*

Overlooking Hadrian's Wall, this stone-built rural inn attracts
loyal locals and tourists alike. Old horse brasses and open
fires are a feature of the beamed bar and dining-room,
complete with resident ghost. The walled gardens enjoy
spectacular views. There is a long-standing tradition of home-
made pies and casseroles - wild boar and duckling - or
smoked fish pie, braised ham shank in balsamic gravy and
steak and kidney pudding. Vegetarian alternatives and
sandwiches (at lunchtime only), and a more formal dining
menu.
OPEN: 12–2.30 6.30–11 **BAR MEALS:** Lunch served: all week
Dinner served: all week 12–2 6.30–9 Av main course £6

continued

RESTAURANT: Lunch served: Sun 12–2 Dinner served: Wed–Sat
7–8.30 Av 3 course à la carte £17 **BREWERY/COMPANY:** Free
House **PRINCIPAL BEERS:** Northumberland Castle, Carlsberg-Tetley
Tetley Bitter, Jennings Cumberland Ale, Wylam Turbinia.
FACILITIES: Garden: Views over Hadrians Wall, food served ouside
NOTES: Parking 30

HAYDON BRIDGE   Map 11 NY86

The General Havelock Inn
Ratcliffe Rd NE47 6ER ☎ 01434 684376 ☐ 01434 684283
e-mail: GeneralHavelock@aol.com
Dir: *On A69, 7m west of Hexham*

Built as a private house in 1840, but licensed since 1890, this
pub occupies a pleasant riverside setting not far from
Hadrian's Wall. Its name comes from a British Army officer
who fought in India in the 19th century. The restaurant is in a
converted barn that overlooks the River Tyne. The food is all
home-made and largely local, and the wide-ranging menu
offers cullen skink, poached fillet of cod with mussels and
parsley liquor, Cumberland sausages, chicken, leek and
Cheddar pie, and beef and Guinness stew with wild
mushrooms.
OPEN: 12–2.30 7–11 **BAR MEALS:** Lunch served: Tues–Sun 12–2
Dinner served: Tues–Sat 7–9 Av main course £6
RESTAURANT: Lunch served: Tue–Sun 12–2 Dinner served: Tue–Sat
7–9 Av 3 course à la carte £17.95 **BREWERY/COMPANY:** Free
House **PRINCIPAL BEERS:** Greene King Old Speckled Hen, Exmoor
Gold, Jennings Cumberland Ale, Timothy Taylor Landlord.
FACILITIES: Children welcome Garden: Patio, food served outside
Dogs allowed

HEDLEY ON THE HILL   Map 11 NZ05

Pick of the Pubs

The Feathers Inn
NE43 7SW ☎ 01661 843607 ☐ 01661 843607
From its hilltop position, this small stone-built free house
overlooks the splendid adventure country of the Cheviots.
The three-roomed pub is well patronized by the local
community, but strangers, too, are frequently charmed by
its friendly and relaxed atmosphere. Families are
welcome, and a small side room can be booked in
advance if required. Old oak beams, coal fires and rustic
settles set the scene and there's a good selection of
traditional pub games like shove ha'penny and bar
skittles. The stone walls are decorated with local
photographs of rural life. Although the pub has no
garden, food and drinks can be served at tables on the
green in good weather. The menus change regularly, and
the imaginative home cooking includes an extensive

continued

HEDLEY ON THE HILL continued

choice of vegetarian meals. Expect salmon steak with Thai sauce, honey roast ham with mango chutney, beef and pigeon casserole with a fresh herb pastry crust and chilli minced steak tortilla. An appetising range of puddings.
OPEN: 12-3 6-11 Closed: Dec 25 **BAR MEALS:** Lunch served: Sat-Sun 12-2.30 Dinner served: Tue-Sun 7-9 Av main course £6.75 **BREWERY/COMPANY:** Free House
PRINCIPAL BEERS: Mordue Workie Ticket, Big Lamp Bitter, Fuller's London Pride, Yates Bitter. **FACILITIES:** Children welcome Children's licence Dogs allowed **NOTES:** Parking 12

HEXHAM   Map 11 NY96

Pick of the Pubs

Dipton Mill Inn
Dipton Mill Rd NE46 1YA ☎ 01434 606577
Dir: *2m S of Hexham on HGV route to Blanchland (B6306)*
Originally part of a farmhouse, the inn has been here since the 1800s. Enjoy a delightful walk through the woods to Hexham racecourse and back before relaxing with a pint of home-brewed Hexhamshire ale in the low-ceilinged bar. Freshly prepared food utilises ingredients from local suppliers; rolls are made by a local baker and the inn offers a good selection of local cheeses. Sample steak and kidney pie, mince and dumplings, dressed crab salad or tomato, bean and vegetable casserole from the enterprising menu.
OPEN: 12-2.30 6-11 (Sun 12-4, 7-10.30) Closed: 25 Dec
BAR MEALS: Lunch served: all week Dinner served: all week 12-2.30 6.30-8.30 Av main course £5.75
BREWERY/COMPANY: Free House
PRINCIPAL BEERS: Hexhamshire Shire Bitter, Devil's Water, Devil's Elbow & Whapweasel. **FACILITIES:** Children welcome Children's licence Garden: Stream, food served outdoors, patio No credit cards

Miners Arms Inn
Main St, Acomb NE46 4PW ☎ 01434 603909
Dir: *17 miles W of Newcastle on A69, 2 miles W of Hexam.*
Close to Hadrian's Wall in a peaceful village, this charming 18th-century pub has recently come under new management, although changes have been few. Real ales are a speciality, as is good homecooked food. There is no jukebox or pool table, so visitors will have to entertain themselves with conversation, and some choices from a menu that includes curry, Italian chicken, steak and kidney pie, and a special trifle. Good setting for cyclists and walkers.
OPEN: 12-3 5-11 **BAR MEALS:** Lunch served: all week Dinner served: all week 12-2 5-9 Av main course £4.75
RESTAURANT: Lunch served: all week Dinner served: all week 12-2 5-9 Av 3 course fixed price £9 **BREWERY/COMPANY:** Free House **PRINCIPAL BEERS:** Miners Lamp, Yates, Black Sheep Best, Northumberland Smooth. **FACILITIES:** Children welcome Garden: Outdoor eating, patio/terrace Dogs allowed (water) No credit cards

The Rose & Crown Inn ◆◆◆ 🏠 ⬦
Main St, Slaley NE47 0AA ☎ 01434 673263 📠 01434 673305
e-mail: rosecrowninn@supanet.com
A 200-year-old listed building combining the charm of a traditional country inn with modern service and comfort. Conveniently situated for exploring Keilder Forest and the delights of the Borders, as well as the Roman sites of Vindolanda and Howsteads. Handy, too, for fishing, horse-riding, hunting, sailing and shooting. Appetising food is on offer and among the dishes on the menu you might find beef casserole, turkey and ham pie, poached chicken breast and salmon and mushroom tagliatelle.
OPEN: 11.30-3 6-11 **BAR MEALS:** Lunch served: all week Dinner served: all week 12-2.15 6.30-9.30 **RESTAURANT:** Lunch served: all week Dinner served: all week 12-2.15 6.30-9.30 Av 3 course à la carte £16 **BREWERY/COMPANY:** Free House
PRINCIPAL BEERS: Black Sheep Special, Theakston Best, Timothy Taylor Landlord, Greene King Ruddles County. **FACILITIES:** Children welcome Garden: Food served outside **NOTES:** Parking 36
ROOMS: 3 bedrooms 3 en suite from s£32.50 d£45

LONGFRAMLINGTON   Map 11 NU10

Granby Inn ⬦
Front St NE65 8DP ☎ 01665 570228 📠 01665 570736
Dir: *On A697, 11m N of Morpeth*

Situated at the heart of Northumberland, between the Cheviots and the coast, this 200-year-old coaching inn is a family-run business which retains much of its original character. Expect rump steak with a peppercorn sauce, entrecote bordelaise, sizzling king prawns with Szechuan sauce, seafood platter, steak pie, and a choice of salads. Good range of traditional desserts.
OPEN: 11-3 6-11 Closed: 25-26 Dec **BAR MEALS:** Lunch served: all week Dinner served: all week 11.30-2 6-9.30 Av main course £7.50
RESTAURANT: All week 11.30-2 6-9.30 Av 3 course à la carte £15
BREWERY/COMPANY: Free House **FACILITIES:** Children welcome **NOTES:** Parking 20 **ROOMS:** 5 bedrooms 5 en suite from s£29.50 d£56

LONGHORSLEY   Map 11 NZ19

Linden Tree Bar & Grill ★ ★ ★ 🏠🏠 ⬦
Linden Hall NE65 8XF ☎ 01670 500033 📠 01670 500001
e-mail: stay@lindenhall.co.uk
Dir: *Off the A1 on the A697 1m N of Longhorsley*
Originally two large cattle byres, this popular bar takes its name from the linden trees in the grounds of Linden Hall Hotel, an impressive Georgian mansion offering smartly furnished bedrooms. Straightforward meals range from aubergine and broccoli bake, braised lamb shank, or medallions of pork, to grilled salmon, or poached smoked cod fillets.

continued

OPEN: 11–11 (Sun 12–10.30) Closed: 1 Jan **BAR MEALS:** Lunch served: all week Dinner served: all week 12–2 6–9.30 Av main course £8.50 **BREWERY/COMPANY:** Free House
PRINCIPAL BEERS: Black Bull, Ruddles Best, John Smiths.
FACILITIES: Children welcome Garden: Food served outside, courtyard **NOTES:** Parking 200 **ROOMS:** 50 bedrooms 50 en suite

---

LOW NEWTON BY THE SEA — Map 11 NU22

The Ship
The Square NE66 3EL ☎ 01665 576262
e-mail: forsythchristine@hotmail.com
Dir: NW from A1 at Alnwick

The village of Low Newton was purpose-built as a fishing village in the 18th century and is in the shape of an open-sided square. The unspoilt Ship overlooks the green and is just a stroll away from the beach. Bustling in summer and a peaceful retreat in winter, it offers a menu that includes plenty of fresh, locally caught fish and shellfish, venison rump steaks, Greek salad with houmous, and maybe Ship Inn trifle with ratafia and Madeira to finish.
OPEN: 11–4 6.30–11 (During school holidays open all day)
BAR MEALS: Lunch served: all week 12–2.30 6.30–8 Av main course £7.50 **BREWERY/COMPANY:** Free House
PRINCIPAL BEERS: Original Northumberland, Black Sheep Special.
FACILITIES: Children welcome Garden: Food served outside Dogs allowed (water provided) No credit cards

---

MATFEN — Map 11 NZ07

The Black Bull
NE20 0RP ☎ 01661 886330
Dir: Leave A69 at Corbridge, join B6318. 2m N sign to Matfen
A 200-year-old, creeper-covered inn fronting the village green, which has a river running through it. The comfortable restaurant and carpeted bar have low beams and open fires.

NEWTON ON THE MOOR — Map 11 NU10

Cook and Barker Inn 🛏 ♀
NE65 9JY ☎ 01665 575234 📠 01665 575234
Dir: 0.5m from A1 S of Alnwick

This warm and friendly, very traditional English pub is easily located just off the A1, slightly north of Morpeth. There is a good selection of real ales and a long list of wines to accompany the extensive bar menus, which suit a wide range of tastes and pockets. Seafood selections include chargrilled sardines, seared tuna loin with ratatouille and pan-fried halibut with baked aubergine and garlic cream. From 'forest and fields' come hoi sin-style pork cutlet with fresh lime, coriander and egg noodles, wood pigeon with bacon, wild mushrooms and port and redcurrant jus and beef fillet with sun-dried tomato, prawn and basil stuffing. Set lunch and dinner alternatives are legion with consistently pleasing results, while for simpler tastes, there's a 'grills and roasts' selection. Those fortunate enough to turn this into an overnight stay are rewarded in the morning with fine Northumbrian coastal views.
OPEN: 12–3 6–11 **BAR MEALS:** Lunch served: all week Dinner served: all week 12–2 6–9 **RESTAURANT:** Lunch served: all week Dinner served: all week 12–2 7–9 Av à la carte £25 Av 3 course fixed price £18.50 **BREWERY/COMPANY:** Free House
PRINCIPAL BEERS: Timothy Taylor Landlord, Theakstons Best Bitter, Fuller's London Pride, Batemans XXXB. **FACILITIES:** Children welcome Garden: Beer garden, food served outside
NOTES: Parking 60 **ROOMS:** 5 bedrooms 5 en suite from s£37.50 d£70

ROWFOOT — Map 11 NY66

The Wallace Arms 🛏
NE49 0JF ☎ 01434 321872 📠 01434 321872
The pub was originally the Railway Inn at Featherstone Halt, on the Haltwhistle-Alston line (now the South Tyne Trail) and is set in beautiful parkland half a mile south of Featherstone Castle. Excellent local ales; great walking country. Look out for the likes of smoked haddock pasta, chicken breast in prawn and garlic sauce, steak and ale pie, or peppered sirloin steak.
OPEN: 11–2.30 4–11 (opening times vary, ring for details)
BAR MEALS: Lunch served: all week Dinner served: all week 12–2 7–9 Av main course £6 **RESTAURANT:** Lunch served: all week Dinner served: all week 12–2 7–9 Av 3 course à la carte £15
BREWERY/COMPANY: Free House **PRINCIPAL BEERS:** Four Rivers Hadrian Legion, Hook Norton Old Hooky, Timothy Taylor Landlord, Young's Special. **FACILITIES:** Children welcome Garden: Beer garden, food served outdoors, BBQ Dogs allowed
NOTES: Parking 30 No credit cards

England

SEAHOUSES   Map 11 NU23

The Olde Ship Hotel ★ ★ 🛏 ♀
9 Main St NE68 7RD ☎ 01665 720200 🖹 01665 721383
e-mail: theoldeship@seahouses.co.uk
Dir: lower end of main street above harbour
Sitting above a tiny bustling harbour, this historic hotel has
been managed by the same family for over 90 years.
Originally a farmhouse and then licensed in 1812, there is a
strong nautical theme to the cosy, comfortable bars, with lots
of seafaring memorabilia. Expect tip-top ales, and home-
cooked food like bosun's fish stew, game pie, beef stovies,
and spicy lamb stew. Ideal for a weekend break, with bracing
country walks.
OPEN: 11–11 **BAR MEALS:** Lunch served: all week Dinner served:
all week 12–2 7–8.30 Av main course £6.95 **RESTAURANT:** Lunch
served: all week Dinner served: all week 12–2 7–8.30 Av 5 course fixed
price £17 **BREWERY/COMPANY:** Free House
PRINCIPAL BEERS: Scottish Courage John Smith's, Theakston Best,
Interbrew Bass, McEwans. **FACILITIES:** Children welcome Garden:
Grassed area with summer house **NOTES:** Parking 18 **ROOMS:** 18
bedrooms 18 en suite from s£37 d£74

WARDEN   Map 11 NY96

The Boatside Inn 🛏
NE46 4SQ ☎ 01434 602233
*Dir: Just off A69 west of Hexham, follow signs to Warden Newborough &
Fourstones*

The name comes from the rowing boat that ferried people
across the River Tyne before the bridge was built. This
attractive stone pub nestles beneath Warden Hill Iron Age fort,
a popular destination for walkers, and promises real ale and
good food cooked from local produce. Expect interesting
sandwiches and snacks, plus halibut with crayfish in butter
sauce, chicken cobbler, Cumberland sausage, and tagine of
lamb. Plenty of art and antiques for sale.
OPEN: 11–3 6–11 **BAR MEALS:** Lunch served: all week Dinner
served: all week 12–2 6.30–9.30 Av main course £8
RESTAURANT: Lunch served: all week Dinner served: all week 12–2
6.30–9.30 Av 3 course à la carte £15 **BREWERY/COMPANY:** Free
House **PRINCIPAL BEERS:** Theakston Best, Scottish Courage
Courage Directors & John Smith's. **FACILITIES:** Children welcome
Garden: Patio with lawned area, food served outdoors
NOTES: Parking 70

> 🏵 **For a list of pubs with**
> **AA Rosette Awards for food see pages 12 & 13.**

WARENFORD   Map 11 NU12

Pick of the Pubs

Warenford Lodge 🛏 ♀
NE70 7HY ☎ 01668 213453 🖹 01668 213453
e-mail: warenfordlodge@aol.com
Dir: 100yds E of A1, 10M N of Alnwick
Near the old toll bridge over Warren Burn, at the heart of
some fine walking country, this 200-year-old coaching inn is
just a stone's throw from the A1. The interior is characterised
by its thickset exposed stone walls and open fireplaces,
where welcoming open fires burn on colder days. It is a
popular venue for both visitors and locals who enjoy the
country atmosphere and award-winning Northumbrian
dishes. You can expect dishes such as Seahouses fish
chowder, made with local fish and home-cured bacon and
served with garlic bread, or potted crabmeat with pink crab
mayonnaise. Mains range between fillet of beef with
Lindisfarne oyster dumplings, and a vegetarian option of
leek roly poly with vegetable casserole. Baked lemon
pudding served with thick cream is a house speciality,
alongside apple fritters with apple strudel ice cream, and the
Northumberland cheese platter is also worthy of note.
OPEN: 12–2 7–11 Closed: 25/26 Dec, 1 Jan
BAR MEALS: Lunch served: Sat–Sun 12–1.30 Dinner served:
Tues–Sun 7–9.30 Av main course £8.10 **RESTAURANT:** Lunch
served: Sat–Sun 12–1.30 Dinner served: Tues–Sun 7–9.30 Av 3
course à la carte £15.10 **BREWERY/COMPANY:** Free House
PRINCIPAL BEERS: Scottish Courage john Smith's.
FACILITIES: Children welcome Garden: **NOTES:** Parking 60

NOTTINGHAMSHIRE

BEESTON   Map 09 SK53

Pick of the Pubs

Victoria Hotel ♀
Dovecote Ln NG9 1JG ☎ 0115 925 4049 🖹 0115 922 3537
*Dir: M1 J25 take A52 E. R at Nursuryman PH & R opp Rockaway
Hotel into Barton St 1st L*
The original hotel came to life in the hey-day of the railways
and the large patio garden is still handy for a touch of train-
spotting. Almost derelict, with trees growing out of the roof,
in the early 1990s, the unpretentious brick building has
been restored and transformed into a great pub with a
traditional atmosphere, popular with ale drinkers and those
who appreciate freshly cooked food. In addition to the 12
well-kept real ales, farm ciders and 150 malt whiskies, the
attraction is the single, daily-changing menu. Dishes might
include duck liver and apricot pâté with melba toast,
Portuguese pork casserole with chorizo sausage, black
pudding, broad beans, pimento and fresh herbs, and tarte
de Santiago. The vegetarian option might be fresh basil
crêpes stuffed with roasted vegetables and melted
Mozzarella. Every summer the pub hosts a Festival of Ale,
Food and Music, which gets bigger and better each year.
OPEN: 11–11 **BAR MEALS:** Lunch served: all week Dinner
served: all week 12–8.45 Av main course £6.95
RESTAURANT: Lunch served: all week Dinner served: all week
12–8.45 **BREWERY/COMPANY:** Tynemill Ltd
PRINCIPAL BEERS: Batemans XB, Caledonian Deuchers IPA,
Castle Rock Hemlock, Everards Tiger. **FACILITIES:** Garden:
Food served outside, patio Dogs allowed **NOTES:** Parking 10

CAUNTON
Map 09 SK76

Caunton Beck 🐷 ♀
NG23 6AB ☎ 01636 636793 📠 01636 636828
Dir: 5m NW of Newark on A616

Set amid herb gardens and a dazzling rose arbour, this
civilised pub-restaurant has been constructed around a single
16th-century cottage. Food is available from 8am to around
midnight, so you can look in for breakfast, a sandwich, and a
full meal with a decent wine list - or just enjoy a quiet drink
and a read of the paper. Favourites are classic Caesar salad,
braised pork and sage faggots, and chocolate and orange
bread and butter pudding.
OPEN: 8am-midnight **BAR MEALS:** Lunch served: all week Dinner
served: all week 8am-midnight Av main course £5.75
RESTAURANT: Lunch served: all week Dinner served: all week Av 3
course à la carte £20 Av 3 course fixed price £12
BREWERY/COMPANY: Free House **PRINCIPAL BEERS:** Greene
King Ruddles Best & Ruddles County, Interbrew John Smith's.
FACILITIES: Children welcome Garden: Food served outside Dogs
allowed **NOTES:** Parking 40

CAYTHORPE
Map 09 Sk 64

Black Horse Inn
NG14 7ED ☎ 0115 966 3520
Three generations of the same family have run this small,
beamed country pub where old-fashioned hospitality is
guaranteed. In winter, coal fires burn, and if the toilets are
outside (that is changing!), at least there are no slot machines
or music. The inn has its own small brewery, producing Dover
Beck Bitter, and food ranges from crispy bacon sandwiches to
fresh fish specials, mixed grill, and seafood salad.
OPEN: 12-3 5.30-11 **BAR MEALS:** Lunch served: Tue-Sat 12-2
Dinner served: Mon-Sat 7-8.30 Av main course £7
RESTAURANT: Lunch served: Tue-Sat Dinner served: Mon-Sat Av 3
course à la carte £21.50 **BREWERY/COMPANY:** Free House
PRINCIPAL BEERS: Interbrew Bass, Exmoor Gold, Adnams Bitter,.
FACILITIES: Garden: Food served outdoors Dogs allowed (water)
NOTES: Parking 30 No credit cards

COLSTON BASSETT
Map 09 SK73

Pick of the Pubs

The Martins Arms Inn 🐷 ♀
School Ln NG12 3FD ☎ 01949 81361 📠 01949 81039
Dir: M1 J22, Take A50 then A46 North towards Newark. Colston
Bassett is situated East of Cotgrave.
During the middle years of the 19th century, Squire
Martin created this village inn from a 17th-century

continued

farmhouse. Nowadays the Grade II listed building has
something of county house feel, with period furnishings,
traditional hunting prints and seasonal fires in the
Jacobean fireplace. The acre of landscaped grounds
includes a herb garden and well-established lawns, ideal
for outside eating in the summer. The best regional
ingredients are a feature of the menu, with a belter of a
ploughman's lunch comprising Melton Mowbray pork pie,
Colston Bassett Stilton, home-baked ham, house pickles
and a crusty warm baguette. On the dinner menu, you'll
find similarly substantial fare: roasted pheasant breast
with chestnut and pork sausage, rösti potato and thyme
jus on a roast root vegetable, or pork fillet medallions
stacked with braised fennel and sun blushed tomato
compote and smoked Mozzarella. The old stables now
house Martins Arms Antiques and Interiors.

OPEN: 12-3 6-11 **BAR MEALS:** Lunch served: all week 12-2
Dinner served: Mon-Sat 6-10 Av main course £13
RESTAURANT: Lunch served: all week Dinner served: Mon-Sat
12-2 6-9.30 Av 3 course à la carte £25
BREWERY/COMPANY: Free House
PRINCIPAL BEERS: Marston's Pedigree, Interbrew Bass, Greene
King Abbot Ale, Timothy Taylor Landlord. **FACILITIES:** Children
welcome Garden: Food served outside **NOTES:** Parking 35
ROOMS: 2 bedrooms 1 en suite

EASTWOOD
Map 09 SK44

The Nelson & Railway Inn
12 Station Rd, Kimberley NG16 2NR ☎ 0115 938 2177
Dir: One mile north of junction 26 M1
This unusual 17th-century village pub, with various Victorian
and 20th-century additions, has an eccentric atmosphere,
nurtured by the landlord who has been there for over thirty
years. Nearby, the two competing railway stations that once
gave the inn its major business are now derelict and next door
is the Hardy & Hanson brewery that supplies the bar with
many of its beers. A hearty menu includes steak and kidney
pie, cod in batter, lasagne, monster mixed grill, stir-fry egg
noodles and seafood platter.
OPEN: 10.30-3 5-11 (Summer (May-Sept) open all day)
BAR MEALS: Lunch served: all week Dinner served: all week
12-2.30 5.30-9 Av main course £5 **RESTAURANT:** Lunch served: all
week Dinner served: all week 12-2.30 5.30-9 Av 3 course à la carte
£10 **BREWERY/COMPANY:** Hardy & Hansons
PRINCIPAL BEERS: Hardys, Hansons Best Bitter, Classic, Cool &
Dark. **FACILITIES:** Children welcome Garden: Food served
outdoors, patio/terrace Dogs allowed (water provided)
NOTES: Parking 50 **ROOMS:** 3 bedrooms from s£24 d£39

England

ELKESLEY   Map 09 Sk 67

Pick of the Pubs

Robin Hood Inn 🐷 ♀
High St DN22 8AJ ☎ 01777 838259
See Pick of the Pubs on page 353

LAXTON   Map 09 SK76

The Dovecote Inn ♀
Moorhouse Rd NG22 0NU ☎ 01777 871586 ▤ 01777 871586
e-mail: dovecoteinn@yahoo.co.uk
Set in the only village that still uses the '3 field system', (pop into the local Visitor Centre to find out what that is), this 18th-century pub is an ideal stopping point for walkers, who can relax over a pint in the large front and rear gardens. A typical menu mixes grills, salads and light bites with other dishes such as mushroom Stroganoff, cottage pie, seafood platter, steak in Guinness pie, and lasagne.
OPEN: 11.30-3 6.30-11.30 **BAR MEALS:** Lunch served: all week Dinner served: all week 12-2 6.30-9.30 Av main course £6.25
RESTAURANT: 12-2 6.30-9.30 **BREWERY/COMPANY:** Free House **PRINCIPAL BEERS:** Mansfield Smooth, Banks Smooth, Marston's Pedigree. **FACILITIES:** Children welcome Garden: Food served outside Dogs allowed **NOTES:** Parking 45
ROOMS: 2 bedrooms 2 en suite from s£35 d£45

MAPLEBECK   Map 09 SK76

The Beehive
NG22 0BS ☎ 01636 636306
Nestling down a country lane, this popular family pub is by a stream and has a play area in the garden. Mansfield beers. Claims to be the smallest pub in the county of Nottinghamshire.

NORMANTON ON TRENT   Map 09 SK75

The Square & Compass ♀
Eastgate NG23 6RN ☎ 01636 821439 ▤ 01636 822794
e-mail: greatnorthen@ukgateway.net
Dir: Off A1 & B1164 N of Newark-on-Trent
Full of charm and character, this beamed pub is almost 500 years old, and is said to be haunted by the ghost of a traveller who was hung for stealing. A typical menu includes stuffed woodland mushrooms, seafood platter, game casserole, and roulade of chicken. The pub also owns the Maypole Brewery, which produces real ales for local hostelries. A new building nearby houses three bedrooms.
OPEN: 12-3 5-11 **BAR MEALS:** Lunch served: all week Dinner served: all week 12-3 6-10 Av main course £6.50
RESTAURANT: Lunch served: all week Dinner served: all week 12-3 6-11 Av 3 course à la carte £16 **BREWERY/COMPANY:** Free House **PRINCIPAL BEERS:** Timothy Taylor Landlord, Wells Bombadier, Shepherd Neame Spitfire. **FACILITIES:** Children welcome Garden: **NOTES:** Parking 80 **ROOMS:** 3 bedrooms 3 en suite from s£40 d£40

NOTTINGHAM   Map 09 SK54

Fellows Morton & Clayton 🐷 ♀
54 Canal St NG1 7EH ☎ 0115 950 6795 ▤ 0115 953 9838
e-mail: info@fellowsmortonandclayton.co.uk
Atmospheric city centre pub, originally a warehouse belonging to the brewers Samuel Fellows and Matthew Clayton, with a cobbled courtyard overlooking the canal. It has been a pub and restaurant since 1981 and a regular Nottingham in Bloom award winner (flowers on display from the end of May to mid September). Favourite dishes are home-made steak and kidney pie, and Moby Dick haddock weighing approximately 16oz.
OPEN: 11-11 (Sun 12-10.30) **BAR MEALS:** Lunch served: all week Dinner served: Tue-Sat 11.30-10 Av main course £5.50
RESTAURANT: Lunch served: all week 11.30-2.30 Dinner served: Tue-Sat 5.30-9.30 Av 3 course à la carte £13.50 Av 2 course fixed price £4.99 **BREWERY/COMPANY:** Free House
PRINCIPAL BEERS: Timothy Taylor Landlord, Fuller's London Pride, Catle Eden Ale, Mallard Bitter. **FACILITIES:** Garden: Food served outdoors, Patio **NOTES:** Parking 4

Lincolnshire Poacher
161-163 Mansfield Rd NG1 3FR ☎ 0115 941 1584
Dir: M1 J26.Town centre
Traditional wooden-floored town pub with settles and sturdy wooden tables. Bustles with real ale fans in search of the 12 real ales on tap - regular brewery evenings and wine tastings. Also, good cider and 70 malt whiskies - a great drinkers pub. Large summer terrace.

Ye Olde Trip to Jerusalem
1 Brewhouse Yard, Castle Rd NG1 6AD
☎ 0115 947 3171 ▤ 0115 950 1185
Travellers, it is said, will always find their way to the quaint old inn below Castle Rock. With so many relics of bygone days, it feels like a museum too. In Middle English, a 'trip' was a resting place - hence what began as a refreshment stop for Richard the Lionheart's Holy Land-bound Crusaders in 1189. Before that, the inhabitants of William the Conqueror's castle used caves here for brewing, ale being considerably healthier than water. Indeed, the first bar is a cave, with sandstone walls. Giant meat-filled Yorkshire puddings, steak and kidney pudding, 6oz pork banger and mash, and cod, chips and mushy peas, and Kimberley pie are popular main courses. There's a good vegetarian selection, as well as salads, jacket potatoes, burgers, sandwiches and a Young Crusaders menu. In the Rock Lounge look for the 'cursed galleon'; the last three people to clean it all died mysteriously!
OPEN: 11-11 (Sun 12-10.30) **BAR MEALS:** Food served: all week 11-6 Av main course £4.99 **PRINCIPAL BEERS:** Kimberley Best Bitter, Best Mild, Classic, & Guest beers. **FACILITIES:** Children welcome

SOUTHWELL   Map 09 Sk 65

French Horn
Main St, Upton NG23 5ST ☎ 01636 812394
This 18th-century former farmhouse is handy for those visiting the racecourse and nearby Southwell Minster. Real ales and wines. Children welcome. Snacks all day & dining menus.

OPEN: 11.30–3 6.30–11
BAR MEALS: L served all week.
D served Mon–Sat. 12–2 7–9.30
Av main course £8
RESTAURANT: L served all week.
D served Mon–Sat. 12–2 7–9.30
Av cost 3 course £18.50
BREWERY/COMPANY:
WHITBREAD
PRINCIPAL BEERS: Interbrew
Flowers IPA & Boddingtons Bitter,
Marston's Pedigree, Carlsberg-
Tetley Tetley Bitter
FACILITIES: Garden: Beer garden,
food served outdoors
NOTES: Parking 40

Robin Hood Inn

Recent complete refurbishments have breathed new life into
this attractive but unassuming pub located just four miles
south of Retford. Run by an enthusiastic landlord/chef, Alan
Draper, it's a destination well worth making a detour off the A1.

High Street, Elkesley DN22 8AJ
☎ 01777 838259

The new decor manages to retain a traditional feel appropriate for a building that in parts dates back to the 14th
century, but there's a refreshing brightness about the place. Ceilings and floors are deep red, whilst the walls are
green and adorned with foodie pictures. Bar meals range from filled baguettes and sandwiches through to traditional
main meals such as local free-range pork sausages served with mashed potato, onion gravy and apple sauce, fried
fillet of haddock with chips and minted mushy peas, or seafood omelette served 'open' topped with a mornay sauce
and glazed under the grill. If you're after something more
substantial, seek out the main menu, which is complemented by
a daily changing specials board. Starters include moules marinére,
crispy pork, Caesar salad with crispy bacon and marinated
chargrilled Mediterranean vegetables with goat's cheese fondant.
Follow these with the likes of chargrilled Tamil coconut and
chicken served with basmati rice and tomato, red onion and
coriander salsa or roast fillet of cod on steamed greens with
chorizo and new potatoes. Follow with a platter of English
regional cheeses or an impressive array of puddings including
chocolate and hazelnut truffle with vanilla ice cream, crisp apple
galette with raspberries, or coconut and lime brûlée. A great port
of call for anyone wishing to visit the adjacent 14th – century
church, the village pottery or nearby Clumber Park (a National
Trust property).

THURGARTON   Map 09 SK64

The Red Lion
Southwell Rd NG14 7GP ☎ 01636 830351
Dir: On A612 between Nottingham & Southwell
The 16th-century inn that was once a monk's alehouse. Try
not to be put off your meal by the 1936 Nottingham Guardian
cutting on the wall that tells of the murder of a previous
landlady, Sarah Ellen Clarke, by her niece! A new parlour has
been added, and the interior has been recently completely
refurbished. Not far from Thurgarton Priory. The kitchen has a
good local reputation.
OPEN: 11.30–2.30 6.30–11 **BAR MEALS:** All week 12–2 7–10
RESTAURANT: All week 12–2 7–10 **BREWERY/COMPANY:** Free
House **PRINCIPAL BEERS:** Interbrew Bass, Greene King Ruddles
Best & Abbot Ale, Marston's Pedigree, Carlsberg-Tetley Tetley Bitter
FACILITIES: Children welcome Garden: Food served outside
NOTES: Parking 40

TUXFORD   Map 09 SK77

The Mussel & Crab 🍴 ♀
NG22 0PJ ☎ 01777 870491 📠 01777 871096
e-mail: musselandcrab1@hotmail.com
Dir: From the Ollerton/Tuxford Junction of the A1 & the A57 go N on the
B1164 to SibthorpeHill and the pub is 800 yds on the R

As its name suggests, fish and seafood dominate the menu
at this quirky pub. You can play liar dice, watch the fish in
the gents' toilets, and ponder over the large carved wooden
hands in the bar area. The large selection of blackboard
dishes is less idiosyncratic: smoked fish platter, salmon and
pesto fishcakes, oven-baked swordfish, and grilled Torbay
sole ('witch'), plus pork Wellington, Gressingham duck, and
a vegetarian combination of three curries.
OPEN: 11.30–2.30 6–11 **BAR MEALS:** Lunch served: all week
Dinner served: all week 11.30–2 6.30–10 Av main course £12
RESTAURANT: Lunch served: all week Dinner served: all week 12–2
6.30–9 Av 3 course à la carte £19 **BREWERY/COMPANY:** Free
House **PRINCIPAL BEERS:** Carlsberg-Tetley Tetley Smooth, Tetley
Cask. **FACILITIES:** Garden: Food served outside, patio area Dogs
allowed **NOTES:** Parking 74

WALKERINGHAM   Map 09 SK78

The Three Horse Shoes
High St DN10 4HR ☎ 01427 890959
e-mail: johnturner@barbox.net
A quiet village pub festooned with hanging baskets and some
10,000 bedding plants, all grown and tended by the owner.
There's also an aviary, and a Japanese water garden. Medallions

continued

of pork in a white wine herb mustard and cream sauce, roast
stuffed breast of lamb, spinach and courgette lasagne, or home-
made steak and kidney pie may be on today's menu.

OPEN: 11.30–3 7–11 (from June 5–11) **BAR MEALS:** Lunch served:
all week 12–2 Dinner served: Mon–Sat 7–9.30 Av main course £7.50
RESTAURANT: Lunch served: Sun 12–2 Dinner served: Mon–Sat
7–9.30 Av 3 course à la carte £13 **BREWERY/COMPANY:** Free
House **PRINCIPAL BEERS:** Stones, Bass, Worthington.
FACILITIES: Children welcome Garden: **NOTES:** Parking 40

WELLOW   Map 09 SK66

Olde Red Lion
Eakring Rd NG22 0EG ☎ 01623 861000
Dir: From Ollerton on the A616 to Newark after 2 miles, Wellow village
turn L.
400-year-old pub opposite the maypole in a quiet
Nottinghamshire village; popular with walkers. Unspoilt
atmosphere; traditional pub food.

WEST LEAKE   Map 09 SK52

Star Inn 🍴
Melton Ln LE12 5RQ ☎ 01509 852233
e-mail: lcollins1@ntlworld.com
Dir: A6 toward Loughborough, 0.33m L to Kingston, over canal, R to Sutt
Bonn, over crossroad, 1m Star on L

Whitewashed walls and flowering window boxes and tubs add
a touch of colour to this picturesque inn, which was once used
for housing cows and chickens. Look out for the cock-fighting
prints and foxes' masks on the ochre-painted walls in the
public bar. Straightforward yet appetising pub food includes
casseroles, roasts, pies, pasta bakes, and fresh fish and chips.
Evening specials include Burgundy chicken breast, tuna
provençale, and Dijon pork.
OPEN: 11–2.30 6–11 (Sun 12–4, 7–10.30) **BAR MEALS:** Lunch
served: all week 12.15–2 Dinner served: Tue–Sat 6.30–8.30 Av main
course £6 **RESTAURANT:** Lunch served: all week 12.15–2 Dinner

continued

served: Tue–Sat 6.30–8.30 Av 3 course à la carte £10.50
BREWERY/COMPANY: Enterprise Inns
PRINCIPAL BEERS: Interbrew Bass, Adnams Broadside, Greene King IPA, Fullers London Pride. **FACILITIES:** Children welcome Garden: Terrace, Food served outside Dogs allowed **NOTES:** Parking 40
ROOMS: 2 bedrooms 2 en suite from s£45 d£45

OXFORDSHIRE

ABINGDON   Map 04 SU49

The Merry Miller
Cothill OX13 6JW ☎ 01865 390390 📠 01865 390040
e-mail: rob@merrymiller.fsbusiness.co.uk
Dir: 1m from the Marcham interchange on the A34
Former 17th-century granary situated in a quiet village close to Oxford. Beams, flagstones, log fires and pine furnishings characterise the tastefully refurbished bar and restaurant. Snack or main meals may be taken in either bar or restaurant, and include a range of fresh-filled baguettes as well as fish and chips, half shoulder of lamb, or fish risotto.
OPEN: 12–11 (Sun 12–10.30) **BAR MEALS:** Lunch served: all week Dinner served: all week 12–2.45 6.30–9.45 Av main course £10.95
RESTAURANT: Lunch served: all week Dinner served: all week 12–2.45 6.30–9.45 Av 3 course à la carte £18
BREWERY/COMPANY: Greene King **PRINCIPAL BEERS:** Greene King IPA & Old Speckled Hen. **FACILITIES:** Children welcome Dogs allowed **NOTES:** Parking 60

ADDERBURY   Map 06 SP43

The Red Lion
The Green OX17 3LU ☎ 01295 810269 📠 01295 811906
Civilised old stone coaching inn on the Banbury to Oxford road. Once known as the King's Arms it had a tunnel in the cellar used by Royalists in hiding during the Civil War. Expect a rambling, beamed interior, daily papers, good wines and a varied menu. Comfortable bedrooms.

ARDINGTON   Map 04 SU48

Pick of the Pubs

The Boars Head ⚲
Church St OX12 8QA ☎ 01235 833254 📠 01235 833254
e-mail: bruce-buchan@theboarshead.freeserve.co.uk
Dir: Off A417 W of Wantage
The Boars Head is an attractive 400-year-old timbered pub set beside the church in a timeless estate village. Chef/patron Bruce Buchan has been here for a couple of years now, having established a fine reputation at several Oxfordshire dining pubs. There's a series of rooms, easy on the eye, and mainly given over to eating, though there is still a locals' bar. Log fires, evening candlelight and fresh flowers set the stage for an innovative choice of pub food. A short menu lists simply described dishes based on fresh local produce. Starters range from creamy smoked haddock chowder to salad of smoked goose with melon in Sauternes, foie gras and walnut dressing, with equally interesting mains like pan-fried sweetbreads with chorizo and scallops, or fillet of halibut with aubergine confit and champagne gratin. You can finish in some style with hot Grand Marnier soufflé with iced chocolate cream.
OPEN: 12–3 6.30–11 **BAR MEALS:** Lunch served: all week Dinner served: all week 12–2.30 7–10 Av main course £8.50

RESTAURANT: Lunch served: all week Dinner served: all week 12–2.30 7–10 Av 3 course à la carte £27
BREWERY/COMPANY: Free House
PRINCIPAL BEERS: Brakspear Bitter, Hook Norton Old Hooky, West Berkshire Berwery Dr. Hexter's. **FACILITIES:** Children welcome Patio, food served outdoors Dogs allowed
NOTES: Parking 10 **ROOMS:** 3 bedrooms 3 en suite from d£65

ASTHALL   Map 06 SP21

The Maytime Inn ♦♦♦ 🛏 ⚲
OX18 4HW ☎ 01993 822068 📠 01993 822635
Dir: A361 from Swindon, R onto A40 then onto B4047 to Asthall

Traditional Cotswold pub in the Windrush valley, near the former home of the famous Mitford sisters (Nancy wrote *Love in a Cold Climate*). The present owners acquired the then derelict local in 1975 and set about transforming it into a character inn. Daily menus listed on the blackboard may include roast fillet of salmon, crab cakes, roast duck with ginger and pineapple sauce, and breast of chicken stuffed with brie. Comfortable, well-equipped bedrooms with modern en suite facilities.
OPEN: 11–3 6–11 **BAR MEALS:** Lunch served: all week Dinner served: all week 12.30–2.15 7–9.30 Av main course £8.95
RESTAURANT: Lunch served: all week Dinner served: all week 12.30–2.15 7–9.30 Av 3 course à la carte £15
BREWERY/COMPANY: Free House
PRINCIPAL BEERS: Interbrew Bass, Fuller's London Pride, Greene King Old Speckled Hen. **FACILITIES:** Children welcome Garden: patio/terrace, food served outside Dogs allowed (water)
NOTES: Parking 100 **ROOMS:** 6 bedrooms 6 en suite from s£52.50 d£69.50

BAMPTON   Map 06 SP30

The Romany ♦♦♦
Bridge St OX18 2HA ☎ 01993 850237 📠 01993 852133
e-mail: romany@barbox.net
A shop until 20 years ago, The Romany is housed in an 18th-century building of Cotswold stone with a beamed bar, log fires and intimate dining room. Food ranges from ploughmans' to steaks, with home-made specials like hot pot or steak and ale pie. Regional singers provide live entertainment a couple of times a month.
OPEN: 11–11 **BAR MEALS:** Lunch served: all week Dinner served: all week 11–11 Av main course £4 **RESTAURANT:** Lunch served: all week Dinner served: all week 11–11 Av 3 course à la carte £10
BREWERY/COMPANY: Free House **PRINCIPAL BEERS:** Archers Village, Bass,. **FACILITIES:** Children welcome Garden: Food served outside Dogs allowed (water) **NOTES:** Parking 8
ROOMS: 11 bedrooms 11 en suite from s£22.50 d£35

continued

BAMPTON continued

The Vines ♀
Burford Rd OX18 2PF ☎ 01993 843559 ▤ 01993 840080
e-mail: thevinesbb@aol.com
Dir: *From A40 Whitney, take A4095 to Faringdon, then 1st R after Bampton to Black Bourton*

Mediterranean-style restaurant in a tiny village pub designed by BBC *Real Rooms* personality John Cregg, with hand-painted murals themed on Bacchus. The menu offers a choice of light bites, salads and pasta in addition to main meals. Favourite dishes are pan fried veal escalope, chicken breast stuffed with goats cheese, Cajun style salmon, duck breast marinated in Chinese five spice and cherry brandy, and chunky vegetable and water chestnut stew.
OPEN: 11–2.30 6–11 (Sun 12–10.30) **BAR MEALS:** Lunch served: Tue–Sun Dinner served: Tue–Sun 12–2 6.30–9.30 Av main course £9
RESTAURANT: Lunch served: Tue–Sun Dinner served: Tue–Sun 12–2 6.30–9.30 Av 3 course à la carte £18 **BREWERY/COMPANY:** Free House **PRINCIPAL BEERS:** Greene King IPA, Marston's Pedigree, Tetley Smooth. **FACILITIES:** Garden: Food served outside. Orchard Dogs allowed (in the garden only) **NOTES:** Parking 70

BANBURY   Map 06 SP44

The George Inn 🛏
Lower St, Barford St Michael OX15 0RH ☎ 01869 338226 ▤ 01869 337804
Handy for both Banbury and Oxford, this 300-year-old thatched village pub features old beams, exposed stone walls and open fireplaces. It stands in a large garden, with a patio and orchard, overlooking open countryside. Live music is an established tradition, and the pub hosts a variety of rock, folk and solo artists. There's a good choice of real ales, and options from the single menu include baguettes, baked potatoes, pasta, pies, and fish and chips.
OPEN: 12–3 7–11 **BAR MEALS:** Lunch served: Sat–Sun 12–2 Dinner served: 7–9 Av main course £6 **BREWERY/COMPANY:** Free House **PRINCIPAL BEERS:** Hook Norton Best, Greene King Abbot Ale, Old Speckled Hen, Badger Tanglefoot + guest ales.
FACILITIES: Children welcome Garden: Patio, orchard, food served outside Dogs allowed **NOTES:** Parking 20 No credit cards

Ye Olde Reine Deer Inn ♀
47 Parsons St OX16 5NA ☎ 01295 264031 ▤ 01295 264018
Dir: *One mile from M40 J11, in town centre just off market square*
Oliver Cromwell once held court in the oak-panelled Globe Room at this historic town centre pub that dates from 1570. Nowadays visiting and local diners can enjoy the wood-panelled splendour of this room, where popular lunchtime bar food and some tasty evening meals are served. Daily specials like chicken in lime and coriander, pork and Stilton casserole, mushrooms in cider and cheese, and corned beef hash supplement the likes of chilli con carne, and shepherd's pie.

OPEN: 11–11 Closed: 25 Dec, BHs, **BAR MEALS:** Lunch served: Mon–Sat 11–2 Dinner served: Tues–Thur 6–9 **RESTAURANT:** Lunch served: Mon–Sat 11–2 Dinner served: Tues–Thur 6–9 Av 3 course fixed price £12 **BREWERY/COMPANY:** Hook Norton
PRINCIPAL BEERS: Hook Norton, Best , Mild, Old Hooky.
FACILITIES: Garden: Patio, food served outside Dogs allowed (water) **NOTES:** Parking 14

Pick of the Pubs

Wykham Arms 🛏 ♀
Sibford Gower OX15 5RX ☎ 01295 788808 ▤ 01295 788013
e-mail: james@moodycow.co.uk

Picture-postcard 17th-century village pub, built of mellow Hornton stone with a thatched roof and overlooking rolling Oxfordshire countryside. The owners also run The Moody Cow in Herefordshire (qv). Although there is a smart, modern feel throughout the rambling series of five rooms, visitors can still expect original features such as slate floors, exposed stone, sturdy pine furnishings, tasteful prints and open fires. Interesting, home-made food, freshly prepared from local produce, matches the style of the place. From starters like tempura battered king prawns, goat's cheese on ciabatta, and pasta bolognese, the choice extends to freshly battered cod and chips, bangers and mash with onion gravy, The Moody Cow Pie (steak and kidney with gravy), canon of lamb with chicken and herb mousse and rosemary jus, and daily fish specials (whole plaice with herb and parmesan crust). Puddings include gooey chocolate pudding. South-facing terrace.
OPEN: 12–2.30 6.30–11 **BAR MEALS:** Lunch served: all week Dinner served: all week 12–2 6.30–9.30 Av main course £8.95
RESTAURANT: Lunch served: all week Dinner served: all week 12–2 6.30–9.30 Av 3 course à la carte £16
BREWERY/COMPANY: Free House
PRINCIPAL BEERS: Hook Norton Best, Flowers IPA, Wadsworth 6X. **FACILITIES:** Children welcome Garden: Food served outside Dogs allowed (water provided)
NOTES: Parking 30

continued

PUB WALK

Oxford
Turf Tavern

Oxford's history, beauty and tradition are admired all over the land. A stroll through the streets of Oxford, 'that sweet city with her dreaming spires', is a memorable experience.

From the inn turn right towards the Christopher Wren's Sheldonian Theatre, then left at the junction for the Radcliffe Camera. Cross Radcliffe Square towards Brasenose College and turn right into Brasenose Lane. Go along to Turl Street, then veer right between Jesus College and Exeter College and head for Broad Street (visit the world-famous Blackwell's Bookshop). Turn left along Broad Street to St Giles, where Charles I drilled his men during the Civil War. Turn back towards Broad Street but continue ahead along Cornmarket Street to the Carfax Tower where Charles II was proclaimed King in 1660. Keep ahead into St Aldates to the entrance (on the left) to Christ Church, founded in

1525 and the largest college in Oxford. This is also the city's Cathedral. Leave Christ Church by the Meadows exit and walk straight ahead down the tree-lined New Walk. At the River Thames, swing left along the towpath. Don't cross the arched footbridge spanning the River Cherwell; instead follow the tree-lined path between meadows and sports fields. Leave the riverbank and pass into Rose Lane via wrought-iron gates. At the main road turn right towards Magdalen Bridge. On the right is the University Botanic Garden; at over 300 years old, it is the oldest in Britain. With your back to Magdalen College bell tower, turn right up the High Street, then right into Queen's Lane. Continue into New College Lane, to the Bridge of Sighs, a 1914 replica of its Venice namesake. Ahead is the Sheldonian Theatre. Go right and right again to find the entrance to the Turf Tavern.

TURF TAVERN
4 Bath Place, off Holywell Street OXFORD OX1 3SU
Tel:1865 243235
Directions: Off Holywell Street, near the Broad Street end, on R
In the heart of Oxford, approached through hidden alleyways this, very popular, pub lies in the shadow of the colleges. In the summer relax in the sheltered courtyards. Eleven real ales are served daily along with some typical pub fare.
Open: 11-11 (Sun 12-10.30)
Bar meals: 12-8
Garden.

Distance: 2 1/4 miles (3.6km)
Map: OS Landranger 164; preferably a good street map
Terrain: Cityscape
Paths: Pavements, firm paths and towpath
Gradient: Level ground - no hills

Walk submitted and checked by Nick Channer

England

Pick of the Pubs

The Boot Inn ♀
OX29 6XE ☎ 01865 881231 ▤ 01865 882119
e-mail: boot@traditionalfreehouses.com
Dir: off the A40 between Witney & Eynsham

For reasons unexplained, the good-and-famous who have donated footwear to this extraordinary Cotswold stone pub include Ian Botham, George Best, Eddie Irvine, The Bee Gees and Sir Ranulph Fiennes: the licensees have pledged to continue the tradition, adding recently the coveted boots that once belonged to Sir Stanley Matthews. Set back from the hum-drum of the busy A40 and surrounded by open fields and hedgerows, the accent here is on brasserie-style pub food in a modern idiom. Smart and civilised interior with a spacious quarry-tiled bar and attractively decorated dining areas either side. A typical meal may begin with classic Caesar salad, smoked mackerel and crab fishcakes, or tagliatelle, followed by seared tuna niçoise, calves' liver and back bacon, chargrilled breast of guinea fowl with a kumquat compot, or 'Lamboot' - slow-roasted lamb shank with mashed roots, with beetroot and mint jus. Interesting list of wines; 12 by the glass.
OPEN: 11–3 6–11 **BAR MEALS:** Lunch served: all week 12–2.30 Av main course £7 **RESTAURANT:** Lunch served: all week Dinner served: all week 12–2.30 7–9.30 Av 3 course à la carte £20 **BREWERY/COMPANY:** Free House
PRINCIPAL BEERS: Hook Norton Best Bitter.
FACILITIES: Children welcome Courtyard, **NOTES:** Parking 30

The George and Dragon

As England's patron saint, St George figures frequently on inn signs, often with the dragon whose defeat was his most celebrated exploit. According to the legend, he killed it to save a beautiful princess who would otherwise have been given to the monster. Alternatively, the George is the jewel of the Order of the Garter, England's premier order of knighthood, which was founded by King Edward III in the 14th century. An allied name is the Star and Garter, which also refers to the order's insignia. Or again, the George can mean any of the six kings of that name since the Hanoverian dynasty succeeded to the throne.

Bottle & Glass ♀
RG9 4JT ☎ 01491 575755
Dir: N of B4155 between Reading & Henley

Located near the glorious Chilterns, this 15th-century thatched and timbered inn is reputedly where sheep and cattle drovers stopped for a 'bottle and glass' en route to market. There is a cosy beamed bar with an open fire and scrubbed tables to retreat to after one of the spectacular nearby walks. Freshly prepared dishes include beef Oxford (diced rump steak cooked with red wine and apricots), and Cumberland sausage with egg and chips.
OPEN: 11–3.30 6–11 Closed: Dec 25 **BAR MEALS:** Lunch served: all week Dinner served: Mon–Sat 12–1.45 7–9.30 Av main course £7.75 **BREWERY/COMPANY:** Brakspear **PRINCIPAL BEERS:** Brakspear Bitter, Old Ale & Special. **FACILITIES:** Garden: Beer garden, food served outdoors Dogs allowed (garden only, water) **NOTES:** Parking 30

Pick of the Pubs

Blewbury Inn ◎◎
London Rd OX11 9PD ☎ 01235 850496 ▤ 01235 850496
See Pick of the Pubs on page 359

The Elephant & Castle
OX15 4LZ ☎ 01295 720383
e-mail: elephant.bolxham@bt.internet.com
Dir: Just off A361
The arch of this 15th-century Cotswold-stone coaching inn still straddles the former Banbury to Chipping Norton turnpike. Locals play darts or shove-ha'penny in the big wood-floored bar, whilst the two-roomed lounge boasts a bar-billiards table and a large inglenook fireplace. The reasonably priced menu starts with a range of sandwiches and crusty filled baguettes, whilst hot dishes include pub favourites like steak and kidney pie, lasagne, haddock, and rump steak.
OPEN: 10–3 5–11 **BAR MEALS:** Lunch served: Mon–Sat 12–2 Av main course £4 **RESTAURANT:** Lunch served: Mon–Sat 12–2 Dinner served: all week Av 3 course à la carte £6.50
BREWERY/COMPANY: Hook Norton **PRINCIPAL BEERS:** Hook Norton Best Bitter. **FACILITIES:** Children welcome Garden: Beer garden, food served outdoors, patio **NOTES:** Parking 20

Blevobury   May 99 [signature]

OPEN: 12-3 6-11
BAR MEALS: L served Tues-Sun.
D served Tues-Sun. 12-2 7-9
Av main course £14
RESTAURANT: L served
Tue-Sun 12-2. D served Tues-Sat.
6-11 Av cost 3 courses £0
BREWERY/COMPANY: FREE
HOUSE
PRINCIPLE BEERS: Hook Norton
Best, Old Hooky, Generation,
Wadworth 6X, Timothy Taylor
Landlord, Batemans
FACILITIES: Dogs welcome.
Garden: Food served outside
NOTES: Parking 20
ROOMS: 2 en suite Double room
from £50 Single room from £40

Blewbury Inn

★ ◎◎
London Road OX11 9PD
☎ 01235 850496 📠 01235 850496
Dir: At the junction of the A417 & B4016
below Didcot.

An appealing though modest, white-painted 200-year-old pub set beside the A417 on the edge of Blewbury, a rambling village nestling beneath the Oxfordshire Downs. Justifiably popular among local diners for Franck Peigné's inventive menus with a distinct Gallic flavour, reflecting his Brittany origins.

The once very homely interior has been given a 'modern' makeover, the decor in the single bar and intimate restaurant now featuring a light seafaring theme. At lunchtimes, the atmosphere is relaxed and the menu light and simple, perhaps including Parma ham, Brie de Meaux and apple and cider chutney on a grilled bagel or Cornish mussel soup with chervil and fennel. In the evening though, the real emphasis is on dining, with the bar serving as an area for pre-dinner drinks (although you're welcome to pop in for a pint at the bar). Booking is advisable and a fixed-price menu offers three choices at each course. Starter may include salad of marinated Cajun chicken with Feta cheese, pickled cucumber and winter leaves, or Capricorn goat's cheese tartlet with red onion marmalade. A choice of main courses could be medallions of lamb fillet with pesto mash, ragout of white beans and chorizo, roast cod with ratatouille, or confit of duck leg with Toulouse sausage, apple and potato rösti, Puy lentil jus. Round off with coffee crème brûlée with toffee ice cream, prune and Armagnac parfait with panettone, or French regional cheeses. Regular theme nights – Brasserie, Irish, Game – and a Gourmet Club with monthly set four-course dinners, wine and whisky tastings are popular. Accommodation in two en suite bedrooms.

BRIGHTWELL BALDWIN   Map 04 SU69

Pick of the Pubs

The Lord Nelson Inn ♀
OX9 5NP ☎ 01491 612330 612497 ▤ 01491 612118
e-mail: diane@lordnelsoninn.fsnet.co.uk
Dir: Off the B4009 between Watlington & Benson
Having been closed for 66 years, this impressive 300-year-old inn was re-opened on 21st October 1971 - Trafalgar Day. Originally a thatched cottage and extended in the late-18th century, the Lord Nelson boasts a splendid inglenook fireplace - the perfect antidote after an invigorating country walk in the fresh air. During summer, the pretty garden with its weeping willow and rear terrace prove to be a popular attraction. Brakspears real ale is served in the attractive beamed bar, there is a comprehensive wine list and all food is freshly cooked to order by the inn's experienced chefs. Interesting, well designed specials include the likes of wild rabbit casserole with parsnip and potato mash and pan-fried foie gras, baked brill with grilled whole artichoke and pea sauce and salmon and herb fishcakes. Imaginative Sunday lunch menu.
OPEN: 11–3 6–11 **BAR MEALS:** Lunch served: all week Dinner served: all week 12–3 6–10 Av main course £9.50
RESTAURANT: Lunch served: all week Dinner served: all week 12–3 6–10 Av 3 course à la carte £25
BREWERY/COMPANY: Free House
PRINCIPAL BEERS: Brakspears. **FACILITIES:** Garden: beer garden, patio, outdoor eating **NOTES:** Parking 20

BRITWELL SALOME   Map 04 SU69

Pick of the Pubs

The Goose ◉ ♀
OX49 5LG ☎ 01491 612304 ▤ 01491 614822
e-mail: barberwhitehart@aol.com
Dir: 1.5 from Watlington on B4009 towards Benson & Wallingford
Owned and run by the Barber family, the Goose is an 18th-century building of traditional brick and flint. The simple bar is hung with local artworks and there is an intimate dining room painted in bottle green. Chris Barber does the cooking, presenting a regularly changing menu which specialises in local, wild and organic produce of the highest possible standard, including vegetables and fruit grown in the family's own organic, walled garden. The no-choice, set-price, three-course lunch and dinner menus offer good value. A typical set dinner comprises Parmesan fritters with parsley and lemon, pan-fried organic salmon with braised cabbage, mash and tarragon sauce, and crème brûlée. The carte lists fish of the day and seasonal game dishes along with slow roast belly of pork with gratin of spinach and apple jus, or breast of chicken with truffled bread sauce and broccoli.
OPEN: 12–3 6–11 **BAR MEALS:** Lunch served: Tues-Sun 12–2 Dinner served: Tues-Sat 6.30–9 Av main course £15
RESTAURANT: Lunch served: Tues-Sun 12–2 Dinner served: Tues-Sat 6.30–9 Av 3 course à la carte £25 Av 3 course fixed price £17.50 **BREWERY/COMPANY:** Free House
PRINCIPAL BEERS: Brakspear Bitter. **FACILITIES:** Children welcome Garden: Food served outside Dogs allowed (water) **NOTES:** Parking 20

BURCOT   Map 04 SU59

The Chequers ♀
OX14 3DP ☎ 01865 407771 ▤ 01865 407945
Dir: On A415 (Dorchester/Abingdon rd)
Partly dating back to the 16th century and originally a staging post for barges on the Thames. A varied menu includes dishes such as bacon, mushroom and pine nut salad, seared salmon with charred potatoes, braised leek, orange and ginger, braised shank of lamb, panfried duck breast with red cabbage and garlic mash, and grilled cod with chive mash and mild curry cream.
OPEN: 11–3 6–11 (Sun 7–10.30) **BAR MEALS:** Lunch served: all week Dinner served: all week 12–2 6.30–9.30 Av main course £11
RESTAURANT: Lunch served: all week Dinner served: all week 12–2 6.30–9.30 Av 3 course à la carte £22 **BREWERY/COMPANY:** Free House **PRINCIPAL BEERS:** Brakspear Bitter, Fuller's London Pride.
FACILITIES: Children welcome Garden: Patio, food served outside Dogs allowed **NOTES:** Parking 40

BURFORD   Map 06 SP21

Golden Pheasant ★ ★
91 High St OX18 4QA ☎ 01993 823223 ▤ 01993 822621
Dir: Leave M40 at junction 8 and follow signs A40 Cheltenham into Burford
Attractive, honey-coloured, 15th-century stone inn situated in the centre of Burford. Expect an informal atmosphere, comfortable bedrooms and a wide range of food. Old English Inns.

Pick of the Pubs

The Inn for All Seasons ★ ★ ★
The Barringtons OX18 4TN
☎ 01451 844324 ▤ 01451 844375
e-mail: sharp@innforallseasons.com
See Pick of the Pubs on page 361

Skills and Crafts
Inns with names like the Bricklayers Arms and the Masons Arms hark back to the days when groups of craftsmen and tradesmen met regularly in the local hostelry. The trade union movement originally grew up in pubs in this way and a 'local' can mean either a pub or a union branch. Itinerant craftsmen would expect a welcome at these houses, too, and pick up news of work. The Axe and Compasses is a carpenters' badge, the Three (or more) Horseshoes a device of smiths, the Wheatsheaf of bakers and the Beetle and Wedge of builders, while quite a few pubs display the Oddfellows Arms. The Shoulder of Mutton could signify that the landlord doubled as a butcher.

OPEN: 11–2.30 6–11
(Sun 12–3, 7–10.30)
BAR MEALS: L served all week.
D served all week. 11.30–2.20
6.30–9.30 Av main course £8.50
RESTAURANT: L served all week.
D served all week. 11.30–2.30
6.30–9.30 Av cost 3 course £19.50
BREWERY/COMPANY:
FREE HOUSE
PRINCIPAL BEERS: Wadworth 6X,
Interbrew Bass
FACILITIES: Children welcome,
dogs allowed. Garden: Food served
outdoors
NOTES: Parking 80
ROOMS: 10 en suite Double room
from £75 Single room from £35

The Inn for All Seasons

Some three miles west of Burford on the A40, this engaging 16th-century Grade II listed mansion has lost nothing of its charm following conversion into a 10-bedroom country inn. It reveals a treasure-trove of ancient oak beams, original fireplaces and complementary period furniture.

★ ★ ★ ⊛ ♀
The Barringtons OX18 4TN
☎ 01451 844324 📠 01451 844375
e-mail: sharp@innforallseasons.com
Dir: 3 miles W of Burford on the A40.

Residents are assured of a warm and friendly welcome in en suite bedrooms that are both spacious and comfortably furnished, with a hint of romance thrown in for good measure. Close by is the National Trust's Sherborne Estate with its remarkable collection of early spring flowers - snowdrops, winter aconites and wild daffodils - a joy to behold in the course of a bracing walk. There are a number of guest ales and always a Wychwood beer from nearby Witney to accompany a simple bar snack or a more formal restaurant meal. Menus plough an 'all-seasons' furrow, taking in

curried leeks wrapped in smoked salmon or braised shank of Cotswold lamb with a bean ragout, whilst vegetarians can take comfort in a hot tart of mixed vegetables or tagliatelle with oyster mushrooms and white asparagus. Pride of place undoubtedly goes to the selection of fish, fresh from Brixham, delivering the likes of grilled sardines with garlic and parsley butter, lobster and lemon rice sauced with sweet mustard and brandy or turbot fillet bEarnaise with tarragon potatoes. For dessert try lemon tart with blackcurrant coulis or, for a lighter snack, plump for the hand-raised pork pie with home-made chutney or the locally-sourced farmhouse cheeses that underline the Inn's all-round quality.

BURFORD continued

Pick of the Pubs

The Lamb Inn ★ ★ ★ ◎ 🕮 ♀
Sheep St OX18 4LR ☎ 01993 823155 🖹 01993 822228
Dir: from M40 J8 follow signs for A40 & Burford, off High Street
The Lamb is a traditional coaching inn built with honey-coloured Cotswold stone quarried at nearby Taynton. It is situated on Sheep Street, away from the bustle of the centre but close enough to the shops. Inside you'll find numerous log fires, gleaming brass and copper, and highly polished antique furniture. In summer you can visit the walled cottage garden, admire the herbaceous borders and perhaps take lunch on the lawn. The comprehensive bar lunch menu ranges through sandwiches, brill and shrimp fishcakes and grilled rib eye steak with peppercorn sauce. Robust dishes figure among the house favourites, with options like roast partridge with red cabbage and chestnut confit and juniper berry sauce, or braised oxtail with caramelised shallots and smoked bacon lardons. Candlelit dinner in the pretty pillared restaurant is a set-price two or three course affair, as is Sunday lunch, which begins with a glass of Buck's Fizz.
OPEN: 11–2.30 6–11 (Sun 12–2.30 7–10.30) Closed: 25-26 Dec
BAR MEALS: Lunch served: Mon-Sat 12-2 Av main course £9
RESTAURANT: Lunch served: Sun 12.30-1.45 Dinner served: all week 7-9 Av 3 course fixed price £27
BREWERY/COMPANY: Free House
PRINCIPAL BEERS: Wadworth 6X, Hook Norton Best, Badger Dorset Bitter. **FACILITIES:** Garden: walled cottage garden, food served outside Dogs allowed (water) **NOTES:** Parking 5
ROOMS: 15 bedrooms 15 en suite from s£70 d£110

CHADLINGTON   August 2006   Map 06 SP32

The Tite Inn ♀
Mill End OX7 3NY ☎ 01608 676475 🖹 0870 7059308
e-mail: willis@titeinn.com
Dir: 3m S of Chipping Norton
Delightful Cotswold inn which takes its name from the constantly running stream, or tite, beneath it. Roses clambering up the stone walls attract customers in summer, while log fires and mulled wine help create a cosy atmosphere in winter. Troops stopped here en route to the Battle of Edge Hill. Varied choice of locally brewed ales and a menu offering dishes such as Brazil nut roast, caramelised onion and goat's cheese tart, lamb kidneys braised in red wine, salmon fishcakes with hollandaise sauce, and sweet and spicy meatloaf.
OPEN: 12–2.30 6.30–11 (Sun 12-3, 7-10.30) Closed: Dec 25-26
BAR MEALS: Lunch served: Tue-Sun Dinner served: Tue-Sun 12-2 7-9 Av main course £7.95 **RESTAURANT:** Lunch served: Sun 12-2 Dinner served: Tue-Sat 6.30-11 Av 3 course à la carte £16.95
BREWERY/COMPANY: Free House **PRINCIPAL BEERS:** Fullers, Youngs, Guest Beers, Brakspears. **FACILITIES:** Children welcome Garden: Food served outside. Large garden area Dogs allowed (water provided) **NOTES:** Parking 30

> Most of the pubs in this guide book pride themselves on the quality of their food. This may take a little time to prepare.

CHALGROVE   Map 04 SU69

Pick of the Pubs

The Red Lion Inn 🕮 ♀
The High St OX44 7SS ☎ 01865 890625 🖹 01865 890795
Dir: B480 from Oxford Ring rd, thru Stadhampton, L then R at mini-rdbt, at Chalgrove Airfield R fork into village

A traditional inn set back from the road beside a running brook in the delightful village of Chalgrove. The lovely cream-painted pub dates from the 11th century, and has been owned by the parish church since 1637. It enjoys a good local following both from the village teams it continues to support, and an upmarket clientele drawn to the imaginative food. Expect a civilised atmosphere in the beamed and tastefully refurbished bar and dining area, where perennial pub favourites are given a welcome modern twist alongside more serious dishes. Lunchtime fare ranges from filled ciabatta and baguettes to traditional Oxford sausages, Thai red chicken curry, and spicy vegetable couscous. Evening specials might include oven-roasted Banbury duck, or mille-feuille of salmon and cod, while the menu offers stilton and leek brûlée, beef bourguignon, and chocolate tart with coconut ice cream. There's a lovely rear garden for summer visitors.
OPEN: 12-3 6-11 (Sun 7-10.30) Closed: 25 Dec
BAR MEALS: Lunch served: all week 12-2 Dinner served: Mon-Sat 7-9 Av main course £8.50 **RESTAURANT:** Lunch served: all week 12-2 Dinner served: Mon-Sat 7-9 Av 3 course à la carte £15 **BREWERY/COMPANY:** Free House
PRINCIPAL BEERS: Fuller's London Pride, Adnams Best + changing guest beers. **FACILITIES:** Garden: Large, award winning Dogs allowed (water) **NOTES:** Parking 20

CHARLBURY   Map 06 SP31

Pick of the Pubs

The Bull Inn 🕮
Sheep St OX7 3RR ☎ 01608 810689
See Pick of the Pubs on page 363

CHECKENDON   Map 04 SU68

Pick of the Pubs

The Highwayman 🕮 ♀
Exlade St RG8 0UA ☎ 01491 682020 🖹 01491 682229
e-mail: info@thehighwaymancheckendon.co.uk
See Pick of the Pubs on page 364

OPEN: 12–2.30 7–11
BAR MEALS: L served Tues–Sun.
D served Tues–Sat. 12–2 7–9
Av main course £10
RESTAURANT: L served Tues–Sun
12–1.30 booking only. D served
Tues–Sat. 7–9 Av cost 3 courses £20
BREWERY/COMPANY: FREE
HOUSE
PRINCIPLE BEERS: Greene King
IPA, Abbot Ale, Ruddles County
FACILITIES: Garden: Terrace, food
served outside
NOTES: Parking 14
ROOMS: 3 en suite. Double room
from £60. Single room from £50

The Bull Inn

Sheep Street OX7 3RR
☎ 01608 810689
Dir: A40 at Oxford R to Woodstock, thru
Woodstock & after 1.5m L to Charlbury.

Good old-fashioned hospitality is guaranteed at this friendly pub in the main street of an handsome, unspoilt Cotswold town. The Bull dates from the 16th century, and is surrounded by excellent walking country including the Blenheim and Cornbury estates.

The smart stone exterior is matched inside by a tastefully furnished lounge and dining room, and a friendly, traditional bar featuring wooden floors and Greene King ales. Music and fruit machines have been banned for a relaxing atmosphere, enhanced by comfortable sofas and a cosy inglenook fireplaces. Roy and Suzanne Flynn aided by their son and daughter, are highly personable hosts, and have created a most appealing inn that attracts many discerning visitors from Oxford and the Cotswolds. The quality home-made food can be enjoyed in the restaurant, with full service and a menu of adventurous dishes, or from a more traditional choice in the bar. Seafood features on the restaurant menu in the guise of Mediterranean fish stew, seared tuna loin on warm salad niçoise, and smokey fish pie. Otherwise expect dishes such as boned rack of lamb with gratin dauphinoise, half a boned Gressingham duck with honey, lime and ginger sauce, or wild mushroom risotto. Puddings include bread and butter pudding with prunes and Armagnac. There is an attractive vine-covered terrace for the summer and overnight accommodation is available in three en suite bedrooms.

OPEN: 12-3 6-11
BAR MEALS: L served all week.
D served all week. 12-2.30 7-9.30
Av main course £6.95
RESTAURANT: L served all week.
D served all week. 12-2.30 7-9.30
Av cost 3 courses £27.50
BREWERY/COMPANY:
FREE HOUSE
PRINCIPAL BEERS: Gales HSB,
Fuller's London Pride, Black Sheep
Best, Young's Special, Shepherds
Neame Spitfire Premium Ale
FACILITIES: Children welcome,
dogs allowed. Garden: Beer garden,
food served outdoors, patio
NOTES: Parking 30
ROOMS: 4 en suite Double room
from £70 Single room from £55

The Highwayman

Exlade Street RG8 0UA
☎ 01491 682020 📠 01491 682229
e-mail:
info@thehighwaymancheckendon.co.uk
Dir: On A4074 Reading to
Wallingford Rd.

From its position overlooking open fields on the edge of the wooded Chiltern Hills, the 300-year-old Highwayman exudes a wonderful welcome. Its rambling interior is packed with curios and old artefacts, and at night there is dining at sunken tables by glimmering candlelight.

The character bar, with its warm atmosphere, is just the place to relax with a pint of Black Sheep or any of the other of the selection of real ales on offer here. The inter-connecting dining rooms have been tastefully furnished, as has the adjoining conservatory – creating exactly the right atmosphere to place to enjoy imaginative pub food. It has had a reputation for good food for some years and the current owners have striven to maintain food standards here to support the reputation. The kitchen uses the best and freshest ingredients even for simple dishes such as ploughman's lunches, a selection of sandwiches and home-made soups on the bar menu. More substantial meals can be eaten in the dining rooms and could perhaps be a choice of smoked haddock on a chive mash or salad of roasted peppers and tomato. Main courses might be calves' liver with rocket mash, spiced onion and lemon potatoes, or roast chump of lamb on Mediterranean vegetables with red wine gravy. There is usually a selection of fish dishes, which may include salmon fillet with lobster sauce and vegetarian alternatives. The attractive rear garden is popular for summer imbibing and peaceful overnight accommodation is available in four comfortable en suite bedrooms.

CHINNOR   Map 06 SP70

Pick of the Pubs

Sir Charles Napier ⊚⊚ ♀
Spriggs Alley OX9 4BX ☎ 01494 483011 🖹 01494 485311
Dir: *M40 J6 to Chinnor. Turn R at rdbt carry on straight up hill to Spriggs Alley*

Despite its helipad and a serious approach to cooking, this remains a genuine peoples' pub, with its excellent real ales and welcoming atmosphere. Inside there's an eclectic mix of unmatching old chairs and tables, huge log fires and exhibition sculptures, while outside the terrace shaded by vines and wisteria makes an attractive spot for lunch. Dishes range from Thai mussel soup, and rillette of pork with fig salad, to navarin of lamb, and roast quail with grape sauce. In the evening expect starters such as pan-fried foie gras, and Stilton soufflé with walnut dressing, followed by monkfish with casserole of baby vegetables, guinea fowl with caramelised lime and ginger, and baked Cornish lobster. Some highly recommended wines from an exhaustive list make a match for any dish. Surrounded by beech woods and fields in the Chiltern Hills.

OPEN: 12–2.30 6.30–10 (closed Mon) Closed: 25/26 Dec
BAR MEALS: Lunch served: Tue–Sat Dinner served: Tues–Thurs 12–2.30 7–9 Av main course £10.50 **RESTAURANT:** Lunch served: Tue–Sun Dinner served: Tue–Sat 12–2.30 7–10 Av 0 course fixed price £16 **BREWERY/COMPANY:** Free House
PRINCIPAL BEERS: Wadworth 6X. **FACILITIES:** Children welcome Garden: Food served outside **NOTES:** Parking 50

CHIPPING NORTON   Map 06 SP32

Chequers 🍴 ♀
Goddards Ln OX7 5NP ☎ 01608 644717 🖹 01608 646237
e-mail: enquiries@chequers-pub.co.uk
Dir: *Town centre, next to theatre*

continued

This old coaching inn is next door to the renowned theatre. An alehouse in the 16th century, it also provided lodgings for stonemasons working on the local church. The cosy bar has log fires, low ceilings and soft lighting, while the restaurant is a bright and airy. Well kept real ale, good wines and decent coffee are served along with freshly prepared dishes – a daily curry, Thai fishcakes, pork and leek sausages, and a good choice for vegetarians.
OPEN: 11–11 (Sun 11–10.30) Closed: 25 Dec **BAR MEALS:** Lunch served: all week 12–2.30 Dinner served: Mon–Sat 6–9 Av main course £7 **RESTAURANT:** Lunch served: all week 12–2.30 Dinner served: Mon–Sat 6–9 Av 3 course à la carte £15
BREWERY/COMPANY: Fullers **PRINCIPAL BEERS:** Fuller's Chiswick Bitter, London Pride & ESB.

The Plough
High St, Finstock OX7 3BY ☎ 01993 868333
Great pub for walkers and those with dogs. Some ales served from cask. Children not allowed in bar. Bedrooms.

CHISLEHAMPTON   Map 04 SU59

Coach And Horses Inn ♦♦♦ 🍴 ♀
Watlington Rd OX44 7UX ☎ 01865 890255 🖹 01865 891995
e-mail: david-mcphillips@lineone.net

A 16th-century former coaching inn situated in quiet countryside within a short distance of Oxford city centre. It retains plenty of character, with its beams, large fireplaces, old bread oven and well, and is believed to haunted by Alice, a young girl killed during the Civil War. Set price and carte menus are available, and speciality dishes include pheasant Burgundy, chicken Camembert and medallions of pork fillet Dijon.
OPEN: 11.30–3 6–11 **BAR MEALS:** Lunch served: all week 12–2 Dinner served: Mon–Sat 7–10 Av main course £10
RESTAURANT: Lunch served: all week 12–2 Dinner served: Mon–Sat 7–10 Av 3 course à la carte £20 Av 2 course fixed price £13
BREWERY/COMPANY: Free House **PRINCIPAL BEERS:** Hook Norton Best, Interbrew Flowers Original. **FACILITIES:** Children welcome Garden: Food served outside Dogs allowed
NOTES: Parking 40 **ROOMS:** 9 bedrooms 9 en suite from s£49.50 d£60

> **Restaurant and Bar Meal times indicate the times when food is available. Last orders may be approximately 30 minutes before the times stated.**

England

CHURCH ENSTONE   Map 06 SP32

Crown Inn ⊚
Mill Ln OX7 4NN ☎ 01608 677262

A 17th-century free house in a village setting on the edge of the Cotswolds. All dishes are home cooked, and may include Gressingham duck breast with plum sauce, liver and bacon, or fresh halibut.

OPEN: 12–3 6–11 (Sun 7–10.30) **BAR MEALS:** Lunch served: Tue–Sun 12–2 Dinner served: Tue–Sat 7–9 Av main course £8
RESTAURANT: Dinner served: Mon–Sat 7–9
BREWERY/COMPANY: Free House
PRINCIPAL BEERS: Everards. **FACILITIES:** Children welcome Garden: Dogs allowed **NOTES:** Parking 10
ROOMS: 4 bedrooms 3 en suite from s£35 d£45

CHURCH HANBOROUGH   Map 06 SP41

Pick of the Pubs

The Hand & Shears 🐕 ⌐
OX8 8AB ☎ 01993 88337 🖹 01993 883060
e-mail: handandshears@traditionalfreehouses.com
Dir: From A40 Eynsham rdbt follow signs for The Hanboroughs. Turn L at sign for church Hanborough follow road through village, pub is on R opposite church.

Stylishly refurbished pub-restaurant drawing discerning diners from far and wide for innovative brasserie-style food served in an informal pub atmosphere. Pop in for a pint of Hook Norton or a decent glass of wine and tuck into a warm bacon and Brie on tomato ciabatta sandwich or Caesar salad. Alternatively, relax over three courses, beginning perhaps, with melon and Parma ham, or pan-fried tiger prawns, then move on to local sausages with cheese mash and onion gravy, traditional steak and kidney pudding, or fan tailed pork fillet with cider and mushroom cream sauce. Leave room for good home-made puddings.

OPEN: 11–3 6–11 **BAR MEALS:** Lunch served: all week 12–3 Dinner served: Mon–Sat 6.30–10 Av main course £11
RESTAURANT: Lunch served: all week 12–3 Dinner served: Mon–Sat 6–10 Av 3 course à la carte £17 **PRINCIPAL BEERS:** Hook Norton Best Bitter, Interbrew Bass. **FACILITIES:** Food served outdoors Dogs allowed (water) **NOTES:** Parking 40

CLIFTON   Map 06 SP43

Duke of Cumberland's Head
OX15 0PE ☎ 01869 338534 🖹 01869 338643
Dir: A4260 from Banbury, then B4031 from Deddington
Stone and thatch pub situated in the hamlet of Clifton, between the historic villages of Deddington and Aynho. It was

built in 1645, originally as cottages, and is named after Prince Rupert who led the king's troops at the battle of Edge Hill. A good range of food is offered from sandwiches and deep-fried haddock to substantial dishes of rabbit in cream and bacon sauce, and boeuf bourguignon.

OPEN: 12–2.30 (w/end 12–3) 6.30–11 Closed: Nov 1–Easter
BAR MEALS: Lunch served: all week 12–2 Dinner served: Mon–Sat 6–9 Av main course £8.50 **RESTAURANT:** Lunch served: Wed–Sun 12–2 Dinner served: Wed–Sat 7–9.30 Av 3 course à la carte £18 Av 2 course fixed price £15 **PRINCIPAL BEERS:** Hook Norton, Adnams, Wadworth 6X, Jennings.. **FACILITIES:** Children welcome Children's licence Garden: beer garden, outdoor eating, BBQ Dogs allowed **NOTES:** Parking 20 **ROOMS:** 7 bedrooms 5 en suite from s£35 d£60

CLIFTON HAMPDEN   Map 04 SU59

Pick of the Pubs

The Plough Hotel & Restaurant ⌐
Abingdon Rd OX14 3EG ☎ 01865 407811 🖹 01865 407136
e-mail: admin@the-ploughinn.co.uk

A pretty, thatched and beamed 17th-century inn with inglenook fireplaces and oodles of charm. Set close to the River Thames with its peaceful riverside walks, it is owned and run along traditional lines by Yuksel Bektas, a Turk whose tail-coated presence guarantees the inn's hallmark of courteous hospitality. This delightful country pub has a cosy, heavily beamed main bar (watch your head when entering), and a smart dining room featuring check tiled floor and polished wooden tables. Good food is guaranteed in both rooms, with interesting menus: from the carte expect starters like smoked duck breast salad, avocado and William pear, and warm baby brioche filled with wild mushroom and whisky ragout, followed perhaps by roast fillet of venison, escalopes of pork fillet, and supreme of chicken. Tasteful overnight accommodation is offered in eight en suite bedrooms, many furnished with antiques.

continued

continued

OPEN: Open all day **BAR MEALS:** Lunch served: all week Dinner served: all week 11–11 Av main course £12.95 **RESTAURANT:** Lunch served: all week Dinner served: all week Av 3 course à la carte £22.50 **BREWERY/COMPANY:** Free House **PRINCIPAL BEERS:** Scottish Courage John Smith's, Courage Best & Directors. **FACILITIES:** Children welcome Children's licence Garden: Beer garden, patio, food served outdoors **NOTES:** Parking 35 **ROOMS:** 11 bedrooms 11 en suite from s£67.50 d£82.50

CUMNOR Map 06 SP40

Pick of the Pubs

Bear & Ragged Staff ⚲
28 Appleton Rd OX2 9QH
☎ 01865 862329 ▯ 01865 865947
e-mail: gavinmansfield@hotmail.com
Dir: *A420 from Oxford, R to Cumnor on B4017*

A 700-year-old pub dating back to Cromwell's days, and allegedly haunted by the mistress of the Earl of Warwick. Cromwell's brother Richard is believed to have chiselled out the royal crest from above one of the fireplaces. The wooden décor, including beams and floors, and two of the original massive fireplaces add to the atmosphere, and the appeal is enhanced by soft furnishings and warm colours. The pub caters for a wide cross section of locals as well as being a popular destination for lovers of good food. Freshly-prepared meals with full service might produce starters like smoked duck breast on a mixed leaf salad, or timbale of salmon, crab and prawns, followed by monkfish in smoked bacon with saffron sauce, or Thai chicken curry, and perhaps profiteroles with Chantilly cream and a rich chocolate sauce. A good range of Havana cigars, ports and brandies.
OPEN: 12–11 (Sun 12–10.30) **BAR MEALS:** Lunch served: all week Dinner served: all week 12–3 6–10 Av main course £10 **RESTAURANT:** Lunch served: all week Dinner served: all week 12–3 6–10 Av 3 course à la carte £17 **BREWERY/COMPANY:** Morrells **PRINCIPAL BEERS:** Morrells Varsity & Oxford Blue, Everards Tiger, Fuller's London Pride. **FACILITIES:** Children welcome Garden: Food served outdoors, patio, BBQ Dogs allowed (water, toys) **NOTES:** Parking 60

The Vine Inn
11 Abingdon Rd OX2 9QN ☎ 01865 862567 ▯ 01865 863302
Dir: *A420 from Oxford, R onto B4017*
Country village pub-restaurant dating from 1743 and situated just off the A420 south-west of Oxford. Vine-covered stone

façade, homely main bar with a relaxing atmosphere and a modern rear dining room. Typical menus include paper bag trout, chargrilled tuna steak with wholegrain mustard sauce, duck legs in blackcurrant and rosemary jus, beef in brandy with rice, and a selection of baguettes, platters, and jacket potatoes.
OPEN: 11–2.30 6–11 (Sun 12–4, 7–10.30) **BAR MEALS:** Lunch served: all week 12.30–2.15 Dinner served: Mon–Sat 6.30–9.15 Av main course £5 **RESTAURANT:** Lunch served: all week 12.30–2.15 Dinner served: Mon–Sat 6.30–9.15 Av 3 course à la carte £19 **BREWERY/COMPANY:** Punch Taverns **PRINCIPAL BEERS:** Adnams Bitter, Carlsberg-Tetely Tetely Bitter, Wadworth 6X + guest beers. **FACILITIES:** Children welcome Garden: Food served outside Dogs allowed (water) **NOTES:** Parking 45

DEDDINGTON Map 06 SP43

Pick of the Pubs

Deddington Arms ★ ★ ★ ◉ ⚲
Horsefair OX15 0SH ☎ 01869 338364 ▯ 01869 337010
e-mail: deddarms@aol.com
Dir: *A43 to Northampton, B4100 to Aynho, B4031 to Deddington. M40 J11 to Banbury. Follow signs for hospital, then towards Adderbury & Deddington, on A4260.*

The Deddington Arms has a long history of providing hospitality for travellers, with over 400 years of warm welcomes and comfortable accommodation. It continues to offer shelter of a high standard – the spacious en suite bedrooms enjoy all modern conveniences today, though their charm and character has not been compromised. In the traditional bar, timbers, open fires and village views are of interest, while high standards prevail here too with innovative food based on fresh produce being served from a carte menu in the smart restaurant. Begin a meal with duet of pigeon and duck with black pudding risotto, or tempura tiger prawns, and follow on with Thai steamed sea bream with a lime and coriander risotto, or perhaps medallions of beef with oxtail. The wine list features labels from all around the world, and there is a good range of real ales.
OPEN: 11–11 **BAR MEALS:** Lunch served: all week Dinner served: all week 12–2 6.30–8 Av main course £8.50 **RESTAURANT:** Lunch served: all week Dinner served: all week 12–2 6.30–10.00 Av 3 course à la carte £22 **BREWERY/COMPANY:** Free House **PRINCIPAL BEERS:** Carlsberg-Tetleys Tetleys Bitter, Marston's Pedigree. **FACILITIES:** Children welcome **NOTES:** Parking 36 **ROOMS:** 27 bedrooms 27 en suite from s£75 d£80

continued

DORCHESTER-ON-THAMES   Map 04 SU59

Pick of the Pubs

The George ★ ★ ★ ◎ ♀
25 High St OX10 7HH ☎ 01865 340404 📄 01865 341620
Dir: From M40 J7 take A329 S to A4074 at Shillingford. Follow signs to Dorchester.From M4 J13 take A34 to Abingdon then A415 E to Dorchester

Historic features throughout this 15th-century hostelry, the centrepiece of the village, include the inglenook fireplaces of Potboys Bar and a fine vaulted ceiling in the hotel restaurant. Bar menus change daily with a weather eye to high quality fresh produce from near and far. Starters might include roast plum tomato soup and rabbit confit with mustard sauce, followed by boar and apple sausages with chive mash, wild mushroom and basil tagliatelle, and grilled salmon fillet with sauce vierge. Dinner menus offer chargrilled scallops with pancetta, roast peppered saddle of lamb, home-made blueberry ice cream and commendable British farmhouse cheeses.

OPEN: 11-11 **BAR MEALS:** Lunch served: all week Dinner served: all week 12-2.30 6.30-9.30 Av main course £7.50
RESTAURANT: Lunch served: all week Dinner served: all week 12-2.30 6.30-9.30 Av 3 course à la carte £22.50
BREWERY/COMPANY: Free House
PRINCIPAL BEERS: Greene King, Marstons Pedigree,.
FACILITIES: Children welcome **NOTES:** Parking 28
ROOMS: 24 bedrooms 24 en suite from s£69 d£79

OPEN: 11.30-11 (Sun 12-10.30) **BAR MEALS:** Lunch served: all week Dinner served: all week 12-2.15 7-9.45 Av main course £13 **RESTAURANT:** Lunch served: all week Dinner served: all week 12-2.15 7-9.45 Av 3 course à la carte £22
BREWERY/COMPANY: Free House
PRINCIPAL BEERS: Brakspear. **FACILITIES:** Children's licence Garden: **NOTES:** Parking 150 **ROOMS:** 18 bedrooms 18 en suite from s£65 d£85

Pick of the Pubs

The White Hart ★ ★ ★ ◎ ♀
High St OX10 7HN ☎ 01865 340074 📄 01865 341082
e-mail: whitehartdorches@aol.com
Dir: A4074 Oxford to Reading, 5M J7 M40 A329 to Wallingford

Privately-owned hotel situated in one of Oxfordshire's most famous villages. The Romans built a town here, though its ramparts are now only faintly recognisable. The abbey, at the heart of Dorchester, dates back to the 12th century and the adjoining gatehouse is now a museum. A perfect base for exploring the Cotswolds and the Chilterns, taking a cruise on the Thames or visiting Oxford, the historic White Hart offers the chance to relax and dine in comfortably furnished surroundings. Food ranges from sandwiches and hot bar meals, to imaginative dishes and a weekly-changing menu. Expect venison steak with sweet potato farls and roasted vegetable ratatouille, braised lamb shank with rosemary and port wine sauce, and pan-fried calves' liver on horseradish mash with cassis sauce.

DUNS TEW   Map 06 SP42

The White Horse Inn
OX25 6JS ☎ 01869 340272 📄 01869 347732
Dir: M40 J11, A4260, follow signs to Deddington and then onto Duns Tew
Dating back to the 17th century, this Cotswold coaching inn has a wealth of charming features, including log fires, oak panelling and flagstone floors.

EAST HANNEY   Map 04 SU49

The Black Horse ♀
Main St OX12 0JE ☎ 01235 868212 📄 01235 868989
e-mail: bhhoxon@onetel.net.uk

Bavarian home-cooked specialities reflect the origin of this traditional pub's chef/proprietor, whose schnitzels come in various guises. Lighter eclectic selections include chicken korma, fish 'n' chips, and lasagne grande, as well as baguettes, ploughmans' and salads. Main courses include peppered pork steak, duck in a port wine demiglace sauce, spinach ricotta cannelloni and mushroom Stroganoff. German apfelkuchen to finish.
OPEN: 12-2.30 6-11 **BAR MEALS:** Lunch served: Tue-Sun Dinner served: Tue-Sun 12-2 6-9 Av main course £8.60
RESTAURANT: Lunch served: Tue-Sun Dinner served: Tue-Sun 12-2 6-9 **BREWERY/COMPANY:** Free House **PRINCIPAL BEERS:** Hook Norton, Brakspear, Vale Brewery-Wychert, London Pride (Fullers).

continued   *continued*

FACILITIES: Children welcome Garden: Food served outside. Terrace garden (Guide dogs only) **NOTES:** Parking 10

EAST HENDRED
Map 04 SU48

The Wheatsheaf ♀
Chapel Square OX12 8JN ☎ 01235 833229
Dir: *2m from the A34 Milton interchange*
Two miles from the Ridgeway path in a pretty village of thatched properties, this 16th-century beamed pub was formerly the magistrates' court. Freshly prepared food includes steak-and-kidney pie and home-made puds. Specials such as home-smoked local trout and English beef steaks. Sunday lunch.
OPEN: 12–3 6–11 (Sun 7–10.30) **BAR MEALS:** Lunch served: all week 12–2 Dinner served: Mon-Sat 7–9.30 Av main course £6.75
BREWERY/COMPANY: Greene King **PRINCIPAL BEERS:** Greene King Abbot Ale, IPA, plus guest ales. **FACILITIES:** Children welcome Garden: patio/terrace, outdoor eating, aviary Dogs allowed
NOTES: Parking 10

FARINGDON
Map 04 SU29

Pick of the Pubs

The Lamb at Buckland ◉ ☜ ♀
Lamb Ln, Buckland SN7 8QN
☎ 01367 870484 🖷 01367 870675
Dir: *Just off A420 3m E of Faringdon*
Quietly situated just off the Oxford to Swindon road, this civilised little 18th-century inn stands on the very edge of the Cotswolds, with spectacular views across the Thames flood plain. Inside the charming stone building, the tastefully furnished bar and restaurant subtly reinforce the brand image with sheep prints and models, and even the carpet has a specially woven Lamb motif! Peta and Paul Barnard have earned an enviable reputation for their real ales, restaurant quality food and decent wine list. The varied and imaginative menu makes good use of the finest quality local ingredients, and food can be served in either the bar or restaurant areas. There's a garden, too, for alfresco dining and family barbecues on summer Sunday evenings. Lighter meals include dependable ploughman's lunches and baked seafood pancakes, whilst boiled beef and carrots, roast grouse, and grilled fresh tuna satisfy heartier appetites. Finish with summer pudding, hot poached dates, or the intriguing dieters' despair. Useful overnight accommodation in four en suite upstairs bedrooms.
OPEN: 10.30–3pm 5.30–11pm Closed: 25–26 Dec
BAR MEALS: Lunch served: all week Dinner served: all week 12–2 6.30–9.30 Av main course £15.95 **RESTAURANT:** Lunch served: all week Dinner served: all week 12–2 6.30–9.30 Av 3 course à la carte £27 **BREWERY/COMPANY:** Free House
PRINCIPAL BEERS: Hook Norton, Adnams Broadside, Arkells 3Bs.
FACILITIES: Children welcome Children's licence Garden: Food served outside. Dogs allowed (in the garden only) **NOTES:** Parking 50 **ROOMS:** 4 bedrooms 4 en suite from s£47.50 d£42.50

Pick of the Pubs

The Trout at Tadpole Bridge ♀
Buckland Marsh SN7 8RF ☎ 01367 870382
e-mail: info@trout-inn.co.uk
Dir: *Halfway between Oxford & Swindon on the A420, take rd signed Bampton, pub is approx 2m down it.*
Originally a coal storage house, this 17th-century building was converted into cottages, and then into an inn towards the end of the 19th century. It is situated on the banks of the River Thames with a pretty riverside garden, ideal for summer drinking. The refurbished interior has a light, modern and airy feel, with polished wooden tables, oak beams and a roaring log fire in winter. Above average pub food, cooked with style using fresh local produce, is the key to the success of the Trout. Diners beat a path to the door to sample such delights as Maryland crab cakes with spicy salsa, and roast guinea fowl with a chestnut stuffing on a bed of roasted vegetables with a cider and honey sauce. If it's a snack you're after, how about grilled butterflied breast of chicken topped with Welsh rarebit.
OPEN: 11.30–3 6–11 Closed: 25 Dec–1 Jan
BAR MEALS: Lunch served: all week 12–2 Dinner served: Mon-Sat 7–9 Av main course £11.95 **RESTAURANT:** Lunch served: all week 12–2 Dinner served: Mon-Sat 7–9 Av 3 course à la carte £22.95 **BREWERY/COMPANY:** Free House
PRINCIPAL BEERS: Archers Village Bitter & Golden Bitter, Fuller's London Pride,. **FACILITIES:** Children welcome Garden: Overlooking River Thames, food served outside Dogs allowed (water) **NOTES:** Parking 70 **ROOMS:** 6 bedrooms 6 en suite from s£55 d£80

FIFIELD
Map 06 SP21

Merrymouth Inn ☜ NEW
Stow Rd OX7 6HR ☎ 01993 831652 🖷 01933 830840
e-mail: alan.fiaherty@btclick.com
Dir: *Situated on the A424 between Burford (3M) and Stow on the Wold (4M)*
A 13th-century inn, hunting lodge and farm have been combined to form the bar, restaurant and letting rooms at the Merrymouth. Formerly owned by the monks of Bruern Abbey, the inn takes its name from the Murimuth family who acquired the village of Fifield six centuries ago. Pride is taken in the standard of the food produced here, using superior ingredients, local wherever possible. Fresh fish is a feature and the home-made puddings are very popular.
OPEN: 12–2.30 6–10.30 (Closed Sun eve in winter)
BAR MEALS: Lunch served: all week Dinner served: all week 12–2 6.30–9 Av main course £8.50 **RESTAURANT:** Lunch served: all week Dinner served: all week 12–2 6.30–9 Av 3 course à la carte £16
BREWERY/COMPANY: Free House **PRINCIPAL BEERS:** Hook Norton Best, Wychwood Hobgoblin. **FACILITIES:** Children welcome Garden: Dogs allowed **NOTES:** Parking 70 **ROOMS:** 9 bedrooms 9 en suite from s£45 d£60

FRINGFORD
Map 06 SP62

The Butchers Arms
OX27 8EB ☎ 01869 277363
Boasting a mention in Flora Thompson's novel *Lark Rise to Candleford*, this traditional village pub has a wide range of ales on offer. From the patio you can watch cricket matches in progress during the summer.
OPEN: 12–3 6–11 (Sat/Sun open all day) **BAR MEALS:** Lunch served: Tue-Sat Dinner served: Tue-Sat 12–2 7–10
RESTAURANT: Lunch served: Tue-Sat Dinner served: Tue-Sat 12–2 7–10 **BREWERY/COMPANY:** Pubmaster
PRINCIPAL BEERS: Youngs Bitter, Jennings Cumberland, Adnams Broadside. **FACILITIES:** Children welcome Dogs allowed No credit cards

---

Pubs offering a good choice of fish on their menu

continued

England

FYFIELD

Map 04 SU49

The White Hart 🛏 ♀
Main Rd OX13 5LW ☎ 01865 390585 🗎 01865 390671
Dir: Just off A420, 8m SW of Oxford

A wonderful old chantry house erected in 1442 to house five people engaged to pray for the soul of the lord of Fyfield manor. It has retained many original features, but now offers succour of a different kind. Food ranges from lunchtime sandwiches to main courses such as braised shank of lamb with leek and potato gratin and rosemary jus or seared escalope of salmon in orange butter sauce. The extensive gardens include a children's play area.
OPEN: 11–3 6–11 **BAR MEALS:** Lunch served: all week Dinner served: all week 12–2 7–10 Av main course £8.50
RESTAURANT: Lunch served: all week Dinner served: all week 12–2 7–10 Av 3 course à la carte £18 Av 3 course fixed price £18
BREWERY/COMPANY: Free House **PRINCIPAL BEERS:** Hook Norton, Wadworth 6X, Theakstons Old Peculier, London Pride.
FACILITIES: Children welcome Garden: Food served outside, large gardens Dogs allowed (water provided) **NOTES:** Parking 40

GORING

Map 04 SU68

Miller of Mansfield 🛏 ♀
High St RG8 9AW ☎ 01491 872829 🗎 01491 874200
Dir: From Pangbourne A329 to Streatley, then R on B4009, 0.5m to Goring

Historic ivy-clad pub in a sprawling riverside village, set between the Chilterns and the Berkshire Downs. The pub is close to the River Thames and handy for both the Ridgeway national trail and the Thames Path. Snacks are served in the oak-beamed bar, and there is a full restaurant menu. Typical dishes are pork fillet with Calvados and apple, peppered steaks, baked cod and Thai chicken.
OPEN: 11–11 (Sun 12–10.30) **BAR MEALS:** Lunch served: all week Dinner served: all week 12–2 6.30–10 Av main course £6.50
RESTAURANT: Lunch served: all week Dinner served: all week 12–2 7–10 Av 3 course à la carte £16 **BREWERY/COMPANY:** Free House

PRINCIPAL BEERS: Scottish Courage Courage Best, Greene King Old Speckled Hen, Brakspear Bitter. **FACILITIES:** Children welcome Dogs allowed (water) **NOTES:** Parking 8 **ROOMS:** 10 bedrooms 10 en suite from s£57.50 d£75

GREAT TEW

Map 06 SP33

Pick of the Pubs

The Falkland Arms ♀
OX7 4DB ☎ 01608 683653 🗎 01608 683656
e-mail: sjcourage@btconnect.com
Dir: Off A361 1.25m, signposted Great Tew

This 500-year-old inn takes its name from Lucius Carey, 2nd Viscount Falkland, who inherited the manor of Great Tew in 1629. Nestling at the end of a charming row of Cotswold stone cottages, the Falkland Arms is a classic; flagstone floors, high-backed settles and an inglenook fireplace characterise the intimate bar, where a huge collection of beer and cider mugs hangs from the ceiling. Home-made specials such as beef and ale pie or salmon and broccoli fishcakes supplement the basic lunchtime menu, served in the bar or the pub garden. In the evening, booking is essential for dinner in the small, non-smoking dining room. Expect parsnip soup or grilled goats' cheese salad, followed by chicken breast with bacon and mushrooms in shallot sauce; salmon and prawns with lemon and dill sauce; or mushroom and herb stroganoff. An old spiral staircase leads up to six delightful cottage-style en suite bedrooms.
OPEN: 11.30–2.30 6–11 (Summer Sat 11.30–11.30, Sun 12–10.30)
BAR MEALS: Lunch served: all week 12–2 Av main course £7.75
RESTAURANT: Lunch served: all week 12–2 Dinner served: Mon–Sat 7–8 Av 3 course à la carte £17
BREWERY/COMPANY: Wadworth
PRINCIPAL BEERS: Wadworth 6X & Henry's IPA.
FACILITIES: Garden Food served outside Dogs allowed (on lead, water) **ROOMS:** 6 bedrooms 6 en suite from s£40 d£65

HAILEY

Map 06 SP31

Pick of the Pubs

Bird in Hand 🛏 ♀
Whiteoak Green OX29 9XP
☎ 01993 868321 🗎 01993 868702
Dir: Leave A40 for Witney town centre, onto B4022, through Hailey, inn 1m N

Expect a warm welcome at this 17th-century Cotswold stone inn where the heavily beamed bars have an ageless charm. The focal point of the oldest room is a huge

continued

continued

inglenook fireplace where logs blaze on winter days. In the summer the garden is a pleasant place to sit, and the splendid modern English food can be served here or anywhere else in the pub, including the stylish, subtly-lit restaurant. Renowned for good quality cooking of fresh ingredients, it offers a choice of bar meals like creamy seafood pasta, wild boar and apple sausages, and hot baguettes. Blackboard specials might include rack of lamb with garlic mash, and Cajun chicken breast, and from the menu the likes of sautéed chicken livers followed by Banbury duck breast. Several quiet bedrooms surround a grass courtyard.

OPEN: 11-11 **BAR MEALS:** Lunch served: all week Dinner served: all week 12-2.30 7-9.30 Av main course £12.95
RESTAURANT: Lunch served: all week Dinner served: all week 12-2.30 7-9.30 Av 3 course à la carte £20
BREWERY/COMPANY: Heavitree
PRINCIPAL BEERS: Worthingtons, Brakespear, Adnams.
FACILITIES: Children welcome Garden: Food served outside. Patio & lawn areas Dogs allowed (in the garden only)
NOTES: Parking 100 **ROOMS:** 16 bedrooms 16 en suite from s£55 d£68

HENLEY-ON-THAMES   Map 04 SU78

Pick of the Pubs

The Five Horseshoes 🌳 🍷
Maidensgrove RG9 6EX ☎ 01491 641282 📠 01491 641086
e-mail: info@totalevents.co.uk
Dir: A4130 from Henley, onto B480

There are breathtaking views over the valley below from this 17th-century vine-covered inn located high above Henley. Deer from nearby Stonor Park can be spotted from the garden, while red kites regularly soar overhead. This idyllic spot is just 10 minutes drive from the town up a twisting road, and the low-beamed bar is worth a visit

just to see its fascinating collection of curios from old tools and banknotes to firearms and brasses. With its wood-burning stove and rustic stripped tables it exudes old world charm, just the place to try a pint of Brakspear Special or a glass of wine with some superior food. The menu changes regularly, listing perhaps prawn and crab galette, or creamy Stilton soup, followed by pan-fried lambs' liver and bacon, Thai-spiced lamb shank, or beef and vegetable stir-fry. Motley desserts like pain au chocolate and spotted dick with custard.
OPEN: 11.30-3 6-11 **BAR MEALS:** Lunch served: all week Dinner served: all week 12-2 7-10 Av main course £7.95
RESTAURANT: Lunch served: all week Dinner served: all week 12-2 7-9 Av 3 course à la carte £29 Av 3 course fixed price £14.75
BREWERY/COMPANY: Brakspear
PRINCIPAL BEERS: Brakspear Ordinary & Special.
FACILITIES: Children welcome Garden: 2 gardens lovely views, food served outside Dogs allowed (water) **NOTES:** Parking 85

The Golden Ball 🌳 🍷
Lower Assendon RG9 6AH ☎ 01491 574157 📠 01491 576653
e-mail: Golden.Ball@theseed.net
Dir: A4130, R onto B480, pub 300yrds on L
Dick Turpin hid in the priest hole at this 400-year-old building tucked away in the Stonor Valley close to Henley. It has a traditional pub atmosphere with well-used furnishings, open fire, exposed timbers, brasses and a collection of old bottled ales. Well-kept beer and home-cooked food are served, and there's a south-facing garden with plenty of garden furniture and undercover accommodation. Favourite fare includes sausage and mash, fish pie and lasagne.
OPEN: 11-3 6-11 **BAR MEALS:** Lunch served: all week Dinner served: all week 12-2.15 7-9.30 Av main course £7.25
BREWERY/COMPANY: Brakspear **PRINCIPAL BEERS:** Brakspear Bitter & Special. **FACILITIES:** Children welcome Garden: beer garden, food served outdoors Dogs allowed on lead only
NOTES: Parking 50

The Little Angel 🌳 🍷
Remenham Ln RG9 2LS ☎ 01491 574165 📠 01491 411879
e-mail: info@thelittleangel.com
Dir: from M4, pub is on the R at bottom of hill as you arrive in Henley

Grade II listed building reputedly haunted by Mary Blandy who poisoned her father in 1751, was found guilty and hanged. The unfortunate woman took refuge here after being pursued by an angry mob. The pub overlooks Henley Cricket Club and is the place to go for the Regatta and the Henley Festival. The Spanish proprietor has introduced a warm Mediterranean feel to the decor and a tapas menu to run alongside the bar snacks and brasserie restaurant carte. Dishes include seared scallops, dim sum, steak and mushroom

continued   *continued*

HENLEY-ON-THAMES continued

pie, and chargrilled tuna fillet with cherry tomatoes and olive tapenade.
OPEN: 11–3 6–11 (Sun 12–3 7–10.30) **BAR MEALS:** Lunch served: all week Dinner served: all week 12–2.30 7–10 Av main course £7.95 **RESTAURANT:** Lunch served: all week Dinner served: all week 12.30–2.30 7–10 Av 3 course à la carte £22
BREWERY/COMPANY: Brakspear **PRINCIPAL BEERS:** Brakspear Ordinary Bitter, Special Bitter Seasonal Ales. **FACILITIES:** Garden: Food served outdoors **NOTES:** Parking 40

HENTON   Map 06 SP70

Peacock Inn
OX9 4AH ☎ 01844 353519
Black and white timbered inn in quiet village setting. Patio with outdoor eating facilities. Children welcome. Bedrooms. Look out for the peacocks!

HOOK NORTON   Map 06 SP33

The Gate Hangs High ♀
Whichford Rd OX15 5DF ☎ 01608 737387
Dir: Off A361 SW of Banbury
Originally a toll house on the road to Banbury market, this charming country pub in picturesque ironstone country is well worth finding. 'The gate hangs high and hinders none, Refresh and pay, and travel on,' reads the sign outside. Handy for exploring the Cotswolds and visiting Broughton Castle or nearby Upton House. Just down the lane is the famous Hook Norton Brewery from where the pub sources its tip-top ales. Imaginative and traditional home cooking ranges from duck with a cider apple and sage sauce to chargrilled noisettes of lamb and oven-baked salmon supreme. Good wine list and a range of malt whiskies.
OPEN: 12–3 6–11 Closed: 25 & 26 Dec **BAR MEALS:** Lunch served: all week Dinner served: all week 12–2 6–10 Av main course £7.50 **RESTAURANT:** Lunch served: all week Dinner served: all week 12–2 6–10 Av 3 course à la carte £20 **BREWERY/COMPANY:** Hook Norton **PRINCIPAL BEERS:** Hook Norton - Best, Old Hooky, Haymaker & Generation. **FACILITIES:** Children welcome Garden: Beer garden, outdoor eating, patio, Dogs allowed allowed in garden **NOTES:** Parking 20

Sun Inn ♀
High St OX15 5NH ☎ 01608 737570 🖷 01608 730770
e-mail: enquiries@the-sun-inn.com

Traditional, extended pub in good walking country close to the Oxfordshire/Warwickshire border. Hook Norton is a sizeable village and close by is the famous, old-established Hook Norton Brewery. Festooned with hops, the candlelit bar has a

cosy log fire and relaxed atmosphere. Fresh food is cooked to order and among the imaginative specials you may find loin of venison, chilli- and herb-crusted monkfish with roasted shallots and a thyme sauce, and saddle of venison with redcurrant and red wine sauce. Appetising bar menu for those popping in for a pint and a light snack. Combine a visit with a tour of the brewery.
OPEN: 11.30–3 6–11.30 **BAR MEALS:** Lunch served: all week Dinner served: all week 12–2 7–9.30 Av main course £6.50 **RESTAURANT:** Lunch served: all week Dinner served: all week 12–2 7–9.30 Av 3 course à la carte £19.50 **BREWERY/COMPANY:** Hook Norton **PRINCIPAL BEERS:** Hook Norton Best Bitter, Old Generation, Mild & Double Stout. **FACILITIES:** Children welcome Garden: Food served outside **NOTES:** Parking 20
ROOMS: 5 bedrooms 5 en suite from s£35 d£50

KELMSCOT   Map 04 SU29

The Plough Inn
GL7 3HG ☎ 01367 253543 🖷 01367 252514
Dir: From M4 onto A419 then A361 to Lechlade & A416 to Faringdon, pick up signs to Kelmscot

Peacefully situated in an unspoilt village close to Kelmscot Manor and the Thames, the 17th-century Plough is a favoured refreshment stop among the walking and boating fraternity. Good home-made food includes traditional snacks and decent specials like venison casserole, beef stew and dumplings, grilled sea bass, bouillabaisse, and game pie.
OPEN: 11–3 7–11 (Sun 12–3, 7–10.30) Closed: 6–20 Jan **BAR MEALS:** Lunch served: all week Dinner served: all week 12–2 7–9 Av main course £9 **RESTAURANT:** Lunch served: all week Dinner served: all week 12–2.30 7–9 Av 3 course à la carte £20 **BREWERY/COMPANY:** Free House **PRINCIPAL BEERS:** London Pride, Hook Norton, Guest beers. **FACILITIES:** Children welcome Children's licence Garden: Food served outside Dogs allowed (water provided) **NOTES:** Parking 10 **ROOMS:** 8 bedrooms 8 en suite from s£45 d£65

KINGSTON LISLE   Map 04 SU38

The Blowing Stone Inn 🛏
OX12 9QL ☎ 01367 820288 🖷 01367 820288
Dir: B4507 from Wantage toward Ashbury/Swindon, after 6m R to Kingston Lisle
Situated in a pretty village in the Vale of the White Horse. The name of the inn comes from a local legend that King Alfred used a sarsen stone pierced with holes to summon his troops. Open fires and warm hospitality make this a great place to relax, where the Sunday roast is carved at your table, and freshly-prepared fish dishes are a speciality (Dover sole, salmon, scallops, crab and lobster).
OPEN: 11–2.30 6–11 **BAR MEALS:** 11–2.30 6.30–9.30

continued   continued

RESTAURANT: Lunch served: Tues–Sun 12–2 Dinner 7–9 Av 3 course à la carte £20 **BREWERY/COMPANY:** Free House **PRINCIPAL BEERS:** Wadworth 6X, Scottish Courage Courage Best, Fuller's London Pride. **FACILITIES:** Children welcome Garden: food served outside Dogs allowed **NOTES:** Parking 30 **ROOMS:** 3 bedrooms 3 en suite from d£40

LEWKNOR   Map 04 SU79

The Leathern Bottel ♀
1 High St OX9 5TW ☎ 01844 351482

Run by the same family for 25 years, this 16th-century coaching inn is set in the foothills of the Chilterns. Walkers with dogs, families with children, parties for meals or punters for a quick pint are all made equally welcome. In winter there's a wood-burning stove, a good drop of Brakespears ale, nourishing specials and a quiz on Sunday. Summer is the time for outdoor eating, the children's play area, Pimms and morris dancers.
OPEN: 10.30–3 6–11 **BAR MEALS:** Lunch served: all week Dinner served: all week 12–2 7–9.30 Av main course £6.95 **BREWERY/COMPANY:** Brakspear **PRINCIPAL BEERS:** Brakspear Ordinary, Special, Old Ale. **FACILITIES:** Children welcome Children's licence Garden: Food served outside, large lawn Dogs allowed (water) **NOTES:** Parking 35

LOWER WOLVERCOTE   Map 06 SP41

The Trout Inn ♀
195 Godstow Rd OX2 8PN ☎ 01865 302071
Dir: From A40 at Wolvercote rdbt (N of Oxford) follow signs for Wolvercote

A riverside inn which has associations with Matthew Arnold, Lewis Carroll and Colin Dexter's Inspector Morse. Constructed in the 17th century from the ruins of Godstow Abbey, its rich history includes being torched by Parliamentarian troops. A good choice of food offers baked whole trout with garlic mushrooms and cheddar mash, lemon chicken, beef,

continued

mushroom and Bass pie, or Cumberland sausage wrapped in Yorkshire pudding, with liver and bacon.
OPEN: 11–11 **BAR MEALS:** Lunch served: all week Dinner served: all week **BREWERY/COMPANY:** Vintage Inns **PRINCIPAL BEERS:** Interbrew Bass, Fuller's London Pride. **FACILITIES:** Garden: Patio, food served outside **NOTES:** Parking 100

MARSTON   Map 06 SP50

Victoria Arms
Mill Ln OX3 0PZ ☎ 01865 241382
Dir: From A40 follow signs to Old Marston, sharp R into Mill Lane, pub lane 500yrds on L
Friendly country pub situated on the banks of the River Cherwell, occupying the site of the old Marston Ferry that connected the north and south of the city. The old ferryman's bell is still behind the bar. Popular destinations for punters, and fans of TV sleuth Inspector Morse, as the last episode used this as a location. Typical menu includes lamb cobbler, steak and Guinness pie, spicy pasta bake, battered haddock, and ham off the bone.
OPEN: 11.30–11 **BAR MEALS:** Lunch served: all week Dinner served: all week 12–2 6.30–9.30 Av main course £7.50 **BREWERY/COMPANY:** Wadworth **PRINCIPAL BEERS:** Wadworth 6X, Henrys IPA, Badger Tanglefoot, Wadworth JCB. **FACILITIES:** Children welcome Garden: Food served outside. Patio & lawn area Dogs allowed **NOTES:** Parking 70

MIDDLETON STONEY   Map 06 SP52

Pick of the Pubs

The Jersey Arms ♀
OX25 8AD ☎ 01869 343234 ▤ 01869 343565
e-mail: jerseyarms@bestwestern.co.uk
Charming family-run hotel, formerly a coaching inn with the original courtyard housing spacious and comfortable bedrooms which are quieter than main building rooms. Cosy bar offering good range of popular bar food with the extensive menu supplemented by daily blackboard specials, including soups, pâtés, pasta dishes and traditional main courses like steak and kidney pie. Beamed and panelled restaurant with Mediterranean terracotta decor and cosmopolitan brasserie-style menu.
OPEN: 12–11 **BAR MEALS:** Lunch served: all week Dinner served: all week 12–2.15 6.30–9.30 Av main course £7.95 **RESTAURANT:** Lunch served: all week Dinner served: all week 12–2.15 6.30–9.30 Av 3 course à la carte £21 **BREWERY/COMPANY:** Free House **PRINCIPAL BEERS:** Interbrew Flower, Boddingtons. **FACILITIES:** Children welcome Garden: Food served outside, courtyard **NOTES:** Parking 50 **ROOMS:** 20 bedrooms 20 en suite from s£81 d£95

MURCOTT   Map 06 SP51

The Nut Tree ♀
Main St OX5 2RE ☎ 01865 331253 ▤ 01865 331977
Dir: off B4027 NE of Oxford via Islip and Charlton-on-Moor
14th-century thatched pub set in six acres of gardens, including a duck pond. There are donkeys, geese, peacocks and chickens, which supply the pub with eggs. Beamed interior with inglenooks and woodburning stoves. Conservatory serves as a non-smoking restaurant. Comprehensive menu specialises in fish and traditional dishes with a modern twist.

NETTLEBED   Map 04 SU68

The White Hart Hotel ◎◎ NEW
High St RG9 5DD ☎ 01491 642145 ⬚ 01491 649018
Beautifully restored brick and flint building dating from 17th century, with a stylish bar containing many cosy nooks and crannies for a quiet drink, and a quality restaurant. Chris Barber, former private chef to the Prince of Wales, serves his own version of classic pub cooking at affordable prices. A typical meal might be penne with field and wild mushrooms (also as a main course), sausages and mash with onion gravy, and pear and almond tart. Separate restaurant menu. No credit cards

NORTH MORETON   Map 04 SU58

The Bear ◎ ♀
High St OX11 9AT ☎ 01235 813236
Dir: Off A4130 between Didcot & Wallingford
15th-century inn on the village green, with exposed beams, open fireplaces and a cosy, relaxed atmosphere. Hook Norton ales.

NUFFIELD   Map 04 SU68

The Crown ♀
RG9 5SJ ☎ 01491 641335 ⬚ 01491 641335
Dir: Follow Henley signs, then Wallingford rd on L past turning for village
Heavily beamed 17th-century pub, originally a waggoners' inn. Located in the wooded country of the Chilterns, on the route of the Ridgeway long-distance trail. Inglenook fireplace and beams inside. Good choice of dishes with full restaurant facilities and bar meals.

OXFORD   Map 06 SP50

The Anchor
2 Hayfield Rd, Walton Manor OX2 6TT ☎ 01865 510282
Dir: A34 Oxford Ring Road(N), exit Peartree Roundabout, 1.5m then R at Polstead Rd, follow rd to bottom, pub on R
Local resident T E Lawrence (of Arabia) once frequented this friendly 1930s pub. Nowadays you'll find a relaxed atmosphere, good food and drink, and plenty to do. The wide-ranging menu offers pub favourites such as steak and ale pie, bangers and mash, burgers, scampi, and crispy battered haddock, whilst the daily specials always include vegetarian and fish options. There's a regular Tuesday quiz night, too.
OPEN: 12-3 6-11 (Mon-Sat 12-11, Sun 12-10.30)
BAR MEALS: Lunch served: all week Dinner served: all week 12-2.30 6-9 Av main course £4.95
BREWERY/COMPANY: Wadworth
PRINCIPAL BEERS: Wadworth 6X, Henrys IPA.
FACILITIES: Garden: Large patio, BBQ, food served outdoors Dogs allowed (water) **NOTES:** Parking 15

Turf Tavern ♀
4 Bath Place, off Holywell St OX1 3SU ☎ 01865 243235
Situated in the heart of Oxford, approached through hidden alleyways and winding passages, this famous pub lies in the shadow of the city wall and the colleges. It is especially popular in the summer when customers can relax in the sheltered courtyards. Eleven real ales are served daily, from a choice of around 500 over a year, along with some typical pub fare. The pub has been featured in TV's *Inspector Morse*, and was frequented by JRR Tolkien.
OPEN: 11-11 (Sun 12-10.30) **BAR MEALS:** Lunch served: all week Dinner served: all week 12-8 Av main course £4.95
BREWERY/COMPANY: Whitbread **FACILITIES:** Garden: Food served outside

See Pub Walk on page 357

The White House
2 Botley Rd OX2 0AB ☎ 01865 242823 ⬚ 01865 793331
Dir: 2 minutes walk from rail station
Set back from a busy road, this pub was once a tollhouse where people crossed the river to enter Oxford. The menu may include roast fillet of salmon with roast peppers and fresh herbs, sauteed calves' liver with onion sauce, pork cutlets cooked in beer with cabbage and bacon, or wild mushroom ravioli.
OPEN: 11-11 **BAR MEALS:** Lunch served: all week Dinner served: all week 12-2.30 6-9.30 Av main course £5 **RESTAURANT:** Lunch served: all week Dinner served: all week 12-2.30 6-9.30 Av 3 course à la carte £20 **BREWERY/COMPANY:** Punch Taverns
PRINCIPAL BEERS: Wadworth 6X, Greene King Abbot Ale, Bass, Fullers London Pride. **FACILITIES:** Children welcome Garden: Dogs allowed **NOTES:** Parking 15

PISHILL   Map 04 SU78

Pick of the Pubs

The Crown Inn ◎ ♀
RG9 6HH ☎ 01491 638364 ⬚ 01491 638364
e-mail: robin@crownpishill.fsnet.co.uk
Dir: On B480 off A4130, NW of Henley-on-Thames

A long-standing favourite, close to the magnificent parkland of Stonor House, this 15th-century brick and flint coaching inn (with one bedroom!) has origins that well date back to the 11th century. At the top of a steep climb for horse-drawn carriages from Henley to the Chilterns and on to Oxford, ostlers would water the horses while everyone else refreshed themselves: it is arguable that the village was once spelled with an extra 's' in the middle. In about four acres of grounds, its 400-year-old thatched barn has been renovated to cater for private functions and weddings. Fixed-price Winter Warmer and Shoot Lunch menus are available at lunchtime, though the regular menus offer greater variety. Main course options range from fresh haddock in Brakspear batter with pea purée and chips, to loin of suckling pig stuffed with apricots, peanuts and couscous, served on a bubble and squeak potato cake with ratatouille.
OPEN: 11.30-2.30 6-11 (Sun 12-3, 7-10.30) Closed: 25-26 Dec, 1 Jan **BAR MEALS:** Lunch served: all week Dinner served: all week 12-2 7-9.30 Av main course £7.50 **RESTAURANT:** Lunch served: all week Dinner served: all week 12-2 7-9.30 Av 3 course à la carte £22 **BREWERY/COMPANY:** Free House
PRINCIPAL BEERS: Brakspear Bitter, Fuller's.
FACILITIES: Children welcome Garden: Large sheltrd garden with seating **NOTES:** Parking 60 **ROOMS:** 1 bedroom 1 en suite from d£85

See Pub Walk on page 375

PUB WALK

Pishill
The Crown Inn

A glorious walk offering classic Chiltern scenery – rolling hills, steep valleys and dense woodland. Visit the 257-acre Warburg Nature Reserve which provides habitats for butterflies, birds and plants, as well as numerous species of fungi.

From the Crown, turn right and walk safely along wide grass verges. As the road begins to bend left, turn left onto a dirt track known as Pishill Bank. Follow it to a path and pass beside Walnut Tree Cottage, climbing steadily through woodland. As the path levels out, turn left to join a waymarked path (PS20). Keep to the main path across the top of the valley until it joins a track before reaching a field. Cross over another track into the field, still following the PS20 signs. On the far side of the field, follow the path into more woodland and descend into a valley, down to the bottom and up the other side to a stile. Emerge from the woods and follow a fenced path between fields. At a stile, join a concrete drive which, in turn, meets a gravel drive to Maidensgrove Farm. Pass through a white gate on the right and follow a

drive round the edge of Russells Water Common. At the lane, turn right and cross the common to reach a waymarked track on your left. Follow it down into a valley and look for a sign for the Warburg Nature Reserve. Turn left at a junction, entering the reserve car park. Enter the main gate and turn left over a stile. Soon the path ascends steeply up through the valley. As you near the top, avoid a track on the left and go ahead to join the Oxfordshire Way. Bear left along the path and then turn right after a few paces into a farmyard. Veer left to join a waymarked bridleway, still on the Oxfordshire Way, and on reaching a field, follow a track along the left edge. When the track dwindles to a path, follow it into woodland and maintain your route along its left edge. Cross a lane and still on the Way, follow the white arrows on tree trunks. Veer left at a fork (PS17) down into a steep valley. At the bottom cross a track and go ahead, along the right edge of a field. At the lane, turn right past Pishill Church. Bear left at the junction back to the inn.

THE CROWN
Pishill, Henley-on-Thames
RG9 6HH
Tel: 01491 638364
Directions: On B480 off A4130, NW of Henley-on-Thames
A long-standing favourite at the top of a steep hill from Henley to Oxford - maybe the village name once had an extra 's' in the middle. In about four acres of grounds, its 400-year-old thatched barn has been renovated for functions and weddings.
Open:11.30-2.30 6-11
Bar Meals: 12-2 7-9.3
Children welcome. Garden and parking available.

Distance: 3 3/4 miles (6km)
Map: OS Landranger 175
Terrain: Stunning Chiltern valleys
Paths: Field and woodland paths and tracks, some country road walking
Gradient: Some climbing

Walk submitted and checked by The Crown, Pishill

England

RAMSDEN

Map 06 SP31

The Royal Oak ♀

High St OX7 3AU ☎ 01993 868213 ▤ 01993 868864

Dir: From Witney take B4022 toward Charlbury, then turn R before Hailey, and go through Poffley End.

The Royal Oak was built as a 16th-century coaching inn on a junction of the old Roman road and the main London to Hereford stagecoach route. The restaurant has been refurbished and the kitchen is run by a French and Spanish chef, so in addition to the modern British cooking there are many regional French and Spanish dishes. It is an excellent base for walking, handy for Blenheim Palace and the Wychwood Forest.
OPEN: 11.30-3 6.30-11 Closed: Dec 25 **BAR MEALS:** Lunch served: all week Dinner served: all week 12-2 7-10 Av main course £6
RESTAURANT: Lunch served: all week Dinner served: all week 12-2 7-10 Av 3 course à la carte £22 **BREWERY/COMPANY:** Free House **PRINCIPAL BEERS:** Hook Norton Old Hooky, Best, Fuller's ESB, Adnams Broadside. **FACILITIES:** Courtyard, food seved outside Dogs allowed (water) **NOTES:** Parking 20
ROOMS: 4 bedrooms 4 en suite

ROKE

Map 04 SU69

Home Sweet Home ◌

OX10 6JD ☎ 01491 838249

Dir: Just off the B4009 from Benson to Watlington, signed posted on B4009

Long ago converted from adjoining cottages by a local brewer, this pretty 15th-century inn stands in a tiny hamlet surrounded by lovely countryside. A wealth of oak beams and the large inglenook fireplace dominate a friendly bar with an old-fashioned feel. There is a friendly home-from-home menu with reasonably priced traditional pub food and a pint of top-class ale. Cornish crab tart, liver and crispy bacon and various steaks are typical choices.
OPEN: 11-3 6-11 (Sun 12-3 closed Sun eve) Closed: Dec 25-26 **BAR MEALS:** Lunch served: all week 12-2 Dinner served: Mon-Sat 6-9 Av main course £7.95 **RESTAURANT:** Lunch served: Mon-Sun 12-2 Dinner served: Mon-Sat 7-9 Av 3 course à la carte £11
BREWERY/COMPANY: Free House
PRINCIPAL BEERS: Brakspear. **FACILITIES:** Children welcome Children's licence Garden: Patio/terrace, food served outdoors Dogs allowed (water) **NOTES:** Parking 60

ROTHERFIELD PEPPARD

Map 04 SU78

The Greyhound

Gallowstree Rd RG9 5HT ☎ 0118 9722227 ▤ 0118 9722227
e-mail: thegreyhoundpub@hotmail.com
Dir: 4 miles from Henley on Thames
Picture-postcard pretty brick and timber village inn with a wonky tiled roof and splendid front garden decked with

wooden tables and cotton parasols. The inn, complete with classic beamed bar, woodblock floor, and open brick fireplace, is under new management. The adjacent restaurant is housed in a beautifully converted pitched-roof barn. A sample menu includes thyme scented chicken breast with chorizo sausage and Parma ham, beer battered cod, lamb chump with ginger and honey, and fillet of beef with Stilton or peppercorn sauce.
OPEN: 12-3 5.30-11 (Sat till 12 Sun till 8) closed Mon & 25-28 Dec
BAR MEALS: Lunch served: Tue-Sun 12-2.30 Dinner served: Tue-Sat 7-9.30 Av main course £10 **RESTAURANT:** Lunch served: Tue-Sun 12-2.30 Dinner served: Tue-Sat 7-9.30 Av 3 course à la carte £18.50 Av 2 course fixed price £10.90 **BREWERY/COMPANY:** Free House
PRINCIPAL BEERS: Brakspear, Fuller's London Pride.
FACILITIES: Children welcome Garden: Food served outside Dogs allowed **NOTES:** Parking 40 **ROOMS:** 12 bedrooms 12 en suite from s£60 d£80

SHENINGTON

Map 06 SP34

The Bell ◌

OX15 6NQ ☎ 01295 670274
e-mail: thebell@shenington.co.uk
Dir: M40 J11 take A422 towards Stratford. Village is signposted 3m N of Wroxton
Nestling amid mellow stone houses, a classic village green and a church with an impressive Tudor tower, the comfortable and welcoming 300-year-old Bell has an open log fire burning in winter, and tables outside in the summer. The pub promises home-cooked food prepared with fresh local ingredients. Expect duck in port and black cherries, braised beef with Madeira and medley of mushrooms, pork loin in apple cider and pineapple, plus soups and devilled sausages on toast.
OPEN: 12-2.30 7-11 **BAR MEALS:** Lunch served: all week Dinner served: all week 12-2 7-11 Av main course £7.95
RESTAURANT: Lunch served: all week Dinner served: all week 12-2 7-11 Av 3 course à la carte £12.50 **BREWERY/COMPANY:** Free House **PRINCIPAL BEERS:** Hook Norton,Flowers.
FACILITIES: Children welcome Garden: Beer garden, outdoor eating, Dogs allowed (water) **ROOMS:** 3 bedrooms 1 en suite from s£20 d£40

SHIPTON-UNDER-WYCHWOOD

Map 06 SP21

The Lamb Inn

High St OX7 6DQ ☎ 01993 830465 ▤ 01993 832025
Dir: 4m N of Burford on the A361
A delightful old Cotswold-stone inn, in which the rustic beamed bar with its stone walls, wooden floor and sturdy furniture make a fine setting for enjoying a wholesome meal. Interesting dishes on the blackboard menu may include game terrine, calves' liver in Pernod, poached salmon, chargrilled tuna with Mediterranean vegetables, and chocolate truffle torte.
OPEN: 11-11 (Sun 12-10.30) **BAR MEALS:** Lunch served: all week Dinner served: all week 12-2 7-9.30 Av main course £10
RESTAURANT: Lunch served: Sun 12-2 Dinner served: Tues-Sat 7-9.30 Av 3 course à la carte £22.50 **BREWERY/COMPANY:** Old English Inns **PRINCIPAL BEERS:** Ruddles, Old Speckled Hen.
FACILITIES: Children welcome Garden: Dogs allowed
NOTES: Parking 15 **ROOMS:** 5 bedrooms 5 en suite from s£65 d£75

continued

Pick of the Pubs

The Shaven Crown Hotel
High St OX7 6BA ☎ 01993 830330 🖹 01993 832136
Dir: On A361, halfway between Burford and Chipping Norton opposite village green and church
A beautiful honey-coloured stone building, originally a late 14th-century hospice for monks of Bruern Abbey, and internment centre for the notorious fascist Oswald Moseley during the war. Recorded as one of the ten oldest inns and hotels in the country, it became a hostelry in 1571. Visitors never fail to be impressed by its original gateway, medieval hall with double-collar braced roof, mullioned windows and central courtyard garden. In places it has the feel of a baronial hall or stately home. Make for the convivial Monks Bar which offers a very popular and extensive menu including venison sausages in rich gravy, duck breast with blackcurrant coulis, and Cotswold lamb cutlets. Or dine in the intimate candlelit restaurant on the likes of smoked duck and orange salad, grilled sea bass with pink peppercorn sauce, and pannacotta with fresh fruit.
OPEN: 11.30-2.30 5-11 **BAR MEALS:** Lunch served: all week
Dinner served: all week 12-2 5.30-9.30 Av main course £8.50
RESTAURANT: Lunch served: Sun 12-2 Dinner served: all week
7-9 Av 3 course à la carte £21 Av 3 course fixed price £25
BREWERY/COMPANY: Free House
PRINCIPAL BEERS: Hook Norton Best, Greene King Abbot Ale,
Fuller's London Pride. **FACILITIES:** Children welcome Garden:
Enclosed courtyard, food served outside Dogs allowed (water)
NOTES: Parking 15 **ROOMS:** 9 bedrooms 9 en suite from s£55
d£85

SOUTH MORETON   Map 04 SU58

The Crown Inn
High St OX11 9AG ☎ 01235 812262
Dir: From Didcot take A4130 towards Wallingford. Village on R
This friendly pub runs a regular fun quiz on Monday nights. The building dates from around 1870, and features antique furnishings to complement the rustic cottage-style decor. Expect roast half shoulder of lamb, various steaks, fresh chicken Kiev and lasagne. Fish dishes include fresh cod mornay, scampi, sole, fresh salmon hollandaise, and a fish platter.
OPEN: 11-3 5.30-11 (Sun 12-3 7-10.30) Closed: Dec 25-26
BAR MEALS: Lunch served: all week Dinner served: all week 12-2
7-9.30 Av main course £7.50 **RESTAURANT:** Dinner served: all week
12-2 7-9.30 Av 3 course à la carte £14.50
BREWERY/COMPANY: Wadworth **PRINCIPAL BEERS:** Badger
Tanglefoot, Adnams Best , Wadworth 6X & Henrys IPA.
FACILITIES: Children welcome Garden: Food served outdoors
Dogs allowed (water) **NOTES:** Parking 30

SOUTH STOKE   Map 04 SU58

The Perch and Pike
RG8 0JS ☎ 01491 872415 🖹 01491 875852
e-mail: perchandpike@hotmail.com
Dir: Between Goring and Wallingford just off B4009
Set among acres of farmland, with the Ridgeway Path going past the door and surrounded by the Chilterns, this 18th-century pub is in a lovely location. Choose from a menu that may include pot roast partridge with Toulouse sausage, rump of lamb with truffle mash, chargrilled catfish with avocado or smoked salmon and fresh prawn salad.

continued

OPEN: 11-3 6-11 **BAR MEALS:** Lunch served: All week 12-2.30
Dinner served: Mon-Sat 7-9.45 Av main course £10.95
RESTAURANT: Lunch served: all week 12-2.30 Dinner served:
Mon-Sat 7-9.45 Av 3 course à la carte £27
BREWERY/COMPANY: Brakspear **PRINCIPAL BEERS:** Brakspear
Bitter, Special, Old, Mild. **FACILITIES:** Children welcome Garden:
Food served outside Dogs allowed **NOTES:** Parking 30
ROOMS: 4 bedrooms 4 en suite from s£65 d£65

STADHAMPTON   Map 04 SU69

Pick of the Pubs

The Crazy Bear ♦♦♦♦
Bear Ln OX44 7UR ☎ 01865 890714 🖹 01865 400481
e-mail: sales@crazybearhotel.co.uk
Dir: M40 J7 L on A329
Just 15 minutes drive from Oxford is an unusual small hotel full of surprises. A flamboyant refurbishment has resulted in this rural 16th-century property having two separate dining rooms, one embracing fine English dining, and the other offering a Thai-style brasserie. Menus from both restaurants are also available in the bar along with open Swiss sandwiches and exotic salads. The choice of food is extensive, and can be sample in the likes of dry-roasted tournedos of monkfish, sauté sesame sea bass, and grilled fillet of cod, plus starters like king sea scallops, and marinated duckling. Nearly 50 Thai dishes best tasted from good-value set menus. No Thai desserts, but classic English offerings might include chocolate marquise, or the ubiquitous sticky toffee pudding. Art deco bedrooms and extravagant suites.
OPEN: 12-11 **BAR MEALS:** Lunch served: all week Dinner
served: all week 12-10 Av main course £10.50
RESTAURANT: Lunch served: all week Dinner served: all week
12-3 7-10 Av 3 course à la carte £32.50 Av 3 course fixed price
£13.50 **BREWERY/COMPANY:** Free House
PRINCIPAL BEERS: Greene King IPA, Ruddles County & Abbot
Ale. **FACILITIES:** Garden: Patio, food served outside
NOTES: Parking 30 **ROOMS:** 12 bedrooms 12 en suite from
s£60 d£80

STANDLAKE   Map 06 SP30

The Bell at Standlake
21 High St OX29 7RH ☎ 01865 300784
Dir: Off the A415
Unpretentious, 300-year-old, half-timbered pub nestling in the heart of pretty Standlake. The small, simply furnished front bar is the venue for a daily changing blackboard menu of specials, along with a selection of French stick or doorstep

continued

England

STANDLAKE continued

sandwiches, ploughmans' and jacket potatoes. Pies are a speciality.
OPEN: 12–11 **BAR MEALS:** Lunch served: all week 12-4 Dinner served: Mon–Sat 6-9 Av main course £6 **RESTAURANT:** 12-2 6-9.30
BREWERY/COMPANY: Greene King **PRINCIPAL BEERS:** Greene King Morland Original, Interbrew Bass, Flowers Original, Wadworth 6X.
FACILITIES: Children welcome Garden: Food served outside Dogs allowed (water) **NOTES:** Parking 40

STANTON ST JOHN   Map 06 SP50

Star Inn ♀
Middle Rd OX33 1EX ☎ 01865 351277
Dir: At A40/Oxford ring road rdbt take Stanton exit, follow rd to T junct, R to Stanton, 3rd L, pub on L 50yds

Although the Star is only fifteen minutes drive from the centre of Oxford, it still retains a distinctly 'village' feel. The oldest part of the pub dates from the early 17th century, and in the past, the building has been used as a butcher's shop and an abattoir. The garden is peaceful and secluded. Typical menu features rib-eye steak, moussaka, vegetarian cannelloni, and shoulder of lamb.
OPEN: 11–2.30 6.30–11 **BAR MEALS:** Lunch served: all week Dinner served: all week 12-2 6.30-9.30 Av main course £6.95
BREWERY/COMPANY: Wadworth
PRINCIPAL BEERS: Wadworth 6X & Henrys IPA.
FACILITIES: Children welcome Garden: Food served outside Dogs allowed (water bowl)s **NOTES:** Parking 50

Pick of the Pubs

The Talk House ♀
Wheatley Rd OX33 1EX ☎ 01865 351648 📠 01865 351085
e-mail: thetalkhouse@traditionalfreehouses.com
Dir: Stanton-St-John signed from the Oxford ring road
The Talk House is a cleverly converted 17th-century inn located within easy reach of Oxford and the A40 and well worth seeking out. It comprises three bar and dining areas, all with a Gothic look and a welcoming atmosphere. Business, wedding and function bookings are catered for, and The Snug is ideal for private parties of eight to fifteen, with its own fireplace and private bar. The menu offers something for everyone, from pub-style favourites like steak, kidney and real ale pie, and ham, egg and chips, to more high falutin' dishes such as baked red snapper fillet topped with lobster herb butter, or half a shoulder of lamb with rosemary and honey sauce. Bed and breakfast accommodation is also offered in four chalet-style rooms situated around the attractive rear courtyard.

OPEN: 12–3 5.30–11 **BAR MEALS:** Lunch served: all week Dinner served: all week 12-2 7-10 Av main course £10
RESTAURANT: Lunch served: all week Dinner served: all week 12-2 7-10 Av 3 course à la carte £20
BREWERY/COMPANY: Free House
PRINCIPAL BEERS: Hook Norton Best Bitter, Greene King Old Speckled Hen, Fuller's London Pride, Wadworth 6X.
FACILITIES: Children welcome Garden: Fountain, food served outside **NOTES:** Parking 60 **ROOMS:** 4 bedrooms 4 en suite from s£40 d£60

STEEPLE ASTON   Map 06 SP42

Red Lion
South Side OX25 4RY ☎ 01869 340225
Dir: Off A4260 between Oxford & Banbury
The art of conversation and the enjoyment of fresh food is positively encouraged at this traditional pub. The 17th-century building comprises a bar, separate dining room, library and floral terrace. Typical dishes include Arbroath smokies en cocotte, jugged hare with forcemeat balls, and a soufflé of fresh lime.
OPEN: 11–3 6–11 (Sun 12-3, 7-10.30) **BAR MEALS:** Lunch served: Mon–Sat 12-2 Av main course £4.80 **RESTAURANT:** Dinner served: Tue–Sat 7.30-9.15 Av 3 course à la carte £23.50
BREWERY/COMPANY: Free House **PRINCIPAL BEERS:** Hook Norton. **FACILITIES:** Garden: Floral terrace Dogs allowed none **NOTES:** Parking 15

STEVENTON   Map 04 SU49

The Cherry Tree
33 High St OX13 6RS ☎ 01235 831222
Dir: Leave A34 at Milton Interchange, follow signs for Steventon, go into village, over railway bridge, pub on R
Inviting roadside tavern, full of old world charm. Home made specials feature on the varied menu. Wadworth ales.

STOKE ROW   Map 04 SU68

Pick of the Pubs

Crooked Billet ♀
RG9 5PU ☎ 01491 681048 📠 01491 682231
See Pick of the Pubs on page 379

continued

OPEN: 12–11 (Sun 12–10.30)
RESTAURANT: L served all week.
D served all week. 12–2.30 7–10 Av
cost 3 course £12
BREWERY/COMPANY:
BRAKSPEAR
PRINCIPAL BEERS: Brakspear
Bitter
FACILITIES: Children Welcome.
Garden: Food served outside
NOTES: Parking 50

Crooked Billet

RG9 5PU
☎ 01491 681048 📠 01491 682231
Dir: From Henley to Oxford A4130.
Turn L at Nettlebed for Stoke Row

A rustic country gastro-pub hidden away down a single-track lane in deepest Oxfordshire. Now very food driven, with a casual, informal atmosphere and friendly service. Built in 1642, and once the hideout of the notorious highwayman Dick Turpin who courted Bess the landlord's daughter, it retains all the original, old world charm of the true country pub.

A rustic country gastro-pub hidden away down a single-track lane in deepest Oxfordshire. Now very food driven, with a casual, informal atmosphere and friendly service. Built in 1642, and once the hideout of the notorious highwayman Dick Turpin who courted Bess the landlord's daughter, it retains all the original, old world charm of the true country pub. Delightfully unspoilt inside with low beams, ancient tiled floors, open fires and simple furnishings, it attracts well-heeled folk and local celebrities - Kate Winslet had her wedding reception here - for some first-class dining. The award-winning food from chef/proprietor Paul Clerehugh is created from local produce and organic fare including beef, lamb and free-range chicken from the village. An extensive choice includes a popular, daily-changing set lunch menu (grilled Craster kipper and scrambled egg, lambs' liver with mashed potatoes, and passion fruit mousse gateau with plum sorbet), a separate vegetarian menu with a choice of four or so main courses (perhaps roast Mediterranean vegetables with nutty green herb couscous), and a lengthy carte. From the latter try Chinese-marinated duck confit to start, or pan-fried partridge breast, followed by crispy-skinned salmon escalope or roast goose breast. There is a tempting selection of desserts such as rum baba with caramel banana, vanilla ice cream and crème anglaise. To accompany the meals there is bitter from Brakspear and an award-winning selection of 80 wines, including 10 by the glass. There are regular live music nights and the pub is very popular so booking is always advised.

England

STRATTON AUDLEY　　　　　Map 06 SP62

The Red Lion 🐾 ♀
Church St OX27 9AG ☎ 01869 277225 📠 01869 277225
e-mail: robtalbotcooper@talk21.co.uk
Dir: 2 Miles N of Bicester, just off the Buckingham Road

A charming thatched country pub with a warm and friendly
atmosphere and cosy interior brightened by open fires. Low
beams, stone walls and antique posters create a congenial
setting for a pint or two of Hook Norton or a meal from wide-
ranging menus. 'Bob's ballistic baltis' and a dozen 'giant
gourmet burgers' share space with barbecue rack of ribs,
vegetarian sausages with colcannon and chargrilled tuna
steak. The fillet steak with mushrooms is a full half-pound cut.
OPEN: 12-3 6-11 (all Sat-Sun) **BAR MEALS:** Lunch served: all
week 12-2 Dinner served: Mon-Sat 6.30-9 Av main course £8.95
PRINCIPAL BEERS: Hook Norton Best, Greene King Ruddles Best.
FACILITIES: Garden: Patio, seating, food served outside Dogs
allowed (water)

SUTTON COURTENAY　　　　　Map 04 SU59

Pick of the Pubs

The Fish 🐾 ♀
4 Appleford Rd OX14 4NQ
☎ 01235 848242 📠 01235 848014
e-mail: mike@thefish.co.uk
Dir: From A415 in Abingdon take B4017 then L onto B4016 to village

Unassuming, late 19th-century brick-built pub located a
short stroll for the Thames in the heart of this beautiful
and historic village - where Asquith and George Orwell
are buried. Very much a dining pub-restaurant although
drinkers are welcome at the bar. Good value bistro
lunches are served in the front bar-cum-dining area and
in the attractive garden and patio when fine: dishes are
modern versions of classic French and English dishes with
a strong emphasis on fresh seafood. Typical choices
include pan-seared scallops with chilli vinaigrette,
carpaccio of tuna with mooli, mint and black olives, sea
bass on a leek and potato sauce with caviar butter, and
roast monkfish with chorizo cassoulet and saffron sauce.
Further options may be crispy duck confit with taboulet
and sun-dried tomato jam and calves' liver and bacon
with shallot confit, with almond tart with vanilla ice cream
or dark chocolate marquise with coffee bean syrup to
follow. Set-price and à la carte dinners.
OPEN: 12-3.30 6-11 Closed: 2 days between Xmas & New Year
BAR MEALS: Lunch served: all week 12-2
RESTAURANT: Lunch served: all week Dinner served: all week
12-2 7-9.30 Av 3 course à la carte £25 Av 3 course fixed price
£19.95 **BREWERY/COMPANY:** Greene King

PRINCIPAL BEERS: Greeen King IPA. **FACILITIES:** Garden:
Patio, food served outside Dogs allowed (water) **NOTES:** Parking
30 **ROOMS:** 2 bedrooms 2 en suite from s£36 d£45

SWALCLIFFE　　　　　Map 06 SP33

Stag's Head 🐾 ♀
OX15 5EJ ☎ 01295 780232 📠 01295 788977
e-mail: stagsheadswalcliffe@dial.pipex.com
Dir: 6M W of banbury on the B4035

Pretty thatched pub dating back to the late 15th century or
even earlier. With its picture postcard look and picturesque
village setting, it's not suprising this ancient inn draws a broad
range of customers. Among the better dining pubs in
Oxfordshire, the Stags Head offers an eclectic range of dishes,
from traditional steaks and pot-roasted lamb, to lamb tikka
massala and Thai green chicken curry. Vegetarian options
might include cheddar, leek and spring onion pasta or roasted
peppers and goats' cheese. Dine or enjoy a decent pint
alfresco in the landscaped garden.
OPEN: 11.30-2.30 6.30-11 **BAR MEALS:** Lunch served: Tues-Sun
12-2.15 Dinner served: Tues-Sat 7-9.30 Av main course £9
RESTAURANT: Lunch served: Tues-Sun 12-2.15 Dinner served:
Tues-Sat 7-9.30 **BREWERY/COMPANY:** Free House
PRINCIPAL BEERS: Brakspears PA, Hook Norton Best, Wychwood
Seasonal, Spinning Dog Brewery. **FACILITIES:** Children welcome
Garden: Food served outside Dogs allowed (water, biscuits)
ROOMS: s£30 d£60

SWERFORD　　　　　Map 06 SP33

Pick of the Pubs

The Mason's Arms 🐾
OX7 4AP ☎ 01608 683212 📠 01608 683105
e-mail: masonsarms@ox74ap.fsnet.co.uk
Set in 3 acres overlooking the Swere Valley on the edge of
the Cotswolds, the Masons is a lovely, 300-year-old stone
pub that has been stylishly redesigned throughout in
country-farmhouse style to provide a modern dining
venue without destroying the traditional charm of a village
inn. In addition to wonderful views and a relaxed,
informal atmosphere, fresh produce is sourced locally to
create the imaginative, modern pub dishes listed on the
eclectic menu available in the bar. From starters like South
Coast mussels, or Thai fishcakes with seasonal leaves and
sweet chilli sauce, main course options range from pub
favourites - pork and chive sausages with creamy mash,
traditional steak and kidney pudding - given a modern
makeover, to chicken supreme with lime and coriander
salsa, roasted pepper, caramelised red onion and Brie

continued

continued

England

tartlet, or fillet of salmon topped with a herb crust. Hook Norton Best on tap, a select list of wines, and popular themed evenings.
OPEN: 12–3 6–11 **BAR MEALS:** Lunch served: all week Dinner served: all week 12–2.30 7–9.30 Av main course £9.95
RESTAURANT: Lunch served: all week Dinner served: all week 12–2.30 7–10 Av 3 course à la carte £19
BREWERY/COMPANY: Free House
PRINCIPAL BEERS: Hook Norton Best. **FACILITIES:** Children welcome Garden: Food served outside Dogs allowed (water provided) **NOTES:** Parking 50

SWINBROOK   Map 06 SP21

The Swan Inn
OX18 4DY ☎ 01993 822165
Dir: Take the A40 towards Burford & Cheltenham at the end of the dual carrage way is a rdbt, straight over the turn R for Swinbrook the pub can be found over the bridge on the left side

With its flagstone floors, antique furnishings and open fires, the 400-year-old Swan is full of charm and character and sits next to the River Windrush, a setting that cannot fail to impress. Plenty of scenic walks and popular tourist attractions close by. Choose cottage pie, spaghetti bolognese or deep fried whitebait with horseradish from the snack menu, followed perhaps by sirloin steak, Norfolk chicken cooked with tarragon or pan-fried trout with dried fruits.
OPEN: 11.30–3 6.30–11 Closed: Dec 25 **BAR MEALS:** Lunch served: all week 12–2 Dinner served: Mon–Sat 7–9 Av main course £8.95 **RESTAURANT:** Lunch served: all week 12–2 Dinner served: Mon–Sat 7–9 Av 3 course à la carte £16
BREWERY/COMPANY: Free House **PRINCIPAL BEERS:** Greene King IPA, Old Speckled Hen, Wadworth 6X. **FACILITIES:** Children welcome Garden: Food served outside Dogs allowed (water provided) **NOTES:** Parking 10

TADMARTON   Map 06 SP33

The Lampet Arms ♦♦♦
Main St OX15 5TB ☎ 01295 780070 ▯ 01295 788066
Dir: take the B4035 from Banbury to Tadmarton for 5m

Victorian-style building named after Captain Lampet, the local landowner who built it. The captain mistakenly believed he could persuade the council to have the local railway line directed through the village, thereby increasing trade. Typical menu choices include the likes of salmon in lime and coriander, casserole, vegetable lasagne, salmon steak and fish pie.
OPEN: 11.30–3 5–11 (Sun 12–3, 7–10.30) **BAR MEALS:** Lunch served: all week Dinner served: all week 12–2.30 6.30–9.30 Av main course £3 **RESTAURANT:** Lunch served: all week Dinner served: all week 12–2 6.30–9.30 **BREWERY/COMPANY:** Free House
PRINCIPAL BEERS: Interbrew Flowers IPA, Boddingtons, Marston's Pedigree, Fuller's London Pride. **FACILITIES:** Children welcome Garden: Terrace, outdoor eating Dogs allowed **NOTES:** Parking 18
ROOMS: 4 bedrooms 4 en suite from s£39 d£60

THAME   Map 06 SP70

The Swan Hotel
9 Upper Hight St OX9 3ER ☎ 01844 261211 ▯ 01844 261954
e-mail: swanthame@hotmail.com
Former coaching inn dating from the 16th century, overlooking the market square at Thame. The Tudor-painted ceiling is a feature of the upstairs restaurant, while

downstairs in the cosy bar there is an open fire. Daily specials served here include duck and sweet chilli, lazy aged rump steak with pepper or mustard sauce, and veal sausage with mash and onion gravy. Several real ales always on tap.

OPEN: 11–11 Closed: 25–26 Dec **BAR MEALS:** Lunch served: all week Dinner served: all week 12–2.30 7–9 Av main course £6.25 **RESTAURANT:** Lunch served: Wed–Sun 12–2 Dinner served: Tues–Sat 7–9.30 Av 3 course à la carte £24
BREWERY/COMPANY: Free House **PRINCIPAL BEERS:** Hook Norton, Timothy Taylor Landlord, Brakspears, Shepherd Neame Spitfire. **FACILITIES:** Dogs allowed (water) **NOTES:** Parking 200
ROOMS: 7 bedrooms 7 en suite from s£50 d£80

WANTAGE   Map 04 SU38

The Hare
Reading Rd, West Hendred ☎ 01235 833249 ▯ 01235 833268
Dir: Situated at West Hendred on A417 Between Wantage (3 M W)and didcot (5 M E)

A late 19th-century inn mid-way between Wantage and Didcot, modernised in the 1930s by local brewers, Morland, and featuring a colonial-style verandah and colonnade. Inside it retains the more original wooden floors, beams and open fire. A brasserie-style menu delivers fillets of salmon, chumps of lamb and char-grilled rib-eye steaks. More serious diners might try bouillabaisse terrine, pan-seared venison black cherry rösti and French yellow-plum tart or home-made ice creams.
OPEN: 11.30–2.30 5.30–11 (Fri-Sun 11.30–11) Closed: 1 Jan
BAR MEALS: Lunch served: all week Dinner served: all week 12–2 7–9 **RESTAURANT:** Lunch served: all week Dinner served: all week 12–2 7–9 Av 3 course à la carte £20.25 Av 2 course fixed price £15
BREWERY/COMPANY: Greene King **PRINCIPAL BEERS:** Greene King Abbot Ale, IPA, Morland Original. **FACILITIES:** Garden: Food served outside Dogs allowed (water, during the day)
NOTES: Parking 37

continued

WANTAGE continued

The Star Inn ♦♦♦♦
Watery Ln, Sparsholt OX12 9PL ☎ 01235 751539 & 751001
01235 751539
e-mail: star.inn@amserve.net
Dir: Sparsholt is 4m west of Wantage, take the B4507 Wantage to Ashbury road and turn off R to the village, the Star Inn is signposted
Four miles out of town in downland country close to The Ridgeway, this 300-year-old village pub is popular with the local horseracing fraternity. Log fires, attractive prints and daily papers lend the pub special character. Fresh fish is often highlighted on the specials board. Look otherwise for prawn platter, home-cooked ham and eggs, chicken creole and grilled steaks, culminating in a gargantuan mixed grill with fresh, hand-cut chips.
OPEN: 12-3 6-11 (Sat 12-11,Sun 12-10.30) Closed: Dec 25
BAR MEALS: Lunch served: Tue-Sun 12-2 Dinner served: Mon-Sat 7-9 Av main course £8 **RESTAURANT:** Lunch served: Tue-Sun 12-2 Dinner served: Mon-Sat 7-9 **BREWERY/COMPANY:** Free House
PRINCIPAL BEERS: Greene King Morland Original, Butts Bitter.
FACILITIES: Children welcome Garden: Food served outside Dogs allowed **NOTES:** Parking 20 **ROOMS:** 8 bedrooms 8 en suite from s£80 d£60

WATLINGTON
Map 04 SU69

The Fox and Hounds NEW
Christmas Common OX49 5HL ☎ 01491 612599
Dir: Junct 5 off M40 22 miles to Christmas Common (On road to Henley)

Following its latest make-over by new proprietors, it brags four cosy bar areas and a non-smoking restaurant to seat up to 50. The lunchtime bar menu includes Welsh rarebit - a 'very posh cheese on toast' - doorstep sandwiches and perhaps whole kippers with crusty bread. At night traditional 'Britishness' is reflected by starters of Stilton potato cake or preserved duck leg with speciality home dressing, followed by 8oz haggis burger or vegetarian suet pudding.
OPEN: 10.30-3 6-11 (all day Sun) **BAR MEALS:** Lunch served: all week 12-2.30 Dinner served: Mon-Sat 6-10 Av main course £10.95
RESTAURANT: Lunch served: all week 12-2.30 Dinner served: Mon-Sat 7-9.30 Av 3 course à la carte £20
BREWERY/COMPANY: Brakspear **PRINCIPAL BEERS:** Brakspear Bitter, Special, Old Ale, Mild. **FACILITIES:** Garden: Dogs allowed (water) **NOTES:** Parking 30

WESTCOTT BARTON
Map 06 SP42

The Fox Inn
Enstone Rd OX7 7BL ☎ 01869 340338
e-mail: sarnett@ukonline.co.uk
Original flagstone floors, oak beams and a roaring fire in the ancient inglenook are among the attractions at this welcoming

17th-century Cotswold village pub. New licensees serve a changing variety of dishes including cold platters, salads and traditional bar snacks, and have introduced a new restaurant menu. Typical dishes here include medallions of venison and chargrilled steak with pepper and cognac sauce.
OPEN: 12-2.30 5-11 (Sun 12-10.30) **BAR MEALS:** Lunch served: all week Dinner served: all week 12-2 7-9 Av main course £6.50
RESTAURANT: Lunch served: all week 12-2 Dinner served: Mon-Sat 7-9 Av 3 course à la carte £21 **BREWERY/COMPANY:** Enterprise Inns **PRINCIPAL BEERS:** Hook Norton Best, Theakston XB, Greene King Old Speckled Hen. **FACILITIES:** Children welcome Garden: Food served outisde Dogs allowed (water) **NOTES:** Parking 20

WESTON-ON-THE-GREEN
Map 06 SP51

The Chequers 🍴 ♈
Northampton Rd OX25 3QH ☎ 01869 350319 📠 01869 350024
e-mail: rchequers@aol.com
Dir: 2M from M40 J9
17th-century coaching inn built of Cotswold stone. The bar offers a traditional menu (burgers, lasagne, scampi), while the restaurant is devoted to Thai food. The menu includes kwaitiew noodle dishes, pad (stir-fry), kaeng (Thai curry), khoa (rice dishes), and pla (fish and seafood).
OPEN: 11.30-3 6-11 **BAR MEALS:** Lunch served: all week Dinner served: all week 12-2.30 7-10.30 Av main course £7.75
RESTAURANT: Lunch served: all week Dinner served: all week 12-2.30 7-10.30 Av 3 course à la carte £7.75
BREWERY/COMPANY: Fullers **PRINCIPAL BEERS:** Fullers London Pride, Fullers ESB. **FACILITIES:** Children welcome Garden: Food served outside Dogs allowed (water provided)
NOTES: Parking 45

WHEATLEY
Map 06 SP50

Bat & Ball Inn ♦♦♦ 🍴
28 High St OX44 9HJ ☎ 01865 874379 📠 01865 873363
Dir: Pass thru Wheatley towards Garsington, take only L turn, signed Cuddesdon
As you might have guessed from its name, this former coaching inn has a cricketing theme. The bar is absolutely packed with cricketing memorabilia and the seven letting rooms are named after famous cricketers. A good choice of hand-pulled ales is served, and there's a comprehensive menu supplemented by daily specials. Expect the likes of smoked salmon fishcakes, smothered chicken breast with bacon, onions and mushrooms, and braised half shoulder of lamb.
OPEN: 11-11 **BAR MEALS:** Lunch served: all week Dinner served: all week 12-2.45 6.30-9.45 Av main course £10
RESTAURANT: Lunch served: all week Dinner served: all week 12-2.45 6.30-9.45 Av 3 course à la carte £22.50
BREWERY/COMPANY: Marstons **PRINCIPAL BEERS:** Marston's Pedigree & Original. **FACILITIES:** Children welcome Garden: Patio, food served outdoors Dogs allowed **NOTES:** Parking 15
ROOMS: 7 bedrooms 7 en suite from s£43 d£50

WITNEY
Map 06 SP31

The Bell 🍴 ♈
Standlake Rd, Ducklington OX8 7UP
☎ 01993 702514 📠 01993 706822
Dir: One mile south of Witney in Ducklington village off A415 Abingdon road.
This popular village local was completed in 1315 as a hostel for builders of the adjacent church. Much extended over the years, the pub was upgraded in 1995 and now includes the former William Shepheards brewery, which closed in 1886.

continued

continued

Many original features - and a collection of some 500 bells - add to the pub's strongly traditional character. The freshly prepared menu includes various meat pies, pasta, Thai curry, and fresh fish dishes as available.
OPEN: 12-3 5-11 **BAR MEALS:** Lunch served: all week 12-2 Dinner served: Mon-Sat 6-9 Av main course £8.50 **RESTAURANT:** Lunch served: all week 12-2 Dinner served: Mon-Sat 6-9 Av 3 course à la carte £17 **PRINCIPAL BEERS:** Greene King Ruddles Best, IPA & Old Speckled Hen. **FACILITIES:** Children welcome Garden: Food served outdoors, patio **NOTES:** Parking 12 **ROOMS:** 7 bedrooms 7 en suite from s£35 d£55

WOODSTOCK — Map 06 SP41

Pick of the Pubs

Kings Head Inn ◆◆◆◆ ◎ ⌂ ♀
Chapel Hill, Wootton OX20 1DX ☎ 01993 811340
e-mail: t.fay@kings-head.co.uk
Dir: On A44 2m N of Woodstock then R to Wootton. Inn near church on Chapel Hill

A traditional country inn with a warm atmosphere, built in the 17th century of mellow Cotswold stone, and later sensitively modernised. In the beamed bar, a civilised mix of wooden tables, old settles and soft seating help to create a relaxed, informal mood. Seasonal variety comes with winter log fires and summer meals in the peaceful garden. Comfortable bedrooms offer well-equipped accommodation for those who decide to stay over and explore the Cotswolds and Oxfordshire. Imaginative meals are served in both the non-smoking restaurant and the bar, based on modern British ideas with some Mediterranean and New World influences. Starters like toasted goats' cheese, warm duck salad, and seared pigeon breast might be followed by wild mushroom risotto, roast rack of lamb, chargrilled pork fillet medallions, and steamed breast of chicken.
OPEN: 11-2 6.30-11 Closed: Dec 25 **BAR MEALS:** Lunch served: all week 12-2 Dinner served: Mon-Sat 7-9 Av main course £10.95 **RESTAURANT:** Lunch served: all week 12-2 Dinner served: Mon-Sat 7-9 Av 3 course à la carte £21 **BREWERY/COMPANY:** Free House **PRINCIPAL BEERS:** Wadworth 6X, Greene King Triumph. **FACILITIES:** Garden: Beer garden, food served outdoors Dogs allowed (ex guide dogs) **NOTES:** Parking 8 **ROOMS:** 3 bedrooms 3 en suite from s£60 d£75

WOOLSTONE — Map 04 SU28

The White Horse ◆◆◆◆ ♀
SN7 7QL ☎ 01367 820726 📠 01367 820566
e-mail: whorseuffington@aol.com
Attractive beamed and thatched 16th-century village inn, just five minutes' walk from the Uffington White Horse and Ancient Monument. Bar food includes salads, ploughman's lunches and freshly cooked cod and chips. In the restaurant expect calves' liver, rack of lamb, steaks, and baked swordfish.
OPEN: 11-3 6-11 (Sun 12-3 7-10.30) **BAR MEALS:** Lunch served: all week Dinner served: all week 11-3 6-11 **RESTAURANT:** 12-3 7-10 **BREWERY/COMPANY:** Free House **PRINCIPAL BEERS:** Arkells, Fuller's, Hook Norton Best, Wadworth. **FACILITIES:** Children welcome Garden: **NOTES:** Parking 80 **ROOMS:** 6 bedrooms 6 en suite

WOOTTON — Map 06 SP41

The Killingworth Castle Inn
Glympton Rd OX20 1EJ ☎ 01993 811401 📠 01993 811401
e-mail: wiggiscastle@aol.com
Dir: Exit A34 onto B4027, cross over A4260, pub on N edge of Wootton

Built in 1637 as a coaching inn on the former Worcester to London 'highway', its tradition lives on in the conversion of former stables into up-to-date bedroom accommodation. At the popular end, bar food strays little from beef and ale pie and Toad-in-the-hole backed up by burgers, baguettes and baked potatoes. A dining menu more adventurously adds tortellini al pesto, chicken Dijonaise and Thai green curry with spinach. Classic pub games and folk evenings.
OPEN: 12-2.30 6.30-11 (Sun 12-3, 7-10.30) **BAR MEALS:** All week 12-2 7-9 Av main course £8. **BREWERY/COMPANY:** Greene King **PRINCIPAL BEERS:** Greene King Morland Original, Ruddles Best, IPA **FACILITIES:** Family room Garden: Food served outside Dogs welcome **NOTES:** Parking 80 **ROOMS:** 4 bedroom 4 en suite from £55

WYTHAM — Map 06 SP40

White Hart
OX2 8QA ☎ 01865 244372
Dir: Just off A34 NW of Oxford
In the pretty, thatched village of Wytham (owned by Oxford University), this attractive, creeper-covered gastro-pub has flagstone floors, open fires and an Italian/modern English menu. It has frequently been used in the television series *Inspector Morse*.
OPEN: 11.30-2.30 6-11 (Summer-Sat 11.30-11, Sun 12-10.30) **BAR MEALS:** All week 12-2 7-9 Av main course £8. **BREWERY/COMPANY:** Allied Domecq **PRINCIPAL BEERS:** Tetley, Adnams **FACILITIES:** Children welcome Garden: Walled **NOTES:** Parking 80

Water and Steam
Many attractive pubs today stand on the banks of rivers and canals. The riverside ones reflect the fact that for centuries the quickest, safest and cheapest way to move people and goods about was by river, not by road. The 18th century saw the construction of artificial rivers, the canals, and hostelries quickly sprang up for boatmen and travellers on them too. Again, when the railways spread across the country from the 1840s om, pubs near stations proudly called themselves the Railway or the Railway Arms to cater for the new system.

England

RUTLAND

BARROWDEN
Map 06 SK90

Exeter Arms ♀
LE15 8EQ ☎ 01572 747247
e-mail: info@exeterarms.com
Once a smithy, then the village dairy, the Exeter Arms was also a coaching inn before it became the village pub. Nestling in the picturesque Welland Valley overlooking the village green and duck pond, this 17th-century inn now offers cosy, character bars where the home-brewed family of Boys beers is served. Tours of the brewery, housed in a nearby stone barn, can be arranged by appointment. A good reputation has been built up locally around the food, which is all cooked to order and shown on a daily-changing menu. Specialities include fish and game when seasonally available, and a choice of traditional roast dishes on Sundays. Nearby is the Cecil family seat of Burghley House at Stamford, whose heraldry appears on the inn sign. Ideally placed for walking in Rockingham Forest, and visiting Rutland Water, England's largest man-made lake.
OPEN: 12-2 6-11 (Sun & BHs 7-10.30) **BAR MEALS:** Lunch served: Tue-Sun 12-2 Dinner served: Tue-Sat 7-9 Av main course £8.50 **RESTAURANT:** Lunch served: all week Dinner served: all week 12-2 7-9 Av 3 course à la carte £15 **PRINCIPAL BEERS:** Own Beers. **FACILITIES:** Garden: Food served outside Dogs allowed (water) **NOTES:** Parking 15 **ROOMS:** 3 bedrooms 3 en suite from s£30 d£55

CLIPSHAM
Map 09 SK91

Pick of the Pubs

The Olive Branch 🏠 ◎◎
Main St LE15 7SH ☎ 01780 410355 📠 01780 410000
e-mail: olive@work.gb.com
Dir: *2 miles off A1 at Ram Jam Inn junction, 10 miles north of Stamford*

A traditional village pub, well worth seeking out, run by three local entrepreneurs who, with locals, friends and family, rescued it from closure in 1999, since when it has gone from strength to strength - this year gaining an AA 2-rosette award for its food. An attractive front garden and terrace, and an interior full of locally made furniture and artists' works - all for sale - help to engender a spirit that complements the reputation for fine food. Add open log fires, mulled wine and chestnuts in winter, and barbecues, Morris dancing and garden skittles in summer, and you have something special. Local produce governs the menus: honey roast parsnip soup, duck fillet brochette with couscous and yoghurt dressing, roast fillet of turbot

with olive mash, baby leeks and white wine sauce, apple and cinnamon crumble. Hot sandwiches include tuna, red pepper and rocket melt. A wide choice of wines by the glass and real ales from Oakham's Grainstore brewery.
OPEN: 12-3.30 (Sun 12-6 only) 6-11 Closed: 26 Dec 1 Jan
BAR MEALS: Lunch served: all week 12-2 Dinner served: Mon-Sat 7-9.30 Av main course £10.50 **RESTAURANT:** Lunch served: all week 12-2 Dinner served: Mon-Sat 7-9.30 Av 3 course à la carte £19.50 Av 3 course fixed price £10.50
BREWERY/COMPANY: Free House
PRINCIPAL BEERS: Grainstore 1050 & Olive Oil, Fenland, Brewster's. **FACILITIES:** Children welcome Garden: Food served outside. Patio area Dogs allowed **NOTES:** Parking 15

COTTESMORE
Map 09 SK91

The Sun Inn 🏠
25 Main St LE15 7DH ☎ 01572 812321

Dating back to 1647, this whitewashed pub has recently been re-thatched in its original style. Stone and quarry tiled floors, oak beams and a cosy fire in the bar add to the charm. Handy for visiting Rutland Water and historic Oakham. Expect traditional fish and chips, steak and venison pie, half a roast duck in an orange liqueur sauce and home-made fish cakes among many popular dishes on the varied menu.
OPEN: 11-2.30 6-11 **BAR MEALS:** Lunch served: Tue-Sun 12-2 Dinner served: Tue-Sat 7-9 Av main course £6.95
RESTAURANT: Lunch served: Tue-Sun 12-2 Dinner served: Tue-Sat 7-9 Av 3 course à la carte £15 **BREWERY/COMPANY:** Everards Brewery **PRINCIPAL BEERS:** Adnams Bitter, Everards Tiger, Marston's Pedigree, Scottish Courage Courage Directors.
FACILITIES: Garden: Food served outdoors Dogs allowed
NOTES: Parking 15

EMPINGHAM
Map 06 SK90

White Horse Inn 🏠 ♀
Main St LE15 8PS ☎ 01780 460221 📠 01780 460521
Dir: *From A1 take A606 signed Rutland Water*
Set in a lovely village, this stone-built 17th-century former farmhouse is just a long cast from Rutland Water, whose wild trout regularly feature on the extensive menu. Among the dishes may be Lincolnshire sausages with onion and mushroom gravy, sea bream with fresh herb butter, seafood pancakes or char-grilled steaks with optional peppered sauce - followed by sweets such as prune and port fool 'home-made by Auntie June'. Some of the bedrooms are in a converted stable block across the courtyard beside a conference centre.
OPEN: 8-11 **BAR MEALS:** Lunch served: all week Dinner served: all week 12-2.15 7-9.45 Av main course £8.50 **RESTAURANT:** Lunch

continued

continued

served: all week Dinner served: all week 12–2.15 7.15–10 Av 3 course à la carte £18 **PRINCIPAL BEERS:** Scottish Courage Courage Directors & John Smith's, Greene King Old Speckled Hen & Ruddles County, Marston's Pedigree. **FACILITIES:** Children welcome Children's licence Garden: Beer garden, food served outdoors, patio **NOTES:** Parking 60 **ROOMS:** 13 bedrooms 13 en suite from s£50 d£65

EXTON   Map 09 SK91

Fox & Hounds 🍽️
LE15 8AP ☎ 01572 812403
Fine old coaching inn close to Rutland Water and Viking Way. Pretty lawns. Bedrooms.

LYDDINGTON   Map 06 SP89

Pick of the Pubs

Old White Hart ♀
51 Main St LE15 9LR ☎ 01572 821703 📠 01572 821965
e-mail: theoldwhitehart@hotmail.com
Honey-coloured 17th-century stone pub standing by the green in an attractive village high above the Welland Valley, close to good walks and Rutland Water. Interesting, freshly prepared food is served in the cosy main bar, with its heavy beams, dried flower arrangements, traditional furnishings and splendid log fire, and in the adjoining dining areas. Good blackboard specials may include warm salad of smoked bacon, black pudding and cherry tomatoes topped with grilled Slipcote cheese and balsamic dressing and grilled sardines with garlic toast for starters, followed by deep-fried Grimsby haddock, whole Dover sole, herb-crusted cod with pesto dressing, wild mushroom and asparagus risotto, home-made Gloucester Old Spot sausages, and confit neck of lamb on mash. Ambitious evening carte. Good selection of real ales and wines by the glass. Flower-filled rear garden with 10 pétanque pitches.
OPEN: 12–3 6.30–11 Closed: 25 Dec **BAR MEALS:** Lunch served: all week Dinner served: all week 12–2 6.30–9 Av main course £10 **RESTAURANT:** Lunch served: all week Dinner served: all week 12–2 6.30–9 Av 3 course à la carte £17 Av 3 course fixed price £12.95 **BREWERY/COMPANY:** Free House **PRINCIPAL BEERS:** Greene King IPA & Abbot Ale, Timothy Taylor Landlord. **FACILITIES:** Garden: Beer garden, patio, outside eating **NOTES:** Parking 25 **ROOMS:** 5 bedrooms 5 en suite from s£45 d£65

MARKET OVERTON   Map 08 SK81

Black Bull 🍽️
2 Teigh Rd LE15 7PW ☎ 01572 767677 📠 01572 767291
Since the 15th century this thatched and beamed pub has stood opposite the stocks on the green of a picture postcard village. The long-serving chef's daily specials are strong on fresh fish dishes such as seafood casserole and zander fillet with salmon, prawns and mashed potato. Lunchtime offers whitebait with lemon mayonnaise, pan-fried liver in rich gravy and home-cooked ham and eggs. More elaborate evening dishes might include oriental duck pancakes, 'Boozi Beef' in brandy, port and cream sauce and an eye-catching tray of home-made desserts.
OPEN: 11.30–2.30 6–11 (Sun 12–2.30, 7–10.30)
BAR MEALS: Lunch served: all week Dinner served: all week 12–1.45

6.30–9.45 Av main course £10.50 **RESTAURANT:** Lunch served: all week Dinner served: all week 12–1.45 6.30–9.45
BREWERY/COMPANY: Free House **PRINCIPAL BEERS:** Hook Norton, Theakston Black Bull, Greene King IPA, Charles Wells Bombardier. **FACILITIES:** Dogs allowed (water) **NOTES:** Parking 20 **ROOMS:** 2 bedrooms 2 en suite from s£30 d£45

OAKHAM   Map 06 SK80

Barnsdale Lodge Hotel ★ ★ ★ ◉ 🍽️ ♀
The Avenue, Rutland Water, North Shore LE15 8AH
☎ 01572 724678 📠 01572 724961
e-mail: barnsdale.lodge@btconnect.com
A distinctive Edwardian-style hotel overlooking Rutland Water in the heart of this picturesque little county. Its rural connections go back to its origins as a 17th-century farmhouse, but nowadays the Barnsdale Lodge offers modern comforts and hospitality. Real ales including local brews are served in the bar, with dishes such as saffron and poppyseed linguini, and Barnsdale cheese fondue. There is also a gourmet menu, and well-decorated and furnished overnight accommodation.
OPEN: 7–11 **BAR MEALS:** Lunch served: all week Dinner served: all week 12.15–2.15 7–9.45 Av main course £8.95
RESTAURANT: Lunch served: all week Dinner served: all week 12.15–2.15 7–9.45 Av 3 course à la carte £30
BREWERY/COMPANY: Free House **PRINCIPAL BEERS:** Rutland Grainstore, Marstons Pedigree, Scottish Courage Courage Directors, Theakston Best Bitter. **FACILITIES:** Children welcome Garden: Food served outdoors, patio, BBQ Dogs allowed (water) **NOTES:** Parking 280 **ROOMS:** 45 bedrooms 45 en suite from s£65 d£89

The Blue Ball
6 Cedar St, Braunston-in-Rutland LE15 8QS ☎ 01572 722135
Dir: From A1 take A606 to Oakham.Village SW of Oakham
Thatched and beamed village inn, formerly called The Globe, dating from the 1600s, and reputedly Rutland's oldest pub. A warm and friendly welcome and traditional pub food awaits from new licensees.

Pick of the Pubs

The Finch's Arms ♀
Oakham Rd, Hambleton LE15 8TL
☎ 01572 756575 📠 01572 771142
See Pick of the Pubs on page 387

The Grainstore Brewery
Station Approach LE15 6RE ☎ 01572 770065 📠 01572 770068
e-mail: grainstorebry@aol.com
Founded in 1995, Davis's Brewing Company is housed in the three-storey Victorian grain store next to Oakham railway station. Finest quality ingredients and hops are used to make the beers that can be sampled in the pub's Tap Room. Filled baguettes and Stilton and pork pie ploughman's are of secondary importance, but very tasty all the same. Go for the brewery tours and blind tastings; rustic wooden floors and furniture that attract walkers by the score.
OPEN: 11–3 5–11 **BAR MEALS:** Lunch served: all week 11–3
BREWERY/COMPANY: Free House
PRINCIPAL BEERS: Grainstore Cooking Bitter, Triple B, Ten Fifty, Steaming Billy Bitter. **FACILITIES:** Dogs allowed (water, biscuit) **NOTES:** Parking 8 No credit cards

continued

OAKHAM continued

Pick of the Pubs

The Old Plough 🐾 ♀
2 Church St, Braunston LE15 8QY
☎ 01572 722714 📠 01572 770382
e-mail: oldplough@rutnet.co.uk

An old coaching inn that has kept its traditional identity despite being tastefully modernised. This genteel and very popular country pub dates back to 1783, and its village location makes it handy for visiting the lovely Georgian town of Oakham, as well as touring the rest of the old county of Rutland. Owners Claire and David host lots of speciality evenings and various weekend entertainments, and their enthusiasm for good food extends to candle-lit dinners in the picturesque conservatory, as well as light lunches on the terrace. Expect favourites like liver, bacon and onions, and Cajun chicken, as well as steak and kidney pudding, Braunston chicken stuffed with creamy cheese, trio of sausages with mustard mash and Calvados sauce, mushroom Stroganoff, salmon en croûte, and beer-battered cod fillet. Regular guest ales are always available.

OPEN: 11–3 6–11 (Sat 11–11, Sun 12–10.30)
BAR MEALS: Lunch served: all week Dinner served: all week 12–2 6–10 Av main course £6 **RESTAURANT:** Lunch served: all week Dinner served: all week 12–2.30 6–10 Av 3 course à la carte £16 **BREWERY/COMPANY:** Free House
PRINCIPAL BEERS: Boddingtons, Bass Cask.
FACILITIES: Children welcome Garden: Food served outside, garden terrace Dogs allowed (Not overnight in bedrooms)
NOTES: Parking 30 **ROOMS:** 1 bedrooms 1 en suite from s£39.95 d£49.95

STRETTON　　　　　　　Map 09 SK91

Pick of the Pubs

Ram Jam Inn ★ ★ ⊛ 🐾
The Great North Rd LE15 7QX
☎ 01780 410776 📠 01780 410361
e-mail: rji@rutnet.co.uk
Dir: On A1 northbound carriageway past B1668 turn off, through service station into hotel car park

On a lonely stretch of the A1 (northbound) between Stamford and Grantham, this family-run inn is somewhat of a legend. Once the Winchelsea Arms, its long-standing name change derived from an 18th-century landlord whose roadside sign advertised 'Fine Ram Jam'. What it was no one knows now – but the moniker remains. Today, its informal yet stylish café-bar and bistro exudes warmth, while bright, spacious bedrooms with up-to-date en suite bathrooms make this a tempting overnight stop. Wide-ranging all-day menus offer virtually anything from hot and cold sandwiches to clotted cream teas and more elaborate three-course meals. Everything is home-made, from bread to the tempting desserts that grace the comprehensive menus. Try a toasted ciabatta with roast peppers and melted Brie or rich rabbit stew in red wine while the children delight in Ram Jam ices. Despite its somewhat rustic

presentation, the quality of produce is consistently high – as in the smoked halibut rarebit appetiser and wild boar sausages with mash and Cumberland sauce. Irresistible!
OPEN: 7am–11pm Closed: 25 Dec **BAR MEALS:** Lunch served: all week Dinner served: all week 12–9.30 Av main course £6.95 **RESTAURANT:** Lunch served: all week Dinner served: all week 12–9.30 Av 3 course à la carte £16.50
BREWERY/COMPANY: Free House
PRINCIPAL BEERS: Fuller's London Pride, Scottish Courage John Smith's. **FACILITIES:** Children welcome Garden: beer garden, patio, food served outdoors Dogs allowed
NOTES: Parking 64 **ROOMS:** 7 bedrooms 7 en suite from s£47 d£57

WHITWELL　　　　　　Map 06 SK90

Noel Arms Inn
Main St LE15 8BW ☎ 01780 460334 📠 01780 460531
Dir: From A1 take A606 to Oakham

Country pub near Rutland Water with a cosy lounge in the original thatched building and a more modern bar. Dishes range from bangers and mash at lunchtime, to roast monkfish with sauté potatoes, spinach and braised leek, and rack of English lamb with Mediterranean vegetables and rosemary and lentil jus.
OPEN: 11–11 (Breakfast 7.30–9.30) **BAR MEALS:** Lunch served: all week Dinner served: all week 12–9.30 Av main course £7.95 **RESTAURANT:** Lunch served: all week Dinner served: all week 12–9.30 Av 3 course à la carte £18 **BREWERY/COMPANY:** Free House **PRINCIPAL BEERS:** Marstons Pedigree, Adnams Broadside, Flowers Original. **FACILITIES:** Children welcome Garden: BBQ Dogs allowed **NOTES:** Parking 60 **ROOMS:** 10 bedrooms 10 en suite from s£30 d£49.50

WING　　　　　　　　Map 06 SK80

The Cuckoo Inn
3 Top St LE15 8SE ☎ 01572 737340
Dir: A6003 from Oakham, turn R then L

Four miles from Rutland Water, a part-thatched 17th-century coaching inn noted for unusual guest ales from micro-breweries: the pub has a rose garden and barbecue. Home-cooked food is notably good value: steak and kidney pie; lamb casserole – supplemented by some authentic Indian dishes such as chicken Madras and lamb rogan josh.
OPEN: 11.30–3 (Sun 12–4, 7–10.30) 6.30–11 (closed Tue lunch)
BAR MEALS: Lunch served: Wed–Mon Dinner served: Wed–Mon 11.30–2.30 7–10 Av main course £6 **BREWERY/COMPANY:** Free House **PRINCIPAL BEERS:** Marston's Pedigree.
FACILITIES: Children welcome Garden: BBQ, outdoor eating, floral display Dogs allowed **NOTES:** Parking 20 No credit cards

Pick of the Pubs

Kings Arms ♦♦♦♦ ♀
Top St LE15 8SE ☎ 01572 737634 📠 01572 737255
e-mail: enquiries@thekingsarms-wing.co.uk
See Pick of the Pubs on page 388

continued

OPEN: 10.30–3 6–11.30
BAR MEALS: L served all week.
D served all week. 12–2.30 7–9.30
RESTAURANT: L served all week.
D served all week. 12–2.30 7–9.30
Av cost 3 course £17
BREWERY/COMPANY:
FREE HOUSE
PRINCIPAL BEERS: Greene King
Abbot Ale, Theakston Best Bitter,
Timothy Taylor Landlord
FACILITIES: Children welcome.
Garden: Overlooking lake
NOTES: Parking 40
ROOMS: 6 en suite

The Finch's Arms

♀
Oakham Road Hambleton LE15 8TL
☎ 01572 756575 📄 01572 771142

Well- run by experienced publicans Colin and Celia Crawford this stone-built 17th-century inn, set in a sleepy village on a narrow strip of land jutting into Rutland Water, offers interesting Mediterranean-style food in a relaxed atmosphere.

Once the pub would have looked out over a valley and the little village of Lower Hambleton, but these days the pub has stunning views over Rutland Water. Lower Hambleton has disappeared beneath its waters, but luckily for us Upper Hambleton and the Finch's Arms escaped this fate. During the time they have been here, the Crawfords have tastefully refurbished the pub developing a stylish restaurant, with cane furnishings and open fires, and the neat summer terrace. From both locations diners can enjoy stunning views across Rutland Water while tucking into such dishes as bouillabaise, confit of pork chump on Puy lentils, Savoy cabbage and fondant potato, pan-seared gurnard with basil broth or smoked salmon lasagne. The menu changes constantly and range from some imaginative snack dishes to more serious dishes. Starters might include chicken liver parfait with red onion marmalade, crab soufflé and warm Stilton brûlée with wild mushroom compote. The comfortable bar area has warm yellow rag-washed walls, stripped pine, wooden floors and open fires. Here you will find a selection of well-kept cask ales, well-chosen wines and decent coffee. Comfortable accommodation is supplied in six individually furnished en suite bedrooms.

OPEN: 12–3 6–11 (Fri–Sun 12–12)
BAR MEALS: L served Tue–Sun 12–2. D served all week. 6.30–9.30 Av main course £8
RESTAURANT: L served Tue–Sun 12–2. D served all week. 6.30–9.30 Av cost 3 courses £15
BREWERY/COMPANY: FREE HOUSE
PRINCIPLE BEERS: Grainstore, Oakham Ales
FACILITIES: Children Welcome Garden: Patio, beer garden, food served outdoors
NOTES: Parking 25
ROOMS: 8 en suite Double room from £55 Single room from £45

Kings Arms

◆◆◆◆ ♀🐖

Top Street LE15 8SE
☎ 01572 737634 🖨 01572 737255
e-mail:
enquiries@thekingsarms-wing.co.uk
Dir: 1m off A6003 between Uppingham & Oakham.

Comfortable accommodation and good food make this family-run inn a fine base for exploring England's smallest county. Built from local stone in 1649 and roofed with slate from nearby Collyweston, the Kings Arms stands in a quaint village just two miles from Rutland Water.

The bar offers frequently changing guest ales with nearby Oakham's Grainstore brewery well represented. With its flagstone floors, low beams and winter fires, the Kings Bar is the oldest part of the building. Here, large chalkboards list the daily specials, with particular emphasis on steaks and varieties of fish. The snack menu might include a three-cheese ploughman's board; fresh spaghetti with a cream, chive and smoked salmon sauce; or a trio of local sausages with garlic mash and red wine jus. In summer the large garden comes into its own, with scattered tables and chairs as well as a children's play area. The garden also makes an ideal venue for weddings and private parties, held in a marquee on the lawn. Back indoors, each of the marble-topped tables in the lively, informal restaurant has its own candle lamp. Chef Simon Richards is renowned for creating mouthwatering meals from fresh ingredients. Starters of salmon tortellini on mixed leaves with basil dressing, or warm fresh asparagus with pesto oil precede daily alternatives. These might include modern British dishes such as pan-fried monkfish with vegetable couscous timbale and roasted pepper coulis, or roast lamb noisette with summer black truffle risotto and a rosemary and tomato jus or the more traditional rib-eye steak with tomato, onion rings, mushrooms and chips. Half of the cottage-style en suite bedrooms are built in the old village bakery, and the largest room includes a suite that features the original bread ovens.

SHROPSHIRE

ALBRIGHTON
Map 08 SJ41

The Horns of Boningale
WV7 3DA ☎ 01902 372347 📠 01902 372970
e-mail: horns@boningale.freeserve.co.uk
Dir: *From Wolverton, follow the A41 to Oaken, turn L at traffic lights onto the Holyhead Road towards Shifnal. The Horns is on the L, 2miles from Oaken.*
This 300 year-old free house was formerly popular as a 'ham and eggery' with Shropshire cattlemen, and the dish is still available. Now completely refurbished as a civilised dining pub, the main bar is divided into three cosy rooms. There's also a large formal restaurant, leading out to landscaped gardens and an ornamental fishpond. Expect, steak and ale pie, Thai curry, savoury bean tartlet, and halibut mornay.
OPEN: 12-3 5.30-12 **BAR MEALS:** Lunch served: all week 12-2 Dinner served: Mon-Sat 6-9.30 Av main course £7
RESTAURANT: Lunch served: all week 12-2 Dinner served: Mon-Sat 6-9.30 Av 3 course à la carte £15 Av 3 course fixed price £6.50
PRINCIPAL BEERS: Hook Norton Old Hooky, Bass Bitter, Enville Ale, Worthington. **FACILITIES:** Children welcome Garden: Food served outside Dogs allowed **NOTES:** Parking 50

BISHOP'S CASTLE
Map 08 SO38

Boars Head ♦♦♦ 🍴 ♀
Church St SY9 5AE ☎ 01588 638521 📠 01588 630126
e-mail: sales@boarsheadhotel.co.uk
Granted its first licence in 1642, this old coaching inn was once the centre of one of England's most Rotten Boroughs; its former stable block - known as 'The Curly Tail' - now accommodating overnighters in considerable comfort. Inside, look for the recently uncovered priest hole in one of the chimneys and settle in the popular beamed bar, a focus of village life, where food, accurately described as traditional, takes in trout with almonds and steaks in various guises.
OPEN: 11.30-2.30 6.30-11 **BAR MEALS:** Lunch served: all week Dinner served: all week 12-2 6.30-9.30 Av main course £6.50
RESTAURANT: Lunch served: all week Dinner served: all week 12-2 6.30-9.30 Av 3 course à la carte £12.50
BREWERY/COMPANY: Free House **PRINCIPAL BEERS:** Scottish Courage Courage Best & Courage Directors, Theakstons Best.
FACILITIES: Children welcome Children's licence Dogs allowed Bedrooms only **NOTES:** Parking 20 **ROOMS:** 4 bedrooms 4 en suite from s£35 d£55

The Castle Hotel
The Square SY9 5BN ☎ 01588 638403 📠 01588 638403
Built on the site of the old castle keep, this 18th-century coaching inn retains its character and includes open fires, a fine example of a Georgian staircase and a garden with lovely views over the town and valley beyond. Strong emphasis on freshly prepared food, a good selection of sweets and a wide choice of malt whiskies.
OPEN: 12-2.30 6.30-11 **BAR MEALS:** Lunch served: all week Dinner served: all week 12-1.30 6.30-9 Av main course £7.95
BREWERY/COMPANY: Free House
PRINCIPAL BEERS: Hobson's, Bass, Black Sheep.
FACILITIES: Children welcome Garden: Beer garden, patio Dogs allowed **NOTES:** Parking 30 **ROOMS:** 5 bedrooms 5 en suite from s£37.50 d£65

The Three Tuns Inn ♀
Salop St SY9 5BW ☎ 01588 638797 📠 01588 638081
e-mail: info@thethreetunsinn.co.uk
Dir: *22m SW of Shrewsbury*

Late 16th-century timbered-framed pub in the centre of the village serving tip-top ales brewed across the courtyard, and home-cooked food prepared from fresh local produce. Expect rich fish soup, beef in Three Tuns ale, seafood pancakes, goats' cheese with red onion marmalade, game pie and decent sandwiches. Added attractions include a small brewing museum and en suite bedrooms in the converted stables.
OPEN: 12-11 (Sun 12-10.30) **BAR MEALS:** Lunch served: all week Dinner served: all week 12-2.30 7-9.30 Av main course £8
BREWERY/COMPANY: Free House **PRINCIPAL BEERS:** Tuns Offa's Ale, & Tuns XXX. **FACILITIES:** Children welcome Garden: Beer garden, patio, outdoor eating Dogs allowed **NOTES:** Parking 6 **ROOMS:** 4 bedrooms 4 en suite from s£35 d£65

BRIDGNORTH
Map 08 SO79

The Bear ♀
Northgate WV16 4ET ☎ 01746 763250
Dir: *From High Street (Bridgnorth) go through Northgate (sandstone archway) and the pub is on the L*

Traditional Grade II listed hostelry in one of the loveliest of the Severn-side towns. The way it clings to the top of a high sandstone cliff gives it an almost continental flavour. A former coaching inn, the award-winning Bear boasts two carpeted bars which are characterised by whisky-water jugs, gas-type wall lamps and wheelback chairs. Good quality, appetising menu offers the likes of ham, egg and chips, braised lamb shank, wild mushroom and spinach risotto, and salmon and herb fishcakes. Daily-changing real ales and a choice of seven malts.
OPEN: 11-3 5-11 (Sun 7-10.30) **BAR MEALS:** Lunch served: all week 12-2 Av main course £5.50 **BREWERY/COMPANY:** Free House **PRINCIPAL BEERS:** Changing guest ales.
FACILITIES: Garden: Food served outside **NOTES:** Parking 18 **ROOMS:** 3 bedrooms 3 en suite from s£35 d£52 No credit cards

BRIDGNORTH continued

The Lion O'Morfe 🛏 ♀
Upper Farmcote WV15 5PS ☎ 01746 710678 📠 01746 710678
Dir: Off A458(Bridgnorth/Stourbridge) 2.5m from Bridgnorth follow signs for Claverley on L,0.5m up hill on L

Friendly pub dating from the early 1850s when the owner took advantage of the Duke of Wellington's Beer House Act of 1830, and paid two guineas to Excise for change of use from a Georgian farmhouse to an inn. The name 'Morfe' is derived from the Welsh for 'marsh'. A sample evening menu offers traditional pub food dishes such as steak and kidney pie, battercrisp cod, chicken curry, tuna salad, or gammon steak.
OPEN: 12–2.30 7–11 Spring & Summer 6–11 **BAR MEALS:** Lunch served: all week 12–2 Dinner served: Mon–Sat 7–10
RESTAURANT: Lunch served: all week 12–2 Dinner served: Mon–Sat 7–10 Av 3 course à la carte £10 **BREWERY/COMPANY:** Free House
PRINCIPAL BEERS: Banks, Bass, Woods, Wye Valley.
FACILITIES: Children welcome Garden: Food served outside. Orchard & play area Dogs allowed (water provided)
NOTES: Parking 40

BURLTON 10/7/05 Map 08 SJ42

Pick of the Pubs

The Burlton Inn 🛏
SY4 5TB ☎ 01939 270284 📠 01939 270204
e-mail: bean@burltoninn.co.uk
Dir: 8M N of Shrewsbury on A528 towards Ellesmere

This classy 18th-century inn, close to the old London to Holyhead coaching route, promises a quiet pint in neat, well furnished cottagey rooms, free of music and amusement machines. The best available market produce is used to create dishes listed on daily specials boards, and a typical month's menu lists rosemary-skewered monkfish with pancetta and ciabatta, pan-cooked pork steak with creamed cabbage and cider gravy. or venison casserole with red wine, port and juniper berries. There are vegetarian options like leek and Gruyère filo bundles and grilled Halloumi. Sandwiches might include hot open ciabattas of minute steak with fried red onion and sliced chicken breast with curried mayonnaise or fresh baguettes with roast ham and home-made chutney, tuna and spring onion or soft Brie with grapes. Six adjacent en suite bedrooms in a converted outbuilding.
OPEN: 11–3 6–11 (Sun 12–3 7–10.30) Closed: Dec 25–26 Jan 1
BAR MEALS: Lunch served: all week Dinner served: all week 12–2 6.30–9.45 Av main course £9.50 **RESTAURANT:** Lunch served: all week Dinner served: all week 12–2 6.30–9.45 Av 3

course à la carte £18.50 **BREWERY/COMPANY:** Free House
PRINCIPAL BEERS: Banks, Greene King Abbot Ale, Wye Valley Bitter. **FACILITIES:** Garden: Food served outdoors
NOTES: Parking 40 **ROOMS:** 6 bedrooms 6 en suite from s£45 d£70

CHURCH STRETTON Map 08 SO49

The Royal Oak 🛏
Cardington SY6 7JZ ☎ 01694 771266
Reputedly the oldest pub in Shropshire, dating from 1462, this Grade II listed pub is all atmosphere and character. Nestling in the out-of-the-way village of Cardington, the pub, with its low beams, massive walls and striking inglenook, is a great place to seek out on cold winter days. In the summer it is equally delightful with its peaceful garden and patio. New proprietors have made great strides with the introduction of packed lunches on request and a free walkers' guide to the area.
OPEN: 12–3 7–11 (Sun 12–3, 7–10.30) **BAR MEALS:** Lunch served: Tue–Sun Dinner served: Tue–Sun 12–2 7.30–9 Av main course £4.75
RESTAURANT: Lunch served: Tue–Sun Dinner served: Tue–Sun 12–2 7.30–9 Av 3 course à la carte £15 **BREWERY/COMPANY:** Free House **PRINCIPAL BEERS:** Hobsons Best Bitter, Wood Shropshire Lad, Interbrew Bass,. **FACILITIES:** Children welcome Children's licence Garden: Patio, food served outdoors Dogs allowed
NOTES: Parking 40

CLEOBURY MORTIMER Map 08 SO67

Pick of the Pubs

The Crown at Hopton ♦♦♦♦ ◉
Hopton Wafers DY14 0NB ☎ 01299 270372 📠 01299 271127
Dir: On A4117 8m west of Ludlow, 2m east of Cleobury Mortimer
Located in a sleepy hollow, this former coaching inn is surrounded by immaculate gardens and has its own duck pond. The 16th-century free house was once owned by a nearby estate, and the informal Rent Room bar recalls the days when rents were collected here from the local tenants. The inn, which has been lovingly restored to a high standard, boasts two inglenook fireplaces, exposed timbers and an elegant dining room. Bedrooms are individually furnished to maximum guest comfort and, in addition to occasional period furniture, all offer en suite facilities. Altogether a perfect base for exploring this magnificent area. The chef, Barry Price, creates imaginative dishes using fresh seasonal ingredients. Roast avocado with garlic and bacon, or grilled Feta cheese with prosciutto might precede beef Wellington, loin of lamb, chicken en croûte, or roast monkfish wrapped in bacon. Leave room for the pastry chef's home-made desserts.
OPEN: 12–3 6–11 **BAR MEALS:** Lunch served: all week Dinner served: all week 12–2.30 6–9.30 Av main course £9.95
RESTAURANT: Lunch served: Sun 12–3 Dinner served: Tue–Sat 7–9.30 Av 3 course à la carte £21.95
BREWERY/COMPANY: Free House
PRINCIPAL BEERS: Marstons Pedigree, Timothy Taylor Landlord. **FACILITIES:** Children welcome Garden: Patio area, Food served outside **NOTES:** Parking 40
ROOMS: 7 bedrooms 7 en suite from s£44 d£70

continued

The Kings Arms Hotel 🛏 ♀
DY14 8BS ☎ 01299 270252 🖷 01299 271968
Dir: take A456 from Kidderminster the A4117 to Cleobury Mortimer

Simple victuals have given way to steak and kidney pie, and braised duck breast in Grand Marnier, and the home-brewed ales are nowadays from Youngs and Greene King as this 18th-century inn has moved with the times. The oak floors, exposed beams and fine inglenook fireplace remain a pleasant setting for popular choices of food that might also include fish pie, battered haddock, and various home-made pâtés.
OPEN: 11.30-11 (Sun 12-10.30) **BAR MEALS:** Lunch served: all week Dinner served: Mon-Wed, Fri-Sat 11.30-3.30 6.30-9 Av main course £6 **RESTAURANT:** Lunch served: all week Dinner served: Mon-Wed, Fri-Sat 12-3 7-9 **PRINCIPAL BEERS:** Hobsons Best, Youngs Special, Greene King Abbot Ale. **FACILITIES:** Children welcome Garden: Food served outside. Dogs allowed
NOTES: Parking 4 **ROOMS:** 5 bedrooms 5 en suite from s£25 d£45

CRAVEN ARMS   Map 08 SO48

The Plough ♀
Wistanstow SY7 8DG ☎ 01588 673251 🖷 01588 672419
e-mail: plough@bartender.net
Home of the Woods Brewery, this country pub is well worth the short diversion off the A49. Sample a pint of Woods Special, Shropshire Lad or Parish in the welcoming bar with its simple furnishings and roaring log fires. The seasonal menu offers the likes of pan-fried black pudding with home-made apple conserve, venison sausages in a Port gravy, beery beef casserole with herb dumplings and grilled goat's cheese salad.
OPEN: 11.30-2.30 6.30-11 **BAR MEALS:** Lunch served: all week 12-2 Dinner served: Tues-Sat 6.30-9 Av main course £7.50
PRINCIPAL BEERS: Wood Parish Special, Shropshire Lad, Timothy Taylor Landlord. **NOTES:** Parking 50

The Sun Inn 🛏 ♀
Corfton SY7 9DF ☎ 01584 861239 & 861503
e-mail: thesun@corfton.co.uk
Dir: on the B4368 7m N of Ludlow
In beautiful Corvedale, a friendly, family-owned pub that dates back to 1613. Numerous awards include those to its home-brewed cask beer that features at various summer beer festivals, and landlady Teresa Pearce's home-cooked meals. Typical dishes include hand-made sausages flavoured with the Sun's own real ale, leek and ham bake and haddock with prawns and pasta. Good facilities for families and the disabled.
OPEN: 12-2.30 6-11 **BAR MEALS:** Lunch served: all week Dinner served: all week 12-2 6-9.30 Av main course £6.50
RESTAURANT: Lunch served: all week Dinner served: all week 12-2

7-9.30 Av 3 course à la carte £10 **BREWERY/COMPANY:** Free House **PRINCIPAL BEERS:** Corvedale Normans Pride, Secret Hop, Dark & Delicious. **FACILITIES:** Children welcome Children's licence Garden: Food served outdoors, patio Dogs allowed (water)
NOTES: Parking 30

CRESSAGE   Map 08 SJ50

Pick of the Pubs

The Cholmondeley Riverside Inn ♦♦♦♦ ♀
Cound SY5 6AF ☎ 01952 510900 🖷 01952 510980
Dir: On A458 Shrewsbury-Bridgnorth rd
In three acres of garden alongside the River Severn, this extensively refurbished coaching inn offers river view dining both outdoors and in a modern conservatory. The single menu serves both dining areas and spacious bar, furnished and decorated in haphazard country style. Traditional pub dishes include hot crab pâté and mushrooms with Shropshire blue cheese, followed by local lamb noisettes with parsnip chips, and salmon fishcakes with hollandaise. Exotic alternatives follow the lines of Peking duck pancakes with hoisin sauce, 'Pee-kai' chicken breasts with satay sauce, and spinach, sorrel and Mozzarella parcels.
OPEN: 11-3 7-11 Closed: 25 Dec **BAR MEALS:** Lunch served: all week Dinner served: all week 12-2.30 7-10 Av main course £7.50 **RESTAURANT:** Lunch served: all week Dinner served: all week 12-2.30 7-10 Av 3 course à la carte £23
BREWERY/COMPANY: Free House
PRINCIPAL BEERS: Riverside Ale, guest beers.
FACILITIES: Children welcome Garden: beer garden, patio, outdoor eating Dogs allowed **NOTES:** Parking 100
ROOMS: 7 bedrooms 7 en suite from s£50 d£70

On the Inside

The earliest pubs were people's homes and were furnished and decorated accordingly. It was not until the 1820s that the bar-counter made its appearance, but already a distinction had grown up between the taproom for labourers and poorer customers, and the parlour began to sport carpets, pictures of the royal family and cases of butterflies or stuffed birds. The Victorian gin palaces introduced an altogether plushier style. The big brewing chains have intruded a fake and regimental note into pub decor, but many pubs still nostalgically display Toby jugs or horse-brasses, agricultural bygones, ornamental brass plates or gleaming copper pans. Some maintain their individuality with collections of oddities that have taken the landlord's fancy - police equipment or cigarette cards, neckties or man traps, or even fossilised hot cross buns.

continued

England

HAMPTON LOADE — Map 08 SO78

The Lion Inn ☜ ♀ NEW
WV15 6HD ☎ 01746 780263 ▤ 01746 780263
Dir: 5m S of Bridgnorth, 8m N of Kidderminster, 1m off the A442
The resident ghost is not the only person who can't stay away from the Lion. This ever popular pub has a long and fascinating history of hospitality. It started life as a 16th-century cider and perry mill but was later extended to provide beer, bed and female company to the bargees who passed back and forth on the River Severn. Today it can still be visited by boat, whilst those arriving by car could try out the last working chain ferry on the River Severn. Run by the same family since 1958, its charms include over 20 country wines and food lovingly prepared by the owner and his son. Try traditional style bar snacks or home-made main meals such as Jamaican chicken breast stuffed with banana, wrapped in bacon then cooked in curry sauce or venison pot roast with bacon shallot and mushroom in a rich birch wine sauce.
OPEN: 12-2.30 7-11 Closed: 25 Dec **BAR MEALS:** Lunch served: Tue-Sun Dinner served: Tue-Sun 12-2 7-9.30 Av main course £7
RESTAURANT: Lunch served: Tue-Sun 12-2 Dinner served: Tue-Sat 7-9 Av 3 course à la carte £15 Av 3 course fixed price £15
BREWERY/COMPANY: Free House **PRINCIPAL BEERS:** Hook Norton Old Hooky, Warfield Shropshire Pride, Enville White, Lion Inn Brewery Ferryman's Bitter. **FACILITIES:** Children welcome Food served outdoors Dogs allowed (water, dog chews) **NOTES:** Parking 118 No credit cards

HODNET — Map 08 SJ62

The Bear Hotel ★ ★ ☜
TF9 3NH ☎ 01630 685214 ▤ 01630 685787
e-mail: info@bearhotel.org.uk
Dir: Junction A53 & A442 on sharp corner in middle of small village
An illuminated cellar garden, once a priest hole, is one of the more unusual attractions at this 16th-century coaching inn. There was also a bear pit in the car park until 1970. Hodnet Hall Gardens are close by. Extensive menu includes bar snacks and restaurant meals. Look out for various steaks, fidget pie, Thai red chicken with vegetable stir fry, prawn curry, steak and ale pie, and baked salmon en croute.
OPEN: 10.30-11 (Sun 12-10.30) **BAR MEALS:** Lunch served: all week Dinner served: all week 12-2 6.30-9.30 Av main course £5.50
RESTAURANT: Lunch served: all week Dinner served: all week 12-2 6.30-9.30 Av 3 course à la carte £17 **BREWERY/COMPANY:** Free House **PRINCIPAL BEERS:** Theakston, John Smiths, Courage Directors. **FACILITIES:** Children welcome Garden: Food served outside. Lawns with shrubs Dogs allowed (in the garden only)
NOTES: Parking 70 **ROOMS:** 8 bedrooms 8 en suite from s£42.50 d£60

> Room prices show the minimum double and single rates charged. Room rates in hotels and B&B's often vary depending on the facilities, so be sure to check prices with the establishment before booking.

IRONBRIDGE — Map 08 SJ68

Pick of the Pubs

The Malthouse ♀
The Wharfage TF8 7NH ☎ 01952 433712 ▤ 01952 433298
e-mail: enquiries@malthousepubs.co.uk
The Malthouse is situated on the banks of the River Severn in Ironbridge, a village renowned for its spectacular natural beauty and award-winning museums, and now a designated UNESCO World Heritage Site. It has been an inn since the turn of the 20th century, and before that a malthouse. The building has recently been extensively refurbished; to one side there is a bar with its own menu and kitchen - a popular music and dining venue - and on the other a restaurant, the two styles of food and decor completely different. Fresh fish is a speciality, and while the bar offers cod in beer batter with fries, the restaurant has tempura battered monkfish with curried chickpeas, spinach and coriander dressing. A new concept is Art at the Malthouse, launched to provide free space for artists. The only condition is that the owners like the work and the artist helps hang the exhibition.
OPEN: 11-11 (Sun 12-3 6-10.30) Closed: 25-26 Dec
BAR MEALS: Lunch served: all week Dinner served: all week 12-2.30 6-9.30 Av main course £8 **RESTAURANT:** Lunch served: all week Dinner served: all week 12-2 6.30-9.45 Av 3 course à la carte £20 **BREWERY/COMPANY:** Inn Partnership **PRINCIPAL BEERS:** Flowers Original, Boddingtons, Tetley. **FACILITIES:** Children welcome Garden: Food served outside. Front courtyard **NOTES:** Parking 15 **ROOMS:** 6 bedrooms 6 en suite from s£55 d£65

LLANFAIR WATERDINE — Map 08 SO27

Pick of the Pubs

The Waterdine ☺☺
LD7 1TU ☎ 01547 528214 ▤ 01547 529992
See Pick of the Pubs on page 393

LUDLOW — Map 08 SO57

The Charlton Arms ♦♦♦ ☜ ♀
SY8 1PJ ☎ 01584 872813 ▤ 01584 879120
Dir: Situated on Ludford Bridge on the Hereford road, South exit Ludlow town centre
In a spectacular riverside setting beside the medieval packhorse bridge over the River Teme, here is a family-run free house that features six local real ales and home cooking that relies on fresh seasonal produce. Main courses are created from fresh fish and organic beef, lamb and pork from local suppliers - the high points of the ever-popular Sunday lunches. Modest en suite bedrooms offer a great base for exploring both the town and the Welsh Marches.
OPEN: 11-11 **BAR MEALS:** Lunch served: all week Dinner served: all week 12-2 7-9 Av main course £6.50
BREWERY/COMPANY: Free House **PRINCIPAL BEERS:** Hobsons Best Bitter, Wye Vally Butty Bach, Woods Shropshire Lad. **FACILITIES:** Garden: Food served outside **NOTES:** Parking 40 **ROOMS:** 6 bedrooms 6 en suite from s£30 d£45

OPEN: 12–2 7–11
BAR MEALS: L served Tue-Sun.
D served Tue-Sat. 12–2 7–9
Av main course £12
RESTAURANT: L served Tue-Sun.
D served Tue-Sat. 12–1.45 7–9
Av cost 3 course £22
BREWERY/COMPANY:
FREE HOUSE
PRINCIPAL BEERS:
Woodhampton Jack Snipe, Wood
Shropshire Legends, Parish Bitter
& Shropshire Lad
FACILITIES: Garden: Food served
outdoors, river
NOTES: Parking 12
ROOMS: 3 en suite Double room
from £80 Single room from £45

The Waterdine

 ◆◆

LLANFAIR WATERDINE LD7 1TU
☎ 01547 528214 📄 01547 529992
Dir: 4m NW of Knighton, just off the
Newtown road, turn R in Lloyney, over
bridge, follow road up to village, last on
left opposite church

Set above the River Teme, which runs along the foot of the
garden, in peaceful, beautiful countryside with superb views.
This former drovers' inn dating from about 1550 is an
original Welsh longhouse located not far from Offa's Dyke
Path, and stands in lovely mature gardens which are ideal for
summer use.

The Waterdine's main claim to fame is that Lord Hunt planned his
Everest expedition in the lounge bar when he lived in the valley. The property is heavily beamed throughout, and
boasts three large inglenook fireplaces fitted with wood-burning stoves bringing warmth and comfort to the public
rooms. In the summer the south-facing building enjoys the sun all day. Owner Ken Adams is the inspiration behind
the food, much of which is sourced from the inn's own very
productive vegetable and fruit gardens. Mr Adams, an internationally
renowned chef who has the distinction of having opened the first
restaurant in Ludlow (The Oaks), applies his impeccable pedigree to
menus which are based on well-sourced local produce. Meals are
served in the two dining rooms, one a bright conservatory with
breathtaking views of the hills. A typical meal might include cheese
soufflé with pickled damsons, or whole quail roasted in cardamom
and herb butter, followed by hare with celeriac shallots and wild
mushrooms, or pot-roasted fillet of Black Hall beef, and chocolate
gateau with passion fruit sorbet, or crisp lemon tart. Individually-
designed bedrooms are well furnished and decorated, offering
excellent facilities for the weary traveller

LUDLOW continued

The Church Inn ♦♦♦
Buttercross SY8 1AW ☎ 01584 872174 🖥 01584 877146
Dir: Town centre
Occupying one of the oldest sites in Ludlow, going back at least seven centuries, the Church Inn is an ideal base for exploring the beautiful Welsh Marches. Good range of real ales.

The Cookhouse ♀ NEW
Bromfield SY8 2JR ☎ 01584 856565 & 856665 🖥 01584 856661

Once a farmhouse occupied by the soldier and colonial ruler 'Clive of India', the Cookhouse now offers something for everyone. Try the lounge bar for local ales, a large selection of wines or even tea, coffee and snacks. The stylish café-bar and restaurant offer everything from kids' snacks to more formal, award winning dinners. Dishes could include roast duckling with spicy plums and red cabbage or fillet of plaice filled with salmon mousse and coated in mandarin sauce. Everything is home made.
OPEN: 11–11 (Sunday 12–10.30) **BAR MEALS:** Lunch served: all week Dinner served: all week 12–3 6–10 Av main course £7.95 **RESTAURANT:** Lunch served: all week Dinner served: all week 12–3 6–10 Av 3 course à la carte £22.50 **BREWERY/COMPANY:** Free House **PRINCIPAL BEERS:** Hobsons Best Bitter & Town Crier, Interbrew Worthington Cream Flow. **FACILITIES:** Children welcome Garden: Food served outdoors **NOTES:** Parking 100

Pick of the Pubs

The Roebuck Inn ♦♦♦♦ 🍴🍴 ♀
Brimfield SY8 4NE ☎ 01584 711230 🖥 01584 711654
e-mail: dave@roebuckinn.demon.co.uk
Dir: Just off the A49 between Ludlow & Leominster
A classy country inn offering comfortable bedrooms, a bright and airy dining room and traditional bars with inglenooks and wood panelling. An impressive range of home-produced fare is prepared from first-class ingredients. Large boards display fresh fish and seasonal dishes like fresh turbot with grape and vermouth sauce and mixed game terrine with red onion marmalade. The British cheese board is recommended and tempting alternatives include glazed citrus tart or pear, rhubarb and ginger Charlotte.
OPEN: 11.30–3 6.30–11 (Sun 12–3, 7–10.30)
BAR MEALS: Lunch served: all week Dinner served: all week 12–2.30 7–9.30 Av main course £12.50 **RESTAURANT:** Lunch served: all week Dinner served: all week 12–2.30 7–9.30 Av 3 course à la carte £23 **BREWERY/COMPANY:** Free House **PRINCIPAL BEERS:** Carlsberg-Tetley Tetley, Woods, Wadworth 6X. **FACILITIES:** Children welcome **NOTES:** Parking 24 **ROOMS:** 3 bedrooms 3 en suite from s£45 d£70

Pick of the Pubs

Unicorn Inn 🍴 ♀
Corve St SY8 1DU ☎ 01584 873555
Dir: A49 to Ludlow
A traditional beamed and panelled inn dating in part from the Elizabethan age, set beside the River Corve on the edge of town. This family-run hostelry, rescued from dereliction over a decade ago, prides itself on its high quality home-cooked food and friendly atmosphere. It no longer offers accommodation, but the pub thrives on a combination of local and tourist trade, with log fires in the winter and a riverside summer terrace both offering instant appeal. Probably unsung in comparison with some of its grander neighbours, but still a venue for good food lovers – those without expense accounts. The best of the day's offerings are served in the candlelit and atmospheric dining room. Start perhaps with bacon, ham and Stilton terrine or whitebait with devil sauce, followed by lamb, port and redcurrant hotpot, or sea bass with moules marinière. Bar food is memorable too: typically rabbit casserole, and spicy meatballs.
OPEN: 12–2.30 Sun 12–3.30, 7–10.30 6–11 Closed: Dec 25
BAR MEALS: Lunch served: all week Dinner served: all week 12–2.15 6–9.15 Av main course £6.50 **RESTAURANT:** Lunch served: all week Dinner served: all week 12–2.15 6–9.15 Av 3 course à la carte £16.50 **BREWERY/COMPANY:** Free House **PRINCIPAL BEERS:** Interbrew Bass, Hancocks HB. **FACILITIES:** Garden: Beer garden, terrace, food served outdoors Dogs allowed (water) **NOTES:** Parking 3

MADELEY   Map 08 SJ60

The New Inn
Blists Hill Victorian Town, Legges Way TF7 5DU
☎ 01952 588892 🖥 01952 243447
e-mail: rhamundy@btinternet.com
Dir: Between Telford & Broseley
In the Victorian town of Ironbridge Gorge Open Air Museum, this pub was re-located brick by brick from the Black Country but remains basically as it was in 1890. Customers buy old currency at the bank, then exchange it for traditionally brewed beer at five-pence farthing per pint – equal to about £2.10 today. Mostly traditional food options include home-made steak and ale casserole with Yorkshire pudding and chicken sauced with white wine and cream: but what would our forbears have made of the lasagne and creamily-sauced vegetable pancakes?
OPEN: 11–4 Closed: Dec 24–25, Nov–Mar closed Thu–Fri
BAR MEALS: Lunch served: all week 12–2.30 Av main course £4 **RESTAURANT:** Lunch served: all week 12–2.30 Av 3 course fixed price £8.25 **BREWERY/COMPANY:** Ironbridge Gorge Museums **PRINCIPAL BEERS:** Banks Bitter **FACILITIES:** Children welcome Garden: Food served outside **NOTES:** Parking: 300

MARKET DRAYTON   Map 08 SJ63

The Hinds Head 🍴 NEW
Norton in Hales TF9 4AT ☎ 01630 653014 🖥 01630 653014
Dir: Norton in Hales is about 3miles NE of Market Drayton
An 18th-century coaching inn by the parish church, much extended with a conservatory built out over the old courtyard. The original bars have open fires feature old prints. Fresh local ingredients are cooked to order with a great variety of seafood and popular favourites like Shrewsbury lamb and

continued

medallions of beef fillet smothered in wild mushrooms. Charcoal grills, low-cost lunchtime specials, vegetarian options and sticky home-made desserts make this inn an excellent choice.
OPEN: 12–2 6.30–11 **BAR MEALS:** Lunch served: all week 12–2 Dinner served: Mon–Sat 6–9 Av main course £10
RESTAURANT: Lunch served: all week 12–2 Dinner served: Mon–Sat 6–9 Av 3 course à la carte £19 **BREWERY/COMPANY:** Free House
PRINCIPAL BEERS: Wells Bombadier, Scottish Courage Theakstons Best, John Smith's. **NOTES:** Parking 15

MINSTERLEY   Map 08 SJ30

The Stables Inn
Drury Ln, Hopesgate SY5 0EP ☎ 01743 891344
Dir: From Shrewsbury A488 turn L at r'about in Mimsterely. At Plox Green x-roads turn R. Pub approx 3m.
In a peaceful hamlet of just eight houses, the Stables was built in 1680 to serve the drovers travelling between Montgomery and Shrewsbury markets. Overlooking scenic pastureland, its beamed bar warmed by an open fire is the place to settle over a beer and contemplate a traditional menu that majors in steaks and home-made casseroles. Fresh daily soups precede chicken curry, chilli con carne, vegetable korma and sausages with mash and onion gravy.
OPEN: 12–3 (Sat–Sun) 7–11 (Sat–Mon 7–11) Closed: 1 Jan
BAR MEALS: Lunch served: Sat–Sun 12–1.45 Dinner served: Tue–Sun 7–9.30 Av main course £7.50 **RESTAURANT:** Lunch served: Sat–Sun 12–1.45 Dinner served: Tue–Sun 7–9.30 Av 3 course à la carte £13.50 **BREWERY/COMPANY:** Free House
PRINCIPAL BEERS: Interbrew Worthington Bitter, Greene King IPA, Adnams Best Bitter. **FACILITIES:** Children welcome Garden: Beer Garden:, food served outdoors **NOTES:** Parking 40 No credit cards

---

MORVILLE   Map 08 SO69

Acton Arms
WV16 4RJ ☎ 01746 714209
e-mail: acton-arms@madasfish.com
Dir: On A458, 3m W of Bridgnorth
Believed to be England's most frequently haunted inn, with three resident spooks, the Acton Arms, a former coaching inn, is situated close to Upper Cresset Hall.

MUCH WENLOCK   Map 08 SO69

The Feathers
Brockton TF13 6JR ☎ 01746 785202
Stylish dining in beamed, stone-lined rooms with Mediterranean-style decor and atmosphere; seasonally-changing menus - reports please!

The George & Dragon
2 High St TF13 6AA ☎ 01952 727312
Dir: on A458 halfway between Shrewsbury & Bridgnorth
Adjacent to the market square, Guildhall and ruined priory, this historic, Grade II listed building houses an amazing collection of brewery memorabilia, including over 500 water jugs hanging from the ceiling, one of the largest collections in the country. The inn's cosy and inviting atmosphere makes this an obvious choice for locals and visitors. Expect a good range of popular dishes, including perhaps roast beef and Yorkshire pudding or Thai chicken curry. Jacket potatoes, sandwiches, and ploughman's lunches are also available.
OPEN: 12–3 (wknds all day) 6–11 (Summer all day)
BAR MEALS: Lunch served: Thur–Tues Dinner served: Thur–Tues

12–2.15 6–9.15 Av main course £7.95 **RESTAURANT:** Lunch served: Thur–Tues Dinner served: Thur–Tues12–2.15 6.30–9.15 Av 3 course à la carte £15 **BREWERY/COMPANY:** Free House
PRINCIPAL BEERS: Greene King Abbot Ale, Old Speckled Hen & IPA, Adnams Broadside, Interbrew Bass. **FACILITIES:** Children welcome **ROOMS:** 2 bedrooms from s£25 d£50

Longville Arms
Longville in the Dale TF13 6DT ☎ 01694 771206 🖷 01694 771742
e-mail: longvillearms@aol.com
Dir: From Shrewsbury take A49 to Church Stretton, then B4371 to Longville
Prettily situated in a scenic corner of Shropshire, ideally placed for walking and touring, this welcoming country inn has been carefully restored and now includes a 60-seat dining room. Solid elm or cast-iron-framed tables, oak panelling and wood-burning stoves are among the features which help to generate a warm, friendly ambience inside. Favourite main courses on the wide-ranging bar menu and specials board include fresh haddock, steak and ale pie, breast of chicken and a selection of steaks and balti dishes.
OPEN: 12–3 7–11 (Sat–Sun 12–3 6–11) **BAR MEALS:** Lunch served: all week Dinner served: all week 12–2.30 7–9.30 Av main course £6.95
RESTAURANT: Lunch served: all week Dinner served: all week 12–2.30 7–9.30 Av 3 course à la carte £12.50
BREWERY/COMPANY: Free House **PRINCIPAL BEERS:** Scottish Courage Courage Directors, John Smith's & Courage Best, Theakstons Best, Wells Bombardier. **FACILITIES:** Children welcome Garden: Beer garden, food served outdoors Dogs allowed Not in garden
NOTES: Parking 40 **ROOMS:** 4 bedrooms 4 en suite from s£30 d£48

The Talbot Inn
High St TF13 6AA ☎ 01952 727077 🖷 01952 728436
e-mail: maggie@talbotinn.dps.co.uk

Dating from 1360, the Talbot may have been a hostel for travellers and a centre for alms giving. Delightful courtyard which was used in the 1949 film Gone to Earth. Daily specials highlight the varied menu, which may include steak and kidney pie, fresh salmon, Shropshire pie and cod mornay.
OPEN: 11–3 (Sun 12–3, 7–10.30) 6.15–11 Closed: 25 Dec
BAR MEALS: Lunch served: all week Dinner served: all week 12–2.30 7–9.30 Av main course £12 **RESTAURANT:** Lunch served: all week Dinner served: all week 12–2.30 7–9.30 Av 3 course à la carte £20 **BREWERY/COMPANY:** Free House
PRINCIPAL BEERS: Bass. **FACILITIES:** Children welcome Garden: Food served outside. Courtyard Dogs allowed (in the garden only)
NOTES: Parking 5 **ROOMS:** 6 bedrooms 6 en suite from s£32.50 d£32.50

continued

MUCH WENLOCK continued

Pick of the Pubs

Wenlock Edge Inn
Hilltop, Wenlock Edge TF13 6DJ ☎ 01746 785678 📠 01746 785285
Dir: *4.5m from Much Wenlock on B4371*

Beside a quiet road near one of the high points of Wenlock Edge's dramatic wooded ridge, this row of original 17th-century quarrymen's cottages has been a long-standing favourite since its rescue from dereliction by the Waring family in 1984. The small country-style dining-room and bars, one with a wood-burning stove, are cosy, friendly and relaxed: those who prefer privacy to conversation and jovial banter may not benefit fully from its unique atmosphere. Hobson's ales provide a suitable accompaniment to the Shrewsbury lamb, venison or steak-and-mushroom pies and chicken and apricot quiche that define the inn's home-cooking. Vegetable-based soups might be ham with asparagus in spring or an autumnal cock-a-leekie, with pan-fried fresh fish, local beef steaks and roast lamb legs to follow. Sponges, tarts and crumbles are all made on the premises, while a hearty country breakfast is appreciated by the walking types who stay overnight.
OPEN: 11.30–2.30 6.30–11 Closed: 24-26 Dec
BAR MEALS: Lunch served: all week Dinner served: all week 12–2 7–9 Av main course £7.50 **RESTAURANT:** Lunch served: all week Dinner served: all week 12–2 7–9 Av 3 course à la carte £14.75 **BREWERY/COMPANY:** Free House
PRINCIPAL BEERS: Hobsons Best & Town Crier.
FACILITIES: Children welcome Garden: Food served outside. Patio area Dogs allowed (water), toys **NOTES:** Parking 50
ROOMS: 3 bedrooms 3 en suite from s£45 d£70

MUNSLOW   Map 08 SO58

The Crown Country Inn ♦♦♦♦ 🍴
SY7 9ET ☎ 01584 841205 📠 01584 841255
e-mail: admin@crowncountryinn.co.uk
Dir: *On B4368 between Craven Arms & Much Wenlock*

A Shropshire Hundred house dating back to Tudor times, where judge Jeffries is said to have presided, the inn has massive oak beams, inglenook fireplaces and flagstone floors. A warm welcome and seriously good food are today's hallmarks. Try griddled black pudding with crispy bacon or fresh Devon Bay mackerel to start with. Main meals offer Shetland salmon with crab bisque sauce or Hereford beef

steaks. Freshly prepared desserts and carefully selected cheeses follow.
OPEN: 12-2.30 7-11 **BAR MEALS:** Lunch served: Tues-Sun 12-2 Dinner served: Tues-Sat 7-9 Av main course £7.50
RESTAURANT: Lunch served: Tues-Sun 12-2 Dinner served: Tues-Sat 7-9 Av 3 course à la carte £18
BREWERY/COMPANY: Free House **PRINCIPAL BEERS:** Holden's Black Country Bitter, Black Country Mild, Golden Glow & Special Bitter.
FACILITIES: Children welcome Garden: Beer garden, patio, food served outside Dogs allowed (water) **NOTES:** Parking 20
ROOMS: 3 bedrooms 3 en suite from s£35 d£55

NESSCLIFFE   Map 08 SJ31

The Old Three Pigeons Inn 🍴 ♀
SY4 1DB ☎ 01743 741279 📠 01743 741259
e-mail: dillon@threepigeons.fsnet.co.uk
Dir: *On A5 London road, 8 Miles W of Shrewsbury*

A 600-year-old inn built of sandstone, ship's timbers and wattle and daub, situated in two acres of land looking towards Snowdonia and the Bretton Hills. There is a strong emphasis on fish, with a choice of many seasonal dishes and it is a venue for gourmet club and lobster evenings. Characteristic dishes include lamb shank casserole, beef and ale pie, sirloin steak, home-cured Irish gammon and lobster thermidor.
OPEN: 11.30-3 7-11 (closed Mon) **BAR MEALS:** Lunch served: Tue-Sun Dinner served: Tue-Sun 11.30-3 6-9.30 Av main course £12
RESTAURANT: Lunch served: Tue-Sun Dinner served: Tue-Sun 11.30-3 7-9 Av 3 course à la carte £20 **BREWERY/COMPANY:** Free House **PRINCIPAL BEERS:** Scottish Courage John Smith's, Moles Best Bitter, Matston's Pedigree, Interbrew Flowers Original.
FACILITIES: Children welcome Garden: Food served outside Dogs allowed **NOTES:** Parking 50

NEWPORT   Map 08 SJ71

The Swan at Forton 🍴 ♀
TF10 8BY ☎ 01952 812169 📠 01952 812722
e-mail: mailtheswan@forton.co.uk

On the border between Shropshire and Staffordshire, a family-run free house with an extensive menu served throughout the two large, comfortable bars and non-smoking restaurant. The coach house has been converted into comfortable, well-equipped bedrooms. Regular evenings featuring home-made pies or curries are a great success, while other popular dishes include a steak and kidney pies, poacher's chicken and treacle tart. At the weekends a sumptuous four-course carvery is the focal point.
OPEN: 12-3 6-11 (Sun 12-10.30) **BAR MEALS:** Lunch served: all week Dinner served: all week 12-2.30 6-10 Av main course £5.95
RESTAURANT: Lunch served: all week Dinner served: all week 12-2 6-10 Av 3 course à la carte £17.50 Av 4 course fixed price £10.95
PRINCIPAL BEERS: Interbrew Bass, Flowers IPA & Boddingtons Bitter, Greene King Abbot Ale, Charles Wells Bombardier.
FACILITIES: Children welcome Garden: Patio, food served outside
NOTES: Parking 67 **ROOMS:** 9 bedrooms 5 en suite from s£25 d£40

NORTON   Map 08 SJ70

Pick of the Pubs

Hundred House Hotel ★ ★ 🏵🏵 🍴 ♀
Bridgnorth Rd TF11 9EE ☎ 01952 730353 📠 01952 730355
e-mail: hundredhouse@lineone.net

See Pick of the Pubs on page 397

continued

OPEN: 11-3 6-11(Sun 11-10.30)
BAR MEALS: L served all week.
D served all week. 12-2.30 6-10
Av main course £7
RESTAURANT: L served all week.
D served Mon-Sat 12-2.30 6-10 Av
cost 3 course £28
BREWERY/COMPANY: FREE
HOUSE
PRINCIPAL BEERS: Smiles
Heritage, Wood Shropshire Lad,
Everards Tiger, Charles Wells
Bombardier
FACILITIES: Children welcome.
Garden: Food served outside,
large beer garden
NOTES: Parking 40
ROOMS: 10 en suite Double room
from £99 Single room from £69

The Hundred House Hotel

★ ★ ⊚⊚ ♀
Bridgnorth Road Norton TF11 9EE
☎ 01952 730353 📠 01952 730355
e-mail: hundredhouse@lineone.net
Dir: On A442 6m N of Bridgnorth

'Excellent people, rooms, food. Epitomises hospitality' is the sort of guest comment that this very special hotel has come to expect. This creeper-clad hotel may appear predictably traditional, but inside it offers a unique experience that is always a hit with guests.

Everything stands out, from the staff to the interior decor, and from the accommodation to the food, the result of a tremendous human as well as an economic investment. The oldest part of this hotel dates from the 14th century, but the main building is Georgian with many additions over the past few centuries. In the bedrooms there are swings hanging from the ceiling, which apparently encourage even the most staid of overnighters to let their hair down. The bars and restaurant are filled with fresh flowers; and herbs drying from the rafters, both the product of the gardens, which are tended with dedication. And it is these herbs that are in part responsible for the distinctive flavour that emanates from the kitchen. There's an extensive choice at lunchtime and in the evening, made even greater by a specials list, and everything is home made. Consider fish specials like chargrilled John Dory, and fresh Dover sole, perhaps preceded by terrine of smoked salmon and leeks, and followed by pears poached in red wine. Or from the carte, griddled scallops with sweet pepper coulis, and pan-fried venison steak stuffed with mushrooms and rowanberry jelly. A brasserie menu widens the scope yet further, with the choice of bruschetta topped with tomato, tapenade and basil, Cajun chicken, and hot potato cakes. The intimate atmosphere is relaxing, and there's a peaceful garden.

OSWESTRY
Map 08 SJ22

The Bear Hotel ◆◆◆◆ ♀
Salop Rd SY11 2NR ☎ 01691 652093 ▤ 01691 679996
e-mail: pub@bearhotel.net
This former 19th-century temperance hotel is today renowned for its collection of over 130 single malts. Converted in the 1930s, it has been in the same hands since 1979. The family take pride is offering a warm welcome and quality food. Lunchtime bar food of brunches and burgers, ploughman's, omelettes and sandwiches are augmented by specials such as beef stroganoff and chump of lamb with mustard sauce. The thriving restaurant at night is a la carte.
OPEN: 11-3 7-11 (Sun 7-11 only) Closed: Dec 25, 1 Jan
BAR MEALS: Lunch served: Mon-Sat Dinner served: Mon-Sat 12-2 7-9.30 Av main course £5 **RESTAURANT:** Dinner served: Mon-Sat 7-9.30 Av 3 course à la carte £15 **PRINCIPAL BEERS:** Marston's Pedigree, Mansfield Riding Bitter. **FACILITIES:** Dogs allowed
NOTES: Parking 25 **ROOMS:** 10 bedrooms 5 en suite from s£25 d£40

Pick of the Pubs

The Bradford Arms ◆◆◆◆ ♀
Llanymynech SY22 6EJ ☎ 01691 830582 ▤ 01691 830728
e-mail: bradfordarmshotel.com
Dir: On A483 in village centre

Originally a coaching inn and 'Victorianised' in 1901, this carefully-upgraded property is stylish and comfortable. Meals can be enjoyed in the spacious conservatory, the more formal dining room, or the inviting bar, while the lounge is the perfect place for a pre- or after-dinner drink, with its soft lighting and open fire helping to generate an intimate atmosphere. Everything except ice cream is made on the premises, and inn offers an enterprising modern English and European menu. Expect devilled crab tartlet, and spinach and feta cheese parcels among the imaginative starters, while main choices may include Moroccan beef kebab, red sea bream with pine nut crust and orange sauce, and ravioli with roasted artichoke and red peppers. Banana and butterscotch crêpe, and rum and blackcurrant cheesecake are typical desserts, but the pièce de résistance is the huge selection of international cheeses. Five en suite bedrooms are available.
OPEN: 11-3 7-11 Closed: 2wks Sept, 25-26 Dec, 2 wks Jan
BAR MEALS: Lunch served: Tues-Sun Dinner served: Tues-Sun 12-2 7-10 Av main course £10 **RESTAURANT:** Lunch served: Tues-Sun Dinner served: Tues-Sun 12-2 7-10 Av 3 course à la carte £18 **BREWERY/COMPANY:** Free House
PRINCIPAL BEERS: Greene King Abbot Ale, Shepherd Neame Bishops Finger,. **NOTES:** Parking 20 **ROOMS:** 5 bedrooms 5 en suite from s£35 d£55

The Horseshoe
Llanyblodwel SY10 8NQ ☎ 01691 828969
Timbered Tudor inn by the River Tanat on the Powys border, close to the Offa's Dyke path. Oak-panelled dining room; varied menus.

Pick of the Pubs

The Old Mill Inn
Candy SY10 9AZ ☎ 01691 657058 ▤ 01691 680918
e-mail: theoldmill.inn@virgin.net
Dir: from B4579 turn L after bridge, follow signs for Trefonen, through traffic lights, take first R after Ashford Hotel, first R
Peacefully situated in the Candy Valley, the Old Mill has been a pub for over 20 years. Not easily accessible but well worth the effort. The famous Offa's Dyke Path, one of Britain's most popular national trails, is just a yard or two from the main door and the River Morda runs beside the inn. On winter days, the pub's cosy interior is the obvious place to be, with a spacious conservatory overlooking extensive gardens, a cracking log fire and a welcoming ambience enhancing the pleasant surroundings. Ever-changing menu includes bar meals, vegetarian dishes, classic specialities and healthy options. A wide-ranging selection of starters, including trio of chicken kebabs with lemon sauce and baked salmon ring, sets the tone for dinner which varies from roast half duckling with autumn berry sauce to roasted Tuscan red pepper with vegetables, potatoes or chips. Make a point of trying the sticky toffee pudding with whipped Devon cream, toffee sauce and vanilla ice cream - one of several appetising desserts for which the pub is known in the area.
OPEN: 12-3 (Wed-Thur, Sun 12-3, 7-10.30) 7-11 (6-11 Fri Sat)
BAR MEALS: Lunch served: Wed-Sun Dinner served: Wed-Sun 12-2 7-9 Av main course £6 **RESTAURANT:** Lunch served: Wed-Sun Dinner served: Wed-Sun 12-2.30 6-9.30 Av 3 course à la carte £12 **BREWERY/COMPANY:** Free House
PRINCIPAL BEERS: Greene King Old Speckled Hen, Carlsberg-Tetley Tetleys Bitter & Friary Meux Bitter. **FACILITIES:** Children welcome Children's licence Garden: Beer garden, food served outdoors, patio, Dogs allowed (water) **NOTES:** Parking 200
ROOMS: 5 bedrooms from s£120 d£40

The Walls
Welsh Walls SY11 1AW ☎ 01691 670970 ▤ 01691 653820
Large busy pub with an almost eccentric atmosphere. Licenced for civil weddings. Located in a former Victorian church school.

PICKLESCOTT
Map 08 SO49

Bottle & Glass Inn
SY6 6NR ☎ 01694 751345 ▤ 01694 751348
Dir: Turn off A49 at Dorrington between Shrewsbury & Church Stretton
This traditional country inn serves all kinds of people but locals always come first. It is situated in beautiful countryside on the slopes of the Longmynd in the heart of South Shropshire hill country. The emphasis is on local ales and local produce. Straightforward dishes including steaks, cod, and gammon off the bone, and there is a popular Sunday carvery.

continued

England

OPEN: 12-2 7-11 Closed: Winter Closed week days
BAR MEALS: Lunch served: Sat & Sun 12-2 Dinner served: Mon-Sat 7-8.45 Av main course £5.50 **RESTAURANT:** Lunch served: Sun 12-2 Dinner served: Fri-Sat 7-8.45 Av 3 course à la carte £13
BREWERY/COMPANY: Free House **PRINCIPAL BEERS:** Woods Parish, Shropshire Gold Salopians, guest ale. **FACILITIES:** Children welcome Children's licence Garden: patio Dogs allowed bar only, Water **NOTES:** Parking 20 **ROOMS:** 3 bedrooms 3 en suite from s£35 d£50

SHIFNAL   Map 08 SJ70

Odfellows Wine Bar ♀
Market Place TF11 9AU ☎ 01952 461517 📠 01952 463855
e-mail: matt@odley.co.uk
Dir: 3rd exit from Mway rdbt, at next rdbt take 3rd exit, past petrol station, round bend under railway bridge, bar on L
This single room wine bar with high ceilings, an elevated dining area and a conservatory started life as a private house in Queen Ann's day. Over 40 wines are available from around the globe - many by the glass.
OPEN: 12-2.30 5.30-11 (Sun & Fri open all day) Closed: Dec 25-26, Jan 1 **BAR MEALS:** Lunch served: all week Dinner served: all week 12-2 7-9.30 Av main course £9.50 **RESTAURANT:** Lunch served: all week Dinner served: all week 12-2 7-10
BREWERY/COMPANY: Free House
PRINCIPAL BEERS: Bathams, Timothy Taylor Landlord, Enville, Holdens. **NOTES:** Parking 35 **ROOMS:** 7 bedrooms 7 en suite from s£37.50 d£47.50

SHREWSBURY   Map 08 SJ41

Pick of the Pubs

The Armoury 🍴 ♀
Welsh Bridge, Victoria Quay SY1 1HH
☎ 01743 340525 📠 01743 340526
The site has had a chequered history; granted to the friars of St Augustine by Henry III in 1255, it was destroyed at the Dissolution. The 1806 Armoury burnt down in 1882 but was at last restored for its present use in 1995. All-day opening, regular guest ales and modern food prove as popular as ever. Ploughman's and granary sandwiches are offered alongside dishes like spicy crab and spring onion cake or a half shoulder of lamb with glazed root vegetables.
OPEN: 12-11 (Sun 12-10.30) Closed: 25-26 Dec
BAR MEALS: Lunch served: all week Dinner served: all week 12-2.30 6-9.30 Av main course £8.95 **RESTAURANT:** Lunch served: all week Dinner served: all week
BREWERY/COMPANY: Free House
PRINCIPAL BEERS: Wood Shropshire Lad, Wadworth 6X, Interbrew Boddingtons.

Braby's Bar NEW
16 Castle Gates SY1 2AB ☎ 01743 358807
e-mail: george.mitchell@virgin.net
Dir: From S: M6, M54, A5. From N: M6, A49
An early 19th-century ale house, the Braby's Bar has a roof garden and nestles beneath the shadow of Shrewsbury Castle. Bedrooms.

The Plume of Feathers
Harley SY5 6LP ☎ 01952 727360 📠 01952 728542
Many original features still survive at this historic inn which started life as a pair of cottages around 1620. The name of the inn was recorded in 1842. Open fires, antique furniture and old beams give the interior a cosy, inviting atmosphere.
OPEN: 12-3 (Sat/Sun 12-11) 5.30-11 **BAR MEALS:** Lunch served: all week 12-2 Dinner served: Mon-Sat 6-9 Av main course £7.95
RESTAURANT: Lunch served: all week 12-3 Dinner served: Mon-Sat 6-9 Av 3 course à la carte £18 **BREWERY/COMPANY:** Free House
PRINCIPAL BEERS: Courage Directors, guest beers.
FACILITIES: Children welcome Dogs allowed No credit cards

White Horse Inn
Pulverbatch SY5 8DS ☎ 01743 718247
Dir: 7m past the Nuffield Hospital
Some 8 miles south of Shrewsbury off the A49, a cruck-structured building - reputedly 13th century - houses this fine old inn. Up to 40 main dishes are on offer every day, ranging from salmon, plaice and haddock in various guises to home-made steak and ale pie, whole lamb shanks and half a dozen speciality curries. Grills include chicken, gammon and various cuts of steak: a daily special might be beef bourguignonne.
OPEN: 12-2.30 7-11 **BAR MEALS:** Lunch served: all week Dinner served: all week 12-2 7-9.30 Av main course £6
RESTAURANT: Lunch served: all week Dinner served: all week 12-2 7-9.30 **BREWERY/COMPANY:** Whitbread
PRINCIPAL BEERS: Shepherd Neame Spitfire,.
FACILITIES: Children welcome Garden: **NOTES:** Parking 50

TELFORD   Map 08 SJ71

The Grove Inn ♦♦♦
10 Wellington Rd, Coalbrookdale TF8 7DX
☎ 01952 433269 📠 01252 433269
e-mail: frog@fat-frog.co.uk
A former coaching inn in the Ironbridge Gorge offering a taste of France amongst hand-painted murals and a huge collection of frogs. Downstairs there's a French restaurant complete with check table cloths and café music, serving traditional French country food like pork medallions provençale, mignons of beef béarnaise, duck in blackcurrant sauce, and wild mushroom ravioli. Also a seafood and wine bar offering six different chicken dishes, and hot baguettes.
OPEN: 12-2.30 (Sun 12-5.30) 5.30-11 **BAR MEALS:** Lunch served: all week 12.30-2 Dinner served: Mon-Sat 6.30-8.30 Av main course £6.95 **RESTAURANT:** Lunch served: all week 12.30-2 Dinner served: Mon-Sat 7-9.30 Av 3 course à la carte £19.50
BREWERY/COMPANY: Free House **PRINCIPAL BEERS:** Banks Original, Traditional, Marston's Pedigree. **FACILITIES:** Children welcome Garden: Patio, food served outside Dogs allowed (water, food if required) **NOTES:** Parking 12 **ROOMS:** 5 bedrooms 5 en suite from s£30 d£45

England

WENTNOR
Map 08 SO39

The Crown Inn
SY9 5EE ☎ 01588 650613 ᵈ 01588 650436
e-mail: crowninn@wentnor.com
*Dir: From Shrewsbury A49 to Church Stretton, follow signs over Long
Mynd to Asterton, R to Wentnor*

Standing in the shadow of the famous Long Mynd, in an area
with vast potential for walking and other outdoor pursuits, the
Crown is a traditional, unspoilt 17th-century coaching inn with
log fires, beams and horse brasses. Sophisticated meals are
served in the bar and non-smoking restaurant: pork
tenderloin filled with marinated fruits, pan-fried breast of duck
with a burnt orange sauce, and grilled sea bass with couscous
are typical of the choices.
OPEN: 12-3 7-11 (Sat 12-3 6-11) Closed: Dec 25
BAR MEALS: Lunch served: all week Dinner served: all week 12-2
7-9 Av main course £9 **RESTAURANT:** Lunch served: all week
Dinner served: all week 12-2 7-9 Av 3 course à la carte £16
BREWERY/COMPANY: Free House
PRINCIPAL BEERS: Hobsons, Interbrew Worthington Bitter, Greene
King Old Speckled Hen, Salopian Shropshire Gold.
FACILITIES: Children welcome Garden: Beer garden, food served
outdoors **NOTES:** Parking 20 **ROOMS:** 3 bedrooms 2 en suite
from s£27 d£50

WESTON HEATH
Map 08 SJ71

Pick of the Pubs

The Countess's Arms
TF11 8RY ☎ 01952 691123 ᵈ 01952 691660
Owned by the Earl of Bradford and re-opened in 1998
after extensive refurbishment, this popular rural
Shropshire pub sports a spacious, wooden-floored bar
and first-floor gallery where customers can look down on
the blue glass mosaic tiled bar below. The pub is situated
one mile from Weston Park, the family seat of the Earls of
Bradford, and a short drive from Boscobel House, where
Charles II sought refuge from Cromwell's soldiers after the
Battle of Worcester. There has been recent a change of
hands which has resulted in an innovative fresh food
menu in the large modern restaurant and bar. Live jazz on
Friday nights adds to the buzzy atmosphere.
OPEN: 11-11 (Sun 12-10.30) **BAR MEALS:** Lunch served: all
week Dinner served: all week 12-2.30 6-9.45 Av main course £9
RESTAURANT: Lunch served: all week Dinner served: all week
12-2.30 6-9.45 Av 3 course à la carte £18
BREWERY/COMPANY: Free House
PRINCIPAL BEERS: Banks's, Boddingtons, Flowers Original.
FACILITIES: Children welcome Children's licence Garden:
Food served outside. **NOTES:** Parking 100

WHITCHURCH
Map 08 SJ54

The Horse & Jockey
Church St SY13 1LB ☎ 01948 664902 ᵈ 01948 664902
e-mail: andy.thelwell@onmail.co.uk
Dir: In town centre next to church

This coaching inn was built and extended from the 17th to the
19th centuries, with exposed beams and open fire, was built
on Roman ruins. An extensive menu offers everything from
sandwiches to chicken and sweetcorn pie, battered cod fillet
and vegetable cheese fritters. In addition, there are such
favourites as best end of lamb and poached fillet of halibut
served with lemon and prawn sauce. There is a garden and
barbecue for the summer,
OPEN: 11.30-2.30 6-11 **BAR MEALS:** Lunch served: Tues-Sun
Dinner served: Tues-Sun 11.30-2.30 6-10 Av main course £4
RESTAURANT: Lunch served: Tues-Sun Dinner served: Tues-Sun
11.30-2.30 6-10 Av 3 course à la carte £14.55
BREWERY/COMPANY: Pubmaster **PRINCIPAL BEERS:** Interbrew
Worthington, Scottish Courage John Smith's. **FACILITIES:** Children
welcome Garden: Patio, food served outside **NOTES:** Parking 10

Willey Moor Lock Tavern
Tarporley Rd SY13 4HF ☎ 01948 663274
Dir: 2m N of Whitchurch on A49 (Warrington/Tarporley)
A former lock keeper's cottage idyllically situated beside the
Llangollen Canal. Low-beamed rooms are hung with a novel
teapot collection, there are open log fires and a range of real
ales. Deep-fried fish and a choice of grills rub shoulders with
traditional steak pie, chicken curry and vegetable chilli. Other
options include salad platters, children's choices and gold rush
pie for dessert.
OPEN: 12-2.30 6-11 (Sun 12-2.30 7-10.30) Closed: 25 Dec
BAR MEALS: Lunch served: all week Dinner served: all week 12-2
6-9.30 **RESTAURANT:** Lunch served: all week Dinner served: all
week 12-2 7-9.30 **BREWERY/COMPANY:** Free House
PRINCIPAL BEERS: Theakston. **FACILITIES:** Children welcome
Garden: Beer garden by the canal, food served outside
NOTES: Parking 50 No credit cards

WOORE
Map 08 SJ74

Swan at Woore
Nantwich Rd CW3 9SA ☎ 01630 647220
*Dir: A51 Stone to Nantwich road 10 miles from Nantwich in the village of
woore wich is between Stone and Nantwich*
Refurbished 19th-century dining inn by the A51 near Stapley
Water Gardens. Four separate eating areas lead off from a
central servery. Daily specials boards supplement the menu,
which might include crispy confit of duck, slow roast knuckle
of lamb, roasted salmon on vegetable linguine, or red onion
and garlic 'Tarte Tatin'. There's a separate fish menu - grilled

continued

red mullet fillets, perhaps, or seared tuna on roasted sweet peppers.
OPEN: 12–3 5–11 **BAR MEALS:** Lunch served: all week Dinner served: all week 12–2.30 6.30–9.30 Av main course £6.50
RESTAURANT: Lunch served: all week Dinner served: all week 12–2.30 6.30–9.30 Av 3 course à la carte £14.50
BREWERY/COMPANY: Inn Partnership
PRINCIPAL BEERS: Interbrew Bass, Marston's Pedigree.
FACILITIES: Children welcome Children's licence Garden: Food served outside, Small lawn **NOTES:** Parking 40

WORFIELD   Map 08 SO79

The Dog Inn & Davenport Arms 🥂
Main St WV15 5LF ☎ 01746 716020 📠 01746 716050
e-mail: thedog@tinyworld.co.uk
Dir: On the Wolverhampton road turn L opposite the Wheel pub over the bridge and turn R in to the village of Worfield the Dog is on the L. Tourist signs on the A454 & A442
The Dog is an ancient pub nestling in a picturesque village of handsome houses close to the River Worfe. Spick-and-span with a tiled floor and light pine furnishings inside, it offers tip-top Butcher's Ales (brewed at the Munslow Arms) and a short menu listing home-cooked dishes. Choose from a varied menu that offers dishes such as pork with caramelised apple and crispy sage, Hungarian lamb with leek and paprika, steak and kidney pie, or classic lobster thermidor.
OPEN: 12–2.30 7–11 **BAR MEALS:** Lunch served: all week Dinner served: all week 12–2 7–9.30 Av main course £9
RESTAURANT: Lunch served: all week Dinner served: all week 12–2 7–9.30 Av 3 course à la carte £14 **BREWERY/COMPANY:** Free House **PRINCIPAL BEERS:** Courage Directors, Wells Bombardier, Highgate Mild, Courage Best. **FACILITIES:** Children welcome Garden: Food served outside Dogs allowed (please ask staff before – resident terrier) **NOTES:** Parking 8

SOMERSET

APPLEY   Map 03 ST02

Pick of the Pubs

The Globe Inn 🥂
TA21 0HJ ☎ 01823 672327
Dir: From M5 J6 take A38 towards Exeter. Village signposted in 5m
It may be a bit off the beaten track down tortuous lanes, but well worth a visit. The rambling 500-year-old slate and cob-built pub can be found in glorious countryside with plenty of signed footpaths for the energetic. Inglenook fires warm the four cosy rooms in winter, and each one has its own themed memorabilia such as Corgi and Dinky cars, and ephemera from the 1930s. An extensive choice of food, from specials like grilled breast of duck, Dragon's Breath Beef (hot with chilli!), and baguette filled with onion and pepper salsa, to a good fish choice - seafood pancake, grilled salmon, and garlic king prawns - and perhaps venison pie, and lamb curry. For a novel dessert don't miss Terry's chocolate orange crêpes with Cointreau and clotted cream, and a pint of Cotleigh ale won't go amiss.
OPEN: 11–3 6.30–11 (closed Mon) **BAR MEALS:** Lunch served: Tue–Sun Dinner served: Tue–Sun 12–2 7–10 Av main course £9 **RESTAURANT:** Dinner served: Tue–Sun 7–10 Av 3 course à la carte £15 **BREWERY/COMPANY:** Free House **PRINCIPAL BEERS:** Cotleigh Tawny, Palmers IPA, Palmers 200.

FACILITIES: Children welcome Garden: Food served outside. Large garden with views Dogs allowed (garden only)
NOTES: Parking 30
See Pub Walk on page 403

ASHCOTT   Map 03 ST43

Ring O Bells 🥂
High St TA7 9PZ ☎ 01458 210232 📠 01458 210880
e-mail: info@ringobells.com
Dir: From M5 follow signs A39 & Glastonbury. turn north off A39 at post office follow signs to church and village hall
Traditional village pub, recipient of many awards for its quality ales, good food, and friendly service. A pleasant blend of original 18th-century building and modern function room and skittle alley. Fresh local ingredients go into typical blackboard specials like Yorkshire pudding filled with steak and kidney, and Mexican tortilla stuffed with spicy vegetables in peanut sauce. An interesting collection of old bells and horse brasses.
OPEN: 12–3 7–11 (Sun 7–10.30) Closed: 25 Dec
BAR MEALS: Lunch served: all week Dinner served: all week 12–2.30 7–10 Av main course £5.50 **RESTAURANT:** 12–2.30 7–10 Av 3 course à la carte £11.50 **BREWERY/COMPANY:** Free House **PRINCIPAL BEERS:** Regular guest ales. **FACILITIES:** Children welcome Garden: Beer garden, food served outside, patio **NOTES:** Parking 25

ASHILL   Map 03 ST31

Square & Compass 🥂
Windmill Hill TA19 9NX ☎ 01823 480467
Dir: Turn off A358 at stewley cross service station (ashill) 1M along Wood Road, behind service station
Beautifully located overlooking the Blackdown Hills in the heart of rural Somerset, a traditional country pub with a warm, friendly atmosphere. Lovely gardens make the most of the views, and the refurbished bar area features hand-made settles and tables. Very extensive choice of food includes pasta, steaks, fish such as breaded plaice, battered cod, and seafood crêpes, and specials like duck with red wine and wild berry sauce. A good range of West Country ales.
OPEN: 12–3 6.30–11 (Sun 7–11) **BAR MEALS:** Lunch served: all week Dinner served: all week 12–2.30 7–10
BREWERY/COMPANY: Free House **PRINCIPAL BEERS:** Exmoor Ale & Gold Moor Withy Cutter, Wadworth 6X, Branscombe Bitter.
FACILITIES: Children welcome Garden: Food served outside Dogs allowed **NOTES:** Parking 30

AXBRIDGE   Map 03 ST45

Lamb Inn
The Square BS26 2AP ☎ 01934 732253
Rambling town-centre inn on the square, opposite King John's hunting lodge. Comfortable bars with log fires. Good range of Butcombe ales and farm ciders. Skittle alley and large terraced garden.

> **Restaurant and Bar Meal times indicate the times when food is available. Last orders may be approximately 30 minutes before the times stated.**

continued

SOMERSET

AXBRIDGE continued

The Oak House ♀
The Square BS26 2AP ☎ 01934 732444 📠 01934 733112
e-mail: info@oakhousehotel.com
Dir: From M5 J22, take A38 to Bristol. Turn onto A371 to Cheddar/Wells, then L at Axbridge. Town centre
Parts of the house date back to the 11th century, with exposed beams, massive inglenook fireplaces and an ancient well linked to the Cheddar Caverns. The bar is small and intimate, while in the bistro food is served in an informal atmosphere. Sirloin and gammon steaks, Cumberland sausages and Cajun chicken share the menu with 'family favourites' comprising fisherman's pie, pork and cider casserole, leek and potato bake and specials on the chalkboard.
OPEN: 12–3 7–11 Closed: 25 Dec, 1 Jan **BAR MEALS:** Lunch served: all week Dinner served: all week 12–3 6.30–9 Av main course £6.95 **RESTAURANT:** Lunch served: Thur–Sat 12–3 7–9 Av 3 course à la carte £10.95
PRINCIPAL BEERS: Carlsberg-Tetley Tetley Bitter.
ROOMS: 8 bedrooms 8 en suite from s£29.95 d£49.95

BATH   Map 03 ST76

The Olde Green Tree 🐾 ♀
12 Green St BA1 2JZ ☎ 01225 448259
Dir: Town centre
Three-roomed, oak-panelled pub, loved for its faded splendour, dim and atmospheric interior and a front room decorated with World War II Spitfires. Menus include basic pub fare - soup, bangers and mash ('probably the best sausages in Bath'), rolls and salads, steak and ale pie, and daily vegetarian specials. Often six or seven real ales are served, along with German lager, local cider, and an array of malts, wines and good coffee.
OPEN: 11–11 (Sun 12–10.30) Closed: 25-26 Dec, 1 Jan
BAR MEALS: Lunch served: Mon–Sat 12–2.15 Av main course £5
BREWERY/COMPANY: Phoenix Inns
PRINCIPAL BEERS: Changing guest beers. **FACILITIES:** Dogs allowed (manager's discretion only) No credit cards

Pack Horse Inn 🐾
Southstoke Ln, South Stoke BA2 7DU
☎ 01225 832060 📠 01225 830075
e-mail: packhorseinn@utgateway.net
Dir: 2.5m from Bath city centre, via the A367(A37). Turn onto B3110 towards Frome. South Stoke turning on R.
Dating back to 1489, this historic pub was built by monks to provide shelter for pilgrims and travellers. Views from the garden over rolling Somerset countryside. Original bar and inglenook fireplace inside. Well known locally for its traditional cider, including Taunton Traditional and Thatcher Cheddar Valley. Light snacks, baguettes and burgers and dishes such as sherry chicken and steak Diane typify the menu.
OPEN: 11.30-2.30 6–11 (sun all day) **BAR MEALS:** Lunch served: all week 12–2 Dinner served: Tues-Sat 6–9 Av main course £6.95
PRINCIPAL BEERS: Ushers Best, Scottish Courage Courage Best, Wadworth 6X. **FACILITIES:** Children welcome Children's licence Garden: Food served outside Dogs allowed (water)

Richmond Arms ♀
7 Richmond Place BA1 5PZ ☎ 01225 316725
e-mail: cunifletch@aol.com
A mile from the city centre in a long Georgian terrace with a south-facing garden, the pub has been sympathetically

refurbished. Attention turns rapidly to inventive food with a modern touch: pheasant braised with pancetta, cloves, cinnamon and chestnuts, lamb shank with sweet sherry and fresh thyme, Thai style pork curry, and tagliatelle.
OPEN: 12-3 6–11 **BAR MEALS:** Lunch served: Tue–Sun 12–2 Dinner served: Tue-Sat 6-8.30 Av main course £10
PRINCIPAL BEERS: Bass, Butconbe, Courage Best.
FACILITIES: Garden: Food served outside Dogs allowed (non food eve only) No credit cards

BATHAMPTON   Map 03 ST76

The George Inn ♀
Mill Ln BA2 6TR ☎ 01225 425079
Dir: M4 J18 onto A46 L at traffic lights & follow signs for Bathampton
A traditional wisteria-clad country pub on the Kennet and Avon Canal in a quiet village location just a mile from Bath. Believed to have once been a monastery, with mysterious tunnels that link the pub to St Nicholas' church opposite. Run by the same family since the 1970s. Home-cooked food using fresh local produce includes such hearty dishes as chicken wrapped in bacon with cider and Stilton sauce, steak and Guinness pie, roasted duck breast with honey on spicy fruit couscous, and deepfried cod in a soda and lime batter.
OPEN: 11–3 (Sun 12–5) 6–10.30 (Summer Sat 11–11, Sun 12–10.30) **BAR MEALS:** Lunch served: all week Dinner served: all week 12–2 6.30–9.30 Av main course £8 **PRINCIPAL BEERS:** Wadworth 6X, Scottish Courage Courage Best. **FACILITIES:** Children welcome Garden: Food served outdoors Dogs allowed **NOTES:** Parking 500

BECKINGTON   Map 03 ST85

Pick of the Pubs

Woolpack Inn
BA11 6SP ☎ 01373 831244 📠 01373 831223
Dir: Just off A36 near junction with A361
Relaxing 16th-century coaching inn featuring an attractive, flagstoned bar and various cosy dining areas. Noted locally for good food, the wide range of freshly prepared dishes may include pan-fried calamari with almonds and saffron, crab cakes with red Thai curry sauce, sea bass on squid with Parma ham, pan-fried pork fillet with roast baby sweet potatoes and Drambuie reduction, and caramelised pear mille feuille with coffee and caramel sauce.
OPEN: 11–11 (Sun 12–10.30) **BAR MEALS:** Lunch served: all week 12-2.30 Av main course £7 **RESTAURANT:** Lunch served: all week Dinner served: all week 12-2.30 6.30–9.30 Av 3 course à la carte £25 **BREWERY/COMPANY:** Old English Inns
PRINCIPAL BEERS: Greene King IPA, Wadworth 6X, Brains SA, Old Speckled Hen. **FACILITIES:** Children welcome Dogs allowed **ROOMS:** 11 bedrooms 11 en suite from s£60 d£80

BLAGDON   Map 03 ST55

The New Inn 🐾 ♀
Church St BS40 7SB ☎ 01761 462475 📠 01761 463523
e-mail: the.new-inn@virgin.net
Dir: From Bristol take A38 S then A368 towards Bath
Open fires, traditional home-cooked food, and magnificent views across fields to Blagdon Lake are among the attractions at this welcoming 17th-century inn, tucked away near the church. A hearty pub food menu offers lamb chops, Mexican chilli, battered cod and chips, grilled rainbow trout, chicken

continued

continued

402

PUB WALK

Appley
The Globe Inn

THE GLOBE INN,
APPLEY Nr Wellington
TA21 0HJ
Tel:1823 672327
Directions: From M5 J6 take
A38 towards Exeter. Village
signposted in 5m.
Rambling old pub hidden in a
secluded hamlet and reached
via tortuous, narrow lanes.
Return from your walk to a
decent pint of Cotleigh ale
and a good pub meal.
Excellent Sunday lunches.
Open: 11-3 6.30-11
Bar meals: 12-2 7-10
Children welcome. Garden
and parking available.

Distance: 3 miles (4.8km)
Map: OS Landranger 181
Terrain: Undulating countryside
bisected by the River Tone
Paths: Mainly field paths and
country lanes
Gradient: Some gentle climbing

Walk submitted and checked by
Elizabeth Burt of
The Globe Inn, Appley

Explore the gentle countryside near Appley on this enjoyable Somerset ramble, crossing the River Tone to visit the gardens at Cothay Manor.

On leaving the Globe, cross the road and take the footpath opposite the pub, crossing three fields alongside a hedge. The path then heads diagonally across the next field and to the right in the next. On reaching a metal gate and stile, go across the footbridge over the river and along the edge of the next field to a gate. Go out to the lane, turn right and make for the entrance to Cothay Manor. One of Britain's finest small manor houses, Cothay Manor dates from about 1481, though there are later additions. Inside are exceptional 15th-century wall paintings which were found under several layers of plaster and wall-paper. The gardens of Cothay Manor are open between May and September (groups by appointment). Follow the lane up the hill and along to Elworthy Farm on the right. At this point leave the road and join a footpath running through the farmyard and down the side of a barn. Follow the path up the bank and across the field, keeping over to the right to a stile. Join a towpath running beside an abandoned canal and eventually you reach the lane at Greenham. Turn right and follow it to Appley Cross (about three quarters of a mile, 1.2km). Turn right and head down the lane to the Globe in Appley.

England

BLAGDON continued

curry, and a selection of filled rolls, jacket potatoes, ploughmans' and basket meals.
OPEN: 11.30–2.30 7–10.30 (times vary, contact for details)
BAR MEALS: Lunch served: all week Dinner served: all week 12–2 7–9 Av main course £7.25 **BREWERY/COMPANY:** Wadworth
PRINCIPAL BEERS: Wadworth 6X, Henry's IPA & Butcombe Best.
FACILITIES: Children welcome Garden: Food served outside. Picnic benches Dogs allowed (in the garden only) **NOTES:** Parking 40

BRADFORD-ON-TONE — Map 03 ST12

White Horse Inn 🛏 🍷
TA4 1HF ☎ 01823 461239 🖷 01823 461872
Dir: N of A38 between Taunton & Wellington
A stone-built country pub, the White Horse is situated in the centre of the village opposite the church. Expect a friendly welcome and good value food, including bar snacks, a restaurant menu (also available in the bar) and daily specials from the blackboard. Favourites are salmon fishcakes, half shoulder of lamb with redcurrant jus, chicken stuffed with smoked cheese, and beer battered cod.
OPEN: 11.30–3.00 (Summer Sat–Sun open all day) 5.30–11
BAR MEALS: Lunch served: all week Dinner served: Mon–Sat 12–2 6.30–9.30 **RESTAURANT:** Lunch served: all week Dinner served: all week 12–2 6.30–9.30 Av 3 course à la carte £16
BREWERY/COMPANY: Enterprise Inns
PRINCIPAL BEERS: Butcombe Bitter, Marston's Pedigree, Cotleigh Tawney, Scottish Courage John Smith's. **FACILITIES:** Garden: Food served outdoors Dogs allowed none **NOTES:** Parking 20

BRIDGWATER — Map 03 ST33

Ashcott Inn 🍷
50 Bath Rd, Ashcott TA7 9QQ ☎ 01458 210282 🖷 01458 210282
Dir: M5 J23 follow signs for A39 to Bridgwater
Dating back to the 16th century, this former coaching inn has an attractive bar with beams and stripped stone walls, as well as quaint old seats and an assortment of oak and elm tables. Outside is a popular terrace and a delightful walled garden. The new licensees have introduced a new changing menu, perhaps offering many Cumberland sausages with caramelised red onions, supreme of salmon with a spinach and rocket salad, swordfish with black pepper and lime, and chargrilled tuna loin. Try one of the interestingly filled wraps or ciabatta rolls.
OPEN: 11–11 **BAR MEALS:** Lunch served: all week Dinner served: all week 12–2.45 5.30–9.30 Av main course £8
RESTAURANT: Lunch served: all week Dinner served: all week 12–2.45 5.30–9.30 Av 3 course à la carte £15
BREWERY/COMPANY: Heavitree **PRINCIPAL BEERS:** Abbot, Greene King Old Speckled Hen,. **FACILITIES:** Garden: Sheltered, Food served outside **NOTES:** Parking 50

BRUTON — Map 03 ST63

The Claire De Lune ♦♦♦♦ 🍷
2–4 High St BA10 0AA ☎ 01749 813395 🖷 01749 813395
e-mail: drew.beard@virgin.net
Dir: 6 miles off the A303 on the B3081, situated on the eastern end of Bruton High St
A modern bar and bistro and comfortable bedrooms housed in a large double-jettied building dating from 1500. Weekly dinner menus are cooked to order from high quality local ingredients. Starters might include monkfish

with saffron cream or red onion and goats' cheese tart, followed by fresh fish bouillabaisse or fillet of beef with shallot and port gravy. Desserts, local cheese and speciality teas and coffee follow. Opening times vary, especially out of season.
OPEN: 11–2 7–11 Closed: 1 Jan–31 Jan **BAR MEALS:** Lunch served: Fri 12–2 Av main course £10 **RESTAURANT:** Lunch served: Tue–Sun Dinner served: Tue–Sat 12–2 7–9 Av 3 course à la carte £17.50
BREWERY/COMPANY: Free House **FACILITIES:** Children welcome Children's licence Garden: Patio, food served outside
ROOMS: 3 bedrooms 3 en suite from s£35 d£47.50

BUTLEIGH — Map 03 ST53

The Rose & Portcullis
Sub Rd BA6 8TQ ☎ 01458 850287 🖷 01458 850120

A 16th-century freehouse, drawing its name from the local lord of the manor's coat of arms. Thatched bars and an inglenook fireplace are prominent features of the cosy interior. Large and varied bar and dining-room menus are on offer daily. Typical hot food choices include cottage pie, chicken breast in mild curry sauce and the gamut of grills. Vegetarian dishes include pasta with pine kernels: various omelettes, hot baguettes and junior choices are also on offer.
OPEN: 12–3 6–11 **BAR MEALS:** 12–2 7–9 **RESTAURANT:** 12–2 7–9 **BREWERY/COMPANY:** Free House
PRINCIPAL BEERS: Interbrew Flowers IPA, Butcombe Bitter, Wadworth 6X. **FACILITIES:** Children welcome Garden: Children's play area, food served outside Dogs allowed **NOTES:** Parking 50

CASTLE CARY — Map 03 ST63

The George Hotel ★ ★ 🍷
Market Place BA7 7AH ☎ 01963 350761 🖷 01963 350035
Dir: From A303 take A371 at Wincanton, then N to Castle Cary
Built of stone and thatch, this lovely 15th-century inn is under new management. Blending perfectly into this pretty, historic market town, it offers spacious bedrooms and cosy bars. An imaginative range of dishes is available, making good use of fresh local produce, and including, perhaps, a half shoulder of lamb with garlic and mint jus, or crispy duck confit with plum sauce.
OPEN: 11–11 **BAR MEALS:** Lunch served: all week Dinner served: all week 12–2.30 5.30–9.30 Av main course £4.95
RESTAURANT: Lunch served: Sun 12–2 Dinner served: all week 5.30–9.30 Av 3 course à la carte £15 **BREWERY/COMPANY:** Old English Inns **PRINCIPAL BEERS:** Otter, Wadworth 6X, Greene King IPA, Ruddles County. **FACILITIES:** Children welcome
NOTES: Parking 10 **ROOMS:** 14 bedrooms 14 en suite from s£50 d£75

continued

Horse Pond Inn ◆◆◆ 🛏 ♀

The Triangle BA7 7BD ☎ 01963 350318 📠 01963 351764
e-mail: horsepondinn@aol.com

Modernised and extended 16th-century inn, with en suite motel-style accommodation, situated in the historic country town of Castle Cary. Comfortable bar offering a range of real ales and an extensive menu of traditional pub food. For a lighter meal choose from omelettes, salads, jacket potatoes, or sandwiches. More substantial main courses include vegetable Kiev, sweet and sour pork in batter with noodles and onions, sole filled with scallops and crabmeat, Horse Pond chicken special, or a variety of pies.
OPEN: 10.30-11 (Sun 12-3, 7-10.30) **BAR MEALS:** Lunch served: all week 12-2 Dinner served: Tue-Sun 7-9 Av main course £4.50 **RESTAURANT:** Dinner served: all week 7-9 Av 3 course à la carte £12 Av 3 course fixed price £11 **BREWERY/COMPANY:** Free House **PRINCIPAL BEERS:** Scottish Courage Courage Best, Directors, John Smiths, Greene King Ruddles Best. **FACILITIES:** Children welcome Garden: Food served outdoors Dogs allowed (water)
NOTES: Parking 28 **ROOMS:** 5 bedrooms 5 en suite from s£35 d£45

CHARD — Map 03 ST30

The Happy Return 🛏

East St TA20 1EP ☎ 01460 63152
Dir: From M5 Taunton J, take Ilminster rd then follow signs to Chard, L at junct with A30 into East Street. Pub on R
A 17th-century friendly local with a warm welcome and straightforward selection of bar food. Be sure to sample the pies. The chef has twice been Steak and Kidney Pie Champion, and also won Pie of the Century in 2000. Other meal options include shank of lamb with sage and onion sauce, beef curry, pork chop in apple and brandy sauce, and the 'alternative' sandwich. These last have intriguing titles such as 'Green & Pleasant', 'Lap Dancer', 'Ike & Tina Tuna', and 'Burning Istanbul'.
OPEN: 12-2.30 Open all day Sat 7-11 **BAR MEALS:** Lunch served: all week Dinner served: all week 12-2 7-9.30 Av main course £6.50 **RESTAURANT:** Lunch served: all week Dinner served: all week 12-2 7-9.30 Av 3 course à la carte £15 Av 3 course fixed price £11.50 **BREWERY/COMPANY:** Free House **PRINCIPAL BEERS:** Draught Bass. **FACILITIES:** Garden: food served outside. Patio garden Dogs allowed (in the garden only) **NOTES:** Parking 10 **ROOMS:** 2 bedrooms from s£30 d£42

CHEW MAGNA — Map 03 ST56

Pony & Trap 🛏 ♀

Newtown BS40 8TQ ☎ 01275 332627
Refurbished 200-year-old rural pub enjoying a peaceful hillside location with beautiful views across the Chew Valley

from the rear garden. Good informal pubby atmosphere, a warm welcome and traditional home-cooked food await in the bar. Typical dishes range from beef casserole, fish pie, and chicken and mushroom pie, to salmon in white wine sauce, and fillet steak.
OPEN: 11-3 7-11 **BAR MEALS:** Lunch served: all week Dinner served: all week 12-2 7-9.30 Av main course £8 **RESTAURANT:** Lunch served: all week Dinner served: all week 12-2 7-9.30 **BREWERY/COMPANY:** Ushers **PRINCIPAL BEERS:** Ushers Best, Butcombe Bitter.
FACILITIES: Children welcome Garden: Food served outside. Panoramic views Dogs allowed **NOTES:** Parking 50

CHURCHILL — Map 03 ST45

Pick of the Pubs

Crown Inn

The Batch, Skinners Ln BS25 5PP ☎ 01934 852995
Dir: Take A38 S of Bristol. Turn R at Churchill traffic lights, then 1st L

Totally unspoilt gem of a stone-built pub situated at the base of the Mendip Hills and close to invigorating local walks. Originally a coaching stop on the old Bristol to Exeter route, it once housed the village grocer's and butcher's shop before real ale became its main commodity. Today, an ever-changing range of local brews are tapped straight from the barrel in the two rustic stone-walled and flagstone-floored bars. Bag a table by the open fire and sample, perhaps, a pint of RCH PG Steam Bitter from Weston-super-Mare. Freshly prepared food is served at lunchtime only, the blackboard listing rare beef sandwiches, filled jacket potatoes, cauliflower cheeses, locally-caught trout and popular casseroles. Peaceful front terrace for summer alfresco sipping.
OPEN: 12-11 **BAR MEALS:** Lunch served: all week 12-2.30 Av main course £4.50 **BREWERY/COMPANY:** Free House **PRINCIPAL BEERS:** Bass, Palmers IPA, guest ales.
FACILITIES: Children welcome Garden: Food served outside Dogs allowed **NOTES:** Parking 20 No credit cards

CHURCHINFORD — Map 03 ST21

The York Inn ◆◆◆ 🛏

Honiton Rd TA3 7RF ☎ 01823 601333
Dir: Exit M5 J26, towards Wellington for 0.5m, 1st L at rdbt. 1m L onto Ford St, 2m at top of hill L, 4m phone box, R to Inn
Traditional inn with beams and an inglenook fireplace, dating from around 1600 and located in an Area of Outstanding Natural Beauty. There is a lively locals bar serving freshly prepared snacks and a separate dining room, where the emphasis is on fresh seafood and locally supplied game.

continued

continued

England

CHURCHINFORD continued

Options include king scallops with garlic butter, mussels marinière, and turbot fillets with seafood sauce.
OPEN: 12–3 6–11 **BAR MEALS:** Lunch served: Tue–Sun 12–3 Dinner served: Mon–Sat 7–11 Av main course £5.50 **RESTAURANT:** Lunch served: Tue–Sun 12–3 Dinner served: Mon–Sat 7–11 Av 3 course à la carte £22 **BREWERY/COMPANY:** Free House
PRINCIPAL BEERS: Otter Bitter. **FACILITIES:** Children welcome Garden: flowered courtyard, Food served outside Dogs allowed
NOTES: Parking 12 **ROOMS:** 3 bedrooms 3 en suite from s£40 d£60

CLEVEDON
Map 03 ST47

The Black Horse
Clevedon Ln, Clapton-in-Gordano BS20 7RH ☎ 01275 842105

A traditional country inn that specialises in real ales from the cask and ciders. Built in the 14th-century, it still has flagstone floors and a large open fireplace and is genuinely unspoilt. The pub, tucked down country lanes close to the M5 (J19) was once used as the village lock-up and one room still has prison bars on the window. The bar food is simple and there is a large beer garden with a children's play area.
OPEN: 11–3 5–11 (Fri–Sat open all day) **BAR MEALS:** Lunch served: Mon–Sat 12–2 Av main course £4.50
BREWERY/COMPANY: Unique **PRINCIPAL BEERS:** Scottish Courage Best, Smiles Best, Interbrew Bass, Fuller's London Pride
FACILITIES: Children allowed Garden: Food served outside, patio Dogs allowed **NOTES:** Parking 40

CLUTTON
Map 03 ST65

The Hunters Rest
King Ln, Clutton Hill BS39 5QL
☎ 01761 452303 📠 01761 453308
e-mail: info@huntersrest.co.uk
Dir: Follow signs for Wells A37 go through village of Pensford untill large Rdbt turn L towards Bath. After 100 metres turn R into country lane pub 1m up hill

This inn, built as a hunting lodge for the Earl of Warwick around 1750, later became a smallholding and tavern for the

local north Somerset coal-mining community. The coal is long gone and the new clientele can now expect starters of smoked haddock, salmon and trout in cheese sauce or chicken tikka with mint yoghurt, progress to Hunters 'Oggies' (giant filled pasties), grills and Somerset faggots. Comfortable en suite bedrooms have recently been added on the pub's upper floor.
OPEN: 11.30–3 (All day Sun) 6.30–11 **BAR MEALS:** Lunch served: all week Dinner served: all week 12–2 6.30–9.45 Av main course £7
BREWERY/COMPANY: Free House
PRINCIPAL BEERS: Interbrew Bass, Smiles Best, Emoor Ale, Wadworth 6X. **FACILITIES:** Children welcome Garden: Food served outside Dogs allowed (water) **NOTES:** Parking 80
ROOMS: 4 bedrooms 4 en suite from s£50 d£75

COMBE HAY
Map 03 ST75

Pick of the Pubs

The Wheatsheaf ♦♦♦♦
BA2 7EG ☎ 01225 833504 📠 01225 833504
e-mail: silkwinp@aol.com
Dir: Take A369 Exeter rd from Bath to Odd Down, turn L at park towards Combe Hay. Follow lane for approx 2m to thatched cottage & turn L

Nestling on a hillside overlooking a peaceful valley, 2 miles south of Bath off the A367, the 17th-century Wheatsheaf is a pretty, black and white timbered pub, adorned with flowers in summer, and featuring an attractively landscaped terraced garden, an ideal spot for summer imbibing. Peter Wilkins took over in November 2000 and has maintained the unspoilt character of the rambling bar, complete with massive solid wooden tables, sporting prints and open log fire. Food on the varied carte features home-cooked dishes, notably local game in season and fresh fish. Typical choices may include ploughman's lunches, terrines, and locally caught trout, in addition to roast rack of lamb, breast of pheasant stuffed with cream cheese, mushrooms and garlic, and chicken filled with crab and prawns and wrapped in bacon. Comfortable overnight accommodation in a converted stable block.
OPEN: 11–2.30 6–10.30 (Sun 12–3,7–10.30) Closed: 25–26 Dec, Jan 1 **BAR MEALS:** Lunch served: all week Dinner served: all week 12–2 6.30–9.30 Av main course £10 **RESTAURANT:** Lunch served: all week Dinner served: all week 12–2 6.30–9.30 Av 3 course à la carte £18 **BREWERY/COMPANY:** Free House
PRINCIPAL BEERS: Courage Best, John Smith, Old Speckled Hen,. **FACILITIES:** Children welcome Children's licence Garden: Food served outside. Terraced garden Dogs allowed on leads **NOTES:** Parking 100 **ROOMS:** 3 bedrooms 3 en suite from s£50 d£75

continued

COMPTON MARTIN — Map 03 ST55

Ring of Bells
Main St BS40 6JE ☎ 01761 221284
e-mail: roger@ring47.freeserve.co.uk
Village pub with views of the Mendip Hills and the coast.
Family-friendly; good ales (Butcombe); bar food and daily
specials using local produce.

CRANMORE — Map 03 ST64

Strode Arms ♀
BA4 4QJ ☎ 01749 880450 📠 01749 880823
Dir: S of A361, 3.5m E of Shepton Mallet, 7.5m W of Frome
Rambling, mostly 15th-century building, formerly a
farmhouse and coaching inn, with a splendid front terrace
overlooking the village duck pond. Spacious bar areas are
neatly laid-out with comfortable country furnishings and
warmed by open log fires. Both the varied printed menu and
daily specials draw local diners and visitors to the nearby
East Somerset Railway. From the board order, perhaps,
smoked haddock and cod fishcakes, peppered rib of beef
with a shallot and red wine sauce, braised lambs' heart with
lemon and lime stuffing and, for pudding, a home-made
coconut and orange tart.
OPEN: 11.30-2.30 5.30-11.30 **BAR MEALS:** Lunch served: all week
12-2 Dinner served: Mon-Sat 7-9.30 Av main course £8
RESTAURANT: Lunch served: all week 12-2 Dinner served: Mon-Sat
7-9.30 Av 3 course à la carte £13.50
BREWERY/COMPANY: Wadworth **PRINCIPAL BEERS:** Henry's
IPA, Wadworth 6X, JCB. **FACILITIES:** Children welcome Garden:
Beer garden, patio, outdoor eating Dogs allowed **NOTES:** Parking
24

CREWKERNE — Map 03 ST40

The Manor Arms ♦♦♦ ♀
North Perrott TA18 7SG ☎ 01460 72901 📠 01460 72901
Dir: From A30 (Yeovil/Honiton rd) take A3066 towards Bridport, N Perrott
1.5m further on

On the Dorset-Somerset border, this 16th-century Grade II
listed pub and its neighbouring hamstone cottages overlook
the village green. The popular River Parrett trail runs by the
door. The inn has been lovingly restored and an inglenook
fireplace, flagstone floors and oak beams are among the
charming features inside. Bar food includes fillet steak
medallions, pan-fried whole plaice, shank of lamb, and
salmon darn. Most of the bedrooms are located in a
converted coach house.
OPEN: 11.30-2.30 (Sun 12-2.30 7-10.30) 6.45-11.00
BAR MEALS: Lunch served: all week Dinner served: all week 12-1.45
7-9 Av main course £5.25 **RESTAURANT:** Lunch served: all week

continued

Dinner served: all week 12-1.45 7-9 Av 3 course à la carte £18
BREWERY/COMPANY: Free House
PRINCIPAL BEERS: Butcombe, Otter. **FACILITIES:** Children
welcome Children's licence Garden: Beer garden, outdoor eating
NOTES: Parking 20 **ROOMS:** 8 bedrooms 8 en suite from s£35
d£42

CROSCOMBE — Map 03 ST54

The Bull Terrier ♦♦♦ 🐾
Long St BA5 3QJ ☎ 01749 343658
e-mail: barry.vidler@bullterrierpub.co.uk
Dir: half way between Wells & Shepton Mallet on the A371
One of Somerset's oldest pubs, formerly the Rose & Crown,
first licensed in 1612. The building dates from the late 15th
century, though the fireplace and ceiling in the inglenook bar
were added in the 16th century. One menu is offered
throughout, including steak and kidney pie, fresh trout and
almonds, mushroom and cashew pasta, and English lamb
steak.
OPEN: 12-2.30 7-11 (Sun 12-2.30, 7-10.30) **BAR MEALS:** Lunch
served: all week Dinner served: all week 12-2 7-9 Av main course £6
RESTAURANT: Lunch served: all week Dinner served: all week 12-2
7-9 Av 3 course à la carte £11 **BREWERY/COMPANY:** Free House
PRINCIPAL BEERS: Butcombe, Courage Directors, Marstons
Pedigree, Greene King Old Speckled Hen. **FACILITIES:** Garden:
Food served outside Dogs allowed **NOTES:** Parking 3
ROOMS: 2 bedrooms 2 en suite from s£30 d£50

DINNINGTON — Map 03 ST41

Rose & Crown Inn
TA17 8SX ☎ 01460 52397
Dir: So/A303 between South Petherton And Ilminster
Licensed for over 250 years, this traditional village pub is
situated on the old Fosse Way, and has a very relaxed
atmosphere and friendly locals. An ideal location for cycling
and walking. Local beers available.

DITCHEAT — Map 03 ST63

The Manor House Inn ♦♦♦♦ 🐾 ♀
BA4 6RB ☎ 01749 860276
e-mail: manorhouseinn@onetel.net.uk
Dir: from Shepton Mallet take the Castle Cary road, after 3m R to Ditcheat

Over the years since its first appearance as The White Hart,
this red-brick pub has had a number of names, but the
current owners choose to subtitle it 'The Heart of Somerset
Hospitality.' There are flagstone floors, en suite bedrooms in a
nearby cottage, and a menu that offers the likes of lamb and
mint sausages, grilled calves liver with bacon on bubble and
squeak cake, wild mushroom and brandy risotto, and

continued

DITCHEAT continued

individual aubergine charlotte with spicy vegetable filling.
There are also light luncheons, ciabattas, and specials.
OPEN: 12–2.30 6.30–11 (Sun 7–10.30) **BAR MEALS:** Lunch served:
all week Dinner served: all week 12–2 7–9.30 Av main course £6.95
RESTAURANT: Lunch served: all week Dinner served: all week 12–2
7–9.30 Av 3 course à la carte £22.50 **BREWERY/COMPANY:** Free
House **PRINCIPAL BEERS:** Butcombe, Scottish Courage John
Smith's. **FACILITIES:** Garden: Food served outside Dogs allowed
(water, toys) **NOTES:** Parking 25 **ROOMS:** 3 bedrooms 3 en suite
from s£45 d£65

EAST COKER   Map 03 ST51

The Helyar Arms ♦♦♦♦
Moor Ln BA22 9JR ☎ 01935 862332 📠 01935 864129
e-mail: info@helyar-arms.co.uk
Dir: from Yeovil, take A30 or A37, follow signs for East Coker

A Grade II listed country inn and restaurant, parts of which
date back to 1460, that owes its name to Archdeacon Helyar, a
chaplain to Queen Elizabeth I. En suite bedrooms are
furnished to a high standard with period appeal. Log fires
warm the old world bar, while the separate restaurant was
restored from an original apple loft. In new hands this year,
meals are prepared from fresh market produce covering a
wide range of local specialities.
OPEN: 11.30–3 (Sun 12–3,6–10.30) 6–11 **BAR MEALS:** Lunch
served: all week Dinner served: all week 12–2.30 6.30–9.30 Av main
course £7 **RESTAURANT:** Lunch served: all week Dinner served: all
week 12–2.30 6.30–9.30 Av 3 course à la carte £15
BREWERY/COMPANY: Inn Partnership **PRINCIPAL BEERS:** Bass,
Flowers Original, Fullers London Pride, Greene King IPA.
FACILITIES: Garden: Outdoor eating, BBQ **NOTES:** Parking 40
ROOMS: 6 bedrooms 6 en suite from s£59 d£70

EXFORD   Map 03 SS83

Pick of the Pubs

The Crown Inn ★★★ 🏵🏵 ♀
TA24 7PP ☎ 01643 831554 📠 01643 831665
e-mail: info@crownhotelexmoor.co.uk
*Dir: From M5 J25 follow signs for Taunton. Take A358 then B3224 via
Wheddon Cross to Exford*
A charming coaching inn dating back to the 16th century
situated in the heart of Exmoor National Park, with
Exford's village green to the front and a spacious, mature
water and terrace garden to the rear where outdoor
eating is a pleasure in summer. Hotel bedrooms are both
comfortable and well equipped, many with pretty views
out over this pretty moorland village. The cosy bar and a

smart dining-room set with crisp white table linen each
have their own menus bristling with imaginative ideas and
making full use of local produce. In the bar at lunch or in
the evening look for pressed terrine of venison with apple
and saffron chutney and flat mushroom, spinach and
goats' cheese Pithivier before baked halibut with
asparagus, spring onions and sage oil, herb-encrusted
chicken with ratatouille and olive oil mash and calves'
liver with pea purée and pancetta; rounding off with dark
chocolate delice or West Country cheeses. More formal
dinners and Sunday lunch are served at fixed prices in the
restaurant.
OPEN: 11–3 6–11 **BAR MEALS:** Lunch served: all week Dinner
served: all week 12–2 6.30–9.30 Av main course £7.50
RESTAURANT: Lunch served: Sun 12–2 Dinner served: all week
7–9 Av 3 course à la carte £25 Av 4 course fixed price £32.50
BREWERY/COMPANY: Free House
PRINCIPAL BEERS: Exmoor Ale, Guest ales.
FACILITIES: Children welcome Garden: Beer garden, outdoor
eating, patio, Dogs allowed (water) **NOTES:** Parking 20
ROOMS: 17 bedrooms 17 en suite from s£47.50 d£95

FAULKLAND   Map 03 ST75

The Faulkland Inn
BA3 5UH ☎ 01373 834312
e-mail: enquiries@faulkland-inn.co.uk
*Dir: On the A366 between Radstock and Trowbridge, 17M from Bristol &
the M4/M5*

Family-run coaching inn set in a village complete with a green,
stocks, standing stones and pond. The style of cooking is
unique to the area, with a modern international approach,
utilising local fish, game and cheese. Weekly menus range
through various platters, pasta, curry and chargrilled steaks in
the bar, and restaurant dishes such as noisettes of wild boar,
haggis and red onion tart with brandy and peppercorn sauce.
OPEN: 12–3 6–11 **BAR MEALS:** Lunch served: all week Dinner
served: all week 12–2 7–10 Av main course £5.50
RESTAURANT: Lunch served: all week Dinner served: all week 12–2
7–9.30 Av 3 course à la carte £20 **BREWERY/COMPANY:** Free
House **PRINCIPAL BEERS:** Bass & guest ales.
FACILITIES: Children welcome Garden: Food served outside
NOTES: Parking 30 **ROOMS:** 3 bedrooms 3 en suite from s£30
d£35

Tuckers Grave
Faulkland BA3 5XF ☎ 01373 834230
Tapped ales and farm cider in Somerset's smallest pub. Tiny
atmospheric bar with old settles. Lunchtime sandwiches and
ploughman's lunches.

continued

FITZHEAD
Map 03 ST12

Fitzhead Inn ♦♦♦ 🛏️
TA4 3JP ☎ 01823 400667
Expect a relaxed atmosphere, good real ales – including local varieties – and appetising home-cooked food at this 250-year-old pub hidden away in the Vale of Taunton. One can expect to encounter daily specials such as roast duck breast, fillet steak filled with Stilton and an array of fish and seafood that can extend to a spectacular seafood platter if ordered in advance. The four bedrooms are all en suite, but note that credit cards are not taken.
OPEN: 12–2 7–11 **BAR MEALS:** Lunch served: Wed–Sun 12–2 Dinner served: all week 7–9.45 Av main course £7
RESTAURANT: Lunch served: Wed–Sun 12–2 Dinner served: all week 7–9.45 Av 3 course à la carte £18
BREWERY/COMPANY: Free House **PRINCIPAL BEERS:** Cotleigh Tawny, Fuller's London Pride, Juwards Ales, Interbrew Bass.
FACILITIES: Children welcome Garden: Food served outside Dogs allowed **ROOMS:** 4 bedrooms 4 en suite No credit cards

FRESHFORD
Map 03 ST76

The Inn at Freshford 🛏️ ☂
BA3 6EG ☎ 01225 722250 📠 01225 723887
e–mail: dwill60632@aol.com
Dir: *1m from A36 between Beckington & Limpley Stoke*
Traditional 15th-century inn with log fires, located in the Limpley Valley. The area is ideal walking country, especially down by the Kennet & Avon Canal. Extensive gardens. A typical menu includes salmon, monkfish, trout, duck, venison, lamb, pork tenderloin, and swordfish.
OPEN: 11–3 6–11 **BAR MEALS:** Lunch served: all week Dinner served: all week 12–2 6–9 **RESTAURANT:** Lunch served: all week Dinner served: all week 12–2 6–9 Av 3 course à la carte £13
BREWERY/COMPANY: Latona Leisure
PRINCIPAL BEERS: Wadworth 6X, Marston's Pedigree.
FACILITIES: Children welcome Garden: Food served outside Dogs allowed **NOTES:** Parking 60

FROME
Map 03 ST74

Pick of the Pubs

The Horse & Groom ☂
East Woodlands BA11 5LY ☎ 01373 462802 📠 01373 462802
e–mail: horse.and.groom@care4free.net
Dir: *Just off Frome by-pass (A361 Shepton Mallet/Devizes rd)*

Peaceful 17th-century inn adorned with colourful hanging baskets, found at the end of a narrow lane opposite a farmhouse. As much a 'local' as a watering hole for visitors, the bar is furnished with stripped pine pews and

continued

settles on a flagstone floor. The comfortable little lounge has an inglenook fireplace and wood-burning stove, with easy chairs and sofas for relaxing. A huge range of food is served from the bar menu, and the restaurant carte and daily specials. Snacks include various filled baguettes, plus pasta carbonara, lambs' liver and bacon in gravy, and gammon steak with pineapple. A typical meal in the restaurant might be aubergine cheesecake or Halloumi stuffed peppers, pheasant breast with claret and orange sauce, or seared Aylesbury duck breast, and chocolate bread and butter pudding.
OPEN: 11.30–2.30 (Sun 12–3, 7–10) 6.30–11 **BAR MEALS:** Lunch served: Tue–Sun 12–2 Dinner served: Tue–Sat 6.30–9 Av main course £7 **RESTAURANT:** Lunch served: Tue–Sun 12–2 Dinner served: Tue–Sat 6.30–9 Av 3 course à la carte £15
PRINCIPAL BEERS: Wadworth 6X, Butcombe Bitter, Branscombe Branoc, Brakspear Bitter. **FACILITIES:** Garden: Food served outside Dogs allowed (water) **NOTES:** Parking 20

Pick of the Pubs

The Talbot Inn ♦♦♦♦
High St, Mells BA11 3PN ☎ 01373 812254 📠 01373 813599
e–mail: roger@talbotinn.com
See Pick of the Pubs on page 410

The White Hart 🛏️
Trudoxhill BA11 5DP ☎ 01373 836324 📠 01373 836566
Home of the Ash Vine Brewery (visits by arrangement). Bustling village pub with open-plan bar, extensive menu, farm cider and country wines. Menu includes pan-fried sea bass, fillet steak with red wine jus, steak and kidney pudding, vegetarian cottage pie, and braised lamb shank with tomato and basil.
OPEN: 12–3 5.30–11 **BAR MEALS:** Lunch served: all week Dinner served: all week 12–2 6.30–9.30 Av main course £6.95
RESTAURANT: Lunch served: all week 12–2.30 6.30–9.30 Av 3 course à la carte £7.95 **BREWERY/COMPANY:** Free House
PRINCIPAL BEERS: Butcombe, Hewish IPA, Wadworth 6X.
FACILITIES: Children welcome Garden: Food served outside. Enclosed garden **NOTES:** Parking 40

GLASTONBURY
Map 03 ST53

The Who'd a Thought It Inn ☂
17 Northload St BA6 9JJ ☎ 01458 834460 📠 01458 831039
e–mail: restaurant@whodathoughtit.co.uk
Dir: *Bottom of High St, 100yds from Abbey ruins*
18th-century building with lots of local artefacts and interesting memorabilia. One wall is covered in old photographs and there is even an award-winning gents loo. Large patio can fit up to 30 people. Typical menu includes steak and ale pie, spinach and Stilton lasagne, lamb steak and minty gravy, and a selection of roasts.
OPEN: 11–11 (Sun 12.30–2.45, 7–10.30) (Winter 11–3, 5–11) Closed: 25 Dec **BAR MEALS:** Lunch served: all week Dinner served: all week 12–2.15 5–9.15 **RESTAURANT:** Lunch served: all week Dinner served: all week 12–2.15 5.45–9.15 Av 3 course à la carte £13
BREWERY/COMPANY: Palmers Brewery
PRINCIPAL BEERS: Palmers IPA & 200 Premium Ale.
FACILITIES: Children welcome Garden: Patio, food served outside Dogs allowed **NOTES:** Parking 10 **ROOMS:** 5 bedrooms 5 en suite from sE40 dE58

OPEN: 12–2.30 6–11
BAR MEALS: L served all week.
D served all week. 12–2.30 7–12 Av
main course £5.50
RESTAURANT: L served all week.
D served all week. 12–2.30 7–12 Av
cost 3 course £20
BREWERY/COMPANY: FREE
HOUSE
PRINCIPAL BEERS: Interbrew
Bass, Butcombe Bitter, Fuller's
London Pride, Scottish Courage
Courage Best
FACILITIES: Children welcome,
dogs allowed. Garden: Cottage
garden, food served outdoors
NOTES: Parking 10
ROOMS 8 en suite Min price
double room £65 Min price single
room £45

The Talbot 15th-Century Coaching Inn

A rambling 15th-century coaching inn at the heart of this timeless feudal village noted for a magnificent manor house, splendid church and several unspoilt cottages made from traditional stone.

◆◆◆◆
High Street Mells BA11 3PN
☎ 01373 812254 ▤ 01373 813599
e-mail: roger@talbotinn.com
Dir: From A36(T), R onto A361 to Frome,
then A362 towards Radstock, 0.5m then
L to Mells 2.5m.

Built from the same materials, the friendly inn has loads of character and a pleasant, buzzy atmosphere. Lots of little stone-flagged and beamed bars and eating areas are charmingly decorated with terracotta-painted walls and country prints. These make a charming setting for some excellent real ales and, undisputed star of the show, the reliable home-cooked food. For lunch, hot tomato and Mozzarella tartlet, toasted goats' cheese ciabatta, and tagliatelle, along with

Mediterranean sandwich made from regional breads and different daily fillings from the blackboard, curry of the day with basmati rice and all the trimmings, and various ploughmans (ham, Stilton, Cheddar or pâté. The evening carte picks up the pace with starters like fresh crab mousse wrapped in smoked salmon, mussels cooked in white wine and cream, and terrine of seasonal Somerset game. The main courses are also full of interest, with pan-fried breast and confit leg of Gressingham duck with a blackcurrant and orange sauce, wild mushroom and asparagus tagliatelle in a herb cream sauce, and full rack of barbecued ribs served with fries and salad. From the chargrill come a selection of steaks with choice of sauce, and fish specials delivered daily from Brixham. For those who want the evening to go on and on, there is well-furnished and comfortable accommodation.

HASELBURY PLUCKNETT   Map 03 ST41

Pick of the Pubs

The Haselbury Inn ♀
North St TA18 7RJ ☎ 01460 72488 📠 01460 72488
e-mail: howard@haseluburyinn.fsnet.co.uk
Dir: *Just off A30 between Crewkerne & Yeovil on B3066*

This extended village inn started life as a rope factory for the old ports of West Bay and Lyme Regis. It now boasts a comfortable bar with exposed stone and brickwork and open fires, and a separate dining-room. Circular pub walks details are available from the bar. Great British roasts on Sunday are a highlight, other choices range from filo tartlet of bacon and mushrooms in blue cheese sauce to steaks and grills, daily blackboard selections and vegetarian dishes.
OPEN: 11.45–2.30 6–11 (closed Mon) **BAR MEALS:** Lunch served: Tue–Sun Dinner served: Tue–Sun 12–2 6.30–9.30 Av main course £8 **RESTAURANT:** Lunch served: Tue–Sun 12–2 6.30–9.30 Av 3 course à la carte £17 Av 3 course fixed price £15 **BREWERY/COMPANY:** Free House **PRINCIPAL BEERS:** Palmers IPA, Fuller's London Pride, Greene King Old Speckled Hen, Adnams Broadside.
FACILITIES: Garden: Food served outside, Dove cote **NOTES:** Parking 50

See Pub Walk on page 417

HINTON BLEWETT   Map 03 ST55

Ring O'Bells ♀ NEW
BS39 5AN ☎ 01761 452239
Dir: *11 miles S of Bristol on A37 toward Wells, small road signed in Clutton & Temple Cloud*
A 200-year-old pub with a traditional log fire in winter months, and a cosy, warming atmosphere. The pub boasts several sports teams, including cricket, rugby, golf and shove ha'penny. It serves a wide choice of real ales, and concentrates on good value food. Typical dishes include beef in Guinness served in a giant Yorkshire pudding, chicken stuffed with Stilton, and lamb shank in a port and rosemary sauce.
OPEN: 11–3.30 (Sat 11–4, 6–11 Sun 12–4, 7–10.30) 5–11
BAR MEALS: Lunch served: all week Dinner served: all week 12–2 6.30–10 Av main course £6.50 **BREWERY/COMPANY:** Free House
PRINCIPAL BEERS: Abbey Ales Bellringer, Wadworth 6X, Fuller's London Pride, Wickwar BOB. **FACILITIES:** Children welcome Garden: Small garden with lovely views Dogs allowed (water) **NOTES:** Parking 20

HINTON ST GEORGE   Map 03 ST41

The Lord Poulett Arms ♦♦♦♦ 🛏 ♀
High St TA17 8SE ☎ 01460 73149
e-mail: lordpoulett@aol.com
Dir: *2m N of Crewkerne, 1.5m S of A303*
17th-century thatched Hamstone inn with sunny beer garden and a roaring fire in the bar during winter months. Facilities include a private dining/meeting room and four letting bedrooms. Regular folk and blues evenings. Strong emphasis on home-cooked food with seasonal produce used in the regularly-changing menus and specials board. Plenty of fish from the Dorset coast (scallops, mussels, sea bass) with perhaps red mullet and ginger sauce, plaice stuffed with prawns, and local steak and pork dishes.
OPEN: 11.30–2.30 6.30–11 (Sun 12–2.30, 7–10.30)
BAR MEALS: Lunch served: Tue–Sun Dinner served: Tue–Sun 12–2 7–9 **RESTAURANT:** Lunch served: Tue–Sun Dinner served: Tue–Sun 12–2 7–9 **BREWERY/COMPANY:** Free House
PRINCIPAL BEERS: Butcombe Bitter, Palmers IPA + Guest Beers.
FACILITIES: Children welcome Garden: Secluded, food served outside Dogs allowed (water) tap **NOTES:** Parking 10
ROOMS: 4 bedrooms 4 en suite from s£28 d£48

ILCHESTER   Map 03 ST52

Ilchester Arms 🛏 ♀
The Square BA22 8LN ☎ 01935 840220 📠 01935 841353
e-mail: info@ilchesterarmshotel.co.uk
Dir: *From A303 take A37 to Ilchester/Yeovil, L towards Ilchester at 2nd sign marked Ilchester. Hotel 100yds on R*
Dominating the old town square, an elegant Georgian building that still sports flagstone floors and open fires. Brasserie-style meals in the bar, and a more serious approach in the dining room, show a penchant for Caribbean cuisine alongside more traditional fare. Chef's specials list avocado and plantain salad and coconut prawns and 'Jammin' Jamaican chicken'! There's a great choice of wines by the glass to wash down the more conservative garlic mushroom parcels, pork fillet with cider and apple sauce.
OPEN: 11–11 **BAR MEALS:** Lunch served: all week Dinner served: all week 12–2.30 7–10 Av main course £9.50 **RESTAURANT:** Dinner served: Wed–Sat 7–9.30/10 Av 3 course à la carte £24 Av 3 course fixed price £17.95 **BREWERY/COMPANY:** Free House
PRINCIPAL BEERS: Regularly changing ales from local breweries.
FACILITIES: Children welcome Garden: Patio, food served outside
NOTES: Parking 25 **ROOMS:** 8 bedrooms 8 en suite from s£40 d£60

ILMINSTER   Map 03 ST31

New Inn
Dowlish Wake TA19 0NZ ☎ 01460 52413
Dir: *From Ilminster follow signs for Kingstone then Dowlish Wake*
A 350-year-old stone-built pub tucked away in a quiet village close to Perry's thatched cider mill. There are two bars with woodburning stoves, bar billiards and a skittle alley. The menu features local produce and West Country specialities, including fish, steaks and home-made pies.
OPEN: 11–3 (Sun 12–3, 7–10.30) 6–11 **BAR MEALS:** Lunch served: all week 12–2.30 Dinner served: Mon–Sat 7–9.30 Av main course £6.50 **BREWERY/COMPANY:** Free House
PRINCIPAL BEERS: Butcombe Bitter + guest beers.
FACILITIES: Children welcome Garden: Beer garden, Food served outdoors Dogs allowed **NOTES:** Parking 50

KILVE — Map 03 ST14

The Hood Arms ◆◆◆◆ 🛏

TA5 1EA ☎ 01278 741210 ▤ 01278 741477
e-mail: Mattbri@tinyworld.co.uk
Dir: Off A39 between Bridgwater & Minehead
Traditional 17th-century coaching inn, set among the Quantock
Hills, and a popular watering hole for walkers. Kilve Beach is
within a short walking distance, past an old priory thought to
have been the haunt of smugglers, and is famous for its
strange 'moonscape' landscape and fossils. A typical menu
includes steak and ale pie, salmon on spinach and tarragon
mash, duck with black cherry sauce, and trout with apple and
almond butter. Accommodation includes two self-catering
cottages.
OPEN: 11-3 6-11 **BAR MEALS:** Lunch served: all week Dinner
served: all week 12-3 6-9.30 Av main course £6.45
RESTAURANT: Lunch served: all week Dinner served: all week 12-3
6-9.30 Av 3 course à la carte £15.95 **BREWERY/COMPANY:** Free
House **PRINCIPAL BEERS:** Wadworth 6X, Otter Ale, Exmoor Fox,
Cotleigh Tawney Ale. **FACILITIES:** Children welcome Children's
licence Garden: Beer garden, food served outdoors, patio Dogs
allowed Some areas, Water **NOTES:** Parking 12
ROOMS: 6 bedrooms 6 en suite from s£38 d£52

KINGSDON — Map 03 ST52

Pick of the Pubs

Kingsdon Inn 🛏 ♀
TA11 7LG ☎ 01935 840543
See Pick of the Pubs on page 413

LANGLEY MARSH — Map 03 ST02

The Three Horseshoes 🛏
TA4 2UL ☎ 01984 623763 ▤ 01984 623763
*Dir: M5 J25 take B3227 to Wiveliscombe. From square follow signs for
Langley Marsh. 1m*
Handsome 300-year-old red sandstone village inn, full of old
motoring memorabilia, banknote collections, model
aeroplanes and beer mats. This unspoilt pub has a lively
locals' bar with traditional games, decent ales and local
farmhouse cider. Food is genuinely made to order, with
vegetables from the garden, and no chips or fried food. Expect
daily specials like roasted guinea fowl, rabbit casserole,
pigeon breasts in red wine, home-made pies (fish or steak
and kidney), and chilli con carne.
OPEN: 12-2.30 7-11 (closed Mon Oct-Mar) **BAR MEALS:** Lunch
served: all week Dinner served: all week 12-2 7-9.30 Av main course
£5.50 **RESTAURANT:** Lunch served: all week Dinner served: all
week 12-2 7-9.30 **BREWERY/COMPANY:** Free House
PRINCIPAL BEERS: Palmer IPA, Otter Ale, Fuller's London Pride,
Adnams Southwold. **FACILITIES:** Garden: Beer garden, food served
outdoors **NOTES:** Parking 6

LANGPORT — Map 03 ST42

Pick of the Pubs

The Halfway House
Pitney TA10 9AB ☎ 01458 252513
Dir: on B3153 between Langport and Somerton
This is a pub largely dedicated to the promotion of real
ale as produced by the many excellent micro-breweries in

Somerset, Devon and Wiltshire. There are always six to
ten real ales available in tip-top condition. There is also an
excellent choice of bottled Continental beers. This
delightfully old-fashioned rural pub draws customers from
a huge area and it has been the winner of numerous
national awards. Three homely rooms boast open fires,
books and games; no music or electronic games. Home-
cooked meals (except Sundays when it is too busy with
drinkers) include soups, sausages, sandwiches and a good
selection of curries in the evening.
OPEN: 11.30-3 5.30-11 Closed: 25 Dec **BAR MEALS:** Lunch
served: Mon-Sat Dinner served: Mon-Sat 12-2 7-9.30 Av main
course £3.50 **BREWERY/COMPANY:** Free House
PRINCIPAL BEERS: Butcombe Bitter, Teignworthy, Otter Ale,
Cotleigh Tawny Ale. **FACILITIES:** Children welcome Garden: 3
acres, seating, food served outside Dogs allowed (water)
NOTES: Parking 30

Rose & Crown
Huish Episcopi TA10 9QT ☎ 01458 250494
Boasting a licensee who was born on the premises, this
thatched pub is probably better known in the area as 'Eli's' -
the name of the owner's father who ran the Rose & Crown for
55 years. In the same family for 130 years, few changes have
taken place here and the pub still has a thatched roof,
flagstones and a wide selection of old pub games. Local farm
cider and cider brandy accompany dishes such as steak and
ale pie, chicken curry, and various ploughman's lunches.
OPEN: 11.30-2.30 5.30-11 (Fri-Sat 11.30-11, Sun 12-10.30)
BAR MEALS: Lunch served: all week Dinner served: all week 12-2
6-8.30 Av main course £6 **BREWERY/COMPANY:** Free House
PRINCIPAL BEERS: Teignworthy Reel Ale, Interbrew Bass, Hop Back
Summer Lightning, Butcombe Bitter. **FACILITIES:** Children welcome
Garden: Beer garden, food served outdoors Dogs allowed (water)
NOTES: Parking 50 No credit cards

The River Parrett Trail
The River Parrett Trail was devised to link the
gentle hill country of the Dorset border with the
fragile wetlands of the Somerset Levels and
Moors. The final stretch follows the winding river
towards Bridgwater Bay and the Bristol Channel.
Taking you to the heart of this unspoilt corner of
England, the 50-mile trail can be completed either
as a comfortable walk over three or four days, or
as a series of shorter rambles which allow time to
discover and explore the varied landscapes en
route. Along the way you'll find old mills,
medieval churches and historic sites, as well as
the withy beds and willow plantations at the heart
of Somerset's willow-growing and basket-making
industry. Ideally-placed pubs on the route of the
trail include the delightful 16th-century Manor
Arms at North Perrott, the 400-year-old Royal
Oak at Over Stratton, and the cottage-style
Rose & Crown at Stoke St Gregory.

continued

OPEN: 11-3 6-11

BAR MEALS: L served all week.
D served Mon-Sat. 12-2 7-10
Av main course £5.50

BREWERY/COMPANY:
FREE HOUSE

PRINCIPAL BEERS: Cotleigh Barn Owl, Otter Bitter, Cottage Golden Arrow, Fullers London Pride

FACILITIES: Children Welcome. Garden: Beer garden, food served outside

NOTES: Parking 16

Kingsdon Inn

A delightful 300-year-old cottage at the end of a flower-edged path, prettily thatched in picture postcard style. Located just a few minutes drive from the A303 in an attractive village, it makes an ideal staging post where weary travellers can relax over a good home-cooked lunch or supper.

KINGSDON TA11 7LG
☎ 01935 840543
Dir: From A303 take A372 towards Langport then B3151 toward Street, 1st R and R again.

Peaceful pastoral views make the front garden a pleasant spot in summer, while the rambling bars create a charming ambience all year round. The older, original front rooms have low beamed ceilings, a huge stone inglenook now for decorative purposes only, scrubbed pine and old stripped tables and chairs and a warm decor, while on cooler days there is a blazing log fire on a raised hearth in the lower bar. In this welcoming, convivial atmosphere the food is presented on separate evening and lunchtime menus, with daily-changing choices featuring fresh fish and game in

season. Good value dishes include lamb's liver with bacon and onions, poached salmon with parsley butter, ham and mushroom tagliatelle, garlic chicken and bacon salad, and beefsteak and kidney pie, with lighter choices or starters such as Greek salad, Guinness and stilton p,tÈ, and soused herring fillet. In the evening expect kidneys in Madeira sauce, crab and prawn mornay, and Mediterranean vegetable parcels followed by wild rabbit in Dijon mustard sauce, half a roast duck in scrumpy sauce, and roast whole shank of pork. Desserts should not be missed: lemon brioche pudding, banana fudge pie, and chocolate truffle torte should go down well with Cotleigh Barn Owl, Butcombe Bitter, and various other well-kept West Country ales.

LEIGH UPON MENDIP
Map 03 ST64

The Bell Inn ♀
BA3 5QQ ☎ 01373 812316 ▤ 01373 812163
Dir: head for Bath, then twrds Radstock following the Frome Rd, turn twrds Mells and then Leigh-on-Mendip

Situated on the old pilgrims' route to Glastonbury, this historic inn has a fireplace dating back to 1687, built by the same stonemasons who constructed the church. Traditional pub grub includes steak and kidney pie, pork, leek and cider sausages, chicken, ham and leek pie, and scampi with salad. More adventurous dishes include prime beef fillet with roasted shallot and Guinness sauce, osso bucco of lamb, wild rice risotto with woodland mushrooms, and oven-roast chicken supreme with port and raisin sauce.
OPEN: 12–3 6.30–11 **BAR MEALS:** Lunch served: all week Dinner served: all week 12–2 6.30–9 Av main course £7
RESTAURANT: Lunch served: all week Dinner served: all week 12–2 6.30–9 Av 3 course à la carte £15 **BREWERY/COMPANY:** Free House **PRINCIPAL BEERS:** Wadworth 6X, Bass, Butcombe Bitter.
FACILITIES: Children welcome Garden: Beer garden, patio, outdoor eating **NOTES:** Parking 20

LITTON
Map 03 ST55

The Kings Arms
BA3 4PW ☎ 01761 241301

Full of nooks and crannies, this 15th-century local at the heart of the Mendips has a large garden with a stream running through it, and boasts a separate children's play area and outdoor eating. Menus offer smoked haddock fish pie, homemade chilli, and steak, mushroom and Guinness pie. Kings Arms Platters include Pigman's Platter – jumbo pork Lincolnshire sausage with eggs and chips.
OPEN: 11–2.30 6–11 **BAR MEALS:** Lunch served: all week Dinner served: all week 12–2.30 6.30–10 Av main course £8
BREWERY/COMPANY: Free House **PRINCIPAL BEERS:** Bass, Butcombe, Wadworth 6X, Flowers. **FACILITIES:** Children welcome Garden: Dogs allowed (In garden only. On lead at all times)
NOTES: Parking 50

LOWER VOBSTER
Map 03 ST74

Vobster Inn
BA3 5RJ ☎ 01373 812920
e-mail: vobsterinn@bt.com
Set in four acres in rolling countryside close to Bath, the Vobster Inn is a 17th-century Mendip stone building with a large garden featuring a popular summer barbecue and boules pitch. In addition to chicken breast stuffed with apple smoked cheese, wrapped in Parma ham, and various steaks, the interesting menu may list seafood such as pan-fried Newlyn plaice fillet, Sicilian swordfish, or oven roasted fillet of mahi mahi. Puddings might include tiramisù, poached pears in Marsala, and sticky pineapple sponge.
OPEN: 12–3 7–11 **BAR MEALS:** Lunch served: all week Dinner served: all week 12–2 7–10 Av main course £8.50
RESTAURANT: Lunch served: all week Dinner served: all week 12–2 7–11 Av 3 course à la carte £18 **BREWERY/COMPANY:** Free House **PRINCIPAL BEERS:** Butcombe, Scottish Courage Courage Best, Wadworth 6X. **FACILITIES:** Children welcome Garden: Food served outside **NOTES:** Parking 45

LUXBOROUGH
Map 03 SS93

Pick of the Pubs

Royal Oak Inn 🛏
TA23 0SH ☎ 01984 640319 ▤ 01984 641561
e-mail: royaloakof.luxborough@virgin.net
Dir: From A38 (Taunton/Minehead) at Washford take minor rd S thru Roadwater

A very rural and unspoilt 14th-century inn at the heart of local community and farming life in a small Exmoor hamlet. In previous incarnations it has been an abattoir, a butchers and a tailors, and the Blazing Stump bar refers to a parsimonious landlord who fed the fire only one log at a time. A recent renovation has left the rustic character intact, with a large open fireplace, low beams and slate floor in the main bar, and tastefully decorated dining areas. In this cosy atmosphere the fine food and well-kept real ales have gained a well-earned reputation. Typical lunch dishes include smoked haddock and leek fishcake, mixed game casserole, and steak and ale pie, with dinner extending to whole grilled trout, roast tail of monkfish, confit of lamb casserole, and onion and thyme tartlet.
OPEN: 12–2.30 6–11 **BAR MEALS:** Lunch served: all week Dinner served: all week 12–2.30 7–9 Av main course £12
RESTAURANT: Lunch served: all week Dinner served: all week 12–2.30 6–9 Av 3 course à la carte £25
BREWERY/COMPANY: Free House **PRINCIPAL BEERS:** Tawney, Palmers 200, Exmoor Gold, Palmers Dorset Gold.
FACILITIES: Children welcome Garden: Food served outside, courtyard garden Dogs allowed (water provided) **NOTES:** Parking 18 **ROOMS:** 12 bedrooms 11 en suite from s£45 d£55

MIDFORD
Map 03 ST76

Hope & Anchor 🐾 ♀
BA2 7DD ☎ 01225 832296 📠 01225 832296
Dir: *A367 from Bath to Radstock, L onto B3110 to Frome/Midford. Pub on bottom of hill under railway bridge*

Unassuming stone pub set hard beside the busy B3110 in the Cam Valley, three miles south of Bath. The comfortably furnished bar and dining area, with bare boards, open stone fireplace and a warm decor, is the setting for some enjoyable pub food. In the bar, order the tapas selection, salmon fishcakes, or pork and garlic sausages, while restaurant fare may include fillet of venison, chicken satay or pan-fried skate wings with artichoke and chilli salsa.
OPEN: 11.30–2.30 6.30–11 Closed: Dec 25–26 **BAR MEALS:** Lunch served: all week Dinner served: all week 12–2 6.30–9.30 Av main course £6 **RESTAURANT:** Lunch served: all week Dinner served: all week 12–2 6.30–9.30 Av 3 course à la carte £22
BREWERY/COMPANY: Free House
PRINCIPAL BEERS: Deuchars IPA, Bass, Butcombe, London Pride.
FACILITIES: Garden: Food served outside. Terraced garden Dogs allowed (in the garden only) **NOTES:** Parking 30

MIDSOMER NORTON
Map 03 ST65

Old Station
Wells Rd, Hallatrow, nr Paulton ☎ 01761 452228
Eccentric pub full of bric-à-brac and curios, offering a good range of West Country ales, interesting food in both bars and dining room, and en suite bedrooms.

MONKSILVER
Map 03 ST03

Pick of the Pubs

The Notley Arms ♀
TA4 4JB ☎ 01984 656217
The pub is situated on the edge of Exmoor in a small hamlet with a population of approximately 90 souls, whose winter trade contributes largely to the success of the coach-house skittle alley that graces the pub car park. It is the second pub in the village, the other is the thatched cottage opposite. All are inter-connected with Old Cleeve Abbey, and started as many village pubs did as a 'resting place' for visiting monks. The daily blackboard menu, amended at each session, offers a good choice of home-made fare: soup, coarse country-style pâté, and smoked mackerel, and special dishes such as bacon, leek and cider pudding; aubergine tagine with dates, almonds and couscous, or red mullet fillets Mediterranean style with orange and capers. Old-fashioned puddings include treacle tart with clotted

cream, and Somerset apple cake. In winter a roast is served at Sunday lunchtime.
OPEN: 11.30–2.30 6.30–11 **BAR MEALS:** Lunch served: all week Dinner served: all week 12–2 7–9.30 Av main course £5
BREWERY/COMPANY: Unique Pub Co
PRINCIPAL BEERS: Exmoor Ale, Wadworth 6X, Smiles Best.
FACILITIES: Children welcome Garden: Food served outside. Pretty garden Dogs allowed On lead, water provided
NOTES: Parking 26

MONTACUTE
Map 03 ST41

Kings Arms Inn 🐾 ♀
TA15 6UU ☎ 01935 822513 📠 01935 826549
Dir: *Turn off A303 at A3088 roundabout signposted Montacute. Hotel by church in village centre*
In a picturesque village near to the National Trust's Montacute House, the location of the 1995 movie Sense and Sensibility, this delightful 17th-century Hamstone inn offers a relaxed, country house atmosphere. There is an ever-changing menu of freshly cooked main meals, which can be enjoyed in the restaurant or bar. Expect sausage and bean casserole or lamb hot pot at lunchtime, as well as a good selection of sandwiches. The à la carte menu includes spinach risotto and baked duck breast.
OPEN: 11–11 (Sun 12–10.30) **BAR MEALS:** Lunch served: all week Dinner served: all week 12–2.30 7–9 Av main course £9
RESTAURANT: Lunch served: all week Dinner served: all week 12–2.30 7–9 Av 3 course à la carte £25 Av 3 course fixed price £19.95
BREWERY/COMPANY: Greene King **PRINCIPAL BEERS:** Scottish Courage Courage Directors, Greene King Abbot Ale.
FACILITIES: Children welcome Garden: Large lawn, orchard, food served outside Dogs allowed (water) **NOTES:** Parking 12
ROOMS: 15 bedrooms 15 en suite from s£55 d£70

The Phelips Arms 🐾 ♀
The Borough TA15 6XB ☎ 01935 822557
e-mail: thephelipsarms@aol.com
Dir: *From Cartgate roundabout on A303 follow signs for Montacute*

A 17th-century listed hamstone building overlooking the village square and close to historic Montacute House (NT) features a secluded rear garden and comfortable bars. Well-kept real ales and wines are served in a convivial atmosphere to accompany confidently home-cooked food. Freshly prepared ingredients, using local produce wherever possible, supplement baguettes and jacket potatoes at lunchtime with queen scallops in garlic butter, local ham, egg and chips and Greek salad of goats' cheese, olives and vinaigrette.
OPEN: 11.30–2.30 6–11 Closed: 25 Dec **BAR MEALS:** Lunch served: all week Dinner served: all week 12–2 6–9 Av main course £7

continued

continued

RESTAURANT: Lunch served: all week Dinner served: all week 12–2 6–9 **BREWERY/COMPANY:** Palmers
PRINCIPAL BEERS: Palmers IPA & 200 Premium Ale.
FACILITIES: Garden: Food served outside Dogs allowed (water)
NOTES: Parking 40 **ROOMS:** 4 bedrooms 4 en suite from s£27 d£50

NETHER STOWEY   Map 03 ST13

The Cottage Inn
Keenthorne TA5 1HZ ☎ 01278 732355
Dir: M5 J23 follow A39 signs for Cannington/Minehead. Inn on A39
Dating from the 16th century, the Cottage is an old coaching inn and traditional cider house where cider was made until about 15 years ago. The walls of the bar are original cob-stone and wattle around one metre thick at its base. Hearty eating options include a carvery with four roasts and five veg, cottage pies, curries, steaks, and Thai green curry.
OPEN: 11–11 **BAR MEALS:** Lunch served: all week 12–2.30 Dinner served: Tue–Sun 6–9.30 Av main course £5.95
RESTAURANT: Lunch served: all week 12–2.30 Dinner served: Tue–Sun 6–9.30 Av 3 course à la carte £13
BREWERY/COMPANY: Free House
PRINCIPAL BEERS: Worthington, Bass, Otter.
FACILITIES: Children welcome Garden: Food served outside. Patio area Dogs allowed (in the garden only) **NOTES:** Parking 60

NORTH CURRY   Map 03 ST32

The Bird in Hand
1 Queen Square TA3 6LT ☎ 01823 490248
A friendly 300-year-old village inn with large stone inglenook fireplaces, flagstone floors, exposed beams and studwork. Cheerful staff make you feel at home. Blackboard specials concentrate on local produce.
OPEN: 12–3 7–11 **BAR MEALS:** Lunch served: Tues–Sun Dinner served: Tues–Sun 12–2 7–9.30 Av main course £5
RESTAURANT: Lunch served: Tue–Sun Dinner served: Tue–Sun 12–2 7–9.30 Av 3 course à la carte £20 **BREWERY/COMPANY:** Free House **PRINCIPAL BEERS:** Badger Tanglefoot, Exmoor Gold, Otter Ale, Cotleigh Barn Owl. **FACILITIES:** Children welcome Dogs allowed **NOTES:** Parking 20

NORTON ST PHILIP   Map 03 ST75

Pick of the Pubs

George Inn ♀
High St BA3 6LH ☎ 01373 834224 🖹 01373 834861
e-mail: georgeinn@aol.com
Dir: From Bath take A36 to Warminster, after 6m take A366 on R to Radstock, village 1m
This handsome old inn has been lovingly restored by Wadworth. Originally built in the late 14th century as a monastic guest house, the stone and timber-framed building is among the finest surviving medieval inns in the land. The George has featured in movies and TV series including *Moll Flanders* and *The Remains of the Day*. With its galleried courtyard, soaring timber roofs and 15th-century stair tower it merits a day-time detour or an overnight stay in one of the skilfully-added en suite bedrooms. Well-kept real ales and a decent wine list complement lunchtime snacks and a full carte. Bar food includes home-made soup and sandwiches, game terrine, steak and ale pie and perhaps home-made chicken Kiev. The carte has substantial versions of traditional dishes like

mushroom and Stilton pepperpot, and half shelled mussels marinière-style as precursors to baked cod with prawn and cream sauce, pan-fried duck breast with cherry brandy sauce and individual beef Wellington.

OPEN: 11–2.30 (summer only) 5.30–11 **BAR MEALS:** Lunch served: all week Dinner served: all week 12–2.30 7–9.30 Av main course £6.95 **RESTAURANT:** 12–2.30 7–9.30 Av 3 course fixed price £15.95 **BREWERY/COMPANY:** Wadworth
PRINCIPAL BEERS: Wadworth 6X, Henrys IPA.
FACILITIES: Garden: Food served outside Dogs allowed By Arrangement **NOTES:** Parking 26 **ROOMS:** 8 bedrooms 8 en suite from s£60 d£80

NUNNEY   Map 03 ST74

The George at Nunney ★ ★
Church St BA11 4LW ☎ 01373 836458 🖹 01373 836565
Dir: 0.5m N off A361, Frome/Shepton Mallet
The garden was used in the Middle Ages as a place of execution, and the pub is reputedly haunted, but this rambling old coaching inn is deservedly popular. Set in a historic conservation village opposite a romantic, ruined 13th-century castle, it serves a wide choice of food. Big steaks, mixed grill, steak and ale pie, and double chicken breasts with choice of sauces, plus a separate fish menu including sea bass, hake, bream and fresh dressed crabs.
OPEN: 12–3 6.30–11 **BAR MEALS:** 12–2 7–9
RESTAURANT: 12–2 7–9 **BREWERY/COMPANY:** Free House
PRINCIPAL BEERS: Highgate Saddlers Brewery, Wadworth 6X, Intervbrew Bass. **FACILITIES:** Children welcome Garden:
NOTES: Parking 30 **ROOMS:** 9 bedrooms 8 en suite from s£40 d£50

OTHERY   Map 03 ST33

Rose & Crown
East Lyng TA3 5AU ☎ 01823 698235
e-mail: derek.mason@btinternet.com
Set among the Somerset Levels, this 13th-century coaching inn serves a range of real ales, and offers a relaxed atmosphere. The menu includes a variety of ploughmans', omelettes, and salads, as well as vegetarian dishes such as country style vegetable kiev and vegetable curry. Meat-based main dishes include steak chasseur and liver and bacon casserole.
BAR MEALS: Lunch served: all week Dinner served: all week 12–2 7–9.15 Av main course £6.25 **RESTAURANT:** Lunch served: all week Dinner served: all week 12–2 7–9.15 Av 3 course à la carte £12
BREWERY/COMPANY: Free House
PRINCIPAL BEERS: Butcombe Bitter, Gold, Palmer 200 Premium Ale,. **FACILITIES:** Garden Food served outside **NOTES:** Parking 40
ROOMS: 2 bedrooms 2 en suite from s£30 d£50

continued

PUB WALK

Haselbury Plucknett
Haselbury Inn

Explore scenic countryside on the Somerset/Dorset border on this easy walk. The 12th-century squire Wulfric, who become an eccentric hermit dressed permanently in chain mail, lived in this area.

With the inn on your right, follow Frog Lane, keeping the car park on your right. Cross a stream and a stile and turn sharp right into a field. Keep the stream on your right, cross a stile to another field and over to the next stile. At the next stile cross a stream and join an enclosed track. At the end go forward over Claycastle Lane and up a track on the left side of Tarqua House, signposted North Perrott. At the end of the track enter a field and walk with the hedge on your right to a stile in the field corner. Cross over, turn sharp right and keep ahead for a short distance to another stile leading to a short, enclosed path. Beyond it is another stile giving access to a small enclosure, the other side of which is a stile into a field. Cross it and go left up the hill to a point about half

way along the top side of the field. Just to the left of the gate is a stile. Keep children and dogs under control here as the North Perrott road is just ahead. The road is narrow and visibility is poor. Cross the road to a stile Go diagonally left to an opening in the corner of the field, pass through and turn sharp right. Follow the field edge, with the hedge on your right, to the corner. Turn left, again following the field edge. After a few paces look for some steps and join an enclosed path, with two stiles, running up to the top of Swan Hill. Turn left, then right down a track marked 'private road, no lorries.' Look for an enclosed path on your right and at the bottom another path joins from the right. Swing left and soon you will see Haselbury church. Go right at the end of the path into 'The Gardens' and on to the end of the wall in front of the church. Turn left onto an enclosed path, with the church on your left. Pass into a field, round to the right and follow the path into North Street opposite the inn.

HASELBURY INN,
North Street HASELBURY PLUCKNETT Crewkerne TA18 7RJ
Tel: 01460 72488
Directions: Just off A30 between Crewkerne & Yeovil on B3066
An attractive village in an attractive village on the Dorset/Somerset border, originally used for the manufacture of sails and flax for ships. Comfortable, open plan bar with exposed stone and brickwork and open fires; separate restaurant.
Open: 11.45-2.30 6-11
Bar meals: 12-2 6.30-9.30
Garden and parking available.

Distance: 1 1/4 miles (2km)
Map: OS Landranger 193
Terrain: Rolling farmland on the Somerset/Dorset border
Paths: Mainly field paths. Quite a few stiles
Gradient: Undulating

Walk submitted and checked by Nick Bullock

England

OVER STRATTON
Map 03 ST41

The Royal Oak 🛏 ♀
TA13 5LQ ☎ 01460 240906 📠 01460 242421
Dir: A3088 from Yeovil, L onto A303, Over Stratton on R after S Petherton
Built out of warm Ham stone, its thatched roofing dating back
to the 16th century, a warmly welcoming old inn full of
blackened beams, flagstones, log fires, pews and settles - with
the added attraction of garden, children's play area and
barbecue. Real ales from the owning brewery and world-wide
selections of wines supplement traditional menus of fish pie,
salmon with saffron hollandaise and game cobblers with chive
and horseradish scones.
OPEN: 11-3 6-11 (wkds all day) **BAR MEALS:** Lunch served: all
week Dinner served: all week 12-2.30 7-9.30 **RESTAURANT:** Lunch
served: all week Dinner served: all week 12-2.30 7-9.30
BREWERY/COMPANY: Woodhouse Inns
PRINCIPAL BEERS: Badger Best, Tanglefoot. **FACILITIES:** Children
welcome Children's licence Garden: Food served outside Dogs
allowed (water) **NOTES:** Parking 70

PORLOCK
Map 03 SS84

The Ship Inn 🛏 ♀
High St TA24 8QD ☎ 01643 862507 📠 01643 863224
e-mail: mail@shipinnporlock.co.uk
Dir: A358 to Williton, then A39 to Porlock

Dating from the 13th century, the Ship has welcomed many
travellers, including Wordsworth, Coleridge and even Nelson's
press gang. Nestling at the foot of Porlock's notorious hill,
where Exmoor tumbles into the sea, it is now undergoing
'considered restoration'. All food is home made, including
seasonal soups, venison casserole, roast vegetable lasagne,
Welsh rarebit, Somerset mussels cooked in local cider, and
whitebait. A weekend fish special could be salmon on roasted
Mediterranean vegetables.
OPEN: 11-11 (Sun 12-11) **BAR MEALS:** Lunch served: all week
Dinner served: all week 12-2 6.30-9.00 Av main course £5.95
RESTAURANT: Lunch served: Sun 12-2 Dinner served: all week 7-9
Av 3 course à la carte £12.50 **BREWERY/COMPANY:** Free House
PRINCIPAL BEERS: Cotleigh Barn Owl, Bass, Courage Best,.
FACILITIES: Children welcome Garden: Food served outside. Sun
terrace Dogs allowed (water provided) **NOTES:** Parking 40
ROOMS: 10 bedrooms 8 en suite from s£22 d£22

PRIDDY
Map 03 ST55

New Inn 🛏 ♀
Priddy Green BA5 3BB ☎ 01749 676465 📠 01749 679463
e-mail: hatton-newinn@virgin.net
Dir: From M4 J18 take A39 R to Priddy 3m before Wells. From J19 through
Bristol onto A39. From M5 J21 take A371 to Cheddar, then B3371
Overlooking the village green high up in the Mendip Hills, this
15th-century former farmhouse is popular among walkers,

riders and pot-holers, and once served beer to the local lead
miners. The Priddy Sheep Fayre is held on the village green,
as it has been since the 14th century. Typical menu features
lamb cutlets in mint butter, cod and chips, spinach and
mushroom lasagne, New Inn pie and a variety of jacket
potatoes, omelettes and toasties. Skittle alley.
OPEN: 11.30-2.30 (Sun & Mon 12-2.30) 7-11 **BAR MEALS:** Lunch
served: all week Dinner served: all week 12-2 7-9.30 Av main course
£6 **RESTAURANT:** Lunch served: all week Dinner served: all week
12-2 7-9.30 Av 3 course à la carte £15 **BREWERY/COMPANY:** Free
House **PRINCIPAL BEERS:** Interbrew Bass, Fuller's London Pride,
Wadworth 6X. **FACILITIES:** Children welcome Garden: Patio, food
served outside Dogs allowed **NOTES:** Parking 30
ROOMS: 6 bedrooms 2 en suite from s£25 d£36

RUDGE
Map 03 ST85

The Full Moon at Rudge 🛏 ♀
BA11 2QF ☎ 01373 830936 📠 01373 831366
e-mail: fullmoon@lineone.net
Dir: From A36 (Bath/Warminster rd) follow signs for Rudge
Standing at the crossroads of old drovers' routes, there's been
a coaching inn or hostelry on this site since the early 1700s. The
inn retains its small rooms, scrubbed tables and stone floors.
Daily-changing fish board offers the likes of fillet of brill with
seared oranges and spring onions, and king prawns and
scallops with grilled black pudding. Other options might include
shoulder of lamb, fillet steak and leek and asparagus tart.
OPEN: 11-11 **BAR MEALS:** Lunch served: all week Dinner served:
all week 12-3 6.30-9.30 Av main course £5.95 **RESTAURANT:** Lunch
served: all week Dinner served: all week 12-3 6.30-9.30 Av 3 course à
la carte £22.50 **BREWERY/COMPANY:** Free House
PRINCIPAL BEERS: Butcombe Bitter, Interbrew Worthington Bitter,
Wadworth 6X. **FACILITIES:** Garden: Food served outdoors Dogs
allowed **NOTES:** Parking 90 **ROOMS:** 5 bedrooms 5 en suite from
s£40 d£65

SHEPTON MALLET
Map 03 ST64

Pick of the Pubs

The Three Horseshoes 🛏 ♀
Batcombe BA4 6HE ☎ 01749 850359 📠 01749 850615
Dir: Take A359 from Frome to Bruton. Batcombe signed on R

A honey-coloured stone, 16th-century coaching inn tucked
away in a pretty village in the heart of the very rural
Batcombe Vale. Terracotta painted walls, exposed stripped
beams, attractive stencilling, and a fine stone inglenook
with log fire characterise the long and low-ceilinged main
bar. There is a good range of real ales and the menu
offers a wide range of interesting home-cooked dishes
that attract discerning diners from far and wide. A typical

continued

continued

sample includes wild mushroom risotto, chicken strips with tagliatelle, chicken breast stuffed with bacon and Brie, calves' liver, pork fillet stuffed with apricots and pistachio nuts, and grilled salmon on a herb risotto. Steaks and pies are also on offer. There is a lovely rear garden with play area and views of the parish church. **OPEN:** 12–3 6.30–11 Closed: 25–26 Dec **BAR MEALS:** Lunch served: all week Dinner served: all week 12–2 7–9.30 Av main course £9 **RESTAURANT:** Lunch served: all week Dinner served: all week 12–2 6.30–9.30 Av 3 course à la carte £16 **BREWERY/COMPANY:** Free House **PRINCIPAL BEERS:** Butcombe Bitter, Wadworth 6X, Adnams Bitter, Interbrew Bass. **FACILITIES:** Children welcome Garden: Food served outside Dogs allowed (water) **NOTES:** Parking 25

Pick of the Pubs

The Waggon and Horses
Frome Rd, Doulting Beacon BA4 4LA
☎ 01749 880302 🖷 01749 880602
e-mail: fcardona@onetel.com
Dir: 1.5m N of Shepton Mallet at crossroads with Wells-Frome road

The Colombian-born landlord of this 18th-century coaching inn, Francisco Cardona, is a widely travelled and cultured man who has put his pub at the centre of the community's artistic life. The pub hosts regular art exhibitions and an impressive concert programme of classical music – events that delight the customers and support local artists. He also has a passion for horses and has bred an Olympic competitor. The pub is in a small village setting, but customers travel quite a distance to enjoy the good food and real ale. The cosmopolitan menu ranges from traditional pub fare to more exotic dishes, including plenty of fish – seafood kebabs, hake steaks

continued

Galician style, Mediterranean fish stew – and the likes of chicken cacciatore (an Italian-style casserole), navarin of lamb, and wild boar chops. Produce is locally sourced, including free-range chicken and game in season. Local wines and Somerset Royal Cider Brandy are also featured. **OPEN:** 11–3 6–11.20 (Sun 12–3, 7–11) **BAR MEALS:** Lunch served: all week Dinner served: all week 12–2.30 6.30–9.30 Av main course £8.90 **RESTAURANT:** Lunch served: all week Dinner served: all week 12–2 6.30–10 Av 3 course à la carte £15 **BREWERY/COMPANY:** Ushers **PRINCIPAL BEERS:** Ushers Best, Founders. **FACILITIES:** Garden: Beer garden, patio, food served outdoors Dogs allowed on lead please **NOTES:** Parking 40

SHEPTON MONTAGUE   Map 03 ST63

The Montague Inn
Shepton Montague BA9 8JW ☎ 01749 813213
Dir: R off A371 between Wincanton & Castle Cary toward Shepton Montague
This comfortably refurbished, stone-built village inn nestling in rolling unspoilt Somerset countryside on the edge of sleepy Shepton Montague just came under new management as this guide went to press. Tastefully decorated throughout, including the three well-appointed rear bedrooms, with the homely bar featuring old dark pine and an open log fire; cosy, yellow-painted dining room. Attractive summer terrace with rural views for summer sipping. **OPEN:** 12–2.30 6.30–11 (closed Mon lunch) **BAR MEALS:** Lunch served: Tue–Sun 12–2.30 Av main course £7 **RESTAURANT:** Lunch served: Sun Dinner served: Tue–Sat 6.30–9 Av 3 course à la carte £25 **BREWERY/COMPANY:** Free House **PRINCIPAL BEERS:** Butcombe Bitter, Greene King IPA. **FACILITIES:** Children welcome Garden: Dogs allowed **NOTES:** Parking 30 **ROOMS:** 3 bedrooms 3 en suite from s£45 d£70

SOMERTON   Map 03 ST42

Devonshire Arms
Long Sutton TA10 9LP ☎ 01458 241271
Old-fashioned gabled stone inn. Bedrooms.

The Globe
Market Square TA11 7LX ☎ 01458 272474 🖷 01458 274789
Dir: 4m from A303
Fresh fish at weekends and hearty English cooking draw local diners to this 17th-century former coaching inn in the market square.

From Gin Shop to Gin Palace
As the alehouses moved further up in the world in the 18th century, new drinking-houses filled the vacant space at the foot of the social ladder. These were the gin shops (or dram shops, for brandy). Gin was cheap and strong, it was adulterated with anything from turpentine to sulphuric acid, and in the slums of London and other towns the poor could get 'drunk for a penny, dead drunk for twopence' as the slogan went, in squalid cellars, hovels and back alleys. The scenes of drunkenness and degradation – vividly depicted in Hogarth's 'Gin Lane' – were so appalling that in the 1750s Parliament made spirits more expensive. Following the sharp rise in beer prices at the end of the century, gin made a comeback in the industrial slums and from the 1820s on the distillers made a bid for working-class custom by opening gin palaces of ostentatious grandeur. The brewers followed this lead, hence the creation of magnificent Victorian and Edwardian pubs opulently provided with mahogany panelling, tiles and gilt, engraved mirrors and decorated glass, ornate gas lamps and richly elaborate ceilings. A few of them survive.

SPARKFORD
Map 03 ST62

The Sparkford Inn
High St BA22 7JH ☎ 01963 440218 📠 01963 440358
e-mail: sparkfordinn@sparkford.fsbusiness.co.uk
Dir: just off A303, 400yds from rdbt at Sparkford

A picturesque 15th-century former coaching inn characterized
by its popular garden, beamed bars and fascinating old prints
and photographs. Nearby are the Haynes Motor Museum and
the Yeovilton Fleet Air Arm Museum. A varied menu offers a
selection of traditional meals and home-cooked favourites,
including cottage pie, chicken and leek casserole, lasagne,
chilli con carne, deep fried breaded plaice, double jumbo
sausages and Cajun chicken and a good lunchtime carvery.
OPEN: 11-11 **BAR MEALS:** Lunch served: all week Dinner served:
all week 12-2.15 7-9.30 Av main course £6 **RESTAURANT:** Lunch
served: all week Dinner served: all week 12-2 7-9.30 Av 3 course à la
carte £13 **BREWERY/COMPANY:** Free House
PRINCIPAL BEERS: Interbrew Bass, Otter Ale, Butcombe Butter.
FACILITIES: Children welcome Garden: Beer garden , food served
outside Dogs allowed **NOTES:** Parking 50 **ROOMS:** 10 bedrooms
10 en suite from s£35 d£49.50

STANTON WICK
Map 03 ST66

Pick of the Pubs

The Carpenters Arms
BS39 4BX ☎ 01761 490202 📠 01761 490763
e-mail: carpenters@dial.pipex.com
*Dir: From A37(Bristol/Wells rd) take A368 towards Weston-S-Mare
take 1st R*

A converted row of honey-stoned former miners' cottages
in a tiny hamlet overlooking the Chew Valley. Beyond the
pretty façade with its climbing roses and colourful flower
tubs is a comfortable stone-walled bar with low beams,
warming open fire and a chatty, music-free atmosphere.
Comfortable, cottage-style bedrooms are a particular

continued

draw for harassed business types and weekenders. The
Cooper's Parlour, with an extensive daily chalkboard, is
the focus of imaginative snacks and bar food. Starters
range from goats' cheese gratin with roasted peppers to
crispy duck and baby spinach salad. Main offerings
include dishes like roast salmon fillet with stir-fried
vegetables and flamed pork medallions with bacon,
mushrooms and cream. Chef's daily recommendations in
the dining-room offer smoked haddock fillets Mornay,
pheasant breast marinated in red wine, orange and
juniper and perhaps pan-fried ostrich fillet in field
mushroom and red onion gravy.
OPEN: 11-11 Closed: 25/26 Dec **BAR MEALS:** Lunch served: all
week Dinner served: all week 12-2 7-10 Av main course £9
RESTAURANT: Lunch served: Sun 12-2 Dinner served: Mon-Sat
7-10 Av 3 course à la carte £20 **BREWERY/COMPANY:** Buccaneer
Holdings **PRINCIPAL BEERS:** Interbrew Bass, Butcombe Bitter,
Scottish Courage Courage Best, Wadworth 6X.
FACILITIES: Children welcome Garden: Beer garden, patio, food
served outdoors **NOTES:** Parking 200 **ROOMS:** 12 bedrooms 12
en suite from s£62 d£84.50

STAPLE FITZPAINE
Map 03 ST21

The Greyhound Inn ♦♦♦♦
TA3 5SP ☎ 01823 480227 📠 01823 481117
*Dir: From M5, take A358 E, signed Yeovil, after 4m follow sign to R, signed
Staple Fitzpaine*
Nestling in a picturesque village, this Grade II listed coaching
inn has four en suite bedrooms. Taking its name from men
known as Greyhounds, who dispatched news on horseback
before the Royal Mail, the pub is within easy reach of the coast.
A series of rambling, connecting rooms, characterised by
flagstone floors, old timbers and natural stone walls, greets the
visitor, with a good selection of traditional ales and seasonal,
freshly prepared dishes, including pork steak topped with apple
and Somerset cheddar, honey roasted rack of lamb, and deep-
fried Somerset Camembert. A range of omelettes, doorsteps,
homemade pies and special desserts are also available.
OPEN: 12-3 6-11 (Summer open all day) **BAR MEALS:** Lunch
served: all week Dinner served: all week 12-2 7-9.30 Av main course
£9.50 **RESTAURANT:** Dinner served: Thur-Sat 7 Av 3 course à la
carte £17.50 **BREWERY/COMPANY:** Free House
PRINCIPAL BEERS: Otter, Exmoor, London Pride.
FACILITIES: Children welcome Children's licence Garden: Food
served outside. Large patio area Dogs allowed On leads. Water
provided **NOTES:** Parking 60 **ROOMS:** 4 bedrooms 4 en suite
from s£49.95 d£66

STOGUMBER
Map 03 ST03

The White Horse
High St TA4 3TA ☎ 01984 656277 📠 01984 656277
Dir: Opposite the church in the centre of the village
Tucked away on the edge of the Quantock Hills, this
traditional village local is located opposite the church, and
includes the historic village market hall. The West Somerset
railway is about one mile from Stogumber. The White Horse
specialises in steaks, including gammon, sirloin, and pork. All
meats locally sourced.
OPEN: 11.30-2.30 6.30-11 **BAR MEALS:** Lunch served: all week
Dinner served: all week 12-2 7-9.30 Av main course £5
BREWERY/COMPANY: Free House **PRINCIPAL BEERS:** Cotleigh
Tawny Bitter, Exmoor Fox, Juwards Bitter, Branscombe Vale Branoc.
FACILITIES: Garden: Food served outside Dogs allowed (water)
NOTES: Parking 5 **ROOMS:** s£27 d£40

STOKE ST GREGORY
Map 03 ST32

Rose & Crown 🐕 ♀
Woodhill TA3 6EW ☎ 01823 490296 📠 01823 490996
e-mail: ron.browning@virgin.net
Dir: M5 J25, A358/A378 then 1st L through North Curry to Stoke St Gregory church on R. Pub 0.5m on L
Close to the famous Somerset Levels and handy for Wells and Glastonbury, this 17th-century picturesque cottage-style pub includes a 60-ft well and an attractive dining room recently converted from the inn's old skittle alley. Fresh local produce and fish from Brixham are used and there is a good selection of real ales and guest beers. Grilled skate wings, mixed grill and lamb cutlets are popular in the bar, and restaurant dishes might include grilled pork valentine with apple sauce, scrumpy chicken and local trout.
OPEN: 11-3 7-11 **BAR MEALS:** Lunch served: all week Dinner served: all week 12.30-2 7-10 Av main course £8.50
RESTAURANT: Lunch served: all week Dinner served: all week 12.30-2 7-10 Av 3 course à la carte £15
BREWERY/COMPANY: Free House **PRINCIPAL BEERS:** Hardy Royal Oak & Hardy Country, Exmoor Ale. **FACILITIES:** Children welcome Garden: Food served outside **NOTES:** Parking 20
ROOMS: 6 bedrooms 3 en suite from s£27.50 d£40

TAUNTON
Map 03 ST22

Pick of the Pubs

The Blue Ball ♀
Triscombe, nr Crowcombe TA4 3HE
☎ 01984 618242 📠 01984 618371
Dir: 9M from Taunton on the Minehead A358 road, turn L signposted Triscombe the pub is 1.5M along this road
Unspoilt 18th-century thatched pub hidden away along a narrow lane amid the Quantock Hills, offering imaginative pub food, Somerset ales, decent wines and an informal dining atmosphere to a well heeled and discerning clientele. Carpeted main bar with rustic, country-style furnishings, sporting prints, and daily-changing blackboard menus above the huge inglenook fireplace. Locally sourced produce feature in tea-smoked Quantock duck breast with port and redcurrant sauce, pheasant with Calvados and caramelised apples, lamb loin stuffed with apricots and pistachio nuts, and Dunster Beach codling with Puy lentils and salsa verde. Starters may include spicy carrot, coconut and coriander soup and terrine of ham and foie gras, while for pudding try the prune and Armagnac tart or a plate of West Country cheeses. Impressive list of 400 wines; any under £20 available by the glass. Super terraced garden with view over the Vale of Taunton. Footpaths lead into the Quantocks and miles of breezy walks.
OPEN: 12-3 7-11 **BAR MEALS:** Lunch served: all week 12-1.45 Av main course £7.50 **RESTAURANT:** Lunch served: all week Dinner served: all week 12-1.45 7-9.30 Av 3 course à la carte £18
BREWERY/COMPANY: Free House **PRINCIPAL BEERS:** Cotleigh Tawny, Youngs Special, Hop Back Summer Lightning.
FACILITIES: Children welcome Garden: Food served outside Dogs allowed (water) **NOTES:** Parking 20 No credit cards

Queens Arms 🐕
Pitminster TA3 7AZ ☎ 01823 421529
A pub since the mid-1800s, although the building began life as a mill 800 years earlier. Under new ownership since 2001, at least four, mostly local, real ales are available, as well as a

continued

wide choice of locally sourced, home-cooked meals. Fresh fish Mornay is cooked in home-made lobster sauce, salmon steak is poached in lime. Liver, bacon and onions is served with red wine gravy, and chicken breast comes with home-made orange and tarragon sauce.
OPEN: 11-11 (Sun 12-10.30) Closed: 25 Dec **BAR MEALS:** Lunch served: all week Dinner served: all week 12-2 7-9 Av main course £6.95 **BREWERY/COMPANY:** Enterprise Inns
PRINCIPAL BEERS: Butcombe Bitter, Butcombe Gold, Cotleigh Tawny, Otter Bitter. **FACILITIES:** Children welcome Garden: Food served outside. Lawn & patio area Dogs allowed (water bowl) in bar **NOTES:** Parking 20

WAMBROOK
Map 03 ST20

The Cotley Inn
TA20 3EN ☎ 01460 62348 📠 01460 68833
e-mail: cotley70@freeserve.co.uk
Traditional stone-built inn located in an area renowned for good walks. A warm welcoming atmosphere awaits inside and the walls are lined with works by local artists. Cosy bar and adjoining dining room offer a good choice of meals and snacks prepared with fresh produce. Expect mushroom fritters with garlic mayonnaise and Brie filo with a fruit sauce among the starters, while 'big meaty eats' might feature rump steak garni, devilled kidneys with rice and salad, deep fried plaice and chicken cordon bleu.
OPEN: 11-3 7-11 **BAR MEALS:** Lunch served: all week Dinner served: all week 12-3 7-11 **RESTAURANT:** Lunch served: all week Dinner served: all week 12-3 7-11 **BREWERY/COMPANY:** Free House **PRINCIPAL BEERS:** Otter Ale, Interbrew Boddingtons Bitter. **FACILITIES:** Children welcome Garden: Food served outside Dogs allowed **NOTES:** Parking 40 **ROOMS:** 2 bedrooms from s£30 d£45

WASHFORD
Map 03 ST04

The Washford Inn ◆◆◆
TA23 0PP ☎ 01984 640256

The steam railway between Minehead and Bishop's Lydeard near Taunton runs directly behind this pleasant family inn, which is well situated for many enjoyable walking routes and offers home-made, locally produced food. Lasagne, prawn platter, 10oz gammon steak, mussels in garlic and roast lamb shank are among the appetising dishes.
OPEN: 12-11 (Winter 12-3, 5-11) **BAR MEALS:** Lunch served: all week Dinner served: all week 12-9 Av main course £4.99
RESTAURANT: Lunch served: all week Dinner served: all week 12-2.30 6-9 Av 3 course à la carte £12 9
BREWERY/COMPANY: Free House
PRINCIPAL BEERS: Butcombe Gold, Courage Directors, Wadworth 6X, Bass. **FACILITIES:** Children welcome Children's licence Garden: Beer garden, outdoor eating, patio Dogs allowed **NOTES:** Parking 40 **ROOMS:** 7 bedrooms 7 en suite from s£24 d£48

WATERROW
Map 03 ST02

The Rock Inn ♦♦♦ ♀
TA4 2AX ☎ 01984 623293 ▤ 01984 623293
Dir: From Taunton take B3227. Waterrow approx 14m W

400-year-old former coaching inn built into the rock face, in a lovely green valley beside the River Tone. Sit in the peaceful bar, with winter log fire and traditional furnishings, and sample the appetising menu. Recently taken over by new management, who replace the self-proclaimed 'Most Miserable Landlord in Somerset'!
OPEN: 7.30-3 6-12 Closed: 25-26 Dec **BAR MEALS:** Lunch served: all week Dinner served: all week 11-2.30 6-10.30 Av main course £5 **RESTAURANT:** Lunch served: all week Dinner served: all week 11-2.30 6-10.30 **BREWERY/COMPANY:** Free House **PRINCIPAL BEERS:** Cotleigh Tawny, Exmoor Gold, monthly guest ales. **FACILITIES:** Children welcome **NOTES:** Parking 20 **ROOMS:** 7 bedrooms 7 en suite from s£22 d£22

WELLS
Map 03 ST54

Pick of the Pubs

The Fountain Inn/Boxers Restaurant 🍴 ♀
1 St Thomas St BA5 2UU ☎ 01749 672317 ▤ 01749 670825
e-mail: adrian@finnwells.demon.co.uk
See Pick of the Pubs on page 423

The Pheasant Inn
Worth, Wookey BA5 1LQ ☎ 01749 672355
Dir: W of Wells on the B3139
Set at the foot of the Mendips, with impressive views, this popular country pub has a traditional public bar where walkers can enjoy a pint of real ale beside a welcoming log fire. There is a bar snack menu and a carte with a distinctly Italian flavour, offering a good choice of home-made pasta dishes, including a vegetarian choice. Scampi Pietro is a house speciality, and other favourites are home-made minestrone, chicken Piedmontese, and tiramisù.
OPEN: 11-3 (Sun 12-3) 6-11 (Sun 7-9) Closed: Dec 26, Jan 1 **BAR MEALS:** Lunch served: all week Dinner served: all week 12-2 6.30-9.30 Av main course £6.25 **RESTAURANT:** Lunch served: all week Dinner served: all week 12-2 6.30-9.30 Av 3 course à la carte £12.50 **BREWERY/COMPANY:** Free House **PRINCIPAL BEERS:** Butcombe Gold, Jenning's Cumberland Ale, Timothy Taylor Landlord, Wadworth 6X. **FACILITIES:** Children welcome Garden: Food served outdoors, BBQ Dogs allowed **NOTES:** Parking 28

WEST CAMEL
Map 03 ST52

The Walnut Tree 🍴
Fore St BA22 7QW ☎ 01935 851292 ▤ 01935 851292
Dir: Off A303 between Sparkford & Yeovilton Air Base
This well-kept inn in a quiet village has good accommodation in a modern extension. The cosily carpeted bar and lounge and a choice of dining areas entice the hungry with prominently displayed blackboards. Fresh fish from Poole and snack lunches are on offer in a decidedly chip-free zone.
OPEN: 11-3 (Closed Sun eve, Mon lunch) 6.30-11.30 **BAR MEALS:** Lunch served: Tue-Sun 12-2 Dinner served: Mon-Sat 7-9.30 Av main course £10 **RESTAURANT:** Lunch served: Tue-Sun 12-2 Dinner served: Mon-Sat 7-9.30 Av 3 course à la carte £22 **BREWERY/COMPANY:** Free House **PRINCIPAL BEERS:** Butcombe Bitter. **FACILITIES:** Garden: **NOTES:** Parking 40 **ROOMS:** 13 bedrooms 13 en suite from s£88 d£80

WEST HUNTSPILL
Map 03 ST34

Crossways Inn 🍴 ♀
Withy Rd TA9 3RA ☎ 01278 783756 ▤ 01278 781899
e-mail: crossways.inn@virgin.net
Dir: On A38 3.5m from M5 J22/23
A relaxing atmosphere pervades this 17th-century coaching inn on the old Taunton to Bristol route. Sash windows and part-panelled walls with a large fireplace in the central bar set the tone. Bar meals that include Singapore prawn curry, Greek lamb and apricots and Thai fish cakes add an eclectic touch to the more usual beef and Guinness pie, liver and bacon casserole and stuffed chicken breast with tarragon cream sauce. There is a family room and safe rear garden.
OPEN: 10.30-3 5.30-11 Closed: 25 Dec **BAR MEALS:** Lunch served: all week Dinner served: all week 12-2 6.30-9 Av main course £5.20 **RESTAURANT:** Lunch served: all week Dinner served: all week 12-2 6.30-9.00 Av 3 course à la carte £10.50 **BREWERY/COMPANY:** Free House **PRINCIPAL BEERS:** Interbrew Bass, Flowers Original & Flowers IPA, Fuller's London Pride, Greene King Abbot Ale. **FACILITIES:** Children welcome Garden: Seating, food served outside Dogs allowed **NOTES:** Parking 60 **ROOMS:** 3 bedrooms 3 en suite from s£24 d£34

WHEDDON CROSS
Map 03 SS93

The Rest and Be Thankful Inn ♦♦♦♦ ♀
TA24 7DR ☎ 01643 841222 ▤ 01643 841813
e-mail: enquiries@restandbethankful.co.uk
Dir: 5m S of Dunster
Weary travellers must have named this old coaching inn, located in the highest village on Exmoor. Old world charm blends with friendly hospitality in the cosy bar and spacious restaurant, where both traditional and contemporary food is served every day. Grilled rib-eye steak, poached Scottish salmon, peppered pork and deep-fried trout from the specials board, or bar meals like chicken Kiev, duckling a l'orange, and scampi. Pretty bedrooms, some with great views of Dunkery Beacon.
OPEN: 9.30-3 6.30-11 **BAR MEALS:** Lunch served: all week Dinner served: all week 12-2 7-10 Av main course £6.50 **RESTAURANT:** Lunch served: all week Dinner served: all week 12-2 7-10 Av 3 course à la carte £16 **BREWERY/COMPANY:** Free House **PRINCIPAL BEERS:** Exmoor Ale, Interbrew Bass & Worthington Bitter, Fuller's London Pride,. **FACILITIES:** Children welcome Garden: Patio, food served outdoors **NOTES:** Parking 50 **ROOMS:** 5 bedrooms 5 en suite from s£26 d£52

OPEN: 10.30–2.30 6–11 (Sun 12–3, 7–10.30)

BAR MEALS: L served all week. D served all week. 12–2.30 6–10 Av main course £6

RESTAURANT: L served all week. D served all week. 12–2.30 6–10 Av cost 3 course £17.50

BREWERY/COMPANY: INNSPIRED

PRINCIPLE BEERS: Butcombe Bitter, Interbrew Bass, Scottish Courage Courage Best

FACILITIES: Children welcome

NOTES: Parking 24

The Fountain Inn

1 St Thomas Street BA5 2UU
☎ 01749 672317 📠 01749 670825
e-mail: adrian@finnwells.demon.co.uk
Dir: City centre, at junc of A371 & B3139

Situated no more than 50 yards from Wells Cathedral, this 16th-century inn takes its name from the spring that feeds the conduit in the city. It is reputed to have housed the labourers who helped to build the cathedral, but since the great church was completed by 1465, the tale is probably apocryphal.

More likely is that it supplied shelter for maintenance workers. In no doubt at all, though, is its reputation for good quality food and wines. This side of the business has been built up by the present owners, who fell in love with the place when they visited Wells 20 years ago. The Fountain is just around the corner from Vicars' Close, a row of medieval houses built specially for the Vicars' Choral, and it's hardly surprising that it has long been a favourite haunt of the cathedral choir. Nowadays its popularity has spread much further afield, fuelled in part by the locally brewed Butcombe Bitter and other decent ales which are served in the unpretentious ground-floor bar complete with winter fires. An extensive range of home-cooked food is served in the bar, with typical dishes like beef, ale and mushroom pie, fruity chicken curry, and fresh cod cooked in beer batter. The same quality ingredients go into the menu upstairs in Boxer's Restaurant, where spinach and wild rice cakes, Greek salad, and seared carpaccio of beef might be followed by baked guinea fowl, Parma-wrapped chicken breast, and roasted rump of lamb in a herb crust.

WINCANTON
Map 03 ST72

Bull Inn 🕸 ♀
Hardway, nr Bruton BA10 0LN ☎ 01749 812200
17th-century former coaching inn on the famous Somerset
Levels, close to Bruton, Stourhead Gardens and Wincanton
Racecourse. Frequented by cast members of leading stage
musicals, jockeys and soap stars. Impressive outside staircase.
Full range of bar meals and restaurant dishes, including
smoked haddock wrapped in bacon, avocado and wild
mushroom Stroganoff, and cod, prawn and dill bake.
OPEN: 11.30-2.30 6-11 **BAR MEALS:** Lunch served: all week 12-2
Dinner served: Mon-Sat 6-10 Av main course £8
RESTAURANT: Lunch served: all week 12-2 Dinner served: Mon-Sat
7-9.30 Av 3 course à la carte £18.95 **BREWERY/COMPANY:** Free
House **PRINCIPAL BEERS:** Butcombe Bitter, Greene King IPA & Old
Speckled Hen, Shepherd Neame-Spitfire. **FACILITIES:** Children
welcome Garden: Food served outside Dogs allowed (water) tap
outside **NOTES:** Parking 30

The George Inn NEW
Mill St BA9 9AP ☎ 01963 32185
Real log fires and comfortable sofas contribute to the
pleasantly relaxing atmosphere at this Grade II listed pub.
Located in one of Wincanton's oldest streets, the newly
refurbished inn offers food to suit all tastes. Scallops with
asparagus, game casserole, calves' liver with wild mushrooms,
peppered fillet of wild boar with brandy sauce, and escalope
of veal with lemon and brown nut butter shows the range.
BREWERY/COMPANY: Free House No credit cards

WINSFORD
Map 03 SS93

Pick of the Pubs

The Royal Oak Inn ★ ★ ★
TA24 7JE ☎ 01643 851455 ▤ 01643 851009
e-mail: enquiries@royaloak-somerset.co.uk
Dir: M5 South, J27, at Tiverton roundabout North on A396.
A charming 12th-century inn with inglenook fireplaces and
oak beams, the Royal Oak Inn is set in the heart of a
beautiful Exmoor village. It is popular with locals as well
as the hunting, shooting and fishing set, and is an
excellent base for walking on Exmoor. Country-house-style
accommodation is available and good country cooking in
both the convivial bar and smart dining room. Options in
the bar range from soups, salads and sandwiches to
specials like lamb shank with spring onion and bacon
mash and red wine jus. From the dinner carte you can
expect dishes like smooth chicken liver parfait served with
Melba toast and spiced pear chutney, and seared fillet of
sea bass with braised chicory and aubergine caviar,
finished with a lightly curried sauce vierge. There's a
choice of home-made puddings, or a selection of West
Country cheeses to finish.
OPEN: 11-3 6-11 **BAR MEALS:** Lunch served: all week 12-2
Dinner served: all week 7-9.30 Av main course £8.50
RESTAURANT: Lunch served: Sun 12.15-2.30 Dinner served: all
week 7.30-9 Av 3 course à la carte £27.50
BREWERY/COMPANY: Free House
PRINCIPAL BEERS: Cotleigh Barn Owl Bitter, Exmoor Ale.
FACILITIES: Children welcome Garden: Dogs allowed
NOTES: Parking 20 **ROOMS:** 14 bedrooms 14 en suite from
s£78 d£98

WITHYPOOL
Map 03 SS83

Pick of the Pubs

Royal Oak Inn ★ ★ 🛏 🕸
TA24 7QP ☎ 01643 831506 ▤ 01643 831659
e-mail: enquiries@royaloakwithypool.co.uk
Dir: From M5 thru Taunton on B3224, then B3223 to Withypool

With an ever-growing reputation as a sporting hotel for its
hunting, shooting, walking and activity holidays in the
Exmoor National Park, this old inn has a long and
colourful history – R D Blackmore stayed here whilst
writing the classic *Lorna Doone*. The Rod Room is chock-
full of fishing memorabilia and in both beamed bars,
warmed by open fires, a wealth of good food created
from local produce, evidenced by a range of daily
specials, accompanies real Exmoor ales and guest beers.
Light dishes include baked ham and lemon chicken
sandwiches, filled jacket potatoes and specials perhaps of
honey-glazed confit duck leg and shank of lamb with
garlic mash. Enhanced by the carefully selected wine list,
the Acorn restaurant weighs in with king prawns in lager
batter, chicken and bean cassoulet and peppered sirloin
steak, followed by sticky toffee pudding and lemon tart
with raspberry compote.
OPEN: 11-3.30 6-11 **BAR MEALS:** Lunch served: all week
Dinner served: all week 12-2 6.30-9.30 Av main course £10
RESTAURANT: Lunch served: Sun 12-2 Dinner served: all week
7-9 Av 3 course à la carte £25 Av 3 course fixed price £25
BREWERY/COMPANY: Free House
PRINCIPAL BEERS: Exmoor Ale & Fox Bitter, Carlsberg-Tetley
Tetley Bitter, Oakhill Yeoman. **FACILITIES:** Children welcome
patio, outdoor eating Dogs allowed Kennels if needed
NOTES: Parking 20 **ROOMS:** 8 bedrooms 8 en suite from
s£38 d£76

WOOKEY
Map 03 ST54

The Burcott Inn 🛏 ♀
Wells Rd BA5 1NJ ☎ 01749 673874
A convenient stop for visitors to Wells or the Mendip Hills, this
stone-built roadside inn sits opposite a working water mill,
and is characterised by beams, open fires, pine tables and
settles. Freshly prepared food is available in the bars,
restaurant or large garden, and over 70 guest beers are
served each year. The menu includes such dishes as chicken
korma, smoked salmon and prawn gratin, steak and ale pie,
mixed grill, roast duck breast with black cherries, trout
marinara, and Spanish quiche. Try your hand at the traditional
pub games.
OPEN: 11.30-2.30 6-11 Closed: 25/26 Dec, 1 Jan

continued

BAR MEALS: Lunch served: all week 12–2.30 Dinner served: Tue–Sat 6.30–9.30 Av main course £6.50 **RESTAURANT:** Lunch served: all week 12–2.30 Dinner served: Tue–Sat 6.30–9.30 Av 3 course à la carte £15 **BREWERY/COMPANY:** Free House
PRINCIPAL BEERS: Timothy Taylor Landlord, Greene King Abbot Ale, Cotleigh Barn Owl Bitter, RCH Pitchfork. **FACILITIES:** Children welcome Garden: Food served outside. Large garden
NOTES: Parking 30

WOOLVERTON — Map 03 ST75

Red Lion 🐷 ⚐
Bath Rd BA2 7QS ☎ 01373 831050 830350 ▤ 831050
Dir: *On the A36 between Bath & Warminster*
Once a court room, with possible connections to Hanging Judge Jeffries, this 400-year-old building has a lovely stone floor and an open fire. It is decorated in Elizabethan style and is, of course, haunted. Good home cooking is served, ranging from sandwiches to steaks. Look out for beef and ale pie, roasted lamb shoulder, poached salmon, smoked trout and prawn salad, beef lasagne, baked chicken, and lamb chops. Recently sensitively refurbished. Convenient for Bath, Trowbridge, Frome and Longleat.
OPEN: 11.30–11 (Sun 12–10.30) **BAR MEALS:** Lunch served: all week Dinner served: all week 12–2.30 6–9 Av main course £6.50
BREWERY/COMPANY: Wadworth
PRINCIPAL BEERS: Wadworth 6X 7 Henry's IPA.
FACILITIES: Children welcome Garden: Food served outdoors Dogs allowed **NOTES:** Parking 40

STAFFORDSHIRE

ABBOTS BROMLEY — Map 09 SK02

The Royal Oak
Bagot St WS15 3DB ☎ 01283 840117
There is a friendly village atmosphere at this black and white pub, with its open fires, beamed ceilings and oak-panelled restaurant.

ALREWAS — Map 09 SK11

The Old Boat 🐷
DE13 7DB ☎ 01283 791468 ▤ 01283 792886

Situated on the Trent and Mersey Canal, the pub was originally a watering hole for canal construction workers, and later for bargemen. The snug at the far end of the bar used to be the cellar; casks of ale were rolled off the barges into the room and kept cool in up to two feet of water. Typical dishes are fishcakes with home-made tartar sauce, and black pudding with local sausage, mushrooms and port gravy.

continued

OPEN: 11.30–3.30 6.30–11.30 Closed: 25 Dec, 31Dec
BAR MEALS: Lunch served: all week Dinner served: all week 12–2.30 7–10 Av main course £4.50 **RESTAURANT:** Lunch served: all week Dinner served: all week 12–2.30 7–10 Av 3 course à la carte £17.50 Av 3 course fixed price £14.95 **PRINCIPAL BEERS:** Ushers Bitter & Founders Ale. **FACILITIES:** Children welcome Garden: Food served outside **NOTES:** Parking 40

ALTON — Map 09 SK04

Bulls Head Inn ♦♦♦
High St ST10 4AQ ☎ 01538 702307 ▤ 01538 702065
e-mail: janet@alton.freeserve.co.uk
Traditional beers, home cooking and well-equipped accommodation are provided in the heart of Alton, less than a mile from Alton Towers theme park. Oak beams and an inglenook fireplace set the scene for the old world bar, the cosy snug (where children can sit) and the country-style restaurant. Menus offer the likes of sirloin steak, deep fried breaded plaice, lasagne verdi, steak, ale and mushroom pie, and hunters chicken.
BAR MEALS: Lunch served: Mon–Fri 12–2 Dinner served: all week 6.30–9.30 Av main course £7 **RESTAURANT:** Dinner served: all week 6.30–9.30 Av 3 course à la carte £13
BREWERY/COMPANY: Free House **PRINCIPAL BEERS:** Bass, Worthington, London Pride. **FACILITIES:** Children welcome Children's licence Food served outside. Patio area **NOTES:** Parking 15 **ROOMS:** 6 bedrooms 6 en suite from s£45 d£55

BURTON UPON TRENT — Map 09 SK22

Burton Bridge Inn ⚐
24 Bridge St DE14 1SY ☎ 01283 536596
With its own brewery at the back, this is one of the oldest pubs in the area. The unspoilt old-fashioned interior has oak panelling, feature fireplaces, and a distinct lack of electronic entertainment. A full range of Burton Bridge ales is on tap, and the menu includes straightforward meals like roast pork or beef cobs, as well as traditional filled Yorkshire puddings.
OPEN: 11–2.30 5–11 **BAR MEALS:** Lunch served: all week 11.30–2 Av main course £3 **BREWERY/COMPANY:** Burton Bridge **PRINCIPAL BEERS:** Pilgrim Porter, Gale's Festival Mild, Burton Bridge Golden Delicious & Bridge Bitter **FACILITIES:** Children welcome Garden: Patio Dogs allowed

Pins & Firkins
Brewing has a rich store of technical terms and old-fashioned measures. The conventional container for draught beer – for centuries made of wood, but nowadays of metal – is called a cask. A barrel in brewing terminology is a 36-gallon cask, and a keg is a sealed metal container for beer that has been filtered, sterilised and pressurised before leaving the brewery. British beer in pubs still comes in pints or half-pints and pubs still order their beer using the old-style cask measures, which follow a scale of nine
pin – 4.5 gallons   **firkin** – 9 gallons
kilderkin – 18 gallons   **barrel** – 36 gallons
hogshead – 54 gallons
Two obsolete cask sizes are the butt of 108 gallons and the tun, which held varying quantities above 200 gallons. A yard of ale is a glass tube 3ft long and containing up to 3 pints, now only used in drinking contests.

BUTTERTON
Map 09 SK05

The Black Lion Inn
ST13 7SP ☎ 01538 304232
Dir: From A52 (between Leek & Ashbourne) take B5053

This charming, 18th-century village inn lies on the edge of the Manifold valley, in the heart of the Peak District's walking and cycling country. Winter fires glint on the comfortable clutter of old brass and china, adding to the pleasure of a well-kept pint. The popular bar menu includes pies and steaks, as well as lamb casserole, spinach and ricotta cannelloni, and plenty of interesting fish dishes. Three upstairs bedrooms provide a comfortable base from which to explore the National Park.
OPEN: 12-3 7-11 **BAR MEALS:** Lunch served: Tues-Sun 12-2 Dinner served: all week 7-9 Av main course £8
RESTAURANT: Lunch served: Tues-Sun 12-2 Dinner served: all week 7-9.30 Av 3 course à la carte £15 **BREWERY/COMPANY:** Free House **PRINCIPAL BEERS:** Theakston Best, Marston's Pedigree, Whim Arbor light.. **FACILITIES:** Children welcome Children's licence Garden: Dogs allowed **NOTES:** Parking 30 **ROOMS:** 3 bedrooms 3 en suite from d£50

CHEADLE
Map 09 SK04

The Queens At Freehay ⬡ NEW
Counslow Rd, Freehay ST10 1RF
☎ 01538 722383 ▤ 01538 722383
The Queens, located near Cheadle and some 3.5 miles from Alton Towers, opened in October 1999. Previously a run down pub, it was extensively renovated and transformed into a popular and award-winning eating house. Three full-time chefs are kept busy preparing freshly cooked meals, including fish and game in season, maybe lemon sole roulade, filled with spinach and tiger prawns and served with fish velouté, or roast duckling with port and wild berry sauce.
OPEN: 12-2.30 6-11 Closed: 25-26 Dec, 31 Dec
BAR MEALS: Lunch served: all week Dinner served: all week 12-2 6-9.30 Av main course £9 **RESTAURANT:** Lunch served: all week Dinner served: all week 12-2 6-9.30 Av 3 course fixed price £16 **BREWERY/COMPANY:** Free House
PRINCIPAL BEERS: Draught Bass, Draught Worthington Bitter.
FACILITIES: Children welcome Garden: Food served outside. Lawned area Dogs allowed (guide dogs only) **NOTES:** Parking 30

CRESSWELL
Map 09 SJ93

Izaak Walton Inn ⬡ ♀
Cresswell Ln ST11 9RE ☎ 01782 392265 ▤ 01782 388340
Dir: Just off A50 SE of Stoke-on-Trent
Named after the renowned author of The Compleat Angler, it is said that Isaak himself used to break his journey here to fish

the River Blythe. Believed to date back to the mid 17th century, refurbished in 1999 has recaptured its roots. Surrounded by wood panelling, in front of open fires, diners can choose between exotic Caribbean creole chicken or home-made vegetable masala and traditional three-cheese ploughman's or home-made steak pie. There are super salads and grills with optional special sauces.

OPEN: 12-11 (Sun 12-10.30 Closed: 25 Dec **BAR MEALS:** Lunch served: all week Dinner served: all week 12-10 Av main course £8.50
RESTAURANT: Lunch served: all week Dinner served: all week 12-10 Av 3 course à la carte £16 **BREWERY/COMPANY:** Free House
PRINCIPAL BEERS: Interbrew Bass. **FACILITIES:** Garden: Lawned, food served outside **NOTES:** Parking 80

ECCLESHALL
Map 08 SJ82

The George ⬡ ♀
Castle St ST21 6DF ☎ 01785 850300 ▤ 01785 851452
e-mail: information@thegeorgeinn.freeserve.co.uk

A family-run, 16th-century former coaching inn with its own micro-brewery, where the owners' son produces award-winning Slater's ales. A new chef was expected at the time of preparing this report, but - as a guide - his predecessor's restaurant/bistro menu included medallions of beef fillet on a pâté croûton with Madeira sauce, mussels poached in garlic with cream and herb liquor (optional chilli), Staffordshire leg of lamb with black cherry sauce, and nutty creamed mushroom crumble.
OPEN: 11-11 (12-10.30 Sun) Closed: 25 Dec **BAR MEALS:** Lunch served: all week Dinner served: all week 12-2.30 6-9.45 Av main course £9.95 **RESTAURANT:** Lunch served: all week Dinner served: all week 12-2.30 6-9.45 Av 3 course à la carte £20
BREWERY/COMPANY: Free House **FACILITIES:** Children welcome Dogs allowed **NOTES:** Parking 30
ROOMS: 10 bedrooms 10 en suite from s£30 d£60

continued

PUB WALK

Norbury Junction
The Junction Inn

The outward leg of this attractive walk skirts an extensive area of woodland before joining the towpath of the Shropshire Union Canal, returning to Norbury Junction along a leafy stretch of the canal, with views of the Wrekin.

Turn right outside the pub and cross the Shropshire Union Canal. Pass the maintenance yard where the scene is alive with moored narrow boats. Walk ahead along the road passing the entrance to Norbury Manor on the left. Continue down the lane towards the woodland. The canal embankment, known as Shelmore Great Bank, can be seen on the right. Follow the road between the trees, passing a white cottage on the right. As the road bends sharp right, go straight on to follow a track running along the edge of Shelmore Wood. Further on join a firm track running alongside a row of oak trees. Soon you reach a junction with a concrete drive. Continue ahead, with the outline of Norbury Park on the left. Shortly you reach a brick and stone cottage by the road. Turn right and walk down through the woodland. Go through the tunnel under the canal and then bear immediately left over a stile. A flight of steps takes you to the towpath of the Shropshire Union Canal. Turn left and follow the canal along the top of the embankment. This is Shelmore Great Bank, built to avoid the canal having to cut through Lord Anson's estate at Norbury Park. Lord Anson reared pheasants for shooting, which he did not want disturbed, and he probably use his influence on the route of the canal. To the west is the distinctive outline of the Wrekin, Shropshire's highest hill. Continue on the towpath, passing an iron milepost, then cross a stone bridge at the junction of the Shropshire Union Canal and the remains of a defunct canal to Newport. Just beyond it is the Junction Inn.

THE JUNCTION INN
NORBURY JUNCTION Stafford
ST20 0PN
Tel: 01785 284288
Directions: From M6 take road for Eccleshall, L at Gt Bridgeford & head for Woodseaves, L there & head for Newport, L for Norbury Junct
Near the Shropshire Union Canal, this pub was originally built in the heyday of canal traffic. It as the junction of the Shropshire and the now disused Shrewsbury and Newport Canals. Traditional Pub fare and real ales.
Open: 11-11 (Sun 12-10.30)
Bar meals: 12-9
Children welcome and dogs allowed outside. Garden and parking available.

Distance: 2 3/4 miles (4.4km)
Map: OS Landranger 127
Terrain: Farmland and woodland
Paths: Country lanes, tracks and canal towpath
Gradient: Gently undulating, no steep hills

Walk submitted and checked by Nick Channer

England

HIMLEY
Map 09 SO89

Crooked House
Coppice Mill DY3 4DA ☎ 01384 238583 ⊟ 01384 214911
Former farmhouse dating from 1765, condemned after
collapsing mines underneath caused severe subsidence.
Restored but still showing signs of its past - one side is 4ft
lower than the other, and several optical illusions like wonky
grandfather's clock and bottles rolling uphill are unsettling
after a few pints! Wholesome food like Cajun chicken, red
pepper lasagne, bangers and mash, and steak and kidney pie,
and familiar puds like Bramley apple pie, and blackberry and
apple crumble.
OPEN: 11.30-11 (Winter 11.30-2.30, 6-11) **BAR MEALS:** Lunch
served: all week Dinner served: all week 12-2 6-8.30 Av main course
£6 **PRINCIPAL BEERS:** Bank's Original & Bitter, Marston's Pedigree.
FACILITIES: Children welcome Children's licence Garden: Patio,
food served outdoors Dogs allowed **NOTES:** Parking 50

LEEK
Map 09 SJ95

Abbey Inn 🛏
Abbey Green Rd ☎ 01538 382865 ⊟ 01538 398604
e-mail: martin@abbeyinn.co.uk
Set in beautiful countryside on the Staffordshire Moorlands,
this 17th-century inn is on the outskirts of Leek, and handy for
the potteries of Stoke-on-Trent. Modern, well-equipped
bedrooms are in a converted building.

Ye Olde Royal Oak 🛏
Wetton DE6 2AF ☎ 01335 310287 ⊟ 01335 310336
e-mail: royaloak2@compuserve.com
*Dir: A515 twrds Buxton, L after 4 miles to Manifold Valley-Alstonfield, follow
signs to Wetton village.*
Formerly part of the Chatsworth estate, this welcoming old
Peak District inn was first licensed in 1760. The popular
Tissington walking and cycling trail is close by, and the pub's
moorland garden includes a camper's croft. Sample the
landlord's collection of over forty single malts, then tuck into
home-made soups, steak and Guinness pie, or hot chicken
salad. There's fresh local trout and pepper-dusted haddock for
fish-fanciers.
OPEN: 12-3 7-11 **BAR MEALS:** Lunch served: Thur-Tue Dinner
served: Thur-Tue 12-2 7-9 Av main course £6.50
RESTAURANT: Lunch served: Thur-Tue Dinner served: Thur-Tue
12-2 7-9 Av 3 course à la carte £12 **BREWERY/COMPANY:** Free
House **PRINCIPAL BEERS:** Greene King Ruddles County, Jennings
Cumberland, BlackSheep Special. **FACILITIES:** Children welcome
Garden: Food served outdoors **NOTES:** Parking 20
ROOMS: 4 bedrooms 4 en suite from s£36 d£43

Three Horseshoes Inn ★ ★ ⊛ 🛏 ♀ NEW
Buxton Rd, Blackshaw Moor ST13 8TW ☎ 01538 300296 ⊟
01538 300320
A sprawling creeper-covered inn geared to catering for visitors
and locals in three smart eating outlets. The bar carvery
focuses on traditional roasts as well as bar snacks and filled
baguettes, and specials like salmon in lemon and chive sauce.
Thai-influenced dishes can be found in the brasserie and
sophisticated restaurant, such as steamed monkfish with
coconut rice, and sautéed duck breast with noodles.
OPEN: 12-3 6-11 **BAR MEALS:** Lunch served: all week Dinner
served: all week 12-2 6.30-9 Av main course £6.95
RESTAURANT: Lunch served: Sun 12.30-1.30 Dinner served: Sun-Fri
6.30-9 Av 3 course à la carte £20 **BREWERY/COMPANY:** Free
House **FACILITIES:** Children welcome Garden: Food served
outdoors **NOTES:** Parking 100 **ROOMS:** 7 bedrooms 7 en suite
from s£40 d£60

NEWCASTLE-UNDER-LYME
Map 08 SJ84

Mainwaring Arms ♀
Whitmore ST5 5HR ☎ 01782 680851 ⊟ 01782 680224

A welcoming old creeper-clad inn on the Mainwaring family
estate. Crackling log fires set the scene at this very traditional
country retreat, where daily blackboard specials support the
popular bar menu. Expect freshly-made sandwiches, home-
made steak and kidney pie, pork and leek sausages with chive
mash, grilled plaice with mustard sauce, or battered cod with
chips and mushy peas.
OPEN: 12-11 **BAR MEALS:** Lunch served: all week Dinner served:
all week 12-2.30 6-8.30 Av main course £5
BREWERY/COMPANY: Free House
PRINCIPAL BEERS: Boddingtons, Marstons Pedigree, Bass, plus
guest ales. **FACILITIES:** Children welcome Dogs allowed only when
food service is over **NOTES:** Parking 60

NORBURY JUNCTION
Map 08 SJ72

The Junction Inn 🛏
ST20 0PN ☎ 01785 284288 ⊟ 01785 284288
*Dir: From M6 take road for Eccleshall, L at Gt Bridgeford & head for
Woodseaves, L there & head for Newport, L for Norb Junct*
Not a railway junction, but a beautiful stretch of waterway
where the Shropshire Union Canal meets the disused Newport
arm. Specials include sizzling platters of beef, prawn or
chicken with fresh mushrooms, peppers, onions, rice and
garlic bread. Fish dishes include beer-battered cod, salmon in
filo and fresh-caught grilled trout with almonds. All are freshly
prepared on the premises. Children's meals from £1.50. Canal
boat hire is available.
OPEN: 11-11 (12-10.30 Sun) **BAR MEALS:** Lunch served: all week
Dinner served: all week 11-9 Av main course £4.50
RESTAURANT: Lunch served: all week Dinner served: all week 12-9
Av 3 course à la carte £9.99 Av 4 course fixed price £9.99
BREWERY/COMPANY: Free House **PRINCIPAL BEERS:** Banks
Mild, Banks Bitter, Junction Ale and guest ales. **FACILITIES:** Children
welcome Garden: Food served outside. Dogs allowed (water
provided) **NOTES:** Parking 100

See Pub Walk on page 427

ONECOTE
Map 09 SK05

Jervis Arms 🛏
ST13 7RU ☎ 01538 304206
Convenient for visitors from Leek or Ashbourne, this
17th century inn set in the Peak National Park has a stream-
side garden kitted out with swings and slides. Some 500 guest
ales have featured over the past five years to accompany
home-cooked steak and ale pie, salmon hollandaise, popular
roasts and T-bone steak weighing in - uncooked - at 20
ounces. Additional menu items to satisfy vegetarians and
undemanding children.

continued

OPEN: 12–2.30 6–11 (open all day Sat–Sun)
BAR MEALS: L served all week. D served all week. 12–2 6–9.30 Av main course £7.95
BREWERY/COMPANY: FREE HOUSE
PRINCIPAL BEERS: Boddingtons, Courage Directors, Bass
FACILITIES: Children welcome, dogs allowed. Garden: Food served outside, lawned area
NOTES: Parking 25

The Hollybush Inn

Set in open countryside close to the Trent and Mersey Canal and just minutes from Stafford, the immaculately thatched Hollybush is Stafford's oldest inn. The pride taken in the very good food is matched only by the warmth of the welcome you can be sure of from the licensees and staff.

Salt Ramsgill ST18 0BX
☎ 01889 508234 📠 01889 508058
e-mail: geoff@hollybushinn.co.uk

The building dates back to the 14th century and was recorded as a hostelry at the time of the Civil War battle at nearby Hopton Heath. The pub regularly wins awards for its summer flower displays - all grown and planted by the landlady – and in summer the large beer garden plays host to jazz concerts and hog roasts, culminating with a Guy

Fawkes Night firework display. Carved heavy beams, open fires, attractive prints and cosy alcoves characterise the comfortably old-fashioned interior. The innovative daily-illustrated menu is allegedly registered at the Post Office as a newspaper, priced sixpence. Lunchtime offerings include triple-decker sandwiches stuffed with bacon, lettuce and tomato, jacket potatoes and toasties, while the main menu takes in the Hollybush favourite steak and ale pie, chargrilled steaks and deep-fried cod in the house beer batter. Look out for the chalkboards listing the fresh speciality dishes of the day, maybe steamed sea bass with mango and ginger chutney, or venison and root vegetable crumble. Here you will also find vegetarian options and the full range of desserts. A list of house wines by the glass supplements the choice of cask ales.

ONECOTE continued

OPEN: 12-3 7-11 (Sun 12-11) **BAR MEALS:** Lunch served: all week Dinner served: all week 12-2 7-10 Av main course £5.45
BREWERY/COMPANY: Free House
PRINCIPAL BEERS: Interbrew Bass, Marston's Pedigree, Titanic Premium, Sarah Hughes Dark Ruby Mild. **FACILITIES:** Children welcome Children's licence Garden: Beer garden, food served outdoors Dogs allowed **NOTES:** Parking 50

ONNELEY

Map 08 SJ74

The Wheatsheaf Inn
Barhill Rd CW3 9QF ☎ 01782 751581 ◻ 01782 751499
e-mail: info@wheatsheaf.ws
Dir: On the A525 between Madeley & Woore, 6.5m W of Newcastle Under Lyme

Overlooking the local golf course and village cricket ground, this recently renovated wayside inn has been a hostelry since 1769. Solid oak beams, roaring log fires and distinctive furnishings are a fine setting for some fine dining. Specials include Chateaubriand roast, steamed halibut steak on buttered spinach, pan-fried kangaroo with herb rosh, and chicken breast in smoked bacon with creamy grape and cheese sauce. Bar meals also available.
OPEN: 12-2.30 6-11 **BAR MEALS:** Lunch served: all week Dinner served: all week 12-2.30 6.30-9.30 Av main course £6
RESTAURANT: Dinner served: all week 6.30-9.30 Av 3 course à la carte £17 **BREWERY/COMPANY:** Free House
PRINCIPAL BEERS: Bass, Worthington, Guest Ales.
FACILITIES: Children welcome Garden: Food served outside Dogs allowed (in the garden only) **NOTES:** Parking 60
ROOMS: 6 bedrooms 6 en suite from s£60 d£70

STAFFORD

Map 08 SJ92

Pick of the Pubs

The Hollybush Inn
Salt ST18 0BX ☎ 01889 508234 ◻ 01889 508058
e-mail: geoff@hollybushinn.co.uk

See Pick of the Pubs on page 429

Pick of the Pubs

The Moat House ★ ★ ★ ★ ◎◎◯♀
Lower Penkridge Rd, Acton Trussell ST17 0RJ
☎ 01785 712217 ◻ 01785 715344
e-mail: info@moathouse.co.uk
Dir: M6 J13 towards Stafford, 1st R to Acton Trussell
This Grade II listed mansion dating back to the 14th century stands behind its original moat. Quality

bedrooms, conference facilities and corporate events are a big attraction, as are the license for weddings and four honeymoon suites. The bar and food trade brings in both the hungry and the curious. 'Moaties' are a popular feature of the lunchtime menu - rustic breads topped typically with honey-baked ham and mustard mayonnaise or smoked salmon with lemon mayonnaise and cucumber, replaced at night by Triyaki pork with soy egg noodles or Thai green chicken curry with savoury rice. Always available are generous salads and the Moat House mixed platter for two. There are generally fresh fish dishes on the specials board, plus grilled steaks with optional sauces and vegetarian dishes such as tagliatelle verdi and roast peppers with provençale risotto. Up-market dining in the canal-side conservatory.

OPEN: 12-11 Closed: Dec 25-26 **BAR MEALS:** 12-2.15 6-9.30
RESTAURANT: 12-2 7-10 Av 3 course fixed price £17.95
BREWERY/COMPANY: Free House
PRINCIPAL BEERS: Bank's Bitter, Marston's Pedigree, Greene King Old Speckled Hen. **FACILITIES:** Children welcome Children's licence Garden: Food served outside
NOTES: Parking 150 **ROOMS:** 32 bedrooms 32 en suite from s£75 d£100

STOKE-ON-TRENT

Map 08 SJ84

Yew Tree Inn
Cauldon, Waterhouses ST10 3EJ ☎ 01538 308348
300-year-old pub with plenty of character and lots of fascinating artefacts, including pianolas, grandfather clocks, a crank handle telephone and a pub lantern. Interesting and varied snack menu consists of hand-raised locally-made pork pies, sandwiches, rolls and quiche. Banana split and home-made fruit crumble feature among the sweets.
OPEN: 10-2.30 6-11 (Sun 12-3, 7-10.30) **BAR MEALS:** Lunch served: Snacks all day **BREWERY/COMPANY:** Free House
PRINCIPAL BEERS: Burton Bridge, Titanic Mild, Interbrew Bass.
FACILITIES: Children welcome Dogs allowed (water)
NOTES: Parking 50 No credit cards

TATENHILL

Map 09 SK22

Horseshoe Inn ♀
Main St DE13 9SD ☎ 01283 564913 ◻ 01283 511314
Dir: From A38 at Branston follow signs for Tatenhill
Historic pub with much of its original character still intact. In the winter visitors are warmed by log fires in the bar and family area. Good local reputation for honest food and a good pint.

continued

PUB WALK

Tutbury
Ye Olde Dog & Partridge

The walk passes romantic castle ruins, pretty farmland and Fauld Crater – formed in 1944 when 4,000 tons of bombs stored in old gypsum mines exploded, killing 70 people and destroying a farm.

From the inn, turn left, then right at the mini roundabout. Head towards the castle, passing the small museum and the Leopard Pub. The road climbs the hill, bending left. A finger post marks a footpath between houses, follow this path down to a little gate by Tutbury Castle. Go straight on to the corner of the field, through a gateway and cross a stile immediately on your left, followed by a bridge. Turn right towards a footbridge in the hedge. Cross this and turn left, looking for a stile and finger post in the hedge. Walk over a large field, keeping straight on when the river winds away to the right. Cross a stile by a hedge corner and go straight ahead in the field to the next stile. Keep ahead until the road at Boundary House. Turn right along the road and then left at the finger post by the Fauld Industrial Estate. Follow the estate road to a stile to the right of some large gates. Descend the bank and go straight on, with the hedge on your right. Cross the next stile and turn left up a track. Beyond the next stile bend slightly right to follow the path with woodland on the left. Cross a stile, turn right to go up hill. Keep the wire fence well to your left and cross a stile to enter the wood. Pass the pheasant enclosure on your left

and at an area of open ground, go right into the trees, then left at a grain hopper. Keep left when the track bends right and climb a steep slope. Go through a kissing gate at the top to reach the crater. Keep walking straight ahead until you, pass a right-hand footpath and continue alongside the hedgerow to where another path joins from the right. Turn sharp left and cross the field to a stile. Keep the hedge on your right, crossing the waymarked stiles past Hare Holes Farm and up to Castle Hayes Farm. Bend slightly left here, past the farm, avoiding two tracks on the left. At an arrow pointing left, follow the track to a stile and keep along hedge to a stile on the right. Veer left and follow the path round to the right. Turn left at the bottom of a slope and follow the path to the road at Owen's Bank. Cross over to the stile and head diagonally across the field, with the castle ahead. Rejoin the path, turn left and return to the pub.

DOG & PARTRIDGE
High Street TUTBURY Burton-on-Trent DE13 9LS
Tel:1283 813030
Directions: On A50 NW of Burton upon Trent(signposted from A50 & A511)
A resplendent half-timbered inn on the old coaching route to London. Nearby are the ruins of Tutbury Castle where Mary Queen of Scots languished. Fish is strong on the menu and roasts for Sunday lunch. Adjacent accommodation is spacious.
Open: 11.45-2 6-11
Bar meals: 11.45-2 6-9.45 (not Monday)
Children welcome. Garden and parking available.

Distance: 5 1/2 miles (8.8km)
Map: OS Landranger 128
Terrain: Undulating country on the Staffordshire/Derbyshire border, to the south of the River Dove
Paths: Paths and tracks
Gradient: Some climbing

Walk submitted and checked by Sue Ellis

OPEN: 11.45–2 6–11
RESTAURANT: L served Tues-Sun.
D served Tues-Sat. 11.45–2 6–9.45
Av cost 3 course £19.95
BREWERY/COMPANY: FREE HOUSE
PRINCIPLE BEERS: Marston's Pedigree
FACILITIES: Children welcome.
Garden: Food served outside
NOTES: Parking 100
ROOMS: 20 en suite Double room from £60 Single room from £55

Ye Olde Dog & Partridge Inn

A beautiful period building resplendent in its timbers and whitewashed walls, with abundant flower displays beneath the windows. The inn has stood in this charming village since the 15th century when Henry IV was on the throne. Its connection with the village sport of bull-running brought it into prominence, and it remains a focus of local activity including the nearby hunt.

★★ ♀
High Street DE13 9LS
☎ 01283 813030 📄 01283 813178
e-mail: info@dogandpartridge.net
Dir: On A50 NW of Burton upon Trent (signposted from A50 & A511).

During the 18th century it became a coaching inn on the route to London. Five hundred years of offering hospitality has resulted in a well-deserved reputation for good food, comfortable accommodation and restful public areas. Bedrooms, including four posters and half testers, are individually furnished and charmingly decorated, and filled with

modern luxuries. Two smart eating outlets ensure that all tastes are catered for. In the Carvery, a grand piano plays while diners choose from an extensive menu; start with a selection from the buffet, or go for fisherman's platter, or woodman's mushrooms, and follow on with a plate of roast meat, or perhaps steak and kidney pie, or ratatouille bake. In the brasserie, with its leather chairs and bare wooden tables, the fixed price menu may lists fallen Dovedale blue cheese soufflé, or terrine of tame and wild duck, followed by chargrilled swordfish loin with mango and chilli salsa, or breast of guinea fowl. Time and space should be found for mouthwatering desserts like chocolate truffle torte, and pear and almond tart.

England

TUTBURY
Map 09 SK22

Pick of the Pubs

Ye Olde Dog & Partridge Inn ★ ★ 🛏 ♀
High St DE13 9LS ☎ 01283 813030 🖹 01283 813178
e-mail: info@dogandpartridge.net

See Pub Walk on page 431
See Pick of the Pubs on page 432

WATERHOUSES
Map 09 SK05

Ye Olde Crown ♦ ♦ 🛏
Leek Rd ST10 3HL ☎ 01538 308204

A traditional village local, Ye Olde Crown dates from around 1648 when it was built as a coaching inn. Sitting on the bank of the River Hamps, it's also on the edge of the Peak District National Park and the Staffordshire moorlands. Inside are original stonework and interior beams, and open fires are lit in cooler weather. Sample menu includes roast beef, steak and kidney pie, chicken tikka masala, battered cod, and tuna pasta bake. Homely accommodation includes an adjacent cottage.
OPEN: 11.30–3 6.30–11 (Sun 12–3, 6.30–11) **BAR MEALS:** Lunch served: all week Dinner served: all week 12–2 7–9.30 Av main course £6 **BREWERY/COMPANY:** Free House **PRINCIPAL BEERS:** Carlsberg-Tetley Tetley Bitter, Burton Ale. **FACILITIES:** Children welcome Children's licence Dogs allowed except overnight by arrangement **NOTES:** Parking 30 **ROOMS:** 7 bedrooms 6 en suite from s£15 d£40

WRINEHILL
Map 08 SJ74

The Crown Inn NEW
Den Ln CW3 9BT ☎ 01270 820472 🖹 01270 820472

A popular drinking hostelry that has prospered since its days as a coaching inn, with a modern reputation for good beer and food. The single bar boasts an inglenook fire which blazes in winter, and exposed oak beams to add to its charm. A really wide choice at lunch and evening including the famous Crown steaks, tuna and black olive penne, seafood basket,

minted lamb shank, plenty of vegetarian dishes, and novel puddings like Dime Bar toffee crunch. No credit cards
OPEN: 12–3 6–11 (Sun 12–4 6–10 Mon 6–11) Closed: Dec 25
BAR MEALS: Lunch served: Tue–Sun Dinner served: Mon–Sun 12–2 6.30–9.30 Av main course £8 **BREWERY/COMPANY:** Free House
PRINCIPAL BEERS: Marston's Pedigree, Adnams & guest beer
FACILITIES: Garden: Seating on lawn, trees and flower beds
NOTES: Parking 35

YOXALL
Map 09 SK11

The Crown
Main St DE13 8NQ ☎ 01543 472551 🖹 01543 473479
Dir: On A515 N of Lichfield
In a picturesque village, this pub is reputedly over 250 years old: its name possibly deriving from its former use as the local courthouse. Within easy reach of Uttoxeter racecourse and Alton Towers it's a great spot to enjoy locally sourced, home-cooked food prepared by the landlord. Expect on the regularly changing menu such lunchtime bites as a breakfast brunch and hot filled baguettes whilst evening options such as steak and Guinness pie are supplemented by offerings posted on the chalkboard.
OPEN: 11.30–3 5.30–11 (Sat–Sun & BHs open all day)
BAR MEALS: Lunch served: all week 12–2 Dinner served: Mon–Sat 6.30–9 Av main course £7 **RESTAURANT:** Lunch served: all week 12–2 Dinner served: Mon–Sat 6.30–9 Av 3 course à la carte £10
BREWERY/COMPANY: Marstons **PRINCIPAL BEERS:** Marston's Pedigree,. **FACILITIES:** Children welcome Garden: Food served outdoors Dogs allowed **NOTES:** Parking 20

SUFFOLK

ALDEBURGH
Map 07 TM45

The Mill Inn 🛏
Market Cross Place IP15 5BJ ☎ 01728 452563 🖹 01728 452028
e-mail: tedmillinn@btinternet.com
Dir: Follow Aldeburgh signs from A12 on A1094. Pub last building on L before sea

Occupying a seafront position, this genuine traditional fisherman's inn is frequented by the local lifeboat crew, those visiting the North Warren bird reserve, or walkers from Thorpness and Orford. Opposite is the 17th-century Moot Hall. Good value food ranges from baguettes, crab salads and sandwiches to seafood lasagne and a choice of steaks. The emphasis is very much on locally caught fish.
OPEN: 11–3 (11–11 summer) 6–11 **BAR MEALS:** Lunch served: all week 12–2 Dinner served: Fri–Wed 7–9 Av main course £6.50
RESTAURANT: Lunch served: all week 12–2 Dinner served: Fri–Wed 7–9 **BREWERY/COMPANY:** Adnams
PRINCIPAL BEERS: Adnams Bitter, Broadside, Regatta & Fisherman.
ROOMS: 4 bedrooms from s£26 d£48

continued

England

BARNBY
Map 07 TM48

Pick of the Pubs

The Swan Inn
Swan Ln NR34 7QF ☎ 01502 476646 📠 01502 562513

Dir: Just off the A146 between Lowestoft and Beccles in the village of Barnby

Arguably one of Suffolk's foremost fish restaurants – the menu lists up to 80 different seafood dishes – the Swan still looks on itself as a traditional village pub with a strong local following. The distinctive pink-painted property dates from 1690, and can be found in the picturesque village of Barnby, which nestles in its rural surroundings. Owned by a family of Lowestoft fish wholesalers, it comprises a village bar that is at the centre of local activities, and the rustic Fisherman's Cove restaurant, with its low beams and nautical memorabilia. The menu is a fish-lovers delight: starters include smoked sprats, smoked trout pâté and Italian seafood salad, while main dishes range from monkfish tails in garlic butter, to crab gratin and whole grilled turbot. Meat lovers are not left out: various steaks are offered along with home-cooked gammon salad.

OPEN: 11-3 6-12 **BAR MEALS:** Lunch served: all week Dinner served: all week 12-2 7-9.30 Av main course £8
RESTAURANT: Lunch served: all week Dinner served: all week 12-2 7-9.30 **BREWERY/COMPANY:** Free House
PRINCIPAL BEERS: Interbrew Bass, Adnams Best, Broadside, Greene King Abbot Ale. **FACILITIES:** Children welcome Garden: Food served outside **NOTES:** Parking 30

BILDESTON
Map 07 TL94

The Crown Hotel
High St IP7 7EB ☎ 01449 740510 📠 01449 740510

Dir: On B1115 between Hadleigh & Stowmarket

A beautiful 15th-century half-timbered former coaching inn with oak-beamed bars and lounge. The formal restaurant, two-acre garden and stylish bedrooms add a touch of extra luxury. Originally a wool merchants, it lays claim to being the most-haunted pub in Britain; only the brave, it's said, will stay in Room 6! A typical meal starts with crab cakes in lobster bisque leading on to grilled gammon, sirloin steak or battered chicken strips with a choice of dips.

OPEN: 11-2.30 6-11 **BAR MEALS:** Lunch served: all week Dinner served: all week 12-2 6.30-9.30 Av main course £7.25
RESTAURANT: Lunch served: all week Dinner served: all week 12-2 6.30-9.30 Av 3 course à la carte £15 **BREWERY/COMPANY:** Free House **PRINCIPAL BEERS:** Adnams, Broadside,.
FACILITIES: Children welcome Garden: Surrounded by trees, food served outside Dogs allowed **NOTES:** Parking 30
ROOMS: 13 bedrooms 13 en suite from s£25 d£55

BLYFORD
Map 07 TM47

Queens Head Inn
Southwold Rd IP19 9JY ☎ 01502 478404

Dir: From A12 after Blythburgh take A145, fork L towards Halesworth, Pub on L opp church

Once used by smugglers, with a secret underground passage linking the inn with the nearby church, this 14th-century thatched building is supposedly haunted by the ghosts of seven smugglers shot in the tunnel by excise men. Undergoing a change of management at time of going to press.

continued

OPEN: 11-3 6-11 (Sun 12-2.30, 7-9.30) **BAR MEALS:** Lunch served: Tue-Sun & BH Dinner served: Tue-Sun & BH 12-2.30 7-9.30 Av main course £6 **BREWERY/COMPANY:** Adnams
PRINCIPAL BEERS: Adnams - Bitter, Broadside.
FACILITIES: Garden: **NOTES:** Parking 50

BRANDESTON
Map 07 TM26

The Queens Head
The Street IP13 7AD ☎ 01728 685307

Dir: From A14 take A1120 to Earl Soham, then S to Brandeston

A village pub dating back 400 years, with wooden panelling, quarry tile floors and open fires. The extensive gardens and play tree are ideal for children, and camping and caravanning facilities are available, with electric hook up, shower and toilet facilities. Adnams ales are served, and a comprehensive menu taking in sandwiches, jacket potatoes, pizza, curries, seafood casserole, and steak and kidney pudding. Every Monday there's a two main meals for the price of one offer.

OPEN: 11.30-3 6-11 (Sun 12-3, 7-10.30) **BAR MEALS:** Lunch served: all week Dinner served: all week 12-2.30 6-9.30
RESTAURANT: Lunch served: all week Dinner served: all week **BREWERY/COMPANY:** Adnams **PRINCIPAL BEERS:** Adnams Broadside, & Bitter seasonal ale. **FACILITIES:** Children welcome Garden: Food served outside Dogs allowed **NOTES:** Parking 30
ROOMS: 3 bedrooms from s£18 d£36

BROCKLEY GREEN
Map 07 TL74

The Plough Inn
CO10 8DT ☎ 01440 786789 📠 01440 786710
e-mail: ploughdave@aol.com

Dir: Take B1061 from A143, approx 1.5m beyond Kedington

In five acres of grounds overlooking the Stour Valley, the Plough has been run by the same family for 45 years. The current landlords have been there for two decades and have worked hard to create a 'traditional country inn' with well-kept ales and comfortable bedrooms. A typical meal may start with pan-fried Greek Halloumi with minted yoghurt and cucumber salad or devilled whitebait, then continue with fillet of sea bass with roasted peppers and lemon grass or spinach cream cheese and walnut pancakes.

OPEN: 12-2.30 5-11 **BAR MEALS:** Lunch served: all week Dinner served: all week 12-2 7-9.30 Av main course £8
RESTAURANT: Lunch served: all week Dinner served: all week 12-2 7-9.30 Av 3 course à la carte £20 Av 3 course fixed price £17.50
BREWERY/COMPANY: Free House **PRINCIPAL BEERS:** Greene King IPA, Adnams Best, Fuller's London Pride, Woodforde's Wherry Best Bitter. **FACILITIES:** Children welcome Garden: Food served outside Dogs allowed (water bowl)s **NOTES:** Parking 50
ROOMS: 8 bedrooms 8 en suite from s£45 d£65

England

BROME
Map 07 TM17

Pick of the Pubs

Cornwallis Arms ★ ★ ★ 🐷 🍽 🍷
IP23 8AJ ☎ 01379 870326 📠 01379 870051
e-mail: info@cornwallis.com
Dir: Just off A140 at Brome

This original Dower House to Brome Hall, set in 21 acres of gardens with fine yew topiary, dates back to 1561. Retaining many original beams, panels, oak and mahogany settles and a 60-foot well, the Tudor Bar is an informal meeting and eating place in front of roaring log fires. No shame here in enjoying a quick bite of roasted Cajun chicken or creamed Yarmouth bloaters, snacking on a panzanella salad of grilled sardines with red wine vinaigrette or splashing out on coq au vin with chourico and honey-glazed parsnips. Equally tempting are mulligatawny soup with saffron cream or grilled fig, Parmesan and rocket salad, followed by cod, salmon and coriander fishcakes and award-winning Brundish Winter Warmer sausages on cheesy bubble-and-squeak; rounding off with warm apple tarte Tatin or a fine selection of English cheeses.
OPEN: 11–11 **BAR MEALS:** Lunch served: all week Dinner served: all week 12–10 Av main course £10
RESTAURANT: Lunch served: all week Dinner served: all week 12–2.30 6.30–9.45 Av 3 course à la carte £24.50
BREWERY/COMPANY: Free House
PRINCIPAL BEERS: Adnams, Broadside, St Peters Best.
FACILITIES: Children welcome Garden: 21 acres of gardens, food served outside Dogs allowed **NOTES:** Parking 400
ROOMS: 16 bedrooms 16 en suite from s£84.50 d£105.50

BURY ST EDMUNDS
Map 07 TL86

The Linden Tree 🐷
7 Out Northgate IP33 1JQ ☎ 01284 754600
Dir: Opposite railway station
A former Victorian station hotel with a charming garden and conservatory. It has a bustling, cheery atmosphere in its stripped pine bar and family dining area with something for everyone on the menu. Family favourites include home-made sausage casserole, chicken curry or steak and mushroom pies and lamb, duck, turkey and beef in various guises from the grill. Linden burgers, leek and mushroom lasagne, assorted salads and children's dishes complete a large repertoire that lives up to its promise.
OPEN: 11–3 5–11 Closed: Xmas for 3 days **BAR MEALS:** Lunch served: all week Dinner served: all week 12–2 6–9.30 Av main course £8 **RESTAURANT:** Lunch served: all week Dinner served: all week

continued

12–2 6–9.30 Av 3 course à la carte £15
BREWERY/COMPANY: Greene King **PRINCIPAL BEERS:** Greene King, IPA, Abbot Ale, Ruddles Country. **FACILITIES:** Children welcome Garden: Large & attractive

The Nutshell
17 The Traverse IP33 1BJ ☎ 01284 764867
Known as the smallest pub in Britain, this novel thatched inn covers an area of 15ft x 7ft 6 inches and features in the Guinness Book of Records.

Six Bells Inn ◆ ◆ ◆ ◆ 🍽 🍷
The Green, Bardwell IP31 1AW
☎ 01359 250820 📠 01359 250820
e-mail: sixbellsbardwell@aol.com
Dir: From A143 take turning marked Six Bells & Bardwell Windmill, premises 1m on L just before village green
This low-beamed 16th-century inn was immortalised in the classic comedy series Dad's Army. The name refers to the number of bells in the village church, which were rung at the impending arrival of a coach. Notable features inside are the inglenook fireplace and old Suffolk range. The daily dinner menu offers dishes like Madeira marinated herring fillets, and roast Suffolk loin of pork with Stilton and pistachio stuffing. Cottage-style accommodation is available in a converted barn.
OPEN: 12–2 (closed Mon-Wed lunch) 6.30–10.30 (Fri-Sat 6–11) Closed: 25-26 Dec **BAR MEALS:** Dinner served: all week 6.15–9 Av main course £7.50 **RESTAURANT:** Dinner served: all week 6.45–9.15 Av 3 course à la carte £17.50 Av 3 course fixed price £17.50
BREWERY/COMPANY: Free House **FACILITIES:** Garden: Food served outdoors **NOTES:** Parking 40 **ROOMS:** 10 bedrooms 10 en suite from s£40 d£55

CAVENDISH
Map 07 TL84

Bull Inn
High St CO10 8AX ☎ 01787 280245
Dir: A134 Bury St Edmunds to Long Melford, then R at green, pub 5m on R
The unassuming Victorian façade of this pub, set in one of Suffolk's most beautiful villages, hides a splendid 15th-century beamed interior. Expect a good atmosphere and decent food, the daily-changing blackboard menu listing, perhaps, curries, shank of lamb, fresh fish and shellfish, and a roast on Sundays.
OPEN: 11–3 (Sun 12–3, 7–10.30) 6–11 **BAR MEALS:** Lunch served: Mon-Sat Dinner served: Mon-Sat 12–2 6.30–9 Av main course £7 **RESTAURANT:** Lunch served: Mon-Sat Dinner served: Mon-Sat 12–2 6.30–9 Av 3 course à la carte £18 **BREWERY/COMPANY:** Adnams **PRINCIPAL BEERS:** Adnams Bitter & Broadside.
FACILITIES: Children welcome Garden: Food served outside Dogs allowed **NOTES:** Parking 30

CHELMONDISTON
Map 07 TM23

Butt & Oyster 🍷
Pin Mill Ln IP9 1JW ☎ 01473 780764 📠 01473 780764
The role of this 16th century pub on the eerie Suffolk coast has always been to provide sustenance for the local bargees and rivermen whose thirst for beer is near legendary. Today, with its character still thankfully intact, the Butt & Oyster is a favourite haunt of locals, tourists and yachtsmen. A mixture of seafood and traditional dishes characterises the menu, including toad in the hole, steak and kidney pie and scampi and chips.
OPEN: 11–11 (Sun 12–10.30) **BAR MEALS:** Lunch served: all week Dinner served: all week 12–2.30 6.30–9.30 Av main course £5.50
BREWERY/COMPANY: Pubmaster **PRINCIPAL BEERS:** Tolly Cobbold. **FACILITIES:** Children welcome Garden: outdoor eating, riverside Dogs allowed Garden: only, Water **NOTES:** Parking 40

435

CHILLESFORD Map 07 TM35

The Froize Inn ♀
The Street IP12 3PU ☎ 01394 450282
Dir: From the A12 (toward Lowestoft) take B1084, Chillesford 5m
Built on the site of Chillesford Friary, this distinctive red-brick building dates back to around 1490 and stands on today's popular Suffolk coast path. Alistair and Joy Shaw who refurbished the inn and were renowned for offering innovative fish and seafood cooking have leased the pub to a small company. Reports on the new regime please.
OPEN: 12-3 6-11 (all day wknd; cl Mon & 3wks Feb/Mar) Closed: 3wks Feb-Mar, 1wk end Sep **BAR MEALS:** Lunch served: Tues-Sun Dinner served: Tues-Sun 12-3 7-9 Av main course £7.50
RESTAURANT: Lunch served: Tues-Sun Dinner served: Tues-Sun 12-3 7-9 Av 3 course à la carte £25 **BREWERY/COMPANY:** Free House **PRINCIPAL BEERS:** Woodforde's, Adnams, St Peter's, Mauldons. **FACILITIES:** Children welcome Garden: Patio, children's area, C&C, beer garden with seating Dogs allowed **NOTES:** Parking 70 **ROOMS:** 2 bedrooms 2 en suite from s£30 d£50 No credit cards

COCKFIELD Map 07 TL95

Three Horseshoes 🍴 ♀
Stow's Hill IP30 0JB ☎ 01284 828177
e-mail: threehorseshoes@tinyworld.co.uk
Dir: A134 towards Sudbury, then L onto A1141 towards Lavenham & Cockfield

This 14th-century thatched inn was formerly a 'Hall House' with vaulted ceilings, heavy oak beams and an ancient King Post. The addition of a conservatory built from Scandinavian timbers, offering fine views over rolling countryside, is a definite bonus. In a warm and inviting bar area hand-pulled ales and chalk board menus are ever-popular. Starters of green-lip mussels and breaded brie wedges lead on to steak and Abbot Ale pie from a family recipe, or Indian curries and traditional grills. Small camping site adjacent.
OPEN: 11-3 6-11 Sun 10.30 Closed: 1st 2 wks in Jan
BAR MEALS: Lunch served: Wed-Mon Dinner served: Wed-Mon 12-2 6-9.30 Av main course £7.45 **RESTAURANT:** Lunch served: Wed-Mon Dinner served: Wed-Mon 12-2 6-9.30
BREWERY/COMPANY: Free House **PRINCIPAL BEERS:** Greene King IPA, Adnams, Nethergate, Interbrew Bass. **FACILITIES:** Children welcome Garden: Enclosed with seating, food served outside Dogs allowed (water) **NOTES:** Parking 40

⊛ **For a list of pubs with**
AA Rosette Awards for food see pages 12 & 13.

COTTON Map 07 TM06

Pick of the Pubs

The Trowel & Hammer Inn 🍴
Mill Rd IP14 4QL ☎ 01449 781234 📠 01449 781765
Dir: From A14 follow signs to Haughley, then Bacton, then turn left for Cotton.
A pub of great renown dating back some 550 years, when merchants and cotton traders heading from the coast to the hills would make this their first port of call. The modern version remains the focal point of village life, especially if newcomers fancy participating in its eclectic entertainments instigated by all-comers from 'rowdy farmers to retired colonels'. Daily changing menus may include baked goats' cheese with red onion marmalade or a plate of freshly caught squid, plaice goujons and whitebait with tartare sauce, followed by rack of lamb, spinach and Ricotta pasta or Norfolk duck breast with wild cherry and orange sauce. Beer is carefully chosen with at least four real ales, two straight from the barrel, and a good wine list with a number of half bottles. Don't stand on ceremony here: just enjoy.
OPEN: 12-3 6-11 (Sat/Sun all day) **BAR MEALS:** Lunch served: all week Dinner served: all week 12-2 6-9.30 Av main course £9 **RESTAURANT:** Lunch served: all week 12-2 Dinner served: Mon-Sat 6-9.30 Av 3 course à la carte £16
BREWERY/COMPANY: Free House
PRINCIPAL BEERS: Adnams Bitter, Greene King IPA & Abbot Ale, Nethergate. **FACILITIES:** Garden: BBQ, beer garden, food served outdoors Dogs allowed (water, biscuits) **NOTES:** Parking 50

DUNWICH Map 07 TM47

Pick of the Pubs

The Ship Inn 🍴
St James St IP17 3DT ☎ 01728 648219 📠 01728 648675
Dir: N on A12 from Ipswich thru Yoxford, R signed Dunwich
At one time a medieval port of some size and importance, the original Dunwich was virtually destroyed by a terrible storm in 1326. Further storms and erosion followed and now the place is little more than a small seaside village beside a shingle beach. Once the haunt of smugglers and seafarers, the Ship is now a popular dining destination attracting many locals and visitors. In new hands but still using fresh local produce, especially fish, the inn offers a varied menu and a good choice of real ales. Choose perhaps from the simple lunchtime menu, which includes the likes of cod and chips, steak and ale casserole and spinach flan, or sample peppered sirloin steak or brill, sole or crab in the restaurant.
OPEN: 11-11 **BAR MEALS:** Lunch served: all week Dinner served: all week 12-5 7-9.15 Av main course £7.95
RESTAURANT: Lunch served: all week Dinner served: all week 12-2 7-9.15 Av 3 course à la carte £16
BREWERY/COMPANY: Free House
PRINCIPAL BEERS: Adnams. **FACILITIES:** Children welcome Garden: Food served outside. Terraced area Dogs allowed **NOTES:** Parking 10 **ROOMS:** 3 bedrooms 3 en suite from s£50 d£60

EARL SOHAM
Map 07 TM26

Victoria
The Street IP13 7RL ☎ 01728 685758
Dir: From the A14 at Stowmarket, Earl Soham is on the A1120
Friendly, down-to-earth village pub with its own brewery
attached to the rear of the building. Traditional pub fare on
offer such as corned beef hash, home-made meat and
vegetarian lasagnes, sausages in red wine, liver and bacon,
and pork and pineapple curry. Home-made desserts include
sponge pudding and treacle and walnut tart.
OPEN: 11.30-3 6-11 (Sun 12-3, 7-10.30) **BAR MEALS:** Lunch
served: all week Dinner served: all week 11.30-2 6-10 Av main course
£5.75 **BREWERY/COMPANY:** Free House
PRINCIPAL BEERS: Earl Soham-Victoria Bitter, Albert Ale, & Gannet
Mild (all brewed on site). Earl Soham Porter, Edward Ale.
FACILITIES: Children welcome Garden: Food serevd outside Dogs
allowed (garden only) **NOTES:** Parking 25 No credit cards

EASTBRIDGE
Map 07 TM46

The Eels Foot Inn
IP16 4SN ☎ 01728 830154
e-mail: theeelsfootinn@aol.com
*Dir: From A12 at Yoxford take B1122 (signed Leiston/Sizewell).Turn L at
Theberton*
An ale house since at least 1533, part of today's pub was a
cobbler's cottage: he used a metal 'eel' to help shape the
ankle-piece on a lady's boot. Right on the river, it has in its
time been a smugglers' pub and a regular stop for
journeymen and drovers. Straightforward menus offer egg
and chips, liver and bacon, salmon, cod and smoked eels.
Regular folk music nights since the 1800s, handy for visitors to
Minsmere Bird Reserve.
OPEN: 12-3 7-11 **BAR MEALS:** Lunch served: all week 12-2
Dinner served: Tues-Sun 7-8.30 Av main course £5
RESTAURANT: Lunch served: all week 12-2 Dinner served: Tues-Sun
7-8.30 **BREWERY/COMPANY:** Adnams
PRINCIPAL BEERS: Adnams Bitter & Broadside, Carlsberg-Tetley
Tetley Bitter. **FACILITIES:** Children welcome Garden: Food served
outside Dogs allowed (water bowls) **NOTES:** Parking 200
ROOMS: 1 bedrooms 1 en suite from s£22 d£22 No credit cards

ERWARTON
Map 07 TM23

The Queens Head
The Street IP9 1LN ☎ 01473 787550
Dir: From Ipswich take B1456 to Shotley
Handsome 16th-century building in traditional Suffolk style,
enjoying fine views of coast and countryside. Low oak-
beamed ceilings, exposed timbers and first class meals make
this a worthwhile destination. Look out for the fascinating
display of navigational maps in the loos. The conservatory
restaurant overlooks the River Stowe. Dishes include prime
English sirloin steak, beef and ale casserole, lamb cutlet
platter, Japanese style prawns, stuffed lemon sole with
crabmeat, and exotic fruit and vegetable curry. Good pudding
menu.
OPEN: 11-3 6.30-11 (Sun 12-3 7-10.30) Closed: 25 Dec
BAR MEALS: Lunch served: all week Dinner served: all week
12-2.45 7-9.30 **RESTAURANT:** Lunch served: all week Dinner
served: all week 12-2.45 7-9.30 **BREWERY/COMPANY:** Free House
PRINCIPAL BEERS: Adnams Bitter & Broadside, Greene King IPA.
FACILITIES: Children welcome Garden: Patio/terrace, food served
outdoors Dogs allowed (guide dogs only) **NOTES:** Parking 30

FRAMLINGHAM
Map 07 TM26

The Station Hotel
Station Rd IP13 9EE ☎ 01728 723455
e-mail: neilpascoe@aol.co.uk
Dir: Bypass Ipswich heading toward Lowestoft on the A12
Since trains stopped coming to Framlingham in 1962 the
buildings of the former station hotel have been put to good
use. One is a vintage motorcycle repair shop, while another is
an antique bed showroom. The hotel has established itself as
a popular destination, with a good reputation for seafood and
locally brewed beers. Check out the menu for roll-mop
herrings, seafood platter, Loch Fyne oysters, smoked trout
salad, greenlip mussels and corn beef hash with a cheese
topping.
OPEN: 12-2.30 5-11 **BAR MEALS:** Lunch served: all week Dinner
served: all week 12-2 7-9.30 Av main course £6
RESTAURANT: Lunch served: all week Dinner served: all week 12-2
7-9.30 Av 3 course à la carte £11 **BREWERY/COMPANY:** Free
House **PRINCIPAL BEERS:** Earl Soham Victoria, Albert & Mild.
FACILITIES: Children welcome Garden: Pond, patio, food served
outdoors Dogs allowed (water, biscuits) **NOTES:** Parking 20

FRAMSDEN
Map 07 TM15

The Dobermann Inn
The Street IP14 6HG ☎ 01473 890461
Dir: S off A1120(Stowmarket/Yoxford)
Previously The Greyhound, the pub was renamed by its
current proprietor, a prominent breeder and judge of
Dobermanns. The thatched roofing, gnarled beams, open fire
and assorted furniture reflect its 16th-century origins. Food
ranges from sandwiches and salads to daily specials such as
supreme of guinea fowl with port and cranberry sauce,
rainbow trout poached in white wine and local venison or
game pie. Vegetarians may feast on mushroom Stroganoff and
spicy nut loaf. Indulge in their legendary banana split!
OPEN: 12-3 7-11 **BAR MEALS:** Lunch served: all week Dinner
served: all week 12-2 7-10 **RESTAURANT:** Lunch served: all week
Dinner served: all week 12-2 7-10 **BREWERY/COMPANY:** Free
House **PRINCIPAL BEERS:** Adnams Bitter & Broadside, Greene King
Abbot Ale, Mauldons Moletrap Bitter. **FACILITIES:** Garden: Food
served outside **NOTES:** Parking 27 **ROOMS:** 1 bedrooms 1 en
suite from d£50 No credit cards

GREAT GLEMHAM
Map 07 TM36

The Crown Inn
IP17 2DA ☎ 01728 663693
*Dir: A12 Ipswich to Lowestoft, in Stratford-St-Andrew L at Shell garage.
Crown 1.5m*
Cosy, extensively renovated 17th-century village pub
overlooking the Great Glemham Estate and within easy reach
of the Suffolk Heritage Coast. Fish dishes include salmon
marinated in lime and coriander, and fresh cod or haddock
cooked in beer batter. Other options are home-made steak
and kidney pie, gammon and lasagne.
OPEN: 11.30-2.30 6.30-11 (closed Mon) **BAR MEALS:** Lunch
served: Tue-Sun Dinner served: Tue-Sun 11.30-2.30 6.30-10 Av main
course £6.95 **BREWERY/COMPANY:** Free House
PRINCIPAL BEERS: Greene King Old Speckled Hen & IPA.
FACILITIES: Children welcome Garden: Food served outdoors
Dogs allowed **NOTES:** Parking 20

HADLEIGH

Map 07 TM04

The Marquis of Cornwallis ♀

Upper St, Layham IP7 5JZ ☎ 01473 822051 📠 01473 822051
e-mail: marquislayham@aol.com

Dir: *From Colchester take A12 then B1070 towards Hadleigh. Layham signed on L, last village before Hadleigh*

This late 16th-century inn is named after a British military commander who was defeated in the American War of Independence, and the candle-lit building is situated in two acres of gardens overlooking the Brett Valley. Dishes are cooked to order from local Suffolk produce, and traditional bar snacks and home-made pies are supplemented by a menu that includes whole baked trout, leek and cheese quiche, Scotch rump steak, or lamb and coconut curry.
OPEN: 12-3 (Sun 7-10.30) 6-11 (Whit-Aug Sat 12-11,Sun 12-10.30) Closed: 25 Dec **BAR MEALS:** Lunch served: all week Dinner served: all week 12-2.30 7-9.30 Av main course £6.50
RESTAURANT: Lunch served: all week Dinner served: all week 12-2.30 7-9.30 Av 3 course à la carte £13.50
BREWERY/COMPANY: Free House **PRINCIPAL BEERS:** Adnams Broadside, Greene King IPA & Abbot Ale. **FACILITIES:** Children welcome Garden: food served outdoors Dogs allowed **NOTES:** Parking 30

HALESWORTH

Map 07 TM37

Pick of the Pubs

The Queen's Head 🏠 ♀

The Street, Bramfield IP19 9HT ☎ 01986 784214 📠 01986 784797
e-mail: qhbfield@aol.com

Dir: *2m from A12 on the A144 towards Halesworth*

One of the first pubs outside London to be recognised for its certified organic menu. Fish from the boats at Dunwich Beach and fresh foods from local organic farms and growers are meticulously sought out. A huge open fire dominates the main bar area with its vaulted ceiling, exposed beams and seating at scrubbed pine tables: old farm tools adorn the walls. Typical of daily-changing meals are River Farm Smokery salmon, Wakelyn's Farm chard and mushroom lasagne, Elm House Farm rare breed pork and leek sausages with apple chutney and Denham Estate venison served with red-currant, port and orange sauce...and so the list goes on: Larchfield Cottage apple crumble with custard and tarte au citron with Village Farm Jersey cream. Tucked away behind the pub is a beautiful garden with an unusual willow dome created by local craftsmen, plenty of bench seating for al fresco enjoyment and lots of space for the children to play.

OPEN: 11.45-2.30 (Sun 12-3, 7-10.30) 6.30-11 Closed: 26 Dec
BAR MEALS: Lunch served: all week Dinner served: all week 12-2 6.30-10 Av main course £7.95
BREWERY/COMPANY: Adnams
PRINCIPAL BEERS: Adnams Bitter & Broadside.
FACILITIES: Children welcome Garden: Enclosed garden with seating Dogs allowed **NOTES:** Parking 15
ROOMS: 2 bedrooms 2 en suite

HARTEST

Map 07 TL85

The Crown

The Green IP29 4DH ☎ 01284 830250

Dir: *On B1066 S of Bury St Edmunds*

Once known as Hartest Hall, this heavily beamed 15th-century building is set on the village green next to the church. One menu is offered throughout, with the emphasis on an impressive range of fresh fish from Lowestoft. Special set meals during the week provide particularly good value.
OPEN: 11-2.30 6-11 **BAR MEALS:** Lunch served: all week Dinner served: all week 12-2 6.30-9.30 Av main course £9
RESTAURANT: Lunch served: all week Dinner served: all week 12-2 6.30-9.30 Av 3 course à la carte £13.50
BREWERY/COMPANY: Greene King **PRINCIPAL BEERS:** Greene King Abbot Ale, Old Speckled Hen & IPA. **FACILITIES:** Children welcome Garden: Dogs allowed **NOTES:** Parking 40

HOLBROOK

Map 07 TM13

The Compasses 🏠

Ipswich Rd IP9 2QR ☎ 01473 328332 📠 01473 327403
e-mail: holbrookcompasses@hotmail.com

Dir: *From A137 S of Ipswich, take B1456/B1080*

Holbrook is bordered by both the rivers Orwell and the Stour and the traditional country pub, dating back to the 17th century, is on the Shotley peninsula. For several decades the inn was a staging post on the road between London and Ipswich and the area is still popular with visitors. The appetising, varied menu ranges from steak and mushroom pie to chicken Alex. Fish dishes include seafood lasagne, salmon wrapped in bacon and battered or grilled cod and haddock.
OPEN: 11-2.30 6-11 Closed: 25-26 Dec **BAR MEALS:** Lunch served: all week Dinner served: all week 11.30-2.15 6-9.30 Av main course £7.50 **RESTAURANT:** Lunch served: all week Dinner served: all week 11.30-2.15 6-9.30 Av 3 course à la carte £14.50
BREWERY/COMPANY: Pubmaster
PRINCIPAL BEERS: Carlsberg-Tetley Tetley Bitter, Greene King IPA, Adnams Bitter, Scottish Courage John Smith's. **FACILITIES:** Children welcome Garden: Food served outside **NOTES:** Parking 30

HONEY TYE

Map 07 TL93

The Lion 🏠 ♀

CO6 4NX ☎ 01206 263434 📠 01206 263434

Dir: *On A134 between Colchester & Sudbury*

Low-beamed ceilings and an open log fire are charming features of this traditional country dining pub on the Essex/Suffolk border. An extensive menu offers lots of interesting choices, including chargrilled swordfish steak, steak and real ale pie, baked supreme of chicken, and roast rack of lamb. Sunday lunch may comprise of creamy tarragon mushrooms, roast loin of pork, and poached supreme of salmon with lemon cream sauce.
OPEN: 11-3 5.45-11 (Sun 12-10.30) **BAR MEALS:** Lunch served:

continued

continued

England

all week Dinner served: all week 12-2 6-9.30 Av main course £7.95
RESTAURANT: Lunch served: all week Dinner served: all week 12-2
6-9.30 **BREWERY/COMPANY:** Free House
PRINCIPAL BEERS: Greene King IPA, Adnams Bitter.
FACILITIES: Children welcome Garden: Patio, Food served outside
Dogs allowed **NOTES:** Parking 40

HORRINGER   Map 07 TL86

Pick of the Pubs

Beehive ♀
The Street IP29 5SN ☎ 01284 735260
e-mail: thebeehive@virginnet.co
*Dir: From A14, 1st turning for Bury St Edmunds, sign for Westley &
Ickworth Park*
Converted from a Victorian flint and stone cottage close to
the National Trust's Ickworth House, one may readily
expect the place to buzz with activity. And so it does in its
succession of cosy dining areas with antique pine tables
and chairs, extending in season to the patio and beer
garden. Over some fifteen years the proprietors have kept
abreast of the times with food that moves with the
seasons and daily changing menus. For starters look for
shellfish chowder with home-made bread or tomato and
roast pepper soup before tucking into a salmon escalope
with herb mustard gratin or peppered rib-eye steak on a
red wine reduction. And there's more: for a tasty snack,
try their home-made pork and apricot sausages and
round off with ginger crème brûlée or orange custard tart.
OPEN: 11.30-2.30 7-11 Closed: Dec 25-26
BAR MEALS: Lunch served: all week 12-2 Dinner served:
Mon-Sat 7-9.45 Av main course £9.95
BREWERY/COMPANY: Greene King
PRINCIPAL BEERS: Greene King IPA & Abbot Ale + guest
beers. **FACILITIES:** Children welcome Garden: Patio, food
served outside **NOTES:** Parking 30

HOXNE   Map 09 TM17

The Swan
Low St IP21 5AS ☎ 01379 668275
Set in a 15th-century Grade II listed building formerly known as
Bishop's Lodge, with large gardens down to the River Dove. Ask
at the bar for the circular pub walk. Lunchtime snacks are filled
jacket potatoes, sandwiches and freshly baked rolls. Main menu
items cooked to order may include baked field mushrooms
followed by Cyril's locally made sausages, baked duck breast
with wild berry sauce, or vegetable suet pudding in cheesy
sauce. Plenty of side orders and things for the youngsters.
OPEN: 11-3 6-11 (Sun 12-10.30) **BAR MEALS:** Lunch served: all
week Dinner served: all week 12-2.30 7-9 Av main course £6.95
RESTAURANT: Lunch served: all week Dinner served: all week
12-2.30 7-9 **BREWERY/COMPANY:** Enterprise Inns
PRINCIPAL BEERS: Adnams Broadside & regular changing ales
FACILITIES: Garden: Large riverside garden, food served outside
Dogs allowed **NOTES:** Parking 20

ICKLINGHAM   Map 07 TL77

Pick of the Pubs

The Red Lion 🐦 ♀
The Street IP28 6PS ☎ 01638 717802 ▤ 01638 515702
e-mail: lizard2020@supernet.com
See Pick of the Pubs on page 440

IXWORTH   Map 07 TL97

Pykkerell Inn 🐦 ♀
38 High St IP31 2HH ☎ 01359 230398 ▤ 01359 230398
Dir: A14 trunk rd/jct Bury St Edmunds central to A143, towards Diss
Attractive 16th-century coaching inn with original beams,
inglenook fireplace, wood-panelled library room, and 14th-
century barn enclosing a patio with barbecue. Menu boards
highlight fresh fish, such as sea bass on basil mash with herb
dressing, alongside steak and ale pie, venison with red wine
and mushroom sauce, and lamb chops.
OPEN: 12-3 6-11 **BAR MEALS:** Lunch served: all week Dinner
served: all week 12-2.30 7-10 Av main course £9.95
RESTAURANT: Lunch served: all week Dinner served: all week
12-2.30 6-10 Av 3 course à la carte £20 Av 3 course fixed price £15
BREWERY/COMPANY: Greene King **PRINCIPAL BEERS:** Greene
King IPA & Abbot Ale. **FACILITIES:** Children welcome Garden:
Food served outside. Courtyard Dogs allowed **NOTES:** Parking 30
ROOMS: 5 bedrooms 5 en suite from s£55 d£75

KERSEY   Map 07 TM04

The Bell Inn 🐦
The Street IP7 6DY ☎ 01473 823229
*Dir: Follow A1171 from Bury St Edmunds thru Lavenham, follow signs for
Kersey*
Surrounded by thatched cottages, the 14th-century Bell stands
next to a ford that crosses the main street of this picturesque
Suffolk village. Largely beamed within, the large winter log fire
is a focal point of village life when tales of the resident ghost
abound. Home-made fare includes warming soups in winter
and pies such as steak and Guinness, fisherman's and chicken
and mushroom. Well-kept cask ales and a warm family-
friendly atmosphere.
OPEN: 12-3 7-11 **BAR MEALS:** Lunch served: all week Dinner
served: all week 12-2 7-9 Av main course £8 **RESTAURANT:** Lunch
served: all week Dinner served: all week 12-2 7-9
BREWERY/COMPANY: Enterprise Inns
PRINCIPAL BEERS: Adnams Bitter & Broadside.
FACILITIES: Children welcome Garden: Double patio, food served
outside **NOTES:** Parking 15

KETTLEBURGH   Map 07 TM26

The Chequers Inn
IP13 7JT ☎ 01728 723760 & 724369
Dir: From Ipswich A12 onto B1116, L onto B1078 then R through Easton
The Chequers is set in beautiful countryside on the banks of
the River Deben. The landlord is a fellow of the British
Institute of Innkeepers and serves a wide range of cask ales
endorsed by the Cask Marque. In addition to snack and
restaurant meals, there is a £3 menu in the bar including local
sausages and ham with home-produced free-range eggs.
OPEN: 12-2.30 6-11 **BAR MEALS:** Lunch served: all week Dinner
served: all week 12-2 7-9.30 Av main course £4
RESTAURANT: Lunch served: all week Dinner served: all week 12-2
7-9.30 Av 3 course à la carte £15 **BREWERY/COMPANY:** Free
House **PRINCIPAL BEERS:** Greene King IPA, Adnams Southwold,
plus two guest ales. **FACILITIES:** Children welcome Garden: Beer
garden, outdoor eating, patio Dogs allowed (as long as under
control) **NOTES:** Parking 40

★ **Indicates AA inspected hotel accommodation**

OPEN: 12–3 6–11
BAR MEALS: L served all week.
D served all week. 12–2.30 6–10
Av main course £9.95
RESTAURANT: L served all week.
D served all week. 12–2.30 6–10
Av cost 3 course £20
BREWERY/COMPANY: GREENE KING
PRINCIPLE BEERS: Greene King Abbot Ale & IPA
FACILITIES: Children welcome. Garden: Patio, food served outdoors
NOTES: Parking 50

The Red Lion

The Street IP28 6PS
☎ 01638 717802 📠 01638 515702
e-mail: lizard2020@supernet.com
Dir: On A1101 between Mildenhall & Bury St Edmunds

Set back from the A1101, with a neat front lawn and a raised rear terrace overlooking the River Lark and open fields, this sympathetically restored 16th-century thatched inn makes a handy refreshment stop following a visit to West Stow Country Park and the Anglo Saxon Village.

Full of exposed beams and warming log fires, rugs on wooden floors, antique furniture and mellow evening candlelight, the Red Lion is a popular dining destination, offering a reliable range of interesting home-cooked food using quality local produce. Thanks to daily deliveries from Lowestoft, it's not unusual for the menu to include up to 20 fish and seafood dishes: perhaps red mullet with garlic butter, fresh oysters grilled with cream, butter, parsley and parmesan or fresh skate wing with caramelised onion and bacon. In season, look out for the fresh game menu, which is particularly extensive at weekends. Typical dishes might include red deer fillet steak with a brandy and tarragon sauce, pheasant breasts with a port and blackcurrant sauce or wild boar fillet steak with a red onion and garlic butter. Simple and appetising bar food ranges from home made soups and pates to old favourites such as Excalibur sausages with mash and onion gravy, prime pork chops with apple and cider sauce or gammon steak with wholegrain mustard sauce. The à la carte' combines the classic (Scottish beef steak; rack of English lamb with a Burgundy and mushroom jus; lamb's liver and kidneys in a Dijon mustard and bacon sauce) with more modern creations such as Norfolk chicken breast with a mild curry and mango sauce and a rice timbale. Follow with comforting home made puddings. At the bar, choose from well-kept Green King Ales, a good range of wines, including country fruit wines, and fruit presses.

LAVENHAM — Map 07 TL94

Pick of the Pubs

Angel Hotel ★ ★ ◉ ☙
Market Place CO10 9QZ ☎ 01787 247388 📠 01787 248344
e-mail: angellav@aol.com
Dir: From A14 take Bury East/Sudbury turn off A143, after 4m take
A1141 to Lavenham, Angel is off the High Street

Originally licensed in 1420, this fine old inn stands amid
some 300 listed buildings in England's best preserved
medieval wool town. Despite its antiquity, the Angel
assumes a thoroughly modern attitude to food in both the
bar and dining room, and consistently attracts a loyal
clientele. Local produce and real ales, along with well-
chosen house wines, appeal to all tastes, balancing
modern ideas, traditional dishes and well-sourced fresh
foodstuffs to good effect. Regularly occurring dishes from
the daily menu include steak and ale pie, roast loin of
lamb, grilled whole plaice with parsley butter, and venison
fillet steak with juniper and wild mushrooms. Fresh fish
and vegetarian options are always available - roast red
pepper with vegetable and herb stuffing for example -
and game in season. In summer lunch can be taken in the
garden. Overnight accommodation is top drawer, for
those who appreciate their creature comforts unsullied by
thoughts of cost.
OPEN: 11–11 (Sun 12–10.30) Closed: 25–26 Dec
BAR MEALS: Lunch served: all week Dinner served: all week
12–2.15 6.45–9.15 Av main course £9 **RESTAURANT:** Lunch
served: all week Dinner served: all week 12–2.15 6.45–9.15 Av 3
course à la carte £17 **BREWERY/COMPANY:** Free House
PRINCIPAL BEERS: Adnams Bitter, Nethergate, Greene King
IPA & Old Speckled Hen. **FACILITIES:** Children welcome
Children's licence Garden: Patio, food served outside,
NOTES: Parking 105 **ROOMS:** 8 bedrooms 8 en suite from
s£45 d£70

LAXFIELD — Map 07 TM27

Pick of the Pubs

The Kings Head
Gorams Mill Ln IP13 8DW ☎ 01986 798395
Virtually unchanged since Victorian times, this charming
inn is known locally as The Low House. Beer is served
from the tap room. There is no bar and customers sit on
original high-backed settles and enjoy traditional Suffolk
music on Tuesday lunchtimes. Home-cooked fare includes
game duck and steak and kidney pie.
OPEN: 11–3 6–11 (11–11 Tues) (Sun 12–3, 7–10.30)

BAR MEALS: Lunch served: all week Dinner served: all week
12–3 7–9 Av main course £7.50
BREWERY/COMPANY: Adnams
PRINCIPAL BEERS: Adnams Best & Broadside, Fullers London
Pride. **FACILITIES:** Garden: Large lawned area Dogs allowed
NOTES: Parking 30 No credit cards

LEISTON — Map 07 TM46

Parrot and Punchbowl 🍴

Aldringham Ln, Aldringham IP16 4PY
☎ 01728 830221 📠 01728 833297
e-mail: graham@parrotpunch.freeserve.co.uk
Just a mile from the Suffolk Heritage Coast - ideal for walking
- this 16th-century pub was once the centre of local smuggling
activities. Inside you can expect plenty of beams, brasses and
good ales on tap, including Adnams, Greene King IPA and
Ruddles County. The wide-ranging bar menu features good
seafood options - maybe seafood platter, dressed crab, whole
plaice, Dover sole and monkfish kebab. Outside there's a
walled garden, boules pitch and children's playground.
OPEN: 11–3 5.30–11 **BAR MEALS:** 12–2 6.30–9.30
RESTAURANT: 12–2 6.30–9.30 **BREWERY/COMPANY:** Whitbread
PRINCIPAL BEERS: Adnams Bitter, Greene King, Woodfordes.
FACILITIES: Garden: Dogs allowed **NOTES:** Parking 60
ROOMS: 3 bedrooms 2 en suite

LEVINGTON — Map 07 TM23

The Ship Inn

Church Ln IP10 0LQ ☎ 01473 659573
Dir: off the A14 towards Felixstowe
Overlooking the River Orwell and neighbouring countryside,
this lovely 14th-century thatched pub is very popular with
walkers, birdwatchers and yachting folk, who seek out the
home-made bar food. Expect fisherman's pie, steak and
kidney pudding, kippers, salmon fishcakes, and pheasant in
white grape sauce - among other interesting dishes.
OPEN: 11.30–3 6.30–11 **BAR MEALS:** Lunch served: all week 12–2
Dinner served: Wed-Sat 7–9 Av main course £6.50
RESTAURANT: Lunch served: all week 12–2 Dinner served: Wed-Sat
7–9 Av 3 course à la carte £11 **BREWERY/COMPANY:** Pubmaster
PRINCIPAL BEERS: Ship Inn Bitter, Greene King IPA, Adnams Best,
Broadside. **FACILITIES:** Children welcome Garden: Beer garden,
patio, outdoor eating **NOTES:** Parking 70

LIDGATE — Map 07 TL75

Pick of the Pubs

Star Inn 🍴
The Street CB8 9PP ☎ 01638 500275
e-mail: tereaxon@aol.com
Dir: From Newmarket, clocktower in High st, follow signs toward
Clare on B1063. Lidgate 7m from Newmarket
A warm, cosy country inn, a unique blend of typical
English pub and Spanish eating house. It has been owned
for many years by a Catalan landlady who has made her
mark on the menu, where Spanish dishes share space
with some imaginative international and British choices.
The pretty pink-painted Elizabethan building is made up
of two cottages with gardens front and rear, and indoors,
two traditionally-furnished bars with heavy oak and pine
furniture lead into a fairly simple dining room. Popular
with trainers on Newmarket race days, and with dealers

continued

continued

England

LIDGATE continued

and agents from all over the world during bloodstock sales. Look out for scampi provençale, scallops Santiago, and paella Valenciana, along with home-grown choices like lamb steaks in blackcurrant, monkfish marinière, wild boar in cranberry sauce, sirloin steak in Stilton sauce and lambs' kidneys in sherry.

Star Inn

OPEN: 11-3 5-11 Closed: 25-26 Dec, 1 Jan
BAR MEALS: Lunch served: all week 12-2 Dinner served: Mon-Sat 7-10 Av main course £12.50 **RESTAURANT:** Lunch served: all week 12-2 Dinner served: Mon-Sat 7-10 Av 3 course à la carte £21 **BREWERY/COMPANY:** Greene King
PRINCIPAL BEERS: Greene King IPA, Abbot Ale, Old Speckled Hen. **FACILITIES:** Children welcome Garden: Food served outside **NOTES:** Parking 12

LONG MELFORD   Map 07 TL84

The Crown Hotel
Hall St CO10 9JL ☎ 01787 377666 📠 01787 379005
e-mail: melfordcrown@btinternet.com
Dir: *from Sudbury take A134 to Bury St Edmunds, at 1st rndbt take 1st L to Long Melford*

At the heart of Constable country, Long Melford's pub was built in 1610 yet retains a Tudor cellar and oak beams. In 1885, the Crown was the last place to hear the Riot Act read in West Suffolk. A hearty bar menu includes salads, ploughmans', jacket potatoes, sandwiches, mixed grill, poached salmon, aubergine and mushroom bake, pizzas, and fisherman's pie. Bedrooms.
OPEN: 11-11 (Sun 12-10.30) **BAR MEALS:** Lunch served: all week Dinner served: all week 12-2.30 7-9.30 Av main course £6
RESTAURANT: Lunch served: all week Dinner served: all week 12-2.30 7-9.30 Av 3 course à la carte £20
BREWERY/COMPANY: Free House **PRINCIPAL BEERS:** Greene

King Old Speckled Hen, IPA. **FACILITIES:** Children welcome Children's licence Garden: Lawn, seating, pond & patio
NOTES: Parking 6 **ROOMS:** 13 bedrooms 13 en suite from s£37.50 d£65

MARKET WESTON   Map 07 TL97

The Mill Inn ♀
Bury Rd IP22 2PD ☎ 01359 221018
e-mail: andrew.leasy@talk21.com
Dir: *A14 Bury St Edmunds, follow A143 to Great Barton & Stanton, L on B1111 thru Barningham, next village M Weston*
Old Chimneys ales from the nearby micro-brewery boost the choice of beers at this Victorian manor house, situated at the centre of the local Windmill Trail. Local produce features in a varied menu that may include pork divan, steak and stout pie, aubergine, tomato and Mozzarella bake, grilled salmon fillet with herb and caper butter, escalope of turkey Columbian, or guinea fowl calvados.
OPEN: 12-3 (Nov-Feb from 12) 7-11 (closed Mon)
BAR MEALS: Lunch served: Tue-Sun Dinner served: Tue-Sun 7-9.30 Av main course £2.95 **RESTAURANT:** Lunch served: Tue-Sun Dinner served: Tue-Sun 12-2 7 Av 3 course à la carte £12.50
BREWERY/COMPANY: Free House **PRINCIPAL BEERS:** Greene King, Adnams Best, Old Chimneys Great Raft & Military Mild.
FACILITIES: Children welcome Garden: beer garden, outdoor eating **NOTES:** Parking 30

MELTON   Map 07 TM25

Wilford Bridge
Wilford Bridge Rd IP12 2PA ☎ 01394 386141
Dir: *Head to the coast from the A12, follow signs to Bawdsey & Orford, cross railway lines, next pub on L*

Chargrills tend to dominate the menu at this much-modernised pub just a short distance from the famous Saxon burial ship at Sutton Hoo. You'll not get burned by the prices of chicken piri-piri marinated in lemon juice or the three lamb cutlets with rosemary jus, even though any fresh vegetables or salads carry a supplementary charge. Round off a filling meal with hot cherries in Madeira or toffee apple and peanut pie. Vegetarian options include cheese and vegetable bake and spinach and Ricotta cannelloni.
OPEN: 11-3 6.30-11 Closed: 25-26 Dec **BAR MEALS:** Lunch served: all week Dinner served: all week 11.30-2 6.30-9.30 Av main course £7 **RESTAURANT:** Lunch served: all week Dinner served: all week 11.30-2 6.30-9.30 Av 3 course à la carte £15
BREWERY/COMPANY: Free House **PRINCIPAL BEERS:** Adnams Best, Broadside, Scottish Courage John Smith's plus guest Ales.
FACILITIES: Children welcome Garden: Patio, food served outdoors
NOTES: Parking 40

continued

MONKS ELEIGH   Map 07 TL94

Pick of the Pubs

The Swan Inn 🛏 ♀
The Street IP7 7AU ☎ 01449 741391
Dir: On the B1115 between Sudbury & Hadleigh
Just across the street from the village green, this attractive,
thatched free house blends easily with Monk Eleigh's
colour-washed cottages, pretty gardens and imposing
church. The village was founded on the prosperous local
wool trade, and the pub dates partly from the 14th
century. Wattle and daub panels were discovered in one
room during renovations, and the dining room boasts a
magnificent beamed ceiling and open fire. The kitchen
uses seasonal local produce to create menus that change
almost daily. Game features heavily during the winter
months, while lobsters, fish and asparagus take pride of
place during summer. An example menu includes sirloin
steak with a mustard and brandy sauce, roast red pepper
with goats' cheese and pesto, whole roast sea bass with
ginger and coriander butter, smoked chicken 'bang bang'
salad, and roast partridge on crispy croûton and a red
wine sauce. All complemented by a good pudding
selection.
OPEN: 12-3 7-11 **BAR MEALS:** Lunch served: Wed-Sun
Dinner served: Wed-Sun 12-2 7-9.30 Av main course £10.50
RESTAURANT: Lunch served: Wed-Sun Dinner served:
Wed-Sun 12-2 7-9.30 Av 3 course à la carte £18.75
BREWERY/COMPANY: Free House
PRINCIPAL BEERS: Greene King IPA, Adnams Bitter &
Broadside. **FACILITIES:** Children welcome Garden:
NOTES: Parking 10

ORFORD   Map 07 TM45

Jolly Sailor Inn 🛏
Quay St IP12 2NU ☎ 01394 450243 📠 0870 128 7874
e-mail: jollyorf@aol.com
Dir: On B1084 E of Woodbridge
Until the 16th century Orford was a bustling coastal port, and
this ancient, timber-framed smugglers' inn stood on the
quayside. But, as Orford Ness grew longer, the harbour silted
up and fell out of use. Nevertheless, the pub still serves
visiting yachtsman, and local fishermen supply the fresh fish
and crabs that feature prominently on the menu. Other dishes
might include home-cooked ham with egg and chips, daily
roasts or pasta with ratatouille.
OPEN: 11.30-2.30 7-11 **BAR MEALS:** Lunch served: all week
Dinner served: all week 12-2 7.15-8.45 Av main course £5.50
BREWERY/COMPANY: Adnams **PRINCIPAL BEERS:** Adnams
Bitter & Broadside. **FACILITIES:** Garden: Food served outside Dogs
allowed on lead only **ROOMS:** 3 bedrooms d£40 No credit cards

King's Head
Front St IP12 2LW ☎ 01394 450271
e-mail: ian-thornton@talk21.com
Dir: From Woodbridge follow signsfor Orford Castle along the B1084
through Butly and Chillesford onto Orford
Modernised Tudor inn overlooking churchyard. Attractive
dining room; Adnams ales and good wines. En suite
bedrooms.

POLSTEAD   Map 07 TL93

Pick of the Pubs

The Cock Inn 🛏 ♀
The Green CO6 5AL ☎ 01206 263150 📠 01206 263150
e-mail: enquiries@the -cock-inn-polstead.fsbusiness.co.uk
Dir: Colchester/A134 towards Sudbury then R, follow signs to Polstead

17th-century pub with a Victorian restaurant extension,
formerly a farmhouse. Occupying a peaceful village green
setting at the heart of Constable country, the Cock Inn
attracts many cyclists and ramblers. Not suprisingly, some
of Suffolk's prettiest landscapes are right on the doorstep.
Inside are quaint oak beams, quarry-tiled floors and plain
painted walls. The eclectic menu changes constantly and
all food is home-made and freshly prepared, using local
ingredients. Sample chargrilled lamb's liver or turkey
escalope in pesto sauce at lunchtime, while in the evening
you may like to try venison steak with horseradish mash
and roasted winter vegetables. Good choice of fish dishes,
including bream, sea bass, lemon sole, halibut, salmon,
trout and monkfish. Families are especially welcome, with
a decent garden for children to play in. On a fine
summer's day, this is the inn's main attraction.
OPEN: 11-3 6-11 **BAR MEALS:** Lunch served: Tues-Sun
11.30-2.30 Dinner served: Tues-Sat 6.30-9.30 Av main course £5
RESTAURANT: Lunch served: Tue-Sun 11.30-2.30 Dinner
served: Tues-Sat 6.30-9.30 Av 3 course à la carte £20
BREWERY/COMPANY: Free House
PRINCIPAL BEERS: Greene King IPA, Scottish Courage John
Smiths. **FACILITIES:** Children welcome Children's licence
Garden: Food served outside Dogs allowed (water)
NOTES: Parking 20

RAMSHOLT   Map 07 TM34

Pick of the Pubs

Ramsholt Arms 🛏
Dock Rd IP12 3AB ☎ 01394 411229
Dir: End of lane on beach at Ramsholt, signed off B1083 Woodbridge
to Bawdsey
Enjoying a glorious, unrivalled postion on a tidal beach
overlooking the River Deben, this 18th-century, pink-
washed former farmhouse, ferryman's cottage and
smugglers' inn is the perfect summer evening destination
for a pint on the terrace to watch the glorious sunset over
the river. Expect a civilised atmosphere, picture windows,
Adnams ales, and good home-cooked food, in particular
fish and seafood in summer and local game in winter.
Blackboard dishes could include cod and chips, local

continued

England

RAMSHOLT continued

lobster, Cromer crab, whole Dover sole, roast partridge and meat pies. Comfortable bedrooms make the most of the view; rewarding riverside walks.

Ramsholt Arms

OPEN: 11.30-11 **BAR MEALS:** Lunch served: all week Dinner served: all week 12-3 6.30-9 Av main course £7.50 **RESTAURANT:** Lunch served: all week Dinner served: all week 12-3 6.30-9 **BREWERY/COMPANY:** Free House **PRINCIPAL BEERS:** Adnams, Greene King, Woodfords, Nethergates. **FACILITIES:** Children welcome Garden: Food served outside. Large garden, estuary Dogs allowed (water provided) **NOTES:** Parking 60 **ROOMS:** 3 bedrooms from s£35 d£70

RATTLESDEN   Map 07 TL95

Brewers Arms
Lower Rd IP30 0RJ ☎ 01449 736377 & 737057 📠 01449 736377 e-mail: rocksue@lineone.net
Dir: From A14 take A1088 toward Woolpit, Rattlesden 2.8m from Woolpit
Enjoy a decent pint of Abbot Ale and relax in the attractive surroundings of this solid 16th-century village hostelry, situated just a short drive from Bury St Edmunds. The dining area was originally the public bar and the lounge bar has book-lined walls and lots of bric-a-brac. Open fires and an old bread oven add to the charm. The well-designed and imaginative menu changes weekly and may feature barracuda steak, cottage pie, salmon and asparagus tart, steak and kidney pie, gamekeeper's pie, poacher's pot, and lamb and coriander burger. Good range of desserts.
OPEN: 11.30-2.30 6.30-11 (closed Mon) **BAR MEALS:** Lunch served: Tue-Sun Dinner served: Tue-Sun 11.30-2 6-9 Av main course £8 **RESTAURANT:** Lunch served: Tue-Sun Dinner served: Tue-Sun 11.30-2 6-9 **BREWERY/COMPANY:** Greene King **PRINCIPAL BEERS:** Greene King IPA, Abbot Ale & Old Speckled Hen. **FACILITIES:** Children welcome Garden: Beer garden , food served outside **NOTES:** Parking 20

REDE   Map 05 TL85

The Plough
IP29 4BE ☎ 01284 789208
Dir: on the A143 between Bury St Edmonds and Haverhill
Picture-postcard thatched 16th-century pub set beside a pond on the village green. Worth the effort in finding for the freshly prepared food served in rambling low-beamed bars. Blackboard-listed dishes may include monkfish Creole, local rabbit in a tarragon and spring onion sauce, and chicken

breast with an orange and kumquat sauce. Recently refurbished.
OPEN: 11-3 6.30-11 **BAR MEALS:** Lunch served: all week 12-2 Dinner served: Mon-Sat 7-9 Av main course £7 **RESTAURANT:** Lunch served: all week 12-2 Dinner served: Mon-Sat 7-9
BREWERY/COMPANY: Greene King **PRINCIPAL BEERS:** Greene King IPA & Abbot Ale, Ruddles Counrty. **FACILITIES:** Children welcome Garden: Beer garden, outdoor eating **NOTES:** Parking 60

RISBY   Map 07 TL86

The White Horse Inn ♀
Newmarket Rd IP28 6RD ☎ 01284 810686 📠 01284 810666 e-mail: whitehorserisby@aol.com
Dir: A14 from Bury St Edmunds
Former coaching inn with a colourful history - as a communications centre in World War II in case of invasion, and for the ghostly spectre of a murdered hanging judge occasionally reflected in the restaurant mirror. The pub is otherwise known for its real ales - up to 15 each week - its extensive carte and freshly produced bar food.
OPEN: 12-3 6-11 (Fri-Sun all day) **BAR MEALS:** Lunch served: all week Dinner served: all week 12-2.30 6.30-9.30 Av main course £5 **RESTAURANT:** Lunch served: all week Dinner served: all week 12-2.30 6.30-9.30 Av 3 course à la carte £20
BREWERY/COMPANY: Free House **PRINCIPAL BEERS:** Fullers London Pride, Shepherd Neame Spitfire, Woodfordes Wherry, Wells Bombardier. **FACILITIES:** Children welcome Garden: Food served outside **NOTES:** Parking 100 **ROOMS:** d£40

ST PETER SOUTH ELMHAM   Map 07 TM38

Pick of the Pubs

St Peter's Hall ◎ 🍴 ♀
NR35 1NQ ☎ 01986 782322 📠 01986 782505 e-mail: beers@stpetersbrewery.co.uk
Dir: From A143/A144 follow brown and white signs to St Peter's Brewery

A magnificent moated building that dominates surrounding farmland, this former medieval monastery dates back to 1280, and was extended in 1539 using architectural salvage from nearby Flixton Priory. As well as a chapel above the porch, expect stone floors, lofty ceilings, a fire blazing in the inglenook fireplace and furnishings dating back to the 17th and 18th centuries. This is also an excellent opportunity to tour the adjacent St Peter's brewery. Menus change weekly and are sensibly short to cater for the weekend (Fri-Sun) opening. For lunch expect dishes such as spiced ale sausages with honey and mustard mashed potato or traditional steak and kidney pudding with St Peter's beer gravy. The

continued

continued

evening menu could include pan fried pork fillet with grain mustard sauce and caramelised apples or fillet of sea bass on crab and mussel pilaf rice with a cream of saffron sauce.
OPEN: 11–11 (Sun 11–11) **BAR MEALS:** Lunch served: Fri-Sun 12.30-2 Dinner served: Fri-Sat 7–10 **RESTAURANT:** Lunch served: Fri-Sun 12.30-2 Dinner served: Fri-Sat 7–10
BREWERY/COMPANY: St Peters Brewery
PRINCIPAL BEERS: St Peters Best. **FACILITIES:** Garden: Moated garden, food served outdoors **NOTES:** Parking 150

SNAPE   Map 07 TM35

Pick of the Pubs

The Crown Inn
Bridge Rd IP17 1SL ☎ 01728 688324
Dir: A12 N to Lowestoft, R to Aldeburgh, then R again in Snape at crossroads by church, pub at bottom hill
There are a wealth of beams and brick floors at this charming, 15th-century smugglers' inn, as well as the 'codgers' – an unusual, semi-circular area of old Suffolk settles clustered around the inglenook fireplace like old men huddling to keep warm. Lying close to the River Alde with its timeless scenery and tranquil coastal bird reserves, the pub and its sheltered garden provides a refuge from gaming machines and piped music. You'll find all the entertainment you need at the nearby Snape Maltings concert venue. The selection of Adnams beers are backed up with an interesting wine list, and a dining room that offers a changing menu emphasising local produce and meat, fish and game in season. Among the choices are fillet steak, warm Mozzarella, sweet pepper, tomato tart, confit of duck with honey glaze on wild mushroom risotto, whole sea bass with garlic tiger prawns, and chicken Thai red curry. For dessert, try the famous sticky toffee pudding.
OPEN: 12–3 6–11 (Sunday 7–10.30) Closed: Dec 25
BAR MEALS: Lunch served: all week Dinner served: all week 12–2 7–9 Av main course £9.50 **RESTAURANT:** Lunch served: all week Dinner served: all week 12–2 7–9 Av 3 course à la carte £17.50 **BREWERY/COMPANY:** Adnams
PRINCIPAL BEERS: Adnams Best & Broadside.
FACILITIES: Garden: Beer garden, food served outdoors
NOTES: Parking 40 **ROOMS:** 3 bedrooms 3 en suite from s£55 d£65

The Golden Key
Priory Ln IP17 1SQ ☎ 01728 688510
Recently extended 15th-century cottage-style pub close to Snape Maltings, well known concert hall. Home-cooked food; Adnams ales; bedrooms; patio garden.

Plough & Sail
Snape Maltings IP17 1SR ☎ 01728 688413 📠 01728 688930
e-mail: enquiries@snapemaltings.co.uk
Part of the Snape Maltings Riverside Centre that incorporates the famous Concert Hall, art gallery and shops, the bustling Plough and Sail is justifiably popular with pre-concert goers. Rambling interior includes a bar and restaurant, while the large terrace provides welcome alfresco seating in summer. Expect good bar food, perhaps including Suffolk egg and ham ciabatta, seared Aldeburgh cod with tomato and cucumber relish, Thai chicken, and lunchtime sandwiches.

continued

OPEN: 11–3 5.30–11 (summer 11–11) **BAR MEALS:** Lunch served: all week Dinner served: all week 12–2.30 7–9 Av main course £5.95 **RESTAURANT:** Lunch served: all week Dinner served: all week 12–2.30 7–9 Av 3 course à la carte £19.50
BREWERY/COMPANY: Free House **PRINCIPAL BEERS:** Adnams Broadside, Woodfordes, Adnams Oyster. **FACILITIES:** Children welcome Children's licence Garden: Patio/terrace, outdoor eating Dogs allowed **NOTES:** Parking 100

SOUTHWOLD   Map 07 TM57

The Angel
High St, Wangford NR34 8RL ☎ 01502 578636 📠 01502 578535
e-mail: enquireis@angelinn.freeserve.co.uk

A traditional green and cream-painted inn with a handsome Georgian façade, set in the heart of the pretty village of Wangford and overlooking the historic parish church. Dating back to the 16th century, and complete with resident ghost, its cosy bar and restaurant are characterised by exposed beams and roaring log fires in winter. Home-made dishes include fresh fish (cod, skate, sole), smoked duck, various steaks, gammon, and steak and ale pie.
OPEN: 12–3 6–11 **BAR MEALS:** Lunch served: Tues-Sun Dinner served: Tues-Sun 12–2 6.30–9 Av main course £7.95
RESTAURANT: Lunch served: Tues-Sun Dinner served: Tues-Sun 12–2 6.30–9 **BREWERY/COMPANY:** Free House
PRINCIPAL BEERS: Adnams Best, Woodfordes Wherry, Greene King Abbot Ale, Brakspear Bitter. **FACILITIES:** Children welcome Garden: Food served outside Dogs allowed **NOTES:** Parking 20
ROOMS: 7 bedrooms 7 en suite from d£59

Pick of the Pubs

Crown Hotel ★ ★
The High St IP18 6DP ☎ 01502 722275 📠 01502 727263
Dir: off A12 take A1094 to Southwold, stay on main road into town centre, hotel on L in High St
Posting inn, dating from 1750, fulfilling the purposes of pub, wine bar, restaurant and small hotel. As flagship for

continued

England

SOUTHWOLD continued

Adnams brewery, it offers excellent ales and wines, and good food in both the bar and restaurant. Typical imaginative dishes in the bar might be smoked haddock and mussel chowder, deep-fried Feta wrapped in Parma ham, pan-fried skate with gremolata butter, and braised lamb shank with pease pudding. In the restaurant look for pork fillet with rosemary polenta and marinated vegetables and glazed lemon tart with chocolate mousse to finish. Bedrooms are attractively decorated with co-ordinated soft furnishings and well equipped.
OPEN: 10.30-3 6-11 **BAR MEALS:** Lunch served: all week Dinner served: all week 12.15-2 7-9.30 Av main course £10
RESTAURANT: Lunch served: all week Dinner served: all week 12.30-2 7.30-9.30 Av 3 course à la carte £27.50 Av 3 course fixed price £27.50 **BREWERY/COMPANY:** Adnams
PRINCIPAL BEERS: Adnams. **FACILITIES:** Children welcome Dogs allowed (guide dogs only) **NOTES:** Parking 18
ROOMS: 13 bedrooms 12 en suite from s£75 d£92

STANTON   Map 07 TL97

The Rose & Crown ⬚
Bury Rd IP31 2BZ ☎ 01359 250236 ▤ 01359 250795
e-mail: roseandcrown@mainline.co.uk
Dir: A14 to Bury St E, then A143. or A140 to Diss, then A143 to Bury St E
The original 17th-century thatched pub has been carefully extended into an old flint barn, to provide a main restaurant, conservatory restaurant, large bar and separate function room. An extensive garden with children's play equipment, including two bouncy castles, is popular for summer use. The main menu is supported by up to ten daily specials – maybe monkfish with lime and crème fraîche, Stilton-stuffed steak with whisky sauce, and porcini ravioli with fresh tomato and basil.
OPEN: 12-11 **BAR MEALS:** Lunch served: all week Dinner served: all week 12-2.15 6-9 Av main course £5 **RESTAURANT:** Lunch served: all week Dinner served: all week 12-2.15 6-9 Av 3 course à la carte £12 **BREWERY/COMPANY:** Pubmaster
PRINCIPAL BEERS: Tetley, Kilkenny, Interbrew Flowers, Greene King Abbot Ale. **FACILITIES:** Children welcome Garden: Food served outside Dogs allowed **NOTES:** Parking 100

STOKE-BY-NAYLAND   Map 07 TL93

Pick of the Pubs

The Angel Inn ♦♦♦♦ ⬚
CO6 4SA ☎ 01206 263245 ▤ 01206 263373
Dir: From A12 take Colchester R turn, then A134, 5m to Nayland. From A12 S take B1068
Set in a landscape immortalised by the paintings of local artist, John Constable, the Angel is a 16th-century inn with beamed bars, log fires and a long tradition of hospitality. In a more modern vein, the pub also has an air-conditioned conservatory, patio and sun terrace. Tables for lunch and dinner may be reserved in The Well Room which has a high ceiling open to the rafters, a gallery leading to the pub's accommodation, rough brick and timber studded walls, and the well itself, fully 52 feet deep. Eating in the bar, by comparison, is on a strictly first-come, first-served basis. The chalkboard menus change daily, with first-class fish options and generous portions of salad or fresh vegetables. Look out for dishes

continued

such as griddled fillet of haddock, chicken and king prawn brochette with yoghurt and mint dip, steak and kidney pudding, roast ballotine of duckling with cassis sauce, or steamed fillets of salmon and halibut with dill sauce.

OPEN: 11-2.30 6-11 Closed: Dec 25-26, Jan 1
BAR MEALS: 12-2 6.30-9 **RESTAURANT:** Lunch served: all week Dinner served: all week 12-2 6.30-9 Av 3 course à la carte £16 **BREWERY/COMPANY:** Free House
PRINCIPAL BEERS: Greene King IPA & Abbot Ale, Adnams Best. **NOTES:** Parking 25 **ROOMS:** 6 bedrooms 6 en suite from s£52.50 d£67.50

STOWMARKET   Map 07 TM05

The Buxhall Crown ⬚
Mill Rd, Buxhall IP14 3BW ☎ 01449 736521 ▤ 01449 737455
e-mail: trevor@buxhallcrown.fsnet.co.uk

Original beams in hidden 15th-century dining pub, offering a warm welcome to families, Greene King ales and pleasant garden. Choose from whole sea bass stuffed with fresh herbs, sautéed lambs' liver on a bed of braised pak choi, winter vegetable stew with dumplings or pan-fried calves' liver, followed by bread and butter pudding or lemon mousse.
OPEN: 12-3 6.30-11 **BAR MEALS:** Lunch served: all week 12-2 Dinner served: Mon-Sat 6.30-9.30 Av main course £9
RESTAURANT: Lunch served: all week 12-2 Dinner served: Mon-Sat 6.30-9.30 Av 3 course à la carte £18
BREWERY/COMPANY: Greene King **PRINCIPAL BEERS:** Greene King IPA, Ruddles County, Woodforde's Wherry, Old Chimneys Mild.
FACILITIES: Children welcome Garden: Patio, food served outside Dogs allowed (water) **NOTES:** Parking 25

♀ **Pubs offering six or more wines by the glass**

SWILLAND   Map 07 TM15

Moon & Mushroom Inn ♀
High Rd IP6 9LR ☎ 01473 785320 ▤ 01473 785320
Dir: *6 miles north of Ipswich taking the Westerfield Rd*

A row of former 16th-century village cottages and a pub since 1721; its current name the result of a locals' competition 250 years later. Real ale is sold by gravity only and home cooking prevails. Venison with haggis, beef with dumplings and haddock mornay are ladelled from tureens with self-served vegetables. **OPEN:** 11–2.30 6–11 (Mon 6–11 only) **BAR MEALS:** Lunch served: Tue–Sat Dinner served: Tue–Sat 12–2 6.30–8.15 Av main course £7.45 **RESTAURANT:** Lunch served: Tue–Sat Dinner served: Tue–Sat 12–2 6.30–8.15 Av 3 course à la carte £10.40 **BREWERY/COMPANY:** Free House **PRINCIPAL BEERS:** Nethergate Umbel, Wolfs Coyote, Wolf Ale, Woodfords Wherry. **FACILITIES:** Garden: Food served outside. Patio area Dogs allowed **NOTES:** Parking 47

THORNHAM MAGNA   Map 07 TM17

The Four Horseshoes ♀
Wickham Rd IP23 8HD ☎ 01379 678777 ▤ 01379 678134
Dir: *From Diss on A140 turn R and follow signs for Finningham, 0.5m turn R for Thornham Magna*
Thornham Magna is a delightful, unspoilt village, close to Thornham Country Park and the interesting thatched church at Thornham Parva. This fine 12th-century inn, with a splendid thatched roof and timber-framed walls, offers varied bar food - home-made steak and ale pie, chicken Kiev, Dover sole, mussels or roasts. **OPEN:** 11.30–11 **BAR MEALS:** Lunch served: all week Dinner served: all week 11.30–6 6–9 Av main course £6.95 **RESTAURANT:** Dinner served: all week 6–9 Av 3 course à la carte £15 **BREWERY/COMPANY:** Greene King **PRINCIPAL BEERS:** Greene King IPA, Abbot, Old Speckled Hen. **FACILITIES:** Children welcome Garden Dogs allowed **NOTES:** Parking 80 **ROOMS:** 8 bedrooms 7 en suite from s£55 d£60

TOSTOCK   Map 07 TL96

Gardeners Arms NEW
IP30 9PA ☎ 01359 270460
Dir: *From A14 follow signs to Tostock (0.5m)*
Parts of this charming pub, at the end of the village green, near the horse chestnut tree, date back 600 years. The basic bar menu - salads, grills, ploughmans', sandwiches, toasties, etc - is supplemented by specials boards that offer six starters and 12 main courses in the evening. Look out for lamb balti,

continued

Thai king prawn green curry, steak and kidney pie, or chicken and Stilton roulade. Large grassy garden. **OPEN:** 11.30–2.30 7–11 **RESTAURANT:** Lunch served: Mon–Sat 12–2 Dinner served: Wed–Sun 7.15–9.30 Av 3 course à la carte £13 **BREWERY/COMPANY:** Greene King **PRINCIPAL BEERS:** Greene King IPA, Greene King Abbot, Greene King seasonal beers. **FACILITIES:** Children welcome Garden: Food served outside, large grass area Dogs allowed **NOTES:** Parking 20

WALBERSWICK   Map 07 TM47

Pick of the Pubs

Bell Inn 🍷 ♀
Ferry Rd IP18 6TN ☎ 01502 723109 ▤ 01502 722728
e-mail: bellinn@btinternet.com
See Pick of the Pubs on page 448

WESTLETON   Map 07 TM46

The Crown at Westleton ★ ★ ⊛⊛
IP17 3AD ☎ 0800 328 6001 ▤ 01728 648239
e-mail: reception@westletoncrown.com
Dir: *Turn off the A12 just past Yoxford Northbound, follow the tourist signs for 2 miles*

Bustling old coaching inn nestling in a quiet village close to the coast and bird reserves. Well established and offering genuine hospitality in a relaxed atmosphere, it also features sound home cooking and good wines and whiskies. Menu choices range from interesting salads and ploughmans' through to roasted rump of lamb with bubble and squeak or slow-roasted belly of pork. **OPEN:** 11–3 6–11 (Sun 7–10.30) **BAR MEALS:** Lunch served: all week Dinner served: all week 12–2.15 7–9.30 Av main course £6.95 **RESTAURANT:** Lunch served: all week Dinner served: all week 12–2.15 7–9.30 Av 3 course à la carte £20 **BREWERY/COMPANY:** Free House **PRINCIPAL BEERS:** Adnams, Greene King IPA. **FACILITIES:** Children welcome Garden Dogs allowed **ROOMS:** 19 bedrooms 19 en suite from s£59.50 d£69.50

OPEN: 11–3 6–11 (11–2.30 Sun, 7–9 Sun-Thurs in winter. End Jul–4 Sep 11–11)
BAR MEALS: L served all week. D served all week. 12–2 6–9 Av main course £6.50
RESTAURANT: D served Fri-Sat 6–9 Av cost 3 course £15
BREWERY/COMPANY: ADNAMS
PRINCIPAL BEERS: Adnams Best, Broadside, Fisherman's & Regatta
FACILITIES: Children and dogs welcome. Garden: Food served outside
NOTES: Parking 10
ROOMS: 6 en suite Double room from £70 Single room from £40

Bell Inn

🍷
Ferry Road P18 6TN
☎ 01502 723109 📠 01502 722728
e-mail: bellinn@btinternet.com
Dir: From A12 take B1387 to Walberswick

Reputedly 600 years old, the Bell is situated at the heart of Walberswick, close to the village green and a stone's throw from the beach and the ancient fishing harbour on the River Blyth. Its peace and tranquillity have attracted many visitors over the years and its atmosphere on Suffolk's sweeping coast is timeless.

The artists Charles Rennie Macintosh and Philip Wilson Steer would have stayed at the Bell, the latter also lodging at Valley Farm next door. Montague Rhodes James wrote one of the best-known ghost stories, 'Whistle and I'll come to you my lad,' while staying at The Bell in 1929. To the north, across the River Blyth, is delightful Southwold, a classic seaside town with a highly individual, old-fashioned air. Reach it either by foot or seasonal ferry. To the south lie the woodland heaths of Dunwich and the Minsmere Bird Sanctuary, while to the west is the famous 'Cathedral of the Marshes' at Blythburgh. Inside the inn, the Bell's low beams, open fires, flagged floors and high wooden settles create a warm, homely welcome - so much so that television and film companies have been attracted by the inn's distinctive appeal. Line in the Sand and an episode of The Knock being the most recent productions. Traditional English pub fare and a seasonal menu are the Bell's hallmarks and among the perennial favourites are whole grilled plaice, traditional beef stew and dumplings, mushroom Stroganoff and chicken supreme. There is good range of vegetarian dishes and sandwiches too, all to be washed down with well-kept Adnams ales or a selection of wines.

WINGFIELD   Map 07 TM27

Pick of the Pubs

De la Pole Arms 🐑 ♀
Church Rd IP21 5RA ☎ 01379 384545 📠 01379 384377
Dir: Opposite Wingfield College

Well worth the effort of finding it, the De la Pole Arms is
hidden away down narrow country lanes and stands
opposite Wingfield Church and Wingfield College. It is
popular with visitors who come by car, foot or bike (this is
a great area for ramblers and cyclists). Inside there are
two bars with stripped wooden tables, quarry-tiled floors
and wood-burning stoves. Excellent St Peter's ales are
served, and you could even go on to visit the brewery,
which is 15-20 minutes' drive away. The quality and
breadth of local produce is reflected in the menus. House
specialities include freshly filleted Lowestoft cod in a
coating of St Peter's beer batter, served with home-made
chips; Gruyère and leek flan served with home-made
chunky tomato relish and salad leaves dressed with
famous De la Pole dressing, and wild rabbit casserole
gently cooked with marjoram, mushrooms, white wine,
wholegrain mustard and cream.

OPEN: 11-3 6-11 (Winter Tue-Thur 11-3, 6.30-11) Closed: Mon Nov
1-Mar 31 **BAR MEALS:** Lunch served: Tues-Sun Dinner served:
Tues-Sun 12-2 7-9 Av main course £8 **RESTAURANT:** Lunch
served: Tues-Sun 12-2 Dinner served: Tues-Sat 7-9 Av 3 course à la
carte £20 **BREWERY/COMPANY:** St Peters Brewery
PRINCIPAL BEERS: St Peters Best, Strong Ale, Fruit Beer, Golden
Ale Aand Wheat beer. **FACILITIES:** Food served outdoors, patio
NOTES: Parking 20

SURREY

ABINGER   Map 04 TQ14

The Volunteer 🐑 ♀
Water Ln, Sutton RH5 6PR ☎ 01306 730798 📠 01306 731621
e-mail: thevolunteer@ukonline.co.uk
Dir: Between Guildford & Dorking, 1m S of A25

Enjoying a delightful rural setting with views over the River
Mole, this popular village pub was originally farm cottages
and first licensed about 1870. An ideal watering hole for
walkers who want to relax over a pint in the attractive pub
garden. Typical fish dishes include lobster thermidor,
Mediterranean squid pasta and fillet of sea bass, while Thai
coconut chicken, partridge with red wine and junipers and
fillet of braised beef on fennel feature among the meat
dishes.

OPEN: 11-3 5-11 (All day Sat & Sun) **BAR MEALS:** Lunch served:
all week Dinner served: all week 12-2.30 7-9.30 Av main course £10
BREWERY/COMPANY: Woodhouse Inns
PRINCIPAL BEERS: Badger Tanglefoot, Dorset Best & King & Barns
Sussex. **FACILITIES:** Garden: Terrace, food served outside Dogs
allowed (water, biscuits) **NOTES:** Parking 30

ALBURY   Map 04 TQ04

The Drummond Arms Inn ♦♦♦
The Street GU5 9AG ☎ 01483 202039 📠 01483 205361
Situated in the pretty village of Albury below the North
Downs, this charming old inn has an attractive garden that
looks over the River Tillingbourne and offers comfortable en
suite accommodation. A varied menu of pub food, served in
the panelled bars, includes home-made steak and kidney
pie, poached smoked haddock, and chicken escalope
Milanese, as well as burgers, jacket potatoes, sandwiches
and freshly baked baguettes.

OPEN: 11-3 6-11 **BAR MEALS:** 12-2 7-9 **RESTAURANT:** Lunch
served: all week 12-2 Dinner served: Mon-Sat 7-9 Av 3 course à la
carte £18 **BREWERY/COMPANY:** Merlin Inns
PRINCIPAL BEERS: Scottish Courage Courage Best, Gales HSB,
Breakspear Bitter. **FACILITIES:** Garden: Riverside, food served
outside **NOTES:** Parking 70 **ROOMS:** 11 bedrooms 11 en suite
from s£45 d£65

William IV
Little London GU5 9DG ☎ 01483 202685
Dir: just off the A25 between Guildford & Dorking

This quaint country pub is only a stone's throw from
Guildford, yet deep in the heart of the Surrey countryside. The
area is great for hiking and the pub is popular with walkers,
partly due to its attractive garden, which is ideal for post-
ramble relaxation. A wide-ranging choice of real ales and a
blackboard menu that changes daily is also part of the
attraction. Expect steak and kidney pie, pot-roast lamb shank,
battered cod and chips, and rib-eye steak.

OPEN: 11-3 5.30-11 (Sun 12-3, 7-10.30) Closed: 25 Dec
BAR MEALS: Lunch served: all week 12-2 Dinner served: Tue-Sat
7-9 Av main course £5.50 **RESTAURANT:** Lunch served: Sun 12-2
Dinner served: Fri-Sat 7-9 Av 3 course à la carte £18
BREWERY/COMPANY: Free House
PRINCIPAL BEERS: Interbrew Flowers IPA, Wadworth 6X, Hall &
Woodhouse, Pilgrim. **FACILITIES:** Garden: Food served outside
Dogs allowed (water) **NOTES:** Parking 15

> 🎖 **For a list of pubs with**
> **AA Rosette Awards for food see pages 12 & 13.**

continued

England

BETCHWORTH — Map 05 TQ25

The Dolphin Inn 🐾 NEW
The Street RH3 7DW ☎ 01737 842288
Dir: Between Reigate and Dorking, off A25
This 400-year-old inn stands opposite a church that appeared in Four Weddings and a Funeral. Inside, the pub is the epitome of country charm, featuring three open fires and bare flagstones in the public bar. The equally traditional menu features dishes such as steak and mushroom pie, ham egg and chips, macaroni cheese or chilli in potato skins. A good selection of fish dishes might include smoked haddock, battered cod or scampi and chips.
OPEN: 11–3 5.30–11 (open all day Sat-Sun) **BAR MEALS:** Lunch served: all week Dinner served: all week 12–3 7–10 Av main course £5.95 **BREWERY/COMPANY:** Youngs
PRINCIPAL BEERS: Young's IPA, Special, Winter Warmer & Waggle Dance. **FACILITIES:** Garden: Food served outdoors, patio Dogs allowed **NOTES:** Parking 25

The Red Lion
Old Reigate Rd RH3 7DS ☎ 01737 843336 📠 01737 845242
Set in 18 acres with a cricket ground and rolling countryside views, this award-winning, 200-year-old pub offers an extensive menu. Beyond baguettes and ploughman's lunches the choice includes sole and smoked salmon, Barbary duck breast, aubergine and broccoli fritters, deep-fried plaice and chips, Toulouse sausage and mash, and steak and ale pie.
OPEN: 11–11 (Sun 12-10.30) Closed: Dec 31-Jan 2
BAR MEALS: Lunch served: all week Dinner served: all week 12–3 6–10 Av main course £10 **BREWERY/COMPANY:** Punch Taverns
PRINCIPAL BEERS: Fullers London Pride, Greene King Old Speckled Hen, Adnams Broadside. **FACILITIES:** Children welcome Garden: Food served outside. Patio area **NOTES:** Parking 50
ROOMS: 6 bedrooms 6 en suite from s£70 d£80

BLACKBROOK — Map 04 TQ14

The Plough at Blackbrook 🐾 ♀
RH5 4DS ☎ 01306 886603
Dir: A24 to Dorking, then toward Horsham, 0.75m from Deepdene rdbt L to Blackbrook
Idyllic countryside surrounds this former coaching inn, much of it visible through the large windows. The striking views can also be enjoyed from the popular cottage garden. A lunchtime snack menu offers the usual favourites plus grilled ham steak with pineapple, and steak sandwich in ciabatta bread. From a list of specials sample ginger and orange lamb with onion rice, and grilled calves' liver with bacon. Good wines and well-kept ales.
OPEN: 11-2.30 6–11 (Sun 12-3, 7-10.30) Closed: 25-26 Dec, 1 Jan
BAR MEALS: Lunch served: all week Dinner served: Tue–Sun 7-9 **BREWERY/COMPANY:** Hall & Woodhouse
PRINCIPAL BEERS: Badger King & Barnes Sussex, Tanglefoot.
FACILITIES: Garden: Secluded graden, patio Dogs allowed (water)
NOTES: Parking 22

BRAMLEY — Map 04 TQ04

Jolly Farmer Inn 🐾 ♀
High St GU5 0HB ☎ 01483 893355 📠 01483 890484
e-mail: accom@jollyfarmer.co.uk
Dir: Onto A3, then A281, Bramley 3m S of Guildford
Originally a coaching inn, this family-run free house has been in existence for over 400 years and still offers accommodation, home-cooked food and a wide choice of ales and lagers to both travellers and locals. Favourites include tacos with hot chilli, cod fillet in beer batter, and steak, mushroom and ale pie. 'The Carnivore Selection' includes Dutch calves' liver with smoked back bacon, while vegetarians can sample savoury-filled aubergine or goats' cheese salad.

OPEN: 11–3 6–11 (Sun 12-3, 7-10.30) **BAR MEALS:** Lunch served: all week Dinner served: all week 12–2 6.30-10 Av main course £8.50 **BREWERY/COMPANY:** Free House **PRINCIPAL BEERS:** Hogs Back TEA, Badger Best, Timothy Taylor Landlord, Hopback Summer Lightning. **FACILITIES:** Children welcome Garden: Food served outside **NOTES:** Parking 22 **ROOMS:** 11 bedrooms 10 en suite from s£45 d£55

CHIDDINGFOLD — Map 04 SU93

Pick of the Pubs

The Crown Inn
The Green GU8 4TX ☎ 01428 682255 📠 01428 685736
Dir: On A283 between Milford & Petworth

Historic inn, dating back over 700 years, with lots of charming features, including ancient panelling, open fires, distinctive carvings and huge beams. Comfortably refurbished by owning brewery Hall and Woodhouse, this striking inn offers individually-styled bedrooms, some with four-poster beds, in a unique setting making it an excellent choice for a relaxing weekend break, especially with Petworth, the famous Devil's Punch Bowl and miles of walking on the scenic South Downs nearby. Reliable food ranges from sausage and mash with onion gravy, chicken tagliatelle, freshly battered fish and chips, and decent sandwiches, warm salads and ploughman's at lunchtime, to Torbay sole, monkfish and tiger prawns pan-fried with ginger and lime cream sauce and served on tagliatelle, and roast duck with sweet plum sauce on the evening menu.

continued
continued

OPEN: 11-11 **BAR MEALS:** Lunch served: all week Dinner served: all week 12-2.30 6.30-9.30 Av main course £8.95 **BREWERY/COMPANY:** Hall & Woodhouse **PRINCIPAL BEERS:** Badger Dorset Best & Tanglefoot, King & Barnes Sussex Ale. **FACILITIES:** Garden: Beer garden, outdoor eating, patio, BBQ Dogs allowed **ROOMS:** 8 bedrooms 8 en suite from s£57 d£67

The Swan Inn & Restaurant ⊙ ♀ NEW
Petworth Rd GU8 4TY ☎ 01428 682073 ▤ 01428 683259
A lovely 14th century village pub whose sympathetic refurbishment has included bare floors, wooden furniture and big leather sofas. The chef makes impressive use of seafood, fish and local game. A meal could include pan-fried sardines with lime salsa and herb salad, followed by roasted guinea fowl with confit of leg, served with stir-fried vegetables, puréed potatoes and a herb cream sauce. Bar snacks are also available.
OPEN: 11-3 (Sun 12-4, 7-10.30) 5.30-11 Closed: First week in Jan **BAR MEALS:** Lunch served: all week Dinner served: all week 12-2.30 6.30-10 Av main course £8 **RESTAURANT:** Lunch served: all week Dinner served: all week 12-2.30 6.30-10 Av 3 course à la carte £24 Av 3 course fixed price £14.50 **BREWERY/COMPANY:** Free House **PRINCIPAL BEERS:** Hogs Back TEA, Ringwood Best, Timothy Taylor Landlord, Fuller's London Pride. **FACILITIES:** Children welcome Garden: Food served outdoors, terrace Dogs allowed (water) **NOTES:** Parking 25 **ROOMS:** 3 bedrooms 3 en suite from s£55 d£65

CLAYGATE   Map 04 TQ16

Swan Inn
Hare Ln KT10 9BT ☎ 01372 462582
Village pub with Edwardian interior. Cricket-team HQ overlooking the village green; hearty bar food.

COBHAM   Map 04 TQ16

The Cricketers ⊙ ♀
Downside KT11 3NX ☎ 01932 862105 ▤ 01932 868186
e-mail: jamesclifton@msn.com
Dir: From A3 take A245 towards Cobham, 2nd r'about turn R, then 1st R opp Waitrose. Pub 1.5m
Dating back to the mid-1500s, this traditional old English pub contains in places original wattle and daub walls of a former abattoir! A daily cold buffet of fresh local fish, home-cooked meats and pies is served in the bar, with blackboard specials adding pork and leek sausages in onion gravy, vegetable spring rolls and salmon with tarragon butter. In summer, enjoy a drink or alfresco meal in the garden overlooking Downside Common.
OPEN: 11-2.30 6-11 Closed: 25 Dec **BAR MEALS:** Lunch served: all week Dinner served: all week 12-2 6.30-10 Av main course £7 **RESTAURANT:** Lunch served: Tue-Sun 12.15-1.45 Dinner served: Tue-Sat 7.15-9.30 Av 3 course à la carte £25 Av 3 course fixed price £16.95 **BREWERY/COMPANY:** Inntrepreneur **PRINCIPAL BEERS:** Wadworth 6X, Young's Bitter, Greene King Old Speckled Hen. **FACILITIES:** Garden: Beer garden, patio, Food served outdoors **NOTES:** Parking 80

COLDHARBOUR   Map 04 TQ14

The Plough Inn ⊙ ♀
Coldharbour Ln RH5 6HD ☎ 01306 711793 ▤ 01306 710055
e-mail: PloughInn@btinternet.com
Dir: M25 J9 - A24 to Dorking. A25 towards Guildford. Coldharbour signposted from the one-way system
Over 300 years old and in the depths of National Trust countryside on Leith Hill, the Plough is much sought after for its ambience and warm welcome. In great walking country, customers arrive on foot, horseback, and bicycle. Major draws include the landlord's home-brewed ales and substantial and unfussy food. Look for king prawns in saffron sauce and chargrilled sea bream, game pie and pork tenderloin with glazed apple and Dijon sauce - and then maybe another pint of Tallywhacker for good measure.
OPEN: 11.30-3 6-11 (Sat-Sun 11.30-11) **BAR MEALS:** Lunch served: all week Dinner served: all week 12-2.30 7-9.30 **RESTAURANT:** Lunch served: all week Dinner served: all week 12-2.30 7-9.30 **BREWERY/COMPANY:** Free House **PRINCIPAL BEERS:** Crooked Furrow, Leith Hill Tallywhacker, Ringwood Old Thumper, Timothy Taylor Landlord. **FACILITIES:** Garden: Well kept, food served outside Dogs allowed **ROOMS:** 6 bedrooms 6 en suite from s£55 d£69.50

COMPTON   Map 04 SU94

The Harrow Inn ⊙ ♀
The Street GU3 1EG ☎ 01483 810379 ▤ 01483 813854
Dir: 3m S of Guildford on A3 then B3000 towards Godalming. Compton on R
Some parts of this beamed pub date back 500 years, so some of the floors and doors are quaintly sloping. In an attractive village, the Harrow Inn has a friendly atmosphere, and is a handy refreshment stop for those travelling on the A3. A varied menu may include fillet of beef Stroganoff, lamb kidneys and baby sausages in sherry and mustard sauce or seared tuna steak on sun-dried tomato risotto.
OPEN: 8-11 (Sun 10-6) **BAR MEALS:** Lunch served: all week 12-3 Dinner served: Mon-Sat 6-10 **RESTAURANT:** Lunch served: Sun 12-3 Dinner served: Mon-Sat 6-10 **BREWERY/COMPANY:** Punch Taverns **PRINCIPAL BEERS:** Greene King IPA, Hogs Back TEA, Marston's Pedigree. **FACILITIES:** Children welcome Garden: Food served outside Dogs allowed **NOTES:** Parking 50 **ROOMS:** 4 bedrooms 4 en suite from s£50 d£55

The Withies Inn ⊙
Withies Ln GU3 1JA ☎ 01483 421158 ▤ 01483 425904
The splendid garden is one of the pub's chief attractions, filled with overhanging weeping willows, apple trees and dazzling flower borders. Inside, the atmosphere is friendly and welcoming, with low beams, 17th-century carved panels and an art nouveau settle, while log fires crackle away in the huge inglenook fireplace. Expect a good choice of bar snacks, filled jacket potatoes and sandwiches, while the restaurant menu offers dishes such as fresh Scottish salmon, half a roast duckling with orange sauce, or suckling pig.
OPEN: 11-3 6-11 (Sun 12-3, 6-11) **BAR MEALS:** Lunch served: all week Dinner served: all week 12-2.30 7-10 Av main course £4.75 **RESTAURANT:** Lunch served: all week 12-2.30 Dinner served: Mon-Sat 7-10 Av 3 course à la carte £30 **BREWERY/COMPANY:** Free House **PRINCIPAL BEERS:** Greene King IPA, Bass, Fullers London Pride, Sussex. **FACILITIES:** Garden: Food served outside Dogs allowed (in the garden only) **NOTES:** Parking 70

DORKING — Map 04 TQ14

Abinger Hatch
Abinger Ln, Abinger Common RH5 6HZ ☎ 01306 730737
Dir: A25 from Guildford, L to Abinger Common
Flagged floors, beamed ceilings and open fires are features of this 18th-century coaching inn, classically located opposite the church and duck pond. It's a free house serving Harveys, Fullers London Pride, Badger Tanglefoot, Youngs, Adnams and Chiswick beers, and home-cooked food prepared by the landlord. Options range from hot and kickin' chicken with BBQ dressing to double-baked loin of lamb with rosemary and red wine sauce.
OPEN: 11.30-2.30 5-11 (all day Sat-Sun) **BAR MEALS:** Lunch served: all week 12-2.15 Dinner served: Tue-Sat 6-9.15 Av main course £5 **RESTAURANT:** Lunch served: all week Dinner served: all week 12-2.15 6-9.15 **BREWERY/COMPANY:** Free House
PRINCIPAL BEERS: Harveys, Fuller's London Pride, Chiswick Bitter, Badger Tanglefoot. **FACILITIES:** Children welcome Children's licence Garden: Food served outside Dogs allowed
NOTES: Parking 35

Pick of the Pubs

The Stephan Langton ♀
Friday St, Abinger Common RH5 6JR ☎ 01306 730775
e-mail: cyraja@tinyworld.co.uk
Dir: Between Dorking & Guildford leave A25 @ Hollow Lane, W of Wootton. Go S for 1.5m then L into Friday Street

A lovely brick and timber inn named after the 13th-century archbishop of Canterbury and local boy who was instrumental in drawing up the Magna Carta. Although it looks much older, and was built on the site of another inn, this secluded hostelry only dates back to 1930. Some of Surrey's loveliest walks are found nearby, including the challenging Leith Hill, and walkers find this a perfect place to recover. The pub is being gradually refurbished to match Jonathan Coomb's upmarket food. The bar choice includes duck confit with Puy lentils and spring greens, and Moroccan-style braised lamb, while the dinner menu offers a short but well-balanced choice: chargrilled squid with chilli and rocket, seared marlin niçoise, and buttermilk pudding with poached rhubarb is a typically appealing meal.
OPEN: 11-3 6-11 Open all day at the weekend in summer **BAR MEALS:** Lunch served: Tues-Sun 12.30-3 Dinner served: Tues-Sat 7-10 Av main course £7 **RESTAURANT:** Lunch served: Tues-Sun 12.30-3 Dinner served: Tues-Sat 7-10 Av 3 course à la carte £20 **BREWERY/COMPANY:** Free House **PRINCIPAL BEERS:** Fuller's London Pride, Adnams, Harveys Sussex Bitter. **FACILITIES:** Children welcome Garden: Food served outside Dogs allowed (water provided) **NOTES:** Parking 20

DUNSFOLD — Map 04 TQ03

The Sun Inn
The Common GU8 4LE ☎ 01483 200242 📄 01483 201141
Dir: A281 thru Shalford & Bramley, take B2130 to Godalming. Dunsfold on L after 2 miles
Heavily timbered coaching inn with open fireplaces and three bar areas, opposite a cricket green. The village boasts seven ponds. Today's menu may include steak and kidney pie, venison sausages, fresh grilled trout and beef Stroganoff.
OPEN: 11-11 (Sun 12-10.30) **BAR MEALS:** Lunch served: all week Dinner served: all week 12-2.15 7-9.15 Av main course £8.95
BREWERY/COMPANY: Punch Taverns
PRINCIPAL BEERS: Knight Barnes Sussex, Ansells Best, Bass, Adnams Broadside. **FACILITIES:** Children welcome Children's licence Garden: Outdoor eating, patio/terrace, BBQ Dogs allowed

EFFINGHAM — Map 04 TQ15

The Plough ♀
Orestan Ln KT24 5SW ☎ 01372 458121 📄 01372 458121
Dir: Between Guildford & Leatherhead on A246
A modern pub with a traditional feel, The Plough provides a peaceful retreat in a rural setting close to Polesden Lacy National Trust House. Home-cooked British dishes include the likes of mushroom and grilled tomato bruschetta, calves' liver mash with carrots and sage butter, and bread and butter pudding.
OPEN: 11-3 5.30-11 **BAR MEALS:** Lunch served: all week Dinner served: all week 12-2.30 7-10 Av main course £7.95
RESTAURANT: Lunch served: all week Dinner served: all week 12-2.30 7-10 Av 3 course à la carte £16
BREWERY/COMPANY: Young & Co **PRINCIPAL BEERS:** Youngs IPA, Special. **FACILITIES:** Garden: Beer garden, patio, outdoor eating **NOTES:** Parking 40

EGHAM — Map 04 TQ07

The Fox and Hounds ♀
Bishopgate Rd, Englefield Green TW20 0XU ☎ 01784 433098 📄 01784 438775
Dir: From village green turn L into Castle Hill Rd, then R into Bishops Gate Rd
The Surrey border once ran through the centre of this good English pub, convenient for walkers and riders. Still used by members of the Household Cavalry who tether their horses outside while they refresh themselves inside. There is a range of daily-changing fish specials as well as menu options such as roast half shoulder of lamb, Dutch calves' liver and Barbary duck breast.
OPEN: 11-11 (Sun 12-10.30) **BAR MEALS:** Lunch served: all week Dinner served: all week 12-2.30 6.30-10 Av main course £5.95
RESTAURANT: Lunch served: all week Dinner served: all week 12-2.30 6.30-10 Av 3 course à la carte £23.95 **BREWERY/COMPANY:** Free House **PRINCIPAL BEERS:** Fullers London Pride, Brakspear.
FACILITIES: Children welcome Garden: Beer garden with seating, patio, BBQ Dogs allowed **NOTES:** Parking 60

ELSTEAD — Map 04 SU94

Pick of the Pubs

The Woolpack 🏠 ♀
The Green GU8 6HD ☎ 01252 703106 📄 01252 703106
Dir: Milford exit off A3
There's plenty of atmosphere in this attractive, tile-hung pub overlooking the village green. Nearby, the River Wey

continued

flows beneath the ancient Elstead Bridge, and there are many good walks in the area. The building was originally constructed as a store for woollen bales, but over the years it has also served as a bicycle repair shop, a band practice hall, a butcher's shop and the local Co-op. Remnants of the woollen industry decorate the bar which also has low beams, open fires and high-backed settles. You'll find good, cask-conditioned ales, and the large blackboard menus are regularly changed. As well as a large selection of salads and ploughman's look out for dishes such as cod, prawn and egg pie, butterfish steak in orange, wine and rosemary sauce, and beef casserole. There's always a large selection of fresh, home-made desserts to choose from, too.

OPEN: 11-2.30 6-11 (Sat & Sun 11-11) Closed: 26 Dec **BAR MEALS:** Lunch served: all week Dinner served: all week 12-2 7-9.45 Av main course £8.50 **RESTAURANT:** Lunch served: all week Dinner served: all week 12-2 7-9.45 Av 3 course à la carte £16 **BREWERY/COMPANY:** Punch Taverns **PRINCIPAL BEERS:** Greene King Abbot Ale, Fuller's London Pride, Carlsberg-Tetley Tetley Bitter **FACILITIES:** Children welcome Garden: Food served outside Dogs allowed (water) **NOTES:** Parking 15

EWHURST   Map 04 TQ04

The Windmill Inn 🞖 ⚲
Pitch Hill GU6 7NN ☎ 01483 277566
Dir: From Cranleigh take B2127, through Ewhurst. At mini rndbt take Shere road. Pub 1.5m on R
Affording far-reaching views across the Weald to the South Downs, this welcoming inn was originally the haunt of 18th-century smugglers. Rebuilt after a fire in 1906. Traditional pub food. Close to a wealth of good walks.

GUILDFORD   Map 04 SU94

Red Lion 🞖 ⚲
Shamley Green GU5 0UB ☎ 01483 892202 🖷 01483 894055
Attractively situated old pub overlooking the village cricket pitch, with summer gardens, winter fires and en suite bedrooms. No less than four varied menus are served in the cosy bar and large, comfortable restaurant. Half crispy roast duck, braised lamb, fish pie, pan-fried pork tenderloin, and giant prawns are typical dishes.
OPEN: 07.30-11 **BAR MEALS:** Lunch served: all week Dinner served: all week 12-3 6.30-10 Av main course £8 **RESTAURANT:** Lunch served: all week Dinner served: all week 12-3 6.30-10 Av 3 course à la carte £19
BREWERY/COMPANY: Pubmaster **PRINCIPAL BEERS:** Adnams Broadside, Marstons Pedigree, Youngs. **FACILITIES:** Children

welcome Garden: Food served outside Dogs allowed (in the garden only) **NOTES:** Parking 30 **ROOMS:** 3 bedrooms 3 en suite from s£45 d£65

HASCOMBE   Map 04 TQ03

The White Horse 🞖
The Street GU8 4JA ☎ 01483 208258 🖷 01483 208200
e-mail: jamesb.ward@virgin.net
Dir: from Godalming take B2130. Pub on L 0.5m after Hascombe
A friendly 16th-century pub situated in picturesque countryside that is a good for walking. The pub is particularly noted in summer for its colourful garden, with hanging baskets and flowers. Restaurant menu and extensive blackboard specials in the bar may offer Thai style salmon and prawn fishcakes, home made steak burger, home made pies, and calves' liver and bacon. Fresh fish is delivered daily.
OPEN: 10-3 5.30-11 (Sat 10-11, Sun 12-10.30) Closed: Dec 25 **BAR MEALS:** Lunch served: all week Dinner served: all week 12-2.20 7-10 **RESTAURANT:** Lunch served: all week 12-2 Dinner served: Mon-Sat 7-10 Av 3 course à la carte £25
BREWERY/COMPANY: Punch Taverns
PRINCIPAL BEERS: Adnams, Fullers London Pride, Hall & Woodhouse Millennium. **FACILITIES:** Children welcome Garden: outdoor eating, patio Dogs allowed **NOTES:** Parking 55

HASLEMERE   Map 04 SU93

The Wheatsheaf Inn ♦♦♦ 🞖 ⚲
Graywood Rd, Graywood GU27 2DE
☎ 01428 644440 🖷 01428 641285
Dir: Leave A3 at Milford, A286 to Haslemere. Graywood approx 1.5m N

In the heart of the county, this Victorian village inn has one of Surrey's loveliest walks right on its doorstep. Nearby is the magnificent viewpoint at Black Down where Alfred, Lord Tennyson lived for 24 years. Freshly prepared, top quality dishes may include rack of lamb on parsnip purée with rosemary gravy, bacon-wrapped breast of chicken stuffed with wild mushrooms in a white wine sauce, and Mediterranean vegetable and brie quiche. Extensive snack menu. Comfortable bedrooms furnished to a good standard.
OPEN: 11-3 6-11 **BAR MEALS:** Lunch served: all week Dinner served: all week 12-2 7-10 Av main course £9.95 **RESTAURANT:** Lunch served: all week Dinner served: all week 12-2 7-10 **BREWERY/COMPANY:** Free House **PRINCIPAL BEERS:** Wadsworth 6X, Fullers London Pride, Harveys Sussex Bitter, Timothy Taylor Landlord. **FACILITIES:** Garden: Patio, food served outside **NOTES:** Parking 20
ROOMS: 7 bedrooms 7 en suite

continued

England

HINDHEAD   Map 04 SU83

Devil's Punchbowl Inn ⚲
London Rd GU26 6AG ☎ 01428 606565 ▨ 01428 605713
Dir: from M25 take A3 to Guildford, from there head toward Portsmouth
The hotel, which dates from the early 1800s, stands 900ft
above sea level with wonderful views as far as London on a
clear day. The 'punchbowl' is a large natural bowl in the
ground across the road. Food ranges from ploughman's
lunches to sandwiches and 16oz steaks and sizzling hot
platters.
OPEN: 7–11 **BAR MEALS:** Lunch served: all week Dinner served:
all week 7–10 Av main course £6.95 **RESTAURANT:** Lunch served:
all week Dinner served: all week 7–10 Av 3 course à la carte £17
BREWERY/COMPANY: Eldridge Pope **PRINCIPAL BEERS:** Bass,
Bombardier. **FACILITIES:** Children welcome Garden: outdoor
eating Dogs allowed **NOTES:** Parking 65 **ROOMS:** 32 bedrooms
32 en suite from s£69 d£89

HOLMBURY ST MARY   Map 04 TQ14

The Royal Oak
The Glade RH5 6PF ☎ 01306 730120
Neatly thatched 18th-century inn tucked away in a picturesque
village on the Surrey downs. Cosy, unpretentious bars with
open fires and beams attracting a loyal local trade. Home-
made traditional pub food.

LEIGH   Map 05 TQ24

The Plough 🐾 ⚲
Church Rd, LEIGH RH2 8NJ ☎ 01306 611348 ▨ 01306 611299
A welcoming country pub overlooking the village green and
situated opposite St Bartholomew's Church. Varied clientele,
good atmosphere and quaint low beams which are
conveniently padded! The comprehensive menu offers a good
choice of sandwiches, snacks and more substantial dishes,
including bangers and mash, various steaks, and liver and
bacon. Cod, salmon and haddock feature among the fish
main courses.
OPEN: 11–11 (Sun 12–10.30) **BAR MEALS:** Lunch served: all week
Dinner served: all week 12–3 7–10 Av main course £6.50
RESTAURANT: Lunch served: all week Dinner served: all week 12–3
7–10 Av 3 course à la carte £15 **BREWERY/COMPANY:** Hall &
Woodhouse **PRINCIPAL BEERS:** Badger Best , Tanglefoot, Sussex
Bitter. **FACILITIES:** Children welcome Garden: Food served outside
Dogs allowed (water) **NOTES:** Parking 6

MICKLEHAM   Map 04 TQ15

Pick of the Pubs

King William IV
Byttom Hill RH5 6EL ☎ 01372 372590
*Dir: Just off A24 (Leatherhead-Dorking), by partly green painted
restaurant, just N of B2289*
Formerly an ale house that catered to the needs of the
staff at Lord Beaverbrook's nearby Cherkley estate, this
popular, family-run free house has steadily built up a
reputation for its good food and well-kept real ales. With
a dedicated proprietor at the helm, this has resulted in the
introduction of popular monthly cookery demonstrations
in the winter months; balanced in summer months by a
special events calendar drawing for numerous walkers
and cyclists. Selections from recent menus include daily
specials such as Moroccan-style lamb kebabs with pilau

rice, and a seafood pie of cockles, mussels, prawn, salmon
and cod - with vegetarian alternatives such as baked
stuffed peppers topped with melted Mozzarella. There are
Sunday roasts, too, and summer barbecues in the
attractive terraced garden. The building itself dates from
1790 with some Victorian additions, displayed to effect in
the panelled Snug and the larger back bar with its open
fire, cast iron tables and grandfather clock.
OPEN: 11–3 6–11 (Sun 12–3, 7–10.30) Closed: 25 Dec,
BAR MEALS: Lunch served: all week Dinner served: all week
12–2 7–9.30 Av main course £7.75 **BREWERY/COMPANY:** Free
House **PRINCIPAL BEERS:** Hogs Back TEA & Hop Garden:
Gold, Badger Best, Adnams Best. **FACILITIES:** Garden: beer
garden, food served outdoors, patio

The Running Horses ⚲
Old London Rd RH5 6DU ☎ 01372 372279 ▨ 01372 363004
e-mail: info@therunninghorses.co.uk
Dir: Off A24 between Leatherhead & Dorking

Providing sustenance for travellers since the 16th century, this
inn is located opposite a Norman church in a pretty village
half a mile away from Box Hill. The bar features a
Highwayman's hideaway and an inglenook fireplace, and
these days there are five en suite bedrooms. Choices from the
menu may include fishes such as smoked haddock and sea
bass, and local venison cooked in red wine or steak and
Guinness pudding.
OPEN: 11.30–3 5.30–11 (Sun 12–3.30, 7–10.30) Closed: Dec 26
BAR MEALS: Lunch served: all week 12–2.30 Dinner served:
Mon-Sat 7–9.30 Av main course £11 **RESTAURANT:** Lunch served:
all week 12–2.30 Dinner served: Mon-Sat 7–9.30 Av 3 course à la carte
£20 **BREWERY/COMPANY:** Punch Taverns
PRINCIPAL BEERS: Fuller's London Pride, Young's Bitter, Greene
King, Adnams Bitter. **ROOMS:** 5 bedrooms 5 en suite from s£80
d£90

Dominoes
Dominoes came to Britain from the Continent at
the end of the 18th century, perhaps brought
back by British soldiers serving in the
Napoleonic Wars. French prisoners-of-war made
sets of dominoes, not only for their own
amusement but to sell to the British. Many
different varieties are played in pubs besides the
standard block game, and some pubs belong to
dominoe leagues.

---

continued

NEWDIGATE Map 04 TQ14

The Six Bells
Village St RH5 5DH ☎ 01306 631276 📠 01306 631793
Dir: 5m S of Dorking (A24), L at Beare Green rdbt, R at T-jct in village

Picturesque timber-framed pub in a quiet village location and reputedly once a smugglers' haunt. Light meals and bar snacks might include the Six Bells club sandwich and a range of baguettes and filled jacket potatoes. Daily-changing blackboard menu may offer rack of lamb and poached salmon.
OPEN: 11-3 6-11 (Sun 12-3, 7-10.30) **BAR MEALS:** Lunch served: Tue-Sun 12-2.30 Dinner served: Mon-Sat 7-9.30 Av main course £6 **RESTAURANT:** Lunch served: Tue-Sun 12-2.30 Dinner served: Tue-Sat 7-9.30 Av 3 course à la carte £20 Av 3 course fixed price £13.90 **BREWERY/COMPANY:** Free House
PRINCIPAL BEERS: Young's Bitter, Fuller's London Pride, Greene King Old Speckled Hen & IPA, Carlsberg-Tetley Tetleys Smooth.
FACILITIES: Children welcome Garden: Patio/terrace, food served outdoors Dogs allowed (water) **NOTES:** Parking 40

The Surrey Oaks
Parkgate Rd RH5 5DZ ☎ 01306 631200 📠 01306 631200
Dir: turn off either A24 or A25 and follow signs to Newdigate, The Surry Oaks is 1M E of Newdigate Village on thew roadtowards Leigh/Charwood
Parts of this country pub date from 1570, the Georgian bar has been converted into a restaurant, and there are two small, beamed bars, one with an inglenook fireplace and stone-flagged floor. It is a renowned real ale pub, and a regular CAMRA award-winner. Restaurant and bar menus offer a good range of dishes plus a daily choice from the blackboard - maybe pheasant breast with apple, sage and bacon, or sea bass with capers and prawns.
OPEN: 11.30-2.30 (Sat-Sun till 3) 5.30-11 **BAR MEALS:** Lunch served: all week 12-2 Dinner served: Tue-Sat 7-9.30 Av main course £6.95 **RESTAURANT:** Lunch served: all week 12-2 Dinner served: Tue-Sat 7.00-9.30 Av 3 course à la carte £15
BREWERY/COMPANY: Punch Taverns
PRINCIPAL BEERS: Adnams, Fuller's London Pride, Wells Bombardier. **FACILITIES:** Children welcome Garden: Beer garden, food served outdoors, patio **NOTES:** Parking 75

OCKLEY Map 04 TQ14

Pick of the Pubs

Bryce's at The Old School House ◉ 🕸 ♀
RH5 5TH ☎ 01306 627430 📠 01306 628274
e-mail: bryces.fish@virgin.net
Dir: 8m S of Dorking on A29
The eponymous Bill Bryce acquired this former boys' boarding school in 1982, converting it into a spacious bar

and restaurant. The building is 17th century and retains the original school bell. The restaurant is housed in the old school gym. The aim here is to provide the freshest fish cooked in the simplest manner - usually grilled, steamed or poached. The range of available fish is limited only by market availability, and Bill prides himself both on its freshness and the simplicity of presentation. Try the Loch Fyne queenie scallops topped with hollandaise and herb salad or home-cured gravad lax on potato pancake with dill and mustard sauce. Other options include chilli salt skate fillets, Cornish monkfish in Parma ham and galette of fresh devilled crab. In addition to fish dishes, there is a selection of bar meals - lasagne bolognese, tagliatelle and home-made egg pasta among them. Good wine list including special cellar vintages.
OPEN: 11-3 6-11 Closed: 25-26 Dec, 1 Jan
BAR MEALS: Lunch served: all week 12-2.30 Dinner served: Mon-Sat 6.30-9.30 Av main course £9 **RESTAURANT:** Lunch served: all week 12-2.30 Dinner served: Mon-Sat 7-9.30 Av 3 course fixed price £25 **BREWERY/COMPANY:** King & Barnes
PRINCIPAL BEERS: Gales HSB,GB, Butser.
FACILITIES: Children welcome Dogs allowed (water)
NOTES: Parking 25

The Kings Arms Inn 🕸
Stane St RH5 5TP ☎ 01306 711224 📠 01306 711224
Dir: From M25 J9 take A24 through Dorking towards Horsham, A29 to Ockley

Heavily beamed 16th-century village inn with welcoming log fires, a priest hole and a friendly ghost who has been responsible for some mysterious happenings. Home-made food is offered in both restaurant and bar, with dishes such as sea bass fillets with mushroom and tarragon sauce, pheasant in cream of mushroom and Armagnac sauce, cottage pie, various roasts, fresh cod in beer batter, and honey and mustard roasted lamb.
OPEN: 11-2.30 (Sun 12-3, 7-10.30) 6-11 **BAR MEALS:** Lunch served: all week Dinner served: all week 12-2 7-9 Av main course £9 **RESTAURANT:** Lunch served: Tue-Sun 12-2 Dinner served: Tue-Sat 7-9 Av 3 course à la carte £25 **BREWERY/COMPANY:** Free House
PRINCIPAL BEERS: Interbrew Flowers Original, Boddingtons, Greene King Old Speckled Hen, Wadworth 6X. **FACILITIES:** Garden: Award winning country garden **NOTES:** Parking 40
ROOMS: 6 bedrooms 6 en suite from s£50 d£70

OXTED Map 05 TQ45

George Inn ♀ NEW
High St RH8 9LP ☎ 01883 713453
A 500-year-old pub and restaurant with a friendly family atmosphere and warmed by log fires under the original oak

continued

continued

England

OXTED continued

beams. Home-made steak and kidney pudding, braised shank of lamb, sardines and salmon fillets from its seasonal menus epitomise the range of carefully sourced and well-cooked fare that is available any day. There are decent wines to accompany, with Badger beers as alternative supping. A committed team let their quality of service speak for itself.
OPEN: 11-11 **BAR MEALS:** Lunch served: all week Dinner served: all week 12-9.30 Av main course £7.50 **RESTAURANT:** Lunch served: all week Dinner served: all week 12-2.30 5-9.30
BREWERY/COMPANY: Woodhouse Inns
PRINCIPAL BEERS: Badger Tanglefoot, Best. **FACILITIES:** Children welcome Garden: Patio, food served outside Dogs allowed
NOTES: Parking 25

PIRBRIGHT   Map 04 SU95

The Royal Oak
Aldershot Rd GU24 0DQ ☎ 01483 232466
Dir: *M3 J3 take A322 towards Guildford, then A324 towards Aldershot*
Tudor cottage pub with an oak church door, stained glass windows and pew seating. In summer the garden is glorious, while in winter there are welcoming log fires in the rambling bars. No music or fruit machines. Wide choice of real ales, up to nine at any one time. Menu may include wild pink Alaskan salmon, rack of lamb, drunken duck with orange Grand Marnier and blackcurrant Cassis sauce, and leek and Caerphilly tart.
OPEN: 11-11 (Sun 12-10.30) **BAR MEALS:** Lunch served: all week Dinner served: all week 12-2 6.30-9.30 Av main course £7.25
PRINCIPAL BEERS: IPA, Boddingtons. **FACILITIES:** Garden: Food served outside, large water feature Dogs allowed (On leads only) guide dogs allowed inside **NOTES:** Parking 50

REDHILL   Map 05 TQ25

William IV Country Pub
Little Cotton Ln, Bletchingly RH1 4QF ☎ 01883 743278
Dir: *from M25 J6 take A25 towards Redhill. Turn R at top of Bletchingly High Street*
An early Victorian hostelry that comprises a traditional snug, lounge and dining-room. Located down a leafy lane past a terraced row of cottages, it is very close to the Pilgrims' Way, which traverses the North Downs. Alfresco eating in the peaceful garden is an additional summer bonus. Home-made specials dot a menu that contains some wicked lunchtime bites and accomplished special dishes that include chicken and leek pie, cheesy leek and potato bake and rib-eye steak.
OPEN: 11.30-3 6-11 (Sun 6.30-10.30) **BAR MEALS:** Lunch served: all week Dinner served: all week 12-2.15 6.45-9.30 Av main course £9
RESTAURANT: Lunch served: all week Dinner served: all week 12-2.15 6.45-9.30 Av 3 course à la carte £14
BREWERY/COMPANY: Punch Taverns
PRINCIPAL BEERS: Adnams Bitter, Young's Bitter, Greene King Old Speckled Hen, Harveys Sussex Best. **FACILITIES:** Garden: Food served outside Dogs allowed **NOTES:** Parking 10

All AA listed accommodation can also be found on the AA's internet site

www.theAA.com

STAINES   Map 04 TQ07

The Swan Hotel
The Hythe TW18 3JB ☎ 01784 452494 ▤ 01784 461593
e-mail: swan.hotel@fullers.co.uk
Dir: *Just off A308, S of Staines Bridge. 12m from M25, M4 & M3. 5m from Heathrow*

On the south bank of the Thames, by Staines Bridge, the 18th-century hotel was once used by river bargemen. Today's interior has two comfortable bars and a riverside conservatory in which to imbibe Fuller's fine ales from the nearby Chiswick brewery. Deep-filled sandwiches, baked potatoes, burgers, home-cooked ham with eggs and steak and ale pie are served in the day. Nightly main courses may include oven-baked duck breast, salmon steak and Thai vegetable red curry.
OPEN: 11-11 **BAR MEALS:** Lunch served: all week Dinner served: all week 12-3 6-9.30 Av main course £7.95 **RESTAURANT:** Lunch served: all week Dinner served: all week 12-3 6-9.30 Av 3 course £15
BREWERY/COMPANY: Fuller Smith Turner PLC
PRINCIPAL BEERS: Fullers London Pride, ESB **FACILITIES:** Children welcome, dogs allowed Garden: Overlooking River Thames, food served outside **ROOMS:** 11 en suite from s£65 d£65

VIRGINIA WATER   Map 04 TQ06

The Wheatsheaf Hotel ★ ★
London Rd GU25 4QF ☎ 01344 842057 ▤ 01344 842932
e-mail: the.wheatsheafhotel@virgin.net
The Wheatsheaf dates back to the second half of the 18th century and is beautifully situated overlooking Virginia Water on the edge of Windsor Great Park. Chalkboard menus offer a good range of freshly prepared dishes with fresh fish as a speciality. Popular options are beer battered cod and chips, roast queen fish with pesto crust, and braised lamb shank on mustard mash.
OPEN: 7-11 **BAR MEALS:** Lunch served: all week Dinner served: all week 12-10 Av main course £9 **RESTAURANT:** Lunch served: all week Dinner served: all week 12-10 Av 3 course à la carte £16
PRINCIPAL BEERS: Courage Best, Directors, Marstons Pedigree, John Smiths. **FACILITIES:** Children welcome Garden: beer garden, patio, outdoor eating **NOTES:** Parking 90 **ROOMS:** 17 bedrooms 17 en suite from s£90 d£95

WALLISWOOD   Map 04 TQ13

The Scarlett Arms
RH5 5RD ☎ 01306 627243
Dir: *S on A29 from Dorking, thru Ockley, R for Walliswood/Oakwood Hill*
Oak beams, a stone floor and a fine open fireplace give a homely feel to this unspoilt, 400-year-old rural pub. Simple country cooking is the perfect complement to the excellent King & Barnes ales on offer.

England

WARLINGHAM — Map 05 TQ35

The White Lion
CR6 9EG ☎ 01883 629011
Listed 15th-century inn with low ceilings and oak beams. The main bar area has a popular inglenook fireplace. Traditional pub grub menu.

WEST CLANDON — Map 04 TQ05

Onslow Arms 🍴 ⏺
The Street GU4 7TE ☎ 01483 222447 📄 01483 211126
Dir: A3 then A247
Dating from 1623, with an inglenook fireplace and a traditional roasting spit, this pub is convenient for both Gatwick and Heathrow airports, and even has its own helipad! There is a popular carvery plus dishes such as poached fillet of salmon with mussels, prawns and mushrooms in a white wine sauce, breast of chicken served with asparagus sauce or Scottish sirloin with pink, green and white peppers. The Cromwell Bar is a favourite with locals, and boasts eight real ales served from hand pumps.
OPEN: 11–11 (Sun 12–10.30) **BAR MEALS:** Lunch served: all week Dinner served: all week 12.15–2.30 7–10 Av main course £6.50 **RESTAURANT:** Lunch served: all week 12.30–2.15 Dinner served: Mon–Sat 7–10 Av 3 course à la carte £24 Av 3 course fixed price £14.95 **BREWERY/COMPANY:** Free House **PRINCIPAL BEERS:** Scottish Courage Courage Best, Young's Bitter, Badger King & Barnes Sussex, Fuller's London Pride.
FACILITIES: Children welcome Garden: Beer garden, patio, food served outside Dogs allowed **NOTES:** Parking 200

WEST END — Map 04 SU96

Pick of the Pubs

The Inn @ West End 🍴 ⏺
42 Guildford Rd GU24 9PW
☎ 01276 858652 📄 01276 485842
e-mail: greatfood@the-inn.co.uk
Dir: On the A322 towards Guildford 3M from J3 of the M3, just beyond the
Having successfully run a pub at nearby Windlesham for some years, Gerry and Ann Price acquired, renamed and totally refurbished this now-stylish pub/restaurant with the e-mail name. Light, modern and airy throughout, the 'Inn' has rapidly become the place to eat in the area, attracting travellers and locals alike for first class food and good wines, (Gerry and Ann also run a wine-importing business) served in a relaxed pub atmosphere. French evenings and wine tastings are a regular feature. A typical menu may offer black pudding with chicken livers, bacon and shallots or pan-fried field mushrooms on toast for starters. Follow on with aubergine ratatouille and goats' cheese mille-feuille with tomato and basil coulis or Cumberland sausages with spinach, mash and gravy, and finish up with banana and walnut bread and butter pudding or apple and almond filo parcel with a mango coulis for dessert.
OPEN: 12–3 5–11 **BAR MEALS:** Lunch served: all week Dinner served: all week 12–2.30 6–9.30 Av main course £12.50 **RESTAURANT:** Lunch served: all week Dinner served: all week 12–2.30 6–9.30 Av 3 course à la carte £22.50 **BREWERY/COMPANY:** Free House **PRINCIPAL BEERS:** Scottish Courage Courage Best, Fuller's London Pride. **FACILITIES:** Garden: **NOTES:** Parking 35

WITLEY — Map 04 SU93

The White Hart
Petworth Rd GU8 5PH ☎ 01428 683695
Dir: From A3 follow signs to Milford, then A283 towards Petworth. Pub 2m on L
16th-century coaching inn with illustrious connections. Richard II used to pub as a hunting lodge and George Elliot based characters in her novel *Middlemarch* on the clientele. Shepherd Neame.

SUSSEX, EAST

ALCISTON — Map 05 TQ50

Pick of the Pubs

Rose Cottage Inn 🍴 ⏺
BN26 6UW ☎ 01323 870377 📄 01323 871440
e-mail: ian@alciston.freeserve.co.uk
Dir: Off A27 between Eastbourne & Lewes
A fiercely traditional pub in a cul-de-sac village close to the South Downs, Rose Cottage has been in the same family ownership for some 40 years and is renowned for it home-cooked food, featuring locally supplied, seasonal fish and game. It's an ideal walkers' retreat and popular with locals looking for a quiet drink, either in the small front garden or one of the rambling rooms within. Bar menus take in salads and sausage and chips, with ploughman's at lunchtime and steaks in the evening, while the restaurant offers shank of Sussex lamb, or grilled sea bass marinated in ginger and soy sauce. Options from the specials board are casserole of Alciston rabbit in cream and mustard, half a Firle pheasant braised in Madeira, and vegetarian spinach pancakes. Comforting home-made puddings include meringues with seasonal fruit, apple pie, and cheesecake with raspberry sauce.
OPEN: 11.30–3 6.30–11 (Sun 12–3 7–10.30) Closed: 25–26 Dec **BAR MEALS:** Lunch served: all week Dinner served: all week 12–2 7–9.30 Av main course £9 **RESTAURANT:** Dinner served: Mon–Sat 7–9 Av 3 course à la carte £20 **BREWERY/COMPANY:** Free House **PRINCIPAL BEERS:** Harveys Best. **FACILITIES:** Garden: Food served outside. Grass paddock Dogs allowed (water provided) **NOTES:** Parking 25 **ROOMS:** 1 bedrooms 1 en suite from d£45

The Birds of the Air
Pride of place among bird signs is taken by the Swan, often adopted by inns close to a river. The eccentric Swan with Two Necks probably began as a swan with two nicks in its beak. The Cock may be related to cock-fighting or to St Peter. Geese and chickens appear alone or keeping dangerous company with the Fox. The Bird in Hand comes from falconry and the Dog and Duck either from fowling or from the amusement of setting a dog on a pinioned duck. The Eagle is from Heraldry and the Magpie and Stump from the countryside, while rarities include the Parrot and the Peahen.

England

ALFRISTON
Map 05 TQ50

George Inn ♀
High St BN26 5SY ☎ 01323 870319 ▤ 01323 871384
e-mail: george_inn@hotmail.com
A splendid flint and half-timbered building with 13th-century foundations and a network of smugglers' tunnels leading from its cellars. The Grade II listed inn is set in one of the area's loveliest villages, and boasts an interior featuring heavy oak beams and an ancient inglenook fireplace. The menus change regularly, with fresh ingredients going into beef braised in red wine with shallots, roasted vegetable lasagne, and sausage and mash.
OPEN: 11-11 Closed: Dec 25 **BAR MEALS:** Lunch served: all week Dinner served: all week 12-2.30 7-9 Av main course £6 **RESTAURANT:** Lunch served: all week Dinner served: all week 12-2.30 7-9 Av 3 course à la carte £25 **BREWERY/COMPANY:** Greene King **PRINCIPAL BEERS:** Greene king Old Speckled Hen, Abbot Ale, Ruddles Country,. **FACILITIES:** Children welcome Garden: Food served outside Dogs allowed **ROOMS:** 7 bedrooms 6 en suite from s£40 d£60

The Sussex Ox ⌂ ♀ NEW
Milton St BN26 5RL ☎ 01323 870840 ▤ 01323 870715
e-mail: sussexox@aol.com
Dir: Off the A27 between Polegate and Lewes, Signed to Milton Street

Idyllically situated pub, tucked away down a meandering country lane. There are two restaurants here, The Sty family room leading out to the garden, and the peaceful Front Room restaurant with candlelit tables and soft background music. Favourite food includes Sussex Ox burger, Sussex pie, fresh crab, Sussex smokie, and game in season. There are also fresh pasta dishes, curries, and loin of lamb in white onion sauce.
OPEN: 11-3 6-11 (Sun 12-3, 6-10.30) **BAR MEALS:** Lunch served: all week Dinner served: all week 12-2.30 6-9 Av main course £7 **RESTAURANT:** Lunch served: all week Dinner served: all week 12-2.30 6-9 Av 3 course à la carte £14 **BREWERY/COMPANY:** Free House **PRINCIPAL BEERS:** Hop Back Summer Lightning, Harveys Best, Youngs Bitter. **FACILITIES:** Children welcome Garden: Large, with seating,wonderful views Dogs allowed (water) **NOTES:** Parking 60

ARLINGTON
Map 05 TQ50

Old Oak Inn ⌂
BN26 6SJ ☎ 01323 482072
e-mail: arnllo@yahoo.com
Dir: N of A27 between Polegate & Lewes
Originally the village almshouse, dating from 1733, which became a pub in the early 1900s. Opposite Abbots Wood, an ideal area for walking. Typical bar dishes include filled baguettes and ploughmans, as well as pasta and curries. In

the restaurant expect the likes of roast duck, fresh grilled trout, lamb steaks in rosemary, duck with citrus and ginger, fresh salmon and crab salad, and home made steak and kidney pudding.
OPEN: 11-3 6-11 **BAR MEALS:** Lunch served: all week 12-2 Dinner served: Tue-Sat 7-9 Av main course £6.50 **RESTAURANT:** Lunch served: all week 12-2 Dinner served: Tue-Sat 7-9 Av 3 course à la carte £15 **BREWERY/COMPANY:** Free House **PRINCIPAL BEERS:** Harveys, Badger, Adnams Broadside & guest ales. **FACILITIES:** Garden: Food served outside Dogs allowed (water provided). To be kept on lead **NOTES:** Parking 30

ASHBURNHAM PLACE
Map 05 TQ61

Ash Tree Inn ⌂
Brownbread St TN33 9NX ☎ 01424 892104
The Ash Tree is a friendly old pub with three open fires, plenty of exposed beams and a traditional local atmosphere. Bar food includes ploughman's, salads and sandwiches, while the restaurant may be serving steaks, local lamb, steak and ale pie, or salmon in a variety of sauces.
OPEN: 12-4 7-11 (Summer 7-11.30) **BAR MEALS:** 12-2 7-9 Av main course £8 **RESTAURANT:** Lunch served: all week 12-2 Dinner served: Tues-Sun 7-9 Av 3 course à la carte £12 **BREWERY/COMPANY:** Free House **PRINCIPAL BEERS:** Harveys Best, Greene King Old Speckled Hen, Brakspear Bitter + guest ales. **FACILITIES:** Children welcome Garden: Dogs allowed **NOTES:** Parking 20

BARCOMBE
Map 05 TQ41

The Anchor Inn ♀
Anchor Ln BN8 5BS ☎ 01273 400414 ▤ 01273 401029
Dir: From A26 (Lewes/Uckfield rd)

In an unspoiled part of rural Sussex on the banks of the River Ouse, the Anchor started life in 1790, catering for bargees who travelled from Newhaven to Slaugham, but the last commercial barge moored here in 1861. Recently two new bars have been added using oak from a French priory. A typical meal may start with chicken and coconut wontons or kaffir lime mussels with warm ciabatta, continue with veal and wild mushroom roulade or pan-seared Barbary duck with caramelised pears, and finish up with rum and raisin pudding or lemon and orange crème brûlée.
OPEN: 11-11 (Sun 12-10.30) Closed: 25 & 31 Dec **BAR MEALS:** Lunch served: all week Dinner served: all week 12-3 6-9 Av main course £4.50 **RESTAURANT:** Lunch served: all week Dinner served: all week 12-3 6-9 Av 3 course à la carte £16.95 **BREWERY/COMPANY:** Free House **PRINCIPAL BEERS:** Harvey Best, Badger Tanglefoot. **FACILITIES:** Children welcome Garden: Patio, Beer Garden:, food served outdoors **NOTES:** Parking 300 **ROOMS:** 3 bedrooms 1 en suite from s£35 d£55

continued

BERWICK
Map 05 TQ50

Pick of the Pubs

The Cricketers Arms ♀
BN26 6SP ☎ 01323 870469 🖷 01323 871411
Dir: Off A27 between Polegate & Lewes (follow signs for Berwick
Church)

Just off the A27, this handy watering hole for walkers
hiking the South Downs Way is an unspoilt, 500-year
old building that was originally a terrace of flint cottages
that became an ale-house some 200 years ago.
Delightfully unpretentious inside, its three charming
rooms sport half-panelled walls, open fires, scrubbed
tables and a nice chatty atmosphere free from
background music, fruit machines and pool tables.
Harvey's ales tapped straight from the cask and a short
menu listing home made, traditional food such as garlic
mushrooms, local pork and chive sausages, local cod in
batter, T-bone steaks and vegetarian dishes 'prepared
by local expert'. A stunning cottage garden for use in
the summer.
OPEN: 11-3 6-11 Closed: 25 Dec **BAR MEALS:** Lunch served:
all week Dinner served: all week 12-2.15 6.30-9.00 Av main
course £6 **BREWERY/COMPANY:** Harveys of Lewes
PRINCIPAL BEERS: Harveys Best, PA + seasonal ales.
FACILITIES: Garden: Cottage style, food served outside Dogs
allowed **NOTES:** Parking 25

BLACKBOYS
Map 05 TQ52

The Blackboys Inn
Lewes Rd TN22 5LG ☎ 01825 890283
Dir: On B2192 between Holland and Heathfield
Rambling, black-weatherboarded 14th-century inn set in large
gardens overlooking an iris- and lily-covered pond. It has a
splendid beamed interior, complete with resident ghost. A
wide range of fresh home-cooked dishes is served from the
bar snack menu, restaurant carte and blackboard specials.
Expect the likes of hot seafood platter (for two), Thai lamb
salad, and fillet steak with mushroom, cream and brandy
sauce.
OPEN: 11-3 (Sun 12-3, 7-10.30) 6-11 Closed: Jan 1
BAR MEALS: Lunch served: all week Dinner served: all week
12-3.00 6.30-10.30 Av main course £6 **RESTAURANT:** Lunch
served: all week 12-1.45 Dinner served: Mon-Sat 7-10 Av 3 course à
la carte £20 **BREWERY/COMPANY:** Harveys of Lewes
PRINCIPAL BEERS: Harveys Best, Harveys Pale Bitter, Harveys
Old. **FACILITIES:** Children welcome Garden: pond, trees, food
served outside Dogs allowed in public bar (Water)
NOTES: Parking 40

BRIGHTON
Map 05 TQ30

The Greys
105 Southover St BN2 9UA ☎ 01273 680734
e-mail: mike@greyspub.com
A well-known music pub that also provides restaurant quality
food in an informal atmosphere. Live entertainment is
provided twice a week - Sunday and Monday evening - and
more often than not these events are sold out. Typical dishes
are pâté de campagne (so coarse it's nearly vulgar), coquilles
de fruits de mer, entrecôte Dijonnaise, and a vegetarian
pipperoni with cracked wheat tortilla. Finish with chocolate
Edwardian trifle, a concoction of sherry, Cognac and amaretti
biscuits.
OPEN: 11-3 5.30-11 (Sat-Sun 11-11) **BAR MEALS:** Lunch served:
Tue-Sun 12-2 Dinner served: Tue-Sat 7-9.30 Av main course £9.25
RESTAURANT: 12-2 7-9.30 Av 3 course à la carte £17.95 Av 3 course
fixed price £17 **BREWERY/COMPANY:** Whitbread
PRINCIPAL BEERS: Timothy Taylor Landlord, Itchen Valley
Godfathers. **FACILITIES:** Dogs allowed on leads **NOTES:** Parking
16 No credit cards

CHIDDINGLY
Map 05 TQ51

The Six Bells ♀
BN8 6HE ☎ 01825 872227
Dir: E of A22 between Hailsham & Uckfield(turn opp Golden Cross PH)
Inglenook fireplaces and plenty of bric-a-brac are to be found
at this large characterful free house which is where various
veteran car and motorbike enthusiasts meet on club nights.
The jury in the famous onion pie murder trial sat and
deliberated in the bar before finding the defendant guilty. Live
music at weekends. Exceptionally good value bar food
includes such dishes as shepherds pie, steak and kidney pie,
tuna pasta bake, buttered crab with salad and chicken curry
with rice.
OPEN: 11-3 6-11 **BAR MEALS:** Lunch served: all week Dinner
served: all week 11-2.30 6-10.30 Av main course £4
BREWERY/COMPANY: Free House **PRINCIPAL BEERS:** Courage
Directors, John Smiths, Harveys Best. **FACILITIES:** Children welcome
Garden: Dogs allowed **NOTES:** Parking 60

COWBEECH
Map 05 TQ61

Merrie Harriers
BN27 4JQ ☎ 01323 833108 🖷 01323 833845
e-mail: merrieharriers@talk21.com
Dir: Off A271, between Hailsham & Herstmonceux
A 17th-century clapboarded coaching inn within easy reach of
atmospheric Pevensey Levels and the fascinating
Hertsmonceux Castle and Science Park. Inside the pub are
low-beamed ceilings, a traditional high-backed settle and
open fires. Extensive lunch menu includes baked broccoli and
cauliflower cheese, Cajun chicken, and 'Sussex Smokie' (large
smoked haddock). Lighter meals range from sausages and
mash to home-cooked ham, egg and chips, and desserts
include baked lime cheesecake, banoffee pie and hot treacle
sponge pudding.
OPEN: 11.30-2.30 6.15-11 **BAR MEALS:** Lunch served: all week
Dinner served: all week 12 6.30 **RESTAURANT:** 12-2 6.30-9 Av 2
course fixed price £7.95 **BREWERY/COMPANY:** Free House
PRINCIPAL BEERS: Harveys Best, Horsham Best.
FACILITIES: Garden: Food served outside **NOTES:** Parking 20

England

England

DANEHILL   Map 05 TQ42

Pick of the Pubs

The Coach and Horses
RH17 7JF ☎ 01825 740369
Dir: *From E Grinstead travel S through Forest Row on A22 to J with A275 Lewes Road turn R on A275 for 2 M untill Danehill turn l on school lane 1/2 M pub is on the L*
A 19th-century cottagey pub built of local sandstone with former stables now forming part of the restaurant. Homely winter fires and neatly tended gardens add plenty of character and colour to the picturesque surroundings, and half-panelled walls, highly polished wooden floorboards and vaulted beamed ceilings give the place a charming, timeless feel. In an age when the traditional village local is coming under increasing threat, the Coach and Horses proves that some classic hostelries can survive in any climate. Food plays a key role in the pub's success, with a good selection of lunchtime snacks and a constantly changing evening menu. Expect grilled smoked haddock with buttered spinach and poached egg, pork and leek sausages with red wine jus and onion marmalade, and honey roast duck confit with creamed white cabbage. Leave room for a dessert, which might be iced banana parfait or vanilla crème brûlée with lemon shortbread.
OPEN: 11.30–3 6–11 **BAR MEALS:** Lunch served: all week Dinner served: all week 12–2 7–9 Av main course £8.95
RESTAURANT: Lunch served: all week Dinner served: all week 12–2 7–9 Av 3 course à la carte £17
BREWERY/COMPANY: Free House
PRINCIPAL BEERS: Harveys Best, Harveys Old Ale, Hook Norton. **FACILITIES:** Garden: Food served outside Dogs allowed (water) **NOTES:** Parking 30

DITCHLING   Map 05 TQ31

The Bull ♀
2 High St BN6 8TA ☎ 01273 843147 🖳 01273 857787
Dir: *A23 N from Brighton, then A27 E towards Lewes, after 1m turn L following signs to Ditchling*
Dating from 1569, with its first known license being given in 1636, The Bull has a long history which includes a stint as a court house. Public areas are heavily beamed and furnished with antiques.

EAST CHILTINGTON   Map 05 TQ31

Pick of the Pubs

The Jolly Sportsman ♀
Chapel Ln BN7 3BA ☎ 01273 890400 🖳 01273 890400
e-mail: thejollysportsman@mistral.co.uk
Dir: *From Lewes take Offham/Chailey rd A275, L at Offham onto B2166 towards Plumpton, take Novington Ln, after approx 1m L into Chapel Ln*
Sympathetically upgraded to a character Victorian-style dining inn by respected restaurateur Bruce Wass from Thackerays in Tunbridge Wells, this isolated pub enjoys a lovely garden setting on a quiet dead-end road looking out to the South Downs. The nearby Rectory Brewery (run by a vicar) supplies some of the beers drawn from the cask in the small atmospheric bar, with its stripped wooden floor and mix of comfortable furniture. Well

sourced food shines on daily-changing menus, served throughout the bar and smart, yet informal restaurant, from a wide range of eclectic disciplines: haggis, neeps and tatties, ciabatta with pesto, tomato and goats' cheese, and a five-cheese ploughman's rub shoulders with poached organic salmon fillet with butter sauce and Cornish mussels, cockles, winkles and clams. Fennel and mustard soup, seared herbed and spiced tuna steak, corn-fed Goosnargh chicken with oyster mushrooms and venison with braised red cabbage develop the theme. Follow with exotic fruit-filled shortbread, hot rice pudding with prunes and port, or a plate of British farmhouse cheeses.

OPEN: 12–2.30 6–11 (Sun 12–4) Closed: 25/26 Dec
BAR MEALS: Lunch served: Tue–Sun 12.30–2.30 Dinner served: Tue–Sat 7–9 Av main course £9.75 **RESTAURANT:** Lunch served: Tue–Sun 12.30–2.30 Dinner served: Tue–Sat 7–9 Av 3 course à la carte £20 Av 3 course fixed price £13.75
BREWERY/COMPANY: Free House
PRINCIPAL BEERS: Changing guest beers.
FACILITIES: Children welcome Children's licence Garden: Beer garden, patio, outdoor eating Dogs allowed
NOTES: Parking 30

EAST DEAN   Map 05 TV59

Pick of the Pubs

The Tiger Inn ♀
BN20 0DA ☎ 01323 423209 🖳 01323 423209
Dir: *Signed from A259 heading to the coast*
Rose-covered flint-built pub on the village green, popular with walkers for its real ales and home-cooked food – from steak and ale pie to whole lobster. Candle-lit in the evenings, offering an intimate and cosy environment. Quality wines are offered from a blackboard, as many as ten by the glass. In summer you can choose from 20 different ploughmans', featuring 13 English cheeses. Bookings are not taken and it can get very busy.
OPEN: 11–3 6–11 (Sat 11–11, Sun 12–10.30)
BAR MEALS: Lunch served: all week Dinner served: all week 12–2.00 6.30–9 Av main course £6
BREWERY/COMPANY: Free House
PRINCIPAL BEERS: Harvey Best, Flowers Original, Taylor Landlord, Adnams Best. **FACILITIES:** Dogs allowed No credit cards

continued

England

EWHURST GREEN
Map 05 TQ72

The White Dog Inn
Village St TN32 5TD ☎ 01580 830264
Dir: Between Staplecross & Bodiam off B2165 & B2244
A 16th-century country inn enjoying a quiet village location
with splendid views across the Rother Valley to Bodiam Castle.
Homely bar and restaurant with polished tiled floors and
inglenook fireplace.

EXCEAT
Map 05 TV59

The Golden Galleon 🐄 ⟡
Exceat Bridge BN25 4AB ☎ 01323 892247 🗎 01323 892555
e-mail: stef@goldengalleon.co.uk
Dir: On A259, 1.5m E of Seaford

Real ale on tap at this popular 18th-century inn comes from
the pub's own micro-brewery - Cuckmere Haven Brewery, as
well as up to eight other breweries. The inn is believed to
have inspired Rudyard Kipling's 'Song of the Smugglers'. A
wide-ranging menu includes dishes such as pork loin in a
ginger and honey glaze, garlic and wine mussels, wild
mushroom and truffle spaghetti, and some excellent pizzas.
OPEN: 10.30-11 (closed Sun evening Sep-May)
BAR MEALS: Lunch served: all week 12-2 Dinner served: Mon-Sat
6-9 Av main course £7 **RESTAURANT:** Lunch served: all week
12-2.30 Dinner served: Mon-Sat 6-9 Av 3 course à la carte £15
BREWERY/COMPANY: Free House
PRINCIPAL BEERS: Cuckmere Haven, Harvey, Greene King.
FACILITIES: Children welcome Garden: Food served outside, patio
& grass area Dogs allowed **NOTES:** Parking 60

FIRLE
Map 05 TQ40

The Ram Inn ⟡
BN8 6NS ☎ 01273 858222
e-mail: michael@thecusp.fsnet.co.uk
Dir: R off A27 3m E of Lewes

The inn is part of the Firle Estate, seat of the Gage family who
recently celebrated 500 years of occupancy. The oldest part of
the Ram dates from 1542, and though added to many times,
boasting 18 rooms and 14 staircases, it has changed little in
many years - note the original red lino on the bar floor. Food
ranges through baguettes and jacket potatoes to fish and
chips, steak and kidney pudding, and vegetarian specials.
OPEN: 11.30-11 (Sun 12-10.30) **BAR MEALS:** Lunch served: all
week Dinner served: all week 12-9 **BREWERY/COMPANY:** Free
House **PRINCIPAL BEERS:** Harveys Best plus regular changing ales.
FACILITIES: Children welcome Children's licence Garden: Food
served outside, play area Dogs allowed (water) **NOTES:** Parking 10

FLETCHING
Map 05 TQ42

Pick of the Pubs

The Griffin Inn 🐄 ⟡
TN22 3SS ☎ 01825 722890 🗎 01825 722810
*Dir: M23 J10 to East Grinstead then A22 then A275. Village signed on
L. 10m from M23*

In an unspoilt country village close to the Ashdown Forest,
this fine pub makes best use of its location and the two-
acre garden, with its south-facing sheltered terrace, comes
into its own on warm summer days. Old beams, wainscot
walls, open fires and a motley collection of old pews and
wheel-back chairs characterise the main bar that leads to
a separate locals' bar and a prettily decorated rear
restaurant. Both the restaurant and bar menus change
daily, with an emphasis on freshly prepared, locally
sourced foodstuffs - much of it organic. Fish from
Newhaven is delivered daily, and might include diver-
caught king scallops, roasted halibut fillet on curried
coconut leeks, skate wings with tomato and onion salsa or
smoked haddock brandade with spinach and poached
egg. Traditional Sunday lunch is an excellent showpiece
with home produced puddings served with real ales and
fine wines. The refurbished en suite bedrooms are now
quoted as 'up to speed - whatever happened to scratch?'!
OPEN: 12-3 6-11 Closed: 25 Dec **BAR MEALS:** Lunch served:
all week Dinner served: all week 12-2.30 7-9.30 Av main course
£8.50 **RESTAURANT:** Lunch served: all week Dinner served:
Mon-Sat 12.15-2.30 7.15-9.30 Av 3 course à la carte £25
BREWERY/COMPANY: Free House
PRINCIPAL BEERS: Harvey Best, Badger Tanglefoot, Thomas
Hardy Hardy Country. **FACILITIES:** Children welcome Garden:
2 large lawns, food served outside Dogs allowed
NOTES: Parking 20 **ROOMS:** 8 bedrooms 8 en suite from
s£50 d£85

continued

England

GUN HILL
Map 05 TQ51

The Gun Inn
TN21 0JU ☎ 01825 872361 📠 01825 873081
Dir: *From A22 London-Eastbourne, Golden Cross (3m N of Hailsham) L past Esso station, 1.5m down lane on L*

Originally a 15th-century farmhouse, the Gun Inn is situated in a tiny hamlet amid rolling Sussex countryside. It got its name from the cannon foundries that were located at Gun Hill. The pub also served as the courthouse for hearings in the 'Onion Pie Murder', a local crime of passion. Resplendent in summer with its pretty gardens and flower-adorned façade, it offers fresh grilled plaice, steak and kidney pie, smoked haddock in cheese and mustard sauce, and seafood platter. No onion pie.
OPEN: 11.30-3 6-11 (Sun Close10:30) Closed: Dec 25-26
BAR MEALS: Lunch served: all week Dinner served: all week 12-2 6-9.30 Av main course £7 **BREWERY/COMPANY:** Free House
PRINCIPAL BEERS: Wadworth 6X, Adnams Best, Harvey Best.
FACILITIES: Children welcome Children's licence Garden: Food served outside Dogs allowed (water provided) **NOTES:** Parking 55

HARTFIELD
Map 05 TQ43

Anchor Inn
Church St TN7 4AG ☎ 01892 770424
Dir: *On B2110*
On the edge of Ashdown Forest, at the heart of 'Winnie the Pooh' country, stands this old inn dating back to the 14th-century, complete with stone floors and a large inglenook. A couple of en suite bedrooms are an added draw for walkers and Pooh fans alike. Sandwiches, ploughman's, baked potatoes are among the bar snacks or try Tandoori spare ribs and prawn and mango curry for a starter or snack and main dishes such as venison steak with port and redcurrant sauce.
OPEN: 11-11 **BAR MEALS:** Lunch served: all week Dinner served: all week 12-2 6-10 Av main course £6 **RESTAURANT:** Lunch served: all week 12-2 Dinner served: Tue-Sat 7-9.30 Av 3 course à la carte £20 Av 3 course fixed price £20 **BREWERY/COMPANY:** Free House
PRINCIPAL BEERS: Fuller's London Pride, Harveys Best, Interbrew Flowers IPA, Flowers Original & Bass. **FACILITIES:** Children welcome Garden: Food served outdoors Dogs allowed (water)
NOTES: Parking 30 **ROOMS:** 2 bedrooms 2 en suite from s£40 d£60

Do you have a favourite pub
that we have overlooked?
Please use the Reader's Report forms at
the back of this guide to tell us all about it.

Pick of the Pubs

The Hatch Inn
Coleman's Hatch TN7 4ET
☎ 01342 822363 📠 01342 822363
e-mail: Nilkad@bigfoot.com
Dir: *A22 14 iles, L at Forest Row rdbt, follow for 3 miles until Colemans Hatch and turn R*

Classic 15th-century inn which was originally a row of three cottages reputed to date back to 1430 and thought to have been built to house workers at the local water-driven hammer mill. Previously known as the Cock Inn, the Hatch takes its name from the original coalman's gate leading onto Ashdown Forest. Frequently seen on television in various dramas and adverts and possibly a haunt of smugglers at one time, the inn is only minutes away from the famous, restored Pooh Bridge, immortalised in A.A. Milne's Winne the Pooh stories. Good quality food includes fresh grilled Dover sole with lemon and parsley butter, chargrilled ostrich steak with a timbale of braised red cabbage and wild mushroom sauce, and home-made steak and kidney pie with shortcrust pastry.
OPEN: 11.30-3 5.30-11 (Open all day Sun Open all day Sat May-Sept) Closed: Dec 25 **BAR MEALS:** Lunch served: all week 12-2.30 Dinner served: Tue-Sat 7-9.15 Av main course £8 **RESTAURANT:** Lunch served: all week 12-2.30 Dinner served: Tue-Sat 7-9.15 Av 3 course à la carte £25
BREWERY/COMPANY: Free House
PRINCIPAL BEERS: Harveys, Fuller's London Pride,.
FACILITIES: Garden: Beer garden, food served outdoors, terrace Dogs allowed (water)

HEATHFIELD
Map 05 TQ25

Three Cups Inn
Three Cups TN21 9LR ☎ 01435 830252
Unspoilt rural pub dating from 1700. Located on a ridge in the High Weald, close to many good walks. Bar food.

ICKLESHAM
Map 05 TQ18

Pick of the Pubs

The Queen's Head
Parsonage Ln TN36 4BL ☎ 01424 814552 📠 01424 814766
Dir: *Between Hastings & Rye on A259*
There's always a warm welcome beneath the high beamed ceilings of this distinctive, tile-hung pub, which is renowned for its hearty home-cooked meals and good selection of well-kept ales. The 17th-century building has

continued

been licensed since 1831 and enjoys spectacular views across the Brede Valley to the historic town of Rye. Large inglenook fireplaces, church pews and a clutter of old farm implements all add to the relaxed character of this bustling, independent free house. A full menu is served all day at weekends and the printed selection is supplemented by fresh fish and daily specials listed on the blackboard. Meals range from ploughman's to fillet steak, and there is a popular daily curry. Typical dishes include home-made soup, pâté, or soft herring roes on toast as starters, and main courses of steak, ale and mushroom pie, or a vegetarian sticky rice with wild mushrooms.
OPEN: 11–11 (Sun 12–10.30) **BAR MEALS:** Lunch served: all week Dinner served: all week 12–2.45 6.15–9.45 Av main course £6.95 **RESTAURANT:** Lunch served: all week Dinner served: all week **BREWERY/COMPANY:** Free House **PRINCIPAL BEERS:** Rother Valley Level Best, Greene King Abbot Ale, Ringwood Old Thumper, Woodforde Wherry. **FACILITIES:** Children welcome Garden: Beer garden, BBQ, food served outdoors **NOTES:** Parking 50

KINGSTON (NEAR LEWES) Map 05 TQ30

The Juggs ♀
The Street BN7 3NT ☎ 01273 472523 📠 01273 483274
Dir: E of Brighton on A27
Named after the women who walked from Brighton with baskets of fish for sale, this rambling, tile-hung 15th-century cottage, tucked beneath the South Downs, offers an interesting selection of freshly cooked food.
OPEN: 11–3 6–11 (11–11 summer) **BAR MEALS:** Lunch served: all week Dinner served: all week 12–2 6–9.30 Av main course £6.95 **RESTAURANT:** Lunch served: all week Dinner served: all week 12–2 6–9.30 Av 3 course à la carte £15 **BREWERY/COMPANY:** Shepherd Neame **PRINCIPAL BEERS:** Harveys Beer. **FACILITIES:** Children welcome Garden: Patio, beer garden, food served outdoors Dogs allowed on lead **NOTES:** Parking 30

LEWES Map 05 TQ41

The Snowdrop ♀
South St BN7 2BU ☎ 01273 471018

In 1836 this was the site of the UK's biggest avalanche. Hence the pub's deceptively gentle name. Proudly vegetarian for over ten years, the menu offers constantly changing specials, including Sunday roasts. Entertainment is a big feature here, from jazz on a Monday evening, or bands on a Saturday night, to the annual 'Alternative Miss Snowdrop' contest.
OPEN: 11–11 Closed: 25 Dec **BAR MEALS:** Lunch served: all week Dinner served: all week 12–3 6–9 Av main course £5.95 **BREWERY/COMPANY:** Free House **PRINCIPAL BEERS:** Harveys Best, Summer Lightning, Old Thumper. No credit cards

---

LITLINGTON Map 05 TQ50

Plough & Harrow
BN26 5RE ☎ 01323 870632 📠 01323 870632
Dir: S of A27 between Lewes & Polegate
Gloriously situated on the edge of the South Downs, this Grade II listed thatched building lies in a small village on the scenic Cuckmere Haven. Only minutes from historic Alfriston and the Sussex coast. Good, wholesome pub fare includes ploughman's, home-made pie, fresh cod, quiche, Litlington beef, steak and swordfish.
OPEN: 11–3 6–11 (Sun 12–3, 7–10.30) **BAR MEALS:** Lunch served: all week Dinner served: all week 12–2.30 6.30–9.30 Av main course £8.95 **RESTAURANT:** Lunch served: all week Dinner served: all week 12–2.30 6.30–9.30 Av 3 course à la carte £18 **BREWERY/COMPANY:** Free House **PRINCIPAL BEERS:** Harveys Best, Badger Best & Tanglefoot. **FACILITIES:** Children welcome Garden: Beer garden, outdoor eating Dogs allowed not in restaurant **NOTES:** Parking 50

MAYFIELD Map 05 TQ52

Pick of the Pubs

The Middle House 🍴 ♀
High St TN20 6AB ☎ 01435 872146 📠 01435 873423
Dir: E of A267, S of Tunbridge Wells

Listed Grade I and described as 'one of the finest timber framed buildings in Sussex', the Middle House was built in 1575 for Sir Thomas Gresham, founder of the London Stock Exchange. It is a fine example of Elizabethan architecture whose charms include wattle and daub, a restaurant panelled with carved oak and a Grinling Gibbons fireplace in the lounge. Outside, attractive south-facing gardens look over the vale of Heathfield. Dine in the relaxing bar, where many fine ales are served on draught and the inglenook fireplace provides a weekly spit roast, or in the smart restaurant. Here, the menu offers dishes ranging from traditional favourites - perhaps steak, Guinness and mushroom pie or chargrilled sirloin with pepper sauce - through to internationally inspired dishes such as Cajun marinated chicken with rice noodles, nacho chips and Cajun cream sauce or Thai chicken curry with noodles and crispy leeks.
OPEN: 11–11 **BAR MEALS:** Lunch served: all week Dinner served: all week 12–2.30 7–9.30 Av main course £9 **RESTAURANT:** Lunch served: all week Dinner served: all week 12–2 7–9.30 Av 3 course à la carte £24.50 Av 3 course fixed price £19.95 **BREWERY/COMPANY:** Free House **PRINCIPAL BEERS:** Harvey Best, Greene King Abbott Ale, Black Sheep Best, Theakston Best. **FACILITIES:** Children welcome Garden: Food served outside **NOTES:** Parking 25 **ROOMS:** 6 bedrooms 6 en suite from s£45 d£65

MAYFIELD continued

Rose & Crown Inn
Fletching St TN20 6TE ☎ 01435 872200 📠 01435 872200
Attractive 16th-century village inn with splendid front patio
and a rambling interior with low beams, open fires and an
unspoilt atmosphere. Consult the blackboard for the day's
selection of fresh fish or home-made dishes such as fishcakes,
shank of lamb or Thai-style steak. For a lighter snack, try a
Sussex Smokie, or an Italian ciabatta sandwich.
OPEN: 11–3 5.30–11 (Sun 12–10.30) **BAR MEALS:** Lunch served:
Mon-Sat 12–2.30 Av main course £6.25 **RESTAURANT:** Lunch
served: Tue-Sat Dinner served: Tue–Sat 12–2 7–9 Av 3 course à la carte
£20 **PRINCIPAL BEERS:** Harveys Sussex Best, Youngs Special.
FACILITIES: Children welcome Garden: Dogs allowed (not in
restaurant) **NOTES:** Parking 15 **ROOMS:** 4 bedrooms 4 en suite
from s£39.95 d£59.95

OFFHAM
Map 05 TQ14

The Blacksmith's Arms
London Rd BN7 3QD ☎ 01273 472971
A busy 200-year-old roadside pub with a reputation for good
local produce freshly cooked by its chefs. Pan-fried venison
steak on a honeyed parsnip mash; Sussex smokie; duck and
pheasant pâté with gooseberry and apple chutney;
mushroom, cranberry and Brie in a filo pastry parcel; and
roasted tuna loin steak on sun dried tomato and olive confit
demonstrate the versatility of the kitchen. Tempting dessert
menu.
OPEN: 12–3 6.30–11 Closed: Dec 25-26 **BAR MEALS:** Lunch served:
all week 12–2.30 Dinner served: Mon-Sat 7–9 Av main course £9
RESTAURANT: Lunch served: all week 12–2 Dinner served: Mon–Sat
7–9 Av 3 course à la carte £17.50 **BREWERY/COMPANY:** Free House
PRINCIPAL BEERS: Harveys Ales. **FACILITIES:** Garden: Food
served outside. Patio area Dogs allowed **NOTES:** Parking 22

OLD HEATHFIELD
Map 05 TQ52

Pick of the Pubs

Star Inn
Church St TN21 9AH ☎ 01435 863570 📠 01435 862020
e-mail: heathfieldstar@cs.com
Dir: Take A21 from M25 towards Hawkhurst, R towards Broadoak, L
to Battle (B267), R into Heathfield
Built as an inn for the stonemasons who constructed the
church in the 14th century, this creeper-clad, honey-stone
building has a wonderful, award-winning summer garden
that abounds with colourful flowers and unusual picnic
benches and affords impressive views across the High
Weald; a view once painted by Turner. Equally appealing
is the atmospheric, low-beamed main bar with its huge
inglenook fireplace and cosy dining ambience. Good bar
food focuses on fresh fish from Billingsgate or direct from
boats in Hastings. Specialities include cod and chips, red
mullet served with squid ink linguine, large cock crabs,
bouillabaisse and mussels in wine, garlic and cream. For
those favouring meat, you will find home-made steak and
kidney pie, marinated duck breast, Highland steaks and
local venison on menu. Generous ploughman's lunches
and excellent Harveys and Shepherd Neame brews on
handpump.
OPEN: 11.30–3 5.30–11 **BAR MEALS:** Lunch served: all week
Dinner served: all week 12–2.15 7–9.30 Av main course £7
RESTAURANT: Lunch served: all week Dinner served: all week

12–2.15 7–9.30 Av 3 course à la carte £20
BREWERY/COMPANY: Free House
PRINCIPAL BEERS: Harvey Best, Shepherds Neame, Master
Brew, Bishops Finger. **FACILITIES:** Children welcome Garden:
picnic tables, Food served outside Dogs allowed
NOTES: Parking 20

POYNINGS
Map 05 TQ21

Royal Oak Inn ♀ NEW
The Street BN45 7AQ ☎ 01273 857389 📠 01273 857787
Dir: N on the A23 just outside Brighton, take the A281 (signed for Henfield
& Poynings), then follow signs into Poynings village
Nestling at the foot of the South Downs, close to the famous
Devil's Dyke, this white-painted village pub is popular on
summer weekends for its excellent barbecue facilities. Also
very popular with walkers, it offers good ales and a varied
menu, including the Poynings (pronounced Punnings locally)
grill, bangers and mash, poached fillet of salmon Hollandaise,
chicken, leek and mushroom pie, and a variety of sandwiches,
baked potatoes and ploughman's.
OPEN: 11–11 (Sun 12–10.30) **BAR MEALS:** Lunch served: all week
Dinner served: all week 12–2.30 6–9.30 Av main course £7.50
BREWERY/COMPANY: Free House **PRINCIPAL BEERS:** Harveys
Sussex, Courage Directors, Greene King Morland Old Speckled Hen.
FACILITIES: Children welcome Garden: Beer garden, outdoor
eating, patio, Dogs allowed **NOTES:** Parking 35

RINGMER
Map 05 TQ41

The Cock ♀
Uckfield Rd BN8 5RX ☎ 01273 812040 📠 01273 812040
Dir: On A26 approx 2m N of Lewes(not in Ringmer village)

This atmospheric old inn has been a thriving meeting place
since the 16th-century and was a mustering point during the
Civil War siege of Arundel. With its 40-seater restaurant added
in the mid-1980s, it offers today a warm welcome. The same
menu is served throughout with main dishes and house
specials such as salmon in cream and watercress sauce,
Florentine chicken in cheese sauce and spinach, Ricotta and
chestnut parcels to follow perhaps deep fried Brie or
marinated anchovies.
OPEN: 11–3 6–11 Closed: Dec 25 **BAR MEALS:** Lunch served: all
week Dinner served: all week 12–2 6.30–9.30 Av main course £7.50
RESTAURANT: Lunch served: all week 12–2
6.30–9.30 Av 3 course à la carte £15 **BREWERY/COMPANY:** Free
House **PRINCIPAL BEERS:** Harveys Best, Old & Mild, Greene King
Ruddles County, Fuller's London Pride. **FACILITIES:** Children
welcome Garden: Food served outdoors, terrace Dogs allowed Dog
chews **NOTES:** Parking 20

continued

RUSHLAKE GREEN · Map 05 TQ61

Horse & Groom ♀
TN21 9QE ☎ 01435 830320 📠 01435 830320
e-mail: chappellhatpeg@aol.com
Grade II listed building on the village green with pleasant views from the well-cultivated gardens. Dishes are offered from blackboard menus in the cosy bars. Steak, kidney and Guinness pudding and smoked salmon with home-made tagliatelle are favourites, along with the excellent fresh fish choice - perhaps monkfish in filo with vanilla and ginger or fresh loin of tuna on Bombay potatoes with lime and coriander dressing.
OPEN: 11.30-3 5.30-11 **BAR MEALS:** Lunch served: all week Dinner served: all week 12-2.30 7-9.30 Av main course £11
RESTAURANT: Lunch served: all week Dinner served: all week 12-2.30 7-9.30 Av 3 course à la carte £22 **BREWERY/COMPANY:** Free House
PRINCIPAL BEERS: Harveys Master Brew, Shepherd Neame Spitfire.
FACILITIES: Children welcome Garden: Food served outside Dogs allowed **NOTES:** Parking 20

RYE · Map 05 TQ92

Pick of the Pubs

Mermaid Inn ★ ★ ★ ☺ ☜ ♀
Mermaid St TN31 7EY ☎ 01797 223065 📠 01797 225069
e-mail: mermaidinnrye@btclick.com
Destroyed by the French in 1377 and rebuilt in 1420, this famous smugglers' inn is steeped in history. Timbers hewn from ancient ships' timbers, secret passageways and log fires are all part of the enchantment, and the Giant's Fireplace Bar has a priest hole as well as its enormous inglenook. Both traditional bar food and restaurant fare are offered, favourites including pan-fried crab cakes; baked tomato, pesto and olive tart, and steak and kidney pudding.
OPEN: 11-11 (Sun 12-11) **BAR MEALS:** Lunch served: all week 12-2.15 Dinner served: Sun-Fri 7-9.15 Av main course £8
RESTAURANT: Lunch served: all week Dinner served: all week 12-2.15 7-9.15 Av 3 course à la carte £32
BREWERY/COMPANY: Free House
PRINCIPAL BEERS: Greene King Old Speckled Hen, Scottish Courage Courage Best. **FACILITIES:** Children welcome Garden: Patio, food served outside, fountain **NOTES:** Parking 26
ROOMS: 31 bedrooms 31 en suite from s£70 d£140

Pick of the Pubs

The Ypres Castle Inn ☜ ♀
Gun Garden TN31 7HH ☎ 01797 223248
An attractive weather boarded building, dating in part from 1640, the Ypres Castle is in a wonderful location next to the 13th-century Ypres Tower and Gun Gardens, with views to the coast and marshes. The inn is named after Sir John Ypres and was once something of a smuggling centre. Regular Friday live music nights are a draw, featuring local and regional blues, jazz and rock bands. There's a large garden including a boules pitch, and inside traditional pub games like shove ha'penny are available. A good range of beers includes Harveys, Youngs, Adnams, Bass and Bombardier, and seafood is well represented on the carte, with grilled Rye Bay plaice, Dungeness crab, and fresh cod in home-made beer batter. Other options are rack of salt marsh lamb with mint and redcurrant glaze, or Gloucester Old Spot pork

continued

steak with apple and cider sauce. A full bar menu is also available at lunchtime.
OPEN: 12-11 (Jan-Mar Mon-Fri 12-3, 6-11, Sat 12-4 6-11 Sun 12-4, 7-10.30) **BAR MEALS:** Lunch served: all week Dinner served: all week 12-2.30 7-10.30 Av main course £8
RESTAURANT: Lunch served: all week Dinner served: all week 12-2.30 7-10.30 Av 3 course à la carte £18
BREWERY/COMPANY: Free House
PRINCIPAL BEERS: Harveys Best, Youngs, Adnams Broadside, Bass. **FACILITIES:** Children welcome Garden: Food served outside Dogs allowed (water)

THREE LEG CROSS · Map 05 TQ63

The Bull
Dunster Mill Ln TN5 7HH ☎ 01580 200586 📠 01580 201289
Dir: *From M5 exit at Sevenoaks toward Hastings, R at x-rds onto B2087, R onto B2099 through Ticehurst, R for Three Legged Cross*

In a peaceful hamlet setting, the Bull is a real country pub, with oak beams and large open fires, based around a Wealden hall house built around 1385. Food choice ranges from Shrewsbury lamb and Javanese beef, to venison in red wine, poached salmon, and vegetable and leek crumble.
OPEN: 11-11 Closed: Dec 25, 26 (evening) **BAR MEALS:** 11-2.30 6.30-9.30 **RESTAURANT:** 11-2.30 6.30-9.30
BREWERY/COMPANY: Free House **PRINCIPAL BEERS:** Harveys, Interbrew Bass. **FACILITIES:** Children welcome Garden: Duck pond, play area, food served outside Dogs allowed **NOTES:** Parking 80 **ROOMS:** 4 bedrooms 4 en suite from s£30 d£50

UPPER DICKER · Map 05 TQ50

The Plough ☜ ♀
Coldharbour Rd BN27 3QJ ☎ 01323 844859
Dir: *Off A22, W of Hailsham*
Following major refurbishment this 17th-century former farmhouse, which has been a pub for over 200 year, now comprises two bars and two restaurants. Excellent wheelchair facilities, a large beer garden and a children's play area add to the appeal, and the Plough is also a handy stop for walkers. Expect such fish dishes as whole baked lemon trout, salmon and sea bass, while other options include shoulder of lamb, honey roast duck and mushroom, leek and Stilton bake.
OPEN: 11-3 6-11 (Sun 11-3, 7-10.30, Summer wknd 11-11)
BAR MEALS: Lunch served: all week Dinner served: all week 12-2.30 6.30-9.30 Av main course £8 **RESTAURANT:** Lunch served: all week Dinner served: all week 12-2.30 6.30-9.30 Av 3 course à la carte £16 **BREWERY/COMPANY:** Shepherd Neame
PRINCIPAL BEERS: Shepherd Neame Spitfire Premium Ale, Best & Bishop's Finger. **FACILITIES:** Children welcome Garden: Food served outdoors Dogs allowed **NOTES:** Parking 40

WARBLETON
Map 05 TQ61

The Warbill in Tun Inn
Church Hill TN21 9BD ☎ 01435 830636 🖹 01435 830636
e-mail: warbillintun@ic24.net
The pub is approximately 400 years old - maybe more - and was long associated with the smuggling trade. Brian Epstein owned a house nearby, and the Beatles often used to visit. Old locals tell tales of meetings with Lennon, McCartney and others, including the resident ghost. Beers fielded are Harvey's Sussex Best, Shepherd Neame's Bishops Finger, Everard's Tiger and guests, and as far as food is concerned, steaks are a speciality, and home-made dishes like double lamb chops.
OPEN: 12–3 7–11 **BAR MEALS:** Lunch served: all week Dinner served: all week 12–1.45 7–9.30 Av main course £4.95
RESTAURANT: Lunch served: all week Dinner served: all week 12–1.45 7–9.30 Av 3 course à la carte £12
BREWERY/COMPANY: Free House **PRINCIPAL BEERS:** Harveys Best, Crown Inn Ironmaster, Warbleton Winter Ale.
FACILITIES: Children welcome Garden: Beer garden Dogs allowed (water) **NOTES:** Parking 20

WINCHELSEA
Map 05 TQ91

The New Inn
German St TN36 4EN ☎ 01797 226252
Rambling 18th-century inn of some character enjoying a delightful village setting close to Rye and the Sussex coast. Georgian decor; fine views; bedrooms.

WITHYHAM
Map 05 TQ43

Pick of the Pubs

The Dorset Arms
TN7 4BD ☎ 01892 770278 🖹 01892 770195
e-mail: jep@dorset-arms.co.uk
See Pick of the Pubs on page 467

SUSSEX, WEST

AMBERLEY
Map 04 TQ01

Black Horse
High St, Amberley BN18 9NL ☎ 01798 831552
A traditional tavern with a lively atmosphere, in a beautiful South Downs village. There is a display of sheep bells donated by the last shepherd to have a flock on the local hills. Good food served in the large restaurant and bar, including extensive vegetarian choice and children's menu. Expect rack of lamb, beef Wellington, and salmon steak with a lime and hollandaise sauce. Lovely gardens, and good local walks.
OPEN: 11–11 (Sun 12–10.30) **BAR MEALS:** Lunch served: all week Dinner served: all week 12–3 6–9 Av main course £10
PRINCIPAL BEERS: Greene King Old Speckled Hen, Carlsberg-Tetley Friary Meux Bitter. **FACILITIES:** Garden: Food served outdoors

The Bridge Inn
Houghton Bridge BN18 9LR ☎ 01798 831619
Dir: 5m N of Arundel on B2139
The Bridge Inn dates from 1650, and has a Grade II listing. It is very popular with cyclists and walkers, and is only a two minute walk from the Amberley chalk pits and museum. Special features are the open fires and display of original oil

and watercolour paintings. Campers can arrange pitches in the garden. The menu offers a comprehensive fish choice plus dishes such as braised lamb shank, rack of pork ribs, leek and Stilton crepes, and Lincolnshire sausage.
OPEN: 11–11 (Sun 12–10.30) **BAR MEALS:** Lunch served: all week Dinner served: all week 12–2.30 7–9.30 Av main course £9.50
RESTAURANT: Lunch served: See bar Dinner served: See bar 12–2.30 7–9.30 Av 3 course à la carte £17
BREWERY/COMPANY: Free House **PRINCIPAL BEERS:** Flowers Original, Harveys Sussex, Fullers London Pride, Tanglefoot.
FACILITIES: Children welcome Garden: Food served outside. Well kept garden Dogs allowed (water provided) **NOTES:** Parking 20

ARDINGLY
Map 07 TQ32

The Gardeners Arms
Selsfield Rd RH17 6TJ ☎ 01444 892328 🖹 01444 892331
e-mail: gardenersarms.ardingly.wi@freshnet.co.uk
Dir: On B2028 between Haywards Heath and Turners Hill, follow signs to Wakehurst Place

Reputedly the home of a former magistrate who often conducting hangings on the front lawn, this pub dates back over 400 years. No such grisly scenes today in the inviting interior with its open fires, oak beams and panelling, antique furniture, and charming nooks and crannies. Straightforward bar food, grills and blackboard specials produce steak, mushroom and ale pie, Sussex smokies with prawns and cheese sauce and roast aubergine with Mediterranean vegetables, hearty bread and butter pudding, and rhubarb and apple crumble.
OPEN: 11.30–3 6–11 **BAR MEALS:** Lunch served: all week Dinner served: all week 12–2 6.30–9.30 Av main course £9.95
RESTAURANT: Lunch served: all week Dinner served: all week 12–2 6.30–9.30 Av 3 course à la carte £18.50
BREWERY/COMPANY: Woodhouse Inns
PRINCIPAL BEERS: Badger Best, Tanglefoot, Champion Ale, Sussex Bitter. **FACILITIES:** Garden: Patios, food served outside Dogs allowed (water) **NOTES:** Parking 60

Bar Billiards
The ingenious blend of billiards and skittles is a relative newcomer to the pub scene. It was introduced here from Belgium in the 1930s, with support from billiard table manufacturers. The game caught on rapidly, especially in the South and Midlands, and leagues had been organised by the time the Second World War began. Its much more recent rival is pool, which came here from America in the 1960s in the wake of the Paul Newman film The Hustler.

---

continued

OPEN: 11.30-3 5.30-11
BAR MEALS: L served all week.
D served Tue-Sat. 12-2 7.30-9.30
Av main course £6.50
RESTAURANT: L served all week.
D served Tue-Sat. 12-2 7.30-9.30
Av cost 3 course £16.50
BREWERY/COMPANY: HARVEYS
OF LEWES
PRINCIPLE BEERS: Harveys
Sussex Best & seasonal beers
FACILITIES: Dogs allowed. Garden:
Patio, food served outdoors
NOTES: Parking 20

The Dorset Arms

Historic, white weather-boarded 15th-century inn on the borders of Kent and Sussex close to Ashdown Forest and Royal Tunbridge Wells. Although the building itself dates from around the reigns of Henry VI and Edward IV, the name comes from the arms of the Sackville family from nearby Buckhurst Park.

TN7 4BD
☎ 01892 770278 📄 01892 770195
e-mail: jep@dorset-arms.co.uk
Dir: 4m W of Tunbridgewells on B2110 between Groombridge and Hartfield.

Records show that it became an inn by the turn of the 18th century, prior to which it would have been an open-halled farmhouse with soot-covered rafters and an earthen floor. Many interesting Tudor and later period features remain, such as the massive wall and ceiling beams in the restaurant, an ice cave buried in the hillside behind the pub, and a bar with Sussex oak floor and magnificent open log fire. In these splendid surroundings visitors might understandably ""expect some decent food, and they would not be disappointed. There's plenty of choice, from the tempting blackboard specials to the wide-ranging bar menu, a fixed-price dining room menu, and another one for

Sunday lunch. Eat in style with starters like chicken liver pâté, smoked salmon, or breaded Camembert with port and redcurrant jelly, then move on to the likes of steak Tournedos, escalope of veal with mushrooms in Marsala sauce, or king prawns in garlic and wine. Specials such as crispy-topped cottage pie, barbecued chicken breast, and lamb chop in a rich Shrewsbury sauce might entice diners away from light meals like spinach and feta goujons, or cod and chips. The home-made desserts are for irresistible for everyone: meringues with pears and chocolate sauce, steamed raisin and apple pudding, and luxury bread and butter pudding offer the same good value as the rest of the food. Locally brewed real ales of quality from Harveys Brewery in Lewes are always available.

England

ASHURST
Map 04 TQ11

The Fountain Inn 🛏 ♀
BN44 3AP ☎ 01403 710219 📠 01403 710219
Dir: On B2135 N of Steyning
A 16th-century free house located in a peaceful village. Local resident Laurence Olivier frequented the pub and Paul McCartney made the video for 'White Christmas' in the bar. The Fountain has its own 16th-century cider press used for apple pressing and scrumpy-making. Sample Sussex smokie, grilled goats' cheese salad or chargrilled fillet of salmon or sea bass, and finish with sticky toffee pudding or French apple tart.
OPEN: 11.30–2.30 6–11 (Sun 12–3, 7–10.30) **BAR MEALS:** Lunch served: all week 11.30–2 Dinner served: Tue–Sat 6–9.30 Av main course £8.95 **BREWERY/COMPANY:** Free House
PRINCIPAL BEERS: Harveys Sussex, Shepherd Neame Master Brew, Fullers London Pride Adnams Best, Black Sheep Best.
FACILITIES: Garden: Food served outside, large garden Dogs allowed (water provided) **NOTES:** Parking 50 No credit cards

BILLINGSHURST
Map 04 TQ02

The Blue Ship
The Haven RH14 9BS ☎ 01403 822709
Victorian brick and tile-hung rural cottage, with 15th-century interior, hidden down a country lane off the A29. The games room features bar billiards, darts and shove ha'penny. Newfoundland dogs are particularly welcome as the owners have many of their own. Home-made pub grub includes ham, egg and chips, steak and onion pie and cottage pie.
OPEN: 11–3 6–11 **BAR MEALS:** Lunch served: all week 12–2 Dinner served: Tues–Sat 7–9.15 Av main course £5
BREWERY/COMPANY: Hall & Woodhouse
PRINCIPAL BEERS: Badger King & Barnes Sussex Bitter, Badger Best. **FACILITIES:** Children welcome Garden: Food served outside Dogs allowed (water) **NOTES:** Parking 9 No credit cards

Cricketers Arms ♀
Loxwood Rd, Wisborough Green RH14 0DG ☎ 01403 700369
A traditional village pub dating from the 16th century with oak beams, wooden floors and open fires. Idyllic location overlooking the village green with views of cricket matches and hot-air-balloon rides. A full bar menu is served, ranging from snacks to three course meals and Sunday roasts, and there is a large selection of specials. Typical dishes include, seared tuna steak, home-battered cod and chips and Cricketers' chicken and Cricketers' burger.
OPEN: 11.30–2.30 5.30–11 **BAR MEALS:** 12–2 6.30–9.30
RESTAURANT: 12–2 6.30–9.30 **BREWERY/COMPANY:** Whitbread
PRINCIPAL BEERS: Fuller's London Pride, Wadworth 6X, Interbrew Flowers Original,. **FACILITIES:** Children welcome Garden: Food served outside Dogs allowed (water)

Ye Olde Six Bells
76 High St RH14 9QS ☎ 01403 782124
Dir: On the A29 between London & Bognor, 17m from Bognor
Attractive timbered town pub dating back to 1436 and featuring flagstone floors and an inglenook fireplace. Noted for the legend of a cursed tunnel leading to the nearby church. Good King and Barnes ales, a pretty roadside garden, and traditional pub food, including brunch, steak and kidney pudding, gammon steak and home-made cauliflower cheese.
OPEN: 11–2.30 5.30–11 (Sun 12–3, 7–10.30) **BAR MEALS:** Lunch served: all week 12–2 Dinner served: Mon–Sat 7–9 Av main course £4.50 **BREWERY/COMPANY:** Hall & Woodhouse

PRINCIPAL BEERS: Badger Tanglefoot, Best and Sussex Ale.
FACILITIES: Children welcome Garden: Play area, patio, outdoor eating, BBQ Dogs allowed on a lead **NOTES:** Parking 15

BURPHAM
Map 04 TQ00

Pick of the Pubs

George & Dragon 🏵 🛏
BN18 9RR ☎ 01903 883131
Dir: Off A27 1m E of Arundel, signed Burpham, 2.5m pub on L
An old smuggling inn located in a peaceful village at the foot of the South Downs, where there are lovely walks alongside the nearby River Arun. The interior features beamed ceilings and walls hung with a variety of modern prints. It is very much a dining pub, with informal but attentive service, attracting a sociable local clientele. A bar menu is available at lunch and supper, offering sandwiches, jacket potatoes and light meals, such as Selsey crab pâté with wholemeal toast. The main menu evolves with the seasons, fish making a good showing with the likes of seafood platter, or red bream fillet with red pepper and balsamic dressing. Game too is featured with options of half a pheasant with juniper and thyme jus, or fillet of venison wrapped in bacon with brandy and peppercorn sauce.
OPEN: 11–2.30 6–11 Closed: 25 Dec **BAR MEALS:** Lunch served: all week 12–2 Dinner served: Mon–Sat 7–9.30 Av main course £6.95 **RESTAURANT:** Dinner served: Mon–Sat 7–9.30 Av 3 course à la carte £30 Av 3 course fixed price £24.95
BREWERY/COMPANY: Free House
PRINCIPAL BEERS: Harvey Best, Brewery-on-Sea Spinnaker Bitter, Fuller's London Pride. **NOTES:** Parking 40

CHILGROVE
Map 04 SU81

The White Horse at Chilgrove 🏵 🛏 ♀
High St PO18 9HX ☎ 01243 535219 📠 01243 535301
Dir: On B2141 between Chichester & Petersfield

Picture if you will a picturesque South Downs hostelry, dating from 1756, with a team of French chefs and a celebrated yet user-friendly wine list in a very British setting conducive to the enjoyment of its understated charm. In essence a gastronomic inn, The White Horse pre-dates a myriad of trendy imitators with style and confidence, many of its long-serving staff greeting the host of regular diners as members of the family. Today's food styles may have changed, yet in this case the fusion of French cuisine and English hospitality has remained unchanged. Bar lunches do give way to the restaurant's greater clout, yet the selection will still impress; chicken, avocado and bacon salad, Selsey crab and fresh rock oysters, roast young

continued *continued*

grouse or partridge and braised local hare staying true to the inn's former roots. Italian-style open sandwiches and a glass of real ale are equally worth the detour for those not wishing to go the whole hog. Chicken liver parfait with apple chutney, confit duck on raspberry jus and strawberry brûlée with tuille biscuit in the restaurant well live up to expectations.
OPEN: 11–3 6–11 **BAR MEALS:** 11–3 6–11 **RESTAURANT:** 11–3 Dinner from 6 **BREWERY/COMPANY:** Free House
FACILITIES: Children welcome Garden: Dogs allowed
NOTES: Parking 100 **ROOMS:** 8 bedrooms 8 en suite

COMPTON
Map 04 SU71

Coach & Horses
The Square PO18 9HA ☎ 02392 631228
Dir: On B2146 S of Petersfield
The pub stands beside the square of this prettiest of downland villages. The original timber-framed 16th-century dining room and the pine-clad Victorian extension create an evocative ambience enjoyedd by villagers and visitors alike. Well known locally for its rib-eye steaks with multifarious sauces – mushroom and brandy, Stilton, garlic and peppered – the menu also includes a good fresh fish selection. Hearty bar snacks can accompany a good choice of real ales. There is also a skittle alley and sheltered rear garden.
OPEN: 12–3 6–11 **BAR MEALS:** Lunch served: all week Dinner served: all week 12–2 6–9 Av main course £6 **RESTAURANT:** Lunch served: Tues-Sun 12–2 Dinner served: Tue-Sat 6–9 Av 3 course à la carte £20 **BREWERY/COMPANY:** Free House
PRINCIPAL BEERS: Fuller's ESB, Ballard's Best, Cheriton Diggers Gold. **FACILITIES:** Children welcome Garden: Patio, food served outside Dogs allowed **NOTES:**

COPTHORNE
Map 05 TQ33

Hunters Moon Inn
Copthorne Bank RH10 3JF ☎ 01342 713309 ▤ 01342 714399
e-mail: enquiries@huntersmooninn.co.uk
Dir: M23, J10 Copthorne Way to roundabout, 1st L, then R into Copthorne Bank
Once associated with poachers and smugglers, this village pub has comfortable lounges, open log fireplace and a walled patio garden. A varied menu offers salmon in sorrel, white wine and cream, whole plaice with lemon and caper butter, beef stew with dumplings, duck breast with orange and Cointreau sauce, and sea bass with roasted peppers and basil. Good wine list
OPEN: 12–11 Closed: Dec 26 **RESTAURANT:** Lunch served: Tues-Sun 12–2 Dinner served: all week 7–9.30 Av 3 course à la carte £19.50 **BREWERY/COMPANY:** Free House
PRINCIPAL BEERS: Badger Best, Fuller's London Pride.
FACILITIES: Garden: Patio, food served outside Dogs allowed
NOTES: Parking 100 **ROOMS:** 10 bedrooms 10 en suite from d£45

DUNCTON
Map 05 SU91

The Cricketers
GU28 0LB ☎ 01798 342473 ▤ 01799 342473
e-mail: tamzin@thecricketersinn.co.uk
Attractive white-painted pub situated in spectacular walking country at the western end of the South Downs. Delightful and very popular garden with extensive deck seating and weekend barbecues. Rumoured to be haunted, the inn has changed little over the years. Full range of meat, fish and salad dishes, with main courses including half shoulder of lamb, bangers and mash, and Cornish scallops.

OPEN: 11–3.00 6–11 **BAR MEALS:** Lunch served: all week 12–2.30 Dinner served: Mon -Sat 7–9.30 Av main course £10 **RESTAURANT:** Lunch served: all week 12–3 Dinner served: Mon–Sat 7–9.30 Av 3 course à la carte £20 **BREWERY/COMPANY:** Free House **PRINCIPAL BEERS:** Youngs Bitter, Archers Golden, London Pride, Harvey Sussex. **FACILITIES:** Garden: Food served outside Dogs allowed Must be on lead. Water provided **NOTES:** Parking 30

EARTHAM
Map 04 SU90

The George Inn
PO18 0LT ☎ 01243 814340 ▤ 01243 814725
e-mail: thegeorgeinn@hotmail.com
Dir: From A27 at Tangmere r'about follow signs for Crockerhill/Eartham

Built in the 18th century as an ale house for local estate workers, the pub has a village bar with a flagstone floor (walkers and dogs welcome), and a cosy lounge with an open fire and patio doors leading to a delightful garden. Exposed ships' timbers are a feature of the candlelit restaurant, where the regularly changing menu might offer liver and bacon, grilled sea bass with lemon and ginger butter, and imaginative vegetarian dishes.
OPEN: 11–3 6–11 **BAR MEALS:** Lunch served: all week Dinner served: all week 12–2 6–9 Av main course £7 **RESTAURANT:** Lunch served: all week Dinner served: all week 12–2 6–9 Av 3 course à la carte £15 **BREWERY/COMPANY:** Free House
PRINCIPAL BEERS: Greene King Abbot Ale + guest beers.
FACILITIES: Children welcome Garden: Large, food served outside Dogs allowed (water) **NOTES:** Parking 30

EAST DEAN
Map 05 TV59

The Hurdlemakers
Main Rd PO18 0JG ☎ 01243 811318 ▤ 01243 821294
The name of this old village pub recalls a once-thriving rural craft which employed several men from East Dean. Nowadays this unspoilt village inn, built from traditional Sussex flint, is popular with walkers on the nearby South Downs Way. Various pub specials and an evening menu, with steak and

continued

continued

England

EAST DEAN continued

mushroom pie, seafood in garlic butter, poached plaice in lemon and herbs, and fish pie, plus home-made desserts like gooseberry and ginger cheesecake.
OPEN: 11-2.30 (wknds 11-3) 6-11 (open all day Sundays spring/summer) **BAR MEALS:** Lunch served: all week Dinner served: all week 12-2.15 6.30-9.30 Av main course £6
RESTAURANT: Lunch served: all week Dinner served: all week 12-2.15 6.30-9.30 Av 3 course à la carte £18
BREWERY/COMPANY: Free House **PRINCIPAL BEERS:** Gales HSB, Wadworth 6X, King & Barnes Sussex, Adnams Best.
FACILITIES: Children welcome Garden: Beer garden, food served outdoors, patio, BBQ Dogs allowed (water) **NOTES:** Parking 10
ROOMS: 2 bedrooms from s£25 d£25

ELSTED　　　　　　　　　　　　　　　Map 04 SU81

Pick of the Pubs

The Elsted Inn ♀
Elsted Marsh GU29 0JT ☎ 01730 813662
Dir: From Midhurst take A272 W. After 4m L signed 'Elsted & Harting' (NB Elsted Marsh also known as Lower Elsted)
New owners at this unpretentious Victorian roadside pub are maintaining the style of cooking that made this rural retreat so popular. So expect hearty country cooking based on quality local produce, notably venison, free-range eggs, hand-made bread and sausages, and locally grown vegetables. Also expect local Ballard's Best to wash down Sussex bacon pudding, venison casserole, pork in cider, whole grilled plaice, delicious home-made soups, hand-cut sandwiches and ploughman's lunches. For the sweet-toothed there is bread-and-butter pudding and home-made ice creams. Homely, wooden-floored bars with log fires and a pine-furnished rear dining area. Changing blackboard menus; summer barbeques; comfortable bedrooms in rear converted coach house.
OPEN: 11.30-3 5.30-11 (Sun 12-3, 6-11) **BAR MEALS:** Lunch served: all week Dinner served: all week 12-2.00 7-9.30 Av main course £4.95 **RESTAURANT:** Lunch served: all week Dinner served: all week 12-2 7-9.30 Av 3 course à la carte £15.50
BREWERY/COMPANY: Free House
PRINCIPAL BEERS: Fullers London Pride.
FACILITIES: Children welcome Garden: Beer garden, patio, BBQ, outdoor eating Dogs allowed food and water bowls
NOTES: Parking 8 **ROOMS:** 4 bedrooms 4 en suite from s£40 d£59.99

Pick of the Pubs

The Three Horseshoes
GU29 0JY ☎ 01730 825746
Dir: A272 from Midhurst to Petersfield, after 2m L to Harting & Elsted, after 3m pub on L
Nestling below the South Downs in a peaceful, out-of-the-way village, the Three Horseshoes, a 16th-century former drovers' ale house, is, in many ways, the quintessential English country pub. Full of rustic rural charm, the unspoilt cottagey bars feature worn tiled floors, low-beamed ceilings, latch doors, a vast inglenook with winter log fire, and a motley mix of wooden furniture. On fine days the extensive rear garden, complete with roaming chickens and stunning South Downs views, is a popular attraction. In addition, tip-top real ales are drawn from the

cask and a daily-changing blackboard menu offers some robust country cooking. Good hearty dishes may include roasted red pepper with garlic, basil and anchovies, baked Brie with cranberry sauce, steak, kidney and Murphy's pie, braised lamb with apples and apricots, calves' liver and bacon, crab and lobster in summer, and excellent ploughman's lunches with unusual cheeses, including the local Gospel Green cheddar. Equally substantial puddings such as lemon meringue roulade and bread-and-butter pudding.
OPEN: 11-2.30 6-11 **BAR MEALS:** Lunch served: all week Dinner served: all week 12-2 7-9.30 Av main course £8.95
RESTAURANT: Lunch served: all week Dinner served: all week 12-2 7-9.30 Av 3 course à la carte £20
BREWERY/COMPANY: Free House
PRINCIPAL BEERS: Cheriton Pots Ale, Ballards Best, Fuller's London Pride, Ringwood Fortyniner. **FACILITIES:** Garden: Food served outside Dogs allowed **NOTES:** Parking 30

FERNHURST　　　　　　　　　　　　　Map 04 SU82

Pick of the Pubs

The King's Arms ♀
Midhurst Rd GU27 3HA ☎ 01428 652005 📠 01428 658970
Dir: On A286 between Haslemere and Midhurst, 1m S of Fernhurst

An original 17th-century barn conversion set in 22 acres of orchard and gardens. The Sussex stone pub and outbuildings, flower-decked in summer, comprise a cosy, beamed bar with inglenook to one side and to the other an informal dining area with wine memorabilia, leading to a patio whose pergola supports living vines and ivy. An emigré from the frenetic London scene, Michael Hurst reflects current cooking trends that what he describes as a fusion of modern and traditional British cooking. Everything is home-made and menus change monthly to take into account seasonal changes in ingredients, so expect to find local butcher's sausages and cod in beer batter rubbing shoulders with salmon and dill fishcakes with tomato and basil sauce and beef rib-eye with hand-cut chips. Blackboard specials of roast monkfish with curried aubergine and grilled chicken Caesar salad are further proof of his impeccable pedigree. Real ales and a good selection of wines by the glass complement the food.
OPEN: 11.30-3 5.30-11 Closed: 25 Dec, 1st 2 wks in Jan
BAR MEALS: Lunch served: all week 12-3 Dinner served: Mon-Sat 7-11 Av main course £6 **RESTAURANT:** Lunch served: all week 12-2.30 Dinner served: Mon-Sat 7-10 Av 3 course à la carte £21.50 **BREWERY/COMPANY:** Free House
PRINCIPAL BEERS: Timothy Taylor Landlord, Fuller's London Pride, Gale's HSB, RCH Pitchfork. **FACILITIES:** Children

continued

continued

welcome Garden: Patio, food served outside Dogs allowed (water) **NOTES:** Parking 45

The Red Lion
The Green GU27 3HY ☎ 01428 653304 📠 01428 661120
e-mail: redlionzzz@aol.com
Dir: *From A3 at Hindhead take A287 to Haslemere, then A286 to Fernhurst*
This 500-year-old building, reputedly the oldest pub in the village, overlooks the village green and has a striking sandstone exterior, old oak beams and open fires. Recent change in management.
OPEN: 12–3.20 5–11.20 (Open all day during summer) Closed: 25 Dec **BAR MEALS:** Lunch served: all week 12–2 Dinner served: Tue–Sat 6.30–9.30 Av main course £7 **RESTAURANT:** Lunch served: all week 12–2 Dinner served: Tue–Sat 6.30–9.30 Av 3 course à la carte £20 **BREWERY/COMPANY:** Free House
PRINCIPAL BEERS: King & Barnes Sussex Best, Marston's Pedigree, Interbrew Flowers Original, Hogs Back TEA. **FACILITIES:** Garden: Food served outside Dogs allowed (water) **NOTES:** Parking 50

HALNAKER   Map 04 SU90

Anglesey Arms 🏠
PO18 0NQ ☎ 01243 773474
Dir: *4m E from centre of Chichester on A285 (Petworth Road)*
Traditional village inn, run by the same landlord for over 30 years. It is close to 'glorious Goodwood', the Downs and Chichester Harbour, and the village itself is famous for its windmill, immortalised in a poem by Hilaire Belloc. The menu has a good choice of steaks, Selsey crab, locally smoked salmon, Goodwood raised lamb, home-made fishcakes, and home-made puddings like treacle tart and custard.
OPEN: 11–3 6–11 Closed: 25 Dec **BAR MEALS:** Lunch served: all week Dinner served: all week 12–2 7–10 Av main course £8.50 **RESTAURANT:** Lunch served: all week Dinner served: all week 12–2 7.30–10 Av 3 course à la carte £18.50
BREWERY/COMPANY: Pubmaster **PRINCIPAL BEERS:** Burton Ale, Young's Bitter. **FACILITIES:** Children welcome Garden: Food served outside Dogs allowed (water) **NOTES:** Parking 50

HAMMERPOT   Map 04 TQ00

The Woodman Arms 🏠
BN16 4EU ☎ 01903 871240 📠 01903 871240
e-mail: landlord@thewoodmanarms.co.uk
Dir: *E of Arundel, off the A27*
Built to accommodate local woodmen in the 16th century, today's thatched pub with low beams and an award-winning garden is a long-standing favourite on account of its consistently good food and friendly service. On the edge of the South Downs, it is ideally placed for spectacular downland rambles (maps provided free of charge). In addition to lunchtime soup and sandwiches, evening menus include a daily curry, Scotch beef fillets with optional pepper sauce, cod fillets in beer batter, fresh dressed crab salad or treacle pudding and custard.
OPEN: 11–3 6–11 (Sun 12–3, 7–10.30) **BAR MEALS:** Lunch served: all week 12–2.15 Dinner served: Mon–Sat 6.45–9 Av main course £6 **RESTAURANT:** Lunch served: all week 12–2.15 Dinner served: Mon–Sat 6.45–9 Av 3 course à la carte £12.50
BREWERY/COMPANY: Gales **PRINCIPAL BEERS:** Gales HSB, Gales Butser, Gales GB. **FACILITIES:** Children welcome Children's licence Garden: Award winning, food served outside Dogs allowed **NOTES:** Parking 30

HAYWARDS HEATH   Map 05 TQ32

The Sloop 🏠 ♀
Sloop Ln, Scaynes Hill RH17 7NP ☎ 01444 831219
e-mail: nigel.cannon@lineone.net

The Sloop is located next to the tranquil River Ouse, surrounded by beautiful countryside, and has been a pub since 1815, though the older part of the building (originally two lock-keepers cottages) dates back centuries before. It offers well-kept ales, an impressive wine list and an interesting menu with a New England flavour, specialities of the house including New Hampshire fish stew and bread pudding with maple syrup.
OPEN: 12–3 6–11 (Sun 12–10.30) **BAR MEALS:** Lunch served: all week Dinner served: all week 12–2.15 6.30–9.15 Av main course £9 **RESTAURANT:** Lunch served: all week Dinner served: all week 12–2.15 6.30–9.15 Av 3 course à la carte £18
BREWERY/COMPANY: Greene King **PRINCIPAL BEERS:** Greene king IPA, Abbot Ale, Ruddles county, XX Dark Mild & Guest beers.
FACILITIES: Children welcome Garden: Food served outside Dogs allowed **NOTES:** Parking 75

HORSHAM   Map 04 TQ02

The Black Jug 🏠 ♀
31 North St RH12 1RJ ☎ 01403 253526 📠 01403 217821
Dir: *100yrds from Horsham railway station, almost straight opp Horsham Art Centre*
Relaxed, light and airy town pub with stripped wood floors, darkwood furnishings, and a spacious rear conservatory. An interesting menu includes dishes such as smoked haddock and salmon fishcakes with salad garnish, pan fried Barbary duck breast on braised savoy cabbage, seafood chowder, Black Jug pie, mussels in creamy white wine and garlic sauce, pork, honey and rosemary sausages and mash, and pan fried snapper on braised haricot beans and chorizo sausage.
OPEN: 11–11 (Sun 12–10.30) Closed: 26 Dec **BAR MEALS:** Lunch served: all week Dinner served: all week 12–10 12–10 Av main course £9.95 **RESTAURANT:** Lunch served: all week Dinner served: all week 12–10 Av 3 course à la carte £20 **PRINCIPAL BEERS:** Courage Directors, Marstons Pedigree, Wadworth 6X, Harveys Best.
FACILITIES: Children welcome Garden: Food served outside. Heated garden area Dogs allowed **NOTES:** Parking 9

England

England

KIRDFORD   Map 04 TQ02

Pick of the Pubs

The Half Moon Inn ☜
RH14 0LT ☎ 01403 820223 ▤ 01403 820224
e-mail: halfmooninn.kirdford@virgin.net
See Pick of the Pubs on page 473

LICKFOLD   Map 04 SU92

Pick of the Pubs

Lickfold Inn ◉ ♀
GU28 9EY ☎ 01798 861285 ▤ 01798 861342
Dir: *From A3 take A283, through Chiddingfold, 2m on R signed
'Lurgashall Winery', pub in 1m*

Quiet country lanes deep in the heart of the South Downs lead to this up-market brick and wood fronted inn, which dates back to 1460. It is popular with the rambling fraternity and handy for Goodwood races and the National Trust's magnificent Petworth House. The interior is characterised by Georgian settles, Tudor oak beams, moulded panelling and open fires. An enormous inglenook with a spit is the centrepiece downstairs. Food is freshly prepared and a serious approach to cooking is evident in a carte that offers oven roasted strawberry grouper with dill butter and salad, or rabbit with a tarragon and mustard sauce set on creamy mashed potato. Breads are home made, as are the interesting choice of puddings, encompassing chargrilled banana with coconut ice cream and maple syrup, and steamed chocolate pudding with fudge sauce.
OPEN: 11–3.30 6–11.30 Closed: 25 Dec **BAR MEALS:** Lunch served: all week Dinner served: all week 12–2.30 7–9.30 Av main course £12 **RESTAURANT:** Lunch served: all week Dinner served: all week 12–2.30 7–9.30 Av 3 course à la carte £26
BREWERY/COMPANY: Free House **PRINCIPAL BEERS:** Ballard Best, Hogs Back Hair of the Hog,. **FACILITIES:** Children welcome Children's licence Garden: Beer garden, patio, food served outdoors, BBQ Dogs allowed (water bowl) **NOTES:** Parking 50

LODSWORTH   Map 04 SU82

Pick of the Pubs

The Halfway Bridge Inn
Halfway Bridge GU28 9BP ☎ 01798 861281 ▤ 01798 861878
e-mail: mail@thesussexpub.co.uk
Dir: *On A272*
A rambling, red-brick coaching inn dating back to around 1740, standing mid-way between Midhurst and Petworth

continued

and now offering up-market bedroom accommodation to meet 21st-century expectations. Locally popular, especially with the polo set from nearby Cowdray Park – and handy for travellers on the busy A272 – the pub offers an interesting variety of fresh food throughout its tastefully furnished rooms. Real fires offer a warm winter welcome and in summer there is a sheltered rear patio and a lawn. Lunch and evening menus share a preference for traditional pub food such as risotto fish cakes with spicy dipping sauce, followed by steak, kidney, mushroom and Guinness pudding at generous prices. Alternative main dishes on offer might include seared tuna steak with tapenade, and carnivores' choices such as home-made duck confit with garlic, honey and thyme jus. Puddings are in similar vein – banana toffee pie and the intriguing 'Chocolate Thingy' that is above reproach but defies any accurate description.
OPEN: 11–3 6–11 Closed: 25 Dec **BAR MEALS:** Lunch served: all week Dinner served: all week 12–2 7–10 Av main course £9
RESTAURANT: Lunch served: all week Dinner served: all week 12–2 7–10 Av 3 course à la carte £17.50
BREWERY/COMPANY: Free House
PRINCIPAL BEERS: Gales HSB, Cheriton Pots Ale, Fuller's London Pride, Harveys Best. **FACILITIES:** Garden: Patio, food served outside Dogs allowed (water) **NOTES:** Parking 30
ROOMS: 8 bedrooms 8 en suite from s£45 d£75

LOWER BEEDING   Map 05 TQ22

The Crabtree Inn ☜ ♀
Brighton Rd RH13 6PT ☎ 01403 891273
Dir: *On A281, 4m SE of Horsham.1/2mile south of Leonardslee Gardens*

Writer Hilaire Belloc enjoyed drinking in this pub, which was once used by smugglers on their way from the coast to London. It is said to be linked by tunnels to a nearby monastery. New owners have quickly built a strong following with good beers and their broad traditional-cum-modern dishes. Start with gingered crab cakes or chicken and ham beignets, before moving on to saltimbocca, fresh fish of the day, or vegetable terrine.
OPEN: 11–3 6–11 **BAR MEALS:** Lunch served: all week Dinner served: all week 12–2 7–9.45 **RESTAURANT:** Lunch served: all week Dinner served: all week 12–2 7–9.30 Av 3 course à la carte £23
BREWERY/COMPANY: Hall & Woodhouse
PRINCIPAL BEERS: King & Barnes Sussex, Hall & Woodhouse Badeer Best, Stowfold Press. **FACILITIES:** Children welcome Garden: Food served outside. Large garden Dogs allowed
NOTES: Parking 30

◉ **For a list of pubs with
AA Rosette Awards for food see pages 12 & 13.**

OPEN: 11-3 6-11
BAR MEALS: L served all week.
D served all week. 11-2.30 7-9.30
Av main course £9
RESTAURANT: L served all week.
D served all week. 11-2.30 7-9.30
Av cost 3 course £18.20
BREWERY/COMPANY: LAUREL
PUB PARTNERSHIPS
PRINCIPAL BEERS: Fuller's
London Pride, Young's Special
FACILITIES: Children welcome.
Garden: Food served outside
NOTES: Parking 12
ROOMS: 2 Min price double room
£120

The Half Moon Inn

Kirdford RH14 OLT
☎ 01403 820223 🖶 01403 820224
e-mail: halfmooninn.kirdford@virgin.net
Dir: Off A272 between Billingshurst &
Petworth. At Wisborough Green follow
signs 'Kirdford'

The pretty red-tiled building of this 16th-century village inn, its façade covered by climbing rose bushes, sits directly opposite the church in this unspoilt Sussex village near the River Arun. Although drinkers are welcome The Half Moon Inn is mainly a dining pub.

Former TV commercial maker Patrick Burfield and his barrister wife Francesca abandoned their careers a couple of years ago to take over the pub. Since then, the interior, with its low beams and log fires has been fully redecorated, and there are two letting rooms with a shared bathroom. Well-presented cask ales and lagers are on offer, as well as a varied wine list featuring four house choices available by the glass. A young kitchen team specialises in 'British food with a twist'. Lunch choices might include starters of warm oyster mushroom and bacon salad, a trio of pâté or chicken liver risotto with melted goats' cheese followed by mains such as escalope of veal Milanese, grilled whole lemon sole with prawns and capers and the chef's chicken curry. Vegetarians are well catered for with at least two starters and two main choices always available (perhaps a roasted vegetable flan topped with Cambozola, a spinach and nutmeg risotto, tortellini with a pesto cream or a red onion and goats' cheese tart). Home-made desserts take in the likes of fruits of the forest crumble, lemon tart, chocolate and crème de menthe mousse or a simple mango sorbet, while the cheeseboard is impressive. At dinner, the menu is broadly similar, although the atmosphere changes, with candlelight, tablecloths and polished glassware. Well-tended gardens, a small children's play area and a boules pitch are an added draw in the summer, while for the more energetic, a pamphlet featuring local country walks is available.

England

LURGASHALL
Map 04 SU92

The Noah's Ark ♀
The Green GU28 9ET ☎ 01428 707346 🖹 01428 707742
e-mail: wija@btinternet.com
Dir: Off A283 N of Petworth
This charming 16th-century inn is the perfect grandstand for
cricket on the village green. When the nights draw in, settle
down by the log fire for a game of cribbage or dominoes. The
snack menu includes hot wraps and jacket potatoes, but for
more substantial fare try swordfish with vegetable stir-fry and
salsa verde, rack of lamb with rosemary crust, or fillet steak
with green peppercorn sauce.
OPEN: 11-3 6-11 Closed: Dec 25 **BAR MEALS:** Lunch served: all
week 12-2.30 Dinner served: Mon-Sat 7-10 Av main course £7
RESTAURANT: Lunch served: all week Dinner served:
Mon-Sat 7-10.00 Av 3 course à la carte £20 Av 3 course fixed price
£20 **BREWERY/COMPANY:** Greene King
PRINCIPAL BEERS: Greene King IPA ,Old Speckled Hen & Ruddles
County. **FACILITIES:** Children welcome Children's licence Garden:
Beer garden, food served outdoors **NOTES:** Parking 20

MIDHURST
Map 04 SO82

The Angel Hotel
North St GU29 9DN ☎ 01730 812421 🖹 01730 815928
Much extended Tudor coaching inn with Georgian frontage
close to Cowdray Castle in an attractive small town. New
owners and now more civilised hotel and restaurant than inn,
although there is a popular bar and bistro.
OPEN: 11-3 6.30-10 **BAR MEALS:** Lunch served: all week 12-2.30 6-9.30
RESTAURANT: Lunch served: all week Dinner served: all week 12-2.30
6.30-9.30 Av 3 course à la carte £25 **BREWERY/COMPANY:** Free
House **PRINCIPAL BEERS:** HSB. **FACILITIES:** Children welcome
Garden: Food served outside Dogs allowed **NOTES:** Parking 42
ROOMS: 28 bedrooms 28 en suite from s£65 d£110

NUTHURST
Map 04 TQ12

Pick of the Pubs

Black Horse Inn ◌ ♀
Nuthurst St RH13 6LH ☎ 01403 891272 🖹 01403 892656
e-mail: merlin66@supanet.com

An old 17th-century smugglers' hideout, still hidden
away up a quiet backwater and half-masked by its
impressive window boxes, the pub has stone-flagged
floors and a large inglenook for blazing winter fires.
Built of clay tiles and mellow brick it was originally a
row of cottages with a forge in the adjoining barn.
Beside a babbling stream, there is a delightful garden
and surrounding the pub the stunning countryside
offers numerous walks.

continued

OPEN: 11-3 6-11 (Sat-Sun all day) **BAR MEALS:** Lunch
served: all week 12-2.30 Dinner served: Mon-Sat 6-9.30 Av main
course £6.25 **RESTAURANT:** Lunch served: all week 12-2.30
Dinner served: Mon-Sat 6-9.30 **BREWERY/COMPANY:** Free
House **PRINCIPAL BEERS:** Harveys Sussex, Fuller's London
Pride. **FACILITIES:** Garden: Food served outside Dogs allowed
NOTES: Parking 26

OVING
Map 04 SU90

The Gribble Inn ◌ ♀
PO20 2BP ☎ 01243 786893 🖹 01243 786893
e-mail: brianelderfield@hotmail.com
Dir: From A27 take A259. After 1m L at roundabout, 1st R, 1st L to Oving
A fine thatched 16th-century inn with secluded garden, two
enormous log fires, low wooden beams, and settle seating in
the character main bar. Beers are brewed on the premises.
The pub was named after Rose Gribble, a local schoolteacher
and poetess. A sample menu features braised lamb's liver and
bacon casserole, cottage pie, Sussex scrumpy chicken,
trawlerman's fish pie, aubergine and bean layer cake, and
Petherton pork steak with cider and horseradish.
OPEN: 11-3 5.30-11 (Sun 12-3, 7-10.30) **BAR MEALS:** Lunch served:
all week Dinner served: all week 12-2.30 6-9.30 Av main course £7.75
RESTAURANT: Lunch served: all week Dinner served: all week 12-2.30
6-9.30 Av 3 course fixed price £15 **BREWERY/COMPANY:** Woodhouse
Inns **PRINCIPAL BEERS:** Gribble Ale, Plucking Pheasant, Fursty Ferret,
Reg's Tipple. **FACILITIES:** Children welcome Garden: Food served
outside. Secluded garden Dogs allowed Toys & water provided
NOTES: Parking 40

PETWORTH
Map 04 SU92

Badgers ◌ NEW
Station Rd GU28 0JF ☎ 01798 342651 🖹 01798 343649
A country dining pub nestling in the South Downs, Badgers
was previously the Railway Tavern, serving Petworth's old
railway station. It has plenty of charm, with open fires inside
and a pretty courtyard area outside, overlooking the small
garden, carp pond and stream. The menu specialises in fish
during the summer and game during the winter,
complemented by a selection of wines. Typical options are
zarzuela (Spanish fish casserole) and flamed pork fillet.
OPEN: 11-3 5.30-11 Closed: Bank holidays **BAR MEALS:** Lunch
served: all week Dinner served: all week 12-2 7-9 Av main course
£10.95 **RESTAURANT:** Lunch served: all week Dinner served: all
week 12-2 7-9 Av 3 course à la carte £25
BREWERY/COMPANY: Free House **PRINCIPAL BEERS:** Badgers,
Sussex, Carlsberg, Becks. **FACILITIES:** Children welcome Garden:
Food served outside, courtyard **NOTES:** Parking 20 **ROOMS:** d£75

The Black Horse ◌
Byworth GU28 0HL ☎ 01798 342424 🖹 01798 342868
An unspoilt pub built on the site of an old priory in a beautiful
garden. The three-storey, brick and stone, Georgian frontage
hides a much older interior dating back to the 14th century.
Wooden floors and furniture, half-panelled walls and open
fires characterise the three rustic rooms. Good ales and
traditional home-cooked food includes trout with hazelnuts,
smoked duck salad, chestnut pâté en croûte, and tuna with
red pepper relish. Busy in summer.
OPEN: 11-2.30 6-11 **BAR MEALS:** Lunch served: Tue-Sun 12-2
Dinner served: all week 7-9 Av main course £6.25
RESTAURANT: Lunch served: Tue-Sun 12-2 Dinner served: all week
7-9 Av 3 course à la carte £13 **PRINCIPAL BEERS:** Fuller's London
Pride, Arundel Gold, Cheriton Pots Ale. **FACILITIES:** Garden: Food
served outside Dogs allowed (water) **NOTES:** Parking 24

England

Welldiggers Arms
Polborough Rd GU28 0HG ☎ 01798 342287
Dir: 1m E of Petworth on the A283
Welldiggers once occupied this rustic, 300-year-old roadside pub, which boasts low-beamed bars with open log fires and huge oak tables. It is conveniently located for racing at Goodwood and Fontwell, as well as a visit to Sir Edward Elgar's cottage. Dishes on the menu may include English steaks, butchered on the premises, fresh scallops, lobster and crab and cod with home-made chips.
OPEN: 11-3 6.30 Closed: Dec 25 **BAR MEALS:** Lunch served: all week 12-2 Dinner served: Tues-Sat 6.30-9.30 Av main course £8.50 **RESTAURANT:** Lunch served: all week 12-2 Dinner served: Tues-Sat 6.30-9.30 Av 3 course à la carte £13.50 **BREWERY/COMPANY:** Free House **PRINCIPAL BEERS:** Youngs. **FACILITIES:** Children welcome Garden: Large lawn & patio, food served outside Dogs allowed **NOTES:** Parking 35

ROWHOOK   Map 04 TQ13

Pick of the Pubs

The Chequers Inn
RH12 3PY ☎ 01403 790480
Dir: Off A29 NW of Horsham

A 15th-century Grade II listed building of great character with original beams and Horsham flagstones, the bars warmed by open fires. The landlord is a member of the Master Chefs of Great Britain and the emphasis is on fresh, seasonal produce. Inventive dishes include pan-fried Irish diver scallops with vermouth cappuccino, game terrine with Savoy cabbage and wild mushrooms and vanilla roasted breast of wild duck with confit and cassis jus.
OPEN: 11-3 6-11 **BAR MEALS:** Lunch served: all week 12-2 Dinner served: Mon-Sat 7-9.30 Av main course £6 **RESTAURANT:** Lunch served: all week 12-2 Dinner served: Mon-Sat 7-9.30 Av 3 course à la carte £25 Av 3 course fixed price £15 **BREWERY/COMPANY:** Punch Taverns **PRINCIPAL BEERS:** Harvey's Sussex Ale, Young's Special, Fuller's London Pride. **FACILITIES:** Garden: Beer garden, patio, outdoor eating Dogs allowed (water) **NOTES:** Parking 40

RUDGWICK   Map 04 TQ03

The Fox Inn
Guildford Rd, Bucks Green RH12 3JP
☎ 01403 822386 ☐ 01403 823950
e-mail: seafood@foxinn.co.uk
Dir: situated on A281 midway between Horsham and Guildford
'Famous for Fish!' is the claim of this attractive 16th-century inn, a message borne out by the extensive menu. Long food hours take in all-day breakfast and afternoon tea, while the

continued

bar menu focuses on seafood. Whole grilled sea bass with sesame and chilli dressing, smoked haddock on buttered spinach, Thai fish curry, and seafood platter are some of the choices, along with sausage and mash, chicken supreme, and sizzling beef stir fry.
OPEN: 11-11 (Sun 12-10.30) **BAR MEALS:** Lunch served: all week Dinner served: all week 12-10 Av main course £12.50 **RESTAURANT:** 12-10 Av 3 course à la carte £22.50 **BREWERY/COMPANY:** Hall & Woodhouse **PRINCIPAL BEERS:** King & Barnes Sussex, Badger Tanglefoot, Best. **FACILITIES:** Children welcome Garden: Food served outdoors Dogs allowed (water) **NOTES:** Parking 30

SHIPLEY   Map 04 TQ12

George & Dragon
Dragons Green RH13 7JE ☎ 01403 741320
Dir: Signposted off A272 between Coolham and A24
A 16th-century, tile-hung cottage that provides welcome peace and quiet, especially on balmy summer evenings when the peaceful garden is a welcome retreat. Its interior is all head-banging beams and character inglenook fireplaces where a pint of Badger or Tanglefoot will not come amiss. The food is home made using fresh vegetables and 'real' chips and offers dishes such as roasts of lamb and crispy coated chicken breast with sweet-and-sour sauce. Shipley is famous for its smock mill.
OPEN: 11-3 6-11 (Sun-Sun & BHs open all day) **BAR MEALS:** Lunch served: all week Dinner served: all week 12-2 6.45-9.30 Av main course £6.50 **RESTAURANT:** Lunch served: all week Dinner served: all week 12-2 6.45-9 Av 3 course à la carte £11.50 Av 3 course fixed price £10 **BREWERY/COMPANY:** Hall & Woodhouse **PRINCIPAL BEERS:** Badger Best, Tanglefoot & Sussex Best. **FACILITIES:** Children welcome Children's licence Garden: Beer garden, food served outdoors, BBQ Dogs allowed **NOTES:** Parking 20 No credit cards

SIDLESHAM   Map 04 SZ89

Crab & Lobster
Mill Ln PO20 7NB ☎ 01243 641233
Dir: Off B2145 between Chichester & Selsey
Well-kept pub situated close to the shores of Pagham Harbour, a noted nature reserve. Popular with walkers and twitchers who fill the cosy bars (open fires) in winter, and the pretty rear garden with mudflat views in summer.
OPEN: 11-3 6-11 **BAR MEALS:** Lunch served all week 12-12.30 Dinner served Tue-Sat 7-9.45 Av main course £6.50 **RETAURANT MEALS:** Lunch served all week 12-2.30 Dinner served Tue-Sat 7-9.45 Av 3-course meal £12.50 **BREWERY/COMPANY:** Free House **PRINCIPAL BEERS:** Timothy Taylor Landlord. Itchen Valley Fagins, Cheriton Pots Ale **FACILITIES:** Children welcome Garden: Food served outside Dogs allowed (water provided) **NOTES:** Parking 12

SINGLETON
Map 04 SU81

The Fox and Hounds 🐾 NEW
PO18 0EY ☎ 01243 811251
The building probably dates from the 16th century, when it would have been part of a huge hunting park owned by the Fitzalan family, Earls of Arundel. Today, it is popular with walkers enjoying the rolling Sussex countryside and visitors to Goodwood for motor and horse-racing. A menu of typical pub fare includes liver and bacon, steak and ale pie, open sandwiches and home-made puddings.
OPEN: 11.30–3 6–11 **BAR MEALS:** Lunch served: all week Dinner served: all week 12–2 6.30–9 Av main course £8 **RESTAURANT:** Lunch served: all week Dinner served: all week 12–2 6.30–9 Av 3 course à la carte £15 **BREWERY/COMPANY:** Enterprise Inns
PRINCIPAL BEERS: Interbrew Bass, Hancocks HB, Greene King IPA.
FACILITIES: Garden: Dogs allowed (water) **NOTES:** Parking 40

Pick of the Pubs

The Fox Goes Free 🐾 ♀
Charlton PO18 0HU ☎ 01243 811461 🖥 01243 811461
Dir: A286 6m from Chichester, towards Midhurst 1m from Goodwood racecourse
Built in 1588, the pub was a favoured hunting lodge of William III; more recently, it also hosted the first Women's Institute meeting in 1915. The lovely old brick and flint building still nestles in unspoilt countryside, and is handy for the Weald and Downland Museum and nearby Goodwood races. With its two huge fireplaces, old pews and brick floors, the pub simply exudes charm and character. But this is an inn for all seasons as the outdoor bar and barbecue make good use of the lovely flint-walled herb garden and apple trees. Four welcoming bedrooms make The Fox an ideal country retreat, whilst the menu marries traditional and modern styles. Typical dishes include rump of English lamb with red wine, honey and balsamic vinegar; duck breast with Roquefort and port; red mullet with red onion, peppers and pesto; or sea bass with a lemon and olive oil jus.
OPEN: 11–3 6–11 (Sat-Sun all day in summer)
BAR MEALS: Lunch served: all week Dinner served: all week 12–2.30 6.30–10.30 Av main course £9 **RESTAURANT:** Lunch served: all week Dinner served: all week 12–2.30 6–10.30 Av 3 course à la carte £16 **BREWERY/COMPANY:** Free House
PRINCIPAL BEERS: Ringwood Best, Ballards Best, Fox Bitter, Interbrew Bass. **FACILITIES:** Garden: Food served outside Dogs allowed (water) **NOTES:** Parking 8
ROOMS: 4 bedrooms 3 en suite from s£35 d£50

SOUTHBOURNE
Map 04 SU70

The Old House at Home 🐾 ♀
Cot Lane, Chidham, nr Southbourne PO18 8SU
☎ 01243 572477 🖥 01243 574978
e-mail: thebar@theoldhouseathome.com
Sleepy Chidham is situated on a low-lying peninsula jutting out into Chichester Harbour, close to wonderful scenic walks and

continued

┌─────────────────────────────────────┐
│ 🏵 **For a list of pubs with**   │
│ **AA Rosette Awards for food see pages 12 & 13.** │
└─────────────────────────────────────┘

wildlife-rich marshes. Often filled with walkers and twitchers, the 17th-century Old House at Home offers a warm welcome, traditional ales and wines from its own vineyards. Hearty dishes like braised rabbit, oxtail and pork medallions with flageolet beans sit alongside grilled halibut steak with caper butter sauce and watercress, potato and roasted pine nut salad.

OPEN: 11.30–2.30 6–11 (Sun 12–3 7–10.30) **BAR MEALS:** Lunch served: all week Dinner served: all week 12–2 6.30–9.30 Av main course £5.95 **RESTAURANT:** Lunch served: all week Dinner served: all week 12–2 6.30–9.30 **BREWERY/COMPANY:** Free House
PRINCIPAL BEERS: Interbrew Flowers IPA & Bass, Greene King Abbot Ale, Fuller's London Pride,. **FACILITIES:** Garden: Food served outside, patio Dogs allowed (water) **NOTES:** Parking 30

SOUTH HARTING
Map 04 SU71

The Ship Inn 🐾
GU31 5PZ ☎ 01730 825302
Dir: From Petersfield take B2146 towards Chichester
17th-century inn made from a ship's timbers, hence the name. Home-made pies are a feature, and other popular dishes include fresh sea bass, fish pie, calves' liver, rack of lamb, ham and asparagus mornay, and hot beef Hungarian goulash. A range of vegetarian dishes and bar snacks are also available.
OPEN: 11–11 (Oct-Mar 12–3, 6–11) **BAR MEALS:** Meals served: Mon-Sat 12–2.30 7–9.30 Av main course £8 **RESTAURANT:** All week 12–2.30 7–9.30 Av 3 course à la carte £25
BREWERY/COMPANY: Free House **PRINCIPAL BEERS:** Palmer IPA, Cheriton Pots Ale, Ringwood Fortyniner. **FACILITIES:** Garden: Food served outdoors Dogs allowed (water) **NOTES:** Parking 5

STEDHAM
Map 04 SU82

Hamilton Arms/Nava Thai Restaurant 🐾
Hamilton Arms School Ln GU29 0NZ
☎ 01730 812555 🖥 01730 817459
e-mail: hamiltonarms@hotmail.com
Dir: Off A272 between Midhurst & Petersfield

continued

Named after Emma Hamilton, Nelson's mistress, the Hamilton Arms is renowned for its traditional Thai cuisine, friendly ambience and dazzling display of floral hanging baskets. Handy for the magnificent walking country of the South Downs. Expect Scottish rainbow trout topped with curry pasta and coconut milk, vegetable tempora, Nava Thai roast duck, and squid with garlic, chillis and french beans among many dishes.
OPEN: 11-3 6-11 Closed: 1 Week Jan **BAR MEALS:** Lunch served: Tues-Sun Dinner served: Tues-Sun 12-2.30 6-10.30 Av main course £6.50 **RESTAURANT:** Lunch served: Tues-Sun Dinner served: Tues-Sun 12-2.30 6-10.30 Av 3 course à la carte £20
BREWERY/COMPANY: Free House **PRINCIPAL BEERS:** Ballard's Best, Fuller's London Pride,. **FACILITIES:** Children welcome Garden: Food served outside Dogs allowed (water) **NOTES:** Parking 40

SUTTON
Map 04 SU91

Pick of the Pubs

White Horse Inn ♦♦♦
The Street RH20 1PS ☎ 01798 869221 🖹 01798 869291
Dir: Turn off A29 at foot of Bury Hill. After 2m pass Roman Villa on R. 1m to Sutton

Pretty Georgian inn tucked away in a sleepy village at the base of the South Downs. Neat bars and dining room, and comfortable en suite accommodation. Expect imaginative food, the daily-changing choice featuring perhaps Stilton and broccoli soup, baked sea bass with lemon basil and tomato, confit of duck, lamb shank with tomatoes and red wine, and French lemon tart.
OPEN: 11-3 6-11 **BAR MEALS:** Lunch served: all week Dinner served: all week 12-2 7-9 Av main course £6.40
RESTAURANT: Lunch served: all week Dinner served: all week 12-2 7-9 Av 3 course à la carte £22.50
BREWERY/COMPANY: Free House
PRINCIPAL BEERS: Wadworth 6X, Youngs PA, Shepherd Neame Spitfire, Courage Best. **FACILITIES:** Children welcome Garden: Dogs allowed **NOTES:** Parking 10
ROOMS: 6 bedrooms 5 en suite from s£55 d£65

TILLINGTON
Map 04 SU92

Pick of the Pubs

The Horse Guards Inn 🍴 ♀
GU28 9AF ☎ 01798 342332 🖹 01798 344351
e-mail: mail@horseguardsinn.co.uk
Dir: On A272 1m W of Petworth. Inn next to church
Once a regular watering hole for the horse guards who travelled from London to Portsmouth transporting gold bullion or dealing with smugglers, this 18th-century inn

continued

nestles on a hillside on the edge of Petworth Park. Converted from three cottages, its rambling series of tastefully refurbished rooms feature stripped beams, open fires, pine panelling and antique furnishings. The restaurant and many of the bedrooms enjoy views across the Rother valley to the South Downs. The restaurant occupies three levels, and becomes a cosy candlelit setting in the evenings. There is an emphasis on fine quality fresh produce, which is used to create dishes ranging from classic to exotic. Typical main courses include roast saddle of lamb with confit tomatoes and garlic mash, crispy duck-leg confit with tomato and white bean cassoulet, and tournedos of Scottish beef with crispy stir-fried noodles and a soy and red wine jus.
OPEN: 11-3 6-11 **BAR MEALS:** Lunch served: all week Dinner served: all week 12-2 7-9 Av main course £8.50
RESTAURANT: Lunch served: all week Dinner served: all week 12-2 7-9 Av 3 course à la carte £22.50
BREWERY/COMPANY: Free House
PRINCIPAL BEERS: London Pride, Fullers IPA.
FACILITIES: Children welcome Garden: Food served outside. Secluded garden Dogs allowed **NOTES:** Parking 5
ROOMS: 3 bedrooms 3 en suite from s£65 d£65

WALBERTON
Map 04 SU90

Oaks Bar 🍴 ♀
Yapton Ln BN18 0LS ☎ 01243 552865 🖹 01243 553862
e-mail: reservations@oakslodge.co.uk
Dir: on A27 between Arundel & Fontwell

This fine 18th-century coaching inn, which has served the needs of many generations of travellers, has been fully renovated in a light contemporary style. It's an award-winning pub, serving good food in a relaxed atmosphere. Dishes are based on fresh local produce - maybe crispy oriental duck on a wild roquette and crisp vegetable salad with chilli jam, or panache of seared scallops with herb crushed potatoes, crispy chorizo, wilted greens and roast plum tomato sauce.
OPEN: 11.30-3 6-11 Closed: 26-29 Dec **BAR MEALS:** Lunch served: all week Dinner served: all week 12-3 6-10 Av main course £8 **RESTAURANT:** Lunch served: all week 12-3 Dinner served: Mon-Sat 6-10 Av 3 course à la carte £20 **BREWERY/COMPANY:** Free House **PRINCIPAL BEERS:** Speckled Hen, London Pride, Youngs Special, John Smiths. **FACILITIES:** Children welcome Garden: Food served outside. Colourful garden Only guide dogs allowed **NOTES:** Parking 30 **ROOMS:** 4 bedrooms 4 en suite from s£45 d£70

★ **Indicates AA inspected hotel accommodation**

WARNHAM — Map 04 TQ13

The Greets Inn
47 Friday St RH12 3QY ☎ 01403 265047 📠 01403 265047
Dir: Off A24 N of Horsham

A fine Sussex hall house dating from about 1350 and built for Elias Greet, a local merchant. Magnificent inglenook fireplace and head-crackingly low beams in the flagstone-floored bar. There is a rambling series of dining areas where specialities such as lemon sole with lemon and dill butter, sea bass with red wine and rosemary, and calf's liver with bacon are served. There is also traditional pub food and in summer weekend barbecues. **OPEN:** 11–2.30 6–11 (Sun 12–2, 7–10.30) **BAR MEALS:** Lunch served: all week Dinner served: all week 12–2 7–9 Av main course £8 **RESTAURANT:** Lunch served: all week Dinner served: all week 12–2 7–9 Av 3 course à la carte £20 **PRINCIPAL BEERS:** Interbrew Flowers Original, Fuller's London Pride, Harvey's Sussex. **FACILITIES:** Children welcome Children's licence Garden: Large, food served outside Dogs allowed (water) **NOTES:** Parking 30

WEST HOATHLY — Map 05 TQ33

The Cat Inn 🍷
Queen's Square RH19 4PP ☎ 01342 810369
Sixteenth-century village inn situated opposite an historic 11th-century church. Seating outside on the sunny front terrace. High beamed ceiling and huge inglenook fireplace inside. Bar food includes rack of lamb and sausage and mash. Try the vegetable, mushroom and Stilton special, the 'casserole of the week' or venison steak from the wholesome restaurant menu. **OPEN:** 12–2.30 5.30–11 **BAR MEALS:** Lunch served: all week Dinner served: all week 12–2.30 7–9.30 Av main course £10 **RESTAURANT:** Lunch served: all week Dinner served: all week 12–2.30 7–9.30 Av 3 course à la carte £20 **BREWERY/COMPANY:** Free House **PRINCIPAL BEERS:** Harveys Best, Adnams, Southwold. **FACILITIES:** Food served outside. Patio area **NOTES:** Parking 30

WINEHAM — Map 05 TQ21

The Royal Oak
BN5 9AY ☎ 01444 881252 📠 01444 881530
This delightful, 14th-century, black and white timbered cottage has been dispensing ale for over 200 years and continues to maintain the traditional, unspoilt character that many village pubs lost long ago. A true ale house, so expect head-cracking low beams, a huge inglenook with winter log fire, wooden and flagged floors, rustic furnishings and real ale straight from the cask. Extensive summer gardens and a limited menu of decent sandwiches, home-made soup and ploughman's

OPEN: 11–2.30 5.30–11 (Sun 12–3, 7–10.30) **BAR MEALS:** All week 11–2.30 5.30–11 **BREWERY/COMPANY:** Inn Business **PRINCIPAL BEERS:** Harveys best Bitter, Marston's Pedigree, Fuller's London Pride, Wadworth 6X. **FACILITIES:** Garden: Food served outside Dogs allowed (water) **NOTES:** Parking 40 No credit cards

TYNE & WEAR

NEWCASTLE UPON TYNE — Map 11 NZ26

Cooperage
The Close, Quayside NE1 3RF ☎ 0191 232 8286
Set on the waterfront under the city's famed bridges, the Cooperage is one of the oldest pubs in the area. Lots of real ale choice.

Crown Posoda
31 The Side, Dean St NE1 3JE ☎ 0191 232 1269
Complete with Victorian stained glass screens, this friendly old pub also boasts gilt mirrors and candelabra. Real ale. Lunchtime pub grub. No children.

Shiremoor House Farm
Middle Engine Ln, New York NE29 8DZ ☎ 0191 257 6302

Located in what were once derelict farm buildings, this pub offers large bars, plenty of ale choice, and tables in the courtyard. Pub grub. Children welcome.

WHITLEY BAY — Map 11 NZ37

The Waterford Arms 🍷
Collywell Bay Rd, Seaton Sluice NE26 4QZ
☎ 0191 237 0450 & 0191 296 5287
Dir: From A1 N of Newcastle take A19 at Seaton Burn then follow signs for A190 to Seaton Sluice
The building dates back to 1899 and is situated close to the small local fishing harbour, overlooking the North Sea. Splendid beaches and sand dunes are within easy reach, and the pub is very popular with walkers. Seafood dishes are the

continued

continued

WHITLEY BAY continued

speciality, including a whale-sized cod or haddock and chips, seafood feast, and salmon.
OPEN: 12–11 (Sun 12–11) **BAR MEALS:** Lunch served: all week Dinner served: all week 12–9 Av main course £4 **RESTAURANT:** Lunch served: all week Dinner served: all week 12–9 Av 3 course à la carte £8.50 **BREWERY/COMPANY:** Pubmaster **PRINCIPAL BEERS:** Tetleys, Worthington, plus guest.
FACILITIES: Children welcome Food served outside
NOTES: Parking 90 **ROOMS:** 5 bedrooms 5 en suite from s£30 d£45

WARWICKSHIRE

ALDERMINSTER   Map 04 SP24

Pick of the Pubs

The Bell ♦♦♦♦ ⌂ ♀
CV37 8NY ☎ 01789 450414 🖷 01789 450998
e-mail: thebellald@aol.com
Dir: On A3400 3.5M S of Stratford-upon-Avon

Within easy reach of Stratford-upon-Avon and Warwick Castle, you'll find a relaxed atmosphere at this former coaching inn. Fresh flowers enhance the friendly, welcoming bars, and the spacious conservatory looks out across a delightful old courtyard garden towards the rolling Stour Valley beyond. The Conservatory offers the perfect venue for a special occasion or private function and the Bell provides an impressive range of entertainment – from themed food evenings and musical suppers. Drop in at any time for a regularly changing menu or something from the choice of daily blackboard specials. Start with creamy field mushrooms or grilled goats' cheese and then graduate to pan-fried lambs' liver with bubble and squeak and crispy bacon, grilled lemon sole fillets on carrot and onion salsa or the Bell's home-made curry with spiced rice and assorted side dishes. The pub is well placed for touring the Cotswolds, and offers accommodation in seven individually furnished rooms.
OPEN: 12–2.30 7–11 **BAR MEALS:** Lunch served: all week Dinner served: all week 12–2 7–9.30 Av main course £9 **RESTAURANT:** Lunch served: all week Dinner served: all week 12–2 7–9.30 Av 3 course à la carte £18 **BREWERY/COMPANY:** Free House **PRINCIPAL BEERS:** Greene King IPA & Ruddles County.
FACILITIES: Children welcome Garden: Food served outside Dogs allowed (water) **NOTES:** Parking 70 **ROOMS:** 6 bedrooms 4 en suite from s£25 d£40

ARDENS GRAFTON   Map 03 SP15

Pick of the Pubs

The Golden Cross ⌂ ♀
B50 4LG ☎ 01789 772420 🖷 01789 773697
Nestling in the heart of Shakespeare country west of Stratford, with views across a rolling Warwickshire landscape, the Golden Cross is a stylishly refurbished rural inn offering imaginative, freshly prepared food in an informal pub atmosphere. Relax with a pint in the beamed bar, with its rug-strewn stone floor mellow decor and scrubbed pine tables, or dine in style in the light and airy, high-ceilinged dining-room. Extensive menus successfully blend traditional pub favourites (given a modern twist) with more inventive dishes. Start with confit duck leg with ginger and vanilla-scented rice, cream of roast tomato and rosemary soup or chicken liver parfait with orange and lime confit. To follow, choices include braised lamb shank with celeriac mash and redcurrant sauce, steak, ale and root vegetable pie, and spiced chicken breast with ratatouille couscous and red pepper jus. At lunch accompany a pint of Hook Norton with an avocado and smoked bacon ciabatta or marmalade glazed ham, egg and chips. Home-made puddings.
OPEN: 11–3 5–11 (all day Sat–Sun) **BAR MEALS:** Lunch served: all week Dinner served: all week 12–2.30 7–9.30 Av main course £9.95 **RESTAURANT:** Lunch served: all week Dinner served: all week 12–2.30 7–9.30 Av 3 course à la carte £14
PRINCIPAL BEERS: Hook Norton, Bass, Guest ales.
FACILITIES: Children welcome Garden: Food served outside Dogs allowed (in the garden only) **NOTES:** Parking 80

ASTON CANTLOW   Map 03 SP16

Pick of the Pubs

King's Head ⌂ ♀
21 Bearley Rd B95 6HY ☎ 01789 488242 🖷 01789 488137
Pretty black and white Tudor pub in an ancient village deep in the heart of Shakespeare country. Flanked by a huge spreading chestnut tree, and oozing old-world atmosphere, this impressive building has been sensitively refurbished in a modern style. Tastefully rustic inside, with huge polished flagstones, exposed original beams, old scrubbed pine tables, painted brick walls, open log fires and scatter cushions on pew benches and antique settles. Expect a laid-back atmosphere and approach to dining – sit where you want and eat what you want from a diverse menu with the accent firmly on flavours from around the world. On the home front though, local game and the famous Aston Cantlow duck suppers are a must. Enjoy the piped jazz and sample one of the first-rate real ales with, perhaps, smoked haddock and wild mushroom frittata with shaved fennel salad, followed by braised lamb shank with Desirée potato, red onion and rosemary gratin or wild sea bass on a pesto mash. There is a smart rear terrace for alfresco summer dining.
OPEN: 12–3 5.30–11 (Summer open all day)
BAR MEALS: Lunch served: all week Dinner served: all week 12–2.30 7–10 Av main course £8 **RESTAURANT:** Lunch served: all week Dinner served: all week 12–2.30 7–10 Av 3 course à la carte £16 **PRINCIPAL BEERS:** Greene King Abbot Ale, Fuller's London Pride. **FACILITIES:** Children welcome Garden: Food served outside Dogs allowed **NOTES:** Parking 60

England

PUB WALK

Withybrook
The Pheasant

THE PHEASANT
Main Street WITHYBROOK Nr
Coventry CV7 9LT
Tel:01455 220480
Directions: Off B4112 NE of
Coventry
Charming 17th-century coaching inn
next to the brook from which the
village takes its name. The interior is
characterised by an inglenook
fireplace, farm implements and
horse racing photographs. An
extensive menu.
Open:12–3 6–11
Bar meals: 12–2 6.30–10
Children welcome and dogs
allowed. Garden and parking
available.

A pretty country ramble exploring unspoilt open countryside between Coventry and Rugby. The route returns to Withybrook along the Oxford Canal, which dates back to the 18th century.

Turn left on leaving the pub and follow the road towards Rugby and Pailton. Keep the brook on your right. When the road bends left, go straight on towards Shilton and follow the lane past Hopsford Spring Farm on the right and Hopsford Old Hall Farm on the left. Pass Lynton House, a white house with a well in the garden, and descend the slope. As you begin to go up the other side, turn left on to a concrete track running alongside a copse. There are telegraph poles here. On the left is the site of the medieval village of Hopsford. Follow the track, veer right at the fork by the car park sign and cross a cattle-grid. Over to the left is a large fishing

lake. The fields here are ridged an furrowed and the line of the ol Oxford Canal can still be traced on th ground. Proceed towards farr outbuildings and silos at Hopsfor Hall Farm, keep them on your left an continue on the track towards th railway. Go through a gate and ahea now is a small viaduct carrying th London to Manchester railway line Pass under it, to quickly arrive at th Oxford Canal. Look for a gentle slop taking you up to the towpath. Go le and about 200 yards (183m) alon the canal, look for a bridge. Make th steep climb up the bank. Turn left t cross the bridge and head toward Mobbs Wood Farm. Follow the pat and as you near the farm swing le and pick up the Centenary Way whic is clearly waymarked. Turn left an walk along a leafy track for about ha a mile (800m). Pass through a gat and walk ahead, following the roa back towards the Pheasant.

Distance: 3 1/2 miles (5.7km)
Map: OS Landranger 140
Terrain: Undulating farmland
bisected by the Oxford Canal
Paths: Towpath, tracks, paths , road.
Winter: sections prone to flooding
Gradient: Gentle climbing and several
short, steep ascents

*Walk submitted and checked by Alan
Bean of The Pheasant, Withybrook*

England

BROOM
Map 03 SP05

Broom Tavern
High St B50 4HL ☎ 01789 773656 ▤ 01789 772983
e-mail: richard@distinctivepubs.freeserve.co.uk
Dir: N of B439 W of Stratford-upon-Avon

Charming brick and timber 16th-century inn, reputedly haunted by a cavalier killed on the cellar steps. The same menu is offered in the bar and restaurant. 'Tavern Favourites' include home-made steak and kidney pie and the Tavern duck supper, while 'From Around the Globe' there might be seafood fettucine, Chinese stir-fry or the Tavern balti. Legend has it that William Shakespeare and friends fell asleep under a tree outside the Broom, after losing a drinking contest nearby.
OPEN: 11.30-2.30 5-11 **BAR MEALS:** Lunch served: all week Dinner served: all week 12-2 6.30-9 Av main course £8 **RESTAURANT:** Lunch served: all week Dinner served: all week 12-2 6.30-9 Av 3 course à la carte £15 **BREWERY/COMPANY:** Greene King **PRINCIPAL BEERS:** Green King IPA, Adnams Bitter. **FACILITIES:** Children welcome Garden: Food served outside **NOTES:** Parking 30

EDGEHILL
Map 04 SP34

The Castle Inn
OX15 6DJ ☎ 01295 670255 ▤ 01295 670521
e-mail: castleedghill@msn.com
Dir: M40 then A422. 6m until Upton House, then turn next R 1.5m
Standing on the summit of a beech-clad ridge, 700ft above sea level, this is one of the most unusual pubs in the country. Built as a battlemented folly to commemorate the centenary of the Battle of Edgehill, and opened on the anniversary of Cromwell's death, the inn was first licensed in 1822. Traditional, home-cooked dishes such as breaded haddock fillet, beef and ale pie, and lamb chop with tomato and egg. Selection of ploughman's lunches, sandwiches, jacket potatoes and snacks in a basket.
OPEN: 11.15-2.30 6.15-11 **BAR MEALS:** Lunch served: all week Dinner served: all week 12-2 6.30-9 Av main course £6 **BREWERY/COMPANY:** Hook Norton **PRINCIPAL BEERS:** Hook Norton Best, Old Hooky & Generation. **FACILITIES:** Garden: Food served outside Dogs allowed **NOTES:** Parking 40 **ROOMS:** 3 bedrooms 3 en suite from s£37.50 d£57.50

ETTINGTON
Map 04 SP24

The Houndshill ♦♦♦
Banbury Rd CV37 7NS ☎ 01789 740267 ▤ 01789 740075
Dir: On A422 SE of Stratford-upon-Avon
Attractive traditional family-run inn set at the Heart of England, making it the ideal base for visits to Stratford-upon-Avon and the Cotswolds. The Houndshill has a pleasant tree-lined garden and is very popular with families. Typical dishes include grilled sirloin steak, seared swordfish, pan-fried fillet of salmon, lamb cutlets and haddock kiev. Lots of light bites.

continued

OPEN: 12-3 7-11 (Sun 12-3, 7-10.30) Closed: Dec 25-28
BAR MEALS: Lunch served: all week Dinner served: all week 12-2 7-9.30 Av main course £8.50 **RESTAURANT:** 12-2 7-9.30 Av 3 course à la carte £13 **BREWERY/COMPANY:** Free House **PRINCIPAL BEERS:** Hook Norton Best, Marston's Pedigree. **FACILITIES:** Children welcome Garden: Beer garden, Food served outdoors Dogs allowed
NOTES: Parking 50 **ROOMS:** 8 bedrooms 8 en suite from s£40 d£60

GREAT WOLFORD
Map 04 SP23

Pick of the Pubs

Fox & Hounds Inn
CV36 5NQ ☎ 01608 674220 ▤ 01608 684871
See Pick of the Pubs on page 482

HENLEY-IN-ARDEN
Map 03 SP16

The Crab Mill NEW
Preston Bagot B95 5EE ☎ 01926 843342 ▤ 01926 843989
Crab apple cider was once made at this 15th-century hostelry, now restored though still showing some original features, and appealing to generally well-heeled customers. The pub is set in beautiful surroundings, and serves good home-cooked food: monkfish and chorizo kebab with mixed leaves, cod in red wine, duck with lemon, tarragon and honey, and warm salad of chicken livers, pear and blue cheese. No credit cards

ILMINGTON
Map 04 SP24

Pick of the Pubs

Howard Arms
Lower Green CV36 4LT ☎ 01608 682226 ▤ 01608 682226
e-mail: howard.arms@virgin.net
Dir: Off A429 or A34

Occupying an idyllic spot on the village green, this mellow Cotswold stone inn has been welcoming

continued

OPEN: 12–2.30 6–11
BAR MEALS: L served Tue-Sun.
D served Tue-Sat. 12–2 7–9 Av main
course £10
RESTAURANT: L served Tue-Sun.
D served Tue-Sat. 12–2 7–9 Av cost
3 course £15
BREWERY/COMPANY:
FREE HOUSE
PRINCIPAL BEERS: Shepherd
Neame Spitfire, Hook Norton Best,
Black Sheep Best, Fuller's London
Pride, Timothy Taylor Landlord,
Adnams Broadside
FACILITIES: Children and dogs
welcome. Garden: Food served
outside
NOTES: Parking 15
ROOMS: 3 en suite Double room
from £55 Single room from £35

Fox & Hounds Inn

Licensed since 1540 and an ideal base for exploring the glorious Cotswolds, the Fox & Hounds exudes plenty of character and old-world charm. Good food, good beer, exceptional whiskies and an inviting atmosphere. Old settles, Tudor inglenook fireplaces and solid ceiling beams adorned with jugs or festooned with hops create a welcoming ambience.

♀
CV36 5NQ
☎ 01608 674220 📠 01608 684871
e-mail: enquiries@yorke-arms.co.uk
Dir: Off A44 NE of Moreton-in-Marsh.

Fascinating features recall the history of this Cotswold stone building down the years - for example, the bar entrance is a double-hinged 'coffin door' which allowed coffins to be brought in and laid out prior to the funeral service. Supposedly, a secret tunnel, along which bodies were sometimes carried, linked the cellar with the nearby church and the inn abounds with colourful tales of poltergeists and ghostly sightings. The Warwickshire Hunt meets at the inn and, appropriately, the highly amusing, though somewhat controversial, pub sign depicts Tony Blair confronting a pack of hounds with several foxes behind him blowing raspberries. In addition to a range of traditional ales, the bar also offers a staggering selection of almost 200 fine whiskies. The bar menu is characterised by traditional bar food, including soup, sandwiches and baguettes, there is a good choice of vegetarian dishes and the well-planned specials board is imaginative and impressive. Expect slow roasted lamb shank on colcannon with caramelised shallots and rosemary jus, smoked haddock with cheese and leek croquettes and a tarragon dressing, roast corn-fed chicken and Mediterranean vegetable tartlet. To follow, there is banana Pavlova with warm chocolate rum sauce and lemon and ricotta cheesecake with a compote of fresh oranges.

LMINGTON continued

travellers and local customers for over 300 years. Three comfortable and tastefully appointed upstairs bedrooms encourage visitors to stay, while the excellent food provides another delightful temptation. Robert and Gill Greenstock have successfully created a civilised dining pub where the varied weekly-changing menus offer freshly prepared dishes cooked to a high standard. Against a backdrop of period charm and character including stone floors, open fires and heavy timbers, enjoy starters like crab fritters with a coriander sauce, oak smoked salmon with warm potato cake, or leek and Roquefort tart. Main choices range from the ever-popular beef and ale to duck breast with apple and prune compote, vegetarian moussaka, filo-wrapped lamb cutlets, and chargrilled marlin. Home-made puddings follow the same interesting trend, as in warm blueberry and marzipan Bakewell tart with clotted cream. Good cask ales and keg beers, including Old Speckled Hen.

OPEN: 11–3 6–11 (Sun 7–10.30) Closed: 25 Dec
BAR MEALS: Lunch served: all week Dinner served: all week 12–2 7–9 Av main course £11 **BREWERY/COMPANY:** Free House **PRINCIPAL BEERS:** Everards Tiger Best, North Cotswold Genesis, Greene King Old Speckled Hen, Timothy Taylor landlord. **FACILITIES:** Garden: Beer garden, patio, food served outdoors Dogs allowed (guide dogs only) **NOTES:** Parking 25 **ROOMS:** 3 bedrooms 3 en suite from s£48 d£78

KENILWORTH
Map 09 SP27

Clarendon House ★ ★ ☺ NEW
High St CV8 1LZ ☎ 01926 857668 ▤ 01926 850669
e-mail: info@clarendonhousehotel.com
Dir: From A452 pass castle, turn L into Castle Hill and continue into High Street

The timber-framed tavern at the heart of this hotel dates back to 1430, when it was built around an old oak tree. The tree and the original well, 40 feet deep, remain, although the current owners have also installed large comfy sofas and a patio with heaters. Food is a considerable draw, ranging from steak & caramelised onion baguettes, tapas and cream teas in the bar to the modish Modern British-style dishes in the brasserie.
OPEN: 11–11 (Sun 12–10.30) Closed: 25-26 Dec
BAR MEALS: Lunch served: all week Dinner served: all week 12-10 Av main course £9.95 **RESTAURANT:** Lunch served: all week Dinner served: all week 12-10 Av 3 course à la carte £17
BREWERY/COMPANY: Free House **PRINCIPAL BEERS:** Greene King Abbot Ale, IPA, Hook Norton Best,. **FACILITIES:** Children welcome Garden: Patio, food served outside Dogs allowed
NOTES: Parking 35 **ROOMS:** 22 bedrooms 22 en suite from s£57.50 d£79.50

LAPWORTH
Map 07 SP17

Pick of the Pubs

The Boot ☺ ♀
Old Warwick Rd B94 6JU ☎ 01564 782464 ▤ 01564 784989
Within easy travelling distance from the M42 (J4), Birmingham, Solihull and Warwick, is a country pub and restaurant that exudes a lively and convivial atmosphere. Standing beside the Grand Union Canal in the unspoilt village of Lapworth, this 16th-century former coaching inn is well worth seeking out. Apart from its smartly refurbished interior, it is the modern brasserie-style food and interesting global wine list that draw the most attention. Wide-ranging menus promise – and deliver – home produced dishes in a delightful, modern style. This might include 'first plates' of mixed seafood cannelloni with Newburg sauce and goats' cheese or chargrilled fennel with Parma ham and Greek yoghurt, followed by 'seconds' typified by calves' liver with black pudding and leek mash, teriyaki salmon with cucumber noodles or spaghetti with broccoli, Parmesan and basil. Side orders offer frites, olive oil mash and mixed leaf salads, while the 'Puds and Stickies' list a chocolate and Mocha slice, washed down, perhaps, with Beaumes de Venise sold by the glass from the extensive wine list.
OPEN: 11–3 5.30–11 (Summer Open all day) Closed: Dec 25
BAR MEALS: Lunch served: all week Dinner served: all week 12–2.30 7–10 Av main course £10 **RESTAURANT:** Lunch served: all week Dinner served: all week 12–2.30 7–10 Av 3 course à la carte £18.95 Av 4 course fixed price £21.95
PRINCIPAL BEERS: Greene King Old Speckled Hen, Wadworth 6X, Scottish Courage John Smith's. **FACILITIES:** Children welcome Children's licence Garden: Food served outside Dogs allowed (water) **NOTES:** Parking 200

LONG ITCHINGTON
Map 06 SP46

The Two Boats
Southam Rd CV47 8QZ ☎ 01926 812640
Dir: Located on Grand Union canal next to the Coventry to Banbury Rd (A423)
Popular pub located on a beautiful stretch of the Grand Union Canal. Canalside garden, 3 real ales and traditional pub food.

LOWER BRAILES
Map 04 SP33

The George Hotel ♀
High St OX15 5HN ☎ 01608 685223 ▤ 01608 685916
e-mail: thegeorgehotel@speed-e-mail.com
Dir: B4035 toward Shipston on Stour

continued

LOWER BRAILES continued

Originally built for the stonemasons building the 12th-century church nearby, the George still oozes history and atmosphere in its refurbished bedrooms, bars and dining room. The original out-houses have even been re-built to provide stabling for carriage or riding horses. Work up an appetite with a dozen or so walks around the village and return for 'Regular Nights' such as blues music and curry on Monday. Menus pay homage to Chinese, Mexican, Italian and Indian influences. Impossible to pigeon-hole, but full of imagination and fun for real ale drinkers and foodies.
OPEN: 11-11 (Sun 12-10.30) **BAR MEALS:** Lunch served: all week Dinner served: all week 12-2 7-9.30 Av main course £8
RESTAURANT: Lunch served: all week Dinner served: all week 12-2 7-9.30 Av 3 course à la carte £14 **BREWERY/COMPANY:** Hook Norton **PRINCIPAL BEERS:** Hook Norton - Generation, Mild, Hooky Best, Old Hooky. **FACILITIES:** Garden: Patio, food served outside Dogs allowed (water) **NOTES:** Parking 60
ROOMS: 7 bedrooms 7 en suite from s£30 d£60

LOWSONFORD   Map 03 SP16

Fleur De Lys ♀
Lapworth St B95 5HJ ☎ 01564 782431 ▤ 01564 782431
Dir: A34 (Birmingham to Stratford)

Converted from three cottages and a mortuary and located alongside the Stratford-upon-Avon Canal, this 17th-century pub boasts a galleried dining room and atmospheric bars with low beams and real log fires. Fleur de Lys pies were originally made here. The style is casual dining with steak and Guinness pie, free-range sausages with bubble and squeak and traditional fish and chips among the wholesome dishes.
OPEN: 11-11 (Sun 12-10.30) **BAR MEALS:** Lunch served: all week Dinner served: all week 12-2.30 6-9.30 Av main course £7.95
BREWERY/COMPANY: Whitbread **PRINCIPAL BEERS:** Flowers Original, Wadworth 6X, Marstons Pedigree, Greene King Old Speckled Hen. **FACILITIES:** Children welcome Garden: Beer garden, outdoor eating Dogs allowed (water) **NOTES:** Parking 150

MONKS KIRBY   Map 04 SP48

The Bell Inn 🛏
Bell Ln CV23 0QY ☎ 01788 832352 ▤ 01788 832352
Dir: Off the Fosseway Intersection with B4455

The Spanish owners of this quaint, timbered inn, originally a priory gatehouse and brewhouse cottage, describe it as 'a corner of Spain in the heart of England'. Not surprisingly, there's a strong emphasis on Mediterranean cuisine and an extensive tapas menu. Sample paella Valencia, chicken with chorizo or Chateaubriand Spanish style, or perhaps choose from the wide-ranging selection of seafood dishes - hake with shellfish, grilled sea bass, whole lobster and prawn piri piri among them.
OPEN: 12-2.30 7-11 Closed: 26 Dec, 1 Jan **BAR MEALS:** Lunch served: Tue-Sun 12-2.30 Dinner served: all week 7-11 Av main course £4.50 **RESTAURANT:** Lunch served: Tue-Sun 12-2.30 Dinner served: all week 7-11 Av 3 course à la carte £18
BREWERY/COMPANY: Free House
PRINCIPAL BEERS: Interbrew Flowers IPA & Boddingtons.
FACILITIES: Children welcome Garden: Food served outside

PRINCETHORPE   Map 04 SP47

The Three Horseshoes ♀
Southam Rd CV23 9PR ☎ 01926 632345
Dir: On A423 at X of B4455 & B4453
Traditional coaching inn, built about 1856, on the Fosse Way. It has a large garden with a range of children's play equipment overlooking open countryside. Beams, horse brasses and log fires characterise the bar, where a blackboard menu of home-cooked food is available.

RATLEY   Map 04 SP34

The Rose and Crown
OX15 6DS ☎ 01295 678148
Dir: Follow Edgehill signs, 7 miles N of Banbury or 13m SE of Stratford-On-Avon on A422.
Following the Battle of Edgehill in 1642, a Roundhead was discovered in the chimney of this 11th-century pub and beheaded in the hearth. His ghost reputedly haunts the building. Enjoy the peaceful village location and the traditional pub food, perhaps including beef and ale pie, scampi and chips, chicken curry and the Sunday roast.
OPEN: 12-2.30 6.30-11 **BAR MEALS:** Lunch served: all week Dinner served: all week 12-2 7-9 Av main course £6.95
RESTAURANT: Dinner served: Wed-Sat 7-9.30 Av 3 course fixed price £10.15 **BREWERY/COMPANY:** Free House
PRINCIPAL BEERS: Wells Bombardier & Eagle IPA, Greene King Old Speckled Hen. **FACILITIES:** Children welcome Garden: Patio, food served outdoors Dogs allowed **NOTES:** Parking 4
ROOMS: 2 bedrooms 2 en suite from s£30 d£49

England

RUGBY   Map 09 SP57

Golden Lion Inn ★ ★ 🛏 ♇
Easenhall CV23 0JA ☎ 01788 832265 ▤ 01788 832878
e-mail: goldenlioninn@aol.com
Dir: from Rugby School take A426 towards Leicester
Run by the same family since 1931 – now in the third
generation – this 16th-century village inn offers traditional
ales, a log fire, home-cooked bar food and a candlelit
restaurant. Accommodation is also available for those who
wish to stay over. Catch of the day from the blackboard might
be steamed fillet of sea bass with chive butter sauce, and an
alternative could be lambs' liver, black pudding and bacon in
rich onion gravy.
OPEN: 11-11 **BAR MEALS:** Lunch served: all week Dinner served:
all week 12-2 6-9.45 Av main course £6.50 **RESTAURANT:** Lunch
served: Tue-Sun 12-2 Dinner served: Mon-Sun 6-9.45 Av 3 course à
la carte £18.75 Av 3 course fixed price £22.50
BREWERY/COMPANY: Free House **PRINCIPAL BEERS:** Greene
King Abbot Ale, Ruddles Best Bitter, IPA. **FACILITIES:** Children
welcome Garden: Food served outdoors, patio, **NOTES:** Parking 80
ROOMS: 12 bedrooms 12 en suite from s£49 d£50

SHIPSTON ON STOUR   Map 04 SP24

The Red Lion ♦♦♦♦ 🛏 ♇
Main St, Long Compton CV36 5JS
☎ 01608 684221 ▤ 01608 684221
e-mail: redlionnot@aol.com
Dir: On A3400 between Shipston on Stour & Chipping Norton
A Grade II listed stone-built coaching inn dating from 1748,
located in an area of outstanding natural beauty on the edge
of the Cotswolds. Inside are stone walls, sturdy beams and log
fires. The menu include home-made steak and kidney pie,
lasagne, pork tenderloin with Calvados and cream, and stuffed
flat mushrooms with Boursin cheese. An ideal base for
exploring and touring the area and visiting Stratford, Blenheim
Palace and Warwick Castle.
OPEN: 11-2.30 6-11 (Sun 12-3, 7-10.30) **BAR MEALS:** Lunch
served: all week Dinner served: all week 12-2 7-9 Av main course
£7.50 **RESTAURANT:** Lunch served: all week Dinner served: all week
12-2 7-9 Av 3 course à la carte £13 **BREWERY/COMPANY:** Free
House **PRINCIPAL BEERS:** Hook Norton Best, Websters Bitter,
Theakston Best. **FACILITIES:** Children welcome Garden: Beer
garden, food served outdoors Dogs allowed **NOTES:** Parking 60
ROOMS: 5 bedrooms 5 en suite from s£30 d£50

White Bear Hotel ♇
High St CV36 4AJ ☎ 01608 661558 ▤ 01608 662612
e-mail: whitebearhot@hotmail.com

This former coaching inn, parts of which date from the 16th-
century, has a Georgian façade overlooking the market place.

continued

The Bear, as it is known to locals, is a lively pub serving good
food and fine ales, and the two beamed bars are full of
character. A typical menu might include halibut on sweet
potato mash with tomato and capers, and slow-roasted oxtail
casserole on mustard mash.
OPEN: 11-11 (Sun 12-10.30) **BAR MEALS:** 12-2 6.30-9.30
RESTAURANT: 12-2 6.30-9.30 **BREWERY/COMPANY:** Punch
Taverns **PRINCIPAL BEERS:** Marstons Pedigree, Interbrew Bass &
Guest Ales. **FACILITIES:** Children welcome Garden: Patio, food
served outside Dogs allowed (water) **NOTES:** Parking 20
ROOMS: 10 bedrooms 10 en suite from s£30 d£50

STRATFORD-UPON-AVON   Map 03 SP25

The Dirty Duck
Waterside CV37 6BA ☎ 01789 297312 ▤ 01789 293441
Frequented by members of the Royal Shakespeare Company
from the nearby theatre, this traditional, partly Elizabethan inn
has a splendid front terrace with peaceful views across the
River Avon.

Pick of the Pubs

The Fox and Goose Inn ♦♦♦♦ 🖾 🛏 ♇
Armscote CV37 8DD ☎ 01608 682293 ▤ 01608 682293

Look for Armscote close to the River Stour mid-way
between Stratford and Shipston to find this stylish
pub/restaurant-with-rooms that has been transformed by
local entrepreneur Sue Gray. Two old cottages and a
former blacksmith's forge have been converted to create a
buzzy, cosmopolitan atmosphere. The deep red-walled
bar and brightly painted dining room, along with slightly
eccentric, luxury en suite bedrooms have proven an
instant hit since their opening just two years ago.
Matching the decor and ambience is a daily-changing
menu from a team of young chefs whose overall talent
belies their years. Seared scallops on wilted pak choi with
sweet chilli dressing and home-made tagliatelle with roast
peppers, goats' cheese and pepper essence, and calves'
liver and bacon on bubble and squeak with red wine
gravy; followed perhaps by dark chocolate torte illustrate
the point. Regular monthly fish nights and summer
barbecues on a decked terrace in the garden.
OPEN: 11-3 6-11 Closed: 25-26 Dec **BAR MEALS:** Lunch
served: all week Dinner served: all week 12-2.30 7-9.30 Av main
course £10 **RESTAURANT:** Lunch served: all week Dinner
served: all week 12-2.30 7-9.30 Av 3 course à la carte £20
BREWERY/COMPANY: Free House
PRINCIPAL BEERS: Hook Norton Old Hooky, Greene King Old
Speckled Hen, Wells Bombardier, Fuller's London Pride.
FACILITIES: Garden: Wooden deck coverd by pergola
NOTES: Parking 20 **ROOMS:** 4 bedrooms 4 en suite from
s£35 d£70

TEMPLE GRAFTON   Map 04 SP15

The Blue Boar 🍺 🍷
B49 6NR ☎ 01789 750010 🖹 01789 750635
e-mail: blueboar@covlink.co.uk
Dir: *Take left hand turn to Temple Grafton off A46 (from Stratford to Alcester). The pub is situated on the first crossroads.*

An inn since the early 1700s, with records of every landlord since 1776. Nearly two hundred years earlier, William Shakespeare married Ann Hathaway in the village church. On offer may be fresh Greenland halibut with caper and anchovy sauce, vegetarian frittata, a complete Spanish menu, and a choice of sweets. Water from the glass-covered well was long used for brewing. Open fires in winter, and views of the Cotswolds from the patio garden.
OPEN: 11-11 **BAR MEALS:** Lunch served: all week Dinner served: all week 12-3 6-10 Av main course £8 **RESTAURANT:** Lunch served: all week Dinner served: all week 12-3 6-10 Av 3 course à la carte £18
BREWERY/COMPANY: Free House **PRINCIPAL BEERS:** Hook Norton, Morland Old Speckled Hen, Theakston XB.
FACILITIES: Children welcome Garden: Food served outside. Patio area Dogs allowed (guide dogs only) **NOTES:** Parking 500
ROOMS: 15 bedrooms 15 en suite from s£40 d£50

WARWICK   Map 04 SP26

Pick of the Pubs

The Tilted Wig 🍺
11 Market Place CV34 4SA
☎ 01926 410466 411534 🖹 01926 495740
Dir: *From M40 J15 follow A429 into Warwick, after 1.5m L into Brook St on into Market Place*

Overlooking the market square, this attractive pine-furnished hostelry combines the atmosphere of a brasserie, wine bar and restaurant all rolled into one. Originally a coaching inn and now a Grade II listed building. The name stems from its proximity to the Crown

continued

Court. A wide range of cask-conditioned ales and a good menu offering quality, home-cooked dishes, which might include cottage pie, tuna steak, whole-tailed scampi, Barnsley chop, chilli con carne, liver, bacon and onions, and tagliatelle.
OPEN: 11-11 (Sun 12-10.30) Closed: Dec 25
BAR MEALS: Lunch served: all week 12-3 Dinner served: Mon-Sat 6-9 Av main course £6.95 **BREWERY/COMPANY:** Punch Taverns
PRINCIPAL BEERS: Carlsberg-Tetley Tetely Bitter, Adnams Broadside. **FACILITIES:** Children welcome Garden: Food served outside, patio **NOTES:** Parking 6 **ROOMS:** 4 bedrooms 4 en suite from s£58 d£58

WHATCOTE   Map 04 SP24

Royal Oak 🍺
CV36 5EF ☎ 01295 680319
Dir: *11 miles from Stratford on Avon. 11 miles from Banbury. Just off A422, signposted Whatcote*
Historic 12th-century inn built for workers building churches in the area. Cromwell reputedly stopped here for a drink after the Battle of Edge Hill. Sample menu includes lamb shank in red wine gravy, sausage and chips, lasagne verdi, vegetable Stroganoff, oriental fishcakes, chicken and cheese with mushrooms, and hot and spicy chicken goujons.
OPEN: 12-3 5.30-11 (closed Mon lunch) **BAR MEALS:** Lunch served: Tue-Sun 12-2 Dinner served: all week 6-9.30 Av main course £6.50 **RESTAURANT:** Lunch served: Tue-Sun 12-2 Dinner served: all week 6-9.30 Av 3 course à la carte £13
BREWERY/COMPANY: Hook Norton **PRINCIPAL BEERS:** Hook Norton, Theakston, Stowford Press. **FACILITIES:** Children welcome Garden: Food served outside. Dogs allowed (On a lead). Water provided **NOTES:** Parking 25

WITHYBROOK   Map 04 SP48

The Pheasant
Main St CV7 9LT ☎ 01455 220480 🖹 01455 220633
Dir: *Off B4112 NE of Coventry*

Charming 17th-century coaching inn located next to the brook from which the village takes its name. The interior is characterised by an inglenook fireplace, farm implements and horse racing photographs. The extensive menu encompasses fish and seafood; steak, chicken and grills; game; omelettes; cold meats; cheeses and sandwiches or rolls. All this plus daily specials on the blackboard.
OPEN: 12-3 6-11 (Sun 12-10.30) Closed: 25-26 Dec
BAR MEALS: Lunch served: all week Dinner served: all week 12-2 6.30-10 **BREWERY/COMPANY:** Free House
PRINCIPAL BEERS: Courage Directors, Theakstons Best.
FACILITIES: Children welcome Garden: Dogs allowed (garden only at manager's discretion) **NOTES:** Parking 55

See Pub Walk on page 479

WOOTTON WAWEN · Map 04 SP16

The Bulls Head
Stratford Rd B95 6BD ☎ 01564 792511
Dir: On A3400
There is plenty of atmosphere at this picturesque inn, originally two large cottages. Low beams, flagstones and old pews can be found inside. A variety of dishes is available and the blackboard changes daily. Fillet of plaice on a chive and cheese crust, or Indian spicy lamb and roast aubergine may be on the menu. **OPEN:** 12–3 6–11 **BAR MEALS:** 12–2.30 7–10 **RESTAURANT:** 12–2.30 7–10 **BREWERY/COMPANY:** W'hampton & Dudley **PRINCIPAL BEERS:** Marston's Pedigree, Banks Bitter plus guest ales. **FACILITIES:** Children welcome Garden **NOTES:** Parking 30

WEST MIDLANDS

BARSTON · Map 09 SP27

Pick of the Pubs

The Malt Shovel ◉ 🍽 ♀
Barston Ln B92 0JP ☎ 01675 443223 📠 01675 443223
Bustling, award-winning country pub and restaurant converted, about four years ago, from an early 20th-century mill where malt was ground. Inside is a welcoming bar and relaxed atmosphere, with a popular barn for more formal eating. The latter features light green wooden panelling, peach coloured walls and original timbers. Cask-conditioned ales, imported beers and good wines are on offer along with a well-planned, imaginative menu using plenty of fresh fish. A good choice of starters, including seared chicken livers on crostini with a poached egg, salad of rocket leaves and Parmesan, and carpaccio of tuna with rocket. Main courses range from grilled sirloin steak with garlic roasted potatoes and Gorgonzola sauce to rosemary studded pork on spiced pear with Dolcelatte, turnip and Parma ham. Try glazed lime tart with ginger ice cream or a plate of Stilton, mature Cheddar and baby goats' cheese, grapes, celery and apple chutney to follow.
OPEN: 12–3 5.30–11 (Sun 12–10.30) **BAR MEALS:** 12–2.30 6.30–9.45 **RESTAURANT:** 12–2.30 7–9.45
BREWERY/COMPANY: Free House
PRINCIPAL BEERS: Greene King Old Speckled Hen, Interbrew Bass. **FACILITIES:** Garden: Food served outside, patio **NOTES:** Parking 30

BIRMINGHAM · Map 09 SP08

The Peacock 🍽 NEW
Icknield St, Forhill, nr King's Norton B38 0EH
☎ 01564 823232 📠 01564 829593
Despite its out of the way location, at Forhill just outside Birmingham, the Peacock keeps very busy serving nine traditional ales and a varied menu, (booking essential). Expect the likes of minted half shoulder of lamb with roasted parsnips and mint and redcurrant jus, or monkfish wrapped in pancetta on a bed of asparagus. Several friendly ghosts are in residence, and one of their tricks is to disconnect the taps from the barrels.
OPEN: 12–11 (Sat 12–3, 7–11 Sun 12–3, 7–10.30)

continued

BAR MEALS: Lunch served: Mon–Sat 12–3 Av main course £7.95 **RESTAURANT:** Lunch served: all week Dinner served: all week 12–3 6.30–9.30 **BREWERY/COMPANY:** Scottish & Newcastle **PRINCIPAL BEERS:** Hobsons Best Bitter, Theakstons Old Peculier,. **FACILITIES:** Garden: Patio at front, food served outside Dogs allowed (water) **NOTES:** Parking 100

COVENTRY · Map 09 SP37

The Rose and Castle
Ansty CV7 9HZ ☎ 024 76612822
Dir: From junc of M6/M69 at Walsgrave follow signs for Ansty.0.75m to pub
The canal runs through the garden at this small family friendly pub. Inside, exposed beams and a varied menu that includes smoked haddock in a creamy sauce with cheese and mashed potato topping, garden pancake, chicken curry, a variety of grills and steaks, and filled giant Yorkshire puddings. The Burger Collection includes such odd-named items as The Godiva Burger, The Great Dane and The Italian Job.
OPEN: 12–3 6–11 (BHs 12–11) **BAR MEALS:** Lunch served: all week Dinner served: all week 12–3 6–11 **BREWERY/COMPANY:** Free House **PRINCIPAL BEERS:** Interbrew Bass, Hook Norton Best Bitter. **FACILITIES:** Children welcome Garden: Food served outside, lawn, view over canal **NOTES:** Parking 50

OLDBURY · Map 09 SO98

Waggon & Horses
17a Church St B69 3AD ☎ 0121 5525467
A listed back bar, copper ceiling and original tilework are among the character features to be found at this real ale pub in the town centre. Traditional pub food includes filled baguettes, toasties, jacket potatoes, and main meals such as fish and chips, and faggots and mash with mushy peas and gravy.
OPEN: 12–3 5–11 (Sun 12–3, 7–10.30) **BAR MEALS:** Lunch served: Mon–Sat 12–2 Dinner served: Wed–Fri 6–8 Av main course £3.95 **PRINCIPAL BEERS:** Marston's Pedigree, Enville White, Holden Special, Brains Bitter. **FACILITIES:** Children welcome Children's licence **NOTES:** Parking 3

Royal State
The Crown is one of the commonest inn names, for patriotic reasons and sometimes because the inn stood on royal land. The Rose and Crown celebrates Henry VII's achievement in ending civil war by reconciling the rival roses of York and Lancaster in the crown. The King's Head, King's Arms and Queen's Arms are equally familiar, often with Henry VIII on the sign, roughly after Holbein. Elizabeth I, the Georges, Queen Victoria and Prince Albert make their appearances, too, and many pubs are names after childen of George III or Queen Victoria (the Duke of York, Duke of Clarence, Duke of Edinburgh, etc). Others honour the Prince of Wales or his badge of the Feathers, while the Fleur de Lys recalls the fact that down to 1801 the kings of England claimed to be kings of France as well.

SEDGLEY   Map 09 SO99

Beacon Hotel
129 Bilston St DY3 1JE ☎ 01902 883380
This traditional Victorian pub has an attached brewery, which
has been operation for some 150, with a thirty-year break
between 1957 and 1987. Brewery tours are available, but only
by appointment. The current owner is the grandson of Sarah
Hughes, who bought the Beacon back in 1920.
OPEN: 12–2.30 5.30–10.45 **BREWERY/COMPANY:** Free House
PRINCIPAL BEERS: Sarah Hughes Dark Ruby, Sarah Hughes
Surprise. **FACILITIES:** Children welcome Children's licence Garden:
Dogs allowed (water) **NOTES:** Parking 50 No credit cards

WEST BROMWICH   Map 08 SP09

The Vine
Roebuck St B70 6RD ☎ 0121 5532866 ▤ 0121 5255450
e-mail: suki@sukis.co.uk

In the surroundings of a typically Victorian ale house, today's
clientele congregates in the front bar to appreciate the quality
and range of Suki Patel's eclectic cooking. Traditional English
cooking of ham, eggs, chips and peas rubs shoulders with
Indian dishes. Real ale or the local mild go down well with
lamb bhuna or Jeera chicken cooked before your eyes in the
bright and cheerful veranda restaurant. Additionally there's a
barbecue menu served throughout the day at weekends.
OPEN: 11.30–2.30 5–11 (Fri–Sun all day) **BAR MEALS:** Lunch
served: all week Dinner served: all week 12–2 5–10.30 Av main course
£3.75 **RESTAURANT:** Dinner served: all week 5–10.30
BREWERY/COMPANY: Free House **PRINCIPAL BEERS:** 8–12
changing real ales. **FACILITIES:** Children welcome Garden: Food
served outside

Drays and Horses

A few breweries still engagingly use Shire
horses and old-style drays to deliver their as in
days of yore. The older 18th-century drays were two-
wheeled wagons drawn by a pair of horses in
tandem, with the driver sitting on one of the barrels.
From this developed the more familiar four-wheeled
dray, drawn by two horses abreast, with the driver
perched up on a high seat. Some of them had open
sides, other rails or low boards, while some had iron
stanchions supporting chains. Strong, hardy and
weighing in at about a ton, Shire horses trace their
ancestry from the vast, tank-like warhorses of the
Middle Ages, which rumbled into battle at a
ground-shaking trot. Their descendants
today rumble through the streets on
more peaceful and merciful
errands.

WIGHT, ISLE OF

ARRETON   Map 04 SZ58

Hare and Hounds 🍴
Downend Rd PO30 2NU ☎ 01983 523446 ▤ 01983 523378
Next to Robin Hill Country Park with fine downland views, an
old historic thatched pub with a long, colourful history that
has been much extended and opened up in recent years. Day-
long menus cater for a variety of tastes. Good walking area.
Greene King. Family friendly.

The White Lion 🍴
PO30 3AA ☎ 01983 528479 ▤ 01983 528479
e-mail: cthewhitelion@aol.com

A 300-year-old former coaching inn with oak beams, polished
brass, open fires and added summer attractions in the
children's playground and aviary. Popular locally for its cosy
atmosphere, well-priced bar food and the starting point for
the Isle of Wight ghost hunt. Curious visitors can stoke up on
a seafood platter for two, veal escalope in wine and onion
gravy or creamy peppered pork medallions before departing
bravely into the unknown – or so 'tis said.
OPEN: 11–12 (Sun 11–10.30) **BAR MEALS:** Lunch served: all week
Dinner served: all week 12–9 Av main course £6.50
PRINCIPAL BEERS: Badger Best, Fuller's London Pride,Interbrew
Flowers IPA,. **FACILITIES:** Children welcome Garden: Food served
outside Dogs allowed (water)

BEMBRIDGE   Map 04 SZ68

The Crab & Lobster Inn 🍴 ♀
32 Foreland Fields Rd PO35 5TR
☎ 01983 872244 ▤ 01983 873495
e-mail: alansi.o.w@aol.com
Clifftop inn with a large patio area affording magnificent views
across the Solent and English Channel. Locals and tourists
alike seek out the friendly atmosphere in the nautically
themed bars, and walkers find the cliffs particularly rewarding.
As the name suggests, local seafood is the speciality, with
warm hors d'oeuvre of lobster, scallops, shrimps, mussels,
prawns and crab, and locally caught lobster served grilled,
thermidor or with salad. Comfortable bedrooms.
OPEN: 11–3 6–11 (Wknds & summer all day) **BAR MEALS:** Lunch
served: all week Dinner served: all week 12–2.30 6.30–9.30 Av main
course £7.50 **RESTAURANT:** Lunch served: all week Dinner served:
all week 12–2.30 7–10 Av 3 course à la carte £17.50
BREWERY/COMPANY: Whitbread **PRINCIPAL BEERS:** Interbrew
Flowers Original, Goddards Fuggle-Dee-Dum. **FACILITIES:** Children
welcome Garden: Food served outside Dogs allowed (water)
NOTES: Parking 40 **ROOMS:** 5 bedrooms 5 en suite from s£30
d£40

PUB WALK

Seaview
Seaview Hotel

With its many miles of footpaths, well-signposted trails and stunning scenery, the Isle of Wight is perfect for walking. This varied route follows the Barnsley Trail through open countryside.

From the hotel turn left towards the seafront. Keep the coastline on your right and follow the Isle of Wight Coastal Path towards Ryde. As the trail rejoins the main road on a bend, turn left, pass Bluett Avenue and turn right at the junction with Fairey Road. Follow the track to the B3330 road at Nettlestone Hill. Turn right, through the Barnsley Valley, and take the first track on the left, as the road swings to the right. This rural stretch through the valley is an interesting feature. Originally, the sea reached as far inland as the Park and Longlands copses and this type of inlet was greatly favoured by the Romans. During the medieval period the inlet developed into Barnsley Harbour,

and although itt was prone to silting, like most of the creeks along the north shore of the island, there was sufficient depth to allow larger ships to sail up to the mill just south of the B3330. The mill pond banks are still visible. Follow the bridleway through the fields to Park Farm. Just before the farm, veer left to join a footpath running through the fields to meet up with the B3330 again. Cross over into Priory Drive and follow it along to the Coastal Path. Turn left, following the trail back to Seaview and the hotel. This final stretch allows you access to St Helen's Duver, a slender spit protruding into Bembridge Harbour. National Trust land, this peaceful haven of grassland, sand dunes and rare flowers has more than 200 different species of wild plants, including tree lupin, evening primrose and sea thrift. Nearby is the ruined tower of St Helen's Church. Once a priory, all but the tower has been ravaged by the sea over the years.

SEAVIEW HOTEL
High Street SEAVIEW PO34 5EX
Tel: 01983 612711
Directions: B3330 Ryde-Seaview rd, turn L via Puckpool along seafront Duver road, hotel is situated on left hand side adjacent to the sea
Open: 11–2.30 6–11
Bar Meals: 12–2 7–9.30
Children welcome and dogs allowed. Garden and parking available.

Distance: 4 miles (6.4km)
Map: OS Outdoor Leisure 29
Terrain: Country and urban areas
Paths: Isle of Wight Coastal Path, bridleways, footpaths, some road
Gradient: Undulating countryside

Walk submitted and checked by Seaview Hotel and Nettlestone and Seaview Parish Council

England

BONCHURCH
Map 04 SZ57

The Bonchurch Inn
Bonchurch Shute PO38 1NU ☎ 01983 852611 📠 01983 856657
e-mail: gillian@bonchurch-inn.co.uk
Dir: South coast of the Island
17th-century coaching inn with cobbled courtyard, located in picturesque island village where Charles Dickens wrote part of David Copperfield. Italian specialities feature heavily on the menu, including cannelloni with spinach, risotto Milanese, pizza Napolitana, and spaghetti bolognese. More traditional dishes are also on the menu, such as ploughman's lunches, grilled fillet steak, breaded plaice, and chicken kiev.
OPEN: 11–3.30 6.30–11 Closed: 25 Dec **BAR MEALS:** Lunch served: all week Dinner served: all week 11–2.15 6.30–9 Av main course £7 **RESTAURANT:** Dinner served: all week 6.30–9.30 Av 3 course à la carte £17 **BREWERY/COMPANY:** Free House **PRINCIPAL BEERS:** Scottish Courage Courage Directors & Courage Best. **FACILITIES:** Children welcome Dogs allowed (water) **NOTES:** Parking 7 **ROOMS:** 2 bedrooms 1 en suite from d£60

CHALE
Map 04 SZ47

Clarendon Hotel & Wight Mouse Inn ★ ★
PO38 2HA ☎ 01983 730431 📠 01983 730431
e-mail: info@wightmouseinns.co.uk
Dir: On B3399 next to St Andrews church, Chale
This 17th-century coaching inn overlooks West Wight's superb coastline and is handy for Blackgang Chine and lovely sandy beaches. The family-friendly theme is being developed and the 'chilled mouse' self-contained shop unit in the garden is especially popular, while the adjacent pub has log fires, a welcoming atmosphere and over 350 malt whiskies. Straightforward bar menu that might include lemon and herb butterfly chicken breast, T-bone steak, and seafood au gratin.
OPEN: 11–midnight (Sun 12–10.30) **BAR MEALS:** Lunch served: all week Dinner served: all week 12–10 Av main course £6 **RESTAURANT:** Dinner served: all week 6–10 Av 3 course à la carte £15 **PRINCIPAL BEERS:** Six real ales including Badger Best. **FACILITIES:** Children welcome Children's licence Garden: Beer garden, patio, outdoor eating Dogs allowed **NOTES:** Parking 200 **ROOMS:** 12 bedrooms 12 en suite from s£39 d£78

COWES
Map 04 SZ49

The Folly
Folly Ln PO32 6NA ☎ 01983 297171 📠 01983 297444
e-mail: Follyinn.whippingham@whitbread.com
Reached by both land and water and very popular with the Solent's boating fraternity, the Folly is one of the island's more unusual pubs. Timber from an old sea-going French barge was used in the construction and wood from the hull can be found in the nautical theme of the bar. Extensive specials board menu ranging from 'Crewpot' casserole – beef goulash, lamb and vegetable or spicy sausage – to plaice, mackerel trout and salmon.
OPEN: 9–23.00 (BHs & Cowes Week late opening) **BAR MEALS:** Lunch served: all week Dinner served: all week 12–9.30 Av main course £7 **PRINCIPAL BEERS:** Interbrew Flowers Origional, IPA, Greene King Old Speckled Hen, Gales HSB. **FACILITIES:** Children welcome Garden: Food served outside Dogs allowed (water) **NOTES:** Parking 30

FRESHWATER
Map 04 SZ38

Pick of the Pubs

The Red Lion
Church Place PO40 9BP ☎ 01983 754925 📠 01983 754925
Dir: In Freshwater follow signs for parish church

This civilised inn attracts the yachting fraternity from nearby Yarmouth, who are drawn by the interesting food as much as the picturesque setting in an old village just a short stroll from the tidal River Yar. The pub's origins date from the 11th century, though the current red brick building is much newer. The open-plan bar is comfortably furnished with country kitchen-style tables and chairs, plus relaxing sofas and antique pine. Order early to guarantee your chosen dishes from the blackboard menu, as demand soon exceeds supply. Everything is freshly made from tried and tested recipes, with the likes of herring roes on toast, or spicy-coated sardines followed by Red Lion fish pie, chicken Madras curry, and baby leg of lamb for two. Puddings include Cointreau and orange trifle, lemon meringue pie, and citrus cheesecake, and to wash it all down there are four real ales, including the island's Goddard Best.
OPEN: 11.30–3 5.30–11 (Sun 12–3 7–10.30)
BAR MEALS: Lunch served: all week Dinner served: all week 12–2 6.30–9 Av main course £9
BREWERY/COMPANY: Whitbread
PRINCIPAL BEERS: Interbrew Flowers Original, Fuller's London Pride, Goddards. **FACILITIES:** Garden: Food served outside Dogs allowed **NOTES:** Parking 20

NITON
Map 04 SZ57

Buddle Inn
St Catherines Rd PO38 2NE ☎ 01983 730243
e-mail: buddleinn@aol.com
Dir: Take A3055 from Ventnor. In Niton take 1st L signed 'to the lighthouse'
One of the island's oldest hostelries, a cliff-top farmhouse in the 16th century, which abounds with local history and tales of smuggling and derring-do. Popular with hikers and ramblers (dogs and muddy boots welcome), the interior is characterised by stone flags, oak beams and a large open fire. Specialising in real ale, wines and good company, home-cooked food includes local crab and lobster, daily pies and curries, ploughman's and steaks.
OPEN: 11–11 (Sun 12–10.30) **BAR MEALS:** Lunch served: all week Dinner served: all week 11.30–2.45 6–9.30 Av main course £10 **PRINCIPAL BEERS:** Interbrew Flowers Original & Bass, Greene King Abbot Ale, Adnams best. **FACILITIES:** Garden: Food served outside Dogs allowed (water) **NOTES:** Parking 50

ROOKLEY | Map 04 SZ58

The Chequers
Niton Rd PO38 3NZ ☎ 01983 840314 ▤ 01983 840820
Overlooking rolling farmland, this family-friendly pub was used to collect parish taxes in the 18th century. Today it provides plenty of entertainment for children and is a meeting place for walkers. A simple but hearty menu includes pork medallions, mixed grills, fresh cod and plaice fillets, and chicken curry.
OPEN: 11-11 **BAR MEALS:** Lunch served: all week Dinner served: all week 12-10 Av main course £7.95 **RESTAURANT:** Lunch served: all week Dinner served: all week 12-10 **BREWERY/COMPANY:** Free House **PRINCIPAL BEERS:** Gale's HSB, Greene King Old Speckled Hen,Scottish Courage John Smiths, Courage Directors.
FACILITIES: Children welcome Garden: Food served outside Dogs allowed (water) **NOTES:** Parking 70

SEAVIEW | Map 04 SZ69

Pick of the Pubs

Seaview Hotel & Restaurant ★★★ ◉◉◉ ♀
High St PO34 5EX ☎ 01983 612711 ▤ 01983 613729
e-mail: reception@seaviewhotel.co.uk
Dir: B3330 Ryde-Seaview rd, turn L via Puckpool along seafront duver road, hotel is situated on left hand side adjacent to the sea

Seaview's picturesque sailing village is one of the island's best-loved spots, and the jewel in its crown has to be this pub-cum-restaurant. Built in 1795, there are stunning views across the sea to Portsmouth naval dockyard. Both navies - merchant and royal - are commemorated in the fascinating collection of artifacts displayed throughout the pub and the different restaurants, including classic ship models, letters from the Titanic, and bills from the Queen Mary. In amongst this homage to the sea is another tribute, this time to the fish and seafood freshly caught and brought to the table by local fishermen. Skate wing with lemon and caper noisette, fillet of brill, and monkfish tail are likely to appear on the restaurant menu, along with loin of island pork, and breast of corn fed chicken stuffed with wild mushrooms and spinach. From the bar menu expect hot crab ramekin, smoked duck breast salad, and braised lamb shank.
OPEN: 11-2.30 6-11 Closed: Dec 24-27 **BAR MEALS:** Lunch served: all week Dinner served: all week 12-2 7-9.30 Av main course £8.95 **RESTAURANT:** Lunch served: all week 12-2 7.30-9.30 Av 3 course à la carte £25
BREWERY/COMPANY: Free House
PRINCIPAL BEERS: Goddards, Greene King Abbot Ale.
FACILITIES: Children welcome Garden: Courtyard/patio, Food served outside Dogs allowed **NOTES:** Parking 12
ROOMS: 16 bedrooms 16 en suite from s£55 d£70
See Pub Walk on page 489

SHALFLEET | Map 04 SZ48

Pick of the Pubs

The New Inn ⌂ ♀
Mill Ln PO30 4NS ☎ 01983 531314 ▤ 01983 531314
e-mail: martin.bullock@virgin.net

Dating back to 1753 and one of the Isle of Wight's best-known watering holes, the New Inn is conveniently located on the 65-mile coast path, near the National Trust's Newtown River and Nature Reserve. The interior tells of its long past with its beamed ceilings, open fireplaces and flagstone floors. During recent years the New Inn has developed an enviable reputation for its seafood and use of local produce. Expect whole crab salad, local sea bass, crab and lobster. Thai-style swordfish and halibut topped with tiger prawns, cod fillet in a prawn and peppercorn sauce or tuna steak with lime and coriander are among the fish dishes that may be on offer on the constantly changing menu. Not all the dishes are fish, of course, and in addition to steak Diane and chicken supreme local game is used in the winter. Wide-ranging international wine list with about 60 wines and plenty of well-kept real ales.
OPEN: 11-3 6-11 (Jul-Aug all day) **BAR MEALS:** Lunch served: all week Dinner served: all week 12-2.30 6-10 Av main course £9.50 **RESTAURANT:** 12-2.30 6-10
PRINCIPAL BEERS: Interbrew Bass, Flowers Bitter, Greene King IPA, Marston's Pedigree. **FACILITIES:** Garden: Elevated lawn area at rear of pub Dogs allowed (water) **NOTES:** Parking 20

SHANKLIN | Map 04 SZ58

Fisherman's Cottage ♀
Shanklin Chine PO37 6BN ☎ 01983 863882 ▤ 01983 874215
Situated right on Appley beach, the recently re-thatched cottage was built in 1817 by Shanklin's first operator of covered 'bathing machines'. Inside the low-beamed bar, the pub's history is recorded in the period pictures that line the walls. The simple menu includes sandwiches, salads, jacket potatoes and popular favourites like battered cod and jumbo sausages. The pub is closed from November to February.
OPEN: 11-3 7-11 (Mar-Oct all day every day) Closed Nov-Feb **BAR MEALS:** Lunch served: all week Dinner served: all week 11-2 7-9 Av main course £5 **BREWERY/COMPANY:** Free House **PRINCIPAL BEERS:** Courage Directors, John Smiths Smooth.
FACILITIES: Children welcome Garden: Large patio, food served outdoors Dogs allowed (water) No credit cards

England

SHORWELL   Map 04 SZ48

The Crown Inn
Walkers Ln PO30 3JZ ☎ 01983 740293 ▤ 01983 740293
Dir: From Newport to Carisbrooke High St, then L at rdbt at top of hill,
take B3323 to Shorwell

Opposite the church in the centre of the village, this 17th-
century pub is set in award-winning gardens complete with a
play area, stream, huge trout and a colony of mallards. The
resident ghost disapproves of card games. Food is offered
from a bar menu and specials board with local fish and
options such as spicy vegetable schnitzel, lasagne, jumbo
sausage and egg, chicken burger, and fisherman's pie.
OPEN: 10.30-3.00 (Sun 12-3.00) 6-11 (sun eve 6-10:30) Closed:
none **BAR MEALS:** Lunch served: all week Dinner served: all week
12-2.30 6-9.30 Av main course £6.95
BREWERY/COMPANY: Whitbread **FACILITIES:** Children welcome
Garden: Dogs allowed (on lead) **NOTES:** Parking 60

VENTNOR   Map 04 SZ57

The Spyglass Inn 🛏
The Esplanade PO38 1JX ☎ 01983 855338 ▤ 01983 855220
Dir: Town centre

The huge collection of seafaring memorabilia fascinates
visitors to this popular 19th-century pub, which is located at
the western end of Ventnor Esplanade. An extensive terrace
overlooking the sea is ideal for summer drinks and meals.
Seafood is the speciality, including Ventnor Bay lobsters and
crabs. Daily changing specials board may offer crab tart, beef
braised in beer, sweet and sour pork, or seafood casserole.
Live music is provided most evenings - country, folk or jazz.
OPEN: 10.30-3 (Sun 12) 6.30-11 (May-Oct 10.30-11, open all day)
BAR MEALS: Lunch and Dinner served: all week 12-2.15 7-9.30 Av
main course £5.50 **RESTAURANT:** Lunch and Dinner served: all
week 12-2.15 7-9.30 **BREWERY/COMPANY:** Free House
PRINCIPAL BEERS: Badger Dorset Best, Tanglefoot & King & Barnes
Sussex Best, Ventnor Golden. **FACILITIES:** Children welcome
Garden: Terrace over looking sea, Food served outside Dogs allowed
NOTES: Parking 10 **ROOMS:** 3 bedrooms 3 en suite from d£45

WILTSHIRE

ALDERBURY   Map 03 SU12

The Green Dragon
Old Rd SP5 3AR ☎ 01722 710263
Dir: 1m off A36 (Southampton/Salisbury rd)
There are fine views of Salisbury Cathedral from this 14th-
century pub. Dickens wrote Martin Chuzzlewit here, and
called the pub the Blue Dragon. An interesting and daily
changing menu features home-made meat and vegetarian
dishes using locally sourced produce.
OPEN: 11.30-2.30 6-11 (Sun 12-3, 7-10.30) **BAR MEALS:** Lunch
served: all week Dinner served: all week 12-2 Av main course £5
RESTAURANT: Dinner served: all week 7-9 Av 3 course à la carte
£16 **BREWERY/COMPANY:** Hall & Woodhouse
PRINCIPAL BEERS: Badger Dorset Best & Tanglefoot, King & Barnes.
FACILITIES: Children welcome Garden: BBQ, beer garden, outdoor
eating Dogs allowed outside on lead **NOTES:** Parking 10

ALVEDISTON   Map 03 ST92

Pick of the Pubs

The Crown 🛏
SP5 5JY ☎ 01722 780335 ▤ 01722 780836
Dir: 2.5m off A30 approx half-way between Salisbury and Shaftesbury

Tucked away in the Ebble Valley between Salisbury and
Shaftesbury, the Crown, with its pink-washed walls,
thatched roof and creepers serves entirely home-made
food with particular emphasis on fresh local produce. Its
old world setting, characterised by head-cracking low
beams, two inglenook fireplaces and comfortable
furnishings sets the scene for food that can range from a
simple sandwich to fresh fish and rib-eye steaks - a steal
on Tuesday nights for just a fiver. Listed daily on
chalkboards, expect to find salmon fillet with home-made
tartare sauce, chargrilled red snapper with stir-fried
vegetables, lambs' liver with smoked bacon and pork fillet
in Dijon mustard sauce. Cosily inviting letting rooms
provide a handy base for splendid local walks and visits to
Salisbury Cathedral and Stonehenge.
OPEN: 11.30-3 6-11 (Sun 12-3, 7-10.30) **BAR MEALS:** Lunch
served: all week Dinner served: all week 12-2 6.30-9 Av main
course £5 **RESTAURANT:** Lunch served: all week Dinner
served: all week 12-2 6.30-9.30 Av 3 course à la carte £19
BREWERY/COMPANY: Free House
PRINCIPAL BEERS: Ringwood Best, Wadworth 6X.
FACILITIES: Children welcome Garden: Food served outdoors,
patio, Dogs allowed (water) **NOTES:** Parking 40
ROOMS: 3 bedrooms 3 en suite from d£23.75

PUB WALK

Salisbury
The Old Mill at Harnham

OLD MILL,
Town Path, West Harnham
SALISBURY SP2 8EU
Tel: 01722 327517
Directions: near city centre, on River Avon
Open: 11-11
Bar meals: 12-2.30 7-9
Children welcome and dogs allowed. Garden and parking available.

This easy, undemanding walk along the Nadder to Salisbury Cathedral offers an assortment of riches and scenic delights, taking you right to the heart of the city. Stroll by the Avon and visit the magnificent Close before beginning the return leg across the famous watermeadows.

Turn right from the inn and follow Town Path and the road to the junction with Lower Street. Bear right here and follow Middle Street. Through an opening join a parallel path running across Middle Street Meadow, a native wildlife meadow. Look for a gap in the hedge at the end of the football pitch and rejoin the road. Turn right and walk to Upper Street. As the road bends left, swing right at a footpath sign to Bemerton. Follow the clear path through the trees until you reach a footbridge. Keep right here, cross the Nadder and follow the enclosed path between fields, meadows and trees towards

Salisbury. Cross a wooden footbridge by a brick cottage and head for several more bridges. At the entrance to a farm, turn right and follow the road towards the city centre. At a roundabout, turn right and pass the entrance to Fisherton Island; the road soon reaches some detached villas on the left. Keep right at this point and cross the grass, avoiding the footbridge over the Nadder. With the river on your right, make for a footbridge, crossing a feeder stream, ahead. Go over, turn right and take the riverside path along to where the Nadder and the Avon meet. Keep left and follow the path along to the next road bridge. Turn right along Crane Street to the junction with High Street. Bear right here to Salisbury Cathedral and the Close. Retrace your steps along Crane Street to the bridge and follow the riverside path to the second footbridge. Cross over and take Town Path across the meadows towards Harnham, returning to the Old Mill.

Distance: 4 miles (6.4km)
Map: OS Landranger 184
Terrain: Meadows and woodland, city streets and thoroughfares
Paths: Roads, pavements, meadow and woodland paths
Gradient: Level ground - no hills

Walk submitted and checked by Nick Channer

493

England

AXFORD
Map 04 SU27

Red Lion Inn 🏠 ♀
SN8 2HA ☎ 01672 520271 🖥 01672 520271
Dir: M4 J15, A246 Marlborough centre. Follow signs for Ramsbury. Inn 3m
A 17th-century brick and flint inn with peaceful views across the unspoilt beauty of the Kennet Valley. Fresh fish and game (in season) feature strongly on the regularly changing menu. Typical dishes include grilled scallops with Italian cured ham and Parmesan, pork and game pâté, fillet steak forestière and baked turbot with sun-dried tomato, anchovy and black olive tapenade.
OPEN: 11–3 6.30–11 **BAR MEALS:** Lunch served: all week Dinner served: all week 12–2 7–9 Av main course £6 **RESTAURANT:** Lunch served: all week Dinner served: all week 12–2 7–9 Av 3 course à la carte £20 **BREWERY/COMPANY:** Free House
PRINCIPAL BEERS: Hook Norton Best, Wadworth 6X plus guest beers. **FACILITIES:** Children welcome Garden: **NOTES:** Parking 30

BARFORD ST MARTIN
Map 03 SU03

Barford Inn
SP3 4AB ☎ 01722 742242 🖥 01722 743606
e-mail: ido@barfordinn.co.uk
Dir: on A30 5m W of Salisbury
Just five miles from Salisbury is this 16th-century former coaching inn with welcoming lounge, lower bar area and intimate snug. During WW II the Wiltshire Yeomanry dedicated a tank to the pub, then known as The Green Dragon. Specials may include confit of duck legs, pan-fried escalope of veal, grilled whole plaice or cheddar and leek bake. Friday night is Israeli BBQ night. The bright, well-appointed bedrooms are in an annexe.
OPEN: 11–11 Closed: Dec 25 **BAR MEALS:** Lunch served: all week Dinner served: all week 12–2.30 7–9.30 Av main course £9
RESTAURANT: Lunch served: all week Dinner served: all week 12–2.30 7–9.30 Av 3 course à la carte £16
BREWERY/COMPANY: Hall & Woodhouse
PRINCIPAL BEERS: Badger Dorset Best, Tanglefoot.
FACILITIES: Children welcome Garden: Food served outside
NOTES: Parking 40 **ROOMS:** 4 bedrooms 4 en suite from s£50 d£50

BECKHAMPTON
Map 03 SU06

Waggon & Horses ♀
SN8 1QJ ☎ 01672 539418
A beautiful thatched coaching inn dating back some 400 years, located close to Avebury's stone circles. Charles Dickens stayed at the pub on one time and wrote part of The Pickwick Papers here. The straightforward menu includes dishes such as beef and Stilton pie, chicken breast, Brie and ham, and lamb shank with minted gravy.

Nine Men's Morris
A certain eeriness clings to one of the world's oldest games, which was played in Ancient Egypt 3,000 years ago and in Ireland in prehistoric times. It involves moving pegs or counters to form rows of three on a board or playing surface with 24 holes marked on it in an intricate pattern.

BERWICK ST JAMES
Map 03 ST92

Pick of the Pubs

The Boot Inn 🏠
High St SP3 4TN ☎ 01722 790243 🖥 01722 790243

The Boot is an attractive, 16th-century stone and flint inn with a village setting and award-winning gardens, complete with a summer house, colourful borders and hanging baskets. The interior is traditional in style, and the atmosphere warm and friendly. Real ales are served – Wadworth 6X, Bass and Henrys IPA – and a regularly changing menu of good quality, home-cooked food. Fresh local produce, including herbs and vegetables from the garden, appear in dishes of roast shoulder of lamb with mint gravy; beef, mushroom and red wine stew, and oven baked goats' cheese set on salad leaves with date compote. Fresh fish is offered according to availability, and game in season. Favourites are a warm salad of scallops with crispy smoked bacon, and home-made fishcakes. For a more exotic flavour, there's Thai curry or chilli con carne.
OPEN: 12–3 6–11 **BAR MEALS:** Lunch served: Tues–Sun Dinner served: Tues–Sun 12–2.30 6.30–9.30 Av main course £8.95 **BREWERY/COMPANY:** Wadworth
PRINCIPAL BEERS: Wadsworth 6x, Bass, Henrys IPA.
FACILITIES: Garden: Food served outside Dogs allowed (water)
NOTES: Parking 18

BERWICK ST JOHN
Map 03 ST92

Talbot Inn 🏠 NEW
The Cross, Berwick St John SP7 0HA ☎ 01747 828222
e-mail: easontalbot@hotmail.com
Dir: 4 miles E of Shaftesbury signed off A30 towards Wilton
Standing in the beautiful Chalke Valley, a haven for wildlife with many wonderful walks, the Talbot's roaring log fires create a cosy winter atmosphere. Food is freshly cooked to order on a menu that traverses the world in adventurous guises such as Vietnamese pak choi and chicken soup and hake fillets in tempura batter. Equally popular are locally smoked trout, salmon fishcakes, wild boar sausages and home-made steak and kidney pudding. Round off with spotted Dick or apple and blackberry crumble.
OPEN: 12–2.30 6.30–11 **BAR MEALS:** Lunch served: Tue–Sun 12–2.15 Dinner served: Tue–Sat 6.30–9.15 **RESTAURANT:** Lunch served: Tue–Sun 12–2.15 Dinner served: Tue–Sat 6.30–9.15
BREWERY/COMPANY: Free House
PRINCIPAL BEERS: Wadworth 6X, Hop Back Summer Lightning & Guest Beers. **FACILITIES:** Garden: Patio area with hanging baskets Dogs allowed (water) **NOTES:** Parking 14

England

he Quarrymans Arms 🐑 ♀
ox Hill SN13 8HN ☎ 01225 743569
mail: John@quarrymans-arms.co.uk
ir: *Phone the pub for accurate directions*

300-year-old miners' pub tucked away up a narrow hillside
ne. Really splendid views over the Colerne Valley – great for
alkers, cavers, potholers and cyclists. It is on the Macmillan
'ay, a long distance footpath, and offers accommodation and
ggage transfer. The interior is packed with mining
iemorabilia, and you can hear and feel the trains taking trips
own the stone mines. Popular dishes are Greek-style lamb
hank, Thai crab cakes, and pork Dijonnaise.
PEN: 11-3.30 6-11 (all day Fri-Sun) **BAR MEALS:** Lunch served:
l week Dinner served: all week 11-3 6.30-10.30 Av main course £6
ESTAURANT: Lunch served: all week Dinner served: all week 11-3
30-10.30 **BREWERY/COMPANY:** Free House
RINCIPAL BEERS: Butcombe Bitter, Wadworth 6X, Moles.
ACILITIES: Children welcome Garden: Food served outside Dogs
'lowed **NOTES:** Parking 25 **ROOMS:** 3 bedrooms 1 en suite from
£25 d£45

RADFORD-ON-AVON   Map 03 ST86

he Dandy Lion 🐑 ♀
5 Market St BA15 1LL ☎ 01225 863433 📠 01225 869169

17th-century terraced building whose interior decor reflects
he town's busy antique trade, and offers both convivial pub
ining and exclusivity in an upper restaurant. Light bites and
asta with daily specials – spaghetti matriciana, salmon fillet,
pinach and Ricotta cannelloni, Lion's Mushrooms,
andwiches, ploughman's, jacket potatoes – by day. Wild
nushroom risotto, pork Normandy, or self-cooked steaks on
ot stones at night.
PEN: 10.30-3 6-11 (Sun 11.30-3, 7-10.30) **BAR MEALS:** Lunch
erved: all week 12-2.15 Dinner served: Mon-Thu Av main course
9.50 **RESTAURANT:** Lunch served: Sun Dinner served: all week
2-2.15 7-9.30 Av 3 course à la carte £17.50
REWERY/COMPANY: Wadworth
RINCIPAL BEERS: Butcombe, Wadworth 6X, Henrys IPA,
'adworth Seasonal Ales. **FACILITIES:** Children welcome Children's
cence

Pick of the Pubs

The Kings Arms ♀
Monkton Farleigh BA15 2QH
☎ 01225 858705 📠 01225 858999
e-mail: enquiries@kingsarms-bath.org.uk
Dir: *Follow A4 from Bath to Bradford, At Bathford join A363, turning L
to Monkton Farleigh*

In a most attractive conservation village only five minutes'
drive from Bradford-on-Avon, this historic Bath stone and
pan-tiled building dates back to the 11th century and was
originally a monks retreat attached the nearby and now
ruined monastery. Converted into a public house in the
17th century, its many features include stone mullion
windows and flagged floor in the Chancel Bar and a vast
inglenook in the medieval-style restaurant, hung with
tapestries and pewter plates. Approached by way of an
arboreal courtyard, the pub leads through an enclosed
garden with parasolled tables and an aviary of golden
pheasants and lovebirds. Bar food at lunch only includes
traditional dishes such as roast beef and horseradish
sandwich and home-cooked ham, two egg and chips.
Dinner promises chef's own chicken Kiev served on a bed
of creamed spinach, chargrilled Barnsley lamb chop with
butter-fried mushrooms, grilled tomato and fresh mint
sauce and hot treacle tart and custard.
OPEN: 11-11 (Sun 11-10.30) **BAR MEALS:** Lunch served: all
week Dinner served: all week 12-3 5.30-9.30 Av main course
£5.60 **RESTAURANT:** Lunch served: all week Dinner served: all
week 12-3 5.30-9.30 Av 3 course à la carte £19
PRINCIPAL BEERS: Interbrew Bass, Wadworth 6X, Buttcombe
Bitter,. **FACILITIES:** Children welcome Children's licence
Garden: Dogs allowed **NOTES:** Parking 45

Top of the Tree
Pubs called the Royal Oak were originally named in loyal remembrance of the day in
1651 when the youthful King Charles II hid in an oak tree at Boscobel in Shropshire, while
Roundhead soldiers unsuccessfully searched the woods for him. The Royal Oak sign often shows
simply the oak tree, or the king is shown perched among the branches - in plain view from all
directions, but conventionally accepted as invisible to the purblind Parliamentarian troops.
Sometimes, more subtly, the tree has a large crown among the foliage. Rarer variants
include the king holding an oak spray with acorns, or acorns below a crown.

BRINKWORTH   Map 03 SU08

Pick of the Pubs

The Three Crowns 🐦 🍷
SN15 5AF ☎ 01666 510366 📠 01666 510303
Dir: A3102 to Wootton Bassett, then B4042, 5m to Brinkworth
A 200-year-old inn standing on the village green by the
church in this quiet village. Deceptively small from the
outside, it opens into a large, bright conservatory, garden
room and a heated patio where the popular food can be
sampled in comfort. The traditional bars, complete with
lots of brass, have tables made from giant converted
bellows and, in winter, an open log fire to add to the
homely atmosphere. Meals can be chosen from the
regularly changing blackboards, and include unusual
(kangaroo, crocodile) and often ambitious choices
alongside the more traditional. Lunchtime snacks like
ploughman's, filled rolls and jacket potatoes come in huge
portions, but for a more serious meal expect various
steaks, duck supreme, rack of lamb, roast partridge,
Somerset wild boar, chicken korma pie, and seafood pie.
Round things off with chocolate bread and butter
pudding, iced ginger parfait, or banana haystacks.
OPEN: 11–3 6-11 Closed: 25-26 Dec **BAR MEALS:** Lunch
served: all week 12-2 Av main course £5 **RESTAURANT:** Lunch
served: all week Dinner served: all week 12-2 6.15-9.30 Av 3
course à la carte £20.25 **PRINCIPAL BEERS:** Wadworth 6X,
Boddingtons, Castle Eden, Fullers London Pride.
FACILITIES: Children welcome Children's licence Garden:
Food served outside, patio area Dogs allowed
NOTES: Parking 40

BROAD CHALKE   Map 03 SU02

The Queens Head Inn 🍷
1 North St SP5 5EN ☎ 01722 780344 📠 01722 780344
Dir: Take A354 from Salisbury toward Blandford Forum, at Coome Bissett
turn R toward Bishopstone, follow rd for 4m
Attractive 15th-century inn with friendly atmosphere and low-
beamed bars, once the village bakehouse. Sample steak pie,
home-made chicken and mushroom pie, or Spanish casserole
from the appealing menu. Alternatively, try one of the
seasonal game dishes, such as pheasant and bacon, jugged
hare or rabbit, from the specials board.
OPEN: 11–3 6-11 (Sun 12-3, 7-10.30) **BAR MEALS:** Lunch served:
all week Dinner served: all week 12-2 7-9 Av main course £7.50
RESTAURANT: Lunch served: all week Dinner served: all week 12-2
7-9 Av 3 course à la carte £15 **BREWERY/COMPANY:** Free House
PRINCIPAL BEERS: Greene King IPA & Old Speckled Hen,
Wadworth 6X. **FACILITIES:** Children welcome Garden: Patio
garden, food served outdoors **NOTES:** Parking 30
ROOMS: 4 bedrooms 4 en suite from s£35 d£60

The Birds of the Air
Pride of place among bird signs is taken by the Swan,
often adopted by inns close to a river. The eccentric Swan
with Two Necks probably began as a swan with two nicks
in its beak. The Cock may be related to cock-fighting or to
St Peter. Geese and chickens appear alone or keeping
dangerous company with the Fox. The Bird in Hand comes
from falconry and the Dog and Duck either from fowling
or from the amusement of setting a dog on a pinioned
duck. The Eagle is from Heraldry and the Magpie and
Stump from the countryside, while rarities include the
Parrot and the Peahen.

BROMHAM   Map 03 ST96

The Greyhound Inn
SN15 2HA ☎ 01380 850241
Dir: Chippenham rd from Devizes for 4m. L into Bromham
New proprietors welcome visitors to this 300-year-old pub,
which has an inside artesian well, beamed ceilings, and an
open fireplace. Large garden and skittle alley.

BURTON   Map 03 ST87

The Old House at Home 🍷
SN14 7LT ☎ 01454 218227 📠 01454 218865
Dir: On B4039 NW of Chippenham
A soft stone, ivy-clad pub with beautiful landscaped gardens
and a waterfall. Inside there are low beams and an open fire.
Overseen by the same landlord for over fifteen years. The
kitchen offers a good fish choice, vegetarian and pasta dishes,
and traditional pub meals. Favourites include lamb cutlets
with champ, salmon and asparagus, Woodland duck breast
with stuffing, and king scallops in Cointreau.
OPEN: 11.30-2.30 (w/end 11.30-3) 7-11 (Sun 7-10.30) Closed Tue
lunch **BAR MEALS:** 12-2 7-10 **BREWERY/COMPANY:** Free
House **PRINCIPAL BEERS:** Wadworth 6X, Smiles Best, Interbrew
Bass. **FACILITIES:** Children welcome Garden: **NOTES:** Parking 25

CALNE   Map 03 ST97

Lansdowne Arms 🍷
Derry Hill SN11 9NS ☎ 01249 812422

Coaching house dating from 1843, with scenic views along the
Avon Valley and close to Bowood House. An interesting menu
includes grills such as Scrumpy pork, minted lamb béarnaise,
and honey glazed gammon. Specials may include seared tuna
with Thai sauce, lamb's liver with onions and bacon, spinach,
mushroom and pepper parcel, and old favourites like steak
and kidney pie, breaded plaice fillet, broccoli and Swiss
cheese quiche. 'Sandwedges', jacket potatoes, and
ploughmans' also available.
OPEN: 11.30-2.30 6-11 (Sun 12-3, 7-10.30) **BAR MEALS:** Lunch
served: all week 12-2 Dinner served: Mon-Sat 7-9 Av main course
£7.50 **BREWERY/COMPANY:** Wadworth
PRINCIPAL BEERS: Wadworth 6X, IPA, Summersault, JCB.
FACILITIES: Children welcome Garden: Food served outside Dogs
allowed **NOTES:** Parking 50

All AA listed accommodation can also be found on the AA's internet site
www.theAA.com

England

White Horse Inn ◆◆◆◆

Compton Bassett SN11 8RG ☎ 01249 813118 📠 01249 811595
e-mail: white.horse.inn@btclick.com
A rustic inn at the heart of a picturesque village in pretty countryside. The cosy oak-beamed bar offers a variety of real ales and ciders to enjoy with a wide-ranging choice of meals and snacks. Lunches and lighter options include Thai chicken curry, smoked fish tart with crème fraîche and tagliatelle with spinach, pesto and Parmesan. Main dishes encompass pan-fried kidneys with grain mustard, oven-baked cod with bubble and squeak and a grill selection that includes a 20-oz T-bone. Comfortable bedrooms.
OPEN: 11–3 5–11 Closed: 25 Dec **BAR MEALS:** Lunch served: all week Dinner served: all week 12–2 7–9.30 Av main course £9
RESTAURANT: Lunch served: all week Dinner served: all week 12–2 7–9.30 Av 3 course à la carte £15 **BREWERY/COMPANY:** Free House **PRINCIPAL BEERS:** Wadworth 6X, Hook Norton, Badger Tanglefoot,. **FACILITIES:** Garden: Food served outside Dogs allowed **NOTES:** Parking 75 **ROOMS:** 7 bedrooms 7 en suite from s£45 d£65

CASTLE COMBE   Map 03 ST87

The White Hart ♀

SN14 7HS ☎ 01249 782295
Dir: Centre of village
Historic, part-timbered 14th century pub in a classic village which film fans will recognise as Puddleby-on-the-Marsh in the movie version of Doctor Doolittle. Many charming features inside the inn, including low ceilings, beams and a cosy log fire. Pleasant patio gardens, sunny conservatory and sheltered courtyard also attract customers. Extensive menu offers the likes of cod and chips, mixed grill and steak and ale pie.
OPEN: 11–11 (Sun 12–10.30) **BAR MEALS:** Lunch served: all week Dinner served: all week 12–2.45 6.30–9 Av main course £5.95
RESTAURANT: Lunch served: all week Dinner served: all week 12–2.45 6.30–9 Av 3 course à la carte £12
BREWERY/COMPANY: Wadworth
PRINCIPAL BEERS: Wadworth 6X, Henry's Original IPA, plus guest ales. **FACILITIES:** Children welcome Garden: Beer garden, outdoor eating Dogs allowed

CHILMARK   Map 03 ST93

Pick of the Pubs

The Black Dog ♀

SP3 5AH ☎ 01722 716344 📠 01722 716124

Set beside the B3089 west of Salisbury in the pretty village of Chilmark, the 15th-century stone-built Black Dog is a great country pub. First and foremost, it is the village local, yet successfully combines its unspoilt historic charm

continued

with an appealing modern decor, tip-top local ales, a warm, friendly welcome, and offers excellent contemporary pub food. Classic main bar with red and black tiled floor, a huge table topped with unusual dried flower arrangements, and a chatty atmosphere; adjoining beamed and cosy dining areas. Good, popular food ranges from Black Dog burger, imaginatively filled baguettes and venison in red wine casserole at lunchtime, to modern, well presented evening dishes listed on the interesting carte. For starters, try lime and basil marinated salmon with hollandaise or smoked chicken and asparagus Caesar salad with Parmesan shaving, followed by grilled Torbay sole, roast monkfish on lightly curried mussels with cream, coconut and lime, or a prime fillet steak with cracked black pepper, Dijon mustard, brandy and cream. Huge rear garden for summer imbibing.
OPEN: 11–3 6–11 **BAR MEALS:** Lunch served: all week Dinner served: all week 12–2.30 6–9.30 **RESTAURANT:** Lunch served: all week Dinner served: all week 12–2.30 6–9.30 Av 3 course à la carte £20 **PRINCIPAL BEERS:** Bass, Wadworth 6X,.
FACILITIES: Children welcome Garden: Food served outside Dogs allowed **NOTES:** Parking 30

CHRISTIAN MALFORD   Map 03 ST97

The Rising Sun

Station Rd SN15 4BL ☎ 01249 721571 📠 01249 721571
e-mail: risingsun@tesco.net
Dir: From M4 J 17 take B4122 towards Sutton Benger, turn L on to the B4069, pass through Sutton Benger after 1M you come into Christian Malford, turn R into the village (station road) the pub is the last building on the L
Since taking over some three years ago the Hutchens family have preserved the essence of a convivial, unspoilt country inn, whist bringing a refreshing approach to pub food. Wherever possible all dishes are cooked from fresh, using local ingredients and organic produce. Particularly popular are the slow-cooked braised steaks and casseroles. Look out for dinner specials such as pheasant or venison in the winter months; while peppered steak with mustard mash or rabbit in white wine with bubble-and-squeak will tease the taste buds at any time.
OPEN: 12–2.30 6.30–11 **BAR MEALS:** Lunch served: Tues-Sun Dinner served: Tues-Sun 12–2 6.30–11 Av main course £7
RESTAURANT: Lunch served: Tues-Sun Dinner served: Tues-Sun 12–2 6.30–10 Av 3 course à la carte £18
BREWERY/COMPANY: Free House **PRINCIPAL BEERS:** Hook Norton plus guest ale. **FACILITIES:** Garden: Food served outside, lawn Dogs allowed (water) **NOTES:** Parking 15

Darts

Although darts is now regarded as the archetypal pub game, its history is shrouded in almost total mystery and it may not have entered the pub scene until well into the 19th century. The original board may have been the end of a barrel, with the doubles ring as its outer ring. The accepted arrangement of numbers round the rim dates from the 1890s, but there are variant types of board in different areas of the country. The Yorkshire board, for instance, has no trebles ring. Nor does the Lancashire or Manchester board, which has a very narrow doubles ring and is customarily kept soaked in beer when not in use.

COLLINGBOURNE DUCIS — Map 04 SU25

The Shears Inn & Country Hotel ⌂ ♀
The Cadley Rd SN8 3ED ☎ 01264 850304 ▤ 01264 850220
Dir: On A338 NW of Andover & Ludgershall

A 16th-century pub, once a crossroad shearing shed for sheep off to market, now a thriving country inn serving good food, beer and wine. Thatched, with beams and brick floors, and handy for Salisbury and Marlborough. The carte, plus blackboard for fish specials, ranges over whole grilled sole with lemon butter, sea bass fillets on baby spinach, roasted trio of pheasant, duck breast and venison, and chicken stuffed with crab in a light mustard sauce.
OPEN: 11–3 5.30–11 **BAR MEALS:** Lunch served: all week Dinner served: all week 12–2.30 6.30–9.30 Av main course £6.95 **RESTAURANT:** Lunch served: all week Dinner served: all week 12–2.30 6.30–9.30 Av 3 course à la carte £20
BREWERY/COMPANY: Free House
PRINCIPAL BEERS: Theakstons Best, Marston's Pedigree, Gales HSB, Wadworth 6X. **FACILITIES:** Children welcome Garden: Food served outdoors Dogs allowed **NOTES:** Parking 50
ROOMS: 6 bedrooms 6 en suite from s£39.50

CORSHAM — Map 03 ST87

Methuen Arms Hotel ⌂
2 High St SN13 0HB ☎ 01249 714867 ▤ 01249 712004
e-mail: methuenarms@lineone.net
Dir: Town centre,on A4 between Bath & Chippenham
Dating back in part to the 14th century with Georgian additions and mullioned windows, this building started out as a nunnery. The fine Cotswold stone façade conceals a welcoming lounge and public bar where appetising meals are served, and the candlelit Winter's Court Restaurant. Choices include grilled tuna steak with lemongrass and salsa, darne of salmon in herb butter, crispy aromatic duck, and braised lambs' liver. Expect good old-fashioned service.
OPEN: 11–11 **BAR MEALS:** Lunch served: all week Dinner served: all week 12–2.15 6–9.15 Av main course £5.95 **RESTAURANT:** Lunch served: all week 12–2 Dinner served: Mon–Sat 7–9.45 Av 3 course à la carte £21 Av 3 course fixed price £16.95
BREWERY/COMPANY: Latona Leisure
PRINCIPAL BEERS: Wadworth 6X, Interbrew Boddingtons Bitter & Bass, Scottish Courage Courage Best. **FACILITIES:** Children welcome Garden: adjoins Corsham Park, food served outdoors Dogs allowed **NOTES:** Parking 60 **ROOMS:** 24 bedrooms 24 en suite from s£40 d£60

CORSLEY HEATH — Map 03 ST84

The Royal Oak Inn
BA12 7PR ☎ 01373 832238
Dir: On A362 between Warminster & Frome
Situated on the edge of the Longleat estate, this 16th-century inn was built on the site of a 15th-century monk's retreat and is owned by the Marquis of Bath.

CORTON — Map 03 ST94

Pick of the Pubs

The Dove Inn ♦♦♦♦ ⌂ ♀
BA12 0SZ ☎ 01985 850109 ▤ 01985 851041
e-mail: info@thedove.co.uk
Dir: Between Salisbury & Warminster on minor rd (parallel to A36)
A thriving, traditional pub tucked away in a beautiful Wiltshire village close to the River Wylye. A dramatic central fireplace is a feature of the refurbished bar, and the large garden is the site of summer barbecues, and ideal for a drink on warm days. The award-winning food is based firmly on West Country produce, with many ingredients coming from within just a few miles. Popular lunchtime bar snacks give way to a full evening carte, featuring starters like Thai crab cakes, duck confit, and smoked halibut, followed by calves' liver, pheasant risotto, and braised lamb. A good range of well-kept real ales includes Oakhill, Wadworth, Fullers and Hopback. Five en suite bedrooms built around a courtyard make The Dove an ideal touring base, with Bath and Salisbury within easy range.
OPEN: 12–3 6.30–11 (Sat-Sun 12–3.30 Sat 7–11 Sun 7–10.30)
BAR MEALS: Lunch served: all week Dinner served: all week 12–2.30 7–9.30 Av main course £6.50 **RESTAURANT:** Lunch served: all week Dinner served: all week 12–3 7–9.30 Av 3 course à la carte £24 **BREWERY/COMPANY:** Free House
PRINCIPAL BEERS: Oakhill Best Bitter, Brakspear, Wadworth 6X, Fuller's London Pride. **FACILITIES:** Children welcome Garden: Beer garden, patio, food served outdoors Dogs allowed (water) **NOTES:** Parking 24 **ROOMS:** 5 bedrooms 5 en suite from s£45 d£80

DEVIZES — Map 03 SU06

The Bear Hotel ★ ★ ★ ⌂ ♀
The Market Place SN10 1HS ☎ 01380 722444 ▤ 01380 722450
e-mail: beardevizes@aol.com
This attractive coaching inn dates from at least 1559, and now combines modern facilities with the kind of old-fashioned hospitality that was once offered to George III and Queen Charlotte. You'll find oak beams, log fires and fresh flowers throughout the hotel's comfortable lounges and bars. Expect an extensive choice of baguettes, omelettes, sandwiches and grills, as well as interesting restaurant fare that includes Parmesan crusted chicken breast with roast cherry tomatoes, noisettes of lamb served with pesto mash, and pan-fried king prawns. The bedrooms vary in size, but all are well equipped and most have refurbished bathrooms.
OPEN: 9.30–11 Closed: 25-26 Dec **BAR MEALS:** Lunch served: all week Dinner served: all week 11–2.30 7–9.15 Av main course £3.95
RESTAURANT: Lunch served: Sun 12.15–1.45 Dinner served: Mon–Sat 7–9.15 Av 3 course à la carte £24.95
BREWERY/COMPANY: Wadworth
PRINCIPAL BEERS: Wadworth 6X, Wadworth IPA.
FACILITIES: Children welcome Food served outside. Courtyard Dogs allowed **ROOMS:** 24 bedrooms 24 en suite from s£45 d£75

The Elm Tree ⚑
Long St SN10 1NJ ☎ 01380 723834 & 722446 🖹 01380 723834
e-mail: theelmtree@btinternet.com
16th-century town centre coaching inn with a sheltered
courtyard and a menu specialising in Italian cooking. Wadworth.

Fox & Hounds
Nursteed Rd SN10 3HJ ☎ 01380 723789 🖹 01380 723789
Dir: On A342 between Devizes & Andover, 1m from Devizes town
boundary
Thatched former farmhouse located near its owning brewery –
customers are guaranteed a tip-top pint of Wadworth 6X.

The Raven Inn 🖙
Poulshot Rd SN10 1RW ☎ 01380 828271 🖹 01380 828271
e-mail: pjh@raveninn.co.uk
Dir: Take A361 out of Devizes towards Trowbridge, turn L at sign for
Poulshot
A traditional part-timbered, 18th-century inn situated just
beyond the northern edge of the expansive village green.
From here you can enjoy classic Kennet and Avon Canal
towpath walking beside the famous Caen Hill locks. Speciality
dishes include herby salmon with stir-fried leeks and spinach,
sausage and bacon hotpot, and vegetable curry. Home-made
soups, pâté and puddings are also an attraction.
OPEN: 11–2.30 6.30–11 **BAR MEALS:** Lunch served: all week
Dinner served: all week 12–2 7–9.30 Av main course £6.75
RESTAURANT: Lunch served: all week Dinner served: all week 12–2
7–9.30 Av 3 course à la carte £15
BREWERY/COMPANY: Wadworth
PRINCIPAL BEERS: Wadworth 6X, Greene King IPA, Summersault.
FACILITIES: Garden: Beer garden, food served outdoors
NOTES: Parking 20

EAST KNOYLE   Map 03 ST83

The Fox and Hounds
The Green SP3 6BN ☎ 01747 830573 🖹 01747 830865
Dir: Off A303 onto A350 for 200yds, then R. Pub 1 0.5m on L
Originally three cottages, dating from the late 15th century, this
thatched pub overlooks the Blackmore Vale with fine views for
up to 20 miles. East Knoyle is the birthplace of Sir Christopher
Wren, and was also home to Lady Jayne Seymour.

EBBESBOURNE WAKE   Map 03 ST92

Pick of the Pubs

The Horseshoe
Handley St SP5 5JF ☎ 01722 780474
Reflecting the rural charm of the village in which it
stands, the 17th-century Horseshoe Inn nestles into the
folds of the Wiltshire Downs, close to the meandering
River Ebble. The small building was originally the
stables for the old stagecoach road that ran along the
ridge not more than two miles away. These days it is a
homely and traditional local, adorned with climbing
roses. Outside there is a pretty, flower-filled garden
and inside there is a central servery dispensing ale
from the barrel to two rooms, both filled with simple
furniture, old farming implements and country
bygones. Good value bar food is freshly prepared from
local produce and meals are accompanied by plenty of
vegetables. Hearty meals include pheasant and
cranberry or steak and kidney pies, fresh fish bake,
honey roasted duckling, and lambs' liver and bacon
casserole.
OPEN: 12–3 6.30–11 **BAR MEALS:** Lunch served: Tue–Sun
12–2 Dinner served: Tue–Sat 7–9.30 Av main course £8.95
RESTAURANT: Lunch served: Tue–Sun 12–2 Dinner served:
Tue–Sat 7–9.30 Av 3 course à la carte £20
BREWERY/COMPANY: Free House
PRINCIPAL BEERS: Wadworth 6X, Ringwood Best, Adnams
Broadside, Butcombe Best. **FACILITIES:** Garden: Food served
outside, three goats **NOTES:** Parking 20 **ROOMS:** 2 bedrooms
2 en suite from s£35 d£60

FONTHILL GIFFORD   Map 03 ST93

Pick of the Pubs

Beckford Arms ◆◆◆◆
SP3 6PX ☎ 01747 870385 🖹 01747 870385
e-mail: beck.ford@ukonline.co.uk
See Pick of the Pubs on page 500

The Kennet & Avon Canal
Following the towpath of the 87-mile Kennet & Avon Canal is the best way to
appreciate its varied wildlife, luxuriant flora and fauna and colourful boating activity,
and there is a varied assortment of canalside pubs where you can take a break from
the trail. Walking from east to west, you may like to try the 16th-century Royal Oak at
Wootton Rivers, the historic French Horn at Pewsey, and the Bridge Inn at Horton. On
reaching Devizes, home of the famous Wadworth Brewery, take a stroll through the
town and stop off at the Bear Hotel in the Market Place or the Elm Tree in Long Street.
Beyond Devizes, take a detour to the George and Dragon at Rowde or the Raven Inn at
Poulshot before following the towpath to the colourful Barge Inn at Seend and the
delightful 16th-century Hop Pole at Limpley Stoke. Along the way you may like to
explore the quaint old streets of Bradford-on-Avon, perhaps popping into the terraced
Dandy Lion in Market Street. The Georgian delights of Bath await you at the end of
the trail, where you might like to relax at the Richmond Arms or the Olde
Green Tree.

OPEN: 12–11 (Sun 12–10.30)
BAR MEALS: L served all week.
D served all week. Av main course
£8.95
RESTAURANT: L served all week.
D served all week. Av cost 3 course
£18.95
BREWERY/COMPANY: FREE
HOUSE
PRINCIPAL BEERS: Hop Back Best,
Timothy Taylor Landlord, Abbot,
Hopback Summer Lightning, Old
Speckled Hen
FACILITIES: Children and dogs
welcome. Garden: Food served
outside
NOTES: Parking 40

The Beckford Arms

Substantial 18th-century stone-built inn peacefully situated opposite the Fonthill Estate and providing a good base from which to explore the unspoilt Nadder Valley. Eddie and Karen Costello have transformed this rural retreat since arriving here two years ago.

◆◆◆◆
FONTHILL GIFFORD SP3 6PX
☎ 01747 870385 📠 01747 870385
e-mail: beck.ford@ukonline.co.uk
Dir: 2m from A303 (Fonthill Bishop turning) halfway between Hindon & Tisbury at crossroads next to Beckford Estate.

Beyond the basic locals' bar, you will find a rambling main bar, adjoining dining area and an airy conservatory all decorated in a tastefully rustic style, complete with scrubbed plank tables topped with huge candles, and warm terracotta-painted walls. Expect a roaring log fire in winter, a relaxed, laid-back atmosphere, and interesting modern pub menus. From ciabatta sandwiches, hearty soups, salads, salmon and prawn fishcakes with basil and lime reduction, or a Thai curry at lunchtime, the choice of well presented dishes extends, perhaps, to rack of lamb with tomatoes, wine and Italian herbs, sautÈed medallions of Wiltshire pork with caramelised apple, Calvados and cider, and salmon with Vermouth glaze in the evening. Generous bowls of fresh vegetables, colourful plates and friendly service all add to the dining experience here. Sun-trap patio and a delightful garden - perfect for summer sipping. Good value overnight accommodation.

FORD Map 03 ST87

Pick of the Pubs

The White Hart ⚲
SN14 8RP ☎ 01249 782213 📄 01249 783075
Dir: *From M4 J17 take A429 then A420, Ford is situated alongside A420*

In a sleepy village deep in the Bybrook Valley, this 16th-century coaching inn stands by a babbling trout stream. Within, it combines a traditional bar food and excellent real ale section with a more intimate beamed dining-room with wooden tables candlelit by night. Most of the bedrooms are in converted stables and hayloft across the lane, well-fitted with modern appointments with a peaceful night's rest promised. The pleasant atmosphere and relaxed, friendly atmosphere are decidedly country inn and suitably informal. Fixed-price lunch selections include smoked salmon, braised lamb shank with colcannon and lemon cheesecake with strawberry ice cream. Alternatives in the bar might be Thai chicken curry, grilled plaice with lemon and chive butter and macaroni cheese with mushrooms, spinach and grain mustard. Further dining options run to breast of duck with honey, peppercorns and couscous and fillet of salmon on pasta nero with buttered spinach and samphire accompanied by a wine list of commendable variety.
OPEN: 11–3 7–11 **BAR MEALS:** Lunch served: all week Dinner served: all week 12-2 6.30-9.30 Av main course £5.95
RESTAURANT: Lunch served: all week Dinner served: all week 12-2 7–9.30 Av 3 course à la carte £25.50 Av 3 course fixed price £13.95 **BREWERY/COMPANY:** Lionheart
PRINCIPAL BEERS: Marstons Pedigree, Wadsworth 6X, Bass, Courage Directors. **FACILITIES:** Children welcome Garden: outdoor eating, patio, riverside Dogs allowed by arragement
NOTES: Parking 80 **ROOMS:** 11 bedrooms 11 en suite from s£64 d£84

GREAT HINTON Map 03 ST95

Pick of the Pubs

The Linnet ⚲
BA14 6BT ☎ 01380 870354 📄 01380 870354
Dir: *Just off the A361 Devizes to Trowbridge rd*
A quiet village local that has been given a new lease of life by chef/landlord Jonathan Furby, and is among a line of Wiltshire pubs that have become, dining pubs of repute, with comfortably spaced tables neatly laid and flower-adorned. Everything is freshly home-made, from a range of breads to pasta and ice cream. Purchasing of

continued

fresh ingredients, local wherever possible, shows on menus that are kept sensibly short and supplemented daily by whatever is available at market. An example of a set lunch at the Linnet could start with chicken liver and black pudding parfait with a redcurrant and sage chutney, continue with pan-fried cod fillet on a saffron and prawn sauce with crispy fried spinach, and finishes up with cherry Pavlova ice cream. Alternatively try smoked trout in coriander and yoghurt with lobster oil, and lamb sausages on wild mushrooms with mustard and rosemary sauce. Presentation is top-class and the service is pleasantly relaxed and informal.
OPEN: 11–2.30 6.30-11 (Sun 12-3, 7-10.30) Closed: 1 Jan
BAR MEALS: Lunch served: Tue–Sun Dinner served: Tue–Sun 12-2 6.30-9.30 Av main course £10.95 **RESTAURANT:** Lunch served: Tue–Sun Dinner served: Tue–Sun 12-2 6.30-9.30 Av 3 course à la carte £19 **BREWERY/COMPANY:** Wadworth
PRINCIPAL BEERS: Wadworth 6X & Henrys IPA.
FACILITIES: Garden: Large patio area, food served outside
NOTES: Parking 45

GRITTLETON Map 03 ST88

The Neeld Arms ⚲
The Street SN14 6AP ☎ 01249 782470 📄 01249 782168
e-mail: neeldarms@zeronet.co.uk

Just 5 minutes' drive from the M4 (J 17) this 17th-century Cotswold stone pub stands at the centre of a pretty village in lush Wiltshire countryside. Its half dozen bedrooms are highly commended for comfort. Quality real ales and freshly prepared food are an equal draw to diners who will eagerly tuck in to lamb shanks, pheasant casserole, steak and kidney pie or local venison when available. Children are welcome and the small garden is especially popular for alfresco eating in fine weather.
OPEN: 12-3 5.30-11 **BAR MEALS:** Lunch served: all week Dinner served: all week 12-2 6-9.30 Av main course £9
BREWERY/COMPANY: Free House
PRINCIPAL BEERS: Wadworth 6X, Buckleys Best, Brakspear Bitter.
FACILITIES: Children welcome Garden: Patio, food served outside Dogs allowed **NOTES:** Parking 12 **ROOMS:** 6 bedrooms 6 en suite from s£38.50 d£53.50

HEYTESBURY Map 03 ST94

Pick of the Pubs

The Angel Inn ◆◆◆◆
High St BA12 0ED ☎ 01985 840330 📄 01985 840931
e-mail: Angelheytesbury@aol.com
See Pick of the Pubs on page 503

England

HINDON   Map 03 ST93

Pick of the Pubs

Angel Inn ★ ★ ◎◎ ⚐ ♀
SP3 6DJ ☎ 01747 820696 🖹 01747 820869
e-mail: eat@the-angel-inn.co.uk
See Pick of the Pubs on page 504

Pick of the Pubs

The Lamb at Hindon ★ ★ ◎ ♀
High St SP3 6DP ☎ 01747 820573 🖹 01747 820605
e-mail: the-lamb@demon.co.uk
Dir: *1m from A303 & B3089 in the centre of the village*

Situated in picturesque Hindon, this 17th-century posting
inn is a handy refreshment stop for A303 travellers. A
weekly market was held here until 1862, with business
transactions conducted in the bar. A relaxing restaurant
serves local produce, including game in season, while bar
food may feature hearty ploughman's lunches, venison
and mushroom casserole, and whole Dover sole. Cold
food is served in the bar until 12.30, tea and scones are
served throughout the afternoon too.
OPEN: 11–11 (Sun 12–10.30) **BAR MEALS:** Lunch served: all
week Dinner served: all week 12–2.30 7–10 Av main course £7.95
RESTAURANT: Lunch served: all week Dinner served: all week
12–1.45 7–9.30 Av 3 course à la carte £19.95 Av 3 course fixed
price £19.95 **BREWERY/COMPANY:** Free House
PRINCIPAL BEERS: Wadworth 6X, Hampshire Ironside and
King Alfred, Stonehenge Pigswill, Everards Tiger.
FACILITIES: Children welcome Garden: outdoor eating, patio,
beer garden Dogs allowed **NOTES:** Parking 25
ROOMS: 14 bedrooms 14 en suite from s£35 d£75

HOLT   Map 03 ST86

Pick of the Pubs

The Tollgate Inn ⚐ ♀
BA14 6PX ☎ 01225 782326 🖹 01225 782805
See Pick of the Pubs on page 506

HORNINGSHAM   Map 03 ST84

The Bath Arms ♀
BA12 7LY ☎ 01985 844308 🖹 01985 844150
Dir: *Off B3092 S of Frome*
Purchased from Glastonbury Abbey and converted into a pub
in 1763, the Bath Arms is an impressive, creeper-clad stone

continued

inn occupying a prime position at one of the entrances to
Longleat Estate. Recently acquired by Young's Brewery, it has
been comfortably refurbished and features a fine beamed bar
with settles and old wooden tables, and a terracotta painted
dining-room with open fire. Promising early menus offer
traditional fish and chips, tuna with mango salsa and herb oil,
poussin with bacon and braised Savoy cabbage, rib-eye steak
with red wine jus, and snacks like Longleat ploughman's. New
rear terrace.
OPEN: 12–3 6–11 (Closed Sun eve in Winter) (May–Oct open all day)
BAR MEALS: Lunch served: all week 12–2.30 Dinner served:
Mon-Sat 7–9.30 Av main course £6.50 **RESTAURANT:** Lunch
served: all week 12–2.30 Dinner served: Mon-Sat 7–9.30 Av 3 course à
la carte £13.95 **BREWERY/COMPANY:** Young & Co
PRINCIPAL BEERS: Youngs Bitter, Special, Triple AAA.
FACILITIES: Children welcome Garden: Food served outside Dogs
allowed **NOTES:** Parking 15 **ROOMS:** 6 bedrooms 6 en suite from
s£45 d£65

HORTON   Map 03 SU06

The Bridge Inn ⚐ ♀
Horton Rd SN10 2JS ☎ 01380 860273 🖹 01380 860273
e-mail: manager@thebridgeinn.freeserve.co.uk
Dir: *A361 from Devizes, R at 3rd roundabout*
Spacious renovated pub, with well furnished bars, log fires,
welcoming atmosphere, and a large garden with barbecue.
Built originally as a small farm and bakery, it stands next to
the Kennet and Avon Canal, and visitors can still watch
narrow boats passing by. Today's menu may include trout
stuffed with mushrooms and prawns, butterflied chicken
breast with chasseur sauce, Mediterranean vegetable bake
with a cheesy topping, or lemon and tarragon chicken.
OPEN: 12–3 6.30–11 **BAR MEALS:** Lunch served: all week Dinner
served: all week 12–2.15 7–9.15 Av main course £5
BREWERY/COMPANY: Wadworth
PRINCIPAL BEERS: Wadworth Henry's original IPA, 6X.
FACILITIES: Children welcome Garden: Food served outside Dogs
allowed (water) **NOTES:** Parking 20

KILMINGTON   Map 03 ST73

The Red Lion Inn
KILMINGTON BA12 6RP ☎ 01985 844263
Dir: *B3092 off A303 N towards Frome. Pub 2.5m from A303 on R on
B3092 just after turning to Stourhead Gardens*
A 14th-century coaching inn that once regularly provided two
spare horses to assist in the climb up nearby White Sheet Hill.
The interior, unchanged over a quarter of a century, features
flag stone floors, oak beams, antique settles and two blazing
log fires. As well as being a champion of real ale, the long-
standing landlord supervises his kitchen to ensure that all
produce – much of it local – is saved in prime condition.
Home-made chicken, lamb and apricot and creamy fish pies
are a speciality.
OPEN: 11.30–2.30 6.30–11 (Sun 12–3 7–10.30) **BAR MEALS:** Lunch
served: all week 12–1.50 Av main course £4.45
BREWERY/COMPANY: Free House
PRINCIPAL BEERS: Butcombe Bitter, Jester. **FACILITIES:** Children
welcome Garden: Large, food served outside Dogs allowed
NOTES: Parking 25 **ROOMS:** 2 bedrooms from s£25 d£35 No
credit cards

◆ **Indicates AA inspected
bed & breakfast accommodation**

OPEN: 11.30-3 6.30-11
BAR MEALS: L served all week.
D served all week. 12-2 7-9.30
Av main course £9.50
RESTAURANT: L served all week.
D served all week. 12-2 7-9.30
BREWERY/COMPANY: FREE HOUSE
PRINCIPLE BEERS: Ringwood Best
FACILITIES: Children and dogs welcome
NOTES: Parking 12
ROOMS: 9 en suite. Double room from £65. Single room from £50

The Angel Inn

◆◆◆◆
High Street BA12 0ED
☎ 01985 840330 📠 01985 840931
e-mail: Angelheytesbury@aol.com
Dir: From A303 take A36 toward Bath, 8m, Heytesbury on L.

A dining pub in the modern idiom, the Angel preserves all the charm and character of a traditional coaching inn. You'll find it tucked away in a tiny village in the lovely Wylye Valley on the edge of Salisbury Plain, just a few minutes' drive from Warminster.

Well placed for exploring Bath, Salisbury and the nearby Longleat Estate. There's a reassuringly civilised atmosphere within, the long beamed bar featuring scrubbed pine tables, warmly decorated walls and an attractive fireplace with a wood-burning stove. A separate lounge area with squashy sofas and easy chairs leads through to the neatly furnished rear dining room. In summer, guests spill out into the secluded courtyard garden, which is furnished with hardwood tables and cotton parasols. Relaxed and friendly service makes for a pleasurable dining experience. Comprehensive seasonal menus are based on good quality produce approached with flair and imagination. Lighter/starter dishes include the chef's soup of the day, a game terrine, or chargrilled smoked salmon on a bed of leaves with shallot and juniper dressing. For something more substantial maybe Wiltshire pork medallions cooked in a sauce of brandy, Dijon mustard and cream, or pan-fried breast of chicken with lemon pepper sauce, all served with a panache of seasonal vegetables. Wild berry and ginger crumble with créme anglaise, and date and orange pudding with hot dark chocolate sauce figure among the sumptuous puddings packed with flavours. New rooms have augmented the range of accommodation available, which is proving popular with business guests and tourists alike. Small functions and private dinner parties can also be catered for.

OPEN: 11-3 7-11
BAR MEALS: L served all week. week. D served Mon-Sat. 12-2 7-9. Av main course £7.25
RESTAURANT: L served all week. week. D served Mon-Sat. 12-2 7-9. Av cost 3 courses £20
BREWERY/COMPANY: FREE HOUSE
PRINCIPAL BEERS: Wadworth 6X, Bass, Wadworth Henry's Original IPA
FACILITIES: Children welcome, dogs allowed. Garden: Patio area, food served outside
NOTES: Parking 20
ROOMS: 7 en suite. Double room from £55. Single room from £45.

Angel Inn

★ ★ ⊛⊛ ♀
Hindon, Wiltshire SP3 6DJ
☎ 01747 820696 📄 01747 820869
e-mail: eat@the-angel-inn.co.uk
Dir: 1.5m from A303, on B3089 towards Salisbury

A name change – formerly the Grosvenor Arms – and an extensive and sympathetic refurbishment, has done credit to this handsome coaching inn. Totally fresh produce, much of it organic, forms the basis of contemporary dishes and the owners are enthusiastic about their wines and ales.

Standing opposite the parish church in Hindon, which is a particularly attractive and unspoilt Georgian village in the most rural part of Wiltshire, the pub was originally named the Angel in its medieval past. The current Georgian building was erected on the ruins of the original Angel. The inn is approached though a pleasant, enclosed, tree-filled courtyard, which buzzes with life in the summer months when it is prettily lit and food is served outside. The interior is a warm red and has open fires gracing the three bars, a stylish sitting room and old beams and flagstone-flooring. Coir flooring and fresh flowers grace the airy restaurant, which was created from the former stable block. Fresh mainly organic produce are used to create contemporary dishes, from the likes of garlic field mushrooms on toast and baked crottin of goat's cheese with pesto to grilled brochette of lamb's kidneys, pancetta and black pudding with parsnip purèe, shallot and sherry vinegar sauce. Fish from Brixham, meats from Aubrey Allen and cheeses from Neal's Yard underpin the kitchen's credentials. Some sample dishes include rabbit confit and roast quail terrine with poached quail eggs and roast plum tomato and dressing, and roast saddle of venison with braised red cabbage, beetroot and will mushrooms in a port and juniper jus. The wine list is carefully selected and offers 14 wines by the glass and a good selection of half bottles.

LACOCK Map 03 ST96

The George Inn
4 West St SN15 2LH ☎ 01249 730263
Dir: M4 J17 take A350 S
The inn is situated in a beautiful National Trust village, often used as a film and television location. The George dates from 1361 and boasts many classic features, including a medieval fireplace, a low-beamed ceiling, mullioned windows, flagstone floors and an old treadwheel by which a dog would drive the spit. Dishes include sea bass filled with Mediterranean vegetables on a shellfish base, steaks, wild boar, and duck with plum and ginger sauce.
OPEN: 10–2.30 5–11 **BAR MEALS:** Lunch served: all week Dinner served: all week 12–2 6–10 Av main course £7.50
RESTAURANT: Lunch served: all week Dinner served: all week 12–2 6–10 Av 3 course à la carte £12 **BREWERY/COMPANY:** Wadworth
PRINCIPAL BEERS: Wadworth 6X, Henrys IPA, Old Timer & Farmers Glory. **FACILITIES:** Children welcome Garden: Food served outside Dogs allowed **NOTES:** Parking 40 **ROOMS:** 3 bedrooms 3 en suite

Red Lion Inn 🐾 ♀
1 High St SN15 2LQ ☎ 01249 730456 ▤ 01249 730766
Dir: just off A350 between Chippenham & Melksham
Set in a National Trust village immortalised in many a TV and film recording, the Red Lion dates from the 1700s. The older part of the building has exposed timbers and a large open fire. The same menu is offered throughout, and the bestselling dishes are the home-made pies, casseroles and vegetarian items. Fishy dishes include whole tail scampi, breaded cod, red snapper and fisherman's platter.
OPEN: 11.30–3 6–11 **BAR MEALS:** Lunch served: all week Dinner served: all week 12–2.30 6–9 Av main course £6.95
RESTAURANT: Lunch served: all week Dinner served: all week 12–2.30 6–9 Av 3 course à la carte £15
BREWERY/COMPANY: Wadworth
PRINCIPAL BEERS: Wadworth Henry's IPA & 6X.
FACILITIES: Children welcome Garden: Patio, food served outdoors Dogs allowed **NOTES:** Parking 70 **ROOMS:** 6 bedrooms 6 en suite from s£45 d£65

The Rising Sun ♀ NEW
32 Bowden Hill SN15 2PP ☎ 01249 730363
The pub is located close to the National Trust village of Lacock, on a steep hill, providing spectacular views over Wiltshire from the large garden. Live music and quiz nights are a regular feature, and games and reading material are provided in the bar. Five to six real ales are served and a good selection of wines and whiskies. Thai curries and stir-fries are popular options, alongside traditional liver, bacon and onions.
OPEN: 12–3 6–11 (Sun all day) Closed: 1 Jan **BAR MEALS:** Lunch served: all week 12–2 Dinner served: Wed-Sat 7–9 Av main course £6
BREWERY/COMPANY: Free House **PRINCIPAL BEERS:** Moles Best, Moles Molennium, Molecatcher, Tap Bitter.
FACILITIES: Children welcome Garden: Food served outside Dogs allowed (water) **NOTES:** Parking 25

LIMPLEY STOKE Map 03 ST76

The Hop Pole Inn 🐾
Woods Hill, Lower Limpley Stoke BA3 6HS
☎ 01225 723134 ▤ 01225 723199
e-mail: latonahop@aol.com
Dir: Off A36 (Bath to Warminster road)
The Hop Pole dates from 1580, the name coming from the hop plant that still grows outside the pub. Set in the beautiful

Limpley Stoke Valley, it offers a tranquil resting place. Eagle-eyed film fans may recognise it as the pub in the 1992 film *Remains of the Day*, starring Emma Thompson and Anthony Hopkins. A hearty menu includes home-made pies, Stilton chicken, tournedos Rossini, duck with orange and ginger, local fresh trout, and a vegetarian selection.
OPEN: 11–2.30 6–11 (Sun 12–3, 7–10.30) Closed: 25 Dec
BAR MEALS: Lunch served: all week Dinner served: all week 12–2.15 6.30–9.15 Av main course £7.50 **RESTAURANT:** Lunch served: all week Dinner served: all week 12–2.15 6.30–9.15 Av 3 course à la carte £15 **BREWERY/COMPANY:** Free House
PRINCIPAL BEERS: Scottish Courage Courage Best, Butcombe Bitter, Interbrew Bass. **FACILITIES:** Children welcome Garden: Patio, food served outside Dogs allowed **NOTES:** Parking 20

LITTLE CHEVERELL Map 03 ST95

The Owl 🐾 ♀
Low Rd SN10 4JS ☎ 01380 812263
e-mail: jamie@theowl.info
Dir: A344 from Stonehenge, then A360, after 10m L onto B3098, R after 0.5m, Owl signposted
Cosy 19th-century local situated well off-the-beaten-track in a tiny hamlet and surrounded by farmland and views of Salisbury Plain. Pretty split-level garden that runs down to the Cheverell Brook. Typical menu includes steak and ale pie, salmon steak with a cracked black crust and hollandaise sauce, roasted sweet peppers stuffed with rice, mushrooms and creamy Stilton sauce, red snapper with caper sauce, and smoked salmon pasta.
OPEN: 11–3 6.30–11 (Sun 12–3, 7–10.30) **BAR MEALS:** Lunch served: all week Dinner served: all week 12–3 7–10 Av main course £6.95 **RESTAURANT:** Lunch served: all week Dinner served: all week 12–3 7–10 Av 3 course à la carte £9.95
BREWERY/COMPANY: Free House
PRINCIPAL BEERS: Wadworth 6X, Interbrew Flowers IPA, Scottish Courage Courage Best. **FACILITIES:** Children welcome Garden: Food served outside Dogs allowed (water) **NOTES:** Parking 16 **ROOMS:** 3 bedrooms 2 en suite

LOWER CHICKSGROVE Map 03 ST92

Pick of the Pubs

Compasses Inn 🐾 ♀
SP3 6NB ☎ 01722 714318 ▤ 01722 714318
e-mail: thecompassesinn@tinyworld.co.uk
Dir: A30 W from Salisbury, after 10m R signed Chicksgrove
A timeless air of peace and tranquillity pervades within this attractive 16th-century thatched inn, set in the unspoilt Nadder Valley. Landlord Jonathan Bold is running a successful establishment and attracting people out to this remote rural pub. Imaginative, well-presented food is the key. Diners are now negotiating the narrow lanes and walking down the old cobbled path that leads to the latched door and into the long and low-beamed bar, with its bare stone walls, worn flagstone floors, large inglenook with wood-burning stove, and an assortment of traditional furniture. In addition to a warm welcome and local real ales, they find an ever-changing blackboard menu, which may feature roasted monkfish with lemon and thyme, scallops with grain mustard and sun-dried tomato, rare pieces of beef fillet with Madeira and mushrooms or steak and kidney pie. Good puddings. Overnight accommodation in four en suite bedrooms; one tucked beneath the heavy thatch.

continued
continued

OPEN: 11.30–2.30 6.30–11
BAR MEALS: L served
Tue-Sun 12–2. D served Tue-Sat.
7–9.30 Av main course £10.50
RESTAURANT: L served
Tue-Sun 12–2. D served Tue-Sat.
7–9.30 Av cost 3 course £18
BREWERY/COMPANY:
FREE HOUSE
PRINCIPAL BEERS: Bath Ale
Gem, Tisbury Brewery Best, Abbey
Ales Bellringer, Shepherds Neame
Spitfire, Timothy Taylor Landlord
FACILITIES: Dogs allowed (garden
only). Garden: food served
outside. Patio area
NOTES: Parking 40

The Tollgate Inn

♀
Holt Wiltshire BA14 6PX
☎ 01225 782326 📠 01225 782805
Dir: On B 3105 between Bradford on
Avon and Melksham M4 J18, A46
towards Bath, then A363 to Bradford
on Avon then B3105 Melksham, pub on
the R handside

Since being renovated and revived two years ago, this traditional roadside inn has kept its charm while plenty of modern comforts have been added and the quality of both the food and wine has been constantly upgraded and rewarded with numerous commendations. In the 16th century, it was a weaving shed, while the upstairs restaurant, in and adjoining building was a Baptist chapel for the weavers, and still has the original chapel windows and stone steps.

The welcoming bars include squashy comfy sofas, daily papers and glossy magazines around a welcoming log fire. Also upstairs some bed and breakfast accommodation has been created with four en suite bedrooms with private dining facilities. The quality of the food continues to attract plenty of customers. The kitchen is helped by a supply of meat, game and poultry from nearby farms, locally grown fruit and vegetables, and the pick of the Cornish catch delivered daily. There are plenty of original dishes on the carte, such as pan-fried sea bass with oriental spices, bok choy and ginger, hake with red pepper salsa and aÔoli or confit of Barbary duck with a bitter sweet honey dressing. Among starters you could find Mediterranean vegetable terrine with a Greek salad or red pepper and chill soup with a a coriander pesto and among the main courses, chicken cafrael, tomato and chilli relish, pineappple chat and kachumber or blue cheese ravioli, walnut, celery and endive and a walnut dressing. For dessert try home-made ice cream or lemon and ginger pudding with lemon curd sauce or a selection of top-quality British cheeses. Outside there is a terrace for alfresco dining and facilities are being created for weddings.

LOWER CHICKSGROVE continued

OPEN: 12–3 6–11 Closed: Tue after BH Mon
BAR MEALS: Lunch served: Tue–Sun 12–2 Dinner served:
Tue–Sat 7–9 Av main course £9.95 **RESTAURANT:** Lunch
served: Tues–Sun 12–2 Dinner served: Tues–Sat 7–9 Av 3 course à
la carte £20 **BREWERY/COMPANY:** Free House
PRINCIPAL BEERS: Interbrew Bass, Wadworth 6X, Tisbury
Stonehenge, Chicksgrove Churl. **FACILITIES:** Children welcome
Garden: Patio/terrace, Food served outside Dogs allowed
(water) **NOTES:** Parking 30 **ROOMS:** 4 bedrooms 4 en suite
from s£40 d£55

LOWER WOODFORD   Map 03 SU13

The Wheatsheaf 🐕 ⟂
SP4 6NQ ☎ 01722 782203 ▤ 01722 782203
e-mail: wheatsheafwoodford.wi@freshnet.uk.com
Dir: Take A360 N of Salisbury. Village signposted 1st R

Once a farm and brewhouse, now a thriving country pub in
the Avon Valley. Major refurbishment in 2002 has resulted in
rustic decor with a contemporary twist. Expect dishes such as
seared tuna steak with lemon and coriander butter, salmon
and dill fishcakes, and traditional cod and chips. Steak and
Tanglefoot ale pie, Cumberland sausage and mash, and slow-
roasted lamb shank should also be available.
OPEN: 11–3.00 (Sun 12–3) 6.30–11 (Fri & Sat 6.00–11, Sun 7–11)
BAR MEALS: Lunch served: all week Dinner served: all week
12–2.30 7–9.30 Av main course £6.95 **RESTAURANT:** Lunch served:
all week Dinner served: all week 12–2.30 7–9.30
BREWERY/COMPANY: Hall & Woodhouse
PRINCIPAL BEERS: Badger Dorset Best & Tanglefoot, King & Barnes
Sussex Ale. **FACILITIES:** Children welcome Garden: Food served
outside. Enclosed garden Dogs allowed (in the garden only)
NOTES: Parking 50

Dominoes
Dominoes came to Britain from the Continent at
the end of the 18th century, perhaps brought
back by British soldiers serving in the Napoleonic
Wars. French prisoners-of-war made sets of
dominoes, not only for their own amusement but
to sell to the British. Many different varieties are
played in pubs besides the standard block game,
and some pubs belong to dominoe leagues.

LUDWELL   Map 03 ST92

Grove Arms Inn ♦♦♦♦ 🐕
SP7 9ND ☎ 01747 828328 ▤ 01747 828960
Dir: On main A30 Shaftsbury to Salisbury Rd 3 M from Shaftsbury

Grade II listed thatched inn, completely refurbished and
offering well-kept accommodation in six letting rooms. Home-
cooked pub food includes steaks (up to 40oz!), smoked
haddock in creamy sauce, cod in batter, steak and kidney
pudding, and chicken curry, all cooked 'just like mum does'.
The owners pride themselves on their Sunday roast, and
delicious desserts like Spotted Dick, sherry trifle, apple pie,
and peach melba.
OPEN: 12–11.30 **BAR MEALS:** Lunch served: all week Dinner
served: all week 12–2.30 6–9.30 Av main course £6.95
RESTAURANT: Lunch served: all week Dinner served: all week
12–2.30 6–9.30 **BREWERY/COMPANY:** Free House
PRINCIPAL BEERS: Ringwood Best, Ringwood Fortyniner (49er),
Scottish Courage Courage Best. **NOTES:** Parking 60
ROOMS: 6 bedrooms 6 en suite from s£40 d£50

MALMESBURY   Map 03 ST98

Pick of the Pubs

Horse & Groom ♦♦♦♦♦ ◎ ⟂
The Street, Charlton SN16 9DL
☎ 01666 823904 ▤ 01666 823390
Dir: from M4 head toward Malmesbury, 2nd rdbt go R towards
Cricklade on B4040, premises through the village on the left

A small, relaxed and civilised 16th-century coaching inn
set back from the road in a pleasant garden that features
with a duck-pond. Sympathetic conversion has brought
the three bedrooms and two bars and dining-room up to
modern expectations without any detriment to the inn's
inherent character: log fires burn in winter and drinks and
snacks are served outdoors in fine weather. Menus appeal
to all tastes and pockets with starters or light snacks that

continued

MALMESBURY continued

include salmon tagliatelle, grilled Brie slices with Cumberland sauce, stuffed toasted mushrooms and fillets of plaice meunière: all is cooked to order and subject to availability of fresh produce. Main dishes balance the traditional beer-battered haddock with home-made chips and beef, Stilton and Guinness pie with more up-to-date interpretations of ballotine of duck with apricots and basil and escalope of monkfish with red pepper sauce. For dessert, lemon shortbread tartlets, blueberry fritters and genuine Cotswolde ice creams. Well-chosen real ales attract a loyal local following.
OPEN: 12-3 7-11 (all day Wknds) Closed: 25-26 Dec
BAR MEALS: Lunch served: all week Dinner served: all week 12-2 7-10 Av main course £4.50 **RESTAURANT:** Lunch served: all week Dinner served: all week 12-2 7-10 Av 3 course à la carte £20 **BREWERY/COMPANY:** Free House
PRINCIPAL BEERS: Wadworth 6X, Archers Village, Smiles Best, Uley Old Spot. **FACILITIES:** Garden: Food served outside Dogs allowed (water) **NOTES:** Parking 40
ROOMS: 3 bedrooms 3 en suite from s£60 d£80

The Smoking Dog ♀
62 The High St SN16 9AT ☎ 01666 825823 ▤ 01666 829137
Log fires, solid wooden floors and a relaxed atmosphere greet visitors to this refined 18th-century stone-built pub, right in the heart of Malmesbury. There's an expanding range of real ales that features continually changing guest beers, and the pub has a good reputation for interesting, freshly-cooked food. Expect a daily choice of home-made soup and hot-pot, plus cod brochettes, smoked salmon and home-made burgers.
OPEN: 11.30-11 (Sun 12-10.30) **BAR MEALS:** Lunch served: all week Dinner served: all week 12-2 7-9.30 Av main course £10.95
RESTAURANT: Lunch served: all week Dinner served: all week 12-2 7-9.30 Av 3 course à la carte £18.95 **PRINCIPAL BEERS:** Wadworth 6X, Archers Best, Brains Bitter, SA & Reverend James.
FACILITIES: Children welcome Garden: Dogs allowed (water, biscuits)

Pick of the Pubs

The Vine Tree ☺ ♀
Foxley Rd, Norton SN16 0JP
☎ 01666 837654 ▤ 01666 838003
e-mail: info@thevinetree.co.uk
See Pick of the Pubs on page 509

MARTEN   Map 04 SU26

The Windmill ☺ ♀
SN8 3SH ☎ 01264 731372
Dir: 6m SW of Hungerford om A338
At the time of going to press, this free house, close to Stonehenge and Hungerford, had just changed hands. The new owners changed the name, from The Tipsy Miller, and now specialise in locally sourced, and mainly organic food. Recent refurbishment includes a new children's play area, paved outside eating area, and an extensive wine list. Menu includes seared scallops, charred venison, and braised pheasant.
OPEN: 11-2.30 6.30-11 (Thur-Fri 5.30-11) (Sun 12-3, 7-10.30)
Closed: 25 Dec **BAR MEALS:** Lunch served: Tues-Sun 12-2.30 Dinner served: Tues-Sat 6.30-10 Av main course £16
RESTAURANT: Lunch served: Tues-Sun 12-2.30 Dinner served: Tues-Sat 6.30-9.15 Av 3 course à la carte £25 Av 3 course fixed price

£17.50 **BREWERY/COMPANY:** Free House **FACILITIES:** Children welcome Garden: Food served outside, paved terrace Dogs allowed **NOTES:** Parking 25

MELKSHAM   Map 03 ST96

Kings Arms Hotel
Market Place SN12 6EX ☎ 01225 707272 ▤ 01225 792986
Dir: In the town centre opposite Lloyds Bank
Once an important coaching house on the London to Bath route, warmth and hospitality are offered by this traditional market place inn.

MERE   Map 03 ST83

Old Ship Inn
Castle St BA12 6JE ☎ 01747 860258 ▤ 01747 860501
Dir: W of Stonehenge just off A303
You are assured of a warm welcome at this 16th-century coaching inn. Architectural features include stone walls, flagstone floors and an original elm stairway. Home-cooked dishes are served in the bar, and there is a full carte in the oak-beamed restaurant.

Talbot Hotel ♦♦♦ ☺
The Square BA12 6DR ☎ 01747 860427 ▤ 01747 861978
Dir: follow signs from A303 into village
Newly refurbished 16th-century coaching inn, where the restaurant has been recently been re-launched as Taps. The Talbot is now able to offer a full à la carte menu on Friday and Saturday evenings in both the restaurant and bars. Examples from the menu are salmon supreme, oven roasted rump of lamb, and aubergine and Mozzarella gateau. Many attractions are within easy reach, including Longleat, Salisbury, Wincanton Racecourse and Sherborne Castle.
OPEN: 11-11 (Mon-Tue 11-3 6-11, Sun 12-3, 7-10.30)
BAR MEALS: Lunch served: all week Dinner served: all week 12-2.30 6.30-9.30 Av main course £6.50 **RESTAURANT:** Lunch served: all week Dinner served: all week 12-2.30 6.30-9.30 Av 3 course à la carte £14
BREWERY/COMPANY: Hall & Woodhouse
PRINCIPAL BEERS: Dorset Best, Champion Ale, Badger IPA.
FACILITIES: Children welcome Garden: Terrace, Food served outside **NOTES:** Parking 20 **ROOMS:** 7 bedrooms 7 en suite from s£32.50 d£65

NEWTON TONEY   Map 04 SU24

The Mallet Arms ♀ **NEW**
SP4 0HF ☎ 01980 629279 ▤ 01980 629459
e-mail: Malet@doghouse.co.uk
Dir: 8 miles SE of Salisbury on A338, 5 miles SW of A303
Built around 350 years old, the Malet stands on the banks of the River Bourne, originally the bake house for a long gone Elizabethan manor. It's a village pub with a lively bar scene, an enthusiastic cricket team, and a 'Flying Malet' facility providing outside catering and beer tents for local events. Food is all home made - beef burgers, fish, curries and lots of game in season, and special culinary evenings are a regular occurrence.
OPEN: 11-3 6-11 Closed: 26 Dec, 1 Jan **BAR MEALS:** Lunch served: all week Dinner served: all week 12-2.30 6.30-10 Av main course £7.50 **RESTAURANT:** Lunch served: all week Dinner served: all week 12-2.30 6.30-10 Av 3 course à la carte £20
BREWERY/COMPANY: Free House
PRINCIPAL BEERS: Wadworth 6X, Stonehenge Heelstone, Butts Barbus Barbus & local guest ales. **FACILITIES:** Garden: Paved with seating area, large paddock Dogs allowed (water) **NOTES:** Parking 30

continued

OPEN: 12–2.30 6.30–11 (Sun 12–10.30)
BAR MEALS: L served all week. D served all week. 12–2.30 7–9.30
RESTAURANT: L served all week. D served all week. 12–2.30 7–9.30
BREWERY/COMPANY: FREE HOUSE
PRINCIPAL BEERS: Youngs P.A., Wychwood Fiddlers Elbow
FACILITIES: Children welcome, dogs allowed. Garden: Food served outside. Terrace with fountain
NOTES: Parking 100

The Vine Tree

The essence of a quality village free house in the heart of Wiltshire's countryside, The Vine Tree is a converted 16th century mill house. Come here for interesting, modern pub food and memorable summer alfresco dining.

Foxley Road Norton SN16 0JP
☎ 01666 837654 🖹 01666 838003
e-mail: info@thevinetree.co.uk

Close to Malmesbury, Tetbury and Westonbirt Arboretum, it is well worth the drive. The Vine Tree's tranquil sun-trap terrace includes a fountain, rose beds, pagodas, trailing vines and the newly developed barbecue area. Another development this year is two boules pitches – an appropriate addition in a village which hosts the biggest boules competition in England. There's also a two-acre garden with a play area to keep the kids entertained. If the weather isn't up to it, be consoled by the log fire in the main bar and a warm welcome from licensee Tiggi Wood. Try a meal

in one of the recently redecorated, pine-furnished dining areas or for liquid refreshment, a pint of the locally brewed Archers village bitter, a glass of wine from the carefully selected list, or decent cappuccino and espresso coffee. Cooking is modern British in style. A particularly popular choice is moules marinére made with white wine, garlic, shallots, cream and leeks and accompanied by home made mini loaves. Other dishes might include cutlet of pork with honey and apple gravy, green pea and black pudding mash or marinated medallion of yellow fin tuna with seaweed and Chinese egg noodles. All are freshly prepared using quality ingredients, including local game. The imaginative Sunday menu includes the traditional roast alongside plenty of tempting alternatives – perhaps pan-fried cod with a Tuscan mixed-bean casserole.

NUNTON   Map 03 SU12

The Radnor Arms 🍴 ⟡
SP5 4HS ☎ 01722 329722
Dir: From Salisbury ring road take A338 to Ringwood. Nunton signposted on R

A popular pub in the centre of the village dating from around 1750. In 1855 it was owned by the local multi-talented brewer/baker/grocer. Bought by Lord Radnor in 1919. Bar snacks are supplemented by an extensive fish choice and daily specials, which might include steamed turbot, seared salmon or braised lamb shank, all freshly prepared. Fine summer garden with rural views.
OPEN: 11-3 6-11 (Sun 12-3 7-10.30) **BAR MEALS:** Lunch served: all week 12-2.30 Dinner served: Mon-Sat 7-9.30 Av main course £7
RESTAURANT: Lunch served: all week 12-2.30 Dinner served: Mon-Sat 7-9.30 Av 3 course à la carte £18.50
BREWERY/COMPANY: Hall & Woodhouse
PRINCIPAL BEERS: Badger Tanglefoot, Badger Best, Badger Golden Champion. **FACILITIES:** Children welcome Children's licence Garden: Food served outside Dogs allowed **NOTES:** Parking 40

PEWSEY   Map 03 SU16

The French Horn 🍴 ⟡
Marlborough Rd SN9 5NT ☎ 01672 562443 ▤ 01672 562785
e-mail: info@french-horn-pewsey.co.uk
Dir: A338 thru Hungerford, at Burbage take B3087 to Pewsey
Popular local pub set beside historic Pewsey Wharf on the Kennet & Avon Canal, busy with walkers and cyclists. Napoleonic prisoners of war working on the canal were summoned to the inn for meals by the sound of a French horn. Quality food is served in the restaurant - confit of Barbary duck leg, smoked haddock rarebit, pan-fried rib eye steak, and the bar - vegetable quiche, beef stew and dumplings, ploughman's platter.
OPEN: 12-2.30 6.30-11 **BAR MEALS:** Lunch served: all week Dinner served: all week 12-2.15 7-9.15 Av main course £4.95
RESTAURANT: Lunch served: all week Dinner served: all week 12-2.15 7-9.15 Av 3 course à la carte £20
BREWERY/COMPANY: Wadworth **PRINCIPAL BEERS:** Wadworth 6X & Henry's Original IPA. **FACILITIES:** Garden: Beer garden, food served outdoors Dogs allowed (water) **NOTES:** Parking 20

Pick of the Pubs

The Seven Stars 🍴 ⟡
Bottlesford SN9 6LU ☎ 01672 851325 ▤ 01672 851583
e-mail: sevenstars@dialin.net
Dir: Off A345
Thatched and creeper-clad 16th-century building tucked away down narrow lanes in the heart of the Pewsey Vale.

Best approached from the A345 at North Newnton (follow signs for Woodborough, then Bottlesford), it is well worth the effort for the splendid 7-acre garden, complete with lake and rural views to the White Horse on Pewsey Down. Delightful rambling interior of beams and black oak panelling in which to sample locally-made cider, West Country real ales and some good food prepared by French chef/landlord Philippe Cheminade. Gallic-inspired dishes such as smoked salmon Niçoise, moules marinière, and fillet of beef bourguignon are well executed, as one would expect, but so are more traditional offerings like roast mallard with wild mushrooms, sirloin steak, and grilled seabass. Decent sandwiches, filled baguettes and ploughman's lunches for those popping in for just a snack.
OPEN: 12-3 6-11 (closed Sun eve & all Mon) Closed: 1 Wk after New Year **BAR MEALS:** Lunch served: Tue-Sun 12-2 Dinner served: Tue-Sat 7-9.30 Av main course £7.25
RESTAURANT: Lunch served: Tue-Sun 12-2 Dinner served: Tue-Sat 7-9.30 Av 3 course à la carte £20
BREWERY/COMPANY: Free House
PRINCIPAL BEERS: Wadworth 6X, Badger Dorset Best, Stonehenge Ales Pigwill. **FACILITIES:** Children welcome Garden: Food served outside. Front terrace **NOTES:** Parking 50

The Woodbridge Inn 🍴
North Newnton SN9 6JZ ☎ 01980 630266 ▤ 01980 630457
e-mail: woodbridgeinn@btconnect.com
Dir: 2m SW on A345
Variously a toll house, bakery and brewhouse, this Grade II-listed, 16th-century building is situated in over four acres of beautiful riverside grounds. Fish dishes include Mediterranean bream, local trout, salmon and black marlin, while specials include sizzling beef, prawn, pork and chicken stir-fry specials, steak and ale pie. There is also a selection of Mexican dishes: fajitas, tortillas, enchiladas, and black beans, with onions, jalapeños and melted cheese among the many items on the bar menu.
OPEN: 12-11.30 Closed: Jan 1 **BAR MEALS:** Lunch served: all week Dinner served: all week 12-10 Av main course £6.95
RESTAURANT: Lunch served: all week Dinner served: all week 12-10 Av 3 course à la carte £20 **BREWERY/COMPANY:** Wadworth **PRINCIPAL BEERS:** Wadworth 6X, Henrys IPA, Summersault & Old Timer. **FACILITIES:** Children welcome Garden: Food served outside. Enclosed garden area Dogs allowed (in the garden only) **NOTES:** Parking 60 **ROOMS:** 4 bedrooms 3 en suite from s£35 d£50

PITTON   Map 04 SU23

Pick of the Pubs

The Silver Plough ⟡
White Hill SP5 1DU ☎ 01722 712266 ▤ 01722 712266
Dir: From Salisbury take A30 towards Andover, Pitton signposted (approx 3m)
At the heart of a village full of thatched houses, surrounded by rolling countryside and a peaceful garden, this popular pub was converted from a farmstead around 60 years ago. It is handy for visiting the New Forest and within easy reach of many lovely downland and woodland walks. Inside are black beams strung with numerous antique bootwarmers, toby jugs, painted clogs, glass rolling pins and various other artefacts. Dishes are prepared from local produce and the sauces and

continued   *continued*

England

puddings are home made. The range of food is extensive and varied. Lunchtime offerings include Caesar salad, crispy baked bruschetta, chargrilled steaks, and Plough Pudding - speciality sausage served with Yorkshire pudding, grain mustard and fresh herb mashed potato. Among the à la carte options are home-made chicken liver pâté with tomato and red onion confit and home-made walnut bread, and oven roast duck breast, cooked pink, and set on fresh raspberry jus.
OPEN: 11-3 6-11 (Sun 12-3, 6-10.30) **BAR MEALS:** Lunch served: all week Dinner served: all week 12-2.30 7-9.30 Av main course £8 **RESTAURANT:** Lunch served: all week Dinner served: all week 12-2.30 7-9.30 Av 3 course à la carte £20 **BREWERY/COMPANY:** Hall & Woodhouse **PRINCIPAL BEERS:** Badger Tanglefoot, Dorset Best, IPA & King & Barnes Sussex. **FACILITIES:** Children welcome Garden: Beer garden, outdoor eating Dogs allowed (water) **NOTES:** Parking 50

RAMSBURY   Map 04 SU27

Pick of the Pubs

The Bell
The Square SN8 2PE ☎ 01672 520230
Recently refurbished in a light and contemporary style, The Bell is in the centre of Ramsbury and has a pretty garden to the rear. The chef provides a fresh and innovative menu, described as 'northern with a southern twist'. Strong flavours and imaginative combinations using local produce. Desserts are also a speciality. The well-kept cellar offers good real ales while the constantly changing wine list offers a colourful journey around the world's vineyards.
OPEN: 12-3 6-11 **BAR MEALS:** Lunch served: Tue-Sun 12-2 Dinner served: Tue-Sat 7-9 **RESTAURANT:** Lunch served: all week 12-2 Dinner served: Mon-Sat 7-9 **BREWERY/COMPANY:** Free House **PRINCIPAL BEERS:** Butts, Wadworth 6X, Henrys IPA. **FACILITIES:** Children welcome Garden Dogs allowed **NOTES:** Parking 20

REDLYNCH   Map 04 SU22

Kings Head 🐾
SP5 2JT ☎ 01725 510420
An attractive country pub, dating from the 17th century, with low beams, open fires and hanging baskets in the summer months. It's a three-time winner of the Pubs in Bloom award and has similar accolades for its food. Seafood crêpes, herb-crusted salmon, chicken breast stuffed with asparagus and smoked cheese, and ham hock glazed in honey are favourite dishes. The pub is conveniently situated for exploring the New Forest and Avon Valley.
OPEN: 11-4 6-11 **BAR MEALS:** Lunch served: all week Dinner served: all week 12-3 6-10 Av main course £7.95 **BREWERY/COMPANY:** Ushers **PRINCIPAL BEERS:** Ushers Best, Spring Fever & Founders. **FACILITIES:** Children welcome Garden: Spacious, food served outside Dogs allowed (water) **NOTES:** Parking 30 **ROOMS:** 2 bedrooms 2 en suite from d£50

ROWDE   Map 03 ST96

Pick of the Pubs

The George and Dragon 🐑 🐾 ♀
High St SN10 2PN ☎ 01380 723053 🖹 01380 724738
e-mail: gd-rowde@lineone.net

A hostelry has stood here since the 14th century, but today's building dates back to 1675 - still retaining its outside gents' loo! Within is a treasure trove of antiquity in the panelled bars and dining room that are seasonally warmed by log fires. Tim Withers's daily-changed menus have shown remarkable consistency over the years, with pristine fresh fish from Cornwall occupying centre stage. Provençale fish soup with rouille, Gruyère and garlic croûtons is a perennial favourite alongside faultless fishcakes with hollandaise and cheese soufflé baked with Parmesan and cream that come in starter or main portions. The elongated fish menu is likely to include Scottish langoustines, organic Glenarm salmon with rhubarb and ginger and a classic dish of skate wings with capers and black butter. The list of bottled continental beers and generously priced wines exhibits a similar attention to detail: similarly the plate of West Country cheeses with cucumber pickle and perhaps a port or pudding wine offered by the glass.
OPEN: 12-3 7-11 Closed: 25 Dec, 1 Jan **BAR MEALS:** Lunch served: Tues-Sat Dinner served: Tues-Sat 12-2 7-10 Av main course £10 **RESTAURANT:** Lunch served: Tues-Sat Dinner served: Tues-Sat 12-2 7-10 Av 3 course à la carte £25 Av 3 course fixed price £12.50 **BREWERY/COMPANY:** Free House **PRINCIPAL BEERS:** Hop Back Summer Lightning, Butcombe Bitter, Milk Street Brewery, Bath Ales. **FACILITIES:** Children welcome Garden: Food served outside Dogs allowed (water) **NOTES:** Parking 10

SALISBURY   Map 03 SU12

The Coach & Horses 🐾
Winchester St SP1 1HG ☎ 01722 336254 🖹 01722 414319
Many changes have taken place in its 500-year history, but the black and white timbered facade of Salisbury's oldest inn remains. Slate-floored bar and cobbled courtyard. Bedrooms.

The Old Mill at Harnham ♀
Town Path, West Harnham SP2 8EU
☎ 01722 327517 🖹 01722 333367
Dir: near city centre, on River Avon
Listed building which became Wiltshires first papermaking mill in 1550. Tranquil meadow setting with classic views of Salisbury Cathedral. Crystal clear water diverted from the River Nadder cascades through the restaurant. Bedrooms.
See Pub Walk on page 493

SEEND Map 03 ST96

The Barge Inn 🏨 ⛾
Seend Cleeve SN12 6QB ☎ 01380 828230 📠 01380 828972
Dir: Off A365 between Melksham & Devizes

Delightfully situated Victorian barge-style pub, converted from a wharf house, on the Kennet and Avon Canal between Bath and Devizes. Note the delicately painted Victorian flowers adorning the ceilings and upper walls. In addition to the lunchtime menu of snacks and hot dishes (wharfman's purse and navvie's pie, for example), there's a seasonal carte supported by blackboard specials with daily vegetarian, meat and fish options.
OPEN: 11–3 6–11 **BAR MEALS:** Lunch served: all week Dinner served: all week 12–2 7–9.30 Av main course £9
RESTAURANT: Lunch served: all week Dinner served: all week 12–2 7–9.30 Av 3 course à la carte £16
BREWERY/COMPANY: Wadworth
PRINCIPAL BEERS: Wadworth 6X & Henry's IPA, Badger Tanglefoot, Butcombe Bitter. **FACILITIES:** Children welcome Garden: Large canal side garden, food served outside Dogs allowed (water)
NOTES: Parking 50

Bell Inn 🏨
Bell Hill SN12 6SA ☎ 01380 828338
e-mail: Bellseend@aol.com
Local tradition has it that Oliver Cromwell and his troops breakfasted at the inn on 18 September 1645 when advancing from Trowbridge to attack Devizes Castle. The pub has recently been extended to include the old brewhouse, now a two-floor restaurant with wonderful views over the valley. House specialities include Thai green chicken, venison casserole, breaded cod, and spinach and Ricotta cannelloni.
OPEN: 11–3 5.30–11 **BAR MEALS:** Lunch served: all week Dinner served: all week 11.45–2.15 6.15–9.30 Av main course £6.75
RESTAURANT: 11.45–2.15 6.15–9.30
BREWERY/COMPANY: Wadworth
PRINCIPAL BEERS: Wadworth 6X, Henry's IPA, Henrys Smooth.
FACILITIES: Children welcome Garden: Food served outside Dogs allowed **NOTES:** Parking 30

SHERSTON Map 03 ST88

The Rattlebone Inn ⛾
Church St SN16 0LR ☎ 01666 840871 📠 01666 840871
Dir: M4 J18 take A46 towards Stroud,then R onto B4040 through Acton Turville & onto Sherston. Or N from M4 J17 & follow signs
According to legend, this 16th-century village inn stands where local hero John Rattlebone died of his wounds after the Battle of Sherston in 1016. The pub is due for refurbishment after a recent takeover by Youngs, but the rambling series of beamed rooms will keep their existing character. A good choice of imaginative dishes includes Welsh lamb noisettes, stuffed chicken breasts, and chargrilled swordfish steak.
OPEN: 12–11 **BAR MEALS:** Lunch served: all week Dinner served: all week 12–2 7–9 Av main course £6.50 **RESTAURANT:** Lunch served: all week Dinner served: all week 12–2 7–9 Av 3 course à la carte £17.50 **BREWERY/COMPANY:** Young & Co
PRINCIPAL BEERS: Youngs Special, Bitter, Smiles Best, Youngs Triple A. **FACILITIES:** Children welcome Garden: Food served outside

STOURHEAD Map 03 ST73

Spread Eagle Inn 🏨 ⛾
BA12 6QE ☎ 01747 840587 📠 01747 840954
e-mail: rthespreadeagle@aol.com
Dir: N of A303 off B3092
Fine 18th-century brick inn peacefully located in the heart of Stourhead Estate (NT), just yards from the magnificent landscaped gardens, enchanting lakes and woodland walks. Popular all day with visitors seeking refreshment, it offers traditional pub food, including lasagne, steak and kidney pie and sandwiches.
OPEN: 9–11 **BAR MEALS:** Lunch served: all week Dinner served: all week 12–3 6–9 Av main course £5.50 **RESTAURANT:** Dinner served: all week 6–9 Av 3 course à la carte £15
BREWERY/COMPANY: Free House **PRINCIPAL BEERS:** Scottish Courage Courage Best, Butcombe Gold, Marston's Pedigree.
FACILITIES: Children welcome Garden **NOTES:** Parking 200
ROOMS: 5 bedrooms 5 en suite from s£60 d£85

SWINDON Map 03 SU18

The Sun Inn 🏨 ⛾ NEW
Lydiard Millicent SN5 3LU ☎ 01793 770425 📠 01793 778287
e-mail: bleninns@clara.net
Dir: 3 miles to the W of Swindon, 1.5 miles from Junct 16 of M4

Completely restored over the last year, this 18th-century inn is situated in the conservation area of Lydiard Millicent. Two separate restaurants have been created from the old cellars at ground level, and exposed beams, open fires and antique furnishing feature throughout. The gardens are particularly attractive, with mature trees, a large grassed area and heated patio. Light snacks, full meals and daily specials are offered, including slow roasted lamb shank and Jamaican-style chicken.
OPEN: 11.30–2.30 5.30–11 **BAR MEALS:** Lunch served: all week Dinner served: all week 12–2.30 7–9.30 Av main course £6
RESTAURANT: Lunch served: all week Dinner served: all week 12–2.30 7–9.30 Av 3 course à la carte £14
BREWERY/COMPANY: Free House **PRINCIPAL BEERS:** Hook Norton Best, Fuller's London Pride, Interbrew Flowers original.
FACILITIES: Children welcome Garden: Patio, food served outside Dogs allowed (water) **NOTES:** Parking 50

continued

TOLLARD ROYAL — Map 03 ST91

King John Inn 🛏
SP5 5PS ☎ 01725 516207
Dir: On B3081 (7m E of Shaftesbury)
A Victorian building, opened in 1859, the King John is a friendly and relaxing place. Nearby is a 13th-century church, and it is also a good area for walkers. Typical menu offers casseroled rump and kidney, lamb with cranberry and orange, plaice goujons, garlic king prawns, and beer battered cod. Bedrooms.

UPPER CHUTE — Map 04 SU25

The Cross Keys
SP11 9ER ☎ 01264 730295 📠 01264 730889
Dir: Near Andover
Located in a walkers' paradise on top of the North Wessex Downs, this welcoming free house enjoys commanding views from its south-facing terrace and large garden. Traditional pub favourites like cheese ploughman's or ham, eggs and chips are supported by home-cooked specials including chicken and mushroom casserole, steak and ale pie, grilled sea bass, and Sunday roasts.
OPEN: 11–3 6–11 Closed: 26 Dec, 1 Jan **BAR MEALS:** Lunch served: all week Dinner served: all week 12–2.15 6–9.30 Av main course £7.25 **RESTAURANT:** Lunch served: all week Dinner served: all week 12–2.15 6–9.30 Av 3 course à la carte £14
BREWERY/COMPANY: Free House **PRINCIPAL BEERS:** Fullers London Pride, Wadworth Henrys IPA, Hampshire King Alfred.
FACILITIES: Children welcome Garden: Food served outside Dogs allowed **NOTES:** Parking 40

UPTON LOVELL — Map 03 ST94

Prince Leopold 🛏 ♀
BA12 0JP ☎ 01985 850460 📠 01985 850737
e-mail: Princeleopold@Lineone.net
Dir: S of A36 between Warminster & Salisbury
Built in 1887 as the local general store and post office, the inn is named after Queen Victoria's youngest son, who was a frequent visitor when he lived at nearby Boyton. The River Wylye runs through the garden, which offers some fine views across the valley. Balti dishes, authentically prepared from whole spices, are a speciality, along with a good choice of fresh fish, slow cooked leg of lamb and steak Leopold.
OPEN: 12–3 7–11 **BAR MEALS:** Lunch served: Tue–Sun Dinner served: Tue–Sun 12–2.30 7–10 Av main course £6.50
RESTAURANT: Lunch served: Tue–Sun Dinner served: Tue–Sun 12–2.30 7–10 Av 3 course à la carte £17
BREWERY/COMPANY: Free House
PRINCIPAL BEERS: Ringwood Best, Scottish Courage John Smith's.
FACILITIES: Children welcome Garden: River, patio, food served outdoors **NOTES:** Parking 20 **ROOMS:** 6 bedrooms 6 en suite from s£34 d£42

WARMINSTER — Map 03 ST84

Pick of the Pubs

The Angel Inn ♦♦♦♦♦ 🏵 🛏 ♀
Upton Scudamore BA12 0AG
☎ 01985 213225 📠 01985 218182
Comfortably refurbished old whitewashed inn situated in a small village north of Warminster, offering a relaxed and unpretentious atmosphere, freshly prepared food and

continued

well appointed bedrooms – the perfect base from which to explore Wiltshire and Bath. Interesting dishes include rack of lamb with crispy leeks and a Lyonnaise sauce, fillet steak with roasted artichokes and foie gras with a Madeira jus, pan fried Caribbean gumbo cakes with a salad and mango dressing, and breast of chicken poached in a wild mushroom tea. Walled terrace garden with upmarket furniture and brollies.
OPEN: 12–3 6–11 Closed: 25 Dec **BAR MEALS:** Lunch served: all week Dinner served: all week 12–2 7–9.30 Av main course £6.95 **RESTAURANT:** Lunch served: all week Dinner served: all week 12–2 7–9.30 Av 3 course à la carte £20
BREWERY/COMPANY: Free House
PRINCIPAL BEERS: Wadworth 6X, Butcombe.
FACILITIES: Children welcome Garden: Food served outside Paved terrace area Dogs allowed (water provided) **NOTES:** Parking 30 **ROOMS:** 10 bedrooms 10 en suite from s£55 d£75

The Cross Keys NEW
Lyes Green, Corsley BA12 7PB
☎ 01373 832406 📠 01373 832934
Near the attractions of Longleat, this popular pub was until recently part of the nearby farm. Although extended over the years, it retains much of its original charm and character. Among the features are quarry-tiled floors, open log fires and quaint beams. Local meat and game form part of the interesting, monthly-changing menu and all dishes are home-made. Roast haunch of venison with braised red cabbage, juniper and thyme sauce and chargrilled supreme of chicken are among the popular main courses.
BREWERY/COMPANY: Wadworth No credit cards

The George Inn ♦♦♦♦
BA12 7DG ☎ 01985 840396 📠 01985 841333

The hub of local activity in the small village of Longbridge Deverill, the George is a picturesque 200-year-old inn in two acres of engaging riverside setting. The ten bedrooms have recently had a makeover to meet modern-day expectations. Bar snacks feature home-made pâté, steak pie and lasagne plus daily specials, while the restaurant promises the likes of medallions of beef fillet and shanks of lamb supplied by the village butcher. There's a patio and beer garden, and a separate function suite.
OPEN: 11–11 **BAR MEALS:** Lunch served: all week Dinner served: all week 12–2.30 6.30–9.30 Av main course £6.95 **RESTAURANT:** Dinner served: all week 12–2.30 6.30–9.30 Av 3 course à la carte £20
BREWERY/COMPANY: Free House **PRINCIPAL BEERS:** Scottish Courage John Smith's, Wadworth 6X. **FACILITIES:** Garden: Food served outdoors, river, terrace **NOTES:** Parking 50 **ROOMS:** 10 bedrooms 10 en suite from s£40 d£60

England

WESTBURY
Map 03 ST85

The Duke of Bratton ♦♦ 🏠 ♀
Melbourne St, Bratton BA13 4RW
☎ 01380 830242 📠 01380 831239
Dir: from Westbury follow B3098

A 'Country Inn with Rooms and Restaurant' fairly describes this pub in the centre of a picturesque village beneath the famous White Horse just three miles east of Westbury. Built up from virtually nothing by its current licensees, its reputation for fine fresh fish and prime local produce continues to grow. Menus evolve with the seasons with special dishes such as spicy Creel prawns with garlic dip, followed by succulent Scotch beef, breast of Wiltshire chicken in various guises and hand-carved Wiltshire ham.
OPEN: 11.30-3 7-11 **BAR MEALS:** Lunch served: Tues-Sun Dinner served: Tues-Sun 12-2 7-9 Av main course £6.50
RESTAURANT: Lunch served: Tues-Sun Dinner served: Tues-Sun 12-2 7-9 Av 3 course à la carte £18.75 **BREWERY/COMPANY:** Free House **PRINCIPAL BEERS:** Moles Best, Scottish Courage Courage Best, Interbrew Bass. **FACILITIES:** Garden: Food served outside
NOTES: Parking 30 **ROOMS:** 3 bedrooms from s£30 d£50

WHITLEY
Map 03 ST86

Pick of the Pubs

The Pear Tree Inn 🏠 🏠 ♀
Top Ln SN12 8QX ☎ 01225 709131 📠 01225 702276
Dir: A365 from Melksham toward Bath, at Shaw R on B3353 into Whitley, 1st L in lane, pub is at end of lane.

The Pear Tree is a pub/restaurant in a rural setting, surrounded by parkland studded with great oak trees. The gardens are well planted and there is an extensive patio area with solid teak furniture and cream parasols. At the front there's a large boules piste, and the inn annually fields a team for the Bath Boules Competition. The original part of the pub dates back to 1750 when it was a

farmstead, and the bar is a comfortable domain for locals with four real ales on hand pump. For those who want to eat, a high standard of food is produced from as much locally sourced produce as possible. A selection of breads is baked from locally milled stoneground flour, and ice creams and sorbets are made daily on site. Example dishes are baked monkfish on fennel cassoulet, and roast best end of lamb with sweet potato mash.
OPEN: 11-3 6-11 Closed: 25/26 Dec, 1 Jan
BAR MEALS: Lunch served: all week Dinner served: all week 12-2 6.30-9.30 Av main course £9 **RESTAURANT:** Lunch served: all week Dinner served: all week 12-2 6.30-9.30 Av 3 course à la carte £22.50 **BREWERY/COMPANY:** Free House **PRINCIPAL BEERS:** Wadworth 6X, Oakhill Best, Bath Gem Bitter, Smiles Best. **FACILITIES:** Children welcome Garden: Beer garden, patio, food served outdoors **NOTES:** Parking 60

WINTERBOURNE BASSETT
Map 03 SU07

The White Horse Inn 🏠
SN4 9QB ☎ 01793 731257 📠 01793 731257
e-mail: ckstone@btinternet.com

Food is served in both the bar and conservatory restaurant of this village pub on the Marlborough Downs, two miles north of the legendary Avebury stone circle. The extensive menu may feature seared salmon with fried garlic and spring onions; oven baked red snapper with herb crust; pork fillet Somerset; and oriental vegetable curry. The pub is noted for its constantly changing range of sauces, devised to accompany the main dishes.
OPEN: 11-3 7-11 **BAR MEALS:** Lunch served: all week Dinner served: all week 12-2.30 7-10 Av main course £5.75
RESTAURANT: Lunch served: all week Dinner served: all week 12-2.30 7-10 **BREWERY/COMPANY:** Wadworth
PRINCIPAL BEERS: Wadworth 6X, IPA, Hophouse Brews.
FACILITIES: Garden: Food served outdoors **NOTES:** Parking 25

WOODFALLS
Map 03 SU12

The Woodfalls Inn ♦♦♦♦ 🏠 ♀
The Ridge SP5 2LN ☎ 01725 513222 📠 01725 513220
e-mail: woodfallsi@aol.com
Dir: B3080 to Woodfalls
Built in 1868 as an ale house and coaching inn on the northern edge of the New Forest, this attractively refurbished inn offers well equipped bedrooms and a good range of food. A typical example includes pan-fried chicken with bacon topped with cheese, steak and ale pie, swordfish steak in Thai sauce, and salmon steak.
OPEN: 11-11 **BAR MEALS:** Lunch served: all week Dinner served: all week 12-2.15 6.30-9.30 Av main course £9 **RESTAURANT:** Lunch

continued

continued

served: all week Dinner served: all week 12-2.15 6.30-9 Av 3 course à
la carte £17.50 **BREWERY/COMPANY:** Free House
PRINCIPAL BEERS: Courage Directors & Best, HSB, Hopback's GFB,
John Smiths. **FACILITIES:** Children welcome Garden: Food served
outside. Patio area Dogs allowed (Toys & water provided)
NOTES: Parking 40 **ROOMS:** 10 bedrooms 10 en suite from s£45
d£69.90

WOOTTON RIVERS   Map 03 SU16

Royal Oak ⌂ ♀
SN8 4NQ ☎ 01672 810322 🖥 01672 811168
Dir: 3m S from Marlborough

A thatched and timbered 16th-century inn situated 100 yards
from the Kennet and Avon Canal in one of Wiltshire's prettiest
villages. It is close to Savernake Forest - a wonderful area for
canal and forest walks. Menus are flexible to suit every
occasion, with light dishes, a full carte and fixed-price options.
Representative main courses are roast beef with horseradish,
oven baked sea bass with lime leaves, and spinach and red
pepper tart.
OPEN: 10.30-3.30 6-11 **BAR MEALS:** Lunch served: all week
Dinner served: all week 11.30-2.30 6-9.30 Av main course £7.50
RESTAURANT: Lunch served: all week Dinner served: all week
11.30-2.30 6-9.30 Av 3 course à la carte £12.50
BREWERY/COMPANY: Free House
PRINCIPAL BEERS: Wadworth 6X + guest ales.
FACILITIES: Children welcome Garden: Dogs allowed
NOTES: Parking 20 **ROOMS:** 6 bedrooms 3 en suite from s£25
d£40

WYLYE   Map 03 SU03

The Bell Inn ♦♦♦ ♀
High St, Wylye BA12 0QP ☎ 01985 248338 🖥 01985 248389
e-mail: lk.thebell@wylye2.freeserve.co.uk

There's a wealth of old oak beams, log fires and an inglenook
fireplace at this 14th-century coaching inn, situated in the

continued

pretty Wylye Valley. Quick meals in the bar range from freshly
cut sandwiches to fresh Dorset mussels in white wine and
cream or smoked Wiltshire ham with free-range eggs and
chips. Items from the main carte are seared fillet of beef with
bacon, wild mushrooms and Madeira sauce, or wild
mushroom and vegetable crumble.
OPEN: 11.30-2.30 (Sun 12-3, 7-10.30) 6-11 **BAR MEALS:** Lunch
served: all week Dinner served: all week 12-2 6-9.30 Av main course
£7.50 **RESTAURANT:** Lunch served: all week Dinner served: all week
12-2 6-9.30 Av 3 course à la carte £25 **BREWERY/COMPANY:** Free
House **PRINCIPAL BEERS:** Regularly changing beers.
FACILITIES: Children's licence Garden: Food served outside Dogs
allowed (water) **NOTES:** Parking 20 **ROOMS:** 3 bedrooms 3 en
suite from s£30 d£45

WORCESTERSHIRE

ABBERLEY   Map 03 ST76

Manor Arms Country Inn ♦♦♦ ♀
WR6 6BN ☎ 01299 896507 🖥 01299 896723
e-mail: manorarms@abberley.com

Set just across the lane from the Norman church of St
Michael, the interior of this 300-year-old inn is enhanced by
original oak beams and a log-burning fire. A modern
extension at the back has added a restaurant, en-suite
bedrooms and conference room. Expect a wide choice of grills
and roasts, plus alternatives such as poached haddock with a
poached egg and chive and butter sauce, or cheese and lentil
terrine on smooth tomato coulis.
OPEN: 12-3 6-11 (closed Mon lunchtime in winter)
BAR MEALS: Lunch served: all week Dinner served: all week
12-2.00 7-9.00 Av main course £6.50 **RESTAURANT:** Dinner served:
all week 7-9.30 Av 3 course fixed price £14
BREWERY/COMPANY: Enterprise Inns
PRINCIPAL BEERS: Fuller's London Pride, Theakstons Best Bitter,
Scottish Courage John Smith's & Courage Directors.
FACILITIES: Children's licence Garden: Patio/terrace, food served
outdoors **NOTES:** Parking 25 **ROOMS:** 10 bedrooms 10 en suite
from s£40 d£50

BEWDLEY   Map 08 SO77

Pick of the Pubs

Horse & Jockey ⌂ ♀
Far Forest DY14 9DX ☎ 01299 266239 🖥 01299 266227
e-mail: suzanne-st@hotmail.com
See Pick of the Pubs on page 517

Little Pack Horse 🛏 ♀
31 High St DY12 2DH ☎ 01299 403762 🖷 01299 403762
e-mail: littlepackhorse@aol.com
Historic timber-framed inn with low beams and an elm timber bar, located in one of the Severn Valley's prettiest towns. The interior is warmed by a cosy woodburning stove and candlelit at night. Full of eccentricities and oddities. Expect oriental tiger prawn chow mein, Moroccan vegetable and chicpea couscous, casserole of king prawns and monkfish tails flamed with Pernod and leeks, roast rack of lamb glazed with a herb crust, or mushroom, spinach and sweetpepper Stroganoff on the menu.
OPEN: 12-3 6-11 (Sat-Sun 12-11) **BAR MEALS:** Lunch served: all week Dinner served: all week 12-2.15 6.30-9.30 Av main course £6 **PRINCIPAL BEERS:** Ushers - Best, Four Seasons, Burton Ale.
FACILITIES: Children welcome Garden: Food served outside, patio area Dogs allowed

---

BRANSFORD   Map 03 SO75

The Bear & Ragged Staff 🛏 ♀
Station Rd WR6 5JH ☎ 01886 833399 🖷 01886 833106
e-mail: bearragged@aol.com
Dir: 3m from centre of Worcester off the A4103 (Hereford Rd) Or 3m from the centre of Malvern off A449, turning L just before Powick Village. signpost for Bransford.

Mid-way between Worcester and the Malvern Hills, this smart dining pub has an enviable reputation for its imaginative menus and fresh Cornish fish. The name comes from the family crest of the Earl of Warwickshire. Lunchtime bar meals include brunch rolls, Cajun-spiced salmon, and five cheese tortellini. It's wise to book for the restaurant at weekends, when starters like avocado, crab and tomato pancake might precede ribeye steak with shallots and red wine sauce, roast cod on butter bean mash, or fillet of venison on puree of aubergine and rich redcurrant sauce flavoured with chocolate.
OPEN: 12-2.30 6.30-10.30 **BAR MEALS:** Lunch served: all week Dinner served: Sun- Fri 12-2.00 6.30-8 Av main course £6 **RESTAURANT:** Lunch served: all week Dinner served: all week 12-2 7-9 Av 3 course à la carte £20 **BREWERY/COMPANY:** Free House **PRINCIPAL BEERS:** Bass, Highgate Special Bitter, Worthington.
FACILITIES: Garden: Food served outside Dogs allowed (in the garden only, water provided) **NOTES:** Parking 40

BREDON   Map 03 SO93

Fox & Hounds Inn & Restaurant ♀
Church St GL20 7LA ☎ 01684 772377 🖷 01684 772377
Dir: M5 J9 into Tewkesbury take B4080 towards Pershore. Bredon 3m
Pretty 16th-century thatched pub, resplendent with colourful, over-flowing hanging baskets in summer, close to the River Avon. There is a wide-ranging menu available throughout,

plus blackboard specials and lunchtime bar snacks. Favourite dishes include home-made pies, fresh game in season, crispy duck, and the daily fresh fish selection.
OPEN: 11.30-3 6-11 (Sun 12-3, 6.30-10.30) **BAR MEALS:** Lunch served: all week Dinner served: all week 12-2 6.30-9.30 Av main course £6.95 **RESTAURANT:** Lunch served: all week Dinner served: all week 12-2 6.30-9.30 Av 3 course à la carte £17 **BREWERY/COMPANY:** Whitbread **PRINCIPAL BEERS:** Banks, Marstons Pedigree, Greene King Old Speckled Hen.
FACILITIES: Children welcome Garden: Beer garden, patio, outdoor eating, BBQ Dogs allowed (guide dogs only) **NOTES:** Parking 35

BRETFORTON   Map 03 SP04

Pick of the Pubs

The Fleece Inn 🛏 ♀
The Cross WR11 7JE ☎ 01386 831173
Dir: B4035 from Evesham

An extraordinary slice of history, this 17th-century inn stayed in the same family until Lola Taplin bequeathed it to the National Trust in 1977. It has remained largely unchanged over the centuries, providing the contemporary customer with an extraordinary experience. The pub's pewter room is a notable example, where a fine collection of pewter has been displayed for over 300 years. Local tradition has it that Lola still watches over the pub, which was her home for 77 years, in the form of an owl perched on the thatched roof of the barn next door. Cask ale and honest home-cooked food are served. Local produce is featured, and options range from snacks to main meals. Home-made pies and farmhouse hot pots are house specialities, there's daily fresh fish according to availability and traditional puddings and gateaux. Children's meals are offered and vegetarian options include a popular cheese, leek and potato bake.
OPEN: 11-3 6-11 **BAR MEALS:** Lunch served: all week Dinner served: all week 12-2 6.30-9 Av main course £5 **RESTAURANT:** Lunch served: all week Dinner served: all week 12-2 6.30-9 Av 3 course à la carte £5.50 **BREWERY/COMPANY:** Free House **PRINCIPAL BEERS:** Uley Beer, Hook Norton Best, Woods.
FACILITIES: Children welcome Garden: Food served outside, large

---

DROITWICH   Map 03 SO86

The Chequers
Cutnall Green WR9 0PJ ☎ 01299 851292 🖷 01299 851744
Well maintained traditional inn with lots of exposed beams inside. Interesting and varied menu. Cosy atmosphere.

continued

OPEN: 12–3 6–11 (Sun 12–10.30)
BAR MEALS: L served all week.
D served all week. 12–2.30 6–9.30
Av main course £7
RESTAURANT: L served Sun.
D served all week. 12–4 6–9.30
Av cost 3 courses £20
BREWERY/COMPANY:
FREE HOUSE
PRINCIPAL BEERS: Hobsons
Original, Hobsons Town Crier,
Morland Old Speckled Hen,
Shropshire Lad
FACILITIES: Children welcome
Garden: Food served outside.
Large lawn
NOTES: Parking 50

Horse & Jockey

A peaceful country pub dedicated to maintaining traditional practices of hospitality, serving genuinely fresh food sourced from local farms and cooked with imagination. thanks to the owners focus and dedication it is now a deservedly successful dining destination.

Far Forest Bewdley DY14 9DX
☎ 01299 266239 📠 01299 266227
e-mail: suzanne-st@hotmail.com

The family owners, Shadia, Suzanne and Richard, bought the Horse and Jockey as a dilapidated and failing business and have put life back into it. The pub was first licensed in 1838 to serve cider to farmworkers on the large local estate. A major restoration a few years ago uncovered oak beams, floorboards and an inglenook fireplace, and the much-extended original building incorporates a glass-covered well which locals remember being in the garden. In this charming environment, the quality cooking is a bonus. The regularly changing menus incorporate a selection of beef and lamb from a local farm, typically braised ox heart in red wine, sirloin topped with home-made pâté, and lamb chops with a peppercorn cream. Fresh fish delivered for the weekend might result in sautéed shark loin, seafood jambalaya, and red snapper with a chilli, coconut and coriander chowder. From the main menu expect pan-fried duck breast, venison steak in a port and red wine jus, and sweet potato, aubergines and smoked cheese galette, and oven-roasted salmon on an olive oil mash. The accomplished pace is maintained with desserts like lemon and lime torte, blueberry cheesecake, and an irresistible assiette of chocolate. Up-dated interpretations of traditional pub food come with beef pie, pan-fried chicken supreme, and home-baked ham with double egg and chips.

DROITWICH continued

Old Cock Inn

Friar St WR9 8EQ ☎ 01905 774233
This charming old pub has three stained-glass windows rescued from the local church after it was destroyed during the Civil War The stone carving above the front entrance is believed to be of Judge Jeffreys who presided over the local magistrates' court. Various snacks and light meals feature on the menu, while more substantial fare includes rump steak, steak and Guinness pie, pan-fried duck breast and fillet of lamb with artichoke, wild mushrooms, mint, peppercorns and wine sauce.
OPEN: 12–3 6–11 **RESTAURANT:** Lunch served: all week Dinner served: Mon–Sat 12–2.30 5.30–9.30 Av 3 course à la carte £25

FLADBURY   Map 03 SO94

Chequers Inn

Chequers Ln WR10 2PZ ☎ 01386 860276 ▤ 01386 861286
e-mail: chequers_inn_fladbury@hotmail.com
Dir: Off A4538 between Evesham and Pershore
14th-century inn tucked away in a pretty village with views of the glorious Bredon Hills. Inside are lots of old beams and a cosy fire. Under new management, the Chequers uses fresh local produce in its home-made dishes and offers a changing monthly menu in addition to daily specials. Expect rack of lamb with port wine and redcurrant sauce and sweet and sour monkfish among other dishes.
OPEN: 11–3 6–11 **BAR MEALS:** Lunch served: all week Dinner served: Mon–Sat 12–2 6.30–10 Av main course £7
RESTAURANT: Lunch served: all week Dinner served: Mon–Sat 12–2 6.30–10 Av 3 course à la carte £18 **BREWERY/COMPANY:** Free House **PRINCIPAL BEERS:** Hook Norton Best, Courage Directors, Fullers London Pride, Piddle In The Wind. **FACILITIES:** Children welcome Garden: Food served outside **NOTES:** Parking 28
ROOMS: 8 bedrooms 8 en suite from s£55 d£60

FLYFORD FLAVELL   Map 03 SO95

The Boot Inn ♦♦♦♦

Radford Rd WR7 4BS ☎ 01386 462658 ▤ 01386 462547
Dir: Take Evesham rd, L at 2nd rdbt onto A422, Flyford Flavell signed after 3m
Family-run inn, dating from c1350, situated in a lovely village on the Wychavon Way, well placed for the Cotswolds and Malvern Hills. There are gardens front and back, with a heated patio and quality wooden furniture. Home-cooked food, from an extensive carte and specials board, includes noisettes of spring lamb with redcurrant and mint sauce, poached salmon, and cod in beer batter. Award-winning accommodation is provided in the converted coach house.
OPEN: 11–2.30 6.30–11 **BAR MEALS:** Lunch served: all week 12–2 6.30–10 **RESTAURANT:** Lunch served: all week Dinner served: all week 12–2 6.30–10 **BREWERY/COMPANY:** Free House **PRINCIPAL BEERS:** Interbrew Boddingtons, Wadworth 6X, Greene King Old Speckled Hen, Marston's Pedigree. **FACILITIES:** Children welcome Garden: Patio, food served outside Dogs allowed **NOTES:** Parking 30 **ROOMS:** 5 bedrooms 5 en suite from s£45 d£55

HONEYBOURNE   Map 03 SP14

The Thatched Tavern

WR11 5PQ ☎ 01386 830454 ▤ 01386 833842
e-mail: timandjane@thethatchedtavern.co.uk
Dir: 6 miles from Chipping Campden
Good as its name, this charming old 13th-century inn nestles under a thatched roof. Flagstone floors and open fires add to the cheerful atmosphere of a genuine village pub. Well-kept ales accompany good value meals that range from brunch and bar snacks to midweek specials and Sunday brunch. Everything from home-made pies and steaks to pizza, haddock smokies and Portuguese sardines come with the same friendly service.
OPEN: 11–3 6–11 **BAR MEALS:** Lunch served: all week Dinner served: all week 12–2.30 7–10 Av main course £9
RESTAURANT: Lunch served: all week Dinner served: all week 12–2.30 7–10 Av 3 course à la carte £20
BREWERY/COMPANY: Punch Taverns
PRINCIPAL BEERS: Adnams Broadside, Interbrew Bass, Fuller's London Pride, Marston's Pedigree. **FACILITIES:** Garden: Food served outside **NOTES:** Parking 25 **ROOMS:** 3 bedrooms from s£20 d£25

KEMPSEY   Map 03 SO84

Pick of the Pubs

Walter de Cantelupe Inn

Main Rd WR5 3NA ☎ 01905 820572 ▤ 01905 820572
e-mail: walter.depub@fsbdial.co.uk
Dir: 4m S of Worcester City centre, on A38 in the centre of village

The pub's name is taken from the mid-13th-century Bishop of Worcester, though the building (originally three cottages) dates from the 16th century. The blackboard menu offers a good choice of dishes, and a popular annual event is the outdoor Paella Party, the Spanish-made paella pan yielding 200 portions, requiring six people to hold it when full. Recently introduced en suite accommodation is popular with visitors to historic Worcester, the Malvern Hills and Severn Vale.
OPEN: 12–2 6–11 Closed: Dec 25–26 **BAR MEALS:** Lunch served: Tue–Sat 12–2 Dinner served: Tue–Sun 6.30–9.30 Av main course £6.85 **RESTAURANT:** Lunch served: Tue–Sun 12–2 Dinner served: Tue–Sun 7–9 Av 3 course à la carte £18
BREWERY/COMPANY: Free House
PRINCIPAL BEERS: Timothy Talyor Landlord, Malvern Hill's Black Pear, Everards Beacon Bitter. **FACILITIES:** Garden: Food served outside Dogs allowed **NOTES:** Parking 24
ROOMS: 2 bedrooms 2 en suite from s£29 d£40

England

Pick of the Pubs

The Talbot at Knightwick ♀
WR6 5PH ☎ 01886 821235 📠 01886 821060
e-mail: admin@the-talbot.co.uk
Dir: A44 through Worcester, 8m W turn onto B4197

Now here's a 15th-century inn that really justifies the word 'local'; four hand-pumped real ales are brewed on the premises from hops grown in the parish. The food, too, has a domestic flavour as most of the ingredients are sourced locally, or grown in the pub's 'chemical free' garden. Over the years, Annie and Wiz Clift have developed their own unique style, firmly rooted in the traditions and seasonal produce of the Teme Valley. There are lunchtime rolls and ploughman's, as well as set-price menus. Starters like spiced red lentil soup or devilled kidneys might precede roast wild boar loin with rosemary and chilli, whole lemon sole, or timbale of garden vegetables. Save room for a special rice pudding with cinnamon shortcake or sticky date and toffee pudding. Old beams, winged settles and log fires complete the picture, with a charming patio and riverside lawn for summer drinking.
OPEN: 11–11 (Sun 12–10.30) **BAR MEALS:** Lunch served: all week Dinner served: all week 12–2 6.30–9.30 Av main course £8 **RESTAURANT:** Lunch served: all week Dinner served: all week 12–2 6.30–9.30 Av 3 course à la carte £25 Av 3 course fixed price £22.95 **BREWERY/COMPANY:** Free House **PRINCIPAL BEERS:** Teme Valley This, That , T'Other, City of Cambridge Hobsons Choice. **FACILITIES:** Children welcome Garden: Riverside, food served outside Dogs allowed **NOTES:** Parking 50 **ROOMS:** 10 bedrooms 10 en suite from s£38.50 d£69.50

Farmers Arms
Birts St, Birtsmorton WR13 6AP ☎ 01684 833308
e-mail: farmersarmsbirtsmorton@yahoo.co.uk
Dir: On B4208 S of Great Malvern
Expect a friendly welcome at this 15th-century black and white timbered pub, in a quiet parish close to the Malvern Hills. It serves decent ales and homely bar food in its low-beamed rooms, including cottage pie, macaroni cheese, Hereford pie and a variety of jacket potatoes, Vienna rolls and sandwiches.
OPEN: 11–2.30 (Sun 12–2.30, 7–11) 6–11 **BAR MEALS:** Lunch served: all week Dinner served: all week 11–2 6–9.30 Av main course £4 **BREWERY/COMPANY:** Free House **PRINCIPAL BEERS:** Hook Norton Best & Old Hooky. **FACILITIES:** Children welcome Garden: Patio, food served outside Dogs allowed (water) **NOTES:** Parking 30 No credit cards

Admiral Rodney Inn ♦♦♦♦ 🛏 NEW
Berrow Green WR6 6PL ☎ 01886 821375 📠 01886 821375
Dir: From M3 Junc 7, take A44 signed Bromyard & Leominster. After approx 7m at Knightwick turn R onto B4197, Inn 1.5m on L at Berrow Green

Early 17th-century inn which originally doubled as a farmhouse and alehouse serving travellers on the nearby Worcester Way Walk. From its lofty position it has great views of the city and Malvern Hills, and modern visitors can enjoy a pint of Wye Valley or Hook Norton Bitter with good pub grub. Grills like wild boar, ostrich and rump steak, a list of specials like medallions of beef, and breast of duck, plus various pasta dishes and jacket potatoes.
OPEN: 12–2 6.30–11 **BAR MEALS:** Lunch served: Tues-Sat Dinner served: Tues-Sat 12–2 7–9 Av main course £6 **RESTAURANT:** Lunch served: Tues-Sun Dinner served: Tues-Sat 12–2 7–9 Av 3 course à la carte £15 **BREWERY/COMPANY:** Free House **PRINCIPAL BEERS:** Wye Valley Bitter, Hook Norton Bitter, Scottish Courage John Smith's Smooth, Greene King Old Speckled Hen. **FACILITIES:** Children welcome Garden: Food served outside Dogs allowed (water) **NOTES:** Parking 40 **ROOMS:** 3 bedrooms 3 en suite

Pick of the Pubs

Crown & Sandys Arms 🛏 ♀
Main Rd WR9 0EW ☎ 01905 620252 📠 01905 620769
e-mail: richardeverton@crownandsandys.co.uk

What was once a rather drab and dated pub on the village High Street has been transformed into a classy bistro-style pub since its purchase by local wine merchant Richard Everton.. The building itself belongs to Lord Sandys of Ombersley's estate and now sports a trendy open-plan bar and bistro and an up-to-date restaurant sponsored by

continued

England

OMBERSLEY continued

a famous champagne house. Dishes change every week, offering the likes of green-lip mussel and prawn marinière or spinach, mushroom and herb tagliatelle in two sizes according to one's appetite. Main dishes list up to 20 fish dishes (including a fruits de mer platter for two given 24 hours' notice) and impressive main courses from slow-roast lamb rack with bubble-and-squeak to Malaysian curry with pineapple chutney and chargrilled banana. Regular 'wine dinners' and theme evenings add to its appeal for the regulars.

OPEN: 11–2.30 5–11 **BAR MEALS:** Lunch served: all week Dinner served: all week 11.30–2.30 6–10 Av main course £6.95
RESTAURANT: Lunch served: all week Dinner served: all week 11.30–2.30 6–10 Av 3 course à la carte £20
BREWERY/COMPANY: Free House
PRINCIPAL BEERS: Adnams Bitter, Marston's Pedigree, Greene King Abbot Ale, Woods Parish Bitter plus Guest beers.
FACILITIES: Children welcome Garden: Food served outside, Japanese style terrace **NOTES:** Parking 100
ROOMS: 3 bedrooms 3 en suite from s£55 d£65

Pick of the Pubs

The Kings Arms 🍺 ♀
Main Rd WR9 0EW ☎ 01905 620142 📠 01905 620142
Dir: Just off A449
Dating back to 1411, this wonderful black and white timbered inn was reputedly King Charles II's first stop after fleeing the Battle of Worcester in 1651. The inviting, dimly lit interior welcomes visitors with intimate nooks and crannies, flagstone floors and three blazing winter fires. On warmer days, customers spill out into the pretty walled garden for alfresco eating on tables set amid the summer flowers. A tempting array of modern pub food is available, with a daily blackboards election of fresh fish and seafood. Expect flaked smoked haddock in a spinach and cheese sauce; deep-fried brie with date and apple chutney or leek and goat's cheese tart. Follow on with oxtail braised in Guinness; shepherd's pie with cheese crusted leeks; chargrilled pork chop with herby potatoes, roast roots and winter pears, or broccoli and Stilton strudel. Lemon tart, or apple and winter berry crumble are typical pudding choices.
OPEN: 11–3 5.30–11 (Sun all day) Closed: 25 Dec
BAR MEALS: Lunch served: all week Dinner served: all week 12–2.15 6–10 Av main course £9.50 **RESTAURANT:** Lunch served: all week Dinner served: all week 12–2.15 6–10 Av 3 course à la carte £16.50 **BREWERY/COMPANY:** Free House
PRINCIPAL BEERS: Banks's Bitter, Marston's Pedigree, Cannon Royall Arrowhead, Morrells Varsity. **FACILITIES:** Children welcome Garden: Patio, food served outside **NOTES:** Parking 60

PENSAX   Map 03 SO76

The Bell Inn ♀
WR6 6AE ☎ 01299 896677
Dir: From Kidderminster A456 to Clows Top, B4202 towards Abberley, pub 2m on L
Friendly rural local offering five real ales by the jug at weekends to extend the choice available. There's also a beer festival held at the end of June. Home-made dishes are

prepared from seasonal local produce – steaks, liver and onions, and home-cooked ham with free-range eggs. Superb views are enjoyed from the garden, and great local walks. Walkers and cyclists are welcome, and there's a registered caravan/campsite opposite.

OPEN: 12–2.30 5–11 **BAR MEALS:** Lunch served: Tues–Sun 12–2 Dinner served: all week 6–9 Av main course £6
RESTAURANT: Lunch served: Tue–Sun 12–2 Dinner served: all week 6–9 **BREWERY/COMPANY:** Free House
PRINCIPAL BEERS: Enville Best, Timothy Taylor Best Bitter, Hobsons Best, Hook Norton Best. **FACILITIES:** Children welcome Garden: Food served outside Dogs allowed **NOTES:** Parking 20

POWICK   Map 03 SO85

The Halfway House 🍺
Bastonford WR2 4SL ☎ 01905 831098
Dir: From A15 J7 take A4440 then A449

Situated on the A449 between Worcester and Malvern, this delightful family-run pub is just a few minutes' drive from the picturesque spa town of Malvern, a popular centre for exploring the Malvern Hills. All dishes are listed on blackboards and the choice ranges from lamb shank and Herefordshire rib-eye steak to seafood platter and pan-fried Gressingham duck breast. Other options might include honey-baked ham, trio of pork and leek sausages and mushroom Stroganoff.
OPEN: 12–3 6–11 (Mon closed all afternoon) **BAR MEALS:** Lunch served: Tue–Sun 12–2.30 Dinner served: Mon–Sat 6–9 Av main course £10 **RESTAURANT:** Lunch served: Tue–Sun 12–2.30 Dinner served: Mon–Sat 6–9 Av 3 course à la carte £20
BREWERY/COMPANY: Free House
PRINCIPAL BEERS: Marston's Pedigree, St Georges Bitter.
FACILITIES: Children welcome Garden: Food served outdoors **NOTES:** Parking 30

continued

SHATTERFORD   Map 08 SO78

The Bellmans Cross ☺ ♀
Bridgnorth Rd DY12 1RN ☎ 01299 861322 ▤ 01299 861047
Dir: on A442 5m outside Kidderminster

A warm and friendly atmosphere pervades this French-owned inn standing by the A442. The 150-year-old, black and white building has been revived recently. Menus are seasonal and the food is freshly prepared with a mix of British and Continental dishes. A distinctly Gallic air pervades the restaurant 'carte' with a keen eye to fresh local produce, while from the bar menu offers the more traditional liver and onions, black pudding tart, fresh haddock and generous salads.
OPEN: 11–3 6–11 (Open all day on Sat & BHs)
BAR MEALS: Lunch served: all week Dinner served: all week 12–2.15 6–9.30 Av main course £10 **RESTAURANT:** Lunch served: all week Dinner served: all week 12–2.15 6–9.30 Av 3 course à la carte £20
BREWERY/COMPANY: Free House
PRINCIPAL BEERS: Interbrew Bass, Greene King Old Speckled Hen, Worthington, Carlsberg-Tetley Tetley Bitter. **FACILITIES:** Children welcome Garden: Patio, food served outdoors Dogs allowed (Guide dog only) **NOTES:** Parking 30

Red Lion Inn ☺ ♀
Bridgnorth Rd DY12 1SU ☎ 01299 861221
Dir: N from Kidderminster on the A442
This largely 'non-smoking' free house enjoys panoramic views towards the Clee Hills and Severn Valley, and you're as welcome to drop in for a pint and a sandwich as you are for a bottle of Chablis and rack of lamb. Popular hot and cold bar meals provide a simpler alternative to the restaurant menu, which includes duck breast with orange and Cointreau, fresh trout with capers and white wine, as well as a selection of grills.
OPEN: 11.30–2.30 6.30–11 (Sun 12–3, 7–10.30) Closed: Dec 25
BAR MEALS: Lunch served: all week Dinner served: all week 11.30–2 6.30–9.30 Av main course £7 **RESTAURANT:** Lunch served: all week Dinner served: all week 11.30–2 6.30–9.30 Av 3 course à la carte £15
BREWERY/COMPANY: Free House
PRINCIPAL BEERS: Bathams, Banks' Mild, Shropshire Lad, Wye Valley Butty Bach. **FACILITIES:** Children welcome Garden: Food served outdoors, patio, **NOTES:** Parking 50

TENBURY WELLS   Map 03 SO56

Pick of the Pubs

The Fountain Inn ☺ ♀
Oldwood, St Michaels WR15 8TB
☎ 01584 810701 ▤ 01584 819030
e-mail: miamifountaininn@aol.com
Dir: 1M out of Tenbury Wells on the A4112 Leominster Road
Few pubs can offer live sharks as part of their decor, and the Fountain must surely be the only inn whose chef

continued

found fame for having been bitten by one of them. If you missed the media coverage, you can at least visit the culprit, Miami, and other exotic creatures including a Red Sea ray, in the tank that nestles incongruously by the roaring log fire. The rest of the interior is more traditional, as you would expect from a 19th-century beer and cider house. Hand pulled guest beers and the exclusive Fountain Ale complement the short snack menu and an extensive selection of daily specials. There's a good selection of seafood dishes, including whitebait, baked tuna steak and poached salmon hollandaise. Other dishes might include authentic vegetable curry, Mediterranean lamb, beef and ale pie or local partridge with apple sauce.

OPEN: 9–11 **BAR MEALS:** Lunch served: all week Dinner served: all week 9–8pm 9–8pm Av main course £7.25
RESTAURANT: Lunch served: all week Dinner served: all week 12.00–10pm 21–10pm Av 3 course à la carte £13.95
BREWERY/COMPANY: Free House
PRINCIPAL BEERS: Interbrew Bass, Black Sheep Best, Charles Wells Bombardier, Fuller's London Pride. **FACILITIES:** Children welcome Garden: Food served outside Dogs allowed (guide dogs only) **NOTES:** Parking 60

Pick of the Pubs

Peacock Inn ♦♦♦♦ ◎ ☺ ♀
WR15 8LL ☎ 01584 810506 ▤ 01584 811236
e-mail: jvidler@fsbdial.co.uk
Dir: A456 from Worcester then A443 to Tenbury Wells. Inn is 1.25m E of Tenbury Wells

Nestling in the Teme Valley, famous for its orchards and hopyards, and with impressive views across the river, this 14th-century coaching inn has been sympathetically extended and a wealth of pretty shrubs, ivy and colourful hanging baskets help create a splendidly welcoming exterior. Oak beams and open log fires enhance the relaxing bars and oak-panelled restaurant. Local market

continued

England

produce plays a key role in the Peacock's menus, and
dishes range from traditional steak and kidney pie in a
rich gravy to English sirloin steak with a choice of sauce or
melting blue cheese. Other options might include freshly
battered cod and chips in a beer batter, braised duck leg
on a bed of spring onion mash and a thyme-flavoured jus,
and escalope of fresh salmon with a red pesto crust and a
lime butter sauce. Quality overnight accommodation in
spacious, well-equipped and attractive bedrooms; two
with four-poster beds.
OPEN: 12.30–3 6–11 **BAR MEALS:** Lunch served: all week
Dinner served: all week 12–2.15 6.30–9.30 Av main course £10
RESTAURANT: Lunch served: all week Dinner served: all week
12–2.15 7–9.30 Av 3 course à la carte £22
BREWERY/COMPANY: Free House
PRINCIPAL BEERS: Hobsons Best Bitter, Timothy Taylor
Landlord, Wood Shropshire Lad. **FACILITIES:** Children welcome
Garden: Food served outside Dogs allowed **NOTES:** Parking
30 **ROOMS:** 3 bedrooms 3 en suite from s£45 d£55

WYRE PIDDLE
Map 03 SO94

The Anchor Inn ♀
Main St WR10 2JB ☎ 01386 552799 📠 01386 552799
Dir: From M5 J6 take A4538 S towards Evesham

An impressive half-timbered inn on the banks of the Avon,
standing in gardens that overlook the pleasure craft moored
by the water's edge. Old world in style, the 400-year-old
building features a cosy lounge with original low-timbered
ceiling, old coaching prints around the walls and an inglenook
fireplace decorated with horse brasses. Menus featuring local
produce include Evesham asparagus from May to July and
prime game dishes over the winter months.
OPEN: 11–2.30 (Sat-Sun 12–3) 6–11 (Sun 7–10.30)
BAR MEALS: Lunch served: all week Dinner served: all week 12–2.15
7–9.15 Av main course £10.50 **RESTAURANT:** Lunch served: all
week 12–2.15 Dinner served: Mon-Sat 7–9.15 Av 3 course à la carte
£15 **BREWERY/COMPANY:** Whitbread
PRINCIPAL BEERS: Interbrew Flowers Original, Flowers IPA &
Boddingtons Bitter, Marston's Pedigree. **FACILITIES:** Children's
licence Garden: Beer garden, Food served outdoors
NOTES: Parking 10

YORKSHIRE, EAST RIDING OF

BEVERLEY
Map 09 TA03

White Horse Inn
22 Hengate HU17 8BN ☎ 01482 861973 📠 01482 861973
Dir: A1079 from York to Beverly
A classic 16th-century local with atmospheric little rooms
arranged around the central bar. Gas lighting, open fires,
antique cartoons and high-backed settles add to the charm.
John Wesley preached in the back yard in the mid-18th
century. Traditional bar food includes many popular dishes –
among them chicken Kiev, wholetail scampi, jumbo haddock,
chilli con carne, spinach and Ricotta pasta and a choice of
fresh salads. Toasted sandwiches and roast beef baguettes
also feature.
OPEN: 11–11 (Sun 12–10.30/no food Mon lunch)
BAR MEALS: Lunch served: Tue–Sun 12–2 Av main course £4.25
BREWERY/COMPANY: Samuel Smith
PRINCIPAL BEERS: Samuel Smith Old Brewery Bitter & Soveriegn
Bitter. **FACILITIES:** Children welcome Garden: beer garden, food
served outdoors Dogs allowed (on leads only, water)
NOTES: Parking 30 No credit cards

BRANDESBURTON
Map 09 TA14

The Dacre Arms ♀
Main St YO25 8RL ☎ 01964 542392 📠 01964 542392
This popular village inn is the home of the Franklin Dead
Brief. The society was started in 1844 and currently has 300
members. Each one pays 20p on the death of a member and
the landlord is always the treasurer. An extensive range of
quality pub food includes large filled Yorkshire puddings,
steak and ale pie, lasagne and curries.
OPEN: 11.30–2.30 6–11 (open all day wknds) Closed: 25 Dec
BAR MEALS: Lunch served: all week Dinner served: all week 12–2
6–10 Av main course £5.45 **RESTAURANT:** Dinner served: all week
7–9 Av 3 course à la carte £16 Av 4 course fixed price £12.75
BREWERY/COMPANY: Free House **PRINCIPAL BEERS:** Black
Sheep Best, Scottish Courage John Smith's, Theakston's Old Peculier.
FACILITIES: Garden: Beer garden, food served outdoors, BBQ
NOTES: Parking 60

DRIFFIELD
Map 09 TA05

The Bell ★ ★ ★
46 Market Place YO25 6AN ☎ 01377 256661 📠 01377 253228
e-mail: bell@bestwestern.co.uk
Dir: Enter town from A164, turn R at traffic lights. Car park 50yrds on L
behind black railings
Furnished with antiques, this is a delightful 18th-century
coaching inn. The oak-panelled bar serves cask beers and 300
whiskies. Food ranges from grilled salmon steak with
hollandaise sauce and poached halibut with white wine and
spring onions, to strips of chicken cooked with honey,
mustard and cream served with rice, and breast of duckling
served on a lake of plum sauce. Bedrooms, snooker room,
swimming pool and squash court are available.
OPEN: 10–2.30 6–11 Closed: Dec 25 **BAR MEALS:** Lunch served:
all week Dinner served: all week 12–1.30 7–9.30 Av main course £5.50
RESTAURANT: Lunch served: all week 12–1.30 Dinner served:
Mon-Sat 7–9.30 Av 3 course à la carte £20 Av 3 course fixed price
£15.95 **BREWERY/COMPANY:** Free House
PRINCIPAL BEERS: Daleside Old Leg Over, Green grass, Hambleton
Stud, Stallion. **FACILITIES:** Children's licence **NOTES:** Parking 18
ROOMS: 16 bedrooms 16 en suite from s£79 d£108

FLAMBOROUGH

Map 09 TA27

The Seabirds Inn ♀
Tower St YO15 1PD ☎ 01262 850242 🖂 01262 850242
Dir: *On B1255 E of Bridlington*

Just down the road from the RSPB's spectacular Bempton
Cliffs bird sanctuary and the stunning cliffs at Flamborough
Head. This aptly named pub has a reputation for fresh fish
dishes, including paupiettes of plaice filled with salmon and
prawn mousse, smoked haddock with tomato, onion and
mushroom sauce, and smoked haddock and broccoli pie.
Other options include beef Wellington, and pork and Stilton
sausages on a bed of apple mash with redcurrant and red
onion gravy.
OPEN: 11–3 7–11 (Sat 6.30–11) **BAR MEALS:** 12–2 7–9
RESTAURANT: Lunch served: all week 12–2 Dinner served: Mon-Sat
7–9 Av 3 course à la carte £15 **BREWERY/COMPANY:** Free House
PRINCIPAL BEERS: Scottish Courage John Smith's, Interbrew
Boddingtons Bitter. **FACILITIES:** Garden: Beer Garden: with seating
Dogs allowed (water) **NOTES:** Parking 20

HOLME UPON SPALDING MOOR

Map 09 SE83

Ye Olde Red Lion Hotel 🐷 ♀
Old Rd YO43 4AD ☎ 01430 860220 🖂 01430 861471
e-mail: benwalsh@redlion.prestel.co.uk
Dir: *off A1079 (York/Hull road). At Market Weighton take A614*
A historic 17th-century coaching inn with a friendly
atmosphere, oak beams and a cosy fire. There has been a
hostelry on this site since Doomsday and this building once
provided hospitality for weary travellers who were helped
across the marshes by monks. Good quality home-cooked bar
food and an international menu covering dishes from many
countries. Restaurant main courses include fresh chicken fillet,
roast rack of lamb garni, Aylesbury honey roast duckling and
seafood mornay.
OPEN: 11.30–2.30 6–11 (Sun 12–3 7–10.30) **BAR MEALS:** Lunch
served: all week Dinner served: all week 12–1.45 6.45–9.45 Av main
course £7 **RESTAURANT:** Lunch served: all week Dinner served: all
week 12–1.30 7.15–9.30 Av 3 course à la carte £15
BREWERY/COMPANY: Free House
PRINCIPAL BEERS: Carlsberg-Tetley Tetley Bitter, Interbrew Bass.
FACILITIES: Children welcome Garden: Patio, food served outside
NOTES: Parking 60 **ROOMS:** 8 bedrooms 8 en suite from s£36
d£58

HUGGATE

Map 09 SE85

The Wolds Inn ♦♦♦ 🐷
YO42 1YH ☎ 01377 288217
e-mail: hudggate@woldsinn.freeserve.co.uk
Dir: *S Of A166 between York & Driffield*

Probably the highest inn on the Yorkshire Wolds, this
venerable village local, close to the parish church, also claims
16th-century origins. Beneath a huddle of tiled roofs and
white-painted chimneys, it sports an interior of wood
panelling, gleaming brassware and open fires. Baguettes and
sandwiches and bar main dishes of gammon and egg, Whitby
seafood and a Sunday roast. Restaurant specials move on to
salmon goujons, steak pie and roast duckling with orange
sauce.
OPEN: 12–2 6.45–11 **BAR MEALS:** Lunch served: Tues-Sun Dinner
served: Tues-Sun 12–2 7–9.30 Av main course £5.20
RESTAURANT: Lunch served: Tues-Sun Dinner served: Tues-Sun
12–2.30 7–9.30 Av 3 course à la carte £17.20
BREWERY/COMPANY: Free House
PRINCIPAL BEERS: Carlsberg-Tetley Tetley Bitter, Timothy Taylor
Landlord, Greene King Old Speckled Hen,. **FACILITIES:** Children
welcome Garden: Enclosed with seating and large lawned area
NOTES: Parking 50 **ROOMS:** 3 bedrooms 3 en suite from s£24.50
d£35

HULL

Map 09 TA02

The Minerva Hotel
Nelson St, Victoria Pier HU1 1XE
☎ 01482 326909 🖂 01482 326909
Dir: *M62 onto A63, then Castle St, turn R at signpost for Fruit Market into
Queens St at the top of Queenes St on R hand side of the pier*
Built in 1831 and famous in the area for its nautical
memorabilia, a handsome riverside pub with old-fashioned
rooms and cosy snugs. Within walking distance are fifteen
more pubs on the Hull Ale Trail! In addition to the pubs
annual beer festivals, there is always a good choice on offer.
Simple yet appetising bar food includes filled Yorkshire
puddings, beef cobbler, curries and jumbo-sized fresh
haddock fillets; followed by bread-and-butter pudding.
Alfresco eating in summer.
OPEN: 11–11 (Sun 12–10.30) Closed: Dec 25 **BAR MEALS:** Lunch
served: all week 12–2 Dinner served: Mon-Thu 6–9 Av main course
£4.50 **RESTAURANT:** 12–2 6–9 **PRINCIPAL BEERS:** Carlsberg-
Tetley Tetley Bitter, Timothy Taylor Landlord, Black Sheep Best,
Roosters. **FACILITIES:** Children welcome Garden: Food served
outside, Promenade with tables

KILHAM   Map 09 TA06

The Old Star
Church St YO25 4RG ☎ 01262 420619 ▤ 01262 420712
e-mail: oldstarkilham@ntlbusiness.com
A sympathetically restored 17th-century inn retaining its
essential character whilst providing comfortable, modern
facilities. Standing opposite Kilham's parish church, it remains
the hub of the local community. Seasonal produce from local
suppliers, interesting guest ales and house wines all indicate
an interest in the customer. A typical Gourmet Weekend menu
lists spiced lamb fillet salad, fillet of ling with a herb crumble
topping, and baked chocolate Mascarpone cheesecake - in all
good food at generous prices.
OPEN: 11-2 6-11 (Sat 11-11, Sun 11-10.30) **BAR MEALS:** Lunch
served: all week 12-2 Dinner served: Wed-Sun 7-9.30 Av main course
£5.95 **RESTAURANT:** Lunch served: all week 12-2 Dinner served:
Wed-Sun 7-9.30 Av 3 course à la carte £14.95 Av 2 course fixed price
£13.95 **BREWERY/COMPANY:** Free House
PRINCIPAL BEERS: Theakstons XB, Scottish Courage John Smiths.
FACILITIES: Children welcome Garden: Food served outside Dogs
allowed **NOTES:** Parking 5

LUND   Map 09 SE94

Pick of the Pubs

Wellington Inn ♀
19 The Green YO25 9TE ☎ 01377 217294 ▤ 01377 217192
Dir: On B1284 NE of Beverley
Opposite the picture-postcard village green, the
Wellington is a focal point: completely renovated by the
present owners, its clientele is drawn from far afield for
decent bar lunches and impressive à la carte dining.
Traditional soups and sandwiches supplement a
frequently changed lunch menu that offers fresh crab
salad and country pâté with crab apple and herb jelly
before main courses such as seafood linguini. cassoulet of
pork and chorizo, and beef cooked in Guinness with root
vegetables and Irish colcannon. At night, expect queen
scallop and chorizo tart with red pepper sauce, baked cod
fillet on potatoes sautéed with smoked salmon and served
with orange and coriander hollandaise, and roasted duck
breast with parsnip purée, caramelised apple and
Calvados jus. Puddings range from raspberry crème
brûlée to three-tier chocolate terrine. Good list of wines
with useful tasting notes.
OPEN: 12-3 6.30-11 **BAR MEALS:** Lunch served: all week
Dinner served: all week 12-2 7-9 Av main course £9
RESTAURANT: Dinner served: all week 7-9.30 Av 3 course à la
carte £23 **BREWERY/COMPANY:** Free House
PRINCIPAL BEERS: Timothy Taylor Landlord, Dark Mild, Black
Sheep Best, John Smiths. **FACILITIES:** Children welcome
Garden: Courtyard, food served outside **NOTES:** Parking 40

SLEDMERE   Map 09 SE96

The Triton Inn ♦♦♦ ♀
YO25 3XQ ☎ 01377 236644
e-mail: thetritoninn@seldmere.fsbusiness.co.uk
Dir: leave A166 at Garton on the Wolds, take B1252 to Sledmere
Still restored to post horses, this 18th-century coaching inn is
set in the shadow of historic Sledmere House, halfway
between York and the coast on the scenic route to Bridlington.
It makes an ideal base for touring the wolds, moors and coast.

A log fire burns in the oak-panelled bar and home-made food
is freshly prepared to order. Options range from sandwiches
and baked potatoes to Thai prawns in batter, lemon chicken,
and brandy peppered steak.
OPEN: 11.30-2.30 7-11 Closed: Mons 1 Oct-31 Mar
BAR MEALS: Lunch served: Tues-Sun Dinner served: Wed-Sun 12-2
7-9 Av main course £5.95 **RESTAURANT:** Lunch served: Sun Dinner
served: Wed-Sun 12-2 7-9 Av 3 course à la carte £14.50
BREWERY/COMPANY: Free House
PRINCIPAL BEERS: Carlsberg-Tetley Tetley Bitter, Scottish Courage
John Smith's.. **FACILITIES:** Children welcome Garden: Food served
outside **NOTES:** Parking 35 **ROOMS:** 5 bedrooms 2 en suite from
s£24 d£44

YORKSHIRE, NORTH

ACASTER MALBIS   Map 09 SE54

The Ship Inn
Moor End YO23 2UH
☎ 01904 705609 & 703888 ▤ 01904 705971
Dir: from York take A1036 south after Dringhouses take follow signs for
Bishopthorpe and then Acaster Malbis
17th-century coaching house with a relaxing riverside garden
very pleasant for watching the colourful boats and barges.
Acaster Malbis is the site of a Roman fort. Traditional bar food
is on offer, including steak in ale pie, and battered haddock
fillet.

AKEBAR   Map 09 NZ19

The Friar's Head ⌂
Akebar Park DL8 5LY ☎ 01677 450201 ▤ 01677 450046
Dir: Take A684 from Leeming Bar Motel (on A1). W towards Leyburn for
7m. Friar's Head is in Akebar Park
A typical stone-built Yorkshire Dales pub in Lower
Wensleydale at the entrance to the National Park. Originally a
farm and adjoining cottages, the pub has a well-stocked bar,
hand-pulled Yorkshire ales and a blazing log fire to relax by
after an invigorating walk in the hills. Alternatively, on a
summer's day enjoy a game of bowls, croquet or petanque on
the lawn. Food is freshly cooked to order, using mainly local
produce in season. Try breast of duck or Friar's fishcakes.
OPEN: 10-2.30 6-11.30 (Sun 7-10.30) **BAR MEALS:** Lunch served:
all week Dinner served: all week 12-2.30 6-11 Av main course £7
RESTAURANT: Lunch served: all week Dinner served: all week
12-2.30 6-11 Av 3 course à la carte £18
BREWERY/COMPANY: Free House **PRINCIPAL BEERS:** Scottish
Courage John Smith's, Theakston Best Bitter, Black Sheep Best.
FACILITIES: Children welcome Garden: Food served outdoors
NOTES: Parking 60

APPLETREEWICK   Map 09 SE06

The Craven Arms
BD23 6DA ☎ 01756 720270 ▤ 01756 720270
Dir: From Skipton take A59 towards Harrogate, B6160 N. Village signed on
R. (Pub just outside village)
Old world Dales pub with beams, a Yorkshire range and log
fires, and spectacular views of the River Wharfe and Simon's
Seat. Old artefacts and notes are displayed on the bar ceiling.
Steak and kidney pie, game pie and Cumberland sausage are
among the traditional dishes.
OPEN: 11.30-3 (Sun 12-3,7-10.30) 6.30-11 **BAR MEALS:** Lunch
served: all week Dinner served: all week 12-2 7-9.30 Av main course

continued

continued

PUB WALK

Clapham
New Inn

NEW INN,
CLAPHAM nr Settle LA2 8HH
Tel: 015242 51203
Directions: On A65 in Yorkshire
Dale National Park
Family-run 18th-century coaching
inn beneath Ingleborough, one of
Yorkshire's most famous summits.
Plenty of walks from the pub,
including one to Ingleborough
Show Cave, open all year at
weekends and on Bank Holidays.
Wholesome food.
Open: 11-11
Bar Meals: 12-2 6.30-9
Children welcome and dogs
allowed. Garden and parking
available.

A spectacular walk exploring the wild Yorkshire landscape of the Three Peaks. This is potholing adventure country: a subterranean world of passages, caves and waterlogged caverns.

From the inn turn right and follow the road alongside Clapham Beck. At the church turn right, signposted Austwick, and follow the lane through the tunnels, up the hill, to the top. Turn right (Thwaite Lane) towards Austwick. Continue down the lane, with views ahead towards the North Craven Fault. Climb the ladder-stile on your left and follow the path alongside the wall running below Norber Brow. When the wall turns right, follow the path up to the left to what is known as Norber 'erratics' – large boulders lifted by glaciers from Crummockdale and deposited on the limestone shelves of Norber Brow. Go over the ladder-stile and down to the lane. Turn left on the lane, pass the entrance to Sowerthwaite Farm and up to Crummock Farm. Through the stile to the waymark and take the springy green path sweeping up to the left. At a point where the path levels and Ingleborough Massive appears on the skyline, look for a path turning to the left – a good point to admire the all-round views. Go down the broad, grassy track, over a ladder-stile and down to the top of Long Lane. Go down the lane to a ladder-stile on your right. Clamber over and descend the short, steep path to a wide track. Turn left, down to an old packhorse bridge and past the entrance to Ingleborough Cave. Continue to Clapham Woods and the start of a nature trail. The trail was established in 1970 to commemorate the life and work of Reginald Farrer, a botanist and plant collector specialising in alpines and rhododendrons. Further along the narrow path on your left you reach the edge of a bank where rhododendrons grow in acid soil. Pass alongside a lake and when you reach the sawmill and yard, turn left into the village and return to the inn.

Distance: 6 1/2 miles (10.4km)
Map: OS Outdoor Leisure 2 -
Yorkshire Dales Western area
Terrain: Spectacular limestone
country of the Western Dales
Paths: Paths, tracks and lanes
Gradient: Some climbing

*Walk submitted and checked
by the New Inn, Clapham*

£5.50 **BREWERY/COMPANY:** Free House
PRINCIPAL BEERS: Black Sheep, Tetley. **FACILITIES:** Children
welcome Garden: Beer garden, food served outdoors
NOTES: Parking 35

ASENBY   Map 09 SE37

Pick of the Pubs

Crab & Lobster
YO7 3QL ☎ 01845 577286 ▤ 01845 577109
See Pick of the Pubs on page 527

ASKRIGG   Map 09 SD99

Kings Arms Hotel
Market Place DL8 3HQ ☎ 01969 650817 ▤ 01969 650856
e-mail: kingsarms@askrigg.fsnet.co.uk
Dir: N off A684 between Hawes & Leyburn
At the heart of the Yorkshire Dales, Askrigg is surrounded by
stunning scenery against a backdrop of Pennine hills: its pub,
built in 1762 as racing stables, was converted to an inn in
1860. Bar and bistro specialities include traditional Yorkshire
country cooking as well as oriental dishes. Try fillet of sea bass
with a pesto and black olive crust, braised lamb shank with
mash and leek gravy, or whole baby chicken with peppers
and chorizo.
OPEN: 11–3 6–11 (Sat 11–11, Sun 12–10.30) **BAR MEALS:** Lunch
served: all week Dinner served: all week 12–2 6.30–9 Av main course
£10 **RESTAURANT:** Dinner served: Fri–Sat 7–9 Av 3 course à la carte
£19 **BREWERY/COMPANY:** Free House
PRINCIPAL BEERS: John Smiths, Black Sheep, Theakston Cool Cask,
Guest Ales. **FACILITIES:** Children welcome Garden: Food served
outside, flagged courtyard Dogs allowed (water provided)

AUSTWICK   Map 08 SD76

The Game Cock Inn NEW
The Green LA2 8BB ☎ 015242 51226 ▤ 015242 51028
e-mail: r.lord@totalise.co.uk
Five miles north of Settle in a pretty limestone village known
as 'Cuckoo Town', a cosy family-run pub whose stock-in-trade
revolves around real ales and freshly cooked food. An open
log fire in winter, outside to the rear is a large garden with
play area and an aviary. A vast menu runs literally to pages,
with extra specials daily whose choice includes Morecambe
Bay potted shrimps, whole stuffed poussin and rack of lamb
with mint mash.
OPEN: 11.30–3 6–11 (All Sun) **BAR MEALS:** Lunch served: all week
Dinner served: all week 10.30–2 6–9 Av main course £8.50
RESTAURANT: Lunch served: all week Dinner served: all week
11.30–2 6–9 Av 3 course à la carte £15 **PRINCIPAL BEERS:** Thwaites
Best Bitter, Smooth. **FACILITIES:** Children welcome Garden: Large
with a childrens play area **NOTES:** Parking 6

AYSGARTH   Map 09 SE08

The George & Dragon Inn
DL8 3AD ☎ 01969 663358 ▤ 01969 663773
Beautifully situated near Aysgarth Falls in the heart of Herriot
country, the owners of this attractive 17th century free house
continue the long tradition of Yorkshire hospitality. Beamed
ceilings and open fires set the scene for freshly cooked daily
specials like breast of chicken with smoked ham, prawns and
fresh herb velouté, beef Stroganoff with basmati rice, poached

escalope of Scottish salmon with almond and lemon butter,
and roast topside of beef with Yorkshire pudding.

OPEN: 11–11 **BAR MEALS:** Lunch served: all week Dinner served:
all week 12–2 6–9 Av main course £9.50 **RESTAURANT:** Lunch
served: all week Dinner served: all week 12–2 6–9 Av 3 course à la
carte £18 Av 3 course fixed price £10.95
BREWERY/COMPANY: Free House **PRINCIPAL BEERS:** Black
Sheep Best, Scottish Courage John Smith's, Theakstons Bitter.
FACILITIES: Children welcome Garden: Patio, food served outside
Dogs allowed (water) **NOTES:** Parking 35
ROOMS: 7 bedrooms 7 en suite from s£34.50 d£59

BAINBRIDGE   Map 09 SD99

Rose & Crown Hotel ★ ★
DL8 3EE ☎ 01969 650225 ▤ 01969 650735
e-mail: stay@theprideofwensleydale.co.uk
Dir: On A684 in centre of village

Overlooking the village green, this traditional 500-year-old
coaching inn is home to the forest horn, blown each evening
from Holy Rood (September 27th) to Shrovetide to guide
travellers safely to the village. Appetising choice of starters
and light snacks, while main courses include steak and kidney
pudding, glazed breast of duckling, ragout of wild mushroom,
sweet Wensleydale cheese and onion tart, and fillet of salmon
on olive oil mash.
OPEN: 11–11 (Sun 12–10.30) **BAR MEALS:** Lunch served: all week
Dinner served: all week 12–2.15 6–9.30 Av main course £7.50
RESTAURANT: Lunch served: all week Dinner served: all week
12–2.15 7–9.30 Av 3 course à la carte £18.50 Av 4 course fixed price
£19.95 **BREWERY/COMPANY:** Free House
PRINCIPAL BEERS: Websters Bitter, Black Sheep Best, Scottish
Courage John Smith's. **FACILITIES:** Children welcome Children's
licence Garden: Food served outside Dogs allowed
NOTES: Parking 65 **ROOMS:** 12 bedrooms 12 en suite from s£26
d£52

continued

OPEN: 11.30-3 6.30-11
BAR MEALS: L served all week.
D served all week. 12-2.30 6.30-10
Av main course £11.50
RESTAURANT: L served all week.
D served all week. 12-2.30 7-10
Av cost 3 course £25
BREWERY/COMPANY: FREE HOUSE
PRINCIPAL BEERS: Black Sheep Best, Interbrew Worthington Bitter, Theakston Best, Carlsberg-Tetley Tetley Bitter
FACILITIES: Children and dogs welcome. Garden: 7 acre mature gardens, food served outdoors
NOTES: Parking 50
ROOMS: 12 en suite Double room from £120

Crab & Lobster

◆◆◎◎ ♀
Asenby,North Yorkshire YO7 3QL
☎ 01845 577286 ▤ 01845 577109
Dir: From A1(M) junc take A168 towards Thirsk

Amid seven acres of garden, lake and streams stands this unique 17th-century thatched pub and adjacent small hotel that have been the consuming passion of owners David and Jackie Barnard for all of a decade. Renowned for the quality of the food and the unusual accommodation.

At the Crab & Lobster, an Aladdin's Cave of themed bric-a-brac and antiques, low beams, ledges and windowsills in both the cosy bar and brasserie diningroom is covered with pots, pans, parasols and puppets and old fishing nets housing mock crabs. Equally well known for excellent food, notably their innovative fish dishes, menus are rather less cluttered but just as inventive, embracing culinary influences from France and Italy, with a nod towards Asia thrown in for good measure. From the famous fish club sandwich (lunch only) through an array of chunky fish soup, hand carved Craster salmon and lobster, asparagus and Brie spring rolls feature among starters alone. Typical main dishes feature brill fillet with crab and wilted spinach, posh fish and chips with minted mushy peas and salmon, clams, scallops and mussels in tarragon butter sauce. All is not lost for carnivores, who can tuck into oriental beef pancakes followed by braised lamb shank and crispy confit duck with toffee apples and oranges. Alfresco eating and summer barbecues, good real ales and extensive wine list – and a pavilion open all day for food, drinks, coffees and relaxing. The adjacent Crab Manor is delightfully eccentric, standing apart from the pub in well-manicured gardens, with opulent, individually furnished bedrooms, including three in a thatched tropical beach house, named after famous hotels world-wide.

England

BEDALE · Map 09 SE28

Freemasons Arms
Nosterfield DL8 2QP ☎ 01677 470548
Cluttered with curios and memorabilia, this inviting, long and low whitewashed building, formerly a row of 18th-century cottages, features English cooking that uses local produce. Booking is essential.

BILBROUGH · Map 09 SE54

Pick of the Pubs

The Three Hares Inn & Restaurant ⊚⊚ ⓘ ♀
Main St YO23 3PH ☎ 01937 832128 📠 01937 834626
e-mail: info@thethreehares.co.uk
See Pick of the Pubs on page 529

BOROUGHBRIDGE · Map 09 SE36

Pick of the Pubs

The Black Bull Inn ♀
6 St James Square YO51 9AR
☎ 01423 322413 📠 01423 323915
Dir: from J48 A1(M) take B6265 for 1mile E

Grade II listed building, 800 years old in parts and reputedly haunted, which has always been an inn. Typical dishes on the interesting menus range from crab and salmon fishcakes, and mushroom and bacon ragout, to sea bass with pesto butter sauce, venison with shallot and port sauce, and beef in creamy whisky sauce.
OPEN: 11-11 (Sun 12-10.30) **BAR MEALS:** Lunch served: all week Dinner served: all week 12-2 6-9.30 Av main course £6 **RESTAURANT:** Lunch served: all week Dinner served: all week 12-2 6-9.30 Av 3 course à la carte £15 **BREWERY/COMPANY:** Free House **PRINCIPAL BEERS:** Black Sheep, John Smiths, guest. **FACILITIES:** Children welcome Dogs allowed **NOTES:** Parking 4 **ROOMS:** 4 bedrooms 4 en suite from s£40.50 d£54

BREARTON · Map 08 SE36

Pick of the Pubs

Malt Shovel Inn ⓘ ♀
HG3 3BX ☎ 01423 862929
Dir: From A61 (Ripon/Harrogate) take B6165 towards Knaresborough. Turn at Brearton - 1.5m.
The Malt Shovel has been at the heart of this small farming community since 1525 - the oldest building in a

very old village, which has some good examples of ancient strip farming. The setting is very rural, surrounded by rolling farmland, yet it is only 15 minutes' from Harrogate and in easy reach of Knaresborough and Ripon. There area clutter of beer mugs, horse brasses and hunting scenes in the heavily-beamed rooms leading off the carved oak bar, and you can enjoy a quiet game of dominoes or shoveha'penny without any electronic intrusions. The blackboard menu has something for everyone, with the likes of pan-fried sea bass with herb butter, chargrilled liver with red wine and onion gravy, Thai chicken curry, and goats' cheese and leek tart. The dishes are all home made, including the puddings, such as cloutie dumpling, lemon tart and fresh fruit brûlée.
OPEN: 12-2.30 6.45-11 (Sun 12-2.30, 7-10.30)
BAR MEALS: Lunch served: Tue-Sun 12-2 Dinner served: Tue-Sat 7-9 Av main course £6.50 **BREWERY/COMPANY:** Free House **PRINCIPAL BEERS:** Daleside Nightjar, Durham Magus, Black Sheep Best, Theakston Masham. **FACILITIES:** Children welcome Garden: Patio, heated garden **NOTES:** Parking 20 No credit cards

BROUGHTON · Map 09 SD95

Bull Inn ♀
BD23 3AE ☎ 01756 792065
Dir: On A59 4m from Skipton coming from M6
A friendly welcome awaits at this real country pub, resting on the edge of the Yorkshire Dales at the front of Broughton Hall, yet accessibly on the main A59. There's a Junior Menu for children.

PUBS AT WAR
With its reputation for long opening hours and drunken behaviour, the British pub was viewed as a serious threat to the war effort during the dark days of the First World War. The Prime Minister, David Lloyd George, who in 1915 commented 'we are fighting Germany, Austria and drink, and the greatest of these foes is drink,' drastically curtailed opening hours and even considered prohibition. It was only after the war that the situation gradually improved. The storm clouds had passed and people looked optimistically to the future. 20 years later, however, in September 1939, the British pub once again faced the uncertainty of war. But instead of locking its doors and turning away custom, the traditional local became a social focal point at the heart of the community, where service men and women, air raid wardens, fire-watchers, grocers and butchers could relax and forget, albeit briefly, the terrible effects of bombs and bullets. The writer AP Herbert described the British pub during the Second World War as 'the one place where, after dark, the collective heart of the race could be seen and felt, beating resolute and strong.' Many inns were frequented by British and American airmen based nearby, and if you happen to visit the splendid 17th-century Eagle pub in Cambridge, have a look at their signatures scrawled on the pub's high red ceiling.

continued

OPEN: 12-3 7-11
BAR MEALS: 12-2 7-9.15 Av main course £8.95
RESTAURANT: L served Tue-Sun. D served Tue-Sat 12-2 7-9.15 Av cost 3 course £22
BREWERY/COMPANY: FREE HOUSE
PRINCIPAL BEERS: Timothy Taylors Landlord, Black Sheep, Guest ales each week
FACILITIES: Dogs allowed. Garden: food served outside. Terrace area
NOTES: Parking 30

The Three Hares

Located in a peaceful village near the historic city of York, an inviting 18th-century dining pub whose restaurant incorporates the old village forge. Recently refurbished the bar boasts hand-pulled, cask conditioned ales, including a guest beer that changes every week, and a good list of wines by the glass.

★★
Main Street, Bilbrough YO23 3PH
☎ 01937 832128 🖷 01937 834626
e-mail: info@thethreehares.co.uk
Dir: Bilbrough can be reached from either direction on the A64.

Meals available from the immaculately written blackboards, changed regularly according to market availability, display imagination and attention to detail. Well-made country soups, such as nettle and chive, seared squid and chorizo sausage with herb liguine well indicate the style of starters; followed by pan-fried fillet of sea bream with blue cheese mash, or beef and Guinness sausages with a parsley mash. Restaurant choices may include chicken liver pâté with apple chutney, roast cod with Puy lentils and lamb chump with roast garlic and sweetbreads: potatoes and seasonal vegetables come as extras for two people.

England

BUCKDEN   Map 09 SD97

Pick of the Pubs

The Buck Inn ★ ★ @@
BD23 5JA ☎ 01756 760228 📠 01756 760227
e-mail: thebuckinn@buckden.yorks.net
Dir: From Skipton take B6265, then B6160

An inn for all seasons facing south across the village green in this unspoilt part of the Dales. The old Georgian coaching inn is backed by the famous Buckden Pike, which rises a dramatic 2,300ft, and surrounded by picturesque stone cottages and panoramic views. The cosy bar has lots of old world charm and character, where real ales like the Theakston range, Black Bull and Old Peculiar are hand pulled. A wide choice of imaginative dishes is served in the pretty restaurant, where a carte offers a daily-changing choice based on Dales meat, fresh fish and local vegetables. Start with the likes of sea bass and red pepper terrine, or breaded fishcake, move on to roast hock of lamb with garlic mash, or baked breast of pheasant with fondant mash, and save plenty of space for dark chocolate tart, sticky toffee pudding, and lemon tart. Several en suite bedrooms are available.
OPEN: 8-11 **BAR MEALS:** Lunch served: all week Dinner served: all week 12-5 6.30-9 Av main course £7.95
RESTAURANT: Dinner served: all week 6.30-9 Av 3 course à la carte £23.95 Av 4 course fixed price £23.95
BREWERY/COMPANY: Free House
PRINCIPAL BEERS: Theakston Best, Black Bull, & Old Peculiar, Scottish Courage John Smith's. **FACILITIES:** Children welcome Dogs allowed **NOTES:** Parking 40 **ROOMS:** 14 bedrooms 14 en suite from s£36 d£72

BURNSALL   Map 09 SE06

Pick of the Pubs

The Red Lion ★ ★ @ 🐾 ♀
By the Bridge BD23 6BU ☎ 01756 720204 📠 01756 720292
e-mail: redlion@daelnet.co.uk
Dir: From Skipton take A59 east take B6160 towards Bolton Abbey, Burnsall 7m
Set on the banks of the River Wharfe in the heart of the Dales, a 16th-century ferryman's inn in a beautiful unspoilt village. Old world charm abounds inside and out, with grounds running down to the water (fishing available), and a cosy interior of old armchairs, sofas and wood-burning stoves. Pride is taken in the seasonal menus based on fresh local produce which offer an extensive choice. Light lunches might be speciality salads

continued

and sandwiches, or seared fillet of beef on Parmesan, rocket, and roasted red onions, while the evening bar menu runs to roasted calves' liver, and baked goats' cheese topped with a herb crust. A separate specials list offers tantalising choices like traditional cassoulet with ciabatta, local venison with garlic roasted potatoes and a cranberry and chestnut sauce, and brochette of monkfish and king scallops. Bedrooms, upstairs or in an annexe, offer comfy accommodation.

OPEN: 08.00-11.30 (Sun closes 10.30) **BAR MEALS:** Lunch served: all week Dinner served: all week 12-2.30 6-9.30 Av main course £9.95 **RESTAURANT:** Lunch served: all week Dinner served: all week 12-3.00 7-9.30 Av 3 course à la carte £26.95 Av 3 course fixed price £24.95 **BREWERY/COMPANY:** Free House **PRINCIPAL BEERS:** Theakston Black Bull, Greene King Old Speckled Hen, Timothy Taylor Landlord, Scottish Courage John Smith's. **FACILITIES:** Children welcome Children's licence Garden: Beer garden, patio, food served outdoors Dogs allowed **NOTES:** Parking 70 **ROOMS:** 11 bedrooms 11 en suite from s£53 d£107

BYLAND ABBEY   Map 09 SE57

Pick of the Pubs

Abbey Inn 🐾 ♀
YO61 4BD ☎ 01347 868204 📠 01347 868678
e-mail: jane@nordli.freeserve.co.uk
See Pick of the Pubs on page 531

SHADES & GRADES OF BEER
A distinction between beer and ale used to be drawn centuries ago. Ale was the old British brew made without hops. In the 15th century the use of hops spread to Britain from the Continent and this bitterer drink was called beer. Ale is no longer made and the two words are now used indiscriminately. Bottled beer is distinguished from draught beer from a cask or keg, but a better dividing line is the one between real ale, which matures in the cask, and keg or bottled beer that doesn't. Bitter is the British draught beer, with plenty of hops. Mild, less hops and less sharp in taste, is often found in the Midlands and the North West. Old ale usually means stronger mild, matured longer. Light ale or pale ale is bottled beer of a lightish colour. Lager is lighter and blander. Brown ale is darker, richer bottled beer, and porter is richer still. Stout is the blackest and richest of all.

OPEN: 11.30–3 6.30–11
BAR MEALS: L served
Tue–Sun 12–2.
D served Mon–Sat. 6.30–9.
Av main course £7.50
RESTAURANT: L served
Tue–Sun 12–2. D served Mon–Sat.
6.30–9 Av cost 3 course £20
BREWERY/COMPANY:
FREE HOUSE
PRINCIPLE BEERS: Black Sheep
Best, Carlsberg-Tetley Bitter
FACILITIES: Children welcome.
Garden: Patio area
NOTES: Parking 30
ROOMS: 3 en suite. Double room
from £80

Abbey Inn

In an isolated rural position midway between Wass and Coxwold, the rambling, stone-built Abbey Inn stands, as its name suggests, in the shadow of the hauntingly beautiful ruins of Byland Abbey. Worth locating for modern pub food, individual decor and superior pub accommodation.

♀
Byland Abbey, North Yorkshire YO61 4BD
☎ 01347 868204 ▤ 01347 868678
e-mail: jane@nordli.freeserve.co.uk
Dir: From A19 Thirsk/York follow signs to Byland Abbey/Coxwold.

Completed by Benedictine monks from nearby Ampleforth during the 19th century, the plain, creeper-clad façade conceals a highly distinctive interior. Four splendid dining areas are decorated in eclectic style and are full of charm and character. Each features either bare board or flagstone floors strewn with rugs, open fireplaces and an interesting mix of furnishings, from huge settles with scatter cushions to Jacobean-style chairs and oak and stripped deal tables topped with large, Gothic candlesticks. Fine tapestries, stuffed birds, dried flowers and unusual objets d'arts complete the stylish decor. One of the chief attractions at the Abbey Inn

is the enterprising range of modern British food offered on a seasonally changing menu and daily specials board. At lunchtime choose chef's home-made lamb and mint pie, oven-baked sea bass with a hazelnut butter or venison and blackberry casserole with herb dumpling. The evening menu may list peppered rib-eye steak with onion rings, lamb shoulder marinated in garlic and rosemary, and grilled fillet of mackerel with champ potatoes, black pudding and caviar vinaigrette. Traditional puddings include lemon passett with fresh raspberries and white chocolate créme brûlée. Commendable list of wines; half-bottle bin ends and eight by the glass. A lovely summer terrace and garden, excellent food and charming surroundings make a visit to the Abbey Inn well worthwhile and a peaceful night here is assured in superbly appointed en suite bedrooms that overlook the floodlit Abbey.

England

CARLTON   Map 09 SE08

Foresters Arms ♀
DL8 4BB ☎ 01969 640272
e-mail: jane@theforestersarms.freeserve.co.uk
Dir: S of Leyburn off A684 or A6108
A Grade II listed building dating back to the 1600s and
situated in a picturesque Dales village at the heart of the
National Park. Ideal for visiting Middleham Castle, Aysgarth
Falls and historic Bolton Castle, famous for its association with
Mary Queen of Scots. Fine open fireplace, flagged floors and
beamed ceilings. Good choice of cask conditioned Yorkshire
ales and an imaginative menu offering the likes of fillet of
black bream, pan-fried breast of chicken and lobster
thermidor.
OPEN: 12–3 6.30–11 **BAR MEALS:** Lunch served: Wed-Sun 12-2
Dinner served: Tues-Sat 7-9 Av main course £7.90
RESTAURANT: Dinner served: Tue-Sat 7-9.30 Av 3 course à la carte
£25 **BREWERY/COMPANY:** Free House
PRINCIPAL BEERS: Scottish Courage John Smith's, Theakston Bitter,
Black Sheep Best, Greene King Ruddles County.
FACILITIES: Children welcome Dogs allowed (water)
NOTES: Parking 15 **ROOMS:** 3 bedrooms 3 en suite from s£40
d£75

CARTHORPE   Map 09 SE38

Pick of the Pubs

The Fox & Hounds ♀
DL8 2LG ☎ 01845 567433 ▤ 01845 567155
*Dir: Off A1, signposted on both northbound & southbound
carriageways*
Tucked away just off the A1 in a mercifully peaceful spot,
a neat 200-year-old inn whose dining-room was once the
village smithy, adorned today with the original anvil and
tools of the trade. Numerous prints of Whitby adorn the
comfortable interior of this family-run pub. The kitchen is
manned by landlord Howard, assisted by his daughter,
Helen (who makes all the sweets, petit fours and ice
creams) while front-of-house is cheerily overseen by
Bernadette Fitzgerald. A single menu is served both at
lunch and evening and blackboard menus offer fresh crab
tartlet or duck-filled filo parcels, followed by roast cod
steak with spinach and mustard mash and pan-fried pork
fillet with black pudding and apple butter sauce. For
pudding, try raspberry and almond tart or banana
cheesecake. There is a midweek set-price dinner; and
there are an astonishing 48 wines available by the glass.
OPEN: 12-2.30 7-11 Closed: 1st wk Jan **BAR MEALS:** Lunch
served: Tue-Sun Dinner served: Tue-Sun 12-2 7-10 Av main
course £9 **RESTAURANT:** Lunch served: Tue-Sun Dinner
served: Tue-Sun 12-2 7-9.30 Av 3 course à la carte £16 Av 3
course fixed price £12.95 **BREWERY/COMPANY:** Free House
PRINCIPAL BEERS: Black Sheep Best, Interbrew Worthington
Bitter. **FACILITIES:** Children welcome **NOTES:** Parking 22

**Restaurant and Bar Meal times indicate
the times when food is available.
Last orders may be approximately
30 minutes before the times stated.**

CLAPHAM   Map 08 SD76

New Inn 🕯
LA2 8HH ☎ 015242 51203 ▤ 015242 51496
e-mail: info@newinn-clapham.co.uk
Dir: On A65 in Yorkshire Dale National Park

Family-run 18th-century coaching inn located in a peaceful
Dales village beneath Ingleborough, one of Yorkshire's most
famous summits. There are plenty of good walks from the
pub, including one to Ingleborough Show Cave, open to the
public at weekends and on Bank Holidays throughout the
year. Honest, wholesome food includes breaded haddock,
Cumberland sausage, crusty steak pie and baked minted lamb
fillet.
OPEN: 11-11 (Winter open 11-3, 6.30-11) **BAR MEALS:** Lunch
served: all week Dinner served: all week 12-2 6.30-9 Av main course
£7.95 **RESTAURANT:** Lunch served: all week Dinner served: all week
12-2 6.30-8.30 Av 3 course à la carte £16.50 Av 4 course fixed price
£16.50 **BREWERY/COMPANY:** Free House
PRINCIPAL BEERS: Black Sheep Best, Carlsberg-Tetley Tetley Bitter,
Dent Fullback, Daleside Bitter. **FACILITIES:** Children welcome
Garden: Riverside, waterfall, food served outside Dogs allowed
(water) **NOTES:** Parking 35 **ROOMS:** 19 bedrooms 19 en suite
from s£34 d£58

See Pub Walk on page 525

COXWOLD   Map 09 SE57

Pick of the Pubs

The Fauconberg Arms 🕯
Main St YO61 4AD ☎ 01347 868214 ▤ 01347 868172
e-mail: fanconbergarms@aol.co.uk
*Dir: Take A19 S from Thirsk, 2m turn L, signposted alternative route for
caravans/heavy vehicles. 5m to village*
The pub's name comes from the Fauconberg family, who
were given the village and estate by Henry VIII. The
current landlords took over in 2001 and serve an
imaginative menu that includes dishes such as deep-fried
skate wing on stir-fried vegetables, roast duck breast with
plum and ginger sauce and steamed egg noodles,
butternut squash ravioli with asparagus and vegetable
broth, and roasted lamb rump with a port and beetroot
jus and haricot beans.
OPEN: 11-2.30 6.30-11 (Summer all day) **BAR MEALS:** Lunch
served: all week Dinner served: all week 12-2.30 6.30-9 Av main
course £8 **RESTAURANT:** Lunch served: Sun 12-4 Dinner
served: Wed-Sat 6.30-9.30 Av 3 course à la carte £25 Av 3 course
fixed price £17 **BREWERY/COMPANY:** Free House
PRINCIPAL BEERS: Theakston Best, Carlsberg-Tetley Tetley
Bitter, Scottish Courage, John Smith's. **NOTES:** Parking 25
ROOMS: 4 bedrooms 4 en suite from s£35 d£60

CRAY   Map 09 S097

The White Lion Inn 🐾 ♀

Cray BD23 5JB ☎ 01756 760262 📠 01756 761024
e-mail: admin.whitelion@btinternet.com

Nestling beneath Buckden Pike, and the highest pub in Wharfedale, this traditional Dales inn is a 'tiny oasis' of hospitality. The tastefully restored former drovers' hostelry remains faithful to its origins with old beams, log fires and stone-flagged floors. Hand-pulled ales and home-cooked food complete the picture: try venison casserole, Boursin chicken, Madeira pork, and steak and mushroom pie, along with various lighter bites at lunchtime.
OPEN: 11-11 Closed: 25 Dec **BAR MEALS:** Lunch served: all week Dinner served: all week 12-2.15 5.45-8.45 Av main course £8.50
BREWERY/COMPANY: Free House **PRINCIPAL BEERS:** Roosters Yankee, Moorhouse Pendle witches Brew, Premier Bitter, Timothy Taylor Landlord. **FACILITIES:** Children welcome Garden: Food served outside Dogs allowed (water) **NOTES:** Parking 20
ROOMS: 10 bedrooms 8 en suite from s£32.50 d£45

CROPTON   Map 09 SE78

The New Inn 🐾 ♀

YO18 8HH ☎ 01751 417330 📠 01751 417310
e-mail: newinn@cropton.fsbusiness.co.uk
With the award-winning Cropton micro-brewery in its own grounds, this family-run free house on the edge of the North York Moors National Park is popular with locals and visitors alike. Meals are served in the newly restored village bar, and in the elegant Victorian restaurant not to mention the brewery's own visitor centre!
OPEN: 11-11 **BAR MEALS:** Lunch served: all week Dinner served: all week 12-2 6-9.30 Av main course £6 **RESTAURANT:** Lunch served: all week Dinner served: all week 12-2 6-9.30 Av 3 course à la carte £15 **BREWERY/COMPANY:** Free House
PRINCIPAL BEERS: Cropton Two Pints, Monkmans Slaughter, Backwoods, Thwaites Best Bitter. **FACILITIES:** Children welcome Garden: Food served outside **NOTES:** Parking 50
ROOMS: 9 bedrooms 9 en suite from s£32 d£29

DACRE BANKS   Map 09 SE16

The Royal Oak Inn 🐾

Oak Ln HG3 4EN ☎ 01423 780200
e-mail: enquiries@theroyaloak.uk.com
Dir: From A59(Harrogate/Skipton) take B6451 towards Pateley Bridge
According to its dated doorway lintel, the Royal Oak has just passed its 250th anniversary. At the heart of Nidderdale, this family-run free house draws a wealth of tourists, anglers and hikers for some fine Yorkshire ales and home-cooked meals. From an extensive menu that includes baguettes and club

sandwiches, house specialities include swordfish steak with garlic butter and king prawns, whole roast pheasant with game chips and steak, red wine and mushroom short-crust pie.
OPEN: 11.30-3 5-11 (Sun 11.30-3, 7-10.30) **BAR MEALS:** Lunch served: all week Dinner served: all week 11.30-2 6.30-9 Av main course £8.95 **RESTAURANT:** Lunch served: all week Dinner served: all week 11.30-2 6.30-9 Av 3 course à la carte £18 Av 3 course fixed price £12.95 **BREWERY/COMPANY:** Free House
PRINCIPAL BEERS: Rudgate Yorkshire Dales, Black Sheep Best, Interbrew Worthington Bitter. **FACILITIES:** Children welcome Garden: Food served outdoors, patio **NOTES:** Parking 15
ROOMS: 3 bedrooms 3 en suite from s£30 d£50

DANBY   Map 11 NZ70

Duke of Wellington Inn 🐾

YO21 2LY ☎ 01287 660351
e-mail: landlord@dukeofwellington.freeserve.co.uk
Dir: From A171 between Guisborough & Whitby take rd signed 'Danby & Moors Centre'

The Duke's cast-iron plaque can be seen above the fireplace of this traditional stone-built pub, commemorating its use by local regiments during the Napoleonic Wars. Today's landlords welcome an altogether more leisurely type of tourist, drawn by its selection of ales and good home-cooked food. Venison stew with bubble-and-squeak, beef in stout and home-made Whitby crab cakes keep drawing them back in number to its homely bars and refurbished dining-room.
OPEN: 11-3 7-11 **BAR MEALS:** Lunch served: all week Dinner served: all week 12-2 7-9 Av main course £7 **RESTAURANT:** 12-2 7-9 **BREWERY/COMPANY:** Free House
PRINCIPAL BEERS: Scottish Courage John Smith's, Cameron's Strongarm,. **FACILITIES:** Children welcome Garden: Terrace, food served outside Dogs allowed (water) **NOTES:** Parking 12
ROOMS: 9 bedrooms 9 en suite from s£33 d£60

EAST WITTON   Map 09 SE18

Pick of the Pubs

The Blue Lion 🐾 ♀

DL8 4SN ☎ 01969 624273 📠 01969 624189
e-mail: bluelion@breathemail.net
See Pick of the Pubs on page 534

continued

England

OPEN: 11–11
BAR MEALS: L served all week.
D served all week. 12–2 7–9
Av main course £12.95
RESTAURANT: L served Sun.
D served all week. 12–2 7–9 Av cost
3 course £24.75
BREWERY/COMPANY: FREE
HOUSE
PRINCIPAL BEERS: Black Sheep
Riggwelter, Theakston Old Peculier
FACILITIES: Children and dogs
welcome. Garden: Beer garden,
patio, food served outdoors
NOTES: Parking 30
ROOMS: 12 en suite. Double room
from £69 Single room from £53.50

The Blue Lion

Self-promoted as a "country retreat" and tastefully restored over the years, this 18th-century former coaching inn that once attracted trade from drovers and travellers on their journeys through Wensleydale remains today the focal point of East Witton village.

EAST WITTON DL8 4SN
☎ 01969 624273 📠 01969 624189
e-mail: ebluelion@breathemail.net
Dir:

Charming, individually decorated bedrooms are well equipped to meet the expectations of today's more discerning visitors, while the bar with its flagstone floor and open fire and a dining-room that glimmers with soft candle-light of an evening create a romantic setting for the enjoyment of predominantly local fresh foods cooked with care and not a little enthusiasm. Bar food is in no way the poor relation, with starters of roast scallops with Gruyère and lemon risotto or game bird terrine with romesco sauce and walnut pickle followed by fresh tagliatelli tossed in cep sauce

with shaved Parmesan, a sea bass, salmon and cod trio served on a ratatouille tart with tapenade and cassoulet of pork rib, duck and Toulouse sausage served with pancetta and mashed potato. Simpler main dishes might be monkfish fillets with herb crust and langoustine sauce and braised ham hock flavoured with grain mustard, apple and prunes.

EGTON BRIDGE

Map 11 NZ80

Horseshoe Hotel
YO21 1XE ☎ 01947 895245
Dir: From Whitby take A171 towards Middlesborough Village signed in 5m

Right on the banks of the River Esk, its large garden with picnic tables a draw to the local ducks and geese, a residential 18th-century country inn with fishing rights. Inside the bar is a welcoming open fire, oak settles and tables, and local artists' paintings adorning the walls. Imaginative bar food includes such delights as warm tartlet of Brie and wild mushrooms, fish soup with aïoli, chicken breast and crab on a lobster sauce and fillet of lamb with bubble-and-squeak.
OPEN: 11.30–3 6.30–11 All day Sat & Sun in Summer Closed: 25 Dec **BAR MEALS:** Lunch served: all week Dinner served: all week 12–2 7–9 Av main course £8 **RESTAURANT:** Lunch served: all week Dinner served: all week 12–2 7–9 Av 3 course à la carte £14 **BREWERY/COMPANY:** Free House **PRINCIPAL BEERS:** Scottish Courage, John Smiths, Durham, Whitby. **FACILITIES:** Children welcome Garden: Food served outside, patio Dogs allowed (water provided) **NOTES:** Parking 25 **ROOMS:** 6 bedrooms 3 en suite
See Pub Walk on page 537

ELSLACK

Map 09 SD94

The Tempest Arms ♀
BD23 3AY ☎ 01282 842450 ▤ 01282 843331
Dir: From Skipton take A59 towards Gisburn. Elslack signed on L on A56
Peaceful Dales countryside surrounds this essentially English pub, traditionally built from stone and named after a local landowner. The same quality food is served in both the cosy bar with its wing chairs and log fires, and the candle-lit dining room. From an inviting menu expect Eastern spicepot, fish pie, roasted duck, and beef bourguignon, along with sandwiches, nibblies, and puddings like jam roly-poly, twice-baked rice pudding, and old English treacle and orange tart.
OPEN: 7–11 **BAR MEALS:** Lunch served: all week Dinner served: all week 12–2.30 6–9 Av main course £6 **RESTAURANT:** Lunch served: all week Dinner served: all week 12–2.30 6–9 Av 3 course à la carte £14 **BREWERY/COMPANY:** Free House **PRINCIPAL BEERS:** Timothy Taylor Best & Landlord, Black Sheep Best, Theakston Best. **FACILITIES:** Children's licence Garden: Food served outdoors **NOTES:** Parking 120 **ROOMS:** 10 bedrooms 10 en suite from s£52.50 d£65

ESCRICK

Map 09 SE64

Black Bull Inn ♦♦ ♀
Main St YO19 6JP ☎ 01904 728245 ▤ 01904 728154
Dir: From York follow the A19 for 5m, enter Escrick, take second L up main street, premises located on the L
Situated in the heart of a quiet village, this 19th-century pub is within easy reach of York racecourse and the historic city centre. A typical menu may include Moroccan chicken, haddock mornay, steak and ale pie, salmon champagne, fillet steak rossini, or chicken and vegetable pie.

FADMORE

Map 09 SE68

Pick of the Pubs

The Plough Inn ♀
Main St YO62 7HY ☎ 01751 431515
Dir: 1m N of Kirkbymoorside on the A170 Thirsk to Scarborough Rd

A well-established restaurant and country inn located on the edge of the North Yorkshire Moors National Park. From its position overlooking the tranquil village green, the genuinely hospitable Plough enjoys views towards the Vale of Pickering and the Wolds. Snug little rooms and open fires draw local people to this stylishly refurbished pub, and the imaginative food is another attraction. A good selection of home-cooked dishes includes plenty of fresh fish and seafood, and most of the kitchen produce is locally sourced. Among eight seafood dishes expect whole sea bass stuffed with fresh herbs, mussels with wine and cream, and salmon fishcakes. A range of menus, including one for 'early birds', offers starters like duck and mango spring rolls, chicken and walnut pâté, and oven-baked Brie, followed by lamb shank, peppered pork pancake, and smoked bacon escalopes. Well-chosen wines and real Yorkshire ales go down well with bar snacks too.
OPEN: 12–2.30 6.30–11 Closed: 25–26th Dec, 1st Jan **BAR MEALS:** Lunch served: Wed-Mon Dinner served: Wed-Mon 12–2 6.30-8.45 Av main course £10 **RESTAURANT:** Lunch served: Wed-Mon Dinner served: Wed-Mon 12–2 6.30-8.45 Av 3 course à la carte £17 **BREWERY/COMPANY:** Free House **PRINCIPAL BEERS:** Black Sheep Best, Scottish Courage John Smith's + guest beers. **FACILITIES:** Children welcome Garden: patio, Food served outside **NOTES:** Parking 20

Top of the Tree
Pubs called the Royal Oak were originally named in loyal remembrance of the day in 1651 when the youthful King Charles II hid in an oak tree at Boscobel in Shropshire, while Roundhead soldiers unsuccessfully searched the woods for him. The Royal Oak sign often shows simply the oak tree, or the king is shown perched among the branches - in plain view from all directions, but conventionally accepted as invisible to the purblind Parliamentarian troops. Sometimes, more subtly, the tree has a large crown among the foliage. Rarer variants include the king holding an oak spray with acorns, or acorns below a crown.

GIGGLESWICK
Map 08 SD86

Black Horse Hotel ◆◆◆
32 Church St BD24 0BE ☎ 01729 822506
The Black Horse is set in the middle of an attractive village, next to the church and behind the market cross. A good choice of home-cooked meals is served either in the bar or dining room, perhaps lamb hotpot, lasagne (meat or vegetarian), poached salmon, and a selection of pizzas. There are three comfortable en suite bedrooms.
OPEN: 12–2.30 5.30–11 (Sat-Sun all day) **BAR MEALS:** Lunch served: Tue-Sun 12–1.45 Dinner served: all week 7–8.45 Av main course £6.50 **RESTAURANT:** Lunch served: Tue-Sun 12–1.45 Dinner served: all week 7–8.45 Av 3 course à la carte £13
BREWERY/COMPANY: Free House
PRINCIPAL BEERS: Carlsberg-Tetley Tetley Bitter, Jennings Bitter, Timothy Taylor Landlord, Scottish Courage John Smiths.
FACILITIES: Garden: Food served outdoors, patio **NOTES:** Parking 16 **ROOMS:** 3 bedrooms 3 en suite from s£38 d£52

GOATHLAND
Map 11 NZ80

Birch Hall Inn
Beckhole ☎ 01947 896245
e-mail: birchhallinn@beckhole.freeserve.co.uk
Remotely situated between the North York Moors steam railway and the Grosmont Rail Trail walk, this extraordinary little free house comprises two very small rooms separated by a confectionary shop. There's an open fire in the main bar and a tiny family room that leads out into a large garden. Well-kept ales wash down home-baked pies, Beckhole butty sandwiches, home-made scones and buttered beer cake.
OPEN: 11–3 7.30–11 (Sun 12–3, 7.30–10.30) (Summer 11–11, Sun 12–10.30) **BAR MEALS:** Lunch served: all week Dinner served: all week 11–3 7.30–11 Av main course £1.90
BREWERY/COMPANY: Free House **PRINCIPAL BEERS:** Black Sheep Best, Theakstons Black Bull, Cropton Yorkshire Moors Bitter & Honey Gold. **FACILITIES:** Garden: Food served outside, terrace Dogs allowed on leads (Water & dog treat) No credit cards

Mallyan Spout ★ ★
The Common YO22 5AN ☎ 01947 896486 📠 01947 896327
e-mail: Mallyan@ukgateway.net
Dir: Off A169 (Whitby/Pickering rd)
Ivy-clad, stone-built Victorian property with mullioned windows, named after the famous waterfall at the rear of the hotel. Fresh fish from Whitby is a feature of both menus. Bedrooms.

GREAT AYTON
Map 11 NZ51

The Royal Oak Hotel ◆◆◆
123 High St TS9 6BW ☎ 01642 722361 📠 01642 724047
A traditional rural hostelry in the village where Captain Cook grew up. He attended the local school, now housing the Captain Cook Schoolroom Museum. Handy for the Cleveland Hills and the North York Moors, this welcoming pub offers a fine choice of food and ales enhanced by winter log fires, beamed ceilings and plenty of charm. Very extensive bar menu ranges from breast of chicken and double pork chop, to lasagne bolognese and grilled salmon fillet.
OPEN: 11–11 (Sun 12–10.30) Closed: Dec 25 **BAR MEALS:** Lunch served: all week Dinner served: all week 12–2 6.30–9.30
RESTAURANT: Lunch served: all week Dinner served: all week 12–2 7.15–9.15 **BREWERY/COMPANY: FACILITIES:** Children welcome Children's licence **ROOMS:** 5 bedrooms 4 en suite from s£30 d£60

GREAT OUSEBURN
Map 09 SE46

Pick of the Pubs

The Crown Inn 🛏 🍷
Main St YO26 9RF ☎ 01423 330430 📠 01423 331095
Currently listed as one of the country's 'best places to eat seafood', a glance back at its history reveals that Ambrose Tiller founded his world-renowned troupe of dancing girls here, while another regular, Norman Barrett, became ringmaster at Blackpool's Tower Circus. The original brew-house became a dining room where 'House Specials' such as dressed Scottish king scallops with prosciutto, 'Moby Dick' of fresh haddock in Yorkshire beer batter and a hot seafood platter that includes lobster, mussels, prawns and crab claws drenched in garlic butter are served. Bar meals offer battered Brie with fruit coulis, pork and mushroom Stroganoff with home-made chips and sizzling faijitas with sour cream and salsa, supplemented by chargrilled British beef steaks and followed by toffee banana crumble or apple pancakes with butterscotch sauce. Equally notable is the selection of Yorkshire farmhouse cheeses that includes Ribblesdale ewes' milk and Swaledale Blue from celebrated local producers.
OPEN: 12–2 5–11 (Sat 11–11 Sun 12–10.30)
BAR MEALS: Lunch served: Sat-Sun Dinner served: all week 5–9.30 Av main course £12 **RESTAURANT:** Lunch served: Sat-Sun Dinner served: all week 5–9.30 Av 3 course à la carte £20
BREWERY/COMPANY: Free House
PRINCIPAL BEERS: Black Sheep Best, Scottish Courage John Smith's, Timothy Taylor Landlord,. **FACILITIES:** Children welcome Children's licence Garden: Patio, food served outdoors, BBQ **NOTES:** Parking 60

GREEN HAMMERTON
Map 09 SE45

The Bay Horse Inn 🛏 NEW
York Rd YO26 8BN ☎ 01423 330338 & 331113 📠 01423 331279
e-mail: thebayhorseinn@aol.com
An old coaching inn with bags of character located in a small village between the North Yorkshire Moors and Yorkshire Dales National Park, eight miles from either Harrogate or York. It offers traditional bars with log fires, a cosy restaurant, and en suite accommodation. Food is served in both the bar and restaurant, and popular options include beefsteaks - 10oz sirloin and 16oz rump - 16oz gammon and home-made steak and kidney or fisherman's pie.
OPEN: 11.30–2.30 6.30–11 **BAR MEALS:** Lunch served: all week Dinner served: all week 12–2 6.30–9.15 Av main course £6
RESTAURANT: Dinner served: all week 6.30–9.15 Av 3 course à la carte £15.95 **BREWERY/COMPANY:** Free House
PRINCIPAL BEERS: Scottish Courage John Smith's.
FACILITIES: Children welcome Garden: Food served outside Dogs allowed (water) **NOTES:** Parking 40 **ROOMS:** 10 bedrooms 10 en suite from s£35 d£50

**Room prices show the minimum double and single rates charged.
Room rates in hotels and B&B's often vary depending on the facilities, so be sure to check prices with the establishment before booking.**

PUB WALK

Egton Bridge
Horseshoe Hotel

HORSESHOE HOTEL,
EGTON BRIDGE
Whitby YO21 1XE
Tel: 01947 895245
Directions: From Whitby take A171 towards Middlesborough Village signed in 5m
On the banks of the River Esk. Cosy interior with old settles, works by local artists and a log fire. Good home-cooked food. A large garde n with ducks and geese. Fishing is available .
Open: 11.30–3 6–11
Bar Meals: 12–2 7–9
Children welcome and dogs allowed. Garden and parking available.

Distance: 3 miles (4.8km)
Map: OS Landranger 94 or Outdoor Leisure 27
Terrain: North York Moors
Paths: Paved causeways, packhorse routes, field paths and road
Gradient: Undulating with several climbs and descents

Walk submitted and checked by Horseshoe Hotel, Egton Bridge

A very pleasant walk to Beggar's Bridge, a picturesque packhorse bridge spanning the River Esk. There are good views of Glaisdale, once an ironstone mining village with three blast furnaces, and it follows paved causeways, a reminder of the days when Glaisdale was an important trading centre.

On leaving the hotel, follow the drive towards the road and turn left just before it on to a footpath signposted to stepping stones. Cross the river via both sets of stones, pass between houses and turn left at the road. Pass under the railway bridge and take the stile on the left just beyond the farm. Initially follow the fence, then continue through the field to a stream and uphill to a stile. Cross over and climb steeply through woodland. Keep ahead between the trees and across two fields, joining the track to Limber Hill Farm. Pass through the farmyard and turn left at the road. Descend the notoriously steep Limber Hill, a superb viewpoint over Glaisdale and rows of ex-miners' cottages. Veer left along the road at the bottom and follow it for a short distance. Make for the medieval packhorse bridge – Beggar's Bridge – but instead of crossing it, pass under the railway arch and take the footbridge by the ford. There is a signpost here for Egton Bridge. Climb the steps and follow the Coast to Coast waymarks. This long-distance route, extending the width of England between St Bees and Robin Hood's Bay, was pioneered by Alfred Wainwright. He and broadcaster Eric Robson featured the walk in a popular TV series about this legendary outdoor figure. The path follows the old packhorse route, part of the Coast to Coast Walk, for about one mile (1.6km), cutting through Arncliffe Woods to reach a minor road. Bear left, head downhill, cross the ford via the footbridge and the Horseshoe Hotel is a few hundred yards ahead on your left.

England

Pick of the Pubs

The Boars Head Hotel ★ ★ ★ 🏠🏠 🐕
Ripley Castle Estate HG3 3AY
☎ 01423 771888 📠 01423 771509
e-mail: reservations@boarsheadripley.co.uk
Dir: *On the A61 Harrogate/Ripon road, the Hotel is in the centre of Ripley village*

The Boars Head is an old coaching inn on the Ripley Castle Estate, luxuriously refurbished by Sir Thomas and Lady Ingilby. The resident chef/patron offers creative cooking in both the restaurant and bistro from an ever-changing menu. Guests never tire of the selection of beers, and guest beers maintain the regulars' interest. Starter dishes, which can also be taken as mains in a larger portion, include warm salad of white pudding with bacon lardons and chorizo. Options to follow might be balsamic marinated chicken on sweet potato and Madeira jus, and mixed berry crème brûlée topped with vanilla pod ice cream. Long a desirable venue for wedding receptions and other private functions, you can now actually get married here as well. Children and well-behaved dogs are welcome.
OPEN: 11-11 (Winter Mon-Sat 11-3, 5-11) Sun 12-10.30 (Winter Sun 12-3, 5-10.30) **BAR MEALS:** Lunch served: all week Dinner served: all week 12-2.30 6.30-10 Av main course £8.50 **RESTAURANT:** Lunch served: all week Dinner served: all week 12-2 7-9.30 Av 3 course à la carte £22.50 **BREWERY/COMPANY:** Free House **PRINCIPAL BEERS:** Theakston Best, Old Peculier, Daleside Crackshot, White Boar. **FACILITIES:** Children welcome Garden: Food served outside. Courtyard area Dogs allowed Overnight in bedrooms only **NOTES:** Parking 45 **ROOMS:** 25 bedrooms 25 en suite

Board Hotel ♦ ♦ ♦ 🏠 🍷
Market Place DL8 3RD ☎ 01969 667223 📠 01969 667970
e-mail: theboardhotel1@netscapeonline.co.uk
Dir: *M6 J37 - A684 east to Hawes coming down the hill /first public house in your left opposite the market hall*
A typical Dales pub at the heart of spectacular Wensleydale. Directly opposite is the famous cheese factory and close by are numerous stunning walks. In addition, there is plenty of opportunity for cycling, fishing and hang-gliding. Expect a friendly welcome inside and good, hearty pub food. Half roast duck, rainbow trout, sirloin steak and liver and sausage are among the well-established favourites.

OPEN: 11-11 **BAR MEALS:** Lunch served: all week Dinner served: all week 12-2 6.30-9 Av main course £4.75 **RESTAURANT:** 12-2 6.30-9 **BREWERY/COMPANY:** Free House
PRINCIPAL BEERS: Carlsberg-Tetley Tetley Bitter, Black Sheep Best, Theakston Bitter, Marston's Pedigree. **FACILITIES:** Children welcome
NOTES: Parking 10 **ROOMS:** 3 bedrooms 3 en suite from d£50

The Feathers Hotel
YO62 5BT ☎ 01439 770275 📠 01439 771101
e-mail: thefeathers@aol.com
Dir: *From A1(M) Jct 168 to Thursk, then A170 for 14M to Hemsley*
This traditional country inn overlooking the market place was once the home of the local doctor and is one of Helmsley's oldest houses. The beamed Pickwick Bar is popular with locals, and freshly cooked food is served in the Feversham dining room and bar with its Mouseman of Kilburn furniture. Home-made pie and quiche, sausages, mash and onion gravy, mixed grill and 8oz hamburger are among the popular dishes.
OPEN: 10.30-11 **BAR MEALS:** 12-2.30 6-9
RESTAURANT: 12-2.30 6-9 **BREWERY/COMPANY:** Free House
FACILITIES: Children welcome Garden: Food served outside Dogs allowed **NOTES:** Parking 24 **ROOMS:** 14 bedrooms 14 en suite

Pick of the Pubs

The Feversham Arms Hotel ★ ★ ★ 🏠 🍷
1 High St YO62 5AG ☎ 01439 770766 📠 01439 770346
e-mail: info@feversham.com
Dir: *from the A1(M) jct A168 to Thirsk, then A170 for 14m to Helmsley*
Built in 1855, this stylish little hotel was completely transformed by its owners during the second half of 2000. The extensive refurbishment created an intimate new dining room, with a redesigned lounge and bar area. Look, too, for the new 'Brasserie at the Fev' which aims for adventurous contemporary cooking in a relaxed atmosphere. The menu starts with seafood pancake, filo-wrapped goats' cheese or eggs Benedict with air-dried ham. Main courses include pan-seared salmon steak on linguine noodles with a chilli and basil dressing, rich home-made bolognese sauce on a bed of fresh spaghetti with parmesan flakes and rack of lamb on minted potato with rosemary-infused jus. Extensive international wine list and good choice of lunchtime light bites. The accommodation offers seven new suites, and 17 up-graded and redecorated en suite bedrooms. Guests can also avail themselves of the poolside terrace and corner garden, state-of-the-art gym, sauna, heated outdoor pool and tennis court.
OPEN: 10-2.30 6-11 **BAR MEALS:** Lunch served: all week Dinner served: all week 12-2 7-9 **RESTAURANT:** Lunch served:

continued

continued

all week Dinner served: all week 12–2 7–9.30 Av 3 course à la carte £25 **BREWERY/COMPANY:** Free House **PRINCIPAL BEERS:** Theakstons Best, Scottish Courage John Smith's. **FACILITIES:** Children welcome Garden: Food served outside **NOTES:** Parking 50 **ROOMS:** 17 bedrooms 17 en suite from s£70 d£90

Pick of the Pubs

The Star Inn ⊕⊕ ♇
Harome YO62 5JE ☎ 01439 770397 🖩 01439 771833
Dir: From Helmsley take A170 towards Kirkbymoorside. 0.5m turn R for Harome

An old dormitory once used by travelling monks, and a cruck-framed longhouse containing cow byres are two of the fascinating features of this picturesque 14th-century inn. Nowadays the dormitory houses a distinctive coffee loft, while the byres have been converted into a stylish and reputable restaurant. The part-thatched inn also has a separate bar full of the hand-carved furniture of 'Mousey' Thompson, and where fine real ales and carefully-selected house wines by the glass are served. The food uses home-grown herbs from a fragrant, lovingly tended garden, and seasonal exotica chosen from local suppliers. The lunch menu lists an appetising selection like risotto of local pheasant and fresh cranberries, baked wild mushroom quiche with red onion marmalade, and warm duck leg with marinated fresh fig salad, all available as a small or large dish. In the evening expect faggot of local game, and shallow-fried goose galette. There are three self-contained bedrooms nearby.

OPEN: 11.30–3 6.30–11 Closed: 2 wks Jan, 1 wk Nov
BAR MEALS: Lunch served: Tue–Sun Dinner served: Tue–Sun 11.30–2 6.30–10 Av main course £12 **RESTAURANT:** Lunch served: Tue–Sun Dinner served: Tue–Sun 11.30–2 6.30–10 Av 3 course à la carte £25 **BREWERY/COMPANY:** Free House **PRINCIPAL BEERS:** Black Sheep Special, Scottish Courage John Smiths, Theakston Best,. **FACILITIES:** Children welcome Garden: Dogs allowed **NOTES:** Parking 24 **ROOMS:** 3 bedrooms 3 en suite from s£90 d£90

HETTON   Map 09 SD95

Pick of the Pubs

The Angel ⊕⊕ ♇
BD23 6LT ☎ 01756 730263 🖩 01756 730363
e-mail: info@angelhetton.co.uk
Dir: From A59 take B6265 towards Grassington/Skipton

Clocking up 20 years in the same hands, the Angel has a legendary reputation. Genuinely unspoilt, it is a traditional 400-year-old Dales pub with lots of nooks and crannies,

continued

oak beams and roaring log fires in winter. It represents and what the true British pub should be all about; no matter whether your choice is a bowl of soup and a pint of Black Sheep or the full monty, the intention is to make every visit memorable. Throughout, the emphasis is on thoroughly good food prepared from the freshest ingredients – and it shows. Blackboard specials may feature pan-seared sea bass with slow roasted plum tomatoes, rocket, fondant potatoes and balsamic dressing, rack of lamb with pesto mash, confit vegetables and lamb jus, or wild mushroom risotto finished with truffle oil. To follow, try sticky toffee pudding with caramel sauce, and poached pear with cinnamon ice cream. Real ales and many fine wines by the glass. Alfresco lunches can be enjoyed on the terrace with views over Rylestone Fell.

OPEN: 12–3 6–10.30 Closed: Dec 25 **BAR MEALS:** Lunch served: all week Dinner served: all week 12–2 6–9 Av main course £9 **RESTAURANT:** Lunch served: Sun Dinner served: Mon–Sat 6–9 Av 3 course à la carte £25 Av 3 course fixed price £14.50 **BREWERY/COMPANY:** Free House **FACILITIES:** Children welcome Children's licence Garden: **NOTES:** Parking 56

HOVINGHAM   Map 09 SE67

The Malt Shovel
Main St YO62 4LF ☎ 01653 628264 🖩 01653 628264
Dir: 18 miles NE of York, 5 miles from Castle Howard
Friendly village pub retaining many original features, situated in a pretty village close to Castle Howard. Unspoilt atmosphere; good value food. Pubmaster House.

Pick of the Pubs

The Worsley Arms Hotel ★ ★ ★ ⊕⊕ ♇
Main St YO62 4LA ☎ 01653 628234 🖩 01653 628130
e-mail: worsleyarms@aol.com
Dir: From A1 take A64 towards Malton, L onto B1257 signed Slingsby & Hovingham. 2m to Hovingham

At the village centre opposite Hovingham Hall, birthplace of the Duchess of Kent, this 17th-century spa hotel and pub, some 20 minutes' drive north of York, is worth the trip to admire the many family portraits that hang throughout. The separate pub bar is equally of interest to cricket lovers with its long history of matches played on the village green opposite for over 150 years. The Cricketers' Bar menu supplements a wide-ranging sandwich selection with glazed Swaledale goats' cheese with honey and walnut dressing or steamed mussels with shallots, garlic and cream in regular or large portions, and a rib-eye beef steak with green peppercorn sauce and chips for those with healthy appetites. Restaurant menus offer starters such as terrine of Goosnargh duck followed by a classic beef stew with suet

continued

HOVINGHAM continued

dumplings and a range of memorable desserts. Fiercely traditional lounges, comfortable bedrooms and a private garden make this an attractive destination.
OPEN: 12-2.30 7-11 **BAR MEALS:** Lunch served: all week Dinner served: all week 12-2 7-10 Av main course £8.50 **RESTAURANT:** Lunch served: Sun 12-2 Dinner served: all week 7-10 Av 3 course à la carte £25 Av 3 course fixed price £25 **BREWERY/COMPANY:** Free House **PRINCIPAL BEERS:** Scottish Courage John Smith's, Hambleton Stallion. **FACILITIES:** Children welcome Garden: Patio, food served outdoors Dogs allowed **NOTES:** Parking 30 **ROOMS:** 19 bedrooms 19 en suite from s£65 d£95

HUBBERHOLME   Map 09 SD97

The George Inn
BD23 5JE ☎ 01756 760223 ⊟ 01756 760808
e-mail: thegeorge.inn@virgin.net
Dir: At Buckden on B6160 take turn for Hubberholme

The village of Hubberholme has the highest road in Yorkshire running through it, rising to a height of 1,934 feet. Author JB Priestley, who is buried in the local churchyard, regarded the 18th-century George as his favourite watering hole. Stone walls, antique plates, mullion windows and an open fire enhance the pub's character. Good wholesome food ranges from hot and cold snacks to home-made main courses. Expect vegetable curry, fillet of cod, breast of chicken, fish lasagne and Wensleydale pork on the varied menu.
OPEN: 11.30-3 6.30-11 (Summer 11.30-11) Closed: Middle 2 wks in Jan **BAR MEALS:** Lunch served: all week Dinner served: all week 12-2 6.30-8.45 Av main course £7.95 **BREWERY/COMPANY:** Free House **PRINCIPAL BEERS:** Black Sheep Best, Carlsberg-Tetley Tetley Bitter. **FACILITIES:** Garden: Patio, food served outside Dogs allowed (water, biscuits) **NOTES:** Parking 20 **ROOMS:** 7 bedrooms 4 en suite from d£42

KELD   Map 11 NY80

Tan Hill Inn
☎ 01833 628246
Set on the Pennine Way in an isolated position, this hospitable 16th-century inn is the highest in England, at 1,732 feet above sea level. Once at a major trading crossroads, the Tan Hill Inn is now popular with walkers and motorists enjoying the austere beauty of the Pennines.
OPEN: 11-11 **BAR MEALS:** 12-2.30 7-9
BREWERY/COMPANY: Free House
PRINCIPAL BEERS: Theakstons Best, XB, Old Peculiar.
FACILITIES: Children welcome **ROOMS:** 7 bedrooms 7 en suite
No credit cards

KIRBY HILL   Map 11 NZ10

The Shoulder of Mutton Inn ♀
DL11 7JH ☎ 01748 822772 ⊟ 01325 718936
e-mail: info@shoulderofmutton.net
Dir: 4m N of Richmond, 6m from A1 A66 J at Scotch Corner
A 200-year-old traditional inn in an elevated position overlooking Holmedale. Log fires burn in the bar areas, while the separate Stable restaurant retains its original beams. Choose whether to eat here or in the bar from a menu that takes in Kirby Hill half shoulder of lamb, chicken bonne femme and fresh salmon steak hollandaise. Of less classical origin are the steaks, salads and jacket potatoes that complete the picture.
OPEN: 12-3 6-11 **BAR MEALS:** Lunch served: Sat-Sun (summer Mon-Sun) 12-2 Dinner served: all week 7-9.30 Av main course £6.50 **RESTAURANT:** 12-2 6-9.30 **BREWERY/COMPANY:** Free House **PRINCIPAL BEERS:** Scottish Courage John Smiths, Jennings Cumberland Ale, Black Sheep Best. **FACILITIES:** Children welcome Garden: Patio, Food served outside Dogs allowed **NOTES:** Parking 28 **ROOMS:** 5 bedrooms 5 en suite from s£30 d£45

KIRKBYMOORSIDE   Map 09 SE68

Pick of the Pubs

George & Dragon Hotel ★ ★ 👁♀
17 Market Place YO62 6AA ☎ 01751 433334 ⊟ 01751 432933
Dir: Just off A170 between Scarborough & Thirsk in centre of the Market Town

A former coaching dating from the early 17th century, and continuing its long tradition of providing a haven of warmth, refreshment and rest to weary travellers en route from the old Great North Road to the east coast. Sports enthusiasts will enjoy the collection of rugby and cricket memorabilia in the cosy bar, including photographs, autographs, prints and other paraphernalia. Surrounded by exposed beams, and with the warmth of a log fire in winter, visitors can sample hand-pulled real ales like Black Sheep and Tetley as well as wines by the glass. The refurbished Knights' Restaurant in the former brewhouse offer plenty of choice from blackboard lunchtime specials to candlelit dinners. Fish is represented by grilled halibut, pan-fried lemon sole, and salmon steak topped with hollandaise and asparagus sauce, while Caribbean chicken, lamb shank, and game casserole should satisfy meat lovers. Helmsley Castle and Nunnington Hall are easily accessible.
OPEN: 10-11 **BAR MEALS:** Lunch served: all week Dinner served: all week 12-2.15 6.30-9.15 Av main course £10 **RESTAURANT:** Lunch served: all week Dinner served: all week 12-2.15 6.30-9.15 Av 3 course à la carte £25 **BREWERY/COMPANY:** Free House **PRINCIPAL BEERS:** Black Sheep Best. **FACILITIES:** Children welcome Children's licence Garden: Food served outside Dogs allowed **NOTES:** Parking 15 **ROOMS:** 18 bedrooms 18 en suite from £39.50 per person

The Lion Inn

Blakey Ridge YO62 7LQ ☎ 01751 417320 🖹 01751 417717

Dir: From A170 follow signs 'Hutton le Hole/Castleton'. 6m N of Hutton le Hole.

The fourth highest inn in England, the Lion stands 1553ft above sea level and offers breathtaking views over Rosedale and Farndale in the beautiful North York Moors National Park. The cosy interior with original beamed ceilings, 4-ft-thick stone walls and blazing fires in the bars makes up for the isolated location. Typical chef's specials are Old Peculier casserole, chicken curry, mushroom and nut fettuccine and game pie. Deep fried wholetail scampi and prawn salad feature among the fish dishes.

OPEN: 10-11 **BAR MEALS:** Lunch served: all week Dinner served: all week 12-10 Av main course £6.75 **RESTAURANT:** Lunch served: Sun 12-2 Dinner served: all week 7-10 Av 3 course à la carte £17 **BREWERY/COMPANY:** Free House **PRINCIPAL BEERS:** Theakston Blackbull, Bitter & Old Peculier, Scottish Courage John Smith's Bitter, Greene King Old Speckled Hen. **FACILITIES:** Children welcome Garden: Beer garden, food served outdoors Dogs allowed **NOTES:** Parking 200 **ROOMS:** 10 bedrooms 8 en suite from s£17.50 d£50

See Pub Walk on page 543

Pick of the Pubs

Stone Trough Inn 🏠 ♀

Kirkham Abbey YO60 7JS ☎ 01653 618713 🖹 01653 618819
e-mail: info@stonetroughinn.co.uk

Dir: 1 1/2m off A64, between York & Malton

Down a narrow lane high above Kirkham Abbey and the River Derwent, this traditional stone country inn has recently had a major restoration. Lots of beams and cosy rooms add colour and character, and log fires and comfortable furnishings draw a good crowd. Having worked at the renowned Winteringham Fields restaurant in Lincolnshire, chef/landlord Adam Richardson offers impressive, modern pub menus. In the bar may be choices of terrine of potted duck with an orange and apricot chutney and warm thyme toast or freshly prepared soup of the day to start; followed by pork and herb sausages on bubble and squeak with a rich onion gravy or seared fillet of salmon on a bed of stir-fried cabbage with a spicy oriental sauce. Dinner may add rump of lamb on a celeriac fondant with a confit of root vegetables and a rosemary jus, while among desserts may be creamed rice pudding served hot, with mulled fruits and damson purée.

OPEN: 12-2.30 6-11 (Sun 11.45-10.30) Closed: Dec 25 **BAR MEALS:** Lunch served: Tues-Sun Dinner served: Tues-Sun

12-2 6.30-8.30 Av main course £7.95 **RESTAURANT:** Lunch served: Sun 12-2.15 Dinner served: Tue-Sat 6.45-9.30 Av 3 course à la carte £22 **BREWERY/COMPANY:** Free House **PRINCIPAL BEERS:** Carlsberg-Tetley Tetley Bitter, Timothy Taylor Landlord, Black Sheep Best, Guest ales. **FACILITIES:** Children welcome Garden: Food served outside **NOTES:** Parking 100

Pick of the Pubs

The General Tarleton Inn ◉◉ 🏠 ♀

Boroughbridge Rd, Ferrensby HG5 0PZ
☎ 01423 340284 🖹 01423 340288

Dir: On A6055, on crossroads in Ferrensby

A former 18th-century coaching inn within easy reach of the A1, Harrogate and the Yorkshire Dales and under the same ownership as the equally impressive Angel Inn at Hetton (qv). Tastefully refurbished, it sports a rambling, low-beamed bar with open fires, a comfortable mix of furnishings, cosy nooks and crannies; ideal for an intimate dinner chosen from the imaginative brasserie-style menu and interesting daily blackboard additions. Alternatively, dine in the light and airy covered courtyard. Order at the bar; perhaps choosing confit of shoulder of Yorkshire lamb, braised ham shank or tournedos of beef fillet with Yorkshire buffalo blue polenta and salsa Verdi. Fish plays a prominent part in the proceedings; try the lightly smoked haddock with home-made black pudding, poached egg and grain mustard sauce or salmon en croûte stuffed with cheese fondue and baked in filo pastry with lobster sauce. Fixed-price dinner menu in the restaurant. An impressive wine list complements the menu; 20 by the glass. Fourteen well appointed bedrooms are housed in a modern rear extension.

OPEN: 12-3 6-11 Closed: Dec 25 **BAR MEALS:** Lunch served: all week Dinner served: all week 12-2.15 6.00-9.30 Av main course £8.50 **RESTAURANT:** Lunch served: Sun 12-1.30 Dinner served: Mon-Sat 7-9.30 Av 3 course à la carte £30 Av 3 course fixed price £25 **BREWERY/COMPANY:** Free House **PRINCIPAL BEERS:** Black Sheep Best, Carlsberg-Tetley Tetley Bitter, Timothy Taylors Landlord. **FACILITIES:** Children welcome Garden: Beer garden, food served outdoors Dogs allowed (not in bar) **NOTES:** Parking 60 **ROOMS:** 14 bedrooms 14 en suite from s£75 d£85

continued

England

LASTINGHAM
Map 09 SE79

Blacksmiths Arms 🐑
YO62 6TL ☎ 01751 417247
e-mail: blacksmithslastingham@hotmail.com

A stone-built inn dating from 1693 and unspoilt by progress, situated in a beautiful village that is part of a conservation area within the National Park. Furnishings are in keeping with the pub's great age while its ambience is provided by a rich cross-section of folk engaged in lively conversation at the bar. Yorkshire puddings with onion gravy and various home-baked pies form the basis of a menu that remains fiercely traditional. **OPEN:** 12–3.30 6.30–11 (Winter 12–3, 7–11) **BAR MEALS:** Lunch served: Wed-Mon 12–2.30 Dinner served: all week 7–9.15 Av main course £7.25 **RESTAURANT:** Dinner served: all week 12–2 7–9.15 Av 3 course à la carte £15.95 **BREWERY/COMPANY:** Free House **PRINCIPAL BEERS:** Theakstons Best Bitter, Marston's Pedigree, Black Bull Bitter,. **FACILITIES:** Garden: Food served outside, terrace **ROOMS:** 3 bedrooms 3 en suite from d£55

LEYBURN
Map 09 SE19

Pick of the Pubs

Sandpiper Inn ♀
Market Place DL8 5AT ☎ 01969 622206 📠 01969 625367
e-mail: hsandpiper@aol.com
Dir: From A1 take A684 to Leyburn
The oldest building in Leyburn, dating back to around 1640, has been a pub for just 30 years and an outstanding one since its purchase in 1999 by the Harrison family. With a beautiful summer garden, a bar, snug and dining-room within, it is traditional in style yet thoroughly sensible in its approach to food. In addition to the safer options such as fish and chips in real ale batter and Yorkshire ham with eggs and fried potatoes that proliferate on the bar lunch menu, a modern British menu with a hint of Mediterranean flavours is the ever-increasing draw at dinner. Warm goats' cheese on red onion and tomato salad and seared scallops with Jerusalem artichoke purée amongst the starters are indicative of the care taken over fresh produce and balanced flavours. Further evidence comes in main dishes that include pot-roast rabbit with wild mushrooms, a fresh fish selection sauced with saffron and chives and loin of venison with liquorice sauce. Pasta with wilted greens and feta cheese and rib-eye steaks from the grill are amongst the popular alternatives, followed by raspberry and almond tart or iced lemon meringue terrine. Two smart en suite double bedrooms. **OPEN:** 11.30–3 6.30–11 **BAR MEALS:** Lunch served: all week Dinner served: all week 12–2.30 6.30–10 Av main course £7

RESTAURANT: Lunch served: all week Dinner served: all week 12–2.30 6.30–9.00 Av 3 course à la carte £20 **BREWERY/COMPANY:** Free House **PRINCIPAL BEERS:** Black Sheep Best, Dent Aviator, Black Sheep Special, Daleside. **FACILITIES:** Children welcome Garden: Food served outside Dogs allowed **NOTES:** Parking 6 **ROOMS:** 2 bedrooms 2 en suite from s£50 d£60

Wyvill Arms 🐑 ♀
Constable-Burton DL8 5LH ☎ 01677 450581

Situated on the edge of the Yorkshire Dales, this popular inn offers welcoming bars with open fires, beams and flagstones. Takes its name from a local family who converted what was a 1920s farmstead into a pub. Suckling pig on fresh mash with cider and Calvados jus, braised lamb shanks with garlic and rosemary oil, and a wide choice of steaks feature on the appetising menu. **OPEN:** 11–3 5.30–11 **BAR MEALS:** 11.30–2.15 5.30–9.30 **RESTAURANT:** 5.30–9.30 **BREWERY/COMPANY:** Free House **PRINCIPAL BEERS:** Theakston, Blacksheep, John Smiths. **FACILITIES:** Children welcome Garden: Dogs allowed **NOTES:** Parking 40 **ROOMS:** 3 bedrooms 3 en suite from s£34 d£56

LINTON
Map 07 SD96

The Fountaine Inn 🐑
BD23 5HJ ☎ 01756 752210 📠 01756 752210
Dir: From Skipton take B6162 8m turn R for Linton
Located within the magnificent Yorkshire Dales National Park, in a sleepy hamlet beside the River Beck, this 16th-century inn takes its name from a local man who made his fortune in the Great Plague of London in 1665 - burying the bodies! On a more cheerful note, the menu is wholesome and appetising, offering such dishes as steak and ale pie, Cumberland sausages, loin of lamb, sirloin steak, seafood platter, pan-fried calves' liver and goats' cheese tart. **OPEN:** 11–11 (11–3, 5.30–11 in winter) **BAR MEALS:** Lunch served: all week Dinner served: all week 12–5.30 5.30–9 Av main course £5.95 **BREWERY/COMPANY:** Free House **PRINCIPAL BEERS:** Black Sheep Best, Theakston Best, Carlsberg-Tetley Tetley Bitter, Scottish Courage John Smith's. **FACILITIES:** Children welcome Children's licence Garden: Food served outside Dogs allowed **NOTES:** Parking 20

LITTON
Map 09 SD97

Queens Arms
BD23 5QJ ☎ 01756 770208
e-mail: queensarmslitton@mserve.net
Early 16th-century inn located in a remote corner of the Yorkshire Dales, a perfect base for walking and touring. Low

continued

continued

PUB WALK

Blakey Ridge
The Lion

This scenic walk in the magnificent North York Moors National Park offers the chance to escape the pressures of the modern world and savour the region's unique sense of space and distance. Follow the route through spectacular wild country to the remote head of Rosedale.

From the pub car park follow the main road towards Hutton-le-Hole. After about 150 yards (136m) turn left at a waymark and follow the path. On reaching the fence corner, continue straight ahead to join the dismantled railway line. Bear right along the line and after about 100 yards (91m) look for a small cairn on the bank to your left. Leave the line at the cairn and follow the faint track as it descends diagonally across the moor. The path, marked by small cairns, heads towards a shooting butt, close to a large boulder. Just before the butt, bear left down a shallow gully, then head right before descending again via a further gully. The footpath shortcuts the access track to Dale Head Farm, descending directly through bracken to the farm gate. Keep dogs on a lead along this stretch. Turn right in the farmyard and follow the track to the next farm. On reaching the farmyard, pass through a facing gate and follow the waymarks left across the field. Cross a stream by a footbridge, climb the bank and continue across the field towards the farm. Go through several gates and join a minor road. Turn left, then right almost immediately, following the public bridleway to Great Fryup Dale. The bridleway climbs out of the valley, passing through a plantation to join the course of the old East Mines railway. Turn left and follow the route for almost 2 1/2 miles (4km) as it sweeps spectacularly around the dale head and back along the west side of the valley. Return to the inn on the path used at the start of the walk.

THE LION
Blakey Ridge
KIRKBYMOORSIDE YO62 7LQ
Tel: 01751 417320
Directions: From A170 follow signs 'Hutton le Hole/Castleton'. 6m N of Hutton le Hole. The fourth highest inn in England, the Lion offers breathtaking views the North York Moors National Park. Isolated but with a cosy interior with beamed ceilings, 4ft-thick stone walls and blazing fires. Good, sustaining pub food.
Open: 10–11
Bar meals: 12–10pm
Children welcome and dogs allowed. Garden and parking available.

Distance: 4 1/4 miles (6.8km)
Map: OS Outdoor Leisure 26
Terrain: Spectacular wild landscape and rolling moorland of the North York Moors
Paths: Tracks and paths; stretch of disused railway
Gradient: Some climbing

Walk submitted and checked by The Lion, Blakey Ridge.

LITTON continued

ceilings, beams and coal fires give the place a traditional, timeless feel. A good range of food incorporates local produce and international flavours. There's plenty of fish, including fresh halibut with seafood sauce, vegetarian dishes, home-made pies and a generous mixed grill.
OPEN: 11.45–3 6.45–11 (July-Aug Sat–Sun open all day) Closed: 3 Jan–1 Feb **BAR MEALS:** Lunch served: Tue–Sun Dinner served: Tue–Sun 12–2 7–9 Av main course £7 **RESTAURANT:** Lunch served: Tue–Sun Dinner served: Tue–Sun 12–2 7–9 Av 3 course à la carte £15 **BREWERY/COMPANY:** Free House **PRINCIPAL BEERS:** Tetleys. **FACILITIES:** Children welcome Garden: beer garden, outdoor eating, patio Dogs allowed **NOTES:** Parking 10 **ROOMS:** 4 bedrooms 4 en suite from s£40 d£40

LONG PRESTON   Map 08 SD85

Maypole Inn ♀
Maypole Green BD23 4PH ☎ 01729 840219 ▤ 01729 840456
e-mail: landlord@maypole.co.uk
Dir: On A65 between Settle and Skipton
At the heart of the Yorkshire Dales National Park, the Maypole has been plying its trade since 1695: one wonders what founder Ambrose Wigglesworth would think of it today, with its comfortable bedrooms, Yorkshire ales and traditional home cooking. After a good moorland walk, relax in the beamed dining room or cosy bar over a pint and a simple snack, home-made steak pie, fillet of salmon or plain ham and eggs. Daily specials and popular Sunday lunch with cheerful service and a jolly atmosphere.
OPEN: 11–3 6–11 (Sun 12–10.30) (Sat 5–11) **BAR MEALS:** Lunch served: all week Dinner served: all week 12–2 6.30–9 Av main course £6.50 **RESTAURANT:** Lunch served: all week Dinner served: all week 12–2 6.30–9 Av 3 course à la carte £13 9 **BREWERY/COMPANY:** Whitbread **PRINCIPAL BEERS:** Timothy Taylor Landlord, Castle Eden. **FACILITIES:** Children welcome Garden: Outdoor eating Dogs allowed **NOTES:** Parking 30 **ROOMS:** 6 bedrooms 6 en suite from s£29 d£47

MARTON   Map 09 SE78

The Appletree Country Inn
YO62 6RD ☎ 01751 431457 ▤ 01751 430190
e-mail: appletreeinn@supanet.com
Dir: From Kirkby Moorside on A170 turn right after one mile, follow road for two miles to Marton
A former village pub now better termed a dining pub, the Appletree sources most produce locally, including from its own orchard and vegetable garden. Among its representative dishes are griddled king scallops, with orange and samphire salad, chilli jam and crème fraîche, venison suet pudding, with red onion marmalade, juniper and gin sauce, and marbled chocolate pyramid with Bailey's chocolate mousse. Bread, ice cream, petits fours and much else are made on the premises.
OPEN: 12–2.30 Closed: 2 weeks Jan, 2 weeks Oct **BAR MEALS:** Lunch served: Wed–Mon Dinner served: Wed–Mon 12–2 6.30–10 Av main course £10 **RESTAURANT:** Lunch served: Wed–Mon Dinner served: Wed–Mon 12–2 6.30–10 Av 3 course à la carte £22 **BREWERY/COMPANY:** Free House **PRINCIPAL BEERS:** John Smiths Cask, Guest ales; Malton, Cropton, York. **FACILITIES:** Children welcome Garden: Food served outside. Patio area **NOTES:** Parking 30

MASHAM   Map 09 SE28

The Black Sheep Brewery
HG4 4EN ☎ 01765 689227 & 680100 ▤ 01765 689746
e-mail: helen.broadley@blacksheep.co.uk
Dir: Off the A6108 between Ribon & Leyburn, follow brown tourist signs
Schoolboy humour is on the menu at this popular brewery complex on the edge of the Yorkshire Dales. Besides the 'shepherded' brewery tours, 'ewe' can simply call in to eat and drink in the stylish bistro and 'baa...r'. In just ten years, Black Sheep ales have achieved a national reputation, and dishes like lamb shank in Square Ale sauce, and Riggwelter casserole make the most of them. Also lunchtime sandwiches, roast local pheasant, poached salmon, or provençale vegetable tartlet.
OPEN: 11–5.30 7–11 Closed: 25–26 Dec, 2 wks Jan **BAR MEALS:** Lunch served: all week 12–2.30 Dinner served: Wed–Sat 7–9.30 Av main course £6.95 **RESTAURANT:** Lunch served: all week Dinner served: all week 12–2.30 7–9.30 Av 3 course à la carte £18 **PRINCIPAL BEERS:** Black Sheep beers. **FACILITIES:** Children welcome Garden: Food served outside **NOTES:** Parking 25

Kings Head Hotel ★ ★ ⌂ ♀
Market Place HG4 4EF ☎ 01765 689295 ▤ 01765 689070
e-mail: masham.kingshead@snr.co.uk
Overlooking Masham's spacious market square with its cross and maypole, this handsome 18th-century inn was once an excise office. Combines classic Georgian splendour with modern day comforts and is a perfect base for touring the Yorkshire Dales. Expect fish and chips with mushy peas, herb roasted salmon, steak and Stilton pie, or minted lamb shoulder. Bedrooms are well decorated and comfortable.
OPEN: 11–11 **BAR MEALS:** Lunch served: all week Dinner served: all week 12–3 6–10 Av main course £7 **RESTAURANT:** Lunch served: all week Dinner served: all week 12–3 6–10 Av 3 course à la carte £15 **PRINCIPAL BEERS:** Theakstons Best Bitter, Black Bull, Old Peculier, Cool Cask. **FACILITIES:** Children welcome Garden: Food served outside. Victorian courtyard Dogs allowed (in the garden only) **ROOMS:** 10 bedrooms 10 en suite from s£50 d£65

MIDDLEHAM   Map 09 SE18

Black Swan Hotel ⌂ NEW
Market Place DL8 4NP ☎ 01969 622221 ▤ 01969 622221
e-mail: blackswanmiddleham@yahoo.com
Standing in the shadow of Middleham Castle is this welcoming Grade II listed inn dating from 1670. Exposed beams and wooden panelling give character to the stone-built property, which can be found in the centre of this famous horse-training area. Traditional country cooking results in dishes like beef in Old Peculier, game pie, mixed grills, trout with almonds, smoked haddock fish cakes, and various steaks.
OPEN: 11–3.30 6–11 (open all day Sat–Sun summer) **BAR MEALS:** Lunch served: all week Dinner served: all week 12–2 6.30–9 Av main course £5 **RESTAURANT:** Lunch served: all week Dinner served: all week 12–2 6.30–9 Av 3 course à la carte £15 **BREWERY/COMPANY:** Free House **PRINCIPAL BEERS:** Scottish Courage John Smiths, Theakstons Best Bitter, Black Bull & Old Peculier. **FACILITIES:** Children welcome Garden: Food served outdoors, patio/terrace Dogs allowed **ROOMS:** 7 bedrooms 7 en suite from s£25 d£48

continued

The White Swan Hotel 🐾 ♀

Market Place DL8 4PE ☎ 01969 622093 📠 01969 624551

e-mail: whiteswan@easynet.co.uk

Dir: From A1, take A684 toward Leyburn then A6108 to Ripon, 1.5m to Middleton

Traditional Dales coaching inn located on the market square, with beams, flagstone floors and open fires. An ideal place to sit and watch the racehorses riding out in the morning. The emphasis is on quality accommodation and good food. The bar menu offers baked cod in a rarebit sauce, sausage and bubble and squeak with onion gravy, and fillet of salmon on wilted spinach with a tomato and tarragon sauce.

OPEN: 12–3 6.30–11 **BAR MEALS:** Lunch served: all week Dinner served: all week 12–2.15 6.30–9.15 Av main course £8

RESTAURANT: Lunch served: all week Dinner served: all week 12–2.15 6.30–9.15 Av 3 course à la carte £17

BREWERY/COMPANY: Free House **PRINCIPAL BEERS:** Black Sheep Best, Riggwelter, Scottish Courage John Smith's.

FACILITIES: Children welcome Garden: Food served outside Dogs allowed **ROOMS:** 12 bedrooms 12 en suite from s£47.50 d£59

MIDDLESMOOR   Map 09 SE07

Crown Hotel

HG3 5ST ☎ 01423 755204

e-mail: Pamellis@mac.com

The original building dates back to the 17th century; today it offers the chance to enjoy a good pint of local beer by a cosy, roaring log fire, or in a sunny pub garden. Stands on a breezy 900ft hilltop with good views towards Gouthwaite Reservoir. Ideal for those potholing or following the popular Nidderdale Way. Appetising food may include steak and kidney pie, Nidderdale lamb cutlets, fish and chips and salmon, pasta and broccoli bake.

OPEN: 12–2.30 7–11 **BAR MEALS:** Lunch served: Tues–Sun 12–2 Dinner served: Tues–Sat 7–8.30 Av main course £5.50

BREWERY/COMPANY: Free House **PRINCIPAL BEERS:** Black Sheep Best, Scottish Courage John Smith's, Theakstons Bitter,.

FACILITIES: Children welcome Garden: Large lawned area, food served outside Dogs allowed (water) **NOTES:** Parking 20

ROOMS: 7 bedrooms 1 en suite from s£18.50 d£18.50 No credit cards

---

MOULTON   Map 11 NZ20

Pick of the Pubs

Black Bull Inn 🐾

DL10 6QJ ☎ 01325 377289 📠 01325 377422

e-mail: sarah@blackbullinn.demon.co.uk

Dir: 1m S of Scotch Corner off A1

Well-established favourite among a discerning dining clientele and well placed for famished A1 travellers (1 mile south of Scotch Corner) seeking a civilised retreat. Lunchtime meals are served in the characterful, relaxing bar, warmed by a roaring fire in winter, and in the side dark-panelled Fish Bar. An imaginative, seasonally-changing menu lists enviable light snacks such as seafood pancake, linguine with tomato sauce, pancetta and parmesan, Welsh rarebit and bacon, smoked haddock, walnut and Gruyère quiche and various salads and sandwiches. In the evenings, when the pub becomes a fish and seafood restaurant proper, serving shellfish from the Scotland and seafood from the east coast of England, dine in one of the original Pullman carriages, vintage 1932, from the Brighton Belle, or in the attractive

continued

Conservatory restaurant (complete with huge grapevine). Seasonal game and Aberdeen Angus steaks are the featured alternatives on the extensive carte. The Pagenham family have nurtured the restaurant's reputation, which extends far and wide, for 37 years now.

OPEN: 12–2.30 6–10.30 Closed: 24–26 Dec

BAR MEALS: Lunch served: Mon–Fri 12–2 Av main course £5.75

RESTAURANT: Lunch served: Mon–Fri 12–2 Dinner served: Mon–Sat 6.45–10.15 Av 3 course à la carte £25

BREWERY/COMPANY: Free House

PRINCIPAL BEERS: Theakstons Best, John Smiths Smooth,.

FACILITIES: Garden: Food served outside. Patio area

NOTES: Parking 80

MUKER   Map 09 SD99

The Farmers Arms

DL11 6QG ☎ 01748 886297

Dir: From Richmond take A6108 towards Leyburn, turn R onto B6270

Traditional village local at the head of beautiful Swaledale; popular with walkers on the Pennine Way and the Coast to Coast route. Sit by the open fire in the simply furnished main bar and accompany a pint of Theakstons with a decent bar meal. Try home-made steak pie, grilled rainbow trout, spinach and mushroom lasagne or a steak.

OPEN: 11–3.00 7–11 **BAR MEALS:** Lunch served: all week Dinner served: all week 12–2.30 7–8.50 Av main course £6

BREWERY/COMPANY: Free House

PRINCIPAL BEERS: Theakston Best & Old Peculiar, John Smith's, Nimmo's XXXX. **FACILITIES:** Children welcome Garden: Patio, food served outdoors Dogs allowed (water provided) **NOTES:** Parking 6 No credit cards

---

NUNNINGTON   Map 09 SE67

The Royal Oak Inn ♀

Church St YO62 5US ☎ 01439 748271 📠 01439 748271

Dir: Close to church at the opposite end of the village to Nunnington hall(National Trust)

A solid stone pub in this sleepy rural backwater in the Howardian Hills, a short drive from the North Yorkshire Moors. The immaculate open-plan bar is furnished with scrubbed pine and decorated with farming memorabilia, just the place for a pint of Theakstons and a bite to eat. An extensive range of filling bar food plus specials like pork medallion in a cream, white wine and Pernod sauce, and goats' cheese and leek tart.

OPEN: 12–2.30 6.30–11 **BAR MEALS:** Lunch served: Tue–Sun Dinner served: Tue–Sun 12–2 6.30–9.50 Av main course £8

RESTAURANT: Lunch served: Tue–Sun Dinner served: Tue–Sun 12–2 6.30–9 Av 3 course à la carte £17.50 **BREWERY/COMPANY:** Free House **PRINCIPAL BEERS:** Theakston Best, Theakston Old Peculier, Carlsberg-Tetley Tetley Bitter. **NOTES:** Parking 18

Room prices show the minimum double and single rates charged. Room rates in hotels and B&B's often vary depending on the facilities, so be sure to check prices with the establishment before booking.

England

OSMOTHERLEY
Map 09 SE49

Three Tuns Inn ♦♦♦ ◉ 🍽 ☿
South End DL6 3BN ☎ 01609 883301 📠 01609 883301
Dir: Off A19

Perched on the western edge of the North Yorks Moors, Osmotherley is the starting point for the famous 40-mile Lyke Wake Walk. Standing among 17th-century stone cottages, the exterior of the inn is bright with hanging baskets in the summer and there is a rear garden to make the most of the views. The interior is surprisingly modern and the atmosphere relaxed. Fresh seasonal pruduce drives the menus and customers will usually be offered four or more seafood/fish main courses, an example being grilled salmon, foie gras mash, spiced lentils and pineapple syrup.There are vegetarian and meat options such as pot roast lamb rump with roasted Tuscan vegetables. Booking is advisable for Sunday lunch.
OPEN: 12–3 6–11 **BAR MEALS:** Lunch served: all week Dinner served: all week 12–2.30 6–10.30 Av main course £12
RESTAURANT: Lunch served: all week Dinner served: all week 12–2.30 6–9.30 Av 3 course à la carte £22
BREWERY/COMPANY: Free House
PRINCIPAL BEERS: Theakston Best. **FACILITIES:** Children welcome Garden: Food served outside, patio area **NOTES:** Parking 4 **ROOMS:** 7 bedrooms 7 en suite from s£49 d£65

PATELEY BRIDGE
Map 09 SE16

Pick of the Pubs

The Sportmans Arms Hotel ☿
Wath-in-Nidderdale HG3 5PP
☎ 01423 711306 📠 01423 712524
Dir: A39/B6451, restaurant 2m N of Pateley Bridge
Beloved of sportsmen from far and wide, this special pub and small hotel is in a conservation village in one of the most beautiful areas of the Yorkshire Dales. A custom-built kitchen, run by chef/patron Ray Carter for nearly a quarter century, now assisted by his son, lies at the heart of the operation with fresh fish from Whitby daily, local beef, lamb, pork and game all contributing in turn to his seasonal menus. True to the best pub traditions, real ales and fine wines accompany blackboard dishes served in an informal bar and daily restaurant menus that tempt all-comers. Monkfish provençale and fresh pasta and warm goats' cheese on carmelised red onions are typically offered in advance of Scarborough Woof in a mustard and basil crust, breast of ducking with beetroot, ham and tongue. Summer pudding on warm days, sticky toffee on colder ones and a celebrated Wath rarebit with anchovy and capers show that the kitchen has lost none of its flair.

OPEN: 12–2.30 7–11 Closed: 25 Dec **BAR MEALS:** Lunch served: all week Dinner served: all week 12–2 7–9 Av main course £9.50 **RESTAURANT:** Lunch served: all week Dinner served: all week 12–2 7–9.30 Av 3 course à la carte £24
BREWERY/COMPANY: Free House
PRINCIPAL BEERS: Younger, Theakston, John Smiths.
FACILITIES: Children welcome Garden: Food served outside.
NOTES: Parking 30 **ROOMS:** 13 bedrooms 12 en suite from s£50 d£80

PICKERING
Map 09 SE88

Pick of the Pubs

Fox & Hounds Country Inn ♦♦♦♦ ◉ 🍽
Sinnington YO62 6SQ ☎ 01751 431577 📠 01751 432791
e-mail: foxhoundsinn@easynet.co.uk
Dir: 3m W of town, off A170
A village green with a maypole, a little river running through its centre, and banks of daffodils in the spring make Sinnington one of Yorkshire's loveliest villages. The inviting, 18th-century coaching inn with its oak-beamed ceilings, old wood panelling and open fires, blends well into this idyllic spot. All of these factors set the scene for a relaxing meal in the well-appointed dining room where imaginative, well-presented modern cooking is served. From a list of chef's specials expect smoked chicken, beetroot and pinenut salad, grilled whole lemon sole with sautéed herbed prawns, and hazelnut treacle tart. Typical dishes from the carte include pressed ham hock terrine with pineapple and star anise confit, steamed herbed pheasant and venison pudding with a rich port sauce, and chocolate and rosemary torte with Armagnac caramel. Ten comfortable en suite bedrooms ensure a pleasant stay.
OPEN: 12–2 6–11 **BAR MEALS:** Lunch served: all week Dinner served: all week 12–2 6.30–9 Av main course £6.95
RESTAURANT: Lunch served: all week Dinner served: all week 12–2 6.30–9 Av 3 course à la carte £20
BREWERY/COMPANY: Free House
PRINCIPAL BEERS: Camerons Bitter. **FACILITIES:** Children welcome Garden: Beer garden, food served outside Dogs allowed **NOTES:** Parking 30 **ROOMS:** 10 bedrooms 10 en suite from s£44 d£50

Horseshoe Inn
Main St, Levisham YO18 7NL ☎ 01751 460240 📠 01751 460240
e-mail: horseshoeinn@levisham.com
16th-century family-run inn with spacious lounge bar and inviting atmosphere. Situated in a peaceful village, this is an ideal base for walking and touring in the beautiful North York Moors National Park. Very handy for the nearby steam railway which features in the Heartbeat television series. Extensive menu of traditional dishes offers home made steak and kidney pie, poached salmon, Whitby haddock and a good vegetarian selection.
OPEN: 11–3 6–11 Closed: 25 Dec **BAR MEALS:** Lunch served: all week Dinner served: all week 12–2 6.30–9.00 Av main course £7.50
RESTAURANT: Lunch served: AllDinner served: All12–2 6.30–9
BREWERY/COMPANY: Free House
PRINCIPAL BEERS: Theakstons Best Bitter, Scottish Courage John Smiths. **FACILITIES:** Children welcome Garden: Beer garden, food served outside Dogs allowed **NOTES:** Parking 50 **ROOMS:** 6 bedrooms 3 en suite from d£56 No credit cards

continued

Pick of the Pubs

The White Swan ★ ★  ⓢ ♀
Market Place YO18 7AA ☎ 01751 472288 ▤ 01751 475554
e-mail: welcome@white-swan.co.uk
Dir: In the market place between the church and the steam railway station
Attractive stone-built coaching inn located in the centre of Pickering, the largest of Ryedale's four market towns and an ideal base for exploring the riches of the region - the nearby Dalby Forest, the heather moorland of the glorious North York Moors and the natural beauty of Yorkshire's spectacular heritage coastline. Pickering is also served by the North York Moors steam railway; from here passengers can begin an 18-mile train ride through the heart of the National Park. Built as a four-roomed cottage, the White Swan was once the haunt of salt smugglers.
OPEN: 10-3 6-11 **BAR MEALS:** Lunch served: all week Dinner served: all week 12-2 7-9 Av main course £8.50
RESTAURANT: Lunch served: all week Dinner served: all week 12-2 7.30-9 Av 3 course à la carte £25
BREWERY/COMPANY: Free House
PRINCIPAL BEERS: Black Sheep Best & Special.
FACILITIES: Children welcome Garden: Patio garden & small Orchard with seating Dogs allowed **NOTES:** Parking 35
ROOMS: 12 bedrooms 12 en suite from s£70 d£70

PICKHILL   Map 09 SE38

Pick of the Pubs

Nags Head Country Inn ★ ★ ⓢ ♀
YO7 4JG ☎ 01845 567391 ▤ 01845 567212
e-mail: enquiries@nagsheadpickhill.freeserve.co.uk
Dir: 1 E of A1(4m N of A1/A61 junction).W of Thirsk
A former blacksmiths and coaching inn dating from the 16th century, located in the heart of Herriot Country. Inside it's all beamed ceilings, stone-flagged floors and crackling log fires, making it a cosy, traditional country pub. Bar and restaurant meals are chosen from a single menu that changes with the seasons to make the most of available produce. Expect starters like kipper and pink peppercorn terrine, and mains like roast hare fillets in a rich game gravy, crusty-topped rabbit and pheasant pie, and thick piece of cod with roasted cherry tomatoes. Irresistible desserts include black cherry and Drambuie chocolate cup, and Yorkshire curd tart with raspberry coulis and crème frâiche. The tiny village of Pickhill near the River Swale is a handy base for touring the area, and the inn offers modern en suite bedrooms.
OPEN: All day **BAR MEALS:** Lunch served: all week Dinner served: all week 12-2 6-9.30 Av main course £9.95
RESTAURANT: Lunch served: all week Dinner served: all week 12-2 7-9.30 Av 3 course à la carte £20
BREWERY/COMPANY: Free House
PRINCIPAL BEERS: Hambleton Bitter & Goldfield, Black Sheep Best & Special. **FACILITIES:** Children welcome Garden: Food served outside, patio, BBQ, Dogs allowed **NOTES:** Parking 40
ROOMS: 17 bedrooms 17 en suite from s£40 d£60

Pubs offering a good choice of fish on their menu

RAMSGILL   Map 09 SE17

Pick of the Pubs

The Yorke Arms ★ ★  ♀
HG3 5RL ☎ 01423 755243 ▤ 01423 755330
e-mail: enquiries@yorke-arms.co.uk
Dir: Turn off at Pateley Bridge at the Nidderdale filling station on Low Wath rd. Signed to Ramsgill, continue for 34M
The Yorke's foundations date back to the 11th century when it was part of a small monastic settlement producing cheese. This striking building is now more a civilised inn and restaurant than archetypal village pub. All are welcome to relax in the stone-floored bar and lounge with easy chairs and open fires, prior to dining in the bistro or neatly appointed restaurant, to which an alfresco dining area was recently added. It is a comfortable environment in which to enjoy creative Modern English cooking, based on best local produce and majoring increasingly in fine fresh fish. A stunning starter might be seared tuna with artichoke, shrimps and quail's egg salad, followed by roast cod on potato rösti with mussels and Choron sauce. Saddle and braised leg of rabbit with asparagus risotto is similarly accomplished, with rhubarb and strawberry gratin to finish. Fine British cheeses and a comprehensive wine list of notable pedigree.
OPEN: 11-3 (Sun 12-3, 6-10.30) 6-11 **BAR MEALS:** Lunch served: all week Dinner served: Mon-Sat 12-2 7-9 Av main course £14 **RESTAURANT:** Lunch served: all week Dinner served: all week 12-2 7-9 Av 3 course à la carte £28
BREWERY/COMPANY: Free House
PRINCIPAL BEERS: Black Sheep Special, Theakstons Best , Scottish Courage John Smith's. **FACILITIES:** Garden: Patio, food served outside Dogs allowed **NOTES:** Parking 20
ROOMS: 13 bedrooms 13 en suite from d£85

RICHMOND   Map 11 NZ10

Pick of the Pubs

Charles Bathurst Inn ♦♦♦♦ ⓢ
Arkengarthdale DL11 6EN
☎ 01748 884567 & 884265 ▤ 01748 884599
e-mail: info@cbinn.co.uk

Located in glorious Arkengarthdale, the most northerly of the Yorkshire Dales, this tastefully refurbished 18th-century hostelry is known throughout the area as the 'CB Inn'. The pub is named after the son of Oliver Cromwell's physician who once owned lead mines in Arkengarthdale. The bar was originally a hay barn and stable for the horses of guests. Looking very different today, what

continued

England

England

RICHMOND continued

strikes new visitors to this delightful inn is how busy it gets. The re-opening of the Charles Bathurst has transformed the local community, so much so that the pub now employs 30 people, all of whom are local. Excellent fresh fish, locally produced fruit, vegetables and meat, and the 'CB Inn' specialises increasingly in local lamb. Dishes on the ever-changing menu may feature shank of Swaledale lamb on lentil cake with juniper jus, smoked haddock with poached egg on herb mash with mustard and mushroom sauce, and skewered tuna on rice with coconut and chilli sauce.
OPEN: 11-11 **BAR MEALS:** Lunch served: all week Dinner served: all week 12-2 6.30-9 Av main course £8.75
RESTAURANT: Lunch served: all week Dinner served: all week 12-2 6.30-9 Av 3 course à la carte £16
BREWERY/COMPANY: Free House
PRINCIPAL BEERS: Scottish Courage Theakstons, John Smiths Bitter, Smooth, Black Sheep Best & Riggwelter.
FACILITIES: Children welcome Garden: Food served outside Dogs allowed **NOTES:** Parking 50 **ROOMS:** 18 bedrooms 18 en suite from s£45 d£55

ROBIN HOOD'S BAY   Map 11 NZ90

Laurel Inn
New Rd YO22 4SE ☎ 01947 880400
Picturesque Robin Hood's Bay is the setting for this small, traditional pub which retains lots of character features, including beams and an open fire. The bar is decorated with old photographs, and an international collection of lager bottles. This coastal fishing village was once the haunt of smugglers who used a network of underground tunnels and secret passages to bring the booty ashore. Straightforward simple menu offers wholesome sandwiches and soups.
OPEN: 12-11 (Sun 12-10.30) **BREWERY/COMPANY:** Free House
PRINCIPAL BEERS: Scottish Courage Theakston's Black Bull, Theakston's Old Peculiar, John Smiths. **FACILITIES:** Children welcome Dogs allowed No credit cards

---

ROSEDALE ABBEY   Map 09 SE79

Pick of the Pubs

The Milburn Arms Hotel ★ ★ ◎◎ ♀
YO18 8RA ☎ 01751 417312 ▤ 01751 417541
e-mail: info@millburnarms.co.uk
Dir: A170 W from Pickering 3m, R at sign to Rosedale then 7m N

Hidden deep in the folds of the spectacular North York Moors National Park, this charming country house hotel

acts as a perfect retreat from the hustle and bustle of the modern world. Dating back to 1776, the family-run Milburn Arms Hotel offers eleven beautifully furnished en suite bedrooms, with a welcoming bar and log fires in the public rooms. Rosedale, once a centre for ironstone mining, is great for walking and you can quite literally begin a local walk at the front door of the hotel. Also close by are some of Yorkshire's best-loved attractions, including Castle Howard, Rievaulx Abbey and the region's famous steam railway. The Priory Restaurant is known for its quality cuisine. Pan-fried ducks' livers and medley of seafood sharpen the palate for local roast pheasant, grilled halibut steak and roast rack of Yorkshire lamb. Steamed date pudding or strawberry brûlé complete what should be a very enjoyable occasion.
OPEN: 11.30-3 6.30-11 Closed: 25 Dec **BAR MEALS:** Lunch served: all week Dinner served: all week 12-2.15 6.30-9
RESTAURANT: Lunch served: Sun Dinner served: all week 12-2.30 7-9 Av 3 course à la carte £22
BREWERY/COMPANY: Free House
PRINCIPAL BEERS: Black Sheep Best, Carlsberg-Tetely Tetely Bitter, Scottish Courage John Smith's. **FACILITIES:** Children welcome Garden: Food served outside **NOTES:** Parking 60
ROOMS: 11 bedrooms 11 en suite from s£39.50 d£64

Pick of the Pubs

White Horse Farm Hotel ★ ★ ◎ ♀
YO18 8SE ☎ 01751 417239 ▤ 01751 417781
e-mail: sales@whitehorsefarmhotel.co.uk
Dir: Turn off A170, follow signs to Rosedale for approx 7m, hotel sign points up steep hill out of village, hotel 300yds on left
High on the western bank of Rosedale, in popular walking country, this former farm was first licensed 300 years ago when part of the building was turned into a 'tap room' for local miners. Views from up here are worth the climb just to relax in the beer garden over a pint of Black Sheep Bitter. The stonewalled interior with open fires, farming memorabilia and relaxed pubby atmosphere provides the setting for good pub food in generous helpings. Fresh haddock and Whitby scampi regularly feature on a specials board that reflects the day's market availability. Alternatives include giant Yorkshire puddings with sausages and gravy, pie of the day, sirloin steak with a choice of sauces and chicken sizzlers Cajun-style. Bedrooms, some in a rear annexe, all have a share of the view: tables in the restaurant for three- or four-course dinner, and Sunday lunches - booking advised.
OPEN: 12-2.30 (Fri-Sun open all day) 5.30-11
BAR MEALS: Lunch served: All Dinner served: all week 12-2.30 6.30-9.30 Av main course £5 **RESTAURANT:** Lunch served: AllDinner served: all week 12-2 7-12 Av 3 course à la carte £21.95 Av 3 course fixed price £21.95 **BREWERY/COMPANY:** Free House **PRINCIPAL BEERS:** Blacksheep Bitter, Special & Riggwelter, Scottish Courage John Smith's. **FACILITIES:** Children welcome Garden: Beer garden, food served outdoors Dogs allowed Very dog friendly **NOTES:** Parking 100 **ROOMS:** 13 bedrooms 13 en suite from s£72 d£59

Most of the pubs in this guide book pride themselves on the quality of their food. This may take a little time to prepare.

---

continued

SAWLEY Map 09 SE26

The Sawley Arms ◆◆◆◆◆
HG4 3EQ ☎ 01765 620642
Dir: A1-Knaresborough-Ripley, or A1-Ripon B6265-Pateley Bridge

Popular, delightfully old-fashioned 200-year-old pub run by the same welcoming landlady for over 30 years. The author and vet James Herriot was a regular visitor and within walking distance is the renowned Fountains Abbey, a World Heritage Site. Varied menu supplemented by interesting daily specials, freshly-cut sandwiches and wholesome snacks or starters. Corn-fed chicken breast in a creamy mushroom sauce, smoked haddock and various casseroles feature among the favourite dishes. There is a delightful garden and good accommodation.
OPEN: 11.30–3 6.30–10.30 Closed: 25 Dec **BAR MEALS:** Lunch served: all week Dinner served: Tue–Sat 12–2.30 6.30–9 Av main course £7 **RESTAURANT:** Lunch served: all week Dinner served: Tue–Sat 12–2.30 6.30–9 Av 3 course à la carte £18.50 **BREWERY/COMPANY:** Free House **PRINCIPAL BEERS:** Theakston Best, Scottish Courage John Smith's. **FACILITIES:** Garden: Beer garden, food served outdoors **NOTES:** Parking 50 **ROOMS:** 2 bedrooms 2 en suite from s£70 d£80

SCAWTON Map 09 SE58

Pick of the Pubs

The Hare Inn ⚲
YO7 2HG ☎ 01845 597289 🖥 01845 597289

An unusual 17th-century inn close to Rievaulx Abbey, whose probable origins were as a watering hole for the monks. Packed inside with old memorabilia and books, Cornish-ware, prints and bric-à-brac, the wood burning stove adds a warm welcome in the bar whilst an old-fashioned kitchen range is a talking-point in the single dining area. Under low-beamed ceilings are flagstone

floors, old scrubbed pine tables and daily-changed menu boards that proclaim wholesome, freshly cooked food. Expect to find fresh Whitby haddock, queen scallops with Gruyère cheese, duck confit with black pudding and truffle mash - and maybe roast suckling pig with cider gravy and apple sauce. A choice of good beers from Timothy Taylor and Theakstons. There is a garden for outdoor eating, herb garden and dovecote and children are welcome. To eat indoors booking is advised.
OPEN: 12–3 6.30–11 (Sun 12–3.30, 6.30–11) **BAR MEALS:** Lunch served: Tue–Sun Dinner served: all week 12–2.30 6.30–9.30 Av main course £8 **RESTAURANT:** Lunch served: Tue–Sun Dinner served: all week 12–2.30 6.30–9.30 Av 3 course à la carte £13.50 **BREWERY/COMPANY:** Free House **PRINCIPAL BEERS:** Taylor Landlord, Theakstons, John Smiths. **FACILITIES:** Children welcome Garden: outdoor eating, herb garden, dove cote Dogs allowed (garden only) **NOTES:** Parking 18

SETTLE Map 08 SD89

Golden Lion Hotel ◆◆◆◆ ⚲
Duke St BD24 9DU ☎ 01729 822203 🖥 01729 824103
e-mail: bookings@goldenlion.york.net
Dir: in the town centre opposite Barclays bank

Built around 1640, a former coaching inn by the town's open market. A terminus on the old railway from Carlisle, it remains accessible by train across spectacular moorland and offers comfortable accommodation to intrepid explorers. An admirable variety of house and daily specials is posted on large blackboards: typically a trio of salmon, haddock and prawns in hollandaise and saddle of lamb with Cumberland forcemeat, mustard mash and honey-glazed root vegetables.
OPEN: 11–11 **BAR MEALS:** Lunch served: all week Dinner served: all week 12–2.30 6–10 Av main course £7.50 **RESTAURANT:** Lunch served: all week Dinner served: all week 12–2.30 6–10 Av 3 course à la carte £17.50 **BREWERY/COMPANY:** Thwaites **PRINCIPAL BEERS:** Thwaites Bitter & Reward + guest beers. **FACILITIES:** Children welcome **NOTES:** Parking 14 **ROOMS:** 12 bedrooms 10 en suite from s£25.50 d£62

continued

SKIPTON — Map 09 SD95

Devonshire Arms
Grassington Rd, Cracoe BD23 6LA
☎ 01756 730237 📠 01756 730142

The Rhylstone Ladies WI calendar originated at this pub, a convivial 17th-century inn convenient for the Three Peaks. There are also excellent views of Rhylstone Fell. A wide range of cask ales plus extensive wine list will wash down a menu that includes steak and mushroom pie cooked in Jennings Snecklifter ale, lamb Jennings, chicken Diane, and haddock and chips.
OPEN: 11.30–11 (Sun 12–10.30) **BAR MEALS:** Lunch served: all week Dinner served: all week 12–2.30 6.30–9.30 Av main course £7.95 **RESTAURANT:** Lunch served: all week Dinner served: all week 12–2.30 6.30–9.30 Av 3 course à la carte £16 **BREWERY/COMPANY:** Jennings **PRINCIPAL BEERS:** Jennings, Jennings Cumberland, Theakstons. **FACILITIES:** Children welcome Garden: Food served outside Dogs allowed (in the garden only) **NOTES:** Parking 80 **ROOMS:** 6 bedrooms 6 en suite from s£29.50 d£45

STARBOTTON — Map 09 SD97

Fox & Hounds Inn
BD23 5HY ☎ 01756 760367 📠 01756 760862
Dir: on B6160 N of Kettlewell
Situated in a picturesque limestone village in Upper Wharfedale, this ancient pub was originally built as a private house. Much of its trade comes from the summer influx of tourists and those tackling the long-distance Dales Way nearby. Make for the cosy bar, with its solid furnishings and flagstones, and sample a pint of Black Sheep or Theakston ales while you peruse the extensive blackboard menu which offers interesting main courses and good vegetarian meals. Expect steak and mushroom pie, lamb and mint burger in a bap, scampi, and mixed bean and apple casserole.
OPEN: 11.30–2.30 7–10.30 (BHs open lunch only) Closed: Jan–mid Feb **BAR MEALS:** Lunch served: all week Dinner served: all week 12–2 7–9 Av main course £7.50 **BREWERY/COMPANY:** Free House **PRINCIPAL BEERS:** Black Sheep, Timothy Taylor Landlord, Theakston Old Peculier & Black Bull. **FACILITIES:** Children welcome patio Dogs allowed **NOTES:** Parking 15

TERRINGTON — Map 09 SE67

Bay Horse Inn
YO60 6PP ☎ 01653 648416
Homely village pub with a good food trade. Game pie, fresh fish and locally produced steaks and roasts are features of the menu, supported by blackboard specials such as pork chop

continued

with Madeira and mushrooms, pheasant in red wine, and salmon with capers and prawns.
OPEN: 12–3 6.30–11 (Sun 12–3, 6.30–10.30) **BAR MEALS:** Lunch served: all week Dinner served: all week 12–2 7–9 Av main course £6 **RESTAURANT:** Lunch served: all week Dinner served: all week 12–2 7–9 Av 3 course à la carte £12 **BREWERY/COMPANY:** Free House **PRINCIPAL BEERS:** John Smiths, Theakstons, Timothy Taylor Landlord. **FACILITIES:** Children welcome Garden: Picnic tables, **NOTES:** Parking 30

THIRSK

Pick of the Pubs

The Carpenters Arms
YO7 2DP ☎ 01845 537369 📠 01845 537889
Dir: 2m outside Thirsk on the A170
Standing on the site of former carpenters' and blacksmiths' premises, the 18th-century inn is in a quiet rural setting. The bar's low beams are adorned with old tradesmen's tools. The imaginative kitchen brigade produces a comprehensive menu. You might encounter twice-baked soufflé with Shropshire Blue sauce, half-a-dozen Loch Fyne oysters and Thai beef pancake with crispy leeks as starters. Follow then with herb-crusted cod on citrus mash, casseroled game in juniper and ginger wine or spinach and Brie filo parcels with tomato fondue.
OPEN: 11.30–3 6.30–11 **BAR MEALS:** Lunch served: all week Dinner served: all week 12–2 7–9 Av main course £6 **RESTAURANT:** 12–2 7–9 **BREWERY/COMPANY:** Free House **PRINCIPAL BEERS:** Carlsberg-Tetley Tetelt Bitter, Timothy Taylor Landlord, Greene King Old Speckled Hen. **FACILITIES:** Children welcome **NOTES:** Parking 50

THORGANBY — Map 09 TF29

The Jefferson Arms
Main St YO19 6DA ☎ 01904 448316 📠 01904 449670

In picturesque surroundings, a beautiful public house dating from 1730 that enjoys a new lease of life under new ownership. It is lavishly decorated in Gothic style reminiscent of an old manor house, and overlooking a patio beer garden with fishpond, fountain and waterfall. Lengthy menus list house specialities such as goats' cheese with Cumberland sauce, salmon en croûte with prawns and a choice of steaks with optional sauces.
OPEN: 12–3 6–11 **BAR MEALS:** Lunch served: Tue–Sun 12–2.30 Dinner served: all week 6–9 Av main course £5.95 **RESTAURANT:** Lunch served: all week Dinner served: all week 12–2.30 6–9 Av 3 course à la carte £18.50 **BREWERY/COMPANY:** Free House **PRINCIPAL BEERS:** Scottish

continued

Courage John Smiths, Black Sheep Best, Theakston Cool Cask, Black Bull. **FACILITIES:** Garden: Food served outdoors, patio **NOTES:** Parking 55 **ROOMS:** 3 bedrooms 3 en suite from s£45 d£60

THORNTON LE DALE — Map 09 SE88

The New Inn
Maltongate YO18 7LF ☎ 01751 474226 📠 01751 477715
e-mail: newinntld@aol.com

A Georgian coaching inn in the centre of a picturesque village complete with beck running beside the main street, and village stocks and market cross. Like the village, the inn retains its old world charm, with its log fires and hand-pulled ales. Freshly cooked food is one of its attractions, with many tempting choices on the menu and specials board: Barbary duck breast, lamb shank, Creole prawns, and pan-seared tuna steak, show the range.
OPEN: 12–2.30 5–11 **BAR MEALS:** Lunch served: all week Dinner served: all week 12–2.30 5.30–9.30 Av main course £7
RESTAURANT: Lunch served: all week Dinner served: all week 12–2.30 5.30–9.30 Av 3 course à la carte £12
BREWERY/COMPANY: Scottish & Newcastle
PRINCIPAL BEERS: Theakston Black Bull, Scottish Courage Courage Directors, John Smith's. **FACILITIES:** Garden: Courtyard, food served outside **NOTES:** Parking 15 **ROOMS:** 6 bedrooms 6 en suite from s£76 d£56

THORNTON WATLASS — Map 09 SE28

Pick of the Pubs

The Buck Inn ★
HG4 4AH ☎ 01677 422461 📠 01677 422447
e-mail: buckwatlass@btconnect.com
Dir: From A1 at Leeming Bar take A684 to Bedale, then B6268. Village 2m on R, hotel by cricket green
After 16 years of running the Buck, Margaret and Michael Fox still strive to maintain the warm welcome and relaxed atmosphere that keeps people coming back. The inn overlooks the village green and cricket pitch (the pub is the boundary), facing the old stone cottages of the village in a peaceful part of Wensleydale, yet is only five minutes' drive from the A1. Cricket isn't the only sport associated with the pub, as quoits are played in the back garden. Live traditional jazz is also a feature on at least two Sundays a month. Five real ales are served, most of them from local independent breweries, and English cooking, freshly prepared on the premises. Specialities are Masham rarebit (Wensleydale cheese with local ale on toast, topped with ham and bacon), deep-fried fresh Whitby cod, and breast of chicken stir-fried in black bean sauce.

OPEN: 11–11 (Sun 12–10.30) **BAR MEALS:** Lunch served: all week Dinner served: all week 12–2 6.30–9.30 Av main course £10
RESTAURANT: Lunch served: all week Dinner served: all week 12–2 6.30–9.30 Av 3 course à la carte £16.50
BREWERY/COMPANY: Free House
PRINCIPAL BEERS: Theakston Best, Black Sheep Best, Scottish Courage John Smith's. **FACILITIES:** Children welcome Garden: Food served outside Dogs allowed (water) **NOTES:** Parking 40 **ROOMS:** 7 bedrooms 5 en suite from s£40 d£60

THRESHFIELD — Map 09 SD96

The Old Hall Inn
BD23 5HB ☎ 01756 752441 📠 01756 753559
Dir: From Skipton north on B6265
Popular Dales inn which takes its name from the 15th-century hall at the rear, built by monks and reputedly the oldest inhabited building in Wharfedale. Good base for excellent walking. The aviary in the garden houses parrots among others. Interesting blackboard menu with lots of fish dishes.

WASS — Map 09 SE57

Wombwell Arms
YO61 4BE ☎ 01347 868280 📠 01347 868039
e-mail: thewombwellarms@aol.com
Dir: From A1 take A168 to A19 jnct. York exit, then L after 2.5m, L at Coxwold to Ampleforth, Wass 2m
The building was constructed in 1620 as a granary, probably using stone from nearby Byland Abbey, and it became an ale house in about 1640. A series of stylishly decorated rooms provide the setting for bistro-style cooking. Local suppliers have been established for all the produce used; at least three vegetarian dishes are offered daily and a good choice of fresh fish, including Whitby cod. Popular options are steak pie and game casserole.
OPEN: 12–2.30 7–11 (closed Sun eve in winter & all Mon)
BAR MEALS: Lunch served: all week Dinner served: all week 12–2 7–9 Av main course £7.95 **RESTAURANT:** Lunch served: all week Dinner served: all week 12–2 7–9 Av 3 course à la carte £17
BREWERY/COMPANY: Free House **PRINCIPAL BEERS:** Black Sheep Best, Timothy Taylor Landlord, Cropton Two Pints.
FACILITIES: Children welcome Food served outside
NOTES: Parking 15 **ROOMS:** 3 bedrooms 3 en suite

Restaurant and Bar Meal times indicate the times when food is available. Last orders may be approximately 30 minutes before the times stated.

continued

WEAVERTHORPE Map 09 SE97

Pick of the Pubs

The Star Country Inn 🐷
YO17 8EY ☎ 01944 738273 📠 01944 738273
e-mail: info@starinn.net
Dir: 12 M E of Malton to Sherborn Village, traffic lights on A64, turn R at the lights weaverthorp4 M Star inn on the Junct facing

In the midst of the Yorkshire Wolds, at the heart of a thriving village community and handy for visiting Castle Howard, Sledmere House and Nunnington Hall. This ascendant Star has expanded over the years to incorporate adjoining cottages that house an extended dining area and comfortable accommodation for overnight guests who will relish the abundant peace and quiet of the place, as well as landlady Susan Richardson's consistently good food. The rustic facilities of bar and dining room, with large open fires and a convivial atmosphere are the perfect complement to food that is based on traditional family recipes combined with the best fresh produce of the area - exciting summer salads and game from the moors in winter. Favourite starters include cheddar rarebit with Yorkshire ale and wholegrain mustard, melon prawn and celery salad and baked creamed spinach with melted cheese and nutmeg. Traditional main courses weigh in with casserole of local game, wild boar with black pudding, brandy and apple cream sauce and locally supplied and reared 8oz fillet steak. Seafood and vegetarian options include smoked haddock fishcakes with leek and spring onion sauce, mixed fish and prawn lattice, chick pea casserole with wild mushrooms and asparagus and spinach pancakes. Sunday lunch and regular special event evenings are especially popular.
OPEN: 12–3 7–11 **BAR MEALS:** Lunch served: Wed–Sun Dinner served: Wed–Sun 12–2 7–9.30 Av main course £9 **RESTAURANT:** Lunch served: Wed–Sun Dinner served: Wed–Sun 12–2 7–9.30 Av 3 course à la carte £15 **BREWERY/COMPANY:** Free House **PRINCIPAL BEERS:** Carlsberg-Tetley Tetley Bitter, Scottish Courage John Smith's, Durham Ales. **FACILITIES:** Garden: Food served outside **NOTES:** Parking 30 **ROOMS:** 3 bedrooms 3 en suite from s£13 d£46

WEST BURTON Map 09 SE08

Fox & Hounds
DL8 4JY ☎ 01969 663279 📠 01969 663111
e-mail: alanfish@fox-hounds.demon.co.uk

Close to the heart of beautiful Wensleydale, this 17th-century coaching inn is attractively located by the pretty green in a totally unspoilt village. Traditional pub food is a feature here. Bedrooms.
OPEN: 11–11 **BAR MEALS:** Lunch served: all week Dinner served: all week 11.30–2 6.30–9 Av main course £6 **RESTAURANT:** Lunch served: all week Dinner served: all week 12–2 6.30–9 Av 3 course à la carte £15 **BREWERY/COMPANY:** Free House **PRINCIPAL BEERS:** Black Sheep, Old Peculier, John Smiths, Tetleys. **FACILITIES:** Children welcome Dogs allowed **NOTES:** Parking 7 **ROOMS:** 7 bedrooms 7 en suite from s£30 d£28

WEST TANFIELD Map 09 SE27

Pick of the Pubs

The Bruce Arms ♦♦♦ 🐷 ♀
Main St HG4 5JJ ☎ 01677 470325 📠 01677 470796
e-mail: iwanttostay@brucearms.com
Dir: On A6108 Ripon/Masham rd, close to A1
Just a few miles' drive north of Ripon, this ivy-clad, stone-built free house is situated in close proximity to the River Ure. Expect to find a well-run and informal inn whose exposed beams, log fires and candle-topped tables complement the traditional décor. Cosy, comfortable bedrooms provide an excellent base for touring the Yorkshire Dales, Jervaulx Abbey, Aysgarth Falls and the Hawes Wensleydale cheese centre. Built in 1820, the premises now run as a 'bistro with bedrooms' following extensive alterations in 1998. An extensive wine list underlines the pubs bistro atmosphere, with a regularly changing blackboard menu that displays a healthy interest in the sourcing of seasonal produce. Twice-baked cheese soufflé or smoked haddock with spinach, poached egg and hollandaise as openers may be followed by roast cod with mustard grain mash or a rack of Dales lamb and fresh tarragon. A choice of home-made desserts or local Yorkshire cheeses promises to round off a memorable meal.
OPEN: 12–2 6.30–11 Closed: 1 Wk Feb **BAR MEALS:** Lunch served: Sat–Sun 12–2 Dinner served: Tues–Sat 6.30–9.30 Av main course £14.50 **RESTAURANT:** Lunch served: Sat–Sun 12–2 Dinner served: Tues–Sat 6.30–9.30 Av 3 course à la carte £25 **BREWERY/COMPANY:** Free House **PRINCIPAL BEERS:** Black Sheep Best. **FACILITIES:** Children welcome Garden: Terrace, food served outside **NOTES:** Parking 15 **ROOMS:** 3 bedrooms 3 en suite from s£35 d£50

WEST WITTON
Map 09 SE08

Pick of the Pubs

The Wensleydale Heifer Inn ★ ★ ◎ ♀
DL8 4LS ☎ 01969 622322 🖹 01969 624183
e-mail: heifer@daelnet.co.uk
Dir: A684, at West end of village.
In the heart of Wensleydale and the Yorkshire Dales
National Park. Dating from 1631, the heart of this old inn
is still in its kitchen, where the new owners oversee
preparation of a wide range of dishes, including
vegetarian. Game comes from the moors, fish from
Scotland and the East Coast, beef and lamb from the
dales - all supplemented by local vegetables and fresh
garden herbs. Puddings and bread are baked daily.
OPEN: 9-11 **BAR MEALS:** Lunch served: all week Dinner
served: all week 12-2 6-9 Av main course £7.50
RESTAURANT: Dinner served: all week 12-2 6.30-9.00 Av 3
course à la carte £20 **BREWERY/COMPANY:** Free House
PRINCIPAL BEERS: Theakston Best Bitter, Scottish Courage
John Smith's, Black Sheep Best. **FACILITIES:** Children welcome
Garden: Beer garden, food served outdoors Dogs allowed
NOTES: Parking 30 **ROOMS:** 9 bedrooms 9 en suite from
s£60 d£72

WHITBY
Map 11 NZ81

The Magpie Cafe ♀
14 Pier Rd YO21 3PU ☎ 01947 602058 🖹 01947 601801
e-mail: ian@magpiecafe.co.uk

More a licensed restaurant than a pub, this has been the
home of North Yorkshire's best-ever fish and chips since 1937.
The 250-year-old building is in a magnificent setting below the
ruined abbey, which is 199 steps up the cliff. Serving local real
ales to accompany extensive menus with some three dozen
fishy options from seafood brochettes through to lobster
thermidor - with a nod to meat eaters, vegetarians and
weight-watchers thrown in for good measure.
OPEN: 11.30-9 (closed Jan) Closed: closed Jan
BAR MEALS: Lunch served: all week Dinner served: all week 11.30-9
Av main course £7 **RESTAURANT:** Lunch served: all week Dinner
served: all week 11.30-9 Av 3 course à la carte £10
BREWERY/COMPANY: Free House
PRINCIPAL BEERS: Crompton, Scoresby Bitter, Carlsberg-Tetley
Tetley Bitter.. **FACILITIES:** Children welcome

WIGGLESWORTH
Map 08 SD85

The Plough Inn
BD23 4RJ ☎ 01729 840243 🖹 01729 840638
e-mail: Sue@ploughinn.info
*Dir: from A65 between Skipton & Long Preston take B6478 to
Wigglesworth*

A traditional 18th-century country inn ideally situated for
exploring the scenic countryside, bustling market towns and
attractive villages of the Yorkshire Dales. Originally a working
farm and then an RAF billet during World War II. Imaginative
menu draws inspiration from a wide variety of sources,
including English, European and Oriental, and the quality and
presentation of the food here attracts custom from far and
wide. Expect chicken supreme, roasted pork fillet, spicy potato
cakes and mixed bean and lentil casserole.
OPEN: 11-2.30 6.30-11 **BAR MEALS:** Lunch served: all week
Dinner served: all week 12-2 7-9 Av main course £8
RESTAURANT: Lunch served: all week Dinner served: all week 12-2
7-9 Av 3 course à la carte £16 **BREWERY/COMPANY:** Free House
PRINCIPAL BEERS: Carlsberg-Tetley Tetley Bitter, Black Sheep Best.
FACILITIES: Children welcome Garden: Food served outside
NOTES: Parking 70 **ROOMS:** 12 bedrooms 12 en suite from s£45
d£66

YORKSHIRE, SOUTH

BRADFIELD
Map 09 SK29

The Strines Inn ⌂
Bradfield Dale S6 6JE ☎ 0114 2851247
Dir: off A57 between Sheffield toward Manchester
The inn is set amid the grouse moors of the Peak District
National Park, overlooking the Strines Reservoir. Originally a
manor house, it was built in 1275, though most of the present
building dates from the 1550s. It has been an inn since 1771.
Real fires burn in all three rooms and home-made food is
served. Pies are popular, and giant Yorkshire pudding with
prime roast beef. Speciality coffees are also a feature.
OPEN: 10.30-3 6.30-11 (all day Mar-Sep) (Wkds open all day)
Closed: Dec 25 **BAR MEALS:** Lunch served: all week Dinner served:
all week 12-2.30 6.30-9 Av main course £6.95
BREWERY/COMPANY: Free House **PRINCIPAL BEERS:** Marston
Pedigree, Mansfield Ridings Bitter & Cask Ale, Camerons Strongarm.
FACILITIES: Children welcome Garden: Beer garden, patio, food
served outdoors Dogs allowed (water, meat on Sundays)
NOTES: Parking 50 **ROOMS:** 3 bedrooms 3 en suite from s£40
d£65

DONCASTER   Map 09 SE50

Waterfront Inn
Canal Ln, West Stockwith DN10 4ET ☎ 01427 891223
Built in the 1830s overlooking the Trent Canal basin and the
canal towpath, the pub is now popular with walkers. Nearby
is a marina. Real ales and good value food that includes pasta
with home-made ratatouille, broccoli and cheese bake, deep
fried scampi, half honey-roasted chicken, and home-made
lasagne. Serves over 40 real ales and ciders at its annual May
Bank Holiday beer festival.
OPEN: 11-11 **BAR MEALS:** Lunch served: all week Dinner served: all
week 12-2.30 5.30-8.30 Av main course £5.95 **RESTAURANT:** Lunch
served: all week Dinner served: all week 12-2.30 5.30-8.30 Av 3 course
fixed price £12 **BREWERY/COMPANY:** Enterprise Inns
PRINCIPAL BEERS: John Smith Cask, Black Sheep, Timothy Taylors,
Bombardier. **FACILITIES:** Children welcome Garden: Lawned area
Dogs allowed (water provided) **NOTES:** Parking 30
ROOMS: 1 bedrooms 1 en suite from d£16

PENISTONE   Map 09 SE20

Cubley Hall
Mortimer Rd, Cubley S36 9DF ☎ 01226 766086 ▤ 01226 767335
e-mail: cubleyhall@ukonline.co.uk

Cloaked in history, Cubley Hall has evolved through the
centuries from moorland farm to gentleman's residence and
children's home. Many original features have been retained,
including the restaurant converted from an oak-beamed barn.
The menu offers a choice of pizzas, pastas, fish, chargrills and
salads, notably herbed baked salmon, tuna and mixed bean
salad, and bread and butter pudding.
OPEN: 11-11 (Sun 12-10.30) **BAR MEALS:** Lunch served: all week
Dinner served: all week 12-9.30 Av main course £6.95
RESTAURANT: Lunch served: Sun Dinner served: Wknds12-9.30 Av 3
course à la carte £18 **BREWERY/COMPANY:** Free House
PRINCIPAL BEERS: Carlsberg-Tetley Tetley Bitter, Burton Ale, Greene
King Abbot Ale, Young's Special. **FACILITIES:** Children welcome
Garden: Beer garden, patio, food served outdoors **NOTES:** Parking
100 **ROOMS:** 12 bedrooms 12 en suite from s£50.50 d£60

SHEFFIELD   Map 09 SK38

Pick of the Pubs

The Fat Cat
23 Alma St S3 8SA ☎ 0114 249 4801 ▤ 0114 249 4803
e-mail: enquiries@thefatcat.co.uk
So unique is the Fat Cat, dating back to 1855 and now a
listed building, that it defies the opposition of the larger
chain pubs that surround it. The Fat Cat's aims are to
provide a wide range of micro-brewery ales, to be a place

of quiet(ish) relaxation free from music and amusement
machines and to provide good home-cooked food. The
well-kept hand-pumped beers, usually as many as ten,
include some from their own popular brewery (You can
also visit their brewery visitor's centre.) plus guest beers
and a range of bottled beers from Britain and the continent.
The keenly priced food always includes a variety of
vegetarian and gluten-free fare as well as daily specials to
appease its many regular carnivores. Typically on offer are
braised beef and black peppers, tikka mushrooms with rice
and nutty parsnip pie. Consistently one of the top-rated
urban pubs in Britain for many years - and deservedly so.
OPEN: 12-3 5.30-11 (Sun 7-10.30) Closed: Dec 25-26
BAR MEALS: Lunch served: all week 12-2.30 Dinner served:
Mon-Fri 6-7.30 Av main course £2.75
BREWERY/COMPANY: Free House
PRINCIPAL BEERS: Timothy Taylor Landlord, Kelham Island Bitter,
Pale Rider, Pride of Sheffield. **FACILITIES:** Children welcome
Garden: Food served outside Dogs allowed No credit cards

The Trout Inn
33 Valley Rd, Barlow S18 5SL ☎ 0114 2890893 ▤ 0114 2891284
e-mail: trout@traditionalfreehouses.com
Located at the gateway to the Peak district, just five miles out
of the market town of Chesterfield. The inn takes pride in its
freshly-cooked food. At lunchtime there are filled baguettes
with chips, plus braised lamb knuckle, and broccoli and Stilton
bake. For dinner expect various steaks, monster mixed grill,
seared supreme of salmon, and trout pan-fried in sherry.
OPEN: 12-3 6-11 **BAR MEALS:** Lunch served: all week Dinner
served: all week 12-2.30 6-9 Av main course £6.95
RESTAURANT: Lunch served: all week Dinner served: all week
12-2.30 6.30-9.30 Av 3 course à la carte £12.50
BREWERY/COMPANY: Free House **PRINCIPAL BEERS:** Bass,
Wadworth 6X, Abbots Greene King, John Smiths.
FACILITIES: Garden: Food served outside. Patio area Dogs allowed
(in the garden only) **NOTES:** Parking 25

WENTWORTH   Map 09 SK39

Rockingham Arms
8 Main St S62 7TL ☎ 01226 742075 ▤ 01226 361099
Dir: M1 J36 to Hoyland Common then B6090

Attractive ivy-clad village pub on the Wentworth estate with a
large orchard beer garden overlooking the bowling green.
Folk music is a feature on a Friday night and quizzes on a
Tuesday or Sunday.
OPEN: 11-11 (Sun 12-10.30) **MEALS:** Lunch all week 12-2.30
Dinner Mon-Sat 5-9 **FACILITIES:** Beer garden, food served outside
NOTES: Parking 30

continued

YORKSHIRE, WEST

BRADFORD Map 09 SE13

New Beehive Inn
171 Westgate BD1 3AA ☎ 01274 721784 📠 01274 735092
e-mail: newbeehiveinn@talk21.com

Unspoilt Edwardian gem with several rooms, gas lighting, good range of unusual guest ales. Jazz on Wednesday.
OPEN: 12-11 **MEALS:** Lunch only Mon-Sat 12-2
ROOMS: 13 bedrooms 8 en suite

CLIFTON Map 09 SE12

Black Horse Inn ♀
HD6 4HJ ☎ 01484 713862 📠 01484 400582
e-mail: mail@blackhorseclifton.co.uk
Dir: N of Brighouse
A 16th-century coaching inn once used as a meeting place for the loom-wrecking Luddites, it was later a variety club that played host to Roy Orbison and Shirley Bassey. Interior has oak-beamed rooms and open coal fires. Good home-cooked food has been served here for over 50 years, from sandwiches to pork saltimbocca, spinach, Ricotta and pinenut lasagne, and venison haunch steak.
OPEN: 11-11 (Sun 12-3, 5.30-10.30) **BAR MEALS:** Lunch served: all week Dinner served: all week 12-2.15 5.30-9.30 Av main course £7 **RESTAURANT:** Lunch served: all week Dinner served: all week 12-2.15 5.30-9.30 Av 3 course à la carte £19.95
BREWERY/COMPANY: Whitbread **FACILITIES:** Children welcome Garden: Food served outside Dogs allowed **NOTES:** Parking 50
ROOMS: 21 bedrooms 21 en suite from s£39.50 d£60

DEWSBURY Map 09 SE22

West Riding Licensed Refreshment Rooms
Dewsbury Railway Station, Wellington Rd WF13 1HF
☎ 01924 459193 📠 01924 507444

Trains regularly pass this converted Grade II listed railway station built in 1848 and located on the Trans-Pennine route between Leeds and Manchester. The pub supports northern micro-breweries and is linked to an Anglo Dutch brewery in Dewsbury. A daily-changing menu offers such dishes as ham and cottage cheese flan and salad, carrot cakes stuffed in cabbage served with sweet pepper sauce, and mushroom and parsnip crumble.
OPEN: 11-11 Closed: 25 Dec **BAR MEALS:** Lunch served: Mon-Fri 12-3 Dinner served: Tues-Wed 6-9 **BREWERY/COMPANY:** Free House **PRINCIPAL BEERS:** Timothy Taylor Dark Mild & Landlord, Black Sheep Best. **FACILITIES:** Children welcome Garden: Food served outside Dogs allowed **NOTES:** Parking 600 No credit cards

EAST KESWICK Map 09 SE34

The Travellers Rest 🍴
Harewood Rd, East Keswick LS17 9HL ☎ 01937 572766
Dir: 2m from Harewood House on the A659, 4m from the A1/M1
Mid-way between Harewood House and Collingham, an old hostelry dating from 1641 - once the pack-horse route from York to Skipton and beyond. With spectacular views over the Wharfe Valley, it is equally popular with hikers and riders for snacks and starters of Yorky Puds and seafood pancakes that rub shoulders with battered haddock and a daily roast. 'Travellers' pies and daily fish specials: grilled steaks - and on special occasions impishly punned 'Chateau Brian' for two.
OPEN: 12-2.30 5.30-11 (Sunday 12-10.30) **BAR MEALS:** Lunch served: all week Dinner served: all week 12-2 5.30-9 **RESTAURANT:** Lunch served: all week Dinner served: all week 12-6 6-9 Av 3 course fixed price £8.95 **BREWERY/COMPANY:** Punch Taverns **FACILITIES:** Children welcome Garden: Food served outdoors, BBQ **NOTES:** Parking 90
ROOMS: 1 bedroom 1 en suite from s£39.95 d£39.95

HALIFAX Map 09 SE02

The Rock Inn Hotel ★ ★ ★ ♀
Holywell Green HX4 9BS ☎ 01422 379721 📠 01422 379110
e-mail: the rock@dial.pipex.com
Dir: From M62 J24 follow signs for Blackley, L at crossroads, approx 0.5m on L
Substantial modern extensions have transformed this attractive 17th-century wayside inn into a thriving hotel. All-day dining in the brasserie-style conservatory is truly cosmopolitan; kick off with freshly prepared parsnip and apple soup or crispy duck and seaweed, followed by liver and bacon, Thai-style steamed halibut, chicken piri piri or vegetables jalfrezi.
OPEN: 11-11 **MEALS:** All week 12-10
BREWERY/COMPANY: Free House **FACILITIES:** Beer garden, outdoor eating Dogs allowed **ROOMS:** 30 en suite

Pick of the Pubs

Shibden Mill Inn ♦♦♦♦ 🏠 ♀
Shibden Mill Fold HX3 7UL
☎ 01422 365840 📠 01422 362971
e-mail: shibdenmillinn@zoom.co.uk
Nestling in the fold of the Shibden Valley, this low, whitewashed 17th-century inn retains much charm and character. A cosy friendly bar and an intimate candlelit restaurant attract plenty of drinkers and diners and chef Neil Butterworth, having gained experience in some of London's top restaurants, offers a wide and varied selection of dishes. Grilled red mullet, goats' cheese savoury muffin feature among the interesting starters. For main courses there may be grilled calves' liver with a wholegrain mustard sauce, seared salmon fillet with a cider sauce and braised shin of beef with celeriac mash and herb dumpling - among other

continued   *continued*

HALIFAX continued

dishes. Lighter fare includes scrambled eggs with smoked salmon and baby capers, honey roast ham bloomer with home-made salad cream and poached egg and glazed buck rarebit on sun-dried tomato bread. Tasteful en suite bedrooms are thoughtfully equipped.

Shibden Mill Inn

OPEN: 12–2.30 5.30–11 **BAR MEALS:** Lunch served: all week Dinner served: all week 12–2 6–9.30 **RESTAURANT:** Lunch served: all week Dinner served: all week 12–2 6–9.30 Av 3 course à la carte £20 **BREWERY/COMPANY:** Free House **PRINCIPAL BEERS:** John Smiths, Theakston XB, Shibden Mill. **FACILITIES:** Children welcome Garden: Food served outside Dogs allowed In garden only **NOTES:** Parking 200 **ROOMS:** 12 bedrooms 12 en suite

---

HAREWOOD   Map 09 SE34

Harewood Arms Hotel ♀
Harrogate Rd LS17 9LH ☎ 0113 2886566 📠 0113 2886064
e-mail: unwind@theharewoodarmshotel.co.uk
Dir: On A61 S of Harrogate
Built in 1815 this former coaching inn is close to Harewood House, home of the Earl and Countess of Harewood. A good location for those visiting Harrogate, Leeds, York and the Dales. Typical menu includes baked salmon delice, grilled Yorkshire gammon, prime Yorkshire sausages, and nut roast provençale. Lighter meals include salads, sandwiches, baguettes, and omelettes.
OPEN: 11–11 **BAR MEALS:** Lunch served: all week Dinner served: all week 12–3 5–10 Av main course £6.50 **RESTAURANT:** Lunch served: all week Dinner served: all week 12–2 7–10 Av 3 course fixed price £22.50 **BREWERY/COMPANY:** Samuel Smith **PRINCIPAL BEERS:** Sam Smith OBB, Sovereign. **FACILITIES:** Garden: Food served outside Dogs allowed **NOTES:** Parking 90 **ROOMS:** 24 bedrooms 24 en suite from s£62 d£74

HAWORTH   Map 09 SE03

The Old White Lion Hotel ★ ★ 🐷
Main St BD22 8DU ☎ 01535 642313 📠 01535 646222
e-mail: enquiries@oldwhitelionhotel.com
Dir: Turn off A629 onto B6142, hotel 0.5m past Haworth Station
300-year-old former coaching inn located at the top of a cobbled street, close to the Brontë Museum and Parsonage. Traditionally furnished bars offer a welcome respite from the tourist trail. Theakston ales, and a wide range of generously served snacks and meals. A carte features chicken Italia, breast of local pheasant, roasted monkfish, rosemary roasted pork, mix grill Old White Lion style, and cassoulette of field mushrooms among others. Comfortable bedrooms.

continued

OPEN: 11–3 6–11 **BAR MEALS:** Lunch served: all week Dinner served: all week 11.30–2.30 5.30–9.30 Av main course £6 **RESTAURANT:** Lunch served: Sun 12–2.30 Dinner served: all week 7–9.30 Av 3 course à la carte £15 Av 3 course fixed price £13.25 **BREWERY/COMPANY:** Free House **PRINCIPAL BEERS:** Theakstons Best & Black Bull, Carlsberg-Tetley Tetley Bitter, Scottish Courage John Smith's. **FACILITIES:** Children welcome **NOTES:** Parking 9 **ROOMS:** 14 bedrooms 14 en suite from s£46 d£60

HORBURY   Map 09 SE21

Quarry Inn & Cottages 🐷
70 Quarry Hill WF4 5NF ☎ 01924 272523
Dir: On the A642 approx 2.5m from Wakefield
A creeper-clad stone pub with original features, stone walls and beams. Located in the hollow of a disused quarry. Harry Secombe, Roy Castle and members of Wakefield Trinity have visited this traditional pub over the years. Good range of appetising dishes enhanced by daily specials. Expect jumbo battered haddock, home-made steak pie with shortcrust pastry, wholetail scampi and giant Yorkshire pudding among a choice of popular favourites.
OPEN: 11.30–11 (Sun 12–4, 7–10.30) **BAR MEALS:** Lunch served: all week 12–2 Dinner served: Mon-Sat 5.30–8.30 Av main course £3.50 **RESTAURANT:** Lunch served: all week 12–2 Dinner served: Mon-Sat 5.30–8.30 Av 3 course à la carte £7.25 Av 3 course fixed price £7.25 **BREWERY/COMPANY:** Marstons **PRINCIPAL BEERS:** Marston's Pedigree, Mansfield Riding Bitter. **FACILITIES:** Food served outdoors, patio Dogs allowed Food, water, shelter **NOTES:** Parking 36 **ROOMS:** 4 bedrooms 4 en suite from s£25 d£30

LEDSHAM   Map 09 SE42

The Chequers Inn
Claypit Ln LS25 5LP ☎ 01977 683135 📠 01977 680791
Dir: Between A1 & A656 above Castleford
Quaint creeper-covered inn located in an old estate village in the countryside to the east of Leeds. Unusually, the pub is closed on Sunday because the one-time lady of the manor was offended by drunken farm workers on her way to church more than 160 years ago. Inside are low beams and wooden settles, giving the pub the feel of a traditional village establishment.

LEEDS   Map 09 SE23

Whitelocks ♀
Turks Head Yard, Briggate LS1 6HB
☎ 0113 2453950 📠 0113 2423368
Dir: next to Marks & Spencer in Briggate
First licensed in 1715, this wonderfully preserved, city centre pub was originally known as the Turks Head. The current name comes from the family who owned the pub for 90 years

continued

England

until 1944. Inside are all manner of classic features, including a long, narrow bar with polychrome tiles, stained-glass windows and eye-catching advertising mirrors. Look out for the Dickensian style bar at the end of the yard. Popular menu offers steak and Stilton pie, sausage and mash, Cajun chicken, and red pepper lasagne.
OPEN: 11-11 (Sun 12-10.30) Closed: Dec 25-26 Jan 1
BAR MEALS: Lunch served: all week Dinner served: all week 11-8 Av main course £3.95 **RESTAURANT:** Lunch served: all week Dinner served: all week 12-2.30 5.30-7.30 Av 3 course à la carte £9.95
PRINCIPAL BEERS: Theakston Best, Ruddles Best, John Smiths, Guest ales every week. **FACILITIES:** Garden: Food served outside Dogs allowed (guide dogs only)

LINTON   Map 09 SE34

The Windmill Inn ◊ ♀
Main St LS22 4HT ☎ 01937 582209 ▤ 01937 587208
Dir: from A1 exit at Tadcaster/Otley junction and follow Otley signs. In Collingham follow signs for Linton
A coaching inn since the 18th century, the building actually dates back to the 14th century, and originally housed the owner of the long-disappeared windmill. Stone walls, antique settles, log fires and oak beams set the scene in which to enjoy good bar food prepared by enthusiastic licensees. Expect the likes of swordfish on stuffed vegetables, fillet steak and blue cheese melt with mushroom sauce, or salmon Wellington with a tarragon sauce.
OPEN: 11.30-3 5-11 (Summer all day) **BAR MEALS:** Lunch served: all week 12-2.30 Dinner served: Tue-Sat 5.30-9.30 Av main course £5.50 **RESTAURANT:** Lunch served: all week 12-2.30 Dinner served: Tues-Sun 5.30-9.30 Av 3 course à la carte £12
BREWERY/COMPANY: Scottish Courage
PRINCIPAL BEERS: Scottish Courage John Smith's, Theakston Best, Greene King Ruddles County. **FACILITIES:** Children welcome Garden: Food served outside Dogs allowed (water)
NOTES: Parking 60

MYTHOLMROYD   Map 09 SE02

Shoulder of Mutton
New Rd HX7 5DZ ☎ 01422 883165
Dir: A646 Halifax to Todmorden, in Mytholmroyd on B6138, opp train station

Handy for local walks and the popular Calderdale Way, a typical Pennines pub, next to a trout stream, with a reputation for good ales and food undimmed after 26 years of current ownership.It was associated with the infamous Crag Coiners, 18th-century forgers. A menu of home-cooked dishes from fresh ingredients but with few surprises: carvery roasts, beef in ale and filled Yorkshire puddings,. Good guest ales and good company.
OPEN: 11.30-3 7-11 (Sat 11.30-11, 12-10.30) **BAR MEALS:** Lunch

continued

served: all week 12-2 Dinner served: Wed-Mon 7-8 Av main course £3.99 **BREWERY/COMPANY:** Whitbread
PRINCIPAL BEERS: Black Sheep, Boddingtons, Flowers, Taylor Landlord. **FACILITIES:** Children welcome Garden: Outdoor eating, patio, riverside Dogs allowed (water, treats) **NOTES:** Parking 25 No credit cards

---

NEWALL   Map 09 SE14

The Spite ◊
LS21 2EY ☎ 01943 463063
e-mail: sue@bumby62.fsnet.co.uk
'There's nowt but malice and spite at these pubs', said a local who one day did the unthinkable - drank in both village hostelries, renowned for their feuding landlords. The Traveller's Rest, which became The Malice, is long closed, but the Roebuck has survived as The Spite. Salmon mornay, haddock, scampi, steak and ale pie, ostrich fillet and speciality sausages are likely to be on offer.
OPEN: 11.30-3 6-11 **BAR MEALS:** Lunch served: all week 11.30-2 Dinner served: Tue-Sat 6-9 Av main course £6
RESTAURANT: Lunch served: all week 11.30-2 Dinner served: Tue-Sat 6-9 9 **BREWERY/COMPANY:** Unique Pub Co
PRINCIPAL BEERS: John Smiths, Tetleys, Bombardier.
FACILITIES: Children welcome Garden: Food served outside. Lawned area Dogs allowed (water provided) **NOTES:** Parking 50

RIPPONDEN   Map 09 SE01

Old Bridge Inn ♀
Priest Ln HX6 4DF ☎ 01422 822595
Dir: 5m from Halifax in village centre by church

Just beside a cobbled packhorse bridge this friendly 14th-century hostelry is in a picturesque conservation village. Inside are thick stone walls, gnarled beams and antique oak tables, whilst in summer the window boxes outside are awe-inspiring. The mid-week cold buffet and vegetarian options are popular. At night-time, blackboard options may suggest smoked salmon and prawn pâté, pork and apricot tagine, Toulouse sausages with celeriac mash, followed by blackberry and apple crumble or apple and butterscotch meringue .
OPEN: 12-3 5.30-11 **BAR MEALS:** Lunch served: Mon-Fri Dinner served: Mon-Fri 12-2 6.30-9.30 Av main course £5.50
BREWERY/COMPANY: Free House **PRINCIPAL BEERS:** Timothy Taylor Landlord & Golden Best, Black Sheep Best, Moorhouses Premier Bitter. **FACILITIES:** Children welcome Garden: **NOTES:** Parking 40

◆ Indicates AA inspected
bed & breakfast accommodation

England

ROYDHOUSE   Map 09 SE21

Pick of the Pubs

The Three Acres Inn ♀
HD8 8LR ☎ 01484 602606 📠 01484 608411
e-mail: 3acres@globalnet.co.uk
See Pick of the Pubs on page 559

SHELF   Map 09 SE12

Duke of York ⌂ ♀
West St, Stone Chair HX3 7LN ☎ 01422 202056 📠 01422 206618
Dir: M62 J25 to Brighouse.Take A644 N.Inn 500yds on R after Stone Chair r'about

There's a vast array of brassware and bric-a-brac at this 17th-century former coaching inn between Bradford and Halifax, and the atmosphere is lively and friendly. Traditional pub food includes pot roast lamb, hazelnut roasted pork, monkfish with saffron sauce, chicken breast filled with Brie, and escalope of salmon. The pub carries a wide range of cask ales. The bedroom accommodation includes two in converted weavers' cottages.
OPEN: 11.30–11.30 (Sun 12–10.30) **BAR MEALS:** Lunch served: all week Dinner served: all week 12–2.30 5–9.30 Av main course £6.95 **RESTAURANT:** Lunch served: all week Dinner served: all week 12–2.30 5–9.30 Av 3 course à la carte £12 **BREWERY/COMPANY:** Whitbread **PRINCIPAL BEERS:** Taylor Best & Landlord + guest beer.
FACILITIES: Children welcome Garden: Patio, food served outside **NOTES:** Parking 30 **ROOMS:** 7 bedrooms 7 en suite

SOWERBY BRIDGE   Map 09 SE02

Pick of the Pubs

The Millbank at Millbank
HX6 3DY ☎ 01422 825588 📠 01422 822080
e-mail: milbankph@ukonline.co.uk
Dir: A58 from Sowerby Bridge to Ripponden turn R at Triangle
A traditional stone pub and restaurant in a delightful village location with contemporary architect-designed interiors and a growing reputation for the quality of its food. A cosy Tap Room has stone-flagged floors and a range of real ales; the main wooden-floored bar has a contemporary wine bar feel. The dining room, with ex-mill workers' and chapel-goers' seats, complete with prayer-book racks, as dining chairs, has French windows opening on to a raised terrace with stunning views to the gardens and valley beyond. Food here has the emphasis on local fresh produce cooked to bring out its goodness and flavour. Among the popular starters are terrine of venison with chutney and mushroom tagliatelle with truffle oil and Gorgonzola. Main courses are equally imaginative, with the likes of ham hock with colcannon potatoes and mustard sauce and roast breast of Yorkshire pheasant with casserole of leg, bacon, shallots, chestnuts, red wine and Cassis. To follow, try the port and claret jelly in shortbread or the chocolate tart with orange custard. Eclectic wine list and a choice of alternative lighter meals.
OPEN: 12–3 6–11 **BAR MEALS:** Lunch served: Wed–Sun 12–2 Dinner served: Tues–Sat 6–10 Av main course £10.90 **RESTAURANT:** Lunch served: Wed–Sun 12–2 Dinner served: Tues–Sun 6–10 Av 3 course à la carte £20 Av 2 course fixed price £10.95 **BREWERY/COMPANY:** Free House **PRINCIPAL BEERS:** Timothy Taylor Landlord, Carlsberg-Tetley Tetley Bitter. **FACILITIES:** Children welcome Garden: Food served outside Dogs allowed

THORNTON   Map 09 SE03

Pick of the Pubs

Ring O'Bells ⌂ ♀
212 Hilltop Rd BD13 3QL ☎ 01274 832296 📠 01274 831707
e-mail: ringobells@btinternet.com
See Pick of the Pubs on page 560

TODMORDEN   Map 09 SD92

Staff of Life ♦♦♦ ⌂
550 Burnley Rd OL14 8JF ☎ 01706 812929 📠 01706 813773
e-mail: staff.of.life@Talk21.com
Dir: on A646 between Halifax & Burnley

Situated amidst dramatic Pennine scenery, this quaint stone-built inn dates back to 1838 and was once the centre of a thriving mill community. Well known for its wide range of curries. The basic menu is augmented by daily specials and typical dishes include steaks, rack of lamb, Cumberland sausage with egg and chips, teriyaki tuna, or broccoli and cream cheese bake. The pleasant, attractively decorated bedrooms offer value for money accommodation.
OPEN: 12–4 7–11 (Sat 12–11, Sun 12–4, 7–10.30) Closed: 25 Dec **BAR MEALS:** Lunch served: Sat–Sun 12–2.30 Dinner served: Tue–Sun 7–9.30 Av main course £7 **BREWERY/COMPANY:** Free House **PRINCIPAL BEERS:** Taylor Landlord, Golden Best, Best Bitter. **FACILITIES:** Children welcome Garden: Food served outside. Patio area Dogs allowed (water provided) **NOTES:** Parking 26 **ROOMS:** 3 bedrooms 3 en suite from s£24 d£36

THE DALES WAY

Heading for Ribblehead, the 84-mile Dales Way crosses windswept hills and tracts of rugged moorland deep in Pennine adventure country. This is a harsh environment of wild summits and high, breathtaking fells that seems a world away from the softer, more intimate surroundings of the lower Dales. After the long haul, savour a rewarding pint and something to eat perhaps at the Sun Inn in historic Dent, the only village in Dentdale. Next, make for the Dalesman Country Inn in the busy little town of Sedbergh, acknowledged as the western gateway to the Yorkshire Dales. Beyond the M6, the walk skirts Kendal, but you might like to visit the town and take a break at the aptly-named Gateway Inn in Crook Road. Continuing across country, the Dales Way finally comes to a halt at Bowness on the shores of Lake Windermere.

OPEN: 12-3 7-11 (Sat 7-11 only)
BAR MEALS: L served all week.
D served all week. 12-2 7-9.45
Av main course £11.95
RESTAURANT: L served Sun-Fri.
D served all week. 12-2 7-9.45 Av
cost 3 course £25
BREWERY/COMPANY: FREE
HOUSE
PRINCIPAL BEERS: Timothy
Taylor Landlord, Adnams Bitter,
Bank's Bitter
FACILITIES: Children welcome
NOTES: Parking 100
ROOMS: 20 en suite Double room
from £75 Single room from £55

The Three Acres Inn

♀
Roydhouse,
West Yorkshire, HD8 8LR
☎ 01484 602606 🖷 01484 608411
e-mail: 3acres@globalnet.co.uk
Dir: From Huddersfield take A629 then
B6116,take L turn for village

Another long standing favourite, this charming inn has been in the same hands for over thirty years. Located just ten minutes from the M1 (J38), it has commanding views over the Pennines and is noted for its quality food and warm hospitality.

It's a warm, inviting setting – the sort of place you'll want to linger, sampling dishes from a menu that features many delights. Dine in the bar or the restaurant, a charming and elaborately decorated room featuring bare beams, ornamental plates and a corner filled with antique books. All food is freshly prepared to order, and the menu offers an exhaustive selection of dishes ranging from traditional to oriental. Starters might include French onion soup, hot crispy Peking duck with egg noodles and Chinese greens or potted shrimps served with hot buttered soldiers. Main courses are similarly varied: expect the likes of monkfish stir-fry with chilli, ginger, bok choy and oyster sauce, crispy roast half a Gressingham duck with Bramley apple purée and sage and onion stuffing, or deep-fried haddock in beer batter with 'proper chips'. For dessert how about coconut créme brûlée with hot caramelised pineapple and vanilla ice cream or the 'hot sticky pudding of the moment'. On summer days, step onto the front terrace to make the most of the Pennine views. In addition to first - class accommodation in twenty individually decorated bedrooms in several buildings around the car park, guests are invited to sample the delights of 'The Grocer', Truelove and Orme's much-acclaimed delicatessen. This sells the very best British regional produce and many of the delightful ingredients used in the restaurant.

OPEN: 11.30-3.30 5.30-11 (Sun 12-4.30, 6.30-10.30)

BAR MEALS: L served all week. D served all week. 12-2 5.30-9.30 Av main course £9

RESTAURANT: L served all week. D served all week. 12-2 7-9.30 Av cost 3 course £18

BREWERY/COMPANY: FREE HOUSE

PRINCIPLE BEERS: John Smiths, Black Sheep, courage Directors, Green Label, Black Sheep Special

FACILITIES: Children welcome

NOTES: Parking 25

Ring O'Bells

Situated in Thornton, high on the Yorkshire hills above Bradford, the pub offers dramatic views of the Yorkshire Pennines, stretching up to 30 miles on a clear day. It also offers the opportunity to try some good food with traditional and Asian influences. The pub is convenient for visiting Haworth, the village celebrated as the home of the novelist Brontë sisters.

212 Hilltop Road BD13 3QL
☎ 01274 832296 📠 01274 831707
e-mail: ringobells@btinternet.com
Dir: From M62 take A58 for 5m, R at crossroads onto A644, after 4.5m follow signs for Denholme, on to Well Head Rd into Hilltop Rd.

It is less generally known the sisters were actually born in Thornton when their father was curate there. The stone building, very much a town venue, comprises a 19th-century Wesleyan chapel (hence the name) and two mill-workers' cottages. The unusual interior retains many original features and rumour has it that the ghost of a former priest is still in residence. Both the bar and Brontî Restaurant have a good reputation for their food, offering a range of both traditional and imaginative cooking. Some creative effort has gone into the naming of the carte dishes, which include Billy's Blush, Jason's Creation, and Pauline's Treasures - a plate of sinful chocolate delights, and award winning pies are a feature. Fish is a strength with dishes such as grilled black sea bream served on aloo sag with a caper and cucumber yoghurt, or roasted monkfish with caramelised fennel and watercress sauce. There is a good choice of home-made desserts.

WAKEFIELD   Map 09 SE32

Pick of the Pubs

Kaye Arms Inn & Brasserie 🕮 ♀
29 Wakefield Rd, Grange Moor WF4 4BG
☎ 01924 848385 🖺 01924 848977
e-mail: niccola@kayearms.fsbusiness.co.uk
Dir: from M1 follow signs for mining museum, 3m further on (A642)
A family-run dining pub with a refreshing attitude towards food that is matched by good cooking skills. Located within easy reach of the popular National Coal Mining Museum, this long established inn has been run by Brenda and Stuart Coldwell for 30 years, and for most of that time the kitchen has been in the capable hands of their son-in-law Adrian. The imaginative bar menu runs to the likes of cheese soufflé, steak sandwich, and charcuterie plate. While those looking for something more substantial could try the set lunch – perhaps smoked salmon risotto and marinated chicken breast – or from the menu, grilled fillet of sea bass, salmon and prawn fishcake, wild boar and black sheep sausages, and loin of lamb. There's an impressive pudding list: caramelised rice pudding, or treacle and lemon tart, and a serious wine list.
OPEN: 11.30–3 7–11 Closed: Dec 25–Jan 2,
BAR MEALS: Lunch served: Tue–Sun Dinner served: Tue–Sun
12–2 7.15–9.30 **RESTAURANT:** Lunch served: Tue–Sun Dinner served: Tue–Sun 12–2 7.15–9.30 Av 3 course à la carte £19
BREWERY/COMPANY: Free House
PRINCIPAL BEERS: Scottish Courage John Smiths, Theakstons Best. **NOTES:** Parking 50

The Spindle Tree 🕮 ♀
467 Aberford Rd WF3 4AJ ☎ 01924 824810 🖺 01924 824810
Dir: from M62 Eastbound, R at rdbt to Stanley, pub 1m down on R
Traditional pub close to Wakefield town centre serving a varied, good quality pub menu throughout the unpretentious interior. Pubmaster.

WIDDOP   Map 09 SD93

Pack Horse Inn
HX7 7AT ☎ 01422 842803 🖺 01422 842803
Dir: Off A646 & A6033
A converted laithe farmhouse dating from the 1600s, 300 yards from the Pennine Way and popular with walkers. Bedrooms.

THE CHANNEL ISLANDS

GUERNSEY

CATEL

Hotel Hougue du Pommier ★ ★ 🌐 🕮 ♀ NEW
Hougue Du Pommier Rd GY5 7FQ
☎ 01481 256531 🖺 01481 256260
Translated as 'Apple Tree Hill', this lovely inn dating back to 1712 stands amid ten acres of orchards from which cider was once produced. Quiet bedrooms offer a good range of family accommodation overlooking well-kept gardens. Bar food includes lunchtime sandwiches and main dishes such as steak, kidney and ale pie, beer-battered cod and char-flamed prime

sirloin steaks, with the day's specials and desserts displayed on chalkboards.
OPEN: 11–2.15 6–11.45 **BAR MEALS:** Lunch served: all week 12–1.45 Dinner served: Mon–Sun 6.30–8.45 Av main course £7
RESTAURANT: Dinner served: Mon–Sat 6.30–9 Av 3 course à la carte £25 Av 3 course fixed price £17.25 **PRINCIPAL BEERS:** Scottish Courage John Smith's. **FACILITIES:** Children welcome Garden: Food served outside **NOTES:** Parking 60 **ROOMS:** 43 bedrooms 43 en suite from s£34 d£68

JERSEY

ST AUBIN

Old Court House Inn 🕮 NEW
St Aubin's Harbour JE3 8AB ☎ 01534 746433 🖺 01534 745103
e-mail: ochstaubins@jerseymail.co.uk
A combination of 15th-century courthouse and 17th-century merchant's harbourside home, steeped in history and tastefully converted and restored to 21st-century standards. The cosmopolitan restaurant specialises in fresh seafood – Thai tian of crab, local lobster, sea bass, salmon and mussels – while the bistro serves braised shank of lamb, pan-fried medallions of wild venison, and chargrilled steak fillet. There are sunny, sheltered terraces and courtyard for alfresco dining, and smart en suite bedrooms.
BREWERY/COMPANY: Free House No credit cards

ST BRELADE

La Pulente Hotel ♀ NEW
La Route de la Pulente JE3 8HG
☎ 01534 744487 🖺 01534 498846
Dir: West side of the Island, along the 5 mile road.
Amazing sea views, open fires on chilly days and a welcoming atmosphere at all times are promised at this friendly pub. The artistic bar and rustic restaurant are complemented in summer by a balcony and terrace where freshly-caught fish can be enjoyed along with choices from the specials menu: lobster, crab salad, fruits de mer, and perhaps garlic and herb chicken on cracked-pepper mash, green vegetable stew, and Caesar salad.
OPEN: 11–11 **BAR MEALS:** Lunch served: all week 12–2.30 Dinner served: Mon–Sat 6–8.30 **RESTAURANT:** Lunch served: all week 12–2.30 Dinner served: Mon–Sat 6–8.30 Av 3 course à la carte £15 Av 3 course fixed price £12.95 **PRINCIPAL BEERS:** Interbrew Bass Bitter, Scottish Courage Theakstons Best. **FACILITIES:** Children welcome **NOTES:** Parking 30

The AA Hotel Guide **2003**

Britain's best-selling hotel guide for all your business and leisure needs.

 **Lifestyle Guides**   *www.theAA.com*

continued

England

Need to find the perfect place?

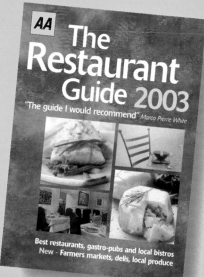

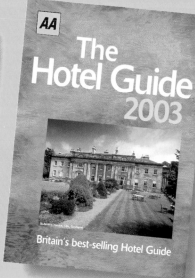

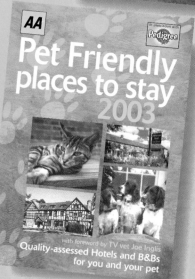

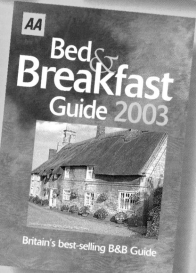

Scotland

Pub of The Year for Scotland

The Old Inn,
Gairloch, Highland

SCOTLAND
ABERDEEN CITY

ABERDEEN   Map 13 NJ90

Old Blackfriars
52 Castle Gate AB11 5BB ☎ 01224 581922 ▤ 01224 582153

Traditional city centre pub with many fascinating features, including stone and wooden interior and original stained glass window display. Built on the site of property owned by Blackfriars Dominican monks. Battered haddock, home-made beefburgers and mixed grills feature among the popular bar meals. Breakfasts, toasted sandwiches and freshly prepared daily specials.
OPEN: 11-12 (Sun 12.30-11) Closed: Dec 25 & Jan 1
BAR MEALS: Lunch served: all week Dinner served: all week 11-9 Av main course £5 **BREWERY/COMPANY:** Belhaven
PRINCIPAL BEERS: Belhaven 80/-, Belhaven St Andrews, Caledonian IPA, Caledonian 80/-. **FACILITIES:** Children welcome Children's licence

Prince of Wales ♀
7 St Nicholas Ln AB10 1HF ☎ 01224 640597
Dir: city centre
Historic city centre pub, dating back to 1850 and boasting the longest bar in Aberdeen, extending to 60 feet. Originally known as the Café Royal, the pub was renamed in 1856. Wide range of real ales, a selection of freshly made soups, filled baguettes and baked potatoes, and home-cooked food that might include breaded haddock, chicken pie, baked potatoes, roast pork with apricot stuffing and local turbot.
OPEN: 10am-midnight (Sunday 12.30-11) **BAR MEALS:** Lunch served: all week 11.30-2 Av main course £4.70
BREWERY/COMPANY: Free House
PRINCIPAL BEERS: Theakstons Old Peculiar, Interbrew Bass, Caledonian 80/-,Timothy Taylor Landlord.

ABERDEENSHIRE

MARYCULTER   Map 13 NO89

Old Mill Inn
South Deeside Rd AB12 5FX ☎ 01224 733212 ▤ 01224 732884
e-mail: Info@oldmillinn.co.uk
Dir: 5m W of Aberdeen on B9077
A 200-year-old country inn on the edge of the River Dee, just 10 minutes' from Aberdeen city centre. Fresh local produce is a feature of the menu, with interesting dishes such as sirloin steak chasseur, supreme of chicken Rob Roy, king prawn jambolaya, or leek and cheese parcels.

continued

OPEN: 11-11 **BAR MEALS:** Lunch served: all week Dinner served: all week 12-2 5.30-9.30 Av main course £5.50 **RESTAURANT:** Lunch served: all week Dinner served: all week 12-2 5.30-9.30 Av 3 course à la carte £15.50 Av 2 course fixed price £5
BREWERY/COMPANY: Free House **PRINCIPAL BEERS:** Interbrew Bass, Caledonian Deuchers IPA. **FACILITIES:** Children welcome Garden: Food served outdoors, patio **NOTES:** Parking 100
ROOMS: 7 bedrooms 7 en suite from s£40 d£50

NETHERLEY   Map 13 NO89

Pick of the Pubs

Lairhillock Inn and Restaurant ♀
AB39 3QS ☎ 01569 730001 ▤ 01569 731175
e-mail: lairhillock@breathemail.net
Dir: From Aberdeen take A90 turn R at Durris turning
For over 200 years the Lairhillock has offered traditional hospitality right in the heart of magnificent countryside, yet nowadays it is only a 15 minute drive south from Aberdeen. The landscape has changed little over the centuries, and there are many opportunities for walking and sightseeing. There are breathtaking views from the pub's recently added conservatory, which is already a favourite with families. The Lairhillock boasts a good choice of well-kept real ales and malt whiskies, and the central log fire is a popular feature in the lounge. Freshly prepared food is served in both bars, with menus based on local produce. Lunchtime brings baguettes, ciabatta steak sandwiches and salads, and there is a children's menu, too. Diners might start with seafood chowder or grilled wood pigeon, followed by steak and ale pie, grilled salmon fillet or crispy vegetable stir-fry.
OPEN: 11-2.30 5-11 (Sat 11-12, Sun 12-11) Closed: 26 Dec, 1-2 Jan **BAR MEALS:** Lunch served: all week Dinner served: all week 12-2 6-9.30 **RESTAURANT:** Lunch served: Sun 12-2 Dinner served: Wed-Mon 7-11 Av 3 course à la carte £25
BREWERY/COMPANY: Free House
PRINCIPAL BEERS: Timothy Taylor Landlord, Marston's Pedigree, Fuller's London Pride. **FACILITIES:** Children welcome Garden: Food served outside Dogs allowed **NOTES:** Parking 100

OLDMELDRUM   Map 13 NJ82

The Redgarth ♀
Kirk Brae AB51 0DJ ☎ 01651 872353
Dir: On A947
There are magnificent views of Bennachie and the surrounding countryside from this friendly establishment, which serves a range of cask conditioned ales along with dishes prepared on the premises using fresh local produce. Examples are Cajun salmon, roast Aberdeen Angus with Yorkshire pudding, mixed game pie, spinach and Ricotta parcel, and poached haddock mornay.
OPEN: 11-2.30 5-11 (Fri-Sat 12pm) Closed: Dec 25-26 Jan 1-3
BAR MEALS: Lunch served: all week Dinner served: all week 12-2 5-9 Av main course £5.25 **RESTAURANT:** Lunch served: all week Dinner served: all week 12-2 5-9 Av 3 course à la carte £15
BREWERY/COMPANY: Free House
PRINCIPAL BEERS: Inveralmond Thrappledouser, Caledonian Deuchers IPA, Taylor Landlord, Burton Ale. **FACILITIES:** Children welcome Children's licence Garden: Beer garden, Outdoor eating **NOTES:** Parking 60 **ROOMS:** 3 bedrooms 3 en suite from s£45 d£55

STONEHAVEN Map 13 NO88

Marine Hotel 🛏 ♀
9/10 Shorehead AB39 2JY ☎ 01569 762155 📠 01569 766691
Dir: 15m south of Aberdeen on A90
Ironically, this harbour-side bar was built, from the remains of Dunnottar Castle as a temperance hotel in the 19th century. A number of 500-year-old gargoyles are visible on the front. A choice of six real ales is offered - 800 different brews over the years - including Dunnottar Ale especially brewed for the establishment. Seasonal dishes feature game, seafood and fish, maybe venison rump with mustard mash, dressed crab with coriander cream, and herring in oatmeal.
OPEN: 11-12 Closed: 25 Dec, 1 Jan **BAR MEALS:** Lunch served: all week Dinner served: all week 12-2 5-9 Av main course £6
RESTAURANT: Lunch served: all week Dinner served: all week 12-2 5-9 Av 3 course à la carte £15 Av 3 course fixed price £10
BREWERY/COMPANY: Free House **PRINCIPAL BEERS:** Timothy Taylor Landlord, Caledonian Deuchars IPA, Fuller's London Pride, Moorhouses Black Cat. **FACILITIES:** Children welcome Children's licence

ANGUS

GLENISLA Map 13 NO26

Pick of the Pubs

The Glenisla Hotel 🛏
PH11 8PH ☎ 01575 582223 📠 01575 582223
e-mail: glenislahotel@sol.co.uk
Dir: On B954

Fine Scottish hospitality is a feature of this lovely whitewashed 17th-century coaching inn, with its six cosy en suite bedrooms. The hotel stands in a magnificent glen on the former route from Perth to Braemar, where the nearby River Isla flows down towards the falls at Reekie Linn. Visitors mingle with locals around a roaring log fire in the convivial, oak-beamed bar where Inveralmond Ales and hearty meals are served to guests at plain wooden tables or in the elegantly furnished dining room. Shooting parties are particularly popular in season, complementing the fresh local produce - venison, pheasant, trout and hill-farmed lamb - that are mainstays of the dining room's adventurous menus. Aberdeen Angus steaks are a permanent feature alongside salmon fishcakes, herb-roasted cod with queenie scallops, game casserole and free-range duck breast with garlic, ginger and soy sauce.
OPEN: 11-11 (Mon-Fri 7 Sun 11-Midnight, Sat 11-1am) Closed: Dec 25-26 **BAR MEALS:** Lunch served: all week Dinner served: all week 12-2.30 6-9 Av main course £11 **RESTAURANT:** Lunch

continued

served: all week Dinner served: all week 12-2.30 6-9.30 Av 3 course à la carte £18 Av 3 course fixed price £15
BREWERY/COMPANY: Free House
PRINCIPAL BEERS: Inveralmond Independence, Thrappledouser & Lia Fail. **FACILITIES:** Children welcome Garden: Barbeque, food served outside Dogs allowed Outside kennels available if required **NOTES:** Parking 20
ROOMS: 6 bedrooms 6 en suite from s£20 d£50

ARGYLL & BUTE

ARDENTINNY Map 10 NS18

Ardentinny Hotel
Loch Long PA23 8TR ☎ 01369 810209 📠 01369 810241
One of the West Coast of Scotland's most enchanting old droving inns, dating back to the early 1700s. Local produce is sourced from the surrounding hills and lochs. Expect some changes from the new management.

ARDFERN Map 10 NM80

Pick of the Pubs

The Galley of Lorne Inn 🛏
PA31 8QN ☎ 01852 500284 📠 01852 500284
e-mail: Joschmodo@aol.com
Dir: 25 S of Oban. A816 then B8002

Just a few minutes' walk from the local marina will bring you to the Galley of Lorne, right on the shores of Loch Craignish and with lovely coastal views towards Jura. Originally an 18th-century drovers' inn, the hotel and restaurant have now expanded into a more modern extension. The blackboard, bar and restaurant menus offer plenty of choice, including sea bass, Islay scallops, venison sausages and rack of lamb.
OPEN: 12-3 5-12 (April-Sept 12-12) Closed: Dec 25
BAR MEALS: Lunch served: all week Dinner served: all week 12-2 6.30-8.30 Av main course £6 **RESTAURANT:** Dinner served: all week 6.30-9.15 Av 3 course à la carte £18
BREWERY/COMPANY: Free House **PRINCIPAL BEERS:** No real ale. **FACILITIES:** Children welcome Garden: Patio, food served outside Dogs allowed (water) **NOTES:** Parking 50
ROOMS: 7 bedrooms 7 en suite from s£37.50 d£27.50

> **For a list of pubs with AA Accommodation**
> ♦ **Awards see pages 645-653** ★

Scotland

ARDUAINE — Map 10 NM71

Pick of the Pubs

Loch Melfort Hotel ★ ★ ★ ◎◎ ⌂
PA34 4XG ☎ 01852 200233 📠 01852 200214
e-mail: LMhotel@aol.com
Dir: on the A816 20m south of Oban

In a stunning loch-side location enjoying views across Asknish Bay and the Sound of Jura, with a panorama of mountains in the background, this is a long-standing favourite of visitors to the West Coast whether by land or sea. The building, originally a private house, sits in 26 acres of grounds. The hotel has its own moorings on the loch, and the National Trust's Arduaine Gardens are literally next door. The Skerry bistro, specialising in local seafood, does a fine line in crumbled cod fillets, hand-dived Mull scallops, salmon and prawn fishcakes and lobsters from Luing. In addition to sandwiches and a 'smaller persons' menu, there is a good alternative selection ranging from cutlets of Speyside lamb grilled with rosemary, sausages in leek mash to grilled Aberdeen Angus sirloin steak, or Highland beefburger. In the restaurant, at dinner only, similar fine ingredients are used in more elaborate guises with a seafood buffet on Sundays.
OPEN: 10.30-11.30 **BAR MEALS:** Lunch served: all week Dinner served: all week 12-2.30 6-9 **RESTAURANT:** Dinner served: all week 7.30-9 **BREWERY/COMPANY:** Free House **FACILITIES:** Children welcome Garden: Food served outside, Sea views Dogs allowed (water) **NOTES:** Parking 50 **ROOMS:** 26 bedrooms 26 en suite

CLACHAN-SEIL — Map 10 NM71

Pick of the Pubs

Tigh an Truish Inn ⌂
PA34 4QZ ☎ 01852 300242
Dir: 14m S of Oban, take A816, 12m turn off B844 toward Atlantic Bridge
Loosely translated, Tigh an Truish is Gaelic for 'house of trousers'. After the Battle of Culloden in 1746, kilts were outlawed and anyone caught wearing one was executed. In defiance of this edict the islanders wore their kilts at home. However, if they went to the mainland, they would stop en route at the Tigh an Truish and change into the hated trews before continuing their journey. Handy for good walks and lovely gardens and particularly popular with tourists and members of the yachting fraternity, the Tigh an Truish offers a good appetising menu based on

the best local produce. Home-made seafood pie, moules marinière, salmon steaks and locally caught prawns feature among the fish dishes, while other options might include meat or vegetable lasagne, beef or nut burgers, steak and ale pie, venison in a pepper cream and Drambuie sauce and chicken curry. Round off your meal by sampling syrup sponge, apple crumble or chocolate puddle pudding.
OPEN: 11-3 5-11 (May-Sept all day) Closed: 25 Dec & Jan 1 **BAR MEALS:** Lunch served: all week Dinner served: all week 12-2 6-8.30 Av main course £5.50 **RESTAURANT:** Lunch served: all week Dinner served: all week 12-2 6-8.30 **BREWERY/COMPANY:** Free House **PRINCIPAL BEERS:** McEwans 80/- plus guest beers. **FACILITIES:** Children welcome Children's licence Garden: Food served outside Dogs allowed **NOTES:** Parking 35 **ROOMS:** 2 bedrooms 2 en suite from d£45 No credit cards

CRINAN — Map 10 NR79

Pick of the Pubs

Crinan Hotel ♀
PA31 8SR ☎ 01546 830261 📠 01546 830292
e-mail: nryan@crinanhotel.com
Lying at the north end of the Crinan Canal that connects Loch Fyne to the Atlantic, this white-painted Scottish baronial hotel is a must. Beside the harbour where the fishing fleet heads in from the Hebrides to land its spectacular catch, it has spectacular views across Loch Fyne to the hills beyond.
OPEN: 11-12 **BAR MEALS:** Lunch served: all week Dinner served: all week 12.30-2.30 6.30-8.30 Av main course £7.50 **RESTAURANT:** Dinner served: all week 7-9 Av 5 course fixed price £37.50 **BREWERY/COMPANY:** Free House **PRINCIPAL BEERS:** Belhaven, Interbrew Worthington Bitter. **FACILITIES:** Children welcome Garden: Food served outside Dogs allowed **NOTES:** Parking 30 **ROOMS:** 20 bedrooms 20 en suite from s£120 d£120

DUNOON — Map 10 NS17

Coylet Inn ⌂
Loch Eck PA23 8SG ☎ 01369 840426 📠 01369 840426
e-mail: coylet@btinternet.com
Comfortable 17th-century coaching inn located on the shores of Loch Eck at the heart of the Argyll Forest Park. Recently renovated in a traditional style that has left its character largely unaltered. The inn was used as a location in the 1994 BBC film *Blue Boy*, a ghost story starring Emma Thompson. Fishing, water-skiing, sailing and speedboats are available on the loch. Local produce forms a major part of a hearty menu that may include grilled salmon, roast venison, smoked haddock and egg pie, or langoustines.
OPEN: 11-2.30 5-12 Closed: 25 Dec **BAR MEALS:** Lunch served: all week Dinner served: all week 12-2 5.30-9.30 **RESTAURANT:** Lunch served: all week Dinner served: all week 12-3 5:30-9:30 Av 3 course à la carte £25 **BREWERY/COMPANY:** Free House **PRINCIPAL BEERS:** McEwans 80/-, Caledonian Deuchars IPA. **FACILITIES:** Garden: Overlooking Loch Eck, food served outisde **NOTES:** Parking 40 **ROOMS:** 4 bedrooms 4 en suite from s£30 d£60

continued

OPEN: 11-11
BAR MEALS: L served all week.
D served all week. 12-2.30 6-9.30
Av main course £9
RESTAURANT: D served all week.
6-9.30 Av cost 3 course £28
BREWERY/COMPANY: FREE
HOUSE
PRINCIPAL BEERS: Bass
FACILITIES: Garden: food served
outside. Patio area
NOTES: Parking 50
ROOMS: 12 en suite Double room
from £80 Single room from £65.50

Cairnbaan Hotel & Restaurant

Built in the late 18th century as a coaching inn to serve fishermen and puffers trading on the Crinan Canal, this hotel now offers smart accommodation and high standards of hospitality. The eleven bedrooms are all furnished and decorated to individual designs, and provide the ideal opportunity to stay in this lovely area and visit the many local places of interest.

★★★
Cairnbaan, LOCHGILPHEAD PA31 8SJ
☎ 01546 603668 ▤ 01546 606045
e-mail: cairnbaan.hotel@virgin.net
Dir: 2m N, take A816 from Lochgilphead,
hotel off B841.

From nearby Oban there are sailings to Mull, Tiree and Colonsay among other islands and Inveraray Castle is well worth a visit, as is Dunadd Fort where the ancient kings of Scotland were crowned. Visitors need not roam away from the hotel to seek their pleasure, however. You can watch the world go by on the canal, or enjoy a meal in the serene restaurant, where the carte specialises in the use of fresh local produce, notably scallops, langoustines and game.

Loch Etive mussels are likely to appear on the starter menu, along with smoked salmon and smoked trout pâté, while mains like breast of pheasant with haggis en croûte, lobster served thermidor or cold with mayonnaise, and fillet of halibut are guaranteed to revitalise any jaded palate. The choice of daily specials might include loin of tuna with pesto sauce, wild mushroom Stroganoff, or tenderloin of pork in sweet ginger. For a lighter meal from the bistro-style menu served in the lounge bar and conservatory, try fish cakes, or grilled goats' cheese to begin, then Cairnbaan fish pie, or perhaps chicken Madras, followed by profiteroles drizzled with warm chocolate sauce.

Scotland

KILBERRY
Map 10 NR76

Pick of the Pubs

Kilberry Inn
PA29 6YD ☎ 01880 770223
e-mail: relax@killberryinn.com
Dir: From Lochgilphead take A83 south. Take B8024 signposted Kilberry
Way off the beaten track, on a scenic single-track road with breathtaking views across Loch Coalisport to Gigha and the Paps of Jura. The Kilberry Inn is a traditional Highland building of the 18th and 19th centuries, converted from a 'Bat 'n' Ben' cottage with quarried walls, beams and log fires. Today it is an established eating house of fine repute, with letting bedrooms that offer full en suite facilities. The food has to be special to encourage travellers to make the journey, and it is. The dining room is warmly welcoming and family friendly, and everything served here, including bread and cakes, preserves and chutneys, is home made. Menu favourites include Kilberry sausage pie, spinach and ricotta pasta, venison game pie, and pan-fried salmon fillet with lime and parsley butter. It also offers a range of Scottish bottled beer, and over 30 malt whiskies, many from the local area.
OPEN: 11-4 5-10.30 Closed: Nov-New Year
BAR MEALS: Lunch served: Tues-Sun Dinner served: Tues-Sun 12.15-2 6.30-9 Av main course £8 **RESTAURANT:** Lunch served: Tues-Sun Dinner served: Tues-Sun 12.30-2 6.30-8.30 Av 3 course à la carte £17.50 Av 2 course fixed price £12
BREWERY/COMPANY: Free House
PRINCIPAL BEERS: Selection of Scottish bottled beers.
FACILITIES: Children welcome Dogs allowed (water)
NOTES: Parking 8 **ROOMS:** 3 bedrooms 3 en suite from s£70 d£70

KILFINAN
Map 10 NR97

Kilfinan Hotel Bar
PA21 2EP ☎ 01700 821201 ▤ 01700 821205
Dir: Near Loch Fyne
Expect a warm Scottish welcome and good, wholesome food at this old coaching inn. Dine in the bistro or bar, on fresh lamb, salmon, steak, pheasant and duck. Popular ceilidhs are regularly held.

LOCHGILPHEAD
Map 10 NR88

Pick of the Pubs

Cairnbaan Hotel & Restaurant ★ ★ ★ ◉ 🕏 ♀
Cairnbaan PA31 8SJ ☎ 01546 603668 ▤ 01546 606045
e-mail: cairnbaan.hotel@virgin.net
See Pick of the Pubs on page 567

PORT APPIN
Map 12 NM94

Pick of the Pubs

Pierhouse Hotel & Restaurant 🕏
PA38 4DE ☎ 01631 730302 ▤ 01631 730400
e-mail: pierhouse@btinternet.com
By the edge of Loch Linnhe, looking out over Lismore Island towards Mull, the Pierhouse started life as the

residence of the Pier Master, who oversaw the passenger and cargo traffic boarding steam boats that went up and down the Loch. The house came into private ownership after the steam trade disappeared, but the property was only granted a liquor licence around 15 years ago. Extensions were built and now the Pierhouse has a strong local reputation for good quality local lobsters, prawns, scallops and salmon caught by local fishermen within sight of the hotel. Lismore oysters, langoustine thermidor, scampi, and mussels extend the options, followed by seafood pasta, and a giant platter sufficient for two. Non-seafood alternatives include venison, pork or chicken stir fry, sirloin steak, beef Stroganoff and vegetable pasta. There is an extensive wine list.
OPEN: 11.30-11.30 (Sun 12-11) Closed: Dec 25
BAR MEALS: Lunch served: all week Dinner served: all week 12.30-2.30 6.30-9.30 Av main course £13
RESTAURANT: Lunch served: all week Dinner served: all week 12.30-2.30 6.30-9.30 Av 3 course à la carte £25
BREWERY/COMPANY: Free House
PRINCIPAL BEERS: Calders Cream, Calders 70/-, Carlsberg-Tetley Tetley Bitter. **FACILITIES:** Children welcome Garden: Food served outdoors, patio Dogs allowed **NOTES:** Parking 20 **ROOMS:** 12 bedrooms 12 en suite from s£45 d£60

STRACHUR
Map 10 NN00

Pick of the Pubs

Creggans Inn ★ ★ ★ ◉
PA27 8BX ☎ 01369 860279 ▤ 01369 860637
e-mail: info@creggans-inn.co.uk
Dir: A82 from Glasgow, at Tarbet take A83 to Cairndow, then A815 down coast to Strachur
A comfortable small hotel standing on the very lip of Loch Fyne that has been a coaching inn since Mary Queen of Scots' day. Views from the hills above take in vistas across the Mull of Kintyre to the Western Isles beyond. It has 14 en suite bedrooms and facilities suitable for all the family including a safe garden and patio for alfresco summer eating. Use of local produce plays its full part in the preparation of seasonal menus likely to include Loch Fyne oysters and mussels, king scallops and local wild game, venison and hill lamb. The brave might plump for a timbale of haggis, neeps and tatties with whisky chasseur sauce, whilst more conservative choices include fresh Tarbert cod in a light batter or locally farmed beef steaks with chips and perhaps a pepper sauce. Lighter snacks follow equally predictable choices such as toasted bacon, lettuce and tomato - with children's options and home-made desserts to follow.
OPEN: 11-11 **BAR MEALS:** Lunch served: all week Dinner served: all week 12-3 6-9 Av main course £6.50
RESTAURANT: Dinner served: all week 7-9 Av 3 course fixed price £26.50 **BREWERY/COMPANY:** Free House
PRINCIPAL BEERS: Interbrew Flowers IPA, Coniston Bluebird Bitter, Scottish Courage Courage Directors, Marston's Pedigree.
FACILITIES: Children welcome Garden: Patio, food served outdoors **NOTES:** Parking 36 **ROOMS:** 14 bedrooms 14 en suite from s£50 d£100

continued

OPEN: 11–2.30 (Summer 11–12, 1am Fri–Sat) 6–11 (Fri–Sat 5–1am, Sun 5–12)
BAR MEALS: L served all week. D served all week. 12–2 6–8 Av main course £7
RESTAURANT: D served all week. 7–9 Av cost 3 course £23
BREWERY/COMPANY: FREE HOUSE
PRINCIPAL BEERS: Calders 70/-, Calders 80/-,
FACILITIES: Children and dogs welcome. Garden: food served outside. Patio area
NOTES: Parking 20

Tayvallich Inn

Converted from an old bus garage in 1971, this 'house in the pass' as it translates, stands by a natural harbour at the head of Loch Sween with stunning views over the anchorage, especially from the picnic tables that front the inn in summer.

TAYVALLICH PA31 8PL
☎ 01546 870282 📠 01546 870333
e-mail: tayvallich.inn@virgin.net
Dir: From Lochgilphead take A816 then B841/B8025.

The cosy bar with a yachting theme and the more formal dining-room feature original works by local artists and large picture windows from which to gaze out over the village and across Tayvallich Bay. Those interested in the works of 19th-century engineer Thomas Telford will find plenty of bridges and piers in the area. Expect a lot of seafood choices, including pan-fried Sound of Jura scallops, Cajun salmon with black butter, or warm salad of smoked haddock with prawns. Meat choices include grilled prime Scottish sirloin steak, chicken curry and honey and mustard glazed rack of lamb. The truly hungry may try the Tayvallich Seafood Platter that combines prawns, mussels, oysters, smoked salmon, pickled herring and crab claws.

Scotland

TARBERT LOCH FYNE   Map 10 NR86

Victoria Hotel ♦♦♦♦ 🏵 🐾
Barmore Rd PA29 6TW ☎ 01880 820236 🖹 01880 820638
e-mail: victoria.hotel@lineone.net

Centrally situated in a picturesque fishing village on the Kintyre peninsula, the Victoria was built as a hotel in the late 18th century. As well as good food, log fires and friendly atmosphere, the hotel is renowned for its restaurant, which enjoys romantic views over Loch Fyne. Stuffed roast pheasant, seafood cluster, chargrilled salmon, or vegetable ragout are just a taste of the hotel's extensive menus. The new patio is great for BBQs, and is often used for live music.
OPEN: 11–12 (Sun 12-12) (Closed 3-5.30 in winter) Closed: 25 Dec
BAR MEALS: Lunch served: all week Dinner served: all week 12–2.30 6–9.30 Av main course £7 **RESTAURANT:** Lunch served: all week Dinner served: all week 12–2.30 6.30–9.30 Av 3 course à la carte £20 Av 3 course fixed price £20 **BREWERY/COMPANY:** Free House
PRINCIPAL BEERS: Interbrew Boddingtons Bitter, John Smith, 80/-.
FACILITIES: Children welcome Garden: Food served outside. Patio area Dogs allowed (water provided) **ROOMS:** 5 bedrooms 5 en suite from s£29 d£29

TAYNUILT   Map 10 NN03

Polfearn Hotel ★ ★ 🐾
PA35 1JQ ☎ 01866 822251 🖹 01866 822251
Dir: turn off A85, continue 1.5m through village down to loch shore

Friendly family-run hotel at the foot of Ben Cruachen, close to the shores of Loch Etive, with stunning all-round views. Whether you're working, walking, cycling, riding, shooting or fishing in the area, the proprietors will store things, dry things, feed, water and warm you with little formality. Dishes are cooked to order from fresh local produce, notably seafood and steak from the local butcher.
OPEN: 12–2 5.30–11 Closed: 25-26 Dec **BAR MEALS:** Lunch served: all week Dinner served: all week 12–1.45 5.30–8.45 Av main course £8.50 **RESTAURANT:** 12–1.45 5.30–8.45 Av 3 course à la

continued

carte £18 **BREWERY/COMPANY:** Free House
PRINCIPAL BEERS: Weekly changing guest ale.
FACILITIES: Children welcome Garden: Food served outside Dogs allowed **NOTES:** Parking 50 **ROOMS:** 14 bedrooms 14 en suite from s£20 d£40

TAYVALLICH   Map 10 NR78

Pick of the Pubs

Tayvallich Inn 🐾
PA31 8PL ☎ 01546 870282 🖹 01546 870333
e-mail: tayvallich.inn@virgin.net
See Pick of the Pubs on page 569

CITY OF EDINBURGH

EDINBURGH   Map 11 NT27

Bennets Bar ♈
8 Leven St EH3 9LG ☎ 0131 229 5143
With its stained glass windows, hand-painted tiles and a traditional brass and wood look, this friendly pub is popular with the actors from the adjacent Kings Theatre. Established in 1839, Bennets keeps over 100 malt whiskies, has a well-kept cellar and serves straightforward home-made food at a reasonable price. Typical menu features roast, steak pie, breaded haddock fillet, macaroni cheese, salads and burgers.
OPEN: 11–12.30 (Sun 12.30–11.30) **BAR MEALS:** Lunch served: Mon–Sat Dinner served: Mon–Sat 12–2 5–8.30 Av main course £3.85
BREWERY/COMPANY: Scottish & Newcastle
PRINCIPAL BEERS: Caledonian Deuchars IPA, McEwans 80/-.

The Bow Bar ♈
80 The West Bow EH1 2HH ☎ 0131 226 7667
Located in the heart of Edinburgh's old town, the Bow Bar reflects the history and traditions of the area. Tables from decommissioned railway carriages and gantry from an old church used for the huge selection of whiskies create interest in the bar, where 140 malts are on tap, and eight cask ales are dispensed from antique equipment. Bar snacks only are served, and there are no gaming machines or music to distract from good conversation.
OPEN: 12–11.30 Mon–Sat (12.30–11 Sun) Closed: 25-26 Dec, 1-2 Jan
BREWERY/COMPANY: Free House
PRINCIPAL BEERS: Deuchars IPA, Belhaven 80/-, Taylors Landlord, Harviestown Bitter & Twisted. **FACILITIES:** Dogs allowed (water provided) No credit cards

Country Matters

Country occupations and pursuits provide many inns with their names. The Wheatsheaf, the Barley Mow, the Haywain, the Dun Cow, the Heifer. the Plough (sometimes the constellation) and the Harrow recall the farming year's immemorial round. Horses, long essential to agriculture, communications and sport, figure frequently - the Black Horse, the Nag's Head, the Grey Mare and many more. The Bull and the Bear are often related to the once popular sport of baiting the animals with dogs. The dog is usually a sporting dog and hunting has supplied many names, from the Fox and Hounds and the Hare and Hounds to numerous deer (also from heraldry), including the Stag and Hounds, the White Hart and the Roebuck. There are signs related to angling, too, such as the Angler and the Trout, and there are Jolly Cricketers and even Jolly Farmers.

PUB WALK

Ratho
Bridge Inn

A fascinating trail around the Midlothian settlement of Ratho, looking at local landmarks and waterside attractions.

From the inn, cross the bridge to the picnic site, turn right and under the bridge to the Old Change House. The large house on the hill is Ratho Hall built in 1800. Keep ahead, past the walled garden; look over the wall to see the spring where water for the original Pop or Pap Inn was drawn. Slightly further on are the remains of the stables. Continue to the old North Quarry on the right – a huge rock climbing and adventure sports area. Proceed along the canal bank for about 10 minutes to a junction. Flowers on the right mark the site of the stables and stableman's cottage for the quarries. The canal widens out here into Wilkies Basin and you can leave the canal by the path on your right or by crossing the aqueduct, taking the rather steep path on your right. Once on the pavement, walk beneath the aqueduct and up the hill.

At the top, take the road on your left and enjoy the panorama over the Forth Valley. Keep ahead for about 10 minutes and look for a crescent area of wild flowers. Cross the road, take the left-hand gate, following the path round the right side of the field to the trees. At the woods turn right and follow the path to a stile. On the top of the hill several stones mark a Neolithic site. Return back down through the trees to the road and turn right. The second buidingd on the right were the school teacher's house and the school. Walk through the village, passing old cottages and Dalmahoy Road on the right. Stay on the main street. No 85, was once the village co-op. Next to it is a house whose garden wall has an 'Alphabet Stone' – spot the error! The next building on the left is the bowling club. During the 1926 General Strike the hunger marchers gathered round the green and every man was given a loaf of bread by the co-op's general manager. As the road bends left, walk down Baird Road to return to the inn.

BRIDGE INN
27 Baird Road RATHO
Edinburgh EH28 8RA
Tel: 0131 3331320
Directions: From Newbridge interchange B7030, follow signs for Ratho
On Union Canal, with a door at either end so boatman could leave their horse walking along the towpath, enter by one door, down a pint and exit by the other to meet his steed! Now thriving at the heart of the city's revived Canal Centre.
Open: 12-11
Bar meals: 12-9
Children welcome. Garden and parking available.

Distance: 6 miles (9.7km)
Map: OS Landranger 65
Terrain: Semi residential, close to the Union Canal to the west of Edinburgh
Paths: Roads and paths, good surfaces
Gradient: Some gentle climbing

Walk submitted and checked by the Bridge Inn, Ratho courtesy of Ron Day

EDINBURGH continued

Doric Tavern ♀
15-16 Market St EH1 1DE ☎ 0131 225 1084 🖥 0131 220 0894

OPEN: 11-11 (Thu-Sat 11-12, Sun 12.30-11) (food wknds 12-9.30)
BAR MEALS: Lunch served: all week Dinner served: all week
12-2.30 6-9.30 Av main course £5 **RESTAURANT:** Lunch served: all
week Dinner served: all week 12-2.30 6-9.30 Av 3 course à la carte
£10 **BREWERY/COMPANY:** Free House
PRINCIPAL BEERS: Belhaven 80/-, Belhaven Sandy Hunters
Traditional, Belhaven St Andrews/Deuchars IPA, Timothy Taylor
Landlord & guests. **FACILITIES:** Children welcome Food served
outside. Patio area Dogs allowed (on leash)

Bustling bistro and pub close to the castle, the haunt of the
city's writers, artists and journalists. Built in 1710 and developed
over the next few hundred years into convivial eating place
with a cheery downstairs pub. Classic favourites and innovative
modern dishes include fillet of venison, various steaks and
pastas, and sweet potato pie, with traditional pub snacks like
bangers and mash, hamburger and chips, and bruschetta.
OPEN: 12-1am Closed: Dec 25-26, Jan 1 **BAR MEALS:** Lunch
served: all week Dinner served: all week 12-4 5-11.30 Av main course
£4.50 **RESTAURANT:** Lunch served: all week Dinner served: all
week 12-6 6-11 Av 3 course à la carte £16 Av 3 course fixed price
£19.95 **BREWERY/COMPANY:** Free House
PRINCIPAL BEERS: Deuchars IPA, Caledonian 80/-.

Royal Ettrick Hotel
13 Ettrick Rd EH10 5BJ ☎ 0131 228 6413 🖥 0131 229 7330
Dir: From W end of street follow Lothian road, turn R onto Gilmor place
for 0.75m, Hotel on R behind Bowling Green
Period mansion, now a hotel, situated in a residential suburb
west of the city. Classic lounge bar with a two-tiered
conservatory extension serving a popular menu, all day, every
day. Bedrooms.

The Ship on the Shore
24/26 The Shore, Leith EH6 6QN ☎ 0131 555 0409
Set in an area of Leith that has benefited from immense
recent refurbishment and investment, the Ship is a cosy bistro-
style bar bedecked with shipping and nautical paraphernalia,
and is regarded as a popular place for romantic dining. As
might be expected, seafood is a speciality and may include
smoked salmon with lemon, chopped onion and capers,
grilled sea bream, salmon in filo pastry and paupiette of sole
and prawns served on braised leek.
OPEN: 12-1 Closed: Dec 25-26, 1-2 Jan **BAR MEALS:** Lunch
served: all week 12-2.30 Dinner served: Mon-Thur 6-9.30 Av main
course £4.95 **RESTAURANT:** Lunch served: all week 12-2.30 Dinner
served: Mon-Sat 6-9.30 Av 3 course fixed price £17.95
BREWERY/COMPANY: Free House
PRINCIPAL BEERS: Deuchars IPA, 80/-, 70/-.

The Starbank Inn ♀
64 Laverockbank Rd EH5 3BZ
☎ 0131 552 4141 🖥 0131 552 4141
Tastefully renovated stone pub situated on the waterfront of
North Edinburgh,affording splendid views over the Firth of Forth
to the Fife coast. The bar menu typically offers roast lamb with
mint sauce, poached salmon, mince and tatties, a vegetarian
dish of the day, and chicken with tarragon cream sauce.

RATHO   Map 11 NT17

Pick of the Pubs

The Bridge Inn 🐿
27 Baird Rd EH28 8RA ☎ 0131 333 1320 🖥 0131 333 3480
e-mail: info@bridgeinn.com
Dir: From Newbridge interchange B7030, follow signs for Ratho

Dating back to about 1750, the Bridge Inn began life as a
farmhouse before becoming a staging-post during the
construction of the Union Canal in 1822. By the mid-1820s
numerous canal travellers stopped here for refreshment.
With a door at either end of the inn, a thirsty boatman
could leave his horse walking along the towpath, enter by
one door, down a pint of ale and exit by the other in time
to meet his plodding steed. The pub was restored during
the 1970s and is now thriving at the heart of the city's
Canal Centre, famous for its fleet of restaurant boats and
sightseeing launches. Local produce, freshly prepared and
served, is the Bridge Inn's hallmark, which has also
specialised in top quality Scottish meat for over 30 years.
Typical dishes on the imaginative menu are shank of
Lothian lamb, roast Barbary duck breast, Thai green curry
and hot beef chilli. For fish lovers, salmon and asparagus
pie topped with puff pastry or duo of sea bass and sea
bream.
OPEN: 12-11 (Sat 11-12, Sun 12.30-11) Closed: 26 Dec, 1 & 2
Jan **BAR MEALS:** Lunch served: all week 12-9 Av main course
£6.95 **RESTAURANT:** Lunch served: all week Dinner served: all

continued   *continued*

Scotland

week 12–2 6.30–9 Av 3 course à la carte £23
BREWERY/COMPANY: Free House
PRINCIPAL BEERS: Bellhaven 80/- & Bellhaven Best.
FACILITIES: Children welcome Children's licence Garden:
beer garden, food served outdoors, patio, Dogs allowed (guide
dogs only) **NOTES:** Parking 60
See Pub Walk on page 571

CITY OF GLASGOW

GLASGOW   Map 10 NS56

Auctioneers ♀
6 North Court, Vincent St G1 2DP
☎ 0141 229 5851 ▤ 0141 229 5852
Once an auction room known as McTears, this city centre pub
still retains its original valuation booths and is decorated with
plenty of eclectic memorabilia. An ideal location for watching
a big screen sporting event. Good pub grub includes haggis,
neeps 'n' tatties, chargrilled Cajun chicken, rump steak,
baguettes and burgers.
OPEN: 12–12 (12.30–11 Sun) Closed: 25 Dec & 1 Jan
BAR MEALS: Lunch served: all week Dinner served: all week 12–8
12–8 Av main course £3.50 **BREWERY/COMPANY:** Bass

Rab Ha's
83 Hutchieson St G1 1SH ☎ 0141 572 0400 ▤ 0141 572 0402
Dir: *City centre*
Victorian building, recently refurbished, housing a pub,
restaurant and bedrooms. Expect a traditional pub
atmosphere and some innovative cooking. Choices include
fajitas, tempura, Thai curries and organic beef burger in the
bar. The restaurant offers fusion cooking with dishes from the
ocean, the earth and from home.
OPEN: 11–12 **BAR MEALS:** Lunch served: all week Dinner served:
all week 12–10 Av main course £5.50 **RESTAURANT:** Dinner served:
all week 5.30–10 Av 3 course à la carte £22.50
BREWERY/COMPANY: Free House
PRINCIPAL BEERS: McEwans 70/- & 80/-. **FACILITIES:** Dogs
allowed **ROOMS:** 4 bedrooms 4 en suite from s£50 d£50

Pick of the Pubs

Ubiquitous Chip ◎◎ ▨ ♀
12 Ashton Ln G12 8SJ ☎ 0141 334 5007 ▤ 0141 337 1302
e-mail: mail@ubiquitouschip.co.uk
Dir: *In the West end of Glasgow, off Byres Road*
Situated in a cobbled lane just off Byres Road, the 'Chip'
centres on a traditional bar with a open coal fire and the
original byres tastefully incorporated. It continues to buzz,
as it has since 1971, when Ronnie Clydesdale opened up
his restaurant in what was once a stable for the
Clydesdale horses. Traditional draught beers, selected
malt whiskies and first class wines by the glass
supplement a menu that is full of refreshingly bright
ideas. Orkney organic salmon is marinated in honey,
tamarind and ginger then served with mash and spinach
sauce; Loch Fyne kipper comes with garlic and scrambled
egg. Other typical dishes include pan-fried Scotch lamb's
liver with Ayrshire bacon and mashed potatoes and
onions in batter or Aberdeen Angus steak with stovies and
wild mushrooms. In a lofty covered courtyard the main
dining area sports plenty of live greenery, while upstairs is

a brasserie-style eating area offering wholesome Scottish
produce at more modest prices.
OPEN: 12–12 Closed: 25 Dec, 1 Jan **BAR MEALS:** Lunch
served: all week Dinner served: all week 12–4 4–11 Av main
course £10 **RESTAURANT:** Lunch served: all week Dinner
served: all week 12–2.30 5.30–11 Av 3 course à la carte £22 Av 3
course fixed price £24.95 **BREWERY/COMPANY:** Free House
PRINCIPAL BEERS: Caledonian 80/- & Deuchars IPA.
FACILITIES: Children welcome

DUMFRIES & GALLOWAY

AULDGIRTH   Map 10 NX98

Auldgirth Inn
DG2 0XG ☎ 01387 740250 ▤ 01387 740694
Dir: *8m NE of Dumfries on A76 Kilmarnock Rd*
This 500-year-old inn was originally a stopping off place for
monks and pilgrims walking across Scotland, and in later
times became Robert Burns' local, as well as being used for a
time as a blacksmiths. It has an unusual large central
chimneystack with a cross on it, and the River Nith runs past
the front door. Making good using of very fresh local produce,
a typical menu includes medallions of pork fillet, beef braised
in ale, pot roast supreme of guinea fowl, and noissettes of
Dumfries-shire lamb. 5 en suite bedrooms.
OPEN: 11.30–2.30 5.30–11 **BAR MEALS:** Lunch served: all week
Dinner served: all week 12–2 6–9 **RESTAURANT:** Lunch served: all
week Dinner served: all week 12–2 6–9
BREWERY/COMPANY: Free House
PRINCIPAL BEERS: Belhavens Best,. **FACILITIES:** Children
welcome Garden: Patio/terrace, food served outdoors Dogs allowed
ROOMS: 5 bedrooms 5 en suite from s£30 d£50

CANONBIE   Map 11 NY37

Pick of the Pubs

Riverside Inn ♀
DG14 0UX ☎ 013873 71512 & 71295 ▤ 013873 71866
e-mail: information@theriversideinn.fsbusiness.co.uk
Dir: *Just across Scottish border on A7, 1st R is Canonbie*

Just within the Scottish borders, this traditional white
painted inn overlooks the River Esk. Here you'll find
comfortable, attractively decorated accommodation that's
ideally situated for traditional outdoor pursuits like
salmon fishing and golf. After a day out, come back to the
cosy residents' lounge, or relax in front of a log fire in the
bar. Food is served here, as well as in the very civilised
dining room and, with menus created from freshest local

continued   *continued*

Scotland

Scotland

CANONBIE continued

ingredients, there's plenty of opportunity to savour the best of Scottish cuisine. Home-made bar meals begin with spicy tomato soup or potted shrimps, backed up by fishcakes and parsley sauce, Galloway scampi, or ham and eggs. In the dining room, smoked chicken Camembert and apple salad or smoked fish pâté precedes venison casserole or thick lamb chops on the three course fixed-price menu. Marmalade bread and butter pudding or chocolate rum cake are typical desserts.
OPEN: 12–2.30 6.30–11 Closed: 25–26 Dec & 1 Jan, 2 wks in Feb **BAR MEALS:** Lunch served: all week Dinner served: all week 12.30–2 7–9 Av main course £7.50 **RESTAURANT:** Dinner served: all week 7–9 Av 3 course à la carte £19.50 Av 3 course fixed price £19.50 **BREWERY/COMPANY:** Free House **PRINCIPAL BEERS:** Yates, Caledonian 80/-. **FACILITIES:** Children welcome Children's licence Garden: Beer garden, Food served outside **NOTES:** Parking 20 **ROOMS:** 7 bedrooms 7 en suite from s£55 d£70

CASTLE DOUGLAS   Map 10 NX76

Douglas Arms Hotel ★ ★
206 King St DG7 1DB ☎ 01556 502231 ▤ 01556 504000 e-mail: doughot@aol.com
Modernised 18th-century coaching inn, one of the oldest buildings in town, where welcoming open fires are lit in the winter months. Chicken curry and fresh haddock in batter are typical bar dishes, while the restaurant might offer supreme of salmon, or medallions of beef in whisky and mustard sauce.
OPEN: 11 **BAR MEALS:** Lunch served: all week Dinner served: all week 12–2 5–9 Av main course £6.50 **RESTAURANT:** Dinner served: all week 6–9 Av 3 course à la carte £19.50 **BREWERY/COMPANY:** Free House **PRINCIPAL BEERS:** Sulwath, Orkney, Caledonian, Broughton. **FACILITIES:** Children welcome Children's licence Dogs allowed **NOTES:** Parking 18 **ROOMS:** 24 bedrooms 24 en suite from s£45 d£69.50

DALBEATTIE   Map 10 NX86

Anchor Hotel
Main St, Kippford DG5 4LN ☎ 01556 620205 ▤ 01556 620205
Dir: A711 to Dalbeattie. follow Solway Coast sign to Kippford
This family-run small hotel overlooks the Marina and Urr Water estuary, and its Seafarers' Bar is a yachtmens' haven. The area is also ideal for walkers and bird watchers. The menu has a definite seafaring theme, and includes such specialities as swordfish steaks, chicken citron, 'Trawlerman's Burgers', 'Captain's Nibbles' and a selection of vegetarian dishes. Most bedrooms are en suite, and some overlook the Marina.
OPEN: 11–3 5–12 Closed: 25 Dec **BAR MEALS:** Lunch served: all week Dinner served: all week 12–2.30 6–9.30 Av main course £6.50 **RESTAURANT:** Lunch served: all week Dinner served: all week 12–2.30 6–9.30 Av 3 course à la carte £12.50 **BREWERY/COMPANY:** Free House **PRINCIPAL BEERS:** Theakstons, Boddingtons, Marstons, Pedigree. **FACILITIES:** Children welcome Children's licence Dogs allowed **ROOMS:** 6 bedrooms 6 en suite from s£30 d£55

EAGLESFIELD   Map 11 NY27

The Courtyard Restaurant
DG11 3PQ ☎ 01461 500215
Dir: 8m N of Gretna
Former draper's shop built of sandstone in 1913, and converted into a bar/restaurant in 1985, the Courtyard is an ideal stopping-off spot for travellers on their way to the Highlands. The cuisine is traditional Scottish with a French influence, and the kitchen prides itself on making good use of local produce. Try duck breast with cranberry sauce, loin of lamb with sherry sauce, or baked cod with a cheese and mustard topping. Comfortable rooms are available.
OPEN: 12–2.30 6.30–12 **BAR MEALS:** Lunch served: all week Dinner served: all week 12–2 6.30–9 Av main course £6.25 **RESTAURANT:** Lunch served: Sun 12–2 Dinner served: all week 7–9 Av 3 course à la carte £15 **BREWERY/COMPANY:** Free House **PRINCIPAL BEERS:** Belhaven Best. **FACILITIES:** Children welcome Garden: Dogs allowed Kennels **NOTES:** Parking 20 **ROOMS:** 3 bedrooms 3 en suite from s£21 d£38

ISLE OF WHITHORN   Map 10 NX43

The Steam Packet Inn 🐷
Harbour Row DG8 8LL ☎ 01988 500334 ▤ 01988 500627 e-mail: Steampacketinn@btconnect.com
Dir: From Newton Stewart take A714,then A746 to Whithorn, then Isle of Whithorn
There are spectacular harbour views from the picture windows in the attractively modernised bar of this 18th-century inn, and a new 40-seat conservatory dining area adds to the charm. The inn makes good use of seafood straight off the boats on its menu with blackboard specials changing twice daily, with basic lunchtime dishes and a more extensive choice in the evening. Expect whole, locally caught lemon and Dover sole or roast breast of pheasant among the main courses.
OPEN: 11–11 (Winter open 11–3, 6–11) Closed: Dec 25 **BAR MEALS:** Lunch served: all week Dinner served: all week 12–2 7–9.30 Av main course £7 **RESTAURANT:** Lunch served: all week Dinner served: all week 12–2 7–9.30 **BREWERY/COMPANY:** Free House **PRINCIPAL BEERS:** Theakston XB, Caledonian Deuchars IPA, Black Sheep Best. **FACILITIES:** Children welcome Garden: Food served outside Dogs allowed **NOTES:** Parking 4 **ROOMS:** 7 bedrooms 7 en suite from s£22.50 d£45

KIRKCUDBRIGHT   Map 10 NX65

Selkirk Arms Hotel ◉◉◉
Old High St DG6 4JG ☎ 01557 330402 ▤ 01557 331639
Traditional white-painted pub on street corner. Nice gardens to rear. Has associations with Scottish poet, Robert Burns.

MOFFAT   Map 10 NT00

Black Bull Hotel 🐷 ♈
Churchgate DG10 9EG ☎ 01683 220206 ▤ 01683 220483 e-mail: hotel@blackbullmoffat.co.uk
The main building dates from the 16th century and was used by Graham of Claverhouse as his headquarters. Graham and his dragoons were sent to quell Scottish rebellion in the late 17th century. Scottish bard Robert Burns was a frequent visitor around 1790. The Railway Bar is the place for drinking and pub games, while the Burns Room or restaurant are for eating or relaxation. Traditional fare includes haggis, Black Bull hotpot, seafood platter, or tagliatelle carbonara.
OPEN: 11–11 (Thu-Sat 11–12) **BAR MEALS:** Lunch served: all week

continued

Dinner served: all week 11.30–2.15 6–9.15 Av main course £5.50
RESTAURANT: Lunch served: all week Dinner served: all week
11.30–2.15 6–9.30 Av 3 course à la carte £10
BREWERY/COMPANY: Free House
PRINCIPAL BEERS: McEwans, Theakston 80/-.
FACILITIES: Children welcome Dogs allowed
ROOMS: 13 bedrooms 13 en suite from s£30 d£39

NEW ABBEY   Map 10 NX96

Criffel Inn 🛏
2 The Square DG2 8BX ☎ 01387 850305 📠 01387 850305
e–mail: criffel-inn@hotmail.com
Dir: M/A74 leave at Gretna, A75 to Dumfries, A710 S to New Abbey
A small, unassuming hotel set on the Solway Coast in a
historic conservation village close to the ruins of the 13th-
century Sweetheart Abbey. Some breathtaking walks nearby,
including Criffel Hill, and an attractive garden for summer
enjoyment. Unchanged for many years, it offers appetising
dishes such as chicken St Andrews, steak Diane, and a good
choice of fish including swordfish, breaded haddock, tuna and
Solway salmon.
OPEN: 12–2.30 5–11 **BAR MEALS:** Lunch served: all week Dinner
served: all week 12–2 5–8 Av main course £7.50
RESTAURANT: Lunch served: all week Dinner served: all week 12–2
5–8 Av 3 course à la carte £18 **BREWERY/COMPANY:** Free House
PRINCIPAL BEERS: Belhaven IPA, Caledonian Deuchars IPA,
Interbrew Flowers Original, Timothy Taylor Landlord.
FACILITIES: Children welcome Garden: Food served outside Dogs
allowed (water) **NOTES:** Parking 8 **ROOMS:** 5 bedrooms 4 en
suite from s£26 d£54

NEWTON STEWART   Map 10 NX46

Pick of the Pubs

Creebridge House Hotel ★ ★ 🏵 ♀
Minnigaff DG8 6NP ☎ 01671 402121 📠 01671 403258
e–mail: info@creebridge.co.uk
Dir: From A75 into Newton Stewart, turn right over river bridge, hotel
200yds on left.
A listed country house hotel dating from 1760, formerly a
shooting lodge and part of the Earl of Galloway's estate.
The River Cree runs nearby, and the hotel nestles in
grounds at the foot of Kirroughtree Forest. The informal
Bridge's bar and brasserie offers a fine selection of malts,
and real ales from a local micro-brewery. Food from a
daily-changing blackboard and a main menu includes
chicken and field mushroom wholemeal pancake, mixed
bean tortilla, and tandoori-style dishes. The Garden
Restaurant overlooking the landscaped grounds offers fine
dining in elegant surroundings. Modern Scottish cooking
on a fixed-price menu might offer quail with Dunsyre blue
cheese and walnut farci, wild lentil and sultana Pithivier,
and steamed fig and banana pudding. The hotel is
frequented by golfers, fishermen, shooters, walkers and
families.
OPEN: 12–2.30 6–11 Closed: 26 Dec **BAR MEALS:** Lunch
served: all week Dinner served: all week 12–2 6–9 Av main course
£8 **RESTAURANT:** 7–9 Av 3 course à la carte £22.50 Av 4
course fixed price £22.50 **BREWERY/COMPANY:** Free House
PRINCIPAL BEERS: Black Sheep Best, Fuller's London Pride.
FACILITIES: Children welcome Children's licence Garden: 3
Acres, food served outside Dogs allowed Kennels
NOTES: Parking 40 **ROOMS:** 19 bedrooms 19 en suite from
s£59 d£94

PORTPATRICK   Map 10 NW95

Pick of the Pubs

Crown Hotel 🛏 ♀
9 North Crescent DG9 8SX ☎ 01776 810261 📠 01776 810551
e–mail: crownhotel@supanet.com

Former fishermen's cottages converted into a bustling
harbourside hotel, with fine views across the Irish Sea.
There is a great atmosphere in the rambling old bar with
its open fire and seafaring displays. Extensive menus are
based on fresh local produce with an emphasis on
seafood – whitebait, langoustine, herring, lobster, crab
and mussels are among the options.
OPEN: 11–12 **BAR MEALS:** Lunch served: all week Dinner
served: all week 12–9.30 **RESTAURANT:** Lunch served: all week
Dinner served: all week 12–2.30 6–9.30
BREWERY/COMPANY: Free House
PRINCIPAL BEERS: Scottish Courage John Smith's, McEwans
80/-. **FACILITIES:** Children welcome Garden: Dogs allowed
ROOMS: 12 bedrooms 12 en suite from s£43 d£72

DUNDEE CITY

BROUGHTY FERRY   Map 11 NO43

Fisherman's Tavern 🛏 ♀
10–16 Fort St DD5 2AD ☎ 01382 775941 📠 01382 477466
e–mail: fishermans.sol.co.uk
Dir: From Dundee City centre follow A930 to Broughty ferry, take a right at
Scottish Tourist Board, road sign for fishermans tavern hotel
This listed 17th-century fisherman's cottage, converted to a
pub in 1827, combines a picturesque coastal setting with
award-winning hospitality and acclaimed bar food. The inn
also offers tastefully decorated en suite bedrooms. The
popular, well-planned menu ranges from light snacks to
traditional wholesome fare and international favourites. After
a stroll along the sands, try Cantonese style stir-fry vegetables,
beef curry Dupiaza, steak and St Andrews Ale pie, or butterfly
grilled chicken marinated in honey and mustard.
OPEN: 11–12 Closed: 1 Jan **BAR MEALS:** Lunch served: all week
11.30–2.30 Av main course £6 **BREWERY/COMPANY:** Free House
PRINCIPAL BEERS: Belhaven, Inveralmond Ossian's Ale, Caledonain
Deuchars IPA, Interbrew Boddingtons Bitter. **FACILITIES:** Children
welcome Garden: Food served outside Dogs allowed (water,
biscuits) **ROOMS:** 11 bedrooms 11 en suite from s£36 d£59

Scotland

BROUGHTY FERRY continued

The Royal Arch Bar
285 Brook St DD5 2DS ☎ 01382 779741
Originally named after the Masonic Arch, the present logo is based on the now-demolished monument commemorating Queen Victoria's visit to Dundee in 1863. With its traditional public bar and art deco lounge, the Royal Arch is renowned for its wide range of cask beers and malt whiskies. Meals are served in either bar; steak pie, chilli con carne and prawn curry typify the main menu, and there are daily specials, too.
OPEN: 11–12 (Sun 12.30–12) Closed: 1 Jan **BAR MEALS:** Lunch served: all week Dinner served: all week 11.30–2.30 5–8 Av main course £5 **RESTAURANT:** Lunch served: all week Dinner served: all week 11.30–2.30 5–8 **BREWERY/COMPANY:** Free House
PRINCIPAL BEERS: McEwans 80/-, Belhaven Best.
FACILITIES: Children welcome Dogs allowed (water, treats)

DUNDEE   Map 11 NO43

Mercantile Bar
100/108 Commercial St DD1 2AJ ☎ 01382 225500 📠 01382 224650
Dir: Town centre
Busy town centre pub serving McEwans ales and traditional bar snacks. Pub supports Dundee's musical talents with a songwriting club. Upstairs restaurant.

EAST AYRSHIRE

DALRYMPLE   Map 10 NS31

The Kirkton Inn ♦♦♦
1 Main St KA6 6DF ☎ 01292 560241 📠 01292 560835
e-mail: kirkton@cqm.co.uk
Dir: Between A77 & A713 approx 5m from Ayr signed from both roads

Village centre inn situated a short stroll from the River Doon where the salmon leap. Well situated for a visit to the Burns Centre and Cottage, the beach at Ayr or Blairquhan Castle. Allegedly haunted by an old landlord who liked it so much he wouldn't leave. Local produce is used in a variety of dishes including roast sirloin of beef and Yorkshire pudding, traditional steak pie, exotic pork with pineapple in a Malibu and cream sauce, lobster thermidor, deep-fried battered haddock, and roast pheasant Kirkton style.
OPEN: 11am–midnight **BAR MEALS:** Lunch served: all week Dinner served: all week 11–9 11–9 Av main course £7.75
RESTAURANT: Lunch served: all week Dinner served: all week 11–9 Av 3 course à la carte £16 Av 3 course fixed price £12.50
BREWERY/COMPANY: Free House
PRINCIPAL BEERS: Belhaven Best, Belhaven St Andrews.

FACILITIES: Children welcome Garden: Food served outside. Picnic benches Dogs allowed (water provided) **NOTES:** Parking 50
ROOMS: 11 bedrooms 11 en suite from s£26 d£46

GATEHEAD   Map 10 NS33

The Cochrane Inn
45 Main Rd KA2 0AP ☎ 01563 570122
Dir: from Glasgow A77 to Kilmarnock, then A759 to Gatehead

The emphasis is on contemporary British food at this village centre pub, just a short drive from the Ayrshire coast. Friendly, bustling atmosphere inside. Good choice of starters may include soused herring and grilled goat's cheese, while main courses might feature stuffed pancake, pan-fried trio of seafood with tiger prawns, or smoked haddock risotto.
OPEN: 11–3 5–12 Closed: 1 Jan **BAR MEALS:** Lunch served: all week Dinner served: all week 12–2 6–9 Av main course £7.25
RESTAURANT: Lunch served: all week Dinner served: all week 12–2 6–9 Av 3 course à la carte £15 **BREWERY/COMPANY:** Free House
PRINCIPAL BEERS: Theakstons. **FACILITIES:** Children welcome Garden: Dogs allowed (guide dogs only) **NOTES:** Parking 30

EAST LOTHIAN

EAST LINTON   Map 11 NT57

Pick of the Pubs

Drovers Inn
5 Bridge St EH40 3AG ☎ 01620 860298
Dir: Off A1 5m past Haddington, follow rd under railway bridge, then L
Herdsmen used to stop here as they drove their livestock to market. Those passing through in the late-19th century would undoubtedly have been aware of the then landlord's son's liking for young Jessie Cowe, daughter of the appropriately named local butcher. The church clock tower in the village square was named Jessie after her. Those old drovers are long gone but the bar, with wooden floors, beamed ceilings and half-panelled walls, retains an old-world charm. Upstairs, though, is more sumptuous with rich colours, low-beamed ceilings and antique furniture. Bistro menus offer Highland haggis with a creamy pepper sauce, shank of Borders lamb with vegetables, and crispy skinned codling on a basil and mustard mash. The chef's daily creations depend on seasonal local produce, while sizzling honey and ginger pie, chargrilled steaks and goats' cheese-filled pastry patties with slow-roasted plum tomatoes, are always popular.
OPEN: 11.30–11 (11.30–1 Thu–Sat) Closed: 25 Dec, 1 Jan
BAR MEALS: Lunch served: all week 11.30–2 Dinner served:

continued
continued

Sun–Fri 6–9.30 Av main course £6.80 **RESTAURANT:** Lunch served: all week Dinner served: all week 11.30–2.00 6–9.30 Av 3 course à la carte £26.50 9.30 **BREWERY/COMPANY:** Free House **PRINCIPAL BEERS:** Adnams Broadside, Caledonian 80/-, Fullers ESB, Wadworths 6X. **FACILITIES:** Children welcome Garden: Food served outside Dogs allowed (in the garden only)

GIFFORD   Map 11 NT56

Goblin Ha' Hotel
EH41 4QH ☎ 01620 810244 ▪ 01620 810718
e-mail: douglasmuir@btconnect.com
Dir: On A846, 100yrds from main village square on shore side of the road

Traditional hotel with a large patio for summer eating, and a good garden with play area and dolls' house for children. A varied range of home-cooked dishes offered in the bar and adjoining conservatory, including duck with plum and ginger sauce, breast of pheasant Caledonia, lasagne, pork fillet with apple and Stilton, and burgers, casseroles and pies.
OPEN: 11–2.30 5–11 **BAR MEALS:** Lunch served: all week Dinner served: all week 12.30–2 6.30–9 Av main course £7
RESTAURANT: Lunch served: all week Dinner served: all week Av 3 course à la carte £13.50 **BREWERY/COMPANY:** Free House **PRINCIPAL BEERS:** Hop Back Summer Lightning, Timothy Taylor Landlord, Caledonian Deuchers IPA, Fuller's ESB.
FACILITIES: Children welcome Children's licence Garden: Food served outdoors, patio Dogs allowed **ROOMS:** 7 bedrooms 6 en suite from s£25 d£50

GULLANE   Map 11 NT48

The Golf Inn
Main St EH31 2AB ☎ 01620 843259 ▪ 01620 842066
e-mail: info@golfinn.co.uk
The inn has 12 golf courses in its vicinity, including the Muirfield Golf Course, host for the 2002 British Open Championship, which is just 500 yards away. Golf is the theme in the public bar with a full-length wall display of trophies and memorabilia. Fish features prominently with dishes such as mussels marinière, gravad lax, fishcakes, and roast monkfish tails with onion and garlic confit. There's also an impressive choice of single malt whiskies.
OPEN: 11–11 **BAR MEALS:** Lunch served: all week Dinner served: all week 12–2.30 6.30–9.30 Av main course £7.50
RESTAURANT: Lunch served: all week Dinner served: all week 12–2.30 6.30–9.30 Av 3 course à la carte £20
BREWERY/COMPANY: Free House
PRINCIPAL BEERS: McEwans 70/-, Belhaven Best.
FACILITIES: Children welcome Garden: Food served outside Dogs allowed **ROOMS:** 14 bedrooms 14 en suite from s£50 d£80

CASTLECARY   Map 10 NS77

Castlecary House Hotel
Castlecary Rd, Castlecary, Cumbernauld G68 0HD ☎ 01324 840233 ▪ 01324 841608
Dir: Off A80 N of Cumbernauld
A friendly hotel complex on the watershed of Scotland's central belt and close to the historic Antonine Wall and Forth & Clyde Canal. 70 bedrooms created mainly in the form of cottages surrounding the main hotel building. Camerons Restaurant is the perfect meeting place for lunch, with 120 covers. From traditional pub food and home-made burgers, the varied menus include seared tuna steak, breast of chicken, collops of Highland venison and roast loin of lamb.
OPEN: 11–11 **BAR MEALS:** Lunch served: all week Dinner served: all week 12–2 6–9 Av main course £5.50 **RESTAURANT:** Lunch served: Mon-Sat Dinner served: Mon-Sat 12–2 7–10 Av 3 course à la carte £18 **BREWERY/COMPANY:** Free House
PRINCIPAL BEERS: Arran Dark, Belhaven 80/-, Sandy Hunter, Interbrew Stones Bitter. **FACILITIES:** Children welcome Children's licence Garden: Dogs allowed **ROOMS:** 70 bedrooms 65 en suite from s£20 d£49.50

ANSTRUTHER   Map 11 NO50

The Dreel Tavern
16 High St West KY10 3DL ☎ 01333 310727 ▪ 01333 311401
Complete with its own strange and satirical 16th-century legend of King James V and the 'Beggar's Benison', the Dreel Tavern has plenty of atmosphere. Its oak beams, open fire and stone walls retain much of the distant past, while home-cooked food and cask-conditioned ales are served to hungry visitors of the present. Expect to savour steak pie, Burgundy lamb, stuffed chicken parcels, deep-fried haddock in batter, Guinness, mushroom and steak pie, and smoked fish pie.
OPEN: 11–12 (Sun 12.30–12) **BAR MEALS:** Lunch served: all week Dinner served: all week 12–2 5.30–9 Av main course £5.95
RESTAURANT: Lunch served: all week Dinner served: all week 12–2 5.30–9 Av 3 course à la carte £11 **BREWERY/COMPANY:** Free House **PRINCIPAL BEERS:** Orkney Dark Island, Taylors Landlord, Harviestoun Bitter & Twisted, Greene King Abbot.
FACILITIES: Children welcome Children's licence Garden: Beer garden, outdoor eating Dogs allowed (water, biscuits)
NOTES: Parking 3

AUCHTERMUCHTY   Map 11 NO21

Forest Hills Hotel
23 High St KY14 7AN ☎ 01337 828318 ▪ 01337 828318
e-mail: lomond-foresthotels@hotmail.com
Popular inn located in the village square, with an oak-beamed bar, Flemish murals, a cosy lounge, and en suite bedrooms. Traditional pub food. The town of Auchtermuchty is well known as home to TV series *Dr Finlay's Casebook*, acoustic duo The Proclaimers, and accordionist extraordinaire Jimmy Shand.

Scotland

BURNTISLAND
Map 11 NT28

Burntisland Sands Hotel ◆◆◆ ☘
Lochie Rd KY3 9JX ☎ 01592 872230
Small, family-run hotel situated just yards from a sandy beach with view across the bay. Popular with families. Good range of traditional pub food.
OPEN: 11–12 **BAR MEALS:** Lunch served: all week Dinner served: all week 12–2.30 6–8.30 Av main course £4.95
RESTAURANT: Lunch served: all week Dinner served: all week 12–2.30 6–8.30 Av 3 course à la carte £12
BREWERY/COMPANY: Free House **PRINCIPAL BEERS:** Two changing guest ales. **FACILITIES:** Children welcome Children's licence Garden: patio/terrace, BBQ, rabbit hutch Dogs allowed
NOTES: Parking 20 **ROOMS:** 4 bedrooms 4 en suite from s£39 d£50

CRAIL
Map 11 NO60

The Golf Hotel ☺
4 High St KY10 3TD ☎ 01333 450206 ▤ 01333 450795
e-mail: thegolfhotel@allglobal.net
With roots in the 14th century, this is the site of one of Scotland's oldest licensed inns, although the current building dates from the early 18th century. The proud current owner is only the fourth since 1928. The golfing connection comes from the Crail Golfing Society, formed here in 1786, at the heart of Scottish golfing life. A hearty menu may include lamb and mint casserole, pasta bake, haddock grilled in Café de Paris butter, braised steak in a rich gravy, and haggis with tatties and turnip.
OPEN: 11–12 **BAR MEALS:** Lunch served: all week Dinner served: all week 12–7 7–9 Av main course £5.95 **RESTAURANT:** Lunch served: all week Dinner served: all week 12–7 7–9 Av 3 course à la carte £17.50 **BREWERY/COMPANY:** Free House
PRINCIPAL BEERS: Scottish Courage McEwans 80/-, 70/-, John Smith's. **FACILITIES:** Children welcome Garden: Dogs allowed
NOTES: Parking 10 **ROOMS:** 5 bedrooms 5 en suite from s£23 d£25

DUNFERMLINE
Map 10 NT08

The Hideaway Lodge & Restaurant ★ ★ ☺ ☘
Kingseat Rd, Halbeath KY12 0UB
☎ 01383 725474 ▤ 01383 622821
e-mail: enquiries@thehideaway.co.uk

Originally built in the 1930s as a miners' welfare institute, this pleasant country inn enjoys a rural setting on the outskirts of Dunfermline. Each room is named after a Scottish loch, and the extensive menu makes good use of fresh local produce. A typical meal may begin with grilled goats' cheese salad or Oban mussels, then move on to chargrilled tuna steak,

Scottish seafood crumble or fillet of Highland venison, and finish with summer fruit pudding or steamed ginger pudding.
OPEN: 12–3 5–11 (Sun 12–10) **BAR MEALS:** Lunch served: all week Dinner served: all week 12–2 5–9.30 Av main course £5
RESTAURANT: Lunch served: all week Dinner served: all week 12–2 5–9.30 Av 3 course à la carte £12 **BREWERY/COMPANY:** Free House **PRINCIPAL BEERS:** Calders 70/- & Cream.
FACILITIES: Children welcome Garden: Food served outdoors
NOTES: Parking 35 **ROOMS:** 8 bedrooms 8 en suite from s£45 d£45

ELIE
Map 11 NO40

Pick of the Pubs

The Ship Inn ☺
The Toft KY9 1DT ☎ 01333 330246 ▤ 01333 330864
e-mail: shipinnelie@aol.com
Dir: Follow A915 & A917 to Elie.Follow signs from High St to Watersport Centre to the Toft.
Just a stone's throw from one of Scotland's finest water-sports centres there's always something happening at this lively free house, right on the waterfront at Elie Bay. The pub's own cricket team plays regularly on the beach, and the annual rugby match against Edinburgh Academicals attracts a huge crowd. A pub since 1838, it has been run for over 20 years by the Philip family whose enthusiasm remains undimmed. Fresh fish takes pride of place on the specials board to supplement a slightly plastic menu offering filled harvester rolls (smoked salmon, prawns and cream cheese perhaps), bangers and mash in 80/- beer gravy or renowned prime Scottish beef steaks, served plain or sauced with haggis and whisky. Alternatively try fresh local haddock in beer batter, scampi tails thermidor and, in summer, a Ship Inn seafood salad that makes best use of the day's catch. There are plenty of children's choices, summer barbecues in the beer garden and accommodation available in the pub's adjacent guest house.
OPEN: 11–11 (Sun 12.30–11) Closed: 25 Dec
BAR MEALS: Lunch served: all week Dinner served: all week 12–2 6–9 **RESTAURANT:** Lunch served: all week Dinner served: all week 12–2 6–9 **BREWERY/COMPANY:** Free House
PRINCIPAL BEERS: Caledonian Deuchars IPA, Belhaven Best, Calders Cream Ale, Interbrew Boddingtons Bitter.
FACILITIES: Children welcome Children's licence Garden: Beer garden, food served outdoors, patio, Dogs allowed (water, biscuits) **ROOMS:** 6 bedrooms 4 en suite from s£30 d£25

KIRKCALDY
Map 11 NT29

Pick of the Pubs

The Old Rectory Inn ☺ ☘
West Quality St, Dysart KY1 2TE
☎ 01592 651211 ▤ 01592 655221
Dir: From Edinburgh take A92 to kirkcaldy, then A907, A955 to Dysart R at Nat trust sign
A delightful old inn with a splendid walled garden set above the harbour. The well-preserved Georgian building, at various times a gentleman's residence, rectory and laundry, has been an inn since the 1980s, and is now a popular destination for lovers of good food. Local produce is a feature of both the bar and restaurant menus where seemingly endless choice is offered. From the carte

continued

continued

come starters like Manhattan clam chowder, grilled, pan-fried or flambéed steaks, the fishy flavours of halibut oriental, and perhaps roast duck with three fruits. The chef might recommend curried egg Madras, and tiger prawns à la Pernod, while from the lunch menu you can try haggis Drambuie, venison and mushroom casserole, and bread and butter pudding. Set meals require further deliberation, along with an evening bar menu with a balanced selection covering seafood, pasta and vegetarian dishes, and yet more Scottish steaks.

OPEN: 12–3 7–12 Closed: 1wk Jan & 2wks mid-Oct, 1 wk early July **BAR MEALS:** Lunch served: Tue-Sun 12–2 Dinner served: Tue-Sat 7–9.30 Av main course £6.85 **RESTAURANT:** Lunch served: Tue-Sun 12–3 Dinner served: Tue-Sat 7–12 Av 3 course à la carte £22.50 **BREWERY/COMPANY:** Free House **PRINCIPAL BEERS:** Calders Cream Ale. **FACILITIES:** Garden: Food served outside. Old fashioned garden Dogs allowed (guide dogs only) **NOTES:** Parking 12

LOWER LARGO   Map 11 NO40

Crusoe Hotel 🛏 ♀
2 Main St KY8 6BT ☎ 01333 320759 🖹 01333 320865
e-mail: relax@crusoe-hotel.co.uk
Dir: A92 to Kirkcaldy East, A915 to Lundin Links, then R to Lower Largo
This historic inn is located on the sea wall in Lower Largo, the birthplace of Alexander Selkirk, the real-life castaway immortalised by Daniel Defoe in his novel, Robinson Crusoe. In the past the area was also the heart of the once-thriving herring fishing industry. Today it is a charming bay ideal for a golfing break. A typical menu may include 'freshly shot' haggis, Pittenweem haddock and a variety of steaks. Accommodation available.
OPEN: 11–12 (Fri 11–1am) (food available 12.30–3, 6–9)
BAR MEALS: Lunch served: all week Dinner served: all week 12–3 6–9 Av main course £5.95 **RESTAURANT:** Dinner served: all week 12–3 6.30–9.00 Av 3 course à la carte £19 Av 3 course fixed price £14.50 **BREWERY/COMPANY:** Free House
PRINCIPAL BEERS: Belhaven 80/-. **FACILITIES:** Children welcome Food served outdoors Dogs allowed **NOTES:** Parking 30
ROOMS: 17 bedrooms 17 en suite from s£45 d£70

MARKINCH   Map 11 NO20

Town House Hotel ◆◆◆◆
1 High St KY7 6DQ ☎ 01592 758459 🖹 01592 755039
Dir: Off A92(Dundee/Kirkcaldy rd) Hotel opp. rail station
Family-run 17th-century coaching inn situated in the heart of town, and offering a fixed-price lunch menu of two or three courses, and a supper carte of imaginative dishes. Expect grilled Gressingham duck breast served with an orange and Cointreau sauce, pan-fried blackened Cajun salmon fillets and cheese or sun-dried tomato tortellini in a tomato and pesto sauce.
OPEN: 12–2 6–11 Closed: 25/26 Dec, 1/2 Jan **BAR MEALS:** Lunch served: Mon-Sat 12–2 Dinner served: all week 6–9 Av main course £8.95 **RESTAURANT:** Lunch served: Mon-Sat 12–2 Dinner served: all week 6–9 Av 3 course à la carte £15 Av 3 course fixed price £8.50 **BREWERY/COMPANY:** Free House **FACILITIES:** Children welcome **ROOMS:** 4 bedrooms 3 en suite from s£30 d£60

ST MONANS   Map 12 NO50

Pick of the Pubs

Seafood Bar & Restaurant 🍴🍴 🛏 ♀
16 West End KY10 2BX ☎ 01333 730327 🖹 01333 730327
e-mail: seafood.resto@aol.com
Dir: Take A595 from St Andrews to Anstruther, then W on A917 through Pittenweem. At St Monans harbour turn R
This little seafood bar and restaurant is perched close to the harbour's edge affords stunning views over St Monans Harbour, the Isle of May, Bass Rock and the Firth of Forth from its harbourside terrace. Below the terrace you can see fascinating examples of rock formations caused by plate movements, plus the resident heron. The bar is housed in a 400-year-old fisherman's dwelling with its own freshwater well. Now located in the adjoining Conservatory restaurant, the well dates back to the time of King David I, who was healed of an arrow wound by the miraculous powers of its water. Seafood specialities include seared scallops with mango and sweet chilli salsa, grilled turbot with red onion marmalade and mustard sauce, and carpaccio of albacore tuna with hoi sin dressing.
OPEN: 12–3 6–11 (June-August open 7 days a week) Closed: 25-26 Dec, 1-3 Jan **BAR MEALS:** Lunch served: Tue-Sun 12–3 Dinner served: Tue-Sat 7–9.30 Av main course £14 **RESTAURANT:** Lunch served: Tue-Sun 12–3 Dinner served: Tue-Sat 7–9.30 Av 3 course à la carte £28 Av 3 course fixed price £18 **BREWERY/COMPANY:** Free House **PRINCIPAL BEERS:** Belhaven Best, Belhaven Extra Cold. **FACILITIES:** Garden: Food served outside, harbourside terrace **NOTES:** Parking 10

Scotland

Hops in Ale
The introduction of hops was stoutly resisted. Henry VIII would drink only hopless ale and the brewers were castigated for ruining the traditional drink. Beer brewed with hops kept better for longer, however, which stimulated the development of large-scale breweries and both inns and alehouses gradually gave up brewing their own.

HIGHLAND

ACHILTIBUIE
Map 12 NC00

Summer Isles Hotel & Bar ◉◉ 🐕
IV26 2YG ☎ 01854 622282 📠 01854 622251
Dir: take A835 N from Ullapool for 10m, Achiltibuie signed on L, 15m to village, hotel 1m on L
The only watering hole in the area for 150 years, this peaceful bar and hotel can be found at the end of a long and winding single track lane that skirts lochs Lurgain, Badagyle and Oscaig. The emphasis is on locally caught and home-produced food, and there's a wide choice of malts and real ale. Langoustine, spiny lobsters, smoked salmon and crab claws all feature on the menu, along with a casserole of the day, and various snacks.
OPEN: 12–11 (4–11 in winter) Closed: Mid Oct–Easter
BAR MEALS: Lunch served: all week Dinner served: all week Av main course £7.50 **RESTAURANT:** Lunch served: all week Dinner served: all week 12.30–2, from 8pm Av 5 course fixed price £41
BREWERY/COMPANY: Free House **PRINCIPAL BEERS:** Orkney Dark Island, Raven & Red Macgregor. **FACILITIES:** Children welcome Garden: Dogs allowed **NOTES:** Parking 20 **ROOMS:** 13 bedrooms 13 en suite from s£52 d£104

ALTNAHARRA
Map 13 NC53

Altnaharra Hotel
IV27 4UE ☎ 01549 411222 📠 01549 411222
e-mail: altnaharra@btinternet.com
Dir: A9 to Bonar Bridge, A336 to Lairg & Tongue
Traditional Highland hotel with a major focus on fishing, set in the middle of fantastic scenery. Lunch and dinner are available on pre-booking, the set-price menus featuring local venison, lamb and fish from Scrabster. Dishes might include smoked trout with pink grapefruit, and duck breast in plum sauce.
OPEN: 12–2.30 5–11 **RESTAURANT:** Lunch served: Sun Dinner served: all week 6–9 Av 3 course à la carte £26.25 Av 2 course fixed price £22 **BREWERY/COMPANY:** Free House
PRINCIPAL BEERS: no real ale. **FACILITIES:** Children welcome Garden: Dogs allowed (garden only) **NOTES:** Parking 60 **ROOMS:** 15 bedrooms 15 en suite from s£69 d£138

APPLECROSS
Map 12 NG74

Pick of the Pubs

Applecross Inn 🐕 ♀
Shore St IV54 8LR ☎ 01520 744262 📠 01520 744400
e-mail: applecrossin@globalnet.co.uk
See Pick of the Pubs on page 582

AVIEMORE
Map 13 NH81

The Old Bridge Inn 🐕 ♀
Dalfaber Rd PH22 1PU ☎ 01479 811137 📠 01479 810270
e-mail: highlandcatering@aol.com
Dir: Exit A9 to Aviemore, 1st L to 'Ski road' then 1st L again - 200m
Cosy and friendly Highland pub overlooking the River Spey. Dine in the relaxing bars or in the attractive riverside garden. A tasty chargrill menu includes lamb chops in redcurrant jelly, Aberdeen Angus sirloin or rib-eye steaks, or butterflied breast of chicken marinated in yoghurt, lime and coriander. Seafood specials include monkfish pan-fried in chilli butter and seafood crumble.

continued

OPEN: 11–11 **BAR MEALS:** Lunch served: all week Dinner served: all week 12–2 6–9 Av main course £5.95 **RESTAURANT:** Lunch served: all week Dinner served: all week 12–2 6–9 Av 3 course à la carte £22 **BREWERY/COMPANY:** Free House
PRINCIPAL BEERS: Caledonian 80/-. **FACILITIES:** Children welcome Garden: Food served outside **NOTES:** Parking 24 **ROOMS:** 8 bedrooms 8 en suite from s£12 d£32

CARRBRIDGE
Map 13 NH92

Dalrachney Lodge Hotel ★ ★ ★
PH23 3AT ☎ 01479 841252 📠 01479 841383
e-mail: stay@dalrachney.co.uk
Dir: A9 onto A938 for 1.5m, through village, pub on R
Sympathetically restored Victorian shooting lodge, with log fires and period furniture, set in 14 acres of mature grounds. Queen Victoria once described the nearby village of Carrbridge as 'the jewel of the North'. An ideal area for riding, hunting and sporting activities of many kinds. Local ingredients, notably Aberdeen Angus beef and Scottish lamb, feature in a varied range of dishes. Choices include casserole of shellfish, medallions of wild venison, grilled rainbow trout and breast of duckling.
OPEN: 12–2 5.30–11 **BAR MEALS:** Lunch served: all week Dinner served: all week 12–2 5.30–11 Av main course £6.50
RESTAURANT: Dinner served: all week 7–8.30 Av 3 course à la carte £25 Av 3 course fixed price £25 **BREWERY/COMPANY:** Free House
FACILITIES: Children welcome Garden: Food served outside Dogs allowed **NOTES:** Parking 40 **ROOMS:** 16 bedrooms 16 en suite

The Fife Coastal Walk

One of Scotland's lesser-known regions and once the home of the country's kings and saints, Fife is a 20-mile-wide peninsula between the Firth of Forth and the Tay. A great way to blend coast and countryside is by following the 94-mile Fife Coastal Walk, which explores a beautiful stretch of the Scottish coastline between Inverkeithing, just north of the Forth Bridge, and Newburgh, near Perth. Discover Fife's fascinating legacy of caves, castles and ancient fishing ports en route and expect a warm welcome at a variety of coastal pubs and waterfront hostelries along the way, including the Georgian Old Rectory Inn at Dysart, the Crusoe Hotel on the sea wall at Lower Largo, the 19th-century Ship Inn at Elie, the Dreel Tavern at Anstruther, and the historic Golf Hotel at Crail, reputed to be one of Scotland's oldest coaching inns.

PUB WALK

Plockton
The Plockton Hotel

Suitable for families, strollers and more ardent hikers, this varied forest walk offers good views towards Skye, one of Scotland's most romantic locations, before passing alongside scenic Loch Lundie.

On leaving the hotel, take the main road out of the village and cross the railway bridge. The road can be busy but there is sufficient verge to walk alongside it. Continue over a road junction, cross a small bridge and keep ahead up the hill. Look to the right for superb views of the Isle of Skye and the Applecross Mountains. At the next junction turn left towards Strome and Duncraig. Once over the cattle-grid look out for a wooden post on the right directing you to the footpath to Achnandarach. Cross the burn by the stepping stones and follow the path. In spring this stretch of the walk dazzles with carpets of primroses and large yellow globe flowers. Keep ahead along a tree-lined path cutting through the forest. Once clear of the woodland, look for two houses, one of which is designed in the Japanese style. At this junction turn left and walk down through the small village of Achnandarach and back to the main road. On reaching the post box, turn right and follow the road alongside picturesque Loch Lundie. At certain times of the year, you may catch sight of heron and other bird life on the water. At the next junction follow the signs for Strome and then look for a gate and post indicating one mile (1.6km). Take this well-maintained path by the railway line and follow it back to Plockton. Pass beneath a small railway bridge and immediately beyond it look out for spectacular views of Plockton and Loch Carron. Turn right at the end of the path and go downhill, back into the village. Return to the pub.

THE PLOCKTON HOTEL
Harbour Street PLOCKTON
IV52 8TN
Tel: 01599 544274
Directions: On A87 to Kyle of Lochalsh take turn at Balmacara. Plockton 7m N. In a National Trust village described as idyllic, the hotel stretches right along the waterfront beside Loch Carron. Garden restaurant. Cooking using Highland produce based on philosophy of keep it simple and do it very well.
Open: 11–11.45 (Sun 12.30–11)
Bar meals: 12–2.15 6–9.15
Children welcome. Garden.

Distance: 5 miles (8km)
Map: OS Landranger 24
Terrain: Forest and loch
Paths: Mainly paths and roads
Gradient: Road has a fairly steep incline, footpaths undulate

Walk submitted and checked by Dot Phoenix

OPEN: 11–11 (Sun 12.30–11)
(Dec–Jan closed Sun 7pm)
BAR MEALS: L served all week.
week. D served all week. 12–9.
Av main course £5.95
RESTAURANT: L served by
appointment, D served all week.
6–9. Av cost 3 course £25
BREWERY/COMPANY: FREE
HOUSE
PRINCIPLE BEERS: Scottish
Courage John Smiths
FACILITIES: Children welcome,
dogs allowed. Garden: beer
garden, food served outdoors,
patio
NOTES: Parking 30
ROOMS: 7 rooms, 3 en suite.
Double room from £50. Single
room from £25

Applecross Inn

Some of the most awe-inspiring scenery is passed on the way to this traditional white-painted inn, and on arrival at its welcoming door it is immediately apparent that the hospitality is just as spectacular.

Shore Street, Applecross IV54 8LR
☎ 01520 744262 ▤ 01520 744400
e-mail: applecrossin@globalnet.co.uk
Dir: From Lochcarron to Kishorn then L onto unclassifed rd to Applecross over 'Bealach Na Ba'.

Judith Fish has been welcoming visitors since 1989, and she is rightly proud of the beautiful location on the shore of Applecross Bay, where the beer garden stretches down to a sandy cove and there are views out towards Skye. Inside, the unspoilt bar has been upgraded and refurbished in keeping with its Highland character, and includes cosy features like the wood-burning stove. The lively kitchen staff have the pick of the rich local produce to create some stunning dishes, including seafood, Aberdeen Angus steaks and game from neighbouring estates. Favourites include king scallops in garlic butter with crispy bacon on rice, local oysters deep fried in tempura batter with sweet chilli sauce, and fresh monkfish and squat lobster in a rich prawn sauce on home-made tagliatelle. Meat eaters will relish the Applecross venison casserole with braised red cabbage on apple and wholegrain mustard mash, and to finish there are puddings to die for: raspberry cranachan, and cardamom pannacotta are just two of these gems. The temptation to stay a while in this secluded, peaceful spot is increased by some well-equipped and romantic bedrooms which enjoy magnificent sea views.

CAWDOR   Map 13 NH85

Pick of the Pubs

Cawdor Tavern 🐷 ♀
The Lane IV12 5XP ☎ 01667 404777 🖹 01667 404777
e-mail: Cawdort@aol.com
Dir: *from A96(Inverness-Aberdeen)take B9006 & follow signs for
Cawdor Castle. Tavern in village centre.*

Located alongside the famous Cawdor Castle in a
picturesque conservation village, this was formerly the
joiners' workshop for the estate. Now decked out in oak
panelling from the castle itself, this refurbished pub draws
discerning diners from far and wide. Roaring log fires
keep the place cosy and warm on long winter evenings,
while the garden patio comes into its own in summer.
Plenty of choice from the lunch carte, like Arbroath
smokie and citrus mousse to start, then the traditional
haggis, neeps and tatties. Grilled garlic mussels might kick
off dinner, followed by fillet of Morayshire pork stuffed
with haggis. A daily specials menu might focus on confit
of pheasant leg on a bed of clapshot, collops of Scottish
beef fillet, and warm banana crêpe with rum butterscotch
cream. More than 100 malt whiskies, and three Scottish
ales including Dark Island from Orkney.
OPEN: 11–3 5–11 (May–Oct 11–11) Closed: 25 Dec, 1 Jan
BAR MEALS: Lunch served: all week Dinner served: all week
12–2 5.30–9 Av main course £7.95 **RESTAURANT:** Lunch
served: all week Dinner served: all week 12–2 6.30–9 Av 3 course
à la carte £19.50 **BREWERY/COMPANY:** Free House
PRINCIPAL BEERS: Tennents 80/-, Black Isle's Redkite,
Tomintool Stag. **FACILITIES:** Children welcome Garden: Food
served outside. Patio area Dogs allowed (water provided).
NOTES: Parking 60

CONTIN   Map 13 NH45

Achilty Hotel ★ ★ 🐷 ♀
IV14 9EG ☎ 01997 421355 🖹 01997 421923
Dir: *On A835, at the northern edge of Contin*
Former drovers' inn, now a cosy, relaxed hotel with the
original stone walls and log fire showing its origins. Set on the
edge of the village near a fast-flowing mountain river, it serves
good Scottish food made from fresh local produce. The
bar/restaurant menu offers extensive choices: seafood
thermidor, scampi Provençal, rack of lamb with garlic crust,
and game pie, plus steaks and vegetarian dishes.
OPEN: 11–11 **BAR MEALS:** Lunch served: all week 12–5 Av main
course £9.95 **RESTAURANT:** Lunch served: all week 12–2.30 Dinner
served: all week 5.30–9 Av 3 course à la carte £20 Av 3 course fixed
price £9.95 **BREWERY/COMPANY:** Free House

PRINCIPAL BEERS: Calders Cream, Calders 70/-.
FACILITIES: Children welcome Garden: **NOTES:** Parking 80
ROOMS: 12 bedrooms 12 en suite from s£35 d£54

DORNOCH   Map 13 NH78

Mallin House Hotel 🐷
Church St IV25 3LP ☎ 01862 810335 🖹 01862 810810
e-mail: mallin.house.hotel@zetnet.co.uk
Dir: *(from Tain (on A9) take A836 to Bonar Bridge, then turn left onto
A949 in direction of Dornoch (approx 10m))*
Mallin House is a modern hotel just 200 yards from the Royal
Dornoch Golf Course. The area is also ideal for angling, pony-
trekking and birdwatching. A single menu, strong on Scottish
cooking is offered throughout, with an emphasis on fresh
seafood, including langoustines in hot garlic butter, and sea
bass with citrus and saffron sauce.
OPEN: 11–2.30 5–11 **BAR MEALS:** Lunch served: Sun 12.30–2
Dinner served: all week 6.30–9 Av main course £6
RESTAURANT: Lunch served: Sun 12.30–2 Dinner served: all week
6.30–9 Av 3 course à la carte £22 **BREWERY/COMPANY:** Free
House **PRINCIPAL BEERS:** Carlsberg-Tetley Tetley Bitter.
FACILITIES: Children welcome Garden: Dogs allowed
NOTES: Parking 22 **ROOMS:** 10 bedrooms 10 en suite from s£29
d£50

DUNDONNELL   Map 12 NH08

Pick of the Pubs

Dundonnell House ★ ★ ★ 🐷🐷 ♀
IV23 2QR ☎ 01854 633204 🖹 01854 633366
e-mail: selbie@dundonnellhotel.co.uk
Dir: *From Inverness W on the A835, at Braemore junct take A382 for
Gairloch*
Sheltering beneath the massive Al Teallach mountain
range, with superb views down Little Loch Broom, this
much-extended former drovers' inn boasted just four
bedrooms when acquired by the Florence family some
forty years ago. Today, in one of Scotland's finest holiday
areas, their acclaimed hotel is a magnet for visitors to
Wester Ross. The Broom Beg ('little broom') bar and
bistro provide a casual atmosphere in which to relax after
a day exploring and enjoy good food, beers and an
extensive range of malt whiskies. It is a long way to the
shops, so local produce plays a full part on a menu
providing batter-crisp haddock fillets, with chips and
tartare sauce, local salmon with prawn, chervil and citrus
butter, chicken fillets and prime Angus steaks from their
own Aberdeenshire butcher. Lunchtime snacks can be as
simple as Orkney Cheddar cheese and apple sauce
sandwiches, beef- or veggie-burgers and local oak-
smoked salmon with dill sauce and brown bread. Dinner
in the spacious restaurant continues to be a key attraction
for residents.
OPEN: 11–11 (Reduced Hrs Nov–Mar please phone)
BAR MEALS: Lunch served: all week Dinner served: all week
12–2.00 6–8.30 Av main course £7.95 **RESTAURANT:** Dinner
served: all week 7–8.30 Av 3 course à la carte £24.50
BREWERY/COMPANY: Free House
PRINCIPAL BEERS: John Smiths,. **FACILITIES:** Children
welcome Children's licence Dogs allowed **NOTES:** Parking 60
ROOMS: 28 bedrooms 28 en suite from s£37.50 d£37.50

continued

Scotland (side tab)

FORT AUGUSTUS
Map 12 NH30

Pick of the Pubs

The Lock Inn 🍺 ♀
Canalside PH32 4AU ☎ 01320 366302
Dir: On the banks of Caledonian Canal in Fort Augustus
Built in 1820, this former bank and post office building,
replete with flagstone floors and original beams, stands
on the banks of the Caledonian Canal close to Loch Ness.
The state-of-the-art kitchen has been recognised by the
Scottish Beef Guild Society for its use of local produce. A
thousand Celtic welcomes are extended to regulars and
visitors who come to enjoy the regular Scottish folk music
evenings when a special dinner features brandied seafood
bisque and Loch an Ora whisky-flavoured game pâté,
followed by seared calves' liver and Angus sirloin steaks.
House specials include Roast Hebridean lamb, loin of
Grampian pork fillet, and Monarch of the Glen venison
casserole. Start perhaps with seafood chowder and round
off with Loch Ness mud pie.
OPEN: 11–11 Closed: 25 Dec, 1 Jan **BAR MEALS:** Lunch
served: all week Dinner served: all week 12–3 6–10 Av main
course £6 **RESTAURANT:** Lunch served: all week Dinner
served: all week 12–3 6–10 Av 3 course à la carte £20
BREWERY/COMPANY: Free House
PRINCIPAL BEERS: Caledonian 80/-, Orkney Dark Island, Black
Isle. **FACILITIES:** Children welcome Children's licence Garden:
Food served outside Dogs allowed (in the garden only)

FORT WILLIAM
Map 12 NN17

Pick of the Pubs

Moorings Hotel ★ ★ ★ 🏵
Banavie PH33 7LY ☎ 01397 772797 📠 01397 772441
e-mail: reservations@moorings-fortwilliam.co.uk
*Dir: from A82 in Fort William follow signs for Mallaig, then L onto
A830 for 1m. Cross canal bridge then 1st R signposted Banavie*

Standing on the banks of the Caledonian Canal beside
Neptune's Staircase - a historic monument comprising
eight lock gates that raise boats by 64 feet. This striking
modern hotel on the west side of town has panoramic
views on clear days towards Ben Nevis and the
surrounding mountains. Most bedrooms share this
stunning outlook, including a new wing that mirrors the
shape of the nearby Thomas Telford house. The Upper
Deck lounge and popular Mariners' Bar share the nautical
theme, and offer an appealing place for a drink or a meal.
The daily-changing bar food has a strong inclination
towards local fish such as West coast haddock, loch

salmon, Angus beef, Grampian chicken and, of course,
haggis served with clapshot and Drambuie sauce. Herb
roast rack of lamb, pan-seared scallops on wilted spinach,
and gently-baked fillet of hake make up the numbers,
along with bangers, burgers, and sandwiches.
OPEN: 12–11.45 **BAR MEALS:** Lunch served: all week Dinner
served: all week 12–9.30 Av main course £7.95
RESTAURANT: Dinner served: all week 7–9.30 Av 4 course fixed
price £26 **BREWERY/COMPANY:** Free House
PRINCIPAL BEERS: Calders 70/- & Sport.
FACILITIES: Children welcome Children's licence Garden:
Small patio, food served outdoors Dogs allowed (water)
NOTES: Parking 80 **ROOMS:** 28 bedrooms 28 en suite from
s£40 d£80

GAIRLOCH
Map 12 NG87

Pick of the Pubs

AA Pub of the Year for Scotland 2003

The Old Inn 🍺 ♀
IV21 2BD ☎ 01445 712006 📠 01445 712445
e-mail: nomadscot@lineone.net
Dir: just off main A832, near harbour at S end of village

Not just old, in fact, but the oldest hotel in Gairloch,
having been built by the Flowerdale Estate around 1792.
Included in the £302.14s cost were two-foot stone walls
and fireplaces, now restored to view after being boarded
over for 25 years. Skye, Rona, Raasay and even the Outer
Hebrides can be seen across Gairloch harbour where
Scottish West Coast seafood, especially lobster, brown
crab, langoustine, mussels, skate and salmon, is landed.
Some will be destined for Mediterranean-style
bouillabaisse, or home-made seafood ravioli. Gairloch
scallops are served with a garlic and ginger butter and
saffron risotto. Another option is Highland game, such as
grilled wild venison steak with chanterelle mushrooms,
garlic and cream sauce, grilled polenta and red cabbage
braised in red wine or perhaps rich port and honey-glazed
ham with seasonal potatoes and vegetables. Desserts
include orange and banana pudding and apricot and
peach crumble. There is an excellent range of real ales
plus plenty of accommodation.
OPEN: 11–12 **BAR MEALS:** 12–2.30 6–9
RESTAURANT: 12–2.30 6–9 **BREWERY/COMPANY:** Free
House **PRINCIPAL BEERS:** Greene King Old Speckled Hen,
Scottish Courage Courage Directors, Isle of Skye Red Cullin Isle of
Skye Blind Piper,Bellhaven St Andrews Ale..
FACILITIES: Children welcome Children's licence Garden:
Food served outside Dogs allowed Rugs **NOTES:** Parking 20
ROOMS: 14 bedrooms 14 en suite from s£25 d£49

continued

GARVE — Map 12 NH36

Inchbae Lodge Hotel
IV23 2PH ☎ 01997 455269 🖷 01997 455207
e-mail: info@inchbae-lodge-hotel.co.uk
Dir: On A835, hotel 6m W of Garve

Originally a 19th-century hunting lodge Inchbae Lodge is situated on the banks of the River Blackwater, with an elegant dining room offering panoramic views. An ideal base for those keen walkers wishing to taking on Ben Wyvis and the Fannich Hills. On the menu alongside venison sausages, smoked salmon, or haggis, neeps and tatties, vegetarians will find vegetarian haggis and lasagne. Comfortable accommodation and a coffee shop.
OPEN: 11-11 Closed: Nov & Dec **BAR MEALS:** Lunch served: all week Dinner served: all week 12-2.30 5-8.30 Av main course £6.50 **RESTAURANT:** Lunch served: Sun 12-2 Dinner served: all week 7-8 Av 3 course fixed price £19.95 **BREWERY/COMPANY:** Free House **PRINCIPAL BEERS:** Belhaven plus guest Scottish ale.
FACILITIES: Children welcome Garden: Food served outdoors Dogs allowed **NOTES:** Parking 30 **ROOMS:** 15 bedrooms 15 en suite from s£35 d£42

GLENCOE — Map 12 NN15

Clachaig Inn
PH49 4HX ☎ 01855 811252 🖷 01855 811679
e-mail: inn@clachaig.com
Dir: In the hart of Glen Coe itself, just off the A82, 20m S of Fort William and 2m E of Glencoe village
Situated at the very heart of Glencoe, this inn has provided hospitality for over 300 years. It is a short forest walk from Signal Rock, where the signal was given for the infamous massacre of 1692. More recently Clachaig has become perhaps the centre of Scottish mountaineering, renowned for its real ales and some 120 malt whiskies. Clachaig surf and turf, crofters salmon, venison burger, and haggis, neeps 'n' tatties are typical of the robust fare. Regular live music.
OPEN: 11-11 (Fri 11-12, Sat 11-11.30, Sun 12.30-11)) **BAR MEALS:** Lunch served: all week Dinner served: all week 12-9 12-9 Av main course £7 **BREWERY/COMPANY:** Free House **PRINCIPAL BEERS:** Isle of Skye Red Cuillin, Orkney Dark Island, Fraoch Heather Ale,Houston Peter's Well. **FACILITIES:** Children welcome Garden: Food served outside **NOTES:** Parking 40 **ROOMS:** 20 bedrooms 17 en suite from s£30 d£29

GLENELG — Map 12 NG81

Pick of the Pubs

Glenelg Inn
IV40 8JR ☎ 01599 522273 🖷 01599 522283
e-mail: christophermain@glenelg-inn.com
Dir: From Shiel Bridge (A87) take unclassified road to Glenelg
Very much a 'home from home' this characterful old village inn occupies a 200-year-old stable mews and commands stunning views across the Glenelg Bay from its splendid waterside garden. Local produce lies at the heart of daily menus and whilst you could always order scampi and chips, it may be more tempting to sample specialities such as fresh scallops pan-fried with organic garlic butter and roast lemon followed by fresh West Coast collops of monkfish, prawns and smoked haddock in flaked pastry with white wine, slow roasted broccoli and dill sauce. For those who prefer meat, how about roast chicken with lime, garlic and chilli on spiced lentils with a citrus sauce. An impressive selection of vegetarian dishes is also available. A truly romantic place to stay, Glenelg remains virtually undiscovered - and many are of the opinion that it should stay so.
OPEN: 12-11 (Bar closed lunchtimes during winter) Closed: End Oct-Etr(ex by arrangement) **BAR MEALS:** Lunch served: all week 12.30-2 Dinner served: Mon-Sat 6-9.30 Av main course £7 **RESTAURANT:** 12.30-2 7.30-9 Av 3 course à la carte £25 **BREWERY/COMPANY:** Free House **FACILITIES:** Children welcome Garden: Large, with trees, Food served outside Dogs allowed **ROOMS:** 6 bedrooms 6 en suite

Skills and Crafts
Inns with names like the Bricklayers Arms and the Masons Arms hark back to the days when groups of craftsmen and tradesmen met regularly in the local hostelry. The trade union movement originally grew up in pubs in this way and a 'local' can mean either a pub or a union branch. Itinerant craftsmen would expect a welcome at these houses, too, and pick up news of work. The Axe and Compasses is a carpenters' badge, the Three (or more) Horseshoes a device of smiths, the Wheatsheaf of bakers and the Beetle and Wedge of builders, while quite a few pubs display the Oddfellows Arms. The Shoulder of Mutton could signify that the landlord doubled as a butcher.

Scotland

KYLESKU   Map 12 NC23

Kylesku Hotel 🛏
IV27 4HW ☎ 01971 502231 ▤ 01971 502313
e-mail: kyleskuhotel@lycos.co.uk
*Dir: 35m N of Ullapool on the A838, turn into Kylesku, hotel is at the end
of the road at Old Ferry Pier*

Ideal for birdwatchers, wildlife enthusiasts, climbers and
walkers, this coaching inn is located on the old ferry slipway
between Loch Glencoul and Loch Glendhu in the Highlands of
Sutherland. Both bar and restaurant menus specialise in
locally caught seafood and venison in season. Dishes might
include local prawns with Marie-Rose sauce, pan-fried fillets of
Lochinver haddock with lemon butter, or venison casserole
cooked in red wine with root vegetables and lardons of
bacon.
OPEN: 11-11.30 (Mon-Sat 10-11.30, Fri 10-12, Sun 12.30-11) Closed:
1 Nov-28 Feb **BAR MEALS:** Lunch served: all week Dinner served:
all week 12-2.30 6-9.30 Av main course £8.50 **RESTAURANT:** All
week 12-2.30 7-8.30 Av 3 course à la carte £21.95 Av 2 course fixed
price £19.95 **BREWERY/COMPANY:** Free House
PRINCIPAL BEERS: Caledonian 80/-. **FACILITIES:** Children
welcome Children's licence Garden: Food served outdoors, patio,
good views Dogs allowed **NOTES:** Parking 50
ROOMS: 8 bedrooms 6 en suite from s£35 d£60

LYBSTER   Map 13 ND23

The Portland Arms Hotel 🛏
KW3 6BS ☎ 01593 721721 ▤ 01593 721722
e-mail: info@portlandarms.co.uk
*Dir: Beside the main A9 road, when travelling from Inverness to Wick,
hotel situated on the left hand side of the road, 200 yrds from the Lybster
sign*
Long a favoured stop-off point between Wick and Thurso, the
Portland Arms dates from the 19th century. Dine in the
informal Jo's Kitchen, the Bistro Bar, or the more formal
Library. In Jo's Kitchen expect toasties, sandwiches, steak pie,
Aga baked ham and pineapple, or salad plates, while the
Library offers trout fillets on sauteed leeks, roast rack of lamb
on potato gallette with apple and apricot compote, or pan-
fried duck breast on goats' cheese gnocchi. Comfortable
accommodation.
OPEN: 7.30-11 Closed: Dec 31-Jan 3 **BAR MEALS:** Lunch served:
all week Dinner served: all week 11.30-3 5-9 Av main course £8
RESTAURANT: Lunch served: all week Dinner served: all week
11.30-3 5-9 Av 3 course à la carte £16 **BREWERY/COMPANY:** Free
House **PRINCIPAL BEERS:** Tennent 70/-. **FACILITIES:** Children
welcome Garden: Food served outside **NOTES:** Parking 20
ROOMS: 22 bedrooms 22 en suite from s£48 d£72.50

NORTH BALLACHULISH   Map 12 NN06

Loch Leven Hotel 🛏
Old Ferry Rd, Onich PH33 6SA
☎ 01855 821236 ▤ 01855 821550
e-mail: reception@lochlevenhotel.co.uk
Dir: off the main A82 at N of Ballachulish Bridge
Over 350 years old, this was a working farm up to 50 years
ago, as well as accommodating travellers from the
Ballachulish ferry. On the northern shore of Loch Leven by the
original slipway, it is ideally placed for touring the Western
Highlands. Local specialities typified by Tobermoray smoked
trout, braised highland lamb shank and chicken stuffed with
haggis underpin a menu of traditional seafood favourites and
an imaginative Oriental selection.
OPEN: 11am-midnight (Thur-Sat 11-1am) **BAR MEALS:** Lunch
served: all week Dinner served: all week 12-3 6-9 Av main course £3
RESTAURANT: 12-3 6-9 Av 3 course à la carte £14 Av 3 course fixed
price £12.50 **BREWERY/COMPANY:** Free House
PRINCIPAL BEERS: Scottish Courage John Smiths, Fountain
McEwan 80/-,. **FACILITIES:** Children welcome Garden: Dogs
allowed (water) **NOTES:** Parking 50 **ROOMS:** 10 bedrooms 10 en
suite from s£20 d£40

ONICH   Map 12 NN06

Pick of the Pubs

Onich Hotel ★ ★ ★ ◉ 🛏
PH33 6RY ☎ 01855 821214 ▤ 01855 821484
e-mail: enquiries@onich-fortwilliam.co.uk
Dir: Beside A82, 2m N of Ballachulish Bridge

Beautifully located hotel on the shores of Loch Linnhe
with spectacular views across to Glencoe and Morvern.
Light meals and hearty bar suppers are served in the
garden lounge, main bar or out on the terrace, alongside
a wide selection of draught beers and malt whiskies.
Typical dishes are ballontine of pheasant and haggis,
breaded Mallaig haddock, and venison casserole.
OPEN: 11-11 **BAR MEALS:** Lunch served: all week Dinner
served: all week 12-10 12-10 Av main course £6.50
RESTAURANT: Dinner served: all week 7-9 Av 4 course fixed
price £26 **BREWERY/COMPANY:** Free House
PRINCIPAL BEERS: Carlsberg-Tetley Tetley Bitter, Calders
Cream, Alloa's 80/- & 70/-. **FACILITIES:** Children welcome
Children's licence Garden: Beer garden, food served outdoors
Dogs allowed (water) **NOTES:** Parking 50
ROOMS: 25 bedrooms 25 en suite

PLOCKTON

Map 12 NG83

Pick of the Pubs

The Plockton Hotel ★ ★
Harbour St IV52 8TN ☎ 01599 544274 🖹 01599 544475
e-mail: sales@plocktonhotel.co.uk
Dir: On A87 to Kyle of Lochalsh take turn at Balmacara. Plockton 7m N.

Stretching along the shores of Loch Carron and looking towards the Applecross Mountains beyond, it is hard to imagine a more lovely spot for a hotel. It was built in 1827 as a private house, but recent developments have resulted in a new garden restaurant and a few more pretty bedrooms in a nearby cottage annexe. The hotel has built its reputation around food, sticking to a successful philosophy of taking produce from the Highland hills and waters, and cooking it simply. Locally-caught langoustines, shellfish from Skye, fresh West Coast fish landed at Gairloch and Kinlochbervie, and Highland beef from Dingwall - all demonstrate the freshest of flavours. Talisker whisky pâté, local queen scallops, and Loch Carron smoked salmon platter starters, poached smoked haddock fillet from the favoured smokehouse at Aultbea, casserole of venison cooked slowly in red wine and juniper berries, and various steaks are all stamped with quality.
OPEN: 11-11.45 (Sun 12.30-11) **BAR MEALS:** Lunch served: all week Dinner served: all week 12-2.15 6-9.15 Av main course £9 **RESTAURANT:** Lunch served: all week Dinner served: all week 12-2.15 6-9.15 Av 3 course à la carte £17
BREWERY/COMPANY: Free House
PRINCIPAL BEERS: Caledonian Deuchars IPA.
FACILITIES: Children welcome Children's licence Garden: Food served outside, waterfront **ROOMS:** 15 bedrooms 15 en suite from s£40 d£30
See Pub Walk on page 581

Pick of the Pubs

Plockton Inn & Seafood Restaurant
Innes St IV52 8TW ☎ 01599 544222 🖹 01599 544487
e-mail: plocktoninn@plocktoninn.freeserve.co.uk
Dir: On A87 to Kyle of Lochalsh take turn at Balmacara. Plockton 7m N

This attractive, stone-built free house stands just 50 metres from the sea, at the heart of the picturesque fishing village that formed the setting for the *Hamish Macbeth* TV series. Formerly a church manse, the

Plockton Inn is now run by a local family. The atmosphere is relaxed and friendly; there are winter fires in both bars, and the prettily decorated en suite bedrooms are comfortable and well-equipped. Local produce takes pride of place on the menu, and locally caught fish and shellfish are prepared in the family's purpose-built smokehouse behind the hotel. At lunch expect freshly made sandwiches, home made soups and hot snacks ranging from jacket potatoes or scampi and chips through to mouthwatering dishes such as a seafood platter from the smokery, haggis with clapshot or moules marinère. A more extensive dinner menu might include cod fillet with tomatoes, olive and parsley or venison collops with bramble and port sauce. Vegetarian options could include baked Camembert or vegetarian haggis.
OPEN: 11-1am **BAR MEALS:** Lunch served: all week Dinner served: all week 12-2.30 5.30-9.30 Av main course £9
RESTAURANT: Lunch served: all week Dinner served: all week 12-2.30 5.30-9.30 Av 3 course à la carte £16
BREWERY/COMPANY: Free House
PRINCIPAL BEERS: Greene King Abbot Ale & Old Speckled Hen, Fuller's London Pride, Isle Of Skye Blaven, Caledonian 80/-.
FACILITIES: Children welcome Garden: Food served outside Dogs allowed **NOTES:** Parking 6 **ROOMS:** 7 bedrooms 6 en suite from s£22.50 d£22.50

SHIELDAIG

Map 12 NG85

Pick of the Pubs

Shieldaig Bar ★  ♀
IV54 8XN ☎ 01520 755251 🖹 01520 755321
e-mail: tighaneileanhotel@shieldaig.fsnet.co.uk

Located right on the loch front in a charming fishing village, this popular bar provides a friendly welcome and stunning views across Loch Torridon to the sea beyond. Visitors and locals mix happily together and the bar is often alive with the sound of local musicians, including the owner Chris Field who can play a pretty exotic selection of instruments. This is a popular rendezvous location throughout the day, so in addition to a full range of alcoholic beverages visitors can order real espresso, coffee, tea and home-baked cakes whilst perusing a ready supply of newspapers and magazines. The menu provides traditional bar food (rib-eye steaks, steak and Guinness pie, smoked haddock omelettes) as well as daily changing specials such as Sheildaig crab bisque with home-made bread or fresh Loch Torridon langoustines with garlic mayonnaise. If you want to stay

continued

continued

SHIELDAIG continued

overnight, take note that the Fields also own the neighbouring Tigh an Eilean hotel.
OPEN: 11–11 (Sun 12.30-10) Closed: Dec 25 & Jan 1
BAR MEALS: Lunch served: all week Dinner served: all week 12–2.30 6–8.30 Av main course £6 **RESTAURANT:** Dinner served: all week 7-8.30 Av 3 course fixed price £27
BREWERY/COMPANY: Free House **FACILITIES:** Children welcome Children's licence Food served outside. Open courtyard Dogs allowed (in the garden only, water provided)
ROOMS: 11 bedrooms 11 en suite from s£49.50 d£110

ULLAPOOL   Map 12 NH19

The Argyll Hotel
Argyll St IV26 2UB ☎ 01854 612422 📠 01854 612522
Traditional family-run hotel just a short stroll from the shores of Loch Broom. Timeless public bar and comfortable main bar, both with open fires and a good choice of malt whiskies to choose from. West Coast scallops and halibut, chicken supreme, venison medallions, and haggis, neeps and tatties feature on the varied menus.
OPEN: 11–11 (Sun 12-11) **BAR MEALS:** Lunch served: all week Dinner served: all week 12–2.30 5.30–9 Av main course £7.50
RESTAURANT: Dinner served: all week 5.30–9 Av 3 course à la carte £13.50 **BREWERY/COMPANY:** Free House
PRINCIPAL BEERS: Calders 70/-, 2 Scottish guest ales.
FACILITIES: Children welcome Dogs allowed **NOTES:** Parking 20
ROOMS: 8 bedrooms 6 en suite from s£30 d£45

Pick of the Pubs

The Ceilidh Place 🌀
14 West Argyle St IV26 2TY
☎ 01854 612103 📠 01854 612886
e-mail: reception@ceilidh.demon.co.uk
Dir: On entering Ullapool, along Shore St, pass pier and take 1st R. Hotel is straight ahead at top of hill

An Ullapool institution for more than 30 years, the Ceilidh Place is set back from the port from where the ferry crosses to Lewis. It is a unique venue comprising an all-day bar, informal dining area, bookshop and a comprehensive display of art for visitors to enjoy at their leisure, all under one roof. Bedrooms in the hotel and bunkhouse are comfortably furnished, if somewhat basic, but the friendly welcome and range of real ales and malt whiskies more than compensate. Locally landed fish is always available in dishes like fillet of cod on garlic mash and rocket purée, or monkfish wrapped in bacon with sauerkraut and chorizo sausage. Regular favourites from

the menu are local haddock, lamb casserole with Heather Ale, and a Mediterranean vegetable pie.
OPEN: 11–11 (Sun 12.30-11) Closed: 2nd Wk in Jan for 2 Wks
BAR MEALS: Lunch served: all week 12–6 6.30–9.30 Av main course £10 **RESTAURANT:** Dinner served: all week 7–9.30 Av 3 course à la carte £22 **BREWERY/COMPANY:** Free House
PRINCIPAL BEERS: Belhaven Best,. **FACILITIES:** Children's licence Garden: Patio, fruit trees & herbs Dogs allowed (garden only) **NOTES:** Parking 20 **ROOMS:** 13 bedrooms 10 en suite from s£40 d£80

Morefield Hotel & Mariners Restaurant
North Rd IV26 2TQ ☎ 01854 612161 📠 01854 612171
Dir: On North Road, on outskirts of town
Popular bar and seafood restaurant, also known for its large selection of malt whiskies and ports. Possible dishes include lobster royale, seafood thermidor, or Achiltibuie salmon and roast scallop terrine. If youre not feeling fishy try Aberdeen Angus prime sirloin, pork fillet Stilton, or something from the vegetarian menu.
OPEN: 11–2.30 5–11 (11–11 summer) **BAR MEALS:** Lunch served: all week Dinner served: all week 12–2 5.30–9.30 Av main course £9
RESTAURANT: Dinner served: all week 6.30–9.30 Av 3 course à la carte £20 **BREWERY/COMPANY:** Free House
PRINCIPAL BEERS: Belhaven, Tennent, 2 guest ales.
FACILITIES: Children welcome Small beer garden **NOTES:** Parking 50 **ROOMS:** 10 bedrooms 10 en suite from s£25 d£40

MIDLOTHIAN

PENICUIK   Map 11 NT25

The Howgate Restaurant 🌀 ♀
Howgate EH26 8PY ☎ 01968 670000 📠 01968 670000
e-mail: Peter@howgate.f9.co.uk
Dir: On A6094, 3m SE of Penicuik
This recently opened restaurant and bistro occupies a long, low 18th-century stable building. Now tastefully refurbished, the atmosphere is warm and welcoming, with winter log fires in the bistro and a slightly more formal ambience in the restaurant. The regularly changing menus offer traditional recipes alongside more adventurous, modern dishes. Chargrilled Borders lamb, Cajun spiced salmon, or sun-dried tomato and woodland mushroom risotto are just a taste of what's on offer.
OPEN: 12–2.30 6–11 Closed: Dec 25-26, 1 Jan **BAR MEALS:** Lunch served: all week Dinner served: all week 12–2.30 6–9.30 Av main course £9 **RESTAURANT:** Lunch served: all week Dinner served: all week 12–2.30 6–9.30 Av 3 course à la carte £25
BREWERY/COMPANY: Free House
PRINCIPAL BEERS: Belhaven Best. **FACILITIES:** Children welcome Children's licence Garden **NOTES:** Parking 45

MORAY

FOCHABERS   Map 13 NJ35

Gordon Arms Hotel 🌀
80 High St IV32 7DH ☎ 01343 820508 📠 01343 820300
e-mail: info@gordonarmshotel.com
This family-run, 18th-century coaching inn retains much of its original character, and the inn's reputation rests on over 200 years of good food and comfortable accommodation. The

continued

continued

public rooms have been carefully refurbished, and the en-suite bedrooms make a good base for walking, or salmon fishing on the nearby River Spey. Tasty lunches and suppers are served in the bar, while the restaurant menus make good use of local venison, lamb and seafood.
OPEN: 11–3 5–11 (Sun 12–3, 6–10.30) **BAR MEALS:** Lunch served: all week Dinner served: all week 12–2 5–7 **RESTAURANT:** Lunch served: all week Dinner served: all week 12–2 7–9 Av 3 course à la carte £18 **BREWERY/COMPANY:** Free House **PRINCIPAL BEERS:** Caledonian Deuchars IPA, Scottish Courage John Smith's Smooth. **FACILITIES:** Children welcome Children's licence Dogs allowed **NOTES:** Parking 40 **ROOMS:** 14 bedrooms 14 en suite from s£45 d£65

PERTH & KINROSS

ABERFELDY
Map 13 NN84

Ailean Chraggan Hotel ♈
Weem PH15 2LD ☎ 01887 820346 📠 01887 829009
Dir: A9 N to jct at Ballinluig then A827 onto Aberfeldy, R onto B846
Small hotel in the heart of Scotland, with views over the River Tay to the hills beyond. Quality local produce is a feature of the menus, notably salmon from the Tay, beef, and game in season. Expect the likes of Loch Etive whole prawn platter, roast Scottish beef with Yorkshire puddings, Gressingham duck breast and blackcurrant sauce, tortellini formaggio, or oatmeal crumb haddock. Large garden and two outside terraces for meals or relaxing.
OPEN: 12–2 6.30–9.30 (8.30 in winter) Closed: 25–26 Dec, 1–2 Jan **BAR MEALS:** Lunch served: all week Dinner served: all week 12–2 6.30–9.30 **RESTAURANT:** Lunch served: all week Dinner served: all week 12–2 6.30–9.30 **BREWERY/COMPANY:** Free House **FACILITIES:** Children welcome Garden: Food served outside Dogs allowed **NOTES:** Parking 40 **ROOMS:** 5 bedrooms 5 en suite from s£42.50 d£75

ALMONDBANK
Map 10 NO02

Almondbank Inn 🍴 ♈
31 Main St PH1 3NJ ☎ 01738 583242 📠 01738 582471
Dir: From Perth take A85 towards Crieff. 3m to Almondbank
Strangers are made very welcome at this small family-run pub, which dates back about 100 years. The resident ghost has been seen on three different occasions. There are fine views from its neat rear garden, as well as walks along the River Almond, which is famous for its fishing. Imaginative pub grub is a speciality, and the extensive dinner menu features steaks, haddock fillet, duck with wild berries, and Mediterranean lamb shank.
OPEN: 11–3 5–11 (All day Mon & Fri, Fri–Sat to 11.45) Closed: Dec, Jan **BAR MEALS:** Lunch served: all week 12–2 Dinner served: Wed–Sun 5–10 Av main course £5 **RESTAURANT:** Lunch served: all week 12–2.30 Dinner served: Wed–Sun 5–10 Av 3 course à la carte £15 **BREWERY/COMPANY:** Free House **PRINCIPAL BEERS:** Broughton Greenmantle, Bellhaven 70/-,. **FACILITIES:** Children welcome Garden: Overlooking River Almond, food served outside Dogs allowed (water, biscuits)

BURRELTON
Map 13 NO23

The Burrelton Park Inn
High St PH13 9NX ☎ 01828 670206
Ideally situated for touring the highlands, this long roadside inn is characterised by its typical Scottish vernacular style. Spacious lounge bar and conservatory offering steamed mussels, braised lambs' liver and farmhouse mixed grill, and a well appointed restaurant featuring stuffed supreme of chicken and vension fillet – among other more elaborate dishes. Fresh catch of the day and special high teas served.
OPEN: 12–2.30 5–11 (Sat–Sun 12–11) **BAR MEALS:** Lunch served: all week Dinner served: all week 12–2 7–8.30 Av main course £6.95 **RESTAURANT:** Lunch served: all week Dinner served: all week 12–2 7–8.30 Av 3 course à la carte £18 **BREWERY/COMPANY:** Free House **PRINCIPAL BEERS:** Changing guest ales. **FACILITIES:** Children welcome Dogs allowed **NOTES:** Parking 30 **ROOMS:** 5 bedrooms 5 en suite from s£30 d£45

CLEISH
Map 10 NT09

Nivingston House ★ ★ ★
KY13 0LS ☎ 01577 850216 📠 01577 850238
e-mail: info@nivingstonhousehotel.co.uk
Dir: 2m W of M90 J5
17th-century converted farmhouse in 14 acres of landscaped grounds. Wonderful views of the Cleish Hills. Lunch and dinner menus change daily and the ingredients used are market fresh every day. Expect rack of Perthshire lamb with rosemary and sherry sauce, Asian style pork chop with orange sate and sesame sauce, spinach and Ricotta cheese parcels baked with red peppers, and grilled Scottish salmon with prawn and lobster sauce among the imaginatively devised dishes.
OPEN: 12–2.30 5.30–11 **BAR MEALS:** Lunch served: all week Dinner served: all week 12–2 7–9 Av main course £10 **RESTAURANT:** Lunch served: all week Dinner served: all week 12–2 7–9 **BREWERY/COMPANY:** Free House **PRINCIPAL BEERS:** Calders. **FACILITIES:** Children welcome Garden: 12 acres, food served outside **NOTES:** Parking 40 **ROOMS:** 17 bedrooms 17 en suite from s£70 d£90

Pins & Firkins
Brewing has a rich store of technical terms and old-fashioned measures. The conventional container for draught beer – for centuries made of wood, but nowadays of metal – is called a cask. A barrel in brewing terminology is a 36-gallon cask, and a keg is a sealed metal container for beer that has been filtered, sterilised and pressurised before leaving the brewery. British beer in pubs still comes in pints or half-pints, and pubs still order their beer using the old-style cask measures, which follow a scale of nine
pin – 4.5 gallons **firkin** – 9 gallons
kilderkin – 18 gallons **barrel** – 36 gallons
hogshead – 54 gallons
Two obsolete cask sizes are the butt of 108 gallons and the tun, which held varying quantities above 200 gallons. A yard of ale is a glass tube 3ft long and containing up to 3 pints, now only used in drinking contests.

GLENDEVON   Map 10 NN90

Pick of the Pubs

Tormaukin Hotel 👁 ♀
FK14 7JY ☎ 01259 781252 🖨 01259 781526
e-mail: enquiries@tormaukin.co.uk
Dir: On A823 between M90 & A9
Surrounded by the Ochil Hills, this 18th-century former
drovers' inn has an idyllic setting in the middle of the
'Hidden Glen', yet hill walks, loch and river fishing and
golf courses are all within easy reach. Sympathetic
refurbishment has retained many original features,
including stone walls, exposed beams and natural timbers.
Bar lunches and suppers, served in front of blazing log
fires in the cosy lounge and bars, cover a range of snacks,
children's choices and daily blackboard specials. Dishes
could include fillet steak with sauté mushrooms and
onions or pork and apple sausages with lamb loin. The
main menu has an equally traditional appeal: expect the
likes of pan-seared fillet of Scottish salmon on mash,
topped with spring onion crackling or breast of cornfed
chicken served on wild mushroom risotto with brandy
cream sauce. Round with desserts such as iced Drambuie
soufflé with marmalade sauce or peach Pavlova served on
a pear coulis.
OPEN: 11–11 (Sun 12–11) Closed: 25 Dec **BAR MEALS:** Lunch
served: all week Dinner served: all week 12–2.15 5.30–9.30
RESTAURANT: Dinner served: all week 6.30–9.30
BREWERY/COMPANY: Free House
PRINCIPAL BEERS: Harviestoun Brooker's Bitter & Twisted,
Timothy Taylor Landlord. **FACILITIES:** Children welcome
Garden: Patio area food served outside **NOTES:** Parking 50
ROOMS: 12 bedrooms 12 en suite

GLENFARG   Map 11 NO11

The Bein Inn 👁 ♀
PH2 9PY ☎ 01577 830216 🖨 01577 830211
e-mail: enquiries@beininn.com

Dating from 1861, this historic inn is a stone's throw from
Balvaird Castle which featured in the 1995 film version of Rob
Roy. Open log fires and a cosy lounge add to the charm, and
the basement bar is decorated with authentic rock music
memorabilia from the 60s and 70s; live music programme
featuring international artists. House specialities include Pa
Mundell's Sirloin Bonnie Prince Charlie in mushroom and
drambuie sauce, grilled fillet of cod on tomato and lentil
casserole, and Highland venison steak.
OPEN: 11–2.30 5–11 **BAR MEALS:** Lunch served: all week Dinner
served: all week 12–2 5–9 Av main course £9.75

RESTAURANT: Lunch served: all week Dinner served: all week 12–2
7–9 Av 3 course à la carte £17 **BREWERY/COMPANY:** Free House
PRINCIPAL BEERS: Belhaven Best. **FACILITIES:** Dogs allowed
NOTES: Parking 30 **ROOMS:** 11 bedrooms 11 en suite from s£25
d£50

KILLIECRANKIE   Map 13 NN96

Pick of the Pubs

The Killiecrankie Hotel ★ ★ ⊚⊚ 👁 ♀
PH16 5LG ☎ 01796 473220 🖨 01796 472451
e-mail: enquiries@killiecrankiehotel.co.uk
Dir: Turn off A9 at Killiecrankie. Hotel 3m N on B8079 on R
Good food together with genuine hospitality and a high
level of personal attention are the hallmarks of this
charming holiday hotel set in mature gardens at the
northern end of the National Trust's Killiecrankie Pass.
Well-presented day rooms include a relaxing lounge and
cosy well-stocked bar with an adjacent conservatory for
informal eating. In new hands, indigenous Scottish
produce is still a notable feature of menus here that
promise sautéed king scallops with crispy air-dried ham
and pesto sauce, pan-fired fillet of Abedeen Angus beef
with Meaux mustard mash and red wine jus. The more
sweet-toothed will enjoy the Drambuie pannacotta with
orange zest syrup and shortbread. An elegant dining
room with striking table appointments, lit candles and
fresh flowers adds a more special location for fixed-price
dinners that allow similarly fine ingredients to speak for
themselves. Bright airy bedrooms are furnished in pine
and well equipped with a wide range of amenities.
OPEN: 11–2.30 5.30–11.00 Closed: All Jan, Mon–Tue in Feb, Mar
& Dec **BAR MEALS:** Lunch served: all week Dinner served: all
week 12.30–2 6.30–8 Av main course £8 **RESTAURANT:** Dinner
served: all week 7–8.30 Av 4 course fixed price £32
BREWERY/COMPANY: Free House **FACILITIES:** Children
welcome Children's licence Garden: Patio, food served
outdoors **NOTES:** Parking 20 **ROOMS:** 10 bedrooms 10 en
suite from s£75 d£150

KINNESSWOOD   Map 11 NN10

Pick of the Pubs

Lomond Country Inn ★ ★ ⊚ 👁 ♀
KY13 9HN ☎ 01592 840253 🖨 01592 840693
e-mail: enquiries@lomondcountryinn.com
Dir: M90 J5, follow signs for Glenrothes then Scotlandwell,
Kinnesswood next village
A small, privately owned hotel on the slopes of the
Lomond Hills that has been entertaining guests for more
than 100 years. It is the only hostelry in the area with
uninterrupted views over Loch Leven to the island on
which Mary Queen of Scots was imprisoned. All the en
suite bedrooms are furnished to a high standard, whilst
cosy public areas offer log fires, a friendly atmosphere,
real ales and a fine collection of single malts. Bar meals
make superb use of local produce such as Pitween
haddock, game casserole or fillet of Tay salmon with herb
and prawn butter. If you want to make the most of the
loch views, choose the AA rosette-winning restaurant, a
relaxing room freshly decorated in country house style.
The menu incorporates dishes available in the bar
alongside daily changing specials such as pan-seared

continued

continued

PUB WALK

Pitlochry
Moulin Hotel

Scotland is great for walking and this invigorating route, starting at the Moulin Hotel just outside Pitlochry, captures the beauty and character of this magical landscape

Rising to the north of Pitlochry is the rocky outcrop of Craigower. This hill, at one time used as a beacon, is now in the care of the National Trust for Scotland who permit access to the summit. Its superb setting provides splendid views over the confluence of the Rivers Tummel and Garry to the north and west, and the valleys of the Tummel and the Tay to the south-east. At the summit there is an annotated photograph highlighting important landmarks in the area, especially the view to the west, which stretches as far as Glencoe. To get there turn left on leaving the pub, following the road signposted to Craigower. Head for the golf course and make sure no-one is playing as you cross it. Continue past a small cottage and on up into some conifer woods on the lower slopes of Craigower. The route through these woods is clearly signposted and should present no real difficulties, although please remember to bear left when crossing the forestry road in order to stay on the direct route to the summit. Near the top this route becomes steep, but if you wish to avoid the steep ascent, there is an alternative. Simply turn right, along the forestry road, for a longer, but more gradual, approach to the summit. This road can also be used as an alternative return route. Retrace your steps to the Moulin Hotel.

MOULIN HOTEL
11-13 Kirkmichael Road, Moulin
PITLOCHRY PH16 5EW
Tel: 01796 472196
Directions: From A9 at Pitlochry take A923. Moulin 0.75m
Under 2,757ft Ben Vrackie, on the old Dunkeld-Kingussie drove road, Moulin's summer courtyard garden and winter log fires and pub games make it popular with walkers, tourists and locals. Real ales from own micro-brewery, and Gaelic fare on big, all-day menu.
Open: 12-11
Bar meals: 12-9.30
Children welcome and dogs allowed. Garden and parking available.

Distance: 3 miles (4.8km)
Map: OS Landranger 43 & 52
Terrain: Tree-clad slopes
Paths: : Forest roads and paths
Gradient: Some steep climbing

Walk submitted and checked by the Moulin Hotel, Pitlochry

KINNESSWOOD continued

breast of pheasant with onion marmalade and black pudding.
OPEN: 11–11 **BAR MEALS:** Lunch served: all week Dinner served: all week 12–2.30 6–9.30 Av main course £8
RESTAURANT: Lunch served: all week Dinner served: all week 12–2.30 6–9.30 Av 3 course à la carte £15
BREWERY/COMPANY: Free House
PRINCIPAL BEERS: Deuchers IPA, Calders Cream, Tetleys, Orkney Dark Island. **FACILITIES:** Children welcome Children's licence Garden: Food served outside. Lawn & landscaping Dogs allowed Kennels **NOTES:** Parking 50 **ROOMS:** 12 bedrooms 12 en suite from s£44 d£49

KINROSS   Map 10 NO10

The Muirs Inn Kinross ♦♦♦ 🐑
49 Muirs KY13 8AU ☎ 01577 862270 ▤ 01577 862270
e-mail: themuirsinn@aol.com
Dir: *from M90 J6 take A922 to T-junction. Inn diagonally opposite on R*
Originally a small farmhouse where the local blacksmith tended to travellers' horses and carriages, this listed inn takes its name from the old Scottish word for moorland. The Mash Tun public bar features rare, hand-etched ornamental glass and mirrors, as well as a custom-built gantry dating back to 1909. There is a good selection of beers and malt whiskies to accompany starters such as smoked haddock chowder and local black pudding, or main dishes of Cajun chicken breast, lamb cutlets or seared snapper.
OPEN: 12–11 **BAR MEALS:** Lunch served: all week Dinner served: all week 12–2.30 5–9 Av main course £3.50 **RESTAURANT:** Lunch served: all week Dinner served: all week 12–2 5–9.30 Av 3 course à la carte £17.95 **BREWERY/COMPANY:** Free House
PRINCIPAL BEERS: Belhaven 80/-, Orkney Dark Island.
FACILITIES: Children welcome Children's licence Garden: Beer garden, patio, food served outside Dogs allowed (water)
NOTES: Parking 8 **ROOMS:** 5 bedrooms 5 en suite from s£37.50 d£55

PITLOCHRY   Map 13 NN95

Pick of the Pubs

Moulin Hotel ★ ★ ♀
11–13 Kirkmichael Rd, Moulin PH16 5EW
☎ 01796 472196 ▤ 01796 474098
e-mail: hotel@moulin.u-net.com
Dir: *From A9 at Pitlochry take A923. Moulin 0.75m*

Half a century before the Jacobite rebellion of 1745, the Moulin Hotel was established at the foot of 2,757ft Ben

Vrackie, on the old drove road from Dunkeld to Kingussie. The modern road runs through nearby Pitlochry, leaving Moulin as an ideal base for walking and touring. The large, white painted pub with its summer courtyard garden is popular with tourists and locals alike, whilst in winter, two blazing log fires set the scene for a game of cards, dominoes or bar billiards. Well-kept real ales come from the pub's own micro-brewery, and there's plenty of Gaelic fare on the big all-day menu. Start with potted hough and oatcakes, or Skye mussels with garlic, before moving on to venison Braveheart, haggis and neeps, or a game casserole McDuff. There's haddock or salmon too, and vegetarians can expect sautéed mushroom pancakes, stuffed peppers, and vegetable goulash. Bedrooms vary in size and style, with on-going refurbishment steadily improving standards of comfort and facilities.
OPEN: 12–11 (Fri-Sat 12–11.45) **BAR MEALS:** Lunch served: all week Dinner served: all week 12–9.30 Av main course £6.50
RESTAURANT: Dinner served: all week 6–9 Av 3 course à la carte £21 Av 4 course fixed price £18.95
BREWERY/COMPANY: Free House
PRINCIPAL BEERS: Moulin Braveheart, Old Remedial, Ale of Atholl & Moulin Light. **FACILITIES:** Children welcome Garden: Food served outside Dogs allowed **NOTES:** Parking 40
ROOMS: 15 bedrooms 15 en suite from s£35 d£40

See Pub Walk on page 591

The Old Mill Inn 🐑 ♀ NEW
Mill Ln PH16 5BH ☎ 01796 474020
e-mail: r@old-mill-inn.com
Dir: *In the centre of Pitlochry, along Mill Lane. Behind the post office.*

Set at the gateway to the Highlands, this converted old mill still boasts a working water wheel, now with a patio overlooking it. Visitors are assured of a good choice of real ales, malts and wine by the glass to accompany an eclectic cuisine: smoked haddock chowder, Stornaway black pudding, steamed mussels, salmon stir-fry, plus burgers, bacon and brie ciabatta, and smoked salmon bagel.
OPEN: 10–11 **BAR MEALS:** Lunch served: all week Dinner served: all week 10–10 Av main course £7.95 **RESTAURANT:** Lunch served: all week Dinner served: all week 10–10 Av 3 course à la carte £15
BREWERY/COMPANY: Free House
PRINCIPAL BEERS: Carlsberg-Tetley Tetley Bitter, Orkney Dark Island, Caledonian 80/-, Kettle Ale. **FACILITIES:** Children welcome Garden: Food served outside **NOTES:** Parking 10
ROOMS: 6 bedrooms 6 en suite from s£55 d£45

continued

Scotland (side tab)

POWMILL · Map 10 NT09

Gartwhinzean Hotel ★ ★ ★
FK14 7NW ☎ 01577 840595 ▤ 01577 840779
Dir: A977 to Kincardine Bridge road, for approx 7m to the vilage of Powmill, hotel at the end of village
Located between two of Scotland's finest cities, Edinburgh and Perth, and handy for exploring the nearby Ochil and Cleish Hills, this attractive hotel overlooks Perthshire's picturesque countryside. A large selection of malt whiskies and a cosy open fire add to the attractions. Traditional steak pie, lightly grilled fillet of salmon and noisettes of lamb feature among the dishes on the interesting, regularly changing menu.
OPEN: 11–11 **BAR MEALS:** Lunch served: all week Dinner served: all week 12–2 5–8.45 Av main course £7 **RESTAURANT:** Lunch served: all week Dinner served: all week 12–2 5–8.45 Av 3 course à la carte £20 Av 3 course fixed price £17.50
BREWERY/COMPANY: Free House **PRINCIPAL BEERS:** Tetley Smoothflow, 70/-. **FACILITIES:** Children welcome Garden: Food served outside **NOTES:** Parking 100 **ROOMS:** 23 bedrooms 23 en suite

RENFREWSHIRE

HOUSTON · Map 10 NS46

Fox & Hounds 🕮 ⌇
South St PA6 7EN ☎ 01505 612448 & 612991 ▤ 01505 614133
e-mail: jonathan@foxandhoundshouston.co.uk
Dir: M8 - Glasgow Airport. A737-Houston
The horse tack decorating the first-floor Huntsman's bar gives this popular, well-kept 18th-century village inn a somewhat English atmosphere. But the extensive, freshly-prepared menu tells a different story. With an emphasis on fresh Scottish produce look for rack of Scottish lamb, seafood platter, pached salmon steak, and veal 'Fox & Hounds'. What's more, you can wash down dishes like chicken rusty nail, fresh peppered tuna steak, or home-made aubergine bake with award-winning ales from the on-site Houston Brewery.
OPEN: 11–11 (11–1am Fri-Sat, 12.30-12 Sun) **BAR MEALS:** Lunch served: all week Dinner served: all week 12–2.30 5.30-10 Av main course £6.95 **RESTAURANT:** Lunch served: all week Dinner served: all week 12–2.30 5.30-10 Av 3 course à la carte £18
BREWERY/COMPANY: Free House **PRINCIPAL BEERS:** St Peters Well, Killelan, Barochan, Texas & Jack Frost. **FACILITIES:** Children welcome Children's licence Dogs allowed **NOTES:** Parking 40

SCOTTISH BORDERS

AUCHENCROW · Map 11 NT86

The Craw Inn NEW
TD14 5LS ☎ 018907 61253
e-mail: info@thecrawinn.co.uk
Ideally located for all country pursuits, this listed 18th century inn is has been cleverly refurbished to preserve its charm: think low beams, delightfully mismatched wooden furniture and exposed areas of floorboards and brick work. The menu reveals a good selection of fish and seafood: perhaps Thai prawns, whole fresh fish or assiette de fruits de mer. Heartier treats after a long walk could include Aberdeen Angus steak, rack of lamb or game.   No credit cards

EDDLESTON · Map 11 NT24

Horse Shoe Inn
EH45 8QP ☎ 01721 730225 ▤ 01721 730268
e-mail: horseshoe@ladon.co.uk
Dir: On A703 S of Edinburgh. From M74 to Biggar, then A72 to Peebles & A703 N to Eddleston
Situated in glorious Border country near historic Peebles and cosmopolitan Edinburgh, this former village smithy was once a coffee shop and a garage. The doors and wooden panelling come from a church. Impressive menu offers such dishes as braised lamb shank, cod in beer batter, mushroom risotto, and Aberdeen Angus beef and ale pie. Interesting selection of lighter bites and puddings, including chilled caramelised apple tart and traditional cranachan. Wide-ranging wine list.
OPEN: 11–3 5.30-12 **BAR MEALS:** Lunch served: Tues-Sun 12–2.30 Dinner served: Tues-Sat 6–9 Av main course £7.95 **RESTAURANT:** Lunch served: all week Dinner served: all week 12–2.30 6–9.30 Av 3 course à la carte £15
BREWERY/COMPANY: Free House
PRINCIPAL BEERS: McEwans 70/-, Scottish Courage John Smith's, Caledonian 80/-. **FACILITIES:** Children's licence Garden: Patio, food served outside **NOTES:** Parking 35 **ROOMS:** 7 bedrooms 7 en suite from s£25 d£25

ETTRICK · Map 11 NT21

Tushielaw Inn 🕮
TD7 5HT ☎ 01750 62205 ▤ 01750 62205
e-mail: Gordon.Harrison@Virgin.net
Dir: At junction of B709 & B711(W of Hawick)
On the banks of Ettrick Water, surrounded by the Border hills, is this 18th-century former coaching inn and drovers' halt. Free trout fishing on Clearburn Loch is provided to residents, and salmon fishing permits are available. The inn appeals to walkers and cyclists with its welcoming open fire and wholesome meals, including steak and stout pie, deepfried breaded haddock, Aberdeen Angus sirloin steaks, grilled Scottish lamb cutlets, and of course, local trout.
OPEN: 12–2.30 6–11 Closed: 25 Dec, 1Jan **BAR MEALS:** Lunch served: Fri-Mon 12–2.15 Dinner served: all week 7–9 Av main course £8 **RESTAURANT:** Lunch served: Fri-Mon 12–2.15 Dinner served: all week 7–9 Av 3 course à la carte £15 **BREWERY/COMPANY:** Free House **FACILITIES:** Children welcome Children's licence Garden: Patio, food served outside Dogs allowed **NOTES:** Parking 8 **ROOMS:** 3 bedrooms 3 en suite from s£30 d£48

GALASHIELS · Map 11 NT43

Abbotsford Arms ★ ★ 🕮
63 Stirling St TD1 1BY ☎ 01896 752517 ▤ 01896 750744
e-mail: abb2517@aol.com
Dir: Turn off A7 down Ladhope Vale, turn L opposite the Bus Station
Ideal for local golf courses and touring the beautiful Borders countryside, this family-run, stone-built 19th-century coaching inn offers comfortable accommodation and traditional bar food. The menu includes steaks, lasagne, swordfish, beef, and chicken dishes. Function room available, holding up to 150.
OPEN: 11–11 Closed: 25 Dec, 2 Jan **BAR MEALS:** Lunch served: all week Dinner served: all week 2–6 6–9 Av main course £6 **RESTAURANT:** Lunch served: all week Dinner served: all week 12–6 6–9 Av 3 course à la carte £14 **BREWERY/COMPANY:** Free House **PRINCIPAL BEERS:** Scottish courage John Smith's, Belhaven 60/-. **FACILITIES:** Children welcome Children's licence Garden: Beer garden, food served outdoors **NOTES:** Parking 10 **ROOMS:** 14 bedrooms 14 en suite from s£40 d£60

Scotland

GALASHIELS continued

Kingsknowles ★ ★ ★ 🐾
1 Selkirk Rd TD1 3HY ☎ 01896 758375 🖳 01896 750377
e-mail: enquiries@kingsknowes.co.uk
Dir: Off A7 at Galashiels/Selkirk rdbt

Splendid baronial mansion set in over three acres of grounds
on the banks of the famous River Tweed. Lovely views of
Eildon Hills and Abbotsford House, Sir Walter Scott's ancestral
home. Only fresh local produce is used and among the typical
specials are the likes of poached Scottish salmon with a light
cheese sauce and Norwegian prawns, and medallions of pork
in a mushroom and tarragon jus.
BAR MEALS: Lunch served: all week Dinner served: all week 11.45-2
5.45-9.30 Av main course £9 **RESTAURANT:** Lunch served: all week
Dinner served: all week 11.45-2 5.45-9.30 Av 3 course à la carte
£19.25 Av 5 course fixed price £19.95 **BREWERY/COMPANY:** Free
House **PRINCIPAL BEERS:** McEwans 80/-, Scottish Courage John
Smith's. **FACILITIES:** Children welcome Garden 3.5 acres, food
served outside Dogs allowed **NOTES:** Parking 60
ROOMS: 11 bedrooms 11 en suite from s£54 d£80

INNERLEITHEN   Map 11 NT33

Traquair Arms Hotel ♦♦♦ 🐾
Traquair Rd EH44 6PD ☎ 01896 830229 🖳 01896 830260
e-mail: traquair.arms@scotborders.com
Dir: 6m E of Peebles on A72. Hotel 100metres from junc with B709
This traditional stone-built inn is in a village setting close to
the River Tweed, surrounded by lovely Borders countryside
and offering en suite bedrooms, a dining room and cosy bar.
Real ales include Traquair Ale from nearby Traquair House,
and the food has a distinctive Scottish flavour with dishes of
Finnan savoury, salmon with ginger and coriander, and fillet
of beef Traquair. Also a selection of omelettes, salads, and
baked potatoes are available.
OPEN: 11-12 Closed: 25 Dec, 1 Jan **BAR MEALS:** Lunch served: all
week Dinner served: all week 12-9 Av main course £6.25
RESTAURANT: Lunch served: all week Dinner served: all week 12-9
Av 3 course à la carte £18 Av 4 course fixed price £20
BREWERY/COMPANY: Free House **PRINCIPAL BEERS:** Traquair
Bear, Broughton Greenmantle & Black Douglas. **FACILITIES:** Children
welcome Garden: Dogs allowed **NOTES:** Parking 75
ROOMS: 15 bedrooms 15 en suite from s£45 d£29

KELSO   Map 11 NT73

Queens Head Hotel ★ ★ 🐾 ♇
Bridge St TD5 7JD ☎ 01573 224636 🖳 01573 224459
Situated between the cobbled square and Rennie's Bridge
over the Tweed, this 18th-century Georgian coaching inn has
historical connections with Kelso Abbey and Bonnie Prince

continued

Charlie. The function room started life as a School of
Callisthenics and Dance in 1833. Home-cooked food with an
international slant, served in the comfortable lounge and
restaurant, includes beef Stroganoff, jambalaya, chow mein,
chimay changa, grilled sardines with Greek salad, and venison
and wild boar sausages.
OPEN: 12-2 Fri-Sat 12-1am 6-11 **BAR MEALS:** Lunch served: all
week Dinner served: all week 12-2 6-9 Av main course £5.95
RESTAURANT: Lunch served: all week Dinner served: all week 12-2
6-9 Av 3 course à la carte £15 **BREWERY/COMPANY:** Free House
PRINCIPAL BEERS: Millers, 70/-, 80/-. Old Speckled Hen, John
Smiths Smooth. **FACILITIES:** Children welcome Dogs allowed
ROOMS: 11 bedrooms 10 en suite from s£40.50 d£43

LAUDER   Map 11 NT54

Lauderdale Hotel
1 Edinburgh Rd TD2 6TW ☎ 01578 722231 🖳 01578 718642
e-mail: Enquiries@lauderdale-hotel.co.uk
Dir: on the main A68 25m S of Edinburgh
Imposing Edwardian building standing in its own extensive
grounds. A cheerful lounge bar and a good range of
generously served food. Abundant floral displays during
summer. Dishes include deep fried chicken fillets, rich beef
gylas, apricot stuffed roast loin of pork, and roast of the day.
Regularly changing specials blackboard.
OPEN: 11-12 (11-1am Fri-Sat) **BAR MEALS:** Lunch served: all
week Dinner served: all week 12-9 Av main course £6.20
RESTAURANT: Lunch served: all week Dinner served: all week 12-9
Av 3 course à la carte £15.50 **BREWERY/COMPANY:** Free House
PRINCIPAL BEERS: Deuchars IPA. **FACILITIES:** Children welcome
Children's licence Garden: Beer garden with seating,food served
outdoors **NOTES:** Parking 50 **ROOMS:** 10 bedrooms 10 en suite
from s£37 d£65

MELROSE   Map 11 NT53

Pick of the Pubs

Burts Hotel 😊😊
Market Square TD6 9PN ☎ 01896 822285 🖳 01896 822870
e-mail: burtshotel@aol.com
Dir: A6091, 2m from A68 3m South of Earlsdon
Family-owned and run for over 30 years, Burts, built in
1722 for a local dignitary, stands on the picturesque
market square of this interesting Borders town. A hunting
and shooting theme extends through the busy bars and
restaurant warmed by winter log fires, where classic
Scottish ales and over 100 malt whiskies are on dispense.
Lunch and bar suppers change in response to market
availability of local produce and come in well-planned
and executed combinations. To start, escabèche of hake
with Niçoise salad and avocado and basil salsa or a filo
tartlet of Stilton, roast red peppers and cherry tomato;
followed by marinated chicken supreme in Thai red curry
with spiced onion and cucumber yoghurt or sole
paupiettes on marinated brocolli and spinach cream.
Scotch Border lamb cutlets, home-made beef-burgers and
Aberdeen Angus steaks for heartier appetites, with warm
treacle tart or Selkirk Bannock pudding and caramel sauce
to follow. Fixed-price restaurant lunches and dinner offer
similar quality ingredients in more elaborate guises,
accompanied by interesting house wines.
OPEN: 11-2.30 5-11 **BAR MEALS:** Lunch served: all week
Dinner served: all week 12-2 6-9.30 **RESTAURANT:** Lunch
served: all week Dinner served: all week 12-2 7-9

continued

BREWERY/COMPANY: Free House
PRINCIPAL BEERS: Caledonian 80/-, Deuchars IPA, Timothy Taylor Ladlord. **FACILITIES:** Children welcome Children's licence Garden: Dogs allowed **NOTES:** Parking 40
ROOMS: 20 bedrooms 20 en suite

ST BOSWELLS   Map 11 NT53

Buccleuch Arms Hotel ★ ★
The Green TD6 0EW ☎ 01835 822243 ▤ 01835 823965
e-mail: bucchotel@aol.com
Dir: on A68, 8m N of Jedburg
Perfectly placed at the heart of the Scottish Borders, this 16th-century inn offers a country welcome in its modern bar. Spacious and comfortable, its varied supper menu includes peppered pork medallions, smoked chicken and avocado, and roast fillet of Scottish lamb. In the restaurant expect roast loin of pork with a whisky and onion sauce, and poached escalope of salmon. Afternoon tea, high tea and a snack menu are also available.
OPEN: 7.30–11 Closed: 25 Dec **BAR MEALS:** Lunch served: all week Dinner served: all week 12–2 6–9 Av main course £6
RESTAURANT: Lunch served: all week Dinner served: all week 12–2 6–9 Av 3 course à la carte £21.95 Av 2 course fixed price £21.95
BREWERY/COMPANY: Free House
PRINCIPAL BEERS: Claders70/-,80/- & Claders Cream Ale, Broughton Greenmantle Ale. **FACILITIES:** Children welcome Garden: Food served outside Dogs allowed **NOTES:** Parking 60
ROOMS: 19 bedrooms 19 en suite from s£30 d£60

SWINTON   Map 11 NT84

Pick of the Pubs

Wheatsheaf Hotel ◆◆◆◆ ⊚⊚ ⌂♈
Main St TD11 3JJ ☎ 01890 860257 ▤ 01890 860688
e-mail: reception@wheatsheaf-swinton.co.uk
Dir: 6m N of Duns on A6112
The Wheatsheaf has been in the same hands for fifteen years, fronted by a chef/patron who is passionate about his use of local produce. Not only does he cook it, he hunts and fishes it too: salmon from the Tweed, game from the Borders and seafood from the Berwickshire coast. In addition to up-graded bedrooms with modern en suite facilities, he's also reverently added a delightful 'fisherman's snug' lounge. Light lunches and snacks, washed down with fine wines or the best Scottish ale, are no less pivotal to his success. Classy dishes such as pheasant and partridge terrine with red onion marmalade rub shoulders with heartier fare, for example braised oxtails with root vegetables and fondant potatoes in a real ale sauce. An à la carte dinner could feature lobster and crayfish bisque laced with brandy, followed by roast loin of highland venison on braised red cabbage with a redcurrant and juniper berry sauce.
OPEN: 11–2.30 (Closed Sun eve in winter) 6–11 (closed Mon) Closed: Last 2 wks Jan, 1 Wk July **BAR MEALS:** Lunch served: Tue–Sun 11.45–2.15 Dinner served: Tue–Sat 6.30–9.30 Av main course £7 **RESTAURANT:** Lunch served: Tue–Sun 11.45–2.15 Dinner served: Tue–Sat 6–9.30 Av 3 course à la carte £25
BREWERY/COMPANY: Free House
PRINCIPAL BEERS: Caledonian 80/- & Deuchers IPA, Broughton Greenmantle Ale. **FACILITIES:** Children welcome Children's licence Garden: Beer garden, food served outdoors, patio, Dogs allowed **NOTES:** Parking 8 **ROOMS:** 8 bedrooms 8 en suite from s£55 d£85

TIBBIE SHIELS INN   Map 11 NT22

Pick of the Pubs

Tibbie Shiels Inn ◆◆◆
St Mary's Loch TD7 5LH ☎ 01750 42231 ▤ 01750 42302
Dir: From Moffat take A708. Inn is 14m on R
Situated on the isthmus between St Mary's Loch and Loch of the Lowes, by the scenic Southern Upland Way, the inn is named after the fine lady who first opened it in 1826 and prospered there for fully 50 years. Its spirit is unchanged, in low-ceilinged, cosy bars full of character and old-world charm, frequented by ramblers and rodsmen – residents fish free of charge. Menus reflect the seasons with winter game and fresh fish, as well as more exotic dishes. A typical menu includes Holy Mole chilli rice, cashew nut loaf with tomato and herb salad, Tibbies mixed grill, and fried haddock with chips or peas. The comfortable bedrooms are all en suite.
OPEN: 11–11 (Sun 12.30–11) **BAR MEALS:** Lunch served: all week Dinner served: all week 12.30–8.30 12–8.30 Av main course £5.25 **RESTAURANT:** Lunch served: all week Dinner served: all week 12–8.30 12.30–8.30 Av 3 course à la carte £11.75
BREWERY/COMPANY: Free House
PRINCIPAL BEERS: Broughton Greenmantle Ale, Belhaven 80/-. **FACILITIES:** Children welcome Children's licence Garden: Lochside location Dogs allowed (guide dogs only)
NOTES: Parking 50 **ROOMS:** 5 bedrooms 5 en suite

TWEEDSMUIR   Map 10 NT12

The Crook Inn
ML12 6QN ☎ 01899 880272 ▤ 01899 880294
e-mail: thecrookinn@btinternet.com

First licensed in 1604, this inn was frequented by none other than Rabbie Burns, national poet. The inn has seen feuds, cattle rustling, kidnappings, and even Jack the Giant Killer. The area is now less dangerous but still breathtaking, and popular with walkers taking on nearby Broad Law. The unusual 1930s art deco interior is a delightful setting to enjoy a menu that includes Borders shepherds pie, Crook haggis, Arbroath haddock fillet, and pan fried sirloin steak.
OPEN: 9–12 Closed: Dec 25 **BAR MEALS:** Lunch served: all week Dinner served: all week 12–2.30 5.30–8.30 Av main course £7 **RESTAURANT:** Lunch served: all week Dinner served: all week 12–2.30 7–9 Av 3 course à la carte £15 Av 4 course fixed price £19.50
BREWERY/COMPANY: Free House **PRINCIPAL BEERS:** Broughton Greenmantle & Best, Scottish Courage John Smith's.
FACILITIES: Children welcome Children's licence Garden: Beer garden, patio, food served outdoors Dogs allowed **NOTES:** Parking 60
ROOMS: 8 bedrooms 8 en suite from s£38.50 d£57

SHETLAND

BRAE

Busta House Hotel
Busta ZE2 9QN ☎ 01806 522506 🖹 01806 522588
Built in 1588, this is the oldest occupied building on Shetland.
The hotel also has some of the few trees on Shetland in its
garden. Seaside location.

SOUTH AYRSHIRE

SYMINGTON   Map 10 NS33

Wheatsheaf Inn 🐑
Main St KA1 5QB ☎ 01563 830307 🖹 01563 830307

This charming 17th-century inn lies in a lovely village setting
close to the Royal Troon golf course, and Seve Ballasteros has
been amongst its celebrity visitors. There has been a hostelry
here since the 1500s; log fires burn in every room, and the
work of local artists is displayed on the walls. Fresh fish such
as sole or red snapper highlights the menu, and alternatives
include duck with plum glaze, and the famous Wheatsheaf
steak pie.
OPEN: 11–12 Closed: 25 Dec, 1 Jan **BAR MEALS:** Lunch served: all
week Dinner served: all week 12-4 4-9.30 Av main course £7
RESTAURANT: Lunch served: all week Dinner served: all week
12-9.30 Av 3 course à la carte £14
BREWERY/COMPANY: Belhaven **PRINCIPAL BEERS:** Belhaven
Best, St Andrews Ale & Belhaven Light. **FACILITIES:** Children
welcome Garden: Food served outside **NOTES:** Parking 20

STIRLING

BALQUHIDDER   Map 10 NN52

Monachyle Mhor ★ ★ 🔘🔘 **NEW**
FK19 8PQ ☎ 01877 384622 🖹 01877 384305
e-mail: info@monachylemhor
Dir: On A84, 11 miles N of Callender, turn right at Kingshouse. Monachyle
Mhor is 6 miles along this road situated between two lochs.
Romantically located farmhouse hotel with dramatic loch and
mountain views. The interior includes open fires, antique
furniture, sporting prints and country fabrics. Don't miss the
award-winning cooking, full of local and home-grown
produce. Dishes could range from seared scallops with
smoked haddock, wild rice kedgeree, steamed garden greens
and wasabi to rack of local lamb and slow roasted shoulder
on crushed olive oil potatoes with shallot, sun blushed tomato
and black olive emulsion.

continued

OPEN: 12 Closed: Jan-14 Feb **BAR MEALS:** Lunch served: all week
Dinner served: all week Av main course £8.50 **RESTAURANT:** Lunch
served: all week Dinner served: all week 12-1.45 7-8.45 Av 4 course
fixed price £32.50 **BREWERY/COMPANY:** Free House
FACILITIES: Garden: Overlooking loch, food served outside
ROOMS: 10 bedrooms 10 en suite from s£60 d£85

CRIANLARICH   Map 10 NN32

Ben More Lodge Hotel ♦♦♦ 🐑
FK20 8QS ☎ 01838 300210 🖹 01838 300218
e-mail: info@ben-more.co.uk
Dir: From Glasgow take A82 to Crianlarich, turn R at T Junc in village in
direction of stirling

Hotel in a beautiful setting at the foot of Ben More (3800 ft)
next to the River Fillan, on the road to the North West
Highlands, offering accommodation in timber-built lodges.
Both bar and restaurant menus feature local salmon and trout
and a good selection of steaks and chops.
OPEN: 11-12 Closed: Dec 25, Mon-Fri in Nov-Mar
BAR MEALS: Lunch served: all week Dinner served: all week
12-2.30 6-8.45 Av main course £7 **RESTAURANT:** Lunch served: all
week Dinner served: all week 12-2.30 6-8.45 Av 3 course à la carte
£16 Av 3 course fixed price £16 **BREWERY/COMPANY:** Free House
FACILITIES: Children welcome Garden: Food served outside Dogs
allowed **NOTES:** Parking 50 **ROOMS:** 11 bedrooms 11 en suite
from s£30 d£50

DRYMEN   Map 10 NS48

Clachan Inn
2 Main St G63 0BG ☎ 01360 660824
Quaint, white-painted cottage, believed to be the oldest
licensed pub in Scotland, situated in a small village on the
West Highland Way. Locate the appealing lounge bar for
freshly-made food, the varied menu listing filled baked
potatoes, salads, fresh haddock in crispy breadcrumbs, spicy
Malaysian lamb casserole, vegetable lasagne, a variety of
steaks, and good daily specials.
OPEN: 11-12 Closed: 25 Dec& 01 Jan **BAR MEALS:** Lunch served:
all week Dinner served: all week 12-4 6-10 Av main course £5.50
RESTAURANT: Lunch served: all week Dinner served: all week 12-4
6-10 **BREWERY/COMPANY:** Free House
PRINCIPAL BEERS: Caledonian Deuchars IPA, Belhaven Best.
FACILITIES: Children welcome Dogs allowed **NOTES:** Parking 2
ROOMS: 3 bedrooms from s£21 d£21

★ **Indicates AA inspected hotel accommodation**

Scotland

KILMAHOG   Map 10 NN60

The Lade Inn NEW
FK17 8HD ☎ 01877 330152 📠 01877 331878
e-mail: steve@theladeinnscotland.freeserve.co.uk

Detached white-painted building set in its own grounds on the Leny Estate west of Callander, named after a mill lade - a stream created from the River Leny to power the mills at Kilmahog. Cosy bar with open fire and collection of brasses, and separate dining area offering real Scottish cooking. Expect haggis, neeps and tatties, Arbroath platter (dressed crab, mackerel fillet, poached salmon and smoked mussels), game casserole and local trout, alongside sandwiches and traditional pub meals.
OPEN: 12-3 5.30-10.30 Closed: 1 Jan **BAR MEALS:** Lunch served: all week Dinner served: all week 12-2.30 5.30-9 Av main course £7.25 **RESTAURANT:** Lunch served: all week Dinner served: all week 12-2.30 5.30-9 Av 3 course à la carte £20 **BREWERY/COMPANY:** Free House **PRINCIPAL BEERS:** Broughton Greenmantle Ale, Caledonian 80/-. **FACILITIES:** Children welcome Garden: Food served outside Dogs allowed **NOTES:** Parking 40

KIPPEN   Map 10 NS69

Cross Keys Hotel 🐾
Main St FK8 3DN ☎ 01786 870293 📠 01786 870293
e-mail: crosskeys@kippen70.fsnet.co.uk

The village of Kippen, situated in the Fintry Hills overlooking the Forth Valley, has strong associations with Rob Roy. The pub dates from 1703, retains its original stone walls, and enjoys real fires in winter. Nearby Burnside Wood is managed by a local community woodland group, and is perfect for walking and nature trails. Look out for hearty dishes such as beefsteak and mushroom pie, grilled salmon with lemon and parsley butter, fish and potato pie, and Moroccan lamb with rice.
OPEN: 12-2.30 5.30-12 (Apr-Sept all day Sat-Sun, Fri-Sat 5.30-1am

Sun 12.30-12) Closed: 1 Jan **BAR MEALS:** Lunch served: all week Dinner served: all week 12-2 5.30-9 Av main course £6 **BREWERY/COMPANY:** Free House **PRINCIPAL BEERS:** Belhaven Best, IPA, 80/-, Harviestoun Brooker's Bitter & Twisted. **FACILITIES:** Children welcome Garden: Beer garden, food served outside Dogs allowed (water, biscuits) **NOTES:** Parking 5 **ROOMS:** 2 bedrooms 2 en suite from d£22.50

STRATHBLANE   Map 10 NS57

Kirkhouse Inn
Glasgow Rd G3 9AA ☎ 01360 771771 📠 01360 771711
Dir: A81 Aberfoyce rd from Glasgow city centre through Bearsden & Milngavie, Strathblane on junct with A891
17th-century coaching inn nestling beneath the jagged scarp of the Campsie Fells, a rolling patchwork of green volcanic hills and picturesque villages. Interesting menu offers international cuisine as well as traditional British dishes.
OPEN: 10-midnight (Fri-Sat 10-1) **BAR MEALS:** Lunch served: all week 12-7 Av main course £7 **RESTAURANT:** Lunch served: all week Dinner served: all week 12-5 5-10 Av 3 course à la carte £17.50 **PRINCIPAL BEERS:** Belhaven. **FACILITIES:** Children welcome **NOTES:** Parking 300 **ROOMS:** 16 bedrooms 16 en suite from s£44.50 d£70

THORNHILL   Map 11 NN60

Lion & Unicorn
FK8 3PJ ☎ 01786 850204
Dir: On A873 Blair Drummond to Aberfoyle
Droving inn dating from 1635, once frequented by Rob Roy MacGregor. These days it has a games room and beer garden, and the most recent addition, three en suite letting rooms, which were under construction as the guide went to press. Home-cooked dishes range from roast beef and Yorkshire pudding in the bar to rack of Persia lamb with apricots and rosemary in the restaurant.
OPEN: 12-12 (Fri-Sat 12-1) **BAR MEALS:** Lunch served: all week Dinner served: all week Av main course £5.50 **RESTAURANT:** Lunch served: all week Dinner served: all week 12-9 Av 3 course à la carte £20 **BREWERY/COMPANY:** Free House **FACILITIES:** Children welcome Garden: Dogs allowed **NOTES:** Parking 25

WEST LOTHIAN

LINLITHGOW   Map 10 NS97

Pick of the Pubs

Champany Inn 🌐🌐
Champany EH49 7LU ☎ 01506 834532 📠 01506 834302
e-mail: reception@champany.com
A collection of buildings dating from the 17th century houses this character hostelry, along with its superior sister, the main restaurant. Both are renowned for the sourcing, handling and cooking of prime Scottish beef, but the Chop and Ale House has its own take on Aberdeen Angus beef. Warm colours in the walls and table linen, and a central chimney with a roaring fire make the former public a smart and welcoming spot, and there is much to gratify the expectant diner. Proper burgers are unlike junk food as possible appear alongside the famous steaks plus the odd lamb, chicken and fish dish, with the likes of marinated smoked duck fillet, and pickled fish to start, and hot waffles, or chocolate and orange tart to finish. A

Scotland

continued
continued

LINLITHGOW continued

short wine list with a good selection from South Africa, and there are rooms for a peaceful night's sleep.

Champany Inn

OPEN: 12–2 6.30–11 (all day w/end) Closed: 25/26 Dec, 1/2 Jan **BAR MEALS:** Lunch served: all week 12–2 Dinner served: all week 6.30–11 Av main course £11.45 **RESTAURANT:** Lunch served: Mon–Fri 12.30–2 Dinner served: Mon–Sat 7–11 Av 3 course à la carte £37.50 **BREWERY/COMPANY:** Free House **PRINCIPAL BEERS:** Belhaven. **FACILITIES:** Children welcome Garden: Patio, food served outdoors **NOTES:** Parking 50 **ROOMS:** 16 bedrooms 16 en suite from s£105 d£105

SCOTTISH ISLANDS
ISLAY, ISLE OF – ARGYLL & BUTE

BALLYGRANT — Map 10 NR36

Ballygrant Inn
PA45 7QR ☎ 01496 840277 🖺 01496 840277
e-mail: info@ballygrant.inn.co.uk
Dir: NE of Isle of Islay, 3m from ferry terminal at Port Askaig

Situated in two and a half acres of grounds, this converted farmhouse offers a warm welcome to tourists, walkers and fishermen alike. Local ales and malt whiskies are served in the bar, along with bar meals that include venison casserole, grilled local scallops, and sirloin steaks. The restaurant menu features crab, lamb cutlets, salmon and grilled trout among others. Many of the ingredients used are locally produced. Occasional folk or blues music.
OPEN: 11–11 (Wkds 11–1am) **BAR MEALS:** Lunch served: all week Dinner served: all week 12–2.30 6–10 Av main course £6.50 **RESTAURANT:** Lunch served: all week Dinner served: all week 12–2.30 6–10 Av 3 course à la carte £17.50

BREWERY/COMPANY: Free House **FACILITIES:** Children welcome Children's licence Garden: outdoor eating, patio Dogs allowed **NOTES:** Parking 35 **ROOMS:** 3 bedrooms 3 en suite from s£22.50 d£45

BOWMORE — Map 10 NR35

Pick of the Pubs

The Harbour Inn 🏵🏵 🗊 ♀
The Square PA43 7JR ☎ 01496 810330 🖺 01496 810990
e-mail: harbour@harbour-inn.com

A gem of an inn, wedged between the square and harbour of the island's capital. It has recently been completely refurbished and extended to provide seven en suite bedrooms and a restaurant looking out from the water's edge across Lochindaal to the peaks of Jura beyond. The most recent addition is a sun lounge serving morning coffee and all day snacks. A full range of Islay single malt whiskies is served in the small bar, and the menu offered in the award-winning restaurant is constructed around shellfish, locally fished and collected from the quay to ensure freshness, and beef, lamb and game from Islay or Jura. The dinner carte might offer local crab sushi with avocado chilli and lime vinaigrette, and beef fillet with haggis and rolls of Bruichladdich smoked beef surrounded by whisky sauce. A lighter bistro-style menu is available at lunchtime.
OPEN: 11–1 **BAR MEALS:** Lunch served: Mon–Sat 12–2.30 Dinner served: all week 6–9 Av main course £6.50
RESTAURANT: Lunch served: Mon–Sat 12–2.30 Dinner served: all week 6–9 Av 3 course à la carte £25
BREWERY/COMPANY: Free House **FACILITIES:** Garden: Dogs allowed **ROOMS:** 7 bedrooms 7 en suite from s£45 d£85

NORTH UIST – WESTERN ISLES

CARINISH — Map 12 NF86

Carinish Inn
PA82 5EJ ☎ 01876 580673 🖺 01876 580665
e-mail: carinishinn@macinnesbros.co.uk
Modern-style refurbished inn at Carinish, North Uist, convenient for the RSPB Balranald Nature Reserve and local archaeological sites. Fish features prominently on the set-price menu, including roast fillet of West Coast salmon, stuffed monkfish tail wrapped in bacon with stewed tomatoes and polenta, and seafood casserole in a creamy wine and herb sauce. Local artists perform every Saturday night.
OPEN: 11–11 (Thu–Sat 11–1am, Sun–Wed 11–11)

continued

continued

BAR MEALS: Lunch served: all week Dinner served: all week 12-2.30 6.30-9.30 Av main course £6.50 **RESTAURANT:** Lunch served: all week Dinner served: all week 12-2.30 6.30-9.30 Av 3 course à la carte £15 **BREWERY/COMPANY:** Free House **FACILITIES:** Children welcome **NOTES:** Parking 50 **ROOMS:** 8 bedrooms 8 en suite from s£50 d£70

SKYE, ISLE OF - HIGHLAND

ARDVASAR   Map 12 NG60

Ardvasar Hotel ★ ★ NEW ♀
IV45 8RS ☎ 01471 844223 📄 01471 844495
Dir: From ferry terminal, 50yds & turn L
The second oldest inn on Skye, this well-appointed white-painted cottage-style hotel offers a warm, friendly welcome and acts as an ideal base for exploring the island, spotting the wildlife and enjoying the stunning scenery. Overlooking the Sound of Sleat, the Ardvasar is within walking distance of the Clan Donald Centre and the ferry at Armadale. Popular menus offers freshly-caught seafood, as well as baked venison in peppers and port wine pie, lamb and leek potato hot pot and savoury vegetable crumble. Straightforward basket meals are a perennial favourite.
OPEN: 12-12 **BAR MEALS:** Lunch served: all week Dinner served: all week 12-2.30 5.30-9.30 Av main course £8.50 **RESTAURANT:** Dinner served: all week 7.30-9 Av 3 course à la carte £15.50 **BREWERY/COMPANY:** Free House **PRINCIPAL BEERS:** 80/-, Deuchars. **FACILITIES:** Children welcome Garden: Food served outside Dogs allowed **NOTES:** Parking 30 **ROOMS:** 10 bedrooms 10 en suite from s£50 d£80

CARBOST   Map 12 NG33

The Old Inn 🐷
IV47 8SR ☎ 01478 640205 📄 01478 640450
e-mail: oldinn@carbost.f9.co.uk
Once a croft house, this Highland inn is a perfect base for hill walkers and climbers. Rents used to be collected here and a local dentist pulled teeth in one of the upstairs rooms! The patio offers splendid views of the loch and the Cuillins, while inside is a charming mix of wooden floors and original stone walls. Traditional bar food includes the likes of Scottish sausage hotpot, pasta bake, 8oz sirloin steak garni, poached salmon, and lemon sole.
OPEN: 11-12 (hours change in winter please ring) **BAR MEALS:** Lunch served: all week Dinner served: all week 12-2 6.30-10 Av main course £7 **BREWERY/COMPANY:** Free House **FACILITIES:** Children welcome Children's licence Garden: Food served outdoors, patio Dogs allowed **NOTES:** Parking 20 **ROOMS:** 6 bedrooms 6 en suite from s£28 d£46

ISLE ORNSAY   Map 12 NG71

Pick of the Pubs

Hotel Eilean Iarmain ★ ★ ⑩⑩
IV43 8QR ☎ 01471 833332 📄 01471 833275
e-mail: hotel@eilean-iarmain.co.uk
Dir: A851, A852 right to Isle Ornsay harbour front
A very special, 19th-century award-winning Hebridean hotel overlooking Isle Ornsay harbour - well-known to fans of Flora MacDonald - that enjoys spectacular sea views. Poets and artists are drawn here by its unique

heritage and the Celtic hertiage typified by the Celtic-speaking staff. Morag Mac Donald claims that her guests will leave with their lives enriched: they will undoubtedly depart with well-satisfied appetites! Look first to the specials board for the likes of brandied crab and lobster bisque, roast monkfish tails with mushroom duxelle and tomato salsa and tian of raspberry tuiles served on a wild berry coulis. Bar meals can be as simple as peppered mackerel with creamed horseradish, roast baby chicken with red wine and onion jus and hot apple sponge crumble with rum and raisin ice cream.

OPEN: 12-12 (Winter Mon-Sun 12-2.30, 5-12) **BAR MEALS:** Lunch served: all week Dinner served: all week 12.30-2.30 6.30-9.30 Av main course £8 **RESTAURANT:** Lunch served: all week Dinner served: all week 12.30-2 7.30-9 Av 3 course à la carte £25 Av 5 course fixed price £31 **BREWERY/COMPANY:** Free House **PRINCIPAL BEERS:** McEwans 80/-. **FACILITIES:** Children welcome Garden: Food served outside Dogs allowed **NOTES:** Parking 30 **ROOMS:** 12 bedrooms 12 en suite from s£90 d£120

SOUTH UIST - WESTERN ISLES

LOCHBOISDALE   Map 12 NF71

Polochar Inn
Polochar HS8 5TT ☎ 01878 700215 📄 01878 700768
Dir: From Lochboisdale travel W & take B888. Hotel at end of road
Overlooking the sea towards the islands of Eriskay and Barra, this superbly situated 18th-century inn enjoys beautiful sunsets. The bar menu offers fresh seafood dishes and steaks with various sauces, while restaurant fare includes venison, fresh scallops or steak pie.
OPEN: 11-11 (Fri 11-1, Sat 11-11.30 Sun 12.30-11) **BAR MEALS:** Lunch served: all week Dinner served: all week 12.30-2.30 6-9 Av main course £8 **RESTAURANT:** Lunch served: all week Dinner served: all week 12.30 6-9 Av 3 course à la carte £15 **BREWERY/COMPANY:** Free House **PRINCIPAL BEERS:** no real ale. **FACILITIES:** Children welcome Garden: barbecue **NOTES:** Parking 40 **ROOMS:** 11 bedrooms 11 en suite from s£35 d£55

continued

Scotland

How can I have a break without breaking the bank?

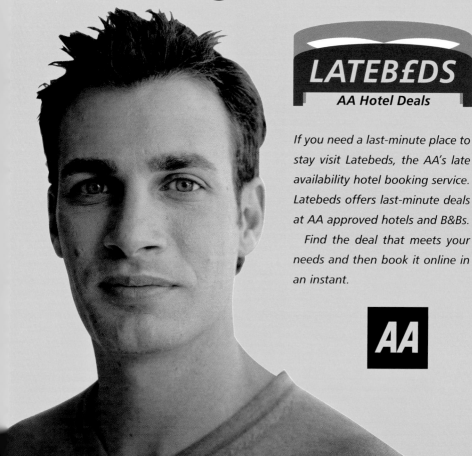

LATEBEDS
AA Hotel Deals

If you need a last-minute place to stay visit Latebeds, the AA's late availability hotel booking service. Latebeds offers last-minute deals at AA approved hotels and B&Bs.
   Find the deal that meets your needs and then book it online in an instant.

AA

Latebeds
www.theAA.com

Wales

Pub of The Year for Wales

*The Bell at Skenfrith,
Skenfrith, Monmouthshire*

WALES

BRIDGEND

KENFIG Map 03 SS88

Prince of Wales Inn ♈
CF33 4PR ☎ 01656 740356
Dir: *M4 J37 into North Cornelly & follow signs for nature reserve, Kenfig*
Dating from 1440, this stone-built inn has been many things in its time including a school, guildhall and courtroom. Why not sup some real cask ale in the bar by an inviting log fire? Typical menu includes steak and onion pie, lasagne, chicken and mushroom pie, and a variety of fish dishes. Look out for today's specials on the blackboard.
OPEN: 11.30–4 6–11 (Sat & Sun all day) **BAR MEALS:** Lunch served: all week 12–2.30 Dinner served: Tue–Sat 7–9.30 Av main course £5.75 **RESTAURANT:** Lunch served: all week 12–2.30 Dinner served: Tue–Sat 7–9.30 Av 3 course à la carte £14
BREWERY/COMPANY: Free House **PRINCIPAL BEERS:** Bass Triangle, Worthington Best, Felinfoel Double Dragon, Thomas Watkin OSB. **FACILITIES:** Children welcome Garden: Food served outside Dogs allowed (water, toys) **NOTES:** Parking 30

MAESTEG Map 03 SS89

Old House Inn 🐑 ♈
Llangynwyd CF34 9SB ☎ 01656 733310 📠 01656 737337

Dating back to 1147, The Old House can lay claim to being one of the oldest in the country. It has huge gnarled beams and stone walls over three feet thick and lots of Welsh antiques and bric-a-brac. A conservatory and dining terrace overlooking the garden have been sympathetically added without detracting from its atmosphere. Blackboard specials change every day, majoring in fresh fish. Other menus include traditional pub food, from garlic mushrooms and barbecue-style pork ribs to chicken chasseur.
OPEN: 11–11 **BAR MEALS:** Lunch served: all week Dinner served: all week 11–2.30 6–10 Av main course £8 **RESTAURANT:** 11–2.30 6–10 Av 3 course à la carte £14 **BREWERY/COMPANY:** Whitbread **PRINCIPAL BEERS:** Interbrew Flowers Original, Flowers IPA, Brains Bitter. **FACILITIES:** Children welcome Children's licence Garden: Food served outside **NOTES:** Parking 150

> We endeavour to be as accurate as possible but changes to times and other information can occur after we have gone to press

CARDIFF

CARDIFF Map 03 ST17

Buff's Wine Bar & Restaurant
8 Mount Stuart Square CF10 5EE
☎ 029 20464628 📠 029 20480715
Housed in a listed building at the heart of the former docklands – now being restored as Cardiff Bay's commercial centre – business executives here lunch on game terrine with Cumberland sauce, deep-fried goats' cheese with onion marmalade, and fish cakes in mild curry sauce. A la carte lunches above and evening dinner parties by arrangement.
OPEN: 11–7 Closed: BHs **BAR MEALS:** Lunch served: Mon–Fri 11.30–3.30 Av main course £6 **RESTAURANT:** Lunch served: Mon–Fri 12–2.30 Av 3 course à la carte £18
BREWERY/COMPANY: Free House **PRINCIPAL BEERS:** Only keg beers. **FACILITIES:** Garden: patio, outdoor eating

Cayo Arms
36 Cathedral Rd CF11 9HL ☎ 029 20391910
e-mail: celticinns@twpubs.co.uk
Dir: *From Cardiff take Kingsway West turn R into Cathedral Road*
Wales's newest brewery company has moved into Cardiff at this nationally-known bi-lingual pub on a leafy thoroughfare leading to the new stadium and city centre. In front is a large patio garden with umbrella-ed tables and patio heaters that add to the draw on Match Days of Tomos Watkins's ales. The same brew is used in a steak and ale pie and the batter for their celebrated fish and chips. Bedroom accommodation, though modest, is useful to know in the area.
OPEN: 12–11 **BAR MEALS:** Lunch served: all week Dinner served: all week 12–8 Av main course £5.95 **PRINCIPAL BEERS:** Watkins Brewery Bitter, OSB, Whoosh, Merlin Stout. **FACILITIES:** Children welcome Garden: Food served outside Dogs allowed **NOTES:** Parking 30

CREIGIAU Map 03 ST08

Pick of the Pubs

Caesars Arms 🏅 🐑 ♈
Cardiff Rd CF15 9NN ☎ 029 20890486 📠 029 20892176
Dir: *1m from M4 J34*

Some ten miles out of Cardiff, yet easily accessible from the M4 (J34), a sprawling pub down winding lanes that attracts a well-heeled clientele to its heated patio and terrace looking over the gardens and surrounding countryside. Head chef Emma Ward bravely undertakes responsibility for the vast selection of fresh fish, seafoods, meat and game enticingly displayed in shaven-ice display cabinets. To begin are Bajan fish cakes, crispy laver balls,

continued

tiger prawns in garlic and scallops with leeks and bacon, followed by cuts of monkfish and crawfish tails priced by weight. Welsh beef steaks, honeyed crispy duck and roast rack of Welsh lamb satisfy the most ardent meat eaters: meanwhile help yourself from brimming bowls full of assorted salads. All in a friendly and relaxed atmosphere, draught ales are somewhat overshadowed by a massive wine list with many selections by the glass.
OPEN: 12–4.30 7–12.00 Closed: 25 Dec **BAR MEALS:** Lunch served: all week Dinner served: all week 12–2.30 7–10.30 Av main course £5 **RESTAURANT:** Lunch served: all week 12–4.30 Dinner served: Mon–Sat 7–10.30 Av 3 course à la carte £20 **BREWERY/COMPANY:** Free House
PRINCIPAL BEERS: Hancocks. **FACILITIES:** Children welcome Garden: Food served outside, terrace **NOTES:** Parking 100

CARMARTHENSHIRE

ABERGORLECH
Map 02 SN53

The Black Lion
SA32 7SN ☎ 01558 685271
Dir: From Carmarthan take A40 eastwards,then B4310 signposted Brechfa & Abergorlech

A 17th-century coaching inn in the Brechfa Forest, with a beer garden overlooking the Cothi River and a stone, arched packhorse bridge. Flagstoned floors, settles and a grandfather clock grace the antique-furnished bar, while the modern dining room is welcoming in pink and white. Try home-made game pie, beef bourguignon, steak, ale and mushroom pie and various fish dishes. Miles of forest and riverside walks are easily reached from the pub.
OPEN: 12–3.30 7–11 **BAR MEALS:** Lunch served: Tue–Sun Dinner served: Tue–Sun 12–2.30 7–9.30 Av main course £5.50 **RESTAURANT:** Lunch served: Tue–Sun Dinner served: Tue–Sun 12–2.30 7–9.30 Av 3 course à la carte £12
BREWERY/COMPANY: Free House **PRINCIPAL BEERS:** Brains Reverend James. **FACILITIES:** Children welcome Garden: Food served outdoors Dogs allowed (water) **NOTES:** Parking 20

BRECHFA
Map 02 SN53

Forest Arms
SA32 7RA ☎ 01267 202339 ▤ 01267 202339
Grade II-listed, early 19th-century stone-built inn in a pretty village in the beautiful Cothi Valley. A mile or so away, its own stretch of river yields salmon, sea and brown trout, which sometimes feature on the specials menu. Battered cod and scampi, and home-made chicken curry, spaghetti Bolognese, chilli con carne, and steak and mushroom pie are usually

available. Fly-fishing mementoes adorn the unspoilt, traditional bars. The rear garden is a registered helipad.
OPEN: 12–2 6.30–11 (closed Sun) **BAR MEALS:** Lunch served: all week 12–2 Dinner served: Mon–Sat 6.30–9 Av main course £5.75 **RESTAURANT:** Lunch served: Mon–Sat Dinner served: Mon–Sat 12–2 6–9 **BREWERY/COMPANY:** Free House
PRINCIPAL BEERS: Dylan's, Brains Buckleys Best, Buckleys Dark.
FACILITIES: Children welcome Garden: Food served outdoors
NOTES: Parking 15 **ROOMS:** 4 bedrooms from s£18 d£36 No credit cards

LLANARTHNE
Map 02 SN52

Golden Grove Arms
SA32 8JU ☎ 01558 668551 ▤ 01558 668069
Dir: From end M4 take A48 toward Carmarthen, then R at Pantyeynon, 2 or 3m to Llanarthne
Visitors to the Towy Valley and Wales's National Botanic Gardens will find Llanarthne mid-way between Carmarthen and Llandeilo. Up-to-date country accommodation and facilities in a natural setting draw the crowds to both bars and the restaurant for home-cooked traditional and vegetarian cooking. Extensive choices encompass curries, grills, and catch of the day like cod in batter, red snapper Thai style, and salmon en croûte, plus beef Stroganoff, shank of lamb and a menu of 'lite bites'.
OPEN: 11–11 **BAR MEALS:** Lunch served: all week Dinner served: all week 11.30–2.30 6–9 Av main course £5.10 **RESTAURANT:** Lunch served: all week Dinner served: all week 11.30–2.30 6–9 Av 3 course à la carte £13.50 **BREWERY/COMPANY:** Free House
PRINCIPAL BEERS: Brains Buckleys Best, Reverend James Original Ale, Smooth Bitter & Dark Smooth. **FACILITIES:** Children welcome Garden: Beer garden, food served outdoors, patio **NOTES:** Parking 40 **ROOMS:** 6 bedrooms 6 en suite from s£35 d£45

LLANDDAROG
Map 02 SN51

White Hart Inn
SA32 8NT ☎ 01267 275395 ▤ 01267 275395
Dir: 6m E of Carmarthen towards Swansea, just off A48 on B4310, signed Llanddarog
Built in 1371, this thatched, stone pub originally housed the stone masons who built their first church next door. Heavy beams, stone fireplaces, and a wide-ranging menu. Cole's Family Brewery produces 'Cwrw Blasus', or 'tasty ale', which uses water from the pub's own deep bore well. The hand-carved furniture is thought to have been made by a joiner who was sacked by Winchester Cathedral for his drinking. The work was paid for in beer. Menu includes pies, roasts, Welsh black beef steaks, swordfish in leek and whisky sauce, and old-fashioned puddings.
OPEN: 11.30–3 6.30–11 (Sun 12–3, 7–10.30) Closed: Dec 25/26 **BAR MEALS:** Lunch served: all week Dinner served: all week 11.30–2 6.30–10 Av main course £11 **RESTAURANT:** Lunch served: all week Dinner served: all week 11.30–2 6.30–10 Av 3 course à la carte £17.50 **BREWERY/COMPANY:** Free House **PRINCIPAL BEERS:** White Hart Brewery: Cwrw Blasus, Black Stag, Roasted Barley Stout, To Gwellt. **FACILITIES:** Children welcome Garden: patio/terrace, food served outdoors, BBQ Dogs allowed (only guide dogs, or in garden) **NOTES:** Parking 50

continued

The Angel Inn 🏨 ♀
Salem SA19 7LY ☎ 01558 823394 📠 01558 823371
Dir: A40 then B4302, turn L 1m after leaving A40 then turn R at T.Junct and travel 0.25m to Angel Inn. Located on the right hand side
A two-bar village pub with a 100-seater restaurant, characterised by beamed ceilings and a large collection of fascinating artefacts. There is popular bar food, a children's menu, a selection of vegetarian dishes and daily local specials such as grilled fillet of Welsh beef, charred breast of St David's duckling, and sea trout. Desserts include roast banana with dill parfait and caramel sauce.
OPEN: 12–2.30 6–11 **BAR MEALS:** Lunch served: Tue–Sun 12–2 Dinner served: Tue–Sat 6.45-9.30 Av main course £7
RESTAURANT: Lunch served: Tue–Sun 12–2 Dinner served: Tue–Sat 6.45-9.30 Av 3 course à la carte £19 **BREWERY/COMPANY:** Free House **FACILITIES:** Garden: Food served outside. Grass area & benches Dogs allowed (in the garden only, water provided)
NOTES: Parking 60

The Castle Brewery 🏨
113 Rhosmaen St SA19 6EN ☎ 01558 823446 📠 01558 824256
e-mail: castle@twpubs.co.uk
19th-century Edwardian-style hotel within easy reach of Dinefwr Castle and wonderful walks through classic parkland. Charming tiled and partly green-painted back bar attracts plenty of locals, while the front bar and side area offer smart furnishings and the chance to relax in comfort over a drink. Enclosed rear courtyard is the venue for music and art throughout the year. Extensive range of Tomas Watkins ales available and good quality bar and restaurant food prepared with the finest of fresh local ingredients. Expect hearty dishes such as medallions of beef, Rhydlewis oak smoked salmon platter, and Tomas Watkins steak and stout pie.
OPEN: 12–11 (Sun 12–10.30) **BAR MEALS:** Lunch served: all week Dinner served: all week 12–2.30 6.30-9 Av main course £4.50
RESTAURANT: Lunch served: all week Dinner served: all week 7–9 Av 3 course à la carte £15 **PRINCIPAL BEERS:** Watkins Best, Watkins OSB, Celtic Bitter, Worthington Draught.
FACILITIES: Children welcome Garden: Food served outside. Patio area Dogs allowed (guide dogs only)

The Cottage Inn ♀
Pentrefelin SA19 6SD ☎ 01558 822890 📠 01558 823309
Dir: On main A40 between Brecon & Carmarthen, 1.5 miles W of Llandeilo
Formerly the Nags Head Inn, this timbered coaching inn is just 1.5 miles from Aberglasney Gardens and six miles from the National Botanical Gardens. Choose from the extensive bar menu or the à la carte selection, including the good range of fish.
OPEN: 12–3 6–12.30 Closed: Dec 25 **BAR MEALS:** Lunch served: all week Dinner served: all week 12–2.30 6–10 Av main course £6
RESTAURANT: Lunch served: all week Dinner served: all week 12–2.30 6–10 Av 3 course à la carte £16
BREWERY/COMPANY: Free House **PRINCIPAL BEERS:** Tomas Watkins, Boddingtons, Wadsworth 6X, Double Dragon.
FACILITIES: Children welcome Garden: Food served outside
NOTES: Parking 60 **ROOMS:** 5 bedrooms 5 en suite

♀ **Pubs offering six or more wines by the glass**

Neuadd Fawr Arms 🏨 ♀
SA20 0ST ☎ 01550 721644 📠 01550 721644
Dir: On the A40 take the A483 Builth Wells Rd, after 300 meters turn L at the crossroads continue along this rd for 3M and take 2nd l over river Bridge, continue to Cilycwm pub is on R
Traditional local peacefully set next to the church in a picturesque village, with character slate floors, quarry tiles and oak boards. It lies on the route of an old drovers' trail, and is handy for exploring the Cambrian Mountains and the Towy Valley. A good range of wines and real ales, and a varied menu with freshly-cooked options. Popular Sunday roasts, plus fresh fish on Friday, and steak and ale pie, or braised lamb shank.
OPEN: 11–3 (open all day Fri–Sun) 6–11 **BAR MEALS:** Lunch served: all week Dinner served: all week 12–2.30 6.30-9 Av main course £8 **RESTAURANT:** Lunch served: all week Dinner served: all week 12–2.30 6.30-9 Av 3 course à la carte £14
BREWERY/COMPANY: Free House **PRINCIPAL BEERS:** Tomos Watkin Whoosh, Brains Reverend James, Felinfoel Double Dragon.
FACILITIES: Children welcome Garden: Food served outside, over looking river **NOTES:** Parking 15 **ROOMS:** 3 bedrooms 3 en suite from s£27.50 d£45

The Red Lion Inn
SA18 3JB ☎ 01269 851202
Almost 300 years old, this historic inn retains the atmosphere and feel of the original pub. Several fireplaces and other original features remain to generate a friendly, welcoming environment in which to relax and enjoy good food and well kept real ales. The menu is created by a team of enthusiastic and professional chefs who have many years' experience between them. Dishes range from fillet of salmon with roast potato and spinach, to breast of chicken stuffed with Mozzarella and wrapped in Parma ham.
OPEN: 12–3 6–11 **BAR MEALS:** Lunch served: all week Dinner served: all week 12–2 6–9 Av main course £5.50
RESTAURANT: Lunch served: all week Dinner served: all week 12–2 6–9 Av 3 course à la carte £20 **PRINCIPAL BEERS:** Worthington, Tomos Watkin. **FACILITIES:** Children welcome Garden: Food served outside **NOTES:** Parking 50

Pick of the Pubs

The Salutation Inn 🏨
Pont-ar-Gothi SA32 7NH ☎ 01267 290336
Dir: On A40 between Carmarthen & Llandeilo. 5mins from National Botanical Gardens
The 'Sal', as it is affectionately known to the locals, has long been pulling them in from as far away as Swansea and Llanelli. Partly, this can be put down to the lure of the Towy Valley, with its excellent fishing, but the Salutation has long had a reputation for food that has strengthened under the stewardship of Richard and Sera Porter. It's a pub with character and a loyal following of colourful locals who congregate in the bar where Felinfoel Double Dragon is the preferred ale. Stripped floors, bare tables and candles are the defining features of both bar and restaurant areas where generous blackboards offer a selection of broadly modern British dishes. Among the starters are crispy crab cake with avocado salad and a

continue▶

mild curry dressing or Pembrokeshire fish pie with parsley and cheddar crust. Robust mains might include loin of pork stuffed with apples and apricots on bubble and squeak or halibut wrapped in Parma ham with sauce vierge
OPEN: 12–3 6–12 **BAR MEALS:** Lunch served: all week Dinner served: all week 12–2 6–9.30 Av main course £6
RESTAURANT: Lunch served: all week Dinner served: all week 12–2 6–9.30 Av 3 course à la carte £19.50
BREWERY/COMPANY: Felinfoel
PRINCIPAL BEERS: Felinfoel - Double Dragon, Dragon Bitter, Dragon Dark. **FACILITIES:** Children welcome Garden: Food served outside **NOTES:** Parking 15

RHANDIRMWYN   Map 03 SN74

The Royal Oak Inn ◆◆◆
SA20 0NY ☎ 01550 760201 🖥 01550 760332
e-mail: royaloak@rhandirmwyn.com
Attractive 17th-century hillside inn, formerly Earl Cawdor's hunting lodge, in the hamlet of Rhandirmwyn, due north of Llandovery, and famed for its fine views over the upper Towy Valley. The Dinas bird reserve is literally on the doorstep. Stone interiors warmed by log fires, half-a-dozen real ales, home-cooked bar meals and beer garden. A typical menu includes Welsh fillet steak, beef strips in pepper sauce and leek and mushroom crumble.
OPEN: 11.30–3 6–11 **BAR MEALS:** 12–2.30 6–9.30
BREWERY/COMPANY: Free House **PRINCIPAL BEERS:** Greene King Abbot Ale, Wadworth 6X, Burtons. **FACILITIES:** Children welcome Garden: Lawn, food served outside Dogs allowed **NOTES:** Parking 20 **ROOMS:** 5 bedrooms 3 en suite from s£22.50 d£28

RHOS   Map 02 SN33

Lamb of Rhos ♀
SA44 5EE ☎ 01559 370055
Country inn with flagstone floors, beamed ceilings and open fires – as well as its own jail and the 'seat to nowhere'. A menu of traditional pub fare includes steaks, chops, mixed grill, vegetarian and vegan dishes all cooked on the premises.
OPEN: 12–11 **BAR MEALS:** Lunch served: all week Dinner served: all week 12–2 6–9 Av main course £5.50 **RESTAURANT:** Lunch served: Sun 12–2 Dinner served: Fri-Sat 7–9 Av 3 course à la carte £16
BREWERY/COMPANY: Free House
PRINCIPAL BEERS: Worthington Cream Flow, Banks Original.
FACILITIES: Children welcome Garden: Beer garden, outdoor eating, patio Dogs allowed By arrangement only **NOTES:** Parking 50 **ROOMS:** 5 bedrooms 5 en suite from s£30 d£40 No credit cards

CEREDIGION

CARDIGAN   Map 02 SN14

Black Lion Hotel 🐾
High St SA43 1HJ ☎ 01239 612532
e-mail: manager@blacklion.plus.com
Dir: On the A487 through Cardigan, 20 miles north of Fishguard
Established as a one-room 'grogge shoppe' in 1105, the Black Lion lays claim to being one of Wales' oldest coaching inns. Today, this family-run hotel offers comfortable town centre accommodation in an evocative atmosphere opposite the historic castle. Tomas Watkin Welsh Ales accompany

sandwiches, coachman's platters and hot dishes in the spacious lounge bar, whilst restaurant diners can expect Welsh lamb or pan-fried duck, backed up with grills, seafood and vegetarian dishes.
OPEN: 10–11 **BAR MEALS:** Lunch served: all week Dinner served: all week 12–2.30 6–9 Av main course £4.95 **RESTAURANT:** Lunch served: all week Dinner served: all week 12–2.30 6–9 Av 3 course fixed price £11.50 **BREWERY/COMPANY:** Tomos Watkin & Sons
PRINCIPAL BEERS: Tomos Watkins Woosh, OSB.
FACILITIES: Children welcome **NOTES:** Parking 20
ROOMS: 14 bedrooms 14 en suite from s£30 d£40

Webley Hotel ◆◆◆
Poppit Sands SA43 3LN ☎ 01239 612085
Dir: A484 from Carmarthen to Cardigan, then to St Dogmaels, turn R in village centre to Poppit Sands
Located on the coastal path, and within walking distance of Poppit Sands, this hotel overlooks the Teifi Estuary and Cardigan Island. Bar food ranges from haddock and trout, to daily specials like pork with lemongrass and ginger, chicken in cream and mustard sauce, or beef barolo.
OPEN: 11.30–3 6.30–11.30 Closed: 25 Dec **BAR MEALS:** Lunch served: all week Dinner served: all week 11.30–2 6.30–9 Av main course £5.80 **BREWERY/COMPANY:** Free House
PRINCIPAL BEERS: Bass, Brains Buckleys Bitter.
FACILITIES: Children welcome Garden: Food served outside Dogs allowed (garden only) **NOTES:** Parking 60 **ROOMS:** 8 bedrooms 5 en suite from s£32.50 d£55 No credit cards

---

LLWYNDAFYDD   Map 02 SN35

Crown Inn & Restaurant
SA44 6BU ☎ 01545 560396 🖥 01545 560857
e-mail: anthony.ames@virgin.net
Dir: Off A487 NE of Cardigan
Traditional 18th-century Welsh longhouse with original beams and open fireplaces, close to Cardigan Bay. The delightful, award-winning garden is one of the pub's main attractions, its tree-sheltered setting, pond and colourful flowers attracting many customers. From the inn it's an easy walk down the lane to a cove where there are caves and National Trust cliffs. Plenty to choose from among the bar specials, including beef steak braised in red wine and mushrooms and grilled whole lemon sole with anchovy, caper and lemon butter. Extensive bar menu and wine list.
OPEN: 12–3 6–11 **BAR MEALS:** Lunch served: all week Dinner served: all week 12–2 6–9 Av main course £6.50
RESTAURANT: Lunch served: By appointment only Dinner served: all week 6.30–9 Av 3 course à la carte £20
BREWERY/COMPANY: Free House
PRINCIPAL BEERS: Interbrew Flowers Original & Flowers IPA , Tomos Watkins OSB, Greene King Old Speckled Hen.
FACILITIES: Children welcome Garden: Food served outside **NOTES:** Parking 80

Wales

continued

CONWY

ABERGELE
Map 08 SH97

Kinmel Arms 🛏 ♀
St George LL22 9BP ☎ 01745 832207 🖨 01745 832207
e-mail: lynn@watzat.co.uk
Dir: *from Bodelwyddan towards Abergele take slip road at St George. Take 1st L and Kinmel Arms is on L at top of hill*
In a village conservation area on the edge of Kinmel Estate, this 17th century coaching inn has a prime position with panoramic views over the countryside and sea. The pub has changed hands and after a major refurbishment programme has re-opened as a gourmet pub. Reports please.
OPEN: 12–3 7–11 **BAR MEALS:** Lunch served: all week Dinner served: all week 12–2 7–9 Av main course £8 **RESTAURANT:** Lunch served: all week Dinner served: all week 12–2 7–9 Av 3 course à la carte £14.50 Av 3 course fixed price £13.95
BREWERY/COMPANY: Free House
PRINCIPAL BEERS: Marston's Bitter & Pedigree, Thwaites Bitter.
FACILITIES: Children welcome Garden: Food served outdoors, patio, BBQ Dogs allowed **NOTES:** Parking 40

BETWS-Y-COED
Map 08 SH75

Ty Gwyn Hotel ♦♦♦♦ 🛏 ♀
LL24 0SG ☎ 01690 710383 & 710787 🖨 01690 710383
e-mail: mrate/1050@aol.com
Dir: *At Juction of A5/A470, 100 yards S of Waterloo Bridge.*

Former coaching inn with old world characteristics situated overlooking the River Conwy amid marvellous mountain scenery. Good home-cooked food includes grilled sea bass steak with lobster and prawn sauce, wild mushroom and pine nuts Stroganoff, breast of chicken California, chargrilled rump steak, fresh Conway salmon with dill and Dubonnet butter sauce, and king prawns Adelphi wrapped in bacon, lobster and prawn velouté.
OPEN: 12–2 7–9.30 **BAR MEALS:** Lunch served: all week Dinner served: all week 12–2 7–9 Av main course £5.95
RESTAURANT: Lunch served: all week Dinner served: all week 12–2 7–9 Av 3 course à la carte £17.95 **BREWERY/COMPANY:** Free House **PRINCIPAL BEERS:** Wadworth 6X, Welsh Smooth, Interbrew Boddingtons. **FACILITIES:** Children welcome **NOTES:** Parking 12 **ROOMS:** 12 bedrooms 9 en suite from d£35

CAPEL CURIG
Map 08 SH75

Cobdens Hotel ★ ★ 🛏
LL24 0EE ☎ 01690 720243 🖨 01690 720354
e-mail: info@cobdens.co.uk
Dir: *On A5, 4m N of Betws-Y-Coed*
Situated at the foot of Moel Siabod in the heart of Snowdonia, this 250-year-old inn is a popular centre for outdoor pursuits.

continued

The new management are continuing the emphasis on wholesome food prepared from fresh local ingredients. Look out for oven roasted chicken tandoori, pink pepper crusted leg of lamb steak, grilled Welsh black sirloin steak, or tagliatelle primavera 'with a twist'. Light bites and sandwiches also available. Comfortable en suite bedrooms.
OPEN: 11–11 (Sun 12–10.30) Closed: 25 Dec, Jan
BAR MEALS: Lunch served: all week Dinner served: all week 12–2.30 6–9 Av main course £9 **RESTAURANT:** Lunch served: all week Dinner served: all week 12–2 6–9 Av 3 course à la carte £14
BREWERY/COMPANY: Free House **PRINCIPAL BEERS:** Greene King Old Speckled Hen, Brains Bitter plus Guest beers.
FACILITIES: Children welcome Garden: Snowdonia National Park, food served ouside Dogs allowed **NOTES:** Parking 35
ROOMS: 16 bedrooms 16 en suite from s£34 d£68

CONWY
Map 08 SH77

The Groes Inn ★ ★ ★ 🛏 ♀
LL32 8TN ☎ 01492 650545 🖨 01492 650855
Dir: *Off A55 to Conwy, L at mini r'about by Conwy castle onto B5106, 2 1/2m inn on R*
Built around 500 years ago in the River Conwy Valley, the Groes Inn gained its licence in 1573, reputedly making it the first Licenced House in Wales. Beamed ceilings, rambling rooms with nooks and crannies, roaring fires, and flower-decked gardens. The focus is on local fish - try the popular seafood platter and finish with one of the delicious home-made ice creams. Other options include country chicken supreme, tavern beef and onions, bangers and mash, steak and kidney pot with thyme dumplings, and crispy roast duckling dinner.
OPEN: 12–3 6.30–11 **BAR MEALS:** Lunch served: all week Dinner served: all week 12–2.15 6.30–9 Av main course £9
RESTAURANT: Lunch served: all week Dinner served: all week 12–2.15 6.30–9 Av 3 course fixed price £25
BREWERY/COMPANY: Free House **PRINCIPAL BEERS:** Tetley, Burton Ale. **FACILITIES:** Garden: Food served outside. Very picturesque **NOTES:** Parking 90 **ROOMS:** 14 bedrooms 14 en suite from s£68 d£85

GWYTHERIN
Map 08 SH86

Lion Inn ♀
LL22 8UU ☎ 01745 860244
Dir: *3m off A548 (Llanrwst/Abergale rd) on B5384*
The original inn dates back some 300 years, but has been gradually extended over the last century. It is located in a historic village surrounded by beautiful countryside. Food ranges from snacks and beer-battered cod in the bar, to Anglesey eggs and fillet steak in the restaurant.
OPEN: 12–3 7–11 (Times may vary ring for details)
BAR MEALS: Lunch served: Tue–Sun Dinner served: Tue–Sun 12–2 7–9 Av main course £6 **RESTAURANT:** Lunch served: Tue–Sun Dinner served: Tue–Sun 12–2 7–9 Av 3 course à la carte £12 Av 3 course fixed price £12 **BREWERY/COMPANY:** Free House
PRINCIPAL BEERS: Marstons Pedigree. **FACILITIES:** Children welcome Children's licence Garden: Beer garden, patio, outdoor eating, Dogs allowed Dog basket, Food, water, Blankets
NOTES: Parking 15 **ROOMS:** 6 bedrooms 6 en suite from s£28 d£41

LLANDUDNO JUNCTION — Map 08 SH87

Pick of the Pubs

The Queens Head 🍴 ♈

Glanwydden LL31 9JP ☎ 01492 546570 🖹 01492 546487
Dir: Take A470 from A55 towards Llandudno, at 3rd roundabout R towards Penrhyn Bay, then 2nd R into Glanwydden, pub on L

A short drive inland from the sea-front, the Curetons' celebrated pub is well worth seeking out for its range of good food that relies in large part on local Welsh produce served in imaginative guises. Daily fish dishes relying on Conwy salmon, fresh local mussels and scallops are some of the highlights of a lengthy menu that also includes braised Welsh Black beef, possibly in a wild mushroom and Madeira sauce, and grilled venison sausages with red wine and onion gravy. Open 'tasty baps' and steak rolls with sautéed onions are a lunchtime feature, supplemented by pasta, salads and vegetarian dishes – typically asparagus and mushroom pancakes with Napoli sauce. The speciality seafood platter of smoked and fresh seafood comes in single or double portions with dipping sauce and new potatoes. In addition to home-made chocolate brandy trifle and hot cherry Bakewell tart, cheeses include local goats' and smoked Cheddar from Llanrwst in the Conwy valley.
OPEN: 11–3 6–11 (Sun 11–10.30) Closed: 25 Dec
BAR MEALS: Lunch served: all week Dinner served: all week 12–2.15 6–9 Av main course £7.95 **RESTAURANT:** Lunch served: all week Dinner served: all week 12–2.15 6–9
BREWERY/COMPANY: Vanguard
PRINCIPAL BEERS: Carlsberg-Tetley Tetley Bitter, Burton Bridge Bridge Bitter. **FACILITIES:** Patio, food served outside
NOTES: Parking 20

LLANNEFYDD — Map 08 SH97

The Hawk & Buckle Inn 🍴

LL16 5ED ☎ 01745 540249 🖹 01745 540316
e-mail: hawkandbuckle@btinternet.com
A 17th-century coaching inn 200m up in the hills, with wonderful views over rolling hills to the sea beyond. Menus offer a good choice of food based on local produce, including grilled plaice with parsley butter, poached salmon in tarragon sauce, roast shoulder of Welsh lamb, with mint and blackcurrant glaze, and roast loin of pork, stuffed with Cumberland sausage, served with wholegrain mustard sauce.
OPEN: 12–2 6–11 Closed: 25–26 Dec **BAR MEALS:** 12–2 6–9.30
RESTAURANT: 6–9.30 **BREWERY/COMPANY:** Free House
PRINCIPAL BEERS: Brains Bitter, Interbrew Boddingtons Bitter.
NOTES: Parking 20 **ROOMS:** 10 bedrooms 10 en suite from s£35 d£45

LLANRWST — Map 08 SH86

White Horse Inn ♦♦♦♦ 🍴 ♈

Capel Garmon LL26 0RW ☎ 01690 710271 🖹 01690 710721
e-mail: whitehorse@supanet.com
A tip for motorists: Capel Garmon perches high up on an escarpment at the Betws-y-Coed end of the Conwy valley: approach from the B5113 south of Llanrwst. The trip is rewarded by a striking collection of Victorian pottery and china hanging from the beams of this 400-year-old inn, worth seeking out for decent real ales and modest accommodation. Fresh local produce underpins a well-thought-out short menu that includes lamb 'Cawl', various steaks and Sunday roasts.
OPEN: 11–3 6–11 Closed: 2 wks Jan **BAR MEALS:** Lunch served: Sat-Sun 12–2 Dinner served: all week 6.30–9.30 Av main course £7.50
RESTAURANT: Lunch served: Sat-Sun 12–2 Dinner served: all week 6.30–9.30 Av 3 course à la carte £20 **BREWERY/COMPANY:** Free House **PRINCIPAL BEERS:** Black Sheep Best, Interbrew Bass.
FACILITIES: Children welcome Food serve outdoors Dogs allowed (water) **NOTES:** Parking 30 **ROOMS:** 6 bedrooms 6 en suite from s£35 d£58

DENBIGHSHIRE

BODFARI — Map 08 SJ07

The Dinorben Arms ♈

LL16 4DA ☎ 01745 710309 🖹 01745 710580
e-mail: info@dinorbenarms.com
Dir: Come off A55 onto B5122 through Caerwys, R onto A541, R after 2.5m in Bodfari. Pub 100yrds of B541 next to church
A heavily beamed 17th-century inn with tiered patios set into a steep hillside that is a blaze of summer colours. Food options encompass Scandinavian-style smörgåsbord, farmhouse buffets and a weekend carvery, supplemented by pan-fried local trout, pot-roast pheasant in season and roast Welsh lamb from the specials menu. Plenty of salads, vegetarian options and smaller portions of all the above for junior gourmands.
OPEN: 12–3 6–11.30 (Sun 12–11) **BAR MEALS:** Lunch served: all week Dinner served: all week 12–3 6–10.30 Av main course £7.50
RESTAURANT: Lunch served: all week Dinner served: all week 12–3 6–10.30 Av 3 course à la carte £15 **BREWERY/COMPANY:** Free House **PRINCIPAL BEERS:** Carlsberg-Tetley Tetley Bitter, Greene King Old Speckled Hen. **FACILITIES:** Children welcome Garden: Beer garden, patio, food served outdoors Dogs allowed (Garden only) **NOTES:** Parking 120

LLANGOLLEN — Map 08 SJ24

The Famous Britannia Inn

Horseshoe Pass LL20 8DW ☎ 01978 860144 🖹 01978 860144
e-mail: brit@globalnet.co.uk
Dir: From Llangollen take A542 N 2m
14th-century coaching inn set in its own award-winning gardens with beautiful views of the Vale of Llangollen. Situated at the foot of the famous Horseshoe Pass.

LLANYNYS — Map 08 SJ16

Cerrigllwydion Arms

LL16 4PA ☎ 01745 890247
Dir: A525 towards Denbigh, R after 1.5m, then L and 1m to pub
This venerable old inn was built in 1400 on land where the parish stables once stood. It was originally for the churchgoers

continued

Wales

LLANYNYS continued

of St Saeran's church. Comfortable dining areas and a garden looking out to the Clwydian Hills make it a popular spot. Menus are traditional so expect steak, kidney and ale pie, popular grills and perhaps salmon with prawn sauce as dining options, with lighter snacks available in the bar.
OPEN: 12–3 7–11 (closed Mon) **BAR MEALS:** Lunch served: Wed–Sun Dinner served: Wed–Sun 12–2 7–9 Av main course £5.50 **RESTAURANT:** Lunch served: Wed–Sun Dinner served: Wed–Sun 12–2 7–9 Av 3 course à la carte £12 **BREWERY/COMPANY:** Free House **PRINCIPAL BEERS:** Interbrew Bass & Worthington Bitter, Carlsberg-Tetley Tetley Bitter,. **FACILITIES:** Children welcome Garden: Food served outdoors **NOTES:** Parking 50

RUTHIN   Map 08 SJ15

Pick of the Pubs

Ye Olde Anchor Inn
2 Rhos St LL15 1DY ☎ 01824 702813 ▤ 01824 703050
e-mail: hotel@anchorinn.co.uk
Dir: at jct of A525 and A494
In the originally medieval town of Ruthin, the Anchor stands out as a base for touring the Conwy coast, Preseli hills and Snowdonia: Chester, Shrewsbury, Llangollen and Caernarfon are all within an easy drive. A relaxed atmosphere permeates the bar and restaurant whose food output is clearly home made. Chicken satay and mushrooms stuffed with spinach and cream cheese are typical starters, followed by scallops with black pudding, chicken breast in Boursin sauce and carpet-bag or Chateaubriand steaks. Crème brûlée, crêpes Suzette and bananas in rum and toffee sauce are typical desserts. Recently extended accommodation offers up-to-date facilities at competitive prices with a hearty breakfast to set overnight guests happily on their way.
OPEN: 12–2 5.30–11 **BAR MEALS:** Lunch served: all week 12–2 Av main course £7 **RESTAURANT:** Dinner served: all week 7–9.30 Av 3 course à la carte £17 **BREWERY/COMPANY:** Free House **PRINCIPAL BEERS:** Bass, Guest ales.
FACILITIES: Children welcome Children's licence Dogs allowed **NOTES:** Parking 20 **ROOMS:** 26 bedrooms 26 en suite from s£37.50 d£52

Pick of the Pubs

White Horse Inn
Hendrerwydd LL16 4LL ☎ 01824 790218
A traditional 17th-century inn nestling in the foothills of the Clwydian Range, and once a stopping place for drovers. From the outside it is nothing special, but step inside and experience the wonderful cooking of Londoner Ruth Vintr, and the warm welcome provided by husband Vit, a Czech emigré. The competent modern European and Celtic food is displayed on an interesting carte and bar menu. Snacks include lamb steak and chips, cod fillet, and a tower of a breakfast; from the main menu choose between banana wrapped in smoked bacon, or split herring with salsa to start, followed by Chinese style trout, witch sole with dry vermouth and litchis, or poussin cooked with red wine. Puddings are adventurous – cherry pancake with cherry brandy and spices, or old favourites like baked rice pudding with strawberry jam. Themed evenings are a speciality.

continued

OPEN: 12–2.30 6–11 **BAR MEALS:** Lunch served: Wed–Sun 12–2.30 Dinner served: Tue–Sun 6–9.30 Av main course £9 **RESTAURANT:** Lunch served: Wed–Sun 12–2.30 Dinner served: Tue–Sun 6–9.30 Av 3 course à la carte £20 **PRINCIPAL BEERS:** Regular changing guest ales. **FACILITIES:** Children welcome Garden: Food served outside Dogs allowed (water) **NOTES:** Parking 50

ST ASAPH   Map 08 SJ07

Pick of the Pubs

The Plough Inn ⓘ ♈
The Roe LL17 0LU ☎ 01745 585080 ▤ 01745 585363
See Pick of the Pubs on page 609

FLINTSHIRE

BABELL   Map 08 SN83

Black Lion Inn ⓘ
CH8 8PZ ☎ 01352 720239
Dir: From Holywell take B5121 towards A541 (Mold to Denbigh road) & take 2nd R to Babell
Some 35 years in the same ownership, this Grade II listed, 13th-century former farmhouse, once used as a drovers' retreat, ploughs a constant furrow. The two comfy bedrooms and a constantly changing dinner menu attract many returning visitors who will have lunched elsewhere, for here there is no such option. A relaxed, yet fairly formal, dinner produces choices of fresh sea bass and game in season, roast duckling with peach and brandy sauce and beef fillet with Stilton cream.
OPEN: 7pm–11pm Open lunch 1st Sun each month **BAR MEALS:** Lunch served: 1st Sun of month Dinner served: Fri–Sat 7.30–9.30 Av main course £8.50 **RESTAURANT:** Lunch served: First Sunday of each month 12–2 Dinner served: Fri–Sat 7.15–9.30 Av 3 course à la carte £13 **BREWERY/COMPANY:** Free House **PRINCIPAL BEERS:** Interbrew Boddingtons Bitter. **FACILITIES:** Children welcome **NOTES:** Parking 80 **ROOMS:** 2 bedrooms 2 en suite from s£22 d£30

CILCAIN   Map 08 SJ16

White Horse Inn
CH7 5NN ☎ 01352 740142 ▤ 01352 740142
e-mail: christine.jeory@btopenworld.com
Dir: From Mold take A541 towards Denbigh. After approx 6m turn L
Situated in a lovely hillside village, the inn is several hundred years old and very popular with walkers, cyclists, horse-riders and people out for a drive in the beautiful surrounding countryside. The dishes are home-made by the landlord's wife using only the best quality ingredients – local wherever possible – including steak and kidney pie, ham and eggs, lamb tajine and various curries.
OPEN: 12–3 6.30–11 (Sat–Sun 12–11) **BAR MEALS:** Lunch served: all week Dinner served: all week 12–2 7–9 Av main course £6 **BREWERY/COMPANY:** Free House **PRINCIPAL BEERS:** Marston's Pedigree, Bank's Bitter, Greene King Abbot Ale, Morrells Varsity. **FACILITIES:** Garden: Patio, food served outdoors Dogs allowed **NOTES:** Parking 12

OPEN: 12–11
BAR MEALS: L served all week.
D served all week. 12–9.30
Av main course £6.95
RESTAURANT: L served all week.
D served all week. 12–3 6–10
Av cost 3 course £14.95
BREWERY/COMPANY:
FREE HOUSE
PRINCIPAL BEERS: Greene King
Old Speckled Hen, Shepherds
Neame Spitfire
FACILITIES: Children welcome.
Garden: outdoor eating, patio,
BBQ
NOTES: Parking 200

The Plough Inn

The Roe St Asaph LL17 0LU
☎ 01745 585080 🖹 01745 585363
Dir: Rhyl/St Asaph turning from A55, L
at rdbt, pub 200yds on L

Unparalleled in the country, the development of this 18th-century former coaching inn over the past two years has been remarkable, and now comprises a real ale bar, up-market bistro, an Italian-themed art deco restaurant and a wine shop.

Standing just out of town on the original Holyhead-to-London road, it buzzes with activity throughout the day and has become a notable dining venue by night - winner of the Welsh Seafood Pub of the Year in 2001. Taking horseracing as its principal theme, the Paddock Bar offers a quick bite menu to accompany beers principally from local micro-breweries while the Racecourse Bistro, with its mural of Chester racecourse, features a fresh fish display, assorted steaks from the chargrill and house specialities from cod in beer batter with real chips to braised shank of Welsh lamb with roasted vegetables and crushed garlic potatoes. An entirely separate menu in Graffiti Italiano offers pizzas and pasta in many guises, in addition to such dishes as veal medallions with mushrooms, cream and herb risotto.

HALKYN

Map 08 SJ27

Britannia Inn

Pentre Rd CH8 8BS ☎ 01352 780272
e-mail: sarah.pollitt@britanniainn.freeserve.co.uk
Dir: Off A55 on B5123
500-year-old stone pub on an old coach route between
Chester and Holyhead, with views over the Dee estuary and
Wirral. It features a family farm with chickens, ducks and
donkeys. Typical dishes are honey lamb steak, poached
salmon fillet, Cumberland sausage, and gammon steak.
OPEN: 11-11 (Sun 12-10.30) **BAR MEALS:** Lunch served: all week
Dinner served: all week 12-2.30 6.30-9 Av main course £6
RESTAURANT: Lunch served: all week Dinner served: all week
12-2.30 6.30-9 Av 3 course à la carte £12
BREWERY/COMPANY: J W Lees **PRINCIPAL BEERS:** J W Lees
Bitter, GM Mild & Moonraker. **FACILITIES:** Children welcome
Garden: Food served outdoors, patio **NOTES:** Parking 40

LIXWM

Map 08 SJ17

The Crown Inn

CH8 8NQ ☎ 01352 781112
Dir: Off the B5121 S of Holywell
An early 17th-century inn in a pretty village not far from the
Clwydian mountain range and Offa's Dyke Path. Hot dishes
include lamb's liver, bacon and onion casserole, chicken
stuffed with pâté, topped with a rich garlic and mushroom
sauce, fillet of cod in real ale batter, and 10oz salmon steaks.
Sirloins and rumps are served with chips or potatoes of the
day, mushrooms, onion rings and grilled tomato.
OPEN: 5.30-11 (6-11 Sun) **BAR MEALS:** Lunch served: Sun
12-2.30 Dinner served: Wed-Sat 6.30-9 Av main course £5.95
RESTAURANT: Lunch served: Sun 12-2.30 Dinner served: Wed-Sun
6.30-9 Av 3 course à la carte £12 Av 4 course fixed price £12
PRINCIPAL BEERS: Tetleys, Robinsons Bitter.
FACILITIES: Children welcome Dogs allowed **NOTES:** Parking 40

MOLD

Map 08 SJ26

The Druid Inn

Ruthin Rd, Llanferres CH7 5SN ☎ 01352 810225
Dir: A494 from Mold, Druid 4 1/2m along road on R
At this 17th-century coaching inn, overlooking the Alyn Valley
and the Craig Harris mountains, a daily blackboard menu
features decent home-cooked food such as braised shoulder
of lamb in red wine, salmon wrapped in bacon with
hollandaise, steak, ale and mushroom pie, and imaginatively-
filled granary baps.
OPEN: 11.30-3 5.30-11 (Sat, Sun & BH all day & food 12-10)
BAR MEALS: Lunch served: all week Dinner served: all week 12-3 6-10
Av main course £8.25 **RESTAURANT:** Lunch served: all week Dinner
served: all week 12-3 6-10 Av 3 course à la carte £14
BREWERY/COMPANY: Burtonwood **PRINCIPAL BEERS:** Burtonwood
Best Bitter & changing guest ale. **FACILITIES:** Children welcome Garden:
Dogs allowed **NOTES:** Parking 40 **ROOMS:** 5 bedrooms 1 en suite
from s£30 d£38.50

NORTHOP

Map 08 SJ26

Pick of the Pubs

Stables Bar Restaurant 🐑 ♀

CH7 6AB ☎ 01352 840577 📠 01352 840382
e-mail: info@soughtonhall.co.uk
Dir: from A55, take A5119 through Northop village
Opened in 1997, this magnificent destination pub was
made from the Grade I listed stables of Soughton Hall, the

former Bishop of Chester's Palace. Superbly converted
under massive oak beams, the building retains a
horseracing theme; the original brick floor and some of
the stalls have been retained, and tables are named after
famous racecourses. The ground floor contains a real ale
bar with an impressive menu, and upstairs diners will find
an open-plan kitchen with an adjacent, fully stocked wine
shop. Choose your own fresh fish, seafood or steaks and
watch them cooked to order, accompanied by fresh
breads, hand-cut chips and a self-served salad. Other
dishes include roast salmon and couscous, Mexican
chicken stir-fry, and chargrilled vegetable kebabs. Right
next door, the Hall itself is a magnificent pile offering
splendid country-house bedrooms, particularly popular
for weddings and special events in a breathtaking setting.

OPEN: 11-3 6-11.30 **BAR MEALS:** Lunch served: all week
Dinner served: all week 12-3 7-10 Av main course £10
RESTAURANT: Lunch served: all week Dinner served: all week
12-3 7-10 Av 3 course à la carte £20 Av 3 course fixed price £25
BREWERY/COMPANY: Free House
PRINCIPAL BEERS: Shepherds Neame Spitfire, Coach House
Dick turpin,. **FACILITIES:** Children welcome Garden: Food
served outdoors, patio, Dogs allowed (water) **NOTES:** Parking
150 **ROOMS:** 14 bedrooms 14 en suite from s£80 d£100

The Church's Sway

Inn signs reflecting the past importance
of the Church include the Cross, the Mitre, the
Adam and Eve, the Angel. The Salutation
commemorates the Annunciation to the Virgin
Mary. The Anchor is not always a nautical sign,
but can be a Christian symbol of hope. The Star
may be the one the three kings followed to
Bethlehem and the Seven Stars are the Virgin
Mary's crown. The Bell is a church bell and
names like the Eight Bells are generally related
to a notable local peal. Inns near a church
dedicated to St Peter may be called the Cross
Keys, which are the saint's keys of heaven and
hell, or the Cock, for the one that crowed twice.
The Lamb and Flag was the badge of the
crusading Knights Templar (and was later
adopted by the Merchant Tailors). The Catherine
Wheel is the Emblem of St Catherine of
Alexandria, who was much venerated in the
crusading period and according to legend
was martyred by being broken on a
spiked wheel.

continued

GWYNEDD

ABERDYFI — Map 08 SN69

Dovey Inn ★ ★
Seaview Ter LL35 0EF ☎ 01654 767332 📠 01654 767996
e-mail: info@doveyinn.com

Historic inn on the estuary of the River Dovey, only 20 yards from the sea and the fine sandy beach. The village clings to the hills above the estuary, once a major slate port and now a sailing centre. An extensive seafood menu includes Thai spiced shark steak, fish pie, Bantry Bay mussels, chargrilled swordfish, and tuna steak with red wine fish gravy. Plenty of other options including sandwiches, light bites, vegetarian, meat dishes, pasta, and pizza.
OPEN: 11-11 (Sun 12-10.30) **BAR MEALS:** Lunch served: all week Dinner served: all week 12-2.30 6-9.30 Av main course £8.50
BREWERY/COMPANY: Free House **PRINCIPAL BEERS:** Hancock HB, Interbrew Bass,. **FACILITIES:** Children welcome Children's licence Patio, Food served outside Dogs allowed **ROOMS:** 8 bedrooms 8 en suite from s£79 d£59

Pick of the Pubs

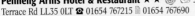

Penhelig Arms Hotel & Restaurant ★ ★
Terrace Rd LL35 0LT ☎ 01654 767215 📠 01654 767690
e-mail: penheligarms@saqnet.co.uk
Dir: On A493 (coastal rd) W of Machynlleth

A relaxed, family-run hotel and restaurant, this jewel of the north-west Wales coastline enjoys spectacular views over the tidal Dyfi estuary. Guests, many returning times over, enjoy a warm and relaxed atmosphere in the bar with its unique central hearth and in fine weather can lounge on the sea wall opposite, awaiting delivery of ever-enticing food. Fresh fish, crabs and lobsters arrive straight from the quay and a solid reliance on such local produce is evident in menus that are updated twice daily. These might include fillets of plaice baked with a Parmesan crust

served with an Italian verde sauce, seared tuna with roast tomato and aïoli, or smoked salmon with a ginger, orange and cream cheese pâté. Pwdin (Welsh desserts) feature wicked and homely creations such as white chocolate cheesecake and bread and butter pudding. 'Other treats include a monthly wine list that never disappoints and beautifully furnished bedrooms.
OPEN: 11.30-3.30 5.30-11 (Sun 12-3.30, 6-10.30) Closed: Dec 25-26 **BAR MEALS:** Lunch served: all week Dinner served: all week 12-2.30 6.30-9.30 Av main course £8.95
RESTAURANT: Lunch served: all week Dinner served: all week 12-2.30 7-9.30 Av 3 course fixed price £24
BREWERY/COMPANY: Free House
PRINCIPAL BEERS: Carlesberg-Tetley Tetley Bitter, Greene King Abbot Ale, Adnams Broadside, Brains Reverend James & SA.
FACILITIES: Children welcome Children's licence Garden: Food served outside Dogs allowed **NOTES:** Parking 12
ROOMS: 14 bedrooms 14 en suite

ABERSOCH — Map 08 SH32

St Tudwal's Inn
High St LL53 7DS ☎ 01758 712539 📠 01758 713701
Dir: take A499 from Pwllheli, follow one way system, pub on R
A Victorian building, now converted to provide two bars and a restaurant, believed to be haunted by a Victorian lady. Steaks are a popular option, alongside dishes such as sea bass poached in sherry with julienne peppers, duck with port, cream and mushroom sauce, and lamb cutlets with wine gravy.
OPEN: 11-11 (Sun 12-10.30) **BAR MEALS:** Lunch served: all week Dinner served: all week 12-2.30 6-9 Av main course £6.25
RESTAURANT: Dinner served: all week 6-9
PRINCIPAL BEERS: Robinsons Best, Hatters Mild.
FACILITIES: Children welcome Garden: Food served outside. Beer patio Dogs allowed (in the garden only) **NOTES:** Parking 20
ROOMS: 5 bedrooms 5 en suite from s£60 d£60

BLAENAU FFESTINIOG — Map 08 SH74

The Miners Arms
Llechwedd Slate Caverns LL41 3NB
☎ 01766 830306 📠 01766 831260
Dir: Blaenau Ffestiniog is 25 miles from Llandudno on the N Wales coast, situated on the A470 to main N-S Trunk Rd
Slate floors, open fires and staff in Victorian costume emphasise the heritage theme of this welcoming pub nestling in the centre of a Welsh village. On the site of Llechwedd Slate Caverns, one of the country's leading tourist attractions, it caters for all comers and tastes: expect steak and ale casserole, pork pie and salad, various ploughman's lunches, and hot apple pie, as well as afternoon tea with scones and cream.
OPEN: 11-5.30 Closed: Nov-Easter **BAR MEALS:** Lunch served: all week 11-5 Av main course £4.50 **BREWERY/COMPANY:** Free House **FACILITIES:** Children welcome Garden: Beer garden, food served outdoors, patio Dogs allowed **NOTES:** Parking 200

★ **Indicates AA inspected hotel accommodation**

Wales

continued

BONTDDU
Map 08 SH61

The Halfway House
LL40 2UE ☎ 01341 430635
Dir: On A436 between Dolgellau & Barmouth

Dating back to 1700, the Halfway House has mellow pine chapel pews and fireplaces, giving the place a welcoming, cosy atmosphere. Situated near the Mawddach estuary, much loved by Wordsworth, the pub is directly on the route of several popular local walks. Good range of cask conditioned ales, several of which are from local breweries. Typical menu includes steak, mushroom and ale pie, wild mushroom and herb capelletti, lamb jalfrezi, and seared salmon on a bed of crispy leeks with soy and ginger sauce.
OPEN: 11–11 (Sun 12–10.30) 6–11 Closed: Dec 25
BAR MEALS: Lunch served: all week Dinner served: all week 12–2.30 6–9.30 Av main course £7 **RESTAURANT:** Lunch served: all week Dinner served: all week 12–2.30 6–9.30
BREWERY/COMPANY: Free House **PRINCIPAL BEERS:** Scottish Courage Courage Directors, Brains Bitter & Reverand James Marston's Pedigree, Theakston Best. **FACILITIES:** Children welcome Garden: Patio, food served outside Dogs allowed (water) **NOTES:** Parking 30

DOLGELLAU
Map 08 SH71

Pick of the Pubs

George III Hotel ★ ★
Penmaenpool LL40 1YD ☎ 01341 422525 ▤ 01341 423565
Dir: 2m West of A493 beyond RSPB Centre

At the edge of the magnificent Mawddach Estuary with splendid views to the Snowdonia National Park, the hotel stands a mile or so out of town, in tranquil waterside meadows inhabited by swans, herons and otters. Part of the accommodation is housed in a former railway station. The Cellar Bar beside the water is ideal for families, cyclists and walkers, while the upper level Dresser Bar, with an unusual bar counter from which it is named, and the main dining rooms are rather more genteel. Noted for local salmon and sea trout, pheasant and wild duck in season, meals are home cooked by the landlord. At one end of the scale are soups, chicken liver pâté or steak and Stilton baps, while the newly added restaurant weighs in with sardines with onion marmalade, rack of Welsh mountain lamb, whole sea bass with prawns and capers, sticky date pudding and cheeses from Harlech and Caws Llyn, a matured Cheddar.
OPEN: 11–11 **BAR MEALS:** Lunch served: all week Dinner served: all week 12–2.30 6.30–9.30 Av main course £6.50
RESTAURANT: Lunch served: Sun 12–2 Dinner served: all week 7–9 Av 3 course à la carte £25 **BREWERY/COMPANY:** Free House **PRINCIPAL BEERS:** Greene King Ruddles Best, Scottish

Courage John Smith's & Courage Directors.
FACILITIES: Children welcome Children's licence Garden: Food served outdoors, patio/terrace Dogs allowed
NOTES: Parking 60 **ROOMS:** 11 bedrooms 11 en suite from s£45 d£80

See Pub Walk on page 613

LLANDWROG
Map 08 SN45

The Harp Inn
Tyn'llan LL54 5SY ☎ 01286 831071 ▤ 01286 830239
e-mail: management@theharp.globalnet.co.uk
Dir: A55 from Chester bypass, signed off A487 Pwllheli rd

A long established haven for travellers, the inn is located in the historic home village of the nearby Glynllifon Estate, between the mountains of Snowdonia and the beautiful beaches of Dinas Dinlle. A proudly Welsh menu offers lob scouse with roll and cabbage, boiled Anglesey eggs on leeky potato mash, breast of chicken filled with orange and coriander pesto, wrapped in Carmarthen ham, Glamorgan sausages with red onion marmalade, and Pembroke fish pie. Welsh language menu supplied.
OPEN: 12–3 6–11 Closed: Jan 1 **BAR MEALS:** Lunch served: Tue–Sun Dinner served: Tue–Sun 12–2 6.30-8.30 Av main course £6.95
RESTAURANT: Dinner served: Tue–Sun 6.30-8.30 Av 3 course à la carte £16 **BREWERY/COMPANY:** Free House
PRINCIPAL BEERS: Interbrew Bass, Black Sheep Best, Wyre Piddle Piddle in the Wind. **FACILITIES:** Children welcome Garden: Food served outside Dogs allowed (water) **NOTES:** Parking 20
ROOMS: 4 bedrooms 1 en suite

LLANENGAN
Map 08 SH22

The Sun Inn
LL53 7LG ☎ 01758 712660
Dir: From Pwllheli take A499 S to Abersoch. Then 1.5m towards Hells Mouth Beach

Friendly and welcoming pub, reputedly haunted, with a wishing well in the garden, and where the locals are likely to burst into song. The changing menu of home-cooked dishes includes steaks, lasagne and chicken breast.
OPEN: 12–2.30 6–11 (open all day Sat) **BAR MEALS:** Lunch served: all week Dinner served: all week 12–3 6–9 Av main course £6.95 **PRINCIPAL BEERS:** Robinson Best, Old Stockport Bitter.
FACILITIES: Children welcome Garden: **NOTES:** Parking 70

continued

PUB WALK

Penmaenpool
George III Hotel

An outstanding linear walk along the banks of the Mawddach Estuary, following the route of the defunct Great Western Railway. The trail, with some of the best views in Wales, runs in front of the hotel along the sea wall. Considered by many to be Europe's most beautiful estuary, this breathtaking corner of the country inspired poets such as Wordsworth and Gerald Manley Hopkins.

Turn left out of the pub front door and head for the sea. The trail is easy to follow, and a half-mile (800m) extension at the end can be added if you continue across the Barmouth railway bridge. There is a charge for crossing the wooden bridge, built in 1865. Small rock promontories jutting out into the river are a feature of the estuary, and the recent addition of benches provide the opportunity to rest before continuing with the walk or turning round and returning to the start point. The trail occasionally passes through Sustrans gates, wide enough for wheelchairs, and easy for bicycles. The trail is now a fully recognised Sustrans cycle route, but still remains an official long-distance footpath mostly maintained by Sustrans grants and the Snowdonia National Park. Look out for RSPB woodlands and wetlands, as well as one of the largest reed-beds in Wales. The river here is home to a variety of birds, including oystercatchers, herons, shellducks, mallards and curlews. The estuary is also renowned for its salmon, sea trout, bass and mullet. Cader Idris stands out to your right, as do the disused slate mines at Arthog. Rhododendrons are also seen in the oak woodland around the river, particularly striking when in bloom.

GEORGE III HOTEL,
Penmaenpool, DOLGELLAU
LL40 1YD
Tel: 01341 422525
Directions: 2m West of Dolgellau on A493 beyond RSPB Centre
In waterside meadows with herons and otters and views to Snowdonia. Part was a former railway station. The bar by Mawddach Estuary suits families, cyclists and walkers, the upper bars are more genteel. Menus noted for local fish and wildfowl.
Open: 11–11
Bar Meals: 12–2.30 6.30–9.30
Children welcome and dogs allowed. Garden and parking available.

Distance: Any distance up to 14 miles (22.5km)
Map: OS Landranger 124
Terrain: Flat with rolled surface. 7 miles (11.3km) vehicle-free
Paths: Footpath, Sustrans cycle trail. Suitable for wheelchairs, a little rough at 3-mile (4.8km) mark
Gradient: No climbing

Walk submitted and checked by George III Hotel

MAENTWROG — Map 08 SH64

Pick of the Pubs

Grapes Hotel
LL41 4HN ☎ 01766 590365 & 590365 ▤ 01766 590654
e-mail: grapeshotel@aol.com
Dir: A5 thru Corwen to Bala, A487 to Maentwrog, onto A496, pub 100yrds in RH side

A Grade II-listed, 17th-century coaching inn with a cellar 400 years older. Long before this area was embraced by the Snowdonia National Park, writer George Borrow 'partook of brandy and water' here, and Lloyd George and Lily Langtry took tea – on separate occasions, allegedly. In the bars, heavily carved pitch-pine, oak and mahogany fittings create a sense of warmth that roaring log fires on wintry days can only accentuate. Specials change twice weekly, but there's always a choice of three/four starters, four fish, two meat and vegetarian dishes. Plaice is always on the menu, and cod, scampi, red mullet and Thai fishcakes also appear. Locals and regulars regard the black ('but not burnt') pork ribs as a must, although the recipe's a secret. Red hot chilli is 'not for the faint-hearted'. All this, a CAMRA award winner and a ghost, too.
OPEN: 11-11 (Sun 12-10.30) Closed: Dec 25
BAR MEALS: Lunch served: all week Dinner served: all week 12-2 6-9 Av main course £6 **BREWERY/COMPANY:** Free House **PRINCIPAL BEERS:** Marstons Pedigree, Greene King Old Speckled Hen, IPA, Wye Valley Butty Bach.
FACILITIES: Children welcome Garden: Dogs allowed Public bar only **NOTES:** Parking 36 **ROOMS:** 8 bedrooms 8 en suite from s£30 d£60

NANTGWYNANT — Map 08 SH56

Pen-Y-Gwryd
LL55 4NT ☎ 01286 870211
Dir: 6m S of Llanberis at head of Gwryd river, close to junction of A4086 & A498
Situated in the magnificent Snowdonia National Park, this cosy climber's pub is the home of British mountaineering. The 1953 Everest team used it as a training base and scrawled their signatures on the ceiling. As well as being an inn, offering shelter and hospitality against a rugged backdrop, it also doubles as a mountain rescue post. Wholesome fare from the daily-changing menu might feature roast Welsh sirloin of beef, roast duck, and lamb in red wine and paprika.
OPEN: 11-11 Closed: Nov to New Year **BAR MEALS:** Lunch served: all week Dinner served: all week 12-2 Av main course £5 **RESTAURANT:** Lunch served: all week Dinner served: all week

7.30-8 Av 3 course à la carte £17 Av 5 course fixed price £19
BREWERY/COMPANY: Free House
PRINCIPAL BEERS: Interbrew Bass & Boddingtons Bitter.
FACILITIES: Children welcome Garden: Beer garden, swimming pool, sauna Dogs allowed **NOTES:** Parking 25
ROOMS: 16 bedrooms 5 en suite from s£26 d£52 No credit cards

PORTHMADOG — Map 08 SH53

The Ship
Lombard St LL49 9AP ☎ 01766 512990
Dir: From A55 take A470 S toward the coast
The oldest pub still operating in Porthmadog, The Ship is located close to the harbour and is mentioned in many maritime books on the area. One menu serves all, with plenty of fresh fish - chargrilled tuna steak, breaded plaice fillet, salmon and spinach in a tarragon sauce, or moules mariniere. Other options include Thai red vegetable curry, lamb chump, steak and kidney pudding, and chicken with wild mushrooms. Over 90 malt whiskies available.
OPEN: 11-11 (Sun 12-10.30) Closed: Dec 25 **BAR MEALS:** 12-2 6.30-9.00 **BREWERY/COMPANY:** Punch Taverns
PRINCIPAL BEERS: Greene King Old Speckled Hen, IPA, Carlsberg-Tetley Tetley Bitter, Burton Ale. **FACILITIES:** Children's licence Dogs allowed

TUDWEILIOG — Map 08 SH23

Lion Hotel
LL53 8ND ☎ 01758 770244 ▤ 01758 770244
e-mail: andrewlee@claramail.com
Dir: A499 from Caernarfon, B4417 Tudweiliog
The Lee family have run this friendly, 300-year-old village inn on the Lleyn Peninsula for 30 years. The large garden and children's play area makes the pub especially popular with cyclists, walkers and families. There is a non-smoking family dining room but food is served throughout, from lunchtime baguettes to traditional favourites such as roast chicken and home-made vegetarian lasagne. The four en suite bedrooms provide a good base for enjoying the area's many outdoor activities.
OPEN: 11.30-11 (Winter 12-2, 7-11 all day Sat, Sun 12-2)
BAR MEALS: Lunch served: all week Dinner served: all week 12-2 6-9 Av main course £6 **RESTAURANT:** Lunch served: all week Dinner served: all week 12-2 6-9 **BREWERY/COMPANY:** Free House **PRINCIPAL BEERS:** Marston's Pedigree, Interbrew Boddingtons, Theakston,. **FACILITIES:** Children welcome Garden: Food served outside Dogs allowed (water) **NOTES:** Parking 40 **ROOMS:** 4 bedrooms 4 en suite from d£44

BEAUMARIS — Map 08 SH67

The Liverpool Arms Hotel
Castle St LL58 8BA ☎ 01248 810362 ▤ 01248 811135
Dir: A5 across the Menai Straits, R onto A545 through Menai Bridge
Historic inn dating back to 1706 when there was a busy trade between Liverpool and Beaumaris - hence the name. Strong nautical theme with timbers from HMS Victory, Nelson's flagship. Popular, daily-changing blackboard menus and a summer salad bar. Expect a choice of fish dishes, as well as scrumpy pork hock in cider sauce, home made steak pie, spinach and ricotta cannelloni.
OPEN: 11.30-11.30 **BAR MEALS:** Lunch served: all week Dinner

continued   *continued*

served: all week 12–2 6–9 Av main course £7
BREWERY/COMPANY: Free House **PRINCIPAL BEERS:** Greene
King Morland Old Speckled Hen, Tetley, Marstons Pedigree.
FACILITIES: Children welcome **NOTES:** Parking 12
ROOMS: 10 bedrooms 10 en suite from s£40 d£59.50

Pick of the Pubs

Ye Olde Bulls Head Inn ★ ★ ◎◎ ♀
Castle St LL58 8AP ☎ 01248 810329 🗎 01248 811294
e-mail: info@bullsheadinn.co.uk
Dir: From Brittannia Road Bridge follow A545
Just a stone's throw from Beaumaris Castle and the Menai
Straits, a traditional watering hole dating back to 1472
whose famous past guests have included Samuel Johnson
and Charles Dickens. The smartly-furnished first-floor
restaurant offers a formal menu based around acclaimed
seafood dishes and a wine connoisseur's ideal list. Sample
seafood sausage with saffron mash, Thai-style scallop
broth, and warm mussel tart, followed perhaps by grilled
local sea bass with Conwy mussel ravioli, steamed black
bream fillet with crab noodles, and pan-fried fillet of cod.
It's not all fish though: smoked beef with pickled walnuts,
and main dish of Hereford duck breast, might be rounded
off with a delectable steamed clementine sponge with
Grand Marnier ice cream. A newer brasserie, complete
with harlequin tiles, ranges through pasta, vegetarian
(shredded vegetable stir fry), spatchcock poussin with a
curried cream sauce, and grilled mullet.
OPEN: 11–11 (Sun 12–10.30) Closed: 25–26 Dec, 1 Jan
BAR MEALS: Lunch served: all week Dinner served: all week
12.00–2.00 6–9.30 Av main course £7.50 **RESTAURANT:** Dinner
served: Mon–Sat 7–9.30 Av 3 course à la carte £29.75
BREWERY/COMPANY: Free House
PRINCIPAL BEERS: Bass, Hancocks, Worthington.
FACILITIES: Children welcome **NOTES:** Parking 10
ROOMS: 13 bedrooms 13 en suite from s£64 d£92

LLANFACHRAETH   Map 08 SH38

Holland Hotel ◆◆◆ ♀
LL65 4UH ☎ 01407 740252
A friendly 18th-century inn within easy reach of the Anglesey
Heritage coastline and Holyhead ferry port. Also convenient
for stunning scenery, safe sandy beaches, and a championship
golf course. Local produce forms the mainstay of menus that
include steak in stout, salads, Indian dishes, a vegetarian
selection, dressed crab and seafood platter.
OPEN: 12–11 **BAR MEALS:** Lunch served: all week Dinner served:
all week 12–9 Av main course £5.50 **RESTAURANT:** Lunch served:
all week Dinner served: all week 12–9 Av 3 course à la carte £10
BREWERY/COMPANY: J W Lees **PRINCIPAL BEERS:** J W Lees.
FACILITIES: Children welcome Garden: Outdoor eating
NOTES: Parking 40 **ROOMS:** 4 bedrooms 4 en suite from s£25
d£50

RED WHARF BAY   Map 08 SH58

Pick of the Pubs

The Ship Inn 🐑 ♀
LL75 8RJ ☎ 01248 852568 🗎 01248 851013
Red Wharf Bay once bustled with the import of coal and
fertilizers, and the then Quay Inn used to serve ale to
sailors from 6am onwards. Nowadays the arrival of the

continued

freshest Conwy Bay fish and seafood at high tide creates
its own stir, and the renamed Ship Inn makes the most of
this catch in its seasonal menus. Renowned for its quality
food, fine wines and real ales, this 18th-century inn boasts
cosy fireside tables and a waterside beer garden that
comes into its own in summer. For a light meal you can
try sautéed woodland mushrooms on a Welsh rarebit
crostini with red pepper sauce, or seared strips of rib-eye
steak on baguettes. For more ceremonial dining there's
seafood casserole, seared king scallops with fennel risotto,
roast goose breast with plum sauce, and roast woodcock.
Farmhouse ice creams, Welsh cheeses, and perhaps
roasted rhubarb and apple crumble make equally fitting
endings.
OPEN: 11–3.30 6.30–11 (Sat 11–11, Sun 12–10.30)
BAR MEALS: Lunch served: all week Dinner served: all week
12–2.30 6.30–9 **RESTAURANT:** Lunch served: Sun 12–2.30
Dinner served: Fri–Sat 7–9.30 Av 3 course à la carte £18 Av 2
course fixed price £16 **BREWERY/COMPANY:** Free House
PRINCIPAL BEERS: Carlsberg-Tetley Friary Meux, Tetley, Burton
Ale, Marston's Pedigree. **FACILITIES:** Children welcome
Garden: Dogs allowed (water) **NOTES:** Parking 45

ABERGAVENNY   Map 03 SO21

Pick of the Pubs

Clytha Arms 🐑 ♀
Clytha NP7 9BW ☎ 01873 840206 🗎 01873 840206
*Dir: From A449/A40 junction (E of Abergavenny) follow signs for 'Old
Road Abergavenny/Clytha'*
A former dower house set in pretty lawned gardens
alongside the old Abergavenny road not far from the
River Usk. Raglan's famous 15th-century castle is a few
miles down the road, and Cardiff with all its attractions is
about 40 minutes drive away. This is an informal pub with
an excellent reputation for good food, and a very flexible
approach to customers' fads and fancies. Bar snacks
encompass the simple yet imaginative, with wild boar
sausages, black pudding with apple and potato mash, leek
and laver rissoles, and crab and avocado salad among the
extensive choices. Interest in the restaurant might focus
on starters like wild boar rillette with red onion chutney,
followed by roast quail with Cognac and strawberries, and
desserts like chocolate pudding with Seville orange ice
cream. A popular festival venue, with en suite
accommodation for those who want to stay a while.
OPEN: 12–3.30 6–11 Closed: 25 Dec **BAR MEALS:** Lunch
served: Tue–Sat 12.30–2.30 Dinner served: Tues–Fri 7–9.30 Av main
course £6 **RESTAURANT:** Lunch served: all week 12.30–2.30
Dinner served: Tue–Sat 7–9.30 Av 3 course à la carte £25 Av 3
course fixed price £17.95 **BREWERY/COMPANY:** Free House
PRINCIPAL BEERS: Bass, Felinfoel Double Dragon, Bullmastiff
Gold. **FACILITIES:** Children welcome Children's licence
Garden: Food served outside, herb garden **NOTES:** Parking 100
ROOMS: 4 bedrooms 4 en suite from s£50 d£50

◎ **For a list of pubs with
AA Rosette Awards for food see pages 12 & 13.**

Wales

ABERGAVENNY continued

Pantrhiwgoch Hotel & Riverside Restaurant ★ ★ 🐾
Brecon Rd NP8 1EP ☎ 01873 810550 🖳 01873 811880
e-mail: info@pantrhiwgoch.co.uk
Dir: On A40 between Abergavenny & Crickhowell
This part-16th-century inn and restaurant perches on a high
bank of the River Usk with splendid views of the valley and
Blorenge Mountain beyond. In addition to two bars,
conservatory and dining room serving the same menu, there
is a fine summer terrace looking down over the river. A
sample lunchtime menu includes pasta bolognese,
breadcrumbed organic pork with sweet red pepper sauce,
lamb's liver with red wine and shallot sauce, vegetable
cassoulet, and fresh hake fillets in light batter. Special gluten-
free options.
OPEN: 11-11 **BAR MEALS:** Lunch served: all week Dinner served:
all week 12-2.30 6.30-9.30 Av main course £10.95
RESTAURANT: Lunch served: all week 12-2.30 Dinner served:
Mon-Sat 6.30-9.30 Av 3 course à la carte £30
BREWERY/COMPANY: Free House **PRINCIPAL BEERS:** Felin
Foel Double Dragon,. **FACILITIES:** Garden: Terrace overlooking
river, **NOTES:** Parking 80 **ROOMS:** 18 bedrooms 18 en suite from
s£63 d£73

The Skirrid Mountain Inn
Lanvihangel Crucorney NP7 8DH ☎ 01873 890258
Ancient, mainly Tudor stone inn, reputedly the oldest inn in
Wales and a courthouse between 1110 and the 17th century.
Nearly 200 people were hanged here and a beam above the
foot of the stairs served as a scaffold. Appetising bar and
restaurant menu offers the likes of local lamb chops, Welsh
Champion sausages and home-made vegetarian Skirrid loaf.
OPEN: 12-3 6-11 (Sat 12-11, Sun 12-10.30) (open all day Jul-Sep)
BAR MEALS: Lunch served: all week 12-2.30 Dinner served:
Mon-Sat 7-9 Av main course £7.95 **RESTAURANT:** Lunch served: all
week 12-2.30 Dinner served: Mon-Sat 7-9 Av 3 course à la carte £12
PRINCIPAL BEERS: Ushers Best, Ushers Founders, Ushers Four
Seasons, Bass. **FACILITIES:** Children welcome Garden:
patio/terrace, BBQ, floral displays Dogs allowed **NOTES:** Parking 20
ROOMS: 3 bedrooms 3 en suite from s£30 d£49 No credit cards

Pick of the Pubs

Walnut Tree Inn 🏵🏵 ♀
Llandewi Skirrid NP7 8AW ☎ 01873 852797 🖳 01873 859764
e-mail: stephenandfrancesco@thewalnuttree.co.uk
Dir: 3m NE of Abergavenny on B4521
Country dining that needs no introduction, so famous has
the Walnut Tree become over the past 40 or so years.
From its humble origins as a pub that served something a
bit more interesting than pie and chips, this Abergavenny
landmark and brainchild of Italian chef Franco Taruschio
has retained its authenticity with new owner, Stephen
Terry. The menu stays true to tradition whilst blazing a
new trail in trendy directions, and it is still worth travelling
miles for. From the seasonal menu comes sea bass with
artichokes and barba di fratti, steamed halibut with
mussels and saffron, grilled tuna with tomatoes and salsa
verde, and roast cod with lentils, bacon and red wine
sauce. Braised shoulder of lamb, and Lady Llanover's salt
duck are also there, with peerless wines to match, and the
kitchen's pacey imagination shows with hot chocolate
fondant and marmalade ice cream. Not a pub for the
casual passer by.
OPEN: 12-4 7-12 Closed: wk at Xmas, **BAR MEALS:** Lunch

continued

served: Tues-Sun Dinner served: Tues-Sun Av main course £14
RESTAURANT: Lunch served: Tue-Sun 12-3 Dinner served:
Tue-Sat 7-11 Av 3 course à la carte £26
BREWERY/COMPANY: Free House **PRINCIPAL BEERS:** no
real ale. **FACILITIES:** Children welcome **NOTES:** Parking 50

BETTWS-NEWYDD   Map 03 SO30

Pick of the Pubs

Black Bear Inn 🐾
NP15 1JN ☎ 01873 880701
Dir: Off B4598 N of Usk
Surrounded by rolling Monmouthshire countryside in a
tiny hamlet, 'cooking by Molineux' here is as spontaneous
as it gets. The bar's oak beams, flagstone floor and open
fire have been left as original as possible with supplies
from local micro-breweries always on tap. Local produce
is used almost entirely in the dining-rooms: salmon and
brown trout are landed from the River Usk less than a
quarter mile away and farmed venison, lamb, beef and
seasonal game are ever in plentiful supply. The greatest
fun for dinner is to choose 'whatever comes from the
kitchen' that could be crispy duck salad with raspberry
vinaigrette, fresh turbot with white wine, mushrooms and
cream, followed by Bailey's Irish Cream cheesecake.
Smaller feasts might include tasty home-made fishcakes,
beef medallions in Madeira sauce and chocolate-and-
orange terrine, all served with minimal formality.
OPEN: 12-2 6-12 **BAR MEALS:** Lunch served: Tue-Sun 12-2
Dinner served: Mon-Sat 6-10 Av main course £10
RESTAURANT: Lunch served: Tue-Sun 12-2 Dinner served:
Mon-Sat 6-10 **BREWERY/COMPANY:** Free House
PRINCIPAL BEERS: Freeminers Speculation, Bath Gem, Fuller's
London Pride, Timothy Taylor Landlord. **FACILITIES:** Children
welcome Garden: Dogs allowed (water) tap **NOTES:** Parking
20 **ROOMS:** 2 bedrooms from s£25 d£50 No credit cards

CHEPSTOW   Map 03 ST59

Pick of the Pubs

The Boat Inn 🐾 ♀
The Back NP16 5HH ☎ 01291 628192 🖳 01291 628193
e-mail: boatinn.co.uk
See Pick of the Pubs on page 617

Castle View Hotel
16 Bridge St NP16 5EZ ☎ 01291 620349 🖳 01291 627397
e-mail: dave@castview.demon.co.uk
Dir: Opposite Chepstow Castle
Built as a private house some 300 years ago, its solid walls up
to five feet thick in places, this hotel is situated opposite the
castle, alongside the River Wye. The regularly changing menu
might offer steaks, breast of chicken stuffed with Stilton, and
cod in beer batter.
OPEN: 12-2.30 6-11 **BAR MEALS:** Lunch served: all week 12-2
Dinner served: Mon-Sat 6.30-9.30 Av main course £4.50
RESTAURANT: Lunch served: Sun Dinner served: Mon-Sat
6.30-9.30 Av 3 course à la carte £15 **BREWERY/COMPANY:** Free
House **PRINCIPAL BEERS:** Carlsberg-Tetley Tetley Bitter.
FACILITIES: Children welcome Garden: beer garden, Outdoor
eating Dogs allowed **NOTES:** Parking 200 **ROOMS:** 13 bedrooms
13 en suite from s£39 d£50

Wales

OPEN: 11–11 Mon–Sat (12–10.30 Sun)
BAR MEALS: L served all week. D served all week. 12–3 6.30–10 Av main course £4.50
RESTAURANT: L served all week. D served all week. 12–3 6.30–10 Av cost 3 course £17
BREWERY/COMPANY: UNIQUE PUB CO LTD
PRINCIPAL BEERS: Interbrew Bass, Smiles, Wadworth 6X
FACILITIES: Children Welcome. Garden: Patio/terrace, food served outdoors
NOTES: Parking 20

The Boat Inn

♀
The Back Chepstow NP16 5HH
☎ 01291 628192 📠 01291 628193
e-mail: boatinn.co.uk

Originally dating from 1795, The Boat stands on the banks of the River Wye. The front terrace is a perfect place to relax on a summer's day and watch the ever-changing scenery. This is a pub which manages to effortlessly combine the virtues of a popular local with an honest approach to providing good bar and restaurant food.

Salmon fisheries were once sited virtually next door: the boats would moor in the tide with deep nets stretching across the tidal flow below Brunel's tubular bridge. Today's revitalised pub is an attractive whitewashed building brightened by hanging baskets of flowers. The newly furnished terrace includes new seats and a barbecue for the summer, but the views can be enjoyed equally well from the first floor restaurant, a romantic setting (candlelit in the evenings) with a large bay window overlooking the river. The ground floor comprises a selection of traditionally furnished rooms decorated with boating memorabilia, and there is a real fire to warm yourself by in the winter months. Lunch is an uncomplicated affair, with fresh soup and filled baguettes available alongside a full-length menu that is available throughout the day. Other simple options include lasagne, curry, steak and jacket potatoes. For those who want something special, a tantalising array of classic and modern dishes could include king scallops on Asian beurre blanc with lentils, fillets of turbot on stir-fried vegetables with oriental fumet, Welsh Black beef tournedos Rossini or shank of Welsh lamb on a bubble and squeak rösti with red wine jus.

LLANDOGO
Map 03 SO50

The Sloop Inn ♦♦♦
NP25 4TW ☎ 01594 530291 📠 01594 530935
Overlooking the River Wye just north of Tintern Abbey, this traditional hostelry offers well maintained accommodation and wide range of bar meals.
OPEN: 12-3 5.30-11 (June-Oct Open all day 12-11)
BAR MEALS: Lunch served: all week Dinner served: all week 12-2 7-9 Av main course £7 **RESTAURANT:** Lunch served: all week Dinner served: all week 12-2 7-9 Av 3 course à la carte £15
BREWERY/COMPANY: Free House **PRINCIPAL BEERS:** Wye Valley Traditional, Wadworth 6X, Fullers London Pride.
FACILITIES: Children welcome Garden: Food served outside Dogs allowed **NOTES:** Parking 40 **ROOMS:** 4 bedrooms 4 en suite from s£29 d£49

LLANTRISANT
Map 03 ST39

Greyhound Inn 🍴 ♀
NP15 1LE ☎ 01291 672505 & 673447 📠 01291 673255
e-mail: enquiry@greyhound-inn.com
Dir: From M4 take A449 towards Monmouth, 1st jct to Usk, L into Usk Sq. Take 2nd L signed Llantrisant. 2.5m to inn
17th-century Welsh longhouse which became a country inn in 1845 and is perfectly situated for exploring miles of stunning Welsh countryside. Award-winning gardens, open log fires and a stone stable block converted into en suite letting rooms add to the charm and character of the place. Good range of home-cooked dishes and tempting daily specials. Try local pheasant in red wine, beef 'n' Guinness, chicken chasseur, luxury fish pie, and Welsh venison and ale pie. Country pine and antique shop across the car park.
OPEN: 11-11 Closed: 25 Dec **BAR MEALS:** Lunch served: all week 12-2.15 Dinner served: Mon-Sat 6-10.30 Av main course £7
RESTAURANT: Lunch served: all week 12-2.15 Dinner served: Mon-Sat 6-10.30 Av 3 course à la carte £13
BREWERY/COMPANY: Free House
PRINCIPAL BEERS: Interbrew Flowers Original & Bass, Marston's Pedigree, Greene King Abbot Ale. **FACILITIES:** Children welcome Garden: Pond with fountain, food served outside Dogs allowed **NOTES:** Parking 60 **ROOMS:** 10 bedrooms 10 en suite from s£49 d£59

LLANVAIR DISCOED
Map 03 ST49

Pick of the Pubs

The Woodland Restaurant & Bar 🍴 ♀
NP16 6LX ☎ 01633 400313
An old inn, extended to accommodate a growing number of diners, the Woodland is located close to the Roman fortress town of Caerwent and Wentworth's forest and reservoir. It remains at heart a friendly village local, serving a good range of beers: Reverend James, Buckley Best and Somerset & Dorset. A varied menu of freshly prepared dishes caters for all tastes from ciabatta bread with various toppings to supreme of chicken filled with smoked bacon, creamed leeks and Welsh farmhouse Cheddar, served with a Bordeaux wine and shallot sauce. Meat is sourced from a local butcher, who slaughters all his own meat, and the fish is mostly from Cornwall, maybe whole roasted baby turbot with capers and black butter. Outside there's a large, well-equipped garden with plenty of bench seating.
OPEN: 11-3 6-11 (Sun 12-3, 7-10.30) **BAR MEALS:** Lunch

continued

served: all week 12-2 Dinner served: Mon-Sat 6.30-10 Av main course £5.95 **RESTAURANT:** Lunch served: all week 12-2 Dinner served: Mon-Sat 6.30-9.30 Av 3 course à la carte £20
BREWERY/COMPANY: Free House
PRINCIPAL BEERS: Buckleys Best, Reverend James, Somerset & Dorset. **FACILITIES:** Children welcome Garden: Food served outside. Well equipped garden Dogs allowed **NOTES:** Parking 30

LLANVAPLEY
Map 03 SO31

Red Hart Inn
NP7 8SN ☎ 01600 780227 📠 01600 780279
e-mail: enquiries@redhartinn.co.uk
Dir: On B4233 E of Abergavenny
Although most of this Severnside pub dates from the 18th century, the oldest part - the restaurant - dates from 1485, when it was built as a hostel for workmen renovating the village church. Much of the produce comes from the Forest of Dean area, including the honey-glazed, fresh Wye salmon, pan-fried venison, and fillet steak Rossini. Crab and king prawn thermidor, on the other hand, is probably sourced from further afield. Three years of national awards for their real ales.
OPEN: 12-2 7-11 (not open Monday) Closed: 25 Dec
BAR MEALS: Lunch served: Sat-Sun 12-2 Dinner served: Tue-Sat 7-9 Av main course £8 **RESTAURANT:** Lunch served: Sat-Sun 12-2 Dinner served: Tue-Sat 7-9 Av 3 course à la carte £13
BREWERY/COMPANY: Free House
PRINCIPAL BEERS: Interbrew Bass, Cottage Brewery Golden Arrow & Best. **FACILITIES:** Children welcome Garden: Food served outdoors, patio Dogs allowed **NOTES:** Parking 30 No credit cards

PENALLT
Map 03 SO51

The Boat Inn
Lone Ln NP25 4AJ ☎ 01600 712615 📠 01600 719120
Dir: From Monmouth take A466.In Redbrook the pub car park is signposted. Park & walk across rail bridge over R Wye
Dating back over 360 years, this riverside pub has served as a hostelry for quarry, mill, paper and tin mine workers, and even had a landlord operating a ferry across the Wye at shift times. Unspoilt slate floor. Excellent real ales.

SHIRENEWTON
Map 03 ST49

The Carpenters Arms
Usk Rd NP16 6BU ☎ 01291 641231
Dir: M48 J2 take A48 to Chepstow then A466I, B4235.Village 3m on L

A 400-year-old hostelry, formerly a smithy and carpenter's shop, with flagstone floors, open fires and a pleasant wooded

continued

valley location near the Wye and Usk valleys. It is now furnished with antiques, and offers straightforward bar food. A typical menu includes steak and mushroom pie, guinea fowl in orange sauce, pheasant casserole, and chicken in leek and Stilton sauce.
OPEN: 11–2.30 6–11 **BAR MEALS:** 12–2 7–9.30
BREWERY/COMPANY: Free House **PRINCIPAL BEERS:** Fuller's London Pride, Wadworth 6X, Marston's Pedigree,Theakston Old Peculier. **FACILITIES:** Dogs allowed **NOTES:** Parking 20 No credit cards

---

SKENFRITH   Map 03 SO42

Pick of the Pubs

AA Pub of the Year for Wales 2003

The Bell at Skenfrith ★ ★ ★ ◉◎ ◌ ♀
NP7 8UH ☎ 01600 750235 🖹 01600 750525
e-mail: enquiries@thebellatskenfrith.com
A recently restored 17th-century coaching inn on the banks of the Monnow, a tributary of the River Wye. An oak bar, flagstones, and old settles provide plenty of character, and there's even somewhere to tether your horse. Opposite is Skenfrith Castle, and nearby is the historic arched bridge that once carried a main route from England to South Wales. Normally two fish courses are available in the bar, and one in the restaurant – perhaps fillet of Dover sole with tagliolini, pistachio and roquette pesto, or fillet of seabass with tagliolini and a herb butter sauce. Often available are confit of duck with celeriac mash and orange, onion and coriander marmalade, and Welsh rack of lamb with smoked garlic polenta and rosemary jus. Real ales and hand-pumped scrumpy. A great place to start (or finish) the 19-mile Three Castles Walk, or the longer Four Castles Cycle Route.
OPEN: Open all day Closed: 1st 2 wks of Feb **BAR MEALS:** Lunch served: all week Dinner served: all week 12–2.30 7–9.30
RESTAURANT: Lunch served: Sun 12–2.30, or by arrangement Dinner served: Fri-Sat 7–9.30 Av 3 course fixed price £30
BREWERY/COMPANY: Free House **PRINCIPAL BEERS:** Freeminer Best Bitter, Hook Norton Best Bitter,. **FACILITIES:** Children welcome Garden: Dogs allowed **NOTES:** Parking 30 **ROOMS:** 8 bedrooms 8 en suite from s£65 d£85

TREDUNNOCK   Map 03 ST39

Pick of the Pubs

The Newbridge Inn ◉ ◌ ♀
NP15 1LY ☎ 01633 451000 🖹 01633 541001
e-mail: thenewbridge@tinyonline.co.uk
See Pick of the Pubs on page 620

TRELLECK   Map 03 SO50

The Lion Inn ◌
NP25 4PA ☎ 01600 860322 🖹 01600 860060
e-mail: lion@web-fanatics.co.uk
Dir: From A40 just south of Monmouth take B4293 and follow signs for Trelleck
This former brew and coach house stands opposite the church and is said to be haunted. Twice winners of the South Wales Argus pub restaurant of the year award, the menu ranges from traditional pub favourites like jacket potatoes or sausage

---

and chips to an innovative selection of home-made vegetarian dishes and Hungarian specials. Pan-fried marlin, peppered sirloin steak and Nagy Mama's stuffed peppers are popular choices.

OPEN: 12–3 6–11 (Mon 7–11; closed Sun eve) **BAR MEALS:** Lunch served: all week 12–2 Dinner served: Mon-Sat 6–9.30 Av main course £7.25 **RESTAURANT:** Lunch served: all week 12–2 Dinner served: Mon-Sat 6–9.30 Av 3 course à la carte £17 Av 3 course fixed price £12.95 **BREWERY/COMPANY:** Free House
PRINCIPAL BEERS: Bath Ales, Wadworth 6X, Fuller's London Pride, Wye Valley Butty Bach. **FACILITIES:** Children welcome Garden: Food served outside, Patio Dogs allowed (water, biscuits)
NOTES: Parking 30

USK   Map 03 SO30

Pick of the Pubs

The Nags Head Inn ♀
Twyn Square NP15 1BH ☎ 01291 672820 🖹 01291 672720
Dir: On A472
Flower-adorned 15th-century inn overlooking the town square, just a short stroll from the River Usk. The village itself has won Wales in Bloom for the last 17 years, and the same family have run the inn for over thirty years. Local game in season, including pheasant cooked in port, and wild Usk salmon are specialities on the menu. Regular dishes include rabbit pie, pheasant in port, whole stuffed partridge, and chicken in red wine.
OPEN: 10–3 5.30–11 Closed: Dec 25 **BAR MEALS:** Lunch served: all week Dinner served: all week 10–2 5.30–10.30
RESTAURANT: Lunch served: all week Dinner served: all week 11.30–2 5.30–10.30 Av 3 course à la carte £15
BREWERY/COMPANY: Free House
PRINCIPAL BEERS: Brains Bitter, Dark, Buckleys Best & Reverend James. **FACILITIES:** Children welcome Garden: Food served outside

---

AA Bed & Breakfast Guide **2003**

Britain's best-selling B&B guide featuring over 3500 great places to stay.

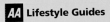 **Lifestyle Guides**   *www.theAA.com*

---

continued

OPEN: 12–3 6–11
BAR MEALS: L served Mon–Sat.
D served Mon–Sat. 12–2.30 6–7.15
Av main course £6
RESTAURANT: L served all week.
D served Mon–Sat. 12–2.30 6–9.45
Av cost 3 courses £25
BREWERY/COMPANY:
FREE HOUSE
PRINCIPAL BEERS: Interbrew
Bass, Hancock's HB, Brains Rev
James,
FACILITIES: Garden: Food served
outside
NOTES: Parking 50

The Newbridge Inn

Set on the southern bank of the River Usk by the 'new' 17th-century bridge, The Newbridge is a gastro-pub re-creation of a classic establishment. Under its high rafters, the whole place shimmering in candlelight is reflected in the river, creating a delightfully romantic setting for an excellent dinner.

Tredunnock Monmouthshire NP15 1LY
☎ 01633 451000 📠 01633 541001
e-mail: thenewbridge@tinyonline.co.uk
Dir: M4 J24 or J26, take Caerleon road to usk Road, follow lane opposite Cwrt Bleddyn Hotel. Through village to river.

The striking interiors are warm and welcoming with wooden floors, subtle lighting and squashy sofas; the walls hung with fine art and hand-decorated blackboards promoting special events. Simply set tables and modern jazz create the mood for informal eating on three levels, with a spiral staircase leading to the top-most floor. Recently awarded an AA Rosette for the food, the flexible menus allow for a limited choice, two or three-course fixed-price lunch or a choice of snacks, like soup of the day, club sandwich or Caesar salad with crispy

bacon. The chef's daily specials reflect a passion for quality produce, with dishes such as pan-fried scallops and pig's trotter galette with a warm potato vinaigrette and crispy pancetta, and slow roasted loin of middle, white pork with piccalilli mashed potatoes and pork braising juices. An interesting choice of 'Gastro Snacks' is served Monday to Friday 6-7.15pm (fish cakes with tartare sauce/steak and kidney pudding). While the full works, from the dinner carte, might include carpaccio of yellowfin tuna, with radish, coriander and sesame, followed by roasted saddle of Welsh lamb with chargrilled vegetables, garlic and basil mash and lamb jus.

ROTH   Map 02 SN10

e New Inn
67 8NW ☎ 01834 812368
: A48 to Carmarthen, A40 to St Clears, A477 to Llanteg then L
400-year-old inn, originally a farmhouse, belonging to
nroth Castle Estate. It has old world charm with beamed
ilings, a Flemish chimney, a flagstone floor and an
glenook fireplace. It is close to the beach, and local lobster
d crab are a feature, along with a popular choice of home-
ade dishes including steak and kidney pie, soup and curry.
PEN: 11.30-3 5.30-11 Closed: Nov-Mar **BAR MEALS:** Lunch
rved: all week Dinner served: all week 12-2 6-9
ESTAURANT: Lunch served: all week Dinner served: all week 12-2
9 **BREWERY/COMPANY:** Free House
RINCIPAL BEERS: Burton, Carlsberg-Tetley Tetley Bitter.
ACILITIES: Children welcome Garden: Beer garden, food served
tdoors Dogs allowed **NOTES:** Parking 100 No credit cards

AREW   Map 02 SN00

arew Inn
A70 8SL ☎ 01646 651267
mail: mandy@carewinn.co.uk
ir: From A477 take A4075. Inn 400yds opp castle & celtic cross
traditional stone-built country inn situated opposite the
arew Celtic cross and Norman castle, which is a regular
enue for activities by The Sealed Knot. A typical menu might
clude tarragon and lime chicken, mushroom and ale parcel,
ork tenderloin with cream and mushrooms, and fillet of trout.
emon meringue pie, Bakewell tart or sticky gingerbread
udding . Live music every Thursday night under the marquee.
PEN: 11.30-2.30 4.30-11 (Summer & wknd 11-11) Closed: Dec 25
AR MEALS: 11.30-2.30 6-9 **RESTAURANT:** 12-2 6-9
REWERY/COMPANY: Free House
PRINCIPAL BEERS: Worthington Best, SA Brains Reverend James.
ACILITIES: Children welcome Garden: Food served outside.
verlooks Carew Castle Dogs allowed (water provided)
NOTES: Parking 20

CILGERRAN   Map 02 SN14

Pick of the Pubs

Pendre Inn
Pendre SA43 2SL ☎ 01239 614223
e-mail: warmak@pendre.fsnet.co.uk
Dir: Off A478 south of Cardigan
An ancient ash tree grows through the pavement in front
of this white stone, thick walled building. Dating back to
the 14th century, the pub is full of memorabilia and
features old beams, slate floors and an inglenook
fireplace. Freshly made meals such as roasted chicken and
onions, mushrooms and mange-tout in honey and pink
peppercorn sauce are impressive with their variety and
value. Home-made desserts are good.
OPEN: 12.00-3.00 6-11 (Sun 7-10.30) **BAR MEALS:** Lunch
served: Mon-Sat 12-2 Dinner served: all week 6-8 Av main
course £4 **RESTAURANT:** Lunch served: Mon-Sat 12-2 Dinner
served: all week 6-8 Av 3 course à la carte £8.95 Av 3 course
fixed price £8.75 **BREWERY/COMPANY:** Free House
PRINCIPAL BEERS: Thomas Watkins. **FACILITIES:** Children
welcome Children's licence Garden: Beer garden, food served
outside, patio, **NOTES:** Parking 6 **ROOMS:** 3 bedrooms 1 en
suite from s£15 d£36 No credit cards

HAVERFORDWEST   Map 02 SM91

Pick of the Pubs

Georges Bar ♀
24 Market St SA61 1NH ☎ 01437 766683 📠 01437 779090
e-mail: llewis6140@aol.com
See Pick of the Pubs on page 622

LAMPHEY   Map 02 SN00

Pick of the Pubs

The Dial Inn 🐨 ♀
Ridgeway Rd SA71 5NU ☎ 01646 672426 📠 01646 672426
Dir: Just off A4139 (Tenby to Pembroke rd)

Built around 1830 as the Dower House for nearby
Lamphey Court, The Dial was converted into a pub in
1966 and immediately established itself as a popular
village local. In recent years the owners have added new
bedrooms and an extension of the dining areas. Food is a
real strength. Choose from traditional bar food, a daily
blackboard menu or the imaginative dining room menu.
Every effort is made to use as much fresh local produce
as possible. Look out for specials such as pan-fried
Scottish haggis dusted with fine oatmeal and served with
freshly made bubble and squeak or Lamphey lamb -
tender chunks of lamb with leeks, apricots and rosemary.
Fish dishes are also a strength and, depending on
availability, could include fresh crab salad, baked local
trout in a piquant tomato sauce or pan-fried fillet of red
mullet with a citrus salad of hot crusty bread.
OPEN: 11-3 6-12 **BAR MEALS:** Lunch served: all week Dinner
served: all week 12-3 6.30-10 Av main course £7
RESTAURANT: Lunch served: all week Dinner served: all week
12-3 6.30-10 **BREWERY/COMPANY:** Free House
PRINCIPAL BEERS: Hancocks, Interbrew Bass, Worthington.
FACILITIES: Children welcome Children's licence Garden:
Food served outside **NOTES:** Parking 50
ROOMS: 4 bedrooms 4 en suite from d£25

Bar Billiards
The ingenious blend of billiards and skittles is a relative
newcomer to the pub scene. It was introduced here
from Belgium in the 1930s, with support from billiard
table manufacturers. The game caught on rapidly,
especially in the South and Midlands, and leagues had
been organised by the time the Second World War
began. Its much more recent rival is pool, which came
here from America in the 1960s in the wake of the
Paul Newman film The Hustler.

Wales

OPEN: Mon–Thur 10.30–5.30.
Fri–Sat 10.30–11
BAR MEALS: L served
Mon–Sat 12–5.30.
D served Fri–Sat. 6–9.45
Av main course £5
RESTAURANT: L served Mon–Sat
12–2.30. D served Fri–Sat. 6–9.30
Av cost 3 courses £20
BREWERY/COMPANY: FREE
HOUSE
PRINCIPLE BEERS: Marston's
Pedigree, Wye Valley Bitter
FACILITIES: Beer garden, patio,
food served outdoors

The Georges Bar

Built on the site of the former George's Brewery, this remarkable 18th-century building incorporates many original features in the restoration of its vaulted wine cellar, numerous eating areas and delightful walled garden that boasts spectacular views over Haverfordwest Castle.

♀
24 Market Street SA61 1NH
☎ 01437 766683 📠 01437 779090
e-mail: llewis6140@aol.com
Dir: on the A40.

Genuine local character is a feature of the all-day café bar and cellar bistro that stays loyal to Welsh tradition with its local produce, freshly prepared food and sheer enthusiasm setting it apart from the norm. In keeping with its brewing heritage, you will find Wye Valley Bitter, Marston's Pedigree and a frequently-changing guest ale on tap, plus a short, global list of wines and monthly wine specials. Including daily specials meal choices must exceed 40 at any one time, from home-made scones and cakes to fish from the Pembrokeshire coast, locally-sourced meats and vegetables, and

fresh herbs from the garden – a minor triumph given its locality. Daily specials featuring real local character might include smoked honey-glazed duck breast salad, goujons of local hake with lime mayonnaise, local seafood chowder with garlic bread, Welsh lamb stew topped with crispy potatoes, and George's turkey, gammon, leek and wild mushroom pie. Amongst possibly a dozen vegetarian options are cheese-topped nut and seed roast in filo pastry, wild mushroom pasta and a hot-and-spicy spinach dahl. Some wicked desserts include crêpes Suzette, chocolate nut Pavlova, old-fashioned treacle tart, and luxury Belgian ice cream sundaes; all contributing to a unique experience that awaits both newcomers and those in the know. For that all important business meeting, there's an airy, fully-equipped private room; free if ten or more are dining in the restaurant.

PEMBROKESHIRE

LANDSHIPPING Map 02 SN01

The Stanley Arms
SA67 8BE ☎ 01834 891227
Dir: Off A40 at Canaston Bridge onto A4075, R at Cross Hands, next to Canastan Bowls

Built as a farmhouse around 1765, the pub has its own mooring on the Cleddau Estuary and is popular with sailors. There's an attractive garden with fine views across the water to Picton Castle, and the area is good for walking. Freshly-cooked pub food includes marinated chicken breast, gammon with egg or pineapple, grilled Milford plaice, salmon with lime and coriander, home-made curries and Welsh steaks, as well as salads and a children's menu.
OPEN: 12–3 6–11 (Sun 7–10.30) (all day Thur–Sun, Jul–Sept 06)
BAR MEALS: Lunch served: all week Dinner served: all week 12–2.30 6–9.30 Av main course £6.50 **RESTAURANT:** Lunch served: all week Dinner served: all week 12–2.30 6–9.30 Av 3 course à la carte £11 **BREWERY/COMPANY:** Free House
PRINCIPAL BEERS: Worthington, Fuller's London Pride, Everards Tiger. **FACILITIES:** Children welcome Children's licence Garden: Food served outdoors Dogs allowed (water) **NOTES:** Parking 20

LETTERSTON Map 02 SM92

The Harp Inn
31 Haverfordwest Rd SA62 5UA
☎ 01348 840061 🖷 01348 840812
Dir: Located on main A40
Following major refurbishment, the pub's restaurant has doubled in size, and there is a new function room. The bar menu is extensive and the restaurant, with its lovely inglenook, has an impressive range of fresh fish. Other options may include venison, steaks, and goose breast with port and pear sauce.
OPEN: 11–3 6–11 **BAR MEALS:** Lunch served: all week Dinner served: all week 12–2.30 6–9.30 Av main course £5.95
RESTAURANT: Lunch served: all week Dinner served: all week 12–2.30 6.30–9.30 Av 3 course à la carte £15
BREWERY/COMPANY: Free House **PRINCIPAL BEERS:** Tetleys, Greene King, Abbot Ale. **FACILITIES:** Children welcome Garden: Dogs allowed **NOTES:** Parking 50

NEVERN Map 02 SN04

Trewern Arms ★ ★
SA42 0NB ☎ 01239 820395 🖷 01239 820173
Dir: On the A487 between Cardigan and Fishguard
Ivy-clad 16th century inn set in attractive grounds astride the River Nevern. The Brew House bar is a popular local, with flagstone floors and old settles. Dishes might include home-

made lasagne, steak and kidney pies and puddings, and lamb shank in red wine sauce, as well as roast pheasant.

OPEN: 11–3 (Sun 12–3,7–10.30) 6–11 Closed: None
BAR MEALS: Lunch served: all week Dinner served: all week 12–2 6–9 Av main course £7.50 **RESTAURANT:** Dinner served: Thu–Sat 7–9 Av 3 course à la carte £18.50
BREWERY/COMPANY: Free House
PRINCIPAL BEERS: Interbrew Flowers Original, Castle Eden Ale, Wadworth 6X. **FACILITIES:** Children welcome Garden: Beer garden, food served outdoors, patio **NOTES:** Parking 80
ROOMS: 10 bedrooms 10 en suite from s£35 d£25

PEMBROKE DOCK Map 02 SM90

Ferry Inn
Pembroke Ferry SA72 6UD ☎ 01646 682947
e-mail: williamsferryinn@aol.com
Dir: A477, off A48, R at garage, signs for Cleddau Bridge, L at roundabout
Creeper-clad 16th-century riverside inn situated on the banks of the Cleddau River, with fine views across the estuary from the nautical themed bar and waterside terrace. Expect good fresh local fish and seafood, perhaps black bream, Dover sole, tuna, brill, sea bass and fried plaice. Other options include sirloin steak, lamb kebabs, beef with caramelised peppercorn sauce, and spinach, Ricotta and goats' cheese cannelloni. At least 20 malt whiskies available.
OPEN: 11.30–2.45 7–11 Closed: 25–26 Dec **BAR MEALS:** Lunch served: all week Dinner served: all week 12–2 7–10 Av main course £5.95 **BREWERY/COMPANY:** Free House
PRINCIPAL BEERS: Interbrew Hancocks HB & Bass.
FACILITIES: Children welcome Garden: riverside terrace Dogs allowed (garden only, water provided) **NOTES:** Parking 12

PORTHGAIN Map 02 SM83

Pick of the Pubs

The Sloop Inn
SA62 5BN ☎ 01348 831449 🖷 01348 831338
e-mail: Matthew@sloop-inn.freeserve.co.uk
Probably the best location in Pembrokeshire belongs to the Sloop Inn, which you'll find by the harbour of a picturesque fishing village. The coastal path drops steeply to the harbour-side, where the pub's south-facing patio makes an ideal spot for drinks or lunch in fine weather. The inn dates from 1743, when it was more of a workers' than a walkers' pub. There are old photos in the main bar of the village as it was when the nearby quarries and village brickworks were still active, before 1930. A row of former workers' cottages, though small on the outside, has been extended within to house a succession of eating areas with a unifying shipping theme. The menu is large

Wales

continued   *continued*

PORTHGAIN continued

and varied and you can choose anything from a bread roll to a three-course special, or just sit and enjoy the company and good beer.
OPEN: 11-11 (Sun 12-4, 5.30-10.30) **BAR MEALS:** Lunch served: all week Dinner served: all week 12-2.30 6-9.30 Av main course £7 **RESTAURANT:** Lunch served: all week Dinner served: all week 12-2.30 6-9.30 Av 3 course à la carte £17.50 **BREWERY/COMPANY:** Free House
PRINCIPAL BEERS: Interbrew Worthington Bitter, Shepherd Neame Bishops Finger, Wadsworth 6X, Brains Reverend James.
FACILITIES: Children welcome Children's licence Garden: beer garden, patio, food served outside, BBQ **NOTES:** Parking 50

SOLVA   Map 02 SM82

The Cambrian Inn
Main St SA62 6UU ☎ 01437 721210
Dir: 13m from Haverfordwest on the St David's Rd
Something of an institution in this pretty fishing village (but park down by the estuary) is a white-painted Grade II listed 17th-century inn that attracts local and returning visitors alike. Fish fresh from the jetty alongside local duck breast in Cointreau and Welsh lamb shank with rosemary are staple dining choices; bar meals inclining more towards prawn and mushroom pancakes, ploughman's and vegetable lasagne.
OPEN: 12-3 6.30-11 (Winter 12:00-2:30, 7pm-11pm) Closed: Dec 25-26 **BAR MEALS:** Lunch served: all week Dinner served: all week 12-2 7-9.30 Av main course £5.50 **RESTAURANT:** Lunch served: all week Dinner served: all week 12-2 7-9.30 Av 3 course à la carte £17.50 **BREWERY/COMPANY:** Free House **PRINCIPAL BEERS:** Reverend James, Brains SA. **FACILITIES:** Children welcome Garden: patio, beer garden, outdoor eating Dogs allowed (garden only) **NOTES:** Parking 12 No credit cards

---

STACKPOLE   Map 02 SR99

Pick of the Pubs

Armstrong Arms
SA71 5DF ☎ 01646 672324
Dir: From Pembroke take B4319 & follow signs for Stackpole
Once the village post office, with its original post box still set in the wall, this 17th-century stone cottage is at the heart of the National Trust's Stackpole Estate, close to the Pembrokeshire coastal path. Exposed ash ceilings, slate floors and bar tops, a log burner and old bread ovens are part of that heritage. Alongside Buckley's ales, local produce plays its full part in the menu with options like rack of Welsh lamb with a herb crust and redcurrant and mint sauce, or fillet of Welsh Black beef with mushroom and Madeira sauce. An extensive fresh fish choice is offered from the daily specials board, with the likes of haddock fillet with creamy wholegrain mustard and leek sauce, or whole black bream with orange.
OPEN: 11-3 6-11 (winter 7-11) **BAR MEALS:** Lunch served: all week Dinner served: all week 12-2 7-9 Av main course £5.50 **RESTAURANT:** Lunch served: all week Dinner served: all week 12-2 7-9 Av 3 course à la carte £14 **BREWERY/COMPANY:** Free House **PRINCIPAL BEERS:** Brains Reverend James, Buckleys Best & IPA, Wadsworth 6X. **FACILITIES:** Children welcome Garden: Beer garden, food served outdoors Dogs allowed (water) **NOTES:** Parking 25

WOLF'S CASTLE   Map 02 SM92

Pick of the Pubs

The Wolfe Inn
SA62 5LS ☎ 01437 741662 ⌨ 01437 741676
e-mail: eat@the-wolfe.co.uk
Dir: On A40 between Haverfordwest and Fishguard
A charming oak-beamed stone-built inn, the Wolfe comprises four distinctive rooms, the Victorian Parlour, Hunters' Lodge, the Brasserie and the Conservatory, together with a secluded patio garden, all reflecting the personal taste of the owner and offering a relaxed and informal atmosphere. The proprietors are members of the Pembrokeshire Product Mark, so only the best and freshest of local produce is used to create the fine and varied choice served in the restaurant and the simplest of dishes in the Brasserie. These range from cutlet of wild boar with forest fruit and nut seasoning served with a rich port wine and blackberry sauce to butcher's bangers with mash and onion gravy. There's always a monthly guest beer, a wide choice of coffees (cappuccino, espresso, machiato, lungo, doppio and filter coffees) and a selection of teas. Self-catering and B&B accommodation is also available.
OPEN: 11-3 6-11 (Sun 11-3 only) **BAR MEALS:** Lunch served: all week Dinner served: all week 12-2 7-9 Av main course £5.95 **RESTAURANT:** Lunch served: all week Dinner served: all week 12-2 7-9 Av 3 course à la carte £24 9 **BREWERY/COMPANY:** Free House **PRINCIPAL BEERS:** Interbrew Worthington Bitter. **FACILITIES:** Children welcome Garden: Food served outdoors, patio, BBQ, rockery, Dogs allowed **NOTES:** Parking 20 **ROOMS:** 3 bedrooms 2 en suite from s£40 d£50

POWYS

BERRIEW   Map 08 SJ10

Lion Hotel
SY21 8PQ ☎ 01686 640452 ⌨ 01686 640604
Dir: 5m from Welshpool on A483, R to Berriew. Centre of village next to church.
Expect a friendly family welcome at this 17th-century timbered black and white inn situated in a pretty village setting. From traditional bar snacks, the bistro menu, supplemented by daily fish options and chef's specials, may offer slow-roasted shoulder of Welsh lamb, sea bass fillets with horseradish mash, or boeuf bourguignon.
OPEN: 11.30-3 5.30-11 (Jan-Apr 11.30-2.30) Closed: Dec 25-26 **BAR MEALS:** Lunch served: all week Dinner served: all week 12-2 7-9 Av main course £8.95 **RESTAURANT:** Lunch served: all week Dinner served: all week 12-2 7-9.00 Av 3 course à la carte £17 **BREWERY/COMPANY:** Free House **PRINCIPAL BEERS:** Interbrew Bass, Worthington Bitter, Greene King Old Speckled Hen, Shepherd Neame Spitfire Premium Ale. **FACILITIES:** Children welcome Garden: Patio, food served outdoors Dogs allowed **NOTES:** Parking 6 **ROOMS:** 7 bedrooms 7 en suite from s£55 d£70

★ **Indicates AA inspected hotel accommodation**

Wales

PUB WALK

Llyswen
The Griffin Inn

A ramble through contrasting Wye Valley landscapes, from a sheltered, shady stretch along the delightful River Wye, to the open, invigorating area around the slopes of Mynydd Forest. Finally, the walk takes in Brechfa Pool with its magnificent views of the Black Mountains and the Brecon Beacons.

From the inn make for the church in Llyswen. On leaving it, turn right along the A470 to reach Bridge End Inn. Turn right, then just before the river bridge (Boughrood Bridge) bear left along a metalled lane by the Wye. Continue ahead on a riverside path for over a mile (1.6km), until reaching the main A470 at Trericket Mill. Turn right along the road for about 100 yards (91m), then go left up a farm road. Climb past the first farm, then at the next, bear left around the barn and shortly turn left down a path by a wall, veering left down to the river. Cross a footbridge and head up the bank opposite, then bear left past a house on the right. After 100 yards

(91m) go through a gate to the road. Turn right, re-passing the house, and proceed uphill to a fork. Keep left, then, where the lane bends right, take a grassy path on the left, running almost parallel with the lane to reach a gate and boundary wall. Follow the wall along and round to a further gate, then continue up the track, which veers right to reach open moor. After about half a mile (0.8km) the track divides into three; take the middle arm so that the boundary wall, still visible, gradually gets nearer. Continue to a minor road, turn right and head for Brechfa Pool and a small chapel. The pool was a favourite with the 19th-century rector Francis Kilvert, whose diary of rural life in this area became a minor classic. Go round the pool clockwise, then turn left along a broad grassy swathe to reach a lane. Cross a cattle-grid, then when the lane bends right, continue ahead following a steeply-descending bridleway to the main road. Bear left and return to Llyswen.

THE GRIFFIN INN,
LLYSWEN Brecon LD3 0UR
Tel: 01874 754241
Directions: On A470 (Brecon to Builth Wells rd)
A hub of the community, this family-run favourite has a friendly atmosphere, traditional comforts and all the sporting benefits of a stay in the glorious upper Wye Valley. Wye salmon, fresh trout, seasonal game, fruit and vegetables locally sourced, often organic.
Open: 10.30–3 7–11
Bar Meals: 12-2 7–9
Dogs allowed. Parking available.

Distance: 7 miles (11.6km)
Map: OS Landranger 161
Terrain: Riverside stretches and hillside walking
Paths: Paved, riverside and woodland paths, wide tracks and grass. Short, steep descent to finish, may be slippery
Gradient: Some climbing

Walk submitted and checked by Nick Channer

Wales

BRECON — Map 03 SO02

The Felin Fach Griffin ◉◉ ♀ NEW
Felin Fach LD3 0UB ☎ 01874 620111 ▤ 01874 620120
e-mail: enquiries@eatdrinksleep.ltd.uk
Dir: 4.5m N of Brecon on the A470 (Brecon to Hay-on-Wye road)
Delightful country inn offering upmarket accommodation and memorable food in an unpretentious atmosphere. Located between the Black Mountains and the Brecon Beacons, it specialises in local produce cooked with distinction. Eggs Benedict and pan-fried calves' liver for lunch perhaps, and in the evening, Polish beetroot soup with wild mushroom ravioli, roasted duck breast with truffled Madeira jus, and glazed lemon tart. Good wines and local ales amidst rural comfort.
OPEN: 12-3 6-11 (Sunday 1-11) Closed: Last week Jan & First week Feb **RESTAURANT:** Lunch served: Tue-Sun Dinner served: Tue-Sun 12.30-2.30 7-9.30 Av 3 course à la carte £15.50 Av 3 course fixed price £22 **BREWERY/COMPANY:** Free House **PRINCIPAL BEERS:** Tomos Watkin OSB, Scottish Courage John Smith's. **FACILITIES:** Garden: Food served outdoors Dogs allowed (water) **ROOMS:** 7 bedrooms 7 en suite from s£47.50 d£72.50

Pick of the Pubs

The Usk Inn ◆◆◆◆ ◉ ◖◗ ♀
Talybont-on-Usk LD3 7JE ☎ 01874 676251 ▤ 01874 676392
e-mail: stay@uskinn.co.uk
Dir: 6m E of Brecon, just off the A40 towards Abergavenny & Crickhowell, if coming through Talybont turn onto Station Rd alongside the railway bridge were 500 yds on the R

This recently refurbished free house has long been welcoming weary travellers with a good range of real ales. Today, visitors arrive on foot from the nearby Taff Trail, as well as on horseback, mountain bike or canal boat. The traditional open fire and flagstone floors remain, but now the inn offers just a little more style. There's a civilised restaurant, with crisp white napery and candlelit tables, and cheerful en suite guest bedrooms featuring locally made pine furniture and patchwork quilts. Food is taken seriously, with imaginative menus that make good use of fresh local produce. Expect twice-cooked lamb shank with minted red wine sauce; beef fillet with goat's cheese; calves' liver with bacon, onions and bubble and squeak; baked sea bass; or roast monkfish on lemon balm. Vegetarian choices include spinach and Ricotta pasta parcels, or beetroot, cherry tomato and red onion tart.
OPEN: 8am-11pm Closed: Dec 25-26 **BAR MEALS:** Lunch served: all week Dinner served: all week 12-3 6.30-10 Av main course £11.95 **RESTAURANT:** Lunch served: all week Dinner served: all week 12-3 7-9.30 Av 3 course à la carte £27.50 Av 2 course fixed price £19.95 **BREWERY/COMPANY:** Free House **PRINCIPAL BEERS:** Brains SA Best, Reverend James & Buckleys

Best, Tomos Watkin OSB, Felinfoel Double Dragon.
FACILITIES: Children welcome Garden: Patio, food served outdoors Dogs allowed (water) **NOTES:** Parking 35 **ROOMS:** 11 bedrooms 11 en suite from s£35 d£65

Pick of the Pubs

White Swan Inn ◉
Llanfrynach LD3 7BZ ☎ 01874 665276
See Pick of the Pubs on page 627

CAERSWS — Map 08 SO09

Pick of the Pubs

The Talkhouse ◆◆◆◆◆ ◉ ♀
Pontdolgoch SY17 5JE ☎ 01686 688919 ▤ 01686 689134
Dir: From Newtown A487 about 5M towards Machynlleth & Dolgellan, turn R onto A470 just before level crossing into caersws carry on about 1 M on A470 inn on the L

If you're hungry or need a break, don't drive past this unassuming stone pub, set hard on the A470. Why? Because refurbishments by Colin and Melanie Dawson have created a beautifully furnished lounge area, complete with soft sofas, and a relaxing bar with a blazing log fire, wooden settles and relaxing music. The adjoining dining room features a good mix of tables topped with candles and an ever-changing blackboard menu listing an imaginative range of freshly prepared dishes. Impressive use is made of local ingredients - some from as nearby as the garden. Typical dishes include chargrilled rib of Welsh black beef with horseradish mash and beetroot fondants, local venison sausages with Puy lentils, vegetables, roasted parsnip purée and home-made quince jelly, or seared fillet of cod with black pudding, bacon and oven dried cherry tomato rösti.
OPEN: 12-2.30 6-11 Closed: 25-26 Dec, last Wk Mar, last Wk Sept **BAR MEALS:** Lunch served: Tue-Sat 12-1.30 Dinner served: Mon-Sat 6-9 Av main course £10 **RESTAURANT:** Lunch served: Tue-Sat 12-1.30 Dinner served: Mon-Sat 6-9 Av 3 course à la carte £20 **BREWERY/COMPANY:** Free House **PRINCIPAL BEERS:** Greene King, Bass. **FACILITIES:** Garden: Food served outside **NOTES:** Parking 30 **ROOMS:** 3 bedrooms 3 en suite from d£65

 Pubs offering a good choice of fish on their menu

continued

OPEN: 12-2 6.30-11
BAR MEALS: L served Wed-Sun.
D served Wed-Sun. 12-2 7-9.30
Av main course £5
RESTAURANT: L served Wed-Sun.
D served Wed-Sun. 12-2 7-9.30
Av cost 3 courses £20
BREWERY/COMPANY:
FREE HOUSE
PRINCIPAL BEERS: Wadsworth
6X, Greene King Old Speckled
Hen, Interbrew Flowers IPA
FACILITIES: Children welcome.
Garden: Food served outside
NOTES: Parking 35

White Swan Inn

Llanfrynach Brecon LD3 7BZ
☎ 01874 665276
Dir: 3 M E of Brecon off the A40 thake
the B4558 and follow the signs to
Llanfrynach

The long, white-painted stone frontage of the White Swan overlooks Llanfrynach churchyard in the heart of the Brecon Beacons National Park. This low, unassuming inn is tucked safely away from the A40, and makes an ideal escape from the frenetic pace of Brecon's Jazz Festival week.

Long renowned as an upmarket local, the pub is particularly popular with walkers and cyclists. Trout fishing is available on the nearby River Usk, and the Monmouthshire and Brecon canal is close by. The building has recently undergone an impressive makeover, with polished floors, exposed oak beams and a vast inglenook fireplace providing much of the pub's character. Well-kept real ales are served in the comfortably furnished and attractively decorated bar, and log fires offer a warm welcome in winter. The lounge and restaurant are equally inviting. Outside there's a secluded rear garden and attractive patio, with stone-topped tables under a plant-swathed trellis. Menus are a careful blend of traditional and modern recipes that make the most of well-chosen, locally produced ingredients. Lunchtime snacks might include a mixed cheese rarebit with barbecued leeks; sweet cured bacon with Pernod potatoes; or Black Mountain sausages with celeriac mash. At dinner, the menu begins with home-made soup; griddled sweet potato and red onion salad; or a chicken, mushroom and spinach stir-fry. A fine wine list accompanies main courses like pepper crusted Trelough duck with chargrilled fennel and potatoes; roast Hereford beef; or tomato pesto risotto with chargrilled vegetables and Parmesan crisps. The chalkboard lists a daily selection of fish dishes.

CARNO Map 08 SN99

Aleppo Merchant Inn
SY17 5LL ☎ 01686 420210 ▤ 01686 420296
e-mail: reception@thealeppo.co.uk
Dir: From Newtown, A489 and A470
Named after his ship by a retired sea captain, this stone-built inn is located in spectacular Welsh countryside between the Snowdonia and Brecon Beacons National Parks. There is a modernised bar with an open fire and straightforward pub food. The menu offers home-made game pie in season, beef carbonnade, Malaysian chicken korma or chicken gulai.
OPEN: 11.30-2.30 7-11 **BAR MEALS:** Lunch served: all week Dinner served: all week 12-2 7-9 Av main course £5.75
RESTAURANT: Lunch served: all week Dinner served: all week 12-2 7-9 Av 3 course à la carte £14 **BREWERY/COMPANY:** Free House
PRINCIPAL BEERS: Interbrew Boddingtons, Wadworth 6X.
FACILITIES: Garden: Food served outside **NOTES:** Parking 50
ROOMS: 6 bedrooms 2 en suite from s£30 d£45

COEDWAY Map 08 SJ31

Ye Old Hand and Diamond
SY5 9AR ☎ 01743 884379 ▤ 01743 884267
e-mail: oldhanddiamond@btconnect.com

Close to the Shropshire border and the River Severn, this 19th-century inn still retains much of its original character. Large open log fires burn in the winter and autumn. Typical menu includes chicken in mushroom and Stilton cream sauce, pork chops with cider and apple sauce, fresh sea bass, roast beef and Yorkshire pudding, and vegetable cannelloni.
OPEN: 11-11 **BAR MEALS:** Lunch served: all week Dinner served: all week 12-10 Av main course £8 **RESTAURANT:** Lunch served: all week Dinner served: all week 12-10 Av 3 course à la carte £15
BREWERY/COMPANY: Free House **PRINCIPAL BEERS:** Bass, Worthington. **FACILITIES:** Children welcome Garden: Food served outside Dogs allowed (guide dogs only) **NOTES:** Parking 90
ROOMS: 7 bedrooms 7 en suite from s£40 d£54

CRICKHOWELL Map 03 SO21

Pick of the Pubs

The Bear ★ ★ ★ ◎ 🛏 ♀
Brecon Rd NP8 1BW ☎ 01873 810408 ▤ 01873 811696
e-mail: bearhotel@aol.com
See Pick of the Pubs on page 629

Pick of the Pubs

Gliffaes Country House Hotel ★ ★ ★ ◎◎
NP8 1RH ☎ 01874 730371 ▤ 01874 730463
e-mail: calls@gliffaeshotel.com
Dir: 1m off the A40, 2.5m W of Crickhowell
Family run for over 50 years, Gliffaes is now in the hands of a third generation with no discernible diminution of standards. With its Italianate towers, this listed 19th-century building stands in 33 acres of gardens and wooded parkland overlooking the River Usk, which the owners claim offers some of the best private fishing in the UK. Each of the 22 sumptuously furnished en suite bedrooms overlook the river or gardens, and dogs are welcome at the hotel's own kennels. Popular bar lunches feature sandwiches, light meals and daily changing specials; chargrilled saddle of lamb, perhaps, or seared fillet of brill with a pesto risotto. The fixed-price dinner menu might start with goujons of sole or a pressed duck and pigeon confit, followed by locally shot pheasant or grilled red mullet. Poppy seed and rum parfait or hot passion fruit soufflé round off the evening.
OPEN: 12-3 6-11 **BAR MEALS:** Lunch served: all week 12-2.30 Av main course £6 **RESTAURANT:** Lunch served: Sun 12.30-2 Dinner served: all week 7.30-9.15 Av 3 course fixed price £28 **BREWERY/COMPANY:** Free House
PRINCIPAL BEERS: Felinfoel Double Dragon Ale.
FACILITIES: Children welcome Garden: Food served outside Dogs allowed in garden, Kennels Water **NOTES:** Parking 30
ROOMS: 22 bedrooms 22 en suite from s£55 d£67

Pick of the Pubs

Nantyffin Cider Mill ◎ ♀
Brecon Rd NP8 1SG ☎ 01873 810775 ▤ 01873 810775
e-mail: info@cidermill.co.uk
Dir: At junction of A40 & A479, 1.5m west of Crickhowell
A genuine all-rounder, this quality pub and restaurant stands in a picturesque garden just across the road from the river Usk. The original cider mill, fully working until the 1960s, has been tastefully incorporated into the main dining room, while the bars are full of character and offer a wide range of real ales and interesting, mainly New World wines. Locally grown produce, much of it organic, forms the basis of imaginative seasonal menus that are supplemented by daily specials including fine market-fresh fish. Kick off with the likes of Pembrokeshire mussels steamed with cider and leeks or seared local pigeon supreme with Puy lentils, parsnip crisps and a red wine glaze. Main courses could include pot roast rabbit with Rosemary, garlic and spices, accompanied by caramelised chicory and bacon or roast fillet of cod with spinach and chive butter sauce.
OPEN: 12-2.30 6-9.30 Closed: 1 Wk Nov, 1wk Jan
BAR MEALS: Lunch served: Tues-Sun Dinner served: Tues-Sun 12-2.30 6.30-9.30 Av main course £13.50
RESTAURANT: Lunch served: Tues-Sun Dinner served: Tues-Sun 12-2.30 7-9.30 Av 3 course à la carte £25
BREWERY/COMPANY: Free House
PRINCIPAL BEERS: Uleys Old Spot, Felinfoel Best Bitter, Marston's Pedigree, Hancocks HB. **FACILITIES:** Children welcome Garden: Food served outdoors, overlooking River Usk **NOTES:** Parking 40

Wales

OPEN: 10–3 6–11
BAR MEALS: L served all week.
D served all week. 12–2 6–10
Av main course £8.95
RESTAURANT: L served all week.
D served Mon–Sat. 12–2 7–9.30
Av cost 3 course £25
BREWERY/COMPANY: FREE
HOUSE
PRINCIPAL BEERS: Interbrew
Bass, Greene King Old Speckled
Hen, Hancocks HB, Brains
Reverend James
FACILITIES: Dogs welcome.
GARDEN: Food served outside
NOTES: Parking 50
ROOMS: 35 en suite. Double
room from £70. Single room from
£54

The Bear

★★★ 🏵 🍽 ♀
Brecon Road, Crickhowell NP8 1BW
☎ 01873 810408 📠 01873 811696
e-mail: bearhotel@aol.com
Dir: On A40 between Abergavenny
& Brecon

Run by the same family for a quarter of a century, The Bear just goes on and on: so popular has it been both locally and country wide that every available nook and cranny has been put to good use as bar, bistro or restaurant space.

A slightly laid-back eccentricity is explained by the owners' regard of the whole house as their own home, treating all-comers with genuine hospitality and supervising the operation with seemingly boundless enthusiasm. Food choices are vast. The bar menu runs from sandwiches and baguettes or light meals such as Thai prawn cakes, Welsh rarebit or home-cured carpaccio of beef, through to satisfying main courses including steamed lamb and suet pudding, tuna and prawn lasagna and casserole of guinea fowl. A selection of bar specials doubles the choice to include dishes such as pan-fried pigeon breast with ginger and orange sauce or fresh potato gnocchi in a rich Neapolitan tomato sauce. Modern, European-inspired fine dining menus include starters such as ravioli of smoked chicken with goats' cheese, artichoke and red pepper coulis or salad of oak smoked duck with wild mushrooms, spinach, Stilton and a pear salsa. For a main course, how about braised shank of Welsh lamb served on leek and bacon mash, confit of belly pork served on egg noodles with a spiced sweet and sour sauce, or baked fillet of sea bass with fresh pasta and a laverbread and orange sauce. Superb desserts and puddings are all home made and a peerless Welsh cheeseboard is accompanied by a range of ports. Add to all this the bedrooms, divided between the main 15th-century inn and coach-house rooms facing the cobbled courtyard, and its fully deserved reputation becomes clear.

CWMDU

Map 03 SO12

Pick of the Pubs

The Farmers Arms 🍴
NP8 1RU ☎ 01874 730464 🖹 01874 730988
e-mail: cwmdu@aol.com

See Pick of the Pubs on page 631

DYLIFE

Map 08 SH89

Star Inn ♦♦♦ 🍴
SY19 7BW ☎ 01650 521345 🖹 01650 521345
Dir: Between Llanidloes & Machynlleth on mountain Rd

Situated at 1300 feet in some of Wales' most breathtaking
countryside, the inn traces its roots back to the 17th century.
The area was a favourite haunt of Dylan Thomas and Wynford
Vaughan Thomas; red kites swoop overhead, and the
magnificent Clywedog reservoir is close by. Varied choice of
wholesome pub fare includes pork in cider and cream sauce;
and aubergine and mushroom nut bake.
OPEN: 12-2.30 7-11 (Ring for opening details during Winter)
BAR MEALS: Lunch served: all week Dinner served: all week
12-2.30 7-11 Av main course £7.50 **RESTAURANT:** 12-2 7-10 Av 3
course à la carte £12.50 **BREWERY/COMPANY:** Free House
PRINCIPAL BEERS: Tetley Smooth, Marston Pedigree.
FACILITIES: Children welcome Garden: Food served outside. Patio
area Dogs allowed on lead at all times **NOTES:** Parking 40
ROOMS: 6 bedrooms 2 en suite from s£18 d£18

ELAN VILLAGE

Map 03 SN96

Elan Valley Hotel 🍴
LD6 5HN ☎ 01597 810448 🖹 01597 810448
e-mail: Hotel@Elanvalley.demon.co.uk
Dir: A44 to Rhayader then B4518 for 2m
Situated below the last of the four reservoirs in the Elan
Valley, this rejuvenated hotel, formerly a Victorian fishing
lodge, stands in the heart of stunning mid-Wales scenery and
is justifiably a popular refreshment stop among visitors to the
area. From snacks like aromatic coriander and mixed bean
curry in the bar to grilled Pencerrig goats' cheese with apple
chutney, fillet of Welsh beef teryaki, or poached halibut with
sautéed oyster mushrooms in the restaurant, perhaps
followed by raspberry meringue roulade.
OPEN: 6-11 (weekends 11-3, 6-11.30) (11-3 Mon-Sun) Closed: 25
Dec **BAR MEALS:** Lunch served: Sat-Sun (winter), Mon-Sun
(summer only) 12-2.30 Dinner served: all week 7-9 Av main course
£5.50 **RESTAURANT:** Dinner served: Thurs-Sat (winter) all
(summer)7-9 Av 3 course à la carte £17
BREWERY/COMPANY: Free House

continued

PRINCIPAL BEERS: Interbrew Hancocks HB, Brains Buckley Best &
Reverand James, Wood Shropshire Lad, Timothy Taylor Landlord.
FACILITIES: Children welcome Garden: Food served outdoors
Dogs allowed **NOTES:** Parking 30 **ROOMS:** 11 bedrooms 11 en
suite from s£35 d£60

GLADESTRY

Map 03 SO25

Royal Oak Inn see Herefordshire p. 244

HAY-ON-WYE

Map 03 SO24

Pick of the Pubs

The Famous Old Black Lion ★ ★ 🔴🍴
Vanessa King HR3 5AD ☎ 01497 820841 🖹 01497 822960
e-mail: info@oldblaclion.co.uk

See Pick of the Pubs on page 632

Kilverts Inn 🍴 🍷
The Bullring HR3 5AG ☎ 01497 821042 🖹 01497 821580
e-mail: info@kilverts.co.uk
Dir: From A50 take A49, then L onto B4348 into Hay-on-Wye. In town
centre near Butter Market

At the heart of Wales's 'bookshop capital' near the Butter
Market - though access and parking can be a little tricky. A
core menu uses local produce, while the bar menu features
pizzas, pasta and other pub favourites. Restaurant dinners
show rather more imagination: lightly spiced parsnip and
sweet potato roulade, served with cream cheese and mint,
pork baton stuffed with peaches, pistachio and sage served
with green ginger wine sauce, or braised hock of Welsh lamb.
OPEN: 9-11 (Sun 12-10.30) Closed: 25 Dec **BAR MEALS:** Lunch
served: all week Dinner served: all week 12-2 7-9.30
RESTAURANT: Dinner served: all week 12-2 7-9.30
BREWERY/COMPANY: Free House
PRINCIPAL BEERS: Hancock's HB, Bass, Worthington Cream Flow.
FACILITIES: Children welcome Garden: Food served outside. Well
kept gardens Dogs allowed before 7pm, water provided if requested
NOTES: Parking 13 **ROOMS:** 11 bedrooms 11 en suite from s£50
d£70

LLANDINAM

Map 08 SO08

The Lion Hotel
SY17 5BY ☎ 01686 688233 🖹 01686 689124
Dir: on the A470 midway between Newton and Llanidloes
Llandinam is perhaps best known as the home of the first
electric light in Wales. The Lion itself is a centre for
international para and hang-gliding. It also occupies an
attractive riverside setting.

OPEN: 12–2.30 6.30–11 (Mon 6.30–11, open BH Mon all day)

BAR MEALS: L served Tue-Sun. D served Tue-Sun. 12–2.15 7–9.30 Av main course £6.95

RESTAURANT: L served Tue-Sun. D served Tue-Sun. 12–2.15 7–9.30 Av cost 3 courses £18.20

BREWERY/COMPANY: FREE HOUSE

PRINCIPAL BEERS: Uley Old Spot Prize Ale, Tomos Watkin OSB, Greene King Old Speckled Hen, Sheperd Neame Spitfire Premium Ale

FACILITIES: Children welcome, dogs allowed. Garden: Beer garden, food served outdoors

NOTES: Parking 30

ROOMS: 2 en suite Double room from £40 Single room from £25

The Farmers Arms

Located in the Brecon Beacons National Park, just on the edge of the Black Mountains, this tiny hamlet stands tucked away in a typically quiet valley of great natural beauty. The Farmers Arms is an increasingly popular inn offering a warm welcome, plenty of good food and comfortable country bedrooms. Inside the emphasis is on traditional charm.

Cwmdu, Powys NP8 1RU
☎ 01874 730464 📠 01874 730988
e-mail: cwmdu@aol.com
Dir: From A40 take A479 signed Builth Wells, Cwmdu is 3m along this road.

The building dates back to the 18th century and the owners have been keen to ensure that it does not fall foul of unsympathetic modern conversions. The unspoilt bar area tempts visitors to linger over good beer, friendly chatter and a game of cards or dominoes, warmed by the cast-iron log burning stove. In the dining room, there's a break from tradition in order to offer a modern, wide-ranging selection of dishes. The best possible local ingredients are used and pretty much any dietary requirements can be catered for on request. Among the starters alone, expect

Welsh specialities such as Welsh Dragon pâté made with venison and chilli or salmon, laverbread and cheese soufflé. Locally sourced main courses range from roast rack of Brecon lamb topped with a herb crust and served with Cumberland sauce to local sea bass with ginger, laverbread and smoked salmon on a chive hollandaise. There's also an inspiring selection of dishes with an international flavour: perhaps Indian spiced chicken fillet on a tomato and parsley couscous with a lemon scented coconut cream, or chargrilled tuna with fresh pesto and chargrilled vegetables. Desserts range from white and dark chocolate truffle mousse to homely jam sponge pudding. There's also commendable selection of real ales.

OPEN: 11-11 (Sun 12-10.30)
BAR MEALS: L served all week.
D served all week. 12-2.30
6.30-9.30 Av main course £8.50
RESTAURANT: D served all week.
6.30-9.30 Av cost 3 course £20
BREWERY/COMPANY: FREE
HOUSE
PRINCIPLE BEERS: Old Black Lion
Ale, Wye Valley & guest ales
FACILITIES: Dogs allowed. Garden:
Patio, food served outside
NOTES: Parking 20
ROOMS: 10 en suite Double room
from £80

The Famous Old Black Lion

In the heart of Hay-on-Wye, celebrated for its second-hand bookshops, this 17th-century coaching inn is filled with lots of original charm. Run by friendly owner, it has an excellent reputation for good food. Hay-on-Wye is a mecca for avid readers and collectors of antiquarian books.

★ ★ ◉ 🐑
Hay-on-Wye HR3 5AD
☎ 01497 820841 📠 01497 822960
e-mail: info@oldblacklion.co.uk
Dir: Town centre.

Its attractive streets, climbing above the River Wye, are filled with bookshops - there's even one in the castle courtyard! Many guests also come to visit the Brecon Beacons, for canoeing or whitewater-rafting or to walk Offa's Dyke Path. The hotel is close to the former Lion Gate entrance to the old walled town. Enjoy a glass of the pub's eponymous real ale in the comfortable King Richard bar, where informal meals are served on candlelit scrubbed pine tables. There's a log burning fire, and exposed oak beams in the Oliver Cromwell restaurant are redolent of the days when the Lord Protector himself is reputed to have lodged here during the siege of Hay Castle. The dining room overlooks the garden terrace. The frequently changing menus have been awarded a number of accolades and uses locally reared meat, organic where possible and seasonal vegetables and herbs from its own garden. The diverse bar menu includes freshly made sandwiches, salads and omelettes, as well as more substantial dishes like sausage and mash, sirloin steak, or fish pie. In the restaurant, duo of minted melon and orange, or confit of duck leg, liven up the palate for rack of Welsh lamb, beef Wellington, or roast monkfish with coriander and lemon. There are ten bedrooms recently refurbished to a high standard.

LLANDRINDOD WELLS Map 03 SO06

The Bell Country Inn 🛏
Llanyre LD1 6DY ☎ 01597 823959 📠 01597 825899
e-mail: dgj.jones@virgin.net
Dir: 1 1/2m NW of Llandrindod Wells on the A4081
Set in the hills above Llandrindod Wells, this former drovers' inn offers comfortable accommodation and a varied menu in the dining room, lounge bar and Stables Restaurant. Seafood from the specials board includes jumbo cod, squid and pan-fried fillet of skate, while favourite alternatives are half a roasted duckling or prime 10oz sirloin steak. There's the Courtyard for outdoor seating, and a play area for children is provided.
OPEN: 11-11 Closed: 25 Dec & 1 Jan **BAR MEALS:** Lunch served: all week 12-2 Dinner served: Mon-Sat 6.30-9.30 Av main course £6.35 **RESTAURANT:** Lunch served: all week 12-2 Dinner served: Mon-Sat 6.30-9.30 Av 3 course à la carte £18.95
BREWERY/COMPANY: Free House
PRINCIPAL BEERS: Worthington, Bass Hancock's HB.
FACILITIES: Children welcome Garden: Food served outside. Patio area Dogs allowed (in the garden only, water provided)
NOTES: Parking 20 **ROOMS:** 9 bedrooms 9 en suite from s£35 d£39.50

LLANFYLLIN Map 08 SJ11

Cain Valley Hotel ★ ★ 🛏
High St SY22 5AQ ☎ 01691 648366 📠 01691 648307
e-mail: info@cainvalleyhotel.co.uk
Dir: from Shrewsbury & Oswestry follow signs for Lake Vyrnwy & onto A490 to Llanfyllin.Hotel on R

Family run coaching inn dating from the 17th century, with a stunning Jacobean staircase, oak-panelled lounge bar and a heavily beamed restaurant, where the walls have been exposed to show off the hand-made bricks. A full bar menu is available at lunchtime and in the evening, alongside a choice of real ales. Home-made soup, mixed seafood, Welsh lamb, steaks and curries are offered. Llanfyllin is set amid green hills, offering wonderful walks and breathtaking views.
OPEN: 11.30-11 (Sun 12-10.30) Closed: 24/25 Dec
BAR MEALS: Lunch served: all week Dinner served: all week 12-2 7-9 Av main course £5 **RESTAURANT:** Lunch served: Sun 12-2 Dinner served: all week 7-9 Av 3 course à la carte £20
BREWERY/COMPANY: Free House
PRINCIPAL BEERS: Carlsberg-Tetley Ansells Best Bitter, Interbrew Bass & Worthingtons. **FACILITIES:** Children welcome Dogs allowed guests bedrooms only **NOTES:** Parking 12 **ROOMS:** 13 bedrooms 13 en suite from s£38 d£62

The Stumble Inn
Bwlch-y-Cibau SY22 5LL ☎ 01691 648860 📠 01691 648955
Dir: A458 to Welshpool, B4393 to Four Crosses and Llansantffraid, A495 Melford, A490 to Bwlch-y-Cibau
Standing opposite the church in a rural farming hamlet in unspoilt mid-Wales countryside close to Lake Vyrnwy, this popular stone-built inn offers a traditional pub atmosphere and food. The menu changes monthly and might feature Thai monkfish, beef goulash, Welsh lamb steak and hake fillet with saffron and prawn cream sauce.
OPEN: 12-3 6-12 Closed: 2 Wks Jan **BAR MEALS:** Lunch served: Sun 12-2 Dinner served: Wed-Sat 6-9 Av main course £7
RESTAURANT: Lunch served: Sun 12-2 Dinner served: Wed-Sat 6-10 Av 3 course à la carte £11 **BREWERY/COMPANY:** Free House
PRINCIPAL BEERS: Carlsberg-Tetley Tetley Bitter plus Changing ales.
FACILITIES: Children welcome Garden: Food served outside
NOTES: Parking 40

LLANGATTOCK Map 03 SO21

The Vine Tree Inn 🛏
The Legar NP8 1HG ☎ 01873 810514 📠 01873 811299
e-mail: s.lennox@virgin.net
Dir: Take A40 W from Abergavenny then A4077 from Crickhowell
The Vine Tree is located in the beautiful Usk Valley overlooking the medieval bridge. It is predominantly a dining pub serving freshly prepared dishes such as chicken Cymru in a creamy white wine, tomato and mushroom sauce, and fillet steak stuffed with pâté in a port wine sauce. There's a vegetarian selection, including nut roast, pasta and curry, and fresh fish dishes - sea bass, sea bream, and monkfish in Pernod and leek sauce.
OPEN: 12-3 6-11 (Sun 7-10.30) **BAR MEALS:** Lunch served: all week Dinner served: all week 12-3 6-10 Av main course £8.01
RESTAURANT: Lunch served: all week Dinner served: all week 12-3 6-10 Av 3 course à la carte £15 **BREWERY/COMPANY:** Free House
PRINCIPAL BEERS: Fuller's London Pride, Castle Eden Ale.
FACILITIES: Children welcome **NOTES:** Parking 27

LLOWES Map 03 SO14

The Radnor Arms 🛏
HR3 5JA ☎ 01497 847460 📠 01497 847460
Dir: A438 Brecon-Hereford Rd between Glasbury & Clyro
The garden of this charming, 400 year-old whitewashed drovers' inn enjoys stunning views across the Wye Valley to the Black Mountains. Local Felinfoel bitter is amongst the superb range of beers served beside blazing winter fires in the cosy bar, and the extensive blackboard menus offer plenty of variety, with good vegetarian options. Expect ham, egg and chips, stir-fried chicken with walnuts, swordfish in white wine sauce, or vegetable and cheese Wellington.
OPEN: 11-2.30 (Sun 12-3) 6.30-10 **BAR MEALS:** Lunch served: Tue-Sun Dinner served: Tue-Sun 12-3 6.30-11 Av main course £7.50
RESTAURANT: Lunch served: Tue-Sun Dinner served: Tue-Sun 12-3 6.30-11 Av 3 course à la carte £12.50 **BREWERY/COMPANY:** Free House **PRINCIPAL BEERS:** Felinfoel, Worthington.
FACILITIES: Children welcome Garden: Beautiful views, seating
NOTES: Parking 50

Wales

LLYSWEN   Map 03 SO13

Pick of the Pubs

The Griffin Inn 🐑 ♀
LD3 0UR ☎ 01874 754241 📠 01874 754592
e-mail: info@griffin-inn.freeserve.co.uk
See Pub Walk on page 625
See Pick of the Pubs on page 635

MONTGOMERY   Map 08 SO29

Pick of the Pubs

The Bricklayers Arms ◎ 🐑
Chirbury Rd SY15 6QQ ☎ 01686 668177
e-mail: robjennings6@hotmail.com
Dir: On entering Montgomery, turn L at the first war memorial 300 yds on L handside
Close to the castle ruins and Offa's Dyke Path, this 13th-century inn stands in the cobbled market square. Drovers once met in the Bricklayers, for here was the main livestock market where animals were sold before heading on towards London. The building still has some black and white timber façade and, throughout the bar and first floor dining room, real open fires and sturdy old floorboards enhance the original rafters and cottage-style furnishings. There's an adequate wine list, and the pub serves some interesting real ales, including Reverend James, now brewed by Brains in Cardiff. The menus feature local meat, game and poultry, and pesticide-free vegetables. Starters might include cauliflower soup with Welsh Cheddar, or Abergavenny smoked chicken with baby leaf salad, followed by Shropshire lamb with mulled apricots, grey mullet with hazelnut, mushroom and tomato crust, or a filo parcel of sweet potato, chick pea and roasted mushroom.
OPEN: 12–2 6–11 Closed: 2 Wks Feb, 1 wk Sept
BAR MEALS: Lunch served: Wed–Sun 12–2 Dinner served: Tue–Sat 6–7 Av main course £10.50 **RESTAURANT:** Lunch served: Tue–Sun Dinner served: Tues–Sun 12–2 7–9
BREWERY/COMPANY: Free House
PRINCIPAL BEERS: Marston's Pedigree, Shepherds Neame Spitfire, Greene King Old Speckled Hen. **FACILITIES:** Children welcome Dogs allowed (water, toys, kennel) **NOTES:** Parking 15

Pick of the Pubs

Dragon Hotel ★ ★ ◎
SY15 6PA ☎ 01686 668359 📠 01686 668287
e-mail: reception@dragonhotel.com
Dir: A483 toward Welshpool, R onto B4386 then B4385, Behind the town hall
With its striking black and white timbered frontage and historic interior, there is much to please the eye at this friendly family-run coaching inn, parts of which date from the mid-1600s. Beams in the bar, lounge and some bedrooms are believed to have come from the castle, which was destroyed by Oliver Cromwell. Outside, an enclosed patio has been created from the former coach entrance. The best available local beef, lamb and fresh fish are featured in the regular menu and daily specials. Steaks are a popular option, and vegetarian dishes such

continued

as mushroom and herb ragout in chasseur sauce. Wide-ranging facilities include en suite bedrooms, an indoor swimming pool and sauna, and a function room.

OPEN: 11–11 **BAR MEALS:** Lunch served: all week Dinner served: all week 12–2 7–9 Av main course £7.50
RESTAURANT: Lunch served: bookings only Dinner served: bookings only 12–2 7–9 Av 3 course à la carte £25 Av 3 course fixed price £19 **BREWERY/COMPANY:** Free House
PRINCIPAL BEERS: Wood Special, Interbrew Boddingtons.
FACILITIES: Children welcome Children's licence Garden: Food served outside **NOTES:** Parking 20 **ROOMS:** 20 bedrooms 20 en suite from s£45 d£75

NEW RADNOR   Map 03 SO26

Red Lion Inn
Llanfihangel-nant-Melan LD8 2TN
☎ 01544 350220 📠 01544 350220
e-mail: enquiries@theredlioninn.net
Dir: A483 to Crossgates then R onto A44

Llanfihangel-nant-Melan may be a bit of a mouthful to the non-Welsh speaking, but it's easy to find being just three miles west of New Radnor. This 16th-century drovers' inn has recently had a new restaurant built to make sure the tradition of hospitality continues. A new Radnor Ale has also been brewed to wash down dishes such as organic salmon on a bed of couscous, chicken supreme with sun-dried tomato sauce, mushroom Stroganoff, and Breconshire beef fillet with green peppercorn sauce. **OPEN:** 12–2.30 6–11 **BAR MEALS:** Lunch served: Wed–Sun Dinner served: Wed–Sun 12–2.15 6.30–9.45 Av main course £6
RESTAURANT: Lunch served: Wed–Sun Dinner served: Wed–Sun 12–2.15 6.30–9.45 Av 3 course à la carte £14.50
BREWERY/COMPANY: Free House **PRINCIPAL BEERS:** Hook Norton Best. **FACILITIES:** Children welcome Garden: Food served outside Dogs allowed **NOTES:** Parking 30
ROOMS: 7 bedrooms 7 en suite from s£30 d£45

Wales

OPEN: 10.30–3 7–11
(Summer 11–11)
BAR MEALS: L served all week.
D served all week. 12–2 7–9
Av main course £7.25
RESTAURANT: L served all week.
D served all week. 1–2.30 7–9
BREWERY/COMPANY: S A
BRAIN
PRINCIPLE BEERS: Brains
Reverand James, SA, Arms Park &
Buckleys Best
FACILITIES: Dogs allowed
NOTES: Parking 20
ROOMS: 7 en suite Double room
from £60 Single room from £35

The Griffin Inn

POWYS LD3 0UR
☎ 01874 754241 📄 01874 754592
e-mail: nfo@griffin-inn.freeserve.co.uk
Dir: On A470 (Brecon to Builth Wells rd)

A family-run favourite for some 17 years, this lovely ivy covered inn provides a relaxed atmosphere, traditional comforts and all the sporting benefits of a stay in the glorious upper Wye valley. It's a hub of the local community, so guests could find themselves engaged in conversation with the local poacher, preacher, the publicans themselves or even the local village bobby.

On a summer's day, sit outside and watch the world go by. In the winter, take refuge in one of the cosy public rooms: perhaps the bar, with its huge open fire, bare tiled floor and fishing memorabilia, the lounge with its charming mixture of chairs and sofas clustered around a log-burning stove, or the dining room, an equally rustic affair with bare beams and blackboard menus. Wye salmon, fresh trout and seasonal game, fruit and vegetables all play their part in the array of home cooked produce. At lunch or dinner diners can choose from dishes such as rack of Welsh lamb, Mediterranean chicken, Welsh black beef daube or Exmoor steak (fillet steak stuffed with stilton, wrapped in bacon and set on a Stilton and port sauce). An impressive array of fresh fish direct from Cornwall could include sea bass, sole, lobster or scallops. Desserts are all home made and might include trifle, bread and butter pudding or mango créme brûlée. Those who fancy a lighter lunch can opt for sandwiches, baguettes or a ploughman's. Seven bedrooms, all en suite, provide comfy, country house style accommodation.

Wales

OLD RADNOR Map 03 SO25

Harp Inn
LD8 2RH ☎ 01544 350655 ▤ 01544 350655
Dir: A44 from Leominster to Gore, then L to Old Radnor
Although this 15th-century pub has been extensively renovated, great care has been taken to retain as much of its original period character as possible. The slate-flagged floor, exposed stone walls and ancient bread oven still remain, as do traditional standards of hospitality and good food. Charles I complained about the food here centuries ago, but he could scarcely do so today. A typical menu includes pork loin steak with creamy mustard sauce, chicken wrapped in bacon in Stilton sauce, and lamb casserole with cranberries.
OPEN: 12-2 6-11 (Sat-Sun 12-3, 6-10.30) **BAR MEALS:** Lunch served: Sat-Sun 12-2 Dinner served: Tue-Sun 6-9 Av main course £7 **RESTAURANT:** Lunch served: Sat-Sun 12-2 Dinner served: Tue-Sun 7-9 Av 3 course à la carte £20 **BREWERY/COMPANY:** Free House **PRINCIPAL BEERS:** Shepherd Neame. **FACILITIES:** Children welcome Garden: Food served outside **NOTES:** Parking 18 **ROOMS:** 5 bedrooms 2 en suite from s£25 d£52

PWLLGLOYW Map 03 SO03

Pick of the Pubs

Seland Newydd
LD3 9PY ☎ 01874 690282
e-mail: seland@newydd.f.business.co.uk
Dir: 4m N of Brecon on B4520 to Builth Wells, 1m before Lower Chapel
This 17th-century coaching inn, originally the Camden Arms, was renamed Seland Newydd, the Welsh translation of New Zealand, by former antipodean owners. The inn enjoys a peaceful village setting in the Brecon Beacons National Park, and comprises a cosy bar and lounge area with a log fire and a separate rear restaurant. Half the building has always been an inn, but the other half was once the local blacksmith's, and the large fireplace in the centre of the room is part of the old forge. Seasonal dining menus are supplemented by a specials board, typically offering braised local lamb with crushed potatoes, oyster mushrooms, fresh asparagus, spinach and Marsala meat jus. Opposite the inn is a short forest walk leading to the river, which the owners reserve for themselves and their guests.
OPEN: 12-3 6-11 **BAR MEALS:** Lunch served: Wed-Sun 12-2 Dinner served: Tue-Sat 7-9 Av main course £10 **RESTAURANT:** Lunch served: Wed-Sun 12-2 Dinner served: Tue-Sat 7-9 Av 3 course à la carte £25 **BREWERY/COMPANY:** Free House **PRINCIPAL BEERS:** Brains Buckleys Best & Dark. **FACILITIES:** Children welcome Garden: Beer garden, food served outdoors Dogs allowed (water) **NOTES:** Parking 30 **ROOMS:** 3 bedrooms 3 en suite from s£42.50 d£50

TALGARTH Map 03 SO13

Castle Inn ◆◆◆
Pengenffordd LD3 0EP ☎ 01874 711353 ▤ 01874 711353
e-mail: castlepen@aol.com
Dir: 4m S of Talgarth on the A479
At just over 1,000 feet above sea level, the pub takes its name from the nearby ancient hill-fort of Castell Dinas. Formerly a hill farm and drovers' inn, the Castle is popular with mountain

walkers and outdoor enthusiasts tramping in the Brecon Beacons. Bunkhouse accommodation is on offer in the neighbouring converted barn. Substantial pub food includes home-made soup, potato skins, pork in cider, and fisherman's pie.
OPEN: 12-3 7-11 (Mon 7-11 only, Sat 12-4, 7-11) Closed: Dec 25 **BAR MEALS:** Lunch served: Wed-Sun 12-2 Dinner served: all week 7-9 Av main course £6.50 **BREWERY/COMPANY:** Free House **PRINCIPAL BEERS:** 2 or 3 regularly changing ales. **FACILITIES:** Children welcome Garden: **NOTES:** Parking 60 **ROOMS:** 5 bedrooms 2 en suite from s£20 d£40

TALYBONT-ON-USK Map 03 SN12

Star Inn ☺ ♀
LD3 7YX ☎ 01874 676635
e-mail: jcoakham@hotmail.com
With its pretty riverside garden, this traditional 200-year-old inn stands in a picturesque village within the Brecon Beacons National Park. The pub has long been known for its constantly changing range of well-kept real ales, and it's an excellent centre for walking and outdoor pursuits. Quiz night on Monday, live bands on Wednesday. Hearty bar food with dishes such as chicken in leek and Stilton sauce, traditional roasts, salmon fish cakes, and vegetarian chilli.
OPEN: 11-3 6.30-11 (Sat All Day) **BAR MEALS:** Lunch served: all week Dinner served: all week 12-2.15 6.30-9.30 Av main course £5.50 **BREWERY/COMPANY:** Free House **PRINCIPAL BEERS:** Felinfoel Double Dragon, Theakston Old Peculiar, Hancock's HB, Bullmastiff Best. **FACILITIES:** Children welcome Garden: Food served outdoors Dogs allowed **ROOMS:** 2 bedrooms 2 en suite from d£45

TRECASTLE Map 03 SN82

Pick of the Pubs

Castle Coaching Inn ♀
LD3 8UH ☎ 01874 636354 ▤ 01874 636457
e-mail: hotel.reservation@btinternet.com
Dir: On A40 W of Brecon

A Georgian coaching inn on the old London-Carmarthen coaching route, now the main A40 trunk road. Family owned and run, the hotel has been carefully restored in recent years, and has lovely old fireplaces and a remarkable bow-fronted bar window. Ten en suite bedrooms are available and a peaceful terrace and garden. Food is served in the bar or more formally in the à la carte restaurant. The evening menu offers dishes from the grill, from the oven and from the ocean. There is also a good vegetarian selection, including cannelloni with goats' cheese, Ricotta and spinach. Welsh lamb from the Brecon Beacons is a feature - rack of lamb or three

continued

continued

succulent lamb chops served with chef's special rosemary and redcurrant sauce – and Welsh black steaks, topped with fried onions, mushrooms and a melting smoked St David's cheese. Complete your meal with dessert or a selection of Welsh farmhouse cheeses.
OPEN: 12–3 6–11 Closed: 25 Dec **BAR MEALS:** Lunch served: Tues-Sun Dinner served: Tues-Sun 12–2 6.30–9.30 Av main course £6.95 **RESTAURANT:** Lunch served: Tues-Sun Dinner served: Tues-Sun 12–2 7–9 Av 3 course à la carte £25
BREWERY/COMPANY: Free House
PRINCIPAL BEERS: Fuller's London Pride, Shepherd Neame Spitfire, Greene King Triumph, Young's Special.
FACILITIES: Children welcome Children's licence Garden: Patio, food served outside Dogs allowed (water, food)
NOTES: Parking 25 **ROOMS:** 10 bedrooms 10 en suite from s£45 d£50

UPPER CWMTWRCH
Map 03 SN71

George VI Inn
SA9 2XH ☎ 01639 830441 🖷 01639 830411
e-mail: marcusrcoles@aol.com
Dir: 2 M from Ystalyfera Rdbt at Upper Cwmtwrch is the George IV inn next to the river
A traditional family-owned pub and restaurant, which occupies a scenic riverside location at the foot of the Black Mountains. Relax by the cosy wood-burner on a cold winter's day or, in summer, make use of the colourful garden and patio for alfresco dining. The pub brews its own beers and offers wholesome fare made from Welsh produce wherever possible. Traditional roasts, sizzling bass in garlic, and Welsh black beef feature on the extensive menu.
OPEN: 11.30–3 6.30–11 (Sun 12–3, 7–10.30) Closed: Jan
BAR MEALS: Lunch served: Wed-Mon Dinner served: Wed-Mon 11.30–2.30 6.30–10 Av main course £8.50 **RESTAURANT:** Lunch served: Wed-Mon Dinner served: Wed-Mon 11.30–2.30 6.30–10 Av 3 course à la carte £15 **BREWERY/COMPANY:** Free House
PRINCIPAL BEERS: White Hart Brewery Cwrw Blasus, Cwrw Cwmtwrch. **FACILITIES:** Children welcome Garden: Food served outside **NOTES:** Parking 40

SWANSEA

LLANSAMLET
Map 03 SS69

Plough and Harrow
57 Church Rd SA7 9RL ☎ 01792 772263
Dir: 2 M from Junct 44 of M4, 5 M from the centre of Swansea near the enterprise park
Sitting in a quiet Swansea suburb next to a church, this Tomos Watkin pub has a roaring log fire and some say, a resident ghost. Cosy relaxed atmosphere with a good local reputation for its food.
OPEN: 12–11 **BAR MEALS:** Lunch served: all week Dinner served: all week 12–2 6–9 Av main course £5 **PRINCIPAL BEERS:** Watkins OSK, Merlins, Whoosh, Worthington Best. **FACILITIES:** Children welcome Dogs allowed No credit cards

PONTARDDULAIS
Map 02 SN50

The Fountain Inn
111 Bologoed Rd SA4 1JP ☎ 01792 882501 🖷 01792 885340
e-mail: bookings@fountaininn.com
Dir: A48 from M4 to Pontlliw then on to Pontarddulais, inn on R

Memorabilia from Swansea's industrial past fill this carefully modernised old free house. The chef uses fresh local ingredients to produce an extensive and interesting range of dishes. Expect cockle, bacon and laverbread crêpe; stuffed Welsh saltmarsh lamb; cheese and leek crusted cod; or hake and monkfish in prawn and watercress sauce. Round off your meal with bara brith bread and butter pudding.
OPEN: 12–2 5.30–11.30 Closed: 25–26 Dec **BAR MEALS:** Lunch served: all week Dinner served: all week 12–2 5.30–9.30 Av main course £9.50 **RESTAURANT:** Lunch served: all week Dinner served: all week 12–2.30 5.30–9.30 Av 3 course à la carte £20 Av 3 course fixed price £9.50 **BREWERY/COMPANY:** Free House
PRINCIPAL BEERS: Greene King Old Speckled Hen, Fuller's London Pride, Batemans XXXX. **FACILITIES:** Children welcome Garden: Food served outside **NOTES:** Parking 30
ROOMS: 9 bedrooms 9 en suite from s£39.95 d£44.95

REYNOLDSTON
Map 02 SS48

King Arthur Hotel
Higher Green SA3 1AD ☎ 01792 390775 🖷 01792 391075
e-mail: info@kingarthurhotel.co.uk
Dir: Just N of A4118 SW of Swansea
This traditional 18th-century country inn stands on the former Swansea to London coaching route. Now in the centre of Britain's first designated Area of Outstanding Natural Beauty, the pub's seven en suite bedrooms make an ideal base for outdoor pursuits and the local shoot. Choose from three different bars with open log fires, chestnut roasters and hot toddies. The varied local menu ranges from cockles and laverbread to Welsh saltmarsh lamb and lots of seasonal fish.
OPEN: 11–11 Closed: 25 Dec **BAR MEALS:** Lunch served: all week Dinner served: all week 12–2.30 6–9.30 Av main course £7 **RESTAURANT:** Lunch served: all week Dinner served: all week 12–2.30 6–9.30 **BREWERY/COMPANY:** Free House
PRINCIPAL BEERS: Felinfoel Double Dragon, Interbrew Worthington Bitter & Bass. **FACILITIES:** Children welcome Garden: Food served outside **NOTES:** Parking 80
ROOMS: 7 bedrooms 7 en suite from s£40 d£55

Wales

VALE OF GLAMORGAN

EAST ABERTHAW
Map 03 ST06

Pick of the Pubs

Blue Anchor Inn
CF62 3DD ☎ 01446 750329 🖥 01446 750077
See Pick of the Pubs on page 639

MONKNASH
Map 03 SS97

The Plough & Harrow 🍺
CF71 7QQ ☎ 01656 890209
e-mail: pugs@publive.com
In a peaceful country setting, on the edge of a small village with views across the fields to the Bristol Channel, this low, state-roofed building was originally built as the chapter house of a monastery, although it has been a pub for 500 of its 600-year existence. Expect an atmospheric interior, open fires, an excellent choice of real ale on tap, and home-cooked food using fresh local ingredients.
OPEN: 12-12 **BAR MEALS:** Lunch served: all week 12-2 Av main course £5 **RESTAURANT:** Dinner served: Mon-Fri 6-9 Av 3 course à la carte £10 **BREWERY/COMPANY:** Free House
PRINCIPAL BEERS: Greene King Abbot, Shepherds Neame Spitfire, Timothy Taylor Landlord, Bass. **FACILITIES:** Garden: Food served outside **NOTES:** Parking 30

PENMARK
Map 03 ST06

Six Bells Inn
CF62 3BP ☎ 01446 710229 🖥 01446 710671
Dir: M4 J33 take A4045,follow signs for 'Cardiff Wales airport' then 'Penmark'
Dating from 1623, this pub has a distinctive Norman archway and takes its name from the bells in the church opposite. Ideally located for Cardiff Wales Airport.

ST HILARY
Map 03 ST07

Pick of the Pubs

The Bush Inn 🍺
CF71 7DP ☎ 01446 772745
Dir: S of A48, E of Cowbridge
In the heart of the Vale nestles the picturesque village of St Hilary, with its 12th-century church and thatched cottages. It is also the home of this 16th-century thatched pub, which has an inglenook fireplace, and an unusual spiral staircase. A typical restaurant menu offers tournedos Rossini, breast of duck with caramelised blackberry and kumquat sauce, rack of Welsh lamb, and goats' cheese and red pesto cappelletti. Very popular puddings. There are also sandwiches and salads in the bar.
OPEN: 11.30-11 (Sun 12-10.30) **BAR MEALS:** Lunch served: all week Dinner served: all week 12-2.30 6.45-9.30 Av main course £5.50 **RESTAURANT:** Lunch served: all week 12-2.30 Dinner served: Mon-Sat 6.45-9.30 Av 3 course à la carte £16.50 Av 3 course fixed price £10.95 **BREWERY/COMPANY:** Punch Taverns **PRINCIPAL BEERS:** Hancocks HB, Greene King Old Speckled Hen, Interbrew Worthington Bitter & Bass.
FACILITIES: Children welcome Garden: Beer garden, food served outdoors **NOTES:** Parking 60

SIGINGSTONE
Map 03 SS97

Victoria Inn
CF71 7LP ☎ 01446 773943
e-mail: mail@victoriainn.plus.com
Dir: Off the B4270 between Llantwit Major and Cowbridge
With an upstairs restaurant and a downstairs lounge, this quiet village inn is decorated with old photographs and prints, and stocked with a fine selection of malt whiskies and good Welsh ales.
OPEN: 11-3 6.30-11 **BAR MEALS:** Lunch served: all week Dinner served: all week 11.45-2 6.30-9.30 Av main course £6.95
RESTAURANT: Lunch served: Sun 12-2 Dinner served: Tues-Sat 6.30-9.30 Av 3 course à la carte £13.95 Av 2 course fixed price £8.95
BREWERY/COMPANY: Free House **PRINCIPAL BEERS:** Tomos Watkins Best Bitter, OSB, Whoosh, Merlin Stout.
FACILITIES: Children welcome Garden: Patio, Food served outside **NOTES:** Parking 60

WREXHAM

HANMER
Map 08 SJ43

Hanmer Arms 🛏 🍺
SY13 3DE ☎ 01948 830532 🖥 01948 830740
e-mail: enquiries@thehamnerarms.co.uk
Dir: Between Wrexham & Whitchurch on A539, off A525

Originally built in the 16th century, this comfortably furnished village hotel is centrally placed in the shadow of St Chad's church. The village bar serves a full range of traditional hand-drawn beers, whilst the first floor restaurant offers commanding views of the Berwyn Mountains and the Cheshire plain. There's a full à la carte menu, plus a daily hot and cold buffet, traditional carvery and themed evening dishes in the Victuals Bar.
OPEN: 12-11 **BAR MEALS:** Lunch served: all week Dinner served: all week 12-10 Av main course £6.95 **RESTAURANTS:** 12-9.30 Av 3 course £10.95 **BREWERY/COMPANY:** Free House
PRINCIPAL BEERS: Carlsberg-Tetley Bitter, Calders
FACILITIES: Children welcome, Dogs allowed Garden: Beer garden **NOTES:** Parking 70 **ROOMS:** 26 en suite from s£45 d£55

> **Restaurant and Bar Meal times indicate the times when food is available. Last orders may be approximately 30 minutes before the times stated.**

Wales

OPEN: 11–11 (Sun 12–10.30)
BAR MEALS: L served Mon–Fri.
D served Mon–Fri. 12–2 6–8
RESTAURANT: L served Sun.
D served Mon–Sat. 12–2.30 7–9.30
BREWERY/COMPANY: FREE HOUSE
PRINCIPAL BEERS: Brains Buckleys Best, Theakston Old Peculiar, Wadworth 6X, Interbrew Boddingtons Bitter, Marston's Bitter
FACILITIES: Children Welcome
NOTES: Parking 70

Blue Anchor Inn

Rumour has it that this pub, which was established over 700 years ago in the 1380s, still retains a secret passage down to the shore, where wreckers and smugglers formerly roamed the wild coastline that looks out across the Bristol Channel. Real ales and good food welcome the lucky traveller.

EAST ABERTHAW
VALE OF GLAMORGAN   CF62 3DD
☎ 01446 750329
🖹 01446 750077

Built of local stone with tiny windows in the ancient style and thickly thatched, the interior is a warren of small rooms separated by thick walls, and with low, beamed ceilings. There are a number of open fires and a large inglenook built in the time when the warmest place to sit was in the fireplace. Outside, ivy softens the grey stone and brightly coloured hanging baskets and flower-tubs grace the frontage in summer. There are also tables and benches for summer use on the courtyard and terrace. There is a path that leads the short distance to the estuary. A number of regular real ales and a couple of guest ales are always available on the handpumps. The food on offer varies from tradi-

tional cottage pie, spicy mince beef kebabs on a tomato and garlic salsa or baked supreme of chicken to a couscous timbale of fresh prawns starter and a sesame glazed breast of duck on the evening menu. Grilled fillet of Grimsby cod with a crunchy peanut crust and baked asparagus and mushroom cheesecake are alternatives while chocolate brioche bread and butter pudding or traditional apple pie with cream are good ways to round a meal off.

LLANARMON DYFFRYN CEIRIOG   Map 08 SJ13

The Hand Hotel NEW
LL20 7LD ☎ 01691 600666 📠 01691 600262
e-mail: handllandc@netscapeonline.co.uk
Darkened beams, open fireplaces and old stone walls
characterise this inviting hotel, tucked away in the twisting
Ceiriog valley. This is a prime centre for walking and pony
trekking, and there are glorious views from the hotel's south
facing beer garden. The menus reflect traditional British tastes,
from lowly bangers and mash or home-made fish cakes,
through lemon sole or vegetarian casserole, to a splendid
venison rump. Finish with cider apple Charlotte or lemon tart.
BREWERY/COMPANY: Free House No credit cards

Pick of the Pubs

The West Arms Hotel ★ ★ ◉ 🐷
LL20 7LD ☎ 01691 600665 📠 01691 600622
e-mail: gowestarms@aol.com
Dir: *Leave A483 at Chirk, follow signs for Ceiriog Valley B4500, hotel
is 11m from Chirk*
Standing at the head of the long, winding Ceiriog Valley,
this 16th-century shooting inn is still very much used by
shooting parties throughout the winter. The Berwyn Hills
form the backdrop to the inn, with its old-world
atmosphere of traditional slate floors, low beamed
ceilings and vast inglenook fireplaces. This has been the
local hostelry for 400 years, and the local's bar is still just
that. But there's a warm welcome for visitors, and the
most popular pastimes include touring, hill walking or
fishing on the hotel's private stretch of river. In the
summer months, light bar lunches are also served in the
hotel's pretty riverside garden. Dinner in the cosy dining
room is an intimate affair at fixed prices, and the short
nightly menu might feature Welsh black beef, Cornish
plaice or baked guinea fowl, followed by Grand Marnier
soufflé, or warm apple and frangipane tart.
OPEN: 8am–11 **BAR MEALS:** Lunch served: all week Dinner
served: all week 12-2 7-9 Av main course £7.95
RESTAURANT: Lunch served: Sun 12-2 Dinner served: all week
7-9 Av 3 course fixed price £24.95
BREWERY/COMPANY: Free House
PRINCIPAL BEERS: Interbrew Flowers IPA, Boddingtons Bitter.
FACILITIES: Children welcome Garden: Food served outside,
spectacular views Dogs allowed (water, 3 kennels)
NOTES: Parking 30 **ROOMS:** 15 bedrooms 15 en suite from
s£52.50 d£95

> **Room prices show the minimum double
> and single rates charged.
> Room rates in hotels and B&B's
> often vary depending on the facilities,
> so be sure to check prices with the
> establishment before booking.**

MARFORD   Map 08 SJ35

Trevor Arms Hotel ♀
LL12 8TA ☎ 01244 570436 📠 01244 570273
Dir: *off A483 onto B5102 then R onto B5445 into Marford*

Haunted 17th-century coaching inn, that was once the scene
of public hangings. Takes its name from Lord Trevor of
Trevallin, who was killed in a duel. This grisly past
notwithstanding, the Trevallin is a charming inn, offering a
varied menu. This may include seared tuna steak with hot
salad, deep-fried battered black pudding on a bacon and
onion mash, grilled supreme of chicken on a casserole of
sweet potatoes and mushrooms, poached fillet of salmon with
roasted cherry tomatoes and asparagus, or a range of specials
from the changing blackboard.
OPEN: 11-11 **BAR MEALS:** Lunch served: all week Dinner served:
all week 11-11 Av main course £6 **RESTAURANT:** Lunch served: all
week Dinner served: all week 11-11 Av 3 course à la carte £15
BREWERY/COMPANY: Scottish Courage
PRINCIPAL BEERS: Greenalls, Courage Directors, Theakstons Old
Peculier, Old Speckled Hen. **FACILITIES:** Children welcome Garden:
patio, beer garden, Food served outside **NOTES:** Parking 70
ROOMS: 29 bedrooms 29 en suite from s£38 d£39.50

WREXHAM   Map 08 SJ35

Pant-yr-Ochain ♀ NEW
Old Wrexham Rd, Gresford LL12 8TY
☎ 01978 853525 📠 01978 853505
The 'Hollow of Lamentation' is a singularly inappropriate
name for this flourishing pub, comprising a 19th-century hall
and much older farmhouse dating from the 16th-century. A
wide ranging menu encompasses sandwiches, ploughman's
and dishes of Welsh black rump steak with creamed spinach,
roast peppers, sauté potatoes and peppercorn sauce, or fillet
of red bream with smoked haddock and spinach risotto.
Interesting vegetarian options include chargrilled aubergine
and roast parsnip timbale with creamy mushroom fricassée.
OPEN: 12-11 (Sun 12-10.30) Closed: 25 Dec **BAR MEALS:** Lunch
served: all week Dinner served: all week 12-9.30 Av main course £7.95
PRINCIPAL BEERS: Timothy Tailor Landlord, Interbrew Flowers
Original & Boddingtons, Shepherd Neame Spitfire Premium Ale,
Fuller's London Pride. **FACILITIES:** Children welcome Garden:
Food served outdoors **NOTES:** Parking 80

continued

Wales

Need to find the perfect place?

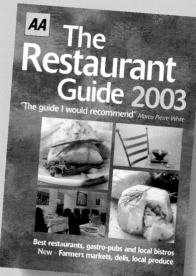

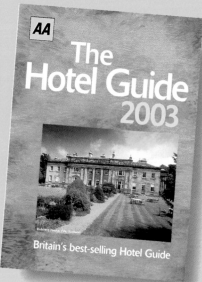

Pick of the Pubs

Pick of the Pubs

This is a list of almost 600 of the top pubs in Britain, these have been selected by the editor and highlighted in the guide with longer descriptions and a tinted background.

Bedfordshire

The Chequers, KEYSOE	24
The Five Bells, STANBRIDGE	25-26

Berkshire

The Bell Inn, ALDWORTH	26
The Crown, BURCHETT'S GREEN	28
Bel and The Dragon, COOKHAM	29
Chequers Inn Brasserie, COOKHAM DEAN	29
Uncle Tom's Cabin, COOKHAM DEAN	29
The Horns, CRAZIES HILL	29
The Pot Kiln, FRILSHAM	30
The Swan Inn, HUNGERFORD	32
The Dundas Arms, KINTBURY	31
Bird In Hand Country Inn, KNOWL HILL	33
The Red House, MARSH BENHAM	33-4
The Yew Tree Inn, NEWBURY	34
The George & Dragon, SWALLOWFIELD	36
The Bladebone Inn, THATCHAM	36
Harrow Inn, WEST ILSLEY	37
Rose & Crown, WINKFIELD	37
The Winterbourne Arms, WINTERBOURNE	38
The Royal Oak Hotel, YATTENDON	38-9

Buckinghamshire

Bottle & Glass, AYLESBURY	40
The Royal Standard of England, BEACONSFIELD	40
Crooked Billet, BLETCHLEY	43
The Ivy House, CHALFONT ST GILES	44
The Red Lion, CHENIES	44
The Crown, CUDDINGTON	45-6
The Walnut Tree, FAWLEY	46
The Dinton Hermit, FORD	47
The Polecat Inn, GREAT MISSENDEN	48
The Rising Sun, GREAT MISSENDEN	48
The Green Dragon, HADDENHAM	49
The Stag & Huntsman Inn, HAMBLEDEN	48
Mole & Chicken, LONG CRENDON	50
The Angel Inn, LONG CRENDON	50
The White Hart, PRESTON BISSETT	50
The Frog, SKIRMETT	51
The Bull & Butcher, TURVILLE	52
The George & Dragon Hotel, WEST WYCOMBE	52
Chequers Inn, WOOBURN COMMON	53

Cambridgeshire

The White Hart, BYTHORN	53
The Black Horse, ELTON	55
The Anchor Inn, ELY	55
The Chequers, FOWLMERE	56
Crown & Punchbowl, HORNINGSEA	58
The Old Bridge Hotel, HUNTINGDON	58
The Pheasant Inn, KEYSTON	59
The Three Horseshoes, MADINGLEY	59
The Queen's Head, NEWTON	59
The Bell Inn, STILTON	60

Cheshire

The Grosvenor Arms, ALDFORD	61
The Bhurtpore Inn, ASTON	62
The Dysart Arms, BUNBURY	63
The Pheasant Inn, BURWARDSLEY	63
The Cholmondeley Arms, CHOLMONDELEY	65
The Dog Inn, KNUTSFORD	66
The Swettenham Arms, SWETTENHAM	68

Cornwall & Isles of Scilly

Trengilly Wartha Inn, CONSTANTINE	72-3
The Halzephron Inn, GUNWALLOE	74-5
Shipwright Arms, HELFORD	75
Royal Oak Inn, LOSTWITHIEL	77
Godolphin Arms, MARAZION	78
The Old Coastguard Hotel, MOUSEHOLE	79
The Pandora Inn, MYLOR BRIDGE	80
The Roseland Inn, PHILLEIGH	81
Port Gaverne Hotel, PORT GAVERNE	82
The Sloop Inn, ST IVES	83-4
The Rising Sun, ST MAWES	84
The Victory Inn, ST MAWES	85
The Port William, TINTAGEL	86
The Springer Spaniel, TREBURLEY	87
The New Inn, TRESCO	87-8
The Gurnards Head Hotel, ZENNOR	89

Cumbria

The Drunken Duck Inn, AMBLESIDE	89
The Royal Oak Inn, APPLEBY-IN-WESTMORLAND	92
Tufton Arms Hotel, APPLEBY-IN-WESTMORLAND	90
The Wheatsheaf at Beetham, BEETHAM	95
The Cavendish Arms, CARTMEL	96
The Punch Bowl Inn, CROSTHWAITE	96-7
The Britannia Inn, ELTERWATER	97
Bower House Inn, ESKDALE GREEN	98
Queens Head Hotel, HAWKSHEAD	99-100
The Horse & Farrier Inn, KESWICK	101
The Kings Head, KESWICK	102
Swan Hotel & Country Inn, KESWICK	101
Pheasant Inn, KIRKBY LONSDALE	104
Snooty Fox Tavern, KIRKBY LONSDALE	103
Three Shires Inn, LITTLE LANGDALE	106
Black Swan Hotel, RAVENSTONEDALE	107
The Fat Lamb Country Inn, RAVENSTONEDALE	107-8
Queens Head Inn, TIRRIL	110
Queens Head Hotel, TROUTBECK	110-1
Farmers Arms, ULVERSTON	111
Brackenrigg Inn, WATERMILLOCK	112
The Yanwath Gate Inn, YANWATH	113

Pick of the Pubs

Pick of the Pubs

Pick of the Pubs

Index of Pub Walks

Pubs with AA Inspected Accommodation

This is a list of the pubs in this guide that have Diamond or Star awards for accommodation. A full listing of AA B&B accommodation can be found in the AA Bed & Breakfast Guide, while Hotels are listed in our AA Hotel Guide. See page 9 for a full explanation of the AA's awards for accommodation.

Bedfordshire
The Old George Hotel SILSOE ♦♦ 25

Berkshire
The Swan Inn HUNGERFORD ♦♦♦♦ 32
The Royal Oak Hotel YATTENDON ★ ★ 38-9

Buckinghamshire
Chequers Inn
  WOOBURN COMMON ★ ★ 53

Cambridgeshire
The Anchor Inn ELY ♦♦♦♦ 55
The Prince of Wales HILTON ♦♦♦♦ 57
The Old Bridge Hotel
  HUNTINGDON ★ ★ ★ 58
The Bell Inn STILTON ★ ★ ★ 60

Cheshire
The Pheasant Inn BURWARDSLEY ★ ★ 63
The Cholmondeley Arms
  CHOLMONDELEY ♦♦♦ 65
The Egerton Arms Hotel
  CONGLETON ♦♦♦ 64
Alvanley Arms Hotel
  COTEBROOK ♦♦♦♦ 64
The Dog Inn KNUTSFORD ♦♦♦♦ 66

Cornwall & Isles of Scilly
The Wellington Hotel BOSCASTLE ★ ★ 70
Trengilly Wartha Inn
  CONSTANTINE ★ ★ 72-3
Coombe Barton Inn
  CRACKINGTON HAVEN ♦♦♦ 73
The Badger Inn LELANT ♦♦♦♦ 77
Ship Inn LOSTWITHIEL ♦♦♦♦ 78
Godolphin Arms MARAZION ★ ★ 78
The Ship Inn MEVAGISSEY ♦♦♦ 79
Ship Inn MOUSEHOLE ♦♦♦ 80
The Old Coastguard Hotel
  MOUSEHOLE ★ ★ 79
Jubilee Inn PELYNT ★ ★ 80
The Victoria Inn PERRANUTHNOE ♦♦♦ 81
Port Gaverne Hotel
  PORT GAVERNE ★ ★ 82
The Crooked Inn SALTASH ♦♦♦♦ 85
The Weary Friar Inn SALTASH ♦♦♦♦ 86
The Old Success Inn SENNEN ★ ★ 86
Driftwood Spars Hotel ST AGNES ♦♦♦ 82-3
The Sloop Inn ST IVES ♦♦♦♦ 83-4
The Wellington Hotel
  ST JUST [NEAR LAND'S END] ♦♦♦ 84
The White Hart ST KEVERNE ♦♦♦ 84
The Rising Sun ST MAWES ★ ★ 84
The Falcon Inn ST MAWGAN ♦♦♦♦ 85
The Farmers Arms ST MERRYN ♦♦♦ 85

The Port William TINTAGEL ♦♦♦♦ 86
Tintagel Arms Hotel TINTAGEL ♦♦♦♦ 86-7
The Edgcumbe Arms TORPOINT ♦♦♦ 87
The New Inn TRESCO ★ ★ 87-8
Swan Hotel WADEBRIDGE ♦♦♦♦ 89

Cumbria
Drunken Duck Inn AMBLESIDE ♦♦♦♦ 89
White Lion Hotel AMBLESIDE ♦♦♦ 89
The Royal Oak Inn
  APPLEBY-IN-WESTMORLAND ★ ★ 92
Tufton Arms Hotel
  APPLEBY-IN-WESTMORLAND ★ ★ ★ 90
The Queen's Head ASKHAM ♦♦♦ 90
Blacksmiths Arms BRAMPTON ♦♦♦ 94
Bridge Hotel BUTTERMERE ★ ★ 96
The Trout Hotel
  COCKERMOUTH ★ ★ ★ 96
The Britannia Inn ELTERWATER ★ 97
Bower House Inn ESKDALE GREEN ★ ★ 98
The Sun Inn HAWKSHEAD ♦♦♦♦ 100
Queens Head Hotel
  HAWKSHEAD ★ ★ 99-100
The Kings Head KESWICK ★ ★ ★ 102
Pheasant Inn KIRKBY LONSDALE ★ ★ 104
Three Shires Inn
  LITTLE LANGDALE ★ ★ 106
Kirkstile Inn LOWESWATER ♦♦♦♦ 105
The Fat Lamb Country Inn
  RAVENSTONEDALE ★ ★ 107-8
Queens Head Hotel
  TROUTBECK ♦♦♦♦ 110-1
Mortal Man Hotel TROUTBECK ★ ★ 110
Brackenrigg Inn WATERMILLOCK ♦♦♦ 112
Eagle & Child Inn WINDERMERE 113

Derbyshire
The Green Man ASHBOURNE ♦♦♦♦ 115
Dog & Partridge Country Inn
  ASHBOURNE ★ ★ 115
The Monsal Head Hotel BAKEWELL ★ ★ 116
The Rutland Arms Hotel
  BAKEWELL ★ ★ ★ 116
Yorkshire Bridge Inn BAMFORD ★ ★ 116
The Queen Anne BUXTON ♦♦♦ 118-9
Miners Arms EYAM ♦♦♦ 120
The Bulls Head Inn FOOLOW ♦♦♦♦ 120
The Maynard Arms
  GRINDLEFORD ★ ★ ★ 121
Millstone Inn HATHERSAGE ♦♦♦♦ 121
The Plough Inn HATHERSAGE ♦♦♦♦ 121

Devon
The Rising Sun ASHBURTON ♦♦♦♦ 124
Sloop Inn BANTHAM ♦♦♦ 126
The Masons Arms BRANSCOMBE ★ ★ 127
Three Crowns Hotel CHAGFORD ★ ★ 129

Pubs with AA Inspected Accommodation

Pubs with AA Inspected Accommodation

Pubs with AA Inspected Accommodation

SCOTLAND

Argyll & Bute

Loch Melfort Hotel ARDUAINE ★ ★ ★	566
Cairnbaan Hotel & Restaurant	
LOCHGILPHEAD ★ ★ ★	567
Creggans Inn STRACHUR ★ ★ ★	568
Victoria Hotel TARBERT ◆◆◆◆	570
Polfearn Hotel TAYNUILT ★ ★	570

Dumfries & Galloway

Douglas Arms Hotel	
CASTLE DOUGLAS ★ ★	574
Creebridge House Hotel	
NEWTON STEWART ★ ★	575

East Ayrshire

The Kirkton Inn DALRYMPLE ◆◆◆	576

Fife

Burntisland Sands Hotel	
BURNTISLAND ◆◆◆	578
The Hideaway Lodge & Restaurant	
DUNFERMLINE ★ ★	578
Town House Hotel MARKINCH ◆◆◆◆	579

Highland

Ardvasar Hotel ARDVASAR ★ ★	599
Dalrachney Lodge Hotel	
CARRBRIDGE ★ ★ ★	580
Achilty Hotel CONTIN ★ ★	583
Dundonnell House	
DUNDONNELL ★ ★ ★	583
Moorings Hotel FORT WILLIAM ★ ★ ★	584
Hotel Eilean Iarmain	
ISLE ORNSAY, Skye ★ ★	599
Onich Hotel ONICH ★ ★ ★	586
Shieldaig Bar SHIELDAIG ★	587-8

Perth & Kinross

Nivingston House CLEISH ★ ★ ★	589
The Killiecrankie Hotel	
KILLIECRANKIE ★ ★	590
Lomond Country Inn	
KINNESSWOOD ★ ★	590-92
The Muirs Inn Kinross KINROSS ◆◆◆	592
Moulin Hotel PITLOCHRY ★ ★	592
Gartwhinzean Hotel POWMILL ★ ★ ★	593

Scottish Borders

Abbotsford Arms Hotel	
GALASHIELS ★ ★	593
Kingsknowes GALASHIELS ★ ★ ★	594
Traquair Arms Hotel	
INNERLEITHEN ◆◆◆	594
Queens Head Hotel KELSO ★ ★	594
Buccleuch Arms Hotel	
ST BOSWELLS ★ ★	595
Wheatsheaf Hotel SWINTON ◆◆◆◆	595
Tibbie Shiels Inn	
TIBBIE SHIELS INN ◆◆◆	595

Stirling

Monachyle Mhor	
BALQUHIDDER ★ ★	596
Ben More Lodge Hotel	
CRIANLARICH ◆◆◆	596

WALES

Carmarthenshire

The Royal Oak Inn	
RHANDIRMWYN ◆◆◆	605

Ceredigion

Webley Hotel CARDIGAN ◆◆◆	605

Conwy

Ty Gwyn Hotel	
BETWS-Y-COED ◆◆◆◆	606
Cobdens Hotel CAPEL CURIG ★ ★	606
The Groes Inn CONWY ★ ★ ★	606
White Horse Inn LLANRWST ◆◆◆◆	607

Gwynedd

Dovey Inn ABERDYFI ★ ★	611
Penhelig Arms Hotel ABERDYFI ★ ★	611
George III Hotel DOLGELLAU ★ ★	612

Isle of Anglesey

Ye Olde Bulls Head Inn	
BEAUMARIS ★ ★	615
Holland Hotel LLANFACHRAETH ◆◆◆	615

Monmouthshire

Pantrhiwgoch Hotel & Riverside Restaurant	
ABERGAVENNY ★ ★	616
The Sloop Inn LLANDOGO ◆◆◆	618
The Bell at Skenfrith SKENFRITH ★ ★ ★	619

Pembrokeshire

Trewern Arms NEVERN ★ ★	623

Powys

The Usk Inn BRECON ◆◆◆◆	626
The Talkhouse CAERSWS ◆◆◆◆◆	626
Gliffaes Country House Hotel	
|CRICKHOWELL ★ ★ ★	628
The Bear CRICKHOWELL ★ ★ ★	629
Star Inn DYLIFE ◆◆◆	630
The Famous Old Black Lion	
HAY-ON-WYE ★ ★	632
Cain Valley Hotel LLANFYLLIN ★ ★	633
Dragon Hotel MONTGOMERY ★ ★	634
Castle Inn TALGARTH ◆◆◆	636

Wrexham

The West Arms Hotel LLANARMON	
DYFFRYN CEIRIOG ★ ★	640

How to Find a Pub in the Atlas Section

Pubs are located in the gazetteer under the name of the nearest town or village. If a pub is in a small village or rural area, it may appear under a town within fives miles of its actual location. The black dots and town names shown in the atlas refer to the gazetteer location in the guide. Please use the directions in the pub entry to find the pub on foot or by car. If directions are not given, or are not clear, please telephone the pub for details.

Key to County Map

The county map shown here will help you identify the counties within each country. You can look up each county in the guide using the county names at the top of each page. Towns featured in the guide use the atlas pages and index following this map.

England
1 Bedfordshire
2 Berkshire
3 Bristol
4 Buckinghamshire
5 Cambridgeshire
6 Greater Manchester
7 Herefordshire
8 Hertfordshire
9 Leicestershire
10 Northamptonshire
11 Nottinghamshire
12 Rutland
13 Staffordshire
14 Warwickshire
15 West Midlands
16 Worcestershire

Scotland
17 City of Glasgow
18 Clackmannanshire
19 East Ayrshire
20 East Dunbartonshire
21 East Renfrewshire
22 Perth & Kinross
23 Renfrewshire
24 South Lanarkshire
25 West Dunbartonshire

Wales
26 Blaenau Gwent
27 Bridgend
28 Caerphilly
29 Denbighshire
30 Flintshire
31 Merthyr Tydfil
32 Monmouthshire
33 Neath Port Talbot
34 Newport
35 Rhondda Cynon Taff
36 Torfaen
37 Vale of Glamorgan
38 Wrexham

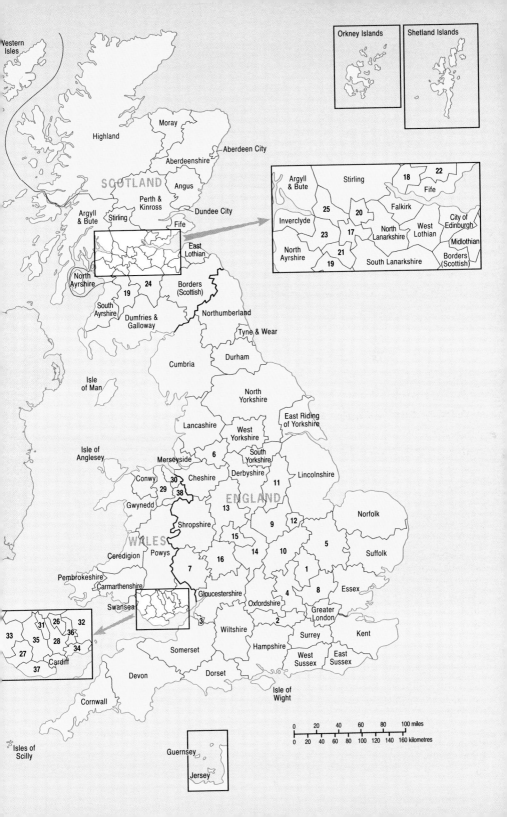

Orkney Islands

Shetland Islands

Western Isles

Highland

Moray

Aberdeenshire

Aberdeen City

SCOTLAND

Angus

Perth & Kinross

Dundee City

Argyll & Bute

Stirling

Fife

East Lothian

North Ayrshire

19

24

Borders (Scottish)

South Ayrshire

Dumfries & Galloway

Northumberland

Tyne & Wear

Cumbria

Durham

Isle of Man

North Yorkshire

Lancashire

East Riding of Yorkshire

West Yorkshire

Isle of Anglesey

Merseyside

6

South Yorkshire

Conwy

30

Cheshire

Derbyshire

Lincolnshire

29

38

11

Gwynedd

ENGLAND

13

Shropshire

9

12

Norfolk

15

Ceredigion

Powys

14

10

5

Suffolk

WALES

16

Pembrokeshire

7

1

Carmarthenshire

Gloucestershire

8

Essex

Swansea

3

Oxfordshire

Greater London

Wiltshire

2

4

Somerset

Surrey

Kent

Hampshire

West Sussex

East Sussex

Devon

Dorset

Isle of Wight

Cornwall

Isles of Scilly

Guernsey

Jersey

Scotland inset:

Argyll & Bute

Stirling

18

22

Fife

Inverclyde

25

20

Falkirk

City of Edinburgh

23

17

North Lanarkshire

West Lothian

Midlothian

North Ayrshire

21

South Lanarkshire

Borders (Scottish)

19

Wales inset:

31

26

32

33

35

36

27

28

34

37

Cardiff

0   20   40   60   80   100 miles

0 20 40 60 80 100 120 140 160 kilometres

How can I get away without the hassle of finding a place to stay?

Booking a place to stay can be a time-consuming process. You choose a place you like, only to find it's fully booked. That means going back to the drawing board again. Why not ask us to find the place that best suits your needs? No fuss, no worries and no booking fee.

Whatever your preference, we have the place for you. From a rustic farm cottage to a smart city centre hotel - we have them all. Choose from around 8,000 quality rated hotels and B&Bs in Great Britain and Ireland.

Hotel Booking Service

0870 50 50 505
accommodation@aabookings.com
www.theAA.com

KEY TO ATLAS

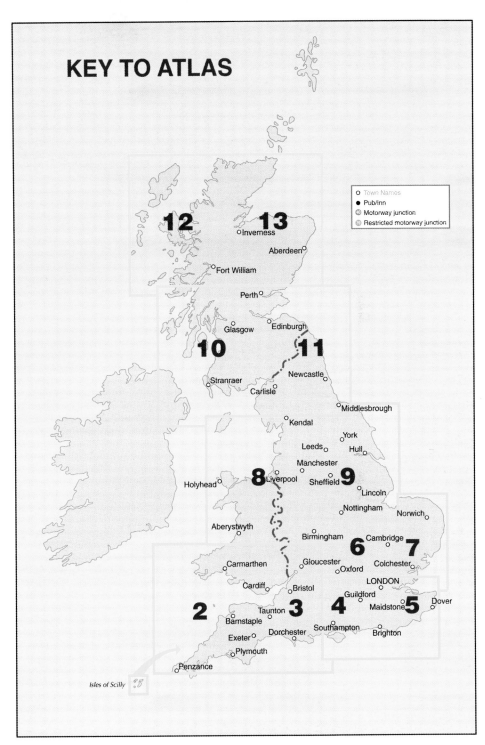

O Town Names
● Pub/Inn
⊕ Motorway junction
⊜ Restricted motorway junction

12 **13**
Inverness

Aberdeen

Fort William

Perth

Glasgow Edinburgh
10 **11**
Stranraer Newcastle
Carlisle
Middlesbrough
Kendal
York
Leeds Hull
Manchester
8 Liverpool Sheffield **9**
Holyhead Lincoln
Nottingham Norwich
Aberystwyth
Birmingham Cambridge
6 **7**
Carmarthen Gloucester Colchester
Oxford
Cardiff Bristol LONDON
Guildford
2 Taunton **3** **4** Maidstone **5** Dover
Barnstaple Brighton
Exeter Dorchester Southampton
Plymouth
Penzance

Isles of Scilly

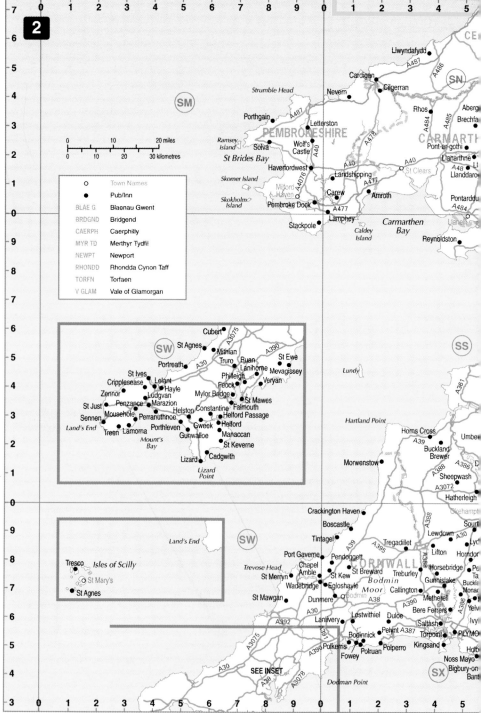

2

For continuation pages refer to numbered arrows

Map legend:

○	Town Names
●	Pub/Inn
BLAE G	Blaenau Gwent
BRDGND	Bridgend
CAERPH	Caerphilly
MYR TD	Merthyr Tydfil
NEWPT	Newport
RHONDD	Rhondda Cynon Taff
TORFN	Torfaen
V GLAM	Vale of Glamorgan

Scale:
0   10   20 miles
0   10   20   30 kilometres

Place labels on map:

Llwyndafydd, Cardigan, Cilgerran, SN, Strumble Head, Nevern, Rhos, Aberg, Brechfa, Porthgain, Letterston, CARMARTH, Pont-ar-gothi, PEMBROKESHIRE, Ramsey Island, Wolf's Castle, Solva, Llanarthne, Ll, St Brides Bay, Haverfordwest, Landshipping, St Clears, A48, Llanddaro, Skomer Island, Milford Haven, Carew, Amroth, Pontarddu, Skokholm Island, Pembroke Dock, Lamphey, Carmarthen Bay, Llanelli, Stackpole, Caldey Island, Reynoldston

SM, SW, SS, SX

Cubert, St Agnes, Milhian, St Ewe, Truro, Ruan, Portreath, Lanihorne, Mevagissey, St Ives, Lelant, Philleigh, Veryan, Cripplesease, Hayle, Feock, Zennor, Ludgvan, Marazion, Mylor Bridge, St Just, Penzance, St Mawes, Sennen, Mousehole, Perranuthnoe, Helston, Constantine, Falmouth, Land's End, Treen, Lamorna, Porthleven, Gweek, Helford, Helford Passage, Mount's Bay, Gunwalloe, Manaccan, St Keverne, Lizard, Cadgwith, Lizard Point

Lundy, Hartland Point, Horns Cross, Umbe, Buckland Brewer, Morwenstow, Sheepwash, Hatherleigh, Crackington Haven, Okehampt, Boscastle, Sourt, Tintagel, Lewdown, Port Gaverne, Tregadillet, Lifton, Horndor, Pendoggett, St Breward, Treburley, Trevose Head, Chapel Amble, St Kew, Gunnislake, Buckla, St Merryn, Bodmin Moor, Callington, Monac, Wadebridge, Egloshayle, A38, Metherell, St Mawgan, Dunmere, Bodmin, Bere Ferrers, Yelv, Lanivery, Lostwithiel, Duloe, Saltash, Ivy, Bodinnick, Pelynt, Torpoint, PLYMO, Polkerris, Polruan, Polperro, Kingsand, Hotb, Fowey, Noss Mayo, Bigbury-on, Bant, SEE INSET, Dodman Point

Tresco, Isles of Scilly, St Mary's, St Agnes, Land's End

CORNWALL, CE

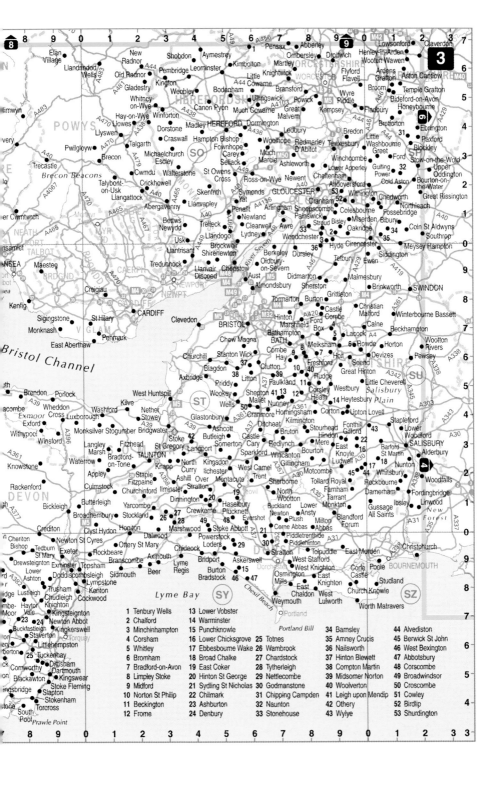

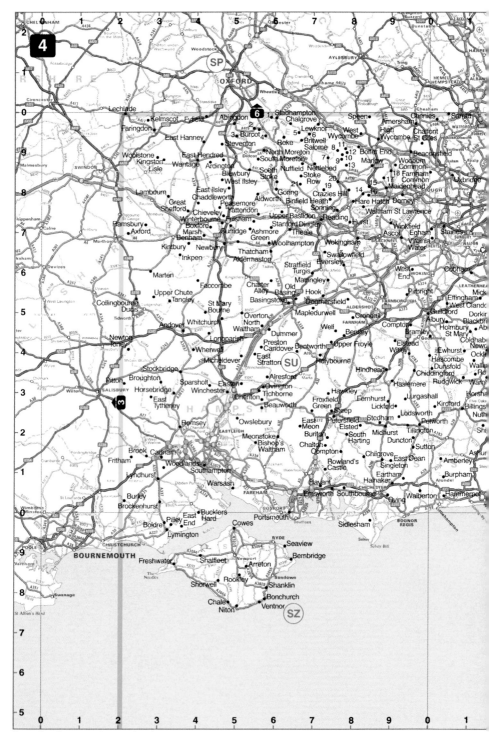

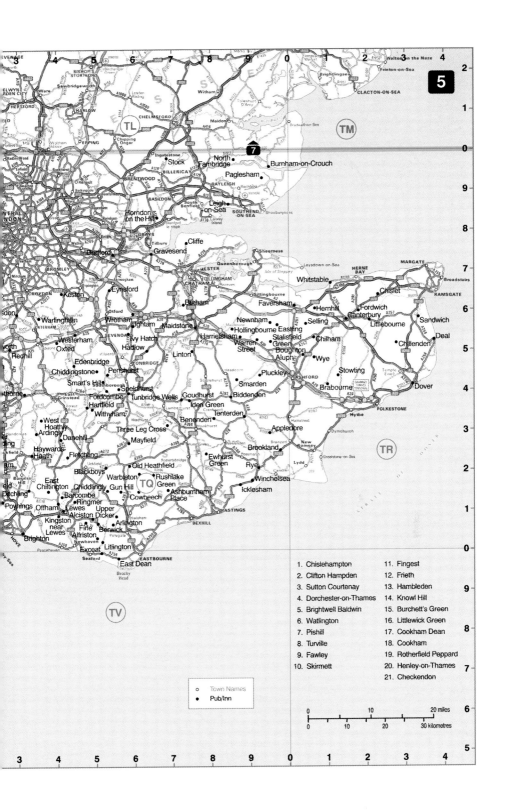

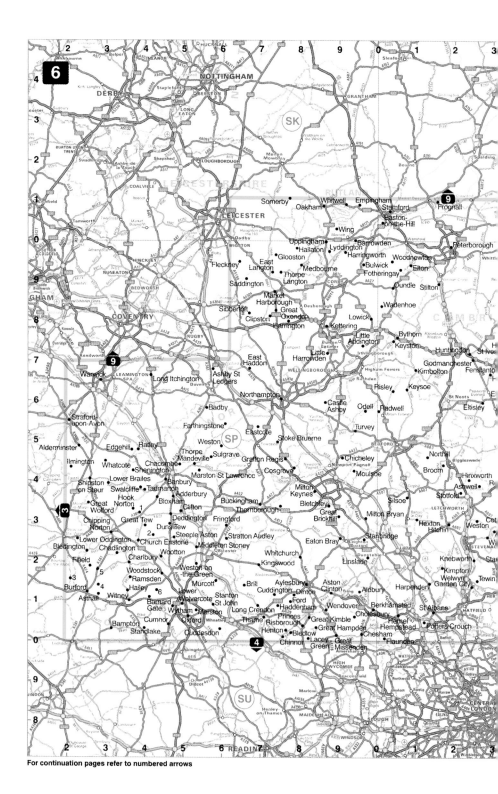

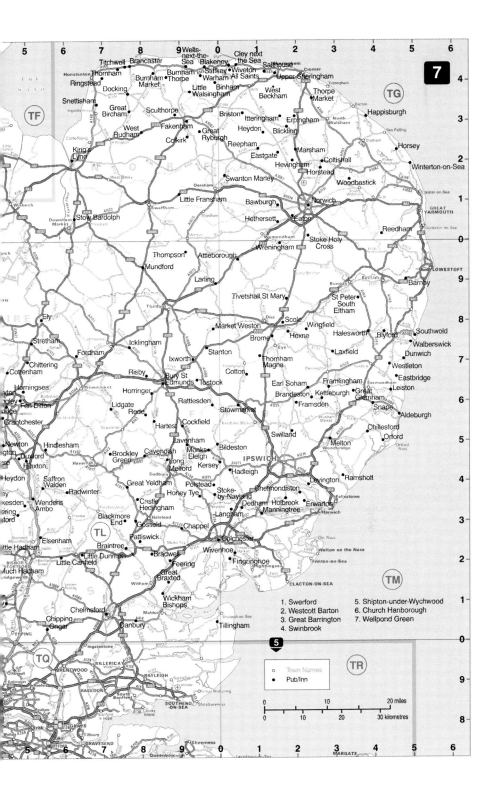

7

TG

TF

1. Swerford
2. Westcott Barton
3. Great Barrington
4. Swinbrook
5. Shipton-under-Wychwood
6. Church Hanborough
7. Wellpond Green

TL

TM

TR

TQ

o	Town Names	
•	Pub/Inn	

0   10   20 miles

0   10   20   30 kilometres

Titchwell Brancaster Wells-next-the-Sea Cley next the Sea Salthouse
Hunstanton Thornham Burnham Stiffkey Wiveton Cromer
Ringstead Burnham Thorpe Warham All Saints Upper Sheringham
Docking Burnham Market Little Walsingham Binham West Beckham Thorpe Market
Snettisham Great Bircham Sculthorpe Briston Itteringham Erpingham North Walsham Happisburgh
West Rudham Fakenham Great Ryburgh Heydon Blickling
King's Lynn Colkirk Reepham Marsham Horsey
Eastgate Hevingham Coltishall Winterton-on-Sea
Swanton Morley Horstead Woodbastick
Little Fransham Bawburgh Norwich
Stow Bardolph Hethersett Eaton Reedham
Ely Swanton Marley Wreningham Stoke Holy Cross
Thompson Attleborough LOWESTOFT
Mundford Barnby
Larling
Tivetshall St Mary St Peter South Eltham
Thetford Diss Southwold
Market Weston Scole Wingfield Walberswick
Stretham Brome Hoxne Halesworth Blyford Dunwich
Icklingham Stanton Laxfield Westleton
Fordham Thornham Magna Eastbridge
Risby Cotton Earl Soham Framlingham Leiston
Ixworth Bury St Edmunds Tostock Brandeston Kettleburgh Great Glemham Snape
Horninger Rattlesden Framsden Aldeburgh
Lidgate Stowmarket Chillesford
Rede Cockfield Swilland Melton Woodbridge Orford
Hartest Lavenham Bildeston IPSWICH
Newton Hindlesham Cavendish Monks Eleigh
Brockley Green Long Melford Kersey Hadleigh Levington Ramsholt
Saffron Walden Sudbury Felixstowe
Radwinter Great Yeldham Polstead Chelmondiston Enwarton
Wenden's Ambo Castle Hedingham Honey Tye Stoke-by-Nayland Dedham Holbrook
Blackmore End Halstead Langham Manningtree Harwich
Elsenham Gosfield Chappel
Little Dunmow Pattiswick Colchester Walton on the Naze
Braintree Bradwell Wivenhoe Fingringhoe Frinton-on-Sea
Little Canfield Feering CLACTON-ON-SEA
Great Braxted Witham
Chelmsford Wickham Bishops
Chipping Ongar Danbury Tillingham
Ingatestone
BILLERICAY
BRENTWOOD RAYLEIGH
BASILDON South Benfleet
SOUTHEND-ON-SEA
GRAVESEND
MARGATE

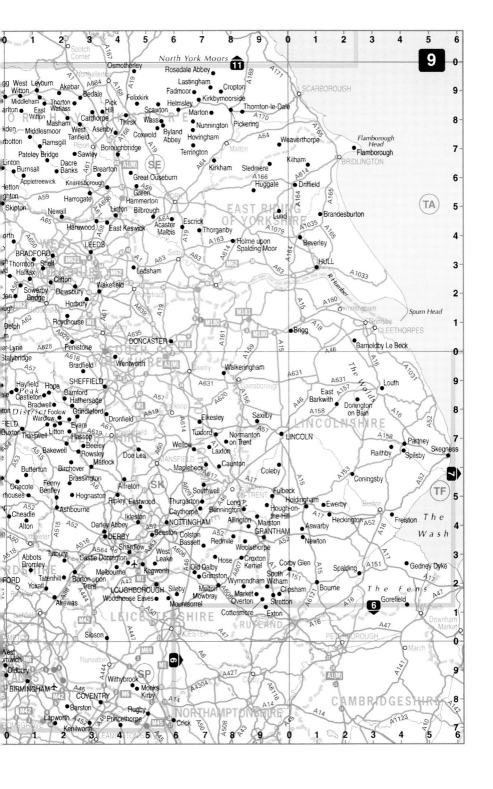

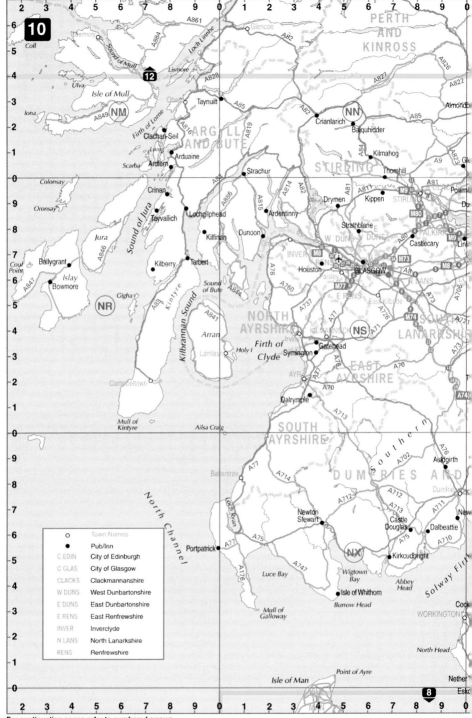

10

Coll
Tobermory
Sound of Mull
A861
Glencoe
A82
PERTH
AND
KINROSS
A884
Loch Linnhe
A826

Lismore
12
A828
A821
A822

Ulva
Isle of Mull
Obar
Taynuilt
A85
A827
Almondb

Iona
NM
A849
Firth of Lorne
A816
Crianlarich
NN
A85
A823
Gle

Colonsay
Clachan-Seil
Luing
A819
Balquhidder
A9

Scarba
Ardfern
Arduaine
ARGYLL
AND BUTE
Kilmahog

Oronsay
Crinan
Strachur
A814
A82
A81
Thornhill
A91

Jura
Tayvallich
A886
A815
Ardentinny
Drymen
Kippen
STIRLING
Powmi
Du

Coul
Point
Ballygrant
A846
Lochgilphead
Kilfinan
Dunoon
Strathblane
A80
Castlecary
M9
Linli

Islay
Bowmore
A83
Kilberry
Tarbert
Sound of Bute
Greenock
W DUNS
DUNS
GLASGOW
A8

NR
Gigha
Kilbrannan Sound
A841
Arran
Lamlash
Holy I
NORTH
AYRSHIRE
KILMARNOCK
Irvine
Gatehead
NS
A71
SOUTH
LANARKSHIRE

Campbeltown
Mull of
Kintyre
Ailsa Craig
Firth of
Clyde
Symington
AYR
EAST
AYRSHIRE
A70

Dalrymple
A713
A70

SOUTH
AYRSHIRE
Southern

Ballantrae
A77
A714
A712
A702
Auldgirth
A76

DUMFRIES
AND
Dumfries

Newton
Stewart
A713
A711
New

Portpatrick
A77
A75
Castle
Douglas
Dalbeattie
A710

NX
Kirkcudbright

Luce Bay
Wigtown
Bay
Abbey
Head
Solway Firt
Cock

North Channel
Isle of Whithorn
Burrow Head
WORKINGTON

Mull of
Galloway
North Head

○	Town Names
●	Pub/Inn
C EDIN	City of Edinburgh
C GLAS	City of Glasgow
CLACKS	Clackmannanshire
W DUNS	West Dunbartonshire
E DUNS	East Dunbartonshire
E RENS	East Renfrewshire
INVER	Inverclyde
N LANS	North Lanarkshire
RENS	Renfrewshire

Isle of Man
Point of Ayre
Nether
8
Esko

For continuation pages refer to numbered arrows
For continuation pages refer to numbered arrows

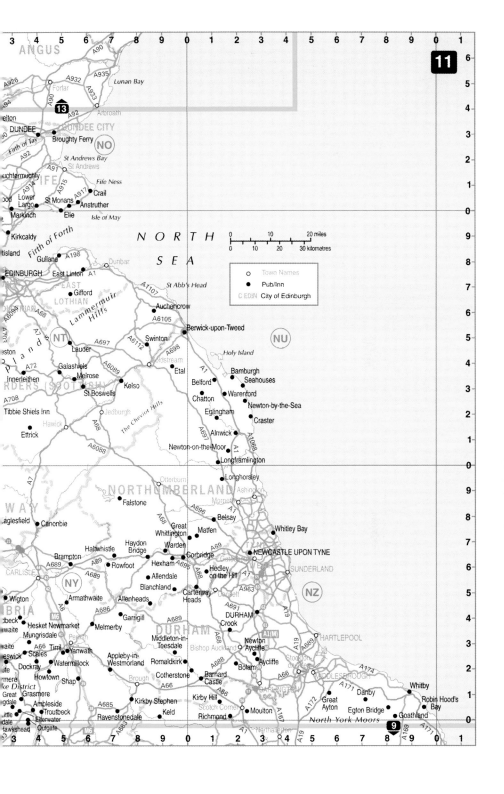

11

ANGUS

A926 A932 A935 Lunan Bay
Forfar
A933
A92
elton Arbroath
DUNDEE
Broughty Ferry NO
Firth of Tay
A92 St Andrews Bay
uchtermuchty A91 St Andrews
FIFE
Fife Ness
A914 A915 A917 Crail
od Lower St Monans Anstruther
Largo
Markinch Elie Isle of May
Kirkcaldy of Forth
Firth of Forth
tisland
Gullane A198 Dunbar
EDINBURGH East Linton A1
EAST
Gifford
LOTHIAN
Lammermuir Hills
A6105
A703 A697 A6112 Swinton
eston Lauder A698
NT
Galashiels A6089 Coldstream
Innerleithen Melrose Etal
A72 St Boswells Kelso
A708
Tibbie Shiels Inn Jedburgh
Hawick
Ettrick A68 The Cheviot Hills
A6088

NORTH
SEA

0   10   20 miles
0   10   20   30 kilometres

○ Town Names
● Pub/Inn
C EDIN City of Edinburgh

Berwick-upon-Tweed

NU

Holy Island

Bamburgh
Belford Seahouses
Warenford
Chatton Newton-by-the-Sea
Eglingham
A697 Craster
Alnwick A1068
Newton-on-the-Moor A1
Longframlington

Longhorsley
Otterburn Ashington
NORTHUMBERLAND Morpeth
Falstone
WAY A696 Belsay
aglesfield Canonbie Great Matfen Whitley Bay
A68 Whittington
Haydon Warden A69
Haltwhistle Bridge NEWCASTLE UPON TYNE
Brampton Rowfoot Hexham A695 Corbridge Gateshead
A689 A69 Hedley A1 SUNDERLAND
CARLISLE A689 Allendale on the Hill A7
NY Blanchland Carterway A963 NZ
Wigton Armathwaite Allenheads Heads Consett A691
BRIA A6 A686 Garrigill A689 DURHAM A19
dbeck Hesket Newmarket Melmerby Crook HARTLEPOOL
waite Mungrisdale Penrith Middleton-in- A1(M)
waite A66 Tirril Teesdale Bishop Auckland Newton STOCKTON
eswick Scales Yanwath A68 Aycliffe A19 A689
ite Dockray Watermillock Appleby-in- Romaldkirk Aycliffe A174
mere Howtown Shap Westmorland Bolam STOCKTON-ON-TEES
ke District Cotherstone A66 DARLINGTON MIDDLESBROUGH
Great Grasmere Brough Barnard A66 A171 Whitby
ggdale Ambleside A685 Castle A66 Danby
ittle Troutbeck Kirkby Stephen Kirby Hill A19 Great Robin Hood's
dale Ellenwater Keld Scotch Corner Ayton Bay
awkshead Outgate Ravenstonedale Kirby Hill Moulton A172 Egton Bridge Goathland
M6 Richmond North York Moors A169 A171
A1 Northallerton 9 A169

Cape Wrath

Rudha Rhobhanais
(Butt of Lewis)

○ Town Names
● Pub/Inn

0   10   20 miles
0   10   20   30 kilometres

NB

Tolsta Head

Handa Island

A857

A838

NA

Gallan
Head

Steornabhagh
(Stornoway)

A858

A866

Broad Bay

Eye Peninsula

Point of
Stoer

A894

A838

Kylesku

A837

WESTERN
ISLES

Scarp

A859

Isle of
Lewis

The Minch

Summer
Isles

Lochinver

Achiltibuie

A835

A837

Taransay

Greenstone
Point

Toe Head

Tairbeart
(Tarbert)

Shiant
Islands

Rudha
Reidh

Ullapool

Pabbay

Sound of Harris

Harris

A832

Dundonnell

Highlands

Uibhist a Tuath
(North Uist)

Beinn na Faoghla
(Benbecula)

Outer Hebrides

A867

Beinn nam Madadh
(Lochmaddy)

Carinish

Dunvegan
Head

The Little Minch

NG

Rona

Sound of Raasay

Shieldaig

Gairloch

A832

A835

A832

NF

Portree

Inner Sound

Applecross

A896

HIGHLAND

Uibhist a Deas
(South Uist)

A865

Rudha Hallagro

Carbost

A863

Raasay

Sconser

Scalpay

A87

Plockton

Kyle of Lochalsh

Domie

North West Highland

A990

A88

Loch Baghasdail
(Lochboisdale)

Isle
of
Skye

Cuillin

Isleornsay

A851

Glenelg

Sound of Sleat

A87

Fort
Auguste

A88

Sound of Barra

Eriskay

Canna

Ardvasar

A87

Barra

A888

Rum

Mallaig

Inner Hebrides

Eigg

Sound of Arisaig

A830

Fort William

A82

NL

Mingulay

Muck

NM

A861

Onich

North Ballachulish

Loch Linnhe

Glencoe

A82

Tiree

Coll

Tobermory

A884

Port
Appin

Ulva

Isle of Mull

10

Lismore

A828

A82

Iona

A849

Firth of Lorne

A816

ARGYLL
AND BUTE

A85

A819

Luing

Scarba

Central London

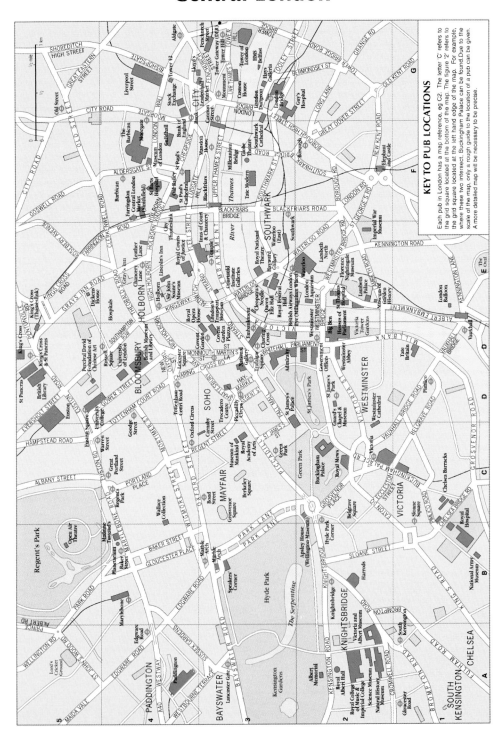

Greater London

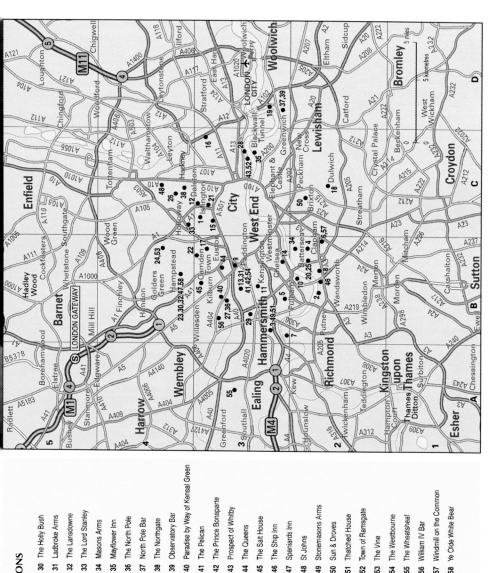

Index

Index

Index

Index

Index

Index

The Pub Guide

Index

Index

Index

Index

Index

Index

Index

Index

Index

Index

Acknowledgements - The Pub Guide 2003
The Automobile Association would like to thank the following for supplying photographs for this book.
The Morritt Arms, Barnard Castle 6b; The Village Pub, Barnsley 4, 6t, 9t, 22bc; The White Horse, Brancaster Staithe 3c; The Mason's Arms, Branscombe 1, 8t, 8c, 8b; Inn for all Seasons, Burford 9bl, 22bl, 22br; The Cholmondeley Arms, Cholmondeley 16bc; The Cleave, Lustleigh 9br; The Three Horseshoes, Maddingly 7tr, 15; Ye Olde Trip to Jerusalem, Nottingham 14t, 15, 16t; The Crown inn, Pishill 15bl; The Bridge Inn, Ratho 7tl; The Barge Inn, Seend 16tc; The Highwayman Inn, Sourton 14b, 16b; The Ring O'Bells, Thornton 15br; The Rising Sun, Umberleigh 2; Percy's Restaurant, Virginstowe 12; The Eagle and Child, Windermere 7b; The Wykeham Arms, Winchester 5r; The Moody Cow, Wykham 5l

The remaining pictures are held in the Association's own library (AA PHOTO LIBRARY) and were taken by:
Adrian Baker 11; Peter Baker 543; Vic Bates 41b; M Birkitt 20t, 22t, 337; Jim Carnie 3tl, 20b; Derek Croucher 221; Steve Day 480, 493b, 591; Eric Ellington 589; Derek Forss 27t, 183b, 283; Caroline Jones 27b; Cameron Lees 276; S&O Mathews 317, 325, 431, 489; Rich Newton 525; Roger Moss 71; Graham Rowatt 179; Karen Ryecart 3c; Peter Sharpe 114; Rick Strange 21, 22t, 41t; Martin Trelawney 297b; Harry Williams 161, 625; Jon Wyand 150; Wyn Voysey 173, 183t

Please send this form to:
  Editor, The Pub Guide,
  Lifestyle Guides,
  The Automobile Association,
  Fanum House,
  Basingstoke RG21 4EA

Readers' Report Form

or fax: 01256 491647
or e-mail: lifestyleguides@theAA.com

Please use this form to tell us about any pub or inn you have visited, whether it is in the guide or not currently listed. We are interested in the quality of food, the selection of beers and the overall ambience of the establishment.

Feedback from readers helps us to keep our guide accurate and up to date. However, if you have a complaint to make during a visit, we do recommend that you discuss the matter with the pub management there and then, so that they have a chance to put things right before your visit is spoilt.

Please note that the AA does not undertake to arbitrate between you and the pub management, or to obtain compensation or engage in protracted correspondence.

Date: ....

Your name (block capitals) ....

Your address (block capitals) ....

....

....

.... Post Code......................

e-mail address: ....

Name of pub: ....

Location ....

Comments ....

....

....

....

(please attach a separate sheet if necessary)

Readers' Report Form

	YES	NO

Have you bought this guide before? ☐ ☐

Do you regularly use any other pub, accommodation or food guides?
If yes, which ones?

....

....

What do you find most useful about The AA Pub Guide?

....

....

....

....

Do you read the editorial features in the guide?...

Do you use the location atlas? ....

Have you tried any of the walks included in this guide?...............................

Is there any other information you would like to see added to this guide?

....

....

....

....

What are your main reasons for visiting pubs (tick all that apply)

food ☐   business ☐   accommodation ☐

beer ☐   celebrations ☐   entertainment ☐

atmosphere ☐   leisure ☐   other ....

How often do you visit a pub for a meal?

more than once a week ☐
one a week ☐
once a fortnight ☐
once a month ☐
once in six months ☐

Please send this form to:
    Editor, The Pub Guide,
    Lifestyle Guides,
    The Automobile Association,
    Fanum House,
    Basingstoke RG21 4EA

or fax: 01256 491647
or e-mail: lifestyleguides@theAA.com

Please use this form to tell us about any pub or inn you have visited, whether it is in the guide or not currently listed. We are interested in the quality of food, the selection of beers and the overall ambience of the establishment.

Feedback from readers helps us to keep our guide accurate and up to date. However, if you have a complaint to make during a visit, we do recommend that you discuss the matter with the pub management there and then, so that they have a chance to put things right before your visit is spoilt.

Please note that the AA does not undertake to arbitrate between you and the pub management, or to obtain compensation or engage in protracted correspondence.

Date: ....

Your name (block capitals) ....

Your address (block capitals) ....

....

....

.... Post Code.............................

e-mail address: ....

Name of pub: ....

Location ....

Comments ....

....

....

....

(please attach a separate sheet if necessary)

We may use information we hold about you to write, e-mail or telephone you about other products and services offered by us and our carefully selected partners. Information may be disclosed to other companies in the Centrica group (including those using the British Gas, Scottish Gas, Goldfish, One-Tel and AA brands) but we can assure you that we will not disclose it to third parties.
Please tick here if you DO NOT wish to receive details of other products or services from the AA. ☐PTO

Readers' Report Form

	YES	NO

Have you bought this guide before? ☐ ☐

Do you regularly use any other pub, accommodation or food guides?
If yes, which ones?

....

....

What do you find most useful about The AA Pub Guide?

....

....

....

....

Do you read the editorial features in the guide?...

Do you use the location atlas? ....

Have you tried any of the walks included in this guide?................................

Is there any other information you would like to see added to this guide?

....

....

....

....

....

What are your main reasons for visiting pubs (tick all that apply)

food ☐   business ☐   accommodation ☐

beer ☐   celebrations ☐   entertainment ☐

atmosphere ☐   leisure ☐   other ....

How often do you visit a pub for a meal?

more than once a week ☐

one a week ☐

once a fortnight ☐

once a month ☐

once in six months ☐

Please send this form to:
    Editor, The Pub Guide,
    Lifestyle Guides,
    The Automobile Association,
    Fanum House,
    Basingstoke RG21 4EA

Readers' Report form

or fax: 01256 491647
or e-mail: lifestyleguides@theAA.com

Please use this form to tell us about any pub or inn you have visited, whether it is in the guide or not currently listed. We are interested in the quality of food, the selection of beers and the overall ambience of the establishment.

Feedback from readers helps us to keep our guide accurate and up to date. However, if you have a complaint to make during a visit, we do recommend that you discuss the matter with the pub management there and then, so that they have a chance to put things right before your visit is spoilt.

Please note that the AA does not undertake to arbitrate between you and the pub management, or to obtain compensation or engage in protracted correspondence.

Date: ....

Your name (block capitals) ....

Your address (block capitals) ....

....

....

.... Post Code....................

e-mail address: ....

Name of pub: ....

Location ....

Comments ....

....

....

....

(please attach a separate sheet if necessary)

Readers' Report Form

YES   NO

Have you bought this guide before? ☐ ☐

Do you regularly use any other pub, accommodation or food guides?
If yes, which ones?

....

....

What do you find most useful about The AA Pub Guide?

....

....

....

....

Do you read the editorial features in the guide?..

Do you use the location atlas? ....

Have you tried any of the walks included in this guide?...............................

Is there any other information you would like to see added to this guide?

....

....

....

....

....

What are your main reasons for visiting pubs (tick all that apply)

food ☐   business ☐   accommodation ☐

beer ☐   celebrations ☐   entertainment ☐

atmosphere ☐   leisure ☐   other ....

How often do you visit a pub for a meal?

more than once a week ☐

one a week ☐

once a fortnight ☐

once a month ☐

once in six months ☐

WIN a MARRIOTT LEISURE BREAK
for two or a DINNER SERVICE
in 5 free prize draws

See overleaf for terms & conditions

We have two of each to give away in each of the
5 prize draws throughout the year. Enjoy a luxury two-night
Leisure Break with Marriott, the winners of the AA Hotel Group
of the Year Award 2001-2, or dine in style with an elegant
Villeroy & Boch dinner service.

For more information on Marriott Leisure Breaks in the UK call
0800 699996 or Villeroy & Boch on 0208 875 6060.

✂ -

HOW TO ENTER
Just complete (in capitals please) and send off this card or alternatively, send your name and
address on a stamped postcard to the address overleaf (no purchase required). Entries are
limited to one per household.
Closing date 4 September 2003.

MR/MRS/MISS/MS/OTHER, PLEASE STATE: _____

NAME: _____

ADDRESS: _____

_____

_____

_____ POSTCODE: _____

TEL. NOS: _____ E-MAIL: _____

Are you an AA Member?   Yes/No
Have you bought this or any other AA Lifestyle Guide before?   Yes/No
If yes, please indicate the year of the last edition you bought:

AA Hotel Guide	____	AA Caravan & Camping (Europe)	____
AA Bed and Breakfast Guide	____	AA Britain Guide	____
AA Restaurant Guide	____	AA Days Out Guide	____
AA Pub Guide	____	AA B&B France	____
AA Caravan & Camping (Britain & Ireland)	____	Other, please state	_____

We may use information we hold about you to write, email or telephone you about other products and
services offered by us and our carefully selected partners. Information may be disclosed to other companies
in the Centrica group (including those using the British Gas, Scottish Gas, Goldfish, One-Tel and AA brands)
but we can assure you that we will not disclose it to third parties. Please tick the box if you do not wish to
receive details of other products and services from the AA ☐

PG03

Terms and Conditions

1. Four winners will be drawn from each of the five prize draws to take place on 03 January, 07 March, 02 May, 04 July and 05 September 2003.

2. Closing date for receipt of entries is midday on the relevant draw date. Final closing date for receipt of entries is 04 September 2003.

3. Entries received after any draw date other than the final one will go forward into the next available draw. Each entry will only be entered in one draw. Only one entry per household accepted.

4. Winners will be notified by post within 14 days of the relevant draw date.

5. Two prizes per draw consist of a Marriott Incentive Voucher Pack containing two B&B vouchers (one per night), two dinner vouchers (for two people). This pack can be used at any Marriott, Courtyard or Renaissance hotel in the UK, with the exception of Hanbury Manor and all London hotels. Two further prizes per draw consist of the Villeroy & Boch 'Twist Alea' dinner service – a 48 piece dinner service of up to 6 place settings.

6. The Leisure Break must be booked within the date specified on reverse of voucher and the prize cannot be used in conjunction with any other promotion or special offer.

7. Marriott provide all hotel accommodation, services and facilities and AA Publishing is not party to your agreement with Marriott in this regard.

8. Prizes are not transferable and there is no cash alternative.

9. No purchase required.

10. The prize draw is open to UK residents over the age of 18, other than employees and agents of the Automobile Association, Marriott or Villeroy & Boch, members of their households or anyone else connected with the promotion.

11. For a list of winners, please send a stamped, self-addressed envelope to AA Lifestyle Guide Winners 2003, AA Publishing, Fanum House (14), Basing View, Basingstoke, Hants, RG21 4EA.

12. Your entry must be sent in with an appropriate stamp.

13. We reserve the right to feature the winners in draw-related publicity.

Please
Affix
Stamp

AA Lifestyle Guide 2003 Prize Draw

AA PUBLISHING
FANUM HOUSE (14)
BASING VIEW
BASINGSTOKE
HANTS RG21 4EA

Fold along this line

Hawkstone Park Hotel
01939 200611

Bear, Hodnet
01630 685214

Mytton & Mermaid
01743-761220

Seal along this edge with sticky tape